INDIANA
RULES OF COURT

VOLUME I – STATE

2014

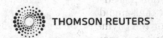

Mat #41258948

This publication was created to provide you with accurate and authoritative information concerning the subject matter covered; however, this publication was not necessarily prepared by persons licensed to practice law in a particular jurisdiction. The publisher is not engaged in rendering legal or other professional advice and this publication is not a substitute for the advice of an attorney. If you require legal or other expert advice, you should seek the services of a competent attorney or other professional.

ISBN: 978-0-314-65395-6

PREFACE

Indiana Rules of Court, Volume I - State, 2014, includes rules and associated material governing practice before the Indiana state courts. It replaces the 2013 edition. It is current with amendments received through November 1, 2013.

For additional information or research assistance call the West reference attorneys at 1-800-REF-ATTY (1-800-733-2889). Contact West's editorial department directly with your questions and suggestions by e-mail at west.editor@thomson.com.

THE PUBLISHER

December 2013

THOMSON REUTERS PROVIEW™

This title is one of many now available on your tablet as an eBook.

Take your research mobile. Powered by the Thomson Reuters ProView™ app, our eBooks deliver the same trusted content as your print resources, but in a compact, on-the-go format.

ProView eBooks are designed for the way you work. You can add your own notes and highlights to the text, and all of your annotations will transfer electronically to every new edition of your eBook.

You can also instantly verify primary authority with built-in links to WestlawNext® and KeyCite®, so you can be confident that you're accessing the most current and accurate information.

To find out more about ProView eBooks and available discounts, call 1-800-344-5009.

TABLE OF CONTENTS

*

INDIANA RULES OF TRIAL PROCEDURE

Effective January 1, 1970

Including Amendments Received Through November 1, 2013

1

I.   SCOPE OF RULES—ONE FORM OF ACTION

Rule 1.   Scope of the rules

Except as otherwise provided, these rules govern the procedure and practice in all courts of the state of Indiana in all suits of a civil nature whether cognizable as cases at law, in equity, or of statutory origin.   They shall be construed to secure the just, speedy and inexpensive determination of every action.

Rule 2.   One form of action

(A) There shall be one [1] form of action to be known as "civil action."

(B) The right of a civil action is not merged in a public offense or a public remedy, but may, in all cases, be sought independently of and in addition to the punishment given or relief granted for the public offense.

II. COMMENCEMENT OF ACTION; SERVICE OF PROCESS, PLEADINGS, MOTIONS AND ORDERS

Rule 3. Commencement of an action

A civil action is commenced by filing with the court a complaint or such equivalent pleading or document as may be specified by statute, by payment of the prescribed filing fee or filing an order waiving the filing fee, and, where service of process is required, by furnishing to the clerk as many copies of the complaint and summons as are necessary.

Amended Dec. 21, 2001, effective April 1, 2002.

Rule 3.1. Appearance

(A) Initiating party. At the time an action is commenced, the attorney representing the party initiating the proceeding or the party, if not represented by an attorney, shall file with the clerk of the court an appearance form setting forth the following information:

(1) Name, address and telephone number of the initiating party or parties filing the appearance form;

(2) Name, address, attorney number, telephone number, FAX number, and e-mail address of any attorney representing the party, as applicable;

(3) The case type of the proceeding [Administrative Rule 8(B)(3)];

(4) A statement that the party will or will not accept service by FAX or by e-mail from:

a. other parties and/or

b. the court under Rule 72(D).

(5) In domestic relations, Uniform Reciprocal Enforcement of Support (URESA), paternity, delinquency, Child in Need of Services (CHINS), guardianship, and any other proceedings in which support may be an issue, the Social Security Identification Number of all family members;

(6) The caption and case number of all related cases;

(7) Such additional matters specified by state or local rule required to maintain the information management system employed by the court;

(8) In a proceeding involving a protection from abuse order, a workplace violence restraining order, or a no-contact order, the initiating party shall provide to the clerk a public mailing address for purposes of legal service. The initiating party may use the Attorney General Address Confidentiality program established by statute; and

(9) In a proceeding involving a mental health commitment, except 72 hour emergency detentions, the initiating party shall provide the full name of the person with respect to whom commitment is sought and the person's state of residence. In addition, the initiating party shall provide at least one of the following identifiers for the person:

(a) Date of birth;

(b) Social Security Number;

(c) Driver's license number with state of issue and date of expiration;

(d) Department of Correction number;

(e) State ID number with state of issue and date of expiration; or

(f) FBI number.

(B) Responding parties. At the time the responding party or parties first appears in a case, the attorney representing such party or parties, or the party or parties, if not represented by an attorney, shall file an appearance form setting forth the information set out in Section (A) above.

(C) Intervening Parties. At the time the first matter is submitted to the court seeking to intervene in a proceeding, the attorney representing the intervening party or parties, or the intervening party or parties, if not represented by an attorney, shall file an appearance form setting forth the information set out in Section (A) above.

(D) Confidentiality of Information Excluded from Public Access. Any appearance form information or record defined as not accessible to the public pursuant to Administrative Rule 9(G)(1) shall be filed in a manner required by Trial Rule 5.

(E) Completion and correction of information. In the event matters must be filed before the information required by this rule is available, the appearance form shall be submitted with available information and supplemented when the absent information is acquired. Parties shall promptly advise the clerk of the court of any change in the information previously supplied to the court.

(F) Forms. The Division of State Court Administration shall prepare and publish a standard format for compliance with the provisions of this rule.

(G) Service. The Clerk of the Court shall use the information set forth in the appearance form for service by mail, FAX, and e-mail under Trial Rule 5(B).

(H) Withdrawal of Representation. An attorney representing a party may file a motion to withdraw representation of the party upon a showing that the attorney has sent written notice of intent to withdraw to the party at least ten (10) days before filing a motion to withdraw representation, and either:

(1) the terms and conditions of the attorney's agreement with the party regarding the scope of the representation have been satisfied, or

(2) withdrawal is required by Professional Conduct Rule 1.16(a), or is otherwise permitted by Professional Conduct Rule 1.16(b).

An attorney filing a motion to withdraw from representation shall certify the last known address and telephone number of the party, subject to the confidentiality provisions of Sections (A)(8) and (D) above, and shall attach to the motion a copy of the notice of intent to withdraw that was sent to the party.

A motion for withdrawal of representation shall be granted by the court unless the court specifically finds that withdrawal is not reasonable or consistent with the efficient administration of justice.

(I) Temporary or Limited Representation. If an attorney seeks to represent a party in a proceeding before the court on a temporary basis or a basis that is limited in scope, the attorney shall file a notice of temporary or limited representation. The notice shall contain the information set out in Section (A) (1) and (2) above and a description of the temporary or limited status, including the date the temporary status ends or the scope of the limited representation. The court shall not be required to act on the temporary or limited representation. At the completion of the temporary or limited representation, the attorney shall file a notice of completion of representation with the clerk of the court.

Adopted Dec. 5, 1994, effective Feb. 1, 1995. Amended July 19, 2002, effective Jan. 1, 2003; Sept. 30, 2004, effective Jan. 1, 2005; July 1, 2005, effective Jan. 1, 2006; Sept. 15, 2009, effective Jan. 1, 2010; Sept. 20, 2011, effective Jan. 1, 2012; Sept. 7, 2012, effective Jan. 1, 2013.

Rule 4. Process

(A) Jurisdiction Over Parties or Persons—In General. The court acquires jurisdiction over a party or person who under these rules commences or joins in the action, is served with summons or enters an appearance, or who is subjected to the power of the court under any other law.

(B) Preparation of summons and praecipe. Contemporaneously with the filing of the complaint or equivalent pleading, the person seeking service or his attorney shall furnish to the clerk as many copies of the complaint and summons as are necessary. The clerk shall examine, date, sign, and affix his seal to the summons and thereupon issue and deliver the papers to the appropriate person for service. Affidavits, requests, and any other information relating to the summons and its service as required or permitted by these rules shall be included in a praecipe attached to or entered upon the summons. Such praecipe shall be deemed to be a part of the summons for purposes of these rules. Separate or additional summons shall, as provided by these rules, be issued by the clerk at any time upon proper request of the person seeking service or his attorney.

(C) Form of summons. The summons shall contain:

(1) The name and address of the person on whom the service is to be effected;

(2) The name, street address, and telephone number of the court and the cause number assigned to the case;

(3) The title of the case as shown by the complaint, but, if there are multiple parties, the title may be shortened to include only the first named plaintiff and defendant with an appropriate indication that there are additional parties;

(4) The name, address, and telephone number of the attorney for the person seeking service;

(5) The time within which these rules require the person being served to respond, and a clear statement that in case of his failure to do so, judgment by default may be rendered against him for the relief demanded in the complaint.

The summons may also contain any additional information which will facilitate proper service.

(D) Designation of Manner of Service. The person seeking service or his attorney may designate the manner of service upon the summons. If not so designated, the clerk shall cause service to be made by mail or other public means provided the mailing address of the person to be served is indicated in the summons or can be determined. If a mailing address is not furnished or cannot be determined or if service by mail or other public means is returned without acceptance, the complaint and summons shall promptly be delivered to the sheriff or his deputy who, unless otherwise directed, shall serve the summons.

(E) Summons and Complaint Served Together—Exceptions. The summons and complaint shall be served together unless otherwise ordered by the court. When service of summons is made by publication, the complaint shall not be published. When jurisdiction over a party is dependent upon service of process by publication or by his appearance, summons and complaint shall be deemed to have been served at the end of the day of last required publication in the case of service by publication, and at the time of appearance in jurisdiction acquired by appearance. Whenever the summons and complaint are not served or published together, the summons shall contain the full, unabbreviated title of the case.

Amended Dec. 21, 2001, effective April 1, 2002.

Rule 4.1. Summons: Service on individuals

(A) In General. Service may be made upon an individual, or an individual acting in a representative capacity, by:

(1) sending a copy of the summons and complaint by registered or certified mail or other public

means by which a written acknowledgment of receipt may be requested and obtained to his residence, place of business or employment with return receipt requested and returned showing receipt of the letter; or

(2) delivering a copy of the summons and complaint to him personally; or

(3) leaving a copy of the summons and complaint at his dwelling house or usual place of abode; or

(4) serving his agent as provided by rule, statute or valid agreement.

(B) Copy Service to Be Followed With Mail. Whenever service is made under Clause (3) or (4) of subdivision (A), the person making the service also shall send by first class mail, a copy of the summons without the complaint to the last known address of the person being served, and this fact shall be shown upon the return.

Amended Dec. 7, 1970, effective Jan. 1, 1971.

Rule 4.2. Summons: Service upon infant or incompetents

(A) Service Upon Infants. Service upon an individual known to be an infant shall be made upon his next friend or guardian ad litem, if service is with respect to the same action in which the infant is so represented. If there is no next friend or guardian ad litem, service shall be made upon his court-appointed representative if one is known and can be served within this state. If there is no court-appointed representative, service shall be made upon either parent known to have custody of the infant, or if there is no parent, upon a person known to be standing in the position of custodian or parent. The infant shall also be served if he is fourteen [14] years of age or older. In the event that service, as provided above, is not possible, service shall be made on the infant.

(B) Service Upon Incompetents. Service upon an individual who has been adjudged to be of unsound mind, otherwise incompetent or who is believed to be such shall be made upon his next friend or guardian ad litem, if service is with respect to the same action in which the incompetent is so represented. If there is no next friend or guardian ad litem, service shall be made upon his court-appointed representative if one is known and can be served within this state. If there is no court-appointed representative, then upon the named party and also upon a person known to be standing in the position of custodian of his person.

(C) Duty to Inform Court—Appearance. Nothing herein is intended to affect the duty of a party to inform the court that a person is an infant or incompetent. An appearance by a court-appointed guardian, next friend or guardian ad litem or his attorney shall correct any defect in service under this section unless such defect be challenged.

Rule 4.3. Summons: Service upon institutionalized persons

Service of summons upon a person who is imprisoned or restrained in an institution shall be made by delivering or mailing a copy of the summons and complaint to the official in charge of the institution. It shall be the duty of said official to immediately deliver the summons and complaint to the person being served and allow him to make provisions for adequate representation by counsel. The official shall indicate upon the return whether the person has received the summons and been allowed an opportunity to retain counsel.

Rule 4.4. Service upon persons in actions for acts done in this state or having an effect in this state.

(A) Acts Serving as a Basis for Jurisdiction. Any person or organization that is a nonresident of this state, a resident of this state who has left the state, or a person whose residence is unknown, submits to the jurisdiction of the courts of this state as to any action arising from the following acts committed by him or her or his or her agent:

(1) doing any business in this state;

(2) causing personal injury or property damage by an act or omission done within this state;

(3) causing personal injury or property damage in this state by an occurrence, act or omission done outside this state if he regularly does or solicits business or engages in any other persistent course of conduct, or derives substantial revenue or benefit from goods, materials, or services used, consumed, or rendered in this state;

(4) having supplied or contracted to supply services rendered or to be rendered or goods or materials furnished or to be furnished in this state;

(5) owning, using, or possessing any real property or an interest in real property within this state;

(6) contracting to insure or act as surety for or on behalf of any person, property or risk located within this state at the time the contract was made;

(7) living in the marital relationship within the state notwithstanding subsequent departure from the state, as to all obligations for alimony, custody, child support, or property settlement, if the other party to the marital relationship continues to reside in the state; or

(8) abusing, harassing, or disturbing the peace of, or violating a protective or restraining order for the protection of, any person within the state by an act or omission done in this state, or outside this state if the act or omission is part of a continuing course of conduct having an effect in this state.

In addition, a court of this state may exercise jurisdiction on any basis not inconsistent with the Constitutions of this state or the United States.

(B) Manner of service. A person subject to the jurisdiction of the courts of this state under this rule may be served with summons:

(1) As provided by Rules 4.1 (service on individuals), 4.5 (service upon resident who cannot be found or served within the state), 4.6 (service upon organizations), 4.9 (in rem actions); or

(2) The person shall be deemed to have appointed the Secretary of State as his agent upon whom service of summons may be made as provided in Rule 4.10.

(C) More convenient forum. Jurisdiction under this rule is subject to the power of the court to order the litigation to be held elsewhere under such reasonable conditions as the court in its discretion may determine to be just.

In the exercise of that discretion the court may appropriately consider such factors as:

(1) Amenability to personal jurisdiction in this state and in any alternative forum of the parties to the action;

(2) Convenience to the parties and witnesses of the trial in this state and in any alternative forum;

(3) Differences in conflict of law rules applicable in this state and in the alternative forum; or

(4) Any other factors having substantial bearing upon the selection of a convenient, reasonable and fair place of trial.

(D) Forum Non Conveniens—Stay or Dismissal. No stay or dismissal shall be granted due to a finding of *forum non conveniens* until all properly joined defendants file with the clerk of the court a written stipulation that each defendant will:

(1) submit to the personal jurisdiction of the courts of the other forum; and

(2) waive any defense based on the statute of limitations applicable in the other forum with respect to all causes of action brought by a party to which this subsection applies.

(E) Order on Forum Non Conveniens—Modification. The court may, on motion and notice to the parties, modify an order granting a stay or dismissal under this subsection and take any further action in the proceeding as the interests of justice may require. If the moving party violates a stipulation required by subsection (D), the court shall withdraw the order staying or dismissing the action and proceed as if the order had never been issued. Notwithstanding any other law, the court shall have continuing jurisdiction for the purposes of this subsection.

Amended Dec. 7, 1970, effective Jan. 1, 1971; amended effective Nov. 10, 1988; amended Dec. 5, 1994, effective Feb. 1, 1995; Amended Dec. 23, 1996, effective March 1, 1997; amended July 19, 2002, effective Jan. 1, 2003.

Rule 4.5. Summons: Service upon resident who cannot be found or served within the state

When the person to be served is a resident of this state who cannot be served personally or by agent in this state and either cannot be found, has concealed his whereabouts or has left the state, summons may be served in the manner provided by Rule 4.9 (summons in in rem actions).

Rule 4.6. Service upon organizations

(A) Persons to be served. Service upon an organization may be made as follows:

(1) In the case of a domestic or foreign organization upon an executive officer thereof, or if there is an agent appointed or deemed by law to have been appointed to receive service, then upon such agent.

(2) In the case of a partnership, upon a general partner thereof.

(3) In the case of a state governmental organization upon the executive officer thereof and also upon the Attorney General.

(4) In the case of a local governmental organization, upon the executive thereof and upon the attorney for the local governmental organization.

(5) When, in subsections (3) and (4) of this subdivision, a governmental representative is named as a party in his individual name or in such name along with his official title, then also upon such representative.

(B) Manner of service. Service under subdivision (A) of this rule shall be made on the proper person in the manner provided by these rules for service upon individuals, but a person seeking service or his attorney shall not knowingly direct service to be made at the person's dwelling house or place of abode, unless such is an address furnished under the requirements of a statute or valid agreement, or unless an affidavit on or attached to the summons states that service in another manner is impractical.

(C) Service at organization's office. When shown upon an affidavit or in the return, that service upon an organization cannot be made as provided in subdivision (A) or (B) of this rule, service may be made by leaving a copy of the summons and complaint at any office of such organization located within this state with the person in charge of such office.

Amended Sept. 30, 2004, effective Jan. 1, 2005.

Rule 4.7. Summons: Service upon agent named by statute or agreement

Whenever an agent (other than an agent appointed to receive service for a governmental organization of this state) has been designated by or pursuant to statute or valid agreement to receive service for the person being served, service may be made upon such agent as follows:

(1) If the agent is a governmental organization or officer designated by or pursuant to statute, service shall be made as provided in Rule 4.10.

(2) If the agent is one other than that described above, service shall be made upon him as provided in Rule 4.1 (service upon individuals) or 4.6 (service upon organizations). If service cannot be made upon such agent, because there is no address furnished as required by statute or valid agreement or his whereabouts in this state are unknown, then his principal shall be deemed to have appointed the Secretary of State as a replacement for the agent and service may be made upon the Secretary of State as provided in Rule 4.10.

Rule 4.8. Summons: Service of pleadings or summons on Attorney General

Service of a copy of the summons and complaint or any pleading upon the Attorney General under these rules or any statute shall be made by personal service upon him, a deputy or clerk at his office, or by mail or other public means to him at such office in the manner provided by Rule 4.1(A)(1), and by Rule 4.11 to the extent applicable.

Rule 4.9. Summons: In rem actions

(A) In general. In any action involving a res situated within this state, service may be made as provided in this rule. The court may render a judgment or decree to the extent of its jurisdiction over the res.

(B) Manner of service. Service under this rule may be made as follows:

(1) By service of summons upon a person or his agent pursuant to these rules; or

(2) By service of summons outside this state in a manner provided by Rule 4.1 (service upon individuals) or by publication outside this state in a manner provided by Rule 4.13 (service by publication) or outside this state in any other manner as provided by these rules; or

(3) By service by publication pursuant to Rule 4.13.

Rule 4.10. Summons: Service upon Secretary of State or other governmental agent

(A)[1] In general. Whenever, under these rules or any statute, service is made upon the Secretary of State or any other governmental organization or officer, as agent for the person being served, service may be made upon such agent as provided in this rule.

(1) The person seeking service or his attorney shall:

(a) submit his request for service upon the agent in the praecipe for summons, and state that the governmental organization or officer is the agent of the person being served;

(b) state the address of the person being served as filed and recorded pursuant to a statute or valid agreement, or if no such address is known, then his last known mailing address, and, if no such address is known, then such shall be stated;

(c) pay any fee prescribed by statute to be forwarded together with sufficient copies of the summons, affidavit and complaint, to the agent by the clerk of the court.

(2) Upon receipt thereof the agent shall promptly:

(a) send to the person being served a copy of the summons and complaint by registered or certified mail or by other public means by which a written acknowledgment of receipt may be obtained;

(b) complete and deliver to the clerk an affidavit showing the date of the mailing, or if there was no mailing, the reason therefor;

(c) send to the clerk a copy of the return receipt along with a copy of the summons;

(d) file and retain a copy of the return receipt.

[1] This rule contains no Subd. (B).

Rule 4.11. Summons: Registered or certified mail

Whenever service by registered or certified mail or other public means by which a return receipt may be requested is authorized, the clerk of the court or a governmental agent under Rule 4.10 shall send the summons and complaint to the person being served at the address supplied upon the summons, or furnished by the person seeking service. In his return the clerk of the court or the governmental agent shall show the date and place of mailing, a copy of the mailed or electronically-transmitted return receipt if and when received by him showing whether the mailing was accepted or returned, and, if accepted, by whom. The return along with the receipt shall be promptly filed by the clerk with the pleadings and become a part of the record. If a mailing by the clerk of the court is returned without acceptance, the clerk shall reissue the summons and complaint for service as requested, by the person seeking service.

Amended Dec. 7, 1970, effective Jan. 1, 1971; amended Sept. 10, 2007, effective Jan. 1, 2008.

Rule 4.12. Summons: Service by sheriff or other officer

(A) In general. Whenever service is made by delivering a copy to a person personally or by leaving a copy at his dwelling house or place of employment as provided by Rule 4.1, summons shall be issued to and served by the sheriff, his deputy, or some person specially or regularly appointed by the court for that purpose. Service shall be effective if made by a person not otherwise authorized by these rules, but proof of service by such a person must be made by him as a witness or by deposition without allowance of expenses therefor as costs. The person to whom the summons is delivered for service must act promptly and exercise reasonable care to cause service to be made.

(B) Special service by police officers. A sheriff, his deputy, or any full-time state or municipal police officer may serve summons in any county of this state if he agrees or has agreed to make the service. When specially requested in the praecipe for summons, the complaint and summons shall be delivered to such officer by the clerk or the attorney for the person seeking service. No agreement with the sheriff or his deputy for such service in the sheriff's own county shall be permitted. In no event shall any expenses agreed upon under this provision be assessed or recovered as costs or affect court costs otherwise imposed for regular service.

(C) Service in other counties. A summons may be served in any county in this state. If service is to be made in another county, the summons may be issued by the clerk for service therein to the sheriff of such county or to a person authorized to make service by these rules.

(D) Service outside the state. Personal service, when permitted by these rules to be made outside the state, may be made there by any disinterested person or by the attorney representing the person seeking such service. The expenses of such person may be assessed as costs only if they are reasonable and if service by mail or other public means cannot be made or is not successful.

Rule 4.13. Summons: Service by publication

(A) Praecipe for summons by publication. In any action where notice by publication is permitted by these rules or by statute, service may be made by publication. Summons by publication may name all the persons to be served, and separate publications with respect to each party shall not be required. The person seeking such service, or his attorney, shall submit his request therefor upon the praecipe for summons along with supporting affidavits that diligent search has been made that the defendant cannot be found, has concealed his whereabouts, or has left the state, and shall prepare the contents of the summons to be published. The summons shall be signed by the clerk of the court or the sheriff in such manner as to indicate that it is made by his authority.

(B) Contents of summons by publication. The summons shall contain the following information:

(1) The name of the person being sued, and the person to whom the notice is directed, and, if the person's whereabouts are unknown or some or all of the parties are unknown, a statement to that effect;

(2) The name of the court and cause number assigned to the case;

(3) The title of the case as shown by the complaint, but if there are multiple parties, the title may be shortened to include only the first named plaintiff and those defendants to be served by publication with an appropriate indication that there are additional parties;

(4) The name and address of the attorney representing the person seeking service;

(5) A brief statement of the nature of the suit, which need not contain the details and particulars of the claim. A description of any property, relationship, or other res involved in the action, and a statement that the person being sued claims some interest therein;

(6) A clear statement that the person being sued must respond within thirty [30] days after the last notice of the action is published, and in case he fails to do so, judgment by default may be entered against him for the relief demanded in the complaint.

(C) Publication of summons. The summons shall be published three [3] times by the clerk or person making it, the first publication promptly and each two [2] succeeding publications at least seven [7] and not more than fourteen [14] days after the prior publication, in a newspaper authorized by law to publish notices, and published in the county where the complaint or action is filed, where the res is located, or where the defendant resides or where he was known last to reside. If no newspaper is published in the county, then the summons shall be published in the county in this state nearest thereto in which any such paper may be printed, or in a place specially ordered by the court. The person seeking the service or his attorney may designate any qualified newspaper, and if he fails to do so, the selection may be made by the clerk.

(D) By whom made or procured. Service of summons by publication shall be made and procured by the clerk, by a person appointed by the court for that purpose, or by the clerk or sheriff of another county where publication is to be made.

(E) Return. The clerk or person making the service shall prepare the return and include the following:

(1) Any supporting affidavits of the printer containing a copy of the summons which was published;

(2) An information or statement that the newspaper and the publication meet all legal requirements applicable to such publication;

(3) The dates of publication.

The return and affidavits shall be filed with the pleadings and other papers in the case and shall become a part of the record as provided in these rules.

Rule 4.14. Territorial limits and service under special order

(A) Territorial limits of effective service. Process may be served anywhere within the territorial limits of this state and outside the state as provided in these rules.

(B) Service under special order of court. Upon application of any party the court in which any action is pending may make an appropriate order for service in a manner not provided by these rules or statutes when such service is reasonably calculated to give the defendant actual knowledge of the proceedings and an opportunity to be heard.

Rule 4.15. Summons: Proof of Service—Return—Amendments—Defects

(A) Return—Form. The person making service shall promptly make his return upon or attach it to a copy of the summons which shall be delivered to the clerk. The return shall be signed by the person making it, and shall include a statement:

(1) that service was made upon the person as required by law and the time, place, and manner thereof;

(2) if service was not made, the particular manner in which it was thwarted in terms of fact or in terms of law;

(3) such other information as is expressly required by these rules.

(B) Return and affidavits as evidence. The return, along with the summons to which it is attached or is a part, the praecipe for summons, affidavits furnished with the summons or praecipe for summons, and all other affidavits permitted by these rules shall be filed by the clerk with the pleadings and other papers in the case and thereupon shall become a part of the record, and have such evidentiary effect as is now provided by law. Copies of such record shall be admissible in all actions and proceedings and may be entered in any public records when certified over the signature of the clerk or his deputy and the clerk's seal.

(C) Proof of filing and issuance dates. The clerk shall enter a filing date upon every praecipe, pleading, return, summons, affidavit or other paper filed with or entered of record by him. The clerk shall also enter an issuance date upon any summons issued, mailed or delivered by him, or other communication served or transmitted by him under these rules. Such filing or issuance date shall constitute evidence of the date of filing or issuance without further authentication when entered in the court records, or when the paper or a copy thereof is otherwise properly offered or admitted into evidence.

(D) Admission of service. A written admission stating the date and place of service, signed by the person being served, may be filed with the clerk who shall file it with the pleadings. Such admission shall become a part of the record, constitute evidence of proper service, and be allowed as evidence in any action or proceeding.

(E) Amendment. At any time in its discretion and upon such terms as it deems just, the court may allow any process or proof of service thereof to be amended unless it clearly appears that material prejudice would result to the substantial rights of the person against whom the process is issued.

(F) Defects in summons. No summons or the service thereof shall be set aside or be adjudged insufficient when either is reasonably calculated to inform the person to be served that an action has been instituted against him, the name of the court, and the time within which he is required to respond.

Rule 4.16. Summons: Duties of persons to aid in service

(A) It shall be the duty of every person being served under these rules to cooperate, accept service, comply with the provisions of these rules, and, when service is made upon him personally, acknowledge receipt of the papers in writing over his signature.

(1) Offering or tendering the papers to the person being served and advising the person that he or she is being served is adequate service.

(2) A person who has refused to accept the offer or tender of the papers being served thereafter may not challenge the service of those papers.

(B) Anyone accepting service for another person is under a duty to:

(1) promptly deliver the papers to that person;

(2) promptly notify that person that he holds the papers for him; or

(3) within a reasonable time, in writing, notify the clerk or person making the service that he has been unable to make such delivery of notice when such is the case.

(C) No person through whom service is made under these rules may impose any sanction, penalty, punishment, or discrimination whatsoever against the person being served because of such service. Any person willfully violating any provision of this rule may be subjected to contempt proceedings.

Amended Oct. 30, 1992, effective Jan. 1, 1993.

Rule 4.17. Summons: Certain proceedings excepted

Rules 4 through 4.16 shall not replace the manner of serving summons or giving notice as specially provided by statute or rule in proceedings involving, without limitation, the administration of decedent's estates, guardianships, receiverships, or assignments for the benefit of creditors.

Rule 5. Service and filing of pleading and other papers

(A) Service: When Required. Unless otherwise provided by these rules or an order of the court, each party and special judge, if any, shall be served with:

(1) every order required by its terms to be served;

(2) every pleading subsequent to the original complaint;

(3) every written motion except one which may be heard ex parte;

(4) every brief submitted to the trial court;

(5) every paper relating to discovery required to be served upon a party; and

(6) every written notice, appearance, demand, offer of judgment, designation of record on appeal, or similar paper.

No service need be made on parties in default for failure to appear, except that pleadings asserting new or additional claims for relief against them shall be served upon them in the manner provided by service of summons in Rule 4.

(B) Service: How made. Whenever a party is represented by an attorney of record, service shall be made upon such attorney unless service upon the party himself is ordered by the court. Service upon the attorney or party shall be made by delivering or mailing a copy of the papers to the last known address, or where an attorney or party has consented to service by FAX or e-mail as provided in Rule 3.1(A)(4), by faxing or e-mailing a copy of the documents to the fax number or e-mail address set out in the appearance form or correction as required by Rule 3.1(E).

(1) Delivery. Delivery of a copy within this rule means

(a) offering or tendering it to the attorney or party and stating the nature of the papers being served. Refusal to accept an offered or tendered document is a waiver of any objection to the sufficiency or adequacy of service of that document;

(b) leaving it at his office with a clerk or other person in charge thereof, or if there is no one in charge, leaving it in a conspicuous place therein; or

(c) if the office is closed, by leaving it at his dwelling house or usual place of abode with some person of suitable age and discretion then residing therein; or,

(d) leaving it at some other suitable place, selected by the attorney upon whom service is being made, pursuant to duly promulgated local rule.

(2) Service by Mail. If service is made by mail, the papers shall be deposited in the United States mail addressed to the person on whom they are being served, with postage prepaid. Service shall be deemed complete upon mailing. Proof of service of all papers permitted to be mailed may be made by written acknowledgment of service, by affidavit of the person who mailed the papers, or by certificate of an attorney. It shall be the duty of attorneys when entering their appearance in a cause or when filing pleadings or papers therein, to have noted in the Chronological Case Summary or said pleadings or papers so filed the address and telephone number of their office. Service by delivery or by mail at such address shall be deemed sufficient and complete.

(3) Service by FAX or e-mail. A party who has consented to service by FAX or e-mail may be served as follows:

a. Service by e-mail shall be made by attaching the document being served in .pdf format. Discovery documents must also be served in accordance with Trial Rule 26(A).

b. Service by FAX shall be deemed complete upon generation of a transmission record indicating the successful transmission of the entire document, except as provided in subparagraph d.

c. Service by e-mail shall be deemed complete upon transmission, except as provided in subparagraph d.

d. Service by FAX or e-mail that occurs on a Saturday, Sunday, a legal holiday, or a day the court or agency in which the matter is pending is closed, or after 5:00 p.m. local time of the recipient shall be deemed complete the next day that is not a Saturday, Sunday, legal holiday, or day that the court or agency in which the matter is pending is not closed.

(C) Certificate of Service. An attorney or unrepresented party tendering a document to the Clerk for filing shall certify that service has been made, list the parties served, and specify the date and means of service. The certificate of service shall be placed at the end of the document and shall not be separately filed. The separate filing of a certificate of service, however, shall not be grounds for rejecting a document for filing. The Clerk may permit documents to be filed without a certificate of service but shall require prompt filing of a separate certificate of service.

(D) Same: Numerous defendants. In any action in which there are unusually large numbers of defendants, the court, upon motion or of its own initiative, may order

(1) that service of the pleadings of the defendants and replies thereto need not be made as between the defendants;

(2) that any cross-claim, counterclaim, or matter constituting an avoidance or affirmative defense contained therein shall be deemed to be denied or avoided by all other parties; and

(3) that the filing of any such pleading and service thereof upon the plaintiff constitutes due notice of it to the parties.

A copy of every such order shall be served upon the parties in such manner and form as the court directs.

(E) Filing.

(1) Except as otherwise provided in subparagraph (2) hereof, all pleadings and papers subsequent to the complaint which are required to be served upon a party shall be filed with the Court either before service or within a reasonable period of time thereafter.

(2) No deposition or request for discovery or response thereto under Trial Rules 27, 30, 31, 33, 34 or 36 shall be filed with the Court unless:

(a) A motion is filed pursuant to Trial Rule 26(C) or Trial Rule 37 and the original deposition or request for discovery or response thereto is necessary to enable the Court to rule; or

(b) A party desires to use the deposition or request for discovery or response thereto for evidentiary purposes at trial or in connection with a motion, and the Court, either upon its own motion or that of any party, or as a part of any pre-trial order, orders the filing of the original.

(3) Custody of original and Period of Retention:

(a) The original of a deposition shall, subject to the provisions of Trial Rule 30(E), be delivered by the reporter to the party taking it and shall be maintained by that party until filed with the Court pursuant to paragraph (2) or until the later of final judgment, agreed settlement of the litigation or all appellate rights have been exhausted.

(b) The original or any request for discovery or response thereto under Trial Rules 27, 30, 31, 33, 34 and 36 shall be maintained by the party originating the request or response until filed with the Court pursuant to paragraph (2) or until the later of final judgment, agreed settlement or all appellate rights have been exhausted.

(4) In the event it is made to appear to the satisfaction of the Court that the original of a deposition or request for discovery or response thereto cannot be filed with the Court when required, the Court may allow use of a copy instead of the original.

(5) The filing of any deposition shall constitute publication.

(F) Filing With the Court Defined. The filing of pleadings, motions, and other papers with the court as required by these rules shall be made by one of the following methods:

(1) Delivery to the clerk of the court;

(2) Sending by electronic transmission under the procedure adopted pursuant to Administrative Rule 12;

(3) Mailing to the clerk by registered, certified or express mail return receipt requested;

(4) Depositing with any third-party commercial carrier for delivery to the clerk within three (3) calendar days, cost prepaid, properly addressed;

(5) If the court so permits, filing with the judge, in which event the judge shall note thereon the filing date and forthwith transmit them to the office of the clerk; or

(6) Electronic filing, as approved by the Division of State Court Administration pursuant to Administrative Rule 16.

Filing by registered or certified mail and by third-party commercial carrier shall be complete upon mailing or deposit

Any party filing any paper by any method other than personal delivery to the clerk shall retain proof of filing.

(G) Filing of Documents and Information Excluded from Public Access and Confidential Pursuant to Administrative rule 9(G)(1). Every document filed in a case shall separately identify information excluded from public access pursuant to Admin. R. 9(G)(1) as follows:

(1) Whole documents that are excluded from public access pursuant to Administrative Rule 9(G)(1) shall be tendered on light green paper or have a light green coversheet attached to the document, marked "Not for Public Access" or "Confidential."

(2) When only a portion of a document contains information excluded from public access pursuant to Administrative Rule 9(G)(1), said information shall be omitted [or redacted] from the filed document, and set forth on a separate accompanying document on light green paper conspicuously marked "Not for Public Access" or "Confidential" and clearly designated [or identifying] the caption and number of the case and the document and location within the document to which the redacted material pertains.

(3) With respect to documents filed in electronic format, the trial court, by local rule, may provide for compliance with this rule in manner that separates and protects access to information excluded from public access.

(4) This rule does not apply to a record sealed by the court pursuant to IC 5–14–3–5.5 or otherwise, nor to records, documents, or information filed in cases to which public access is prohibited pursuant to Administrative Rule (9)(G).

Amended Dec. 11, 1969, effective Jan. 1, 1970; amended Nov. 13, 1979, effective Jan. 1, 1980; Oct. 15, 1986, effective Jan. 1, 1987; Nov. 13, 1990, effective Jan. 1, 1991; Oct. 25, 1991, effective Jan. 1, 1992; Oct. 30, 1992, effective Jan. 1, 1993; Dec. 4, 1998, effective Jan. 1, 1999; Dec. 21, 2001, effective April 1, 2002; July 1, 2003, effective Jan. 1, 2004; Sept. 30, 2004, effective Jan. 1, 2005; amended effective Feb. 11, 2005; July 1, 2005, effective Jan. 1, 2006; Sept. 9, 2008, effective Jan. 1, 2009; Sept. 21, 2010, effective Jan. 1, 2011; Sept. 7, 2012, effective Jan. 1, 2013.

Rule 6. Time

(A) Computation. In computing any period of time prescribed or allowed by these rules, by order of the court, or by any applicable statute, the day of the act, event, or default from which the designated period of time begins to run shall not be included. The last day of the period so computed is to be included unless it is:

(1) a Saturday,

(2) a Sunday,

(3) a legal holiday as defined by state statute, or

(4) a day the office in which the act is to be done is closed during regular business hours.

In any event, the period runs until the end of the next day that is not a Saturday, a Sunday, a legal holiday, or a day on which the office is closed. When the period of time allowed is less than seven [7] days, intermediate Saturdays, Sundays, legal holidays, and days on which the office is closed shall be excluded from the computations.

(B) Enlargement. When an act is required or allowed to be done at or within a specific time by these rules, the court may at any time for cause shown:

(1) order the period enlarged, with or without motion or notice, if request therefor is made before the expiration of the period originally prescribed or extended by a previous order; or

(2) upon motion made after the expiration of the specific period, permit the act to be done where the failure to act was the result of excusable neglect; but, the court may not extend the time for taking any action for judgment on the evidence under Rule 50(A), amendment of findings and judgment under Rule 52(B), to correct errors under Rule 59(C), statement in opposition to motion to correct error under Rule 59(E), or to obtain relief from final judgment under Rule 60(B), except to the extent and under the conditions stated in those rules.

(C) Service of pleadings and Rule 12 motions. A responsive pleading required under these rules, shall be served within twenty [20] days after service of the prior pleading. Unless the court specifies otherwise, a reply shall be served within twenty [20] days after entry of an order requiring it. The service of a motion permitted under Rule 12 alters the time for service of responsive pleadings as follows, unless a different time is fixed by the court:

(1) if the court does not grant the motion, the responsive pleading shall be served in ten [10] days after notice of the court's action;

(2) if the court grants the motion and the corrective action is allowed to be taken, it shall be taken within ten [10] days, and the responsive pleading shall be served within ten [10] days thereafter.

(D) For motions—Affidavits. A written motion, other than one which may be heard ex parte, and notice of the hearing thereof shall be served not less than five [5] days before the time specified for the hearing, unless a different period is fixed by these rules or by order of the court. Such an order may, for cause shown, be made on ex parte application. When a motion is supported by affidavit, the affidavit shall be served with the motion; and, except as otherwise provided in Rule 59(D), opposing affidavits may be served not less than one [1] day before the hearing, unless the court permits them to be served at some other time.

(E) Additional time after service by United States mail. Whenever a party has the right or is required to do some act or take some proceedings within a prescribed period after the service of a notice or other paper upon him and the notice or paper is served upon him by United States mail, three [3] days shall be added to the prescribed period.

(F) Dissolution Actions—Sixty-day waiting period. No cause for dissolution of marriage or for legal separation shall be tried or heard by any court until after the expiration of sixty (60) days from the date of the filing of the petition or from the date of publication of the first notice to a nonresident.

Amended Feb. 25, 1970; amended Dec. 7, 1970, effective Jan. 1, 1971; amended Nov. 3, 1981, effective Jan. 1, 1982; amended effective Nov. 10, 1988; amended Nov. 10, 1988, effective Jan. 1, 1989; Sept. 7, 2012, effective Jan. 1, 2013.

III. PLEADINGS AND MOTIONS

Rule 7. Pleadings allowed—Form of motion

(A) Pleadings. The pleadings shall consist of:

(1) a complaint and an answer;

(2) a reply to a denominated counterclaim;

(3) an answer to a cross-claim;

(4) a third-party complaint, if a person not an original party is summoned under the provisions of Rule 14; and

(5) a third-party answer.

No other pleadings shall be allowed; but the court may, in its discretion, order a reply to an answer or third-party answer. Matters formerly required to be pleaded by a reply or other subsequent pleading may be proved even though they are not pleaded.

(B) Motions and other papers. Unless made during a hearing or trial, or otherwise ordered by the court, an application to the court for an order shall be made by written motion. The motion shall state the grounds therefor and the relief or order sought. The requirement of notice is satisfied by service of the motion.

(C) Demurrers, pleas, etc., abolished. Demurrers, pleas in abatement, and exceptions for insufficiency of a pleading or improper service shall not be used. All objections and defenses formerly raised by such motions shall now be raised pursuant to Rule 12.

Rule 8.   General rules of pleading

(A) Claims for Relief. To state a claim for relief, whether an original claim, counterclaim, cross-claim, or third-party claim, a pleading must contain:

    (1) a short and plain statement of the claim showing that the pleader is entitled to relief, and

    (2) a demand for relief to which the pleader deems entitled. Relief in the alternative or of several different types may be demanded. However, in any complaint seeking damages for personal injury or death, or seeking punitive damages, no dollar amount or figure shall be included in the demand.

(B) Defenses: Form of denials. A responsive pleading shall state in short and plain terms the pleader's defenses to each claim asserted and shall admit or controvert the averments set forth in the preceding pleading. If in good faith the pleader intends to deny all the averments in the preceding pleading, he may do so by general denial subject to the provisions of Rule 11. If he does not intend a general denial, he may:

    (1) specifically deny designated averments or paragraphs; or

    (2) generally deny all averments except such designated averments and paragraphs as he expressly admits.

If he lacks knowledge or information sufficient to form a belief as to the truth of an averment, he shall so state and his statement shall be considered a denial. If in good faith a pleader intends to deny only a part or a qualification of an averment, he shall specify so much of it as is true and material and deny the remainder. All denials shall fairly meet the substance of the averments denied. This rule shall have no application to uncontested actions for divorce, or to answers required to be filed by clerks or guardians ad litem.

(C) Affirmative defenses. A responsive pleading shall set forth affirmatively and carry the burden of proving: accord and satisfaction, arbitration and award, discharge in bankruptcy, duress, estoppel, failure of consideration, fraud, illegality, injury by fellow servant, laches, license, payment, release, res judicata, statute of frauds, statute of limitations, waiver, lack of jurisdiction over the subject-matter, lack of jurisdiction over the person, improper venue, insufficiency of process or service of process, the same action pending in another state court of this state, and any other

matter constituting an avoidance, matter of abatement, or affirmative defense. A party required to affirmatively plead any matters, including matters formerly required to be pleaded affirmatively by reply, shall have the burden of proving such matters. The burden of proof imposed by this or any other provision of these rules is subject to the rules of evidence or any statute fixing a different rule. If the pleading mistakenly designates a defense as a counterclaim or a counterclaim as a defense, the court shall treat the pleading as if there had been a proper designation.

(D) Effect of failure to deny. Averments in a pleading to which a responsive pleading is required, except those pertaining to amount of damages, are admitted when not denied in the responsive pleading. Averments in a pleading to which no responsive pleading is required or permitted shall be taken as denied or avoided.

(E) All pleadings to be concise and direct—Consistency.

    (1) Each averment of a pleading shall be simple, concise, and direct. No technical forms of pleading or motions are required. All fictions in pleading are abolished.

    (2) A pleading may set forth two [2] or more statements of a claim or defense alternatively or hypothetically, either in one [1] count or defense or in separate counts or defenses. When two [2] or more statements are made in the alternative and one [1] of them if made independently would be sufficient, the pleading is not made insufficient by the insufficiency of one or more of the alternative statements. A pleading may also state as many separate claims or defenses as the pleader has regardless of consistency and whether based on legal or equitable grounds. All statements shall be made subject to the obligations set forth in Rule 11.

    (3) Motions and pleadings, joint and several. All motions and pleadings of any kind addressed to two [2] or more paragraphs of any pleading, or filed by two [2] or more parties, shall be taken and construed as joint, separate, and several motions or pleadings to each of such paragraphs and by and against each of such parties. All motions or pleadings containing two [2] or more subject-matters shall be taken and construed as separate and several as to each subject-matter. All objections to rulings made by two [2] or more parties shall be taken and construed as the joint, separate, and several objections of each of such parties.

A complaint filed by or against two [2] or more plaintiffs shall be taken and construed as joint, separate, and several as to each of said plaintiffs.

(F) Construction of pleadings. All pleadings shall be so construed as to do substantial justice, lead to disposition on the merits, and avoid litigation of procedural points.

Amended effective Sept. 16, 1987; amended Dec. 30, 1991, effective Feb. 1, 1992.

Rule 9. Pleading special matters

(A) Capacity. It is not necessary to aver the capacity of a party to sue or be sued, the authority of a party to sue or be sued in a representative capacity, or the legal existence of an organization that is made a party. The burden of proving lack of such capacity, authority, or legal existence shall be upon the person asserting lack of it, and shall be pleaded as an affirmative defense.

(B) Fraud, mistake, condition of the mind. In all averments of fraud or mistake, the circumstances constituting fraud or mistake shall be specifically averred. Malice, intent, knowledge, and other conditions of mind may be averred generally.

(C) Conditions precedent. In pleading the performance or occurrence of promissory or non-promissory conditions precedent, it is sufficient to aver generally that all conditions precedent have been performed, have occurred, or have been excused. A denial of performance or occurrence shall be made specifically and with particularity, and a denial of excuse generally.

(D) Official document or act. In pleading an official document or official act it is sufficient to aver that the document was issued or the act done in compliance with law.

(E) Judgment. In pleading a judgment or decision of a domestic or foreign court, judicial or quasi-judicial tribunal, or of a board or officer, it is sufficient to aver the judgment or decision without setting forth matter showing jurisdiction to render it.

(F) Time and place. For the purpose of testing the sufficiency of a pleading, averments of time and place are material and shall be considered like all other averments of material matter. However, time and place need be stated only with such specificity as will enable the opposing party to prepare his defense.

(G) Special damages—Damages where no answer. When items of special damage are claimed, they shall be specifically stated. The relief granted to the plaintiff, if there be no answer, cannot exceed the relief demanded in his complaint; but, in any other case, the court may grant him any relief consistent with the facts or matters pleaded.

Rule 9.1. Pleading and proof of contributory negligence, assumed risk, res ipsa loquitur, consideration, bona fide purchaser, matters of judicial notice—Answer of distraint

(A) Defense of contributory negligence or assumed risk. In all claims alleging negligence, the burden of pleading and proving contributory negligence, assumption of risk, or incurred risk shall be

upon the defendant who may plead such by denial of the allegation.

(B) Res ipsa loquitur. Res ipsa loquitur or a similar doctrine may be pleaded by alleging generally that the facts connected with the action are unknown to the pleader and are within the knowledge of the opposing party.

(C) Consideration. When an action or defense is founded upon a written contract or release, lack of consideration for the promise or release is an affirmative defense, and the party asserting lack of it carries the burden of proof.

(D) Bona fide purchaser. When the rights of a person depend upon his status as a bona fide purchaser for value or upon similar requirements, such status must be pleaded and proved by the person asserting it, but it may be pleaded in general terms. Once it is established that the person has given any required value, unless such value is commercially unreasonable, and that he has met any requirements of recordation, filing, possession, or perfection, the trier of fact must find that such value was given or such perfection was made in accordance with any requirements of good faith, lack of knowledge, or lack of notice unless and until evidence is introduced which would support a finding of its non-existence.

(E) Presumption—Matters of judicial notice. Neither presumptions of law nor matters of which judicial notice may be taken need be stated in a pleading.

(F) Property distrained—Sufficient answer. In an action to recover the possession of property distrained while doing damage, an answer that the defendant, or person by whose command he acted, was lawfully possessed of the real property upon which the distress was made, and that the property distrained was at the time doing damage thereon, shall be good without setting forth the title of such real property.

Rule 9.2. Pleading and proof of written instruments

(A) When instrument or copy, or an Affidavit of Debt must be filed. When any pleading allowed by these rules is founded on a written instrument, the original, or a copy thereof, must be included in or filed with the pleading. Such instrument, whether copied in the pleadings or not, shall be taken as part of the record. When any pleading allowed by these rules is founded on an account, an Affidavit of Debt, in a form substantially similar to that which is provided in Appendix A–2 to these rules, shall be attached.

(B) Proof of execution of instruments filed with pleadings. When a pleading is founded on a written instrument and the instrument or a copy thereof is included in or filed with the pleading, execution of such instrument, indorsement, or assignment shall be deemed to be established and the instrument, if otherwise admissible, shall be deemed admitted into evidence in the action without proving its execution unless execution be denied under oath in the responsive pleading or by an affidavit filed therewith. A denial asserting that another person who is not a party did execute the instrument, indorsement, or assignment may be made without such oath or affidavit only if the pleader alleges under oath or in an accompanying affidavit that after the exercise of reasonable diligence he was unable to make such person or his representative (subdivision (H)) a party, the reason therefor, and that he is without information as to such execution.

(C) Oath or affidavit of denial of execution must be made upon personal knowledge. An oath or affidavit denying execution as required and made under subdivision (B) of this rule shall be made upon the personal knowledge of the person making it, and, if general in form (Rule 11(B)), shall be deemed to be made upon such personal knowledge.

(D) Burden of proving execution. The ultimate burden of proving the execution of a written instrument is upon the party claiming its validity, but execution is presumed. "Presumed" means that the trier of fact must find the existence of the fact presumed unless and until evidence is introduced which would support a finding of its nonexistence.

(E) Inspection of the original instrument. When a copy of a written instrument is filed with or copied in the pleadings under the provisions of this rule, the pleader shall permit inspection of the original unless it is alleged that the original is lost, whether by destruction, theft or otherwise, or unless it is alleged or established that the instrument is in the possession of another person and out of the control of the pleader or that the duty to allow inspection is otherwise excused. The pleader shall allow inspection promptly upon request of a party, and inspection may be ordered by the court upon motion without a hearing at any time. A party failing to comply with such request or such order shall be subject to the provisions of Rule 37(B). This provision shall not diminish a party's rights under Rules 26 through 38.

(F) Effect of non-compliance—Amendments. Non-compliance with the provisions of this rule requiring a written instrument or an Affidavit of Debt to be included with the pleading may be raised by the first responsive pleading or prior motion of a party. The court, in its sound discretion, may order compliance, the reasons for noncompliance to be added to the pleadings, or allow the action to continue without further pleading. Amendments to correct the omission of a required written instrument, an assignment or indorsement thereof, the omission of a denial of the execution of a written instrument as permitted or required by this rule, or an Affidavit of Debt shall be governed by Rule 15, except as provided by subdivision (A) of this rule.

(G) Exceptions—Infants, incompetents, dead and insolvent persons. The requirement of this rule that execution of a written instrument be denied under oath or otherwise, shall not apply against a party who is not required to file a responsive pleading, or against a party who, at the time the responsive pleading is due or before the pleadings are closed, is or becomes dead, an infant or adjudicated incompetent or is the representative of such person or of a person who is dead, an infant, an adjudicated incompetent, or in insolvency proceedings. Such parties shall be deemed to have denied execution or admissibility without any responsive pleading or denial. The presumption of execution as provided in subdivision (D) of this rule shall not apply to establish execution of a written instrument by a person who, at the time proof is required, is dead, an infant or adjudicated incompetent.

(H) "Execution" of a written instrument. "Execution" of a written instrument includes the following requirements:

(1) That a signature was made with express, implied or apparent authority and was not forged;

(2) That the instrument was properly delivered, including any requisite intent that it be effective;

(3) That the written terms of the instrument have not been materially altered without the express, implied or apparent authority of the person bound thereon;

(4) That the person seeking its enforcement is in possession of the instrument when required; and

(5) That the names or identity of the persons named in the instrument are correct.

(I) "Written instrument": When pleading is founded thereon—When pleading is not founded thereon term includes documents. When a pleading is founded upon a written instrument, any written indorsement or assignment of rights thereof upon which the pleader's title depends is included in the term "written instrument."

Amended Sept. 21, 2010, effective Jan. 1, 2011.

Rule 10.   Form of pleading

(A) Caption—Names of parties. Every pleading shall contain a caption setting forth the name of the court, the title of the action, the file number, and a designation as in Rule 7(A). In the complaint the title of the action shall include the names of all the parties, but in other pleadings it is sufficient to state the name of the first party on each side with an appropriate indication of other parties.

(B) Paragraphs—Separate statements. All averments of a claim or defense shall be made in numbered paragraphs, the contents of each of which shall be limited as far as practicable to a statement of a single set of circumstances, and a paragraph may be referred to by number in all succeeding pleadings. Each claim founded upon a separate transaction or occurrence and each defense other than denials may be stated in a separate count or defense whenever a separation facilitates the clear presentation of the matters set forth.

(C) Adoption by reference—Exhibits. Statements in a pleading may be adopted by reference in a different part of the same pleading or in another pleading or in any motion. A copy of any written instrument which is an exhibit to a pleading is a part thereof for all purposes.

Rule 11. Signing and verification of pleadings

(A) Parties Represented by Attorney. Every pleading or motion of a party represented by an attorney shall be signed by at least one [1] attorney of record in his individual name, whose address, telephone number, and attorney number shall be stated, except that this provision shall not apply to pleadings and motions made and transcribed at the trial or a hearing before the judge and received by him in such form. A party who is not represented by an attorney shall sign his pleading and state his address. Except when specifically required by rule, pleadings or motions need not be verified or accompanied by affidavit. The rule in equity that the averments of an answer under oath must be overcome by the testimony of two [2] witnesses or of one [1] witness sustained by corroborating circumstances is abolished. The signature of an attorney constitutes a certificate by him that he has read the pleadings; that to the best of his knowledge, information, and belief, there is good ground to support it; and that it is not interposed for delay. If a pleading or motion is not signed or is signed with intent to defeat the purpose of the rule, it may be stricken as sham and false and the action may proceed as though the pleading had not been served. For a willful violation of this rule an attorney may be subjected to appropriate disciplinary action. Similar action may be taken if scandalous or indecent matter is inserted.

(B) Verification by affirmation or representation. When in connection with any civil or special statutory proceeding it is required that any pleading, motion, petition, supporting affidavit, or other document of any kind, be verified, or that an oath be taken, it shall be sufficient if the subscriber simply affirms the truth of the matter to be verified by an affirmation or representation in substantially the following language:

"I (we) affirm, under the penalties for perjury, that the foregoing representation(s) is (are) true.

(Signed) _____ "

Any person who falsifies an affirmation or representation of fact shall be subject to the same penalties as are prescribed by law for the making of a false affidavit.

(C) Verified pleadings, motions, and affidavits as evidence. Pleadings, motions and affidavits accompa-

nying or in support of such pleadings or motions when required to be verified or under oath shall be accepted as a representation that the signer had personal knowledge thereof or reasonable cause to believe the existence of the facts or matters stated or alleged therein; and, if otherwise competent or acceptable as evidence, may be admitted as evidence of the facts or matters stated or alleged therein when it is so provided in these rules, by statute or other law, or to the extent the writing or signature expressly purports to be made upon the signer's personal knowledge. When such pleadings, motions and affidavits are verified or under oath they shall not require other or greater proof on the part of the adverse party than if not verified or not under oath unless expressly provided otherwise by these rules, statute or other law. Affidavits upon motions for summary judgment under Rule 56 and in denial of execution under Rule 9.2 shall be made upon personal knowledge.

Amended Oct. 30, 1992, effective Jan. 1, 1993.

Rule 12. Defenses and objections — When and how presented — By pleading or motion — Motion for judgment on the pleadings

(A) When presented. The time allowed for the presentation of defenses and objections in a motion or responsive pleading shall be computed pursuant to the provisions of Rule 6(C).

(B) How presented. Every defense, in law or fact, to a claim for relief in any pleading, whether a claim, counterclaim, cross-claim, or third-party claim, shall be asserted in the responsive pleading thereto if one is required; except that at the option of the pleader, the following defenses may be made by motion:

(1) Lack of jurisdiction over the subject matter,

(2) Lack of jurisdiction over the person,

(3) Incorrect venue under Trial Rule 75, or any statutory provision. The disposition of this motion shall be consistent with Trial Rule 75,

(4) Insufficiency of process;

(5) Insufficiency of service of process;

(6) Failure to state a claim upon which relief can be granted, which shall include failure to name the real party in interest under Rule 17;

(7) Failure to join a party needed for just adjudication under Rule 19;

(8) The same action pending in another state court of this state.

A motion making any of these defenses shall be made before pleading if a further pleading is permitted or within twenty [20] days after service of the prior pleading if none is required. If a pleading sets forth a claim for relief to which the adverse party is not required to serve a responsive pleading, any of the defenses in section (B)(2), (3), (4), (5) or (8) is waived to the extent constitutionally permissible unless made in a motion within twenty [20] days after service of the prior pleading. No defense or objection is waived by being joined with one or more other defenses or objections in a responsive pleading or motion.

When a motion to dismiss is sustained for failure to state a claim under subdivision (B)(6) of this rule the pleading may be amended once as of right pursuant to Rule 15(A) within ten [10] days after service of notice of the court's order sustaining the motion and thereafter with permission of the court pursuant to such rule.

If, on a motion, asserting the defense number (6), to dismiss for failure of the pleading to state a claim upon which relief can be granted, matters outside the pleading are presented to and not excluded by the court, the motion shall be treated as one for summary judgment and disposed of as provided in Rule 56. In such case, all parties shall be given reasonable opportunity to present all material made pertinent to such a motion by Rule 56.

(C) Motion for judgment on the pleadings. After the pleadings are closed but within such time as not to delay the trial, any party may move for judgment on the pleadings. If, on a motion for judgment on the pleadings, matters outside the pleadings are presented to and not excluded by the court, the motion shall be treated as one for summary judgment and disposed of as provided in Rule 56, and all parties shall be given reasonable opportunity to present all material made pertinent to such a motion by Rule 56.

(D) Preliminary determination. Whether made in a pleading or by motion, the defenses specifically enumerated (1) to (8) in subdivision (B) of this rule, and the motion for judgment on the pleadings mentioned in subdivision (C) of this rule shall, upon application of any party or by order of court, be determined before trial unless substantial justice requires the court to defer hearing until trial.

(E) Motion for more definite statement. If a pleading to which a responsive pleading is permitted is so vague or ambiguous that a party cannot reasonably be required to frame a responsive pleading, he may move for a more definite statement before interposing his responsive pleading. The motion shall point out the defects complained of and the details desired. If the motion is granted and the order of the court is not obeyed within twenty [20] days after notice of the order or within such other time as the court may fix, the court may strike the pleading to which the motion was directed or make such order as it deems just.

(F) Motion to strike. Upon motion made by a party before responding to a pleading, or, if no responsive pleading is permitted by these rules, upon motion made by a party within twenty [20] days after the service of the pleading upon him or at any time upon the court's own initiative, the court may order stricken from any pleading any insufficient claim or defense or any redundant, immaterial, impertinent, or scandalous matter.

(G) Consolidation of defenses in motion. A party who makes a motion under this rule may join with it any other motions herein provided for and then available to him. If a party makes a motion under this rule but omits therefrom any defense or objection then available to him which this rule permits to be raised by motion, he shall not thereafter make a motion based on the defense or objection so omitted. He may, however, make such motions as are allowed under subdivision (H)(2) of this rule.

(H) Waiver or preservation of certain defenses.

(1) A defense of lack of jurisdiction over the person, improper venue, insufficiency of process, insufficiency of service of process, or the same action pending in another state court of this state is waived to the extent constitutionally permissible:

(a) if omitted from a motion in the circumstances described in subdivision (G),

(b) if it is neither made by motion under this rule nor included in a responsive pleading or an amendment thereof permitted by Rule 15(A) to be made as a matter of course.

(2) A defense of failure to state a claim upon which relief can be granted, a defense of failure to join an indispensable party under Rule 19(B), and an objection of failure to state a legal defense to a claim may be made in any pleading permitted or ordered under Rule 7(A) or by motion for judgment on the pleadings, or at the trial on the merits.

Amended Oct. 15, 1986, effective Jan. 1, 1987; Aug. 15, 2006, effective Jan. 1, 2007.

Rule 13. Counterclaim and cross-claim

(A) Compulsory counterclaims. A pleading shall state as a counterclaim any claim which at the time of serving the pleading the pleader has against any opposing party, if it arises out of the transaction or occurrence that is the subject-matter of the opposing party's claim and does not require for its adjudication the presence of third parties of whom the court cannot acquire jurisdiction. But the pleader need not state the claim if:

(1) at the time the action was commenced the claim was the subject of another pending action; or

(2) the opposing party brought suit upon his claim by attachment or other process by which the court did not acquire jurisdiction to render a personal judgment on that claim, and the pleader is not stating any counterclaim under this rule.

(B) Permissive counterclaims. A pleading may state as a counterclaim any claim against an opposing party not arising out of the transaction or occurrence that is the subject-matter of the opposing party's claim.

(C) Counterclaim exceeding opposing claim. A counterclaim may or may not diminish or defeat the recovery sought by the opposing party. It may claim relief exceeding in amount or different in kind from that sought in the pleading of the opposing party.

(D) Counterclaim against state. This rule shall not be construed to enlarge any right to assert a claim against the state.

(E) Counterclaim maturing or acquired after pleading. A claim which either matured or was acquired by the pleader after serving his pleading may, with the permission of the court, be presented as a counterclaim by supplemental pleading. A counterclaim or cross-claim which is not due may be asserted against a party who is insolvent or the representative of a party who has been subjected to insolvency proceedings, if recovery thereon will be impaired because of such party's insolvency.

(F) Omitted counterclaim. When a pleader fails to set up a counterclaim through oversight, inadvertence, or excusable neglect, or when justice requires, he may by leave of court set up the counterclaim by amendment.

(G) Cross-claim against co-party. A pleading may state as a cross-claim any claim by one party against a co-party.

(H) Joinder of additional parties. Persons other than those made parties to the original action may be made parties to a counterclaim or cross-claim in accordance with the provisions of Rules 14, 19 and 20.

(I) Separate trials—Separate judgments. If the court orders separate trials as provided in Rule 42(B), judgment on a counterclaim or cross-claim may be rendered in accordance with the terms of Rule 54(B) when the court has jurisdiction so to do, even if the claims of the opposing party have been dismissed or otherwise disposed of. In determining whether or not separate trial of a cross-claim shall be ordered, the court shall consider whether the cross-claim:

(1) arises out of the transaction or occurrence or series of transactions or occurrences that is the subject-matter either of the original action or of a counterclaim therein;

(2) relates to any property or contract that is the subject-matter of the original action; or

(3) claims that the person against whom it is asserted is liable to the cross-claimant for all or part of plaintiff's claim against him.

In addition, the court may consider any other relevant factors.

(J) Effect of statute of limitations and other discharges at law. The statute of limitations, a nonclaim statute or other discharge at law shall not bar a claim asserted as a counterclaim to the extent that:

(1) it diminishes or defeats the opposing party's claim if it arises out of the transaction or occurrence that is the subject-matter of the opposing party's claim, or if it could have been asserted as a counterclaim to the opposing party's claim before it (the counterclaim) was barred; or

(2) it or the opposing party's claim relates to payment of or security for the other.

(K) Counterclaim by and against transferees and successors. A counterclaim may be asserted by or against the transferee or successor of a claim subject to the following provisions:

(1) A successor who is a guardian, representative of a decedent's estate, receiver or assignee for the benefit of creditors, trustee or the like may interpose a claim to which he succeeds against claims or proceedings brought in or outside the court of administration. A claim owing by his predecessor may be interposed against any claim brought by such successor in or outside the court of administration without the necessity of filing such claim or cause of action in the administration proceedings.

(2) A transferee or successor of a claim takes it subject to any defense or counterclaim that is the subject-matter of the opposing party's claim; or that is available to the obligor at the time of the assignment or before the obligor received notice of the assignment.

(3) A surety or party with total or partial recourse upon a claim upon which he is being sued may interpose as a counterclaim:

(a) any claim of his own; and

(b) any claim owned by the person against whom he has recourse who either has notice of the suit, is a party to the suit, is insolvent, has assigned his claim to the surety or party asserting it, or cannot be found.

A counterclaim under subdivision (b) must tend to diminish or defeat the opposing party's claim, or it or the opposing claim must relate to payment of or security for the other, unless the person against whom recourse may be had is a party to the suit or the counterclaim has been assigned to the party asserting it; and if recovery on the counterclaim exceeds the opposing party's claim, any excess recovered shall be held in trust for such person against whom there is a right of recourse.

(4) Subsections (1), (2), and (3), above, are subject to subdivision (L) of this rule.

(L) Counterclaim and cross-claim subject to substantive law principles. Counterclaim and cross-claims are subject to restrictions imposed by other statutes and principles of substantive common law and equity, including rules of commercial law, agency, estoppel, contract and the like. In appropriate cases the court may impose terms or conditions upon its judgment or decree and may enter conditional or noncanceling cross judgments to satisfy such restrictions. This provision is intended to deny or limit counterclaims or cross-claims:

(1) where a creditor will receive an unfair priority because a claim is assigned after insolvency pro-

ceedings, or assigned before such proceedings if it results in an unlawful preference;

(2) where an unfair priority will be allowed if a surety interposing a claim owned in his own right against the creditor suing on the principal's obligation when the principal is solvent and the creditor is not;

(3) where a claim by or against a representative, such as a guardian, receiver, representative of a decedent's estate, assignee for the benefit of creditors, trustee or the like in his individual capacity is asserted against a claim owing or owed by the estate he represents;

(4) where a claim by or against a partnership or two [2] or more obligors is opposed against or by a claim of an individual to the extent that the individual will be allowed unfairly to profit or if it will adversely affect the rights of creditors; or

(5) where a claim is cut off by a holder in due course or a transferee who is protected under principles of commercial law, estoppel, or contract.

(M) Satisfaction of judgment. Satisfaction of a judgment or credits thereon may be ordered, for sufficient cause, upon notice and motion. "Credits" include any counterclaim which tends to diminish or defeat the judgment, or any counterclaim where it or the opposing claim relates to payment of or security for the other.

Amended Dec. 7, 1970, effective Jan. 1, 1971.

Rule 14.   Third-party practice

(A) When defendant may bring in third party. A defending party, as a third-party plaintiff, may cause a summons and complaint to be served upon a person not a party to the action who is or may be liable to him for all or part of the plaintiff's claim against him. The third-party plaintiff must file the third-party complaint with his original answer or by leave of court thereafter with good cause shown. The person served with the summons and the third-party complaint, hereinafter called the third-party defendant, as provided in Rules 12 and 13 may make:

(1) his defenses, cross-claims and counterclaims to the third-party plaintiff's claims;

(2) his defenses, counterclaims and cross-claims against any other defendants or third-party defendants;

(3) any defenses or claims which the third-party plaintiff has to the plaintiff's claim which are available to the third-party defendant against the plaintiff; and

(4) any defenses or claims which the third-party defendant has as against the plaintiff.

The plaintiff may assert any claim against the third-party defendant who thereupon may assert his defenses, counterclaims and cross-claims, as provided in Rules 12 and 13. A third-party defendant may pro-

ceed under this rule against any person not a party to the action who is or may be liable to him for all or part of the claim made in the action against the third-party defendant.

(B) When plaintiff may bring in third party. When a counterclaim or other claim is asserted against a plaintiff, he may cause a third party to be brought in under circumstances, which, under this rule, would entitle a defendant to do so.

(C) Severance—Parties improperly impleaded. With his responsive pleading or by motion prior thereto, any party may move for severance of a third-party claim or ensuing claim as provided in this rule or for a separate trial thereon. If the third-party defendant is a proper party to the proceedings under any other rule relating to parties, the action shall continue as in other cases where he is made a party.

Amended Dec. 7, 1970, effective Jan. 1, 1971.

Rule 15.   Amended and supplemental pleadings

(A) Amendments. A party may amend his pleading once as a matter of course at any time before a responsive pleading is served or, if the pleading is one to which no responsive pleading is permitted, and the action has not been placed upon the trial calendar, he may so amend it at any time within thirty [30] days after it is served. Otherwise a party may amend his pleading only by leave of court or by written consent of the adverse party; and leave shall be given when justice so requires. A party shall plead in response to an amended pleading within the time remaining for response to the original pleading or within twenty [20] days after service of the amended pleading, whichever period may be the longer, unless the court otherwise orders.

(B) Amendments to conform to the evidence. When issues not raised by the pleadings are tried by express or implied consent of the parties, they shall be treated in all respects as if they had been raised in the pleadings. Such amendment of the pleadings as may be necessary to cause them to conform to the evidence and to raise these issues may be made upon motion of any party at any time, even after judgment, but failure so to amend does not affect the result of the trial of these issues. If evidence is objected to at the trial on the ground that it is not within the issues made by the pleadings, the court may allow the pleadings to be amended and shall do so freely when the presentation of the merits of the action will be subserved thereby and the objecting party fails to satisfy the court that the admission of such evidence would prejudice him in maintaining his action or defense upon the merits. The court may grant a continuance to enable the objecting party to meet such evidence.

(C) Relation back of amendments. Whenever the claim or defense asserted in the amended pleading arose out of the conduct, transaction, or occurrence set forth or attempted to be set forth in the original pleading, the amendment relates back to the date of the original pleading. An amendment changing the party against whom a claim is asserted relates back if the foregoing provision is satisfied and, within one hundred and twenty (120) days of commencement of the action, the party to be brought in by amendment:

(1) has received such notice of the institution of the action that he will not be prejudiced in maintaining his defense on the merits; and

(2) knew or should have known that but for a mistake concerning the identity of the proper party, the action would have been brought against him.

The requirement of subsections (1) and (2) hereof with respect to a governmental organization to be brought into the action as defendant is satisfied:

(1) In the case of a state or governmental organization by delivery or mailing of process to the attorney general or to a governmental executive [Rule 4.6(A)(3)]; or

(2) In the case of a local governmental organization, by delivery or mailing of process to its attorney as provided by statute, to a governmental executive thereof [Rule 4.6(A)(4)], or to the officer holding the office if suit is against the officer or an office.

(D) Supplemental pleadings. Upon motion of a party the court may, upon reasonable notice and upon such terms as are just, permit him to serve a supplemental pleading setting forth transactions or occurrences or events which have happened since the date of the pleading sought to be supplemented. Permission may be granted even though the original pleading is defective in its statement of a claim for relief or defense. If the court deems it advisable that the adverse party plead to the supplemental pleading, it shall so order, specifying the time therefor.

Amended Dec. 21, 2001, effective April 1, 2002.

Rule 16. Pre-trial procedure: Formulating issues

(A) When required—Purpose. In any action except criminal cases, the court may in its discretion and shall upon the motion of any party, direct the attorneys for the parties to appear before it for a conference to consider:

(1) the simplification of the issues;

(2) the necessity or desirability of amendments to the pleadings;

(3) the possibility of obtaining admissions of fact and of documents which will avoid unnecessary proof;

(4) a limitation of the number of expert witnesses;

(5) an exchange of names of witnesses to be called during the trial and the general nature of their expected testimony;

(6) the desirability of using one or more types of alternative dispute resolution under the rules therefor;

(7) the desirability of setting deadlines for dispositive motions in light of the date set for trial; and

(8) such other matters as may aid in the disposition of the action.

(B) When called—Notice—Participants. Unless otherwise ordered by the court the pre-trial conference shall not be called until after reasonable opportunity for the completion of discovery.

(1) *Notice.* The clerks shall give at least thirty [30] days' notice of the pre-trial conference unless otherwise directed by the court.

(2) *Participants.* At least one [1] attorney planning to take part in the trial shall appear for each of the parties and participate in the pre-trial conference.

(C) Conference of attorneys. Unless otherwise ordered by the court, at least ten [10] days prior to the pre-trial conference, attorneys for each of the parties shall meet and confer for the following purposes:

(1) *Exhibits.* Each attorney shall mark for identification and provide opposing counsel an opportunity to inspect and copy all exhibits which he expects to introduce at the trial. Numbers or marks placed on such exhibits shall be prefixed with the symbol "P/T", denoting its pre-trial designation. When the exhibit is introduced at the trial of the case, the "P/T" designation will be stricken and the exhibits must also indicate the party identifying same.

Exhibits of the character which prohibit or make impracticable their production at conference shall be identified and notice given of their intended use. Necessary arrangements must be made to afford opposing counsel an opportunity to examine such exhibits.

(2) *Exhibit stipulations.* Written stipulations shall be prepared with reference to all exhibits exchanged or identified. The stipulations shall contain all agreements of the parties with reference to the exchanged and identified exhibits, and shall include, but not be limited to, the agreement of the parties with reference to the authenticity of the exhibits, their admissibility in evidence, their use in opening statements, and the provisions made for the inspection of identified exhibits. The original of the exhibit stipulations shall be presented to the court at the pre-trial conference.

(3) *Fact stipulation.* The attorneys shall stipulate in writing with reference to all facts and issues not in genuine dispute. The original of the stipulations shall be presented to the court at the time of the pre-trial conference.

(4) *Exchange list of witnesses.* Attorneys for each of the parties shall furnish opposing counsel with the written list of the names and addresses of all witnesses then known. The original of each witness list shall be presented to the court at the time of the pre-trial conference.

(5) *Discuss settlement.* The possibility of compromise settlement shall be fully discussed and explored.

(D) Preparation for conference of attorneys and pre-trial. Each attorney shall completely familiarize himself with all aspects of the case in advance of the conference of attorneys and be prepared to enter into stipulations with reference to as many facts and issues and exhibits as possible.

(E) Duty to arrange conference. It shall be the duty of counsel for both plaintiff and defendant to arrange for the conference of attorneys at least ten [10] days in advance of the pre-trial conference.

(F) Refusal to stipulate. If, following the conference of attorneys, either party determines that there are other facts or exhibits that should be stipulated and which opposing counsel refuses to stipulate upon, he shall compile a list of such facts or exhibits and furnish same to opposing counsel at least two [2] days in advance of the pre-trial conference. The original of the list shall be presented to the court at the time of the pre-trial conference.

(G) Witnesses or exhibits discovered subsequent to conference of attorneys and before a pre-trial conference. If, after the conference of the attorneys and before the pre-trial conference, counsel discovers additional exhibits or names of additional witnesses, the same information required to be disclosed at the conference of the attorneys shall be immediately furnished opposing counsel. The original of any such disclosures shall be presented to the court at the time of the pre-trial conference.

(H) More than one pre-trial conference. If necessary or advisable, the court may adjourn the pre-trial conference from time to time or may order an additional pre-trial conference.

(I) Witnesses or exhibits discovered subsequent to pre-trial conference. If, following the pre-trial conference or during trial, counsel discovers additional exhibits or the names of additional witnesses, the same information required to be disclosed at the conference between attorneys shall be immediately furnished opposing counsel. The original of any such disclosure shall immediately be filed with the court and shall indicate the date it was furnished opposing counsel.

(J) Pre-trial order. The court shall make an order which recites the action taken at the conference, the amendments allowed to the pleading, and the agreements made by the parties as to any of the matters considered which limit the issues for trial to those not disposed of by admissions or agreement of counsel, and such order when entered shall control the subsequent course of action, unless modified thereafter to prevent manifest injustice. The court in its discretion may establish by rule a pre-trial calendar on which actions may be placed for consideration as above provided, and may either confine the calendar to jury actions or non-jury actions or extend it to all actions.

(K) Sanctions: Failure to appear. If without just excuse or because of failure to give reasonable attention to the matter, no appearance is made on behalf of a party at a pre-trial conference, or if an attorney is grossly unprepared to participate in the conference, the court may order either one or both of the following:

(1) the payment by the delinquent attorney or party of the reasonable expenses, including attorney's fees, to the aggrieved party; or

(2) take such other action as may be appropriate.

Amended Oct. 25, 1991, effective Jan. 1, 1992; amended Oct. 29, 1991, effective Jan. 1, 1992; Amended July 19, 2002, effective Jan. 1, 2003.

IV. PARTIES

Rule 17. Parties plaintiff and defendant—Capacity

(A) Real party in interest. Every action shall be prosecuted in the name of the real party in interest.

(1) An executor, administrator, guardian, bailee, trustee of an express trust, a party with whom or in whose name a contract has been made for the benefit of another, or a party authorized by statute may sue in his own name without joining with him the party for whose benefit the action is brought, but stating his relationship and the capacity in which he sues.

(2) When a statute provides for an action by this state on the relation of another, the action may be brought in the name of the person for whose use or benefit the statute was intended.

No action shall be dismissed on the ground that it is not prosecuted in the name of the real party in interest until a reasonable time after objection has been allowed for the real party in interest to ratify the action, or to be joined or substituted in the action. Such ratification, joinder, or substitution shall have the same effect as if the action had been commenced initially in the name of the real party in interest.

(B) Capacity to sue or be sued. The capacity of a party to sue or be sued shall be determined by the law of this state, including its conflicts rules, except that a partnership or unincorporated association may sue or be sued in its common name.

(C) Infants or incompetent persons—Unborn, unknown, and unlocated persons. An infant or incompetent person may sue or be sued in any action:

    (1) in his own name;

    (2) in his own name by a guardian ad litem or a next friend;

    (3) in the name of his representative, if the representative is a court-appointed general guardian, committee, conservator, guardian of the estate or other like fiduciary.

The court, upon its own motion or upon the motion of any party, must notify and allow the representative named in subsection (3) of this subdivision, if he is known, to represent an infant or incompetent person, and be joined as an additional party in his representative capacity. If an infant or incompetent person is not represented, or is not adequately represented, the court shall appoint a guardian ad litem for him. The court may, in its discretion, appoint a guardian ad litem or an attorney for persons who are institutionalized, who are not yet born or in being, who are unknown, who are known but cannot be located, or who are in such position that they cannot procure reasonable representation. The court shall make such other orders as it deems proper for the protection of such parties or persons. Persons with claims against the estate of the ward or against the guardian of his estate as such may proceed under this rule or provisions applicable to guardianship proceedings. It shall not be necessary that the person for whom guardianship is sought shall be represented by a guardian ad litem in such proceedings. Nothing herein shall affect the right of a guardian to sue or be sued in his personal capacity.

The court, in its discretion, may honor the infant's or incompetent's choice of next friend or guardian ad litem, but the court may deny approval or remove a person who is not qualified. A next friend or guardian under subsection (C) of this rule may be required by the court to furnish bond or additional bond and shall be subject to the rules applicable to guardians of the estate with respect to duties, terms of the bond required, accounting, compensation and termination.

(D) Sex, marital and parental status. For the purposes of suing or being sued there shall be no distinction between men and women or between men and women because of marital or parental status; provided, however, that this subdivision (D) shall not apply to actions in tort.

(E) Partnerships and unincorporated associations. A partnership or an unincorporated association may sue or be sued in its common name. A judgment by or against the partnership or unincorporated association shall bind the organization as if it were an entity. A money judgment against the partnership or unincorporated association shall not bind

an individual partner or member unless he is named as a party or is bound as a member of a class in an appropriate action (Rules 23 and 23.2).

(F) Unknown persons. When the name or existence of a person is unknown, he may be named as an unknown party, and when his true name is discovered his name may be inserted by amendment at any time.

Rule 17.1. Parties: State as party—Attorney General

If in any action or proceeding involving real property, instituted in any court of this state, it appears from the allegations of any pleading filed therein that the state of Indiana has, or claims to have a lien upon or an interest in such real estate, the state may be made a party defendant to the action, and shall be bound by any judgment or decree rendered thereon. Service of summons shall be made upon the Attorney General as provided in Rule 4.8. It shall be the duty of the Attorney General, in person or by deputy to appear and defend such proceedings or suit, on behalf of the state of Indiana. The Attorney General may, in his discretion, designate the prosecuting attorney of the circuit in which such action is pending as his deputy for the purpose of defending such proceedings or suit on behalf of the state of Indiana. After the prosecuting attorney enters his appearance as such deputy, pleadings under Rule 5 shall be served upon him for and on behalf of the Attorney General. The state may appeal from such judgment or decree, in like manner and under the same terms and conditions as other parties in like cases.

This rule is meant, without limitation, to apply to actions to foreclose a mortgage or other lien on real estate, to subject any real estate to sale, or to partition or quiet title to real estate.

Further, in any case in which the Attorney General represents the State of Indiana, the judge presiding in the case where such cause is pending, shall promptly notify the Attorney General by United States mail, addressed to his office in Indianapolis, Indiana, of any ruling made in such cause or of the fixing of a date for the trial thereof.

Amended April 13, 1971.

Rule 18. Joinder of claims and remedies

(A) Joinder of claims. A party asserting a claim for relief as an original claim, counterclaim, cross-claim, or third-party claim, may join, either as independent or as alternate claims, as many claims, whether legal, equitable, or statutory as he has against an opposing party.

(B) Joinder of remedies—Fraudulent conveyances. Whenever a claim is one heretofore cognizable only after another claim has been prosecuted to a conclusion, the two [2] claims may be joined in a single action; but the court shall grant relief in that action only in accordance with the relative substantive rights of the parties. In particular, a plaintiff may state a claim for money and a claim to have set aside a conveyance fraudulent as to him, without first having obtained a judgment establishing the claim for money.

Rule 19.   Joinder of person needed for just adjudication

(A) Persons to be joined if feasible. A person who is subject to service of process shall be joined as a party in the action if:

(1) in his absence complete relief cannot be accorded among those already parties; or

(2) he claims an interest relating to the subject of the action and is so situated that the disposition of the action in his absence may:

(a) as a practical matter impair or impede his ability to protect that interest, or

(b) leave any of the persons already parties subject to a substantial risk of incurring double, multiple, or otherwise inconsistent obligations by reason of his claimed interest.

If he has not been so joined, the court shall order that he be made a party. If he should join as a plaintiff but refuses to do so, he may be made a defendant.

(B) Determination by court whenever joinder not feasible. Notwithstanding subdivision (A) of this rule when a person described in subsection (1) or (2) thereof is not made a party, the court may treat the absent party as not indispensable and allow the action to proceed without him; or the court may treat such absent party as indispensable and dismiss the action if he is not subject to process. In determining whether or not a party is indispensable the court in its discretion and in equity and good conscience shall consider the following factors:

(1) the extent to which a judgment rendered in the person's absence might be prejudicial to him or those already parties;

(2) the extent to which, by protective provisions in the judgment, by the shaping of relief, or other measures, the prejudice can be lessened or avoided;

(3) whether a judgment rendered in the person's absence will be adequate;

(4) whether the plaintiff will have an adequate remedy if the action is dismissed for nonjoinder.

(C) Pleading nonjoinder. Nonjoinder under this rule may be raised by motion as provided in Rule 12(B)(7).

(D) Exception of class actions. This rule is subject to the provisions of Rule 23.

(E) Parties not indispensable—Joinder of obligors, assignors, and subrogees and subrogors.

(1) *Joint obligors.* Joinder of all the parties to a joint and several obligation and to a joint obligation, including a partnership obligation, shall not be required, and joint or separate action may be brought against one or more of such obligors who shall be subject to permissive joinder as provided in Rule 20. A judgment against fewer than all does not merge or bar the claim against those not made parties for that reason.

(2) *Assignor of claim.* Joinder of the assignor or transferor of a claim or chose in action shall not be required in a suit by the assignee who establishes his title by appropriate pleading and proof, but such assignor or transferor shall be subject to permissive joinder as provided in Rule 20.

(3) *Subrogation.*

(a) A subrogor may enforce the claim to the extent of his interest or in full without joining the subrogee.

(b) The subrogee may enforce the claim to the extent that he establishes his title or interest by appropriate pleading and proof without joining the subrogor.

(c) In such cases the subrogor or subrogee shall be subject to permissive joinder as provided in Rule 20.

Any recovery by the subrogor to the extent that such recovery is owned by a subrogee shall be made as representative and trustee for the subrogee.

(F) Governmental organizations and representatives thereof as parties. Suits by or against a governmental organization or governmental representative relating to the acts, power or authority of such organization or representative, including acts under purported power or authority or color thereof by such organization or representative, shall be governed by this provision.

(1) Suits by or against a governmental organization or against a representative in his official capacity shall be brought in the name of the governmental organization. Suits naming a governmental representative by his official title or by his name along with his official title shall be deemed to name and include the governmental organization which he represents, and suits naming an unofficial branch, office or unit of a governmental organization shall be deemed to name and include the governmental organization of which it is a part; but the court upon its own motion or the motion of any party may require the omitted and proper governmental organization to be included at any time.

(2) Other government organizations and governmental representatives of the same or other governmental organizations may be joined or made parties to suits in which a governmental organization is named as a party in accordance with the provisions of these rules relating to parties. Failure to name, or improper naming of a governmental organization or a governmental representative shall be subject to the provisions of these rules relating to parties.

(3) A judgment for or against a governmental organization shall also bind affected or successive representatives of such organization. When a governmental representative is named as a party in his individual name or in his individual name along with his official title, the judgment, in an appropriate case, may bind him in his individual capacity, but no judgment against him in his individual capacity shall be rendered against him unless he is so named. No action against a governmental organization or against a governmental representative in his official capacity shall be abated, affected or delayed because of the death, incapacity or replacement of a named or unnamed governmental representative, or because of the fact that the name, functions or existence of the governmental organization have been altered or terminated. In either case the action shall proceed without substitution of successors who shall be bound by the judgment in their official capacity.

Rule 20. Permissive joinder of parties

(A) Permissive joinder.

(1) All persons may join in one [1] action as plaintiffs if they assert any right to relief jointly, severally, or in the alternative in respect of or arising out of the same transaction, occurrence, or series of transactions or occurrences and if any question of law or fact common to all these persons will arise in the action.

(2) All persons may be joined in one [1] action as defendants if there is asserted against them jointly, severally, or in the alternative, any right to relief in respect of, or arising out of, the same transaction, occurrence, or series of transactions or occurrences and if any question of law or fact common to all defendants will arise in the action.

A plaintiff or defendant need not be interested in obtaining or defending against all the relief demanded. Judgment may be given for one or more of the plaintiffs according to their respective rights to relief, and against one or more defendants according to their respective liabilities. Unwilling plaintiffs who could join under this rule may be joined by a plaintiff as defendants, and the defendant may make any persons who could be joined under this rule parties by alleging their interest therein with a prayer that their rights in the controversy be determined, along with any counterclaim or cross-claim against them, if any, as if they had been originally joined as parties.

(B) Separate trials. The court may make such orders as will prevent a party from being embarrassed, delayed, or put to expense by the inclusion of a party against whom he asserts no claim and who asserts no claim against him, and may order separate trials of the entire case or separate issues therein, or make other orders to prevent delay or prejudice.

Rule 21. Misjoinder and non-joinder of parties; venue and jurisdiction over the subject-matter

(A) Effect of misjoinder and non-joinder. Misjoinder of parties is not ground for dismissal of an action. Except as otherwise provided in these rules, failure to name another person as a party or include him in the action is not ground for dismissal; but such omission is subject to the right of such person to intervene or of an opposing party to name or include him in the action as permitted by these rules. Subject to its sound discretion and on motion of any party or of its own initiative, the court may order parties dropped or added at any stage of the action and on such terms as are just and will avoid delay. Any claim against a party may be severed and proceeded with separately. Incorrect names and misnomers may be corrected by amendment under Rule 15 at any time.

(B) Effect of venue or jurisdiction over part of case. The court shall have venue and authority over all persons or claims required to be joined or permissively joined, impleaded or included by intervention, interpleader, counterclaim or cross-claim if it has venue or is authorized to determine any claim asserted between any of the parties thereto, notwithstanding any requirement of venue or of jurisdiction over the subject-matter applicable to other claims or other parties. The court may transfer the proceedings to the proper court if it determines that venue or authority of the court is dependent upon a claim, or a claim by or against a particular party which appears from the pleadings, or proves to be a sham or made in bad faith; and if another action is pending in this state by or against a person upon the same claim at the time he becomes a party, the court may dismiss the action as to him, or in its sound discretion, it may order all or part of the proceedings to be consolidated with the first pending action.

Rule 22. Interpleader

(A) Plaintiff or defendant. Persons having claims against the plaintiff may be joined as defendants and required to interplead when their claims are such that the plaintiff is or may be exposed to double or multiple liability. It is not ground for objection to the joinder that the claims of the several claimants or the titles on which their claims depend do not have a common origin or are not identical but are adverse to and independent of one another, or that the plaintiff avers that he is not liable in whole or part to any or all of the claimants. A defendant exposed to similar liability may obtain such interpleader by way of cross-claim or counterclaim. The provisions of this rule supplement and do not in any way limit the joinder of parties permitted in Rule 20.

(B) Extension of statutory interpleader. This rule shall extend, but not diminish or reduce the right to interpleader provided by statute.

(C) Sufficiency of complaint or answer seeking interpleader. A complaint or answer seeking interpleader under Rule 22(A) is sufficient if:

(1) it admits that a liability is owing or it states that a totally or partially unfounded liability is asserted to be owing to either one or more of the parties interpleaded;

(2) it declares that because of such claims the person seeking interpleader is or may be exposed to double or multiple liability; and

(3) it prays that the parties interpleaded assert their claims against the party seeking interpleader and against each other.

The complaint may also show, if such is the fact, that the person seeking interpleader has deposited with the court money, or property, or a bond securing performance. It also may include appropriate prayers for equitable relief, including injunction against other nonpending suits by the parties interpleaded, against the person seeking interpleader or among themselves. Except to the extent that the issues are raised by the pleadings of the person seeking interpleader, the claims of those interpleaded, whether dependent or independent, may be pleaded in the same manner as if the claims were counterclaims or cross-claims under Rule 13 and within the time as prescribed by Rule 6. Incorrectness of the interpleader under Rule 22(A) is grounds for dismissal as provided in Rule 12(B)(6). New service against defaulting parties required by Rule 5(A) shall not apply to the responsive pleadings filed by parties named to interpleader proceedings under Rule 22(A) unless ordered by the court. Trial of the issues may be held at one [1] hearing or in successive stages at the sound discretion of the court and subject to Rule 42.

(D) Release from liability—Deposit or delivery. Any party seeking interpleader, as provided in subdivision (A) of this rule, may deposit with the court the amount claimed, or deliver to the court or as otherwise directed by the court the property claimed, and the court may thereupon order such party discharged from liability as to such claims, and the action continued as between the claimants of such money or property.

Rule 23. Class actions

(A) Prerequisites to a class action. One or more members of a class may sue or be sued as representative parties on behalf of all only if:

(1) the class is so numerous that joinder of all members is impracticable;

(2) there are questions of law or fact common to the class;

(3) the claims or defenses of the representative parties are typical of the claims or defenses of the class; and

(4) the representative parties will fairly and adequately protect the interests of the class.

(B) Class actions maintainable. An action may be maintained as a class action if the prerequisites of subdivision (A) are satisfied, and in addition:

(1) the prosecution of separate actions by or against individual members of the class would create a risk of:

(a) inconsistent or varying adjudications with respect to individual members of the class which would establish incompatible standards of conduct for the party opposing the class, or

(b) adjudications with respect to individual members of the class which would as a practical matter be dispositive of the interest of the other members not parties to the adjudications or substantially impair or impede their ability to protect their interests; or

(2) the party opposing the class has acted or refused to act on grounds generally applicable to the class, thereby making appropriate final injunctive relief or corresponding declaratory relief with respect to the class as a whole; or

(3) the court finds that the questions of law or fact common to the members of the class predominate over any questions affecting only individual members, and that a class action is superior to other available methods for the fair and efficient adjudication of the controversy. The matters pertinent to the findings include:

(a) the interest of members of the class in individually controlling the prosecution or defense of separate actions;

(b) the extent and nature of any litigation concerning the controversy already commenced by or against members of the class;

(c) the desirability or undesirability of concentrating the litigation of the claims in the particular forum;

(d) the difficulties likely to be encountered in the management of a class action.

(C) Determination by order whether class action to be maintained—Notice—Judgment—Actions conducted partially as class actions.

(1) As soon as practicable after the commencement of an action brought as a class action, the court, upon hearing or waiver of hearing, shall determine by order whether it is to be so maintained. An order under this subdivision may be conditional, and may be altered or amended before the decision on the merits.

(2) In any class action maintained under subdivision (B)(3), the court shall direct to the members of the class the best notice practicable under the circumstances, including individual notice to all members who can be identified through reasonable effort. The notice shall advise each member that:

(a) the court will exclude him from the class if he so requests by a specified date;

(b) the judgment, whether favorable or not, will include all members who do not request exclusion; and

(c) any member who does not request exclusion may, if he desires, enter an appearance through his counsel.

(3) The judgment in an action maintained as a class action under subdivision (B)(1) or (B)(2), whether or not favorable to the class, shall include and describe those whom the court finds to be members of the class. The judgment in an action maintained as a class action under subdivision (B)(3), whether or not favorable to the class, shall include and specify or describe those to whom the notice provided in subdivision (C)(2) was directed, and who have not requested exclusion, and whom the court finds to be members of the class.

(4) When appropriate:

(a) an action may be brought or maintained as a class action with respect to particular issues; or

(b) a class may be divided into subclasses and each subclass treated as a class, and the provisions of this rule shall then be construed and applied accordingly.

(D) Orders in conduct of actions. In the conduct of actions to which this rule applies, the court may make appropriate orders:

(1) determining the course of proceedings or prescribing measures to prevent undue repetition or complication in the presentation of evidence or argument;

(2) requiring, for the protection of the members of the class or otherwise for the fair conduct of the action, that notice be given in such manner as the court may direct to some or all of the members of any step in the action, or of the proposed extent of the judgment, or of the opportunity of members to signify whether they consider the representation fair and adequate, to intervene and present claims or defenses, or otherwise to come into the action;

(3) imposing conditions on the representative parties or on intervenors;

(4) requiring that the pleadings be amended to eliminate therefrom allegations as to representation of absent persons, and that the action proceed accordingly;

(5) dealing with similar procedural matters.

The orders may be combined with an order under Rule 16, and may be altered or amended as may be desirable from time to time. The court shall allow reasonable attorney's fees and reasonable expenses incurred from a fund recovered for the benefit of a class under this section and the court may apportion such recovery among different attorneys.

(E) Dismissal or compromise. A class action shall not be dismissed or compromised without the approval of the court, and notice of the proposed dismissal or compromise shall be given to all members of the class in such manner as the court directs.

(F) Disposition of Residual Funds.

(1) "Residual Funds" are funds that remain after the payment of all approved class member claims, expenses, litigation costs, attorneys' fees, and other court-approved disbursements to implement the relief granted. Nothing in this rule is intended to limit the trial court from approving a settlement that does not create residual funds.

(2) Any order entering a judgment or approving a proposed compromise of a class action certified under this rule that establishes a process for identifying and compensating members of the class shall provide for the disbursement of residual funds, unless otherwise agreed. In matters where the claims process has been exhausted and residual funds remain, not less than twenty-five percent (25%) of the residual funds shall be disbursed to the Indiana Bar Foundation to support the activities and programs of the Indiana Pro Bono Commission and its *pro bono* districts. The court may disburse the balance of any residual funds beyond the minimum percentage to the Indiana Bar Foundation or to any other entity for purposes that have a direct or indirect relationship to the objectives of the underlying litigation or otherwise promote the substantive or procedural interests of members of the certified class.

Amended Sept. 21, 2010, effective Jan. 1, 2011.

Rule 23.1. Derivative actions by shareholders

In a derivative action brought by one or more shareholders or members or holders of an interest in such shares or membership, legal or equitable, to enforce a right of a corporation or of an unincorporated association, the corporation or association having failed to enforce a right which may properly be asserted by it, the complaint shall be verified and shall allege that the plaintiff was a shareholder or member or holder of an interest, legal or equitable, in such shares or membership at the time of the transaction or any part thereof of which he complains or that his share or membership thereafter devolved on him by operation of law, and the complaint shall also allege with particularity the efforts, if any, made by the plaintiff, to obtain the action he desires from the directors or comparable authority and the reasons for his failure to obtain the action or for not making the effort. The derivative action may not be maintained if it appears that the plaintiff does not fairly and adequately represent the interests of the shareholders or members similarly situated in enforcing the right of the corporation or association. The action shall not be dismissed or compromised without the approval of the court, and notice of the proposed dismissal or compromise shall be given to shareholders or members in such manner as the court directs.

Rule 23.2. Actions relating to unincorporated associations

In addition to an action brought by or against an unincorporated association under Rule 17(E), an action may be brought against the members of an unincorporated association as a class by naming certain members as representative parties if it appears that the members bringing suit or served with process or the representative parties will fairly and adequately protect the interests of the association and its members. In the conduct of the action the court may make appropriate orders corresponding with those described in Rule 23(D), and the procedure for dismissal or compromise of the action shall correspond with that provided in Rule 23(E).

Rule 24. Intervention

(A) Intervention of right. Upon timely motion anyone shall be permitted to intervene in an action:

(1) when a statute confers an unconditional right to intervene; or

(2) when the applicant claims an interest relating to a property, fund or transaction which is the subject of the action and he is so situated that the disposition of the action may as a practical matter impair or impede his ability to protect his interest in the property, fund or transaction, unless the applicant's interest is adequately represented by existing parties.

(B) Permissive intervention. Upon timely filing of his motion anyone may be permitted to intervene in an action:

(1) when a statute confers a conditional right to intervene; or

(2) when an applicant's claim or defense and the main action have a question of law or fact in common. When a party to an action relies for ground of claim or defense upon any statute or executive order administered by a federal or state governmental officer or agency or upon any regulation, order, requirement, or agreement issued or made pursuant to the statute or executive administrative order, the governmental unit upon timely application may be permitted to intervene in the action. In exercising its discretion the court shall consider whether the intervention will unduly delay or prejudice the adjudication of the rights of the original parties.

(C) Procedure. A person desiring to intervene shall serve a motion to intervene upon the parties as provided in Rule 5. The motion shall state the grounds therefor and set forth or include by reference the claim, defense or matter for which intervention is sought. Intervention after trial or after judgment for

purposes of a motion under Rules 50, 59, or 60, or an appeal may be allowed upon motion. The court's determination upon a motion to intervene shall be interlocutory for all purposes unless made final under Trial Rule 54(B).

Amended Nov. 21, 1980, effective Jan. 1, 1981.

Rule 25. Substitution of parties

(A) Death.

(1) If a party dies and the claim is not thereby extinguished, the court may order substitution of the proper parties. The motion for substitution may be made by the court, any party or by the successors or representatives of the deceased party and, together with the notice of hearing, shall be served on the parties as provided in Rule 5 and upon persons not parties in the manner provided in Rule 4 for the service of summons. Motion for substitution may be made before or after judgment, and if substitution is not reflected in the papers upon which the appeal is based, any party shall, by notice filed with the Clerk of the court on appeal, advise the court on appeal of the substitution of any party. However, if the case is returned to a lower court after the judgment or order upon appeal becomes final, the motion may then be made in such lower court.

(2) In the event of the death of one or more of the plaintiffs or of one or more of the defendants in an action in which the right sought to be enforced survives only to the surviving plaintiffs or only against the surviving defendants, the action does not abate. The death may be suggested upon the record and the action shall proceed in favor of or against the surviving parties.

(B) Incompetency. If a party becomes incompetent, the court upon motion served as provided in subdivision (A) of this rule may allow the action to be continued by or against his representative in the same manner as against a decedent party.

(C) Transfer of interest. In case of any transfer of interest, the action may be continued by or against the original party, unless the court upon motion directs the person to whom the interest is transferred to be substituted in the action or joined with the original party. Service of the motion shall be made as provided in subdivision (A) of this rule.

(D) Persons substituted on death—Personal representative or successors in interest. The proper party or parties to be substituted for the party who dies under subsection (1) of subdivision (A) of this rule includes:

(1) a successor in interest whose rights or obligations do not pass to the representative of the deceased party's estate; or

(2) if the interest passes to or binds the representative of the deceased party's estate, either such representative or, if it is established that the estate

of the deceased party is closed or that opening of such estate is unnecessary, the successor of such estate.

(E) Necessity of filing claims against estate when representative substituted—Proceedings to enforce judgment, execution and judgment liens. A claim based upon a judgment against a party who dies before or after judgment is entered shall be allowed by the court administering his estate even though the claim is not filed with such court if the representative of such estate is substituted as a party within the time when such claim or judgment could have been filed as a claim against the estate under the probate code. Judgments upon an action against a party who dies, whether entered before or after his death shall be satisfied from the assets of his estate by the decedent's representative, and no execution, proceedings supplemental or enforcement orders shall issue on the judgment after the party has died as against his property; but this provision shall not prevent enforcement of execution liens, judgment liens, liens acquired by judicial proceedings, security interests, mortgages, liens or interests in property acquired before his death and being enforced by or under the judgment, subject to any rights of the representative to redeem or stay enforcement as now provided by law.

(F) Public Officers; Death or Separation from Office.

(1) When a public officer is a party to an action or other proceeding in an official capacity and during its pendency dies, resigns, or otherwise ceases to hold office, the action does not abate and the officer's successor is automatically substituted as a party. Proceedings following substitution shall be in the name of the substituted party, but any misnomer not affecting the substantial rights of the parties shall be disregarded. An order of substitution may be entered at any time, but the omission to enter such an order shall not affect the substitution.

(2) A public officer who sues or is sued in an official capacity may be described as a party by the officer's official title rather than by name; but the court may require the officer's name to be added.

Amended Nov. 26, 1997, effective Jan. 1, 1998; amended Feb. 4, 2000, effective Jan. 1, 2001.

V.   DEPOSITIONS AND DISCOVERY

Rule 26.   General provisions governing discovery

(A) Discovery methods. Parties may obtain discovery by one or more of the following methods:

(1) depositions upon oral examination or written questions;

(2) written interrogatories;

(3) production of documents, electronically stored information, or things or permission to enter upon land or other property, for inspection and other purposes;

(4) physical and mental examination;

(5) requests for admission.

Unless the court orders otherwise under subdivision (C) of this rule, the frequency of use of these methods is not limited.

(A.1) Electronic Format. In addition to service under Rule 5(B) or a .pdf format electronic copy, a party propounding or responding to interrogatories, requests for production or requests for admission shall comply with (a) or (b) of this subsection.

(a) The party shall serve the discovery request or response in an electronic format (either on a disk or as an electronic document attachment) in any commercially available word processing software system. If transmitted on disk, each disk shall be labeled, identifying the caption of the case, the document, and the word processing version in which it is being submitted. If more than one disk is used for the same document, each disk shall be labeled and also shall be sequentially numbered. If trans-mitted by electronic mail, the document must be accompanied by electronic memorandum providing the forgoing identifying information.

or

(b) The party shall serve the opposing party with a verified statement that the attorney or party appealing pro se lacks the equipment and is unable to transmit the discovery as required by this rule.

(B) Scope of discovery. Unless otherwise limited by order of the court in accordance with these rules, the scope of discovery is as follows:

(1) *In general.* Parties may obtain discovery regarding any matter, not privileged, which is relevant to the subject-matter involved in the pending action, whether it relates to the claim or defense of the party seeking discovery or the claim or defense of any other party, including the existence, description, nature, custody, condition and location of any books, documents, or other tangible things and the identity and location of persons having knowledge of any discoverable matter. It is not ground for objection that the information sought will be inadmissible at the trial if the information sought appears reasonably calculated to lead to the discovery of admissible evidence.

The frequency or extent of use of the discovery methods otherwise permitted under these rules and by any local rule shall be limited by the court if it determines that: (i) the discovery sought is unreasonably cumulative or duplicative, or is obtainable from some other source that is more convenient, less burdensome, or less expensive; (ii) the party seeking discovery has had ample opportunity by discovery in the action to obtain the information sought or; (iii) the burden or expense of the proposed discovery outweighs its likely benefit, taking into account the needs of the case, the amount in controversy, the parties' resources, the importance of the issues at stake in the litigation, and the importance of the proposed discovery in resolving the issues. The court may act upon its own initiative after reasonable notice or pursuant to a motion under Rule 26(C).

(2) *Insurance agreements.* A party may obtain discovery of the existence and contents of any insurance agreement under which any person carrying on an insurance business may be liable to satisfy part or all of a judgment which may be entered in the action or to indemnify or reimburse for payments made to satisfy the judgment. Information concerning the insurance agreement is not by reason of disclosure admissible in evidence at trial. For purposes of this paragraph, an application for insurance shall not be treated as part of an insurance agreement.

(3) *Trial preparation: Materials.* Subject to the provisions of subdivision (B)(4) of this rule, a party may obtain discovery of documents and tangible things otherwise discoverable under subdivision (B)(1) of this rule and prepared in anticipation of litigation or for trial by or for another party or by or for that other party's representative (including his attorney, consultant, surety, indemnitor, insurer, or agent) only upon a showing that the party seeking discovery has substantial need of the materials in the preparation of his case and that he is unable without undue hardship to obtain the substantial equivalent of the materials by other means. In ordering discovery of such materials when the required showing has been made, the court shall protect against disclosure of the mental impressions, conclusions, opinions, or legal theories of an attorney or other representative of a party concerning the litigation.

A party may obtain without the required showing a statement concerning the action or its subject matter previously made by that party. Upon request, a person not a party may obtain without the required showing a statement concerning the action or its subject matter previously made by that person. If the request is refused, the person may move for a court order. The provisions of Rule 37(A)(4) apply to the award of expenses incurred in relation to the motion. For purposes of this paragraph, a statement previously made is

(a) a written statement signed or otherwise adopted approved by the person making it, or

(b) a stenographic, mechanical, electrical, or other recording, or a transcription thereof, which is a substantially verbatim recital of an oral statement by the person making it and contemporaneously recorded.

(4) *Trial Preparation: Experts.* Discovery of facts known and opinions held by experts, otherwise discoverable under the provisions of subdivision (B)(1) of this rule and acquired or developed in anticipation of litigation or for trial, may be obtained as follows:

(a) (i) A party may through interrogatories require any other party to identify each person whom the other party expects to call as an expert witness at trial, to state the subject matter on which the expert is expected to testify, and to state the substance of the facts and opinions to which the expert is expected to testify and a summary of the grounds for each opinion.

(ii) Upon motion, the court may order further discovery by other means, subject to such restrictions as to scope and such provisions, pursuant to subdivision (B)(4)(c) of this rule, concerning fees and expenses as the court may deem appropriate.

(b) A party may discover facts known or opinions held by an expert who has been retained or specially employed by another party in anticipation of litigation or preparation for trial and who is not expected to be called as a witness at trial, only as provided in Rule 35(B) or upon a showing of exceptional circumstances under which it is impracticable for the party seeking discovery to obtain facts or opinions on the same subject by other means,

(c) Unless manifest injustice would result,

(i) the court shall require that the party seeking discovery pay the expert a reasonable fee for time spent in responding to discovery under subdivision (B)(4)(a)(ii) and (B)(4)(b) of this rule; and

(ii) with respect to discovery obtained under subdivision (B)(4)(a)(ii) of this rule the court may require, and with respect to discovery obtained under subdivision (B)(4)(b) of this rule the court shall require, the party seeking discovery to pay the other party a fair portion of the fees and expenses reasonably incurred by the latter party in obtaining facts and opinions from the expert.

(5) *Claims of Privilege or Protection.*

(a) Information withheld. When a party withholds information otherwise discoverable under these rules by claiming that it is privileged or subject to protection as trial preparation material, the party shall make the claim expressly and shall describe the nature of the documents, communications, or things not produced or disclosed in a manner that, without revealing information itself privileged or protected, will enable other parties to assess the applicability of the privilege or protection.

(b) Information produced. If information is produced in discovery that is subject to a claim of privilege or protection as trial-preparation material, the party making the claim may notify any party that received the information of the claim and the basis for it. After being notified, a party must promptly return, sequester, or destroy the specified information and any copies it has and may not use or disclose the information until the claim is resolved. A receiving party may promptly present the information to the court under seal for a determination of the claim. If the receiving party disclosed the information before being notified, it must take reasonable steps to retrieve it. The producing party must preserve the information until the claim is resolved.

(C) Protective orders. Upon motion by any party or by the person from whom discovery is sought, and for good cause shown, the court in which the action is pending or alternatively, on matters relating to a deposition, the court in the county where the deposition is being taken, may make any order which justice requires to protect a party or person from annoyance, embarrassment, oppression, or undue burden or expense, including one or more of the following:

(1) that the discovery not be had;

(2) that the discovery may be had only on specified terms and conditions, including a designation of the time or place;

(3) that the discovery may be had only by a method of discovery other than that selected by the party seeking discovery;

(4) that certain matters not be inquired into, or that the scope of the discovery be limited to certain matters;

(5) that discovery be conducted with no one present except the parties and their attorneys and persons designated by the court;

(6) that a deposition after being sealed be opened only by order of the court;

(7) that a trade secret or other confidential research, development, or commercial information not be disclosed or be disclosed only in a designated way;

(8) that the parties simultaneously file specified documents or information enclosed in sealed envelopes to be opened as directed by the court. If the motion for a protective order is denied in whole or in part, the court may, on such terms and conditions as are just, order that any party or person provide or permit discovery. The provisions of Trial Rule 37(A)(4) apply to the award of expenses incurred in relation to the motion.

(9) that a party need not provide discovery of electronically stored information from sources that the party identifies as not reasonably accessible because of undue burden or cost. On motion to compel discovery or for a protective order, the party from whom discovery is sought must show that the information is not reasonably accessible because of undue burden or cost. If that showing is made, the court may nonetheless order discovery from such sources if the requesting party shows good cause. The court may specify conditions for the discovery.

(D) Sequence and timing of discovery. Unless the court upon motion, for the convenience of parties and witnesses and in the interests of justice, orders otherwise, methods of discovery may be used in any sequence and the fact that a party is conducting discovery, whether by deposition or otherwise, shall not operate to delay any other party's discovery.

(E) Supplementation of responses. A party who has responded to a request for discovery with a response that was complete when made is under no duty to supplement his response to include information thereafter acquired, except as follows:

(1) A party is under a duty seasonably to supplement his response with respect to any question directly addressed to:

(a) the identity and location of persons having knowledge of discoverable matters, and

(b) the identity of each person expected to be called as an expert witness at trial, the subject-matter on which he is expected to testify, and the substance of his testimony.

(2) A party is under a duty seasonably to amend a prior response if he obtains information upon the basis of which

(a) he knows that the response was incorrect when made, or

(b) he knows that the response though correct when made is no longer true and the circumstances are such that a failure to amend the response is in substance a knowing concealment.

(3) A duty to supplement responses may be imposed by order of the court, agreement of the parties, or at any time prior to trial through new requests for supplementation of prior responses.

(F) Informal Resolution of Discovery Disputes. Before any party files any motion or request to compel discovery pursuant to Rule 37, or any motion for protection from discovery pursuant to Rule 26(C), or any other discovery motion which seeks to enforce, modify, or limit discovery, that party shall:

(1) Make a reasonable effort to reach agreement with the opposing party concerning the matter which is the subject of the motion or request; and

(2) Include in the motion or request a statement showing that the attorney making the motion or request has made a reasonable effort to reach agreement with the opposing attorney(s) concerning

the matter(s) set forth in the motion or request. This statement shall recite, in addition, the date, time and place of this effort to reach agreement, whether in person or by phone, and the names of all parties and attorneys participating therein. If an attorney for any party advises the court in writing that an opposing attorney has refused or delayed meeting and discussing the issues covered in this subsection (F), the court may take such action as is appropriate.

The court may deny a discovery motion filed by a party who has failed to comply with the requirements of this subsection.

Amended Dec. 14, 1970, effective March 1, 1971; amended Nov. 3, 1981, effective Jan. 1, 1982; amended Dec. 5, 1994, effective Feb. 1, 1995; amended July 19, 2002, effective Jan. 1, 2003; amended Sept. 10, 2007, effective Jan. 1, 2008; Sept. 7, 2012, effective Jan. 1, 2013.

Rule 27. Depositions before action or pending appeal

(A) Before action.

(1) *Petition.* A person who desires to perpetuate his own testimony or that of another person regarding any matter that may be cognizable in any court in which the action may be commenced, may file a verified petition in any such court of this state.

The petition shall be entitled in the name of the petitioner and shall state facts showing:

(a) that the petitioner expects to be a party to an action cognizable in a court of this or another state;

(b) the subject-matter of the expected action and his interest therein;

(c) the facts which he desires to establish by the proposed testimony and his reasons for desiring to perpetuate it;

(d) the names or a description of the persons he expects will be adverse parties and their addresses so far as known; and

(e) the names and addresses of the persons to be examined and the substance of the testimony which he expects to elicit from each, and shall ask for an order authorizing the petitioner to take the depositions of the persons to be examined named in the petition, for the purpose of perpetuating their testimony.

(2) *Notice and service.* The petitioner shall thereafter serve a notice upon each person named in the petition as an expected adverse party, together with a copy of the petition, stating that the petitioner will apply to the court, at a time and place named therein, for the order described in the petition. At least twenty [20] days before the date of hearing the notice shall be served in the manner provided in Rule 4 for service of summons; but if such service cannot with due diligence be made upon any expected adverse party named in the petition, the court may make such order as is just

for service by publication or otherwise, and shall appoint, for persons not served in the manner provided in Rule 4, an attorney who shall represent them, and, in case they are not otherwise represented, shall cross-examine the deponent. If any expected adverse party is a minor or incompetent the provisions of Rule 17(C) apply.

(3) *Order and examination.* If the court is satisfied that the perpetuation of the testimony may prevent a failure or delay of justice, it shall make an order designating or describing the persons whose depositions may be taken and specifying the subject-matter of the examination or written interrogatories. The depositions may then be taken in accordance with these rules; and the court may make orders of the character provided for by Rules 34 and 35. For the purpose of applying these rules to depositions for perpetuating testimony, each reference therein to the court in which the action is pending shall be deemed to refer to the court in which the petition for such deposition was filed.

(4) *Use of deposition.* If a deposition to perpetuate testimony is taken under these rules or if, although not so taken, it would be admissible in evidence in the court of the state in which it is taken, it may be used in any action involving the same subject-matter subsequently brought in a court of this state in accordance with the provision of Rule 32.

(B) Pending appeal. If an appeal has been taken from a judgment of any court or before the taking of an appeal if the time therefor has not expired, the court in which the judgment was rendered may allow the taking of the depositions of witnesses to perpetuate their testimony for use in the event of further proceedings in such court. In such case the party who desires to perpetuate the testimony may make a motion in the court for leave to take the depositions, upon the same notice and service thereof as if the action was pending in the court. The motion shall show:

(1) the names and addresses of the persons to be examined and the substance of the testimony which he expects to elicit from each;

(2) the reasons for perpetuating their testimony.

If the court finds that the perpetuation of the testimony is proper to avoid a failure or delay of justice, it may make an order allowing the depositions to be taken and may make orders of the character provided for by Rules 34 and 35, and thereupon the depositions may be taken and used in the same manner and under the same conditions as are prescribed in these rules for depositions taken in actions pending in the court.

(C) Perpetuation by action. This rule does not limit the power of a court to entertain an action to perpetuate testimony.

(D) Filing deposition. The filing or custody of any deposition or evidence obtained under this rule shall be in accordance with Trial Rule 5(E).

Amended Oct. 15, 1986, effective Jan. 1, 1987; amended Sept. 30, 2004, effective Jan. 1, 2005.

Rule 28. Persons before whom depositions may be taken; discovery across state lines; before administrative agencies; and after judgment

(A) Within the United States. Within the United States or within a territory or insular possession subject to the dominion of the United States, depositions shall be taken before an officer authorized to administer oaths by the laws of the United States, or of the state of Indiana, or of the place where the examination is held, or before a person appointed by the court in which the action is pending. A person so appointed has power to administer oaths and take testimony.

(B) In foreign countries. In a foreign country, depositions may be taken:

(1) on notice before a person authorized to administer oaths in the place in which the examination is held, either by the law thereof or by the law of the United States; or

(2) before a person commissioned by the court, and a person so commissioned shall have the power by virtue of his commission to administer any necessary oath and take testimony; or

(3) pursuant to a letter rogatory.

A commission or a letter rogatory shall be issued on application and notice and on terms that are just and appropriate. It is not requisite to the issuance of a commission or a letter rogatory that the taking of the deposition in any other manner is impracticable or inconvenient; and both a commission and a letter rogatory may be issued in proper cases. A notice or commission may designate the person before whom the deposition is to be taken either by name or descriptive title. A letter rogatory may be addressed "To the Appropriate Authority in (here name the country)". Evidence obtained in response to a letter rogatory need not be excluded merely for the reason that it is not a verbatim transcript or that the testimony was not taken under oath or for any similar departure from the requirements for depositions taken within the United States under these rules.

(C) Disqualification for interest. Unless otherwise permitted by these rules, no deposition shall be taken before a person who is a relative or employee or attorney or counsel of any of the parties, or is a relative or employee of such attorney or counsel, or is financially interested in the action.

(D) Scope of discovery outside state—Protective and enforcement orders. A deposition may be taken outside the state as provided in subdivisions (A) and (B) of this rule, and the deponent may be requested to produce documents and things, and may also be requested to allow inspections and copies as provided in Rule 34 to submit to examination under Rule 35. Protective orders may be granted by the court in which the action is pending and by the court where discovery is being made. Enforcement orders may be made by the court where the discovery is sought, and enforcement orders and sanctions may be made by the court where the action is pending as against parties and as against witnesses subject to the jurisdiction of the court. When no action is pending, a court of this state may authorize a deposition to be taken outside this state of any person and upon any matters allowed by Rule 27.

(E) Assistance to tribunals and litigants outside this state. A court of this state may order a person who is domiciled or is found within this state to give his testimony or statement or to produce documents or other things, allow inspections and copies and permit physical and mental examinations for use in a proceeding in a tribunal outside this state. The order may be made upon the application of any interested person or in response to a letter rogatory and may prescribe the practice and procedure, which may be wholly or in part the practice and procedure of the tribunal outside this state, for taking the testimony or statement or producing the documents or other things. To the extent that the order does not prescribe otherwise, the practice and procedure shall be in accordance with that of the court of this state issuing the order. The order may direct that the testimony or statement be given, or document or other thing produced, before a person appointed by the court. The person appointed shall have power to administer any necessary oath. A person within this state may voluntarily give his testimony or statement or produce documents or other things allowing inspections and copies and permit physical and mental examinations for use in a proceeding before a tribunal outside this state.

(F) Discovery proceedings before administrative agencies. Whenever an adjudicatory hearing, including any hearing in any proceeding subject to judicial review, is held by or before an administrative agency, any party to that adjudicatory hearing shall be entitled to use the discovery provisions of Rules 26 through 37 of the Indiana Rules of Trial Procedure. Such discovery may include any relevant matter in the custody and control of the administrative agency.

Protective and other orders shall be obtained first from the administrative agency, and if enforcement of such orders or right of discovery is necessary, it may be obtained in a court of general jurisdiction in the county where discovery is being made or sought, or where the hearing is being held.

(G) Applicability of other laws. This rule does not repeal or modify any other law of this state permitting another procedure for obtaining discovery for use in this state or in a tribunal outside this state, except as expressly provided in these rules.

(H) Discovery after judgment. Discovery after judgment may be had in proceedings to enforce or to challenge the judgment.

Amended Nov. 24, 1975, effective Jan. 31, 1976.

Rule 29. Stipulations regarding discovery procedure

Unless the court orders otherwise, the parties may by written stipulation:

(1) provide that depositions may be taken before any person, at any time or place, upon any notice, and in any manner and when so taken may be used like other depositions, and

(2) modify the procedures provided by these rules for other methods of discovery.

Rule 30.   Depositions upon oral examination

(A) When depositions may be taken. After commencement of the action, any party may take the testimony of any person, including a party, by deposition upon oral examination. Leave of court, granted with or without notice, must be obtained only if the plaintiff seeks to take a deposition prior to the expiration of twenty [20] days after service of summons and complaint upon any defendant except that leave is not required:

(1) if a defendant has served a notice of taking deposition or otherwise sought discovery; or

(2) if special notice is given as provided in subdivision (B)(2) of this rule.

The attendance of witnesses may be compelled by the use of subpoena as provided in Rule 45. The deposition of a person confined in prison may be taken only by leave of court on such terms as the court prescribes.

(B) Notice of examination: General requirements—Special notice—Non-stenographic recording—Production of documents and things—Deposition of organization.

(1) A party desiring to take the deposition of any person upon oral examination shall give reasonable notice in writing to every other party to the action. The notice shall state the time and place for taking the deposition and the name and address of each person to be examined, if known, and if the name is not known, a general description sufficient to identify him or the particular class or group to which he belongs. If a subpoena duces tecum is to be served on the person to be examined, a designation of the materials to be produced thereunder shall be attached to or included in the notice.

(2) Leave of court, when required by subdivision (A) of this rule is not required for the taking of a deposition by plaintiff if the notice:

(a) states that the person to be examined is about to go out of the state or will be unavailable for examination unless his deposition is taken before expiration of the twenty [20] day period; and

(b) sets forth facts to support the statement.

The plaintiff's attorney shall sign the notice, and his signature constitutes a certification by him that to the best of his knowledge, information, and belief the statement and supporting facts are true. The sanctions provided by Rule 11 are applicable to the certification.

If any party shows that when he was served with notice under this subdivision (B)(2) he was unable through the exercise of diligence to obtain counsel to represent him at the taking of the deposition, the deposition may not be used against him.

(3) The court may for cause shown enlarge or shorten the time for taking the deposition.

(4) If a party taking a deposition wishes to have the testimony recorded other than in a manner provided in Rule 74, the notice shall specify the manner of recording and preserving the deposition. The court may require stenographic taking or make any other order to assure that the recorded testimony will be accurate and trustworthy.

(5) The notice to a deponent may be accompanied by a request made in compliance with Rule 34 for the production of documents and tangible things at the taking of the deposition.

(6) A party may in his notice name as the deponent an organization, including without limitation a governmental organization, or a partnership and designate with reasonable particularity the matters on which examination is requested. The organization so named shall designate one or more officers, directors, or managing agents, executive officers, or other persons duly authorized and consenting to testify on its behalf. The persons so designated shall testify as to matters known or available to the organization. This subdivision (B)(6) does not preclude taking a deposition by any other procedure authorized in these rules.

(C) Examination and cross-examination—Record of examination—Oath—Objections. Examination and cross-examination of witnesses may proceed as permitted at the trial under the provisions of Rule 43(B). The officer before whom the deposition is to be taken shall put the witness on oath and shall personally, or by someone acting under his direction and in his presence, record the testimony of the witness. The testimony shall be taken stenographically or recorded by any other means designated in accordance with subdivision (B)(4) of this rule. If requested by one of the parties, the testimony shall be transcribed.

All objections made at the time of the examination to the qualifications of the officer taking the deposition, or to the manner of taking it, or to the evidence presented, or to the conduct of any party, and any other objection to the proceedings, shall be noted by the officer upon the deposition. When there is an objection to a question, the objection and reason therefor shall be noted, and the question shall be answered unless the attorney instructs the deponent not to answer, or the deponent refuses to answer, in which case either party may have the question certified by the Reporter, and the question with the objection thereto when so certified shall be delivered to the party requesting the certification who may then proceed under Rule 37(A). In lieu of participating in the oral examination, parties may serve written questions on the party taking the deposition and require him to transmit them to the officer, who shall propound them to the witness and record the answers verbatim.

(D) Motion to terminate or limit examination. At any time during the taking of the deposition, on motion of any party or of the deponent and upon a showing that the examination is being conducted in bad faith or in such manner as unreasonably to annoy, embarrass, or oppress the deponent or party, the court in which the action is pending or the court in the county where the deposition is being taken may order the officer conducting the examination to cease forthwith from taking the deposition, or may limit the scope and manner of the taking of the deposition as provided in Rule 26(C). If the order made terminates the examination, it shall be resumed thereafter only upon the order of the court in which the action is pending. Upon demand of the objecting party or deponent the taking of the deposition shall be suspended for the time necessary to make a motion for an order. The provisions of Rule 37(A)(4) apply to the award of expenses incurred in relation to the motion.

(E) Submission to witness—Changes—Signing.

(1) When the testimony is fully transcribed, the deposition shall be submitted to the witness for reading and signing and shall be read to or by him, unless such reading and signing have been waived by the witness and by each party. "Submitted to the witness" as used in this subsection shall mean (a) mailing of written notification by registered or certified mail to the witness and each attorney attending the deposition that the deposition can be read and examined in the office of the officer before whom the deposition was taken, or (b), mailing the original deposition, by registered or certified mail, to the witness at an address designated by the witness or his attorney, if requested to do so by the witness, his attorney, or the party taking the deposition.

(2) If the witness desires to change any answer in the deposition submitted to him, each change, with a statement of the reason therefor, shall be made by the witness on a separate form provided by the officer, shall be signed by the witness and affixed to the original deposition by the officer. A copy of such changes shall be furnished by the officer to each party.

(3) If the reading and signing have not been waived by the witness and by each party the deposition shall be signed by the witness and returned by him to the officer within thirty (30) days after it is submitted to the witness. If the deposition has been returned to the officer and has not been signed by the witness, the officer shall execute a certificate of that fact, attach it to the original deposition and deliver it to the party taking it. In such event, the deposition may be used by any party with the same force and effect as though it had been signed by the witness.

(4) In the event the deposition is not returned to the officer within thirty (30) days after it has been submitted to the witness, the reporter shall execute a certificate of that fact and cause the certificate to be delivered to the party taking it. In such event, any party may use a copy of the deposition with the same force and effect as though the original had been signed by the witness.

(F) Certification and Filing—Exhibits—Copies.

(1) The officer shall certify on the deposition that the witness was duly sworn by him and that the deposition is a true record of the testimony given by the witness. He shall then securely seal the deposition in an envelope endorsed with the title of the action and marked "Deposition of (here insert name of witness)" and shall promptly deliver it to the party taking the deposition.

Documents and things, unless objection is made to their production for inspection during the examination of the witness, shall be marked for identification and annexed to and returned with the deposition, and may be inspected and copied by any party, except that:

(a) the person producing the materials may substitute copies to be marked for identification, if he affords to all parties fair opportunity to verify the copies by comparison with the originals; and

(b) if the person producing the materials requests their return the officer shall mark them, give each party an opportunity to inspect and copy them, and return them to the person producing them, and the materials may then be used in the same manner as if annexed to and returned with the deposition.

(2) Upon payment of reasonable charges therefor, the officer shall furnish a copy of the deposition to any party or the deponent.

(3) The officer taking the deposition shall give prompt notice to all parties of its delivery to the party taking the deposition.

(4) The filing of depositions shall be in accordance with the provisions of Trial Rule 5(E).

(G) Failure to attend or to serve subpoena— Expenses.

(1) If the party giving the notice of the taking of a deposition fails to attend and proceed therewith and another party attends in person or by attorney pursuant to the notice, the court may order the party giving the notice to pay to such other party the amount of the reasonable expenses incurred by him and his attorney in so attending, including reasonable attorney's fees.

(2) If the party giving the notice of the taking of a deposition of a witness other than a party fails to serve a subpoena upon him and the witness because of such failure does not attend, and if another party attends in person or by attorney because he expects the deposition of that witness to be taken, the court may order the party giving the notice to pay to such other party the amount of the reasonable expenses incurred by him and his attorney in so attending, including reasonable attorney's fees.

Amended Dec. 7, 1970, effective Jan. 1, 1971; amended Nov. 21, 1980, effective Jan. 1, 1981; amended Dec. 24, 1980, effective Jan. 1, 1981; amended Nov. 3, 1981, effective Jan. 1, 1982; amended Oct. 15, 1986, effective Jan. 1, 1987; amended Nov. 13, 1990, effective Jan. 1, 1991; amended Sept. 30, 2004, effective Jan. 1, 2005.

Rule 31. Deposition of witnesses upon written questions

(A) Serving questions—Notice. After commencement of the action, any party may take the testimony of any person, including a party, by deposition upon written questions. The attendance of witnesses may be compelled by the use of subpoena as provided in Rule 45. The deposition of a person confined in prison may be taken only by leave of court on such terms as the court prescribes.

A party desiring to take a deposition upon written questions shall serve them upon every other party with a notice stating:

(1) the name and address of the person who is to answer them, if known, and if the name is not known, a general description sufficient to identify him or the particular class or group to which he belongs; and

(2) the name or descriptive title and address of the officer before whom the deposition is to be taken.

A deposition upon written questions may be taken of an organization, including a governmental organization, or a partnership in accordance with the provisions of Rule 30(B)(6).

Within twenty [20] days after the notice and written questions are served, a party may serve cross questions upon all other parties. Within ten [10] days after being served with cross questions, a party may serve redirect questions upon all other parties. Within ten [10] days after being served with redirect questions, a party may serve recross questions upon all other parties. The court may for cause shown enlarge or shorten the time.

(B) Officer to take responses and prepare record. A copy of the notice and copies of all questions served shall be delivered by the party taking the deposition to the officer designated in the notice, who shall proceed promptly, in the manner provided by Rule 30(C), (E), and (F), to take the testimony of the witness in response to the questions and to prepare, certify, and deliver the deposition, attaching thereto the copy of the notice and the questions received by him, in accordance with Rule 5(E).

(C) Notice of filing. When the deposition is filed the party taking it shall promptly give notice thereof to all other parties.

Amended Oct. 15, 1986, effective Jan. 1, 1987; amended Sept. 30, 2004, effective Jan. 1, 2005.

Rule 32. Use of depositions in court proceedings

(A) Use of depositions. At the trial or upon the hearing of a motion or an interlocutory proceeding, any part or all of a deposition, so far as admissible under the Rules of Evidence applied as though the witness were then present and testifying, may be used against any party who was present or represented at the taking of the deposition, by or against any party who had reasonable notice thereof or by any party in whose favor it was given in accordance with any one [1] of the following provisions:

(1) Any deposition may be used by any party for the purpose of contradicting or impeaching the testimony of deponent as a witness.

(2) The deposition of a party, or an agent or person authorized by a party to testify or furnish such evidence or of anyone who at the time of taking the deposition was an officer, director, or managing agent, executive officer or a person designated under Rule 30(B)(6) or 31(A) to testify on behalf of an organization, including a governmental organization, or partnership which is a party may be used by an adverse party for any purpose.

(3) The deposition of a witness, whether or not a party, may be used by any party for any purpose if the court finds:

(a) that the witness is dead; or

(b) that the witness is outside the state, unless it appears that the absence of the witness was procured by the party offering the deposition; or

(c) that the witness is unable to attend or testify because of age, sickness, infirmity, or imprisonment; or

(d) that the party offering the deposition has been unable to procure the attendance of the witness by subpoena; or

(e) upon application and notice, that such exceptional circumstances exist as to make it desirable, in the interest of justice and with due regard to the importance of presenting the testimony of witnesses orally in open court, to allow the deposition to be used; or

(f) upon agreement of the parties.

(4) If only part of a deposition is offered in evidence by a party, an adverse party may require him to introduce any other part which ought in context to be considered with the part introduced, and any party may introduce any other parts.

Substitution of parties pursuant to Rule 25 does not affect the right to use depositions previously taken; and, when an action in any court of the United States or of any state has been dismissed and another action involving the same subject-matter is afterward brought between the same parties or their representatives or successors in interest, all depositions lawfully taken and duly filed in the former action may be used in the latter as if originally taken therefor.

(B) Objections to admissibility. Subject to the provisions of Rule 28(B) and subdivision (D)(3) of this rule, objection may be made at the trial or hearing to receiving in evidence any depositions or part thereof for any reason which would require the exclusion of the evidence if the witness were then present and testifying.

(C) Effect of taking or using depositions. A party does not make a person his own witness for any purpose by taking his deposition. The introduction in evidence of the deposition or any part thereof for any purpose other than that of contradicting or impeaching the deponent makes the deponent the witness of the party introducing the deposition, but this shall not apply to the use by an adverse party of a deposition as described in subdivision (A)(2) of this rule. At the trial or hearing any party may rebut any relevant evidence contained in a deposition whether introduced by him or by any other party.

(D) Effect of errors and irregularities in depositions.

(1) *As to notice.* All errors and irregularities in the notice for taking a deposition are waived unless written objection is promptly served upon the party giving the notice.

(2) *As to disqualification of officer.* Objection to taking a deposition because of disqualification of the officer before whom it is to be taken is waived unless made before the taking of the deposition begins or as soon thereafter as the disqualification becomes known or could be discovered with reasonable diligence.

(3) *As to taking of deposition.*

(a) Objections to the competency of a witness or to the competency, relevancy, or materiality of testimony are not waived by failure to make them before or during the taking of the deposition, unless the ground of the objection is one which might have been obviated or removed if presented at that time.

(b) Errors and irregularities occurring at the oral examination in the manner of taking the deposition, in the form of the questions or answers, in the oath or affirmation, or in the conduct of parties and errors of any kind which might be obviated, removed, or cured if promptly presented, are waived unless reasonable objection thereto is made at the taking of the deposition.

(c) Objections to the form of written questions submitted under Rule 31 are waived unless served in writing upon the party propounding them within the time allowed for serving the succeeding cross or other questions and within five [5] days after service of the last questions authorized.

(4) *As to completion and return of deposition.* Errors and irregularities in the manner in which the testimony is transcribed or the deposition is prepared, signed, certified, sealed, indorsed, transmitted, filed, or otherwise dealt with by the officer under Rules 30 and 31 are waived unless a motion to suppress the deposition or some part thereof is made with reasonable promptness after such defect is, or with due diligence might have been, ascertained.

Amended Nov. 3, 1981, effective Jan. 1, 1982; amended Sept. 30, 2004, effective Jan. 1, 2005.

Rule 33. Interrogatories to parties

(A) Availability—Procedures for use. Any party may serve upon any other party written interrogatories to be answered by the party served or, if the party served is an organization including a governmental organization, or a partnership, by any officer or agent, who shall furnish such information as is available to the party. Interrogatories may, without leave of court, be served upon the plaintiff after commencement of the action and upon any other party with or after service of the summons and complaint upon that party.

(B) Format of interrogatory and response. A party who serves written interrogatories under this rule shall provide, after each interrogatory, a reasonable amount of space for a response or an objection. Answers or objections to interrogatories shall include the interrogatory which is being answered or to which an objection is made. The interrogatory which is being answered or objected to shall be placed immediately preceding the answer or objection.

Each interrogatory shall be answered separately and fully in writing under oath, unless it is objected to, in which event the reasons for objections shall be stated in lieu of an answer. The answers are to be signed by the person making them, and the objections signed by the attorney making them.

(C) Time for service, response, and sanctions. The party upon whom the interrogatories have been served shall serve a copy of the answers and objections within a period designated by the party submitting the interrogatories, not less than thirty (30) days after the service thereof or within such shorter or longer time as the court may allow. The party submitting the interrogatories may move for an order under Rule 37(A) with respect to any objection to or other failure to answer an interrogatory.

The party upon whom the interrogatories have been served may object to the failure to follow the Format requirements in subpart (B) by returning the interrogatories to the party who caused them to be served. If this objection is to be made, the interrogatories shall be returned to the party who caused them to be served not later than the seventh (7th) day after they were received. If the interrogatories are not returned in that time, then this objection is waived.

(D) Scope—Use at trial. Interrogatories may relate to any matters which can be inquired into under Rule 26(B), and the answers may be used to the extent permitted by the rules of evidence.

An interrogatory otherwise proper is not objectionable merely because an answer to the interrogatory involves an opinion, contention, or legal conclusion, but the court may order that such an interrogatory be answered at a later time, or after designated discovery has been completed, or at a pre-trial conference.

(E) Option to produce business records. Where the answer to an interrogatory may be derived or ascertained from the business records of the party upon whom the interrogatory has been served or from an examination, audit or inspection of such business records, including a compilation, abstract or summary thereof, and the burden of deriving or ascertaining the answer is substantially the same for the party serving the interrogatory as for the party served, it is a sufficient answer to such interrogatory to specify the records from which the answer may be derived or ascertained and to afford to the party serving the interrogatory reasonable opportunity to examine, audit or inspect such records and to make copies, compilations, abstracts or summaries. A specification shall be in sufficient detail to permit the interrogating party to locate and to identify, as readily as can the party served, the records from which the answer may be ascertained.

Amended Nov. 3, 1981, effective Jan. 1, 1982; amended Dec. 3, 1987, effective Jan. 1, 1988.

Rule 34. Production of documents, electronically stored information, and things and entry upon land for inspection and other purposes

(A) Scope. Any party may serve on any other party a request:

(1) to produce and permit the party making the request, or someone acting on the requester's behalf, to inspect and copy, any designated documents or electronically stored information (including, without limitation, writings, drawings, graphs, charts, photographs, sound recordings, images and other data or data compilations from which information can be obtained or translated, if necessary, by the respondent into reasonably usable form) or to in-

spect and copy, test, or sample any designated tangible things which constitute or contain matters within the scope of Rule 26(B) and which are in the possession, custody or control of the party upon whom the request is served; or

(2) to permit entry upon designated land or other property in the possession or control of the party upon whom the request is served for the purpose of inspection and measuring, surveying, photographing, testing, or sampling the property or any designated object or operation thereon, within the scope of Rule 26(B).

(B) Procedure. The request may, without leave of court, be served upon the plaintiff after commencement of the action and upon any other party with or after service of the summons and complaint upon that party. The request shall set forth the items to be inspected either by individual item or by category, and describe each item and category with reasonable particularity. The request may specify the form or forms in which electronically stored information is to be produced. The request shall specify a reasonable time, place, and manner of making the inspection and performing the related acts. Service is dispensed with if the whereabouts of the parties is unknown.

The party upon whom the request is served shall serve a written response within a period designated in the request, not less than thirty [30] days after the service thereof or within such shorter or longer time as the court may allow. The response shall state, with respect to each item or category, that inspection and related activities will be permitted as requested, unless it is objected to, including an objection to the requested form or forms for producing electronically stored information, stating in which event the reasons for objection shall be stated. If objection is made to part of an item or category, the part shall be specified. If objection is made to the requested form or forms for producing electronically stored information—or if no form was specified in the request—the responding party must state the form or forms it intends to use. The party submitting the request may move for an order under Rule 37(A) with respect to any objection to or other failure to respond to the request or any part thereof, or any failure to permit inspection as requested.

Unless the parties otherwise agree, or the court otherwise orders, a party who produces documents for inspection shall produce them as they are kept in the usual course of business or shall organize and label them to correspond with the categories in the request.

If a request for electronically stored information does not specify the form or forms of production, a responding party must produce the information in a form or forms in which it is ordinarily maintained or in a form or forms that are reasonably usable.

A party need not produce the same electronically stored information in more than one form.

(C) Application to Non-parties:

(1) A witness or person other than a party may be requested to produce or permit the matters allowed by subsection (A) of this rule. Such request shall be served upon other parties and included in or with a subpoena served upon such witness or person.

(2) Neither a request nor subpoena to produce or permit as permitted by this rule shall be served upon a non-party until at least fifteen (15) days after the date on which the party intending to serve such request or subpoena serves a copy of the proposed request and subpoena on all other parties. Provided, however, that if such request or subpoena relates to a matter set for hearing within such fifteen (15) day period or arises out of a *bona fide* emergency, such request or subpoena may be served upon a non-party one (1) day after receipt of the proposed request or subpoena by all other parties.

(3) The request shall contain the matter provided in subsection (B) of this rule. It shall also state that the witness or person to whom it is directed is entitled to security against damages or payment of damages resulting from such request and may respond to such request by submitting to its terms, by proposing different terms, by objecting specifically or generally to the request by serving a written response to the party making the request within thirty (30) days, or by moving to quash as permitted by Rule 45(B). Any party, or any witness or person upon whom the request properly is made may respond to the request as provided in subsection (B) of this rule. If the response of the witness or person to whom it is directed is unfavorable, if he moves to quash, if he refuses to cooperate after responding or fails to respond, or if he objects, the party making the request may move for an order under Rule 37(A) with respect to any such response or objection. In granting an order under this subsection and Rule 37(A)(2) the court shall condition relief upon the prepayment of damages to be proximately incurred by the witness or person to whom the request is directed or require an adequate surety bond or other indemnity conditioned against such damages. Such damages shall include reasonable attorneys' fees incurred in reasonable resistance and in establishing such threatened damage or damages.

(4) A party receiving documents from a non-party pursuant to this provision shall serve copies on all other parties within fifteen (15) days of receiving the documents. If the documents are voluminous and service of a complete set of copies is burdensome, the receiving party shall notify all parties within fifteen (15) days of receiving the documents that the documents are available for inspection at the location of their production by the non-party, or at another location agreed to by the parties. The parties shall agree to arrangements for copying, and any party desiring copies shall bear the cost of reproducing them.

(D) Exception to best evidence rule. When a party or witness in control of a writing or document subject to examination under this rule or Rule 9.2(E) refuses or is unable to produce it, evidence thereof shall be allowed by other parties without compliance with the rule of evidence requiring production of the original document or writing as best evidence.

Amended Nov. 3, 1981, effective Jan. 1, 1982; Dec. 5, 1994, effective Feb. 1, 1995; July 1, 2003, effective Jan. 1, 2004; Sept. 10, 2007, effective Jan. 1, 2008; Sept. 9, 2008, effective Jan. 1, 2009; Sept. 7, 2012, effective Jan. 1, 2013.

Rule 35. Physical and mental examination of persons

(A) Order for examination. When the mental or physical condition (including the blood group) of a party, or of a person in the custody or under the legal control of a party, is in controversy, the court in which the action is pending may order the party to submit to a physical or mental examination by a suitably licensed or certified examiner or to produce for examination the person in his custody or legal control. The order may be made only on motion for good cause shown and upon notice to the person to be examined and to all parties and shall specify the time, place, manner, conditions, and scope of the examination and the person or persons by whom it is to be made.

(B) Report of licensed or certified examiner.

(1) If requested by the party against whom an order is made under Rule 35(A) or the person examined, the party causing the examination to be made shall deliver to him a copy of a detailed written report of the examiner setting out his findings, including results of all tests made, diagnoses and conclusions, together with like reports of all earlier examinations of the same condition. After delivery the party causing the examination shall be entitled upon request to receive from the party against whom the order is made a like report of any examination, previously or thereafter made, of the same condition, unless, in the case of a report of examination of a person not a party, the party shows that he is unable to obtain it. The court on motion may make an order against a party requiring delivery of a report on such terms as are just, and if an examiner fails or refuses to make a report the court may exclude his testimony if offered at the trial.

(2) By requesting and obtaining a report of the examination so ordered or by taking the deposition of the examiner, the party examined waives any privilege he may have in that action or any other involving the same controversy, regarding the testimony of every other person who has examined or may thereafter examine him in respect of the same mental or physical condition.

(3) This subdivision applies to examinations made by agreement of the parties, unless the agreement expressly provides otherwise. This subdivision does not preclude discovery of a report of an examiner or the taking of a deposition of the examiner in accordance with the provisions of any other rule.

Amended Dec. 14, 1970, effective March 1, 1971; Amended Dec. 21, 2001, effective April 1, 2002.

Rule 36. Requests for admission

(A) Request for admission. A party may serve upon any other party a written request for the admission, for purposes of the pending action only, of the truth of any matters within the scope of Rule 26(B) set forth in the request, including the genuineness of any documents described in the request. Copies of documents shall be served with the request unless they have been or are otherwise furnished or made available for inspection and copying. The request may, without leave of court, be served upon the plaintiff after commencement of the action and upon any other party with or after service of the summons and complaint upon that party.

Each matter of which an admission is requested shall be separately set forth. The matter is admitted unless, within a period designated in the request, not less than thirty [30] days after service thereof or within such shorter or longer time as the court may allow, the party to whom the request is directed serves upon the party requesting the admission a written answer or objection addressed to the matter, signed by the party or by his attorney. If objection is made, the reasons therefor shall be stated. The answer shall specifically deny the matter or set forth in detail the reasons why the answering party cannot truthfully admit or deny the matter. A denial shall fairly meet the substance of the requested admission, and when good faith requires that a party qualify his answer or deny only a part of the matter of which an admission is requested, he shall specify so much of it as is true and qualify or deny the remainder. An answering party may not give lack of information or knowledge as a reason for failure to admit or deny unless he states that he has made reasonable inquiry and that the information known or readily obtainable by him is insufficient to enable him to admit or deny or that the inquiry would be unreasonably burdensome. A party who considers that a matter of which an admission has been requested presents a genuine issue for trial may not, on that ground alone, object to the request; he may, subject to the provisions of Rule 37(C), deny the matter or set forth reasons why he cannot admit or deny it.

The party who has requested the admissions may move for an order with respect to the answers or objections. Unless the court determines that an objection is justified, it shall order that an answer be served. If the court determines that an answer does not comply with the requirements of this rule, it may order either that the matter is admitted or that an amended answer be served. The court may, in lieu of these orders, determine that final disposition of the request be made at a pre-trial conference or at a designated time prior to trial. The provisions of Rule 37(A)(4) apply to the award of expenses incurred in relation to the motion.

(B) Effect of admission. Any matter admitted under this rule is conclusively established unless the court on motion permits withdrawal or amendment of the admission. Subject to the provisions of Rule 16 governing amendment of a pre-trial order, the court may permit withdrawal or amendment when the presentation of the merits of the action will be subserved thereby and the party who obtained the admission fails to satisfy the court that withdrawal or amendment will prejudice him in maintaining his action or defense on the merits. Any admission made by a party under this rule is for the purpose of the pending action only and is not an admission by him for any other purpose nor may it be used against him in any other proceeding.

Amended Nov. 3, 1981, effective Jan. 1, 1982.

Rule 37. Failure to make or cooperate in discovery: Sanctions

(A) Motion for order compelling discovery. A party, upon reasonable notice to other parties and all persons affected thereby, may apply for an order compelling discovery as follows:

(1) *Appropriate court.* An application for an order to a party may be made to the court in which the action is pending, or alternately, on matters relating to a deposition or an order under Rule 34, to the court in the county where the deposition is being taken or where compliance is to be made under Rule 34. An application for an order to a deponent who is not a party shall be made to the court in the county where the deposition is being taken.

(2) *Motion.* If a party refuses to allow inspection under Rule 9.2(E), or if a deponent fails to answer a question propounded or submitted under Rule 30 or 31, or an organization, including without limitation a governmental organization or a partnership, fails to make designation under Rule 30(B)(6) or 31(A), or a party fails to answer an interrogatory submitted under Rule 33, or if a party or witness or other person, in response to a request submitted under Rule 34, fails to respond that inspection will be permitted as requested or fails to permit inspection as requested, the discovering party may move for an order compelling an answer, or a designation, or an order compelling inspection in accordance with the request. When taking a deposition on oral examination, the proponent of the question may complete or adjourn the examination before he applies for an order.

If the court denies the motion in whole or in part, it may make such protective order as it would have been empowered to make on a motion made pursuant to Rule 26(C).

(3) *Evasive or incomplete answer.* For purposes of this subdivision an evasive or incomplete answer is to be treated as a failure to answer.

(4) *Award of expenses of motion.* If the motion is granted, the court shall, after opportunity for hearing, require the party or deponent whose conduct necessitated the motion or the party or attorney advising such conduct or both of them to pay to the moving party the reasonable expenses incurred in obtaining the order, including attorney's fees, unless the court finds that the opposition to the motion was substantially justified or that other circumstances make an award of expenses unjust.

If the motion is denied, the court shall, after opportunity for hearing, require the moving party or the attorney advising the motion or both of them to pay to the party or deponent who opposed the motion the reasonable expenses incurred in opposing the motion, including attorney's fees, unless the court finds that the making of the motion was substantially justified or that other circumstances make an award of expenses unjust.

If the motion is granted in part and denied in part, the court may apportion the reasonable expenses incurred in relation to the motion among the parties and persons in a just manner.

(B) Failure to comply with order.

(1) *Sanctions by court in county where deposition is taken.* If a deponent fails to be sworn or to answer a question after being directed to do so by the court in the county in which the deposition is being taken, the failure may be considered a contempt of that court.

(2) *Sanctions by court in which action is pending.* If a party or an officer, director, or managing agent of a party or an organization, including a governmental organization, or a person designated under Rule 30(B)(6) or 31(A) to testify on behalf of a party or an organization, including a governmental organization, fails to obey an order to provide or permit discovery, including an order made under subdivision (A) of this rule or Rule 35, the court in which the action is pending may make such orders in regard to the failure as are just, and among others the following:

    (a) An order that the matters regarding which the order was made or any other designated facts shall be taken to be established for the purposes of the action in accordance with the claim of the party obtaining the order;

    (b) An order refusing to allow the disobedient party to support or oppose designated claims or defenses, or prohibiting him from introducing designated matters in evidence;

    (c) An order striking out pleadings or parts thereof, or staying further proceedings until the order is obeyed, or dismissing the action or proceeding or any part thereof, or rendering a judgment by default against the disobedient party;

    (d) In lieu of any of the foregoing orders or in addition thereto, an order treating as a contempt of court the failure to obey any orders except an order to submit to a physical or mental examination under Rule 35;

    (e) Where a party has failed to comply with an order under Rule 35(A) requiring him to produce another for examination, such orders as are listed in paragraphs (a), (b), and (c) of this subdivision, unless the party failing to comply shows that he is unable to produce such person for examination.

In lieu of any of the foregoing orders or in addition thereto, the court shall require the party failing to obey the order or the attorney advising him or both to pay the reasonable expenses, including attorney's fees, caused by the failure, unless the court finds that the failure was substantially justified or that other circumstances make an award of expenses unjust.

(C) Expenses on failure to admit.

If a party fails to admit the genuineness of any document or the truth of any matter as requested under Rule 36, and if the party requesting the admissions thereafter proves the genuineness of the document or the truth of the matter, he may apply to the court for an order requiring the other party to pay him the reasonable expenses incurred in making that proof, including reasonable attorney's fees. The court shall make the order unless it finds that (1) the request was held objectionable pursuant to Rule 36(A), or (2) the admission sought was of no substantial importance, or (3) the party failing to admit had reasonable ground to believe that he might prevail on the matter, or (4) there was other good reason for the failure to admit.

(D) Failure of party to attend at own deposition or serve answers to interrogatories or respond to requests for inspection.

If a party or an officer, director, or managing agent of a party or an organization, including without limitation a governmental organization, or a person designated under Rule 30(B)(6) or 31(A) to testify on behalf of a party or an organization, including without limitation a governmental organization, fails (1) to appear before the officer who is to take his deposition, after being served with a proper notice, or (2) to serve answers or objections to interrogatories submitted under Rule 33, after proper service of the interrogatories, or (3) to serve a written response to a request for inspection submitted under Rule 34, after proper service of the request, the court in which the action is pending on motion may make such orders in regard to the failure as are just, and among others it may take any action authorized under paragraphs (a), (b), and

(c) of subdivision (B)(2) of this rule. In lieu of any order or in addition thereto, the court shall require the party failing to act or the attorney advising him or both to pay the reasonable expenses, including attorney's fees, caused by the failure, unless the court finds that the failure was substantially justified or that other circumstances make an award of expenses unjust.

The failure to act described in this subdivision may not be excused on the ground that the discovery sought is objectionable unless the party failing to act

has applied for a protective order as provided by Rule 26(C).

(E) Electronically stored information. Absent exceptional circumstances, a court may not impose sanctions under these rules on a party for failing to provide electronically stored information lost as a result of the routine, good faith operation of an electronic information system.

Amended Nov. 3, 1981, effective Jan. 1, 1982; amended Sept. 10, 2007, effective Jan. 1, 2008.

VI. TRIALS

Rule 38. Jury trial of right

(A) Causes triable by court and by jury. Issues of law and issues of fact in causes that prior to the eighteenth day of June, 1852, were of exclusive equitable jurisdiction shall be tried by the court; issues of fact in all other causes shall be triable as the same are now triable. In case of the joinder of causes of action or defenses which, prior to said date, were of exclusive equitable jurisdiction with causes of action or defenses which, prior to said date, were designated as actions at law and triable by jury—the former shall be triable by the court, and the latter by a jury, unless waived; the trial of both may be at the same time or at different times, as the court may direct.

(B) Demand. Any party may demand a trial by jury of any issue triable of right by a jury by filing with the court and serving upon the other parties a demand therefor in writing at any time after the commencement of the action and not later than ten (10) days after the first responsive pleading to the complaint, or to a counterclaim, crossclaim or other claim if one properly is pleaded; and if no responsive pleading is filed or required, within ten (10) days after the time such pleading otherwise would have been required. Such demand is sufficient if indorsed upon a pleading of a party filed within such time.

(C) Same: Specification of issues. In his demand a party may specify the issues which he wishes so tried; otherwise he shall be deemed to have demanded trial by jury for all issues triable as of right by jury. Any other party must file a demand for jury trial to preserve his right to trial by jury:

(1) of issues for which a right to trial by jury was not requested by another party; and

(2) in case a request by another party was improper. But if a proper request for a trial by jury upon issues triable by jury as of right on his behalf is made by any party, such request shall be deemed to have been made on behalf of all parties entitled to a jury trial upon such issues.

(D) Waiver. The failure of a party to appear at the trial, and the failure of a party to serve a demand as required by this rule and to file it as required by Rule 5(E) constitute waiver by him of trial by jury. A

demand for trial by jury made as herein provided may not be withdrawn without the consent of the other party or parties.

The trial court shall not grant a demand for a trial by jury filed after the time fixed in T.R. 38(B) has elapsed except upon the written agreement of all of the parties to the action, which agreement shall be filed with the court and made a part of the record. If such agreement is filed then the court may, in its discretion, grant a trial by jury in which event the grant of a trial by jury may not be withdrawn except by the agreement of all of the parties.

(E) Arbitration. Nothing in these rules shall deny the parties the right by contract or agreement to submit or to agree to submit controversies to arbitration made before or after commencement of an action thereon or deny the courts power to specifically enforce such agreements.

Amended Nov. 10, 1988, effective Jan. 1, 1989; amended Sept. 30, 2004, effective Jan. 1, 2005.

Rule 39. Trial by jury or by the court

(A) By jury. When trial by jury has been demanded as provided in Rule 38, the action shall be designated in the Chronological Case Summary as a jury action. Issues upon which a jury trial is so demanded shall be tried by jury, subject to the following exceptions:

(1) If the parties or their attorneys of record, by written stipulation filed with the court or by oral stipulation made in open court and entered in the record, consent to trial by the court sitting without a jury upon any or all issues triable by jury as of right and so demanded, the court shall try those issues without a jury. The stipulation shall be effective only if filed or made in court before evidence is admitted at the trial or at such later time as the court, in its discretion, may allow.

(2) If a party demands a jury trial on any issue upon which he is entitled to jury trial as of right in the case, the court shall grant it on that issue.

(B) By the court—Advisory jury—Trial by consent. In any case where there are issues upon which a jury trial has not been demanded or has not properly been demanded or upon which there is no right to trial by jury as of right, the court may submit any or all of such issues to a jury for trial. The verdict shall be advisory unless, before the jury retires, the court, with the consent of both parties or their attorneys, orders that the verdict shall have the same effect as if a trial by jury had been a matter of right. Such order shall be granted at the court's discretion, and all issues shall be tried as if subject to jury trial as a matter of right unless the parties' consent is limited to fewer issues, or unless the court limits its order to fewer of those issues upon which consent has been given.

(C) Rulings of the court—Objections. In proceeding under Rules 38 and 39, error may be predicated upon the court's ruling or action without motion or other objection by a party.

(D) Findings in case of advisory jury. Findings of fact shall not be required upon issues to the extent that the judge's decision follows the verdict of a properly selected advisory jury.

Amended Dec. 5, 1994, effective Feb. 1, 1995; Sept. 21, 2010, effective Jan. 1, 2011.

Rule 40. Assignment of cases for trial

(A) [1] **Rules for assignment of cases.** The trial courts shall provide by rule for placing of actions upon the trial calendar:

(1) without request of the parties; or

(2) upon request of a party and notice to the other parties; or

(3) in such manner as the court determines will expedite trials.

Precedence shall be given to actions entitled thereto by any statute of the state, including hearings upon temporary restraining orders, injunctions and receiverships.

[1] This rule contains no subd. (B).

Rule 41. Dismissal of actions

(A) Voluntary dismissal: Effect thereof.

(1) *By plaintiff—By stipulation.* Subject to contrary provisions of these rules or of any statute, an action may be dismissed by the plaintiff without order of court:

(a) by filing a notice of dismissal at any time before service by the adverse party of an answer or of a motion for summary judgment, whichever first occurs; or

(b) by filing a stipulation of dismissal signed by all parties who have appeared in the action.

Unless otherwise stated in the notice of dismissal or stipulation, the dismissal is without prejudice, except that a notice of dismissal operates as an adjudication upon the merits when filed by a plaintiff who has once dismissed in any court of the United States or of any state an action based on or

including the same claim. The provisions of this subdivision shall not apply if the plaintiff in such action could not effectuate service of process, or otherwise procure adjudication on the merits.

(2) *By order of court.* Except as provided in subsection (1) of this subdivision of this rule, an action shall not be dismissed at the plaintiff's instance save upon order of the court and upon such terms and conditions as the court deems proper. If a counterclaim or cross-claim has been pleaded by a defendant prior to the service upon him of the plaintiff's motion to dismiss, the action shall not be dismissed against the defendant's objection unless the counterclaim or cross-claim can remain pending for independent adjudication by the court. Unless otherwise specified in the order, a dismissal under this subsection is without prejudice.

(B) Involuntary dismissal: Effect thereof. After the plaintiff or party with the burden of proof upon an issue, in an action tried by the court without a jury, has completed the presentation of his evidence thereon, the opposing party, without waiving his right to offer evidence in the event the motion is not granted, may move for a dismissal on the ground that upon the weight of the evidence and the law there has been shown no right to relief. The court as trier of the facts may then determine them and render judgment against the plaintiff or may decline to render any judgment until the close of all the evidence. If the court renders judgment on the merits against the plaintiff or party with the burden of proof, the court, when requested at the time of the motion by either party shall make findings if, and as required by Rule 52(A). Unless the court in its order for dismissal otherwise specifies, a dismissal under this subdivision or subdivision (E) of this rule and any dismissal not provided for in this rule, other than a dismissal for lack of jurisdiction, operates as an adjudication upon the merits.

(C) Dismissal of counterclaim, cross-claim, or third-party claim. The provisions of this rule apply to the dismissal of any counterclaim, cross-claim, or third-party claim. A voluntary dismissal by the claimant alone pursuant to subsection (1) of subdivision (A) of this rule shall be made before a responsive pleading is served or, if there is none, before the introduction of evidence at the trial or hearing.

(D) Costs of previously-dismissed action. If a plaintiff who has once dismissed an action in any court commences an action based upon or including the same claim against the same defendant, the court may make such order for the payment of costs of the action previously dismissed as it may deem proper and may stay the proceedings in the action until the plaintiff has complied with the order.

(E) Failure to prosecute civil actions or comply with rules. Whenever there has been a failure to comply with these rules or when no action has been taken in a civil case for a period of sixty [60] days, the court, on motion of a party or on its own motion shall order a hearing for the purpose of dismissing such case. The court shall enter an order of dismissal at plaintiff's costs if the plaintiff shall not show sufficient cause at or before such hearing. Dismissal may be withheld or reinstatement of dismissal may be made subject to the condition that the plaintiff comply with these rules and diligently prosecute the action and upon such terms that the court in its discretion determines to be necessary to assure such diligent prosecution.

(F) Reinstatement following dismissal. For good cause shown and within a reasonable time the court may set aside a dismissal without prejudice. A dismissal with prejudice may be set aside by the court for the grounds and in accordance with the provisions of Rule 60(B).

Amended Nov. 3, 1981, effective Jan. 1, 1982; amended Oct. 29, 1993, effective Jan. 1, 1994.

Rule 42. Consolidation—Separate trials

(A) Consolidation. When actions involving a common question of law or fact are pending before the court, it may order a joint hearing or trial of any or all the matters in issue in the actions; it may order all the actions consolidated; and it may make such orders concerning proceedings therein as may tend to avoid unnecessary costs or delay.

(B) Separate trials. The court, in furtherance of convenience or to avoid prejudice, or when separate trials will be conducive to expedition and economy, may order a separate trial of any claim, cross-claim, counterclaim, or third-party claim, or of any separate issue or of any number of claims, cross-claims, counterclaims, third-party claims, or issues, always preserving inviolate the right of trial by jury.

(C) Submission to Jury in Stages. The Court upon its own motion or the motion of any party for good cause shown may allow the case to be tried and submitted to the jury in stages or segments including, but not limited to, bifurcation of claims or issues of compensatory and punitive damages.

(D) Actions Pending in Different Courts. When civil actions involving a common question of law or fact are pending in different courts, a party to any of the actions may, by motion, request consolidation of those actions for the purpose of discovery and any pre-trial proceedings. Such motion may only be filed in the court having jurisdiction of the action with the earliest filing date and the court shall enter an order of consolidation for the purpose of discovery and any pre-trial proceedings unless good cause to the contrary is shown and found by the court to exist. In the event two or more actions have the same earliest filing date, the motion may be filed only in the court having the lowest court identifier number under Administrative Rule 8(B)(1), which court shall be considered as having the action with the earliest filing date. Upon completion of discovery and any pre-trial proceedings,

each case which has been subject to the order of consolidation shall be ordered returned to the court in which it was pending at the time the order of consolidation was made unless, after notice to all parties and a hearing, the court finds that the action involves unusual or complicated issues of fact or law or involves a substantial question of law of great public importance. In the event the court makes such a finding, it may enter an order of consolidation for the purpose of trial. Except for cause pursuant to IC 34–35–1–1, the right to a change of venue in any action consolidated under this rule shall be suspended during the period of consolidation. Such right shall be reinstated on entry of an order remanding the action to the court in which it was pending at the time of consolidation and the time prescribed for the filing of a motion for change of venue shall be deemed tolled during the period of suspension. Nothing in this Rule shall restrict the equitable discretion of the court having the earliest filed action to dismiss or stay that action. If such an order is entered, that court shall no longer be considered the court in which is pending the action with the earliest filing date for purposes of this Rule. This Subsection (D) shall not apply to actions pending in courts of limited jurisdiction and no such action may be consolidated with another under the provisions of this Subsection (D).

Amended Nov. 13, 1989, effective Jan. 1, 1990; amended Oct. 30, 1992, effective Jan. 1, 1993; amended Sept. 10, 2007, effective Jan. 1, 2008.

Rule 43. Evidence

(A) Form and admissibility. In all trials the testimony of witnesses shall be taken in open court, unless state law, these rules, the Indiana Rules of Evidence, or other rules adopted by the Indiana Supreme Court provide otherwise.

(B) Evidence on motions. When a motion is based on facts not appearing of record the court may hear the matter on affidavits presented by the respective parties, but the court may direct that the matter be heard wholly or partly on oral testimony or depositions.

(C) Interpreters. The court may appoint an interpreter of its own selection and may fix his reasonable compensation. The compensation shall be paid out of funds provided by law or by one or more of the parties as the court may direct, and may be taxed ultimately as costs, in the discretion of the court. Application of this rule shall be in compliance with the Americans with Disabilities Act.

(D) How evidence is presented. The trial shall proceed in the following order, unless the court within its discretion, otherwise directs: First, the party upon whom rests the burden of the issues may briefly state his case and the evidence by which he expects to sustain it. Second, the adverse party may then briefly state his defense and the evidence he expects to offer in support of it. Third, the party on whom rests the burden of the issues must first produce his evidence thereon; the adverse party will then produce his evidence which may then be rebutted.

(E) Public Access. Information filed or introduced in court proceedings is confidential to the extent provided by statutes, rules of court and Indiana Administrative Rule 9(G).

Amended effective May 25, 1994; amended July 1, 2003, effective Jan. 1, 2004; Sept. 15, 2009, effective Jan. 1, 2010.

Rule 44. Proof of official record

The rules concerning proof of official records are governed by the Rules of Evidence.

Amended July 1, 2003, effective Jan. 1, 2004.

Rule 44.1. Determination of foreign law

(A) Foreign law. A party who intends to raise an issue concerning the law of a foreign country shall give notice in his pleadings or other reasonable written notice. The court, in determining foreign law, may consider any relevant material or source, including testimony, whether or not submitted by a party or admissible under Rule 43. The court's determination shall be treated as a ruling on a question of law. It shall be made by the court and not the jury and shall be reviewable.

(B) Law of other states and territories. Judicial notice, proof and notice of intent to offer evidence of the law of another jurisdiction not covered by subdivision (A) of this rule shall be governed by the Uniform Judicial Notice of Foreign Law Act, IC 34–38–4 et seq.

Rule 45. Subpoena

(A) For Attendance of Witnesses—Form—Issuance.

(1) Every subpoena shall:

(a) state the name of the court;

(b) state the title of the action (without naming more than the first named plaintiffs and defendants in the complaint and the case number); and

(c) command each person to whom it is directed to attend and give testimony at a time and place therein specified.

(2) The clerk shall issue a subpoena, or a subpoena for the production of documentary evidence, signed and sealed but otherwise in blank, to a party requesting it or his or her attorney, who shall fill it in before service. An attorney admitted to practice law in this state, as an officer of the court, may also issue and sign such subpoena on behalf of (a) a court in which the attorney has appeared for a party; or (b) a court in which a deposition or production is compelled by the subpoena, if the deposition or production pertains to an action pending in a court where the attorney has appeared for a party in that case.

(B) For production of documentary evidence. A subpoena may also command the person to whom it is directed to produce the books, papers, documents, or tangible things designated therein; but the court, upon motion made promptly and in any event at or before the time specified in the subpoena for compliance therewith, may

(1) quash or modify the subpoena if it is unreasonable and oppressive or

(2) condition denial of the motion upon the advancement by the person in whose behalf the subpoena is issued of the reasonable cost of producing the books, papers, documents, or tangible things.

(C) Service. A subpoena may be served by the sheriff or his deputy, a party or any person. Service of a subpoena upon a person named therein shall be made by delivering a copy thereof to such person. Service may be made in the same manner as provided in Rule 4.1, Rule 4.16 and Rule 5(B).

(D) Subpoena for taking depositions—Place of examination.

(1) Proof of service of a notice to take a deposition as provided in Rules 30(B) and 31(A) constitutes a sufficient authorization for the issuance by the clerk of court for the county in which the deposition is to be taken of subpoenas for the persons named or described therein. The subpoena may command the person to whom it is directed to produce designated books, papers, documents, or tangible things which constitute or contain matters within the scope of the examination permitted by Rule 26(B), but in that event the subpoena will be subject to the provisions of Rule 26(C) and subdivision (B) of this rule.

(2) An individual may be required to attend an examination only in the county wherein he resides or is employed or transacts his business in person, or at such other convenient place as is fixed by an order of court. A nonresident of the state may be required to attend only in the state and county wherein he is served with a subpoena, or within forty [40] miles from the place of service, or at such other convenient place as is fixed by an order of court. A non-resident plaintiff may be required to attend at his own expense an examination in the county of this state where the action is commenced or in a county fixed by the court.

(E) Subpoena for a hearing or trial. At the request of any party subpoenas for attendance at a hearing or trial shall be issued by the clerk of court of the county in which the action is pending when requested, or, in the case of a subpoena for the taking of a deposition, by the clerk of court of the county in which the action is so pending or in the county in which the deposition is being taken. An attorney admitted to practice law in this state, as an officer of the court, may also issue and sign such subpoenas on behalf of the court in which the action is pending or a court of the county in which the deposition is being taken, if the hearing, deposition or production pertains to an action pending in a court where the attorney has appeared for a party in that case. A subpoena may be served at any place within the state; and when permitted by the laws of the United States, this or another state or foreign country, the court upon proper application and cause shown may authorize the service of a subpoena outside the state in accordance with and as permitted by such law.

(F) Contempt. Failure by any person without adequate excuse to obey a subpoena served upon him may be deemed a contempt of the court from which the subpoena issued, or court of the county where the witness was required thereunder to appear or act. The attendance of all witnesses when duly subpoenaed, and to whom fees have been paid or tendered as required by law may be enforced by attachment.

(G) Tender of fees. Service of a subpoena upon a person named therein shall be made by delivering a copy thereof to such person who shall be required to attend outside his county of residence as provided in section (C), and by so tendering to him the fees for one [1] day's attendance and the mileage allowed by law. Such tender shall not be required to be made to a party who is subpoenaed or to an officer, employee, agent or representative of a party which is an organization, including the estate or any governmental organization, who is being examined upon any matter connected in any way with his employment or with duties to the organization.

(H) Proof of service of subpoena—Fees. When a subpoena is served by the sheriff or his deputy, his return shall be proof of service. When served by any other person the service must be shown by affidavit. No fees or costs for the service of a subpoena shall be collected or charged as costs except when service is made by the sheriff or his deputy.

Amended Nov. 30, 1971; amended Oct. 30, 1992, effective Jan. 1, 1993 amended Dec. 5, 1994, effective Feb. 1, 1995; Amended Dec. 21, 2001, effective April 1, 2002.

Rule 46. Exceptions unnecessary

Formal exceptions to rulings or orders of the court are unnecessary; but for all purposes for which an exception has heretofore been necessary it is sufficient that a party, at the time the ruling or order of the court is made or sought, makes known to the court the action which he desires the court to take or his objection to the action of the court and his grounds therefor; and, if a party has no opportunity to object to a ruling or order at the time it is made, the absence of an objection does not thereafter prejudice him.

Rule 47. Jurors and peremptory challenges

(A) Number of jurors in civil cases. In all civil cases, the jury shall consist of six (6) members.

(B) Alternate Jurors. The Court may direct that no more than three (3) jurors in addition to the regular jury be called and impanelled to sit as alternate jurors. Alternate jurors in the order in which they are called shall replace jurors who, prior to the time the jury returns its verdict, become or are found to be unable or disqualified to perform their duties. Alternate jurors shall be drawn in the same manner, shall have the same qualifications, shall be subject to the same examination and challenges, shall take the same oath, and shall have the same functions, powers, facilities and privileges as the regular jurors. An alternate juror who does not replace a regular juror shall be discharged after the jury brings in its verdict. If alternate jurors are permitted to attend deliberations, they shall be instructed not to participate.

(C) Peremptory Challenges.

(1) Each side shall have three (3) peremptory challenges.

(2) In addition to the peremptory challenges under subsection (1), each side is entitled to:

(a) one (1) peremptory challenge if the court directs that one (1) or two alternate jurors are to be impanelled; or

(b) two (2) peremptory challenges if the court directs that three (3) alternate jurors are to be impanelled.

(3) The additional peremptory challenges under subsection (2) may be used only against alternate jurors and the peremptory challenges under subsection (1) may not be used against alternate jurors.

(D) Examination of jurors. The court shall permit the parties or their attorneys to conduct the examination of prospective jurors, and may conduct examination itself. The court's examination may include questions, if any, submitted in writing by any party or attorney. If the court conducts the examination, it shall permit the parties or their attorneys to supplement the examination by further inquiry. The court may impose an advance time limitation upon such examination by the parties or their attorneys. At the expiration of said limitation, the court shall liberally grant additional reasonable time upon a showing of good cause related to the nature of the case, the quantity of prospective jurors examined and juror vacancies remaining, and the manner and content of the inquiries and responses given by the prospective jurors. The court may prohibit the parties and their attorneys from examination which is repetitive, argumentative, or otherwise improper but shall permit reasonable inquiry of the panel and individual prospective jurors.

Amended Dec. 17, 1973, effective Jan. 1, 1974; amended Aug. 17, 1983; amended Nov. 20, 1986, effective Jan. 1, 1987; amended Sept. 2, 1987; amended effective Sept. 24, 1987; amended Dec. 23, 1996, effective March 1, 1997.

Rule 48. Juries of less than six—Majority verdict

The parties may stipulate that the jury shall consist of any number less than six (6) at any time before the jury is selected or that a verdict or a finding of a stated majority of the jurors shall be taken as the verdict or finding of the jury at any time before the verdict has been announced.

Amended Aug. 17, 1983.

Rule 49. Special verdicts and interrogatories

Special verdicts and interrogatories to the jury are abolished.

Rule 50. Judgment on the evidence (Directed verdict)

(A) Judgment on the Evidence—How Raised—Effect. Where all or some of the issues in a case tried before a jury or an advisory jury are not supported by sufficient evidence or a verdict thereon is clearly erroneous as contrary to the evidence because the evidence is insufficient to support it, the court shall withdraw such issues from the jury and enter judgment thereon or shall enter judgment thereon notwithstanding a verdict. A party may move for such judgment on the evidence.

(1) after another party carrying the burden of proof or of going forward with the evidence upon any one or more issues has completed presentation of his evidence thereon; or

(2) after all the parties have completed presentation of the evidence upon any one or more issues; or

(3) after all the evidence in the case has been presented and before judgment; or

(4) in a motion to correct errors; or

(5) may raise the issue upon appeal for the first time in criminal appeals but not in civil cases; or

(6) The trial court upon its own motion may enter such a judgment on the evidence at any time before final judgment, or before the filing of a notice of appeal, or, if a Motion to Correct Error is made, at any time before entering its order or ruling thereon. A party who moves for judgment on the evidence at the close of the evidence offered by an opponent may offer evidence in the event that the motion is not granted, without having reserved the right so to do and to the same extent as if the motion had not been made. A motion for a judgment on the evidence which is not granted or which is granted only as to a part of the issues is not a waiver of trial by jury even though all parties to the action have moved for judgment on the evidence. A motion for judgment on the evidence made at one stage of the proceedings is not a waiver of the right of the court or of any party to make such motion on the same or different issues or reasons at a later stage as permitted above, except that error of the court in denying the motion shall be deemed corrected by evidence thereafter offered or admitted.

(B) Jury trial subject to entry of judgment on the evidence. Every case tried by a jury is made subject to the right of the court, before or after the jury is discharged, to enter final judgment on the evidence, without directing a verdict thereon.

(C) New trial in lieu of judgment on the evidence. When a judgment on the evidence is sought before or after the jury is discharged, the court may grant a new trial as to part or all of the issues in lieu of a judgment on the evidence when entry of a judgment is impracticable or unfair to any of the parties or otherwise is improper, whether requested or not.

(D) Reasons for judgment on the evidence—Partial relief. A motion or request for judgment on the evidence shall state the reasons therefor, but it need not be accompanied by a peremptory instruction or prayer for particular relief. In appropriate cases the court, in whole or in part, may grant to some or all of the parties a judgment on the evidence or new trial in lieu thereof. Unless otherwise specified a motion or request for a judgment on the evidence is general, but the court shall grant such judgment or relief only as is proper.

(E) Motion for judgment notwithstanding verdict, motion in arrest of judgment, demurrer to the evidence and venire de novo abolished. The motion for judgment notwithstanding verdict, motion in arrest of judgment, demurrer to the evidence, and venire de novo are abolished.

Amended Nov. 10, 1988, effective Jan. 1, 1989; amended effective Feb. 16, 1989; Amended February 4, 2000, effective Jan. 1, 2001.

Rule 51. Instructions to jury: Objections, requests: Submission in stages

(A) Preliminary Instructions. When the jury has been sworn the court shall instruct the jury in accordance with Jury Rule 20. Each party shall have reasonable opportunity to examine these preliminary instructions and state his specific objections thereto out of the presence of the jury and before any party has stated his case. (The court may of its own motion and, if requested by either party, shall reread to the jury all or any part of such preliminary instructions along with the other instructions given to the jury at the close of the case. A request to reread any preliminary instruction does not count against the ten [10] instructions provided in subsection (D) below.) The parties shall be given reasonable opportunity to submit requested instructions prior to the swearing of the jury, and object to instructions requested or proposed to be given.

(B) Final Instructions. — The judge shall instruct the jury as to the law upon the issues presented by the evidence in accordance with Jury Rule 26.

(C) Objections and requested instructions before submission. At the close of the evidence and before argument each party may file written requests that the court instruct the jury on the law as set forth in the requests. The court shall inform counsel of its proposed action upon the requests prior to their arguments to the jury. No party may claim as error the giving of an instruction unless he objects thereto before the jury retires to consider its verdict, stating distinctly the matter to which he objects and the grounds of his objection. Opportunity shall be given to make the objection out of the hearing of the jury. The court shall note all instructions given, refused or tendered, and all written objections submitted thereto, shall be filed in open court and become a part of the record. Objections made orally shall be taken by the reporter and thereby shall become a part of the record.

(D) Limit upon requested instructions. Each party shall be entitled to tender no more than ten [10] requested instructions, including pattern instructions, to be given to the jury; however, the court in its discretion for good cause shown may fix a greater number. Each tendered instruction shall be confined to one [1] relevant legal principle. No party shall be entitled to predicate error upon the refusal of a trial court to give any tendered instruction in excess of the number fixed by this rule or the number fixed by the court order, whichever is greater.

(E) Indiana Pattern Jury Instructions (Criminal)/Indiana Model Jury Instructions (Civil). Any party requesting a trial court to give any instruction from the Indiana Pattern Jury Instructions (Criminal)/Indiana Model Jury Instructions (Civil), prepared under the sponsorship of the Indiana Judges Association, may make such request in writing without copying the instruction verbatim, by merely designating the number thereof in the publication.

Amended effective June 8, 1971; Sept. 21, 2010, effective Jan. 1, 2011; Dec. 10, 2010, effective Jan. 1, 2011.

Rule 52. Findings by the Court

(A) Effect. In the case of issues tried upon the facts without a jury or with an advisory jury, the court shall determine the facts and judgment shall be entered thereon pursuant to Rule 58. Upon its own motion, or the written request of any party filed with the court prior to the admission of evidence, the court in all actions tried upon the facts without a jury or with an advisory jury (except as provided in Rule 39[D]) shall find the facts specially and state its conclusions thereon. The court shall make special findings of fact without request

(1) in granting or refusing preliminary injunctions;

(2) in any review of actions by an administrative agency; and

(3) in any other case provided by these rules or by statute.

On appeal of claims tried by the court without a jury or with an advisory jury, at law or in equity, the court on appeal shall not set aside the findings or judgment unless clearly erroneous, and due regard shall be given to the opportunity of the trial court to judge the credibility of the witnesses. The findings of a master, and answers to questions or interrogatories submitted to the jury shall be considered as findings of the court to the extent that the court adopts them. If an opinion or memorandum of decision is filed, it will be sufficient if the findings of fact and conclusions appear therein. Findings of fact are unnecessary on decisions of motions under Rules 12 or 56 or any other motion except as provided in Rule 41(B) (dismissal) and 59(J) (motion to correct errors).

(B) Amendment of findings and judgment—causes therefor. Upon its own motion at any time before a motion to correct errors (Rule 59) is required to be made, or with or as part of a motion to correct errors by any party, the court, in the case of a claim tried without a jury or with an advisory jury, may open the judgment, if one has been entered, take additional testimony, amend or make new findings of fact and enter a new judgment or any combination thereof if:

(1) the judgment or findings are either against the weight of the evidence, or are not supported by or contrary to the evidence;

(2) special findings of fact required by this rule are lacking, incomplete, inadequate in form or content or do not cover the issues raised by the pleadings or evidence;

(3) special findings of fact required by this rule are inconsistent with each other; or

(4) the judgment is inconsistent with the special findings of fact required by this rule.

Failure of a party to move to modify the findings or judgment under this subdivision and failure to object to proposed findings or judgment or such findings or judgment which has been entered of record shall not constitute a waiver of the right to raise the question in or with a motion to correct errors, or on appeal.

(C) Proposed findings. In any case where special findings of facts and conclusions thereon are to be made the court shall allow and may require the attorneys of the parties to submit to the court a draft of findings of facts and conclusions thereon which they propose or suggest that the court make in such a case.

(D) Findings upon part of the issues. The court may make special findings of fact upon less than all the issues in a case when:

(1) special findings of fact are made but are not required under this rule; or

(2) findings are required because of the request of a party or parties who have demanded findings only upon such specified issues.

The court's failure to find upon a material issue upon which a finding of fact is required by this subdivision or this rule shall not be resolved by any presumption and may be challenged under subdivision (B) of this rule; but findings of fact with respect to issues upon which findings are not required shall be recognized as findings only upon the issues or matters covered thereby and the judgment or general finding, if any, shall control as to the other issues or matters which are not covered by such findings.

Amended Nov. 3, 1981, effective Jan. 1, 1982; amended effective Feb. 16, 1989.

Rule 53. Masters

(A) Appointment and compensation. Each trial court with the concurrence of the Supreme Court may appoint a special master in a case pending therein. As used in these rules the word "master" includes without limitation an attorney, a referee, an auditor, an examiner, a commissioner, and an assessor. The compensation to be allowed to a master shall be allowed in the manner and amount paid to judges pro tem and such additional compensation as is fixed by the Supreme Court.

(B) Reference. A reference to a master shall be the exception and not the rule. In actions to be tried by a jury, a reference shall be made only when the issues are complicated; in actions to be tried without a jury, save in matters of account and of difficult computation of damages, a reference shall be made only upon a showing that some exceptional condition requires it. Reference shall be allowed when the parties agree prior to trial as provided by these rules or by statute.

(C) Powers. The order of reference to the master may specify or limit his powers and may direct him to report only upon particular issues or to do or perform particular acts or to receive and report evidence only and may fix the time and place for beginning and closing the hearings and for the filing of the master's report. Subject to the specifications and limitations stated in the order, the master has and shall exercise the power to regulate all proceedings in every hearing before him and to do all acts and take all measures necessary or proper for the efficient performance of his duties under the order. He may require the production before him of evidence upon all matters embraced in the reference, including the production of all books, papers, vouchers, documents, and writings applicable thereto. He may rule upon the admissibility of evidence unless otherwise directed by the order of reference and has the authority to put witnesses on oath and may himself examine them and may call the parties to the action and examine them upon oath. When a party so requests, the master shall make a record of the evidence offered and excluded in the

same manner and subject to the same limitations as provided in Rule 43(C) for a court sitting without a jury.

(D) Proceedings.

(1) *Meetings.* When a reference is made, the clerk shall forthwith furnish the master with a copy of the order of reference. Upon receipt thereof unless the order of reference otherwise provides, the master shall forthwith set a time and place for the first meeting of the parties or their attorneys to be held within twenty [20] days after the date of the order of reference and shall notify the parties or their attorneys. It is the duty of the master to proceed with all reasonable diligence. Either party, on notice to the parties and master, may apply to the court for an order requiring the master to speed the proceedings and to make his report. If a party fails to appear at the time and place appointed, the master may proceed ex parte or, in his discretion, adjourn the proceedings to a future day, giving notice to the absent party of the adjournment.

(2) *Witnesses.* The parties may procure the attendance of witnesses before the master by the issuance and service of subpoenas as provided in Rule 45. If without adequate excuse a witness fails to appear or give evidence, he may be punished as for a contempt and be subjected to the consequences, penalties, and remedies provided in Rules 37 and 45.

(3) *Statement of accounts.* When matters of accounting are in issue before the master, he may prescribe the form in which the amounts shall be submitted and in any proper case may require or receive in evidence a statement by a certified public accountant who is called as a witness. Upon objection of a party to any of the items thus submitted or upon a showing that the form of statement is insufficient, the master may require a different form of statement to be furnished, or the accounts or specific items thereof to be provided by oral examination of the accounting parties or upon written interrogatories or in such other manner as he directs.

(E) Report.

(1) *Contents and filing.* The master shall prepare a report upon the matters submitted to him by the order of reference and, if required by request of any party or the court prior to hearing or the taking of evidence by him to make findings of fact, he shall set them forth in the report. He shall file the report with the clerk of the court and in an action to be tried without a jury, unless otherwise directed by the order of reference, shall file with it a transcript of the proceedings and of the evidence and the original exhibits. The clerk shall forthwith mail to all parties notice of the filing.

(2) *In nonjury actions.* In an action to be tried without a jury the court shall accept the master's decision or his findings of fact unless clearly errone-

ous. Within ten [10] days after being served with notice of the filing of the report any party may serve written objections thereto upon the other parties. Application to the court for action upon the report and upon objections thereto shall be by motion and upon notice as prescribed in Rules 5 and 6. The court after hearing may adopt the report or may reject it in whole or in part or may receive further evidence or may re-commit it with instructions.

(3) *In jury actions.* In an action to be tried by a jury the master shall not be directed to report the evidence. His findings upon the issues submitted to him are admissible as evidence of the matters found and may be read to the jury, subject to the ruling of the court upon any objections in point of law which may be made to the report.

(4) *Stipulation as to findings.* The effect of a master's report is the same whether or not the parties have consented to the reference; but, when the parties stipulate that a master's findings of fact shall be final, only questions of law arising upon the report shall thereafter be considered.

(5) *Draft report.* Before filing his report a master may submit a draft thereof to counsel for all parties for the purpose of receiving their suggestions.

(F) Particular laws not affected. Nothing in this rule shall affect laws providing for the appointment and duties of probate commissioners; and nothing shall prevent any probate or other similar court from appointing a master under this rule.

Rule 53.1. Failure to rule on motion

(A) Time limitation for ruling. In the event a court fails for thirty (30) days to set a motion for hearing or fails to rule on a motion within thirty (30) days after it was heard or thirty (30) days after it was filed, if no hearing is required, upon application by an interested party, the submission of the cause may be withdrawn from the trial judge and transferred to the Supreme Court for the appointment of a special judge.

(B) Exceptions. The time limitation for ruling on a motion established under Section (A) of this rule shall exclude any period after which the case is referred to alternative dispute resolution and until a report on the alternative dispute resolution is submitted to the court. The time limitation for ruling on a motion established under Section (A) of this rule shall not apply where:

(1) The Court, within thirty (30) days after filing, orders that a motion be considered during the trial on the merits of the cause; or

(2) The parties who have appeared or their counsel stipulate or agree on record that the time limitation for ruling on a motion shall not apply; or

(3) The time limitation for ruling has been extended by the Supreme Court as provided by Section (D) of this rule; or

(4) The ruling in question involves a repetitive motion, a motion to reconsider, a motion to correct error, a petition for post-conviction relief, or a ministerial post-judgment act.

(C) Time of ruling. For the purposes of Section (A) of this rule, a court is deemed to have set a motion for hearing on the date the setting is noted in the Chronological Case Summary, and to have ruled on the date the ruling is noted in the Chronological Case Summary.

(D) Extension of time for ruling. A judge may apply to the Supreme Court of Indiana to extend the time limitation set forth under Trial Rule 53.1, 53.2, or 53.3. The application must be filed prior to the filing of a praecipe with the Clerk under Trial Rules 53.1, 53.2, or 53.3, must be verified, must be served on the Clerk and all parties of record, and must set forth the following information:

(1) The nature of the matter under submission;

(2) The circumstances warranting the delay; and

(3) The additional time requested.

The withdrawal of submission under Trial Rule 53.1 or 53.2 or denial of a motion to correct error under Trial Rule 53.3 may not take effect during the pendency of the application for an extension of time to rule. However, if the time limitation expires while the application is pending before the Supreme Court, the jurisdiction of the trial judge shall be suspended at that point pending the action of the Supreme Court.

(E) Procedure for withdrawing submission. Upon the filing by an interested party of a praecipe specifically designating the motion or decision delayed, the Clerk of the court shall enter the date and time of the filing on the praecipe, record the filing in the Chronological Case Summary under the cause, which entry shall also include the date and time of the filing of the praecipe, and promptly forward the praecipe and a copy of the Chronological Case Summary to the Executive Director of the Division of State Court Administration (Executive Director). The Executive Director shall determine whether or not a ruling has been delayed beyond the time limitation set forth under Trial Rule 53.1 or 53.2.

(1) If the Executive Director determines that the ruling or decision has not been delayed, the Executive Director shall provide notice of the determination in writing to the Clerk of the court where the case is pending and the submission of the cause shall not be withdrawn. The Clerk of the court where the case in pending shall notify, in writing, the judge and all parties of record in the proceeding and record the determination in the Chronological Case Summary under the cause.

(2) If the Executive Director determines that a ruling or decision has been delayed beyond the time limitation set forth under Trial Rule 53.1 or 53.2, the Executive Director shall give written notice of the determination to the judge, the Clerk of the trial court, and the Clerk of the Supreme Court of Indiana that the submission of the case has been withdrawn from the judge. The withdrawal is effective as of the time of the filing of the praecipe. The Clerk of the trial court shall record this determination in the Chronological Case Summary under the cause and provide notice to all parties in the case. The Executive Director shall submit the case to the Supreme Court of Indiana for appointment of a special judge or such other action deemed appropriate by the Supreme Court.

(F) Report to Supreme Court. When a special judge is appointed under Trial Rule 53.1 or 53.2, the judge from whom submission was withdrawn shall, within ten (10) days from receipt of the order appointing a special judge, file a written report in the Supreme Court under the cause appointing the special judge. This report shall fully state the nature of the matters held in excess of the time limitations. Additionally, the report may relate any other facts or circumstances which the judge deems pertinent.

(G) Permanent record. The Supreme Court shall maintain a permanent record of special judge appointments under Trial Rules 53.1 and 53.2.

Amended Jan. 18, 1972, effective Jan. 19, 1972; Dec. 17, 1973, effective Feb. 1, 1974; Nov. 1, 1982, effective Jan. 1, 1983; Dec. 5, 1994, effective Feb. 1, 1995; Dec. 21, 2001, effective April 1, 2002; Aug. 15, 2006, effective Jan. 1, 2007; Sept. 21, 2010, effective Jan. 1, 2011; Dec. 10, 2010, effective Jan. 1, 2011; Sept. 20, 2011, effective Jan. 1, 2012; Sept. 7, 2012, effective Jan. 1, 2013.

Rule 53.2. Time for holding issue under advisement; delay of entering a judgment

(A) Time limitation for holding matter under advisement. Whenever a cause (including for this purpose a petition for post conviction relief) has been tried to the court and taken under advisement by the judge, and the judge fails to determine any issue of law or fact within ninety (90) days, the submission of all the pending issues and the cause may be withdrawn from the trial judge and transferred to the Supreme Court for the appointment of a special judge.

(B) Exceptions. The time limitation for holding an issue under advisement established under Section (A) of this rule shall not apply where:

(1) The parties who have appeared or their counsel stipulate or agree on record that the time limitation for decision set forth in this rule shall not apply; or

(2) The time limitation for decision has been extended by the Supreme Court pursuant to Trial Rule 53.1(D).

(C) Time of decision. For the purpose of Section (A) of this rule, a court is deemed to have decided on the date the decision is noted in the Chronological Case Summary.

(D) Extension of time for decision. The procedure for extending the time limitation for decision shall be as set forth in Trial Rule 53.1(D).

(E) Procedure for withdrawing submission. The procedure for withdrawing submission and processing the appointment of a special judge shall be as set forth in Trial Rule 53.1(E).

(F) Report to Supreme Court. Whenever a special judge is appointed pursuant to this rule, the judge from whom submission has been withdrawn shall file a report with the Supreme Court as provided for in Trial Rule 53.1(F).

Amended Jan. 18, 1972, effective Jan. 19, 1972; Nov. 1, 1982, effective Jan. 1, 1983; Dec. 4, 1998, effective July 1, 1999; Sept. 21, 2010, effective Jan. 1, 2011.

Rule 53.3. Motion to correct error: time limitation for ruling

(A) Time limitation for ruling on motion to correct error. In the event a court fails for forty-five (45) days to set a Motion to Correct Error for hearing, or fails to rule on a Motion to Correct Error within thirty (30) days after it was heard or forty-five (45) days after it was filed, if no hearing is required, the pending Motion to Correct Error shall be deemed denied. Any appeal shall be initiated by filing the notice of appeal under Appellate Rule 9(A) within thirty (30) days after the Motion to Correct Error is deemed denied.

(B) Exceptions. The time limitation for ruling on a motion to correct error established under Section (A) of this rule shall not apply where:

(1) The party has failed to serve the judge personally; or

(2) The parties who have appeared or their counsel stipulate or agree on record that the time limitation for ruling set forth under Section (A) shall not apply; or

(3) The time limitation for ruling has been extended by Section (D) of this rule.

(C) Time of ruling. For the purposes of Section (A) of this rule, a court is deemed to have set a motion for hearing on the date the setting is noted in the Chronological Case Summary, and to have ruled on the date the ruling is noted in the Chronological Case Summary.

(D) Extension of time for ruling. The Judge before whom a Motion to Correct Error is pending may extend the time limitation for ruling for a period of no more than thirty (30) days by filing an entry in the cause advising all parties of the extension. Such entry must be in writing, must be noted in the Chronological Case Summary before the expiration of the initial time period for ruling set forth under Section

(A), and must be served on all parties. Additional extension of time may be granted only upon application to the Supreme Court as set forth in Trial Rule 53.1(D).

Added Nov. 1, 1982, effective Jan. 1, 1983. Amended effective Feb. 16, 1989; Feb. 4, 2000, effective Jan. 1, 2001; amended effective Sept. 25, 2002; Sept. 21, 2010, effective Jan. 1, 2011.

Rule 53.4. Repetitive motions and motions to reconsider; time for holding under advisement; automatic denial

(A) Repetitive motions and motions to reconsider ruling on a motion. No hearing shall be required upon a repetitive motion or upon motions to reconsider orders or rulings upon a motion. Such a motion by any party or the court or such action to reconsider by the court shall not delay the trial or any proceedings in the case, or extend the time for any further required or permitted action, motion, or proceedings under these rules.

(B) Effect of court's delay in ruling upon repetitive motion or motion to reconsider ruling on a motion. Unless such a motion is ruled upon within five (5) days it shall be deemed denied, and entry of service of notice of such denial shall not be required. This Rule 53.4 does not apply to an original motion for judgment on the evidence under Rule 50 after the jury is discharged, to amend or make additional findings of fact under Rule 52(B), an original motion to correct errors under Rule 59, or for correction of relief from judgments under Rule 60 or to the original motions to the extent expressly permitted or expressly designated as extending time under these rules.

Formerly Rule 53.3, amended Dec. 7, 1970, effective Jan. 1, 1971; amended Jan. 18, 1972, effective Jan. 19, 1972; renumbered 53.4 and amended Nov. 1, 1982, effective Jan. 1, 1983; amended Nov. 30, 1989, effective Jan. 1, 1990.

Rule 53.5. Continuances

Upon motion, trial may be postponed or continued in the discretion of the court, and shall be allowed upon a showing of good cause established by affidavit or other evidence. The court may award such costs as will reimburse the other parties for their actual expenses incurred from the delay. A motion to postpone the trial on account of the absence of evidence can be made only upon affidavit, showing the materiality of the evidence expected to be obtained, and that due diligence has been used to obtain it; and where the evidence may be; and if it is for an absent witness, the affidavit must show the name and residence of the witness, if known, and the probability of procuring the testimony within a reasonable time, and that his absence has not been procured by the act or connivance of the party, nor by others at his request, nor with his knowledge and consent, and what facts he believes to be true, and that he is unable to prove such facts by any other witness whose testimony can be as readily procured. If, thereupon, the adverse party will consent that, on the trial, the facts shall be taken as true if the absent evidence is written or documentary, and, in case of a witness, that he will testify to said facts as true, the trial shall not be postponed for that cause, and in such case, the party against whom such evidence is used, shall have the right to impeach such absent witness, as in the case where the witness is present, or his deposition is used.

Formerly Rule 53.4, amended Jan. 18, 1972, effective Jan. 19, 1972; amended Nov. 21, 1980, effective Jan. 1, 1981; renumbered 53.5 and amended Nov. 1, 1982, effective Jan. 1, 1983.

VII. JUDGMENT

Rule 54. Judgment; Costs

(A) Definition–Form. "Judgment", as used in these rules, includes a decree and any order from which an appeal lies. A judgment shall contain all matters required by Rule 58 but need not contain a recital of pleadings, the report of a master, or the record of prior proceedings.

(B) Judgment upon multiple claims or involving multiple parties. When more than one [1] claim for relief is presented in an action, whether as a claim, counterclaim, cross-claim, or third-party claim, or when multiple parties are involved, the court may direct the entry of a final judgment as to one or more but fewer than all of the claims or parties only upon an express determination that there is no just reason for delay and upon an express direction for the entry of judgment. In the absence of such determination and direction, any order or other form of decision, however designated, which adjudicates fewer than all the claims or the rights and liabilities of fewer than all

the parties shall not terminate the action as to any of the claims or parties, and the order or other form of decision is subject to revision at any time before the entry of judgment adjudicating all the claims and the rights and liabilities of all the parties. A judgment as to one or more but fewer than all of the claims or parties is final when the court in writing expressly determines that there is no just reason for delay, and in writing expressly directs entry of judgment, and an appeal may be taken upon this or other issues resolved by the judgment; but in other cases a judgment, decision or order as to less than all the claims and parties is not final.

(C) Demand for judgment. A judgment by default shall not be different in kind from or exceed in amount that prayed for in the demand for judgment. Except as to a party against whom a judgment is entered by default, every final judgment shall grant the relief to which the party in whose favor it is rendered is entitled, even if the party has not demanded such relief in his pleadings.

(D) Costs. Except when express provision therefor is made either in a statute or in these rules, costs shall be allowed as of course to the prevailing party unless the court otherwise directs in accordance with any provision of law; but costs against any governmental organization, its officers, and agencies shall be imposed only to the extent permitted by law. Costs may be computed and taxed by the clerk on one [1] day's notice. On motion served within five [5] days thereafter, the action of the clerk may be reviewed by the court.

(E) Judgments severable. Unless otherwise specified therein, judgments against two [2] or more persons or upon two [2] or more claims shall be deemed joint and several for purposes of:

(1) permitting enforcement proceedings jointly or separately against different parties or jointly or separately against their property; or

(2) permitting one or more parties to challenge the judgment (by appeal, motion and the like) as against one or more parties as to one or more claims or parts of claims.

Nothing herein is intended to dispense with notice requirements, or provisions requiring or permitting parties to join or participate in the same appeal.

Amended Nov. 13, 1989, effective permissive prior to Jan. 1, 1991 and mandatory Jan. 1, 1991.

Rule 55. Default

(A) Entry. When a party against whom a judgment for affirmative relief is sought has failed to plead or otherwise comply with these rules and that fact is made to appear by affidavit or otherwise, the party may be defaulted by the court.

(B) Default judgment. In all cases the party entitled to a judgment by default shall apply to the court therefor; but no judgment by default shall be entered against a person (1) known to be an infant or incompetent unless represented in the action by a general guardian, committee, conservator, or other such representative who has appeared therein; or (2) entitled to the protections against default judgments provided by the Servicemembers Civil Relief Act, as amended (the "Act"), 50 U.S.C. appx. § 521, unless the requirements of the Act have been complied with. See Ind. Small Claims Rule 10(B)(3). If the party against whom judgment by default is sought has appeared in the action, he (or, if appearing by a representative, his representative) shall be served with written notice of the application for judgment at least three [3] days prior to the hearing on such application. If, in order to enable the court to enter judgment or to carry it into effect, it is necessary to take an account or to determine the amount of damages or to establish the truth of any averment by evidence or to make an investigation of any other matter, the court may con-

duct such hearing or order such references as it deems necessary and proper and shall accord a right of trial by jury to the parties when and as required.

(C) Setting aside default. A judgment by default which has been entered may be set aside by the court for the grounds and in accordance with the provisions of Rule 60(B).

(D) Plaintiff, counterclaimants, cross-claimants. The provisions of this rule apply whether the party entitled to the judgment by default is a plaintiff, a third-party plaintiff, or a party who has pleaded a cross-claim or counterclaim. In all cases a judgment by default is subject to the limitations of Rule 54(C).

(E) Judgment against governmental organizations. A judgment by default may be entered against a governmental organization.

Amended Dec. 7, 1970, effective Jan. 1, 1971; Sept. 10, 2007, effective Jan. 1, 2008; Oct. 28, 2010, effective Jan. 1, 2011.

Rule 56. Summary judgment

(A) For claimant. A party seeking to recover upon a claim, counterclaim, or cross-claim or to obtain a declaratory judgment may, at any time after the expiration of twenty [20] days from the commencement of the action or after service of a motion for summary judgment by the adverse party, move with or without supporting affidavits for a summary judgment in his favor upon all or any part thereof.

(B) For defending party—When motion not required. A party against whom a claim, counterclaim, or cross-claim is asserted or a declaratory judgment is sought may, at any time, move with or without supporting affidavits for a summary judgment in his favor as to all or any part thereof. When any party has moved for summary judgment, the court may grant summary judgment for any other party upon the issues raised by the motion although no motion for summary judgment is filed by such party.

(C) Motion and proceedings thereon. The motion and any supporting affidavits shall be served in accordance with the provisions of Rule 5. An adverse party shall have thirty (30) days after service of the motion to serve a response and any opposing affidavits. The court may conduct a hearing on the motion. However, upon motion of any party made no later than ten (10) days after the response was filed or was due, the court shall conduct a hearing on the motion which shall be held not less than ten (10) days after the time for filing the response. At the time of filing the motion or response, a party shall designate to the court all parts of pleadings, depositions, answers to interrogatories, admissions, matters of judicial notice, and any other matters on which it relies for purposes of the motion. A party opposing the motion shall also designate to the court each material issue of fact which that party asserts precludes entry of summary judgment and the evidence relevant thereto. The judgment sought shall be rendered forthwith if the designated evidentiary matter shows that there is no genuine issue as to any material fact and that the moving party is entitled to a judgment as a matter of law. A summary judgment may be rendered upon less than all the issues or claims, including without limitation the issue of liability or damages alone although there is a genuine issue as to damages or liability as the case may be. A summary judgment upon less than all the issues involved in a claim or with respect to less than all the claims or parties shall be interlocutory unless the court in writing expressly determines that there is no just reason for delay and in writing expressly directs entry of judgment as to less than all the issues, claims or parties. The court shall designate the issues or claims upon which it finds no genuine issue as to any material facts. Summary judgment shall not be granted as of course because the opposing party fails to offer opposing affidavits or evidence, but the court shall make its determination from the evidentiary matter designated to the court.

(D) Case not fully adjudicated on motion. If on motion under this rule judgment is not rendered upon the whole case or for all the relief asked and a trial is necessary, the court at the hearing of the motion, by examining the pleadings and the evidence before it and by interrogating counsel, shall if practicable ascertain what material facts exist without substantial controversy and what material facts are actually and in good faith controverted. It shall thereupon make an order specifying the facts that appear without substantial controversy, including the extent to which the amount of damages or other relief is not in controversy, and directing such further proceedings in the action as are just. Upon the trial of the action the facts so specified shall be deemed established, and the trial shall be conducted accordingly.

(E) Form of affidavits—Further testimony—Defense required. Supporting and opposing affidavits shall be made on personal knowledge, shall set forth such facts as would be admissible in evidence, and shall show affirmatively that the affiant is competent to testify to the matters stated therein. Sworn or certified copies not previously self-authenticated of all papers or parts thereof referred to in an affidavit shall be attached thereto or served therewith. The court may permit affidavits to be supplemented or opposed by depositions, answers to interrogatories, or further affidavits. When a motion for summary judgment is made and supported as provided in this rule, an adverse party may not rest upon the mere allegations or denials of his pleading, but his response, by affidavits or as otherwise provided in this rule, must set forth specific facts showing that there is a genuine issue for trial. If he does not so respond, summary judgment, if appropriate, shall be entered against him. Denial of summary judgment may be challenged by a motion to correct errors after a final judgment or order is entered.

(F) When affidavits are unavailable. Should it appear from the affidavits of a party opposing the motion that he cannot for reasons stated present by affidavit facts essential to justify his opposition, the court may refuse the application for judgment or may order a continuance to permit affidavits to be obtained or depositions to be taken or discovery to be had or may make such other order as is just.

(G) Affidavits made in bad faith. Should it appear to the satisfaction of the court at any time that any of the affidavits presented pursuant to this rule are presented in bad faith or solely for the purpose of delay, the court shall forthwith order the party employing them to pay to the other party the amount of the reasonable expenses which the filing of the affidavits caused him to incur, including reasonable attorney's fees, and any offending party or attorney may be adjudged guilty of contempt.

(H) Appeal–Reversal. No judgment rendered on the motion shall be reversed on the ground that there is a genuine issue of material fact unless the material fact and the evidence relevant thereto shall have been specifically designated to the trial court.

(I) Alteration of Time. For cause found, the Court may alter any time limit set forth in this rule upon motion made within the applicable time limit.

Amended Oct. 15, 1986, effective Jan. 1, 1987; Dec. 23, 1987, effective Jan. 1, 1988; Dec. 21, 1990, effective Jan. 1, 1991; Dec. 27, 1990, effective Jan. 1, 1991; Oct. 30, 1992, effective Jan. 1, 1993; Dec. 5, 1994, effective Feb. 1, 1995; Sept. 30, 2004, effective Jan. 1, 2005; July 1, 2005, effective Jan. 1, 2006; Sept. 10, 2007, effective Jan. 1, 2008.

Rule 57. Declaratory judgments

The procedure for obtaining a declaratory judgment shall be in accordance with these rules, and the right to trial by jury may be demanded under the circumstances and in the manner provided in Rules 38 and 39. The existence of another adequate remedy does not preclude a judgment for declaratory relief in cases where it is appropriate. Declaratory relief shall be allowed even though a property right is not involved. Affirmative relief shall be allowed under such remedy when the right thereto is established. The court may order a speedy hearing of an action for a declaratory judgment and may advance it on the calendar.

Rule 58. Entry and content of judgment

(A) Entry of judgment. Subject to the provisions of Rule 54(B), upon a verdict of a jury, or upon a decision of the court, the court shall promptly prepare and sign the judgment, and the clerk shall thereupon enter the judgment in the Record of Judgments and Orders and note the entry of the judgment in the Chronological Case Summary and Judgment Docket. A judgment shall be set forth on a separate document, except that a judgment may appear upon the same document upon which appears the court's findings, conclusions, or opinion upon the issues. The entry of the judgment shall not be delayed for the taxing of costs. Attorneys may submit suggested forms of judgment to the court, and upon request of the court, shall assist the court in the preparation of a judgment, but the judgment shall not be delayed to await the resolution of issues by agreement of counsel. The judge failing promptly to cause the judgment to be prepared, signed and entered as provided herein may be compelled to do so by mandate.

(B) Content of judgment. Except in small claims cases, a judgment shall contain the following elements:

(1) A statement of the submission indicating whether the submission was to a jury or to the Court; whether the submission was upon default, motion, cross-claim, counterclaim or third-party complaint; and if the submission was to less than all issues or parties, such other matters as may be necessary to clearly state what issue is resolved or what party is bound by the judgment.

(2) A statement of the appearances at the submission indicating whether the parties appeared in person, by counsel, or both; whether there was a failure to appear after notice; and whether the submission was conducted by telephone conference.

(3) At the court's discretion and in such detail as it may deem appropriate, a statement of the court's jurisdiction over the parties and action and of the issues considered in sufficient particularity to enable any party affected by the judgment to raise in another action the defenses of merger, bar or claim or issue preclusion.

(4) A statement in imperative form which clearly and concisely sets forth the relief granted, any alteration of status, any right declared, or any act to be done or not done.

(5) The date of the judgment and the signature of the judge.

(C) Documents and Information Excluded from Public Access and Confidential Pursuant to Administrative Rule 9(G)(1). Every court that issues a judgment or order containing documents or information excluded from public access pursuant to Administrative Rule 9(G)(1) shall comply with the provisions of Trial Rule 5(G).

Amended Nov. 13, 1989, effective permissive prior to Jan. 1, 1991 and mandatory Jan. 1, 1991; amended Sept. 30, 2004, effective Jan. 1, 2005.

Rule 59.   Motion to correct error

(A) Motion to correct error—When mandatory. A Motion to Correct Error is not a prerequisite for appeal, except when a party seeks to address:

(1) Newly discovered material evidence, including alleged jury misconduct, capable of production within thirty (30) days of final judgment which, with reasonable diligence, could not have been discovered and produced at trial; or

(2) A claim that a jury verdict is excessive or inadequate.

All other issues and grounds for appeal appropriately preserved during trial may be initially addressed in the appellate brief.

(B) Filing of motion. The motion to correct error, if any, may be made by the trial court, or by any party.

(C) Time for filing: Service on judge. The motion to correct error, if any, shall be filed not later than thirty (30) days after the entry of a final judgment is noted in the Chronological Case Summary. A copy of the motion to correct error shall be served, when filed, upon the judge before whom the case is pending pursuant to Trial Rule 5. The time at which the court is deemed to have ruled on the motion is set forth in T.R. 53.3.

(D) Errors raised by motion to correct error, and content of motion.

Where used, a motion to correct error need only address those errors found in Trial Rule 59(A)(1) and (2).

Any error raised however shall be stated in specific rather than general terms and shall be accompanied by a statement of facts and grounds upon which the error is based. The error claimed is not required to be stated under, or in the language of the bases for the motion allowed by this rule, by statute, or by other law.

(E) Statement in opposition to motion to correct error. Following the filing of a motion to correct error, a party who opposes the motion may file a statement in opposition to the motion to correct error not later than fifteen [15] days after service of the motion. The statement in opposition may assert grounds which show that the final judgment or appealable final order should remain unchanged, or the statement in opposition may present other grounds which show that the party filing the statement in opposition is entitled to other relief.

(F) Motion to correct error granted. Any modification or setting aside of a final judgment or an appealable final order following the filing of a Motion to Correct Error shall be an appealable final judgment or order.

(G) Cross errors. If a motion to correct error is denied, the party who prevailed on that motion may, in the appellate brief and without having filed a statement in opposition to the motion to correct error in the trial court, defend against the motion to correct error on any ground and may first assert grounds for relief therein, including grounds falling within sections (A)(1) and (2) of this rule. In addition, if a notice of appeal rather than a motion to correct error is filed by a party, the opposing party may raise any grounds as cross-errors and also may raise any reasons to affirm the judgment directly in the appellate brief, including those grounds for which a motion to correct error is required when directly appealing a judgment under Sections (A)(1) and (2) of this rule.

(H) Motion to correct error based on evidence outside the record.

(1) When a motion to correct error is based upon evidence outside the record, the motion shall be supported by affidavits showing the truth of the grounds set out in the motion and the affidavits shall be served with the motion.

(2) If a party opposes a motion to correct error made under this subdivision, that party has fifteen [15] days after service of the moving party's affidavits and motion, in which to file opposing affidavits.

(3) If a party opposes a motion to correct error made under this subdivision, that party has fifteen [15] days after service of the moving party's affidavits and motion, in which to file its own motion to correct errors under this subdivision, and in which to assert relevant matters which relate to the kind of relief sought by the party first moving to correct error under this subdivision.

(4) No reply affidavits, motions, or other papers from the party first moving to correct errors are contemplated under this subdivision.

(I) Costs in the event a new trial is ordered. The trial court, in granting a new trial, may place costs upon the party who applied for the new trial, or a portion of the costs, or it may place costs abiding the event of the suit, or it may place all costs or a portion of the costs on either or all parties as justice and equity in the case may require after the trial court has taken into consideration the causes which made the new trial necessary.

(J) Relief granted on motion to correct error. The court, if it determines that prejudicial or harmful error has been committed, shall take such action as will cure the error, including without limitation the following with respect to all or some of the parties and all or some of the errors:

(1) Grant a new trial;

(2) Enter final judgment;

(3) Alter, amend, modify or correct judgment;

(4) Amend or correct the findings or judgment as provided in Rule 52(B);

(5) In the case of excessive or inadequate damages, enter final judgment on the evidence for the amount of the proper damages, grant a new trial, or grant a new trial subject to additur or remittitur;

(6) Grant any other appropriate relief, or make relief subject to condition; or

(7) In reviewing the evidence, the court shall grant a new trial if it determines that the verdict of a non-advisory jury is against the weight of the evidence; and shall enter judgment, subject to the provisions herein, if the court determines that the verdict of a non-advisory jury is clearly erroneous

as contrary to or not supported by the evidence, or if the court determines that the findings and judgment upon issues tried without a jury or with an advisory jury are against the weight of the evidence.

In its order correcting error the court shall direct final judgment to be entered or shall correct the error without a new trial unless such relief is shown to be impracticable or unfair to any of the parties or is otherwise improper; and if a new trial is required it shall be limited only to those parties and issues affected by the error unless such relief is shown to be impracticable or unfair. If corrective relief is granted, the court shall specify the general reasons therefor. When a new trial is granted because the verdict, findings or judgment do not accord with the evidence, the court shall make special findings of fact upon each material issue or element of the claim or defense upon which a new trial is granted. Such finding shall indicate whether the decision is against the weight of the evidence or whether it is clearly erroneous as contrary to or not supported by the evidence; if the decision is found to be against the weight of the evidence, the findings shall relate the supporting and opposing evidence to each issue upon which a new trial is granted; if the decision is found to be clearly erroneous as contrary to or not supported by the evidence, the findings shall show why judgment was not entered upon the evidence.

(K) Orders regarding services, programs, or placement of children alleged to be delinquents or alleged to be in need of services. No motion to correct error is allowed concerning orders or decrees issued pursuant to Indiana Code sections 31–34–4–7(e), 31–34–19–6.1(e), 31–37–5–8(f), or 31–37–18–9(b). Appeals of such orders and decrees shall proceed as prescribed by Indiana Appellate Rule 14.1.

Amended Dec. 11, 1969, effective Jan. 1, 1970; Nov. 13, 1979, effective Jan. 1, 1980; Nov. 21, 1980, effective Jan. 1, 1981; Nov. 10, 1988, effective Jan. 1, 1989; amended effective Feb. 16, 1989; amended Jan. 5, 1990, effective Jan. 17, 1990; Dec. 4, 1998, effective Jan. 1, 1999; Feb. 4, 2000, effective Jan. 1, 2001; amended effective Jan. 1, 2009; amended Sept. 21, 2010, effective Jan. 1, 2011; Sept. 20, 2011, effective Jan. 1, 2012.

Rule 60. Relief from judgment or order

(A) Clerical mistakes. Of its own initiative or on the motion of any party and after such notice, if any, as the court orders, clerical mistakes in judgments, orders or other parts of the record and errors therein arising from oversight or omission may be corrected by the trial court at any time before the Notice of Completion of Clerk's Record is filed under Appellate Rule 8. After filing of the Notice of Completion of Clerk's Record and during an appeal, such mistakes may be so corrected with leave of the court on appeal.

(B) Mistake—Excusable neglect—Newly discovered evidence—Fraud, etc. On motion and upon such terms as are just the court may relieve a party or his legal representative from a judgment, including a judgment by default, for the following reasons:

(1) mistake, surprise, or excusable neglect;

(2) any ground for a motion to correct error, including without limitation newly discovered evidence, which by due diligence could not have been discovered in time to move for a motion to correct errors under Rule 59;

(3) fraud (whether heretofore denominated intrinsic or extrinsic), misrepresentation, or other misconduct of an adverse party;

(4) entry of default or judgment by default was entered against such party who was served only by publication and who was without actual knowledge of the action and judgment, order or proceedings;

(5) except in the case of a divorce decree, the record fails to show that such party was represented by a guardian or other representative, and if the motion asserts and such party proves that

(a) at the time of the action he was an infant or incompetent person, and

(b) he was not in fact represented by a guardian or other representative, and

(c) the person against whom the judgment, order or proceeding is being avoided procured the judgment with notice of such infancy or incompetency, and, as against a successor of such person, that such successor acquired his rights therein with notice that the judgment was procured against an infant or incompetent, and

(d) no appeal or other remedies allowed under this subdivision have been taken or made by or on behalf of the infant or incompetent person, and

(e) the motion was made within ninety [90] days after the disability was removed or a guardian was appointed over his estate, and

(f) the motion alleges a valid defense or claim;

(6) the judgment is void;

(7) the judgment has been satisfied, released, or discharged, or a prior judgment upon which it is based has been reversed or otherwise vacated, or it is no longer equitable that the judgment should have prospective application; or

(8) any reason justifying relief from the operation of the judgment, other than those reasons set forth in sub-paragraphs (1), (2), (3), and (4).

The motion shall be filed within a reasonable time for reasons (5), (6), (7), and (8), and not more than one year after the judgment, order or proceeding was entered or taken for reasons (1), (2), (3), and (4). A movant filing a motion for reasons (1), (2), (3), (4), and (8) must allege a meritorious claim or defense. A motion under this subdivision (B) does not affect the finality of a judgment or suspend its operation. This rule does not limit the power of a court to entertain an independent action to relieve a party from a judg-

ment, order or proceeding or for fraud upon the court. Writs of coram nobis, coram vobis, audita querela, and bills of review and bills in the nature of a bill of review, are abolished, and the procedure for obtaining any relief from a judgment shall be by motion as prescribed in these rules or by an independent action.

(C) Appeal—Change of venue. A ruling or order of the court denying or granting relief, in whole or in part, by motion under subdivision (B) of this rule shall be deemed a final judgment, and an appeal may be taken therefrom as in the case of a judgment. No change of venue in such cases shall be taken from the judge or county except for cause shown by affidavit.

(D) Hearing and relief granted. In passing upon a motion allowed by subdivision (B) of this rule the court shall hear any pertinent evidence, allow new parties to be served with summons, allow discovery, grant relief as provided under Rule 59 or otherwise as permitted by subdivision (B) of this rule.

(E) Infants, incompetents, and governmental organizations. Except as otherwise provided herein, this rule shall apply to infants, incompetents, and governmental organizations. The time for seeking relief against a judgment, order or proceeding allowed or recognized under subdivision (B) of this rule or any other statute shall not be tolled or extended as to such persons.

Amended Nov. 13, 1979, effective Jan. 1, 1980; Nov. 21, 1980, effective Jan. 1, 1981; Dec. 4, 1998, effective Jan. 1, 1999; Feb. 4, 2000, effective Jan. 1, 2001; Sept. 9, 2008, effective Jan. 1, 2009.

Rule 60.5. Mandate of funds

(A) Scope of mandate. Courts shall limit their requests for funds to those which are reasonably necessary for the operation of the court or court-related functions. Mandate will not lie for extravagant, arbitrary or unwarranted expenditures nor for personal expenditures (e.g., personal telephone bills, bar association memberships, disciplinary fees). Prior to issuing the order, the court shall meet with the mandated party to demonstrate the need for said funds. At any time in the process, the dispute may be submitted to mediation by agreement of the parties or by order of the Supreme Court or the special judge.

(B) Procedure. Whenever a court, except the Supreme Court or the Court of Appeals, desires to order either a municipality, a political subdivision of the state, or an officer of either to appropriate or to pay unappropriated funds for the operation of the court or court-related functions, such court shall issue and cause to be served upon such municipality, political subdivision or officer an order to show cause why such appropriation or payment should not be made. Such order to show cause shall be captioned "Order for Mandate of Funds". The matter shall be set for trial on the merits of such order to show cause unless the legislative body, the chief executive officer or the affected officer files a waiver in writing of such a trial and agrees to make such appropriation or payment. The trial shall be without a jury, before a special judge of the court that made the order. There shall be no change of venue from the county or from the special judge appointed by the Supreme Court. The court shall promptly notify the Supreme Court of the entry of such order to show cause and the Supreme Court shall then appoint as special judge an attorney who is not a current or former regular judge and who does not reside nor regularly practice law in the county issuing the Order of Mandate of Funds or in any county contiguous thereto. If the appointed judge fails to qualify within seven [7] days after he has received notice of his appointment, the Supreme Court shall follow the same procedure until an appointed judge does properly qualify. Unless expressly waived by the respondent in writing within thirty (30) days after the entering of the trial judge's decree, a decree or order mandating the payment of funds for the operation of the court or court-related functions shall be automatically reviewed by the Supreme Court. Promptly on expiration of such thirty (30) day period, the trial judge shall certify such decree together with either a stipulation of facts or an electronic transcription of the evidence to the Supreme Court. No motion to correct error nor notice of appeal shall be filed. No mandate order for appropriation or payment of funds made by any court other than the Supreme Court or Court of Appeals shall direct that attorney fees be paid at a rate greater than the reasonable and customary hourly rate for an attorney in the county. No mandate order shall be effective unless it is entered after trial as herein provided and until the order has been reviewed by the Supreme Court or such review is expressly waived as herein provided.

Adopted Nov. 1, 1976. Amended Nov. 3, 1981, effective Jan. 1, 1982; Nov. 16, 1984, effective Jan. 1, 1985; Dec. 21, 2001, effective April 1, 2002; amended effective Feb. 4, 2009.

Rule 61. Harmless error

No error in either the admission or the exclusion of evidence and no error or defect in any ruling or order in anything done or omitted by the court or by any of the parties is ground for granting relief under a motion to correct errors or for setting aside a verdict or for vacating, modifying or otherwise disturbing a judgment or order or for reversal on appeal, unless refusal to take such action appears to the court inconsistent with substantial justice. The court at every stage of the proceeding must disregard any error or defect in the proceeding which does not affect the substantial rights of the parties.

Rule 62. Stay of proceedings to enforce a judgment

(A) Execution. Execution may issue upon notation of a judgment in the Chronological Case Summary except as otherwise provided in this rule hereinafter. During the pendency of an appeal the provisions of subdivision (C) of this rule govern the suspending, modifying, restoring, or granting of an injunction, the appointment of a receiver or, to the extent that a stay is not otherwise permitted by law upon appeal, any judgment or order for specific relief other than the payment of money.

(B) Stay of execution. In its discretion and on such conditions for the security of the adverse party as are proper, the court may stay the execution of or any proceedings to enforce a judgment pending the filing and disposition of

(1) a motion to correct error or to alter or amend a judgment made pursuant to Rule 59,

(2) a motion for judgment in accordance with a motion for a judgment on the evidence made pursuant to Rule 50,

(3) a motion for amendment to the findings or for additional findings or for a new trial or judgment made pursuant to Rule 52,

(4) a motion for relief from a judgment or order made pursuant to Rule 60, or

(5) an appeal.

(C) Stay of orders relating to injunctions, appointment of receivers and orders for specific relief. When an appeal is taken from an interlocutory or final judgment granting, dissolving or denying an injunction, the appointment of a receiver or, to the extent that a stay is not otherwise permitted by law upon appeal, from any judgment or order for specific relief other than the payment of money, the court to which the application is made in its sound discretion may suspend, modify, restore, or grant the injunction, the appointment of the receiver or the specific relief during the pendency of the appeal upon such terms as to bond or otherwise as it considers proper for the security of the rights of the adverse party. Nothing in this rule is intended to affect the original jurisdiction of the Supreme Court or the Indiana Court of Appeals.

(D) Stay upon appeal.

(1) *Procedure for obtaining.* No appeal bond or other security shall be necessary to perfect an appeal from any judgment or appealable interlocutory order. Enforcement of a judgment or appealable interlocutory order will be suspended during an appeal upon the giving of an adequate appeal bond with approved sureties, an irrevocable letter of credit from a financial institution approved in all respects by the court, or other form of security approved by the court. The bond, letter of credit, or other security may be given at or after the time of filing the notice of appeal. The stay is effective when the appeal bond, letter of credit, or other form of security is approved by the appropriate court. The trial court or judge shall have jurisdiction to fix and approve the bond or letter of credit and order a stay pending an appeal as well as prior to the

appeal. If the stay is denied by the trial court the appellate tribunal may reconsider the application at any time after denial; and this provision also shall apply to stays or relief allowed under subdivision (C) of this rule. When the stay or relief is granted by the court on appeal, the clerk of the Supreme Court shall issue a certificate thereof to the clerk of the court below who shall file it with the judgment or order below and deliver it to the sheriff or any officer to whom execution or an enforcement order has been issued.

(2) *Form of appeal bond or letter of credit.* Whenever a party entitled thereto desires a stay on appeal, such party may present to the appropriate court for its approval an appeal bond or an irrevocable letter of credit from a financial institution. The bond or letter of credit shall be conditioned for the satisfaction of the judgment in full together with costs, interest, and damages for delay, if for any reason the appeal is dismissed or if the judgment is affirmed, and to satisfy in full such modification of the judgment and such costs, interest, and damages as the appellate court may adjudge and award. When the judgment is for the recovery of money not otherwise secured, the amount of the bond or letter of credit shall be fixed at such sum as will cover the whole amount of the judgment remaining unsatisfied, costs on the appeal, interest, and damages for delay, unless the court after notice and hearing and for good cause shown fixes a different amount or orders security other than a bond or letter of credit. When the judgment determines the disposition of the property in controversy as in real action, replevin, and actions to foreclose liens or when such property is in the custody of the sheriff or when the proceeds of such property or a bond or letter of credit for its value is in the custody or control of the court, the amount of the appeal bond or letter of credit shall be fixed at such sum only as will secure the amount recovered for the use and detention of the property, the costs of the action, costs on appeal, interest, and damages for delay.

(3) *Effect of appeal bond or letter of credit.* Nothing in this subdivision shall be construed as giving the right to stay, by giving such bond or letter of credit, any judgment or order which cannot now be stayed or suspended by the giving of an appeal bond, except as provided in subdivisions (A), (B) and (C) of this rule. The provisions in this rule do not limit any power of an appellate court or of a judge or justice thereof to stay proceedings during the pendency of an appeal or to suspend, modify, restore, or grant an injunction during the pendency of an appeal or to make any order appropriate to preserve the status quo or the effectiveness of the judgment subsequently to be entered.

(E) Stay in favor of governmental organization—Personal representative. When an appeal or review is taken by a governmental organization, or by a court-appointed representative of a decedent's estate, guardian, receiver, assignee for the benefit of creditors, trustee or other court-appointed representative, the operation or enforcement of the judgment shall be stayed as it would as against other persons upon application to the appropriate court, but no bond, obligation or other security shall be required.

(F) Stay of execution under existing laws—Other bonds required before or as a condition to judgment: Money in lieu of bonds—Amount fixed by court. Execution upon a judgment for recovery of money or sale of property may be stayed, and personal property taken in execution may be delivered up as now provided by law. Indiana Acts, ch. 38, §§ 493–506 and §§ 531–536 (Spec.Sess.1881).[1] Nothing in this rule is intended to alter the right of a party to the protection of a surety bond or security or to obtain relief by furnishing a surety bond or security before or as a condition of final judgment, including without limitation such protection or relief in replevin, ejectment, attachment and injunction actions, upon judicial review of administrative action, in suits upon a lost instrument, for costs and the like. In any case where a surety bond, letter of credit, or security is furnished under this rule, the right to furnish money or a check in lieu of a bond shall remain unimpaired. Any requirement that the amount of the bond or letter of credit be fixed and reconsidered by the court in civil actions and proceedings shall remain unaffected by this rule.

(G) Effect of stay or temporary relief when new trial granted. When an appealable judgment or order is entered against a party who has obtained a prior stay or temporary relief by furnishing a surety bond, letter of credit, or other security, including without limitation relief in replevin, ejectment, attachment and injunctive actions, such stay or temporary relief shall lapse except to the extent:

(1) provided in subdivision (A) of this rule; or

(2) a stay is granted as provided or recognized in this rule.

If thereafter the order or judgment is reversed and a new trial or new hearing in fact is ordered or authorized in favor of such party, the original stay or relief shall not be reinstated unless the reversing court orders otherwise or, in the absence of such order, the court on the new trial or new hearing orders otherwise. When a stay or temporary relief is granted to a party seeking reversal of an appealable order or judgment under subdivision (B), (C) or (D) of this rule and a new trial or new hearing in fact is ordered or authorized in favor of such party, the stay or temporary relief shall continue until a final, appealable judgment or order is entered unless the court on review or appeal orders otherwise or, in the absence of such order, the court on the new trial or new hearing orders otherwise. Nothing in this subdivision is intended to limit the liability of the bondsman, the financial institution issuing the letter of credit, or other security or determine the order of liability assumed among different bondsmen or different security furnished in the course of proceedings before judgment, after judgment and after appeal or review.

(H) Stay of judgment as to multiple claims or multiple parties. When a court has ordered a final judgment under the conditions stated in Rule 54(B), the court may stay enforcement of that judgment until the entering of a subsequent judgment or judgments and may prescribe such conditions as are necessary to secure the benefit thereof to the party in whose favor the judgment is entered.

Amended effective March 22, 1971; May 26, 1971; amended Nov. 13, 1979, effective Jan. 1, 1980; Nov. 10, 1988, effective Jan. 1, 1989; amended effective Feb. 16, 1989; amended Feb. 4, 2000, effective Jan. 1, 2001; amended effective Oct. 2, 2007; amended Sept. 21, 2010, effective Jan. 1, 2011.

1 IC 34–55–2–1 to 34–55–2–13 and IC 34–55–5–1 to 34–55–5–6.

Rule 63. Disability and unavailability of a judge

(A) Disability and unavailability after the trial or hearing. The judge who presides at the trial of a cause or a hearing at which evidence is received shall, if available, hear motions and make all decisions and rulings required to be made by the court relating to the evidence and the conduct of the trial or hearing after the trial or hearing is concluded. If the judge before whom the trial or hearing was held is not available by reason of death, sickness, absence or unwillingness to act, then any other judge regularly sitting in the judicial circuit or assigned to the cause may perform any of the duties to be performed by the court after the verdict is returned or the findings or decision of the court is filed; but if he is satisfied that he cannot perform those duties because he did not preside at the trial or for any other reason, he may in his discretion grant a new trial or new hearing, in whole or in part. The unavailability of any such trial or hearing judge shall be determined and shown by a court order made by the successor judge at any time.

(B) Judge pro tempore in case of disability, unavailability, or neglect.

(1) When a judge of a court submits a verified petition and supporting proof to the Supreme Court stating that the judge is or will be unable to perform the duties of the office because of disability or other basis (e.g., order to military active duty), the Supreme Court shall promptly consider the petition.

(2) When a person submits a verified petition to the Supreme Court stating that a judge of a court (a) is unable to perform the duties of the office because of disability or (b) has failed, refused, or neglected to perform these duties, the Supreme Court shall issue an order to the judge, accompanied by the petition, requiring the judge to show cause as to why a judge pro tempore should not be appointed to perform the duties of the office. The order shall set a date for response and indicate that the judge may request a hearing. The order may

include a date for such a hearing on or after the date set for response. The order shall be served at least ten (10) days before the date set for response.

(3) If the Supreme Court is satisfied that a petition submitted under subsection (1) or (2) should be granted, it shall appoint a full-time judge pro tempore to perform the duties of the office until (a) the term of the office is ended, (b) the office becomes vacant, or (c) the judge's ability to resume those duties is established.

(4) A judge who seeks to resume the duties of the office shall submit a verified petition and supporting proof to the Supreme Court. The judge may request a hearing on the petition.

(5) The Supreme Court may order a judge who has submitted a petition under subsection (1) to demonstrate that the judge is or remains unable to perform the duties of the office.

(C) Qualifications and authority of a judge pro tempore. Any judge appointed under this or any other rule or law shall be an attorney in good standing at the bar of the Supreme Court of this state. In the event the Supreme Court of the state shall appoint a judge pro tempore under these provisions, a duly certified copy of the order and judgment of appointment of such judge pro tempore, attested by the chief justice, shall be issued to the person so appointed. If the person so appointed consents to serve, he shall be qualified as other judges are qualified. A certified copy of the order and judgment of appointment shall be filed with the clerk of the named court and entered in the appropriate records of said court. The person so appointed and qualified as a judge pro tempore shall perform the duties of the regular judge of the court, but always shall be subject to the continuing jurisdiction of the Supreme Court. In the event any judge pro tempore, appointed under the provisions of this rule shall fail to qualify and assume the duties of the regular judge of such court, or in the event such judge pro tempore fails to conduct the business of the court as provided by law, the clerk of the court shall notify the Supreme Court in writing of this fact. Upon the receipt of such notification, the Supreme Court may take such action in the premises, in order to further the administration of justice, as such court may deem to be necessary and just.

(D) Compensation of judge pro tempore. A judge pro tempore appointed by the Supreme Court under this rule shall receive a salary computed at the same rate as the regular judge commencing from the date he qualifies. A judge pro tempore appointed locally shall be paid twenty-five dollars $25.00 for each day or part thereof actually served. The judge pro tempore shall be paid out of the respective county, city or town general fund, without an appropriation therefor, upon allowance by the board of county commissioners of the county or council of the city or town in which the court is located. If he is appointed locally, the judge pro tempore shall present a claim to the board of county commissioners specifying the number of days or parts of days actually served, which claim shall be verified by the clerk of the court and the board shall allow the claim. If he is appointed by the Supreme Court, the judge shall present a claim to the board with a copy of his appointment from the Supreme Court, a statement showing the date of his qualification verified by the clerk and a request that he be paid in the same manner thereafter as a regular judge, and thereafter he shall be paid in the same manner as a regular judge. Nothing herein shall be construed to diminish in any manner the compensation of any regular judge so long as such regular judge continues in office.

(E) Judge pro tempore when judge is unable to attend. A judge who is unable to attend and preside at his court for any cause may appoint in writing a judge pro tempore to conduct the business of this court during his absence. The written appointment shall be entered in the records of the court. When duly sworn, or without being sworn if he is a judge of a court of this state, the judge pro tempore shall have the same authority during the period of his appointment as the judge he replaces. A judge appointed under this provision must meet the qualifications prescribed in subdivision (C) of this rule. Such judge shall be allowed the sum of $25.00 for each day or part thereof actually served, per diem as provided in Rule 79(P) and in the manner provided by subdivision (D) of this rule. In his absence or when he shall be unable to make such appointment, the appointment may be made by the clerk of his court, or the deputy clerk assigned to his court or in his absence by any available county officer.

Amended Dec. 22, 2000, effective Jan. 1, 2001; Aug. 15 2006, effective Jan. 1, 2007; amended Sept. 10, 2007, effective Jan. 1, 2008.

Rule 63.1. Lis pendens notice of proceedings avoiding judgments and circumstances tolling and extending statutes of limitations; assignments and discharges in lis pendens and judgment dockets; lis pendens notices in cases involving interest in personal property

(A) Lis pendens notice of avoidance of judgment and tolling of statute of limitations—Effect of failure to file notice thereof. Avoidance of, or proceedings to avoid a final judgment by a subsequent motion for judgment on the evidence (Rule 50), for amendment of the finding or judgment (Rule 52), and to correct errors (Rule 59), by proceedings for relief from a judgment under Rule 60(B) or under the appellate rules and the tolling or extension of the statute of limitations or other bar of a claim to the property shall be ineffective against a purchaser of an interest in land or a purchaser or lien creditor who acquires an interest in personal property and who claims such interest under or because of such judgment, such tolling or such extension if:

(1) the purchaser of land gives value and perfects of record or takes possession of the land in good faith and without notice of the avoidance, tolling or extension while the person against whom he claims is not in possession of the land and before he has filed notice in the lis pendens record of the county where the land is located; or

(2) the purchaser or lien creditor acquiring an interest in personal property, as a buyer, would take priority over an unperfected security interest while the person against whom he claims has not perfected by possession and before he has filed a financing statement containing lis pendens notice as provided in subdivision (C) of this rule.

The lis pendens notice shall be signed by the party or his attorney seeking avoidance of the judgment or the party with the claim asserted to be tolled; identify the judgment by court and docket number; describe the claim in terms which will lead to the records where any evidence thereof is filed or recorded if such is the case; name the parties; in the case of land designate a present record owner thereof if the parties named are not such owner or owners; and describe the land or personal property if the judgment or claim relates to described land or personal property.

(B) Satisfactions and assignments of docketed judgments and matters entered in lis pendens record. A satisfaction, dismissal, release or assignment of claims or matters recorded or filed in the lis pendens record relating to land or of a judgment entered in the judgment docket may be filed or recorded and indexed in the same manner as originally filed, recorded or docketed, and for the same fees provided that such satisfaction, dismissal, release or assignment is:

(1) in writing, describing the judgment by cause number, signed by the person executing it and acknowledged as in the case of a deed; or

(2) in writing certified as entered in his records by the clerk of court where the judgment is entered or the action is pending;

(3) entered in writing upon the margin of the record signed by the person executing it and attested by the clerk's signature.

A satisfaction, continuation, dismissal, release or assignment of a lis pendens notice filed in the case of personal property is sufficient if it meets the requirements of a termination statement, continuation statement, assignment or release of a financing statement.

(C) Constructive notice of lis pendens against personal property and rights of lien creditors. Judicial proceedings brought by a creditor to enforce an unperfected interest in personal property and a lien obtained by judicial proceedings (including tax and other liens through judicial records) in personal property shall not serve as constructive or lis pendens notice thereof until possession is acquired by the creditor or by a court officer, or until notice thereof by the creditor is perfected by filing a financing statement:

(1) naming the defendant as debtor, and the creditor as secured party;

(2) briefly describing the collateral in such words as a "lien upon debtor's personal property by judicial proceedings" and indicating the kind or type of property, along with the court and cause number of the action;

(3) signed by the creditor or judgment creditor; and

(4) in the filing office or offices where a financing statement under a security agreement with respect to the collateral, if filed, would be required to be filed.

Lis pendens notice under this provision is subject to principles of estoppel or commercial law governing negotiable instruments and documents, securities or quasi-negotiable instruments or documents; and to the provisions of Article 9 the Uniform Commercial Code [1] relating to the duration of filing. In an appropriate case the debtor or judgment debtor shall be entitled to a termination statement when judgment in his favor becomes final or when the lien obtained by judicial proceedings is terminated or is satisfied, as in the case of a debtor under a security agreement.

(D) Effect of judgment on lis pendens notice. A properly filed lis pendens notice of a claim against property continues to be perfected with respect to a judgment establishing such claim for the duration of the judgment, subject to the duration of filing under subdivision (C) of this rule.

[1] IC 26–1–9–101 et seq.

VIII. PROVISIONAL AND FINAL REMEDIES AND SPECIAL PROCEEDINGS

Rule 64. Seizure of person or property

(A) Ancillary remedies to assist in enforcement of judgment. At the commencement of and during the course of an action, all remedies providing for seizure of person or property for the purpose of securing satisfaction of the judgment ultimately to be entered in the action are available under the circumstances and in the manner provided by law and existing at the time the remedy is sought. The remedies thus available include, without limitation, arrest, attachment, attachment and garnishment, lis pendens notice, ejectment, replevin, sequestration, and other corresponding or equivalent legal or equitable remedies, however designated and regardless of whether by existing procedure the remedy is ancillary to an action or must be obtained by an independent action. Such remedies are subject to the provisions of this rule, and, except as herein otherwise provided, the action in which any of the foregoing remedies is used shall be commenced and prosecuted pursuant to these rules.

(B) Attachment or attachment and garnishment. Attachment or attachment and garnishment shall be allowed in the following cases in addition to those where such remedies prior to judgment are now permitted by law:

(1) It shall be a cause for attachment that the defendant or one of several defendants is a foreign corporation, a nonresident of this state, or a person whose residence and whereabouts are unknown and cannot be determined after reasonable investigation before the commencement of the action.

(2) Any interest in tangible or intangible property owned by the defendant shall be subject to attachment or attachment and garnishment, as the case may be, if it is subject to execution, proceedings supplemental to execution or any creditor process allowed by law. Wages or salaries shall not be subject to attachment and garnishment under Indiana Acts, ch. 38, §§ 197–244 [1].

(3) Attachment or attachment and garnishment shall be allowed in favor of the plaintiff suing upon a claim for money, whether founded on contract, tort, equity or any other theory and whether it is liquidated, contingent or unliquidated; or upon a claim to determine the rights in the property or obligation attached or garnisheed.

(4) It shall not be objectionable that the property or obligation being attached or garnisheed is in the possession of the plaintiff or is owing by the plaintiff to the defendant or by the defendant to the plaintiff.

(5) A governmental organization, or a representative, including a guardian, receiver, assignee for the benefit of creditors, trustee or representative of a decedent's estate may be named as a garnishee and bound by the duties of a garnishee.

(6) A writ of attachment against the defendant's real estate or his interest therein is effectively served by recordation of notice of the action in the appropriate lis pendens record, and, unless vacant, by serving the writ of attachment or notice thereof upon a person in possession of the land.

(C) Defendant's title raised by denial—Effect of dismissal. In action where the plaintiff is required to establish title to any fund or property, including without limitation any ejectment, replevin, quiet title, partition, equitable, legal or other action, the defendant in his answer may deny the plaintiff's claim of title and thereby place in issue the defendant's title or interest therein. If the defendant prevails under such an answer he shall be entitled to a judgment or decree enunciating his title or interest and any proper negative or affirmative relief against the plaintiff consistent with his proof.

Unless the defendant joins in the notice of dismissal, no voluntary dismissal by the plaintiff in such cases shall be allowed without prejudice after the plaintiff has obtained possession of the property or fund or other relief with respect thereto by posting bond, or after the defendant by answer (whether by denial, affirmative defense, counter-claim or cross-claim) has placed title in issue.

[1] IC 34–1–11–1 to 34–1–11–48.

Rule 65.   Injunctions

(A) Preliminary injunction.

(1) *Notice*.   No preliminary injunction shall be issued without an opportunity for a hearing upon notice to the adverse party.

(2) *Consolidation of hearing with trial on merits*. Before or after the commencement of the hearing of an application for a preliminary injunction, the court may order the trial of the action on the merits to be advanced and consolidated with the hearing of the application.   Even when this consolidation is not ordered, any evidence received upon an application for a preliminary injunction which would be admissible upon the trial on the merits becomes part of the record on the trial and need not be repeated upon the trial.

(3) *Assignment of cases—Judge to act promptly*. Assignment of cases shall not be affected by the fact that a temporary restraining order or preliminary injunction is sought, but such case shall be assigned promptly and the judge regularly assigned to the case shall act upon and hear all matters relating to temporary restraining orders and preliminary injunctions.   The judge shall make himself readily available to consider temporary restraining orders, conduct hearings, fix the manner of giving notice and the time and place for hearings under this rule, and shall act and require the parties to act promptly.

If the party seeking relief or his attorney by affidavit establishes that the judge assigned to the case is not available or cannot be found to consider an application for a restraining order, to conduct a hearing, or to fix the manner of giving notice and the time and place for a hearing under this rule, he may apply to any other judge in the circuit who shall take all further action with respect to any temporary restraining order or preliminary injunction.   If the affidavit establishes that no other judge in the circuit is available or to be found, he may apply to the judge of any adjoining circuit.   Unless an order is entered within ten [10] days after the hearing upon the granting, modifying or dissolving of a temporary or preliminary injunction, the relief

sought shall be subject to the provisions of Rule 53.1.

(4) *Modification of orders—Responsive pleadings*.   Upon the court's own motion or the motion of any party, orders granting or denying temporary restraining orders or preliminary injunctions may be dissolved, modified, granted or reinstated.   Responsive pleadings shall not be required in response to any pleadings or motions relating to temporary restraining orders or preliminary injunctions.

(B) Temporary restraining order—Notice—Hearing—Duration.   A temporary restraining order may be granted without written or oral notice to the adverse party or his attorney only if:

(1) it clearly appears from specific facts shown by affidavit or by the verified complaint that immediate and irreparable injury, loss, or damage will result to the applicant before the adverse party or his attorney can be heard in opposition; and

(2) the applicant's attorney certifies to the court in writing the efforts, if any, which have been made to give notice and the reasons supporting his claim that notice should not be required.

Every temporary restraining order granted without notice shall be indorsed with the date and hour of issuance; shall be filed forthwith in the clerk's office and entered of record; shall define the injury and state why it is irreparable and why the order was granted without notice; and shall expire by its terms within such time after entry, not to exceed ten [10] days, as the court fixes, unless within the time so fixed the order, for good cause shown, is extended for a like period or unless the whereabouts of the party against whom the order is granted is unknown and cannot be determined by reasonable diligence or unless the party against whom the order is directed consents that it may be extended for a longer period.   The reasons for the extension shall be entered of record.   In case a temporary restraining order is granted without notice, the motion for a preliminary injunction shall be set down for hearing at the earliest possible time and takes precedence of all matters except older matters of the same character; and when the motion comes on for hearing the party who obtained the temporary restraining order shall proceed with the application for a preliminary injunction and, if he does not do so, the court shall dissolve the temporary restraining order.   On two (2) days' notice to the party who obtained the temporary restraining order without notice or on such shorter notice to that party as the court may prescribe, the adverse party may appear and move its dissolution or modification and in that event the court shall proceed to hear and determine such motion as expeditiously as the ends of justice require.

(C) Security.   No restraining order or preliminary injunction shall issue except upon the giving of security by the applicant, in such sum as the court deems proper, for the payment of such costs and damages as may be incurred or suffered by any party who is found to have been wrongfully enjoined or restrained. No such security shall be required of a governmental organization, but such governmental organization shall be responsible for costs and damages as may be incurred or suffered by any party who is found to have been wrongfully enjoined or restrained.

The provisions of Rule 65.1 apply to a surety upon a bond or undertaking under this rule.

(D) Form and scope of injunction or restraining order. Every order granting temporary injunction and every restraining order shall include or be accompanied by findings as required by Rule 52; shall be specific in terms; shall describe in reasonable detail, and not by reference to the complaint or other document, the act or acts sought to be restrained; and is binding only upon the parties to the action, their officers, agents, servants, employees, and attorneys, and upon those persons in active concert or participation with them who receive actual notice of the order by personal service or otherwise.

(E) Temporary Restraining Orders—Domestic Relations Cases. Parties wishing protection from domestic or family violence in Domestic Relations cases shall petition the court pursuant to IC 34–26–5. Subject to the provisions set forth in this paragraph, in an action for dissolution of marriage, separation, or child support, the court may issue a Temporary Restraining Order, without hearing or security, if either party files a verified petition alleging an injury would result to the moving party if no immediate order were issued.

(1) Joint Order. If the court finds that an order shall be entered under this paragraph, the court may enjoin both parties from:

    (a) transferring, encumbering, concealing, selling or otherwise disposing of any joint property of the parties or asset of the marriage except in the usual course of business or for the necessities of life, without the written consent of the parties of the permission of the court; and/or

    (b) removing any child of the parties then residing in the State of Indiana from the State with the intent to deprive the court of jurisdiction over such child without the prior written consent of all parties or the permission of the court.

(2) Separate Order Required. In the event a party seeks to enjoin by a temporary restraining order the non-moving party from abusing, harassing, **or** disturbing the peace of the petitioning party or any child or step-child of the parties, or exclude the non-moving party from the family dwelling, the dwelling of the non-moving party, or any other place, and the court determines that an order shall be issued, such order shall be addressed to one person. A joint or mutual restraining order shall not be issued. If both parties allege injury, they

shall do so by separate petitions. The trial court shall review each petition separately and grant or deny each petition on its individual merits. In the event the trial court finds cause to grant both petitions, it shall do so by separate orders.

(3) Effect of Order. An order entered under this paragraph is automatically effective upon service. Such orders are enforceable by all remedies provided by law including contempt. Once issued, such orders remain in effect until the entry of a decree or final order or until modified or dissolved by the court.

(F) Statutory Provision Unaffected by this Rule. Nothing in this rule shall affect provisions of statutes extending or limiting the power of a court to grant injunctions. By way of example and not by way of limitation, this rule shall not affect the provisions of 1967 Indiana Acts, ch. 357, §§ 1–8 [1] relating to public lawsuits, and Indiana Acts, ch. 7, §§ 1–15 [2] providing for removal of injunctive and mandamus actions to the Court of Appeals of Indiana, and Indiana Acts, ch. 12 (1933) [3].

Amended Feb. 25, 1970; amended Jan. 18, 1972, effective Jan. 19, 1972; amended Nov. 30, 1989, effective Jan. 1, 1990; amended Dec. 5, 1994, effective Feb. 1, 1995; amended and effective July 19, 2002.

[1] IC 34–4–17–1 to 34–4–17–8.
[2] IC 34–4–18–1 to 34–4–18–13 (Repealed).
[3] IC 22–6–1–1 to 22–6–1–12.

Rule 65.1. Security: Proceedings against sureties

Whenever these rules or other laws require or permit the giving of security by a party to a court action or proceeding, and security is given in the form of a bond or stipulation or other undertaking with one or more sureties, each surety submits himself to the jurisdiction of the court and irrevocably appoints the clerk of the court as his agent upon whom any papers affecting his liability on the bond or undertaking may be served. His liability may be enforced on motion without the necessity of an independent action. The motion and such notice of the motion as the court prescribes may be served on the clerk of the court, who shall forthwith mail copies to the sureties if their addresses are known. This rule applies to bonds or security furnished on appeal, and enforcement shall be in the court to which the case is returned after appeal.

Rule 66. Receivers, assignees for the benefit of creditors and statutory and other liquidators; claims against such officers

(A) Actions; appointment; procedure. An action wherein a receiver, assignee for the benefit of creditors or statutory, or other liquidator has been appointed shall not be dismissed except by order of the court. Administration of such estates shall be in accordance with the practice heretofore followed. In all other respects the action in which the appointment of such officer is sought or which is brought by or against him is governed by these rules.

(B) Statement of assets and liabilities. Whenever a receiver, assignee for the benefit of creditors, statutory or other liquidator shall have been appointed to take over the business or assets of any person, organization, or partnership, the court appointing such officer may, or upon petition of any interested person shall, fix a time within which the person, or members, owners, agents or officers of the business or assets so placed in the hands of the officer, shall file with the clerk of the court in which such proceedings are had, a full, complete, itemized statement in affidavit form, setting forth in detail all the assets and all the liabilities of such person, organization or partnership including a list of the names and addresses of all known creditors. In case of noncompliance, the statement shall be prepared by the liquidator.

(C) Notice of appointment—Time within which to file claims. After such statement is filed, such officer shall give reasonable notice of his appointment by publication as ordered by the court, and the receiver shall mail a copy of said notice to all creditors listed on the statement so filed or prepared. Said notice shall state the date of appointment of the receiver and the period of time, as shall have been fixed by the court, within which creditors may file claims. Said period of time shall not be less than six [6] months from said date of appointment.

(D) Claims. The procedure for the filing, consideration, allowance or trial of claims in receiverships and assignments for the benefit of creditors, or statutory or other liquidations, shall, insofar as is practicable, conform with the procedure relating to claims in decedents' estates.

(E) Claims which must be paid without filing. A receiver, assignee for the benefit of creditors, statutory or other liquidator shall pay or make distributions according to priorities as required by law upon all claims, whether properly filed or filed within the allowed time after the appointment of the officer, if:

(1) liquidated in amount or capable of liquidation by a mathematical computation;

(2) the claim was owing and could have been filed and proved after the officer's appointment; and

(3) it is shown to be unpaid or owing upon the books or records of the debtor regularly and currently maintained for the purpose of showing the status of claims of such class.

Payment or distribution hereunder may be recovered by the officer or his successor to the extent it was excessive, not owing, or not payable. Upon petition of any interested person or the officer prior to final distribution or along with a petition for final distribution, the court may determine the existence or nonexistence of claims subject to this subdivision and may issue appropriate orders for payment or nonpayment as the case may be.

Rule 67. Deposit in court; payment of judgment

(A) Deposit in court before judgment. Before judgment in an action in which any part of the relief sought is a judgment for a sum of money or the disposition of a sum of money or the disposition of any other thing capable of delivery, a party, upon notice to every other party, and by leave of court, may deposit with the court all or any part of such sum or thing. Payment of all or part thereof may be directed by the court under any judgment or order, or upon motion and hearing to the rightful owners or upon security or agreement of the parties under the direction of the court.

(B) Payment of judgment—Satisfaction entered of record. Unless otherwise directed by the court, payment of money owing under and following a judgment may be made to the judgment creditor or his attorney, to the sheriff holding a writ of execution, or to the clerk of the court where the judgment is rendered. If paid to the clerk, the clerk shall notify the person entitled thereto or his attorney and shall pay such sum to him upon receiving a statement of satisfaction required herein. Money received by the sheriff towards satisfaction of the judgment shall be delivered to the clerk of the court where the judgment is rendered who shall then proceed as if the money were paid to him. A party or person receiving payment or satisfaction of a judgment shall furnish to the sheriff, clerk, party or person making payment a signed statement of total or partial satisfaction and any necessary assignment identifying the judgment by cause number and acknowledged as in the case of a deed which, when acquired or delivered to the clerk shall be entered in the records with the judgment. Such statement or any other entry by the clerk showing an assignment, payment or satisfaction of the judgment when certified by the clerk shall be received as evidence thereof, may be filed in the lis pendens record or judgment docket as provided in Rule 63.1(B) and when so filed shall serve as constructive notice thereof.

Rule 68. Offer of judgment

At any time more than ten [10] days before the trial begins, a party defending against a claim may serve upon the adverse party an offer to allow judgment to be taken against him for the money or property or to the effect specified in his offer, with costs then accrued. If within ten [10] days after the service of the offer the adverse party serves written notice that the offer is accepted, either party may then file the offer and notice of acceptance together with proof of service thereof and thereupon the clerk shall enter judgment. An offer not accepted shall be deemed withdrawn and evidence thereof is not admissible except in a proceeding to determine costs. If the judgment finally obtained by the offeree is not more favorable than the offer, the offeree must pay the costs incurred after the making of the offer. The fact that an offer is made but not accepted does not preclude a subsequent offer. When liability of one party to another has been partially determined by verdict or order of judgment, but the amount or extent of liability remains to be determined by further proceedings, the party adjudged liable may make an offer of judgment, which shall have the same effect as an offer made before trial if it is served within a reasonable time not less than ten [10] days prior to the commencement of hearings to determine the amount or extent of liability.

Rule 69. Execution, proceedings supplemental to execution, foreclosure sales

(A) Execution sales. Process to enforce a judgment or a decree for the payment of money shall be by writ of execution, unless the court directs otherwise and except as provided herein. Notwithstanding any statute to the contrary, real estate shall not be sold until the elapse of six [6] months from the time the judgment or execution thereon becomes a lien upon the property.

Except for any requirement of appraisal and that the property sell for two-thirds (2/3) or more of its appraised value, the sale of real estate shall be conducted under the same rules and the same procedures applicable to foreclosure of mortgages, including subdivision (C) of this rule, without right of redemption after the sale but subject to the judgment debtor's right to care for and remove crops growing at the time the lien attached as in the case of mortgage foreclosure. Unless otherwise ordered by the court, the sheriff or person conducting the sale of any property upon execution shall not be required to offer it for sale in any particular order, in parcels, or first offer rents and profits and shall be required to sell real and personal property separately pursuant to the law applicable. Execution upon any property shall not suspend the right and duty to levy upon other property.

(B) Judgment and execution liens on after-acquired property. In the case of property acquired by the debtor after prior judgment or execution liens have been perfected, such liens shall share pro rata with each other without further levy.

(C) Foreclosure of liens upon real estate. Unless otherwise ordered by the court, judicial foreclosure of all liens upon real estate shall be conducted under the same rules and the same procedures applicable to foreclosure of mortgages upon real estate, including without limitation redemption rights, manner and notice of sale, appointment of a receiver, execution of deed to purchaser and without valuation and appraisement. Judicial lien foreclosures including mortgage foreclosures may be held at any reasonable place stated in the notice of sale. In all cases where a foreclosure or execution sale of realty is not confirmed by the court, the sheriff or other officer conducting the sale shall make a record of his actions therein in his return to be filed promptly with the record of the case and also in the execution docket maintained in the office of the clerk.

(D) Other judicial sales. Unless otherwise ordered by the court all public judicial sales of real estate, other than lien and mortgage foreclosures and execution sales, shall, to the extent possible, be sold in the same manner that real estate is sold in the administration of decedents' estates, and subject to the same rules applicable to the manner and effect thereof. This provision shall apply, without limitation, to judicial sales by trustees, guardians, receivers, assignees for the benefit of creditors and sales in partition proceedings.

(E) Proceedings supplemental to execution. Notwithstanding any other statute to the contrary, proceedings supplemental to execution may be enforced by verified motion or with affidavits in the court where the judgment is rendered alleging generally:

(1) that the plaintiff owns the described judgment against the defendant;

(2) that the plaintiff has no cause to believe that levy of execution against the defendant will satisfy the judgment;

(3) that the defendant be ordered to appear before the court to answer as to his non-exempt property subject to execution or proceedings supplemental to execution or to apply any such specified or unspecified property towards satisfaction of the judgment; and,

(4) if any person is named as garnishee, that garnishee has or will have specified or unspecified nonexempt property of, or an obligation owing to the judgment debtor subject to execution or proceedings supplemental to execution, and that the garnishee be ordered to appear and answer concerning the same or answer interrogatories submitted with the motion.

If the court determines that the motion meets the foregoing requirements it shall, ex parte and without notice, order the judgment debtor, other named parties defendant and the garnishee to appear for a hearing thereon or to answer the interrogatories attached to the motion, or both.

The motion, along with the court's order stating the time for the appearance and hearing or the time for the answer to interrogatories submitted with the motion, shall be served upon the judgment debtor as provided in Rule 5, and other parties and the garnishee shall be entitled to service of process as provided in Rule 4. The date fixed for appearance and hearing or answer to interrogatories shall be not less than twenty [20] days after service. No further pleadings shall be required, and the case shall be heard and determined and property ordered applied towards the judgment in accordance with statutes allowing proceedings supplementary to execution. In aid of the judgment or execution, the judgment creditor or his successor in interest of record and the judgment debtor may utilize the discovery provisions of these rules in the manner provided in these rules for discovery or as provided under the laws allowing proceedings supplemental.

(F) Title opinion or insurance required in all judicial sales of land. In the case of any judicial sale of land, including without limitation mortgage and lien foreclosures, execution sales, sales by receivers, assignees for the benefit of creditors, guardians or trustees, or partition sales, upon motion the court in its discretion may order the judgment creditor, person seeking the sale, or officer conducting the sale to procure a qualified title opinion or a title insurance policy from a title insurance company authorized to do business in Indiana with respect to the interest of the person whose land is being sold. The policy must be conditioned to cover the purchase price at the sale and may be given with any necessary exclusions. The opinion or policy shall run to all parties interested in the litigation and to any purchaser or purchasers at the sale. The opinion or policy or copy thereof shall be available for inspection in the court from which the sale is being conducted or in the office of the court officer conducting the sale at the first notice of sale and shall be made available for inspection at the sale. Expenses of the opinion or policy shall be taxed as costs like other expenses of the sale and paid from the first proceeds of the sale. The opinion or policy shall not cover defects arising in the conduct of the sale.

Rule 70. Judgment for specific acts; vesting title; recordation

(A) Effect of judgment. If a judgment directs a party to execute a conveyance of land, or other property or to deliver deeds or other documents or to perform any other specific act and the party fails to comply within the time specified, the court may direct the act to be done at the cost of the disobedient party by some other person appointed by the court and the act when so done has like effect as if done by the party. On application of the party entitled to performance, the clerk shall issue a writ of attachment, writ of assistance, or sequestration against the property of the disobedient party to compel obedience to the judgment. The court may also in proper cases adjudge the party in contempt and may award damages for disobedience of the order. If real or personal property is involved, the court in lieu of directing a conveyance thereof may enter a judgment divesting the title of any party and vesting it in others and such judgment has the effect of both a judgment and of a conveyance executed in due form of law.

When any order or judgment is for the delivery of possession, the party in whose favor it is entered is entitled to a writ of execution, assistance or order directing the sheriff or other enforcement officer to deliver possession upon application to the clerk. Equitable decrees or orders to pay money shall be enforced as legal judgments to pay money unless otherwise ordered by the court.

(B) Recordation of judgment. A copy of the judgment directing acts or divesting or vesting title of a deed or copy thereof transferring title as provided in subdivision (A) of this rule or other law may be recorded or filed either in the lis pendens records or the deed records of the proper officer and county or place and shall be appropriately indexed. When recorded or filed such record shall constitute constructive notice thereof in transactions with respect to the property under the recording laws, and a copy of such filed or recorded judgment or deed certified by the county recorder or other officer shall constitute prima facie evidence of its validity.

(C) Deed form. A conveyance of land made by a court appointee as authorized by subdivision (A) of this rule may be made in the following form:

"A B by the order (for judgment) of (naming the court), in cause number (state the cause number) entered on (state date order or judgment was entered), in the case of (naming the party plaintiffs) against (naming the party defendants) conveys the (describe the premises, and the interest conveyed if the judgment or order is for less than a fee simple absolute) the title, interest and rights of (name the parties or persons whose title is being conveyed; and the record owner through whom such title was derived if known and if such persons are not record owners), (state with warranty or subject to conditions only if and as provided in the order or judgment). Signed (signature of court appointee, A B), Appointee of above named court to make this conveyance." (Acknowledgment as required in the case of deeds.)

(D) Judicial sales. Property may be sold under judgments and orders in the manner now provided by law subject to these rules, including the sale of the property when specific performance is allowed against the vendee.

Rule 71. Process in behalf of and against persons not parties

When an order is made in favor of a person who is not a party to the action, he may enforce obedience to the order by the same process as if he were a party; and, when obedience to an order may be lawfully enforced against a person who is not a party, he is liable to the same process for enforcing obedience to the order as if he were a party.

IX. TRIAL COURTS AND CLERKS

Rule 72. Trial court and clerks

(A) Trial courts always open. The trial courts shall be deemed always open for the purpose of filing any pleading or other proper paper, of issuing and returning process and of making and directing all interlocutory motions, orders, and rules. Terms of court shall not be recognized.

(B) Trials and hearings—Orders in chambers. All trials upon the merits shall be conducted in open court and so far as convenient in a regular courtroom in or outside the county seat. All other acts or proceedings may be done or conducted by a judge in chambers, without the attendance of the clerk or other court officials and at any place either within or without the circuit; but, no hearing other than one ex parte, shall be conducted outside the state without the consent of all parties affected thereby.

(C) Clerk's office and orders by clerk. The clerk's office with the clerk or a deputy in attendance shall be open during business hours on all days except Saturdays, Sundays, and legal holidays, but the circuit court judge may provide by local rule or order that its clerk's office shall be open for specified hours on Saturdays or particular legal holidays other than New Year's Day, Washington's Birthday, Memorial Day, Independence Day, Labor Day, Veterans Day, Thanksgiving Day, and Christmas Day. All motions and applications in the clerk's office for issuing process, including final process to enforce and execute judgments, and for other proceedings which do not require allowance or order of the court are grantable of course by the clerk; but the clerk's action may be suspended or altered or rescinded by the court upon cause shown.

(D) Notice of Orders or Judgments. Immediately upon the notation in the Chronological Case Summary of a ruling upon a motion, an order or judgment, the clerk shall serve a copy of the entry in the manner provided for in Rule 5(B) upon each party who is not in default for failure to appear and shall make a record of such service. Such service is sufficient notice for all purposes for which notice of the entry is required by these rules; but any party may, in addition, serve a notice of such entry in the manner provided in Rule 5 for the service of papers. In cases of consolidated proceedings involving ten (10) or more parties, the trial judge may provide by order for alternative method of notice to designated liaison parties who undertake responsibility for forwarding notice to all parties.

It shall be the duty of the attorneys when entering their appearance in a case or when filing pleadings or papers therein, to have noted on the Chronological Case Summary and on the pleadings or papers so filed, their mailing address, and service by mail at such address shall be deemed sufficient.

(E) Effect of Lack of Notice. Lack of notice, or the lack of the actual receipt of a copy of the entry from the Clerk shall not affect the time within which to contest the ruling, order or judgment, or authorize the Court to relieve a party of the failure to initiate proceedings to contest such ruling, order or judgment, except as provided in this section. When service of a copy of the entry by the Clerk is not evidenced by a note made by the Clerk upon the Chronological Case Summary, the Court, upon application for good cause shown, may grant an extension of any time limitation within which to contest such ruling, order or judgment to any party who was without actual knowledge, or who relied upon incorrect representations by Court personnel. Such extension shall commence when the party first obtained actual knowledge and not exceed the original time limitation.

Amended Nov. 16, 1984, effective Jan. 1, 1985; Nov. 13, 1989, effective permissive prior to Jan. 1, 1991 and mandatory Jan. 1, 1991; Nov. 26, 1997, effective Jan. 1, 1998; Sept. 10, 2007, effective Jan. 1, 2008; Sept. 21, 2010, effective Jan. 1, 2011; Sept. 7, 2012, effective Jan. 1, 2013.

Rule 73. Hearing of motions

(A) [1] **Hearings upon motions.** Unless local conditions make it impracticable, each judge shall establish regular times and places, at intervals sufficiently frequent for the prompt dispatch of business, at which motions requiring notice and hearing may be heard and disposed of; but the judge at any time or place and on such notice, if any, as he considers reasonable may make order for the advancement, conduct, and hearing of actions. To expedite its business the court may direct the submission and determination of motions without oral hearing upon brief written statements of reasons in support and opposition, or direct or permit hearings by telephone conference call with all attorneys or other similar means of communication.

[1] This rule contains no Subd. (B).

Rule 74. Recording machines; court reports; stenographic report or transcript as evidence

(A) Recording machines—Transcripts. For the purpose of facilitating and expediting the trial of causes and the appeals therefrom, the judge of each circuit, criminal, superior, probate and juvenile court of each and every county of this state may arrange and provide for the recording by electronic or mechanical device, or by stenographic reporting with computer-aided transcription capability of, any and all oral evidence and testimony given in all causes and hearings, including both questions and answers, and all rulings of the judge in respect to the admission and rejection of evidence and objections thereto and the recording of any other oral matters occurring during the hearing in any proceeding. The recording device or the computer aided transcription equipment shall be selected and approved by the court and may be placed under the supervision and operation of the official court reporter or such other person as may be designated by the court. The court may, in its discretion, eliminate shorthand or stenographic reporting of any recorded matter.

A transcript, typewritten or in longhand, made in part or entirely from such recording, shall serve the same purpose as if made from shorthand notes and if certified, as in the case of a transcript of shorthand notes, shall serve the same purpose and be as valid as if made from shorthand notes.

Provided further, that the judge may authorize or direct the court reporter or any other responsible, competent person, in his discretion, to make a transcription from such recordings, and the same shall be certified by the person making said transcriptions in the same manner and have the same effect as if made from shorthand notes.

(B) Reporter may serve as clerk and serve other judges. When the circuit court judge and the judge or judges affected find that such duties will not affect the efficiency of the court, one [1] person may serve both as a court reporter and clerk for a judge or judges whose regular courtroom is located outside the courthouse or its environs; and a court reporter may serve more than one [1] judge. Appointment shall be made by the judge or judges affected and, if they cannot agree, by the circuit court judge.

(C) Pay and duties of court reporters. It shall be the duty of each court reporter whenever required by the judge, to be promptly present in court, and take down in shorthand or by other means the oral evidence given in all causes, including both questions and answers, and to note all rulings of the judge in respect to the admission and rejection of evidence and the objections and exceptions thereto, and write out the instructions of the court in jury trials. The court reporter, when so directed, shall record the proceedings and make a transcript as provided in subdivision (A) of this rule. Reporters shall be paid as provided by 1965 Indiana Acts, ch. 289 [1], but the circuit court judge with the approval of the judge or judges affected may allow the reporter additional pay up to $125 per month for serving more than one [1] judge or function, or serving as both clerk and reporter.

(D) Statutes applicable to reporters and preparation of transcripts. Except as provided otherwise by these rules, the provisions of 1899 Indiana Acts, ch. 169, §§ 2–7, [2] 1939 Indiana Acts, ch. 11, § 1, [3] 1935 Indiana Acts, ch. 218, § 1, [4] 1893 Indiana Acts, ch. 33, § 1, [5] and 1947 Indiana Acts, ch. 89, § 1, [6] relating to court reporters and preparation of transcripts, shall apply to court reporters provided by these rules.

(E) Stenographic report or transcript as evidence. Whenever the testimony of a witness at a trial or hearing which was stenographically reported is admissible on appeal or in evidence at a later trial, proceeding, or administrative hearing, it may be proved by the transcript thereof duly certified by the person who reported the testimony.

Amended effective Nov. 10, 1988.

[1] IC 33–15–26–1 to 33–15–26–9.
[2] IC 33–15–23–2 to 33–15–23–5.
[3] IC 33–15–24–1.
[4] IC 4–22–4–1.
[5] IC 33–1–4–1.
[6] IC 33–15–25–1 [Repealed].

X. VENUE, CHANGE OF VENUE, CHANGE OF JUDGE

Rule 75. Venue requirements

(A) Venue. Any case may be venued, commenced and decided in any court in any county, except, that upon the filing of a pleading or a motion to dismiss allowed by Rule 12(B)(3), the court, from allegations of the complaint or after hearing evidence thereon or considering affidavits or documentary evidence filed with the motion or in opposition to it, shall order the case transferred to a county or court selected by the party first properly filing such motion or pleading if the court determines that the county or court where the action was filed does not meet preferred venue requirements or is not authorized to decide the case and that the court or county selected has preferred venue and is authorized to decide the case. Preferred venue lies in:

(1) the county where the greater percentage of individual defendants included in the complaint resides, or, if there is no such greater percentage, the place where any individual defendant so named resides; or

(2) the county where the land or some part thereof is located or the chattels or some part thereof are regularly located or kept, if the complaint includes a claim for injuries thereto or relating to such land or such chattels, including without limitation claims for recovery of possession or for injuries, to establish use or control, to quiet title or determine any interest, to avoid or set aside conveyances, to foreclose liens, to partition and to assert any matters for which in rem relief is or would be proper; or

(3) the county where the accident or collision occurred, if the complaint includes a claim for injuries relating to the operation of a motor vehicle or a vehicle on railroad, street or interurban tracks; or

(4) the county where either the principal office of a defendant organization is located or the office or agency of a defendant organization or individual to

which the claim relates or out of which the claim arose is located, if one or more such organizations or individuals are included as defendants in the complaint; or

(5) the county where either one or more individual plaintiffs reside, the principal office of a governmental organization is located, or the office of a governmental organization to which the claim relates or out of which the claim arose is located, if one or more governmental organizations are included as defendants in the complaint; or

(6) the county or court fixed by written stipulations signed by all the parties named in the complaint or their attorneys and filed with the court before ruling on the motion to dismiss; or

(7) the county where the individual is held in custody or is restrained, if the complaint seeks relief with respect to such individual's custody or restraint upon his freedom; or

(8) the county where a claim in the plaintiff's complaint may be commenced under any statute recognizing or creating a special or general remedy or proceeding; or

(9) the county where all or some of the property is located or can be found if the case seeks only judgment in rem against the property of a defendant being served by publication; or

(10) the county where either one or more individual plaintiffs reside, the principal office of any plaintiff organization or governmental organization is located, or the office of any such plaintiff organization or governmental organization to which the claim relates or out of which the claim arose is located, if the case is not subject to the requirements of subsections (1) through (9) of this subdivision or if all the defendants are nonresident individuals or nonresident organizations without a principal office in the state.

The pleading or motion permitted by this rule must be filed within the time prescribed for the party making it by Rules 6 and 12 and any other applicable provision of these rules.

(B) Claim or proceeding filed in improper court.

(1) Whenever a claim or proceeding is filed which should properly have been filed in another court of this state, and proper objection is made, the court in which such action is filed shall not then dismiss the action, but shall order the action transferred to the court in which it should have been filed.

(2) The person filing the action shall, within twenty (20) days, pay such costs as are chargeable upon a change of venue and the papers and records shall be certified to the court of transfer in like manner as upon change of venue and the action shall be deemed commenced as of the date of filing the action in the original court.

(3) If the party filing the action does not pay the costs of transfer within twenty (20) days of the order transferring venue, the original court shall dismiss the action without prejudice and shall order payment of reasonable attorney fees to the party making proper objection.

(C) Assessment of costs, traveling expenses and attorneys' fees in resisting venue. When the case is ordered transferred under the provisions of this rule or Rule 21(B) the court shall order the parties or persons filing the complaint to pay the filing costs of refiling the case in the proper court and pay mileage expenses reasonably incurred by the parties and their attorneys in resisting the venue; and if it appears that the case was commenced in the wrong county by sham pleading, in bad faith or without cause, the court shall order payment of reasonable attorneys' fees incurred by parties successfully resisting the venue.

(D) Other venue statutes superseded by this rule. Any provision of these rules and any special or general statute relating to venue, the place of trial or the authority of the court to hear the case shall be subject to this rule, and the provisions of any statute fixing more stringent rules thereon shall be ineffective. No statute or rule fixing the place of trial shall be deemed a requirement of jurisdiction.

(E) Appeal. An order transferring or refusing to transfer a case under this rule shall be an interlocutory order appealable pursuant to Appellate Rule 14(A)(8); provided, however, that the appeal of an interlocutory order under this rule shall not stay proceedings in the trial court unless the trial court or the Court of Appeals so orders.

Amended Nov. 3, 1981, effective Jan. 1, 1982; Dec. 21, 2001, effective April 1, 2002.

Rule 76. Change of venue

(A) In civil actions where the venue may be changed from the county, such change of venue from the county may be had only upon the filing of a verified motion specifically stating the grounds therefor by the party requesting the change. The motion shall be granted only upon a showing that the county where suit is pending is a party or that the party seeking the change will be unlikely to receive a fair trial on account of local prejudice or bias regarding a party or the claim or defense presented by a party. A party shall be entitled to only one change of venue from the county. Denial of a motion for change of venue from the county shall be reviewable only for an abuse of discretion. The Rules of Criminal Procedure shall govern proceedings to enforce a statute defining an infraction.

(B) In civil actions, where a change may be taken from the judge, such change shall be granted upon the filing of an unverified application or motion without specifically stating the ground therefor by a party or his attorney. Provided, however, a party shall be entitled to only one [1] change from the judge. After a final decree is entered in a dissolution of marriage case or paternity case, a party may take only one change of judge in connection with petitions to modify that decree, regardless of the number of times new petitions are filed. The Rules of Criminal Procedure shall govern proceedings to enforce a statute defining an infraction.

(C) In any action except criminal no change of judge or change of venue from the county shall be granted except within the time herein provided. Any such application for change of judge (or change of venue) shall be filed not later than ten [10] days after the issues are first closed on the merits. Except:

(1) in those cases where no pleading or answer may be required to be filed by the defending party to close issues (or no responsive pleading is required under a statute), each party shall have thirty [30] days from the date the case is placed and entered on the chronological case summary of the court as having been filed;

(2) in those cases of claims in probate and receivership proceedings and remonstrances and similar matters, the parties thereto shall have thirty [30] days from the date the case is placed and entered on the chronological case summary of the court as having been filed;

(3) if the trial court or a court on appeal orders a new trial, or if a court on appeal otherwise remands a case such that a further hearing and receipt of evidence are required to reconsider all or some of the issues heard during the earlier trial, the parties thereto shall have ten [10] days from the date the order of the trial court is entered or the order of the court on appeal is certified;

(4) in the event a change is granted from the judge or county within the prescribed period, as stated above, a request for a change of judge or county may be made by a party still entitled thereto within ten [10] days after the special judge has qualified or the moving party has knowledge the cause has reached the receiving county or there has been a failure to perfect the change. Provided, however, this subdivision (4) shall operate only to enlarge the time allowed for such request under such circumstances, and it shall not operate to reduce the period prescribed in subdivisions (C), (C)(1), (C)(2), (C)(3);

(5) where a party has appeared at or received advance notice of a hearing prior to the expiration of the date within which a party may ask for a change of judge or county, and also where at said hearing a trial date is set which setting is promptly entered on the Chronological Case Summary, a party shall be deemed to have waived a request for change of judge or county unless within three days of the oral setting the party files a written objection to the trial setting and a written motion for change of judge or county;

(6) if the moving party first obtains knowledge of the grounds for change of venue from the county or judge after the time above limited, he may file said application, which must be verified personally by the party himself, specifically alleging when the cause was first discovered, how discovered, the facts showing the grounds for a change, and why such cause could not have been discovered before by the exercise of due diligence. Any opposing party shall have the right to file counter-affidavits on such issue within ten [10] days, and the ruling of the court may be reviewed only for abuse of discretion.

(D) Whenever a change of venue from the county is granted, the parties may, within three (3) days from the granting of the motion or affidavit for the change of venue, agree in open court upon the county to which venue shall be changed, and the court shall transfer such action to such county. In the absence of such agreement, the court shall, within two (2) days thereafter, submit to the parties a written list of all counties adjoining the county from which the venue is changed, and the parties within seven (7) days from the date the clerk mails the list to the parties or within such time, not to exceed fourteen (14) days from that date, as the court shall fix, shall each alternately strike off the names of such counties. The party first filing such motion shall strike first, and the action shall be sent to the county remaining not stricken under such procedure. If a party is brought into the action as provided in Trial Rule 14, and that party thereafter files a motion for change of venue which is granted, that party and the plaintiff shall be the parties entitled to strike. A moving party that fails to strike within said time shall not be entitled to a change of venue, and the court shall resume jurisdiction of the cause. If a nonmoving party fails to strike within the time limit, the clerk shall strike for such party.

Amended March 28, 1972; Dec. 18, 1984, effective Jan. 1, 1985; Oct. 15, 1986, effective Jan. 1, 1987; Nov. 27, 1990, effective Jan. 1, 1991; Oct. 25, 1991, effective Jan. 1, 1992; Oct. 29, 1991, effective Jan. 1, 1992; Dec. 6, 1991, effective Feb. 1, 1992; Dec. 12, 1991, effective Feb. 1, 1992; Dec. 20, 1991, effective Feb. 1, 1992; Dec. 5, 1994, effective Feb. 1, 1995; Nov. 26, 1997, effective Jan. 1, 1998; Aug. 15, 2006, effective Jan. 1, 2007; Sept. 9, 2008, effective Jan. 1, 2009.

Rule 77. Court records

(A) Required records. The clerk of the circuit court shall maintain the records for all circuit, superior, county, probate and municipal courts in the county.

(1) The clerk of the circuit court shall maintain any record required by an act of the general assembly or a duly promulgated rule of any state agency, including the following:

(a) Lis pendens record (IC 32–30–11–1);

(b) Record of transcripts and foreign judgments (IC 33–32–3–2(d));

(c) Judgment Docket (IC 33–32–3–2), wherein all orders requiring entry in the judgment docket shall include the term "judgment" in the title and shall set forth the specific dollar amount of the judgment in the body of the order;

(d) Execution docket (IC 33–32–3–5);

(e) Records specified under the probate code; and

(f) Records specified by the state board of accounts as to the fiscal matters relating to the court and clerk.

(2) The clerk of the circuit court shall also maintain the following records as specified under this rule:

(a) Chronological Case Summary;

(b) Case file;

(c) Record of judgments and orders (order book); and

(d) Indexes.

(B) Chronological Case Summary. For each case, the clerk of the circuit court shall maintain a sequential record of the judicial events in such proceeding. The record shall include the title of the proceeding; the assigned case number; the names, addresses, telephone and attorney numbers of all attorneys involved in the proceeding, or the fact that a party appears pro se with address and telephone number of the party so appearing; and the assessment of fees and charges (public receivables). The judge of the case shall cause Chronological Case Summary entries to be made of all judicial events. Notation of judicial events in the Chronological Case Summary shall be made promptly, and shall set forth the date of the event and briefly define any documents, orders, rulings, or judgments filed or entered in the case. The date of every notation in the Chronological Case Summary should be the date the notation is made, regardless of the date the judicial event occurred. The Chronological Case Summary shall also note the entry of orders, rulings and judgments in the record of judgments and orders, the notation of judgments in the judgment docket (IC 33–32–3–2), and file status (pending/decided) under section (G) of this rule. The Chronological Case Summary may be kept in a paper format, or microfilm, or electronically. The Chronological Case Summary shall be an official record of the trial court and shall be maintained apart from other records of the court and shall be organized by case number.

(C) Case file. In each case assigned a case number, the clerk of the circuit court shall maintain a file containing a copy of any order, entry, or judgment in the case and the original of all other documents relating to the case: including pleadings, motions, service of process, return of service, verdicts, executions, returns on executions and, if prepared, certified, and approved, the transcript of the testimony. The original order, entry, or judgment shall be maintained as part of the record of judgments and orders, the file shall contain a copy of such original. Unless necessary to detail the filing chronology, the case file need not include transmittal letters, instructions, envelopes or other extrinsic materials not related to the issues of the case. The file shall contain an index tab listing the case number and an abbreviated designation of the parties and shall note the information required under section (G) of this rule. In the event the court does not maintain a separate evidence file, documents entered into evidence, including depositions, shall be placed into the case file.

(D) Record of judgments and orders (order book). The clerk of the circuit court shall maintain a daily, verbatim, compilation of all judgments of the court, designated orders of the court, orders and opinions of an appellate tribunal relating to a case heard by the court, local court rules under Trial Rule 81, certification of the election of the regular judge of the court, any order appointing a special judge, judge pro tempore, or temporary judge, the oath and acceptance of any judge serving in the court, any order appointing a special prosecutor, and the oath and acceptance of a special prosecutor. The clerk may maintain a separate record of judgments and orders as required for the functional management of the court's business. Except where the record of judgments and orders is maintained electronically, a separate record of judgments and orders for confidential materials shall be maintained.

(E) Indexes. In addition to any index required under the provisions of this rule, state statute, or duly promulgated rule of a state agency, the clerk of the circuit court shall prepare and maintain indexes of all actions and proceedings in the circuit, superior, county, probate, and municipal courts in the County. This index shall be in an alphabetical format which notes the names of all parties, the date on which a party became part of the proceeding, and the case number of the proceeding. In the event courts are not located in the county courthouse, the clerk shall supervise the appropriate preparation of indexes for these courts and provide for the combination of indexes for all courts in the county.

(F) Pleadings and papers: Where filed and entered. All pleadings and papers shall be filed in accordance with Trial Rule 5 with the clerk of the circuit court. In the event a court is not located in the same facility as the clerk of the circuit court, all pleadings and papers shall be filed with the clerk serving that court. If an initial pleading or complaint is assigned to a court not within the facility where the initial pleading or complaint was filed, the clerk shall promptly notify the person filing the pleading and transmit the documents to the clerk serving the court where the matter will be considered and all further papers will be filed with the latter court. In the event an initial pleading or complaint is filed with the clerk of the wrong court, the clerk, upon notice to the person filing the initial pleading or complaint, may transfer the case to the proper court before service of summons or appearance of other parties, or any opposing party may move for transfer as provided for under Trial Rule 12(B) or Trial Rule 75.

(G) Case File Status.

(1) The clerk of the circuit court shall maintain the case files, as set forth under section (C) of this rule, in either a pending or decided status. Pending files, arranged by assigned case number, consist of all cases which have not been decided. Decided files consist of the actions which have been concluded and no further proceedings remain to be conducted as evidenced by the final judgment or other order of the court.

(2) When a case has been decided, the file shall be assigned a disposition date pursuant to Administrative Rule 7 of the Indiana Supreme Court and maintained under the original case number in a location apart from pending files. In the event a decided case is redocketed for consideration by the court, the disposition date shall be deleted from the file and the case file returned to the pending cases in sequence with the case number originally assigned. A disposition date shall be reassigned at the time the case returns to a decided status.

(H) Statistics. The clerk of the circuit court shall establish procedures to determine a statistical count of all actions filed, decided, and reinstated as required by the division of state court administration.

(I) Replacing lost papers. If an original pleading or paper filed with the clerk of the circuit court cannot be located within the recordkeeping system set forth under this rule, the court may authorize a copy of such record to be filed and used as the original.

(J) Method of record keeping. Under the direction of the Supreme Court of Indiana, the clerk of the circuit court may, notwithstanding the foregoing sections, keep records in any suitable media. Records that must be maintained permanently pursuant to Administrative Rule 7 D. (Retention Schedules) (Trial Rule 77 Schedules (10)), must, if maintained electronically, be kept so that a hard copy can be generated at any time. The record keeping formats and systems and the quality and permanency requirements employed for the Chronological Case Summary, the case file, and the record of judgments and orders (order book) shall be approved by the division of state court administration for compliance with the provisions of this rule.

(K) Electronic Posting of Court Records. The clerk, with the consent of the majority of the judges in the courts of record, may make court records, including but not limited to the Chronological Case Summary, record of judgments and orders, index, and case file, available to the public through remote electronic access such as the Internet or other electronic method. The records to be posted, the specific information that is to be included, its format, pricing structure, if

any, method of dissemination, and any subsequent changes thereto must be approved by the Division of State Court Administration under the direction of the Supreme Court of Indiana. Such availability of court records shall be subject to applicable laws regarding confidentiality.

Adopted Dec. 11, 1969, effective Jan. 1, 1970. Amended effective June 8, 1971; amended Nov. 13, 1989, effective permissive prior to Jan. 1, 1991 and mandatory Jan. 1, 1991; Nov. 13, 1990, effective Jan. 1, 1991; Oct. 30, 1992, effective Jan. 1, 1993; amended Dec. 5, 1994, effective Feb. 1, 1995; Dec. 23, 1996, effective March 1, 1997; Dec. 4, 1998, effective Jan. 1, 1999; amended effective Feb. 4, 2000; amended Dec. 21, 2001, effective April 1, 2002.; Sept. 30, 2004, effective Jan. 1, 2005; amended effective Sept. 5, 2006; amended Sept. 10, 2007, effective Jan. 1, 2008; Sept. 9, 2008, effective Jan. 1, 2009; Sept. 21, 2010, effective Jan. 1, 2011; Sept. 7, 2012, effective Jan. 1, 2013.

Rule 78. Jurisdiction pending change from county

Whenever a court has granted an order for a change of venue to another county and the costs thereof have been paid where an obligation exists to pay such costs for such change, either party to the cause may file a certified copy of the order making such change in the court to which such change has been made, and thereupon such court shall have full jurisdiction of said cause, regardless of the fact that the transcript and papers have not yet been filed with such court to which such change is taken. Nothing in this rule shall be construed as divesting the original court of its jurisdiction to hear and determine emergency matters between the time that a motion for change of venue to another county is filed and the time that the court grants an order for the change of venue.

Rule 79. Special judge selection: circuit, superior, and probate courts

(A) Application. When the appointment of a special judge is required under Trial Rule 76, the provisions of this rule constitute the exclusive manner for the selection of special judges in circuit, superior, and probate courts in all civil and juvenile proceedings. Trial Rule 79.1 constitutes the exclusive manner for the selection of special judges in all actions in city, town, and the Marion county small claims courts.

(B) Duty to notify court. It shall be the duty of the parties to advise the court promptly of an application or motion for change of judge.

(C) Disqualification or recusal of judge. A judge shall disqualify and recuse whenever the judge, the judge's spouse, a person within the third degree of relationship to either of them, the spouse of such a person, or a person residing in the judge's household:

(1) is a party to the proceeding, or an officer, director or trustee of a party;

(2) is acting as a lawyer in the proceeding;

(3) is known by the judge to have an interest that could be substantially affected by the proceeding; or

(4) is associated with the pending litigation in such fashion as to require disqualification under the *Code of Judicial Conduct* or otherwise.

Upon disqualification or recusal under this section, a special judge shall be selected in accordance with Sections (D) and (H) of this rule.

(D) Agreement of the parties. Within seven (7) days of the notation in the Chronological Case Summary of the order granting a change of judge or an order of disqualification, the parties may agree to an eligible special judge. The agreement of the parties shall be in writing and shall be filed in the court where the case is pending. Alternatively, the parties may agree in writing to the selection of an eligible special judge in accordance with Section (H). Upon the filing of the agreement, the court shall enter an order appointing such individual as the special judge in the case and provide notice pursuant to Trial Rule 72(D) to the special judge and all parties or appoint a special judge under Section (H).

A judge appointed under this section shall have seven (7) days from the date the appointment as special judge is noted in the Chronological Case Summary to decide whether to accept the case. The filing of an acceptance vests jurisdiction in the special judge. An oath or additional evidence of acceptance of jurisdiction is not required.

This provision shall not apply to criminal proceedings or election contests involving the nomination or election of the judge of the court in which the contest is filed.

(E) [Reserved] Deleted, eff. Jan. 1, 2013.

(F) [Reserved] Deleted eff. Jan. 1, 2013.

(G) [Reserved] Deleted eff. Jan. 1, 2013.

(H) Selection under local rule. In the event the parties do not reach an agreement or the agreed upon judge does not accept the case under Section (D), the appointment of an eligible special judge shall be made pursuant to a local rule approved by the Indiana Supreme Court which provides for the following:

(1) appointment of persons eligible under Section J who: a) are within the administrative district as set forth in Administrative Rule 3(A), or b) are from a contiguous county, and have agreed to serve as a special judge in the court where the case is pending;

(2) the effective use of all judicial resources within an administrative district; and

(3) certification to the Supreme Court of Indiana of cases in which no judge is eligible to serve as special judge or the particular circumstance of a case warrants selection of a special judge by the Indiana Supreme Court.

A person appointed to serve as special judge under a local rule must accept jurisdiction in the case unless the appointed special judge is disqualified pursuant to the Code of Judicial Conduct, ineligible for service under this rule, or excused from service by the Indiana Supreme Court. The order of appointment under the local rule shall constitute acceptance. An oath or additional evidence of acceptance of jurisdiction is not required.

(I) Discontinuation of service or unavailability of special judge.

(1) In the event a special judge assumes jurisdiction and thereafter ceases to act for any reason, except the timely granting of a motion for change of judge, the regular judge of the court where the case is pending shall assume jurisdiction, provided such judge has not previously served in the case and is otherwise eligible to serve. In the event of the timely granting of a motion for a change of judge from a special judge or if the regular judge does not assume jurisdiction under this section, a successor special judge shall be appointed in accordance with Sections (D) and (H) of this rule.

(2) In the event that a special judge assumes jurisdiction and is thereafter unavailable for any reason on the date when a hearing or trial is scheduled:

(a) the special judge may, as appropriate, appoint a judge pro tempore, temporary judge, or senior judge of the court where the case is pending, provided such judge is otherwise eligible to serve and has not previously had jurisdiction of the case removed from them pursuant to the Rules of Trial Procedure, or

(b) the regular judge of the court where the case is pending may assume temporary jurisdiction, provided such judge is otherwise eligible to serve and has not previously had jurisdiction of the case removed pursuant to the Rules of Trial Procedure.

If the regular judge, judge pro tempore, temporary judge, or senior judge does not assume jurisdiction under this section, such hearing or trial shall be reset to a date when the special judge is available.

(J) Eligibility. Any regular judge of a Circuit, Superior, or Probate Court, a senior judge, or a person serving as a full-time judicial officer in a court of record, including a person who has been a member of a panel for selection, is eligible for appointment by a trial court as a special judge unless this judicial official:

(1) has previously served as judge or special judge in the case; except that whenever a court has granted an order for a change of venue to another county, the judge granting the change of venue may be appointed as special judge for that cause in the receiving county if the judge granting the change,

the receiving judge, and all of the parties to the cause agree to such appointment;

(2) is disqualified by interest or relationship; or

(3) is excused from service as special judge by the Indiana Supreme Court.

A special judge need not be a resident of the county where the case is pending, but accessibility should be considered in making the selection. Senior judges shall be eligible for service as special judge only in courts in which the senior judge is currently appointed by the Indiana Supreme Court to serve as senior judge.

(K) Appointment by Indiana Supreme Court. Upon the certification of a request for appointment of a special judge under Trial Rules 53.1, 53.2, 60.5, I.C. 34–13–5–4, as added by P.L. 1–1998, SEC.8, governing public lawsuits, and this rule, the Supreme Court may appoint any person eligible for service under Section (J) or any member of the Bar of this state as special judge. The order of appointment of a special judge by the Indiana Supreme Court shall be noted in the Chronological Case Summary, entered in the Record of Judgments and Orders, and served on all parties in the proceeding in accordance with Trial Rule 72(D) by the Clerk of the trial court. Such order vests jurisdiction in the special judge, and an oath shall only be required for members of the Bar appointed under this Section.

(L) Continuation of Special Judge Jurisdiction. A special judge shall retain jurisdiction of the case, through judgment and post-judgment, including without limitation, proceedings to enforce the judgment or to modify or revoke orders pertaining to custody, visitation, support, maintenance and property dispositions and post-conviction relief unless:

(1) a specific statute or rule provides to the contrary; or

(2) the special judge is unavailable by reason of death, sickness, absence, or unwillingness to serve.

(M) Transfer of Proceeding. In the event the individual selected to serve as special judge in the case is a regular judge of a court within the county and such court has subject matter jurisdiction of the proceeding, such judge may transfer the case without the assessment of costs to that judge's court for all further proceedings. In the event the individual selected is the regular judge of a court outside of the county where the case is pending and such court has subject matter jurisdiction in like cases, the parties and the judge may agree to a change of venue to such judge's court for all further proceedings. Assessment of statutory change of venue fees shall be shared by the parties as agreed or, failing agreement, as ordered by the court.

(N) Place of Hearing.

(1) Absent the transfer of the case as set forth in Section (M), special judges are encouraged to employ procedures such as the use of facsimile transmissions and telephone conferences that reduce the need for travel.

(2) A special judge may entertain motions and perform all administrative tasks and conferences with counsel in his or her own county.

(3) All hearings involving in-person testimony by witnesses shall be conducted in the court where the case is pending unless:

(a) the parties and the judge agree otherwise on the record, or

(b) the hearing is not before a jury and the special judge determines that exceptional circumstances exist such that the matter can only be heard in a timely fashion in his or her own county.

(4) All decisions, orders, and rulings shall be noted promptly in the Chronological Case Summary and, when appropriate, the Record of Judgments and Orders of the court where the case is pending and shall be served in accordance with Trial Rule 72(D). It is the duty of the special judge to effect the prompt execution of this rule. A court is deemed to have ruled on the date the ruling is noted in the Chronological Case Summary.

(5) It is the duty of the judge of the court where the case is pending to assure the availability of facilities and staff for the special judge.

(O) Emergencies. Nothing in this rule shall divest the original court and judge of jurisdiction to hear and determine emergency matters between the time a motion for change of judge is filed and the appointed special judge accepts jurisdiction.

(P) Compensation. A full-time judge, magistrate, or other employee of the judiciary shall not be paid a special judge fee for service as a special judge. A senior judge shall be paid a special judge fee pursuant to Ind.Administrative Rule 5. All other persons serving as special judge shall be paid a special judge fee of twenty-five dollars ($25.00) per day for each jurisdiction served for the entry of judgments and orders and hearings incidental to such entries. Persons residing outside the county where service is rendered shall be entitled to mileage at a rate equal to other public officials as established by state law, hotel accommodations, and reimbursement for meals and other expenses. Compensation for special judge services shall be paid by the State upon presentation of a claim for such services.

Amended Dec. 7, 1970, effective Jan. 1, 1971; amended effective Feb. 15, 1971; amended April 9, 1974, effective June 1, 1974; Nov. 24, 1975, effective Jan. 31, 1976; Dec. 23, 1976, effective Jan. 1, 1977; Nov. 13, 1979, effective Jan. 1, 1980; Nov. 3, 1981, effective Jan. 1, 1982; Nov. 16, 1984, effective Jan. 1, 1985; amended effective May 19, 1987; Oct. 4, 1990; Nov. 13, 1990; amended Nov. 27, 1990, effective Jan. 1, 1991; Dec. 20, 1991, effective Feb. 1, 1992; Oct. 30, 1992, effective Jan. 1, 1993; Oct. 29, 1993, effective Jan. 1, 1994; amended effective July 1, 1995; amended Dec. 15, 1995, effective Feb. 1, 1996; Dec. 23, 1996, effective March 1, 1997; Nov. 26, 1997, effective Jan. 1, 1998; Dec. 21, 2001, effective April 1, 2002; July 1, 2003, effective Jan. 1, 2004; Sept. 30, 2004, effective Jan. 1, 2005; Sept. 15, 2009, effective Jan. 1, 2010; Sept. 21, 2010, effective Jan. 1, 2011; Nov. 18, 2010, effective Jan. 1, 2011; Sept. 7, 2012, effective Jan. 1, 2013; Sept. 13, 2013, effective Jan. 1, 2014.

Rule 79.1. Special judge—selection: city, town, and Marion county small claims courts

(A) Application. The provisions of this rule constitute the exclusive manner for the selection of special judges in all actions in city, town, and Marion county small claims courts.

(B) Duty to notify court. It shall be the duty of the parties to promptly advise the court of an application or motion for change of judge.

(C) Required affidavit. In any action filed in city, town, or the Marion county small claims courts, notwithstanding the provisions of Trial Rule 76(B), a motion for change of judge shall be verified and signed by the party setting forth facts in support of the statutory basis for the change.

(D) Agreement of the parties. In the event it becomes necessary to appoint a special judge in a city, town, or Marion county small claims court, the parties may agree to the appointment of an eligible individual to so serve. Upon being advised of the agreement of the parties, the court shall appoint such individual as the special judge in the case. This provision shall not apply to criminal proceedings. A special judge selected under this section shall have twenty (20) days to accept jurisdiction, appear, and qualify. The individual who serves as special judge under this section is not entitled to the payment of special judge fees as set forth in Trial Rule 79(J).

(E) Selection by court. Absent an agreement by the parties to appoint a specific individual to serve as special judge, the parties may consent to the appointment of a special judge by the judge presiding in the case. A special judge selected under this section shall have twenty (20) days to accept jurisdiction, appear, and qualify. The individual who serves as special judge under this section is not entitled to the payment of special judge fees as set forth in Trial Rule 79(J).

(F) City and town courts. In the event it becomes necessary to appoint a special judge in a city or town court and the parties fail to agree under Section (D) or (E), the case shall be transferred to the appropriate docket of the county, superior, or circuit court of the county in which the city or town court is located and filed without the assessment of additional fees. The judge who receives the case is not entitled to the payment of special judge fees as set forth in Trial Rule 79(J).

(G) Marion county small claims court. In the event it becomes necessary to appoint a special judge in the Marion county small claims court and the parties fail to agree under Section (D) or (E), the procedure set forth in this section shall apply.

(1) *Naming of panel.* Within two (2) days of deciding that a special judge must be appointed under this section, the presiding judge shall submit to the parties for striking a panel of three judges, who, pursuant to IC 33–34–5–6 must be other judges of the Marion county small claims court.

(2) *Striking from panel.* Each party shall be entitled to strike one name from the panel. The moving party shall be entitled to strike first. The parties shall have not less than seven (7) days nor more than fourteen (14) days to strike as the court may allow.

(3) *Failure to strike.* If the moving party fails to timely strike, the presiding judge shall resume jurisdiction of the case. If a non-moving party fails to timely strike, the clerk of court shall strike in such party's stead.

(4) *Transfer of case.* Upon completion of the striking process, the case shall be transferred to the court of the judge remaining on the panel without the assessment of additional costs.

(5) *Inability to transfer.* In the event the case cannot be transferred, for any reason, to the designated special judge, the case shall be transferred to the court having the highest court identifier number, as provided in Administrative Rule 8, of the Marion county small claims court judge who is not disqualified by reason of interest or relationship. No fees will be assessed for such transfer.

(H) Eligibility. Pursuant to IC 33–34–5–6, no person other than a small claims court judge may serve as a special judge in the small claims court. Any regular judge of a circuit, superior, probate, municipal, or county court, a senior judge, or any member of the bar of the state of Indiana is eligible for appointment as a special judge in a city or town court unless this judge or attorney:

(1) has previously served as judge or been a member of a panel for selection as special judge in the case;

(2) is disqualified by interest or relationship; or

(3) is serving as a bailiff, reporter, referee, commissioner, magistrate, or other appointed official of the court where the case is pending, except as expressly authorized by statute.

(I) Continuation of jurisdiction of case. In the event a special judge is appointed or a case is transferred under this rule, the special judge or court shall retain jurisdiction for all future proceedings in the case, including without limitation, proceedings to enforce the judgment and post-conviction relief unless:

(1) a specific statute or rule provides to the contrary; or

(2) the special judge is unavailable by reason of death, sickness, absence, or unwillingness to serve.

Adopted effective Jan. 1, 1994; amended Sept. 10, 2007, effective Jan. 1, 2008.

XI. GENERAL PROVISIONS

Rule 80. Supreme Court Committee on Rules of Practice and Procedure

(A) Creation, members, terms of office, and removal. There is hereby created a committee to be known as the "Supreme Court Committee on Rules of Practice and Procedure." The committee shall consist of nine members appointed by the Supreme Court. All members of the committee shall be members of the bar of the state of Indiana. One member shall be a judge of the Court of Appeals of the state of Indiana, and one member shall be a judge of a trial court of original, general jurisdiction of the state of Indiana.

The term of each member shall be for five years, except that a member appointed to fill the vacancy of an unexpired term shall be appointed only for the remainder of the unexpired term. Any member may be removed by the Supreme Court.

(B) Officers, executive secretary, meetings, quorum, and compensation. The committee annually shall elect from among its members a chairman who shall preside at all meetings, a vice-chairman who shall preside at meetings in the absence of the chairman, and a secretary who shall keep the minutes of the meetings and prepare the agendas for the meetings. The committee, with the prior approval of the Supreme Court, may appoint an executive secretary of the committee who shall be a member of the bar of the state of Indiana and who shall serve at the pleasure of the committee. The executive secretary shall have the right and duty (1) to administer the committee's work, (2) to supervise the maintenance of the committee's records, and (3) to do all other things necessary and proper to carry out his rights and duties under this rule or as delegated to him from time to time by the committee.

The committee shall meet monthly at a time and place designated by the chairman, and the chairman in his discretion may call special meetings of the committee. Five members shall constitute a quorum at any regular or special meeting of the committee. The committee shall act by a vote of a majority of the members present at any regular or special meeting.

The members of the committee shall be allowed their necessary expenses and such reasonable compensation as the Supreme Court shall fix from time to time.

(C) Duties of the committee. The committee shall conduct a continuous study of the Indiana Rules of Procedure and shall submit to the Supreme Court from time to time recommendations and proposed amendments in order to promote simplicity in procedure, the just determination of litigation, and the elimination of unjustified expense and delay. Additionally, the Supreme Court committee on rules of practice and procedure shall serve as the evidence rules review committee as set forth in Rule 1101 of the *Indiana Rules of Evidence*.

The Supreme Court shall consider all recommendations and proposed amendments received from the committee.

(D) Procedure for amending rules. Except in case of an emergency or as otherwise directed by the Supreme Court, the procedure in this section shall be followed in amending the Indiana Rules of Procedure. On or before December 1, the committee shall cause to be published or otherwise made available for comment by the bench, bar, and public the preliminary draft of each amendment that it is considering submitting to the Supreme Court for adoption. The committee shall accept comments on the amendment for a period of sixty (60) days after publication, and may extend the period for comments upon request. Thereafter, the committee shall study all comments received. Only once each year on or before May 1, the committee shall submit to the Supreme Court for adoption the final draft of each amendment published, either as published or as amended further in light of the comments received, along with a complete copy of all comments received, unless the committee determines that the amendment requires further study or that the amendment will not promote the purposes of the Indiana Rules of Procedure. Only once each year on or before July 1, the Supreme Court shall act on each amendment received from the committee. On January 1 of the following year, each amendment adopted shall take effect unless the Supreme Court orders otherwise.

(E) Comments of the bench, bar, and public. All comments on and amendments proposed by the bench, bar, and public of this state to the Supreme Court committee on rules of practice and procedure, whether on or to preliminary drafts of amendments published for comment or otherwise, shall be delivered in writing to the Committee's Executive Secretary, 30 South Meridian Street, Suite 500, Indianapolis, Indiana 46204, for the committee's consideration and recommendation to the Supreme Court.

Adopted effective Jan. 1, 1970. Amended Nov. 30, 1971, effective Jan. 1, 1972; Dec. 23, 1976, effective Jan. 1, 1977; amended effective Nov. 13, 1979; Feb. 16, 1989; Dec. 17, 1991, effective Jan. 1, 1992; amended effective Jan. 21, 1994; Dec. 15, 1995, effective Feb. 1, 1996; amended effective April 21, 1998; Feb. 4, 2000; Feb. 1, 2007; amended Sept. 10, 2007, effective Jan. 1, 2008.

Rule 81. Local court rules

(A) Authority. Courts may regulate local court and administrative district practice by adopting and amending in accordance with this Rule local and administrative district rules not inconsistent with—and not duplicative of—these Rules of Trial Procedure or other Rules of the Indiana Supreme Court. Courts are strongly encouraged to adopt a single set of local rules for use in all courts of record in a county and will be required to do so after January 1, 2007. The single set may reflect different practices due to geographic, jurisdictional and other variables. Courts shall not use standing orders (that is, generic orders not entered in the individual case) to regulate local court or administrative district practice. Local and administrative district rules requiring approval of the Indiana Supreme Court or the Division of State Court Administration are subject to the provisions of this rule.

(B) Notice and comment.

(1) When a court or administrative district proposes to adopt or amend local or administrative district rules, it shall give notice to the bar and public of the content of the proposal, the time period for the bar and public to comment, the address to which comments should be sent, and the proposed effective date. Notice shall include, but not be limited to, transmitting the proposal to the officers of any local county bar association.

(2) The court shall also transmit the proposal to the county clerk and to the Division of State Court Administration in digital format. The county clerk shall post the proposal in the county clerk's office(s) and on the county clerk's website, if any, and the Division of State Court Administration shall post the proposal on the Indiana Judicial Website for public inspection and comment. The court and the Division of State Court Administration shall receive comments for not less than thirty (30) days.

(C) Schedule. The Division of State Court Administration shall establish and publish a uniform annual schedule, similar to the schedule for proposed Supreme Court rules under Rule 80(D), for publishing proposed local and administrative district rules, receiving comment, adopting rules, and the effective date of adopted rules.

(D) Exceptions to the schedule. If a court finds that there is good cause to deviate from the schedule established by the Division of State Court Administration, the court or administrative district may adopt or amend local or administrative district rules at other times. However, a local or administrative district rule shall not take effect unless it has first been posted for thirty (30) days in the county clerk's office(s) and on the county clerk's website, if any, and on the Indiana Judicial Website. The court promptly thereafter shall provide opportunity to comment in the manner provided in subsection (B)(1) above.

(E) Style, format, and numbering. The Division of State Court Administration shall establish and publish a standard format for drafting and amending local and administrative district rules. The format shall include a uniform numbering system which, to the extent practicable, corresponds to the numbering of these Rules of Trial Procedure and other Rules of the Indiana Supreme Court.

(F) Adopted Rules. The court shall cause adopted rules and amendments to be placed in the Record of Judgments and Orders, shall cause the county clerk to post them in the county clerk's office(s) and on the county clerk's website, if any, for public inspection, and shall transmit a copy of the rules in digital format to the Division of State Court Administration for posting on the Indiana Judicial Website.

(G) Availability of local and administrative district rules. All local and administrative district rules, as amended and with any appendices thereto, shall be compiled into one document, which shall be posted and available in the clerk's office at all times for public inspection and on the county clerk's website, if any. They shall be available free of charge on the Indiana Judicial Website.

(H) Suspension of local or administrative district rules. In an individual case the court, upon its own motion or the motion of any party, may waive, suspend or modify compliance with any local or administrative district rule if the interests of justice so require. All such waivers, suspensions or modifications shall be entered in the Chronological Case Summary of the case.

(I) Transition. To continue in effect local and administrative district rules promulgated before the effective date of this Rule, the court shall (1) renumber such rules according to the uniform numbering system established by the Division of State Court Administration under subsection (E) above, (2) cause such rules to be posted and available in the clerk's office as required by subsection (G) above, and (3) transmit a copy of such rules in digital format to the Division of State Court Administration for posting on the Indiana Judicial Website. By January 1, 2007, local rules must be in compliance with the terms of this Rule.

(J) Periodic review and update. Courts and administrative districts should review periodically and change local and administrative district rules as required by changes in statutes, case law, or these Rules of Trial Procedure or other Rules of the Indiana Supreme Court.

Amended effective Jan. 1, 1972; Sept. 30, 2004, effective Jan. 1, 2005; Aug. 15, 2006, effective Jan. 1, 2007.

Rule 81.1. Procedures for cases involving family or household members

(A) Definitions.

(1) An individual is a "family or household member" of another person if the individual:

(a) is or was a spouse of the other person;

(b) is or was living as if a spouse or a domestic partner of the other person, this determination to be based upon:

(i) the duration of the relationship;

(ii) the frequency of contact;

(iii) the financial interdependence;

(iv) whether the two (2) individuals are or previously were raising children together;

(v) whether the two (2) individuals are or previously have engaged in tasks directed toward maintaining a common household; and,

(vi) such other factors as the court may consider relevant.

(c) has a child in common with the other person;

(d) is related by blood or adoption to the other person;

(e) has or previously had an established legal relationship:

(i) as a guardian of the other person;

(ii) as a ward of the other person;

(iii) as a custodian of the other person;

(iv) as a foster parent of the other person; or,

(v) in a capacity with respect to the other person similar to those listed in clauses (i) through (v).

(2) "Family Procedures" entails coordination of proceedings and processes, and information sharing among cases in a court or courts involving family or household members.

(B) Type of Cases. Courts using Family Procedures for a case may exercise jurisdiction over other cases involving the same family or a household member of the family. An individual case to which Family Procedures is being applied may maintain its separate integrity and separate docket number, but may be given a common case number if multiple cases are being heard before one judge. Subject to applicable rules and statutes, the individual cases may all be transferred to one judge or may remain in the separate courts in which they were originally filed.

(C) Notice. A court intending to use Family Procedures for a case must enter an order notifying all parties of the court's intention and, within thirty (30) days after a case is selected, the court shall provide each party with a list of all cases that have been selected to be heard using Family Procedures.

(D) Designation by Court of Intent to Use Family Procedures and Change of Judge for Cause. Within fifteen (15) days after notice is sent that a case has been selected to be heard using Family Procedures, a party may object for cause to the designation or selection of a party's case.

Once notice is sent to the parties that a case has been selected to be heard using Family Procedures, no motion for change of venue from the judge may be granted except to the extent permitted by Indiana Trial Rule 76. A motion for change of venue from the judge in any matter being heard in a court using Family Procedures, or any future cases joined in the court after the initial selection of cases, shall be granted only for cause. If a special judge is appointed, all current and future cases in the court proceeding may be assigned to the special judge.

(E) Concurrent Hearings. A court using Family Procedures may, in the court's discretion, set concurrent hearings on related cases, take evidence on the related cases at these hearings, and rule on the admissibility of evidence for each case separately as needed to adequately preserve the record for appeal.

(F) Judicial Notice. Indiana Evidence Rule 201 shall govern the taking of judicial notice in courts using Family Procedures.

(G) Court Records Excluded from Public Access. In a court using Family Procedures, each party shall have access to all records in cases joined under this Rule, with the exception of court records excluded from public access pursuant to Administrative Rule 9. A party may seek access to such confidential records from another case joined under this Rule by written petition based on relevancy and need. Records excluded from public access shall retain their confidential status and the court using Family Procedures shall direct that confidential records not be included in the public record of the proceedings.

Adopted Sept. 20, 2011, effective Jan. 1, 2012.

Rule 82. Forms

The forms adopted by the Supreme Court shall be sufficient under the rules and are intended to indicate the simplicity and brevity of statement which the rules contemplate.

Rule 83. Definitions

Subject to additional definitions contained herein, and unless the context otherwise requires, in these rules:

(1) "Court on appeal" means the Indiana supreme court or the court of appeals of Indiana.

(2) "Executive" of a governmental organization includes the governor of the state; the officer or individual occupying any office or unit occupied only by one [1] person; the mayor of any city or town; in the case of a governmental unit or agency headed by more than one [1] person, the presiding officer thereof or the secretary thereof, or if none, any member thereof; in the case of a governmental corporation, the president or presiding officer, secretary, or treasurer thereof. "Executive officer" of an organization includes the president, vice president, secretary, treasurer, cashier, director, chairman of the board of directors or trustees, office manager, plant manager, or subdivision manager, partner, or majority shareholder. For purposes of service of process, notice and other papers, the term includes the personal secretary of any of the foregoing persons or any person employed under or with any of the foregoing persons and who is entrusted with responsible handling of legal papers, and any person employed in the organization

if such person promptly delivers the papers served to one of the foregoing.

(3) "Governmental organization" includes the state, or a department, agency, corporation, office or branch thereof; a county, township, municipality or local governmental unit, or a department, agency, corporation, office or branch thereof; or any governmental representative named as such; or any governmental unit.

(4) "Governmental representative" includes an officer, agent, executive or employee of a governmental organization.

(5) "Organization" includes, without limitation, a domestic or foreign corporation, partnership, unincorporated association, business trust, governmental organization or an organization which is a representative.

(6) "Representative" includes, without limitation, a representative of a decedent's estate, guardian, next friend, receiver, assignee for the benefit of creditors, liquidator, trustee or the like.

Amended effective Jan. 1, 1972.

Rule 84.   Effective date

These rules will take effect on January 1, 1970. They govern all proceedings in actions brought after they take effect and also all further proceedings in actions then pending, except to the extent that in the opinion of the court their application in a particular action pending when the rules take effect would not be feasible or would work injustice, in which event the former procedure applies.

Rule 85.   Vacated

Vacated Dec. 5, 1995, effective Feb. 1, 1996.

APPENDICES

Appendix A. Trial Rule 81 Schedule and Format for Local Court Rules

SECOND AMENDED SCHEDULE FOR ALL LOCAL COURT RULES

The Indiana Supreme Court Division of State Court Administration, a statutorily created office of the Chief Justice of Indiana, is charged pursuant to Trial Rule 81 with certain duties regarding the promulgation of local court rules. Those duties include establishing and publishing a uniform annual schedule for adoption and amendments of local rules, and a standard format for drafting, amending, and numbering local rules. In addition, Administrative Rule 1(E), which becomes effective January 1, 2006, requires that the Division establish and publish a schedule for the formation and adoption of local rules for caseload allocation plans.

In order to allow sufficient time for statewide statistical reports to be collected and compiled for use in the local caseload allocation plans and to maintain the same schedule for the promulgation of all local rules, this schedule is amended with additions indicated by underlining and deletions by strikethrough.

Effective January 1, 2007, all local rules in a county must apply in all courts of record in the county. However, after that date local rules may apply only to certain types of cases as long as they apply in all courts.

1. Schedule

Pursuant to Trial Rule 81(C), the following schedule shall apply for local rules promulgated after January 1, 2005, except those that fall under the exception of T.R. 81(D).

Notice of proposed local rules (Includes caseload allocation plans)	June 1
Close of Comment period	July 1
Final approval by local courts	July 2 to July 31
Submission for Supreme Court approval (as to rules specified in Section 8)	August 1
Supreme Court action (as to rules specified in Section 8)	October 1
Revised rules under Section 8 due before Supreme Court	November 1
Final Supreme Court action on resubmitted rules under Section 8	November 15
Effective date of Local Rules	January 1

2. Content of the Notice

Not later than June 1 of each year the courts in any county desiring to adopt or modify local rules shall give notice to the bar and public of the content of any proposed additions, modifications, or deletions to local rules. The notice shall include:

(a) the address to which comments should be sent;

(b) comments by the bar and public will be received until July 1;

(c) the proposals will be adopted, modified, or rejected by July 31;

(d) the rules requiring Supreme Court approval will be submitted to the court by August 1;

(e) that certain local rules (list) may not take effect until approved by the Supreme Court; and

(f) the effective date of the proposed rules shall be January 1 of the following year.

3. Standard Format for Drafting and Amending Local Rules

All proposed local rules not yet effective shall be marked by new text shown by underlining and the deleted text shown by striking. All rule modifications or additions must clearly indicate old and new language.

4. Publication of the Notice

Publication of the notice is accomplished when the courts of a county provide the notice indicating the text of the proposed local rule(s) to the county clerk and to the Division of State Court Administration in digital format. The county clerk shall post the notice in the county clerk's office(s) and on the county clerk's website, if any. The Division of State Court Administration shall post the proposal on the Indiana Judicial Website for public inspection and comment. Notice shall also be given to the president and secretary (or, if none similar officers) of any local bar association.

5. Close of Comment Period

The courts of the county shall accept comments for 45 days, until July 1. After July 1, the courts shall review and study the comments received and make changes to the proposed rules as deemed advisable.

6. Adoption of Local Rules

The court shall adopt the final local rules on or before July 31 of each year.

7. Effective Date of Local Rules

All local rules, whether or not requiring Supreme Court approval, shall become effective January 1 of the following year.

8. Local Rules that Require Supreme Court Approval

(a) Supreme Court approval is required only for local rules within any of the following categories:

i. local rules for special judge selection in civil cases pursuant to T.R. 79(H);

ii. local rules for assignment of criminal cases and selection of successor judges pursuant to Criminal Rule 2.2;

iii. local rules regarding court reporter services pursuant to Administrative Rule 15;

iv. local rules on case reallocation plans pursuant to Administrative Rule 1(E).

All courts of record in each county are required to have a common local rule in each of the above categories.

(b) Not later than August 1 of each year, the court shall submit to the Supreme Court all newly adopted local rules that require Supreme Court approval by sending a Request for Approval of Local Rules to the Clerk of the Indiana Supreme Court. (See Appendix A for a form Request for Approval of Local Rules.) The Clerk shall enter the Request in the Supreme Court Chronological Case Summary and shall forward the Request to the Division of State Court Administration.

(c) The Supreme Court will act upon Requests not later than October 1. The Supreme Court may approve the proposal as submitted, approve a modified version, or reject the proposal.

(d) The Supreme Court order approving the Request for Approval of Local Rules shall be entered of record in the Record of Orders and Judgments of each local court in which it is effective.

(e) A local rule requiring Supreme Court approval is not effective until the Supreme Court enters an order approving it and until the local rule is posted pursuant to T.R. 81(D).

9. Uniform Numbering

The uniform local rule numbers shall consist of five (5) groups of characters. They shall (a) identify the draft as a local rule, (b) the county, (c) the Supreme Court rule set to which the local rule pertains, (d) the Supreme Court rule number to which the local rule refers, and (e) the local sequence. The five sets of characters shall be separated by dashes.

(a) *LR designation.* The first set of characters of a local court rule number shall be "LR" to indicate a local court rule.

(b) *County identifier.* The second set of characters of a local court rule number shall be a two-digit county identifier which comports with the county identifiers found in Administrative Rule 8.

The "LR" designation and county identifier shall be followed by a dash.

(c) *Rule sets and priority for organizing local rules.* The third set of characters of a local court rule number shall indicate the state rule set to which the local rule pertains. The rule set identifier shall consist of two letters and shall be as follows:

Rules of Trial Procedure	TR
Rules of Criminal Procedure	CR
Small Claims Rules	SC
Petitions for Post Conviction Relief	PC
Jury Rules	JR
Administrative Rules	AR
Trial De Novo Rules	DN

As a first preference and to the extent possible, local rules should be correlated to the Indiana Rules of Trial Procedure in content and numbering and should be designated as "TR." Local rules that cannot logically fit within the context of the trial rules may be correlated to one of the remaining Supreme Court rule sets.

Local rules for domestic relations, trust/probate/guardianship and juvenile cases, which cannot logically fit into one of the Indiana Rules of Trial Procedure or one of the foregoing sets of Supreme Court Rules, may be designated as follows:

Family Law	FL
Trust/Probate/Guardianship	PR
Juvenile	JV

A court that proposes to promulgate local rules that cannot logically fall under the foregoing rule set designations should contact the Division of State Court Administration with suggestions and reasons for amendments to the foregoing rule sets.

(d) *State level rule set numbers.* The fourth set of characters of a local court rule number shall identify the state level rule set to which the local rule relates.

In the event a local rule relates to a state rule set but is purely of a local nature and has no corresponding number within the state rule set, the state rule number shall be "00" so that there is no possibility of duplication.

The state level rule set and rule number shall be followed by a dash.

(e) *Local sequence.* The fifth set of characters shall consist of any number of characters assigned by the local courts to indicate a local sequence.

Example of an Adams County rule on criminal case assignment: LR01–CR2.2–1

Example of a Marion County rule on dress code:

LR49–AR00 –1. A local rule regarding dress code would fit under the general context of the state level Administrative Rules (AR). However, because there is no state rule regarding dress code, the fourth set of characters would be "00."

These standards shall remain in effect until amended.

Adopted effective Dec. 13, 2004. Amended effective March 4, 2005; Dec. 22, 2005, effective Jan. 1, 2006.

Appendix A-1. Request for Approval of Local Rules

APPENDIX A

TO LOCAL RULES SCHEDULE UNDER

T.R. 81 AND ADMIN. R.1 (E)

In the
Indiana Supreme Court

IN THE MATTER OF	)
	)
REQUEST FOR APPPROVAL	)
	) Case No.
OF LOCAL RULES	)
	)
FOR COURTS OF RECORD IN	)
	)
_____ COUNTY	)

REQUEST FOR APPROVAL OF LOCAL RULES

The judges of the courts of record of _____ County have

decided to adopt the local rules indicated below and request Supreme Court approval for

the following local rules for which Supreme Court approval is required:

1. ___ Special judge selection rule pursuant to Trial Rule 79(H);

2. ___ Reassignment of criminal cases pursuant to Criminal Rule 2.2;

3. ___ Court reporter rule pursuant to Administrative Rule 15;

4. ___ Caseload allocation rule pursuant to Administrative Rule 1.

_____ The local rule(s) indicated above have been published for comment pursuant

to the schedule established by T.R. 81 (B) for not less than 45 days.

Or

_____ The local rule(s) indicated above are proposed for adoption without first being published for comment because good cause exists for the court(s) to deviate from the schedule established pursuant to T.R. 81. Upon approval by the Supreme Court, these local rules shall be published as required by TR 81 (D) and shall not be effective until so published for comment.

Accordingly, the judges of record of _____ County request approval of the above noted Local Rules.

Submitted this _____ day of _____, _____.

For the Courts of Record of _____ County

_____
Typed name of submitting judge

_____
Signature of submitting judge

Adopted Dec. 22, 2005, effective Jan. 1, 2006.

Appendix A–2. Affidavit of Debt

AFFIDAVIT OF DEBT

Comes now affiant, and states:

I_____ am ☐ Plaintiff
   (Name of Affiant)   OR
           ☐ a designated full-time employee of _____ (Plaintiff).
                                      (Name of Plaintiff)

I am of adult age and am fully authorized by Plaintiff to make the following representations. I am familiar with the record keeping practices of Plaintiff. The following representations are true according to documents kept in the normal course of Plaintiff's business and/or my personal knowledge:

    Plaintiff:
        ☐ is the original owner of this debt.
        OR
        ☐ has obtained this debt from _____and the original owner of this debt
        was _____.

_____, Defendant, has an unpaid balance of $_____ on account _____.
(Name of Defendant)   (last 4 digits of number or id only)
That amount is due and owing to Plaintiff. This account was opened on _____. The last payment from Defendant was received on _____ in the amount of $_____.
The type of account is:
        ☐ Credit card account (i.e. Visa, Mastercard, Department Store, etc.)
        List the name of the Company/Store issuing credit card: _____
        ☐ Account for utilities (i.e. telephone, electric, sewer, etc.)
        ☐ Medical bill account (i.e. doctor, dentist, hospital, etc.)
        ☐ Account for services (i.e. attorney fees, mechanic fees, etc.)
        ☐ Judgment issued by a court (a copy of the judgment is required to be attached)
        ☐ Other: (Please explain) _____
        _____
        _____

    This account balance includes:
        ☐ Late fees in the amount of $_____ as of _____.
                                      (Month, Day, Year)
        ☐ Other (Explain _____)
        ☐ Interest at a rate of _____ % beginning on _____.
                                     (Month, Day, Year)
    Plaintiff:
        ☐ is seeking attorney's fees and additional evidence will be presented to the court prior to entry of judgment on attorney's fees.
        OR
        ☐ is not seeking attorney's fees.

    Plaintiff believes that defendant is not a minor or an incompetent individual.

If the defendant is an individual, plaintiff states and declares that:

☐ Defendant is not on active military service. Plaintiff's statement that Defendant is not on active military service is based upon the following facts:

_____

_____

_____.

OR

☐ Plaintiff is unable to determine whether or not Defendant is not on active military service military service.

("Active military service" includes fulltime duty in the military (including the National Guard and reserves) and, for members of the National Guard, service under a call to active service authorized by the President or Secretary of Defense. For further information, see the definition of "military service" in the Servicemembers Civil Relief Act, as amended, 50 U.S.C.A. Appx. § 521.)

I swear or affirm under the penalties of perjury that the foregoing representations are true.

Dated: _____ Signature of Affiant: _____

Adopted Sept. 21, 2010, effective Jan. 1, 2011. Amended Oct. 28, 2010, effective Jan. 1, 2011.

Appendix B. Appearance by Attorney in Civil Case

STATE OF INDIANA   )   IN THE _____ COURT

) SS:

COUNTY OF _____)   **Case Number:**

                             (To be supplied by Clerk when case is filed.)

(Caption)

APPEARANCE BY ATTORNEY IN CIVIL CASE

This Appearance Form must be filed on behalf of every party in a civil case.

1. The party on whose behalf this form is being filed is:

   Initiating ____   Responding ____   Intervening __; and

   the undersigned attorney and all attorneys listed on this form now appear in this case for the following parties:

   Name of party _____

   Address of party *(see Question # 6 below if this case involves a protection from abuse order, a workplace violence restraining order, or a no-contact order)*

   _____

   _____

   Telephone # of party _____

(List on a continuation page additional parties this attorney represents in this case.)

2. Attorney information for service as required by Trial Rule 5(B)(2)

   Name: _____ Atty Number: _____

   Address: _____

   _____

   Phone: _____

   FAX: _____

   Email Address: _____

   (List on continuation page additional attorneys appearing for above party)

3. This is a _____ case type as defined in administrative Rule 8(B)(3).

4. I will accept service by:

   FAX at the above noted number: Yes ___ No ___

   Email at the above noted address: Yes ___ No ___

5. This case involves child support issues. Yes ___ No ___ *(If yes, supply social security numbers for all family members on a separately attached document filed as confidential information on light green paper. Use Form TCM–TR3.1–4.)*

6. This case involves a protection from abuse order, a workplace violence restraining order, or a no—contact order. Yes ___ No ___ *(If Yes, the initiating party must provide an address for the purpose of legal service but that address should not be one that exposes the whereabouts of a petitioner.)* The party shall use the following address for purposes of legal service:

   _____   Attorney's address

   _____   The Attorney General Confidentiality program address (contact the Attorney General at 1–800–321–1907 or e-mail address is **confidential@atg.state.in.us**).

_____ Another address (provide)

7. This case involves a petition for involuntary commitment. Yes ___ No ___

8. If Yes above, provide the following regarding the individual subject to the petition for involuntary commitment:

   a. Name of the individual subject to the petition for involuntary commitment if it is not already provided in #1 above: _____

   b. State of Residence of person subject to petition: _____

   c. At least one of the following pieces of identifying information:

      (i)   Date of Birth _____
      (ii) Driver's License Number _____
            State where issued _____ Expiration date _____
      (iii) State ID number _____
            State where issued _____ Expiration date _____
      (iv) FBI number _____
      (v)   Indiana Department of Corrections Number _____
      (vi) Social Security Number is available and is being provided in an attached confidential document Yes ___ No ___

9. There are related cases: Yes ___ No ___ _(If yes, list on continuation page.)_

10. Additional information required by local rule: _____

11. There are other party members: Yes ___ No ___ _(If yes, list on continuation page.)_

12. This form has been served on all other parties and Certificate of Service is attached. Yes ___ No ___

_____
Attorney-at-Law
(Attorney information shown above.)

Adopted effective Jan. 1, 2005. Amended Sept. 10, 2007, effective Jan. 1, 2008; amended effective July 17, 2009; Sept. 7, 2012, effective Jan. 1, 2013.

INDIANA RULES OF CRIMINAL PROCEDURE

Adopted Effective January 1, 1970

Including Amendments Received Through November 1, 2013

Rule 1. Statutory rules adopted

Chapter 185, Acts of 1937, has heretofore been abrogated [1]. All other rules of procedure and practice applicable to trial courts adopted by statutory enactment and in effect on January 1, 1970, including the statutes attempted to be repealed by Chapter 185, Acts of 1937, shall continue in full force and effect, except as otherwise provided by the rules of this court.

[1] Repealed by Acts 1963, c. 29, s. 5, "as superseded by rules of the Supreme Court."

Rule 1.1. Documents and information excluded from public access and confidential pursuant to Administrative Rule 9(G)(1)

Documents and information excluded from public access pursuant to Administrative Rule 9(G)(1) shall be filed in accordance with Trial Rule 5(G).

Adopted Sept. 30, 2004, effective Jan. 1, 2005.

Rule 2. Subpoena duces tecum

A subpoena may command the person to whom it is directed to produce the books, documents, or tangible things designated therein; but the court, upon motion made promptly and in any event at or before the time specified in the subpoena for compliance therewith, may:

(1) quash or modify the subpoena if it is unreasonable and oppressive;

(2) condition denial of the motion upon the advancement by the person in whose behalf the subpoena is issued of the reasonable costs of producing the books, papers, documents, or tangible things; or

(3) quash a Grand-Jury subpoena on the ground of privilege against self-incrimination on the motion of a Grand Jury Target Witness.

Amended Nov. 4, 1985, effective Jan. 1, 1986.

Rule 2.1. Appearance

(A) State of Indiana. At the time a criminal proceeding is commenced, the prosecuting attorney for the county where the action is pending shall file an appearance form setting forth the following information:

(1) The name, address, attorney number, telephone number, FAX number, and computer address of the prosecuting attorney representing the State of Indiana, as applicable;

(2) The case type of the proceeding [Administrative Rule 8(B)(3)];

(3) A statement that the State will or will not accept service by FAX;

(4) The number of any arrest report relating to the factual basis underlying the criminal proceeding;

(5) The transaction control number associated with the fingerprints submitted by the arresting agency and the state identification number assigned to the defendant by the Indiana State Police Cen-

tral Records Repository if the defendant has been arrested and processed at the jail; and

(6) Such additional matters specified by state or local rule required to maintain the information management system employed by the court.

(B) Defendant. At the time an attorney for the defendant first appears in the criminal case, the defense attorney shall file an appearance form setting forth the following information:

(1) The name, address, attorney number, telephone number, FAX number, and computer address of the attorney representing the defendant;

(2) The case number assigned to the criminal proceeding;

(3) A statement that the defense attorney will or will not accept service in this case by FAX; and

(4) Such additional matters specified by state or local rule required to maintain the information management system employed by the court.

(C) Defendant-Pro Se. In the event a defendant decides to represent himself or herself in a criminal proceeding without assistance of counsel, the defendant shall file an appearance form setting forth the identifying information required in subsection (B), as applicable.

(D) Completion and Correction of Information. In the event matters must be filed before the information required by this rule is available, the appearance form shall be submitted with available information and supplemented when the absent information is acquired. Attorneys shall promptly advise the clerk of the court of any change in the information previously supplied to the court on the appearance form.

(E) Temporary Appearance. In the event an attorney, different from any specifically identified in a previously filed appearance, is temporarily representing a party in a proceeding before the court, through filing a pleading with the court or in any other capacity including discovery, the new attorney shall file an appearance form. The appearance form shall contain the information set out in Section (A) or (B) above, shall provide the name, attorney number and all contact information of the attorney who has filed the prior appearance in the case, the new attorney's temporary status, and the date the temporary appearance shall end. The court shall not be required to act on the temporary appearance unless the new temporary attorney has not appeared at the request of a party's previously identified counsel.

(F) Forms. The Division of State Court Administration shall prepare and publish a standard format for compliance with the provisions of this rule.

Adopted Dec. 5, 1994, effective Feb. 1, 1995. Amended July 1, 2005, effective Jan. 1, 2006; Sept. 29, 2009, effective Jan. 1, 2010.

Rule 2.2. Assignment of cases

The courts of record in each county shall adopt for approval by the Indiana Supreme Court a local rule by which all felony and misdemeanor cases shall be assigned to each court in the county at the time of filing. Should a county fail to adopt such plan, the Supreme Court shall prescribe a plan for use by the county. The local rule shall include:

(A) provision for non-discretionary assignment of all felony and misdemeanor cases filed in the county to one or more . of the courts and judges with such jurisdiction;

(B) to the extent practical under this mandate for non-discretionary assignment in criminal cases, consideration of the workload of each court in other areas;

(C) provision for the continued assignment of a judge in the event of dismissal; and

(D) pursuant to Ind.Crim.Rule 13(C), provision for the reassignment of the case in the event a change of judge is granted under Ind.Crim.Rule 12 or an order of disqualification or recusal is entered in the case.

Adopted Dec. 5, 1994, effective Feb. 1, 1995; amended effective July 6, 1995.

Rule 2.3 Transfer of cases

(A) Transfer of Cases from City and Town Courts. In all counties where there are circuit, superior, county or juvenile courts, and where there also exist in the same county a city or town court, the judge of the city or town court may, with the consent of the judge of such circuit, superior, county or juvenile court, transfer to the circuit, superior, county or juvenile court any cause of action filed and docketed in such city or town court. Transfer may occur by transferring to the receiving court all original pleadings and documents and bail bonds filed in such cause of action. The cause of action shall be redocketed in the receiving court and disposed as if originally filed with the receiving court, provided that the receiving court has jurisdiction over the matter.

(B) Transfer of Cases to City and Town Courts. The judge of a circuit, superior, county or juvenile court may, with the consent of the judge of a city or town court within the county, transfer to such city or town court any cause of action filed and docketed in the circuit, superior, county or juvenile court, provided that the receiving court has jurisdiction over the matter. Transfer may occur by transferring to the receiving court all original pleadings and documents and bail bonds filed in such cause of action. The cause of action shall be redocketed in the receiving court and disposed as if originally filed with the receiving court.

(C) Transfer of Probation Supervision between Counties after Sentencing. The judge of a circuit, superior, city or town court, when transferring probation supervision to a court of another jurisdiction, may also transfer sanctioning authority for probation violations, including revocation of probation. If the original sentencing court transfers sanctioning authority, the consent of the judge in the receiving court is required.

(D) Fee for Transfer of Probation Supervision. An offender on probation who applies to have the probation supervision transferred to a court in another jurisdiction shall pay a transfer fee of seventy-five dollars ($75) to the receiving court. The receiving court may waive the transfer fee if it finds the offender is indigent.

Adopted Dec. 15, 1995, effective Feb. 1, 1996. Amended Sept. 9, 2008, effective Jan. 1, 2009.

Rule 3. Memorandum to be filed with motion to dismiss

Motion to Dismiss—Memorandum. In all cases where a motion is made to dismiss an indictment or affidavit, a memorandum shall be filed therewith stating specifically the grounds for dismissal. A motion to dismiss shall be based upon such grounds as are provided by law, whether statutory or other legal grounds. A defendant who is in a position adequately to raise more than one (1) ground in support of the motion to dismiss shall raise every ground upon which he intends to challenge the indictment or information. A subsequent motion based upon a ground not properly raised, although available, in the original motion to dismiss may be summarily denied. The court, however, in the interest of justice and for good cause shown, may entertain and dispose of such a motion on the merits. A motion to dismiss based upon lack of jurisdiction over the subject matter may be made at any time.

Amended June 8, 1971; Amended Nov. 4, 1985, effective Jan. 1, 1986.

Rule 4. Discharge for delay in criminal trials

(A) Defendant in Jail. No defendant shall be detained in jail on a charge, without a trial, for a period in aggregate embracing more than six (6) months from the date the criminal charge against such defendant is filed, or from the date of his arrest on such charge (whichever is later); except where a continuance was had on his motion, or the delay was caused by his act, or where there was not sufficient time to try him during such period because of congestion of the court calendar; provided, however, that in the last-mentioned circumstance, the prosecuting attorney shall make such statement in a motion for continuance not later than ten (10) days prior to the date set for trial, or if such motion is filed less than ten (10) days prior to trial, the prosecuting attorney shall show additionally that the delay in filing the motion was not the fault of the prosecutor. Provided further, that a trial court may take note of congestion or an emergency without the necessity of a motion, and upon so finding may order a continuance. Any

continuance granted due to a congested calendar or emergency shall be reduced to an order, which order shall also set the case for trial within a reasonable time. Any defendant so detained shall be released on his own recognizance at the conclusion of the six-month period aforesaid and may be held to answer a criminal charge against him within the limitations provided for in subsection (C) of this rule.

(B)(1) Defendant in Jail—Motion for Early Trial. If any defendant held in jail on an indictment or an affidavit shall move for an early trial, he shall be discharged if not brought to trial within seventy (70) calendar days from the date of such motion, except where a continuance within said period is had on his motion, or the delay is otherwise caused by his act, or where there was not sufficient time to try him during such seventy (70) calendar days because of the congestion of the court calendar. Provided, however, that in the last-mentioned circumstance, the prosecuting attorney shall file a timely motion for continuance as set forth in subdivision (A) of this rule. Provided further, that a trial court may take note of congestion or an emergency without the necessity of a motion, and upon so finding may order a continuance. Any continuance granted due to a congested calendar or emergency shall be reduced to an order, which order shall also set the case for trial within a reasonable time.

(2) In computing the time comprising the seventy (70) calendar days under this Criminal Rule 4(B), each and every day after the filing of such motion for early trial shall be counted, including every Saturday, every Sunday, and every holiday excepting only, that if the seventieth (70th) day should fall upon a Saturday, a Sunday, or a holiday, then such trial may be commenced on the next day thereafter, which is not a Saturday, Sunday, or legal holiday.

(3) The amendment to this Criminal Rule 4(B) shall be effective as to each and every motion for early trial filed on and after June 4, 1974.

(C) Defendant Discharged. No person shall be held on recognizance or otherwise to answer a criminal charge for a period in aggregate embracing more than one year from the date the criminal charge against such defendant is filed, or from the date of his arrest on such charge, whichever is later; except where a continuance was had on his motion, or the delay was caused by his act, or where there was not sufficient time to try him during such period because of congestion of the court calendar; provided, however, that in the last-mentioned circumstance, the prosecuting attorney shall file a timely motion for continuance as under subdivision (A) of this rule. Provided further, that a trial court may take note of congestion or an emergency without the necessity of a motion, and upon so finding may order a continuance. Any continuance granted due to a congested calendar or emergency shall be reduced to an order, which order shall also set the case for trial within a reasonable time. Any defendant so held shall, on motion, be discharged.

(D) Discharge for delay in trial—When may be refused—Extensions of time. If when application is made for discharge of a defendant under this rule, the court be satisfied that there is evidence for the state, which cannot then be had, that reasonable effort has been made to procure the same and there is just ground to believe that such evidence can be had within ninety (90) days, the cause may be continued, and the prisoner remanded or admitted to bail; and if he be not brought to trial by the state within such additional ninety (90) days, he shall then be discharged.

(E) Expiration of time. When any time period established by the rule shall expire on a holiday or during vacation, the time so established shall be extended until the close of the next day when court is in session. This rule supersedes in part Burns' Stat., §§ 9–1402–9–1404 (Repl.1956).[1]

(F) Time periods extended. When a continuance is had on motion of the defendant, or delay in trial is caused by his act, any time limitation contained in this rule shall be extended by the amount of the resulting period of such delay caused thereby. However, if the defendant causes any such delay during the last thirty (30) days of any period of time set by operation of this rule, the State may petition the trial court for an extension of such period for an additional thirty (30) days.

(G) Application. This rule shall apply to all trial courts having criminal jurisdiction in the state of Indiana.

Amended Dec. 17, 1973, effective Feb. 1, 1974; Jan. 2, 1974, effective Feb. 1, 1974; amended effective June 4, 1974; amended Oct. 15, 1986, effective Jan. 1, 1987; amended effective Jan. 26, 1987.

[1] IC 35–1–26–2 [repealed], 35–1–27–1 [repealed], 35–1–27–2 [repealed].

Rule 5. Recording machines: transcripts

Every trial judge exercising criminal jurisdiction of this state shall arrange and provide for the electronic recording or stenographic reporting with computer-aided transcription capability of any and all oral evidence and testimony given in all cases and hearings, including both questions and answers, all rulings of the judge in respect to the admission and rejection of evidence and objections thereto, and any other oral matters occurring during the hearing in any proceeding. The recording device or the computer-aided transcription equipment shall be selected and approved by the court and may be placed under the supervision and operation of the official court reporter or such other person as may be designated by the court. The court may, in its discretion, eliminate shorthand or stenographic reporting of any recorded matter. When computer-aided transcription equipment is used to record oral matters in felony cases, a printed transcript shall be produced and maintained

as a court record for fifty-five years. If a transcription of the recorded matters has not been prepared, certified and filed in the criminal proceeding, the electronic recording of all oral matters, together with a log denoting the individuals recorded and meter location of crucial events, or floppy disk and stenographic paper notes, shall be maintained as a court record for ten years in all misdemeanors or fifty-five years in all felony cases.

The judge of the court in which the oral matters were recorded may direct the court reporter or any other responsible, competent person, in his discretion, to make a transcription of recorded oral matters and certify the accuracy of the transcription. Upon certification, the transcription of recorded oral matters shall have the same effect as if made from shorthand or stenographic notes.

Amended Oct. 15, 1986, effective Jan. 1, 1988; Nov. 10, 1988, effective Jan. 1, 1989; Aug. 15, 2006, effective Jan. 1, 2007.

Rule 6. Exceptions not necessary; offer to prove

The record need not show exceptions to adverse actions, orders or rulings of the court in order to present alleged errors with respect thereto, for the purposes of a motion to correct errors on an appeal. This rule is not intended to affect in any manner the present practice in regard to objections.

Where, on the examination of a witness, an offer to prove is made, the same may be made either before or after the ruling of the trial court on the objection to the question propounded.

Rule 7. Joint and several

All motions of any kind addressed to two [2] or more paragraphs of any pleading, or filed by two [2] or more parties, shall be taken and construed as joint, separate, and several motions to each of such paragraphs and by each of such parties. All motions containing two [2] or more subject matters shall be taken and construed as separate and several as to each subject matter. All objections to rulings made by two [2] or more parties shall be taken and construed as the joint, separate, and several objections of each of such parties.

All motions containing two [2] or more subject matters should be taken and construed as separate and several as to each subject matter.

Rule 8. Instructions; limitations thereon; objections

(A) In addition to instructions given by the Court on its own motion, a party in any cause tried by a jury, before argument, shall be entitled to tender in writing not to exceed ten (10) proposed instructions to be given to the jury. However, the trial court, in its discretion, may fix a greater number in a particular case, which number shall be stated of record by an order book entry made by the court. The number of tendered instructions permitted shall not be reduced by any necessary limiting or cautionary instructions, tendered as final instructions, where a limiting or cautionary instruction has been requested during the course of the presentation of evidence. No party shall be entitled to predicate error upon the refusal of a trial court to give any tendered instruction in excess of the number fixed by the court order, whichever is greater. Each tendered instruction shall be confined to one (1) relevant legal principle.

(B) The court shall indicate on all instructions, in advance of the argument, those that are to be given and those refused. After the court has indicated the instructions to be given, each party shall have a reasonable opportunity to examine such instructions and to state his specific objection to each, out of the presence of the jury and before argument, or specific written objections to each instruction may be submitted to the court before argument. No error with respect to the giving of instructions shall be available as a cause for new trial or on appeal, except upon the specific objections made as above required.

(C) All instructions given or refused, and all written objections submitted thereto, shall be filed in open court and become a part of the record in the cause without a bill of exceptions. Objections made orally shall be taken by the reporter and may be made a part of the record by a general or a special bill of exceptions.

(D) Requested instructions must be reduced to writing (identified as to the party making submission), separately numbered, and accompanied by a cover sheet signed by the party, or his attorney, who requests such instructions and will be deemed sufficiently identified as having been tendered by the parties or submitted by the court if it appears in the record from an order book entry, bill of exceptions, or otherwise, by whom the same were tendered or submitted. Where final instructions are submitted to the jury in written form after having been read by the court, no indication of the party or parties by whom instructions were tendered should appear on any instruction.

(E) The court's action in directing or refusing to direct a verdict shall be shown by order book entry. Error may be predicated upon such ruling or upon the giving or refusing to give a written instruction directing the verdict.

(F) When the jury has been sworn the court shall instruct in writing as to the issues for trial, the burden of proof, the credibility of witnesses, and the manner of weighing the testimony to be received. Each party shall have reasonable opportunity to examine such instructions and state his specific objections thereto out of the presence of the jury and before any party has stated his case.

(G) The court may of its own motion and shall, if requested by either party, reread to the jury the instructions given pursuant to subdivision (F) of this rule along with the other instructions given to the jury at the close of the case.

(H) The manner of objecting to such instructions, of saving questions thereon, and making the same a part of the record shall be the same as in Rule 51(C) of the Rules of Trial Procedure.

Amended Nov. 4, 1985, effective Jan. 1, 1986; amended Oct. 29, 1993, effective Jan. 1, 1994.

Rule 9. Authority of judges

The judge who presides at the trial of a cause shall, if available, rule on the motion to correct errors if one is filed, and shall sign all bills of exceptions, if such are requested. The unavailability of any such trial judge shall be determined and shown by a court order made by the judge then presiding in such court.

Rule 10. Plea of guilty: Record to be made

Whenever a plea of guilty to a felony or misdemeanor charge is accepted from any defendant who is sentenced upon said plea, the judge shall cause the entire proceeding in connection with such plea and sentencing, including questions, answers, statements made by the defendant and his attorney, if any, the prosecuting attorney and the judge to be recorded by an electronic recording device. The court may in its discretion also require the entire proceeding be recorded by the court reporter in shorthand or by stenographic notation.

If a transcription of the recorded matters has not been prepared, certified and filed in the criminal proceeding, the electronic recording of all oral matters, together with a log denoting the individuals recorded and the meter location of crucial events, shall be maintained as a court record for ten years in all misdemeanors or fifty-five years in all felony cases.

Whenever the record of the proceeding is transcribed it shall be prepared in a form similar to that in general use as a transcript of evidence in a trial. When so transcribed, the same shall be submitted to the judge who shall certify that it is a true and complete transcript of such proceedings and shall order the same filed as a part of the record and cause an order book entry of the filing thereof to be made by the clerk.

In any proceeding questioning the validity of such plea of guilty or judgment rendered thereon, such transcription shall be taken and considered as the record of the proceedings transcribed therein and upon appeal the original may be incorporated without copying as a part of the record in such appeal over the certificate of the clerk.

Amended Dec. 23, 1976, effective Jan. 1, 1977; Oct. 15, 1986, effective Jan. 1, 1988; Nov. 10, 1988, effective Jan. 1, 1989; Aug. 15, 2006, effective Jan. 1, 2007.

Rule 10.1. Presence of prosecutor

Except for the initial hearing where evidence is not presented, the Prosecuting Attorney or a deputy prosecuting attorney shall be present at all felony or misdemeanor proceedings, including the presentation of evidence, sentencing or other final disposition of the case.

Adopted Oct. 15, 1986, effective Jan. 1, 1987; amended effective April 28, 1987.

Rule 11. Instructions by judge after sentencing or contested felony probation revocation

Upon entering a conviction, whether the acceptance of a guilty plea or by finding or by verdict, the court shall sentence a defendant convicted in a criminal case within thirty (30) days of the plea or the finding or verdict of guilty, unless an extension for good cause is shown.

Following the sentencing of a defendant after a trial or following a judgment revoking probation of a defendant found to have violated the terms of his probation after a contested felony probation revocation proceeding, the judge shall immediately advise the defendant as follows:

(1) that he is entitled to take an appeal or file a motion to correct error;

(2) that if he wishes to file a motion to correct error, it must be done within thirty (30) days of the sentencing;

(3) that if he wishes to take an appeal, he must file a Notice of Appeal designating what is to be included in the record on appeal within thirty (30) days after the sentencing or within thirty (30) days after the motion to correct error is denied or deemed denied, if one is filed; if the Notice of Appeal is not timely filed, the right to appeal may be forfeited;

(4) that if he is financially unable to employ an attorney, the court will appoint counsel for defendant at public expense for the purpose of filing the motion to correct error and for taking an appeal.

Provided further that when a trial court imposes a death sentence, it shall also advise the defendant at sentencing that the court reporter and clerk will begin immediate preparation of the record on appeal.

The court shall then inquire of the defendant whether or not he wishes to appeal or file a Motion to Correct Error. If the defendant states that he does desire to do so, the court shall forthwith instruct trial counsel for defendant that it is his duty to consult with defendant and with defendant's appeal counsel, if any, on the action to be taken.

The court shall then inquire of the defendant whether or not he is a pauper and has insufficient funds to employ an attorney. If the court finds that he is financially unable to employ counsel for an appeal and the defendant states that he desires an attorney for appeal, the court shall thereupon promptly appoint an attorney to represent the defendant in an appeal and notify the defendant at said time of said action.

The judge shall cause the court reporter to record the entire proceedings in connection with such sentencing or probation revocation, including questions, answers, statements made by the defendant and his attorney, if any, the prosecuting attorney and the judge, and promptly thereafter to transcribe the same in form similar to that in general use as a transcript of evidence in a trial.

Thereafter in any subsequent inquiry into the events occurring at these proceedings, such transcript shall be considered as part of the record on appeal. When properly certified by the clerk, such transcript or a copy thereof may be incorporated as a part of the record in any appeal.

Amended Nov. 30, 1971, effective April 1, 1972; amended effective April 30, 1973; Nov. 4, 1985, effective Jan. 1, 1986; Nov. 10, 1988, effective Jan. 1, 1989; amended effective Feb. 16, 1989; Nov. 30, 1989, effective Jan. 1, 1990; Feb. 4, 2000, effective Jan. 1, 2001; Dec. 21, 2001, effective April 1, 2002; July 1, 2005, effective Jan. 1, 2006.

Rule 12. Change of venue in criminal cases

(A) Change of Venue from the County. In criminal actions and proceedings to enforce a statute defining an infraction, a motion for change of venue from the county shall be verified or accompanied by an affidavit signed by the criminal defendant or the prosecuting attorney setting forth facts in support of the constitutional or statutory basis or bases for the change. Any opposing party shall have the right to file counter-affidavits within ten (10) days, and after a hearing on the motion, the ruling of the court may be reviewed only for abuse of discretion.

(B) Change of Judge—Felony and Misdemeanor Cases. In felony and misdemeanor cases, the state or defendant may request a change of judge for bias or prejudice. The party shall timely file an affidavit that the judge has a personal bias or prejudice against the state or defendant. The affidavit shall state the facts and the reasons for the belief that such bias or prejudice exists, and shall be accompanied by a certificate from the attorney of record that the attorney in good faith believes that the historical facts recited in the affidavit are true. The request shall be granted if the historical facts recited in the affidavit support a rational inference of bias or prejudice.

(C) Change of Judge—Infractions and Ordinance Violations. In proceedings to enforce a statute defining an infraction and in cases involving the prosecution of ordinance violations, a motion for change of judge shall be verified or accompanied by an affidavit signed by the criminal defendant or prosecuting attorney setting forth facts in support of cause for such change of judge. Any opposing party shall have the right to file counter-affidavits within ten (10) days. The decision of the court in such matters shall be reviewed only for abuse of discretion. In the event a motion for change of judge is granted under this provision, the procedure for reassignment of the case as set forth in Criminal Rule 13 shall apply.

(D) Time Period for Filing Request for Change of Judge or Change of Venue. In any criminal action, no change of judge or change of venue from the county shall be granted except within the time herein provided.

(1) *Thirty Day Rule.* An application for a change of judge or change of venue from the county shall be filed within thirty (30) days of the initial hearing. Provided, that where a cause is remanded for a new trial by the court on appeal, such application must be filed not later than thirty (30) days after the the defendant first appears in person before the trial court following remand.

(2) *Subsequently Discovered Grounds.* If the applicant first obtains knowledge of the cause for change of venue from the judge or from the county after the time above limited, the applicant may file the application, which shall be verified by the party specifically alleging when the cause was first discovered, how it was discovered, the facts showing the cause for a change, and why such cause could not have been discovered before by the exercise of due diligence. Any opposing party shall have the right to file counter-affidavits on such issue within ten (10) days, and after a hearing on the motion, the ruling of the court may be reviewed only for abuse of discretion.

(E) Pleadings and Papers. All pleadings, papers and affidavits filed at any hearing held pursuant to this rule shall become a part of the record without further action upon the part of either party.

(F) Reassignment of Case or Selection of Special Judge. Whenever in a criminal action an application for a change of judge has been timely filed and granted, the case shall be reassigned or a special judge shall be selected in accordance with Ind.Crim. Rule 13.

(G) Procedure for Change of Venue from County.

(1) Whenever a change of venue from the county is granted, if the parties to such action shall agree in open court, within three (3) days from the granting of the motion or affidavit for the change of venue, upon the county to which the change of venue shall be changed, it shall be the duty of the court to transfer such action to such county. In the absence of such agreement, it shall be the duty of the court within two (2) days thereafter to submit to the parties a written list of all of the counties adjoining the county from which the venue is changed; provided, however, if it appears to the regular judge or the presiding judge before whom an application for a change of venue from the county is pending that the grounds for such change also exist in one or more of the adjoining

counties to which the case may be venued, such judge shall have the right to eliminate such county or counties from the list of counties to be submitted for striking and to substitute another county or counties where such grounds, in his opinion, do not exist in order that the defendant shall have a fair and impartial trial.

(2) The parties within seven (7) days thereafter, or within such time, not to exceed fourteen (14) days, as the court shall fix, shall each alternately strike off the names of such counties. The party first filing such motion shall strike first, and the action shall be sent to the county remaining not stricken under such procedure. If a moving party fails to so strike within said time, such party shall not be entitled to a change of venue, and the court shall resume general jurisdiction of the cause. If a non-moving party fails to strike off the names of such counties within the time limited, then the clerk shall strike off such names for such party.

(3) Whenever a court has granted an order for a change of venue to another county and the costs thereof have been paid where an obligation exists to pay such costs for such change, either party to the cause may file a certified copy of the order making such change in the court to which such change has been made, and thereupon such court shall have full jurisdiction of said cause, regardless of the fact that the transcript and papers have not yet been filed with such court to which such change is taken. Nothing in this rule shall be construed as divesting the original court of its jurisdiction to hear and determine emergency matters between the time that a motion for change of venue to another county is filed and the time that the court grants an order for the change of venue.

(4) Notwithstanding any provision of these rules or the Indiana Rules of Trial Procedure to the contrary, whenever a court has granted an order for a change of venue to another county, the judge granting the change of venue may be appointed as special judge for that cause in the receiving county if the judge granting the change, the receiving judge, and all of the parties to the cause agree to such appointment.

Amended effective July 1, 1981. Amended Dec. 18, 1984, effective Jan. 1, 1985; Oct. 29, 1993, effective Jan. 1, 1994; Dec. 5, 1994, effective Feb. 1, 1995; Dec. 15, 1995, effective Feb. 1, 1996; Dec. 21, 2001, effective April 1, 2002; Sept. 7, 2012, effective Jan. 1, 2013.

Rule 13. Case reassignment and special judges; selection

(A) Application of Rule. This rule shall apply to the reassignment of the case and the selection of special judges in felony and misdemeanor cases where a change of judge is granted pursuant to Ind.Crim. Rule 12(B) or an order of disqualification or recusal is entered in the case. The reassignment procedure set forth in this rule also shall apply where a change of judge is granted pursuant to Ind.Post–Conviction Remedy Rule 1(4)(b) and in proceedings to enforce a statute defining an infraction and ordinance violation cases where a change of judge is granted for cause pursuant to Crim.R. 12(C).

(B) Duty to Notify Court. It shall be the duty of the parties to promptly advise the court of an application or motion for change of judge.

(C) Selection under Local Rule Adopted by Counties. Upon the granting of a change of judge or the disqualification or recusal of a judge, a successor judge shall be assigned in the same manner as the initial judge. Where this process does not result in the selection of a successor judge, selection shall be made by local rule. The local rule required by Ind. Crim.Rule 2.2 shall include an alternative assignment list of full-time judicial officers from contiguous counties and counties within the administrative district of the court as set forth in Administrative Rule 3(A) and senior judges. The local rule shall take into account the effective use of all judicial resources within an administrative district. Except for those serving pursuant to Criminal Rule 12(G)(4), judges previously assigned to the case are ineligible for reassignment.

A person appointed to serve as special judge under this subsection must accept jurisdiction in the case unless the appointed special judge is disqualified pursuant to the Code of Judicial Conduct, ineligible for service under this Rule, or excused from service by the Indiana Supreme Court.

(D) Appointment by Indiana Supreme Court. A trial court may request the Indiana Supreme Court to appoint a special judge in the following circumstances:

(1) No judge under the local rule is available for appointment: or

(2) The particular circumstance warrants selection of a special judge by the Indiana Supreme Court.

(E) Qualification and Oath. A judge assigned under the provision of this rule shall accept jurisdiction unless disqualified under the *Code of Judicial Conduct* or excused from service by the Indiana Supreme Court. The reassignment of a case or assignment of a special judge shall be entered in the Chronological Case Summary of the case. An oath or special order accepting jurisdiction is not required.

(F) Discontinuance of Service. In the event the case has been reassigned or a special judge assumes jurisdiction and thereafter ceases to act for any reason, further reassignment or the selection of a successor special judge shall be in the same manner as set forth in subsection (C) above.

(G) Compensation. A full-time judge, magistrate, or other employee of the judiciary shall not be paid a special judge fee for serving as a special judge or serving in a case reassigned pursuant to this rule. All other persons serving as special judge shall be paid a special judge fee of twenty-five dollars ($25.00) per day for each jurisdiction served for the entry of judgments and orders and hearings incidental to such entries. All judges, magistrates, and other persons who serve in courts outside of their county of residence shall be entitled to mileage at a rate equal to other public officials as established by state law, hotel accommodations, and reimbursement for meals and other expenses. Senior Judges who serve as special judges shall be paid in accordance with a schedule published by the Executive Director of the division of State Court Administration. At the discretion of the special judge and following consultation with the parties, a special judge or a judge reassigned a case in another court may schedule conferences, entertain motions, and perform all administrative tasks without travel to the court where the case is pending. All hearings involving testimony by witnesses, unless the parties agree to the contrary on record, shall be held in the court where the case is assigned. Special judges are encouraged to employ procedures that reduce the necessity for travel, such as telephone conferences, facsimile exchange of information, and other time-saving measures of communication. Compensation as permitted under this provision shall be paid by the State upon presentation of a claim for such services signed by the special judge.

(H) Continuation of Jurisdiction. A special judge appointed by the Indiana Supreme Court retains jurisdiction of the case for all future proceedings unless:

(1) a specific statute or rule provides to the contrary; or

(2) the judge is unavailable by reason of death, sickness, absence, or unwillingness to serve.

Amended effective Jan. 27, 1970; Feb. 15, 1971; amended April 9, 1974, effective June 1, 1974; Nov. 13, 1979, effective Jan. 1, 1980; Nov. 3, 1981, effective Jan. 1, 1982; Nov. 16, 1984, effective Jan. 1, 1985; amended effective May 9, 1987; amended Oct. 29, 1993, effective Jan. 1, 1994; Dec. 5, 1994, effective July 1, 1995; amended effective July 6, 1995; July 24, 1995; amended Dec. 15, 1995, effective Feb. 1, 1996; Dec. 21, 2001, effective April 1, 2002; July 1, 2003, effective Jan. 1, 2004; Sept. 30, 2004, effective Jan. 1, 2005; Sept. 21, 2010, effective Jan. 1, 2011; amended effective April 5, 2013; April 22, 2013.

Rule 14. Judges pro tempore; appointment

When it shall be made to appear to the Supreme Court of Indiana by satisfactory proof that the judge of any court having criminal jurisdiction is unable because of physical or mental infirmity to perform the duties of his office, and no judge pro tempore has been legally appointed to perform and is performing such duties, the Supreme Court of the state may appoint a judge pro tempore to serve as sole judge of said court for the duration of such infirmity.

The judge so appointed shall be an attorney in good standing in the state of Indiana.

Provided further that when it shall be made to appear to the Supreme Court of Indiana by verified petition supported by affidavit that any judge of any court having criminal jurisdiction fails, refuses, or neglects to perform the duties of his office without good cause, the court shall issue an order to any such judge requiring him to proceed to perform the duties of his office and shall fix a date for said judge to appear and show cause why he has failed to perform such duties, or in the alternative to show cause why a judge or judges pro tempore or commissioner shall not be appointed to complete the performance of the duties of the judge of any such court under order and direction from the Supreme Court of Indiana. In all cases hereunder at least ten [10] days' prior notice, with a copy of such petition, shall be given to the judge concerned that such petition will be presented to the court upon a date named.

Rule 15.   Time limitation for ruling; time limitation for holding issue under advisement

The time limitation for ruling and decision set forth under Trial Rules 53.1, 53.2 and 53.3 shall apply in criminal proceedings.

Amended Nov. 1, 1982, effective Jan. 1, 1983.

Rule 15.1.   Entry of Judgment

Subject to the provisions set forth by statute, upon a verdict of a jury, or upon a decision of the court, the court shall promptly prepare and sign the judgment, and the clerk shall thereupon enter the judgment in the Record of Judgments and Orders and note the entry of the judgment in the Chronological Case Summary. Attorneys shall not submit forms of judgment except upon direction of the court, and these directions shall not be given as a matter of course. The judge, failing promptly to cause the judgment to be prepared, signed, and entered as provided herein, may be compelled to do so by mandate. The provisions of Trial Rule 58(B) relating to the content of a judgment shall not apply in criminal proceedings.

Adopted Nov. 13, 1989, effective permissive prior to Jan. 1, 1991 and mandatory Jan. 1, 1991.

Rule 15.2.   Abstract of Judgment

Upon sentencing a person for any felony conviction, the court shall complete an abstract of judgment in an electronic format approved by the Division of State Court Administration. The Division of State Court Administration will maintain an automated system for purposes of submitting the electronic abstract of judgment.

Adopted May 15, 2012, effective July 1, 2012.

Rule 16.   Motion to Correct Error

Motion to Correct Error within thirty (30) days of sentencing.

(A) When Mandatory. A Motion to Correct Error is not a prerequisite for appeal, except when a party seeks to address newly discovered material evidence, including alleged jury misconduct, capable of production within thirty (30) days after the date of sentencing which, with reasonable diligence, could not have been discovered and produced at trial.

All other issues and grounds for appeal appropriately preserved during trial may be initially addressed in the appellate brief.

(B) Time for Filing; Service on. A Motion to Correct Error, if any, shall be filed within thirty (30) days after the date of sentencing, or the date of notation in the Chronological Case Summary of an order of dismissal or an order of acquittal, and shall be served upon the judge having jurisdiction of the cause. Trial Rule 59 (Motion to Correct Error) and Trial Rule 53.3 (Motion to Correct Error: Time Limitation for Ruling) will apply to criminal proceedings insofar as applicable and when not in conflict with any specific rule adopted by the Indiana Supreme Court for the conduct of criminal procedure.

Amended effective Feb. 16, 1989; amended Nov. 13, 1989, effective permissive prior to Jan. 1, 1991 and mandatory Jan. 1, 1991; Sept. 21, 2010, effective Jan. 1, 2011.

Rule 17.   Affidavits on motion to correct errors; notice; counter-affidavits

When a motion to correct errors is supported by affidavits, notice of the filing thereof shall be served upon the opposing party, or his attorneys of record, within ten [10] days after the filing thereof, and the opposing party shall have twenty [20] days after such service to file counter-affidavits; reply affidavits may be filed within ten [10] days after filing of counter-affidavits, which periods may be extended within the discretion of the court for good cause shown. Such affidavits shall be considered as evidence without the introduction thereof on the hearing on the motion, and shall be a part of the record without a bill of exceptions. If, besides the affidavits, additional evidence is received, the trial court shall cause the court reporter to record all such evidence, and when so transcribed, the same shall be submitted to the judge, who shall certify that it is a true and complete transcript of such evidence, and the same shall be filed with the court and be a part of the record on appeal without being incorporated into any bill of exceptions.

Rule 18.   Service of pleadings, motions and briefs

Unless the court, on motion or of its own initiative orders otherwise, a copy of every pleading and motion, and every brief submitted to the trial court, except trial briefs, shall be served personally or by mail on or before the day of the filing thereof upon each attorney or firm of attorneys appearing of record for each adverse party. Handing a copy to an attorney or leaving it at the attorney's office with the clerk or other person in charge thereof shall be considered as personal service.

It shall be the duty of attorneys when entering their appearance in a cause or when filing pleadings or papers therein, to have noted on the Chronological Case Summary or on said pleadings or papers so filed, their mailing address, and service by mail at such address shall be deemed sufficient.

Amended Nov. 13, 1989, effective permissive prior to Jan. 1, 1991 and mandatory Jan. 1, 1991.

Rule 19. Time within which the appeal must be submitted

The Notice of Appeal designating what is to be included in the record on appeal must be filed within thirty (30) days after the date of sentencing, or the date of notation in the Chronological Case Summary of an order of dismissal or an order of acquittal; provided however that if a Motion to Correct Error is timely filed pursuant to Criminal Rule 16, the Notice of Appeal must be filed within thirty (30) days after the ruling on the Motion to Correct Error is noted in the Chronological Case Summary or the Motion to Correct Error is deemed denied under Trial Rule 53.3, whichever occurs earlier. The time for filing other documents is governed by the Rules of Appellate Procedure. Unless a Notice of Appeal is filed within these time limits the right to appeal may be forfeited.

Amended Nov. 30, 1971, effective April 1, 1972; Nov. 10, 1988, effective Jan. 1, 1989; amended effective Feb. 16, 1989; amended Nov. 30, 1989, effective Jan. 1, 1990; Feb. 4, 2000, effective Jan. 1, 2001; Sept. 21, 2010, effective Jan. 1, 2011.

Rule 20. Extensions of time

Petitions for an extension of time in criminal cases shall contain a concise statement of the status of the case including information as to whether the defendant has been released on bond, whether he is incarcerated and if incarcerated, the name of the institution.

Amended Feb. 4, 2000, effective Jan. 1, 2001.

Rule 21. Application of trial and appellate rules

The Indiana rules of trial and appellate procedure shall apply to all criminal proceedings so far as they are not in conflict with any specific rule adopted by this court for the conduct of criminal proceedings.

Amended Dec. 23, 1996, effective March 1, 1997.

Rule 22. Trial by jury in misdemeanor cases: Demand: Notice: Waiver

A defendant charged with a misdemeanor may demand trial by jury by filing a written demand therefor not later than ten (10) days before his first scheduled trial date. The failure of a defendant to demand a trial by jury as required by this rule shall constitute a waiver by him of trial by jury unless the defendant has not had at least fifteen (15) days advance notice of his scheduled trial date and of the consequences of his failure to demand a trial by jury.

The trial court shall not grant a demand for a trial by jury filed after the time fixed has elapsed except upon the written agreement of the state and defendant, which agreement shall be filed with the court and made a part of the record. If such agreement is filed, then the trial court may, in its discretion, grant a trial by jury.

Adopted Nov. 21, 1980, effective Jan. 1, 1981. Amended Nov. 10, 1988, effective Jan. 1, 1989.

Rule 23. Method of keeping records

Under the direction of the Supreme Court of Indiana, the Clerk of the Circuit Court may, notwithstanding the recordkeeping practices set forth for criminal proceedings, keep records in any suitable media. The recordkeeping formats and systems and the quality and permanency requirements employed for the Chronological Case Summary, the Case File, and the Record of Judgments and Orders (Order Book) shall be approved by the Division of State Court Administration for compliance with applicable requirements.

Adopted Nov. 13, 1989, effective permissive prior to Jan. 1, 1991 and mandatory Jan. 1, 1991.

Rule 24. Capital cases

(A) Supreme Court Cause Number. Whenever a prosecuting attorney seeks the death sentence by filing a request pursuant to Ind.Code § 35–50–2–9, the prosecuting attorney shall file that request with the trial court and with the Court Administrator, Indiana Supreme Court, 315 State House, Indianapolis, Indiana 46204. Upon receipt of same, the Court Administrator shall open a cause number in the Supreme Court and notify counsel.

(B) Appointment of Qualified Trial Counsel. Upon a finding of indigence, it shall be the duty of the judge presiding in a capital case to enter a written order specifically naming two (2) qualified attorneys to represent an individual in a trial proceeding where a death sentence is sought. The provisions for the appointment of counsel set forth in this section do not apply in cases wherein counsel is employed at the expense of the defendant.

(1) *Lead Counsel; Qualifications.* One (1) of the attorneys appointed by the court shall be designated as lead counsel. To be eligible to serve as lead counsel, an attorney shall:

(a) be an experienced and active trial practitioner with at least five (5) years of criminal litigation experience;

(b) have prior experience as lead or co-counsel in no fewer than five (5) felony jury trials which were tried to completion;

(c) have prior experience as lead or co-counsel in at least one (1) case in which the death penalty was sought; and

(d) have completed within two (2) years prior to appointment at least twelve (12) hours of training in the defense of capital cases in a course approved by the Indiana Public Defender Commission.

(2) *Co-Counsel, Qualifications.* The remaining attorney shall be designated as co-counsel. To be eligible to serve as co-counsel, an attorney shall:

(a) be an experienced and active trial practitioner with at least three (3) years of criminal litigation experience;

(b) have prior experience as lead or co-counsel in no fewer than three (3) felony jury trials which were tried to completion; and

(c) have completed within two (2) years prior to appointment at least twelve (12) hours of training in the defense of capital cases in a course approved by the Indiana Public Defender Commission.

(3) *Workload of Appointed and Salaried Capital Counsel.* In the appointment of counsel, the nature and volume of the workload of appointed counsel must be considered to assure that counsel can direct sufficient attention to the defense of a capital case.

(a) Attorneys accepting appointments pursuant to this rule shall provide each client with quality representation in accordance with constitutional and professional standards. Appointed counsel shall not accept workloads which, by reason of their excessive size, interfere with the rendering of quality representation or lead to the breach of professional obligations.

(b) A judge shall not make an appointment of counsel in a capital case without assessing the impact of the appointment on the attorney's workload, including the administrative duties of a chief or managing public defender.

(c) Salaried or contractual public defenders may be appointed as trial counsel in a capital case, if:

(i) the public defender's caseload will not exceed twenty (20) open felony cases while the capital case is pending in the trial court;

(ii) no new cases will be assigned to the public defender within thirty (30) days of the trial setting in the capital case;

(iii) none of the public defender's cases will be set for trial within fifteen (15) days of the trial setting in the capital case; and

(iv) compensation is provided as specified in paragraph (C).

(d) The workload of full-time salaried capital public defenders will be limited consistent with subsection (B)(3)(a) of this rule. The head of the local public defender agency or office, or in the event there is no agency or office, the trial judge, shall not make an appointment of a full-time capital public defender in a capital case without assessing the impact of the appointment on the attorney's workload, including the administrative

duties of a chief or managing public defender. In assessing an attorney's workload, the head of the local public defender agency or office, or in the event there is no agency or office, the trial judge shall be guided by Standard J of the Standards for Indigent Defense Services in Non-Capital cases as adopted by the Indiana Public Defender Commission, effective January 1, 1995, and shall treat each capital case as the equivalent of (40) felonies under the Commission's 'all felonies' category. Appointment of counsel shall also be subject to subsections (B)(3)(c)(ii), (iii) and (iv) of this rule.

(C) Compensation of Appointed Trial Counsel. All hourly rate trial defense counsel appointed in a capital case shall be compensated under subsection (1) of this provision upon presentment and approval of a claim for services detailing the date, activity, and time duration for which compensation is sought. Hourly rate counsel shall submit periodic billings not less than once every thirty (30) days after the date of appointment by the trial court. All salaried capital public defenders compensated under subsection (4) of this provision shall present a monthly report detailing the date, activity, and time duration of services rendered after the date of appointment. Periodic payment during the course of counsel's representation shall be made.

(1) *Hours and Hourly Rate.* Defense counsel appointed at an hourly rate in capital cases filed or remanded after appeal on or after January 1, 2001, shall be compensated for time and services performed at the hourly rate of ninety dollars ($90.00) only for that time and those services determined by the trial judge to be reasonable and necessary for the defense of the defendant. The trial judge's determination shall be made within thirty (30) days after submission of billings by counsel. Counsel may seek advance authorization from the trial judge, ex parte, for specific activities or expenditures of counsel's time.

The hourly rate set forth in this rule shall be subject to review and adjustment on a biennial basis by the Executive Director of the Division of State Court Administration. Beginning July 1, 2002, and July 1st of each even year thereafter, the Executive Director shall announce the hourly rate for defense counsel appointed in capital cases filed or remanded after appeal on or after January 1, of the years following the announcement. The hourly rate will be calculated using the Gross Domestic Product Implicit Price Deflator, as announced by the United States Department of Commerce in its May report, for the last two years ending December 31st preceding the announcement. The calculation by the Executive Director shall be rounded to the next closest whole dollar.

In the event the appointing judge determines that the rate of compensation is not representative of practice in the community, the appointing judge may request the Executive Director of the Division of State Court Administration to authorize payment of a different hourly rate of compensation in a specific case.

(2) *Support Services and Incidental Expenses.* Counsel appointed at an hourly rate in a capital case shall be provided, upon an ex parte showing to the trial court of reasonableness and necessity, with adequate funds for investigative, expert, and other services necessary to prepare and present an adequate defense at every stage of the proceeding, including the sentencing phase. In addition to the hourly rate provided in this rule, all counsel shall be reimbursed for reasonable and necessary incidental expenses approved by the trial judge. Counsel may seek advance authorization from the trial judge, ex parte, for specific incidental expenses.

Full-time salaried capital public defenders shall be provided with adequate funds for investigative, expert, and other services necessary to prepare and present an adequate defense at every stage of the proceeding, including the sentencing phase, as determined by the head of the local public defender agency or office, or in the event there is no agency or office, by the trial judge as set forth above.

(3) *Contract Employees.* In the event counsel is generally employed by the court of appointment to perform other defense services, the rate of compensation set for such other defense services may be adjusted during the pendency of the death penalty case to reflect the limitations of case assignment established by this rule.

(4) *Salaried Capital Public Defenders.* In those counties having adopted a Comprehensive Plan as set forth in I.C. 33–9–15 *et. seq.*, which has been approved by the Indiana Public Defender Commission, and who are in compliance with Commission standards authorized by I.C. 33–9–13–3(2), a full-time salaried capital public defender meeting the requirements of this rule may be assigned in a capital case by the head of the local public defender agency or office, or in the event there is no agency or office, by the trial judge. Salaried capital public defenders may be designated as either lead counsel or co-counsel. Salaried capital lead counsel and co-counsel must be paid salary and benefits equivalent to the average of the salary and benefits paid to lead prosecuting attorneys and prosecuting attorneys serving as co-counsel, respectively, assigned to capital cases in the county.

Each year, by July 1, those counties wishing to utilize full-time salaried capital public defenders for capital cases shall submit to the Executive Director of the Division of State Court Administration the salary and benefits proposed to be paid the capital public defenders for the upcoming year along with the salaries and benefits paid to lead prosecutors and prosecutors serving as co-counsel assigned capital cases in the county in the thirty-six (36) months prior to July 1, or a certification that no such prosecutor assignments were made. The Executive Director shall verify and confirm to the Indiana Public Defender Commission and the requesting county that the proposed salary and benefits are in compliance with this rule. In the event a county determines that the rate of compensation set forth herein is not representative of practice in the community, the county may request the Executive Director to authorize a different salary for a specific year.

(D) Transcription of Capital Cases. The trial or post-conviction court in which a capital case is pending shall provide for stenographic reporting with computer-aided transcription of all phases of trial and sentencing and all evidentiary hearings, including both questions and answers, all rulings of the judge in respect to the admission and rejection of evidence and objections thereto and oral argument, as required by Criminal Rule 5. If the parties agree, on the record, the court may permit electronic recording or stenographic reporting without computer-aided transcription of pre-trial attorney conferences and pre-trial or post-trial non-evidentiary hearings and arguments.

(E) Imposition of Sentence. Whenever a court sentences a defendant to death, the court shall pronounce said sentence and issue its order to the Department of Correction for the defendant to be held in an appropriate facility. A copy of the order of conviction, order sentencing the defendant to death, and order committing the death-sentence inmate to the Department of Correction shall be forwarded by the court imposing sentence to the Indiana Supreme Court Administrator's Office. When a trial court imposes a death sentence, it shall, on the same day sentence is imposed, order the court reporter and clerk to begin immediate preparation of the record on appeal.

(F) Setting of Initial Execution Date—Notice. In the sentencing order, the trial court shall set an execution date one (1) year from the date of judgment of conviction. Copies of said order shall be sent by the trial court to:

(i) the prosecuting attorney of record;

(ii) the defendant;

(iii) the defendant's attorney of record;

(iv) the appellate counsel, if such has been appointed;

(v) the Attorney General;

(vi) the Commissioner of the Department of Correction;

(vii) the Warden of the institution where the defendant is confined; and

(viii) the State Public Defender.

Contemporaneously with the service of the order setting the date of execution to the parties listed in this section, the trial court shall forward to the Supreme Court Administrator's Office a copy of the order, with a certification by the clerk of the court that the parties listed in this section were served a copy of the order setting the date of execution.

(G) Stay of Execution Date. This section governs the stay of execution for defendants sentenced to death.

(1) *Stay of Execution—General.* The Supreme Court shall have exclusive jurisdiction to stay the execution of a death sentence. In the event the Supreme Court stays the execution of a death sentence, the Supreme Court shall order the new execution date when the stay is lifted. A copy of an order to stay an execution or set a new date for execution will be sent to the persons set forth in section (F) of this rule.

(2) *Stay of Initial Execution Date.* Upon petition or on its own motion, the Supreme Court shall stay the initial execution date set by the trial court. On the thirtieth (30th) day following completion of rehearing, the Supreme Court shall enter an order setting an execution date, unless counsel has appeared and requested a stay in accordance with section (H) of this rule. A copy of any order entered under this provision will be sent to the persons set forth in section (F) of this rule.

(H) Post–Conviction Relief—Stay—Duty of Counsel. Within thirty (30) days following completion of rehearing, private counsel retained by the inmate or the State Public Defender (by deputy or by special assistant in the event of a conflict of interest) shall enter an appearance in the trial court, advise the trial court of the intent to petition for post-conviction relief, and request the Supreme Court to extend the stay of execution of the death sentence. A copy of said appearance and notice of intent to file a petition for post-conviction relief shall be served by counsel on the Supreme Court Administrator. When the request to extend the stay is received, the Supreme Court will direct the trial court to submit a case management schedule consistent with Ind.Code § 35–50–2–9(i) for approval. On the thirtieth (30th) day following completion of any appellate review of the decision in the post-conviction proceeding, the Supreme Court shall enter an order setting the execution date. It shall be the duty of counsel of record to provide notice to the Supreme Court Administrator of any action filed with or decision rendered by a federal court that relate to defendants sentenced to death by a court in Indiana.

(I) Initiation of Appeal. When a trial court imposes a death sentence, it shall on the same day sentence is imposed order the court reporter and clerk to begin immediate preparation of the record on appeal.

(J) Appointment of Appellate Counsel. Upon a finding of indigence, the trial court imposing a sentence of death shall immediately enter a written order specifically naming counsel under this provision for appeal. If qualified to serve as appellate counsel

under this rule, trial counsel shall be appointed as sole or co-counsel for appeal.

(1) *Qualifications of Appellate Counsel.* An attorney appointed to serve as appellate counsel for an individual sentenced to die, shall:

(a) be an experienced and active trial or appellate practitioner with at least three (3) years experience in criminal litigation;

(b) have prior experience within the last five (5) years as appellate counsel in no fewer than three (3) felony convictions in federal or state court; and

(c) have completed within two (2) years prior to appointment at least twelve (12) hours of training in the defense of capital cases in a course approved by the Indiana Public Defender Commission.

(2) *Workload of Appointed Appellate Counsel.* In the appointment of Appellate Counsel, the judge shall assess the nature and volume of the workload of appointed appellate counsel to assure that counsel can direct sufficient attention to the appeal of the capital case. In the event the appointed appellate counsel is under a contract to perform other defense or appellate services for the court of appointment, no new cases for appeal shall be assigned to such counsel until the Appellant's Brief in the death penalty case is filed.

(K) Compensation of Appellate Counsel. Appellate counsel appointed to represent an individual sentenced to die shall be compensated under this provision upon presentment and approval of a claim for services detailing the date, activity, and time duration for which compensation is sought. Counsel shall submit periodic billings not less than once every thirty (30) days after the date of appointment. Attorneys employed by appellate counsel for consultation shall be compensated at the same rate as appellate counsel.

(1) *Hours and Hourly rate.* Appellate defense counsel appointed on or after January 1, 2001, to represent an individual sentenced to die shall be compensated for time and services performed at the hourly rate of ninety dollars only for that time and those services determined by the trial judge to be reasonable and necessary for the defense of the defendant. The trial judge's determination shall be made within thirty (30) days after submission of billings by counsel. Counsel may seek advance authorization from the trial judge, *ex parte*, for specific activities or expenditures of counsel's time.

The hourly rate set forth above shall be subject to review and adjustment as set forth in section (C)(1) of this rule.

In the event the appointing judge determines that this rate of compensation is not representative of practice in the community, the appointing judge may request the Executive Director of the Division of State Court Administration to authorize payment of a different hourly rate of compensation in a specific case.

(2) *Contract Employees.* In the event appointed appellate counsel is generally employed by the court of appointment to perform other defense services, the rate of compensation set for such other defense services may be adjusted during the pendency of the death penalty appeal to reflect the limitations of case assignment established by this rule.

(3) *Salaried Capital Public Defenders.* In the event appointed appellate counsel is a salaried capital public defender, as described in section (C)(4) of this rule, the county must comply with, and counsel shall be compensated according to, the requirements of section (C)(4).

(4) *Incidental Expenses.* In addition to the hourly rate or salary provided in this rule, appellate counsel shall be reimbursed for reasonable incidental expenses as approved by the court of appointment.

(L) Briefing on Appeal. In capital cases, counsel may place the verbatim judgment of the trial court and verbatim instructions and the verbatim objections thereto required by Appellate Rule 50B in an Addendum to Brief, and these documents shall not count against the word limit of the brief.

Adopted Nov. 30, 1989, effective Jan. 1, 1990. Amended Oct. 21, 1991, effective Jan. 1, 1992; amended Jan. 22, 1993, effective Feb. 1, 1993; amended effective March 28, 1996; amended Feb. 4, 2000, effective Jan. 1, 2001; amended Dec. 22, 2000, effective Jan. 1, 2001; amended effective March 5, 2001; amended Dec. 21, 2001, effective April 1, 2002; amended Sept. 9, 2008, effective Jan. 1, 2009; amended effective May 29, 2013.

Rule 25.   [Deleted eff. Aug. 17, 2010]

INDIANA RULES FOR SMALL CLAIMS

Adopted Effective January 1, 1976

Including Amendments Received Through November 1, 2013

Rule 1. Scope; citation

(A) Scope. These rules shall apply to all small claims proceedings in all courts of the State of Indiana, including Marion County Small Claims Courts, having jurisdiction over small claims as defined by relevant Indiana statutes.

(B) Citation. These rules may be cited as S.C.

————.

Amended Dec. 23, 1976, effective Jan. 1, 1977; amended Nov. 12, 1993, effective Jan. 1, 1994.

Rule 2. Commencement of action

(A) In General. An action under these rules shall be commenced by the filing of an unverified notice of claim in a court of competent jurisdiction and by payment of the prescribed filing fee or filing an order waiving the filing fee.

(B) Form of Notice of Claim. The notice of claim shall contain:

(1) The name, street address, and telephone number of the court;

(2) The name, address, and telephone number of the claimant and defendant(s);

(3) The place, date, and time when the parties are to appear on the claim, which date shall be set by the court with the objective of dispensing speedy justice between the parties according to the rules of substantive law;

(4) A brief statement of the nature and amount of the claim; and

(a) if the claim arises out of written contract, a copy shall be attached; however, the fact that a copy of such contract is not in the custody of the plaintiff shall not bar the filing of the claim; and

(b) if the claim is on an account, an Affidavit of Debt, in a form substantially similar to Small Claims Appendix A shall be attached;

(5) A statement that the parties may appear either in person or by an attorney;

(6) An instruction to the defendant that the defendant should bring to the trial all documents in the possession of or under the control of the defendant concerning the claim;

(7) A statement that if the defendant does not wish to dispute the claim he may nonetheless appear for the purpose of allowing the court to establish the method by which the judgment shall be paid;

(8) The name, street address and telephone number of the person designated by the court with whom the defendant may communicate if defendant is unable to appear at the time or place designated in the notice;

(9) A statement that a default judgment may be entered against the defendant if he fails to appear on the date specified in the notice of the claim;

(10) Notice of the defendant's right to a jury trial and that such right is waived unless a jury trial is requested within ten (10) days after receipt of the notice of claim; that once a jury trial request has been granted, it may not be withdrawn without the consent of the other party or parties; and within ten (10) days after the jury trial request has been granted, the party requesting a jury trial shall pay the clerk the additional amount required by statute to transfer the claim to the plenary docket or, in the Marion Small Claims Court, the filing fee necessary to file a case in the appropriate court of the county; otherwise, the party requesting a jury trial shall be deemed to have waived the request; and

(11) Any additional information which may facilitate proper service.

(C) Assistance by Clerk. The clerk of the court shall prepare and furnish blank notice of claim forms and the clerk of the court, or other employee of the court as the judge may designate, shall, upon request, assist individual claimants in the preparation thereof, but all attachments to the notice of claim shall be furnished by the claimant.

(D) Number of Claims and Attachments. All claims and attachments thereto shall be filed in such quantity that one copy may remain on file with the clerk, one copy may be delivered to the claimant, and one copy may be served on each defendant.

(E) Documents and Information Excluded from Public Access and Confidential Pursuant to Administrative Rule 9(G)(1). Documents and information excluded from public access pursuant to Administrative Rule 9(G)(1) shall be filed in accordance with Trial Rule 5(G).

Amended Dec. 23, 1976, effective Jan. 1, 1977; amended Nov. 21, 1980, effective Jan. 1, 1981; amended Nov. 10, 1988, effective Jan. 1, 1989; Amended Dec. 23, 1996, effective March 1, 1997; amended Nov. 25, 1997, effective Jan. 1, 1998; amended Dec. 21, 2001, effective April 1, 2002; amended Sept. 30, 2004, effective Jan. 1, 2005; amended Sept. 23, 2008, effective Jan. 1, 2009; amended Sept. 21, 2010, effective Jan. 1, 2011.

Rule 3.   Manner of service

(A) General Provision. For the purpose of service the notice of claim shall also be considered to be the summons. A copy of the notice of claim shall be served upon each defendant. Service may be made by sending a copy by certified mail with return receipt requested, or by delivering a copy to the defendant personally, or by leaving a copy at the defendant's dwelling house or usual place of abode, or in any other manner provided in Trial Rules 4.1 through 4.16. Whenever service is made by leaving a copy at defendant's dwelling house or usual place of abode, the person making the service also shall send by first class mail a copy of the notice of claim to the last known address of the person being served.

(B) Designation of Constable in the Marion County Small Claims Court. Pursuant to Trial Rule 4.12, the Marion County Small Claims Court judge may appoint the elected township constable and deputies as the persons specifically designated by the court to effect service in person. An order with the names of the respective constable and deputies shall be entered in the Record of Judgments and Orders of the particular division of the Small Claims Court.

(C) Designation of Manner of Service in the Marion County Small Claims Court. A person seeking service of a notice of claim filed in the Marion County Small Claims Court, or his or her attorney, may designate upon the notice of claim the manner of service as either in person by the constable or by certified mail or other public means by which a written acknowledgment of receipt may be requested and obtained, as provided in Trial Rule 4.1. The judge of a Marion County Small Claims Court may designate by order an employee as bailiff for the purpose of effecting service of process by certified mail and collecting appropriate fees. If the manner of service is not designated by the person seeking service, the clerk of the court shall note such absence on the notice of claim and shall promptly deliver the notice of claim to the employee appointed by the court as bailiff or to the constable for service by certified mail. The cost for service is set by legislation, and there shall be no additional charge for first class mail delivery required pursuant to T.R. 4.1(B).

(D) Return of Service. The person making service shall comply promptly with the provisions of Trial Rule 4.15. In addition, he or she shall state on the return of service if service was made by delivering a copy to a person, naming such person, or by leaving a copy at the defendant's dwelling or abode, describing the dwelling or abode and noting any unique features, and shall verify that a copy of the notice of claim was sent by first class mail and indicate the address to which the notice was sent. The clerk of court shall note the return of service on the Chronological Case Summary applicable to the case.

Amended Nov. 21, 1980, effective Jan. 1, 1981; Amended Nov. 25, 1997, effective Jan. 1, 1998; amended Sept. 21, 2010, effective Jan. 1, 2011.

Rule 4.   Responsive pleadings

(A) Preservation of Defenses. All defenses shall be deemed at issue without responsive pleadings, but this provision shall not alter the burden of proof.

(B) Entry of Appearance. For the purpose of administrative convenience the court may request that the defendant enter an appearance prior to trial. Such appearance may be made in person, by telephone or by mail but the fact that no appearance is entered by the defendant shall not be grounds for default judgment.

Amended Dec. 23, 1976, effective Jan. 1, 1977.

Rule 5.   Counterclaims

(A) Time and Manner of Filing. If the defendant has any claim against the plaintiff, the defendant may bring or mail a statement of such claim to the small claims court within such time as will allow the court to mail a copy to the plaintiff and be received by the plaintiff at least seven (7) calendar days prior to the trial. If such counterclaim is not received within this time the plaintiff may request a continuance pursuant to S.C. 9. The counterclaim must conform with the requirements of S.C. 2(B)(4).

(B) Counterclaim in Excess of Jurisdiction. Any defendant pursuing a counterclaim to decision waives the excess of the defendant's claim over the jurisdictional maximum of the small claims docket and may not later bring a separate action for the remainder of such claim.

Amended Dec. 23, 1976, effective Jan. 1, 1977; amended Nov. 21, 1980, effective Jan. 1, 1981; amended Nov. 10, 1988, effective Jan. 1, 1989; amended Nov. 13, 1989, effective Jan. 1, 1990; amended effective Jan. 3, 1990; Amended Nov. 25, 1997, effective Jan. 1, 1998.

Rule 6. Discovery

Discovery may be had in a manner generally pursuant to the rules governing any other civil action, but only upon the approval of the court and under such limitations as may be specified. The court should grant discovery only upon notice and good cause shown and should limit such action to the necessities of the case.

Rule 7. Pretrial settlement

All settlements shall be in writing and signed by the plaintiff and defendant. The settlement shall be filed with the clerk and upon approval of the court it shall be entered in the small claims judgment docket and shall have the same effect as a judgment of the court.

Rule 8. Informality of hearing

(A) Procedure. The trial shall be informal, with the sole objective of dispensing speedy justice between the parties according to the rules of substantive law, and shall not be bound by the statutory provisions or rules of practice, procedure, pleadings or evidence except provisions relating to privileged communications and offers of compromise.

(B) Witnesses. All testimony shall be given under oath or affirmation. Witnesses may be called and the court shall have the power to issue subpoenas to compel their attendance. There shall be no additional fee charged for the issuance of subpoenas.

(C) Appearance. Any assigned or purchased claim, or any debt acquired from the real party in interest by a third party cannot be presented or defended by said third party unless this third party is represented by counsel. In all other cases, the following rules shall apply:

(1) *Natural Persons.* A natural person may appear *pro se* or by counsel in any small claims proceeding.

(2) *Sole Proprietorship and Partnerships.* A sole proprietor or partnership may appear by a designated full-time employee of the business in the presentation or defense of claims arising out of the business, if the claim does not exceed one thousand five hundred dollars ($1,500.00). However, claims exceeding one thousand five hundred dollars ($1,500.00) must either be defended or presented by counsel or *pro se* by the sole proprietor or a partner.

(3) *Corporate Entities, Limited Liability Companies (LLC's), Limited Liability Partnerships (LLP's).* All corporate entities, Limited Liability Companies (LLC's), and Limited Liability Partnerships (LLP's) may appear by a designated full-time employee of the corporate entity in the presentation or defense of claims arising out of the business if the claim does not exceed one thousand five hundred dollars ($1,500.00). However, claims exceed-

ing one thousand five hundred dollars ($1,500.00) must be defended or presented by counsel.

(4) *Full–Time Employee Designations—Binding Effect of Designations and Requirements.*

(a) In the event a corporate entity, sole proprietorship, partnership, LLC or LLP designates a full-time employee to appear in its stead, the corporate entity, sole proprietor, partnership, LLC or LLP will be bound by any and all agreements relating to the small claims proceedings entered into by the designated employee and will be liable for any and all costs, including those assessed by reason of contempt, levied by a court against the designated employee.

(b) By authorizing a designated full-time employee to appear under this Rule, the corporate entity, sole proprietorship, partnership, LLC or LLP waives any present or future claim in this or any other forum in excess of one thousand five hundred dollars ($1,500.00).

(c) No person who is disbarred or suspended from the practice of law in Indiana or any other jurisdiction may appear for a corporate entity or on behalf of a sole proprietor, partnership, LLC or LLP under this rule.

(5) *Full–Time Employee Designations—Contents.* Before a designated employee is allowed to appear in a small claims proceeding, the corporate entity, sole proprietorship, partnership, LLC or LLP must have on file with the court exercising jurisdiction of the proceedings, a certificate of compliance with the provisions of this rule, wherein the corporate entity, sole proprietorship, partnership, LLC or LLP must expressly accept, by a duly adopted resolution in the case of a corporate entity, LLC or LLP; or a document signed under oath by the sole proprietor or managing partner of a partnership, the binding character of the designated employee's acts, the liability of the corporate entity, sole proprietorship, partnership, LLC or LLP for assessments and costs levied by a court, and that the corporate entity, sole proprietorship, partnership, LLC or LLP waives any claim for damages in excess of one thousand five hundred dollars ($1,500.00) associated with the facts and circumstances alleged in the notice of claim. Additionally, the designated employee must have on file with the court exercising jurisdiction of the proceedings an affidavit stating that he/she is not disbarred or suspended from the practice of law in Indiana or any other jurisdiction.

Amended Nov. 1, 1982, effective Jan. 1, 1983; amended Dec. 3, 1987, effective Jan. 1, 1988; amended Nov. 30, 1989, effective Jan. 1, 1990; amended Dec. 5, 1994, effective Feb. 1, 1995; amended Sept. 23, 2008, effective Jan. 1, 2009; amended Sept. 21, 2010, effective Jan. 1, 2011.

Rule 9. Continuances

(A) Either party may be granted a continuance for good cause shown. Except in unusual circumstances no party shall be allowed more than one (1) continuance in any case, and all continuances must have the specific approval of the court. Continuances shall be for as short a period as possible, and where feasible the party not requesting the continuance shall be considered in scheduling a new hearing date. The court shall give notice of the continuance and the new date and time of trial to all parties.

(B) Designating Employee. The court may, by a duly executed order recorded in the Record of Judgments and Orders, designate a specifically named employee to be responsible for scheduling hearings under specific directions spelled out by the court in said order.

Amended Nov. 25, 1997, effective Jan. 1, 1998.

Rule 10. Dismissal and default

(A) Dismissal. If the plaintiff fails to appear at the time and place specified in the notice of claim, or for any continuance thereof, the court may dismiss the action without prejudice. If a counterclaim has been filed the court may grant judgment for the defendant after first making an inquiry similar to that required by S.C. 10(B) in the case of default judgments. If the claim is refiled and the plaintiff again fails to appear such claim may be dismissed with prejudice.

(B) Default. If the defendant fails to appear at the time and place specified in the notice of claim, or for any continuance thereof, the court may enter a default judgment against him. Before default judgment is entered, the court shall examine the notice of claim and return thereof and make inquiry, under oath, of those present so as to assure the court that:

(1) Service of notice of claim was had under such circumstances as to establish a reasonable probability that the defendant received such notice;

(2) Within the knowledge of those present, the defendant is not under legal disability and has sufficient understanding to realize the nature and effect of the notice of claim;

(3) Either (a) the defendant is not entitled to the protections against default judgments provided by the Servicemembers Civil Relief Act, as amended (the "Act"), 50 U.S.C. appx. § 521, or (b) the plaintiff has filed with the court, subscribed and certified or declared to be true under penalty of perjury, the affidavit required by the Act (i) stating whether or not the defendant is in military service and showing necessary facts to support the affidavit; or (ii) if the plaintiff is unable to determine whether or not the defendant is in military service, stating that the plaintiff is unable to determine whether or not the defendant is in military service; and

(4) The plaintiff has a prima facie case.

After such assurance, the court may render default judgment and, upon entering such judgment, shall assess court costs against the defendant.

(C) Setting Aside Default. Upon good cause shown the court may, within one year after entering a default judgment, vacate such judgment and reschedule the hearing of the original claim. Following the expiration of one year, the judgment debtor may seek a reversal of the original judgment only upon the filing of an independent action, as provided in Ind. R.Tr.P. 60(B).

Amended Dec. 23, 1976, effective Jan. 1, 1977; amended Nov. 21, 1980, effective Jan. 1, 1981; amended Sept. 23, 2009, effective Jan. 1, 2009; amended Oct. 25, 2010, effective Jan. 1, 2011.

Rule 11. Judgment

(A) Entry and Notice of Judgment. All judgments shall be reduced to writing signed by the court, dated, entered in the Record of Judgments and Orders, and noted in the small claims judgment docket and the Chronological Case Summary. The Marion County Small Claims Court shall forward its judgments to the Clerk of the Circuit Court of Marion County for entry on the Marion County judgment docket. Judgment shall be subject to review as prescribed by relevant Indiana rules and statutes. Notwithstanding the provisions of T.R. 5(A), the court shall send notice of all small claims judgments and all judgments of the Marion County Small Claims Court, whether by default or not, to the attorneys of record, or if a party is appearing *pro se*, to the party of record.

(B) Costs. The party recovering judgment shall also recover costs regardless of the amount.

(C) Method of Payment. Modification. The court may order a judgment paid the prevailing party in any specified manner. If the judgment is not paid as ordered the court may modify its payment order as it deems necessary.

The judgment creditor may seek enforcement of his judgment by any other method provided by law.

(D) Release of Judgment. Upon payment in full, including accrued interest, the clerk shall notify the judgment creditor and shall require him or her to file a release of judgment. If the judgment creditor fails to file a release of judgment within thirty (30) days of the issuance of the notice, the clerk shall note in the Chronological Case Summary that the judgment has been satisfied and that the plaintiff has failed to release judgment pursuant to court directive, and the clerk shall note a release of judgment in the judgment docket.

(E) Deleted, eff. Jan. 1, 1990.

(F) Effect of Judgment. A judgment shall be res judicata only as to the amount involved in the particular action and shall not be considered an adjudication of any fact at issue in any other action or court.

Amended Nov. 21, 1980, effective Jan. 1, 1981; Nov. 13, 1989, effective Jan. 1, 1990; Nov. 13, 1990, effective Jan. 1, 1991.; amended Nov. 25, 1997, effective Jan. 1, 1998; amended Dec. 4, 1998, effective Jan. 1, 1999; amended Sept. 21, 2010, effective Jan. 1, 2011.

Rule 12.   Venue

(A) Proper Venue.

(1) Proper venue for a case filed in the small claims docket of a Circuit or Superior Court shall be in the county where the transaction or occurrence took place, where the obligation was incurred or is to be performed, or where a defendant resides or is employed at the time the complaint is filed.

(2) Except as provided in (3) below, proper venue for a case filed in a small claims court created pursuant to IC 33–34–1–2 shall be in the township where the transaction or occurrence took place, where the obligation was incurred or is to be performed, or where a defendant resides or is employed at the time the complaint is filed.

(3) Proper venue of any claim between landlord and tenant, including but not limited to a claim for rent, possession of real estate, return of property, return of security deposit or for damages filed in a small claims court created pursuant to IC 33–34–1–2 shall be in the township where the real estate is located, unless there is no small claims court in that township.

(B) Motion to Correct Venue. When it appears that the county or township, in the case of small claims courts created pursuant to IC 33–34–1–2 in which the action is pending is not the proper place for the hearing of such action, the court shall, on the motion of a party or upon its own motion, determine the correctness of the venue. If the venue is incorrect the judge shall, at the option of the plaintiff, order the action to be transferred or dismissed without prejudice unless the defendant appears and waives the venue requirement.

(C) No Waiver of Venue. No contract or agreement shall operate as a waiver of the provisions of this rule and the court shall treat any such attempt as being void.

Amended effective March 28, 1990; amended Nov. 18, 1993, effective Jan. 1, 1994; amended Sept. 10, 2007, effective Jan. 1, 2008; Sept. 13, 2013, effective Jan. 1, 2014.

Rule 13.   Small claims litigant's manual

An informative small claims manual shall be formulated by the Judicial Conference of Indiana for distribution to the small claims courts. Each county shall reproduce such manual and shall make it available to every litigant and to such other persons or organizations as the court may deem appropriate.

Amended Nov. 1, 1991, effective Jan. 1, 1992.

Rule 14.   Appointment of referee by circuit judge; compensation

In any circuit court exercising small claims jurisdiction, the circuit judge may appoint a referee to assist the court in performing the "county court functions." Such referee shall be an attorney admitted to practice in Indiana and shall serve at the pleasure of the circuit judge. The referee shall have such authority as the circuit judge shall assign by order. The referee shall be a finder of fact—the decision rendered will be that of the circuit judge.

Such referee shall be paid reasonable compensation, including a mileage allowance to be determined by the appointing circuit court judge. In recommending to the Supreme Court of Indiana appropriate compensation, the appointing circuit court judge shall consider the estimated caseload, the amount of work time needed to fulfill the assigned duties, and any other relevant factors relating to the referee's duties. Compensation shall be reasonably commensurate with the workload assigned. The amount authorized by the Supreme Court to be paid shall be paid by the state.

Amended Dec. 15, 1995, effective Feb. 1, 1996.

Rule 15.   Method of keeping records

Under the direction of the Supreme Court of Indiana, the Clerk of the Circuit Court may, notwithstanding the recordkeeping practices set forth for small claims proceedings, keep records in any suitable media. The recordkeeping formats and systems and the quality and permanency requirements employed for the Chronological Case Summary, the Case File, and the Record of Judgments and Orders (Order Book) shall be approved by the Division of State Court Administration for compliance with applicable requirements.

Adopted Nov. 13, 1989, effective permissive prior to Jan. 1, 1991 and mandatory Jan. 1, 1991.

Rule 16.   Order of possession of real estate

(A) Time for Requesting. An order of possession of real estate shall not be issued if more than thirty (30) days have passed since the judgment was issued. Thereafter, a plaintiff seeking possession may do so by filing a new case.

(B) Duration. An order of possession of real estate shall be effective for no more than thirty (30) consecutive days after its date of issue. The court shall indicate the specific date of expiration on the face of each order of possession.

Adopted Nov. 25, 1997, effective Jan. 1, 1998.

Small Claims Appendix A.   Affidavit of Debt

AFFIDAVIT OF DEBT

Comes now affiant, and states:

I_____ am □ Plaintiff
   (Name of Affiant)   OR
                □ a designated full-time employee of _____ (Plaintiff).
                                               (Name of Plaintiff)

I am of adult age and am fully authorized by Plaintiff to make the following representations. I am familiar with the record keeping practices of Plaintiff. The following representations are true according to documents kept in the normal course of Plaintiff's business and/or my personal knowledge:

    Plaintiff:
           □ is the original owner of this debt.
           OR
           □ has obtained this debt from _____ and the original owner of this debt
           was _____ .

_____ , Defendant, has an unpaid balance of $_____ on account _____ .
(Name of Defendant)   (last 4 digits of number or id only)
That amount is due and owing to Plaintiff. This account was opened on _____ . The last payment from Defendant was received on _____ in the amount of $_____ .
The type of account is:
           □ Credit card account (i.e. Visa, Mastercard, Department Store, etc.)
           List the name of the Company/Store issuing credit card: _____
           □ Account for utilities (i.e. telephone, electric, sewer, etc.)
           □ Medical bill account (i.e. doctor, dentist, hospital, etc.)
           □ Account for services (i.e. attorney fees, mechanic fees, etc.)
           □ Judgment issued by a court (a copy of the judgment is required to be attached)
           □ Other: (Please explain) _____
           _____

This account balance includes:
           □ Late fees in the amount of $_____ as of _____ .
                                             (Month, Day, Year)
           □ Other (Explain _____)
           □ Interest at a rate of _____ % beginning on _____ .
                                         (Month, Day, Year)
Plaintiff:
           □ is seeking attorney's fees and additional evidence will be presented to the court prior to entry
           of judgment on attorney's fees.
           OR
           □ is not seeking attorney's fees.

Plaintiff believes that defendant is not a minor or an incompetent individual.

If the defendant is an individual, plaintiff states and declares that:

□ Defendant is not on active military service. Plaintiff's statement that Defendant is not on active military service is based upon the following facts:

_____

_____

_____.

OR

□ Plaintiff is unable to determine whether or not Defendant is not on active military service military service.

("Active military service" includes fulltime duty in the military (including the National Guard and reserves) and, for members of the National Guard, service under a call to active service authorized by the President or Secretary of Defense. For further information, see the definition of "military service" in the Servicemembers Civil Relief Act, as amended, 50 U.S.C.A. Appx. § 521.)

I swear or affirm under the penalties of perjury that the foregoing representations are true.

Dated: _____ Signature of Affiant: _____

Adopted Sept. 21, 2010, effective Jan. 1, 2011; amended October 25, 2010, effective Jan. 1, 2011.

INDIANA JURY RULES

Adopted December 21, 2001, Effective January 1, 2003

Including Amendments Received Through November 1, 2013

RULE 1. SCOPE

These rules shall govern petit jury assembly, selection, and management in all courts of the State of Indiana. Rules 2 through 10 shall govern grand jury assembly and selection.

Adopted Dec. 21, 2001, effective Jan. 1, 2003; amended July 19, 2002, effective Jan. 1, 2003; amended July 1, 2003, effective Aug. 1, 2003.

RULE 2. JURY POOL

The judges of the trial courts shall administer the jury assembly process. The judges may appoint clerical personnel to aid in the administration of the jury system. Any person appointed to administer the jury assembly process is a jury administrator. The jury administrator shall compile the jury pool annually by selecting names from lists approved by the Supreme Court. In compiling the jury pool, the jury administrator shall avoid duplication of names.

Adopted Dec. 21, 2001, effective Jan. 1, 2003. Amended July 19, 2002, effective Jan. 1, 2003; July 1, 2005, effective Jan. 1, 2006.

RULE 3. RANDOM DRAW

The jury administrator shall randomly draw names from the jury pool as needed to establish jury panels for jury selection. Prospective jurors shall not be drawn from bystanders or any source except the jury pool.

Adopted Dec. 21, 2001, effective Jan. 1, 2003.

RULE 4. NOTICE OF SELECTION FOR JURY POOL AND SUMMONS FOR JURY SERVICE

Not later than seven (7) days after the date of the drawing of names from the jury pool, the jury administrator shall mail to each person whose name is drawn a juror qualification form, and notice of the period during which any service may be performed. The judges of the courts of record in the county shall select, by local rule, one of the following procedures for summoning jurors:

(a) Single tier notice and summons. The jury administrator may send a summons at the same time the jury qualification form and notice is mailed. If so, the jury administrator shall send the jury qualification form and summons to prospective jurors at least six (6) weeks before jury service.

(b) Two tier notice and summons. The jury administrator may send summons at a later time. If the jury administrator sends the jury qualification form and notice first, the jury administrator shall summon prospective jurors at least one (1) week before service.

The summons shall include the following information: directions to court, parking, public transportation, compensation, court policies regarding the use of electronic communication devices (i.e. cell phones, PDAs, smart phones, etc.), attire, meals, and how to obtain auxiliary aids and services required by the Americans with Disabilities Act. The judge may direct the jury administrator to include a questionnaire to be completed by each prospective juror.

A judge may order prospective jurors to appear upon less notice when, in the course of jury selection, it becomes apparent that additional prospective jurors are required in order to complete jury selection.

A judge may authorize the jury administrator to use technological programs for receiving responses to juror qualification forms or to supplement information provided to jurors in the notice of selection and summons. The judge may authorize automated telephone services or web-based programs which include appropriate verification, such as juror identification numbers, PIN numbers, and passwords. The judge must ensure that jurors who are unable or unwilling to use these technological programs are able to complete the proper forms and receive the above-required information by contacting the jury administrator.

Adopted Dec. 21, 2001, effective Jan. 1, 2003. Amended July 19, 2002, effective Jan. 1, 2003; July 1, 2005, effective Jan. 1, 2006; Sept. 21, 2010 to take effect in each county upon the exhaustion of that county's supply of summonses on hand on Sept. 21, 2010.

RULE 5. DISQUALIFICATION

The court shall determine if the prospective jurors are qualified to serve, or, if disabled but otherwise qualified, could serve with reasonable accommodation. In order to serve as a juror, a person shall state under oath or affirmation that he or she is:

(a) a citizen of the United States;

(b) at least eighteen (18) years of age;

(c) a resident of the summoning county;

(d) able to read, speak, and understand, the English language;

(e) not suffering from a physical or mental disability that prevents him or her from rendering satisfactory jury service;

(f) not under a guardianship appointment because of mental incapacity;

(g) not a person who has had rights to vote revoked by reason of a felony conviction and whose rights to vote have not been restored; and

(h) not a law enforcement officer, if the trial is for a criminal case.

Persons who are not eligible for jury service shall not serve. Upon timely advance request from the prospective juror, the court may excuse from reporting for jury service any person whose bona fide religious conviction and affiliation with a religion prevents the prospective juror from performing jury service.

Adopted Dec. 21, 2001, effective Jan. 1, 2003. Amended Aug. 15, 2006, effective Jan. 1, 2007.

RULE 6. EXEMPTION

A person may claim exemption from jury service only if the person (1) has completed a term of jury service in the twenty-four (24) months preceding the date of the person's summons, or (2) is exempt from jury service pursuant to an exemption expressly provided by statute.

Adopted Dec. 21, 2001, effective Jan. 1, 2003. Amended Sept. 30, 2004, effective Jan. 1, 2005; Aug. 15, 2006, effective Jan. 1, 2007; Sept. 21, 2010, effective Jan. 1, 2011.

RULE 7. DEFERRAL

The judge or judge's designee may authorize deferral of jury service for up to one (1) year upon a showing of hardship, extreme inconvenience, or necessity.

Adopted Dec. 21, 2001, effective Jan. 1, 2003; amended July 1, 2003, eff. Aug. 1, 2003; amended Sept. 30, 2004, effective Jan. 1, 2005.

RULE 8. DOCUMENTATION

The facts supporting juror disqualifications, exemptions, and deferrals shall be recorded under oath or affirmation. No disqualification, exemption, or deferral shall be authorized unless the facts support it. These records shall be kept for a minimum of two (2) years.

Adopted Dec. 21, 2001, effective Jan. 1, 2003; amendment July 1, 2003, effective Aug. 1, 2003.

RULE 9. TERM OF JURY SERVICE

(a) A person who appears for service as a petit juror serves until the conclusion of the first trial in which the juror is sworn, regardless of the length of the trial or the manner in which the trial is disposed. A person who appears for service by reporting to the courthouse and being recorded as present for jury service and not deferred but is not selected and sworn as a juror completes the person's service when jury selection is completed; provided, however, jurors who are called for jury service are eligible to serve in any court in that county on the day summoned.

(b) A person who:

(1) serves as a juror; or

(2) serves until jury selection is completed, but is not chosen to serve as a juror;

may not be selected for another jury panel until all nonexempt persons in the jury pool for that year have been called for jury duty.

(c) A person who serves until jury selection is completed, but is not chosen to serve as a juror may be placed back in the jury pool and eligible for additional terms of service upon making a written request to the court.

Adopted Dec. 21, 2001, effective Jan. 1, 2003; amended July 19, 2002, effective Jan. 1, 2003; amended July 1, 2003, eff. Aug. 1, 2003; amended Sept. 30, 2004, effective Jan. 1, 2005.

RULE 10. JUROR SAFETY AND PRIVACY

Personal information relating to a juror or prospective juror not disclosed in open court is confidential, other than for the use of the parties and counsel. The court shall maintain that confidentiality to an extent consistent with the constitutional and statutory rights of the parties.

Adopted Dec. 21, 2001, effective Jan. 1, 2003.

RULE 11. JURY ORIENTATION

Trial courts shall provide prospective jurors with orientation prior to the selection process so they may understand their role in our legal system. Jury orientation shall include a standard presentation recommended by the Indiana Judicial Conference.

Adopted Dec. 21, 2001, effective Jan. 1, 2003.

RULE 12. RECORD SHALL BE MADE

Unless otherwise agreed by the parties, jury selection shall be recorded including all sidebar conferences.

Adopted Dec. 21, 2001, effective Jan. 1, 2003.

RULE 13. JURY PANEL: OATH OR AFFIRMATION BY PROSPECTIVE JURORS

The jury panel consists of those prospective jurors who answered their summons by reporting for jury service. The judge shall administer the following to the prospective jurors of the jury panel: "Do you swear or affirm that you will honestly answer any question asked of you during jury selection?"

Adopted Dec. 21, 2001, effective Jan. 1, 2003.

RULE 14. INTRODUCTION TO CASE

(a) After welcoming the jury panel, the judge shall introduce the panel to the case. Unless sufficiently covered by the jury orientation, the judge's introduction to the case shall include at least the following:

(1) Introduction of the participants;

(2) The nature of the case;

(3) The applicable standard of proof;

(4) The applicable burden(s) of proof;

(5) The presumption of innocence in a criminal case;

(6) The appropriate means by which jurors may address their private concerns to the judge;

(7) The appropriate standard of juror conduct;

(8) The anticipated course of proceedings during trial; and

(9) The rules regarding challenges.

(b) To facilitate the jury panel's understanding of the case, with the court's consent the parties may present brief statements of the facts and issues (mini opening statements) to be determined by the jury.

Adopted Dec. 21, 2001, effective Jan. 1, 2003. Amended Aug. 15, 2006, effective Jan. 1, 2007.

RULE 15. EXAMINATION OF THE JURY PANEL

Examination of jurors shall be governed by Trial Rule 47(D).

Adopted Dec. 21, 2001, effective Jan. 1, 2003.

RULE 16. NUMBER OF JURORS

(a) In all criminal cases, if the defendant is charged with: murder, a Class A, B, or C felony, including any enhancement(s), the jury shall consist of twelve (12) persons, unless the parties and the court agree to a lesser number of jurors. If the defendant is charged with any other crime, the jury shall consist of six (6) persons. The court shall determine the number of alternate jurors to be seated. The verdict shall be unanimous.

(b) In all civil cases, the jury shall consist of six (6) persons, unless the parties agree to a lesser number of jurors before the jury is selected. The verdict shall be unanimous, unless the parties stipulate before the verdict is announced that a verdict or finding of a stated majority of the jurors shall be taken as the verdict or finding of the jury. The number of alternate jurors shall be governed by Trial Rule 47(B).

Adopted Dec. 21, 2001, effective Jan. 1, 2003.

RULE 17. CHALLENGE FOR CAUSE

(a) In both civil and criminal cases the parties shall make all challenges for cause before the jury is sworn to try the case, or upon a showing of good cause for the delay, before the jury retires to deliberate. The court shall sustain a challenge for cause if the prospective juror:

(1) is disqualified under rule 5;

(2) served as a juror in that same county within the previous three hundred sixty-five (365) days in a case that resulted in a verdict;

(3) will be unable to comprehend the evidence and the instructions of the court due to any reason including defective sight or hearing, or inadequate English language communication skills;

(4) has formed or expressed an opinion about the outcome of the case, and is unable to set that opinion aside and render an impartial verdict based upon the law and the evidence;

(5) was a member of a jury that previously considered the same dispute involving one or more of the same parties;

(6) is related within the fifth degree to the parties, their attorneys, or any witness subpoenaed in the case;

(7) has a personal interest in the result of the trial;

(8) is biased or prejudiced for or against a party to the case; or

(9) is a person who has been subpoenaed in good faith as a witness in the case.

(b) In criminal cases the court shall sustain a challenge for cause if the prospective juror:

(1) was a member of the grand jury that issued the indictment;

(2) is a defendant in a pending criminal case;

(3) in a case in which the death penalty is sought, is not qualified to serve in a death penalty case under law; or

(4) has formed or expressed an opinion about the outcome of the case which appears to be founded upon

    a. a conversation with a witness to the transaction;

    b. reading or hearing witness testimony or a report of witness testimony.

(c) In civil cases the court shall sustain a challenge for cause if the prospective juror is interested in another suit, begun or contemplated, involving the same or a similar matter.

Adopted Dec. 21, 2001, effective Jan. 1, 2003.

RULE 18. NUMBER OF PEREMPTORY CHALLENGES

(a) In criminal cases the defendant and prosecution each may challenge peremptorily:

(1) twenty (20) jurors in prosecutions where the death penalty or life without parole is sought;

(2) ten (10) jurors when neither the death penalty nor life without parole is sought in prosecutions for murder, and Class A, B, or C felonies, including enhancements; and

(3) five (5) jurors in prosecutions for all other crimes.

When several defendants are tried together, they must join their challenges.

(b) In civil cases each side may challenge peremptorily three (3) jurors.

(c) In selection of alternate jurors in both civil and criminal cases:

(1) one (1) peremptory challenge shall be allowed to each side in both criminal and civil cases for every two (2) alternate jurors to be seated;

(2) the additional peremptory challenges under this subsection may be used only in selecting alternate jurors; and

(3) peremptory challenges authorized for selection of jurors may not be used in selecting alternate jurors.

(d) If it appears to the court that a particular peremptory challenge may have been used in a constitutionally impermissible manner, the court upon its own initiative may (a) inform the parties of the reasons for its concern, (b) require the party exercising the challenge to explain its reasons for the challenge, and (c) deny the challenge if the proffered basis is constitutionally impermissible.

Adopted Dec. 21, 2001, effective Jan. 1, 2003. Amended Aug. 15, 2006, effective Jan. 1, 2007.

RULE 19. OATH OR AFFIRMATION OF THE JURY

After the jury has been selected, but before commencement of the trial, the judge shall administer the following to the jury, including alternate jurors:

"Do each of you swear or affirm that you will well and truly try the matter in issue between the parties, and give a true verdict according to the law and evidence?"

Adopted Dec. 21, 2001, effective Jan. 1, 2003; amended July 19, 2002, effective Jan. 1, 2003.

RULE 20. PRELIMINARY INSTRUCTIONS

(a) The court shall instruct the jury before opening statements by reading the appropriate instructions which shall include at least the following:

(1) the issues for trial;

(2) the applicable burdens of proof;

(3) the credibility of witnesses and the manner of weighing the testimony to be received;

(4) that each juror may take notes during the trial and paper shall be provided, but note taking shall not interfere with the attention to the testimony;

(5) the personal knowledge procedure under Rule 24;

(6) the order in which the case will proceed;

(7) that jurors, including alternates, may seek to ask questions of the witnesses by submission of questions in writing.

(8) that jurors, including alternates, are permitted to discuss the evidence among themselves in the jury room during recesses from trial when all are present, as long as they reserve judgment about the outcome of the case until deliberations commence. The court shall admonish jurors not to discuss the case with anyone other than fellow jurors during the trial.

(b) The court shall instruct the jurors before opening statements that until their jury service is complete, they shall not use computers, laptops, cellular telephones, or other electronic communication devices while in attendance at trial during discussions, or during deliberations, unless specifically authorized by the court. In addition, jurors shall be instructed that when they are not in court they shall not use computers, laptops, cellular telephones, other electronic communication devices, or any other method to:

(1) conduct research on their own or as a group regarding the case;

(2) gather information about the issues in the case;

(3) investigate the case, conduct experiments, or attempt to gain any specialized knowledge about the case;

(4) receive assistance in deciding the case from any outside source;

(5) read, watch, or listen to anything about the case from any source;

(6) listen to discussions among, or received information from, other people about the case; or

(7) talk to any of the parties, their lawyers, any of the witnesses, or members of the media, or anyone else about the case, including posting information, text messaging, email, Internet chat rooms, blogs, or social websites.

(c) It is assumed that the court will cover other matters in the preliminary instructions.

(d) The court shall provide each juror with the written instructions while the court reads them.

Adopted Dec. 21, 2001, effective Jan. 1, 2003; amended Sept. 30, 2004, effective Jan. 1, 2005; amended Sept. 10, 2007, effective Jan. 1, 2008; amended March 1, 2010, effective July 1, 2010.

RULE 21. OPENING STATEMENT

(a) In criminal cases, the prosecution shall state briefly the evidence that supports its case. The defense may then state briefly the evidence in support of the defense, but has the right to decline to make an opening statement.

(b) In civil cases, the party with the burden of going forward may briefly state the evidence that supports its case. The adverse party may then briefly state the evidence in support of its case.

Adopted Dec. 21, 2001, effective Jan. 1, 2003.

RULE 22. PRESENTATION OF EVIDENCE

Unless the court otherwise directs, the party with the burden of going forward shall produce evidence first, followed by presentation of evidence by the adverse party.

The parties may then respectively offer rebuttal evidence only, unless the court, for good cause shown, permits them to offer evidence upon their original case.

Adopted Dec. 21, 2001, effective Jan. 1, 2003.

RULE 23. JUROR TRIAL BOOKS

In both criminal and civil cases, the court may authorize the use of juror trial books to aid jurors in performing their duties.

Juror trial books may contain:

(a) all given instructions;

(b) information regarding the anticipated trial schedule;

(c) witness lists; and

(d) copies of exhibits admitted for trial.

Adopted Dec. 21, 2001, effective Jan. 1, 2003.

RULE 24. PROCEDURE FOR JUROR WITH PERSONAL KNOWLEDGE IN CRIMINAL CASES

If the court receives information that a juror has personal knowledge about the case, the court shall examine the juror under oath in the presence of the parties and outside the presence of the other jurors concerning that knowledge.

If the court finds that the juror has personal knowledge of a material fact, the juror shall be excused, and the court shall replace that juror with an alternate. If there is no alternate juror, then the court shall discharge the jury without prejudice, unless the parties agree to submit the cause to the remaining jurors.

Adopted Dec. 21, 2001, effective Jan. 1, 2003.

RULE 25. JURY VIEW

When the court determines it is proper, the court may order the jury to view:

(a) the real or personal property which is the subject of the case; or

(b) the place in which a material fact occurred.

The place shall be shown to the jury by a person appointed by the court for that purpose. While the jury is absent for the view, no person, other than the person appointed to show the place to the jury, shall speak to the jury on any subject connected with the trial. Counsel for the parties shall have the right to accompany the jury but shall not speak to the jury.

Adopted Dec. 21, 2001, effective Jan. 1, 2003; amended July 1, 2003, effective Aug. 1, 2003.

RULE 26. FINAL INSTRUCTIONS

(a) The court shall read appropriate final instructions, which shall include at least the following:

(1) the applicable burdens of proof;

(2) the credibility of witnesses; and,

(3) the manner of weighing the testimony received.

The court shall provide each juror with written instructions before the court reads them. Jurors shall retain the written instructions during deliberations. The court may, in its discretion, give some or all final instructions before final arguments, and some or all final instructions after final arguments.

(b) The court shall instruct the bailiff to collect and store all computers, cell phones or other electronic communication devices from jurors upon commencing deliberations. The court may authorize appropriate communications (i.e. arranging for transportation, childcare, etc.) that are not related to the case and may require such communications to be monitored by the bailiff. Such devices shall be returned upon completion of deliberations or when the court permits separation during deliberations. Courts that prohibit such devices in the courthouse are not required to provide this instruction. All courts shall still admonish jurors regarding the limitations associated with the use of such devices if jurors are permitted to separate during deliberations.

Adopted Dec. 21, 2001, effective Jan. 1, 2003. Amended July 1, 2003, effective Aug. 1, 2003; amended March 1, 2010, effective July 1, 2010; Sept. 21, 2010, effective Jan. 1, 2011.

RULE 27. FINAL ARGUMENTS

When the evidence is concluded, the parties may, by agreement in open court, submit the case without argument to the jury.

If the parties argue the case to the jury, the party with the burden of going forward shall open and close the argument. The party which opens the argument must disclose in the opening all the points relied on in the case. If, in the closing, the party which closes refers to any new point or fact not disclosed in the opening, the adverse party has the right to reply to the new point or fact. The adverse party's reply then closes the argument in the case.

If the party with the burden of going forward declines to open the argument, the adverse party may then argue its case. In criminal cases, if the defense declines to argue its case after the prosecution has made opening argument, then that shall be the only argument allowed in the case.

In criminal cases, the party with the burden of going forward is the prosecution. In civil cases, the party with the burden of going forward is the plaintiff.

Adopted Dec. 21, 2001, effective Jan. 1, 2003. Amended Aug. 15, 2006, effective Jan. 1, 2007.

RULE 28. ASSISTING JURORS AT AN IM-PASSE

If the jury advises the court that it has reached an impasse in its deliberations, the court may, but only in the presence of counsel, and, in a criminal case the parties, inquire of the jurors to determine whether

and how the court and counsel can assist them in their deliberative process. After receiving the jurors' response, if any, the court, after consultation with counsel, may direct that further proceedings occur as appropriate.

Adopted Dec. 21, 2001, effective Jan. 1, 2003.

RULE 29. SEPARATION DURING DELIBERA-TION

(a) The court, in its discretion may permit the jury in civil cases to separate during deliberations. However, before the jurors are permitted to separate, the court shall instruct them that while they are separated, they shall:

(1) not discuss the case among themselves or with anyone else;

(2) not talk to the attorneys, parties, or witnesses;

(3) not express any opinion about the case; and

(4) not listen to or read any outside or media accounts of the trial.

(b) The court shall not permit the jury to separate during deliberation in criminal cases unless all parties consent to the separation and the instructions found in section "a" of this rule are given.

Adopted Dec. 21, 2001, effective Jan. 1, 2003.

RULE 30. JUDGE TO READ THE VERDICT

When the jury has agreed upon its verdict, the foreperson shall sign the appropriate verdict form. When returned into court, the judge shall read the verdict. The court or either party may poll the jury. If a juror dissents from the verdict, the jury shall again be sent out to deliberate.

Adopted Dec. 21, 2001, effective Jan. 1, 2003; amended July 1, 2003, effective Aug. 1, 2003.

INDIANA RULES OF EVIDENCE

Adopted Effective January 1, 1994

Including Amendments Received Through November 1, 2013

ARTICLE I

GENERAL PROVISIONS

Rule 101. Scope

(a) **Scope.** These rules apply to proceedings in the courts of this State to the extent and with the exceptions stated in this rule.

(b) **General Applicability.** These rules apply in all proceedings in the courts of the State of Indiana except as otherwise required by the Constitution of the United States or Indiana, by the provisions of this rule, or by other rules promulgated by the Indiana Supreme Court. If these rules do not cover a specific evidence issue, common or statutory law shall apply. The word "judge" in these rules includes referees, commissioners and magistrates.

(c) **Rules of Privilege.** The rules and laws with respect to privileges apply at all stages of all actions, cases, and proceedings.

(d) **Rules Inapplicable.** The rules, other than those with respect to privileges, do not apply in the following situations:

(1) *Preliminary questions of fact.* The determination of a question of fact preliminary to the admission of evidence, where the court determines admissibility under Rule 104(a).

(2) *Miscellaneous proceedings.* Proceedings relating to extradition, sentencing, probation, or parole, issuance of criminal summonses or warrants for arrest or search, preliminary juvenile matters, direct contempt, bail hearings, small claims, and grand jury proceedings.

Adopted effective Jan. 1, 1994. Amended Sept. 13, 2013, effective Jan. 1, 2014.

Rule 102. Purpose

These rules should be construed so as to administer every proceeding fairly, eliminate unjustifiable expense and delay, and promote the development of evidence law, to the end of ascertaining the truth and securing a just determination.

Adopted effective Jan. 1, 1994. Amended Sept. 13, 2013, effective Jan. 1, 2014.

Rule 103. Rulings on Evidence

(a) **Preserving a Claim of Error.** A party may claim error in a ruling to admit or exclude evidence only if the error affects a substantial right of the party and:

(1) if the ruling admits evidence, a party, on the record:

(A) timely objects or moves to strike; and

(B) states the specific ground, unless it was apparent from the context.

(2) If the ruling excludes evidence, a party informs the court of its substance by an offer of proof, unless the substance was apparent from the context.

(b) **Not Needing to Renew an Objection or Offer of Proof.** Once the court rules definitively on the record at trial a party need not renew an objection or offer of proof to preserve a claim of error for appeal.

(c) **Court's Statement About the Ruling; Directing an Offer of Proof.** The court may make any statement about the character or form of the evidence, the objection made, and the ruling. The court may direct that an offer of proof be made in question-and-answer form.

(d) **Preventing the Jury from Hearing Inadmissible Evidence.** To the extent practicable, the court must conduct a jury trial so that inadmissible evidence is not suggested to the jury by any means.

(e) **Taking Notice of Fundamental Error.** A court may take notice of a fundamental error affecting a substantial right, even if the claim of error was not properly preserved.

(f) **Preponderance of Evidence.** When deciding whether to admit evidence, the court must decide any question of fact by a preponderance of the evidence.

Adopted effective Jan. 1, 1994. Amended Sept. 13, 2013, effective Jan. 1, 2014.

Rule 104. Preliminary Questions

(a) In General. The court must decide any preliminary question about whether a witness is qualified, a privilege exists, or evidence is admissible. In so deciding, the court is not bound by evidence rules, except those on privilege.

(b) Relevance That Depends on a Fact. When the relevance of evidence depends on whether a fact exists, proof must be introduced sufficient to support a finding that the fact does exist. The court may admit the proposed evidence on the condition that the proof be introduced later.

(c) Conducting a Hearing So That the Jury Cannot Hear It. The court must conduct any hearing on a preliminary question so that the jury is not present and cannot hear if:

(1) the hearing involves the admissibility of a confession;

(2) a defendant in a criminal case is a witness and so requests; or

(3) justice so requires.

(d) Cross–Examining a Defendant in a Criminal Case. By testifying on a preliminary question, a defendant in a criminal case does not become subject to cross-examination on other issues in the case.

(e) Evidence Relevant to Weight and Credibility. This rule does not limit a party's right to introduce before the jury evidence that is relevant to the weight or credibility of other evidence.

Adopted effective Jan. 1, 1994. Amended Sept. 9. 2008, effective Jan. 1, 2009; Sept. 13, 2013, effective Jan. 1, 2014.

Rule 105. Limiting Evidence that is not Admissible Against Other Parties or for Other Purposes

If the court admits evidence that is admissible against a party or for a purpose—but not against another party or for another purpose—the court, on timely request, must restrict the evidence to its proper scope and instruct the jury accordingly.

Adopted effective Jan. 1, 1994. Amended Sept. 13, 2013, effective Jan. 1, 2014.

Rule 106. Remainder of or Related Writing or Recorded Statements

If a party introduces all or part of a writing or recorded statement, an adverse party may require the introduction, at that time, of any other part—or any other writing or recorded statement—that in fairness ought to be considered at the same time.

Adopted effective Jan. 1, 1994. Amended Sept. 13, 2013, effective Jan. 1, 2014.

ARTICLE II

JUDICIAL NOTICE

Rule
201 Judicial Notice

Rule 201. Judicial Notice

(a) Kinds of Facts That May Be Judicially Noticed. The court may judicially notice:

(1) a fact that:

(A) is not subject to reasonable dispute because it is generally known within the trial court's territorial jurisdiction, or

(B) can be accurately and readily determined from sources whose accuracy cannot reasonably be questioned.

(2) the existence of:

(A) published regulations of governmental agencies;

(B) ordinances of municipalities; or

(C) records of a court of this state.

(b) Kinds of Laws That May Be Judicially Noticed. A court may judicially notice a law, which includes:

(1) the decisional, constitutional, and public statutory law;

(2) rules of court;

(3) published regulations of governmental agencies;

(4) codified ordinances of municipalities;

(5) records of a court of this state; and

(6) laws of other governmental subdivisions of the United States or any state, territory or other jurisdiction of the United States.

(c) Taking Notice. The court:

(1) may take judicial notice on its own; or

(2) must take judicial notice if a party requests it and the court is supplied with the necessary information.

(d) Timing. The court may take judicial notice at any stage of the proceeding.

(e) Opportunity to Be Heard. On timely request, a party is entitled to be heard on the propriety of taking judicial notice and the nature of the fact to be noticed. If the court takes judicial notice before notifying a party, the party, on request, is still entitled to be heard.

(f) Instructing the Jury. In a civil case, the court must instruct the jury to accept the noticed fact as conclusive. In a criminal case, the court must instruct the jury that it may or may not accept the noticed fact as conclusive.

Adopted effective Jan. 1, 1994; amended Sept. 15, 2009, effective Jan. 1, 2010; Sept. 13, 2013, effective Jan. 1, 2014.

ARTICLE III

PRESUMPTIONS IN CIVIL ACTIONS AND PROCEEDINGS

Rule
301 Presumptions in Civil Cases Generally

Rule 301. Presumptions in Civil Cases Generally

In a civil case, unless a constitution, statute, judicial decision, or these rules provide otherwise, the party against whom a presumption is directed has the bur-den of producing evidence to rebut the presumption. But this rule does not shift the burden of persuasion, which remains on the party who had it originally. A presumption has continuing effect even though contrary evidence is received.

Adopted effective Jan. 1, 1994. Amended Sept. 13, 2013, effective Jan. 1, 2014.

ARTICLE IV

RELEVANCY AND ITS LIMITS

Rule
401 Test For Relevant Evidence
402 General Admissibility of Relevant Evidence
403 Excluding Relevant Evidence for Prejudice, Confusion, or Other Reasons
404 Character Evidence; Crimes or Other Acts
405 Methods of Proving Character
406 Habit; Routine Practice
407 Subsequent Remedial Measures
408 Compromise Offers and Negotiations
409 Payment or Offer to Pay Medical or Other Expenses
410 Withdrawn Pleas and Offers
411 Liability Insurance
412 Sex–Offense Cases: The Victim's or Witness's Sexual Behavior or Predisposition
413 Medical Expenses

Rule 401. Test For Relevant Evidence

Evidence is relevant if:

(a) it has any tendency to make a fact more or less probable than it would be without the evidence; and

(b) the fact is of consequence in determining the action.

Adopted effective Jan. 1, 1994. Amended Sept. 13, 2013, effective Jan. 1, 2014.

Rule 402. General Admissibility of Relevant Evidence

Relevant evidence is admissible unless any of the following provides otherwise:

(a) the United States Constitution;

(b) the Indiana constitution;

(c) a statute not in conflict with these rules;

(d) these rules; or

(e) other rules applicable in the courts of this state.

Irrelevant evidence is not admissible.

Adopted effective Jan. 1, 1994. Amended Sept. 13, 2013, effective Jan. 1, 2014.

Rule 403. Excluding Relevant Evidence for Prejudice, Confusion, or Other Reasons

The court may exclude relevant evidence if its probative value is substantially outweighed by a danger of one or more of the following: unfair prejudice, confusing the issues, misleading the jury, undue delay, or needlessly presenting cumulative evidence.

Adopted effective Jan. 1, 1994. Amended Sept. 13, 2013, effective Jan. 1, 2014.

Rule 404. Character Evidence; Crimes or Other Acts

(a) Character Evidence.

(1) *Prohibited Uses.* Evidence of a person's character or character trait is not admissible to prove that on a particular occasion the person acted in accordance with the character or trait.

(2) *Exceptions for a Defendant or Victim in a Criminal Case.* The following exceptions apply in a criminal case:

(A) a defendant may offer evidence of the defendant's pertinent trait, and if the evidence is admitted, the prosecutor may offer evidence to rebut it;

(B) subject to the limitations in Rule 412, a defendant may offer evidence of an alleged victim's pertinent trait, and if the evidence is admitted, the prosecutor may offer evidence to rebut it; and

(C) in a homicide case, the prosecutor may offer evidence of the alleged victim's trait of peacefulness to rebut evidence that the victim was the first aggressor.

(3) *Exceptions for a Witness.* Evidence of a witness's character may be admitted under Rules 607, 608, and 609.

(b) Crimes, Wrongs, or Other Acts.

(1) *Prohibited Uses.* Evidence of a crime, wrong, or other act is not admissible to prove a person's character in order to show that on a particular occasion the person acted in accordance with the character.

(2) *Permitted Uses; Notice in a Criminal Case.* This evidence may be admissible for another purpose, such as proving motive, opportunity, intent, preparation, plan, knowledge, identity, absence of mistake, or lack of accident. On request by a defendant in a criminal case, the prosecutor must:

(A) provide reasonable notice of the general nature of any such evidence that the prosecutor intends to offer at trial; and

(B) do so before trial—or during trial if the court, for good cause, excuses lack of pretrial notice.

Adopted effective Jan. 1, 1994. Amended Sept. 13, 2013, effective Jan. 1, 2014.

Rule 405.   Methods of Proving Character

(a) By Reputation or Opinion. When evidence of a person's character or character trait is admissible, it may be proved by testimony about the person's reputation or by testimony in the form of an opinion. On cross-examination of the character witness, the court may allow an inquiry into relevant specific instances of the person's conduct. If, in a criminal case, a defendant provides reasonable pretrial notice that the defendant intends to offer character evidence, the prosecution must provide the defendant with any relevant specific instances of conduct that the prosecution may use on cross-examination.

(b) By Specific Instances of Conduct. When a person's character or character trait is an essential element of a charge, claim, or defense, the character or trait may also be proved by relevant specific instances of the person's conduct.

Adopted effective Jan. 1, 1994. Amended Sept. 13, 2013, effective Jan. 1, 2014.

Rule 406.   Habit; Routine Practice

Evidence of a person's habit or an organization's routine practice may be admitted to prove that on a particular occasion the person or organization acted in accordance with the habit or routine practice. The

court may admit this evidence regardless of whether it is corroborated or whether there was an eyewitness.

Adopted effective Jan. 1, 1994. Amended Sept. 13, 2013, effective Jan. 1, 2014.

Rule 407.   Subsequent Remedial Measures

When measures are taken that would have made an earlier injury or harm less likely to occur, evidence of the subsequent measures is not admissible to prove:

- negligence;

- culpable conduct;

- a defect in a product or its design; or

- a need for a warning or instruction.

But the court may admit this evidence for another purpose, such as impeachment or—if disputed—proving ownership, control, or the feasibility of precautionary measures.

Adopted effective Jan. 1, 1994. Amended Sept. 13, 2013, effective Jan. 1, 2014.

Rule 408.   Compromise Offers and Negotiations

(a) Prohibited Uses. Evidence of the following is not admissible on behalf of any party either to prove or disprove the validity or amount of a disputed claim or to impeach by a prior inconsistent statement or a contradiction:

(1) furnishing, promising, or offering, or accepting, promising to accept, or offering to accept a valuable consideration in order to compromise the claim; and

(2) conduct or a statement made during compromise negotiations about the claim. Compromise negotiations include alternative dispute resolution.

(b) Exceptions. The court may admit this evidence for another purpose, such as proving a witness's bias or prejudice, negating a contention of undue delay, or proving an effort to obstruct a criminal investigation or prosecution.

Adopted effective Jan. 1, 1994. Amended Sept. 13, 2013, effective Jan. 1, 2014.

Rule 409.   Payment or Offer to Pay Medical or Other Expenses

Evidence of paying, furnishing, promising to pay, or offering to pay:

(a) medical, hospital, or similar expenses resulting from an injury; or

(b) damage to property,

is not admissible to prove liability for the injury or damages.

Adopted effective Jan. 1, 1994. Amended Sept. 13, 2013, effective Jan. 1, 2014.

Rule 410. Withdrawn Pleas and Offers

(a) Prohibited Uses. In a civil or criminal case, evidence of the following is not admissible against the defendant who made the plea or participated in the plea discussions:

(1) a guilty plea or admission of the charge that was later withdrawn;

(2) a nolo contendere plea;

(3) an offer to plead to the crime charged or to any other crime, made to one with authority to enter into or approve a binding plea agreement; or

(4) a statement made in connection with any of the foregoing withdrawn pleas or offers to one with authority to enter into a binding plea agreement or who has a right to object to, approve, or reject the agreement.

(b) Exceptions. The court may admit such a plea, offer, or statement:

(1) in any proceeding in which another statement made during the same plea or plea discussions has been introduced, if in fairness the statements ought to be considered together; or

(2) in a criminal proceeding for perjury or false statement, if the defendant made the statement under oath, on the record, and with counsel present.

Adopted effective Jan. 1, 1994; amended effective Jan. 1, 1994; Sept. 13, 2013, effective Jan. 1, 2014.

Rule 411. Liability Insurance

Evidence that a person was or was not insured against liability is not admissible to prove whether the person acted negligently or otherwise wrongfully. But the court may admit this evidence for another purpose, such as proving a witness's bias or prejudice or proving agency, ownership, or control.

Adopted effective Jan. 1, 1994. Amended Sept. 13, 2013, effective Jan. 1, 2014.

Rule 412. Sex–Offense Cases: The Victim's or Witness's Sexual Behavior or Predisposition

(a) Prohibited Uses. The following evidence is not admissible in a civil or criminal proceeding involving alleged sexual misconduct:

(1) evidence offered to prove that a victim or witness engaged in other sexual behavior; or

(2) evidence offered to prove a victim's or witness's sexual predisposition.

(b) Exceptions.

(1) *Criminal Cases.* The court may admit the following evidence in a criminal case:

(A) evidence of specific instances of a victim's or witness's sexual behavior, if offered to prove that someone other than the defendant was the source of semen, injury, or other physical evidence;

(B) evidence of specific instances of a victim's or witness's sexual behavior with respect to the person accused of the sexual misconduct, if offered by the defendant to prove consent or if offered by the prosecutor; and

(C) evidence whose exclusion would violate the defendant's constitutional rights.

(2) *Civil Cases.* In a civil case, the court may admit evidence offered to prove a victim's sexual behavior or sexual predisposition if its probative value substantially outweighs the danger of harm to any victim and of unfair prejudice to any party. The court may admit evidence of a victim's reputation only if the victim has placed it in controversy.

(c) Procedure to Determine Admissibility.

(1) *Motion.* If a party intends to offer evidence under Rule 412(b), the party must:

(A) file a motion that specifically describes the evidence and states the purpose for which it is to be offered;

(B) do so at least ten (10) days before trial unless the court, for good cause, sets a different time;

(C) serve the motion on all parties; and

(D) notify the victim or, when appropriate, the victim's guardian or representative.

(2) *Hearing.* Before admitting evidence under this rule, the court must conduct an *in camera* hearing and give the victim and parties a right to attend and be heard. Unless the court orders otherwise, the motion, related materials, and the record of the hearing is confidential and excluded from public access in accordance with Administrative Rule 9.

(d) Definition of "Victim." In this rule, "victim" includes an alleged victim.

Adopted effective Jan. 1, 1994. Amended Sept. 13, 2013, effective Jan. 1, 2014.

Rule 413. Medical Expenses

Statements of charges for medical, hospital or other health care expenses for diagnosis or treatment occasioned by an injury are admissible into evidence. Such statements are prima facie evidence that the charges are reasonable.

Adopted effective Jan. 1, 1994. Amended Sept. 13, 2013, effective Jan. 1, 2014.

ARTICLE V

PRIVILEGES

Rule 501. Privileges

(a) **General Rule.** Except as provided by constitution, statute, any rules promulgated by the Indiana Supreme Court, or common law, no person has a privilege to:

(1) refuse to be a witness;

(2) refuse to disclose any matter;

(3) refuse to produce any object or writing; or

(4) prevent another from being a witness or disclosing any matter or producing any object or writing.

(b) **Waiver of Privilege by Voluntary Disclosure.** Subject to the provisions of Rule 502, a person with a privilege against disclosure waives the privilege if the person or person's predecessor while holder of the privilege voluntarily and intentionally discloses or consents to disclosure of any significant part of the privileged matter. This rule does not apply if the disclosure itself is privileged.

(c) **Privileged Matter Disclosed Under Compulsion or Without Opportunity to Claim Privilege.** A claim of privilege is not defeated by a disclosure which was (1) compelled erroneously or (2) made without opportunity to claim the privilege.

(d) **Comment Upon or Inference From Claim of Privilege; Instruction.** Except with respect to a claim of the privilege against self-incrimination in a civil case:

(1) Neither the judge nor counsel may comment upon the claim of a privilege, whether in the present proceeding or on a prior occasion. No inference may be drawn from the claim of a privilege.

(2) In jury cases, the judge, to the extent practicable, must conduct proceedings so as to allow parties and witnesses to claim privilege without the jury's knowledge.

(3) If requested by a party against whom the jury might draw an adverse inference from a claim of privilege, the court must instruct the jury that the jury must not draw an adverse inference from the claim of privilege.

Adopted effective Jan. 1, 1994; amended Sept. 20, 2011, effective Jan. 1, 2012; Sept. 13, 2013, effective Jan. 1, 2014.

Rule 502. Attorney–Client Privilege and Work Product; Limitations on Waiver

The following provisions apply, in the circumstances set out, to disclosure of a communication or information covered by the attorney-client privilege or work-product protection.

(a) **Intentional disclosure; scope of a waiver.** When a disclosure is made in a court proceeding and waives the attorney-client privilege or work-product protection, the waiver extends to an undisclosed communication or information only if:

(1) the waiver is intentional;

(2) the disclosed and undisclosed communications or information concern the same subject matter; and

(3) they ought in fairness to be considered together.

(b) **Inadvertent disclosure.** When made in a court proceeding, a disclosure does not operate as a waiver if:

(1) the disclosure is inadvertent;

(2) the holder of the privilege or protection took reasonable steps to prevent disclosure; and,

(3) the holder promptly took reasonable steps to rectify the error, including (if applicable) following Indiana Rule of Trial Procedure 26(B)(5)(b).

(c) **Controlling effect of a party agreement.** An agreement on the effect of disclosure in a proceeding is binding only on the parties to the agreement, unless it is incorporated into a court order.

(d) **Controlling effect of a court order.** If a court incorporates into a court order an agreement between or among parties on the effect of disclosure in a proceeding, a disclosure that, pursuant to the order, does not constitute a waiver in connection with the proceeding in which the order is entered is also not a waiver in any other court proceeding.

Adopted Sept. 20, 2011, effective Jan. 1, 2012. Amended Sept. 13, 2013, effective Jan. 1, 2014.

ARTICLE VI

WITNESSES

Rule 601. General Rule of Competency

Every person is competent to be a witness except as otherwise provided in these rules or by statute.

Adopted effective Jan. 1, 1994. Amended Sept. 13, 2013, effective Jan. 1, 2014.

Rule 602. Lack of Personal Knowledge

A witness may testify to a matter only if evidence is introduced sufficient to support a finding that the witness has personal knowledge of the matter. A witness does not have personal knowledge as to a matter recalled or remembered, if the recall or remembrance occurs only during or after hypnosis. Evidence to prove personal knowledge may consist of the witness's own testimony. This rule does not apply to a witness's expert testimony under Rule 703.

Adopted effective Jan. 1, 1994. Amended Sept. 13, 2013, effective Jan. 1, 2014.

Rule 603. Oath or Affirmation to Testify Truthfully

Before testifying, a witness must give an oath or affirmation to testify truthfully. It must be in a form designed to impress that duty on the witness's conscience.

Adopted effective Jan. 1, 1994. Amended Sept. 13, 2013, effective Jan. 1, 2014.

Rule 604. Interpreters

An interpreter must be qualified and must give an oath or affirmation to make a true translation.

Adopted effective Jan. 1, 1994. Amended Sept. 13, 2013, effective Jan. 1, 2014.

Rule 605. Judge's Competency as a Witness

The presiding judge may not testify as a witness at the trial. A party need not object to preserve the issue.

Adopted effective Jan. 1, 1994. Amended Sept. 13, 2013, effective Jan. 1, 2014.

Rule 606. Juror's Competency as a Witness

(a) At the Trial. A juror may not testify as a witness before the other jurors at the trial. If a juror is called to testify, the court must give a party an opportunity to object outside the jury's presence.

(b) During an Inquiry into the Validity of a Verdict or Indictment.

(1) *Prohibited Testimony or Other Evidence.* During an inquiry into the validity of a verdict or indictment, a juror may not testify about any statement made or incident that occurred during the jury's deliberations; the effect of anything on that juror's or another juror's vote; or any juror's mental processes concerning the verdict or indictment. The court may not receive a juror's affidavit or evidence of a juror's statement on these matters.

(2) *Exceptions.* A juror may testify about whether:

(A) any juror's drug or alcohol use;

(B) extraneous prejudicial information was improperly brought to the jury's attention;

(C) an outside influence was improperly brought to bear on any juror; or

(D) a mistake was made in entering the verdict on the verdict form.

Adopted effective Jan. 1, 1994. Amended Sept. 13, 2013, effective Jan. 1, 2014.

Rule 607. Who May Impeach a Witness

Any party, including the party that called the witness, may attack the witness's credibility.

Adopted effective Jan. 1, 1994. Amended Sept. 13, 2013, effective Jan. 1, 2014.

Rule 608. A Witness's Character for Truthfulness or Untruthfulness

(a) Reputation or Opinion Evidence. A witness's credibility may be attacked or supported by testimony about the witness's reputation for having a character for truthfulness or untruthfulness, or by testimony in the form of an opinion about that character. But evidence of truthful character is admissible only after the witness's character for truthfulness has been attacked.

(b) Specific Instances of Conduct. Except for a criminal conviction under Rule 609, extrinsic evidence is not admissible to prove specific instances of a witness's conduct in order to attack or support the witness's character for truthfulness. But the court may, on cross-examination, allow them to be inquired into if they are probative of the character for truthfulness or untruthfulness of another witness whose character the witness being cross-examined has testified about.

Adopted effective Jan. 1, 1994. Amended Sept. 13, 2013, effective Jan. 1, 2014.

Rule 609. Impeachment by Evidence of a Criminal Conviction

(a) General Rule. For the purpose of attacking the credibility of a witness, evidence that the witness has been convicted of a crime or an attempt of a crime must be admitted but only if the crime committed or attempted is (1) murder, treason, rape, robbery, kidnapping, burglary, arson, or criminal confinement; or (2) a crime involving dishonesty or false statement, including perjury.

(b) Limit on Using the Evidence After 10 Years. This subdivision (b) applies if more than ten (10) years have passed since the witness's conviction or release from confinement for it, whichever is later. Evidence of the conviction is admissible only if:

(1) its probative value, supported by specific facts and circumstances, substantially outweighs its prejudicial effect; and

(2) the proponent gives an adverse party reasonable written notice of the intent to use it so that the party has a fair opportunity to contest its use.

(c) Effect of a Pardon, Annulment, or Certificate of Rehabilitation. Evidence of a conviction is not admissible if:

(1) the conviction has been the subject of a pardon, annulment, certificate of rehabilitation, or other equivalent procedure based on a finding that the person has been rehabilitated, and the person has not been convicted of a later crime punishable by death or by imprisonment for more than one (1) year; or

(2) the conviction has been the subject of a pardon, annulment, or other equivalent procedure based on a finding of innocence.

(d) Juvenile Adjudications. Evidence of a juvenile adjudication is admissible under this rule only if:

(1) it is offered in a criminal case;

(2) the adjudication was of a witness other than the defendant;

(3) an adult's conviction for that offense would be admissible to attack the adult's credibility; and

(4) admitting the evidence is necessary to fairly determine guilt or innocence.

(e) Pendency of an Appeal. A conviction that satisfies this rule is admissible even if an appeal is pending. Evidence of the pendency is also admissible.

Adopted effective Jan. 1, 1994. Amended Sept. 13, 2013, effective Jan. 1, 2014.

Rule 610. Religious Beliefs or Opinions

Evidence of a witness's religious beliefs or opinions is not admissible to attack or support the witness's credibility.

Adopted effective Jan. 1, 1994. Amended Sept. 13, 2013, effective Jan. 1, 2014.

Rule 611. Mode and Order of Examining Witnesses and Presenting Evidence

(a) Control by the Court; Purposes. The court should exercise reasonable control over the mode and order of examining witnesses and presenting evidence so as to:

(1) make those procedures effective for determining the truth;

(2) avoid wasting time; and

(3) protect witnesses from harassment or undue embarrassment.

(b) Scope of Cross–Examination. Cross-examination should not go beyond the subject matter of the direct examination and matters affecting the witness's credibility. The court may allow inquiry into additional matters as if on direct examination.

(c) Leading Questions. Leading questions should not be used on direct examination except as necessary to develop the witness's testimony. Ordinarily, the court should allow leading questions:

(1) on cross-examination; and

(2) when a party calls a hostile witness, an adverse party, or a witness identified with an adverse party.

Adopted effective Jan. 1, 1994. Amended Sept. 13, 2013, effective Jan. 1, 2014.

Rule 612. Writing or Object Used to Refresh Memory

(a) Right to Inspect

(1) If, while testifying, a witness uses a writing or object to refresh the witness's memory, an adverse party is entitled to have the writing or object produced at the trial, hearing, or deposition in which the witness is testifying.

(2) If, before testifying, a witness uses a writing or object to refresh the witness's memory for the purpose of testifying and the court in its discretion determines that the interests of justice so require, an adverse party is entitled to have the writing or object produced, if practicable, at the trial, hearing, or deposition in which the witness is testifying.

(b) Terms and Conditions of Production and Use.

(1) A party entitled to have a writing or object produced under this rule is entitled to inspect it, to cross-examine the witness thereon, and to introduce in evidence those portions which relate to the testimony of the witness.

(2) If production of the writing or object at the trial, hearing, or deposition is impracticable, the court may order it made available for inspection.

(3) If it is claimed that the writing or object contains matters not related to the subject matter of the testimony, the court must examine the writing or object *in camera*, excise any portions not so related, and order delivery of the remainder to the party entitled thereto. Any portion withheld over objections must be preserved and made available to the appellate court in the event of an appeal.

(c) Failure to Produce or Deliver the Writing or Object. If a writing or object is not produced, made available for inspection, or delivered pursuant to order under this rule, the court must make any order justice requires, but in criminal cases if the prosecution elects not to comply, the order must be one striking the testimony or, if the court in its discretion determines that the interests of justice so require, declaring a mistrial.

Adopted effective Jan. 1, 1994. Amended Sept. 13, 2013, effective Jan. 1, 2014.

Rule 613.   Witness's Prior Statement

(a) Showing or Disclosing the Statement During Examination. When examining a witness about the witness's prior statement, a party need not show it or disclose its content to the witness. But the party must, on request, show it or disclose its contents to an adverse party's attorney.

(b) Extrinsic Evidence of a Prior Inconsistent Statement. Extrinsic evidence of a witness's prior inconsistent statement is admissible only if the witness is given an opportunity to explain or deny the statement and an adverse party is given an opportunity to examine the witness about it, or if justice so requires. This subdivision (b) does not apply to an opposing party's statement under Rule 801(d)(2).

Adopted effective Jan. 1, 1994. Amended Sept. 13, 2013, effective Jan. 1, 2014.

Rule 614.   Calling or Questioning a Witness

(a) Calling by Court. The court may not call a witness except in extraordinary circumstances or as provided for court-appointed experts. All parties are entitled to cross-examine any witness called by the court.

(b) Questioning by Court. The court may question a witness regardless of who calls the witness.

(c) Objections. A party may object to the court's calling or questioning a witness either at that time or at the next opportunity when the jury is not present.

(d) Questioning by Juror. A juror may be permitted to propound questions to a witness by submitting them in writing to the judge. The judge will decide whether to submit the questions to the witness for answer. The parties may object to the questions at the time proposed or at the next available opportunity when the jury is not present. Once the court has ruled upon the appropriateness of the written questions, it must then rule upon the objections, if any, of the parties prior to submission of the questions to the witness.

Adopted effective Jan. 1, 1994. Amended Sept. 13, 2013, effective Jan. 1, 2014.

Rule 615.   Excluding Witnesses

At a party's request, the court must order witnesses excluded so that they cannot hear other witnesses' testimony. Or the court may do so on its own. But this rule does not authorize excluding:

(a) a party who is a natural person;

(b) an officer or employee of a party that is not a natural person, after being designated as the party's representative by its attorney; or

(c) a person whose presence a party shows to be essential to presenting the party's claim or defense.

Adopted effective Jan. 1, 1994. Amended Sept. 13, 2013, effective Jan. 1, 2014.

Rule 616.   Witness's Bias

Evidence that a witness has a bias, prejudice, or interest for or against any party may be used to attack the credibility of the witness.

Adopted effective Jan. 1, 1994. Amended Sept. 13, 2013, effective Jan. 1, 2014.

Rule 617.   Unrecorded Statements During Custodial Interrogation

(a) In a felony criminal prosecution, evidence of a statement made by a person during a Custodial Interrogation in a Place of Detention shall not be admitted against the person unless an Electronic Recording of the statement was made, preserved, and is available at trial, except upon clear and convincing proof of any one of the following:

(1) The statement was part of a routine processing or "booking" of the person; or

(2) Before or during a Custodial Interrogation, the person agreed to respond to questions only if his or her Statements were not Electronically Recorded, provided that such agreement and its surrounding colloquy is Electronically Recorded or documented in writing; or

(3) The law enforcement officers conducting the Custodial Interrogation in good faith failed to make an Electronic Recording because the officers inadvertently failed to operate the recording equipment properly, or without the knowledge of any of said

officers the recording equipment malfunctioned or stopped operating; or

(4) The statement was made during a Custodial Interrogation that both occurred in, and was conducted by officers of, a jurisdiction outside Indiana; or

(5) The law enforcement officers conducting or observing the Custodial Interrogation reasonably believed that the crime for which the person was being investigated was not a felony under Indiana law; or

(6) The statement was spontaneous and not made in response to a question; or

(7) Substantial exigent circumstances existed which prevented the making of, or rendered it not feasible to make, an Electronic Recording of the Custodial Interrogation, or prevent its preservation and availability at trial.

(b) For purposes of this rule, "Electronic Recording" means an audio-video recording that includes at least not only the visible images of the person being interviewed but also the voices of said person and the interrogating officers; "Custodial Interrogation" means an interview conducted by law enforcement during which a reasonable person would consider himself or herself to be in custody; and "Place of Detention" means a jail, law enforcement agency station house, or any other stationary or mobile building owned or operated by a law enforcement agency at which persons are detained in connection with criminal investigations.

(c) The Electronic Recording must be a complete, authentic, accurate, unaltered, and continuous record of a Custodial Interrogation.

(d) This rule is in addition to, and does not diminish, any other requirement of law regarding the admissibility of a person's statements.

Adopted Sept. 15, 2009, effective Jan. 1, 2011. Amended Sept. 13, 2013, effective Jan. 1, 2014.

ARTICLE VII

OPINIONS AND EXPERT TESTIMONY

Rule 701.   Opinion Testimony by Lay Witnesses

If a witness is not testifying as an expert, testimony in the form of an opinion is limited to one that is:

(a) rationally based on the witness's perception; and

(b) helpful to a clear understanding of the witness's testimony or to a determination of a fact in issue.

Adopted effective Jan. 1, 1994. Amended Sept. 13, 2013, effective Jan. 1, 2014.

Rule 702.   Testimony by Expert Witnesses

(a) A witness who is qualified as an expert by knowledge, skill, experience, training, or education may testify in the form of an opinion or otherwise if the expert's scientific, technical, or other specialized knowledge will help the trier of fact to understand the evidence or to determine a fact in issue.

(b) Expert scientific testimony is admissible only if the court is satisfied that the expert testimony rests upon reliable scientific principles.

Adopted effective Jan. 1, 1994. Amended Sept. 13, 2013, effective Jan. 1, 2014.

Rule 703.   Bases of an Expert's Opinion Testimony

An expert may base an opinion on facts or data in the case that the expert has been made aware of or personally observed. Experts may testify to opinions based on inadmissible evidence, provided that it is of the type reasonably relied upon by experts in the field.

Adopted effective Jan. 1, 1994. Amended Sept. 13, 2013, effective Jan. 1, 2014.

Rule 704.   Opinion on an Ultimate Issue

(a) In General—Not Automatically Objectionable. Testimony in the form of an opinion or inference otherwise admissible is not objectionable just because it embraces an ultimate issue.

(b) Exception. Witnesses may not testify to opinions concerning intent, guilt, or innocence in a criminal case; the truth or falsity of allegations; whether a witness has testified truthfully; or legal conclusions.

Adopted effective Jan. 1, 1994. Amended Sept. 13, 2013, effective Jan. 1, 2014.

Rule 705.   Disclosing the Facts or Data Underlying an Expert's Opinion

Unless the court orders otherwise, an expert may state an opinion and give the reasons for it without first testifying to the underlying facts or data. But the expert may be required to disclose those facts or data on cross examination.

Adopted effective Jan. 1, 1994. Amended Sept. 13, 2013, effective Jan. 1, 2014.

ARTICLE VIII

HEARSAY

Rule

Rule 801. Definitions

The following definitions apply under this Article:

(a) Statement. "Statement" means a person's oral assertion, written assertion, or nonverbal conduct if the person intended it as an assertion.

(b) Declarant. "Declarant" means the person who made the statement.

(c) Hearsay. "Hearsay" means a statement that:

(1) is not made by the declarant while testifying at the trial or hearing; and

(2) is offered in evidence to prove the truth of the matter asserted.

(d) Statements That Are Not Hearsay. Notwithstanding Rule 801(c), a statement is not hearsay if:

(1) *A Declarant–Witness's Prior Statement.* The declarant testifies and is subject to cross-examination about a prior statement, and the statement:

(A) is inconsistent with the declarant's testimony and was given under penalty of perjury at a trial, hearing, or other proceeding or in a deposition;

(B) is consistent with the declarant's testimony, and is offered to rebut an express or implied charge that the declarant recently fabricated it or acted from a recent improper influence or motive in so testifying; or

(C) is an identification of a person shortly after perceiving the person.

(2) *An Opposing Party's Statement.* The statement is offered against an opposing party and:

(A) was made by the party in an individual or representative capacity;

(B) is one the party manifested that it adopted or believed to be true;

(C) was made by a person whom the party authorized to make a statement on the subject;

(D) was made by the party's agent or employee on a matter within the scope of that relationship and while it existed; or

(E) was made by the party's coconspirator during and in furtherance of the conspiracy. The statement does not by itself establish the declarant's authority under (C); the existence or scope of the relationship under (D); or the existence of the conspiracy or participation in it under (E).

Adopted effective Jan. 1, 1994; amended effective Jan. 1, 1994; Sept. 13, 2013, effective Jan. 1, 2014.

Rule 802. The Rule Against Hearsay

Hearsay is not admissible unless these rules or other law provides otherwise.

Adopted effective Jan. 1, 1994. Amended Sept. 13, 2013, effective Jan. 1, 2014.

Rule 803. Exceptions to the Rule Against Hearsay—Regardless of Whether the Declarant is Available as a Witness

The following are not excluded by the rule against hearsay, regardless of whether the declarant is available as a witness:

(1) Present Sense Impression. A statement describing or explaining an event, condition or transaction, made while or immediately after the declarant perceived it.

(2) Excited Utterance. A statement relating to a startling event or condition, made while the declarant was under the stress of excitement that it caused.

(3) Then–Existing Mental, Emotional, or Physical Condition. A statement of the declarant's then-existing state of mind (such as motive, design, intent, or plan) or emotional, sensory, or physical condition (such as mental feeling, pain, or bodily health), but not including a statement of memory or belief to prove the fact remembered or believed unless it relates to the execution, revocation, identification, or believed unless it relates to the execution, revocation, identification, or terms of the declarant's will.

(4) Statement Made for Medical Diagnosis or Treatment. A statement that:

(A) is made by a person seeking medical diagnosis or treatment;

(B) is made for—and is reasonably pertinent to—medical diagnosis or treatment; and

(C) describes medical history; past or present symptoms, pain or sensations; their inception; or their general cause.

(5) Recorded Recollection. A record that:

(A) is on a matter the witness once knew about but now cannot recall well enough to testify fully and accurately;

(B) was made or adopted by the witness when the matter was fresh in the witness's memory; and

(C) accurately reflects the witness's knowledge.

If admitted, the record may be read into evidence but may be received as an exhibit only if offered by an adverse party.

(6) Records of a Regularly Conducted Activity. A record of an act, event, condition, opinion, or diagnosis if:

(A) the record was made at or near the time by— or from information transmitted by—someone with knowledge;

(B) the record was kept in the course of a regularly conducted activity of a business, organization, occupation, or calling, whether or not for profit;

(C) making the record was a regular practice of that activity;

(D) all these conditions are shown by the testimony of the custodian or another qualified witness, or by a certification that complies with Rule 902(9) or (10) or with a statute permitting certification; and

(E) neither the source of information nor the method or circumstances of preparation indicate a lack of trustworthiness.

(7) Absence of a Record of a Regularly Conducted Activity. Evidence that a matter is not included in a record described in paragraph (6) if:

(A) the evidence is admitted to prove that the matter did not occur or exist;

(B) a record was regularly kept for a matter of that kind; and

(C) neither the possible source of the information nor other circumstances indicate a lack of trustworthiness.

(8) Public Records.

(A) A record or statement of a public office if:

(i) it sets out:

(a) the office's regularly conducted and regularly recorded activities;

(b) a matter observed while under a legal duty to [observe and] report; or

(c) factual findings from a legally authorized investigation; and

(ii) neither the source of information nor other circumstances indicate a lack of trustworthiness.

(B) Notwithstanding subparagraph (A), the following are not excepted from the hearsay rule:

(i) investigative reports by police and other law enforcement personnel, except when offered by an accused in a criminal case;

(ii) investigative reports prepared by or for a public office, when offered by it in a case in which it is a party;

(iii) factual findings offered by the government in a criminal case; and

(iv) factual findings resulting from a special investigation of a particular complaint, case, or incident, except when offered by an accused in a criminal case.

(9) Public Records of Vital Statistics. A record of a birth, death, or marriage, if reported to a public office in accordance with a legal duty.

(10) Absence of a Public Record. Testimony or a certification under Rule 902 that a diligent search failed to disclose a public record or statement if the testimony or certification is admitted to prove that:

(A) the record or statement does not exist; or

(B) a matter did not occur or exist, if a public office regularly kept a record or statement for a matter of that kind.

(11) Records of Religious Organizations Concerning Personal or Family History. A statement of birth, legitimacy, ancestry, marriage, divorce, death, relationship by blood or marriage, or similar facts of personal or family history, contained in a regularly kept record of a religious organization.

(12) Certificates of Marriage, Baptism, and Similar Ceremonies. A statement of fact contained in a certificate:

(A) made by a person who is authorized by a religious organization or by law to perform the act certified;

(B) attesting that the person performed a marriage or similar ceremony or administered a sacrament; and

(C) purporting to have been issued at the time of the act or within a reasonable time after it.

(13) Family Records. A statement of fact about personal or family history contained in a family record, such as a Bible, genealogy, chart, engraving on a ring, inscription on a portrait, or engraving on an urn, crypt, or burial marker.

(14) Records of Documents That Affect an Interest in Property. The record of a document that purports to establish or affect an interest in property if:

(A) the record is admitted to prove the content of the original recorded document, along with its signing and its delivery by each person who purports to have signed it;

(B) the record is kept in a public office; and

(C) a statute authorizes recording documents of that kind in that office.

(15) Statements in Documents That Affect an Interest in Property. A statement contained in a document that purports to establish or affect an interest in property if the matter stated was relevant to the document's purpose- unless later dealings with the property are inconsistent with the truth of the statement or the purport of the document.

(16) Statements in Ancient Documents. A statement in a document that is at least thirty (30) years old and whose authenticity is established.

(17) Market Reports and Similar Commercial Publications. Market quotations, lists, directories, or other compilations that are generally relied on by the public or by persons in particular occupations.

(18) Statements in Learned Treatises, Periodicals, or Pamphlets. A statement contained in a treatise, periodical, or pamphlet if:

A) the statement is called to the attention of an expert witness on cross-examination or relied on by the expert on direct examination;

(B) the statement contradicts the expert's testimony on a subject of history, medicine, or other science or art; and

(C) the publication is established as a reliable authority by the expert's admission or testimony, by another expert's testimony, or by judicial notice.

If admitted, the statement may be read into evidence but not received as an exhibit.

(19) Reputation Concerning Personal or Family History. A reputation among a person's family by blood, adoption, or marriage—or among a person's associates or in the community—concerning the person's birth, adoption, legitimacy, ancestry, marriage, divorce, death, relationship by blood, adoption, or marriage, or similar facts of personal or family history.

(20) Reputation Concerning Boundaries or General History. A reputation in a community—arising before the controversy—concerning boundaries of land in the community or customs that affect the land, or concerning general historical events important to that community, state, or nation.

(21) Reputation Concerning Character. A reputation among a person's associates or in the community concerning the person's character.

(22) Judgment of a Previous Conviction. Evidence of a final judgment of conviction if:

(A) the judgment was entered after a trial or guilty plea, but not a nolo contendere plea;

(B) the conviction was for a crime punishable by death or by imprisonment for more than a year;

(C) the evidence is admitted to prove any fact essential to the judgment; and

(D) when offered by the prosecutor in a criminal case for a purpose other than impeachment, the judgment was against the defendant.

The pendency of an appeal may be shown but does not affect admissibility.

(23) Judgments Involving Personal, Family, or General History or a Boundary. A judgment that is admitted to prove a matter of personal, family, or general history, or boundaries, if the matter:

(A) was essential to the judgment; and

(B) could be proved by evidence of reputation.

Adopted effective Jan. 1, 1994. Amended Sept. 20, 2011, effective Jan. 1, 2012; Sept. 13, 2013, effective Jan. 1, 2014.

Rule 804. Exceptions to the Rule Against Hearsay—When the Declarant is Unavailable as a Witness

(a) Criteria for Being Unavailable. A declarant is considered to be unavailable as a witness if the declarant:

(1) is exempted from testifying about the subject matter of the declarant's statement because the court rules that a privilege applies;

(2) refuses to testify about the subject matter despite a court order to do so;

(3) testifies to not remembering the subject matter;

(4) cannot be present or testify at the trial or hearing because of death or a then-existing infirmity, physical illness, or mental illness; or

(5) is absent from the trial or hearing and the statement's proponent has not been able, by process or other reasonable means, to procure:

(A) the declarant's attendance, in the case of a hearsay exception under Rule 804(b)(1) or (5); or

(B) the declarant's attendance or testimony, in the case of a hearsay exception under rule 804(b)(2), (3), or (4).

But this subdivision (a) does not apply if the statement's proponent procured or wrongfully caused the declarant's unavailability as a witness in order to prevent the declarant from attending or testifying.

(b) Hearsay Exceptions. The following are not excluded by the hearsay rule if the declarant is unavailable as a witness.

(1) *Former Testimony.* Testimony that:

(A) was given as a witness at a trial, hearing, or lawful deposition, whether given during the current proceeding or a different one; and

(B) is now offered against a party who had—or, in a civil case, whose predecessor in interest had—an opportunity and similar motive to develop it by direct, cross–, or redirect examination.

(2) *Statement Under the Belief of Imminent Death.* A statement that the declarant, while believing the declarant's death to be imminent, made about its cause or circumstances.

(3) *Statement Against Interest.* A statement that that [1] a reasonable person in the declarant's position would have made only if the person believed it to be true because, when made, it was so contrary to the declarant's proprietary or pecuniary interest or had so great a tendency to invalidate the declarant's claim against someone else or to expose the declarant to civil or criminal liability.

A statement or confession offered against the accused in a criminal case, made by a codefendant or other person implicating both the declarant and the accused, is not within this exception.

(4) *Statement of Personal or Family History.* A statement about:

(A) the declarant's own birth, adoption, legitimacy, ancestry, marriage, divorce, relationship by blood or marriage, or similar facts of personal or family history, even though the declarant had no way of acquiring personal knowledge about that fact; or

(B) another person concerning any of these facts, as well as death, if the declarant was related to the person by blood, adoption, or marriage or was so intimately associated with the person's family that the declarant's information is likely to be accurate.

(5) *Statement Offered Against a Party That Wrongfully Caused the Declarant's Unavailability.* A statement offered against a party that has engaged in or encouraged wrongdoing that was intended to, and did, procure the unavailability of the declarant as a witness for the purpose of preventing the declarant from attending or testifying.

Adopted effective Jan. 1, 1994; amended Sept. 9, 2008, effective Jan. 1, 2009; Sept. 13, 2013, effective Jan. 1, 2014.

1 So in original.

Rule 805. Hearsay Within Hearsay

Hearsay within hearsay is not excluded by the rule against hearsay if each part of the combined statements conforms with an exception to the rule.

Adopted effective Jan. 1, 1994. Amended Sept. 13, 2013, effective Jan. 1, 2014.

Rule 806. Attacking and Supporting the Declarant's Credibility

When a hearsay statement—or a statement described in Rule 801 (d)(2)(C), (D), or (E)—has been admitted in evidence, the declarant's credibility may be attacked, and then supported, by any evidence that would be admissible for those purposes if the declarant had testified as a witness. The court may admit evidence of the declarant's inconsistent statement or conduct, regardless of when it occurred or whether the declarant had an opportunity to explain or deny it. If the party against whom the statement was admitted calls the declarant as a witness, the party may examine the declarant on the statement as if on cross-examination.

Adopted effective Jan. 1, 1994. Amended Sept. 13, 2013, effective Jan. 1, 2014.

ARTICLE IX

AUTHENTICATION AND IDENTIFICATION

Rule
901   Authenticating or Identifying Evidence
902   Evidence that is Self–Authenticating
903   Subscribing Witness' Testimony

Rule 901. Authenticating or Identifying Evidence

(a) In General. To satisfy the requirement of authenticating or identifying an item of evidence, the proponent must produce evidence sufficient to support a finding that the item is what the proponent claims it is.

(b) Examples. The following are examples only, not a complete list, of evidence that satisfies the requirement:

(1) *Testimony of a Witness with Knowledge.* Testimony that an item is what it is claimed to be, by a witness with knowledge.

(2) *Nonexpert Opinion About Handwriting.* A nonexpert's opinion that handwriting is genuine, based on a familiarity with it that was not acquired for the current litigation.

(3) *Comparison by an Expert Witness or the Trier of Fact.* A comparison with an authenticated specimen by an expert witness or the trier of fact.

(4) *Distinctive Characteristics and the Like.* The appearance, contents, substance, internal patterns, or other distinctive characteristics of the item, taken together with all the circumstances.

(5) *Opinion About a Voice.* An opinion identifying a person's voice whether heard firsthand or through mechanical or electronic transmission or recording based on hearing the voice at any time under circumstances that connect it with the alleged speaker.

(6) *Evidence About a Telephone Conversation.* For a telephone conversation, evidence that a call was made to the number assigned at the time to:

(A) a particular person, if circumstances, including self-identification, show that the person answering was the one called; or

(B) a particular business, if the call was made to a business and the call related to business reasonably transacted over the telephone.

(7) *Evidence About Public Records.* Evidence that:

(A) a document was recorded or filed in a public office as authorized by law; or

(B) a purported public record or statement is from the office where items of this kind are kept.

(8) *Evidence About Ancient Documents or Data Compilations.* For a document or data compilation, evidence that it:

(A) is in a condition that creates no suspicion about its authenticity;

(B) was in a place where, if authentic, it would likely be; and

(C) is at least thirty (30) years old when offered.

(9) *Evidence About a Process or System.* Evidence describing a process or system and showing that it produces an accurate result.

(10) *Methods Provided by a Statute or Rule.* Any method of authentication or identification allowed by a statute, by the Supreme Court of this State, or by the Constitution of this State.

Adopted effective Jan. 1, 1994. Amended Sept. 13, 2013, effective Jan. 1, 2014.

Rule 902. Evidence that is Self–Authenticating

The following items of evidence are self-authenticating; they require no extrinsic evidence of authenticity in order to be admitted:

(1) Domestic Public Documents That Are Sealed and Signed. A document that bears:

(A) a seal purporting to be that of the United States; any state, district, commonwealth, territory, or insular area of the United States; a political subdivision of any of these entities; or a department, agency, or officer of any entity named above; and

(B) a signature purporting to be an execution or attestation.

(2) Domestic Public Documents That Are Not Sealed but Are Signed and Certified. A document that bears no seal if:

(A) it bears the signature of an officer or employee of an entity named in Rule 902(1)(A); and

(B) another public officer who has a seal and official duties within that same entity certifies under seal -or its equivalent- that the signer has the official capacity and that the signature is genuine.

(3) Foreign Public Documents. A document that purports to be signed or attested by a person who is authorized by a foreign country's law to do so. The document must be accompanied by a final certification that certifies the genuineness of the signature and official position of the signer or attester -or of any foreign official whose certificate of genuineness relates to the signature or attestation or is in a chain of certificates of genuineness relating to the signature or attestation. The certification may be made by a secretary of a United States embassy or legation; by a consul general, vice consul, or consular agent of the United States; or by a diplomatic or consular official of the foreign country assigned or accredited to the United States. If all parties have been given a reasonable opportunity to investigate the document's authenticity and accuracy, the court may, for good cause, either:

(A) order that it be treated as presumptively authentic without final certification; or

(B) allow it to be evidenced by an attested summary with or without final certification.

(4) Certified Copies of Public Records. A copy of an official record -or a copy of a document that was recorded or filed in a public office as authorized by law -if the copy is certified as correct by:

(A) the custodian or another person authorized to make the certification; or

(B) a certificate that complies with Rule 902(1), (2), or (3), a federal statute, or a rule prescribed by the Supreme Court.

(5) Official Publications. A book, pamphlet, or other publication purporting to be issued by a public authority.

(6) Newspapers and Periodicals. Printed material purporting to be a newspaper or periodical.

(7) Trade Inscriptions and the Like. An inscription, sign, tag, or label purporting to have been affixed in the course of business and indicating origin, ownership, or control.

(8) Acknowledged Documents. A document accompanied by a certificate of acknowledgment that is lawfully executed by a notary public or another officer who is authorized to take acknowledgments.

(9) Commercial Paper and Related Documents. Commercial paper, a signature on it, and related documents, to the extent allowed by general commercial law.

(10) Presumptions by a Federal or Indiana Statute. A signature, document, or anything else that a federal or Indiana statute declares to be presumptively or prima facie genuine or authentic.

(11) Certified Domestic Records of a Regularly Conducted Activity. Unless the source of information or the circumstances of preparation indicate a lack of trustworthiness, the original or a copy of a domestic record that meets the requirements of Rule 803(6)(A)–(C), as shown by a certification under oath of the custodian or another qualified person. Before the trial or hearing, the proponent must give an adverse party reasonable written notice of the intent to offer the record—and must make the record and certification available for inspection—so that the party has a fair opportunity to challenge them.

(12) Certified Foreign Records of a Regularly Conducted Activity. The original or a copy of a foreign record that meets the requirements of Rule 902(11), modified as follows:

(A) the certification must be signed in a manner that, if falsely made, would subject the maker to a criminal penalty in the country where the certification is signed; and

(B) the signature must be certified by a government official in the manner provided in Rule 902(2).

The proponent must also meet the notice requirements of Rule 902(11).

Adopted effective Jan. 1, 1994; amended July 1, 2003, effective Jan. 1, 2004; amended Sept. 30, 2004, effective Jan. 1, 2005; Sept. 13, 2013, effective Jan. 1, 2014.

Rule 903. Subscribing Witness' Testimony

A subscribing witness's testimony is necessary to authenticate a writing only if required by the law of the jurisdiction that governs its validity.

Adopted effective Jan. 1, 1994. Amended Sept. 13, 2013, effective Jan. 1, 2014.

ARTICLE X

CONTENTS OF WRITINGS, RECORDINGS, AND PHOTOGRAPHS

Rule 1001. Definitions that Apply to this Article

In this article:

(a) A "writing" consists of letters, words, numbers, or their equivalent set down in any form.

(b) A "recording" consists of letters, words, numbers, sounds, or their equivalent recorded in any manner.

(c) A "photograph" means a photographic image or its equivalent stored in any form.

(d) An "original" of a writing or recording means the writing or recording itself or any counterpart intended to have the same effect by the person who executed or issued it. For electronically stored information, "original" means any printout or other output readable by sight if it accurately reflects the information. An "original" of a photograph includes the negative or a print from it.

(e) A "duplicate" means a counterpart produced by a mechanical, photographic, chemical, electronic, or other equivalent process or technique that accurately reproduces the original.

Adopted effective Jan. 1, 1994. Amended Sept. 13, 2013, effective Jan. 1, 2014.

Rule 1002. Requirement of the Original

An original writing, recording, or photograph is required in order to prove its content unless these rules or a statute provides otherwise. An electronic record of the Indiana Bureau of Motor Vehicles ob-

tained from the Bureau that bears an electronic or digital signature, as defined by statute, is admissible in a court proceeding as if the signature were an original.

Adopted effective Jan. 1, 1994; Amended Dec. 21, 2001, effective April 1, 2002; Sept. 13, 2013, effective Jan. 1, 2014.

Rule 1003. Admissibility of Duplicates

A duplicate is admissible to the same extent as an original unless a genuine question is raised about the original's authenticity or the circumstances make it unfair to admit the duplicate.

Adopted effective Jan. 1, 1994. Amended Sept. 13, 2013, effective Jan. 1, 2014.

Rule 1004. Admissibility of Other Evidence of Contents

An original is not required and other evidence of the content of a writing, recording, or photograph is admissible if:

(a) all originals are lost or destroyed, and not by the proponent acting in bad faith;

(b) an original cannot be obtained by any available judicial process;

(c) the party against whom the original would be offered had control of the original; was at that time put on notice, by pleadings or otherwise, that the original would be a subject of proof at the trial or hearing; and fails to produce it at the trial or hearing; or

(d) the writing, recording, or photograph is not closely related to a controlling issue.

Adopted effective Jan. 1, 1994. Amended Sept. 13, 2013, effective Jan. 1, 2014.

Rule 1005. Copies of Public Records to Prove Content

The proponent may use a copy to prove the content of an official record or of a document that was recorded or filed in a public office as authorized by law if these conditions are met: the record or document is otherwise admissible; and the copy is certified as correct in accordance with Rule 902(4) or is testified to be correct by a witness who has compared it with the original. If no such copy can be obtained by reasonable diligence, then the proponent may use other evidence to prove the content.

Adopted effective Jan. 1, 1994. Amended Sept. 13, 2013, effective Jan. 1, 2014.

Rule 1006. Summaries to Prove Content

The proponent may use a summary, chart, or calculation to prove the content of voluminous writings, recordings, or photographs that cannot be conveniently examined in court. The proponent must make the originals or duplicates available for examination or copying, or both, by other parties at a reasonable time or place. The court may order the proponent to produce them in court.

Adopted effective Jan. 1, 1994. Amended Sept. 13, 2013, effective Jan. 1, 2014.

Rule 1007. Testimony or Statement of a Party to Prove Content

The proponent may prove the content of a writing, recording, or photograph by the testimony, deposition, or written statement of the party against whom the evidence is offered. The proponent need not account for the original.

Adopted effective Jan. 1, 1994. Amended Sept. 13, 2013, effective Jan. 1, 2014.

Rule 1008. Functions of the Court and Jury

Ordinarily, the court determines whether the proponent has fulfilled the factual conditions for admitting other evidence of the content of a writing, recording, or photograph under Rule 1004 or 1005. But in a jury trial, the jury determines in accordance with Rule 104(b) any issue about whether:

(a) an asserted writing, recording, or photograph ever existed;

(b) another one produced at the trial or hearing is the original; or

(c) other evidence of content accurately reflects the content.

Adopted effective Jan. 1, 1994. Amended Sept. 13, 2013, effective Jan. 1, 2014.

ARTICLE XI

MISCELLANEOUS RULES

Rule
1101 Evidence Rules Review Committee

Rule 1101. Evidence Rules Review Committee

(a) The Supreme Court Committee on Rules of Practice and Procedure, as constituted under Ind. Trial Rule 80, serves as the Evidence Rules Review Committee.

(b) The Evidence Rules Review Committee shall conduct a continuous study of the Indiana Rules of Evidence and shall submit to the Supreme Court from time to time recommendations and proposed amendment to such rules. The Committee shall follow the procedure set forth in Ind. Trial Rule 80(D) in amending the Rules of Evidence. The Indiana Supreme Court may suggest amendments or additions in current case law, as may the Indiana General Assembly in legislation. Members of the bench, bar, or public may propose amendments and may comment on published amendments; any such proposals or comments must be submitted in writing to the Committee's Executive Secretary, 30 South Meridian Street, Suite 500. Indianapolis, Indiana 46204.

Adopted effective Jan. 1, 1994; amended Dec. 15, 1995, effective Feb. 1, 1996; amended Sept. 10, 2007, effective Jan. 1, 2008; Sept. 13, 2013, effective Jan. 1, 2014.

INDIANA RULES OF PROCEDURE FOR POST-CONVICTION REMEDIES

Adopted August 1, 1969

Including Amendments Received Through November 1, 2013

Rule
PC 1   Post-Conviction Relief
Appendix to Rule PC 1
PC 2   Belated Notice of Appeal—Belated Motion to Correct
      Error—Belated Appeal

Rule PC 1.   Post-Conviction Relief

Section 1.   Remedy—To whom available—Conditions.

(a) Any person who has been convicted of, or sentenced for, a crime by a court of this state, and who claims:

(1) that the conviction or the sentence was in violation of the Constitution of the United States or the constitution or laws of this state;

(2) that the court was without jurisdiction to impose sentence;

(3) that the sentence exceeds the maximum authorized by law, or is otherwise erroneous;

(4) that there exists evidence of material facts, not previously presented and heard, that requires vacation of the conviction or sentence in the interest of justice;

(5) that his sentence has expired, his probation, parole or conditional release unlawfully revoked, or he is otherwise unlawfully held in custody or other restraint;

(6) that the conviction or sentence is otherwise subject to collateral attack upon any ground of alleged error heretofore available under any common law, statutory or other writ, motion, petition, proceeding, or remedy;

may institute at any time a proceeding under this Rule to secure relief.

(b) This remedy is not a substitute for a direct appeal from the conviction and/or the sentence and all available steps including those under Rule PC 2 should be taken to perfect such an appeal. Except as otherwise provided in this Rule, it comprehends and takes the place of all other common law, statutory, or other remedies heretofore available for challenging the validity of the conviction or sentence and it shall be used exclusively in place of them.

(c) This Rule does not suspend the writ of habeas corpus, but if a person applies for a writ of habeas corpus in the county where the person is incarcerated and challenges the validity of his conviction or sentence, that court shall transfer the cause to the court in which the conviction took place, and the latter court shall treat it as a petition for relief under this Rule.

(d) A petition filed by a person who has been convicted or sentenced for a crime by a court of this state that seeks to require forensic DNA testing or analysis of any evidence, whether denominated as a petition filed pursuant to Ind. Code § 35–38–7–5 or not, is considered a Petition for Post–Conviction Relief.

(e) A petition seeking to present new evidence challenging the person's guilt or the appropriateness of the person's sentence, when brought by a person who has been sentenced to death and who has completed state post-conviction review proceedings, whether denominated as a petition filed pursuant to Ind. Code § 35–50–2–9(k) or not, is considered a Successive Petition for Post–Conviction Relief under Section 12 of this Rule.

Section 2.   Filing.

A person who claims relief under this Rule or who otherwise challenges the validity of a conviction or sentence must file a verified petition with the clerk of the court in which the conviction took place, except that a person who claims that the person's parole has been unlawfully revoked must file a verified petition with the clerk of the court in the county in which the person is incarcerated. Three (3) copies of the verified petition must be filed and no deposit or filing fee shall be required.

The Clerk shall file the petition upon its receipt and deliver a copy to the prosecuting attorney of that judicial circuit. In capital cases, the clerk shall, in addition to delivering a copy of the petition to the prosecuting attorney, immediately deliver a copy of the petition to the Attorney General. If an affidavit of indigency is attached to the petition, the clerk shall call this to the attention of the court. If the court finds that the petitioner is indigent, it shall allow petitioner to proceed in forma pauperis. If the court finds the indigent petitioner is incarcerated in the Indiana Department of Correction, and has requested representation, it shall order a copy of the petition sent to the Public Defender's office.

Section 3.   Contents.

(a) The petition shall be submitted in a form in substantial compliance with the standard form appended to this Rule. The standard form shall be available without charge from the Public Defender's

Office, who shall also see that the forms are available at every penal institution in this State.

(b) The petition shall be made under oath and the petitioner shall verify the correctness of the petition, the authenticity of all documents and exhibits attached to the petition, and the fact that he has included every ground for relief under Sec. 1 known to the petitioner.

(c) Documents and information excluded from public access pursuant to Administrative Rule 9(G)(1) shall be filed in accordance with Trial Rule 5(G).

Section 4. Pleadings.

(a) Within thirty (30) days after the filing of the petition, or within any further reasonable time the court may fix, the state, by the Attorney General in capital cases, or by the prosecuting attorney in noncapital cases, shall respond by answer stating the reasons, if any, why the relief prayed for should not be granted. The court may make appropriate orders for amendment of the petition or answer, for filing further pleadings or motions, or for extending the time of the filing of any pleading.

(b) Within ten [10] days of filing a petition for post-conviction relief under this rule, the petitioner may request a change of judge by filing an affidavit that the judge has a personal bias or prejudice against the petitioner. The petitioner's affidavit shall state the facts and the reasons for the belief that such bias or prejudice exists, and shall be accompanied by a certificate from the attorney of record that the attorney in good faith believes that the historical facts recited in the affidavit are true. A change of judge shall be granted if the historical facts recited in the affidavit support a rational inference of bias or prejudice. For good cause shown, the petitioner may be permitted to file the affidavit after the ten [10] day period. No change of venue from the county shall be granted. In the event a change of judge is granted under this section, the procedure set forth in Ind.Criminal Rule 13 shall govern the selection of a special judge.

(c) At any time prior to entry of judgment the court may grant leave to withdraw the petition. The petitioner shall be given leave to amend the petition as a matter of right no later than sixty [60] days prior to the date the petition has been set for trial. Any later amendment of the petition shall be by leave of the court.

(d) If the petition is challenging a sentence imposed following a plea of guilty, the court shall make a part of the record the certified transcript made pursuant to Rule CR–10.[1]

(e) In the event that counsel for petitioner files with the court a withdrawal of appearance accompanied by counsel's certificate, see Section 9(c), the case shall proceed under these rules, petitioner retaining the right to proceed pro se in forma pauperis if indigent. Thereafter, the court may order the State Public Defender to represent an indigent incarcerated petitioner if the court makes a preliminary finding that the proceeding is meritorious and in the interests of justice.

(f) If the State Public Defender has filed an appearance, the State Public Defender shall have sixty (60) days to respond to the State's answer to the petition filed pursuant to Rule PC 1(4)(a). If the pleadings conclusively show that petitioner is entitled to no relief, the court may deny the petition without further proceedings.

(g) The court may grant a motion by either party for summary disposition of the petition when it appears from the pleadings, depositions, answers to interrogatories, admissions, stipulations of fact, and any affidavits submitted, that there is no genuine issue of material fact and the moving party is entitled to judgment as a matter of law. The court may ask for oral argument on the legal issue raised. If an issue of material fact is raised, then the court shall hold an evidentiary hearing as soon as reasonably possible.

Section 5. Hearing.

The petition shall be heard without a jury. A record of the proceedings shall be made and preserved. All rules and statutes applicable in civil proceedings including pre-trial and discovery procedures are available to the parties, except as provided above in Section 4(b). The court may receive affidavits, depositions, oral testimony, or other evidence and may at its discretion order the applicant brought before it for the hearing. The petitioner has the burden of establishing his grounds for relief by a preponderance of the evidence.

Section 6. Judgment. The court shall make specific findings of fact, and conclusions of law on all issues presented, whether or not a hearing is held. If the court finds in favor of the petitioner, it shall enter an appropriate order with respect to the conviction or sentence in the former proceedings, and any supplementary orders as to arraignment, retrial, custody, bail, discharge, correction of sentence, or other matters that may be necessary and proper. This order is a final judgment.

Section 7. Appeal. An appeal may be taken by the petitioner or the State from the final judgment in this proceeding, under rules applicable to civil actions. Jurisdiction for such appeal shall be determined by reference to the sentence originally imposed. The Supreme Court shall have exclusive jurisdiction in cases involving an original sentence of death and the Court of Appeals shall have jurisdiction in all other cases.

Section 8. Waiver of or failure to assert claims. All grounds for relief available to a petitioner under this rule must be raised in his original petition. Any ground finally adjudicated on the merits or not so raised and knowingly, voluntarily and intelligently waived in the proceeding that resulted in the conviction or sentence, or in any other proceeding the petitioner has taken to secure relief, may not be the basis for a subsequent petition, unless the court finds a ground for relief asserted which for sufficient reason was not asserted or was inadequately raised in the original petition.

Section 9. Counsel.

(a) Upon receiving a copy of the petition, including an affidavit of indigency, from the clerk of the court, the Public Defender may represent any petitioner committed to the Indiana Department of Correction in all proceedings under this Rule, including appeal, if the Public Defender determines the proceedings are meritorious and in the interests of justice. The Public Defender may refuse representation in any case where the conviction or sentence being challenged has no present penal consequences. Petitioner retains the right to employ his own counsel or to proceed pro se, but the court is not required to appoint counsel for a petitioner other than the Public Defender.

(b) In the event petitioner elects to proceed pro se, the court at its discretion may order the cause submitted upon affidavit. It need not order the personal presence of the petitioner unless his presence is required for a full and fair determination of the issues raised at an evidentiary hearing. If the pro se petitioner requests issuance of subpoenas for witnesses at an evidentiary hearing, the petitioner shall specifically state by affidavit the reason the witness' testimony is required and the substance of the witness' expected testimony. If the court finds the witness' testimony would be relevant and probative, the court shall order that the subpoena be issued. If the court finds the proposed witness' testimony is not relevant and probative, it shall enter a finding on the record and refuse to issue the subpoena. Petitioners who are indigent and proceeding in forma pauperis shall be entitled to production of guilty plea and sentencing transcripts at public expense, prior to a hearing, if the petition is not dismissed. In addition, such petitioners shall also be entitled to a record of the post-conviction proceeding at public expense for appeal of the denial or dismissal of the petition.

(c) Counsel shall confer with petitioner and ascertain all grounds for relief under this rule, amending the petition if necessary to include any grounds not included by petitioner in the original petition. In the event that counsel determines the proceeding is not meritorious or in the interests of justice, before or after an evidentiary hearing is held, counsel shall file with the court counsel's withdrawal of appearance, accompanied by counsel's certification that 1) the petitioner has been consulted regarding grounds for relief in his pro se petition and any other possible grounds and 2) appropriate investigation, including but not limited to review of the guilty plea or trial and sentencing records, has been conducted. Petitioner shall be provided personally with an explanation of the reasons for withdrawal. Petitioner retains the right to proceed pro se, in forma pauperis if indigent, after counsel withdraws.

(d) *State.* In non-capital cases, the prosecuting attorney of the circuit in which the court of conviction is situated shall represent the State of Indiana in the court of conviction. In capital cases, the Attorney General shall represent the State of Indiana for purposes of answering the petition, and the prosecuting attorney shall, at the request of the Attorney General,

assist the Attorney General. The Attorney General shall represent the State of Indiana on any appeal pursuant to this Rule.

Section 10. Subsequent Prosecution.

(a) If prosecution is initiated against a petitioner who has successfully sought relief under this rule and a conviction is subsequently obtained, or

(b) If a sentence has been set aside pursuant to this rule and the successful petitioner is to be resentenced, then the sentencing court shall not impose a more severe penalty than that originally imposed unless the court includes in the record of the sentencing hearing a statement of the court's reasons for selecting the sentence that it imposes which includes reliance upon identifiable conduct on the part of the petitioner that occurred after the imposition of the original sentence, and the court shall give credit for time served.

(c) The provisions of subsections (a) and (b) limiting the severity of the penalty do not apply when:

(1) a conviction, based upon a plea agreement, is set aside;

(2) the state files an offer to abide by the terms of the original plea agreement within twenty (20) days after the conviction is set aside; and

(3) the defendant fails to accept the terms of the original plea agreement within twenty (20) days after the state's offer to abide by the terms of the original plea agreement is filed.

Section 11. Definition. Whenever "Public Defender" is mentioned herein, it shall mean the Public Defender of the State of Indiana as defined by statute.

Section 12. Successive Petitions.

(a) A petitioner may request a second, or successive, Petition for Post–Conviction Relief by completing a properly and legibly completed Successive Post–Conviction Relief Rule 1 Petition Form in substantial compliance with the form appended to this Rule. Both the Successive Post–Conviction Relief Rule 1 Petition Form and the proposed successive petition for post-conviction relief shall be sent to the Clerk of the Indiana Supreme Court, Indiana Court of Appeals, and Tax Court.

(b) The court will authorize the filing of the petition if the petitioner establishes a reasonable possibility that the petitioner is entitled to post-conviction relief. In making this determination, the court may consider applicable law, the petition, and materials from the petitioner's prior appellate and post-conviction proceedings including the record, briefs and court decisions, and any other material the court deems relevant.

(c) If the court authorizes the filing of the petition, it is to be (1) filed in the court where the petitioner's first post-conviction relief petition was adjudicated for consideration pursuant to this rule by the same judge if that judge is available, and (2) referred to the State Public Defender, who may represent the petitioner as provided in Section 9(a) of this Rule. Authorization to file a successive petition is not a determination on the merits for any other purpose and does not preclude summary disposition pursuant to Section (4)(g) of this Rule.

Amended Nov. 3, 1981, effective Jan. 1, 1982; Nov. 4, 1985, effective Jan. 1, 1986; Dec. 19, 1985, effective Jan. 1, 1986; Nov. 30, 1989, effective Jan. 1, 1990; Dec. 10, 1990, effective Jan. 1, 1991; Dec. 21, 1990, effective Jan. 1, 1991; Nov. 18, 1993, effective Jan. 1, 1994; Dec. 5, 1994, effective Feb. 1, 1995; Dec. 15, 1995, effective Feb. 1, 1996; amended effective March 28, 1996; Dec. 23, 1996, effective March 1, 1997; Nov. 25, 1997, effective Jan. 1, 1998; Dec. 22, 2000, effective Jan. 1, 2001; amended effective Dec. 21, 2001; Sept. 30 and Oct. 28, 2004, effective Jan. 1, 2005; amended effective Nov. 29, 2005; Sept. 20, 2011, effective Jan. 1, 2012.

1 Criminal Rule 10.

APPENDIX TO RULE PC 1

IN THE _____ COURT OF _____ COUNTY
STATE OF INDIANA

_____Full Name of Movant

_____   Case No. _____
Prison Number (if any)   (To be supplied by the clerk of the court)

v.

State of Indiana, Respondent.

INSTRUCTIONS—READ CAREFULLY

In order for this motion to receive consideration by the court, it shall be in writing (legibly handwritten or typewritten), signed by the petitioner and verified before a person authorized to administer oaths, and it shall set forth in concise form the answers to each applicable question. If necessary, petitioner may furnish his answer to a particular question on the reverse side of the page or an additional blank page. Petitioner shall make it clear to which question any such continued answer refers.

This motion must be filed in the court which imposed sentence.

Under the provisions of Rule PC 1, petitioner is required to include in this motion every ground known to him for vacating, setting aside or correcting his conviction and sentence. Be sure to include every ground.

Since every motion must be sworn to under oath, any false statement of a material fact therein may serve as the basis of prosecution and conviction for perjury. Petitioners should therefore exercise care to assure that all answers are true and correct.

If the motion is taken in forma pauperis, it shall include an affidavit (attached at the back of the form) setting forth information which establishes that petitioner will be unable to pay costs of the proceedings. When the motion is completed, the *original and two copies* shall be mailed to the clerk of the court from which he was sentenced.

1. Place of detention, if detained

_____

_____

If not, present address

_____

_____

2. Name and location of court which, and name of judge who, imposed sentence

_____

3. The case number and the offense or offenses for which sentence was imposed

_____

_____

4. The date upon which sentence was imposed and the terms of the sentence

_____

_____

5. Was the finding of guilty made:

( ) After a plea of guilty? OR

( ) After a plea of not guilty?

6. Did you appeal from the judgment of conviction?

( ) Yes ( ) No

7. If you answered "yes" to (6), list:

(a) The name of the court to which you appealed:

_____

_____

(b) The result in such court and the date of such result:

_____

_____

8. State concisely all the grounds known to you for vacating, setting aside or correcting your conviction and sentence. (See Rule PC 1, Sec. 1a)

(a) _____

_____

_____

(b) _____

_____

_____

(c) _____

_____

_____

(If you have more grounds, use reverse side or separate sheet. However, if this is a successive petition for post-conviction relief, you may submit no more than fifteen (15) additional pages, double-spaced, to provide supporting facts. You may also submit exhibits.)

9. State concisely and in the same order the facts which support each of the grounds set forth in (8).

(a) _____

_____

_____

(b) _____

_____

_____

(c) _____

_____

_____

10. Prior to this petition, have you filed with respect to this conviction:

(a) Any petition for post conviction relief pursuant to Rule PC 1 or PC 2?

( ) Yes ( ) No

(b) Any petitions for habeas corpus in state or federal courts?

( ) Yes ( ) No

(c) Any petitions in the United States Supreme Court for certiorari?

( ) Yes ( ) No

(d) Any other petitions, motions or applications in this or any other court?

( ) Yes ( ) No

11. If you answered "yes" to any part of (10), list with respect to each petition, motion or application:

(a) Its specific nature:

i. _____

ii. _____

iii. _____

(b) The name and location of the court in which each was filed:

i. _____

ii. _____

iii. _____

(c) The disposition of the petition, motion or application and the date of disposition:

i. _____

ii. _____

iii. _____

(d) If known, citations of any written opinions or orders entered pursuant to each disposition:

i. _____

ii. _____

iii. _____

12. Has any ground set forth in (8) been previously presented to this or any other court, *state or federal*, in any petition, motion or application which you have filed?

( ) Yes ( ) No

13. If you answered "yes" to (12), identify:

(a) Which grounds have been previously presented:

i. _____

ii. _____

iii. _____

(b) The proceedings in which each ground was raised:

i. _____

ii. _____

iii. _____

14. Were you represented by an attorney at any time during the course of:

(a) Your preliminary hearing?

( ) Yes ( ) No

(b) Your arraignment and plea?

( ) Yes ( ) No

(c) Your trial, if any?

( ) Yes ( ) No

(d) Your sentencing?

( ) Yes ( ) No

(e) Your appeal, if any, from the judgment of conviction or the imposition of sentence?

( ) Yes ( ) No

(f) Preparation, presentation or consideration of any petitions, motions or applications with respect to this conviction, which you filed?

( ) Yes ( ) No

15. If you answered "yes" to one or more parts of (14), list:

(a) The name and address of each attorney who represented you:

i. _____

ii. _____

iii. _____

(b) The proceedings at which each such attorney represented you:

i. _____

ii. _____

iii. _____

(c) Was said attorney:

( ) Appointed by the court? OR

( ) Of your own choosing?

16. Have you completed service of the challenged sentence?

( ) Yes ( ) No

17. Have you retained an attorney to represent you in this proceeding?

( ) Yes ( ) No

18. If you are without sufficient funds to employ counsel and are incarcerated in the Indiana Department of Correction, the Public Defender may represent you. If you check "NO" you lose the right to representation by the State Public Defender for the duration of this proceeding, including any appeal therefrom.

(a) Do you wish to have the Public Defender represent you?

( ) Yes ( ) No

(b) If yes, have you completed the Affidavit of Indigency attached to this form, stating your salary, if any, amount of savings, and all property owned by you?

( ) Yes ( ) No

_____
Signature of Petitioner

State of _____)
) SS:
County of _____)

I, _____, being duly sworn upon my oath, depose and say that I have subscribed to the foregoing petition; that I know the contents thereof; that it includes every ground known to me for vacating, setting aside or correcting the conviction and sentence attacked in this motion; and that the matters and allegations therein set forth are true.

_____
Signature of Affiant

Subscribed and sworn to before me this _____
day of _____, 19 ___.

_____
Notary Public

My Commission Expires:

_____
(month) (day) (year)

AFFIDAVIT OF INDIGENCY

(See instructions page 1 of this form)

_____
_____
_____
_____
_____
_____

_____
Signature of Petitioner

State of _____)
) SS:
County of _____)

I, _____, being first duly sworn upon my oath, depose and say that I have subscribed to the forego-

ing affidavit; that I know the contents thereof; and that the matters therein set forth are true.

_____
Signature of Affiant

Subscribed and sworn to before me this _____
day of _____, 19 ___.

_____
Notary Public

My Commission Expires:

_____
(month) (day) (year)

FORM FOR SUCCESSIVE POST–CONVICTION
RELIEF RULE 1 PETITIONS

(To Be Filed With Petition For Post–Conviction Relief)

IN THE _____ COURT OF _____ COUNTY

STATE OF INDIANA

_____)
Full Name of Movant   )
)
_____) Cause No._____
Prison Number (if any)   ) (To be supplied by the Clerk of the Court)

```
                                )
        v.                      )
                                )
State of Indiana,               )
                                )
      Respondent                )
```

INSTRUCTIONS—READ CAREFULLY

If you have previously filed a Petition for Post–Conviction Relief directed to this conviction or these convictions and the earlier petition was decided on the merits, you must fill out this form and file it along with your Petition. It must be legibly handwritten or typewritten, signed by the petitioner before a person authorized to take oaths and properly notarized. Since this must be signed under oath, any false statement of a material fact herein may serve as the basis of prosecution and conviction for perjury. Exercise care to be sure all answers are true and correct.

You must mail the original and two copies of this form along with your petition to the Clerk of the Supreme Court and Court of Appeals, 200 West Washington Street, Room 216, Indianapolis, IN 46204–2732. The Clerk will refer your petition to the Supreme Court in death penalty cases and the Indiana Court of Appeals in all other cases. The court will then decide whether your petition may be filed in the trial court where your first Post–Conviction Remedy Rule 1 petition was adjudicated.

NOTE: The court will allow a second or successive petition for post-conviction relief to be filed if the petitioner establishes a reasonable possibility that the petitioner is entitled to post-conviction relief. However, a petitioner does not establish a reasonable possibility that the petitioner is entitled to post-conviction relief, for example, (1) if the petitioner only alleges grounds for relief that are not different from those which have already been decided on the merits, or (2) if the only grounds alleged, even if different, should have been alleged in an earlier proceeding.

In addition to this form, you may submit no more than fifteen (15) pages, double-spaced, to provide supporting facts. You may also submit exhibits. Any citation of authorities should be avoided and is only appropriate if there has been a change in the law since the judgment you were attacking was entered. Your answer(s) should be confined to relevant facts and must not include legal arguments.

1. Were you represented by an attorney on your prior Petition for Post–Conviction Relief?

   Yes ___ No___

   If yes, name(s) and address(es) of attorney(s).

   _____

   _____

   Proceedings at which each attorney represented you:

Drafting Petition for Post–Conviction Relief____
Hearing of Petition for Post–Conviction Relief__
Appeal of denial of Petition for Post–Conviction Relief_____

2. Was there a hearing on your prior Petition?

   Yes ___ No___

3. If the Petition was denied, did you appeal?

   Yes ___ No___

If yes, please state result on appeal, date of decision and citation of case if known:

_____

_____

_____

4. If you are alleging ground(s) for relief which were raised in your previous Petition, explain why you feel consideration is merited:

_____

_____

_____

_____

5. If your Petition raises new grounds which were not included in your prior Petition, explain why you are raising these grounds now. Your explanation should rely on FACTS, not your opinions or conclusions:

_____

_____

_____

_____

_____

Signature of Petitioner

STATE OF _____)
) SS:
COUNTY OF _____)

I, _____, being duly sworn upon my oath, depose and say that I have subscribed to the foregoing; that I know the contents thereof; and that the matters and allegations set forth are true.

Signature of Affiant–Petitioner	Notary Public

Subscribed and sworn to before me, a Notary Public, this _____ day of _____, 20 ___.

Printed Name

My Commission Expires: County   of   Residence:

Amended Dec. 10, 1990, effective Jan. 1, 1991; amended effective Aug. 22, 1991; amended Nov. 18, 1993, effective Jan. 1, 1994; Dec. 22, 2000, effective Jan. 1, 2001; July 19, 2002, effective Jan. 1, 2003; Sept. 21, 2010, effective Jan. 1, 2011.

Rule PC 2. Belated Notice of Appeal—Belated Motion to Correct Error—Belated Appeal

Eligible defendant defined. An "eligible defendant" for purposes of this Rule is a defendant who, but for the defendant's failure to do so timely, would have the right to challenge on direct appeal a conviction or sentence after a trial or plea of guilty by filing a notice of appeal, filing a motion to correct error, or pursuing an appeal.

Appellate court jurisdiction. Jurisdiction of an appeal under this Rule is determined pursuant to Rules 4 and 5 of the Indiana Rules of Appellate Procedure by reference to the sentence imposed as a result of the challenged conviction or sentence.

Section 1. Belated Notice of Appeal

(a) *Required Showings.* An eligible defendant convicted after a trial or plea of guilty may petition the trial court for permission to file a belated notice of appeal of the conviction or sentence if;

(1) the defendant failed to file a timely notice of appeal;

(2) the failure to file a timely notice of appeal was not due to the fault of the defendant; and

(3) the defendant has been diligent in requesting permission to file a belated notice of appeal under this rule.

(b) *Form of petition.* There is no prescribed form of petition for permission to file a belated notice of appeal. The petitioner's proposed notice of appeal may be filed as an Exhibit to the petition.

(c) *Factors in granting or denying permission.* If the trial court finds that the requirements of Section 1(a) are met, it shall permit the defendant to file the belated notice of appeal. Otherwise, it shall deny permission.

(d) *Hearing.* If a hearing is held on a petition for permission to file a belated notice of appeal, it shall be conducted according to Ind. Post–Conviction Rule 1(5).

(e) *Appealability.* An order granting or denying permission to file a belated notice of appeal is a Final Judgment for purposes of Ind. Appellate Rule 5.

(f) *Time and procedure for initiating appeal.* If the court grants permission to file a belated notice of appeal, the time and procedure for filing such notice of appeal is governed by App. R. 9(A).

Section 2. Belated Motion to Correct Error.

(a) *Required Showings.* An eligible defendant convicted after a trial or plea of guilty may petition the court of conviction for permission to file a belated motion to correct error addressing the conviction or sentence, if:

(1) no timely and adequate motion to correct error was filed for the defendant;

(2) the failure to file a timely motion to correct error was not due to the fault of the defendant; and

(3) the defendant has been diligent in requesting permission to file a belated motion to correct error under this rule.

(b) *Merits of motion.* The trial court shall not consider the merits of the motion until it has determined whether the requirements of Section 2(a) are met.

(c) *Hearing.* Any hearing on whether the petition should be granted shall be conducted according to P–C. R. 1(5).

(d) *Factors in granting or denying permission.* If the trial court finds that the requirements of section 2(a) are met, it shall permit the defendant to file the motion, and the motion shall then be treated for all purposes as a motion to correct error filed within the prescribed period.

(e) *Appealability of Denial of Permission.* If the trial court finds that the requirements of Section 2(a) are not met, it shall deny defendant permission to file the motion. Denial of permission shall be a Final Judgment for purposes of App. R. 5.

(f) *Time for initiating appeal.* The time for filing a notice of appeal from denial of permission is governed by App. R. 9(A).

Section 3. Belated Perfection of Appeal.

An eligible defendant convicted after a trial or plea of guilty may petition the appellate tribunal for permission to pursue a belated appeal of the conviction or sentence if:

(a) the defendant filed a timely notice of appeal;

(b) no appeal was perfected for the defendant or the appeal was dismissed for failing to take a necessary step to pursue the appeal;

(c) the failure to perfect the appeal or take the necessary step was not due to the fault of the defendant; and

(d) the defendant has been diligent in requesting permission to pursue a belated appeal.

Amended Dec. 17, 1973, effective Jan. 1, 1974, amended Nov. 10, 1988, effective Jan. 1, 1989; amended and effective Feb. 16, 1989; amended Nov. 18, 1993, effective Jan. 1, 1994; amended Feb. 4, 2000, effective January 1, 2001; amended Sept. 30, 2004, effective Jan. 1, 2005; amended Sept. 10, 2007, effective Jan. 1, 2008; amended Sept. 9, 2008, effective Jan. 1, 2009; Sept. 20, 2011, effective Jan. 1, 2012.

RULES FOR ALTERNATIVE DISPUTE RESOLUTION

Effective March 1, 1997

Including Amendments Received Through November 1, 2013

Rule
    Preamble

Preamble

These rules are adopted in order to bring some uniformity into alternative dispute resolution with the view that the interests of the parties can be preserved in settings other than the traditional judicial dispute resolution method.

RULE 1.   GENERAL PROVISIONS

Rule 1.1.   Recognized Alternative Dispute Resolution Methods

Alternative dispute resolution methods which are recognized include settlement negotiations, arbitration, mediation, conciliation, facilitation, mini-trials, summary jury trials, private judges and judging, convening or conflict assessment, neutral evaluation and fact-finding, multi-door case allocations, and negotiated rulemaking.

Adopted Nov. 7, 1991, effective Jan. 1, 1992; Amended Dec. 23, 1996, effective March 1, 1997.

Rule 1.2.   Scope of These Rules

Alternative dispute resolution methods which are governed by these rules are (1) Mediation, (2) Arbitration, (3) Mini-Trials, (4) Summary Jury Trials, and (5) Private Judges.

Adopted Nov. 7, 1991, effective Jan. 1, 1992; Amended Dec. 23, 1996, effective March 1, 1997.

Rule 1.3.   Alternative Dispute Resolution Methods Described

(A) Mediation. This is a process in which a neutral third person, called a mediator, acts to encourage and to assist in the resolution of a dispute between two (2) or more parties. This is an informal and nonadversarial process. The objective is to help the disputing parties reach a mutually acceptable agreement between or among themselves on all or any part of the issues in dispute. Decision-making authority rests with the parties, not the mediator. The mediator assists the parties in identifying issues, fostering joint problem-solving, exploring settlement alternatives, and in other ways consistent with these activities.

(B) Arbitration. This is a process in which a neutral third person or a panel, called an arbitrator or an arbitration panel, considers the facts and arguments which are presented by the parties and renders a decision. The decision may be binding or nonbinding as provided in these rules.

(C) Mini-Trials. A mini-trial is a settlement process in which each side presents a highly abbreviated summary of its case to senior officials who are authorized to settle the case. A neutral advisor may preside over the proceeding and give advisory opinions or rulings if invited to do so. Following the presentation, the officials seek a negotiated settlement of the dispute.

(D) Summary Jury Trials. This is an abbreviated trial with a jury in which the litigants present their evidence in an expedited fashion. The litigants and the jury are guided by a neutral who acts as a presiding official who sits as if a judge. After an advisory verdict from the jury, the presiding official may assist the litigants in a negotiated settlement of their controversy.

(E) Private Judges. This is a process in which litigants employ a private judge, who is a former judge, to resolve a pending lawsuit. The parties are responsible for all expenses involved in these matters, and they may agree upon their allocation.

Adopted Nov. 7, 1991, effective Jan. 1, 1992; Amended Dec. 23, 1996, effective March 1, 1997.

Rule 1.4 Application of Alternative Dispute Resolution

These rules shall apply in all civil and domestic relations litigation filed in all Circuit, Superior, County, Municipal, and Probate Courts in the state.

Adopted Nov. 7, 1991, effective Jan. 1, 1992; Amended Dec. 23, 1996, effective March 1, 1997; amended Dec. 22, 2000, effective Jan. 1, 2001.

Rule 1.5. Immunity for Persons Acting Under This Rule

A registered or court approved mediator; arbitrator; person acting as an advisor or conducting, directing, or assisting in a mini-trial; a presiding person conducting a summary jury trial and the members of its advisory jury; and a private judge; shall each have immunity in the same manner and to the same extent as a judge in the State of Indiana.

Adopted Nov. 7, 1991, effective Jan. 1, 1992; Amended Dec. 23, 1996, effective March 1, 1997.

Rule 1.6. Discretion in Use of Rules

Except as herein provided, a presiding judge may order any civil or domestic relations proceeding or selected issues in such proceedings referred to mediation, non-binding arbitration or mini-trial. The selection criteria which should be used by the court are defined under these rules. Binding arbitration and a summary jury trial may be ordered only upon the agreement of the parties as consistent with provisions in these rules which address each method.

Adopted Nov. 7, 1991, effective Jan. 1, 1992; Amended Dec. 23, 1996, effective March 1, 1997; amended Dec. 22, 2000, effective Jan. 1, 2001.

Rule 1.7 Jurisdiction of Proceeding

At all times during the course of any alternative dispute resolution proceeding, the case remains within the jurisdiction of the court which referred the litigation to the process. For good cause shown and upon hearing on this issue, the court at any time may terminate the alternative dispute resolution process.

Adopted Nov. 7, 1991, effective Jan. 1, 1992; amended Oct. 30, 1992, effective Jan. 1, 1993; amended Dec. 23, 1996, effective March 1, 1997.

Rule 1.8 Recordkeeping

When a case has been referred for alternative dispute resolution, the Clerk of the court shall note the referral and subsequent entries of record in the Chronological Case Summary under the case number initially assigned. The case file maintained under the case number initially assigned shall serve as the repository for papers and other materials submitted for consideration during the alternative dispute resolution process. The court shall report on the Quarterly Case Status Report the number of cases resolved through alternative dispute resolution processes.

Adopted Nov. 7, 1991, effective Jan. 1, 1992; Amended Dec. 23, 1996, effective March 1, 1997.

Rule 1.9. Service of Papers and Orders

The parties shall comply with Trial Rule 5 of the Rules of Trial Procedure in serving papers and other pleadings on parties during the course of the alternative dispute resolution process. The Clerk of the Circuit Court shall serve all orders, notices, and rulings under the procedure set forth in Trial Rule 72(D).

Adopted Nov. 7, 1991, effective Jan. 1, 1992; amended Dec. 23, 1996, effective March 1, 1997; amended Sept. 30, 2004, effective Jan. 1, 2005.

Rule 1.10. Other Methods of Dispute Resolution

These rules shall not preclude a court from ordering any other reasonable method or technique to resolve disputes.

Adopted Nov. 7, 1991, effective Jan. 1, 1992; Amended Dec. 23, 1996, effective March 1, 1997.

Rule 1.11. Alternative Dispute Resolution Plans.

A county desiring to participate in an alternative dispute resolution program pursuant to IC 33-23-6 must develop and submit a plan to the Indiana Judicial Conference, and receive approval of said plan from the Executive Director of the Indiana Supreme Court Division of State Court Administration.

Adopted July 1, 2003, effective Aug. 1, 2003; amended Sept. 30, 2004, effective Jan. 1, 2005.

RULE 2. MEDIATION

Rule 2.1. Purpose

Mediation under this section involves the confidential process by which a neutral, acting as a mediator, selected by the parties or appointed by the court, assists the litigants in reaching a mutually acceptable agreement. The role of the mediator is to assist in identifying the issues, reducing misunderstanding, clarifying priorities, exploring areas of compromise, and finding points of agreement as well as legitimate points of disagreement. Any agreement reached by the parties is to be based on the autonomous decisions of the parties and not the decisions of the mediator. It is anticipated that an agreement may not resolve all of the disputed issues, but the process can reduce points of contention. Parties and their representatives are required to mediate in good faith, but are not compelled to reach an agreement.

Adopted Nov. 7, 1991, effective Jan. 1, 1992; Amended Dec. 23, 1996, effective March 1, 1997.

Rule 2.2. Case Selection/Objection

At any time fifteen (15) days or more after the period allowed for peremptory change of judge under Trial Rule 76(B) has expired, a court may on its own motion or upon motion of any party refer a civil or domestic relations case to mediation. After a motion referring a case to mediation is granted, a party may object by filing a written objection within seven (7) days in a domestic relations case or fifteen (15) days in a civil case. The party must specify the grounds for objection. The court shall promptly consider the objection and any response and determine whether the litigation should then be mediated or not. In this decision, the court shall consider the willingness of the parties to mutually resolve their dispute, the ability of the parties to participate in the mediation process, the need for discovery and the extent to which it has been conducted, and any other factors which affect the potential for fair resolution of the dispute through the mediation process. If a case is ordered for mediation, the case shall remain on the court docket and the trial calendar.

Adopted Nov. 7, 1991, effective Jan. 1, 1992; amended Oct. 30, 1992, effective Jan. 1, 1993; amended Dec. 23, 1996, effective March 1, 1997.

Rule 2.3. Listing of Mediators: Commission Registry of Mediators

Any person who wishes to serve as a registered mediator pursuant to these rules must register with the Indiana Supreme Court Commission for Continuing Legal Education (hereinafter "Commission") on forms supplied by the Commission. The registrants must meet qualifications as required in counties or court districts (as set out in Ind. Administrative Rule 3(A)) in which they desire to mediate and identify the types of litigation which they desire to mediate. All professional licenses must be disclosed and identified in the form which the Commission requires.

The registration form shall be accompanied by a fee of $50.00 for each registered area (Civil or Domestic). An annual fee of $50.00 shall be due the second December 31st following initial registration. Registered mediators will be billed at the time their annual statements are sent. No fee shall be required of a full-time, sitting judge.

The Commission shall maintain a list of registered mediators including the following information: (1) whether the person qualified under A.D.R. Rule 2.5 to mediate domestic relations and/or civil cases; (2) the counties or court districts in which the person desires to mediate; (3) the type of litigation the person desires to mediate; and (4) whether the person is a full-time judge.

The Commission may remove a registered mediator from its registry for failure to meet or to maintain the requirements of A.D.R. Rule 2.5 for non-payment of fees. A registered mediator must maintain a current business and residential address and telephone number with the Commission. Failure to maintain current information required by these rules may result in removal from the registry.

For the billing of calendar year 2011, when this Rule becomes effective, registered mediators must pay the $50.00 annual fee and a one-time fee of $25.00 for the time period July 1, 2011–December 31, 2011, for a total of $75.00 per registration area. The annual fee shall be $50.00 per calendar year per registration area thereafter.

On or before October 31 of each year, each registered mediator will be sent an annual statement showing the mediator's educational activities that have been approved for mediator credit by the Commission.

Adopted Nov. 7, 1991, effective Jan. 1, 1992. Amended Dec. 23, 1996, effective March 1, 1997; July 1, 2005, effective Jan. 1, 2006; Sept. 21, 2010, effective Jan. 1, 2011; Sept. 13, 2013, effective Jan. 1, 2014.

Rule 2.4. Selection of Mediators

Upon an order referring a case to mediation, the parties may within seven (7) days in a domestic relations case or within fifteen (15) days in a civil case: (1) choose a mediator from the Commission's registry, or (2) agree upon a non-registered mediator, who must be approved by the trial court and who serves with leave of court. In the event a mediator is not selected by agreement, the court will designate three (3) registered mediators from the Commission's registry who are willing to mediate within the Court's district as set out in Admin. R. 3 (A). Alternately, each side shall strike the name of one mediator. The side initiating the lawsuit will strike first. The mediator remaining after the striking process will be deemed the selected mediator.

A person selected to serve as a mediator under this rule may choose not to serve for any reason. At any time, a party may request the court to replace the mediator for good cause shown. In the event a mediator chooses not to serve or the court decides to replace a mediator, the selection process will be repeated.

Adopted Nov. 7, 1991, effective Jan. 1, 1992; Amended Dec. 23, 1996, effective March 1, 1997.

Rule 2.5. Qualifications of Mediators

(A) Civil Cases: Educational Qualifications.

(1) Subject to approval by the court in which the case is pending, the parties may agree upon any person to serve as a mediator.

(2) In civil cases, a registered mediator must be an attorney in good standing with the Supreme Court of Indiana.

(3) To register as a civil mediator, a person must meet all the requirements of this rule and must have either: (1) taken at least forty (40) hours of Commission approved civil mediation training in the three (3) years immediately prior to submission of the registration application, or (2) completed forty (40) hours of Commission approved civil mediation training at any time and taken at least six (6) hours of approved Continuing Mediation Education in the three (3) years immediately prior to submission of the registration application.

(4) However, a person who has met the requirements of A.D.R. Rule 2.5(B)(2)(a), is registered as a domestic relations mediator, and by December 31 of the second full year after meeting those requirements completes a Commission approved civil crossover mediation training program may register as a civil mediator.

(5) As part of a judge's judicial service, a judicial officer may serve as a mediator in a case pending before another judicial officer.

(B) Domestic Relations Cases: Educational Qualifications.

(1) Subject to approval of the court, in which the case is pending, the parties may agree upon any person to serve as a mediator.

(2) In domestic relations cases, a registered mediator must be either: (a) an attorney, in good standing with the Supreme Court of Indiana; (b) a person who has a bachelor's degree or advanced degree from an institution recognized by a U.S. Department of Education approved accreditation organization, e.g. The Higher Learning Commission of the North Central Association of Colleges and Schools. Notwithstanding the provisions of (2)(a) and (b) above, any licensed professional whose professional license is currently suspended or revoked by the respective licensing agency, or has been relinquished voluntarily while a disciplinary action is pending, shall not be a registered mediator.

(3) To register as a domestic relations mediator, a person must meet all the requirements of this rule and must have either: (1) taken at least forty (40) hours of Commission approved domestic relations mediation training in the three (3) years immediately prior to submission of the registration application, or (2) taken at least forty (40) hours of Commission approved domestic relations mediation training at any time, and taken at least six (6) hours of approved Continuing Mediation Education in the

three (3) years immediately prior to submission of the registration application.

(4) However, if a person is registered as a civil mediator and by December 31 of the second full year after meeting those requirements completes a Commission approved domestic relations crossover mediation training program (s)he may register as a domestic relations mediator.

(5) As part of a judicial service, a judicial officer may serve as a mediator in a case pending before another judicial officer.

(C) Continuing Mediation Education ("CME") Requirements for All Registered Mediators. A registered mediator must complete a minimum of six hours of Commission approved continuing mediation education anytime during a three-year educational period. A mediator's initial educational period commences January 1 of the first full year of registration and ends December 31 of the third full year. Educational periods shall be sequential, in that once a mediator's particular three-year period terminates, a new three-year period and six hour minimum shall commence.

Mediators registered before the effective date of this rule shall begin their first three-year educational period January 1, 2004.

Text of Subdivision (D) effective until January 1, 2015. See also text of Subdivision (D) effective January 1, 2015.

(D) Basic and Continuing Mediation Education Reporting Requirements. Within thirty (30) days of presenting a Commission approved basic or continuing mediation education training course, the sponsor of that course must forward a list of attendees to the Commission. This list shall include for each attendee: full name; attorney number (if applicable); residence and business addresses and phone numbers; and the number of mediation hours attended. A course approved for CME may also qualify for CLE credit, so long as the course meets the requirements of Admission and Discipline Rule 29. For courses approved for both continuing legal education and continuing mediation education, the sponsor must additionally report continuing legal education, speaking and professional responsibility hours attended.

Text of Subdivision (D) effective January 1, 2015. See also text of Subdivision (D) effective until January 1, 2015.

(D) Basic and Continuing Mediation Education Reporting Requirements. Subsequent to presenting a Commission approved basic or continuing mediation education training course, the sponsor of that course must forward a list of attendees to the Commission. An attendance report received more than thirty (30) days after a program is concluded must include a late processing fee as approved by the Indiana Supreme Court. *Received*, in the context of an application, document(s), and/or other item(s) which is or are requested by or submitted to the Commission, means delivery to the Commission; mailed to the Commission by registered, certified or express mail return receipt requested or deposited with any third-party commercial carrier for delivery to the Commission within three (3) calendar days, cost prepaid, properly addressed. Sending by registered or certified mail and by third-party commercial carrier shall be complete upon mailing or deposit. This list shall include for each attendee: full name; attorney number (if applicable); residence and business addresses and phone numbers; and the number of mediation hours attended. A course approved for CME may also qualify for CLE credit, so long as the course meets the requirements of Admission and Discipline Rule 29. For courses approved for both continuing legal education and continuing mediation education, the sponsor must additionally report continuing legal education, speaking and professional responsibility hours attended.

Text of Subdivision (E) effective until January 1, 2015. See also text of Subdivision (E) effective January 1, 2015.

(E) Accreditation Policies and Procedures for CME.

(1) *Approval of courses.* The Commission shall approve the course, including law school classes, if it determines that the course will make a significant contribution to the professional competency of mediators who attend. In determining if a course, including law school classes, meets this standard the Commission shall consider whether:

(a) the course has substantial content dealing with alternative dispute resolution process;

(b) the course deals with matters related directly to the practice of alternative dispute resolution and the professional responsibilities of neutrals;

(c) the course deals with reinforcing and enhancing alternative dispute resolution and negotiation concepts and skills of neutrals;

(d) the course teaches ethical issues associated with the practice of alternative dispute resolution;

(e) the course deals with other professional matters related to alternative dispute resolution and the relationship and application of alternative dispute resolution principles;

(f) the course deals with the application of alternative dispute resolution skills to conflicts or issues that arise in settings other than litigation, such as workplace, business, commercial transactions, securities, intergovernmental, administrative, public policy, family, guardianship and environmental, and,

(g) in the case of law school classes, in addition to the standard set forth above the class must be a regularly conducted class at a law school accredited by the American Bar Association.

(2) Credit will be denied for the following activities:

(a) Legislative, lobbying or other law-making activities.

(b) In-house program. The Commission shall not approve programs which it determines are primarily designed for the exclusive benefit of mediators employed by a private organization or mediation firm. Mediators within related companies will be considered to be employed by the same organization or law firm for purposes of this rule. However, governmental entities may sponsor programs for the exclusive benefit of their mediator employees.

(c) Programs delivered by these methods: satellite, microwave, video, computer, internet, telephone or other electronic methods. To be approved courses must provide a discussion leader or two-way communication, classroom setting away from the mediator's offices, opportunity to ask questions, and must monitor attendance.

(d) Courses or activities completed by self-study.

(e) Programs directed to elementary, high school or college student level neutrals.

(3) *Procedures for Sponsors.* Any sponsor may apply to the Commission for approval of a course. The application must:

(a) be submitted to the Commission at least thirty (30) days before the first date on which the course is to be offered;

(b) contain the information required by and be in the form approved by the Commission and available upon request or at the Commission's web site: www.in.gov/judiciary/cle: and

(c) be accompanied by the written course outline and brochure used to furnish information about the course to mediators.

(4) *Procedure for Mediators.* A mediator may apply for credit of a live course either before or after the date on which it is offered. The application must:

(a) contain the information required by and be in the form approved by the Commission and available upon request or at the Commission's web site: www.in.gov/judiciary/cle;

(b) be accompanied by the written course outline and brochure used to furnish information about the course to mediators; and,

(c) be accompanied by an affidavit of the mediator attesting that the mediator attended the course together with a certification of the course Sponsor as to the mediator's attendance. If the application for course approval is made before attendance, this affidavit and certification requirement shall be fulfilled within thirty (30) days after course attendance.

Text of Subdivision (E) effective January 1, 2015. See also text of Subdivision (E) effective until January 1, 2015.

(E) Accreditation Policies and Procedures for CME.

(1) *Approval of courses.* Applications must be accompanied by an application fee as approved by the Indiana Supreme Court. An "application" means a completed application form, with all required attachments and fees, signed and dated by the Applicant. Applications received more than thirty (30) days after the conclusion of a course must include a late processing fee. The Commission shall approve the course, including law school classes, if it determines that the course will make a significant contribution to the professional competency of mediators who attend. In determining if a course, including law school classes, meets this standard the Commission shall consider whether:

(a) the course has substantial content dealing with alternative dispute resolution process;

(b) the course deals with matters related directly to the practice of alternative dispute resolution and the professional responsibilities of neutrals;

(c) the course deals with reinforcing and enhancing alternative dispute resolution and negotiation concepts and skills of neutrals;

(d) the course teaches ethical issues associated with the practice of alternative dispute resolution;

(e) the course deals with other professional matters related to alternative dispute resolution and the relationship and application of alternative dispute resolution principles;

(f) the course deals with the application of alternative dispute resolution skills to conflicts or issues that arise in settings other than litigation, such as workplace, business, commercial transactions, securities, intergovernmental, administrative, public policy, family, guardianship and environmental; and,

(g) in the case of law school classes, in addition to the standard set forth above the class must be a regularly conducted class at a law school accredited by the American Bar Association.

(2) Credit will be denied for the following activities:

(a) Legislative, lobbying or other law-making activities.

(b) In-house program. The Commission shall not approve programs which it determines are primarily designed for the exclusive benefit of mediators employed by a private organization or mediation firm. Mediators within related companies will be considered to be employed by the same organization or law firm for purposes of this rule. However, governmental entities may sponsor programs for the exclusive benefit of their mediator employees.

(c) Programs delivered by these methods: satellite, microwave, video, computer, internet, telephone or other electronic methods. To be approved courses must provide a discussion leader or two-way communication, classroom setting away from the mediator's offices, opportunity to ask questions, and must monitor attendance.

(d) Courses or activities completed by self-study.

(e) Programs directed to elementary, high school or college student level neutrals.

(3) *Procedures for Sponsors.* Any sponsor may apply to the Commission for approval of a course. The application must:

(a) be received by the Commission at least thirty (30) days before the first date on which the course is to be offered;

(b) Include the nonrefundable application fee in order for the application to be reviewed by the Commission. Courses presented by non-profit sponsors which do not require a registration fee are eligible for an application fee waiver. Courses presented by bar associations, Indiana Continuing Legal Education Forum (ICLEF) and government or academic entities will not be assessed an application fee, but are subject to late processing fees.

Applications received less than thirty (30) days before a course is presented must also include a late processing fee in order to be processed by the Commission.

Either the provider or the attendee must pay all application and late fees before a mediator may receive credit.

Fees may be waived in the discretion of the Commission upon a showing of good cause.

(c) contain the information required by and be in the form set forth in the application approved by the Commission and available upon request;

(d) be accompanied by the written course outline and brochure used by the Sponsor to furnish information about the course to mediators; and

(e) be accompanied by an affidavit of the mediator attesting that the mediator attended the course together with a certification of the course Sponsor as to the mediator's attendance. If the application for course approval is made before attendance, this affidavit and certification requirement shall be fulfilled within thirty (30) days after course attendance. Attendance reports received more than thirty (30) days after the conclusion of a course must include a late processing fee.

Course applications received more than (1) one year after a course is presented may be denied as untimely.

(4) *Procedure for Mediators.* A mediator may apply for credit of a live course either before or after the date on which it is offered. The application must:

(a) be received by the Commission at least thirty (30) days before the date on which the course is to be offered if they are seeking approval before the course is to be presented. If the applicant is seeking accreditation, the Sponsor must apply within thirty (30) days of the conclusion of the course.

(b) include the nonrefundable application fee in order for the application to be reviewed by the Commission. Courses presented by non-profit sponsors which do not require a registration fee are eligible for an application fee waiver. Either the provider or the attendee must pay all application and late fees before a mediator may receive credit.

Fees may be waived in the discretion of the Commission upon a showing of good cause.

(c) contain the information required by and be in the form set forth in the application approved by the Commission and available upon request;

(d) be accompanied by the written course outline and brochure used by the Sponsor to furnish information about the course to mediators; and

(e) be accompanied by an affidavit of mediator attesting that the mediator attended the course together with a certification of the course Sponsor as to the mediator's attendance. If the application for course approval is made before attendance, this affidavit and certification must be received by the Commission within thirty (30) days after course attendance. An attendance report received more than thirty (30) days after the conclusion of a course must include a late processing fee. Course applications received more than one (1) year after a course is presented may be denied as untimely.

Text of Subdivision (F) effective until January 1, 2015. See also text of Subdivision (F) effective January 1, 2015.

(F) Procedure for Resolving Disputes. Any person who disagrees with a decision of the Commission and is unable to resolve the disagreement informally, may petition the Commission for a resolution of the dispute. Petitions pursuant to this Section shall be considered by the Commission at its next regular meeting, provided that the petition is received by the Commission at least ten (10) business days before

such meeting. The person filing the petition shall have the right to attend the Commission meeting at which the petition is considered and to present relevant evidence and arguments to the Commission. The rules of pleading and practice in civil cases shall not apply, and the proceedings shall be informal as directed by the Chair. The determination of the Commission shall be final subject to appeal directly to the Supreme Court.

Text of Subdivision (F) effective January 1, 2015. See also text of Subdivision (F) effective until January 1, 2015.

(F) Procedure for Resolving Disputes. Any person who disagrees with a decision of the Commission and is unable to resolve the disagreement informally, may petition the Commission for a resolution of the dispute. Petitions must be received by the Commission within thirty (30) days of notification by the Commission of the Commission's decision and shall be considered by the Commission at its next regular meeting, provided that the petition is received by the Commission at least ten (10) business days before such meeting. The person filing the petition shall have the right to attend the Commission meeting at which the petition is considered and to present relevant evidence and arguments to the Commission. The rules of pleading and practice in civil cases shall not apply, and the proceedings shall be informal as directed by the Chair. The determination of the Commission shall be final subject to appeal directly to the Supreme Court.

(G) Confidentiality. Filings with the Commission shall be confidential. These filings shall not be disclosed except in furtherance of the duties of the Commission or upon the request, by the mediator involved, or as directed by the Supreme Court.

(H) Rules for Determining Education Completed.

(1) *Formula.* The number of hours of continuing mediation education completed in any course by a mediator shall be computed by:

(a) Determining the total instruction time expressed in minutes;

(b) Dividing the total instruction time by sixty (60); and

(c) Rounding the quotient up to the nearest one-tenth (1/10).

Stated in an equation the formula is:

$$\frac{\text{Total Instruction time (in minutes)}}{\text{Sixty (60)}} = \text{Hours completed (rounded up the nearest 1/10)}$$

(2) *Instruction Time Defined.* Instruction time is the amount of time when a course is in session and presentations or other educational activities are in progress. Instruction time does not include time spent on:

(a) Introductory remarks;

(b) Breaks; or

(c) Business meetings

(3) A registered mediator who participates as a teacher, lecturer, panelist or author in an approved continuing mediation education course will receive credit for:

(a) Four (4) hours of approved continuing mediation education for every hour spent in presentation.

(b) One (1) hour of approved continuing mediation education for every four (4) hours of preparation time for a contributing author who does not make a presentation relating to the materials prepared.

(c) One (1) hour of approved continuing mediation education for every hour the mediator spends in attendance at sessions of a course other than those in which the mediator participates as a teacher, lecturer or panel member.

(d) Mediators will not receive credit for acting as a speaker, lecturer or panelist on a program directed to elementary, high school or college student level neutrals, or for a program that is not approved under Alternative Dispute Resolution Rule 2.5(E).

Adopted Nov. 7, 1991, effective Jan. 1, 1992. Amended Dec. 23, 1996, effective March 1, 1997; amended effective July 21, 1997; amended July 19, 2002, effective Jan. 1, 2003; amended effective Sept. 25, 2002; amended July 1, 2003, effective Jan. 1, 2004; Sept. 30 and Oct. 25, 2004, effective Jan. 1, 2005; Sept. 10, 2007, effective Jan. 1, 2008; Sept. 23, 2008, effective Jan. 1, 2009; Sept. 21, 2010, effective Jan. 1, 2011; Sept. 13, 2013, effective Jan. 1, 2015.

Rule 2.6.   Mediation Costs

Absent an agreement by the parties, including any guardian ad litem, court appointed special advocate, or other person properly appointed by the court to represent the interests of any child involved in a domestic relations case, the court may set an hourly rate for mediation and determine the division of such costs by the parties. The costs should be predicated on the complexity of the litigation, the skill levels needed to mediate the litigation, and the litigants' ability to pay. The mediation costs shall be paid within thirty (30) days after the close of each mediation session.

Adopted Nov. 7, 1991, effective Jan. 1, 1992; Amended Dec. 23, 1996, effective March 1, 1997; amended Dec. 22, 2000, effective Jan. 1, 2001.

Rule 2.7.   Mediation Procedure

(A) Advisement of Participants. The mediator shall:

(1) advise the parties of all persons whose presence at mediation might facilitate settlement; and

(2) in child related matters, ensure that the parties consider fully the best interests of the children and that the parties understand the consequences of any decision they reach concerning the children; and

(3) inform all parties that the mediator (a) is not providing legal advice, (b) does not represent either party, (c) cannot assure how the court would apply the law or rule in the parties' case, or what the outcome of the case would be if the dispute were to go before the court, and (d) recommends that the parties seek or consult with their own legal counsel if they desire, or believe they need legal advice; and

(4) explain the difference between a mediator's role and a lawyer's role when a mediator knows or reasonably should know that a party does not understand the mediator's role in the matter; and

(5) not advise any party (i) what that party should do in the specific case, or (ii) whether a party should accept an offer.

(B) Mediation Conferences.

(1) The parties and their attorneys shall be present at all mediation sessions involving domestic relations proceedings unless otherwise agreed. At the discretion of the mediator, non-parties to the dispute may also be present.

(2) All parties, attorneys with settlement authority, representatives with settlement authority, and other necessary individuals shall be present at each mediation conference to facilitate settlement of a dispute unless excused by the court.

(3) A child involved in a domestic relations proceeding, by agreement of the parties or by order of the court, may be interviewed by the mediator out of the presence of the parties or attorneys.

(4) Mediation sessions are not open to the public.

(C) Confidential Statement of Case. Each side may submit to the mediator a confidential statement of the case not to exceed ten (10) pages, prior to a mediation conference, which shall include:

(1) the legal and factual contentions of the respective parties as to both liability and damages;

(2) the factors considered in arriving at the current settlement posture; and

(3) the status of the settlement negotiations to date.

A confidential statement of the case may be supplemented by damage brochures, videos, and other exhibits or evidence. The confidential statement of the case shall at all times be held privileged and confidential from other parties unless agreement to the contrary is provided to the mediator. In the mediation process, the mediator may meet jointly or separately with the parties and may express an evaluation of the case to one or more of the parties or their representatives. This evaluation may be expressed in the form of settlement ranges rather than exact amounts.

(D) Termination of Mediation. The mediator shall terminate mediation whenever the mediator believes that continuation of the process would harm or prejudice one or more of the parties or the children or whenever the ability or willingness of any party to participate meaningfully in mediation is so lacking that a reasonable agreement is unlikely. At any time after two (2) sessions have been completed, any party may terminate mediation. The mediator shall not state the reason for termination except when the termination is due to conflict of interest or bias on the part of the mediator, in which case another mediator may be assigned by the court. According to the procedures set forth herein, if the court finds after hearing that an agreement has been breached, sanctions may be imposed by the court.

(E) Report of Mediation: Status.

(1) Within ten (10) days after the mediation, the mediator shall submit to the court, without comment or recommendation, a report of mediation status. The report shall indicate that an agreement was or was not reached in whole or in part or that the mediation was extended by the parties. If the parties do not reach any agreement as to any matter as a result of the mediation, the mediator shall report the lack of any agreement to the court without comment or recommendation. With the consent of the parties, the mediator's report may also identify any pending motions or outstanding legal issues, discovery process, or other action by any party which, if resolved or completed, would facilitate the possibility of a settlement.

(2) If an agreement is reached, in whole or in part, it shall be reduced to writing and signed by the parties and their counsel. In domestic relations matters, the agreement shall then be filed with the court. If the agreement is complete on all issues, a joint stipulation of disposition shall be filed with the court. In all other matters, the agreement shall be filed with the court only by agreement of the parties.

(3) In the event of any breach or failure to perform under the agreement, upon motion, and after hearing, the court may impose sanctions, including entry of judgment on the agreement.

(F) Mediator's Preparation and Filing of Documents in Domestic Relations Cases. At the request and with the permission of all parties in a domestic relations case, a Mediator may prepare or assist in the preparation of documents as set forth in this paragraph (F).

The Mediator shall inform an unrepresented party that he or she may have an attorney of his or her choosing (1) be present at the mediation and/or (2) review any documents prepared during the mediation. The Mediator shall also review each document drafted during mediation with any unrepresented parties. During the review the Mediator shall explain to unrepresented parties that they should not view or rely on language in documents prepared by the Mediator

as legal advice. When the document(s) are finalized to the parties' and any counsel's satisfaction, and at the request and with the permission of all parties and any counsel, the Mediator may also tender to the court the documents listed below when the mediator's report is filed.

The Mediator may prepare or assist in the preparation of only the following documents:

(1) A written mediated agreement reflecting the parties' actual agreement, with or without the caption in the case, and "so ordered" language for the judge presiding over the parties' case;

(2) An order approving a mediated agreement, with the caption in the case, so long as the order is in the form of a document that has been adopted or accepted by the court in which the document is to be filed;

(3) A summary decree of dissolution, with the caption in the case, so long as the decree is in the form of a document that has been adopted or accepted by the court in which the document is to be filed and the summary decree reflects the terms of the mediated agreement;

(4) A verified waiver of final hearing, with the caption in the case, so long as the waiver is in the form of a document that has been adopted or accepted by the court in which the document is to be filed;

(5) A child support calculation, including a child support worksheet and any other required worksheets pursuant to the Indiana Child Support Guidelines or Parenting Time Guidelines, so long as the parties are in agreement on all the entries included in the calculations;

(6) An income withholding order, with the caption in the case, so long as the order is in the form of a document that has been adopted or accepted by the court in which the document is to be filed and the order reflects the terms of the mediated agreement.

Adopted Nov. 7, 1991, effective Jan. 1, 1992; Amended Dec. 23, 1996, effective March 1, 1997; amended Dec. 22, 2000, effective Jan. 1, 2001; amended Sept. 24, 2009, eff. Jan. 1, 2010.

Rule 2.8   Rules of Evidence

[Former Rule 2.8 relating to neutrals in subsequent proceedings, has been modified, renumbered and moved to Rule 7.6(B)]

With the exception of privileged communications, the rules of evidence do not apply in mediation, but factual information having a bearing on the question of damages should be supported by documentary evidence whenever possible.

Amended Dec. 23, 1996, effective March 1, 1997.

Rule 2.9   Discovery

Whenever possible, parties are encouraged to limit discovery to the development of information necessary to facilitate the mediation process. Upon stipulation by the parties or as ordered by the court, discovery may be deferred during mediation pursuant to Indiana Rules of Procedure, Trial Rule 26(C).

Adopted Nov. 7, 1991, effective Jan. 1, 1992; Amended Dec. 23, 1996, effective March 1, 1997.

Rule 2.10   Sanctions

Upon motion by either party and hearing, the court may impose sanctions against any attorney, or party representative who fails to comply with these mediation rules, limited to assessment of mediation costs and/or attorney fees relevant to the process.

Adopted Nov. 7, 1991, effective Jan. 1, 1992; Amended Dec. 23, 1996, effective March 1, 1997.

Rule 2.11   Confidentiality

Mediation shall be regarded as settlement negotiations as governed by Ind.Evidence Rule 408. For purposes of reference, Evid.R. 408 provides as follows:

Rule 408.   Compromise and Offers to Compromise

Evidence of (1) furnishing or offering or promising to furnish, or (2) accepting or offering or promising to accept a valuable consideration in compromising or attempting to compromise a claim, which was disputed as to either validity or amount, is not admissible to prove liability for or invalidity of the claim or its amount. Evidence of conduct or statements made in compromise negotiations is likewise not admissible. This rule does not require exclusion when the evidence is offered for another purpose, such as proving bias or prejudice of a witness, *negating a contention of undue delay, or proving an effort to obstruct a criminal investigation or prosecution. Compromise negotiations encompass alternative dispute resolution.*[1]

Mediation sessions shall be closed to all persons other than the parties of record, their legal representatives, and other invited persons.

Mediators shall not be subject to process requiring the disclosure of any matter discussed during the mediation, but rather, such matter shall be considered confidential and privileged in nature. The confidentiality requirement may not be waived by the parties, and an objection to the obtaining of testimony or physical evidence from mediation may be made by any party or by the mediators.

Adopted Nov. 7, 1991, effective Jan. 1, 1992; Amended Dec. 23, 1996, effective March 1, 1997.

[1] **Publisher's Note:** The Indiana Rules of Evidence were amended effective January 1, 2014, by order dated September 13, 2013. Evid.R. 408 now reads:

Rule 408.   Compromise Offers and Negotiations

(a) Prohibited Uses. Evidence of the following is not admissible on behalf of any party either to prove or disprove the validity or amount of a disputed claim or to impeach by a prior inconsistent statement or a contradiction:

(1) furnishing, promising, or offering, or accepting, promising to accept, or offering to accept a valuable consideration in order to compromise the claim; and

(2) conduct or a statement made during compromise negotiations about the claim. Compromise negotiations include alternative dispute resolution.

(b) Exceptions. The court may admit this evidence for another purpose, such as proving a witness's bias or prejudice, negating a contention of undue delay, or proving an effort to obstruct a criminal investigation or prosecution.

RULE 3.   ARBITRATION

Rule

Rule 3.1.   Agreement to Arbitrate

At any time fifteen (15) days or more after the period allowed for a peremptory change of venue under Trial Rule 76(B) has expired, the parties may file with the court an agreement to arbitrate wherein they stipulate whether arbitration is to be binding or nonbinding, whether the agreement extends to all of the case or is limited as to the issues subject to arbitration, and the procedural rules to be followed during the arbitration process. Upon approval, the agreement to arbitrate shall be noted on the Chronological Case Summary of the Case and placed in the Record of Judgments and Orders for the court.

Adopted Nov. 7, 1991, effective Jan. 1, 1992; Amended Dec. 23, 1996, effective March 1, 1997.

Rule 3.2   Case Status During Arbitration

During arbitration, the case shall remain on the regular docket and trial calendar of the court. In the event the parties agree to be bound by the arbitration decision on all issues, the case shall be removed from the trial calendar. During arbitration the court shall remain available to rule and assist in any discovery or pre-arbitration matters or motions.

Adopted Nov. 7, 1991, effective Jan. 1, 1992; Amended Dec. 23, 1996, effective March 1, 1997.

Rule 3.3.   Assignment of Arbitrators

Each court shall maintain a listing of lawyers engaged in the practice of law in the State of Indiana who are willing to serve as arbitrators. Upon assignment of a case to arbitration, the plaintiff and the defendant shall, pursuant to their stipulation, select one or more arbitrators from the court listing or the listing of another court in the state. If the parties agree that the case should be presented to one arbitrator and the parties do not agree on the arbitrator, then the court shall designate three (3) arbitrators for alternate striking by each side. The party initiating the lawsuit shall strike first. If the parties agree to an arbitration panel, it shall be limited to three (3) persons.

If the parties fail to agree on who should serve as members of the panel, then each side shall select one arbitrator and the court shall select a third. When there is more than one arbitrator, the arbitrators shall select among themselves a Chair of the arbitration panel. Unless otherwise agreed between the parties, and the arbitrators selected under this provision, the Court shall set the rate of compensation for the arbitrator. Costs of arbitration are to be divided equally between the parties and paid within thirty (30) days after the arbitration evaluation, regardless of the outcome. Any arbitrator selected may refuse to serve without showing cause for such refusal.

Adopted Nov. 7, 1991, effective Jan. 1, 1992; amended Dec. 23, 1996, effective March 1, 1997.

Rule 3.4. Arbitration Procedure

(A) Notice of Hearing. Upon accepting the appointment to serve, the arbitrator or the Chair of an arbitration panel shall meet with all attorneys of record to set a time and place for an arbitration hearing. (Courts are encouraged to provide the use of facilities on a regular basis during times when use is not anticipated, i.e. jury deliberation room every Friday morning.)

(B) Submission of Materials. Unless otherwise agreed, all documents the parties desire to be considered in the arbitration process shall be filed with the arbitrator or Chair and exchanged among all attorneys of record no later than fifteen (15) days prior to any hearing relating to the matters set forth in the submission. Documents may include medical records, bills, records, photographs, and other material supporting the claim of a party. In the event of binding arbitration, any party may object to the admissibility of these documentary matters under traditional rules of evidence; however, the parties are encouraged to waive such objections and, unless objection is filed at least five (5) days prior to hearing, objections shall be deemed waived. In addition, no later than five (5) days prior to hearing, each party may file with the arbitrator or Chair a pre-arbitration brief setting forth factual and legal positions as to the issues being arbitrated; if filed, pre-arbitration briefs shall be served upon the opposing party or parties. The parties may in their Arbitration Agreement alter the filing deadlines. They are encouraged to use the provisions of Indiana's Arbitration Act (IC 34–57–1–1 et seq.) and the Uniform Arbitration Act (IC 34–57–2–1 et seq.) to the extent possible and appropriate under the circumstances.

(C) Discovery. Rules of discovery shall apply. Thirty (30) days before an arbitration hearing, each party shall file a listing of witnesses and documentary evidence to be considered. The listing of witnesses

and documentary evidence shall be binding upon the parties for purposes of the arbitration hearing only. The listing of witnesses shall designate those to be called in person, by deposition and/or by written report.

(D) Hearing. Traditional rules of evidence need not apply with regard to the presentation of testimony. As permitted by the arbitrator or arbitrators, witnesses may be called. Attorneys may make oral presentation of the facts supporting a party's position and arbitrators are permitted to engage in critical questioning or dialogue with representatives of the parties. In this presentation, the representatives of the respective parties must be able to substantiate their statements or representations to the arbitrator or arbitrators as required by the Rules of Professional Conduct. The parties may be permitted to demonstrate scars, disfigurement, or other evidence of physical disability. Arbitration proceedings shall not be open to the public.

(E) Confidentiality. Arbitration proceedings shall be considered as settlement negotiations as governed by Ind.Evidence Rule 408. For purposes of reference, Evid.R. 408 provides as follows:

Rule 408. Compromise and Offers to Compromise

Evidence of (1) furnishing or offering or promising to furnish, or (2) accepting or offering or promising to accept a valuable consideration in compromising or attempting to compromise a claim, which was disputed as to either validity or amount, is not admissible to prove liability for or invalidity of the claim or its amount. Evidence of conduct or statements made in compromise negotiations is likewise not admissible. This rule does not require exclusion when the evidence is offered for another purpose, such as proving bias or prejudice of a witness, negating a contention of undue delay, or proving an effort to obstruct a criminal investigation or prosecution. Compromise negotiations encompass alternative dispute resolution.[1]

(F) Arbitration Determination. Within twenty (20) days after the hearing, the arbitrator or Chair shall file a written determination of the arbitration proceeding in the pending litigation and serve a copy of this determination on all parties participating in the arbitration. If the parties had submitted this matter to binding arbitration on all issues, the court shall enter judgment on the determination. If the parties had submitted this matter to binding arbitration on fewer than all issues, the court shall accept the determination as a joint stipulation by the parties and proceed with the litigation. If the parties had submitted the matter to nonbinding arbitration on any or all issues, they shall have twenty (20) days from the filing of the written determination to affirmatively reject in writing the arbitration determination. If a nonbinding arbitration determination is not rejected, the determination shall be entered as the judgment or accepted as a joint stipulation as appropriate. In the event a nonbinding arbitration determination is rejected, all documentary evidence will be returned to the parties and the determination and all acceptances and rejections shall be sealed and placed in the case file.

Adopted Nov. 7, 1991, effective Jan. 1, 1992; amended Dec. 23, 1996, effective March 1, 1997; amended Sept. 30, 2004, effective Jan. 1, 2005.

[1] **Publisher's Note:** The Indiana Rules of Evidence were amended effective January 1, 2014, by order dated September 13, 2013. Evid.R. 408 now reads:

Rule 408. *Compromise Offers and Negotiations*

*(a) **Prohibited Uses.** Evidence of the following is not admissible on behalf of any party either to prove or disprove the validity or amount of a disputed claim or to impeach by a prior inconsistent statement or a contradiction:*

(1) furnishing, promising, or offering, or accepting, promising to accept, or offering to accept a valuable consideration in order to compromise the claim; and

(2) conduct or a statement made during compromise negotiations about the claim. Compromise negotiations include alternative dispute resolution.

*(b) **Exceptions.** The court may admit this evidence for another purpose, such as proving a witness's bias or prejudice, negating a contention of undue delay, or proving an effort to obstruct a criminal investigation or prosecution.*

Rule 3.5. Sanctions

Upon motion by either party and hearing, the court may impose sanctions against any party or attorney who fails to comply with the arbitration rules, limited to the assessment of arbitration costs and/or attorney fees relevant to the arbitration process.

Adopted Nov. 7, 1991, effective Jan. 1, 1992; Amended Dec. 23, 1996, effective March 1, 1997.

RULE 4. MINI–TRIALS

Rule

Rule 4.1 Purpose

A mini-trial is a case resolution technique applicable in litigation where extensive court time could reasonably be anticipated. This process should be employed only when there is reason to believe that it will enhance the expeditious resolution of disputes and preserve judicial resources.

Adopted Nov. 7, 1991, effective Jan. 1, 1992; Amended Dec. 23, 1996, effective March 1, 1997.

Rule 4.2. Case Selection/Objection

At any time fifteen (15) days or more after the period allowed for peremptory change of venue under Trial Rule 76(B) has expired, a court may, on its own motion or upon motion of any party, select a civil case for a mini-trial. Within fifteen (15) days after notice of selection for a mini-trial, a party may object by filing a written objection specifying the grounds. The court shall promptly hear the objection and determine whether a mini-trial is possible or appropriate in view of the objection.

Adopted Nov. 7, 1991, effective Jan. 1, 1992; Amended Dec. 23, 1996, effective March 1, 1997.

Rule 4.3. Case Status Pending Mini-Trial

When a case has been assigned for a mini-trial, it shall remain on the regular docket and trial calendar of the court. The court shall remain available to rule and assist in any discovery or pre-mini-trial matter or motion.

Adopted Nov. 7, 1991, effective Jan. 1, 1992; Amended Dec. 23, 1996, effective March 1, 1997.

Rule 4.4. Mini-Trial Procedure

(A) Mini-Trial. The court will set a time and place for hearing and direct representatives with settlement authority to meet and allow attorneys for the parties to present their respective positions with regard to the litigation in an effort to settle the litigation. The parties may fashion the procedure as they deem appropriate.

(B) Report of Mini-Trial. At a time set by the court, the attorneys of record shall report to the court the results of the hearing and the possibility of settlement of the issues. Unless otherwise agreed by the parties, the results of the hearing shall not be binding.

(C) Confidentiality. Mini-trials shall be regarded as settlement negotiations as governed by Ind.Evidence Rule 408. For purposes of reference, Evid.R. 408 provides as follows:

Rule 408. *Compromise and Offers to Compromise*

Evidence of (1) furnishing or offering or promising to furnish, or (2) accepting or offering or promising to accept a valuable consideration in compromising or attempting to compromise a claim, which was disputed as to either validity or amount, is not admissible to prove liability for or invalidity of the claim or its amount. Evidence of conduct or statements made in compromise negotiations is likewise not admissible. This rule does not require exclusion when the evidence is offered for another purpose, such as proving bias or prejudice of a witness, negating a contention of undue delay, or proving an effort to obstruct a criminal investigation or prosecution. Compromise negotiations encompass alternative dispute resolution.[1]

Mini-trials shall be closed to all persons other than the parties of record, their legal representatives, and other invited persons. The participants in a mini-trial shall not be subject to process requiring the disclosure of any matter discussed during the mini-trial, but rather, such matter shall be considered confidential and privileged in nature. The confidentiality requirement may not be waived by the parties.

(D) Employment of Neutral Advisor. The parties may agree to employ a neutral acting as an advisor. The advisor shall preside over the proceeding and, upon request, give advisory opinions and rulings. Selection of the advisor shall be based upon the education, training and experience necessary to assist the parties in resolving their dispute. If the parties cannot by agreement select an advisor, each party shall submit to the court the names of two individuals qualified to serve in the particular dispute. Each side shall strike one name from the other party's list. The court shall then select an advisor from the remaining names. Unless otherwise agreed between the parties and the advisor, the court shall set the rate of compensation for the advisor. Costs of the mini-trial are to be divided equally between the parties and paid within thirty (30) days after conclusion of the mini-trial.

Adopted Nov. 7, 1991, effective Jan. 1, 1992; Amended Dec. 23, 1996, effective March 1, 1997.

[1] **Publisher's Note:** The Indiana Rules of Evidence were amended effective January 1, 2014, by order dated September 13, 2013. Evid.R. 408 now reads:

Rule 408. Compromise Offers and Negotiations

(a) Prohibited Uses. Evidence of the following is not admissible on behalf of any party either to prove or disprove the validity or amount of a disputed claim or to impeach by a prior inconsistent statement or a contradiction:

(1) furnishing, promising, or offering, or accepting, promising to accept, or offering to accept a valuable consideration in order to compromise the claim; and

(2) conduct or a statement made during compromise negotiations about the claim. Compromise negotiations include alternative dispute resolution.

(b) Exceptions. The court may admit this evidence for another purpose, such as proving a witness's bias or prejudice, negating a contention of undue delay, or proving an effort to obstruct a criminal investigation or prosecution.

Rule 4.5.   Sanctions

Upon motion by either party and hearing, the court may impose sanctions against a party or attorney who intentionally fails to comply with these mini-trial rules, limited to the assessment of costs and/or attorney fees relevant to the process.

Adopted Nov. 7, 1991, effective Jan. 1, 1992; Amended Dec. 23, 1996, effective March 1, 1997.

RULE 5.   SUMMARY JURY TRIALS

Rule 5.1   Purpose

The summary jury trial is a method for resolving cases in litigation when extensive court and trial time may be anticipated. This is a settlement process, and it should be employed only when there is reason to believe that a limited jury presentation may create an opportunity to quickly resolve the dispute and conserve judicial resources.

Adopted Nov. 7, 1991, effective Jan. 1, 1992; Amended Dec. 23, 1996, effective March 1, 1997.

Rule 5.2.   Case Selection

After completion of discovery, the resolution of dispositive motions, and the clarification of issues for determination at trial, upon written stipulation of the parties, the court may select any civil case for summary jury trial consideration.

Adopted Nov. 7, 1991, effective Jan. 1, 1992; Amended Dec. 23, 1996, effective March 1, 1997.

Rule 5.3.   Agreement of Parties

A summary jury trial proceeding will be conducted in accordance with the agreement of the parties as approved by the court. At a minimum, this agreement will include the elements set forth in this rule.

(A) Completion Dates. The agreement shall specify the completion dates for:

(1) providing notice to opposing counsel of witnesses whose testimony will be summarized and/or introduced at the summary jury trial, proposed issues for consideration at summary jury trial, proposed jury instructions, and verdict forms;

(2) hearing pre-trial motions; and

(3) conducting a final pre-summary jury trial conference.

(B) Procedures for Pre-summary Jury Trial Conference. The agreement will specify the matters to be resolved at pre-summary jury trial conference, including:

(1) matters not resolved by stipulation of counsel necessary to conduct a summary jury trial without numerous objections or delays for rulings on law;

(2) a final pre-summary jury trial order establishing procedures for summary jury trial, issues to be considered, jury instructions to be given, form of jury verdict to be rendered, and guidelines for presentation of evidence; and

(3) the firmly fixed time for the summary jury trial.

(C) Procedure/Presentation of Case. The agreement shall specify the procedure to be followed in the presentation of a case in the summary jury trial, including:

(1) abbreviated opening statements;

(2) summarization of anticipated testimony by counsel;

(3) the presentation of documents and demonstrative evidence;

(4) the requisite base upon which the parties can assert evidence; and

(5) abbreviated closing statements.

(D) Binding Verdict. The parties may stipulate that a unanimous verdict or a consensus verdict shall be deemed a final determination on the merits, and that judgment may be entered by the court.

Adopted Nov. 7, 1991, effective Jan. 1, 1992; Amended Dec. 23, 1996, effective March 1, 1997.

Rule 5.4.   Jury

Jurors for a summary jury trial will be summoned and compensated in normal fashion. Six (6) jurors will be selected in an expedited fashion. The jurors will be advised on the importance of their decision and their participation in an expedited proceeding. Following instruction, the jurors will retire and may be requested to return either a unanimous verdict, a consensus verdict, or separate and individual verdicts which list each juror's opinion about liability and damages. If a unanimous verdict or a consensus verdict is not reached in a period of time not to exceed two (2) hours, then the jurors shall be instructed to return separate and individual verdicts in a period of time not to exceed one (1) hour.

Adopted Nov. 7, 1991, effective Jan. 1, 1992; Amended Dec. 23, 1996, effective March 1, 1997.

Rule 5.5.   Post Determination Questioning

After the verdict has been rendered, the jury will be advised of the advisory nature of the decision and counsel for each side will be permitted to ask general questions to the jury regarding the decisions reached which would aid in the settlement of the controversy. Counsel shall not be permitted to ask specific questions of the jury relative to the persuasiveness of the form of evidence which would be offered by particular witnesses at trial, the effectiveness of particular exhibits, or other inquiries as could convert summary jury trials from a settlement procedure to a trial rehearsal.

Adopted Nov. 7, 1991, effective Jan. 1, 1992; Amended Dec. 23, 1996, effective March 1, 1997.

Rule 5.6.   Confidentiality

Summary jury trials shall be regarded as settlement negotiations as governed by Ind.Evidence Rule 408.   For purposes of reference, Evid.R. 408 provides as follows:

Rule 408.   Compromise and Offers to Compromise

Evidence of (1) furnishing or offering or promising to furnish, or (2) accepting or offering or prom-ising to accept a valuable consideration in compromising or attempting to compromise a claim, which was disputed as to either validity or amount, is not admissible to prove liability for or invalidity of the claim or its amount.   Evidence of conduct or statements made in compromise negotiations is likewise not admissible.   This rule does not require exclusion when the evidence is offered for another purpose, such as proving bias or prejudice of a witness, negating a contention of undue delay, or proving an effort to obstruct a criminal investigation or prosecution.   Compromise negotiations encompass alternative dispute resolution.[1]

Summary jury trials shall be closed to all persons other than the parties of record, their legal representatives, and other invited persons. The participants in a summary jury trial shall not be subject to process requiring the disclosure of any matter discussed during the summary jury trial, but rather, such matter shall be considered confidential and privileged in nature. The confidentiality requirement may not be waived by the parties.

Adopted Nov. 7, 1991, effective Jan. 1, 1992; Amended Dec. 23, 1996, effective March 1, 1997.

[1] **Publisher's Note**: The Indiana Rules of Evidence were amended effective January 1, 2014, by order dated September 13, 2013. Evid.R. 408 now reads:

Rule 408.   Compromise Offers and Negotiations

(a) Prohibited Uses. Evidence of the following is not admissible on behalf of any party either to prove or disprove the validity or amount of a disputed claim or to impeach by a prior inconsistent statement or a contradiction:

(1) furnishing, promising, or offering, or accepting, promising to accept, or offering to accept a valuable consideration in order to compromise the claim; and

(2) conduct or a statement made during compromise negotiations about the claim. Compromise negotiations include alternative dispute resolution.

(b) Exceptions. The court may admit this evidence for another purpose, such as proving a witness's bias or prejudice, negating a contention of undue delay, or proving an effort to obstruct a criminal investigation or prosecution.

Rule 5.7.   Employment Of Presiding Official

A neutral acting as a presiding official shall be an attorney in good standing licensed to practice in the state of Indiana. The parties by agreement may select a presiding official. However, unless otherwise agreed, the court shall provide to the parties a panel of three (3) individuals. Each party shall strike the name of one (1) individual from the panel list. The party initiating the lawsuit shall strike first. The remaining individual shall be named by the court as the presiding official. Unless otherwise agreed between the parties and the presiding official, the court shall set the rate of compensation for the presiding official. Costs of the summary jury trial are to be divided equally between the parties and are to be paid within thirty (30) days after the conclusion of the summary jury trial.

Adopted Dec. 23, 1996, effective March 1, 1997.

RULE 6.   PRIVATE JUDGES

Rule 6.1.   Case Selection

Pursuant to IC 33–38–10–3(c), upon the filing of a written joint petition and the written consent of a registered private judge, a civil case founded on contract, tort, or a combination of contract and tort, or involving a domestic relations matter shall be assigned to a private judge for disposition.

Adopted Nov. 7, 1991, effective Jan. 1, 1992; amended Dec. 23, 1996, effective March 1, 1997; amended Sept. 30, 2004, effective Jan. 1, 2005; amended Sept. 23, 2008, effective Jan. 1, 2009.

Rule 6.2 Compensation of Private Judge and County

As required by IC 33–38–10–8, the parties shall be responsible for the compensation of the private judge, court personnel involved in the resolution of the dispute, and the costs of facilities and materials. At the time the petition for appointment of a private judge is filed, the parties shall file their written agreement as required by this provision.

Adopted Nov. 7, 1991, effective Jan. 1, 1992; amended Dec. 23, 1996, effective March 1, 1997; amended Sept. 30, 2004, effective Jan. 1, 2005.

Rule 6.3.   Trial By Private Judge/Authority

(A) All trials conducted by a private judge shall be conducted without a jury. The trial shall be open to the public, unless otherwise provided by Supreme Court rule or statute.

(B) A person who serves as a private judge has, for each case heard, the same powers as the judge of a circuit court in relation to court procedures, in deciding the outcome of the case, in mandating the attendance of witnesses, in the punishment of contempt, in the enforcement of orders, in administering oaths, and in giving of all necessary certificates for the authentication of the record and proceedings.

Adopted Nov. 7, 1991, effective Jan. 1, 1992; Amended Dec. 23, 1996, effective March 1, 1997.

Rule 6.4.   Place Of Trial Or Hearing

As provided by IC 33–38–10–7, a trial or hearing in a case referred to a private judge may be conducted in any location agreeable to the parties, provided the location is posted in the Clerk's office at least three (3) days in advance of the hearing date.

Adopted Nov. 7, 1991, effective Jan. 1, 1992; amended Dec. 23, 1996, effective March 1, 1997; amended Sept. 30, 2004, effective Jan. 1, 2005.

Rule 6.5   Recordkeeping

All records in cases assigned to a private judge shall be maintained as any other public record in the court where the case was filed, including the Chronological Case Summary under the case number initially assigned to this case. Any judgment or designated order under Trial Rule 77 shall be entered in the Record of Judgments and Orders for the court where the case was filed and recorded in the Judgment Record for the Court as required by law.

Adopted Nov. 7, 1991, effective Jan. 1, 1992; Amended Dec. 23, 1996, effective March 1, 1997.

RULE 7.   CONDUCT AND DISCIPLINE
FOR PERSONS CONDUCTING ADR

Rule 7.0   Purpose

This rule establishes standards of conduct for persons conducting an alternative dispute resolution ("ADR") process recognized by ADR Rule 1, hereinafter referred to as "neutrals."

Adopted Dec. 6, 1994, effective Feb. 1, 1995; Amended December 23, 1996, effective March 1, 1997.

Rule 7.1.   Accountability And Discipline

A person who serves with leave of court or registers with the Commission pursuant to ADR Rule 2.3 consents to the jurisdiction of the Indiana Supreme Court Disciplinary Commission in the enforcement of these standards. The Disciplinary Commission, any court or the Continuing Legal Education Commission may recommend to the Indiana Supreme Court that a registered mediator be removed from its registry as a sanction for violation of these rules, or for other good cause shown.

Adopted Dec. 6, 1994, effective Feb. 1, 1995; Amended Dec. 23, 1996, effective March 1, 1997.

Rule 7.2. Competence

A neutral shall decline appointment, request technical assistance, or withdraw from a dispute beyond the neutral's competence.

Adopted Dec. 6, 1994, effective Feb. 1, 1995; Amended Dec. 23, 1996, effective March 1, 1997.

Rule 7.3. Disclosure and Other Communications

(A) A neutral has a continuing duty to communicate with the parties and their attorneys as follows:

(1) notify participants of the date, time, and location for the process, at least ten (10) days in advance, unless a shorter time period is agreed by the parties;

(2) describe the applicable ADR process or, when multiple processes are contemplated, each of the processes, including the possibility in nonbinding processes that the neutral may conduct private sessions;

(3) in domestic relations matters, distinguish the ADR process from therapy or marriage counseling;

(4) disclose the anticipated cost of the process;

(5) advise that the neutral does not represent any of the parties;

(6) disclose any past, present or known future

    (a) professional, business, or personal relationship with any party, insurer, or attorney involved in the process, and

    (b) other circumstances bearing on the perception of the neutral's impartiality;

(7) advise parties of their right to obtain independent legal counsel; and

(8) advise that any agreement signed by the parties constitutes evidence that may be introduced in litigation.

(B) A neutral may not misrepresent any material fact or circumstance nor promise a specific result or imply partiality.

(C) A neutral shall preserve the confidentiality of all proceedings, except where otherwise provided.

Adopted Dec. 6, 1994, effective Feb. 1, 1995; Amended Dec. 23, 1996, effective March 1, 1997; amended Dec. 22, 2000, effective Jan. 1, 2001.

Rule 7.4. Duties

(A) A neutral shall observe all applicable statutes, administrative policies, and rules of court.

(B) A neutral shall perform in a timely and expeditious fashion.

(C) A neutral shall be impartial and shall utilize an effective system to identify potential conflicts of interest at the time of appointment. After disclosure pursuant to ADR Rule 7.3(A)(6), a neutral may serve with the consent of the parties, unless there is a conflict of interest or the neutral believes the neutral can no longer be impartial, in which case a neutral shall withdraw.

(D) A neutral shall avoid the appearance of impropriety.

(E) A neutral may not have an interest in the outcome of the dispute, may not be an employee of any of the parties or attorneys involved in the dispute, and may not be related to any of the parties or attorneys in the dispute.

(F) A neutral shall promote mutual respect among the participants throughout the process.

Adopted Dec. 6, 1994, effective Feb. 1, 1995; Amended Dec. 23, 1996, effective March 1, 1997.

Rule 7.5. Fair, Reasonable and Voluntary Agreements

(A) A neutral shall not coerce any party.

(B) A neutral shall withdraw whenever a proposed resolution is unconscionable.

(C) A neutral shall not make any substantive decision for any party except as otherwise provided for by these rules.

Adopted Dec. 6, 1994, effective Feb. 1, 1995; Amended Dec. 23, 1996, effective March 1, 1997.

Rule 7.6. Subsequent Proceedings

(A) An individual may not serve as a neutral in any dispute on which another neutral has already been serving without first ascertaining that the current neutral has been notified of the desired change.

(B) A person who has served as a mediator in a proceeding may act as a neutral in subsequent disputes between the parties, and the parties may provide for a review of the agreement with the neutral on a periodic basis. However, the neutral shall decline to act in any capacity except as a neutral unless the subsequent association is clearly distinct from the issues involved in the alternative dispute resolution process. The neutral is required to utilize an effective system to identify potential conflict of interest at the time of appointment. The neutral may not subsequently act as an investigator for any court-ordered report or make any recommendations to the Court regarding the mediated litigation.

(C) When multiple ADR processes are contemplated, a neutral must afford the parties an opportunity to select another neutral for the subsequent procedures.

Adopted Dec. 6, 1994, effective Feb. 1, 1995; Amended Dec. 23, 1996, effective March 1, 1997.

Rule 7.7 Remuneration

(A) A neutral may not charge a contingency fee or base the fee in any manner on the outcome of the ADR process.

(B) A neutral may not give or receive any commission, rebate, or similar remuneration for referring any person for ADR services.

Adopted Dec. 6, 1994, effective Feb. 1, 1995; Amended Dec. 23, 1996, effective March 1, 1997.

RULE 8. OPTIONAL EARLY MEDIATION

Rule

Preamble
8.1   Who May Use Optional Early Mediation
8.2   Choice of Mediator
8.3   Agreement to Mediate
8.4   Preliminary Considerations
8.5   Good Faith
8.6   Settlement Agreement
8.7   Subsequent ADR and Litigation
8.8   Deadlines Not Changed

Form

A: Agreement for Optional Early Mediation

Preamble

The voluntary resolution of disputes in advance of litigation is a laudatory goal. Persons desiring the orderly mediation of disputes not in litigation may elect to proceed under this Rule.

Adopted Dec. 4, 1998, effective Jan. 1, 1999; amended July 19, 2002, effective Jan. 1, 2003.

Rule 8.1. Who May Use Optional Early Mediation

By mutual agreement, persons may use the provisions of this Rule to mediate a dispute not in litigation. Persons may participate in dispute resolution under this Rule with or without counsel.

Adopted Dec. 4, 1998, effective Jan. 1, 1999; amended July 19, 2002, effective Jan. 1, 2003.

Rule 8.2. Choice of Mediator

Persons participating in mediation under this Rule shall choose their own mediator and agree on the method of compensating the mediator. Mediation fees will be shared equally unless otherwise agreed. The mediator is governed by the standards of conduct provided in Alternative Dispute Resolution Rule 7.

Adopted Dec. 4, 1998, effective Jan. 1, 1999; amended July 19, 2002, effective Jan. 1, 2003.

Rule 8.3. Agreement to Mediate

Before beginning a mediation under this Rule, participants must sign a written Agreement To Mediate substantially similar to the one shown as Form A to these rules. This agreement must provide for confidentiality in accordance with Alternative Dispute Resolution Rule 2.11; it must acknowledge judicial immunity of the mediator equivalent to that provided in Alternative Dispute Resolution Rule 1.5; and it must require that all provisions of any resulting mediation settlement agreement must be written and signed by each person and any attorneys participating in the mediation.

Adopted Dec. 4, 1998, effective Jan. 1, 1999; amended July 19, 2002, effective Jan. 1, 2003.

Rule 8.4. Preliminary Considerations

The mediator and participating persons should schedule the mediation promptly. Before beginning the mediation session, each participating person is encouraged to provide the mediator with a written confidential summary of the nature of the dispute, as outlined in Alternative Dispute Resolution Rule 2.7(c).

Adopted Dec. 4, 1998, effective Jan. 1, 1999; amended July 19, 2002, effective Jan. 1, 2003.

Rule 8.5. Good Faith

In mediating their dispute, persons should participate in good faith. Information sharing is encouraged. However, the participants are not required to reach agreement.

Adopted Dec. 4, 1998, effective Jan. 1, 1999; amended July 19, 2002, effective Jan. 1, 2003.

Rule 8.6. Settlement Agreement

If an agreement is reached, to be enforceable, all agreed provisions must be put in writing and signed by each participant. This should be done promptly as the mediation concludes. A copy of the written agreement shall be provided to each participant.

Adopted Dec. 4, 1998, effective Jan. 1, 1999; amended July 19, 2002, effective Jan. 1, 2003.

Rule 8.7. Subsequent ADR and Litigation

If no settlement agreement is reached, put in writing, and signed by the participants, the participants may thereafter engage in litigation and/or further alternative dispute resolution.

Adopted Dec. 4, 1998, effective Jan. 1, 1999; amended July 19, 2002, effective Jan. 1, 2003.

Rule 8.8. Deadlines Not Changed

WARNING: Participation in optional early mediation under this Rule does not change the deadlines for beginning a legal action as provided in any applicable statute of limitations or in any requirement for advance notice of intent to make a claim (for example, for claims against government units under the Indiana Tort Claims Act).

Adopted Dec. 4, 1998, effective Jan. 1, 1999; amended Dec. 22, 2000, effective Jan. 1, 2001; amended July 19, 2002, effective Jan. 1, 2003.

Form A: Agreement for Optional Early Mediation

The undersigned persons, and their undersigned attorneys, if any, agree to mediate their dispute in accordance with the following:

1. _____ will serve as the mediator and will be compensated at the total hourly rate of $ ___. Each participating person is responsible for paying one-half of the mediator's fees and expenses unless

otherwise agreed in writing before or during the mediation.

2. The mediation will be conducted in accordance with Rule 8 — Optional Early Mediation of the Indiana Rules for Alternative Dispute Resolution.

3. Each participant understands and agrees that the mediator is neutral, that the mediator does not represent any participant, and that the mediator's conduct is governed by Alternative Dispute Resolution Rule 7.

4. Each participant agrees that the mediator shall have immunity in the same manner and to the same extent as a judge in the State of Indiana. Each party agrees that any attempt to challenge this immunity in any proceeding shall entitled the mediator to a judgment against the party asserting the challenge for the amount of any resulting judgment plus all reasonable attorney fees, court costs, and all other expenses incurred by the mediator as a result of the challenge.

5. The mediation shall be regarded as settlement negotiations and shall be subject to the same confidentiality protections as provided in Alternative Dispute Resolution Rule 2.11. The participants and the mediator understand and agree that the mediator cannot be compelled to testify regarding any matter discussed during the mediation, which shall be considered confidential and privileged. It is also agreed that the confidentiality requirement may not be waived by any participant or mediator.

6. The participants may agree to settle all or part of the dispute. For a settlement agreement to be binding and enforceable, however, all agreed provi-

sions must be put in writing and signed by each participant and each participating attorney.

7. The mediation shall be conducted in accordance with Indiana Alternative Dispute Resolution Rule 2.7.

8. If the optional early mediation does not result in an agreed full settlement of the dispute, the participants may later use mediation, before or after the filing of any related law suit, and may use the same or a different mediator, as the participants may agree.

9. Either participant may terminate the mediation at any time by a letter to the mediator and a copy to the other participants in the mediation.

10. The mediator may terminate the mediation at any time because of an impasse or if for any reason the mediator deems it improper, unproductive, or unconscionable to continue. The mediator may disclose only to the participants and any participating attorneys the reason(s) for terminating the mediation, but such disclosure is optional at the mediator's sole discretion.

11. The parties agree to mediate in good faith but are not required to reach an agreement.

Participant	date	Participant	date
Attorney (if any)	date	Attorney (if any)	date

Mediator   date

Adopted Dec. 4, 1998, effective Jan. 1, 1999. Amended July 19, 2002, effective Jan. 1, 2003; amended effective May 3, 2006.

INDIANA TAX COURT RULES

Effective July 1, 1986

Including Amendments Received Through November 1, 2013

Rule 1. Scope of the rules

These rules govern the procedure and practice in all actions jurisdictionally cognizable in the Indiana Tax Court. They shall be construed to secure the just, speedy and inexpensive determination of every action. Except to the extent these rules are clearly inconsistent with the Indiana Rules of Trial Procedure ("Trial Rules"), those Trial Rules shall apply to actions in the Tax Court, but nothing herein or in the Trial Rules shall be deemed to extend the jurisdiction of the Tax Court with respect to persons, actions, or claims over which it does not otherwise have authority. In the case of an appeal from a determination of a probate court, the Indiana Rules of Appellate Procedure shall apply.

Amended Dec. 21, 2001, effective Jan. 1, 2002.

Rule 2. One form of action

(A) In the Indiana Tax Court, there shall be one form of action in the nature of a civil action to be known as an "original tax appeal."

(B) An original tax appeal is an action that arises under the tax laws of the State of Indiana by which an initial judicial appeal of a final determination of the Department of State Revenue, the Indiana Board of Tax Review, or the Department of Local Government Finance is sought.

Amended Dec. 21, 2001, effective Jan. 1, 2002.

Rule 3. Commencement of an action

(A) Appeals from final determinations of the Department of State Revenue. An original tax appeal from a final determination of the Department of State Revenue is commenced by filing a petition in the Tax Court.

(B) Appeals from final determinations of the Indiana Board of Tax Review. An original tax appeal from a final determination of the Indiana Board of Tax Review is commenced by filing a petition in the Tax Court and filing a written notice of appeal with the Indiana Board of Tax Review. If the petitioner does not include in the petition a request that the Indiana Board of Tax Review prepare a certified copy of the agency record, the petitioner shall file a separate request for such record under Section (E) of this rule.

(C) Appeals from final determinations of the Department of Local Government Finance. An original tax appeal from a final determination of the Department of Local Government Finance is commenced by filing a petition in the Tax Court.

(D) Copies of petitions. Copies of the petition required under Section B of this rule shall be served upon those persons designated by any applicable statute. A petitioner complies with this rule by serving a copy of the petition in the manner provided by Trial Rule 5(B). Copies of the petition shall be served upon public officers only in their official capacities.

(E) Filing the record of judicial review. In original tax appeals filed under Section (B) of this rule, the petitioner shall request the Indiana Board of Tax Review to prepare a certified copy of the agency record within thirty (30) days after filing the petition. A request included as part of the petition filed under Section (B)(7) of this rule satisfies this requirement. The petitioner shall transmit a certified copy of the record to the Tax Court within thirty (30) days after having received notification from the Indiana Board of Tax Review that the record has been prepared.

(F) Enjoining the collection of a tax. If the petitioner wishes to enjoin the collection of a tax pending the original tax appeal, there must be included with the original tax appeal a petition to enjoin the collection of the tax, which petition must include a summary of the issues that the petitioner will raise in the original tax appeal, and the equitable considerations for which the Tax Court should order the collection of the tax to be enjoined.

(G) Documents and Information Excluded from Public Access and Confidential Pursuant to Administrative Rule 9(G)(1). Documents and information excluded from public access pursuant to Administrative Rule 9(G)(1) shall be filed in accordance with Trial Rule 5(G).

Amended Dec. 21, 2001, effective Jan. 1, 2002; amended Sept. 30, 2004, effective Jan. 1, 2005; amended Sept. 9, 2008, effective Jan. 1, 2009.

Rule 4. Jurisdiction over respondents and service of process

(A) Appeals from final determinations of the Department of State Revenue and the Department of Local Government Finance.

(1) Notwithstanding anything to the contrary herein, the Tax Court acquires jurisdiction over the Department of State Revenue or the Department of Local Government Finance upon the filing of a petition with the clerk of the Tax Court seeking to set aside a final determination of either of such state agencies, as the case may be. The clerk of the Tax Court shall promptly transmit copies of a petition filed in the Tax Court to the Attorney General and to the state agency named as the respondent in such petition and shall state in accompanying transmittal letters: (1) the date on which the petition was filed; (2) the date on which the petition is being mailed to the Attorney General and the respondent state agency; and (3) the time within which these rules require a responsive pleading. Nothing in this rule shall relieve a party from complying with statutory requirements for bringing an original tax appeal.

(2) In original tax appeals of final determinations of the Department of State Revenue or the Department of Local Government Finance, it shall not be necessary to serve summons on the Attorney General, the Department of State Revenue, or the Department of Local Government Finance. Service of summons in accordance with the Trial Rules shall be required for the Tax Court to acquire jurisdiction over any other persons; such service shall be made as provided in Trial Rule 4.11.

(B) Appeals from final determinations of the Indiana Board of Tax Review.

(1) In original tax appeals of final determinations of the Indiana Board of Tax Review, the Tax Court acquires jurisdiction over a party or person who under these rules commences or joins in the original tax appeal, is served with summons or enters an appearance, or who is subjected to the power of the Tax Court under any other law.

(2) In original tax appeals initiated by taxpayers, the named respondent shall be the person or persons designated by statute as parties to judicial review of final determinations of the Indiana Board of Tax Review.

(3) In original tax appeals initiated by a government official or entity, the named respondent shall be the taxpayer who was a party to the proceeding before the Indiana Board of Tax Review.

(4) Service of summons shall be required only with respect to the named respondent and any other person whom the petitioner seeks to join as a party. If the Department of Local Government Finance is a named respondent, service of summons shall be made upon the Commissioner of the Department of Local Government Finance. Service of summons shall be made in accordance with the Trial Rules.

(C) Public Officers in their Official Capacities. Public officers shall only be made parties to original tax appeals in their official capacities.

(D) Substitution of Parties.

(1) When a public officer who is made a party to an original tax appeal in his or her official capacity dies, resigns or otherwise no longer holds the public office, the officer's successor is automatically substituted as a party.

(2) A party shall, by notice filed with the Clerk, advise the Court of the succession in office of any party. The failure of any party to file a notice shall not affect the party's substantive rights.

(3) The death or incompetence of any party on appeal shall not cause the original tax appeal to abate. Successor parties may be substituted for the deceased or incompetent parties.

Amended Dec. 15, 1995, effective Feb. 1, 1996; amended Dec. 21, 2001, effective Jan. 1, 2002; amended effective April 2, 2008.

Rule 5. Time

Time for Response to Petition. In a case in which the clerk of the Tax Court has served a petition in an original tax appeal without service of summons, the period for filing a response to such petition by the State Agency so served shall be thirty (30) days after the mailing of the clerk's transmittal letter. In a case governed by Rule 4(B), the period for filing a response to a petition shall be thirty (30) days after the service of the petition and summons on a named respondent.

Amended Dec. 21, 2001, effective Jan. 1, 2002.

Rule 6. Joinder and intervention

(A) Joinder of Taxpayer in Tax Court Appeals by Government Organization or Representative. In an original tax appeal in the Tax Court brought by a governmental organization or official representative, any person or persons whose liability for, or right to a refund of, taxes would be directly affected by the outcome of such appeal may intervene in the action pursuant to Trial Rule 24 if not already named as a respondent or joined under Trial Rule 20.

(B) Right of Intervention. The Department of Local Government Finance shall have the right to intervene in original tax appeals of final determinations of the Indiana Board of Tax Review when the interpretation of its rules is at issue. This right of intervention shall not extend to settlement of the litigation between the original parties to the tax appeal unless the Department of Local Government Finance was a party to the action before the Indiana Board of Tax Review.

Amended Dec. 21, 2001, effective Jan. 1, 2002.

Rule 7. Failure to make or cooperate in discovery

(A) **Appropriate Court.** An application for an order to a party to compel discovery may be made to the Tax Court, or alternatively, on matters relating to a deposition or an order under Trial Rule 34, to a court in the county where the deposition is being taken or where compliance is to be made. Application for an order to compel discovery directed to a deponent who is not a party shall be made to a court in the county where the deposition is being taken or to the Tax Court.

(B) **Sanctions by the Court in the County Where Deposition Is Taken or by the Tax Court.** If a defendant fails to be sworn or to answer a question after being directed to do so by the court in the county in which the deposition is being taken or by the Tax Court, the failure may be considered a contempt of that court.

Rule 8. Evidentiary hearings

(A) All evidentiary hearings shall be conducted in Allen County, Jefferson County, Lake County, Marion County, St. Joseph County, Vanderburgh County or Vigo County. A taxpayer who appeals to the Tax Court shall, at the time the appeal is filed, file a written election as to the county in which the evidentiary hearings in the appeal shall be conducted. If the taxpayer is an appellee in an appeal to the Tax Court, the taxpayer shall file such written election within thirty (30) days after receiving notice of the appeal. If no such written election is timely filed, evidentiary hearings shall be conducted in Marion County unless otherwise ordered by the Court.

(B) All original tax appeals shall be tried to the Court without a jury.

Rule 9. Subpoena

(A) **Subpoena for Taking Depositions—Place of Examination.** Proof of service of a notice to take a deposition as provided in Trial Rules 30(B) and 31(A) constitutes a sufficient authorization for the issuance by the Tax Court or by the clerk of court for the county in which the deposition is to be taken of subpoenas for the persons named or described therein. The subpoena may command the person to whom it is directed to produce designated books, papers, documents, or tangible things which constitute or contain matters within the scope of the examination permitted by Trial Rule 26(B), but in that event the

subpoena will be subject to the provisions of Trial Rules 26(C) and 45(B).

(B) **Subpoena for a Hearing or Trial.** At the request of any party, subpoenas for attendance at a hearing or trial shall be issued by the clerk of the Tax Court when requested, or, in the case of a subpoena for the taking of a deposition, by the clerk of the Tax Court or by the clerk of the court in the county in which the deposition is being taken. A subpoena may be served at any place within the state; and when permitted by the laws of the United States, this or another state or foreign country, the Court upon proper application and cause shown may authorize the service of a subpoena outside the state in accordance with and as permitted by such law.

(C) **Contempt.** Failure by any person without adequate excuse to obey a subpoena served upon him may be deemed in contempt of the Tax Court or the court from which the subpoena was issued, or of the court of the county where the witness was required thereunder to appear or act. The attendance of all witnesses when duly subpoenaed, and to whom fees have been paid or tendered as required by law may be enforced by attachment.

Amended Dec. 21, 2001, effective Jan. 1, 2002.

Rule 10. Findings by the court

(A) **Effect.** The Court shall determine the facts and judgment shall be entered thereon pursuant to Trial Rule 58. The Court shall render its decisions in writing. The Court shall make special findings of fact without request

(1) in granting or refusing preliminary injunctions, including injunctions against collection of any tax;

(2) in making any final decision after trial; and

(3) in any other case provided by these rules or by statute.

The Court on appeal shall not set aside the findings or judgment of the Tax Court unless clearly erroneous, and due regard shall be given to the opportunity of the Tax Court to judge the credibility of the witnesses. The findings of a master shall be considered as findings of the Court to the extent that the Court adopts them. If an opinion or memorandum of decision is filed, it will be sufficient if the findings of fact and conclusions appear therein. Findings of fact are unnecessary on decisions of motions under Trial Rules 12 or 56 or any other motion except as provided in Trial Rules 41(B) (dismissal) and 59(J) (motion to correct errors).

Rule 11. Court and clerk

(A) **Tax Court Always Open.** The Tax Court shall be deemed always open for the purpose of filing any pleadings or other proper paper, of issuing and returning any process contemplated by these rules, and of making and directing all interlocutory motions, orders and rules. Terms of court shall not be recognized.

(B) Evidentiary Hearings—Orders in Chambers. All evidentiary hearings in connection with an original tax appeal shall be conducted in open court in a regular court or hearing room in the county designated for such hearing by the taxpayer party thereto. In the absence of such designation, such hearings shall be conducted in Marion County. All other acts or proceedings may be done or conducted by the judge in chambers without the attendance of the clerk or other Court officials and at any other place within the State.

(C) Clerk, Clerk's Office and Orders by Clerk. The clerk of the Court is the clerk of the Supreme Court and the Court of Appeals and the address of the clerk's office is State House, Room 216, Indianapolis, Indiana 46204. Except as may be otherwise provided by law, the clerk's office with the clerk or a deputy in attendance shall be open during business hours on all days except Saturdays, Sundays and legal holidays. All motions and applications in the clerk's office for issuing process, for entering defaults or judgments by default, and for other proceedings which do not require allowance or order of the Court are grantable of course by the clerk; but the clerk's action may be suspended or altered or rescinded by the Court upon cause shown.

(D) Notice of Orders or Judgments. The clerk shall give notice of rulings, orders or judgments and with the effect as provided in Trial Rule 72(D).

Amended Sept. 21, 2010, effective Jan. 1, 2011.

Rule 12. Hearings and motions

(A) The judge shall periodically establish times and places, at intervals sufficiently frequent for the prompt dispatch of business at each of the counties designated for the hearing of evidence in original tax appeals, at which motions requiring notice and hearing may be heard and disposed of; but the judge at any time or place and on such notice, if any, as the judge considers reasonable may make order for the advancement, conduct and hearing of actions. To expedite its business, the Court may direct the submission and determination of motions without oral hearing upon brief written statements or reasons in support and opposition, or direct and permit hearings by telephone conference call with all attorneys or other similar means of communications.

(B) Every motion shall be accompanied by a proposed form of order and except in motions for continuance shall include a memorandum of law or a statement of points and authorities, explaining how relevant authorities support the contentions of the moving party.

(C) In matters other than motions for summary judgment (governed by Trial Rule 56), an opposing party may file a written memorandum of law or a statement of authority in response to the matters raised in any motion not later than 10 days from the date of service of the motion, or within such shorter or longer time as the Court may allow.

(D) A reply memorandum, if any, shall be filed within seven days of the service of the responding memorandum, or within such shorter or longer time as the Court may allow.

(E) Oral hearings shall be conducted on motions in the discretion of the Court if requested by either party, or when ordered by the Court. In the motion or response, a party requesting oral hearing shall specify the amount of time required for hearing, whether appearance by telecommunications is requested, the names and telephone numbers of all parties served with the motion or response, and whether official court reporting services are requested for the hearing.

(F) When a petition to enjoin the collection of a tax pending the original tax appeal is filed pursuant to IC 33-3-5-11(b), a hearing will be held as promptly as possible upon request of either party.

(G) If exigent circumstances are present, the petitioning party may wish to consult Trial Rule 65(B).

Amended Nov. 17, 1986, effective Jan. 1, 1987.

Rule 13. Venue

The Tax Court has exclusive statewide jurisdiction over all original tax appeals, and venue of all original tax appeals shall lie only in the Tax Court.

Rule 14. Books and records kept by the clerk and entries

(A) Pleadings and Papers—Where Filed and Entered. All pleadings, papers and rulings, including final judgments and appealable orders, shall be filed with the clerk of the Court who shall file and keep them under a consecutive file number assigned by the clerk to each case.

(B) Docket Book. The clerk of the Court shall keep a docket book of such form that the file number of each case or proceeding shall be noted on the folio of the docket whereon the first entry of the action is made. All papers filed with or transmitted to the clerk, all process issued and returns made thereon, all appearances, orders, verdicts, judgments, enforcement proceedings, execution and returns thereon shall be entered chronologically in the docket on the folio assigned to the action and shall be marked with its file number and the date of filing. Such entries shall be brief but shall show the nature of each paper filed or writ issued and the bare substance of each order or judgment of the Court and of the returns showing execution of process. Each entry shall show the date the filing, return or entry was made, including the date of judgment or order was entered.

(C) Indexes. The clerk under the direction of the judge shall keep suitable indexes of the docket maintained by him.

(D) Calendars. There shall be prepared under the direction of the judge calendars of all actions ready for trial.

(E) Order Book. The clerk shall maintain an order book in such form as the judge may prescribe or may have prescribed by local or other rule. Every ruling, order, or judgment of the judge should be entered or filed in such book verbatim for each day and the judge shall sign the book as to such day's entries. The order book may include such other matters as the judge may direct and shall include such matters as may be required by local or other rule.

(F) Replacing Lost Papers. If an original pleading or paper filed with the clerk be lost, or be withheld by any person, the Court may authorize a copy thereof to be filed and used instead of the original.

(G) Method of Keeping Records. Under the direction of the Supreme Court or the judge, the clerk may, notwithstanding the foregoing sections, keep records in any suitable media, including without limitation, electromagnetic, photographic, electric, electronic, electrostatic and paper media or combinations thereof.

Rule 15. Special judge—Selection

If the judge of the Tax Court is disqualified from hearing a case or is incapable of exercising judicial duties with respect to a case, the Chief Justice of the State of Indiana shall appoint a judge *pro tempore* to sit in place of the disqualified or absent judge.

Rule 16. Small Tax Cases

(A) General. The Small Tax Case Rules set forth the special provisions which are to be applied in the Indiana Tax Court to small tax cases as required by IC 33–3–5–12. Except as otherwise provided in the Small Tax Case Rules, the Indiana Rules for Small Claims are also applicable to such cases. To the extent not inconsistent therewith, the Indiana Tax Court Rules will apply. The term "small tax case" means a case which involves a claim for refund from the Department of State Revenue that does not exceed $5,000 for any year.

(B) Notice of Claim. The notice of claim to be used under Small Claims Rule 2 shall contain:

(1) the name of the Tax Court;

(2) the name, address and telephone number of claimant;

(3) a designation of the type of tax the claim involves;

(4) a statement of the taxable period involved;

(5) a brief statement of the nature of the claim;

(6) a statement of the amount of tax at issue; and

(7) any additional information which may facilitate proper service or processing of the claim.

(C) Manner of Service. For the purpose of service, the notice of claim shall also be considered to be the summons. A copy of the notice of claim shall be served upon the Attorney General by registered or certified mail, return receipt requested.

(D) Appearances for Governmental Defendants. The Attorney General shall be deemed to have entered an appearance for and on behalf of the governmental defendant or defendants.

Adopted Nov. 30, 1989, effective Jan. 1, 1990; Amended Dec. 21, 2001, effective Jan. 1, 2002.

Rule 17. Judgment

All judgments shall be incorporated in written memorandum decisions by the court. Unless specifically designated "For Publication," such written memorandum decisions shall not be published and shall not be regarded as precedent nor cited before any court except for the purpose of establishing the defense of res judicata, collateral estoppel, or the law of the case. Judgment shall be subject to review as prescribed by relevant Indiana rules and statutes.

Adopted Nov. 30, 1989, as Rule 16(E), eff. Jan. 1, 1990; amended Dec. 5, 1994, eff. Feb. 1, 1995; renumbered as Rule 17, eff. Jan. 1, 2002.

Rule 18. Mediation

(A) Purpose. The purpose of a mediation of any matter before the Tax Court is set forth in Rule 2.1 of the Indiana Rules for Alternative Dispute Resolution, which is hereby incorporated by reference.

(B) Mediation Order. At any time, the Tax Court may on its own motion or upon motion of any party refer an original tax appeal to mediation. Any original tax appeal referred to mediation shall be subject to this Rule unless the parties by agreement elect to be subject to the Indiana Rules for Alternative Dispute Resolution without regard to this Rule. At all times during the course of any mediation the appeal remains within the jurisdiction of the Tax Court.

(C) Case Selection/Objection to Mediation Order. After a case has been referred for mediation, a party may object by filing a written objection with the Tax Court within fifteen (15) days after the order of referral is entered. The party must specify the grounds for objection. The Tax Court shall promptly consider the objection and any response and determine whether the litigation should then be mediated or not. In this decision, the Tax Court shall consider the willingness of the parties to mutually resolve their dispute, the ability of the parties to participate in the mediation process, the need for discovery and the extent to which it has been conducted, and any other factors which affect the potential for fair resolution of the dispute through the mediation process. If a case is ordered for mediation, the case shall remain on the court docket and the trial calendar.

(D) Selection of Mediator/Costs of Mediation. Within fifteen (15) days of an order referring a case to mediation, the parties may choose a mediator from the pool of senior judges who have been certified by the Indiana Judicial Nominating Commission. In the event a mediator is not selected by agreement, the court will designate three (3) senior judges who have been certified by the Indiana Judicial Nominating Commission who are willing to mediate cases before the Tax Court. Alternately, each side shall strike the name of one mediator. The side initiating the lawsuit will strike first. The mediator remaining after the striking process will be deemed the selected mediator. The senior judge serving as the mediator shall be paid by the Division of State Court Administration pursuant to Supreme Court Administrative Rule 5. The senior judge serving as the mediator need not be a registered mediator as provided in Indiana Rules for Alternative Dispute Resolution, rule 2. Mediation shall occur at no cost to the parties.

(E) Mediation Procedure, Rules of Evidence, Discovery, Sanctions, Confidentiality. The mediation shall be conducted pursuant to the procedures, rules of evidence, discovery, sanctions, and confidentiality provisions set forth in Rules 2.7, 2.8, 2.9, 2.10, and 2.11 of the Indiana Rules for Alternative Dispute Resolution which are hereby incorporated by reference; provided, however, that the provision of Rule 2.7(B)(2) requiring attorneys or representatives of a party with settlement authority to be present at each mediation shall not apply.

(F) Termination of Mediation. The mediation shall terminate as provided in Rule 2.7(D) of the Indiana Rules for Alternative Dispute Resolution as incorporated by reference in (E) above provided that the Tax Court may, at any time, upon good cause shown and upon a hearing on the issue, terminate the mediation.

Adopted as Rule 16, eff. July 1, 1986; renumbered as Rule 17, eff. Jan. 1, 1990; renumbered as Rule 18, eff. Jan. 1, 2002. Amended Sept. 9, 2008, eff. Jan. 1, 2009.

Rule 19. Special rules

The judge of the Tax Court may from time to time make and amend rules governing practice before it not inconsistent with these rules. In all cases not provided for by rule, the Tax Court may regulate its practice in any manner not inconsistent with these rules. Two (2) copies of all special rules shall be furnished to the clerk and to the Office of the Administrator of State Courts.

Adopted as Rule 16, eff. July 1, 1986; renumbered as Rule 17, eff. Jan. 1, 1990; renumbered as Rule 18, eff. Jan. 1, 2002. Amended Sept. 9, 2008, eff. Jan. 1, 2009.

Rule 20. Effective date

These rules shall be effective as of July 1, 1986, and they shall govern all proceedings in the Tax Court, whether originally commenced in the Tax Court or in another court.

Adopted as Rule 17, eff. July 1, 1986; renumbered as Rule 18, eff. Jan. 1, 1990; renumbered as Rule 19, eff. Jan. 1, 2002. Amended Sept. 9, 2008, effective Jan. 1, 2009.

Rule 21. Title

These rules may be known as the Indiana Tax Court Rules.

Adopted as Rule 19, eff. July 1, 1986; amended Nov. 30, 1989, effective Jan. 1, 1990; renumbered as Rule 20, eff. Jan. 1, 2002; renumbered as Rule 21, eff. Jan. 1, 2009.

NOTICE OF APPEARANCE

IN THE

INDIANA TAX COURT

Case No.

_____)
)
Petitioner,   )
)
v.   )
)
)
)
_____)
)
Respondent.   )

NOTICE OF APPEARANCE

[Party/amicus name], [by counsel/pro se], serves notice of the following [change in] information for purposes of this [appeal/review]:

1. [If this notice is filed by the party initiating the appeal or review, the first rhetorical paragraph must designate the type of tax that is the subject of this appeal. If a review of property tax is sought, specify whether personal property taxes or real property taxes are the subject. Also specify the issue concerned in the appeal, i.e. whether the appeal is concerned with an assessed value or other issue.]

2. [The next rhetorical paragraph must state the relationship of the filing party to the appeal or review; i.e., whether the filing party is the petitioner, respondent, an entity seeking amicus curiae status, or a party not participating in the appeal but seeking to be placed on the service and notice list, etc. Note that any party seeking amicus curiae status must indicate whether amicus curiae status has been previously sought and either granted or refused in connection with this proceeding.]

3. [The next rhetorical paragraph must state the date of the final determination by the administrative agency involved. The character of the determination should also be stated. For example: "This cause is an appeal from a final determination entered by the [agency] on January 2, 1995. "]

4. [As applicable, the name, address, attorney number, telephone number, FAX number, and computer address of the attorney representing the party filing the appearance form. Note that the names and addresses on the appearance form will be used for service from the Clerk's office and will be the names and addresses printed on any written opinion issued by the Indiana Tax Court. A party is reminded of its ongoing obligation to advise the Indiana Tax Court of any changes in appearance information.]

5. [Which, if any, of the listed attorneys are requesting service of orders and opinions by FAX pursuant to Ind.Appellate Rule 26. Service by FAX must be requested in writing on an appearance form.]

6. [As applicable, the name, address, and telephone number of the party filing the appearance form.]

7. [As applicable (i.e. if an appeal from a probate or trial court), or if not previously provided by another party: the name of the lower tribunal from which the appeal or review is sought, the lower cause number, and the name of the presiding judge or agency.]

8. [As applicable, and if not provided by another party: the name, address, and telephone number of the court reporter responsible for the preparation of the transcript.]

signature _____
Attorney or pro se litigant's name,
address and telephone information,
attorney number, party represented

CERTIFICATE OF SERVICE

[The name of each party served with this form should be identified, along with the date and method of service, and the name and signature of the person responsible for initiating service.]

Adopted effective March 13, 1995; Amended Dec. 21, 2001, effective Jan. 1, 2002.

VERIFIED PETITION

IN THE

INDIANA TAX COURT

Case No. ____

_____,)
)
Petitioner,   )
)
v.   )
)
_____,)
)
Respondent.   )

VERIFIED PETITION FOR JUDICIAL REVIEW
OF A FINAL DETERMINATION OF
THE INDIANA BOARD OF TAX REVIEW

The Petitioner, [Name of Petitioner], [with counsel/pro se], ("Petitioner"), for its Petition against Respondent, [Name of Respondent], brings this petition for judicial review of a final determination of the Indiana Board of Tax Review ("Board") and in support thereof alleges as follows:

1. [The name and mailing address of the Petitioner].

2. [The name and mailing address of the Board].

3. [Identification of the Board's final determination at issue, together with a copy, summary, or brief description of the final determination (the "Board's Determination")].

4. [Identification of all persons, as defined in IC 4–21.5–1–11, that were parties to any proceedings that led to the final determination of the Indiana Board of Tax Review].

5. [Specific facts to demonstrate that the Petitioner is entitled to obtain judicial review of the Board's Determination under IC 4–21.5–5–2 including:

a. The standing of the Petitioner under IC 4–21.5–5–3.

b. The exhaustion of the Petitioner's administrative remedies under IC 4–21.5–5–4.

c. The timeliness of the Petitioner's Petition under the applicable statutes.

d. A statement that the Petitioner shall transmit a certified record of the administrative proceedings to the Indiana Tax Court within thirty (30) days after having received notification from the Board that the certified record has been prepared in accordance with IC 6–1.1–15–6.

e. Any other statutory conditions for the availability of judicial review].

6. [At the election of the petitioner, a request that the Indiana Board of Tax Review prepare a certified copy of the agency record. If the petitioner does not include the request in the petition, the petitioner must file a separate request for the record under Rule 3(E).]

7. [Specific facts to demonstrate that the Petitioner has been prejudiced by one or more of the grounds described in IC 33–3–5–14.8].

WHEREFORE, the Petitioner prays for judicial review of the Board's Determination, that the same be vacated and set aside, and that an order be issued remanding this case to the Indiana Board of Tax Review for redetermination in accordance with the Order of this Court, and for all further just and proper relief [and further recite any additional or different relief, specifying the type and extent of relief requested].

/s/

Attorney's Name, Address

and

Indiana Attorney Number

I (we) affirm, under the penalties for perjury, that the foregoing representation(s) is (are) true.

/s/

Adopted Dec. 21, 2001, effective Jan. 1, 2002.

INDIANA RULES OF APPELLATE PROCEDURE

Adopted February 4, 2000, Effective January 1, 2001

Including Amendments Received Through November 1, 2013

APPENDIX SAMPLE FORMS

PILOT PROJECT FOR EXPLORING THE USE OF AN AUDIO/VISUAL RECORD ON APPEAL

TITLE I. SCOPE, DEFINITIONS, FORMS

Rule 1. Scope

These Rules shall govern the practice and procedure for appeals to the Supreme Court and the Court of Appeals. The Court may, upon the motion of a party or the Court's own motion, permit deviation from these Rules.

Adopted Feb. 4, 2000, effective Jan. 1, 2001.

Rule 2. Definitions

In these Rules, the following definitions apply:

A. Administrative Agency. An Administrative Agency is the Worker's Compensation Board, Indiana Civil Rights Commission, Indiana Utility Regulatory Commission, or Review Board of the Department of Workforce Development.

B. [Reserved]

C. Appendix. An Appendix is a compilation of documents filed by a party pertaining to an appeal under Rule 49 and Rule 50.

D. Clerk. The Clerk is the Clerk of the Indiana Supreme Court, Court of Appeals and Tax Court.

E. Clerk's Record. The Clerk's Record is the Record maintained by the clerk of the trial court or the Administrative Agency and shall consist of the Chronological Case Summary (CCS) and all papers, pleadings, documents, orders, judgments, and other materials filed in the trial court or Administrative Agency or listed in the CCS.

F. Court and Court on Appeal. The terms "Court" and "Court on Appeal" shall refer to the Supreme Court and the Court of Appeals.

G. Criminal Appeals. Criminal Appeals are those cases which were designated by the originating court as a Criminal Felony—CF; Class D Felony—DF; Criminal Misdemeanor—CM; Post Conviction Relief—PC; Juvenile Status—JS; Juvenile Delinquency—JD; Infraction—IF; Miscellaneous Criminal—MC; Local Ordinance Violation—OV, and Exempted Ordinance Violation—OE. This definition is for ease of reference and does not change the substantive rights of the parties.

H. Final Judgment. A judgment is a final judgment if:

(1) it disposes of all claims as to all parties;

(2) the trial court in writing expressly determines under Trial Rule 54(B) or Trial Rule 56(C) that there is no just reason for delay and in writing expressly directs the entry of judgment (i) under Trial Rule 54(B) as to fewer than all the claims or parties, or (ii) under Trial Rule 56(C) as to fewer than all the issues, claims or parties;

(3) it is deemed final under Trial Rule 60(C);

(4) it is a ruling on either a mandatory or permissive Motion to Correct Error which was timely filed under Trial Rule 59 or Criminal Rule 16; or

(5) it is otherwise deemed final by law.

I.   Notice of Appeal. The Notice of Appeal initiates the appeal under Rule 9 and replaces the praecipe for appeal.

J.   Petition. The term "Petition" shall mean a Petition for Rehearing, a Petition to Transfer an appeal to the Supreme Court, and a Petition for Review of a Tax Court decision by the Supreme Court. A request for any other relief shall be denominated a "motion."

K.   Transcript. Transcript shall mean the transcript or transcripts of all or part of the proceedings in the trial court or Administrative Agency that any party has designated for inclusion in the Record on Appeal and any exhibits associated therewith.

L.   Record on Appeal. The Record on Appeal shall consist of the Clerk's Record and all proceedings before the trial court or Administrative Agency, whether or not transcribed or transmitted to the Court on Appeal.

M.   Rules. The term "Rule" or "Rules" shall mean these Appellate Rules.

N.   Case Record and Case Records Excluded From Public Access. The term "Case Record" shall mean a record defined by Administrative Rule 9(C)(2). "Case Records Excluded From Public Access" shall mean records identified in Administrative Rule 9(G)(1).

Adopted Feb. 4, 2000, effective Jan. 1, 2001; amended Dec. 21, 2001, effective April 1, 2002; amended Sept. 30, 2004, effective Jan. 1, 2005; amended Sept. 20, 2011, effective Jan. 1, 2012.

Rule 3.   Use Of Forms

Counsel, parties, court reporters, and trial court clerks are encouraged to use the forms published in an Appendix to these Rules.

Adopted Feb. 4, 2000, effective Jan. 1, 2001.

TITLE II. JURISDICTION

Rule 4.   Supreme Court Jurisdiction

A.   Appellate Jurisdiction.

(1) *Mandatory review.* The Supreme Court shall have mandatory and exclusive jurisdiction over the following cases:

(a) Criminal Appeals in which a sentence of death or life imprisonment without parole is imposed under Ind.Code § 35–50–2–9 and Criminal Appeals in post conviction relief cases in which the sentence was death.

(b) Appeals of Final Judgments declaring a state or federal statute unconstitutional in whole or in part.

(c) Appeals involving waiver of parental consent to abortion under Rule 62.

(d) Appeals involving mandate of funds under Trial Rule 60.5(B) and Rule 61.

(2) *Discretionary Review.* The Supreme Court shall have discretionary jurisdiction over cases in which it grants Transfer under Rule 56 or 57 or Review under Rule 63.

(3) *Certain Interlocutory Appeals.* The Supreme Court shall have jurisdiction over interlocutory appeals authorized under Appellate Rule 14 in any case in which the State seeks the death penalty or in life without parole cases in which the interlocutory order raises a question of interpretation of IC 35–50–2–9.

B.   Other Jurisdiction. The Supreme Court shall have exclusive jurisdiction over the following matters:

(1) *The Practice of Law.* Matters relating to the practice of law including:

(a) Admissions to practice law;

(b) The discipline and disbarment of attorneys admitted to the practice of law; and

(c) The unauthorized practice of law (other than criminal prosecutions therefor).

(2) *Supervision of Judges.* The discipline, removal and retirement of justices and judges of the State of Indiana;

(3) *Supervision of Courts.* Supervision of the exercise of jurisdiction by other courts of the State of Indiana, including the issuance of writs of mandate and prohibition; and

(4) *Issuance of Writs.* Issuance of writs necessary or appropriate in aid of its jurisdiction.

Adopted Feb. 4, 2000, effective Jan. 1, 2001; amended Nov. 9, 2000, effective Jan. 1, 2001; amended Sept. 15, 2009, effective Jan. 1, 2010.

Rule 5.   Court Of Appeals Jurisdiction

A.   Appeals From Final Judgments. Except as provided in Rule 4, the Court of Appeals shall have jurisdiction in all appeals from Final Judgments of Circuit, Superior, Probate, and County Courts, notwithstanding any law, statute or rule providing for appeal directly to the Supreme Court of Indiana. See Rule 2(H).

B.   Appeals From Interlocutory Orders. The Court of Appeals shall have jurisdiction over appeals of interlocutory orders under Rule 14 except those appeals described in Rule 4(A)(3).

C.   Appeals From Agency Decisions.

(1) *Jurisdiction.* The Court of Appeals shall have jurisdiction to entertain actions in aid of its jurisdiction and to review final orders, rulings, decisions and certified questions of an Administrative Agency.

(2) *Assignment of Errors.* No party shall file an assignment of errors in the Court of Appeals notwithstanding any law, statute, or rule to the contrary. All issues and grounds for appeal appropriately preserved before an Administrative Agency may be initially addressed in the appellate brief.

Adopted Feb. 4, 2000, effective Jan. 1, 2001. Amended Sept. 15, 2009, effective Jan. 1, 2010.

Rule 6. Appeal Or Original Action In Wrong Court

If the Supreme Court or Court of Appeals determines that an appeal or original action pending before it is within the jurisdiction of the other Court, the Court before which the case is pending shall enter an order transferring the case to the Court with jurisdiction, where the case shall proceed as if it had been originally filed in the Court with jurisdiction.

Adopted Feb. 4, 2000, effective Jan. 1, 2001.

Rule 7. Review Of Sentences

A. Availability. A defendant in a Criminal Appeal may appeal the defendant's sentence. The State may not initiate an appeal of a sentence, but may cross-appeal where provided by law.

B. Scope of Review. The Court may revise a sentence authorized by statute if, after due consideration of the trial court's decision, the Court finds that the sentence is inappropriate in light of the nature of the offense and the character of the offender.

Adopted Feb. 4, 2000, effective Jan. 1, 2001. Amended July 19, 2002, effective Jan. 1, 2003.

Rule 8. Acquisition Of Jurisdiction

The Court on Appeal acquires jurisdiction on the date the Notice of Completion of Clerk's Record is noted in the Chronological Case Summary. Before that date, the Court on Appeal may, whenever necessary, exercise limited jurisdiction in aid of its appellate jurisdiction, such as motions under Rules 18 and 39.

Adopted Feb. 4, 2000, effective Jan. 1, 2001. Amended Sept. 21, 2010, effective Jan. 1, 2011.

TITLE III. INITIATION OF APPEAL

Rule 9. Initiation Of The Appeal

A. Procedure for Filing the Notice of Appeal with the Clerk of the Indiana Supreme Court, Court of Appeals and Tax Court.

(1) *Appeals from Final Judgments.* A party initiates an appeal by filing a Notice of Appeal with the Clerk (as defined in Rule 2(D)) within thirty (30) days after the entry of a Final Judgment is noted in the Chronological Case Summary. However, if any party files a timely motion to correct error, a Notice of Appeal must be filed within thirty (30) days after the court's ruling on such motion is noted in the Chronological Case Summary or thirty (30) days after the motion is deemed denied under Trial Rule 53.3, whichever occurs first.

(2) *Interlocutory Appeals.* The initiation of interlocutory appeals is covered in Rule 14.

(3) *Administrative Appeals.* A judicial review proceeding taken directly to the Court of Appeals from an order, ruling, or decision of an Administrative Agency is commenced by filing a Notice of Appeal with the Clerk within thirty (30) days after the date of the order, ruling or decision, notwithstanding any statute to the contrary.

(4) *Abolition of Praecipe.* The praecipe for preparation of the Record is abolished.

(5) *Forfeiture of Appeal.* Unless the Notice of Appeal is timely filed, the right to appeal shall be forfeited except as provided by P.C.R. 2.

[Grace Period: Effective until January 1, 2014, if an appellant timely files the Notice of Appeal with the trial court clerk or the Administrative Agency, instead of the Clerk as required by App.R. 9(A)(1), the Notice of Appeal will be deemed timely filed and the appeal will not be forfeited.]

B. Death Penalty Cases. When a trial court imposes a death sentence, it shall on the same day sentence is imposed, order the court reporter and trial court clerk to begin immediate preparation of the Record on Appeal.

C. Joint Appeals. If two (2) or more persons are entitled to appeal from a single judgment or order, they may proceed jointly by filing a joint Notice of Appeal. The joined parties may, thereafter, proceed on appeal as a single appellant.

D. Cross-Appeals. An appellee may cross-appeal without filing a Notice of Appeal by raising cross-appeal issues in the appellee's brief. A party must file a Notice of Appeal to preserve its right to appeal if no other party appeals.

E. Payment of Filing Fee. The appellant shall pay to the Clerk the filing fee of $250. No filing fee is required in an appeal prosecuted in *forma pauperis* or on behalf of a governmental unit. The filing fee shall be paid to the Clerk when the Notice of Appeal is filed. The Clerk shall not file any motion or other documents in the proceedings until the filing fee has been paid. A party may proceed on appeal in *forma pauperis* pursuant to Rule 40.

F. Content of Notice of Appeal. The Notice of Appeal shall include the following:

(1) *Party Information.*

(a) Name and address of the parties initiating the appeal, and if a party is not represented by counsel, the party's FAX number, telephone number, and electronic mail address, if any; and

(b) Name, address, attorney number, FAX number (if any), telephone number and electronic mail address of each attorney representing the parties initiating the appeal.

(2) *Trial Information.*

(a) Title of case;

(b) Names of all parties;

(c) Trial court or Administrative Agency;

(d) Case number;

(e) Name of trial judge;

(3) *Designation of Appealed Order or Judgment.*

(a) The date and title of the judgment or order appealed;

(b) The date on which any Motion to Correct Error was denied or deemed denied, if applicable;

(c) The basis for appellate jurisdiction, delineating whether the appeal is from a Final Judgment, as defined by Rule 2(H); an interlocutory order appealed as of right pursuant to Rule 14(A),(C), or (D); an interlocutory order accepted for discretionary appeal pursuant to Rule 14(B); or an expedited appeal pursuant to Rule 14.1; and

(d) A designation of the court to which the appeal is taken.

(4) *Direction for Assembly of Clerk's Record.* Directions to the trial court clerk to assemble the Clerk's Record.

(5) *Request for Transcript.* A designation of all portions of the Transcript necessary to present fairly and decide the issues on appeal. If the appellant intends to urge on appeal that a finding of fact or conclusion thereon is unsupported by the evidence or is contrary to the evidence, the Notice of Appeal shall request a Transcript of all the evidence. In Criminal Appeals, the Notice of Appeal must request the Transcript of the entire trial or evidentiary hearing, unless the party intends to limit the appeal to an issue requiring no Transcript.

(6) *Public Access Information.* A statement whether all or any portion of the court records were sealed or excluded from public access by court order.

(7) *Appellate Alternative Dispute Resolution Information.* In all civil cases, an indication whether Appellant is willing to participate in appellate alternative dispute resolution and, if so, provide a brief statement of the facts of the case.

(8) *Attachments.*

(a) A copy of the judgment or order being appealed (including findings and conclusions in civil cases and the sentencing order in criminal cases);

(b) A copy of the order denying the Motion to Correct Error or, if deemed denied, a copy of the Motion to Correct Error, if applicable;

(c) A copy of all orders and entries relating to the trial court or agency's decision to seal or exclude information from public access, if applicable;

(d) A copy of the order from the Court of Appeals accepting jurisdiction over the interlocutory appeal, if proceeding pursuant to Rule 14(B)(3);

(e) The documents required by Rule 40(C), if proceeding *in forma pauperis.*

(9) *Certification.* A certification, signed by the attorney or pro se party, certifying the following:

(a) That the case does or does not involve an interlocutory appeal or issues of child custody, support, visitation, adoption, paternity, determination that a child is in need of services, termination of parental rights, and all other appeals entitled to priority by rule or statute;

(b) That the attorney or pro se party has reviewed and complied, and will continue to comply, with the requirements of Rule 9(J) and Administrative Rule 9(G)(4), to the extent they apply to the appeal: and

(c) That the attorney or pro se party will make satisfactory payment arrangements for any transcripts ordered in the Notice of Appeal, as required by Rule 9(H).

(10) *Certificate of Filing and Service.* The Certificate of Service required by Rule 24. This Certificate shall also certify the date on which the Notice of Appeal was filed with the Clerk. (See Form # App.R. 9–1)

G. Supplemental Request for Transcript. Any party to the appeal may file with the trial court clerk or the Administrative Agency, without leave of court, a request with the court reporter or the Administrative Agency for additional portions of the Transcript.

H. Payment for Transcript. Within thirty (30) days after the filing of a Notice of Appeal a party must enter into an agreement with the court reporter for payment of the cost of the Transcript. Unless a court order requires otherwise, each party shall be responsible to pay for all transcription costs associated with the Transcript that party requests.

I. Administrative Agency Appeals. In Administrative Agency appeals, the Notice of Appeal shall include the same contents and be handled in the same manner as an appeal from a Final Judgment in a civil case, notwithstanding any statute to the contrary. Assignments of error are not required. See Rule 9(A)(3). (See Form #App.R. 9–1).

J. Documents and Information Excluded from Public Access and Confidential Pursuant to Administrative Rule 9(G). Documents and information excluded from public access pursuant to Administrative Rule 9(G) shall be filed in accordance with Trial Rule 5(G) and Administrative Rule 9(G).

Adopted Feb. 4, 2000, effective Jan. 1, 2001. Amended Dec. 22, 2000, effective Jan. 1, 2001; Dec. 21, 2001, effective April 1, 2002; July 1, 2003, effective Jan. 1, 2004; Sept. 30, 2004, effective Jan. 1, 2005; Oct. 6, 2008, effective Jan. 1, 2009; Sept. 21, 2010, effective Jan. 1, 2011; Sept. 20, 2011, effective Jan. 1, 2012; Sept. 7, 2012, effective Jan. 1, 2013.

Rule 10. Duties Of Trial Court Clerk Or Administrative Agency

A. Notice to Court Reporter of Transcript Request. If a Transcript is requested, the trial court clerk or the Administrative Agency shall give immediate notice of the filing of the Notice of Appeal and the requested Transcript to the court reporter.

B. Assembly of Clerk's Record. Within thirty (30) days of the filing of the Notice of Appeal, the trial court clerk or Administrative Agency shall assemble the Clerk's Record. The trial court clerk or Administrative Agency is not obligated to index or marginally annotate the Clerk's Record.

C. Notice of Completion of Clerk's Record. On or before the deadline for assembly of the Clerk's Record, the trial court clerk or Administrative Agency shall issue and file a Notice of Completion of Clerk's Record with the Clerk and shall serve a copy on the parties to the appeal in accordance with Rule 24 to advise them that the Clerk's Record has been assembled and is complete. The Notice of Completion of Clerk's Record shall include a certified copy of the Chronological Case Summary and shall state whether the Transcript is (a) completed, (b) not completed, or (c) not requested. (See Form # App.R. 10–1). Copies of the Notice of Completion of Clerk's Record served on the parties shall include a copy of the Chronological Case Summary included with the original, but the copies served on the parties need not be individually certified.

D. Notice of Completion of Transcript. If the Transcript has been requested but has not been filed when the trial court clerk or Administrative Agency issues its Notice of Completion of the Clerk's Record, the trial court clerk or Administrative Agency shall issue and file a Notice of Completion of Transcript with the Clerk and shall serve a copy on the parties to the appeal in accordance with Rule 24 within five (5) days after the court reporter files the Transcript. (See Form #App.R. 10–2)

E. Extension of Time to Complete Clerk's Record. The trial court clerk or Administrative Agency may move the Court on Appeal designated in the Notice of Appeal for an extension of time to assemble the Clerk's Record pursuant to Rule 35 (A) and shall state in such motion the factual basis for inability to comply with the prescribed deadline despite exercise of due diligence. (See Form # App.R. 10–3). The trial court clerk shall file an original and one copy of the motion with the Clerk and shall serve a copy of

the motion on the parties to the appeal in accordance with Rule 24. Motions for extension of time in interlocutory appeals, appeals involving worker's compensation, issues of child custody, support, visitation, paternity, adoption, determination that a child is in need of services, and termination of parental rights are disfavored and shall be granted only in extraordinary circumstances.

F. Failure to File Notice of Completion of Clerk's Record. If the trial court clerk or Administrative Agency fails to issue, file, and serve a timely Notice of Completion of Clerk's Record, the appellant shall seek an order from the Court on Appeal compelling the trial court clerk or Administrative Agency to complete the Clerk's Record and issue, file, and serve its Notice of Completion. Failure of appellant to seek such an order not later than fifteen (15) days after the Notice of Completion of Clerk's Record was due to have been issued, filed, and served shall subject the appeal to dismissal.

G. Failure to File Notice of Completion of Transcript. If the trial court clerk or Administrative Agency fails to issue, file, and serve a timely Notice of Completion of Transcript required by Rule 10(D), the appellant shall seek an order from the Court on Appeal compelling the trial court clerk or Administrative Agency to issue, file and serve the Notice of Completion of Transcript. Failure of appellant to seek such an order not later than fifteen (15) days after the Notice of Completion of Transcript was due to have been issued, filed, and served shall subject the appeal to dismissal.

Adopted Feb. 4, 2000, effective Jan. 1, 2001; amended Dec. 22, 2000, effective Jan. 1, 2001; amended Dec. 21, 2001, effective April 1, 2002; amended Sept. 20, 2011, effective Jan. 1, 2012.

Rule 11. Duties Of Court Reporter

A. Preparation of Transcript. The court reporter shall prepare, certify and file the Transcript designated in the Notice of Appeal with the trial court clerk or Administrative Agency in accordance with Rules 28, 29, and/or 30. Preparation of the separately-bound volumes of exhibits as required by Rule 29 is considered part of the Transcript preparation process. The court reporter shall provide notice to all parties to the appeal that the transcript has been filed with the clerk of the trial court or Administrative Agency in accordance with Rules 28, 29, and/or 30. (See Form # App.R. 11–1)

B. Deadline for Filing Transcript. For the period until July 1, 2003, and until revised thereafter, the court reporter or Administrative Agency shall have ninety (90) days after the appellant files the Notice of Appeal to file the Transcript with the trial court clerk or Administrative Agency.

C. Extension of Time to File Transcript. If the court reporter believes the transcript cannot be filed within the time period prescribed by this rule, then the court reporter shall move the Court on Appeal designated in the Notice of Appeal for an extension of time to file the Transcript pursuant to Rule 35 (A) and shall state in such motion the factual basis for inability to comply with the prescribed deadline despite exercise of due diligence. (See Form # App.R. 11–2). The court reporter shall file an original and one copy of the motion with the Clerk and shall serve a copy of the motion on the parties to the appeal in accordance with Rule 24. Motions for extension of time in interlocutory appeals, appeals involving worker's compensation, issues of child custody, support, visitation, paternity, adoption, determination that a child is in need of services, and termination of parental rights are disfavored and shall be granted only in extraordinary circumstances.

D. Failure to Complete Transcript. If the court reporter fails to file the Transcript with the trial court clerk within the time allowed, the appellant shall seek an order from the Court on Appeal compelling the court reporter to do so. The motion to compel shall be verified and affirmatively state that service as required under Rule 24(A)(1) was properly made and that the appellant has complied with the agreement for payment made in accordance with Rule 9(H). Failure of appellant to seek such an order not later than fifteen (15) days after the Transcript was due to have been filed with the trial court clerk shall subject the appeal to dismissal.

Adopted Feb. 4, 2000, effective Jan. 1, 2001; amended Dec. 22, 2000, effective Jan. 1, 2001; amended Dec. 21, 2001, effective April 1, 2002; amended Sept. 20, 2011, effective Jan. 1, 2012.

Rule 12.   Transmittal Of The Record

A. Clerk's Record. Unless the Court on Appeal orders otherwise, the trial court clerk shall retain the Clerk's Record throughout the appeal. A party may request that the trial court clerk copy the Clerk's Record, or a portion thereof, and the clerk shall provide the copies within thirty (30) days, subject to the payment of any usual and customary copying charges.

B. Transcript. In appeals other than Criminal Appeals, the trial court clerk shall retain the Transcript until the Clerk notifies the trial court clerk that all briefing is completed, and the trial court clerk shall then transmit the Transcript to the Clerk. In Criminal Appeals in which the appellant is not represented by the State Public Defender, the Clerk shall notify the trial court clerk when the Appellant's brief has been filed, and the trial court clerk will then transmit the Transcript to the Clerk. In Criminal Appeals in which the appellant is represented by the State Public Defender, the trial court clerk shall transmit the Transcript to the Clerk when the court reporter has completed the preparation, certification and filing in accordance with Rule 11(A). The trial court clerk is entitled to obtain from the appellant reimbursement for the cost of transmitting the Transcript. Any party

may withdraw the Transcript or, at the trial court clerk's option, a copy, at no extra cost, from the trial court clerk for a period not to exceed the period in which the party's brief is to be filed. Any party may move the Court on Appeal to order the trial court clerk to transmit the Transcript at a different time than provided for in this Rule.

C. Access to Record on Appeal. Unless limited by the trial court, any party may copy any document from the Clerk's Record and any portion of the Transcript. After a Transcript or Appendix has been transmitted to or filed with the Clerk, a party to the appeal may arrange to have access to that Transcript or Appendix during the time period that party is working on a brief, subject to any internal rules the Clerk may adopt to provide an accounting for the location of those materials and for ensuring fair access to the Transcript and Appendices by all parties.

D. Appeals from Administrative Agencies. When the appeal is from an Administrative Agency, reference to the "trial court clerk" shall mean the Administrative Agency.

Adopted Feb. 4, 2000, effective Jan. 1, 2001. Amended Dec. 21, 2001, effective April 1, 2002; July 1, 2005, effective Jan. 1, 2006.

Rule 13.   Preparation Of The Record In Administrative Agency Cases

In cases taken directly to the Court of Appeals from the final orders, rulings or decisions and certified questions of an Administrative Agency, the preparation, contents, and transmittal of the Record on Appeal, to the extent possible pursuant to Rules 10, 11 and 12, shall be governed by the same provisions applicable to appeals from Final Judgments in civil cases, including all applicable time periods, notwithstanding any statute to the contrary.

Adopted Feb. 4, 2000, effective Jan. 1, 2001.

Rule 14.   Interlocutory Appeals

A. Interlocutory Appeals of Right. Appeals from the following interlocutory orders are taken as a matter of right by filing a Notice of Appeal with the Clerk within thirty (30) days after the notation of the interlocutory order in the Chronological Case Summary:

(1) For the payment of money;

(2) To compel the execution of any document;

(3) To compel the delivery or assignment of any securities, evidence of debt, documents or things in action;

(4) For the sale or delivery of the possession of real property;

(5) Granting or refusing to grant, dissolving, or refusing to dissolve a preliminary injunction;

(6) Appointing or refusing to appoint a receiver, or revoking or refusing to revoke the appointment of a receiver;

(7) For a writ of habeas corpus not otherwise authorized to be taken directly to the Supreme Court;

(8) Transferring or refusing to transfer a case under Trial Rule 75; and

(9) Issued by an Administrative Agency that by statute is expressly required to be appealed as a mandatory interlocutory appeal.

The Notice of Appeal shall be in the form prescribed by Rule 9, and served in accordance with Rule 9(F)(10).

B. Discretionary Interlocutory Appeals. An appeal may be taken from other interlocutory orders if the trial court certifies its order and the Court of Appeals accepts jurisdiction over the appeal.

(1) Certification by the Trial Court. The trial court, in its discretion, upon motion by a party, may certify an interlocutory order to allow an immediate appeal.

(a) Time for Filing Motion. A motion requesting certification of an interlocutory order must be filed in the trial court within thirty (30) days after the date the interlocutory order is noted in the Chronological Case Summary unless the trial court, for good cause, permits a belated motion. If the trial court grants a belated motion and certifies the appeal, the court shall make a finding that the certification is based on a showing of good cause, and shall set forth the basis for that finding.

(b) Content of the Motion in the Trial Court. A motion to the trial court shall contain the following:

(i) An identification of the interlocutory order sought to be certified;

(ii) A concise statement of the issues to be addressed in the interlocutory appeal; and

(iii) The reasons why an interlocutory appeal should be permitted.

(c) Grounds for Granting Interlocutory Appeal. Grounds for granting an interlocutory appeal include:

(i) The appellant will suffer substantial expense, damage or injury if the order is erroneous and the determination of the error is withheld until after judgment.

(ii) The order involves a substantial question of law, the early determination of which will promote a more orderly disposition of the case.

(iii) The remedy by appeal is otherwise inadequate.

(d) Response to Motion. Any response to a motion for the trial court to certify an interloc-

utory order shall be filed within fifteen (15) days after service of the motion, and computing time in accordance with Trial Rule 6.

(e) Ruling on Motion by the Trial Court. In the event the trial court fails for thirty (30) days to set the motion for hearing or fails to rule on the motion within thirty (30) days after it was heard or thirty (30) days after it was filed, if no hearing is set, the motion requesting certification of an interlocutory order shall be deemed denied.

(2) Acceptance of the Interlocutory Appeal by the Court of Appeals. If the trial court certifies an order for interlocutory appeal, the Court of Appeals, in its discretion, upon motion by a party, may accept jurisdiction of the appeal. The motion shall be accompanied by an appearance as required by Rule 16(H).

(a) Time for Filing Motion in the Court of Appeals. The motion requesting that the Court of Appeals accept jurisdiction over an interlocutory appeal shall be filed within thirty (30) days after the date the trial court's certification is noted in the Chronological Case Summary.

(b) Content of the Motion in the Court of Appeals. The motion requesting that the Court of Appeals accept jurisdiction shall state:

(i) The date of the interlocutory order.

(ii) The date the motion for certification was filed in the trial court.

(iii) The date the trial court's certification of its interlocutory order was noted in the Chronological Case Summary.

(iv) The reasons the Court of Appeals should accept this interlocutory appeal.

(c) Attachments to Motion. The party seeking an interlocutory appeal shall attach to its motion a copy of the trial court's certification of the interlocutory order and a copy of the interlocutory order.

(d) Response to Motion. Any response to a motion requesting the Court of Appeals to accept jurisdiction shall be filed within fifteen (15) days after service of the motion.

(3) Filing of Notice of Appeal. The appellant shall file a Notice of Appeal with the Clerk within fifteen (15) days of the Court of Appeals' order accepting jurisdiction over the interlocutory appeal. The Notice of Appeal shall be in the form prescribed by Rule 9, and served in accordance with Rule 9(F)(10). The appellant shall also comply with Rule 9(E).

C. Interlocutory Appeals From Orders Granting Or Denying Class Action Certification. The Court of Appeals, in its discretion, may accept jurisdiction over an appeal from an interlocutory order granting or denying class action certification under Ind. Trial Rule 23.

(1) Time for Filing Motion. A motion requesting that the Court of Appeals accept jurisdiction over an interlocutory appeal from an order granting or denying class action certification shall be filed within thirty (30) days after the notation of the order in the Chronological Case Summary. The Motion shall be accompanied by an appearance as required by Rule 16(H).

(2) Content of Motion. The motion requesting that the Court of Appeals accept jurisdiction shall state:

(a) The date the order granting or denying class action certification was noted in the Chronological Case Summary.

(b) The facts necessary for consideration of the motion.

(c) The reasons the Court of Appeals should accept the interlocutory appeal.

(3) Attachments to Motion. A copy of the trial court's order granting or denying class action certification shall be attached to the motion requesting that the Court of Appeals accept jurisdiction over the interlocutory appeal.

(4) Response to Motion. Any response to the motion requesting the Court of Appeals to accept jurisdiction shall be filed within fifteen (15) days after service of the motion.

(5) Filing of Notice of Appeal. The appellant shall file a Notice of Appeal with the Clerk within fifteen (15) days of the Court of Appeals' order accepting jurisdiction over the interlocutory appeal. The Notice of Appeal shall be in the form prescribed by Rule 9, and served in accordance with Rule 9(F)(10). The appellant shall also comply with Rule 9(E).

D. Statutory Interlocutory Appeals. Other interlocutory appeals may be taken only as provided by statute.

E. Clerk's Record and Transcript. The Clerk's Record shall be assembled in accordance with Rule 10. The court reporter shall file the Transcript in accordance with Rule 11.

F. Briefing. Briefing in interlocutory appeals shall be governed by Rules 43 and 44.

G. Shortening or Extending Time.

(1) Extensions. Extensions of time to prepare the Transcript or to file any brief in an interlocutory appeal are disfavored and will be granted only upon a showing of good cause. Any motion for extension must comply with Rule 35.

(2) Shortening Deadlines. The Court of Appeals, upon motion by a party and for good cause, may shorten any time period. A motion to shorten time shall be filed within ten (10) days of the filing of either the Notice of Appeal with the Clerk or the motion to the Court of Appeals requesting permission to file an interlocutory appeal.

H. Stay of Trial Court Proceedings. An interlocutory appeal shall not stay proceedings in the trial court unless the trial court or a judge of the Court of Appeals so orders. The order staying proceedings may be conditioned upon the furnishing of a bond or security protecting the appellee against loss incurred by the interlocutory appeal.

I. Death Penalty Cases. In any case in which the State seeks the death penalty or in which the interlocutory order raises a question of interpretation of IC 35–50–2–9, references in this Rule to the Court of Appeals shall refer to the Supreme Court.

Adopted Feb. 4, 2000, effective Jan. 1, 2001. Amended July 19, 2002, effective Jan. 1, 2003; Sept. 10, 2007, effective Jan. 1, 2008; Sept. 9, 2008, effective Jan. 1, 2009; Sept. 21, 2010, effective Jan. 1, 2011; Sept. 20, 2011, effective Jan. 1, 2012.

Rule 14.1. Expedited Appeal for Payment of Placement and/or Services

A. Applicability. This Rule governs appellate review per Indiana Code sections 31–34–4–7(f), 31–34–19–6.1(f), 31–37–5–8(g), and 31–37–18–9(d). All other appeals concerning children alleged to be in need of service or children alleged to be delinquent are not covered by this rule.

B. Notice of Expedited Appeal.

(1) The Department of Child Services ("DCS") shall file a Notice of Expedited Appeal with the Clerk within five (5) business days after the trial court's order of placement and/or services is noted in the Chronological Case Summary. (See Form #App.R. 9–1).

(2) On the same day DCS files the Notice of Expedited Appeal, it shall serve the Notice on the trial court judge, the clerk of the trial court, the court reporter (if a transcript, or any portion of a transcript is requested), the county commissioners, the guardian ad litem, CASA, any juvenile who is the subject of the order if 14 years of age or older, counsel for the juvenile, the parents of the juvenile, the Attorney General, in the case of a juvenile delinquency matter the Chief Probation Officer and Prosecutor, and any other party of record.

(3) The Notice of Expedited Appeal shall include all content required by Rule 9(F).

(4) The certificate of service attached to the Notice of Expedited Appeal shall include (a) the name and address, and (b) the FAX number and e-mail address if known, of every person to whom it was sent.

(5) Any party who has received the Notice of Expedited Appeal shall have five (5) business days from service of the Notice of Expedited Appeal to file an Appearance and request any additional other items to be included in the record. Failure to file an Appearance shall remove that party from the Appeal.

(6) The trial court shall be considered a party to the Appeal if it files a timely appearance.

C. Transcript and Record.

(1) The completion of the Transcript and the Record on Appeal shall take priority over all other appeal transcripts and records. Within ten (10) business days after the filing of the Notice of Appeal is noted in the Chronological Case Summary, the assembly of the Clerk's Record shall be completed and any requested transcript shall be prepared and filed, after which the clerk shall immediately issue and file a Notice of Completion of Clerk's Record (and a separate Notice of Completion of Transcript if assembly of the Clerk's Record is completed before the transcript is filed) and shall immediately serve all parties to the Appeal by both: (i) U.S. mail or third-party commercial carrier; and (ii) personal service, electronic mail, or facsimile.

(2) The Clerk's Record in appeals governed by this rule shall contain the pre-dispositional report and any attachments thereto, in addition to the other records listed in Appellate Rule 2(E). The trial court clerk is not obligated to index or marginally annotate the Clerk's Record, which shall be the responsibility of DCS.

(3) On the eleventh (11th) business day following the filing of the transcript, the trial court clerk shall transmit the transcript to the Clerk without any further notice from the Clerk. Failure to meet this deadline shall require the trial court clerk to show cause to the Court on Appeal why he or she should not be held in contempt. DCS may, but is not required to, file a show cause motion with the Court on Appeal concerning the trial court clerk's failure to meet this deadline.

D. Memoranda.

(1) Any party on Appeal may file a memorandum, which may be in narrative form and need not contain the sections under separate headings listed in Appellate Rule 46(a).

(2) Memoranda shall not exceed ten (10) pages unless limited to 4,200 words and shall adhere to the requirements of Appellate Rules 43(A)–(G), (J), and (K). Memoranda exceeding ten (10) pages in length shall contain the word count certification required by Appellate Rule 44(F). Any factual statement shall be supported by a citation to a page where it appears in the record.

(3) DCS shall have five (5) business days from the notation in the Chronological Case Summary of the filing of the Notice of Completion of Transcript (or the Notice of Completion of Clerk's Record if a transcript was not requested) to file a memorandum stating why the trial court's decision should be reversed. DCS's memorandum shall be accompanied by an Appendix that shall contain copies of all relevant pleadings, motions, orders, entries, and other papers filed, tendered for filing, or entered by the trial court, including but not limited to the pre-dispositional report and all attachments thereto.

(4) Any responding party shall have five (5) business days after DCS has filed its memorandum to file a responsive memorandum stating why the decision should be sustained or reversed, and to file any accompanying supplemental Appendix.

(5) No reply memorandum shall be allowed.

(6) A party shall file its original Memorandum and eight (8) copies.

E. Extensions of Time. Extensions of time are not allowed.

F. Rehearing on Appeal. A party may not seek rehearing of an appellate decision issued under this rule.

G. Outcome of Appeal. If DCS prevails on appeal, payment shall be made in accordance with Indiana Code sections 31–34–4–7(g), 31–34–19–6.1(g), 31–37–5–8(h), or 31–37–18–9(e), as the case may be.

H. Petition to Transfer. A Petition to Transfer must be filed no later than five (5) business days after the adverse decision of the Court of Appeals. A party who files a Petition to Transfer by mail or third-party commercial carrier shall also contemporaneously tender a copy to the Clerk's Office via facsimile. The Petition to Transfer shall adhere to the requirements of Appellate Rules 43(A)–(G), (J), and (K). Appellate Rules 43(H) and (I), 44, and 57 shall not apply. The Petition to Transfer shall not exceed one (1) page in length, excluding the signature block and certificate of service, and shall notify the Supreme Court simply of the party's desire for the Supreme Court to assume jurisdiction over the appeal following the adverse decision of the Court of Appeals. A file-stamped copy of the Court of Appeals' opinion or memorandum decision shall be attached to the Petition to Transfer. No brief in response shall be allowed. The Supreme Court will consider the merits of the Petition to Transfer based on the party's filings submitted to the Court of Appeals and on the Court of Appeals' opinion or memorandum decision.

I. Certification of Opinion. The Clerk shall certify the Court of Appeals' opinion or memorandum decision six (6) business days after it is handed down unless a timely Petition to Transfer has been filed and served in accordance with the preceding section. The Clerk shall certify any opinion of the Supreme Court immediately upon issuance.

J. Service. Service, if by mail or third-party commercial carrier, shall also be by contemporaneous fax or email on all parties whose FAX number or e-mail address is known by the serving party. Parties who are served by contemporaneous FAX or e-mail shall not be entitled to the extension of time set forth in Appellate Rule 25(C). Any party filing an appearance after documents have been served shall promptly be served with all documents not previously provided to the later-appearing party.

Adopted Jan. 1, 2009. Amended Sept. 21, 2010, effective Jan. 1, 2011; Sept. 20, 2011, effective Jan. 1, 2012.

Rule 15. [Abolished, eff. Jan 1, 2012.]

Rule 16. Appearances

A. Initiating Parties. The filing of a Notice of Appeal pursuant to Rule 9 or Notice of Expedited Appeal pursuant to Rule 14.1 satisfies the requirement to file an appearance.

B. Responding Parties. All other parties participating in an appeal shall file an appearance form with the Clerk. (See Form # App.R. 16–1). When the State is appellee in a Criminal Appeal, the Clerk shall enter the appearance of the Attorney General. The appearance form shall be filed within thirty (30) days after the filing of the Notice of Appeal or contemporaneously with the first document filed by the appearing party, whichever comes first. The appearance form shall contain the following:

(1) Name and address of the appearing party, and if the appearing party is not represented by counsel, the party's FAX number, telephone number, and electronic mail address, if any;

(2) Name, address, attorney number, telephone number, FAX number (if any), and electronic mail address of the attorneys representing the parties;

(3) If it is a civil case, whether Appellee is willing to participate in Appellate ADR.

C. Parties to Certified Federal Questions. If the Supreme Court decides to answer a question of law certified by a federal court under Rule 64, parties to the federal proceeding shall file an appearance form with the Clerk setting forth the same information identified in Section (B) of this Rule. Appearance forms shall be filed within thirty (30) days following the order of the Supreme Court granting the federal court's request for an opinion, or contemporaneously with the first document filed by the appearing party, whichever comes first.

D. Amicus Curiae. When moving for leave to file an *amicus curiae* brief under Rule 41, the movant shall file an appearance form with the Clerk containing the following:

(1) Name and address of the movant;

(2) Name, address, attorney number, telephone number, FAX number, and electronic mail address, if any, of the attorneys representing the movant; and

(3) Whether the movant sought *amicus curiae* status in the proceeding before the trial court or Administrative Agency, and if so, whether the request was granted.

E. Correction of Information. Parties shall promptly advise the Clerk of any change in the infor-

mation previously supplied under this Rule and Rule 9.

F. Appearance on Transfer or Review. If an attorney has entered an appearance in a case before the Court of Appeals or the Tax Court, that attorney need not file another appearance in any continuation of that case before the Supreme Court. If an attorney has been granted temporary admission in a case before the Court of Appeals or the Tax Court, that attorney need not again seek temporary admission in any continuation of that case before the Supreme Court.

G. Withdrawal of Appearance. An attorney wishing to withdraw his or her appearance shall seek leave of the court by motion stating the reason that leave is sought. If a new attorney will be replacing the withdrawing attorney, the new attorney's appearance should, if possible, be filed with the motion to withdraw appearance.

H. Appearances in Certain Interlocutory Appeals. In the case of an Interlocutory Appeal under Rules 14(B)(2) or 14(C), a party shall file an appearance setting forth the information required by Rule 16(B) at the time the motion requesting the Court on Appeal to accept jurisdiction over the interlocutory appeal is filed. (See Form # App.R. 16–2).

Adopted Feb. 4, 2000, effective Jan. 1, 2001. Amended July 19, 2002, effective Jan. 1, 2003; Sept. 9, 2008, effective Jan. 1, 2009; Sept. 15, 2009, effective Jan. 1, 2010; Sept. 21, 2010, effective Jan. 1, 2011; Sept. 20, 2011, effective Jan. 1, 2012.

Rule 17. Parties On Appeal

A. Trial Court or Administrative Agency Parties. A party of record in the trial court or Administrative Agency shall be a party on appeal. The Attorney General represents the state in all Criminal Appeals.

B. Death or Incompetence of Party. The death or incompetence of any or all the parties on appeal shall not cause the appeal to abate. The death of the appellant abates a criminal appeal. Successor parties may be substituted for the deceased or incompetent parties.

C. Substitution Of Parties.

(1) *Automatic Substitution for Public Officers in Official Capacities.* When a public officer who is sued in an official capacity dies, resigns or otherwise no longer holds public office, the officer's successor is automatically substituted as a party.

(2) *Substitution of Parties.* A party shall, by notice filed with the Clerk, advise the Court of the succession in office of any party. The failure of any party to file a notice shall not affect the party's substantive rights.

Adopted Feb. 4, 2000, effective Jan. 1, 2001.

Rule 18. Appeal Bonds—Letters of Credit

No appeal bond shall be necessary to prosecute an appeal from any Final Judgment or appealable interlocutory order. Enforcement of a Final Judgment or appealable interlocutory order from a money judgment shall be stayed during appeal upon the giving of a bond, an irrevocable letter of credit, or other form of security approved by a trial court or Administrative Agency. The trial court or Administrative Agency shall have jurisdiction to fix and approve the bond, irrevocable letter of credit, or other form of security, and order a stay prior to or pending an appeal. After the trial court or Administrative Agency decides the issue of a stay, the Court on Appeal may reconsider the issue at any time upon a showing, by certified copies, of the trial court's action. The Court on Appeal may grant or deny the stay and set or modify the bond, letter of credit, or other form of security. No bond, letter of credit, or other form of security shall be required from any party exempted from bond by Trial Rule 62(E). This rule creates no right to a stay where precluded by law.

Adopted Feb. 4, 2000, effective Jan. 1, 2001. Amended Sept. 21, 2010, effective Jan. 1, 2011.

Rule 19.   Court Of Appeals Preappeal Conference

A.   Subjects for Conference. The Court of Appeals may order a preappeal conference upon the motion of any party or on the court's own motion, to consider the following:

(1) the simplification and designation of the issues to be presented on appeal;

(2) obtaining stipulations to avoid the preparation of unnecessary Transcript;

(3) the determination of what Transcript from the trial court is necessary to present properly the issues on appeal;

(4) scheduling;

(5) settlement; and

(6) such other matters as may aid the disposition of the appeal.

B.   Sanctions. If a party fails to appear in person or by counsel at the preappeal conference, without good cause, or if an attorney is unprepared to participate in the conference, the Court of Appeals may impose appropriate sanctions, including attorney fees.

Adopted Feb. 4, 2000, effective Jan. 1, 2001.

Rule 20.   Appellate Alternative Dispute Resolution

The parties in civil cases are encouraged to consider appellate mediation. The Court on Appeal may, upon motion of any party or its own motion, conduct or order appellate alternative dispute resolution.

Adopted Feb. 4, 2000, effective Jan. 1, 2001. Amended Sept. 15, 2009, effective Jan. 1, 2010.

TITLE IV.   GENERAL PROVISIONS

Rule 21.   Order In Which Appeals Are Considered

A.   Expedited Appeals. The court shall give expedited consideration to interlocutory appeals and appeals involving issues of child custody, support, visitation, adoption, paternity, determination that a child is in need of services, termination of parental rights, and all other appeals entitled to priority by rule or statute.

B.   Motion for Expedited Consideration. By motion of any party, other appeals that involve the constitutionality of any law, the public revenue, public health, or are otherwise of general public concern or for other good cause, may be expedited by order of the court.

Adopted Feb. 4, 2000, effective Jan. 1, 2001.

Rule 22.   Citation Form

Unless otherwise provided, a current edition of a Uniform System of Citation (Bluebook) shall be followed.

A.   Citation to Cases. All Indiana cases shall be cited by giving the title of the case followed by the volume and page of the regional and official reporter (where both exist), the court of disposition, and the year of the opinion, e.g., *Callender v. State*, 193 Ind. 91, 138 N.E. 817 (1922); *Moran v. State*, 644 N.E.2d 536 (Ind. 1994). If the case is not contained in the regional reporter, citation may be made to the official reporter. Where both a regional and official citation

exist and pinpoint citations are appropriate, pinpoint citations to one of the reporters shall be provided. Designation of disposition of petitions for transfer shall be included, e.g., *State ex rel. Mass Transp. Auth. of Greater Indianapolis v. Indiana Revenue Bd.*, 144 Ind. App. 63, 242 N.E.2d 642 (1968), *trans. denied by an evenly divided court* 251 Ind. 607, 244 N.E.2d 111 (1969); *Smith v. State*, 717 N.E.2d 127 (Ind. Ct. App. 1999), *trans. denied.*

B.   Citations to Indiana Statutes, Regulations, Court Rules and County Local Court Rules.

1.   Citations to Indiana statutes, administrative materials, and court rules shall comply with the following citation format for initial references and subsequent references:

INITIAL	SUBSEQUENT
Ind. Code § 34–1–1–1 (20xx)	I.C. § 34–1–1–1
34 Ind. Admin. Code 12–5–1 (2004)	34 I.A.C. 12–5–1
29 Ind. Reg. 11 (Oct. 1, 2005)	29 I.R. 11
Ind. Trial Rule 56	T.R. 56
Ind. Crim. Rule 4(B)(1)	Crim. R. 4(B)(1)

INITIAL	SUBSEQUENT
Ind. Post–Conviction Rule 2(2)(b)	P–C.R. 2(2)(b)
Ind. Appellate Rule 8	App. R. 8
Ind. Original Action Rule 3(A)	Orig. Act. R. 3(A)
Ind. Child Support Rule 2	Child Supp. R. 2
Ind. Child Support Guideline 3(D)	Child Supp. G. 3(D)
Ind. Small Claims Rule 8(A)	S.C.R. 8(A)
Ind. Tax Court Rule 9	Tax Ct. R. 9
Ind. Administrative Rule 7(A)	Admin. R. 7(A)
Ind. Judicial Conduct Rule 2.1	Jud.Cond. R. 2.1
Ind. Professional Conduct Rule 6.1	Prof. Cond. R. 6.1
Ind. Alternative Dispute Resolution Rule 2	A.D.R. 2
Ind. Admission and Discipline Rule 23(2)(a)	Admis. Disc. R. (2)(a)
Ind. Evidence Rule 301	Evid. R. 301
Ind. Jury Rule 12	J.R. 12

Effective July 1, 2006, the Indiana Administrative Code and the Indiana Register are published electronically by the Indiana Legislative Services Agency. For materials published in the Indiana Administrative Code and Indiana Register prior to that date, use the citation forms set forth above. For materials published after that date, reference to the appropriate URL is necessary for a reader to locate the official versions of these materials. The following citation format for initial references and subsequent references shall be used for materials published in the Indiana Administrative Code and Indiana Register on and after July 1, 2006:

Initial: 34 Ind. Admin. Code 12–5–1 (2006)

(see http://www.in.gov/legislative/iac/)

Subsequent: 34 I.A.C. 12–5–1

Initial: Ind. Reg. LSA Doc. No. 05–0065 (July 26, 2006)

(see http://www.in.gov/legislative/register/irtoc.htm)

Subsequent: I.R. 05–0065

2. Citations to County Local Court Rules adopted pursuant to Ind. Trial Rule 81 shall be cited by giving the county followed by the citation to the local rule, e.g. Adams LR01–TR3.1–1.

C. References to the Record on Appeal. Any factual statement shall be supported by a citation to the page where it appears in an Appendix, and if not contained in an Appendix, to the page it appears in the Transcript or exhibits, e.g., Appellant's App. p.5; Tr. p. 231–32. Any record material cited in an appellate brief must be reproduced in an Appendix or the Transcript or exhibits. Any record material cited in an appellate brief that is also included in an Addendum to Brief should include a citation to the Appendix or Transcript and to the Addendum to Brief.

D. References to Parties. References to parties by such designations as "appellant" and "appellee" shall be avoided. Instead, parties shall be referred to by their names, or by descriptive terms such as "the employee," "the injured person," "the taxpayer," or "the school."

E. Abbreviations. The following abbreviations may be used without explanation in citations and references: Addend. (addendum to brief), App. (appendix), Br. (brief), CCS (chronological case summary), Ct. (court), Def. (defendant), Hr. (hearing), Mem. (memorandum), Pet. (petition), Pl. (plaintiff), Supp. (supplemental), Tr. (Transcript).

Adopted Feb. 4, 2000, effective Jan. 1, 2001. Amended Dec. 21, 2001, effective April 1, 2002; Aug. 15, 2006, effective Jan. 1, 2007; Sept. 10, 2007, effective Jan. 1, 2008; Sept. 21, 2010, effective Jan. 1, 2011.

Rule 23. Filing

A. Time for Filing. All papers will be deemed filed with the Clerk when they are:

(1) personally delivered to the Clerk (which, when the Clerk's Office is open for business, shall mean personally tendering the papers to the Clerk or the Clerk's designee; and at all other times (unless the Clerk specifies otherwise) shall mean properly depositing the papers into the "rotunda filing drop box" located in the vestibule of the east second-floor entrance to the State House);

(2) deposited in the United States Mail, postage prepaid, properly addressed to the Clerk; or

(3) deposited with any third-party commercial carrier for delivery to the Clerk within three (3) calendar days, cost prepaid, properly addressed.

B. Clerk's Functions. All functions performed by the Clerk are ministerial and not discretionary. The court retains the authority to determine compliance with these Rules.

C. Number of Copies. The following shall be filed:

(1) *Notice of Appeal.* An original and one (1) copy of the Notice of Appeal.

(2) *Appearances.* An original and one (1) copy of any appearance.

(3) *Motions.*

(a) An original and one (1) copy of a motion for extension of time, a motion to withdraw the record, a motion to withdraw appearance, and a motion to file an oversize document.

(b) An original and five (5) copies of all other motions and supporting documents, of all responses and supporting documents, and of all replies and supporting documents.

(4) *Briefs, Addenda to Briefs, Petitions, Additional Authorities.* An original and eight (8) copies of all briefs, Addenda to Briefs, Petitions to Transfer, Petitions for Rehearing, Petitions for Review and notices of additional authorities.

(5) *Authorization or Affidavit In Forma Pauperis Proceedings.* An original and (1) copy of the trial court authorization to proceed in forma pauperis, or an affidavit that the party was permitted to proceed in forma pauperis in the trial court. See Rule 40.

(6) *Appendices.* One (1) copy of any Appendix. See Rule 50.

(7) *Notices by the trial court clerk or Administrative Agency.* One (1) original of the Notice of Completion of Clerk's Record and Notice of Completion of Transcript. See Rules 10(C) and (D).

(8) *Acknowledgement of Oral Argument.* An original and one (1) copy of any acknowledgment of the order setting oral argument. See Rule 52(C).

(9) *Other Documents.* An original and five (5) copies of all other documents filed with the Clerk.

D. Received but not Filed. When the Clerk accepts any document as received but not filed, any time limit for response or reply to that document shall run from the date on which the document is filed. The Clerk shall notify all parties of the date on which any received document is subsequently filed.

E. Signature required. Every motion, petition, brief, appendix, acknowledgment, notice, response, reply, or appearance must be signed by at least one [1] attorney of record in the attorney's individual name, whose name, address, telephone number, and attorney number shall also be typed or printed legibly below the signature. If a party or amicus is not represented by an attorney, then the party or amicus shall sign such documents and type or print legibly the party or amicus's name, address, and telephone number. The signing of the verification of accuracy required by Rule 50(A)(2)(i) or 50(B)(1)(f) satisfies this requirement for appendices.

Adopted Feb. 4, 2000, effective Jan. 1, 2001; amended Dec. 22, 2000, effective Jan. 1, 2001; amended Dec. 21, 2001, effective April 1, 2002; amended Sept. 10, 2007, effective Jan. 1, 2008; amended Sept. 9, 2008, effective Jan. 1, 2009; amended Sept. 20, 2011, effective Jan. 1, 2012; amended Sept. 13, 2013, effective Jan. 1, 2014.

Rule 24. Service Of Documents

A. Required Service.

(1) *Notice of Appeal.* A party filing a Notice of Appeal shall contemporaneously serve a copy upon:

(a) all parties of record in the trial court or Administrative Agency;

(b) the clerk of the trial court or Administrative Agency;

(c) the court reporter;

(d) any persons identified in Rule 14.1, if applicable;

(e) the Attorney General in all Criminal Appeals and any appeals from a final judgment declaring a state statute unconstitutional in whole or in part;

(f) the judge of the trial court or hearing officer of an Administrative Agency before whom the case was heard; and,

(g) any other persons required by statute to be served.

(See Form # App.R. 9–1).

(2) *Documents filed in the thirty-day period following the filing of Notice of Appeal.* A party filing any document in the thirty- day period after a Notice of Appeal is filed shall contemporaneously serve a copy upon:

(a) all parties of record in the trial court or Administrative Agency;

(b) all parties of record who have filed a Notice of Appeal or an appearance with the Clerk;

(c) any persons seeking party status, and,

(d) any persons required by statute to be served.

(3) *Other documents.* Unless otherwise provided by these Rules, all other documents tendered to the Clerk for filing must contemporaneously be served upon:

(a) all parties of record who have filed a Notice of Appeal or an appearance with the Clerk;

(b) any persons seeking party status; and,

(c) any persons required by statute to be served.

(4) *Appendix in Criminal Appeals.* In criminal appeals only, any Appendix or Supplemental Appendix need not be served on the Attorney General.

B. Time for Service. A party shall serve a document no later than the date the document is filed or received for filing.

C. Manner and Date of Service. All papers will be deemed served when they are:

(1) personally delivered;

(2) deposited in the United States Mail, postage prepaid, properly addressed; or

(3) deposited with any third-party commercial carrier for delivery within three (3) calendar days, cost prepaid, properly addressed.

Parties appealing pursuant to Rule 14.1 must comply with the additional requirements found in that Rule.

D.   Certificate of Service.

(1) *Content.* Anyone tendering a document to the Clerk for filing shall:

(a) certify that service has been made;

(b) specifically list the persons served by name;

(c) specify the date and means of service;

(d) include any information required by Rule 14.1, if applicable; and,

(e) if the document is a Notice of Appeal, certify the date on which the Notice of Appeal was filed with the Clerk. (See Form # App.R. 9–1).

(2) *Placement.* The certificate of service shall be placed at the end of the document and shall not be separately filed. The separate filing of a certificate of service, however, shall not be grounds for rejecting a document for filing.

Adopted Feb. 4, 2000, effective Jan. 1, 2001; amended Dec. 21, 2001, effective April 1, 2002; amended Sept. 20, 2011, effective Jan. 1, 2012.

Rule 25.   Computation Of Time

A.   Non–Business and Business Days. For purposes of this rule, a non-business day shall mean a Saturday, a Sunday, a legal holiday as defined by state statute, or a day the Office of the Clerk is closed during regular business hours. A business day shall mean all other days.

B.   Counting Days. In computing any period of time allowed by these Rules, by order of the court, or by any applicable statute, the day of the act, event, or default from which the designated period of time begins to run shall not be included. The last day of the period so computed is to be included unless it is a non-business day. If the last day is a non-business day, the period runs until the end of the next business day. When the time allowed is less than seven (7) days, all nonbusiness days shall be excluded from the computation.

C.   Extension of Time When Served by Mail or Carrier. When a party serves a document by mail or third-party commercial carrier, the time period for filing any response or reply to the document shall be extended automatically for an additional three (3) calendar days from the date of deposit in the mail or with the carrier. This Rule does not extend any time period that is not triggered by a party's service of a document, such as the time for filing a Petition for Rehearing or a Petition to Transfer.

Adopted Feb. 4, 2000, effective Jan. 1, 2001. Amended Sept. 20, 2011, effective Jan. 1, 2012.

Rule 26.   Electronic Transmission By Clerk

A.   Transmission of Orders, Opinions, and Notices to Parties Represented by Attorneys. The Clerk shall transmit orders, opinions, and notices by electronic mail to all parties represented by attorneys.

B.   Transmission of Orders, Opinions, and Notices to Unrepresented Parties. The Clerk shall transmit orders, opinions, and notices by regular U.S. mail or personal delivery to all unrepresented parties unless the party requests electronic mail transmission or FAX transmission. A request to receive electronic mail or FAX transmission must be in writing, provide the electronic mail address or FAX number at which transmission is to be made, and be signed by the unrepresented party making the request. A party requesting electronic mail or FAX transmission may request either, but not both.

C.   Clerk's Functions. When transmission is made by electronic mail, the Clerk shall retain a copy of the sent electronic mail as a record of transmission. When transmission is made by FAX, the Clerk shall retain the machine-generated transmission log as a record of transmission. The Clerk may, without notice, discontinue FAX transmission if the Clerk determines FAX transmission is not practicable. When transmittal is made by electronic mail or FAX, no other transmission will be made.

Adopted Feb. 4, 2000, effective Jan. 1, 2001. Amended Oct. 2, 2009, effective Jan. 1, 2010.

TITLE V.   RECORD ON APPEAL

Rule 27.   The Record On Appeal

The Record on Appeal shall consist of the Clerk's Record and all proceedings before the trial court or Administrative Agency, whether or not transcribed or transmitted to the Court on Appeal. Any provision of these Rules regarding preparation of the Record on Appeal may be enforced by order of the Court on Appeal. The Record of Proceedings is abolished.

Adopted Feb. 4, 2000, effective Jan. 1, 2001.

Rule 28.   Preparation Of Transcript In Paper Format By Court Reporter

A.   Paper Transcript. Except as provided in Rule 30, the court reporter shall prepare a paper Transcript as follows:

(1) *Paper.* The Transcript shall be prepared upon 8½ × 11 inch white paper.

(2) *Numbering.* The lines of each page shall be numbered and the pages shall be numbered at the bottom. Each page shall contain no less than twenty-five (25) lines unless it is a final page. The pages of the Transcript shall be numbered consecutively re-

gardless of the number of volumes the Transcript requires.

(3) *Margins.* The margins for the text shall be as follows:

Top margin: one (1) inch from the edge of the page.

Bottom margin: one (1) inch from the edge of the page.

Left margin: no more than one and one-half (1–½) inch from the edge of the binding.

Right margin: one (1) inch from the edge of the page.

Indented text: no more than two (2) inches from the left edge of the binding.

(4) *Header or Footer Notations.* The court reporter shall note in boldface capital letters at the top or bottom of each page where a witness' direct, cross, or redirect examination begins. No other notations are required.

(5) *Typing.* The typeface shall be no larger than 12-point type. Line spacing shall be no greater than double-spacing.

(6) *Binding.* The Transcript shall have a front and back cover and shall be bound at the left no more than one-half (½) inch from the edge of the page. The Transcript shall be bound using any method which is easy to read and permits easy disassembly for copying. No more than two hundred fifty (250) pages shall be bound into any one volume.

(7) *Title Page and Cover.* The title page of each volume shall conform to Form #App.R. 28–1, and the cover shall be clear plastic.

(8) *Table of Contents.* The court reporter shall prepare a table of contents listing each witness and the volume and page where that witness' direct, cross, and redirect examination begins. The table of contents shall identify each exhibit offered and shall show the Transcript volumes and pages at which the exhibit was identified and at which a ruling was made on its admission in evidence. The table of contents shall be a separately bound volume.

B. Certification. The court reporter shall certify the Transcript is correct, and file the certificate with the trial court clerk or appropriate administrative officer.

C. Copy of Paper Transcript in Electronic Format. All paper Transcripts generated on a word processing system shall be accompanied by a copy of the Transcript in electronic format.

D. Electronic Transcripts in Mandate Cases. In cases arising under Ind. Trial Rule 60.5, the Transcript shall be in an electronic format as set out in Rule 30(A)(2), (6), and (B), or as otherwise ordered pursuant to Rule 61.

Adopted Feb. 4, 2000, effective Jan. 1, 2001; amended Dec. 21, 2001, effective April 1, 2002; amended Sept. 13, 2013, effective Jan. 1, 2014.

Rule 29. Exhibits

A. Documentary Exhibits. Documentary exhibits, including testimony in written form filed in Administrative Agency proceedings and photographs, shall be included in separately-bound volumes that conform to the requirements of Rule 28(A)(6). The court reporter shall also prepare an index of the exhibits contained in the separately-bound volumes, and that index will be placed at the front of the first volume of exhibits.

B. Nondocumentary and Oversized Exhibits. Nondocumentary and oversized exhibits shall not be sent to the Court, but shall remain in the custody of the trial court or Administrative Agency during the appeal. Such exhibits shall be briefly identified in the Transcript where they were admitted into evidence. Photographs of any exhibit may be included in the volume of documentary exhibits.

Adopted Feb. 4, 2000, effective Jan. 1, 2001; amended Dec. 21, 2001, effective April 1, 2002.

Rule 30. Preparation of Transcript in Electronic Format Only

A. Preparation of Electronic Transcript. With the approval of all parties on appeal and the Court on Appeal, the court reporter shall submit only an electronically formatted Transcript in accordance with the following:

(1) *Approval by Court on Appeal.* At the time the Notice of Appeal is filed with the Clerk, all parties to the appeal may jointly move the Court on Appeal to accept only an electronically formatted Transcript.

(2) *Transcription of Evidence.* Consistent with the standards set forth in this rule, the court reporter shall transcribe the evidence on an electronically formatted medium thereby creating an electronic Transcript. The electronic Transcript shall be paginated and the lines sequentially numbered. Marginal notations are not required, but the electronic Transcript shall designate the point at which exhibits, by exhibit number, are considered at trial.

(3) *Technical Standards.* Standards for electronic media, transmission methods, and file format shall be determined by the Division of State Court Administration. The Division of State Court Administration shall publish the established standards and distribute copies of such rules to all trial court clerks and Administrative Agencies. See, Appendix B—Standards for Preparation of Electronic Transcripts Pursuant to Appellate Rule 30.

(4) *Exhibits.* Rule 29 shall govern the submission of exhibits. Exhibits governed by Rule 29(A) shall be arranged in numerical order, indexed and included in a separate bound volume. See Rule 28(A)(6).

(5) *Labeling.* The court reporter shall transcribe the evidence on one or more sequentially numbered

electronic data storage devices for each complete transcription. Each device shall be labeled or tagged to identify the names of the parties and case number in the proceedings in the trial court; the Court on Appeal case number, if known; the device sequence number, if more than one (1) device is required for a complete Transcript; the signature of the court reporter; and whether the device is the official record, official working copy, court reporter's copy or party copy.

(6) Certification of Electronic Record. The signature of the court reporter on the electronic data storage device shall constitute the reporter's certificate.

B. Submission of Electronic Transcript. Following certification of the Transcript, the court reporter shall seal the official record and official working copy in an envelope or package bearing the trial court case number and marked "Transcript". The court reporter shall retain the court reporter's copy of the electronic Transcript and provide each party with the party's copy of the electronic Transcript. The sealed electronic Transcript copies, paper exhibits, and photographic reproductions of oversized exhibits (if included pursuant to Rule 29(a)) shall be filed with the trial court clerk in accordance with Rule 11.

C. Processing of Electronic Transcript by Clerk. Upon receipt of an electronic Transcript, the Clerk shall file stamp the envelope that will be used to store the electronic data storage device; the original envelope submitted by the court reporter may be used for this purpose, if appropriate. The Clerk shall transmit and microfilm the record in a format as directed by the Court. Standards for the microfilm process shall conform to Administrative Rule 6. The official copy will remain in the custody and control of the Clerk pending the appeal. The official working copy will be employed by the Court on Appeal during its review of the case. Following the completion of the case, a paper or microfilm copy of the electronic Transcript shall be indexed as part of the case.

Adopted Feb. 4, 2000, effective Jan. 1, 2001. Amended Dec. 22, 2000, effective Jan. 1, 2001; Dec. 21, 2001, effective April 1, 2002; amended effective Oct. 26, 2005; amended Sept. 21, 2010, effective Jan. 1, 2011; effective Jan. 1, 2012; amended Sept. 13, 2013, effective Jan. 1, 2014.

Rule 31. Statement Of Evidence When No Transcript Is Available

A. Party's Statement of Evidence. If no Transcript of all or part of the evidence is available, a party or the party's attorney may prepare a verified statement of the evidence from the best available sources, which may include the party's or the attorney's recollection. The party shall then file a motion to certify the statement of evidence with the trial court or Administrative Agency. The statement of evidence shall be attached to the motion.

B. Response. Any party may file a verified response to the proposed statement of evidence within fifteen (15) days after service.

C. Certification by Trial Court or Administrative Agency. Except as provided in Section D below, the trial court or Administrative Agency shall, after a hearing, if necessary, certify a statement of the evidence, making any necessary modifications to statements proposed by the parties. The certified statement of the evidence shall become part of the Clerk's Record.

D. Controversy Regarding Action of Trial Court Judge or Administrative Officer. If the statements or conduct of the trial court judge or administrative officer are in controversy, and the trial court judge or administrative officer refuses to certify the moving party's statement of evidence, the trial court judge or administrative officer shall file an affidavit setting forth his or her recollection of the disputed statements or conduct. All verified statements of the evidence and affidavits shall become part of the Clerk's Record.

Adopted Feb. 4, 2000, effective Jan. 1, 2001.

Rule 32. Correction Or Modification Of Clerk's Record Or Transcript

A. Submission of Disagreement Regarding Contents to Trial Court or Administrative Agency. If a disagreement arises as to whether the Clerk's Record or Transcript accurately discloses what occurred in the trial court or the Administrative Agency, any party may move the trial court or the Administrative Agency to resolve the disagreement. The trial court retains jurisdiction to correct or modify the Clerk's Record or Transcript at any time before the reply brief is due to be filed. After that time, the movant must request leave of the Court on Appeal to correct or modify the Clerk's Record or Transcript. The trial court or Administrative Agency shall issue an order, which shall become part of the Clerk's Record, that either:

(1) confirms that the Clerk's Record or Transcript reflects what actually occurred; or

(2) corrects the Clerk's Record or Transcript, including the chronological case summary if necessary; to reflect what actually occurred.

B. Transmission of Order. The trial court clerk shall transmit to the Court on Appeal:

(1) the trial court's order or order of an Administrative Agency and any corrections to the Clerk's Record; and

(2) any corrections to the Transcript by means of a supplemental Transcript. See Rule 9(G). The title of any corrected Transcript shall indicate that it is a corrected Transcript.

Adopted Feb. 4, 2000, effective Jan. 1, 2001.

Rule 33.   Record On Agreed Statement

A.   Applicability. The procedure in this Rule may be used only by the agreement of all the parties that the issues presented by the appeal are capable of resolution without reference to a Clerk's Record or Transcript.

B.   Content. The agreed statement of the record shall set forth only so many of the facts proved or sought to be proved as are essential to a decision of the questions by the court on appeal. The agreed statement shall include:

(1) a copy of the appealed judgment or order;

(2) a copy of the Notice of Appeal with its filing date;

(3) a statement of how the issues arose in the trial court or Administrative Agency; and

(4) the signatures of all parties or their attorneys.

C.   Certification by Trial Court or Administrative Agency. The parties shall submit the agreed statement of the record to the trial court or the Administrative Agency, which shall certify it if it is accurate and adequate for resolution of the issues presented by the appeal. The trial court may amend or supplement the agreed statement with the consent of all parties before certification.

D.   Transmission to the Court on Appeal. The agreed statement of the record shall be a part of the Clerk's Record. The appellant shall include the agreed statement of the record in an Appendix to the appellant's brief. See Rule 50.

E.   Extensions of Time. Use of this procedure does not automatically extend any appellate deadline, but extensions of time may be sought under Rule 35.

Adopted Feb. 4, 2000, effective Jan. 1, 2001.

TITLE VI. MOTIONS

Rule 34.   Motion Practice

A.   Use of Motion. Unless a statute or these Rules provide another form of application, a request for an order or for other relief shall be made by filing a motion in writing.

B.   Motions Subject to Decision Without Response. The Court will not await a response before ruling on the following motions:

(1) to extend time;

(2) to file an oversize Petition, brief or motion;

(3) to withdraw appearance;

(4) to substitute a party; and

(5) to withdraw the record.

The Court will consider any responses filed before it rules on the motion. A response filed after ruling on the motion will automatically be treated as a motion to reconsider; any party may file a motion to reconsider a decision on a motion described in this Section within ten (10) days after the Court's ruling on the motion.

C.   Response. Any party may file a response to a motion within fifteen (15) days after the motion is served. The fact that no response is filed does not affect the Court's discretion in ruling on the motion.

D.   Reply. The movant may not file a reply to a response without leave of the Court. Any reply must be filed with the motion for leave, and tendered within five (5) days of service of the response.

E.   Content of Motions, Responses and Replies. Except for the motions listed in Rule 34(B), a motion, response, or reply shall contain the following, but headings are not required:

(1) *Statement of Grounds.* A statement particularizing the grounds on which the motion, response, or reply is based;

(2) *Statement of Supporting Facts.* The specific facts supporting those grounds, including page citation to the Clerk's Record or Transcript or other supporting material;

(3) *Statement of Supporting Law.* All supporting legal arguments, including citation to authority;

(4) *Other Required Matters.* Any matter specifically required by a Rule governing the motion; and

(5) *Request for Relief.* A specific and clear statement of the relief sought.

F.   Verification of Facts Outside the Record on Appeal. When the motion, response, or reply relies on facts not contained in materials that have been filed with the Clerk, the motion, response, or reply shall be verified and/or accompanied by affidavits or certified copies of documents filed with the trial court clerk or Administrative Agency.

G.   Form of Motions, Responses and Replies.

(1) *Form; Citations; References.* Motions, responses and replies shall conform to the requirements for briefs under Rule 43(B)-(G).

(2) *Length.* Unless the Court provides otherwise, a motion or a response shall not exceed ten (10) pages or 4,200 words, and replies shall not exceed five (5) pages or 2,100 words. If the document exceeds the page limit, it must contain a word count certificate in compliance with Rule 44(F).

H.   Oral Argument. Ordinarily oral argument will not be heard on any motion.

Adopted Feb. 4, 2000, effective Jan. 1, 2001. Amended July 1, 2005, effective Jan. 1, 2006.

Rule 35.   Motion For Extension Of Time

A.   Time for Filing. Any motion for an extension of time shall be filed at least seven (7) days before the expiration of time unless the movant was not then aware of the facts on which the motion is based. No motion for an extension of time shall be filed after the time for doing the act expires.

B. Content.

(1) *Required in All Motions.* All motions shall be verified and state

(a) The date of the appealed judgment or order.

(b) The date any motion to correct error was ruled on or deemed denied.

(c) The date the Notice of Appeal was filed.

(d) The time period that is sought to be extended, and the event which triggered it.

(e) The date the act is to be done, how that date was established, including, if relevant, the means of service, whether the current due date is pursuant to a previous extension of time, and if so, whether final.

(f) The due date requested. This date shall be a business day as defined by Rule 25.

(g) The reason, in spite of the exercise of due diligence shown, for requesting the extension of time, including, but not limited to, the following:

(i) Engagement in other litigation, provided such litigation is identified by caption, number and court;

(ii) The matter under appeal is so complex that an adequate brief cannot reasonably be prepared by the date the brief is due; or

(iii) Hardship to counsel will result unless an extension is granted, in which event the nature of the hardship must be set forth.

(h) If the motion is filed within seven (7) days before the expiration of time, the reasons why counsel was unaware of the need for the extension.

(2) *Criminal Appeals.* A motion in a Criminal Appeal shall also state, if applicable:

(a) the date the trial court granted permission to file a belated Notice of Appeal or a belated motion to correct error;

(b) the date of sentencing;

(c) the sentence imposed; and

(d) a concise statement of the status of the case, including whether the defendant has been released on bond, and whether the defendant has been incarcerated.

C. Proceedings in Which Extensions are Prohibited. No motion for extension of time shall be granted to file a Petition for Rehearing, a Petition to Transfer to the Supreme Court, any brief supporting or responding to such Petitions, or in appeals involving termination of parental rights.

D. Restrictions on Extensions. Motions for extension of time in appeals involving worker's compensation, issues of child custody, support, visitation, paternity, adoption, and determination that a child is in need of services shall be granted only in extraordinary circumstances.

Adopted Feb. 4, 2000, effective Jan. 1, 2001. Amended Aug. 15, 2006, effective Jan. 1, 2007; amended effective May 2, 2008; amended Sept. 21, 2010, effective Jan. 1, 2011.

Rule 36. Motion To Dismiss

A. Voluntary Dismissal. An appeal may be dismissed on motion of the appellant upon the terms agreed upon by all the parties on appeal or fixed by the Court.

B. Involuntary Dismissal. An appellee may at any time file a motion to dismiss an appeal for any reason provided by law, including lack of jurisdiction. Motions to affirm are abolished.

Adopted Feb. 4, 2000, effective Jan. 1, 2001.

Rule 37. Motion To Remand

A. Content of Motion. At any time after the Court on Appeal obtains jurisdiction, any party may file a motion requesting that the appeal be dismissed without prejudice or temporarily stayed and the case remanded to the trial court or Administrative Agency for further proceedings. The motion must be verified and demonstrate that remand will promote judicial economy or is otherwise necessary for the administration of justice.

B. Effect of Remand. The Court on Appeal may dismiss the appeal without prejudice, and remand the case to the trial court, or remand the case while retaining jurisdiction, with or without limitation on the trial court's authority. Unless the order specifically provides otherwise, the trial court or Administrative Agency shall obtain unlimited authority on remand.

Adopted Feb. 4, 2000, effective Jan. 1, 2001.

Rule 38. Motion To Consolidate Appeals

A. Cases Consolidated at Trial or Hearing. When two (2) or more actions have been consolidated for trial or hearing in the trial court or Administrative Agency, they shall remain consolidated on appeal. If any party believes that the appeal should not remain consolidated, that party may file a motion to sever the consolidated appeal within thirty (30) days after the first Notice of Appeal is filed.

B. Cases Consolidated on Appeal. Where there is more than one (1) appeal from the same order or judgment or where two (2) or more appeals involve a common question of law or fact, the Court on Appeal may order a consolidation of the appeals upon its own motion, or upon the motion of any party.

Adopted Feb. 4, 2000, effective Jan. 1, 2001.

Rule 39. Motion To Stay

A. Effect of Appeal. An appeal does not stay the effect or enforceability of a judgment or order of a trial court or Administrative Agency unless the trial court, Administrative Agency or Court on Appeal otherwise orders.

B. Motion in Trial Court or Administrative Agency. Except as provided in (C)(2)(b), a motion for stay pending appeal may not be filed in the Court on Appeal unless a motion for stay was filed and denied by the trial court or by the Administrative Agency if it has authority to grant a stay. If the Administrative Agency does not have such authority, application for stay may be made directly to the Court on Appeal.

C. Motion in Court on Appeal. A motion for a stay pending appeal in the Court on Appeal shall contain certified or verified copies of the following:

(1) the judgment or order to be stayed;

(2) the order denying the motion for stay or a verified showing that (a) the trial court or Administrative Agency has failed to rule on the motion within a reasonable time in light of the circumstances and relief requested; or (b) extraordinary circumstances exist which excuse the filing of a motion to stay in the trial court or Administrative Agency altogether;

(3) other parts of the Clerk's Record or Transcript that are relevant;

(4) an attorney certificate evidencing the date, time, place and method of service made upon all other parties; and

(5) an attorney certificate setting forth in detail why all other parties should not be heard prior to the granting of said stay.

D. Emergency Stays. If an emergency stay without notice is requested, the moving party shall submit:

(1) an affidavit setting forth specific facts clearly establishing that immediate and irreparable injury, loss, or damage will result to the moving party before all other parties can be heard in opposition;

(2) a certificate from the attorney for the moving party setting forth in detail the efforts, if any, which have been made to give notice to the other parties and the reasons supporting his claim that notice should not be required; and

(3) a proposed order setting forth the remedy being requested.

E. Bond. If a stay is granted, the Court on Appeal may fix bond in accordance with Rule 18.

F. Length of Stay. Unless otherwise ordered, a stay shall remain in effect until the appeal is disposed of in the Court on Appeal. Any party may move for relief from the stay at any time.

Adopted Feb. 4, 2000, effective Jan. 1, 2001. Amended Dec. 21, 2001, effective April 1, 2002; July 1, 2003, effective Jan. 1, 2004; Sept. 21, 2010, effective Jan. 1, 2011.

Rule 40. Motion To Proceed In *Forma Pauperis*

A. Appeal From a Trial Court.

(1) *Prior Authorization by the Trial Court.* A party who has been permitted to proceed in the trial court in *forma pauperis* may proceed on appeal in *forma pauperis* without further authorization from the trial court or Court on Appeal. See Rule 9(E).

(2) *Motion to the Trial Court.* Any other party in a trial court who desires to proceed on appeal in *forma pauperis* shall file in the trial court a motion for leave to so proceed, together with an affidavit conforming to Form #App.R. 40–1, showing in detail the party's inability to pay fees or costs or to give security therefor, the party's belief that the party is entitled to redress, and a statement of the issues the party intends to present on appeal. If the trial court grants the motion, the party may proceed without further motion to the Court on Appeal. If the trial court denies the motion, the trial court shall state in a written order the reasons for the denial.

(3) *Revocation of Authorization by the Trial Court.* Before or after the Notice of Appeal is filed, the trial court may certify to or find that a party is no longer entitled to proceed in forma pauperis. The trial court shall state in a written order the reasons for such certification or finding.

(4) *Motion to the Court on Appeal.* If the trial court denies a party authorization to proceed in *forma pauperis* the party may file a motion in the Court on Appeal for leave to so proceed within thirty (30) days of service of the trial court's order. The motion shall be accompanied by a copy of any affidavit supporting the party's request filed in the trial court. If no affidavit was filed in the trial court or if the affidavit filed in the trial court is no longer accurate, the motion shall be accompanied by an affidavit conforming to Form #App.R. 40–1. The motion shall be accompanied by a copy of the order setting forth the trial court's reasons for denying the party in *forma pauperis* status on appeal.

B. Appeal From an Administrative Agency. Any party to a proceeding before an Administrative Agency who desires to proceed in *forma pauperis* on appeal shall file with the Court on Appeal a motion for leave to so proceed, together with an affidavit conforming to Form #App.R. 40–1, showing in detail the party's inability to pay fees or costs or to give security therefor, the party's belief that the party is entitled to redress, and a statement of the issues the party intends to present on appeal.

C. Filings Required in the Court on Appeal. With the first document a party proceeding or desiring to proceed in *forma pauperis* files in the Court on Appeal, the party shall file with the Clerk:

(1) the trial court's authorization to proceed in *forma pauperis* on appeal;

(2) an affidavit stating that the party was permitted to proceed in *forma pauperis* in the trial court and that the trial court has made no certification or finding under Rule 40(A)(3); or

(3) a motion to the Court on Appeal to proceed in *forma pauperis*.

If the trial court subsequently enters an order containing a certification or finding under Rule 40 (A)(3), the party shall promptly file the trial court's order with the Clerk.

D. Effect of In *Forma Pauperis* Status. A party proceeding in *forma pauperis*:

(1) is relieved of the obligation to prepay filing fees or costs in either the trial court or the Court on Appeal or to give security therefor; and

(2) may file legibly handwritten or typewritten briefs and other papers.

Adopted Feb. 4, 2000, effective Jan. 1, 2001; amended Dec. 22, 2000, effective Jan. 1, 2001.

Rule 41. Motion to Appear As *Amicus Curiae*

A. Content. A proposed amicus curiae shall file a motion to appear as an *amicus curiae*. The motion shall identify the interest of the proposed *amicus curiae* and the party with whom the proposed *amicus curiae* is substantively aligned, and it shall state the reasons why an *amicus curiae* brief would be helpful to the court.

B. Time for Filing. The proposed *amicus curiae* shall file its motion to appear within the time allowed the party with whom the proposed *amicus curiae* is substantively aligned to file its brief or Petition. If an entity has been granted leave to appear as an *amicus curiae* in a case before the Court of Appeals or the Tax Court, that entity need not again seek leave to appear as an *amicus curiae* in any continuation of that case before the Supreme Court.

C. Tender of Brief. The proposed *amicus curiae* shall tender or file its *amicus curiae* brief within the time allowed the party with whom the proposed *amicus curiae* is substantively aligned.

D. Belated Filing. The court may permit the belated filing of an *amicus curiae* brief on motion for good cause. If the court grants the motion, the court shall set a deadline for any opposing party to file a reply brief.

E. *Amicus Curiae* Appendix and Addendum to Brief. An entity granted *amicus curiae* status may not file an Appendix or Addendum to the Brief containing documents that are not within the Record on Appeal unless leave to do so has been first granted.

Adopted Feb. 4, 2000, effective Jan. 1, 2001. Amended July 19, 2002, effective Jan. 1, 2003; Sept. 21, 2010, effective Jan. 1, 2011.

Rule 42. Motion To Strike

Upon motion made by a party within the time to respond to a document, or if there is no response permitted, within thirty (30) days after the service of the document upon it, or at any time upon the court's own motion, the court may order stricken from any document any redundant, immaterial, impertinent, scandalous or other inappropriate matter.

Adopted Feb. 4, 2000, effective Jan. 1, 2001.

TITLE VII. BRIEFS

Rule 43. Form Of Briefs And Petitions

A. Applicability. This Rule governs the form of briefs, Petitions for Rehearing (Rule 54), Petitions to Transfer to the Supreme Court (Rule 57), and Petitions for Review of a Tax Court decision (Rule 63) by the Supreme Court.

B. Paper. The pages shall be 8½ by 11 inch white paper of a weight normally used in printing and typing.

C. Production. The document shall be produced in a neat and legible manner using black print. It may be typewritten, printed or produced by a word processing system. It may be copied by any copying process that produces a distinct black image on white paper. Text shall appear on only one side of the paper.

D. Print Size. The font shall be Arial, Baskerville, Book Antigua, Bookman, Bookman Old Style, Century, Century Schoolbook, Courier, Courier New, CG Times, Garamond, Georgia, New Baskerville, New Century Schoolbook, Palatino or Times New Roman and the typeface shall be 12–point or larger in both body text and footnotes.

E. Spacing. All printing in the text shall be double-spaced except lengthy quotes and footnotes shall be single-spaced. Single-spaced lines shall be separated by at least 4-point spaces.

F. Numbering. The pages shall be numbered at the bottom.

G. Margins. All four margins for the text of the document shall be at least one (1) inch from the edge of the page.

H. Cover Colors. The document shall have a front and back cover in the following colors:

Appellant's Brief and Appendix: Blue.

Appellee's Brief and Appendix: Red.

Any reply brief (except as provided below): Gray.

Brief of intervenor or amicus curiae: Green.

Petition for Rehearing: White.

Brief in response to a Petition for Rehearing: White.

Petition to Transfer or for Review: Orange.

Brief in response to a Petition seeking Transfer or Review: Yellow.

Reply brief to brief in response to a Petition seeking Transfer or Review: Tan.

I. Cover Content. The front cover of the document shall conform substantially to Form #App.R. 43–1.

J. Binding. The document shall be bound in book or pamphlet form along the left margin. Any binding process which permits the document to lie flat when opened is preferred.

K. Copy of Document in Electronic Format. All documents may be accompanied by a copy of the document in electronic format. Any electronic format used by the word processing system to generate the document is permissible.

Adopted Feb. 4, 2000, effective Jan. 1, 2001. Amended Dec. 21, 2001, effective April 1, 2002; Aug. 15, 2006, effective Jan. 1, 2007; amended Sept. 10, 2007, effective Jan. 1, 2008; amended effective May 2, 2008.

Rule 44. Brief And Petition Length Limitations

A. Applicability. This Rule governs the length of briefs, Petitions for Rehearing, Petitions to Transfer to the Supreme Court, and Petitions for Review of a Tax Court decision by the Supreme Court.

B. Oversized Brief. A motion requesting leave to file any oversized brief or Petition shall be filed at least fifteen (15) days before the brief or Petition is due. The motion shall state the total number of words requested, not pages.

C. Items Excluded From Length Limits. The text of the following shall not be included in the page or word length limits of this rule:

Cover information

Table of contents

Table of authorities

Signature block

Certificate of service

Word count certificate

Appealed judgment or order of trial court or Administrative Agency, and items identified in Rule 46(A)(10).

Headings and footnotes are included in the length limits.

D. Page Limits. Unless a word count complying with Section E is provided, a brief or Petition may not exceed the following number of pages:

Appellant's brief: thirty (30) pages

Appellee's brief: thirty (30) pages

Reply brief (except as provided below): fifteen (15) pages

Reply brief with cross-appellee's brief: thirty (30) pages

Brief of intervenor or amicus curiae: fifteen (15) pages

Petition for Rehearing: ten (10) pages

Brief in response to a Petition for Rehearing: ten (10) pages

Petition to Transfer: ten (10) pages

Brief in response to a Petition seeking Transfer: ten (10) pages

Reply brief to brief in response to a Petition seeking Transfer: three (3) pages

Brief of intervenor or amicus curiae on transfer or rehearing: ten (10) pages

Petition for Review of a Tax Court decision: thirty (30) pages

Brief in response to a Petition for Review of a Tax Court decision: thirty (30) pages

Reply brief to brief in response to a Petition for Review of a Tax Court decision: fifteen (15) pages

E. Word Limits. A brief or Petition exceeding the page limit of Section D may be filed if it does not exceed, and the attorney or the unrepresented party preparing the brief or Petition certifies that, including footnotes, it does not exceed, the following number of words:

Appellant's brief: 14,000 words

Appellee's brief: 14,000 words

Reply brief (except as provided below): 7,000 words

Reply brief with cross-appellee's brief: 14,000 words

Brief of intervenor or amicus curiae: 7,000 words

Petition for Rehearing: 4,200 words

Brief in response to a petition for Rehearing: 4,200 words

Petition to Transfer: 4,200 words

Brief in response to a Petition seeking Transfer: 4,200 words

Reply brief to brief in response to a Petition seeking Transfer: 1,000 words

Brief of intervenor or amicus curiae on transfer or rehearing: 4,200 words

Petition for Review of a Tax Court decision: 14,000 words

Brief in response to a Petition for Review of a Tax Court decision: 14,000 words

Reply brief to brief in response to a Petition for Review of a Tax Court decision: 7,000 words

F. Form of Word Count Certificate. The following are acceptable word count certifications: "I verify that this brief (or Petition) contains no more than (applicable limit) words," and "I verify that this brief (or Petition) contains (actual number) words." The certification shall appear at the end of the brief or Petition before the certificate of service. The attorney or the unrepresented party certifying a word count may rely on the word count of the word processing system used to prepare the brief or Petition.

Adopted Feb. 4, 2000, effective Jan. 1, 2001. Amended Dec. 21, 2001, effective April 1, 2002; July 1, 2005, effective Jan. 1, 2006; amended effective May 2, 2008; amended Sept. 15, 2009, effective Jan. 1, 2010.

Rule 45. Time For Filing Briefs

A. Applicability. This Rule applies to appeals from Final Judgments and interlocutory orders. Filing deadlines relating to Petitions for Rehearing, to Transfer, and for Review are governed by Rules 54, 57 and 63 respectively.

B. Filing Deadlines.

(1) *Appellant's Brief.* The appellant's brief shall be filed no later than thirty (30) days after:

(a) the date the trial court clerk or Administrative Agency serves its notice of completion of Clerk's Record on the parties pursuant to Appellate Rule 10(C) if the notice reports that the Transcript is complete or that no Transcript has been requested; or

(b) in all other cases, the date the trial court clerk or Administrative Agency serves its notice of completion of the Transcript on the parties pursuant to Appellate Rule 10(D).

Rule 25(C), which grants a three-day extension of time for service by mail or third-party commercial carrier, does not extend the due date for filing the appellant's brief.

(2) *Appellee's Brief.* The appellee's brief shall be filed no later than thirty (30) days after service of the appellant's brief.

(3) *Appellant's Reply Brief; Cross-Appellee's Brief.* Any appellant's reply brief shall be filed no later than fifteen (15) days after service of the appellee's brief. If the reply brief also serves as the cross-appellee's brief, it shall be filed no later than thirty (30) days after service of the appellee's brief.

(4) *Cross-Appellant's Reply Brief.* Any cross-appellant's reply brief shall be filed no later than fifteen (15) days after service of the appellant's reply brief.

C. Extensions of Time. Motions for extensions of time to file any briefs are governed by Rule 35.

D. Failure to File Timely. The appellant's failure to file timely the appellant's brief may subject the appeal to summary dismissal. The appellee's failure to file timely the appellee's brief may result in reversal of the trial court or Administrative Agency on the appellant's showing of *prima facie* error.

Adopted Feb. 4, 2000, effective Jan. 1, 2001. Amended Sept. 21, 2010, effective Jan. 1, 2011.

Rule 46. Arrangement And Contents Of Briefs

A. Appellant's Brief. The appellant's brief shall contain the following sections under separate headings and in the following order:

(1) *Table of Contents.* The table of contents shall list each section of the brief, including the headings and subheadings of each section and the page on which they begin.

(2) *Table of Authorities.* The table of authorities shall list each case, statute, rule, and other authority cited in the brief, with references to each page on which it is cited. The authorities shall be listed alphabetically or numerically, as applicable.

(3) *Statement of Supreme Court Jurisdiction.* When an appeal is taken directly to the Supreme Court, the brief shall include a brief statement of the Supreme Court's jurisdiction to hear the direct appeal.

(4) *Statement of Issues.* This statement shall concisely and particularly describe each issue presented for review.

(5) *Statement of Case.* This statement shall briefly describe the nature of the case, the course of the proceedings relevant to the issues presented for review, and the disposition of these issues by the trial court or Administrative Agency. Page references to the Record on Appeal or Appendix are required in accordance with Rule 22(C).

(6) *Statement of Facts.* This statement shall describe the facts relevant to the issues presented for review but need not repeat what is in the statement of the case.

(a) The facts shall be supported by page references to the Record on Appeal or Appendix in accordance with Rule 22(C).

(b) The facts shall be stated in accordance with the standard of review appropriate to the judgment or order being appealed.

(c) The statement shall be in narrative form and shall not be a witness by witness summary of the testimony.

(d) In an appeal challenging a ruling on a post-conviction relief petition, the statement may focus on facts from the post-conviction relief proceeding rather than on facts relating to the criminal conviction.

(7) *Summary of Argument.* The summary should contain a succinct, clear, and accurate statement of the arguments made in the body of the brief. It should not be a mere repetition of the argument headings.

(8) *Argument.* This section shall contain the appellant's contentions why the trial court or Administrative Agency committed reversible error.

(a) The argument must contain the contentions of the appellant on the issues presented, supported by cogent reasoning. Each contention must be supported by citations to the authorities, statutes, and the Appendix or parts of the Record on Appeal relied on, in accordance with Rule 22.

(b) The argument must include for each issue a concise statement of the applicable standard of review; this statement may appear in the discussion of each issue or under a separate heading placed before the discussion of the issues. In addition, the argument must include a brief statement of the procedural and substantive facts necessary for consideration of the issues presented on appeal, including a statement of how the issues relevant to the appeal were raised and resolved by any Administrative Agency or trial court.

(c) Each argument shall have an argument heading. If substantially the same issue is raised by more than one asserted error, they may be grouped and supported by one argument.

(d) If the admissibility of evidence is in dispute, citation shall be made to the pages of the Transcript where the evidence was identified, offered, and received or rejected, in conformity with Rule 22(C).

(e) When error is predicated on the giving or refusing of any instruction, the instruction shall be set out verbatim in the argument section of the brief with the verbatim objections, if any, made thereto.

(9) *Conclusion.* The conclusion shall include a precise statement of the relief sought and the signature of the attorney and *pro se* party.

(10) *Appealed Judgment or Order.* The brief shall include any written opinion, memorandum of decision or findings of fact and conclusions thereon relating to the issues raised on appeal. When sentence is at issue in a criminal appeal, the brief shall contain a copy of the sentencing order.

(11) *Word Count Certificate* (if necessary). See Rule 44(F).

(12) *Certificate of Service.* See Rule 24(D).

B. Appellee's Brief. The Appellee's Brief shall conform to Section A of this Rule, except as follows:

(1) *Agreement with Appellant's Statements.* The appellee's brief may omit the statement of Supreme Court jurisdiction, the statement of issues, the statement of the case, and the statement of facts if the appellee agrees with the statements in the appellant's brief. If any of these statements is omitted, the brief shall state that the appellee agrees with the appellant's statements.

(2) *Argument.* The argument shall address the contentions raised in the appellant's argument.

(3) *Rule 46(A)(10).* Items listed in Rule 46(A)(10) may be omitted.

C. Appellant's Reply Brief. The appellant may file a reply brief responding to the appellee's argument. No new issues shall be raised in the reply brief. The reply brief shall contain a table of contents, table of authorities, summary of argument, argument, conclusion, word count certificate, if needed, and certificate of service. See Rule 24(D).

D. Cross-Appeals.

(1) *Designation of Parties in Cross-Appeals.* When both parties have filed a Notice of Appeal, the plaintiff in the trial court or Administrative Agency shall be deemed the appellant for the purpose of this Rule, unless the parties otherwise agree or the court otherwise orders. When only one party has filed a Notice of Appeal, that party is the appellant, even if another party raises issues on cross-appeal.

(2) *Appellee's Brief.* The Appellee's Brief shall contain any contentions the appellee raises on cross-appeal as to why the trial court or Administrative Agency committed reversible error.

(3) *Appellant's Reply Brief.* The Appellant's Reply Brief shall address the arguments raised on cross-appeal.

(4) *Cross-Appellant's Reply Brief.* The Cross-Appellant's Reply Brief may only respond to that part of the appellant's reply brief addressing the appellee's cross-appeal.

(5) *Scope of Reply Briefs.* No new issues shall be raised in a reply brief. A reply brief under this section shall contain a table of contents, table of authorities, summary of argument, argument, conclusion, word count certificate, if needed, and certificate of service. See Rule 24(D).

E. Brief of *Amicus Curiae.*

(1) *Preparation.* An amicus curiae brief shall include a table of contents, table of authorities, a brief statement of the interest of the amicus curiae, summary of argument, argument, conclusion, word count certificate, if needed, and certificate of service. See Rule 24(D).

(2) *Avoiding Repetition.* Before completing the preparation of an *amicus curiae* brief, counsel for an *amicus curiae* shall attempt to ascertain the arguments that will be made in the brief of any

party whose position the *amicus curiae* is supporting to avoid repetition or restatement of those arguments in the *amicus curiae* brief.

F. Appendix. Appendices shall be separately bound. See Rule 51.

G. Cases with Multiple Appellants or Appellees. In cases involving more than one appellant or appellee, including cases consolidated for appeal, each party may file a separate brief, more than one party may join in any single brief, or a party may adopt by reference any part of any brief of any party.

H. Addendum to Brief. Any party or any entity granted *amicus curiae* status may elect to file a separately-bound Addendum to Brief. An Addendum to Brief is not required and is not recommended in most cases. An Addendum to Brief is a highly selective compilation of materials filed with a party's brief at the option of the submitting party. Note that only one copy of the Appendix is filed (see Rule 23(C)(6)), but an original and eight copies of any Addendum to Brief must be filed, in accordance with Rule 23(C)(4). If an Addendum to Brief is submitted, it must be filed and served at the time of the filing and service of the brief it accompanies. An Addendum to Brief may include, for example, copies of key documents from the Clerk's Record or Appendix (such as contracts), or exhibits (such as photographs or maps), or copies of critically important pages of testimony from the Transcript, or full text copies of statutes, rules, regulations, etc. that would be helpful to the Court on Appeal but which, for whatever reason, cannot be conveniently or fully reproduced in the body of the brief. An Addendum to Brief may not exceed fifty (50) pages in length and should ordinarily be much shorter in length. The first document in the Addendum to Brief shall be a table of contents, and documents contained in the Addendum to Brief should be indexed or numbered in some manner that facilitates finding the documents referred to therein, preferably with indexed tabs.

The Addendum to Brief shall be bound in book form along the left margin, preferably in a manner that permits the volume to lie flat when opened. The Addendum to Brief shall have a cover that is the same color and similarly styled as the brief it accompanies (see Form App. 43–1), except that it shall be clearly identified as an Addendum to Brief. An Addendum to Brief may not contain argument.

Adopted Feb. 4, 2000, effective Jan. 1, 2001. Amended Dec. 21, 2001, effective April 1, 2002; Sept. 20, 2011, effective Jan. 1, 2012.

Rule 47. Amendment Of Briefs And Petitions

On motion for good cause, the Court may grant leave for a party to amend a brief or Petition. The motion shall describe the nature of and reason for the proposed amendment. The movant shall either tender sufficient copies of an amended brief or Petition (the cover of which shall indicate that it is amended) with its motion or request permission to retrieve the original and all copies of the brief or Petition filed with the Clerk and substitute amended pages. Except as the Court otherwise provides, the amendment of a brief or Petition has no effect on any filing deadlines.

Adopted Feb. 4, 2000, effective Jan. 1, 2001.

Rule 48. Additional Authorities

When pertinent and significant authorities come to the attention of a party after the party's brief or Petition has been filed, or after oral argument but before decision, a party may promptly file with the Clerk a notice of those authorities setting forth the citations. There shall be a reference either to the page of the brief or to a point argued orally to which the citations pertain, with a parenthetical or a single sentence explaining the authority.

Adopted Feb. 4, 2000, effective Jan. 1, 2001.

TITLE VIII. APPENDICES

Rule 49. Filing Of Appendices

A. Time for Filing. The appellant shall file its Appendix with its appellant's brief. The appellee shall file its Appendix, if any, with its appellee's brief. Any party may file a supplemental Appendix without leave of court until the final reply brief is filed. If an appeal is dismissed before an Appendix has been filed and transfer or rehearing is thereafter sought, an Appendix may be filed contemporaneously with the Petition for Rehearing or Transfer and the Briefs in Response.

B. Failure to Include Item. Any party's failure to include any item in an Appendix shall not waive any issue or argument.

Adopted Feb. 4, 2000, effective Jan. 1, 2001. Amended Sept. 21, 2010, effective Jan. 1, 2011.

Rule 50. Contents Of Appendices

A. Appendices in Civil Appeals and Appeals from Administrative Agencies.

(1) *Purpose.* The purpose of an Appendix in civil appeals and appeals from Administrative Agencies is to present the Court with copies of only those parts of the record on appeal that are necessary for the Court to decide the issues presented.

(2) *Contents of Appellant's Appendix.* The appellant's Appendix shall contain a table of contents and copies of the following documents, if they exist:

(a) the chronological case summary for the trial court or Administrative Agency;

(b) the appealed judgment or order, including any written opinion, memorandum of decision, or findings of fact and conclusions thereon relating to the issues raised on appeal;

(c) the jury verdict;

(d) [Deleted, eff. January 1, 2011]

(e) any instruction not included in appellant's brief under Rule 46(A)(8)(e), when error is predicated on the giving or refusing of the instruction;

(f) pleadings and other documents from the Clerk's Record in chronological order that are necessary for resolution of the issues raised on appeal;

(g) any other short excerpts from the Record on Appeal, in chronological order, such as essential portions of a contract or pertinent pictures, that are important to a consideration of the issues raised on appeal;

(h) any record material relied on in the brief unless the material is already included in the Transcript;

(i) a verification of accuracy by the attorney or unrepresented party filing the Appendix. The following is an acceptable verification:

"I verify under penalties of perjury that the documents in this Appendix are accurate copies of parts of the Record on Appeal."

(3) *Appellee's Appendix.* The contents of the appellee's Appendix shall be governed by Section (A)(2) of this Rule, but the appellee's Appendix shall not contain any materials already contained in appellant's Appendix, unless necessary for completeness or context. The Appendix may contain additional items that are relevant to either issues raised on appeal or on cross-appeal.

B. Appendices in Criminal Appeals.

(1) *Contents of Appellant's Appendix.* The appellant's Appendix in a Criminal Appeal shall contain a table of contents and copies of the following documents, if they exist:

(a) the Clerk's Record, including the chronological case summary;

(b) [Deleted, eff. January 1, 2011]

(c) any instruction not included in appellant's brief under Rule 46(A)(8)(e) when error is predicated on the giving or refusing of the instruction;

(d) any other short excerpts from the Record on Appeal, in chronological order, such as pertinent pictures, that are important to a consideration of the issues raised on appeal;

(e) any record material relied on in the brief unless the material is already included in the Transcript;

(f) a verification of accuracy by the attorney or unrepresented party filing the Appendix. The following is an acceptable verification: "I verify under penalties of perjury that the documents

in this Appendix are accurate copies of parts of the Record on Appeal."

(2) *Appellee's Appendix.* The contents of the appellee's Appendix shall be governed by Section (A)(2) of this Rule, but the appellee's Appendix shall not contain any materials already contained in appellant's Appendix, unless necessary for completeness or context. The Appendix may contain additional items that are relevant to either issues raised on appeal or on cross-appeal.

C. Table of Contents. A table of contents shall be prepared for every Appendix. The table of contents shall specifically identify each item contained in the Appendix, including the item's date.

D. Supplemental and Other Appendices. All supplemental and any other appendices shall be governed, to the extent applicable, by Sections A, B, C, E, and F, and shall not duplicate materials contained in other appendices, unless necessary for completeness or context.

E. Cases with Multiple Appellants or Appellees. In cases involving more than one appellant or appellee, including cases consolidated for appeal, each side shall, where practicable, file joint rather than separate appendices to avoid duplication.

F. Transcript. Because the Transcript is transmitted to the Court on Appeal pursuant to Rule 12(B), parties should not reproduce any portion of the Transcript in the Appendix.

Adopted Feb. 4, 2000, effective Jan. 1, 2001. Amended Dec. 21, 2001, effective April 1, 2002; Sept. 21, 2010, effective Jan. 1, 2011.

Rule 51.   Form And Assembly Of Appendices

A. Copying. The copies shall be on 8½ by 11 inch white paper of a weight normally used in printing and typing. The copying process used shall produce text in a distinct black image on only one side of the paper. The left margin shall be wide enough to permit the text to be read after binding . Color copies of exhibits that were originally in color are permitted and encouraged.

B. Order of Documents. Documents included in an Appendix shall be arranged in the order listed in Rule 50.

C. Numbering. All pages of the Appendix shall be numbered at the bottom consecutively, without obscuring the Transcript page numbers, regardless of the number of volumes the Appendix requires.

D. Binding. All Appendices shall be bound separately from the brief. No more than two hundred fifty (250) pages shall be bound into any one Appendix volume. Each volume shall be bound along the left margin. The document shall be bound in book or pamphlet form along the left margin. Any binding process which permits the document to lie flat when opened is preferred. Each volume shall contain a table of contents for the entire Appendix which shall not be included in the page count for that volume.

E. Cover. Each volume of a separately bound Appendix shall have a front and back cover. Each cover of a separately bound Appendix shall be the same color as the brief filed by that party, and the front cover shall state the name of the party submitting the appendix and the brief with which it is submitted, if any. The front cover shall conform substantially to Form #App.R. 51–1.

Adopted Feb. 4, 2000, effective Jan. 1, 2001.

TITLE IX. ORAL ARGUMENT

Rule 52. Setting And Acknowledging Oral Argument

A. Court's Discretion. The Court may, in its discretion, set oral argument on its own or a party's motion. If the Court sets oral argument in a Criminal Appeal, the Clerk shall send the order setting oral argument to the parties and to the prosecuting attorney whose office represented the state at trial.

B. Time for Filing Motion for Oral Argument. A party's motion for oral argument shall be filed no later than seven days after: (1) any reply brief would be due under Rule 45(B), or (2) any reply brief would be due under Rule 57(E) if petitioning to transfer, or (3) any reply brief would be due under Rule 63(E), if petitioning for review.

C. Acknowledgment of Order Setting Oral Argument. Counsel of record and unrepresented parties shall file with the Clerk an acknowledgment of the order setting oral argument no later than fifteen (15) days after service of the order.

Adopted Feb. 4, 2000, effective Jan. 1, 2001; amended Dec. 21, 2001, effective April 1, 2002.

Rule 53. Procedures For Oral Argument

A. Time Allowed. Each side shall have the amount of time for argument set by court order. A party may, for good cause, request more or less time in its motion for oral argument or by separate motion filed no later than fifteen (15) days after the order setting oral argument. A party is not required to use all of the time allowed, and the Court may terminate any argument if in its judgment further argument is unnecessary. A side may not exceed its allotted time without leave of the Court.

B. Order and Content of Argument. Unless the Court's order provides otherwise, the appellant shall open the argument and may reserve time for rebuttal. The appellant shall inform the Court at the beginning of the argument how much time is to be reserved for rebuttal. Failure to argue a particular point shall not constitute a waiver. Counsel shall not read at length from briefs, the Record on Appeal, or authorities.

C. Multiple Counsel and Parties. Unless the Court otherwise provides, multiple appellants or appellees shall decide how to divide the oral argument time allotted to their side. If more than one attorney on a side will participate in oral argument, the first attorney shall inform the Court at the beginning of the argument of the intended allocation of time, but the Court will not separately time each attorney.

D. Cross-Appeals. Unless the Court directs otherwise, if both parties file a Notice of Appeal, the plaintiff in the action below shall be deemed the appellant for purposes of this Rule. Otherwise, the party filing a Notice of Appeal shall be deemed the appellant.

E. Amicus Curiae. An *amicus curiae* may participate in oral argument without leave of the court to the extent that all parties with whom the *amicus curiae* is substantively aligned consent. Otherwise, the Court shall grant leave for an *amicus curiae* to participate in oral argument only in extraordinary circumstances upon motion by the *amicus curiae*.

F. Use of Physical Exhibits at Argument; Removal. If physical objects or visual displays other than handouts are to be used at the argument, counsel shall arrange to have them placed in the court room before the Court convenes for the argument. Counsel shall provide any equipment needed. After the argument, counsel presenting the exhibits shall be responsible for removal of the exhibits from the court room and, if necessary, for return to the trial court clerk.

G. Non-Appearance at Argument. If one or more parties fail to appear at oral argument, the Court may hear argument from the parties who have appeared, decide the appeal without oral argument, or reschedule the oral argument. The Court may sanction non-appearing parties.

H. Appeals Involving Records Excluded From Public Access. In any appeal in which case records are deemed confidential or excluded from public access, the parties and their counsel shall conduct oral argument in a manner reasonably calculated to provide anonymity and privacy in accordance with the requirements of Administrative Rule 9(G)(4).

Adopted Feb. 4, 2000, effective Jan. 1, 2001; amended Oct. 6, 2008, effective Jan. 1, 2009.

TITLE X.   PETITIONS FOR REHEARING

Rule 54.   Rehearings

A.   Decisions From Which Rehearing May be Sought. A party may seek Rehearing from the following:

(1) a published opinion;

(2) a not-for-publication memorandum decision;

(3) an order dismissing an appeal; and

(4) an order declining to authorize the filing of a successive petition for post-conviction relief.

A party may not seek rehearing of an order denying transfer.

B.   Time for Filing Petition. A Petition for Rehearing shall be filed no later than thirty (30) days after the decision. Rule 25(C), which grants a three-day extension of time for service by mail or third-party commercial carrier, does not extend the due date, and no extension of time shall be granted.

C.   Brief in Response. No brief in response to a Petition for Rehearing is required unless requested by the Court, except that the Attorney General shall be required to file a brief in response to the Petition in a criminal case where the sentence is death. A brief in response to the Petition shall be filed no later than fifteen (15) days after the Petition is served or fifteen (15) days after the Court issues its order requesting a response. Rule 25(C), which provides a three-day extension for service by mail or third-party carrier,

may extend the due date; however, no other extension of time shall be granted.

D.   Reply Brief Prohibited. Reply briefs on Rehearing are prohibited.

E.   Content and Length. The Rehearing Petition shall state concisely the reasons the party believes rehearing is necessary. The Petition for Rehearing and any brief in response are governed by Rule 44.

F.   Form and Arrangement. The form and arrangement of the Petition for Rehearing and any brief in response shall conform generally to Rule 43 and shall include a table of contents, table of authorities, statement of issues, argument, conclusion, word count certificate, if needed, and certificate of service.

Adopted Feb. 4, 2000, effective Jan. 1, 2001. Amended Dec. 21, 2001, effective April 1, 2002.

Rule 55.   Transfer And Rehearing Sought By Different Parties

When rehearing is sought by one party, and transfer is sought by another, briefing shall continue under Rule 54 for the Petition for Rehearing and under Rule 57 for the Petition to Transfer. Once the Court of Appeals disposes of the Petition for Rehearing, transfer may be sought from that disposition in accordance with Rule 57 governing Petitions to Transfer.

Adopted Feb. 4, 2000, effective Jan. 1, 2001.

TITLE XI.   SUPREME COURT PROCEEDINGS

Rule 56.   Requests To Transfer To The Supreme Court

A.   Motion Before Consideration by the Court of Appeals. In rare cases, the Supreme Court may, upon verified motion of a party, accept jurisdiction over an appeal that would otherwise be within the jurisdiction of the Court of Appeals upon a showing that the appeal involves a substantial question of law of great public importance and that an emergency exists requiring a speedy determination. If the Supreme Court grants the motion, it will transfer the case to the Supreme Court, where the case shall proceed as if it had been originally filed there. If a filing fee has already been paid in the Court of Appeals, no additional filing fee is required.

B.   Petition After Disposition by the Court of Appeals; Filing Fee. After an adverse decision by the Court of Appeals, a party may file a Petition under Rule 57 requesting that the case be transferred to the Supreme Court. Upon the filing of a Petition to Transfer, the petitioner shall pay a filing fee of $125 to the Clerk. However, no filing fee is required if the Petition is filed by or on behalf of a state or govern-

mental unit, or by a party who proceeded in *forma pauperis* in the Court of Appeals.

Adopted Feb. 4, 2000, effective Jan. 1, 2001.

Rule 57.   Petitions To Transfer And Briefs

A.   Applicability. This Rule applies to Petitions to Transfer an appeal from the Court of Appeals to Supreme Court after an adverse decision by the Court of Appeals.

B.   Decisions From Which Transfer May be Sought. Transfer may be sought from adverse decisions issued by the Court of Appeals in the following form:

(1) a published opinion;

(2) a not-for-publication memorandum decision;

(3) any amendment or modification of a published opinion or a not-for-publication memorandum decision; and

(4) an order dismissing an appeal.

Any other order by the Court of Appeals, including an order denying a motion for interlocutory appeal under Rule 14(B) or 14(C) and an order declining to authorize the filing of a successive petition for post conviction relief, shall not be considered an adverse decision for the purpose of petitioning to transfer, regardless of whether rehearing by the Court of Appeals was sought.

C. Time for Filing Petition. A Petition to Transfer shall be filed:

(1) no later than thirty (30) days after the adverse decision if rehearing was not sought; or

(2) if rehearing was sought, no later than thirty (30) days after the Court of Appeals' disposition of the Petition for Rehearing.

Rule 25(C), which provides a three day extension for service by mail or third-party commercial carrier, does not extend the due date, and no extension of time shall be granted.

D. Brief in Response. A party may file a brief in response to the Petition no later than twenty (20) days after the Petition is served. Rule 25(C), which provides a three-day extension for service by mail or third-party commercial carrier, may extend the due date; however, no other extension of time shall be granted.

E. Reply Brief. The petitioning party may file a reply brief no later than ten (10) days after a brief in response is served. Rule 25(C), which provides a three-day extension for service by mail or third-party commercial carrier, may extend the due date; however, no other extension of time shall be granted.

F. Form and Length Limits. A Petition to Transfer, brief in response, and any reply brief are governed by Rules 43 and 44. No separate brief in support of the Petition to Transfer shall be filed.

G. Content and Arrangement of Petition to Transfer. The Petition to Transfer shall concisely set forth:

(1) *Question Presented on Transfer.* A brief statement identifying the issue, question, or precedent warranting Transfer. The statement must not be argumentative or repetitive. The statement shall be set out by itself on the first page after the cover.

(2) *Table of Contents.* A table of contents containing the items specified in Rule 46(A)(1).

(3) *Background and Prior Treatment of Issues on Transfer.* A brief statement of the procedural and substantive facts necessary for consideration of the Petition to Transfer, including a statement of how the issues relevant to transfer were raised and resolved by any Administrative Agency, the trial court, and the Court of Appeals. To the extent extensive procedural or factual background is necessary, reference may be made to the appellate briefs.

(4) *Argument.* An argument section explaining the reasons why transfer should be granted.

(5) *Conclusion.* A short and plain statement of the relief requested.

(6) *Word Count Certificate,* if necessary. See Rule 44(F).

(7) *Certificate of Service.* See Rule 24(D).

H. Considerations Governing the Grant of Transfer. The grant of transfer is a matter of judicial discretion. The following provisions articulate the principal considerations governing the Supreme Court's decision whether to grant transfer.

(1) *Conflict in Court of Appeals' Decisions.* The Court of Appeals has entered a decision in conflict with another decision of the Court of Appeals on the same important issue.

(2) *Conflict with Supreme Court Decision.* The Court of Appeals has entered a decision in conflict with a decision of the Supreme Court on an important issue.

(3) *Conflict with Federal Appellate Decision.* The Court of Appeals has decided an important federal question in a way that conflicts with a decision of the Supreme Court of the United States or a United States Court of Appeals.

(4) *Undecided Question of Law.* The Court of Appeals has decided an important question of law or a case of great public importance that has not been, but should be, decided by the Supreme Court.

(5) *Precedent in Need of Reconsideration.* The Court of Appeals has correctly followed ruling precedent of the Supreme Court but such precedent is erroneous or in need of clarification or modification in some specific respect.

(6) *Significant Departure From Law or Practice.* The Court of Appeals has so significantly departed from accepted law or practice or has sanctioned such a departure by a trial court or Administrative Agency as to warrant the exercise of Supreme Court jurisdiction.

Adopted Feb. 4, 2000, effective Jan. 1, 2001. Amended Dec. 22, 2000, effective Jan. 1, 2001; Sept. 10, 2007, effective Jan. 1, 2008.

Rule 58. Effect Of Supreme Court Ruling On Petition To Transfer

A. Effect of Grant of Transfer. The opinion or not-for-publication memorandum decision of the Court of Appeals shall be final except where a Petition to Transfer has been granted by the Supreme Court. If transfer is granted, the opinion or not-for-publication memorandum decision of the Court of Appeals shall be automatically vacated except for:

(1) those opinions or portions thereof which are expressly adopted and incorporated by reference by the Supreme Court; or

(2) those opinions or portions thereof that are summarily affirmed by the Supreme Court, which shall be considered as Court of Appeals' authority.

Upon the grant of transfer, the Supreme Court shall have jurisdiction over the appeal and all issues as if originally filed in the Supreme Court.

B. Effect of the Denial of Transfer. The denial of a Petition to Transfer shall have no legal effect other than to terminate the litigation between the parties in the Supreme Court. No Petition for Rehearing may be filed from an order denying a Petition to Transfer.

C. Supreme Court Evenly Divided. When the Supreme Court is evenly divided upon the question of accepting or denying transfer, transfer shall be deemed denied. When the Supreme Court is evenly divided after transfer has been granted, the decision of the Court of Appeals shall be reinstated.

Adopted Feb. 4, 2000, effective Jan. 1, 2001.

Rule 59. Mandatory Appellate Review And Direct Review

A. Mandatory Appeals. All appeals over which the Supreme Court exercises exclusive jurisdiction under Rule 4(A)(1) and where the Supreme Court has accepted jurisdiction under Rule 56(A) shall be appealed in the same manner that cases are appealed to the Court of Appeals.

B. Direct Review. When the Supreme Court Justices participating are evenly divided in such an appeal, the trial court judgment shall be affirmed.

Adopted Feb. 4, 2000, effective Jan. 1, 2001.

Rule 60. Original Actions

Petitions for writ of mandamus or prohibition are governed by the Rules of Procedure for Original Actions.

Adopted Feb. 4, 2000, effective Jan. 1, 2001.

Rule 61. Mandate Of Funds

Supreme Court Review of cases involving the mandate of funds is commenced pursuant to the procedure in Trial Rule 60.5(B). The appeal shall thereafter proceed in accordance with such orders on briefing, argument and procedure as the Supreme Court may in its discretion issue.

Adopted Feb. 4, 2000, effective Jan. 1, 2001.

Rule 62. Appeals Involving Waiver Of Parental Consent To Abortion

A. Applicability. This Rule governs an appeal by a minor or her physician from an adverse judgment or order of a trial court under Indiana Code 16–34–2–4.

B. Permitted Parties. For the purposes of this Rule, the term " physician" shall mean a natural person holding an unlimited license to practice medicine in the State of Indiana. The next friend of the minor shall be a natural person.

C. Appeal by Minor or Her Physician. A minor or her physician wishing to appeal a judgment or order denying the waiver of parental consent to abortion shall file with the trial court, no later than ten (10) days after entry of the order or judgment is noted in the Chronological Case Summary, a written request that the Record on Appeal be prepared and certified. The trial court judge shall promptly certify the judgment or order and summary findings of fact and conclusion of law, together with the Petition initiating the proceeding, and either a stipulation of the facts or an electronic transcription of the evidence taken in the proceeding. These certified documents shall constitute the Record on Appeal. The trial court shall promptly transmit the Record on Appeal to the Clerk. No motion to correct error or Notice of Appeal shall be filed.

D. Appeal by State or Other Party. If the trial court grants the requested consent but the State or any other proper party wishes to appeal and obtains a stay of the trial court's order or judgment, the State or other party shall follow the procedure in Section C.

E. Decision by the Supreme Court. The appeal shall proceed directly to the Supreme Court, which shall decide the appeal on the Record on Appeal without briefs or oral argument, unless the Court otherwise directs. Any party may, however, file a short statement of special points desired to be brought to the attention of the Supreme Court, which statement need not conform to the usual requirements for appellate briefs.

Adopted Feb. 4, 2000, effective Jan. 1, 2001. Amended Sept. 21, 2010, effective Jan. 1, 2011; Sept. 20, 2011, effective Jan. 1, 2012.

Rule 63. Review of Tax Court Decisions

A. Review of Final Judgment or Final Disposition. Any party adversely affected by a Final Judgment of the Tax Court as defined by Rule 2(H), or a final disposition by the Tax Court of an appeal from a court of probate jurisdiction, shall have a right to petition the Supreme Court for review of the Final Judgment or final disposition.

B. Rehearing. Any party adversely affected by a Final Judgment or final disposition may file a Petition for Rehearing with the Tax Court, not a Motion to Correct Error. Rehearings from a Final Judgment or final disposition of the Tax Court shall be governed by Rule 54. A Petition for Rehearing need not be filed in order to seek Review, but when a Petition for Rehearing is used, a ruling or order by the Tax Court granting or denying the same shall be deemed a final decision and 1 Review may be sought.

C. Notice of Intent to Petition for Review. A party initiates a petition for review by filing a Notice of Intent to Petition for Review with the Clerk in accordance with requirements of Rule 9 (except with respect to the filing fee) no later than:

(1) thirty (30) days after the date of entry in the court's docket of the Final Judgment or final disposition if a Petition for Rehearing was not sought; or

(2) thirty (30) days after the date of entry in the court's docket of the final disposition of the Petition for Rehearing if rehearing was sought and such Petition was timely filed by any party.

Rule 25(C), which provides a three-day extension for service by mail or third-party commercial carrier, does not extend the due date for filing a Notice of Intent to Petition for Review, and no extension of time shall be granted.

D. Clerk's Record and Transcript. The Clerk shall give notice of filing of the Notice of Intent to Petition for Review to the Court Reporter and shall assemble the Clerk's Record in accordance with Rule 10. The Court Reporter shall prepare and file the Transcript in accordance with Rule 11. The Clerk shall retain, transmit, and grant access to the Clerk's Record in accordance with Rule 12. Reference to the "trial court clerk" in Rules 10, 11, and 12 shall mean the Clerk.

E. Petition for Review. The petitioning party shall file its Petition for Review no later than thirty (30) days after:

(1) the date of the docket entry of the Clerk's Notice of Completion of Clerk's Record if the Notice reports that the Transcript is complete or that no Transcript has been requested; or

(2) in all other cases, the date of the docket entry of the Clerk's Notice of Completion of Transcript.

F. Brief in Response. A party may file a brief in response to the Petition for Review no later than thirty (30) days after the Petition is served.

G. Reply Brief. The petitioning party may file a reply brief no later than fifteen (15) days after a brief in response is served.

H. Review of Interlocutory Orders. Any party adversely affected by an interlocutory order of the Tax Court may petition the Supreme Court for Review of the order pursuant to Rule 14(B), which shall govern preparation of the Record on Appeal in interlocutory appeals. No Notice of Intent to Petition for Review shall be filed after the Supreme Court accepts a petition for interlocutory review.

I. Form and Length Limits. A Petition for Review, any brief in response, and any reply brief are governed by Rules 43, 44, and 46; provided, that, immediately before the *Argument* section in the Petition for Review and brief in response there shall be a separate section entitled *Reasons for Granting* [or *Denying*] *Review*, which shall concisely explain why review should or should not be granted. Reference to the "appellant's brief," "appellee's brief," and "appellant's reply brief" in Rule 46 shall mean the Petition for Review, brief in response, and reply brief, respectively. No separate brief in support of the Petition shall be filed.

J. Fiscal Impact. Any brief may discuss the fiscal impact of the Tax Court's decision on taxpayers or government.

K. Extensions of Time. Extensions of time may be sought under Rule 35 except that no extension of the time for filing the Notice of Intent to Petition for Review shall be granted.

L. Appendices. Appendices shall be filed in compliance with Rules 49, 50, and 51, Reference to the "appellant's brief" and "appellee's brief" in Rule 49 shall mean the Petition for Review and brief in response, respectively.

M. Considerations Governing the Grant of Review. The grant of review is a matter of judicial discretion. The following provisions articulate the principal considerations governing the Supreme Court's decision whether to grant Review.

(1) *Conflict in Tax Court or Court of Appeals Decisions.* The Tax Court has entered a decision in conflict with another decision of the Tax Court or the Court of Appeals on the same important issue.

(2) *Conflict with Supreme Court Decision.* The Tax Court has entered a decision in conflict with a decision of the Supreme Court on an important issue.

(3) *Undecided Question of Law.* The Tax Court has decided an important question of law or a case of great public importance that should be decided by the Supreme Court.

(4) *Precedent in Need of Reconsideration.* The Tax Court has correctly followed the ruling precedent, but such precedent is erroneous or in need of clarification or modification in some specific respect.

(5) *Conflict with Federal Appellate Decision.* The Tax Court has decided an important federal question in a way that conflicts with a decision of the Supreme Court of the United States or a United States Court of Appeals.

(6) *Significant Departure From Law or Practice.* The Tax Court has so significantly departed from accepted law or practice as to warrant the exercise of the Supreme Court's jurisdiction.

N. Effect of Denial of Review. The denial of a Petition for Review shall have no legal effect other than to terminate the litigation between the parties in the Supreme Court. No Petition for Rehearing may be filed from an order denying a Petition for Review.

O. Effect of Grant of Review. After the Supreme Court grants review, the Tax Court retains jurisdiction of the case for the purpose of any interim relief or stays the parties may seek. The Supreme Court may review the Tax Court's disposition of any request for interim relief or stay.

P. Filing Fee. Upon the filing of a Petition for Review, the petitioner shall pay a fee of $125.00 to the Clerk in addition to any other fees to be paid to the Clerk. However, no filing fee is required if the petition is filed on behalf of a state or governmental unit or by a party who proceeded in *forma pauperis* in the Tax Court.

Q. Applicability of Other Appellate Rules. All other rules of appellate procedure shall apply to Petitions for Review from the Tax Court except as otherwise specifically provided in this Rule.

R. Supreme Court Evenly Divided. Where the Supreme Court is evenly divided, either upon the question of accepting or denying review, or upon the disposition of the case once review is granted, review shall be deemed denied and the decision of the Tax Court shall be final.

Adopted Feb. 4, 2000, effective Jan. 1, 2001. Amended Dec. 21, 2001, effective April 1, 2002; Sept. 12, 2007, effective Jan. 1, 2008; Sept. 21, 2010, effective Jan. 1, 2011; Sept. 20, 2011, effective Jan. 1, 2012.

Rule 64. Certified Questions Of State Law From Federal Courts

A. Applicability. The United States Supreme Court, any federal circuit court of appeals, or any federal district court may certify a question of Indiana law to the Supreme Court when it appears to the federal court that a proceeding presents an issue of state law that is determinative of the case and on which there is no clear controlling Indiana precedent.

B. Procedure. The federal court shall certify the question of Indiana law and transmit the following to the Clerk:

(1) a copy of the certification of the question;

(2) a copy of the case docket, including the names of the parties and their counsel; and

(3) appropriate supporting materials.

The Supreme Court will then issue an order either accepting or refusing the question. If accepted, the Supreme Court may establish by order a briefing schedule on the certified question.

Adopted Feb. 4, 2000, effective Jan. 1, 2001.

TITLE XII. COURT PROCEDURES, POWERS AND DECISIONS

Rule 65. Opinions And Memorandum Decisions

A. Criteria for Publication. All Supreme Court opinions shall be published. A Court of Appeals opinion shall be published if the case:

(1) establishes, modifies, or clarifies a rule of law;

(2) criticizes existing law; or

(3) involves a legal or factual issue of unique interest or substantial public importance.

Other Court of Appeals cases shall be decided by not-for-publication memorandum decision. A judge who dissents from a not-for-publication memorandum decision may designate the dissent for publication if one (1) of the criteria above is met.

B. Time to File Motion to Publish. Within thirty (30) days of the entry of the decision, a party may move the Court to publish any not-for-publication memorandum decision which meets the criteria for publication.

C. Official Reporter. West's Northeastern Reporter shall be the official reporter of the Supreme Court and the Court of Appeals.

D. Precedential Value of Not-For-Publication Memorandum Decision. Unless later designated for publication, a not-for-publication memorandum decision shall not be regarded as precedent and shall not be cited to any court except by the parties to the case to establish *res judicata*, collateral estoppel, or law of the case.

E. Certification of Opinion or Not–For–Publication Memorandum Decision. The Clerk shall serve uncertified copies of any opinion or not-for-publication memorandum decision by a Court on Appeal to all counsel of record, unrepresented parties, and the trial court at the time the opinion or memorandum decision is handed down. The Clerk shall certify the opinion or memorandum decision to the trial court or Administrative Agency only after the time for all Petitions for Rehearing, Transfer, or Review has expired, unless all the parties request earlier certification. If the Supreme Court grants transfer or review, the Clerk shall not certify any opinion or memorandum decision until final disposition by the Supreme Court. The trial court, Administrative Agency, and parties shall not take any action in reliance upon the opinion or memorandum decision until the opinion or memorandum decision is certified.

Adopted Feb. 4, 2000, effective Jan. 1, 2001. Amended Dec. 21, 2001, effective April 1, 2002.

Rule 66. Relief Available On Appeal

A. Harmless Error. No error or defect in any ruling or order or in anything done or omitted by the trial court or by any of the parties is ground for granting relief or reversal on appeal where its probable impact, in light of all the evidence in the case, is sufficiently minor so as not to affect the substantial rights of the parties.

B. Dismissal of Appeals. No appeal shall be dismissed as of right because the case was not finally disposed of in the trial court or Administrative Agency as to all issues and parties, but upon suggestion or discovery of such a situation, the Court may, in its discretion, suspend consideration until disposition is made of such issues, or it may pass upon such adjudicated issues as are severable without prejudice to parties who may be aggrieved by subsequent proceedings in the trial court or Administrative Agency.

C. Disposition of Case. The Court may, with respect to some or all of the parties or issues, in whole or in part:

(1) affirm the decision of the trial court or Administrative Agency;

(2) reverse the decision of the trial court or Administrative Agency;

(3) order a new trial or hearing;

(4) if damages are excessive or inadequate, order entry of judgment of damages in the amount supported by the evidence;

(5) if damages are excessive or inadequate, order a new trial or hearing subject to additur or remittitur;

(6) order entry of Final Judgment;

(7) order correction of a judgment or order;

(8) order findings or a judgment be modified under Ind.Trial Rule 52(B);

(9) make any relief granted subject to conditions; and

(10) grant any other appropriate relief.

D. New Trial or Hearing. The Court shall direct that Final Judgment be entered or that error be corrected without a new trial or hearing unless this relief is impracticable or unfair to any of the parties or is otherwise improper. If a new trial is necessary, it shall be limited to those parties and issues affected by the error unless this would be impracticable or unfair.

E. Damages for Frivolous or Bad Faith Filings. The Court may assess damages if an appeal, petition, or motion, or response, is frivolous or in bad faith. Damages shall be in the Court's discretion and may include attorneys' fees. The Court shall remand the case for execution.

F. Execution From the Court on Appeal. Any execution issued by the Court on Appeal shall be the same as those issued by other courts of record and shall be returnable in the same manner.

Adopted Feb. 4, 2000, effective Jan. 1, 2001. Amended Sept. 15, 2009, effective Jan. 1, 2010.

Rule 67. Costs

A. Time for Filing Motion for Costs. Upon a motion by any party within sixty (60) days after the final decision of the Court of Appeals or Supreme Court, the Clerk shall tax costs under this Rule.

B. Components. Costs shall include:

(1) the filing fee, including any fee paid to seek transfer or review;

(2) the cost of preparing the Record on Appeal, including the Transcript, and appendices; and

(3) postage expenses for service of all documents filed with the Clerk.

The Court, in its discretion, may include additional items as permitted by law. Each party shall bear the cost of preparing its own briefs.

C. Party Entitled to Costs. When a judgment or order is affirmed in whole, the appellee shall recover costs. When a judgment has been reversed in whole, the appellant shall recover costs in the Court on Appeal and in the trial court or Administrative Agency as provided by law. In other cases, the recovery of costs shall be decided in the Court's discretion. Costs against any governmental organization, its officers and agencies, shall be imposed only to the extent permitted by law.

D. Supreme Court Equally Divided. When the Supreme Court justices participating in an appeal are equally divided, neither party shall be awarded costs. See Rule 58(C).

Adopted Feb. 4, 2000, effective Jan. 1, 2001.

Effective Dates

These rules shall take effect as follows:

(A) Appeals and all other proceedings under the Rules of Appellate Procedure initiated on or after January 1, 2001 shall be governed in totality by the revised Rules of Appellate Procedure. Appeals shall be considered initiated either by:

(1) the filing a praecipe for appeal under the former rules (Former Appellate Rule 2), or;

(2) the filing of a notice of appeal under the revised rules (Revised Appellate Rule 9 and 14), or;

(3) in the case of other types of proceedings in which the appellate review process requires the filing of some other form of initiating document, the filing of such document.

(B) If more than one praecipe, notice of appeal, or other initiating document is filed, the appeal or other form of proceeding shall be considered initiated on the date of the filing of the first initiating document.

(C) Appeals initiated prior to January 1, 2001 shall be governed by the former Rules of Appellate Procedure throughout the appeal process except as follows:

(1) Revised Appellate Rule 25(C) provides generally for an automatic three-day extension of time to file responses to documents served by a party by mail. This is a change from former Appellate Rule 12(D), which allowed an automatic five-day extension for such responses. The revised rule shall apply to all responses to documents shown as filed on or after January 1, 2001.

(2) Proceedings on petitions for rehearing shall be governed by the revised rules if the first petition for rehearing is filed on or after January 1, 2001.

(3) Proceedings on petitions to transfer an appeal to the Supreme Court shall be governed by the revised rules if the first petition to transfer is filed on or after January 1, 2001.

(4) Proceedings on petitions for review of a Tax Court decision shall be governed by the revised rules if the first petition for review is filed on or after January 1, 2001.

Adopted Feb. 4, 2000, effective Jan. 1, 2001.

APPENDIX TO INDIANA RULES OF
APPELLATE PROCEDURE

SAMPLE FORMS

Form App. R. 9–1. Notice of Appeal

IN THE INDIANA [SUPREME COURT/COURT OF APPEALS/TAX COURT]

CAUSE NO. _____

NAME,	)	
	)	
[Appellant/Petitioner],	)	[Appeal or Petition] from the
([Plaintiff/Defendant/Claimant/	)	[_____ Court or Administrative
Respondent below]),	)	Agency]
	)	
v.	)	Trial Court [or Administrative
	)	Agency number] Case No.: ___
NAME,	)	
	)	The Honorable _____,
[Appellee/Respondent],	)	Judge.
([Plaintiff/Defendant/Claimant/	)	
Respondent below]).	)	

NOTICE OF APPEAL

[insert whether this is an "expedited" appeal under App. R. 14.1]

(Appearance)

Party Information
Name:

_____

Address:

_____

_____

The following party information *only if not represented by an attorney*:
Tel. No.: _____ Fax No.: _____
E–Mail: _____
Requesting service of orders and opinions of the Court by:
☐ E-mail ☐ FAX or ☐ U.S. Mail (choose one)
In forma pauperis: ☐ Yes ☐ No

Attorney or attorneys representing party filing Notice of Appeal, if any (all fields must be supplied):
Name: _____
Attorney # _____
Address:

_____

_____

Tel. No.: _____ Fax No.: _____
E–Mail: _____

INFORMATION FOR JUDGMENT/ORDER BEING APPEALED
Date of Judgment/Order being appealed: _____
Title of Judgment/Order being appealed: _____
Date Motion to Correct Error denied ☐ or deemed denied ☐, if applicable: ___
If case was heard by a magistrate, date trial judge approved judgment or order:
_____ Basis for Appellate Jurisdiction:

☐ Appeal from a Final Judgment, as defined by Appellate Rule 2(H) and 9(I)
☐ Appeal from an interlocutory order, taken as of right pursuant to Appellate Rule 14(A),(C),(D)

☐ Appeal from an interlocutory order, accepted by discretion pursuant to Appellate Rule 14(B)(3)

☐ Expedited Appeal, taken pursuant to Appellate Rule 14.1

This appeal will be taken to:

☐ Court of Appeals of Indiana, pursuant to Appellate Rule 5

☐ Indiana Supreme Court, pursuant to Appellate Rule 4

   ☐ This is an appeal in which a sentence of death or life imprisonment without parole is imposed under Ind. Code § 35–50–2–9 or a post conviction relief case in which the sentence was death

   ☐ This is an interlocutory appeal authorized under Rule 14 involving the death penalty or a life without parole case raising a question of interpretation of Ind. Code § 35–50–2–9

   ☐ This is an appeal from an order declaring a statute unconstitutional

   ☐ This is an appeal involving a waiver of parental consent to abortion under Rule 62

   ☐ This is an appeal involving mandate of funds

Trial Court Clerk/Administrative Agency/Court Reporter Instructions

Pursuant to Appellate Rule 10 or 14.1(C), the clerk of [insert name of trial court or Administrative Agency] is requested to assemble the Clerk's Record, as defined in Appellate Rule 2(E).

Pursuant to Appellate Rule 11 or 14.1(C), the court reporter of the [insert name of the court or Administrative Agency] is requested to transcribe, certify, and file with the clerk of the [insert name of trial court or Administrative Agency] the following hearings of record, including exhibits:

_____

Public Access

Was the entire trial court or agency record sealed or excluded from public access?

   ☐ Yes ☐ No

Was a portion of the trial court or agency record sealed or excluded from public access?

   ☐ Yes ☐ No

If yes, which provision in Administrative Rule 9(G) provides the basis for this exclusion:

_____

If Administrative Rule 9(G)(1)(c) provides the basis for this exclusion, was the trial court or agency order issued in accordance with the requirements of Administrative Rule 9(H)?

   ☐ Yes ☐ No

Appellate Alternative Dispute Resolution

If civil case, is Appellant willing to participate in Appellate Dispute Resolution?

   ☐ Yes ☐ No

If yes, provide a brief statement of the facts of the case. (Attach additional pages as needed.)

_____

_____

_____

Attachments

The following SHALL be attached to this Notice of Appeal (in all appeals):

   ☐ Copy of judgment or order being appealed

The following SHALL be attached to this Notice of Appeal if applicable (check if applicable):

   ☐ Copy of the trial court or Administrative Agency's findings and conclusion (in civil cases)

☐   Copy of the sentencing order (in criminal cases)

☐   Order denying Motion to Correct Error or, if deemed denied, copy of Motion to Correct Error

☐   Copy of all orders and entries relating to the trial court or agency's decision to seal or exclude information from public access

☐   If proceeding pursuant to Appellate Rule 14(B)(3), copy of Order from Court of Appeals accepting jurisdiction over interlocutory appeal

☐   The documents required by Rule 40(C), if proceeding *in forma pauperis*

Certification

By signing below, I certify that:

(1) This case ☐ does ☐ does not involve an interlocutory appeal; issues of child custody, support, visitation, adoption, paternity, determination that a child is in need of services, termination of parental rights; or an appeal entitled to priority by rule or statute.

(2) I have reviewed and complied, and will continue to comply, with the requirements of Appellate Rule 9(J) and Administrative Rule 9(G)(4) on appeal; and,

(3) I will make satisfactory payment arrangements for any Transcripts ordered in this Notice of Appeal, as required by Appellate Rule 9(H).

Respectfully submitted,

_____

[Insert Name of Attorney or *pro se* party]

_____

Address

_____

Telephone number

_____

Attorney Number(if represented by counsel)

CERTIFICATE OF FILING AND SERVICE

I hereby certify that on this ___ day of _____, 20 ___, the foregoing was filed with the Clerk of the Indiana Supreme Court, Court of Appeals, and Tax Court.

I also certify that on this ___ day of _____, 20 _____, the foregoing was served by [insert specific means of service] upon :

[list names and addresses of:

(1) counsel of record in the trial court/administrative agency;

(2) the trial court clerk/administrative agency clerk;

(3) the parties served as required by Appellate Rule 14.1(B)(2) and (4) (if applicable);

(4) the court reporter;

(5) the Attorney General, if applicable under Rule 9(A)(3);

(6) the judge of the trial court or hearing officer of an Administrative Agency before whom the case was heard; and,

(7) any other persons required by statute.]

_____

[Signature]

Adopted Feb. 4, 2000, effective Jan. 1, 2001. Amended Dec. 22, 2000, effective Jan. 1, 2001; Sept. 21, 2010, effective Jan. 1, 2011; Sept. 20, 2011, effective Jan. 1, 2012; Sept. 13, 2013, effective Jan. 1, 2014.

Form App. R. 9–2. Repealed eff. Jan. 1, 2012.
Form App. R. 10–1. Notice Of Completion Of Clerk's Record
IN THE
INDIANA [SUPREME COURT OR COURT OF APPEALS]
Case No.: _____
[Insert Supreme Court or Court of Appeals number, if known]

_____,	)	Appeal from the _____
	)	Court
	)	
Appellant(s),	)	
	)	Trial Court Case No:
vs.	)	_____
	)	
_____,	)	
	)	The Honorable _____,
Appellee (s).	)	Judge

NOTICE OF COMPLETION OF CLERK'S RECORD

_____, the Clerk of _____ Court, hereby notifies the parties, pursuant to Appellate Rule 10(C), that the Clerk's Record in this case has been assembled and is complete. The Transcript is (circle one):

(a) Completed and filed with this clerk;

(b) Not yet completed;

(c) Not requested in the Notice of Appeal.

Attached to this Notice of Completion is a certified and updated copy of the Chronological Case Summary.

_____

Clerk

_____

Date issued

(*see* Ind. Appellate Rule 45(B)(1))

CERTIFICATE OF SERVICE

I certify that on [insert date] I served a copy of this Notice and a certified copy of the Chronological Case Summary upon the following person(s) by [specify means of service]:

[Separately list name(s) and address(es) of person(s) served]

_____

Clerk

Adopted Feb. 4, 2000, effective Jan. 1, 2001. Amended Dec. 22, 2000, effective Jan. 1, 2001; Sept. 19, 2013, effective Jan. 1, 2014.

Form App. R. 10–2. Notice Of Completion Of Transcript

IN THE INDIANA [SUPREME COURT OR COURT OF APPEALS]

Case No.: _____

[insert Supreme Court or Court of Appeals number, if known]

_____,	)	Appeal from the _____
	)	Court
	)	
Appellant(s),	)	
	)	Trial Court Case No:
vs.	)	
	)	_____
_____,	)	
	)	The Honorable _____,
Appellee (s).	)	Judge

NOTICE OF COMPLETION OF TRANSCRIPT

_____, the Clerk of _____ Court, hereby notifies the parties, pursuant to Appellate Rule 10(D), that the Transcript in this case has been completed.

_____

Clerk

_____

Date issued

(*see* Ind. Appellate Rule 45(B)(1))

CERTIFICATE OF SERVICE

I certify that on [insert date] I served a copy of this document upon the following person(s) by [specify means of service]:

[Separately list name(s) and address(es) of person(s) served]

_____

Clerk

Adopted Feb. 4, 2000, effective Jan. 1, 2001. Amended Dec. 22, 2000, effective Jan. 1, 2001; Sept. 13, 2013, effective Jan. 1, 2014.

Form App. R. 10–3. Clerk's Verified Motion For Extension Of Time To Assemble Clerk's Record
IN THE INDIANA [SUPREME COURT OR COURT OF APPEALS]

Case No.: _____

[insert Supreme Court or Court of Appeals number, if known]

	)	Appeal from the _____
_____,	)	Court
	)	
Appellant(s),	)	
	)	Trial Court Case No:
vs.	)	
	)	_____
	)	
_____,	)	
	)	The Honorable _____,
Appellee(s),	)	Judge

CLERK'S VERIFIED MOTION FOR EXTENSION OF TIME TO ASSEMBLE CLERK'S RECORD

_____, the clerk of _____ court, being first duly sworn upon his/her oath, respectfully petitions the Court for an extension of time in which to prepare the clerk's record in this appeal. In support of this Motion, the clerk shows the Court as follows:

1. The Appellant filed a Notice of Appeal on _____, 20 ___.

2. Pursuant to Appellate Rule 10(B), the clerk's record is due to be assembled thirty days after the Notice of Appeal is filed. Unless this Motion is granted, the record assembly must be completed, and the Notice of Completion of Clerk's Record must be issued no later than _____, 20 ___.

3. This clerk respectfully requests an enlargement of time of _____ (_____) days, to and including _____, ___, in order to assemble the clerk's record and issue its Notice of Completion.

4. An extension of time is needed because: (state reasons specifically including case names and cause numbers)

   _____

   _____

   _____

   _____.

5. This is the (first/second/third) Verified Motion for Extension of Time to Assemble Clerk's Record.

   WHEREFORE, _____, clerk for _____ court respectfully requests an extension of time of _____ (___) days within which to assemble the clerk's record and issue its Notice of Completion of Clerk's Record to _____, 20 ___.

I HEREBY AFFIRM UNDER THE PENALTIES FOR PERJURY THAT THE FOREGOING STATEMENTS ARE TRUE AND CORRECT TO THE BEST OF MY KNOWLEDGE.

_____
Clerk, _____ Court

CERTIFICATE OF SERVICE

I certify that on [insert date] I served a copy of this document upon the following person(s) by [specify means of service]: .

[Separately list name(s) and address(es) of person(s) served]

_____
Clerk

Adopted Feb. 4, 2000, effective Jan. 1, 2001. Amended Dec. 22, 2000, effective Jan. 1, 2001; Sept. 13, 2013, effective Jan. 1, 2014.

Form App. R. 11–1. Notice Of Filing Of Transcript

IN THE INDIANA [SUPREME COURT OR COURT OF APPEALS]

Case No.: _____

[insert Supreme Court or Court of Appeals number, if known]

_____, Appellant(s), vs. _____, Appellee(s).	) Appeal from the _____) Court))) Trial Court Case No:)) _____))) The Honorable _____,) Judge

NOTICE OF FILING OF TRANSCRIPT

_____, the Court Reporter of _____ Court, hereby notifies the parties, pursuant to Appellate Rule 11(A), that the Transcript in this cause has been prepared and certified and is complete. This _____ day of _____, 20 ___, the Transcript was filed with the [clerk of the trial court/ Administrative Agency] in accordance with Appellate Rule[s] [28, 29 and/or 30].

_____

Court Reporter

CERTIFICATE OF SERVICE

I certify that on [insert date] I served a copy of this document upon the following person(s) by [specify means of service]:

[Separately list name(s) and address(es) of person(s) served]

_____

Court Reporter

Adopted Feb. 4, 2000, effective Jan. 1, 2001. Amended Dec. 22, 2000, effective Jan. 1, 2001; Sept. 13, 2013, effective Jan. 1, 2014.

Form App. R. 11–2. Motion for Extension to File Transcript
IN THE
INDIANA [SUPREME COURT OR COURT OF APPEALS]
Case No.: _____
[insert Supreme Court or Court of Appeals number, if known]

```
                                    )   Appeal from the _____
_____,         )   Court
                                    )
Appellant(s),                       )
                                    )   Trial Court Case No:
vs.                                 )   _____
                                    )
_____,         )
                                    )   The Honorable _____,
Appellee(s).                        )   Judge
```

COURT REPORTER'S
VERIFIED MOTION FOR EXTENSION OF TIME
TO FILE TRANSCRIPT

_____, the court reporter for _____ court, respectfully petitions the Court for an extension of time in which to file the transcript in this appeal. In support of this Motion, the court reporter shows the Court as follows:

1. The Appellant filed a Notice of Appeal on _____, 20 ___. The notice of appeal requested the following transcript(s): _____.

2. Pursuant to Appellate Rule 11(B), the transcript is due ninety (90) days after the Notice of Appeal is filed. Unless this Motion is granted, the transcript is due to be filed with the trial court no later than _____, 20 ___.

3. Arrangements have been made to pay for the preparation of the transcript.

OR Satisfactory arrangements have not been made for the preparation of the transcript in that (explain).

4. I estimate the transcript will be _____ pages long and will take _____ hours to prepare.

5. I began work on the transcript on _____ and have completed _____ pages and spent _____ hours.

(OR) I have not yet been able to begin work on the transcript because (state reasons specifically including case names and cause numbers and sizes of other transcripts, nature of case).

(OR) I have not been able to complete the transcript because (state reasons specifically including case names and cause numbers and sizes of other transcripts, nature of case)

6. I anticipate that I will complete the transcript on _____.

7. I request that the time within which to complete the transcript be extended to _____.

8. This is the (first/second/third) Verified Motion for Extension of Time to File Transcript.

WHEREFORE, _____, court reporter for _____ court respectfully requests an extension of time of _____ (_____) days within which to file the transcript to _____, 20 ___.

I HEREBY AFFIRM UNDER THE PENALTIES FOR PERJURY THAT THE FOREGOING STATEMENTS ARE TRUE AND CORRECT TO THE BEST OF MY KNOWLEDGE.

_____
Court Reporter, _____ Court

CERTIFICATE OF SERVICE

I certify that on [insert date] I served a copy of this document upon the following person(s) by [specify means of service]:

[Separately list name(s) and address(es) of person(s) served]

_____

Court Reporter

Adopted Feb. 4, 2000, effective Jan. 1, 2001.   Amended Dec. 22, 2000, effective Jan. 1, 2001;   Sept. 19, 2013, effective Jan. 1, 2014.

Form App. R. 14.1–1. Repealed eff. Jan. 1, 2012.
Form App. R. 15–1. Repealed eff. Jan. 1, 2012.
Form App. R. 16–1. Appellee's Notice of Appearance
IN THE INDIANA [SUPREME COURT/COURT OF APPEALS/TAX COURT]
CAUSE NO. _____

NAME,	)	[Appeal or Petition] from the [_____
[Appellant/Petitioner],	)	Court or Administrative Agency]
([Plaintiff/Defendant/	)	
Claimant/Respondent	)	
below]),	)	Trial Court [or Administrative Agency
	)	number]
	)	Case No.: _____
v.	)	
	)	
NAME,	)	The Honorable _____,
[Appellee/Respondent],	)	Judge.
([Plaintiff/Defendant/	)	
Claimant/Respondent	)	
below]).	)	

APPELLEE'S NOTICE OF APPEARANCE

I. **Party Information**
   Name: _____
   Address: _____
   _____

   The following party information only *if not represented by an attorney*:
   Tel. No.: _____ Fax No.: _____
   E–Mail: _____
   Requesting service of orders and opinions of the Court by:
   ☐ E-mail ☐ FAX or ☐ U.S. Mail (choose one)
   In forma pauperis: ☐ Yes ☐ No

II. **Attorney Information, if applicable (all fields must be supplied):**
   Name: _____
   Attorney # _____
   Address: _____
   _____
   Tel. No.: _____ Fax No.: _____
   E–Mail: _____

III. **Appellate ADR (in all civil cases) (circle one)**
   Appellee ☐ is ☐ is not   willing to participate in Appellate ADR.

   Respectfully submitted,

   Signed: _____

   Printed: _____

   [Insert Name of Attorney or pro se party]

   Address: _____

   _____

   Telephone number: _____

Attorney Number (if applicable): _____

CERTIFICATE OF SERVICE

I hereby certify that on this ____ day of _____, 20 ____, the foregoing was served upon the following persons, by [state exact method of service]:

[List names and address of:

(1) counsel of record or pro se party;

(2) Attorney General, if applicable]

_____
[Signature]

Amended Sept. 20, 2011, effective Jan. 1, 2012; Sept. 7, 2012, effective Jan. 1, 2013.

Form App. R. 16–2.   Notice of Appearance

IN THE INDIANA [SUPREME COURT/COURT OF APPEALS/TAX COURT]
CAUSE NO. _____

NAME,	)	[Appeal or Petition] from the [_____
[Appellant/Petitioner],	)	Court or Administrative Agency]
([Plaintiff/Defendant/	)	
Claimant/Respondent	)	
below]),	)	Trial Court [or Administrative Agency
	)	number]
	)	Case No.: _____
v.	)	
	)	
NAME,	)	The Honorable _____,
[Appellee/Respondent],	)	Judge.
([Plaintiff/Defendant/	)	
Claimant/Respondent	)	
below]).	)	

NOTICE OF APPEARANCE
(in Interlocutory appeals)

I.   **Party Information**
    Name: _____
    Address: _____
    _____

    The following party information only *if not represented by an attorney*:
    Tel. No.: _____   Fax No.: _____
    E–Mail: _____
    Requesting service of orders and opinions of the Court by:
         ☐ E-mail ☐ FAX or ☐ U.S. Mail (choose one)
    In forma pauperis: ☐ Yes ☐ No

II.   **Attorney Information, if applicable (all fields must be supplied):**
    Name: _____
    Attorney # _____
    Address: _____
    _____

    Tel. No.: _____   Fax No.: _____
    E–Mail: _____

III.   **Appellate ADR (in all civil cases) (circle one)**
    Appellee ☐ is ☐ is not   willing to participate in Appellate ADR.

        Respectfully submitted,

        Signed: _____

        Printed: _____

        [Insert Name of Attorney or pro se party]

        Address: _____

        _____

        Telephone number: _____

        Attorney Number (if applicable): _____

CERTIFICATE OF SERVICE

I hereby certify that on this day ___ of _____, 20 ___, the foregoing was served upon the following parties, by [state exact method of service]:

[List names and address of:

(1) counsel of record or pro se party;

(2) Attorney General, if applicable]

_____
[Signature]

Amended Sept. 20, 2011, effective Jan. 1, 2012; Sept. 7, 2012, effective Jan. 1, 2013.

Form App. R. 28–1. Title Page And Cover

[SAMPLE COVER FOR TRANSCRIPT VOLUMES]   App.R. 28-1

Appellate Case No. _____

[Insert Trial Court or Administrative Agency Caption, including
the case number, the names of the parties,
the name of the trial court or administrative agency, and
the name of the presiding judge]

The Transcript [or Supplemental Transcript]

Volume _____ [number of volume] of _____ [total number of volumes]

Pages _____ through _____

Name   Name
Firm (if applicable)   Firm (if applicable)
Address   Address
Telephone number   Telephone number

Attorney for Plaintiff   Attorney for Defendant
[or Pro Se Plaintiff]   [or Pro Se Defendant]

Adopted Feb. 4, 2000, effective Jan. 1, 2001.

Form App. R. 40–1. Affidavit In Support Of Motion To Proceed On Appeal In Forma Pauperis

(SAMPLE AFFIDAVIT IN SUPPORT OF   Form #App. R. 40-1
MOTION TO PROCEED ON APPEAL
IN FORMA PAUPERIS)

IN THE
[INDICATE INDIANA COURT OF APPEALS OR GIVE NAME OF TRIAL COURT]

NO. _____

	)	Appeal from the _____ Court
_____	)	
[Insert name], Appellant,	)	
	)	Trial Court Case No:
vs.	)	_____
	)	
	)	The Honorable _____, Judge
	)	
	)	
_____	)	
[Insert name], Appellee.	)	

AFFIDAVIT IN SUPPORT OF MOTION TO
PROCEED ON APPEAL IN FORMA PAUPERIS

I, _____, state, under penalties of perjury, that I am the [Appellant; Appellee] in the above-entitled case; that in support of my motion to proceed on appeal without being required to prepay fees, costs or give security therefor, I state that because of my poverty I am unable to pay the costs of said proceeding or to give security therefor; that I believe I am entitled to redress; and that the issues which I desire to present on appeal are the following:

_____

_____

[INSERT ISSUES]

I further swear that the responses which I have made to the questions and instructions below relating to my ability to pay the cost of prosecuting the appeal are true.

1.   Are you presently employed? ☐Yes ☐No

    a.   If the answer is yes, state the amount of your salary or wages per month and give the name and address of your employer.

    b.   If the answer is no, state the date of your last employment and the amount of the salary and wages per month which you received.

2.   Have you received within the past twelve months any income from a business, profession or other form of self-employment, or in the form of rent payments, interest, dividends, retirement or disability payments, government benefits or other source? ☐ Yes ☐ No

    a.   If the answer is yes, describe each source of income, and state the amount received from each during the past twelve months.

3.   Do you own any cash or checking or savings account? ☐ Yes ☐ No

    a.   If the answer is yes, state the total value of the items owned.

4.   Do you own any real estate, stocks, bonds, notes, automobiles, or other valuable property (excluding ordinary household furnishings and clothing)?

    a.   If the answer is yes, describe the property and state its approximate value.

5.   List the persons who are dependent upon you for support and state your relationship to those persons.

I understand that a false statement or answer to any questions in this affidavit will subject me to penalties for perjury.

_____

Signature

_____

Date

Adopted Feb. 4, 2000, effective Jan. 1, 2001.

Form App. R. 43–1.   Cover For Briefs And Petitions

[SAMPLE COVER FOR BRIEFS AND PETITIONS]App.R. 43-1

IN THE
INDIANA COURT OF APPEALS [OR SUPREME COURT]

Case No. _____ *

[NAME OF APPELLANT],	)	Appeal [or Interlocutory Appeal,
_____	)	Petition for Review]
Appellant,	)	from the _____
	)	[name of trial court or administrative
	)	agency]
	)	
v.	)	Case No. _____
	)	[Trial court or administrative agency
	)	case no.]
	)	
[NAME OF APPELLEE],	)	Hon. _____
_____	)	[name and title of presiding judge,
Appellee.	)	e.g., judge, special judge, judge pro
	)	tempore]

TITLE [e.g., APPELLANT'S BRIEF]

Name
Firm (if applicable)
Address
Telephone number

Attorney for [Filing Party, e.g., Appellant]**
[or Pro Se Filing Party]

*When seeking or opposing transfer or review, use Court of Appeals or Tax Court case number unless Supreme Court number has been assigned.
**Include information only about the filing party on the cover.

Adopted Feb. 4, 2000, effective Jan. 1, 2001.

Form App. R. 51–1.   Cover For Appendices
<u>[SAMPLE COVER FOR APPENDICES]</u>   App.R. 51-1

IN THE INDIANA COURT OF APPEALS [OR SUPREME COURT]

Case No. _____ *

[NAME OF APPELLANT],	Appeal [or Interlocutory Appeal, Petition for Review]
_____	from the _____
Appellant,	[name of trial court or administrative agency]
v.	Case No. _____
	[Trial court or administrative agency case no.]
[NAME OF APPELLEE],	Hon. _____
_____	[name and title of presiding judge, e.g.
Appellee.	judge, special judge, judge pro tempore]

TITLE [e.g., Appellant's Appendix]
[Title should indicate if appendix is a supplemental appendix]

Volume _____ [number of volume] of _____ [total number of volumes]

Pages _____ through _____

Name
Firm (if applicable)
Address
Telephone number

Attorney for [Filing Party, e.g., Appellant]**
[or Pro Se Filing Party]

*When seeking or opposing transfer or review, use Court of Appeals or Tax Court case number unless Supreme Court number has been assigned.
**Include information only about the filing party on the cover.

Adopted Feb. 4, 2000, effective Jan. 1, 2001.

Appendix B.   Standards for Preparation of Electronic Transcripts Pursuant to Appellate Rule 30

The following standards shall apply when the Court on Appeal grants a motion pursuant to Appellate Rule 30(A)(1) to accept an electronically formatted Transcript.

Standard 1.   The electronic Transcript must comply with all of the requirements set out in Appellate Rule 30.

Standard 2.   The Transcript of the evidence may be prepared in any commercially available word processing software system.

Standard 3.   Pursuant to Appellate Rule 30(A)(5), the court reporter shall transcribe the evidence on one or more sequentially numbered electronic data storage devices for each complete transcription. Approved media for electronic storage include USB flash memory drives, compact discs (CDs), and digital versatile discs (DVDs) specifically formatted to store electronic data in a FAT or FAT–32 file system. Each electronic data storage device shall be prepared and designated as:

a) "Official record"

b) "Official working copy"

c) "Court reporter's copy"

d) "Party copy"

The court reporter must convert the "official record," the "official working copy" and the "party copy" into Portable Document Format (PDF) and transmit these copies in PDF format as set out in Appellate Rule 30.

Standard 4.   Pursuant to Appellate Rule 30(B) the court reporter shall retain a signed, read only "court reporter's copy" of the electronic Transcript in the original word processing version used for the transcription.

Adopted Jan. 31, 2002, effective April 1, 2002. Amended Sept. 21, 2010, effective Jan. 1, 2011.

PILOT PROJECT FOR EXPLORING THE USE OF AN AUDIO/VISUAL RECORD ON APPEAL

INDIANA COURT REPORTING PILOT PROJECT FOR EXPLORING THE USE OF AN AUDIO/VISUAL RECORD ON APPEAL

ORDER ESTABLISHING THE INDIANA COURT REPORTING PILOT PROJECT FOR EXPLORING THE USE OF AN AUDIO/VISUAL RECORD ON APPEAL

After a study of court reporting methods employed in court systems throughout the country, this Court determined that Indiana should explore some of the ways used by other jurisdictions to improve court reporting services. The use of audio/visual recording as the record on appeal is a method our neighbor, Kentucky, has used for more than 25 years to expedite the appellate process. This Order establishes a special court reporting pilot project, which will explore the use of audio/visual recordings as the record on appeal in lieu of paper transcripts. This effort shall be designated as the *Indiana Court Reporting Pilot Project for Audio/Visual Recordings.*

BACKGROUND: Indiana's trial courts use recording equipment, primarily digital, to record the proceedings in their courts. The courts employ county-paid court reporters who help the judge record the proceedings and, when requested to do so, transcribe the recording and create a transcript of the proceedings for submission and use by the Courts on Appeal. Pursuant to Administrative Rule 15, the courts of records in the county adopt, for approval by the Supreme Court, local rules by which all court recording services and charges are governed. The local rules must set the permissible per page fees a court reporter can charge for transcribing the record and must require an annual report of the income generated by each court reporter through the preparation of court transcripts. The 2011 reports indicate that approximately $1,862,000 was collected from the preparation of transcripts, and that $968,000 of that amount was paid from public funds for transcripts in indigent cases. The amounts generated in each county vary depending on the number of appeals and the length of the transcripts. The 2011 total amounts reported by county varied from zero to approximately $320,000 in Marion County, while the county transcript preparation per page charges varied from $2.50 to $7.50.

The Indiana Rules of Appellate Procedure, which were adopted on February 4, 2000, effective January 2, 2001, were the result of a comprehensive undertaking by the Appellate Section of the Indiana State Bar Association, a special Appellate Rules Project, and the Supreme Court Committee on Rules of Practice and Procedure. The proposal tendered to this Court included, among other things, a recommendation that the time for preparation of the transcript be reduced from ninety (90) to sixty (60) days. This Court declined to reduce the 90–day time limit but indicated that further study may be warranted by stating in Appellate Rule 11(B) that the 90–day period will remain "until July 1, 2003, and until revised thereafter."

Consistent with its continuing study and review of how to expedite the appellate process and improve court reporting services, this Court directed the Division of State Court Administration (Division) to conduct a study and report to the court on what other court systems are doing to provide more efficient, more timely and less costly court reporting and transcribing services. The Division reported that among the methods other jurisdictions use to expedite the appellate process, improve court reporting and transcription services, and reduce costs are: (1) the use of audio/visual recordings as the record on appeal; (2) the use of certified professional transcription experts; and, (3) the use of electronic briefing, filing and transmission of appellate documents.

In a separate effort, the Indiana Court of Appeals conducted an analysis of the time that transpired between the filing of the notices of appeal and the completion of transcripts in cases filed with that court. The results indicated that in 2010 there were two thousand two hundred seventy-six (2, 276) appeals in which a transcript was filed. In those cases, the average number of days between the filing of a Notice of Appeal and the filing of the transcript was one hundred fifty-one (151) days. The fewest number of days was eighty-six (86), and the largest was two hundred twenty-nine (229).

In light of the foregoing, this Court decided to direct the Division to undertake a pilot project designed to explore ways for presenting the record on appeal without the preparation of the traditional transcript by a court reporter, and to explore ways to receive and use transcripts in a more timely, efficient, and cost-effective manner. Former Chief Justice Randall Shepard sought and received a pledge of cooperation from the Indiana Court of Appeals, and Chief Judge Margret Robb appointed Judge Cale Bradford, Judge Melissa May, and Judge James

Kirsch as the Court of Appeals judges who will spearhead the project and participate in the review of the selected cases.

IT IS, THEREFORE, ORDERED THAT the Executive Director of the Division of State Court Administration and staff shall work with Chief Judge Robb, the Court of Appeals judges and staff, and the selected trial court judges to conduct a pilot project for a limited period of time, and in a limited number of appealed cases, in three phases to accomplish the following: (1) utilizing audio/visual recordings in lieu of paper transcripts in selected courtrooms; (2) using outside transcript preparation to expedite the process of transcript preparation of lower court proceedings; and, (3) requiring parties on appeal to file in digital format only their appellate briefs and transcript of proceedings. This is one of three (3) Orders concerning this pilot project.

Notwithstanding the procedures set out in the Indiana Rules of Appellate Procedure, this Court authorizes a limited pilot project utilizing audio/visual recordings in lieu of paper transcripts for the preparation of the record and briefing on appeal. During the term of the pilot project, the participating trial courts, trial court clerks, court reporters, and parties shall comply with the Indiana Rules of Appellate and Trial Procedure except as set forth below. Each of the participating courts will utilize the audio/visual equipment installed in its courtroom for this pilot project, while continuing to use its court's existing audio equipment, to record every proceeding in its courtroom during this pilot project. In the cases chosen by the trial courts for this pilot project, participation is mandatory for the parties. Citations to paper transcripts may not be used in the preparation of the appellate briefs in these limited cases.

PILOT PROJECT TERM: This pilot project shall end on December 31, 2013, unless extended by further order of this Court.

PARTICIPATING COURTS: Marion Superior Court, Criminal Division 6 (Major Felony); Tippecanoe Superior Court #3; and Allen Superior Court (Civil).

CASES ON APPEAL: After a Notice of Appeal has been filed, within five (5) business days, the trial court may designate the case as a pilot project case by filing a notice with the appellate clerk, in the form and substance of the attached Exhibit A, with service to the parties. This notice will inform the parties that their appeal must be prepared using the audio/visual recordings in lieu of a paper transcript. Each of the participating trial courts will select fifteen (15) cases being appealed from their courts to the Court of Appeals of Indiana from the following case types: Marion Superior Court—fifteen (15) criminal cases, Tippecanoe Superior Court—fifteen (15) termination of parental rights cases, and Allen Superior Court—fifteen (15) civil cases.

APPELLATE PANEL: During the term of the pilot project, fifteen (15) appeals utilizing audio/visual recordings in lieu of paper transcripts from each of the participating courts will be assigned to a predetermined three-judge panel.

ALTERNATIVE PROCEDURES:

A. *Trial Court Proceedings.* The record of trial court proceedings shall consist of two (2) simultaneously created audio/visual recordings. The recordings shall be made using equipment meeting guidelines established by the Executive Director of the Division of State Court Administration, as approved by this Court.

B. *Method of Identification.* For identification purposes the court reporter, judge or designee shall label each of the two (2) official audio/visual records as follows:

1. line one—the case number assigned in the trial court;

2. line two—a short caption of the proceeding (e.g. Smith v. Jones);

3. line three—the appellate case number assigned by the court on appeal, if known; and,

4. line four—the date and the sequential volume number of the record.

C. *Trial Event Log.* The court reporter, judge or a designee shall keep a Trial Event Log within the accompanying software for the equipment. The Trial Event Log shall indicate:

1. where each witness' direct, cross, or redirect examination begins and ends;

2. where each exhibit is offered into evidence and the court's ruling on the admission of each exhibit begins;

3. where voir dire and jury instructions begin and end, in jury trials;

4. where opening and closing statements begin and end; and,

5. where pre-trial hearings begin and end with a brief synopsis identifying the nature of the hearings.

D. *Access to the Audio/Visual Recording.* Prior to the filing of a Notice of Appeal, parties may request, and at the trial court's discretion, the Court may provide to the parties a copy of the Audio/Visual Recording provided that the parties supply their own media for copying purposes. Such copy shall be provided at no cost to the parties. Notwithstanding the provisions of Ind. Administrative Rule 9 (H) prohibiting public access to court records and pursuant to the authority vested in this Court by the Indiana Access to Public Records Act, I.C. 5–14–3–4(a)(8), the Audio/Visual Recording and any copies shall be deemed confidential and not subject to public access until after the court proceeding has been concluded and all direct appeals have been exhausted.

E. *Certification and Notice of Completion of Audio/Visual Recording.* Within thirty (30) days of the filing of a Notice of Appeal, two (2) of the copies of the Audio/Visual Recording shall be certified by the court reporter and filed with the trial court clerk. The trial court shall retain a copy of the Audio/Visual Recording. Upon the filing of the two (2) certified copies of the Audio/Visual Recording, the trial court clerk shall issue and file a Notice of Completion of Audio/Visual Recording, in the form and substance of Exhibit B, as is provided in Ind. Appellate Rule 10(D) for paper transcripts.

F. *Submission of Audio/Visual Recording.* Following certification of the Audio/Visual Recording, the court reporter shall seal two (2) certified copies in an envelope or package bearing the trial court case number and marked "Audio/Visual Recording." The court reporter shall retain the court reporter's copy of the Audio/Visual Recording and provide a duplicate copy at no cost to each party at the time of filing the Notice of Completion of Audio/Visual Recording (in criminal cases, a copy should be provided to the Attorney General). The court reporter shall file the sealed Audio/Visual Recording, paper exhibits, and photographic reproductions of nondocumentary and oversized exhibits (if included pursuant to Rule 29(a)) with the trial court clerk in accordance with Appellate Rule 11.

G. *Briefs and Other Filings; Filing Deadlines and Citations.*

1. Appellant's Brief. The appellant's brief shall be filed no later than forty-five (45) days after the date the trial court clerk serves its Notice of Completion of the Audio/Visual Recording under section E above. Rule 25 (C), which grants a three-day extension of time for service by mail or third-party commercial carrier, does not extend the due date for filing the appellant's brief, but does apply to the filing of all other briefs.

2. Appellee's Brief. The appellee's brief shall be filed no later than forty-five (45) days after service of the appellant's brief.

3. Appellant's Reply Brief; Cross–Appellee's Brief. Any appellant's reply brief shall be filed no later than fifteen (15) days after service of the appellee's brief. If the reply brief also serves as the cross-appellee's brief, it shall be filed no later than forty-five (45) days after service of the appellee's brief.

4. Cross–Appellant's Reply Brief. Any cross-appellant's reply brief shall be filed no later than fifteen (15) days after service of the appellant's reply brief.

5. Citations to Audio/Visual Recording. Each reference in a brief to a segment of the Audio/Visual Recording (hereinafter A/V Rec.) shall set forth in parentheses "A/V Rec." and include the following: the number of the diskette or tape, and the month, day, year, hour, minute, and second at which the reference begins as recorded in the A/V Rec. For example: (A/V Rec. No. 1; 08/30/86; 09:22:26). Parties may not cite to any paper transcript within briefs, appendices, addendums, and petitions filed with the court on appeal.

6. Other Documents. All briefs, appendices, addendums, and petitions filed with the court on appeal in cases being appealed from a participating court during the term of the pilot project shall be filed in paper format as required under the Rules of Appellate Procedure. Parties are also encouraged to file these documents electronically (see Appellate Rule 43(K)).

ADDITIONAL PROVISION: For this pilot project, the following additional provision shall apply:

In the fifteen (15) criminal cases chosen for this pilot project appealed from Marion Superior Court, Criminal Division 6 (Major Felony), the party filing the Notice of Appeal shall also request and make payment for a paper transcript to be prepared by the court reporter (in accordance with the Rules of Appellate Procedure). Criminal felony cases files must be retained in a permanent medium and microfilmed pursuant to Administrative Rule 6(G)(3) or, if maintained electronically, they must be kept so that a hard copy can be generated at any time. *See Trial Rule 77(J).* The paper transcripts are necessary in order to comply with the current permanency standard for felony case files. However, the parties shall not cite to the paper transcript and are strongly encouraged not to use the paper transcript in the preparation of the briefs on appeal. In these fifteen (15) pilot project criminal cases, these transcripts will be maintained and preserved as part of the appellate record along with the audio and audio/video recordings.

IT IS ORDERED THAT the Clerk of this Court is directed to include a copy of this Order with the case file of each case appealed using the proceedings set out in this Order and to include a reference in the chronological case summary that the appeal is governed by this Order.

Adopted Sept. 18, 2012, effective July 1, 2012.

Exhibit A.   Notice of Designation of Case as an Audio/Visual Recording Pilot Project Case

Exhibit A
IN THE
INDIANA COURT OF APPEALS

Case No.: _____
[insert Court of Appeals number, if known]

_____,	) Appeal from the _____) Court)
Appellant(s),	))
vs.	) Trial Court Case No:)
_____,	) _____)
Appellee(s).	) The Honorable _____,) Judge

NOTICE OF DESIGNATION OF CASE AS AN
AUDIO/VISUAL RECORDING PILOT PROJECT CASE

The undersigned presiding Judge hereby notifies the parties, pursuant to the Indiana Supreme Court Order Establishing the Indiana Court Reporting Pilot Project for Exploring the Use of an Audio/Visual Record on Appeal (Order) in Supreme Court Case No. _____—_____ –MS- _____, that this case is designated as a pilot project case pursuant to the authority vested in me by the above Order. The parties to this appeal must prepare their appellate briefs using only the audio/visual recording in lieu of a paper transcript.

Entered this _____ day of _____, 20 ___.

_____

Judge

_____ Court

Copies to:

Adopted Sept. 18, 2012, effective July 1, 2012.

Exhibit B. Notice of Completion of Audio/Visual Recording

Exhibit B
IN THE
INDIANA COURT OF APPEALS

Case No.: _____

[insert Court of Appeals number, if known]

	)	Appeal from the _____
_____,	)	Court
	)	
Appellant(s),	)	
	)	Trial Court Case No:
vs.	)	
	)	_____
	)	
_____,	)	
	)	The Honorable _____,
Appellee(s).	)	Judge

NOTICE OF COMPLETION OF AUDIO/VISUAL RECORDING

_____, the Court Reporter of _____ Court, hereby notifies the parties, pursuant to the Indiana Supreme Court Order Establishing the Indiana Court Reporting Pilot Project for Exploring the Use of an Audio/ Visual Record on Appeal (Order) in Supreme Court Case No. _____—_____ –MS–_____, that the Audio/Visual Recording in this cause is complete. This ___ day of _____, 20 ___, the Audio/Visual Recording was filed with the clerk of the trial court in accordance with the above Order.

_____

Court Reporter

CERTIFICATE OF SERVICE

I certify that on [insert date] I sent copies of this document to the following parties of record by United States Mail, postage pre-paid. [List parties and their addresses]

_____

Court Reporter

Adopted Sept. 18, 2012, effective July 1, 2012.

RULES OF PROCEDURE FOR ORIGINAL ACTIONS

Including Amendments Received Through November 1, 2013

Rule 1. Scope of Rules

(A) Jurisdiction of Supreme Court Over Original Actions for Writs of Mandamus or Prohibition. The Supreme Court has exclusive, original jurisdiction to supervise the exercise of jurisdiction of all inferior state courts, including the Court of Appeals, by virtue of Indiana Constitution, Article 7, Section 4, and Ind. Appellate Rule 4(B)(3).

(B) Nature of Original Actions Governed by These Rules. Actions commenced in the Supreme Court pursuant to the authority in section (A) above for writs of mandamus or prohibition against inferior state courts and the judge or judges thereof and concerned solely with the question of jurisdiction shall be known as original actions and shall be governed exclusively by these Rules.

(C) Parties to Original Actions. The party who commences an original action is the Relator. The parties against whom an original action is commenced are the Respondents. The Respondents are always an inferior state court and the judge or judges thereof. In rare instances, a court clerk may be an additional Respondent.

(D) Writs Against Administrative Agencies. Complaints filed pursuant to IC 34–27–3–1 et seq. for writs of mandamus or prohibition against administrative agencies and the members thereof are not original actions governed by these Rules. Those complaints are to be filed in the trial court having jurisdiction over the action.

(E) Writs in Aid of Appellate Jurisdiction. Petitions for writs in aid of appellate jurisdiction are not original actions governed by these Rules. Those petitions are to be filed in the court having initial appellate jurisdiction of a pending appeal or of an appeal about to be filed. The authority of the Supreme Court to issue writs in aid of its appellate jurisdiction is Appellate Rule 4(B)(4) and Appellate Rule 8. The authority of the Court of Appeals to issue writs in aid of its appellate jurisdiction is Appellate Rule 8.

(F) Title. These Rules shall be known as the Rules of Procedure for Original Actions and shall be cited in accordance with Ind. Appellate Rule 22(B).

Amended Nov. 20, 1980, effective Jan. 1, 1981; amended Oct. 29, 1993, effective Jan. 1, 1994; amended Dec. 22, 2000, effective Jan. 1, 2001.

Rule 2. Applications for Writs

(A) Conditions Precedent to Making Applications for Writs. Except in original actions involving a change of venue from the judge or county, no application for a writ of mandamus or prohibition will be entertained unless the Relator has raised the jurisdictional question by written motion which the trial court has denied or not ruled upon timely. The motion shall allege the absence of jurisdiction of the respondent court or the failure of the respondent court to act when it was under a duty to act.

(B) Submission of Applications to Supreme Court Administrator. Except for application for emergency writs, all applications for writs of mandamus or prohibition, along with the filing fee, shall be submitted in person or by mail to the Supreme Court Administrator, 315 State House, Indianapolis, Indiana 46204, telephone (317) 232–2540. Relator shall serve Respondents and all interested parties on the same day the Relator's writ application is submitted in person or by mail to the Supreme Court. Delivering a copy of the papers to an interested party's office is personal service on that party within the meaning of these Rules. If emergency relief is requested, Relator must submit the application papers to the Administrator in person after personal service on Respondents and all interested parties. Otherwise, service on the Respondents and interested parties shall be accomplished in the same fashion as service on the Administrator, except that personal service shall always be acceptable.

(C) Filing of Applications. The Supreme Court Administrator shall arrange to have original action applications filed with the Clerk. At the time of filing Relator's filing fee will be deposited.

(D) The Supreme Court Administrator shall submit all original action applications to the Chief

Justice or Acting Chief Justice after filing. If the application is incomplete or in improper form or seeks an unquestionably inappropriate remedy, the Chief Justice or Acting Chief Justice shall enter an order dismissing the application without the intervention of the full Court. In all other cases, the Chief Justice or Acting Chief Justice shall determine whether the case should be immediately set for hearing or referred to the full Court.

If the Chief Justice or the full Court decides to set the case for hearing, the Supreme Court Administrator shall complete and file the notice of hearing. The Supreme Court Clerk shall send copies of the notice of hearing to Relator, Respondents, and all interested parties, including the Attorney General as required by Ind. Original Action 6(D). However, the Court may decide to grant or deny the original action without hearing.

(E) Original Actions Viewed With Disfavor. Original actions are viewed with disfavor and may not be used as substitutes for appeals.

(F) "Application Papers", "Papers", and "Paper" Defined. The words "application papers", "papers", and "paper" as used in these Rules shall mean and include, without limitation, all petitions, records of the proceedings, briefs, notices of hearing, affidavits of emergency, writs, preliminary responses, and returns.

(G) "Parties" and "Party" Defined. The words "parties" and "party" as used in these Rules shall mean and include, without limitation, all Relators, Respondents, parties opposing Relator in the respondent court, and the Attorney General, if service on the Attorney General is required by Orig.Act.R. 6(E).

Amended Nov. 20, 1980, effective Jan. 1, 1981; amended effective June 8, 1988; amended Oct. 29, 1993, effective Jan. 1, 1994; amended Dec. 22, 2000, effective Jan. 1, 2001.

Rule 3. Application Papers

(A) Petition. All applications for writs of mandamus or prohibition shall be made by petition. The petition shall be verified or affirmed and shall state facts showing clearly that:

(1) the Supreme Court has jurisdiction over the application as an original action;

(2) the application is made expeditiously after the jurisdiction of the respondent court became an issue;

(3) the respondent court has exceeded its jurisdiction or the respondent court has failed to act when it was under a duty to act;

(4) the absence of jurisdiction of the respondent court or the failure of the respondent court to act when it was under a duty to act has been raised in the respondent court by a written motion filed therein and brought to the attention of the respondent judge, and the written motion has been denied or not ruled on timely; provided, however, that the petition need not show this in applications involving a change of venue from the judge or county;

(5) the denial of the application will result in extreme hardship; and

(6) the remedy available by appeal will be wholly inadequate. See Form No. 1.

Original action applications which do not include all of the applicable allegations listed above shall be rejected by the Chief Justice or Acting Chief Justice.

(B) Brief. The Relator shall submit a separate supporting brief with Relator's petition. The Relator shall set forth verbatim in the brief, indented and single-spaced, the relevant parts of all cases, statutes, and other authorities relied upon, but need not conform the brief otherwise to the rules applicable to appellate briefs. The brief need not be bound.

(C) Record of Proceedings—Certification. At the time the Relator submits the original action petition, the Relator shall submit a certified record of the proceedings from the respondent court. The record shall contain copies of all relevant pleadings, motions, orders, entries, and other papers filed, tendered for filing, or entered in the respondent court. The record also shall include a current copy of the chronological case summary. In the event a relevant transcript of any evidence in the record exists, it shall be submitted and shall have been certified by the appropriate court reporter and the respondent judge. The last page of the original action record shall be a certificate of the clerk of the respondent court which clearly demonstrates that all the papers contained in the record have been filed, tendered for filing, or entered in the respondent court. The original action record need not be bound like an appellate record, but it should contain a table of contents at the beginning and should be enumerated for purposes of citation to the record.

(D) Filing Fee. Relator shall tender the filing fee of two hundred and fifty dollars ($250) when the Relator submits the original action application to the Supreme Court Administrator. The fee is not applicable in a case prosecuted as a pauper cause or on behalf of a governmental unit. If Relator seeks pauper status, Relator shall submit with the original action papers an affidavit of indigency detailing Relator's assets and financial condition and seeking waiver of the filing fee.

(E) Writs. A Permanent writ form shall be submitted, and an Alternative writ form may also be submitted by the Relator. If emergency relief is sought, an emergency writ form also shall be submitted.

(1) *Emergency Writ.* An Emergency Writ is an order that may be granted prior to a hearing. It must be accompanied by a petition for emergency writ demonstrating that a writ must be issued to maintain the status quo and prevent irreparable injury until the application can be heard. The Emergency Writ operates as a temporary stay of the trial court proceedings until the Supreme Court

hears and rules upon the original action application. All original action applications which include a request for emergency writ shall be presented in person to the Supreme Court Administrator after personal service on the Respondents and all other interested parties. The Administrator shall submit all applications for emergency writ to the Chief Justice, if available, or to the Acting Chief Justice for a determination as to whether or not a sufficient emergency exists to require a stay. If the Chief Justice or Acting Chief Justice grants the emergency writ, the writ shall be filed immediately and the original action may be set for hearing. See Form No. 5. The filing of a petition for emergency writ shall not obviate the need to file the other application papers required by these rules including the petition for writ of mandamus or prohibition.

(2) *Alternative Writ.* An Alternative Writ is an order that requires Respondents to take action (mandamus), to cease action (prohibition), or both. If an Alternative Writ is issued, the Respondents shall file a return with the Court no later than twenty (20) days after the filing of the writ. A "return" is a pleading submitted by the respondent court showing compliance with the writ or stating reasons why the writ should not be made permanent. See Form No. 2. The return shall be submitted in person or by mail to the Supreme Court Clerk for filing.

(3) *Permanent Writ.* A Permanent Writ is an order, issued after the application is made, which is immediately permanent. It dispenses with the general practice of allowing the Respondents to file a return. See Form No. 3.

(F) Notice of Hearing. The Relator shall submit a notice of hearing with Relator's original action petition, leaving the date and time of the hearing blank. See Form No. 4.

(G) Preliminary Response. The Respondents, or any party opposing Relator in the respondent court, or the Attorney General, if service on the Attorney General is required by Orig.Act.R. 6(E), may submit to the Administrator at any time before the hearing a preliminary response showing any factual or legal reason why the original action application should be denied. The Administrator shall have the preliminary response filed with the Clerk of the Supreme Court.

(H) Number of Copies. Each party shall submit to the Administrator the original and five (5) copies of each application paper, including the record.

(I) Production. All application papers shall be typewritten or printed on 8½ × 11 inch white, opaque, unglazed paper of a weight normally used in legal typing and printing, and shall be reproduced by a copying or duplicating process that produces a clear, black image.

(J) Documents and Information Excluded from Public Access and Confidential Pursuant to Ad- ministrative **Rule 9(G)(1).** Documents and information excluded from public access pursuant to Administrative Rule 9(G)(1) shall be filed in accordance with Trial Rule 5(G).

Amended Nov. 20, 1980, effective Jan. 1, 1981; Nov. 16, 1984, effective Jan. 1, 1985; Jan. 18, 1991, effective Jan. 1, 1992; amended effective Jan. 24, 1992; amended Oct. 29, 1993, effective Jan. 1, 1994; Dec. 23, 1996, effective March 1, 1997; Dec. 22, 2000, effective Jan. 1, 2001; Sept. 30, 2004, effective Jan. 1, 2005; Sept. 21, 2010, effective Jan. 1, 2011.

Rule 4. Hearing on Applications

(A) Scheduling of Hearing. The Supreme Court may set the hearing on the application for a date usually not less than one week from the date of submission of the application to the Administrator. An earlier hearing date may be authorized if Relator establishes in Relator's original action petition or emergency writ petition that an extreme emergency exists which necessitates an earlier hearing.

(B) Nature of Hearing. The hearing on the application is only upon the record of the proceedings in the respondent court. No testimonial or documentary evidence shall be offered or received at the hearing.

(C) Time Allowed for Arguments at Hearing. Each side to an original action usually will be allowed thirty (30) minutes for oral argument. A party is not obligated to use all of the allowed time, and the court may terminate the arguments whenever in its judgment further argument is unnecessary. Appearance by the respondent judge or the judge's counsel is not necessary; the party opposing the Relator in the trial court may oppose the original action application. In the event the respondent judge or the judge's counsel appear, the respondent judge or the judge's counsel shall be given an opportunity to speak regardless of whether others opposing the original action have used the 30 minutes allotted to that side.

(D) Order and Content of Argument. The Relator shall open and may conclude the argument by reserving part of the Relator's time for rebuttal before beginning the argument. The parties will not be permitted to read at length from the record of the proceedings, briefs, or authorities during oral argument.

(E) Deliberation After Argument. Upon completion of the oral arguments, the parties will be asked to leave the Supreme Court Conference Room while the Court deliberates. When the Court concludes its deliberation, the parties will be recalled into the Supreme Court Conference Room to learn the Court's decision. In cases where the Court is unable to reach an immediate decision or where a Justice is absent, the Court may delay ruling until such time as agreement is reached or the absent Justice is able to consider the case.

Amended Nov. 20, 1980, effective Jan. 1, 1981; amended Oct. 29, 1993, effective Jan. 1, 1994; amended Dec. 22, 2000, effective Jan. 1, 2001.

Rule 5. Disposition of Applications

(A) Application Granted—Issuance of Writ—Filing With Clerk—Disposition. If the application for writ of mandamus or prohibition is granted, either an alternative or permanent writ will be issued. If the alternative writ is issued, the respondent court shall be given 20 days to file a return. See Orig.Act.R. 3(E)(2). The return shall show compliance with the writ or state reasons why the writ should not be made permanent.

If the return shows compliance with the alternative writ, the Supreme Court will enter an order dismissing the original action as moot.

If the return contests the alternative writ, the Relator shall have five (5) days after service of the return to file a brief in opposition to the return. Any parties opposing the alternative writ other than the respondents also may file a further brief no later than five (5) days after service of the return. For purposes of this rule, Ind.Appellate Rule 23(A) applies but Ind.Appellate Rule 24(D) does not. See Orig.Act.R. 6.

The Supreme Court thereafter will dispose of the original action by written order or opinion without further hearing or the filing of any further papers, unless requested by the Court.

(B) Application Denied. If the application is denied, an order of denial shall be entered expeditiously. The denial of the application will end the proceedings, regardless of whether the Court has conducted a hearing.

(C) Petitions for Rehearing. No petitions for rehearing or motions to reconsider shall be filed after final disposition of the original action.

Amended Nov. 20, 1980, effective Jan. 1, 1981; amended effective June 8, 1988; amended Oct. 29, 1993, effective Jan. 1, 1994; amended effective May 11, 1994; amended Dec. 22, 2000, effective Jan. 1, 2001.

Rule 6. Submission, Filing, and Service of Application Papers

(A) Submission. All application papers or preliminary responses shall be deemed submitted to the Supreme Court Administrator when personally delivered or when deposited with the United States Postal Service or with any properly bonded carrier, properly addressed and with charges prepaid.

(B) Service of Application Papers Submitted Prior to Hearing. A copy of each application paper submitted to the Administrator by the Relator shall be served by the Relator upon the Respondents, upon any party opposing Relator in the respondent court, and upon the Attorney General when required by Orig.Act.R. 6(E). If the papers are submitted to the Administrator in person, such service shall be by personal delivery and accomplished immediately before submission to the Administrator. If the papers are mailed to the Administrator, service on the interested parties may be by mail if simultaneously deposited with the United States Postal Service or with any properly bonded carrier, properly addressed and with charges prepaid.

(C) Service of Preliminary Response. Any preliminary response may be served upon the Relator by personal service or by depositing the same with the United States Postal Service or with any properly bonded carrier, properly addressed and with charges prepaid. The preliminary response shall be served at or before the time of its submission to the Administrator and in all cases service must be effective before a hearing on the original action. Personal delivery shall include leaving a copy of the paper with a responsible person in the office of the party or the attorney of the party served.

(D) Filing and Service of Returns and Briefs After Hearing. Where a hearing on an application has resulted in the granting of an alternative or permanent writ, the filing of any return or briefs shall be directly with the Supreme Court Clerk. Such papers shall also be served on opposing parties at or before the time of filing. Filing with the Clerk and service upon an opposing party shall be deemed accomplished when done personally or upon deposit of the paper with the United States Postal Service or with any properly bonded carrier, properly addressed and with the charges prepaid.

(E) Service on Attorney General—When Required. In all original actions arising out of criminal cases and in all other original actions in which the State of Indiana has or may have an interest, each party shall serve the Attorney General with a copy of each paper submitted to the Administrator or filed with the Clerk.

(F) Proof of Service of All Application Papers Submitted to the Administrator or Filed With Clerk Required. Where personal service is required of Relator or where personal service is made but not required, two copies of the acknowledgment of service or certificate of service shall be submitted as soon as service is accomplished. The certificate of service shall be signed by the person making service. The acknowledgment of service shall be signed by the person served. The acknowledgment or certificate of service shall state the date of service and the address of each person served.

When service is made by mail or carrier, two (2) copies of the receipt from the carrier, the return receipt from the United States Postal Service or the certificate of the person making service as to the deposit with the United States Postal Service or carrier shall be submitted or filed promptly with the Administrator or Clerk, as the case may be. Provided that, the Administrator or Clerk may permit a paper to be submitted or filed without containing or being accompanied by an acknowledgment or certificate of service, but shall require an acknowledgment or certificate of service to be submitted or filed promptly thereafter.

Amended Nov. 20, 1980, effective Jan. 1, 1981; amended Oct. 29, 1993, effective Jan. 1, 1994; amended Dec. 22, 2000, effective Jan. 1, 2001.

FORMS

FORM 1. CAPTION FOR PETITION FOR WRIT

IN THE SUPREME COURT OF INDIANA

NO. _____

STATE OF INDIANA ON THE
RELATION OF JOHN J. JONES,

                          RELATOR,

            v.

THE _____ COURT AND THE
HONORABLE _____, AS
JUDGE THEREOF,

                       RESPONDENTS.

PETITION FOR WRIT OF MANDAMUS

(OR)

PETITION FOR WRIT OF PROHIBITION

(OR)

PETITION FOR WRIT OF MANDAMUS AND WRIT OF PROHIBITION

(OR)

EMERGENCY WRIT OF PROHIBITION

(OR)

PETITION FOR WRIT OF PROHIBITION AND WRIT OF MANDAMUS

(OR)

EMERGENCY PETITION FOR WRIT OF PROHIBITION AND WRIT OF MANDAMUS

Amended Oct. 29, 1993, effective Jan. 1, 1994.

FORM 2. ALTERNATIVE WRIT OF MANDAMUS

IN THE SUPREME COURT OF INDIANA

NO. _____

STATE OF INDIANA ON THE
RELATION OF JOHN J. JONES,

                          RELATOR,

            v.

THE _____ COURT AND THE
HONORABLE _____,
AS JUDGE THEREOF,

                       RESPONDENTS.

ALTERNATIVE WRIT OF MANDAMUS

This original action comes before the Supreme Court on the application of Relator for a writ of mandamus against respondents.

After examining the application and any preliminary response, hearing the oral arguments of counsel, and being advised in the premises, the Court grants the application.

It is therefore ordered that Respondents, the _____ Court and The Honorable _____, as Judge thereof, *[here Relator shall state the precise relief desired];* or in the alternative that Respondents shall file and serve their return, affirmed or verified, on or before the ___ day of _____, 20___, showing cause why this writ of mandamus should not be made permanent.

It is further ordered that the Clerk shall serve a certified copy of this alternative writ of mandamus on Respondents, the _____ Court and The Honorable _____, as Judge thereof, ... *[here Relator shall insert the complete address of the respondent judge for mailing purposes];* ... *[here Relator shall insert the name and complete address for mailing purposes of each party opposing Relator in the respondent court];* and ... *[here Relator shall insert the name, capacity, and complete address for mailing purposes of the Attorney General, if service on the Attorney General is required by Orig. Act. R. 6(D)].*

So ordered this ___ day of _____ 20___.

_____

Chief Justice of Indiana

Amended Oct. 29, 1993, effective Jan. 1, 1994; amended effective May 3, 2006.

FORM 3. PERMANENT WRIT OF MANDAMUS AND PROHIBITION

IN THE SUPREME COURT OF INDIANA

NO. _____

STATE OF INDIANA ON THE
RELATION OF JOHN J. JONES,

                          RELATOR,

            v.

THE _____ COURT AND THE
HONORABLE _____, AS
JUDGE THEREOF,

                       RESPONDENTS.

PERMANENT WRIT OF MANDAMUS AND PROHIBITION

This original action comes before the Supreme Court on the application of Relator for a writ of mandamus and prohibition against Respondents.

After examining the application and preliminary response, hearing the oral arguments of counsel, and being advised in the premises, the court grants the application.

It is therefore ordered that Respondents, the _____ Court and the Honorable _____, as Judge thereof, *[here Relator shall state the precise relief desired].*

It is further ordered that the Clerk shall serve a certified copy of this permanent writ of mandamus and prohibition on Respondents, the _____ Court and the Honorable _____, as Judge thereof, ... *[here Relator shall insert the complete address of the respondent judge for mailing purposes];* ... *[here Relator shall insert the name and complete address for mailing purposes of each party opposing Relator in the respondent court];* and ... *[here Relator shall insert the name, capacity, and complete address for mailing purposes of the Attorney General, if service on the Attorney General is required by Orig. Act. R. 6(D)].*

So ordered this ___ day of _____, 20___.

_____

Chief Justice of Indiana

Amended Oct. 29, 1993, effective Jan. 1, 1994; amended effective May 3, 2006.

FORM 4. EMERGENCY WRIT OF MANDAMUS AND PROHIBITION FORM

IN THE SUPREME COURT OF INDIANA

NO. _____

STATE OF INDIANA ON THE
RELATION OF JOHN J. JONES,

                                        RELATOR,

v.

THE _____ COURT AND THE
HONORABLE _____, AS
JUDGE THEREOF,

                            RESPONDENTS.

EMERGENCY WRIT

This original action comes before the Supreme Court on the application of Relator for a writ of mandamus and prohibition against Respondents.

Relator alleges Relator will be irreparably harmed if this Court does not stay all proceedings in cause number *[insert cause number of underlying action]* until the Court may conduct a hearing on Relator's original action.

Accordingly, it is ordered that Respondents, the _____ Court and the Honorable _____, as Judge thereof, stay all proceedings in cause number ___ until such time as the Court may rule upon Relator's request for writ of mandamus and prohibition.

It is further ordered that the Clerk shall serve a certified copy of this emergency writ of mandamus and prohibition on Respondents, the _____ Court and the Honorable _____, as Judge thereof, ... *[here Relator shall insert the complete address of the respondent judge for mailing purposes];* ... *[here Relator shall insert the name and complete address for mailing purposes of each party opposing Relator in the respondent court];* and ... *[here Relator shall insert the name, capacity, and complete address for mailing purposes of the Attorney General,*

if service on the Attorney General is required by Orig. Act. R. 6(D)(1)].

So ordered this ___ day of _____, 20___.

_____

Chief Justice

Adopted effective Jan. 1, 1994. Amended effective May 3, 2006; amended Sept. 15, 2009, effective Jan. 1, 2010.

FORM 5. NOTICE OF HEARING FORM

IN THE SUPREME COURT OF INDIANA

NO. _____

STATE OF INDIANA ON THE
RELATION OF JOHN J. JONES,

                                        RELATOR,

v.

THE _____ COURT AND THE
HONORABLE _____, AS
JUDGE THEREOF,

                            RESPONDENTS.

NOTICE OF HEARING

To: The _____ Court and The Honorable _____, as Judge thereof, Respondents; ... *[here insert name of each party opposing Relator in the respondent court];* and ... *[here insert name and capacity of Attorney General, if service on the Attorney General is required by Orig. Act. R. 6(D)].*

You are hereby notified that Relator has submitted to the Supreme Court an application for writ of mandamus. A copy of the application papers are served on you with this notice of hearing.

You are hereby notified further that the Supreme Court will hear oral arguments on the application on the ___ day of _____, 20___, at ___ _____.M. Indianapolis time, in the Supreme Court Conference Room, 319 State House, Indianapolis, Indiana. You, or any party opposing Relator in the respondent court, or the Attorney General, if service on the Attorney General is required by Orig. Act. R. 6(D), may appear personally or by counsel at the hearing and be heard on the application.

You are hereby notified further that you, or any party opposing Relator in the respondent court, or the Attorney General, if service on the Attorney General is required Orig. Act. R. 6(D), may submit to the Supreme Court Administrator and serve on all other parties at any time before the hearing a preliminary response showing any factual or legal reason why the application should be denied.

Dated this ___ day of _____, 20___.

_____

Supreme Court
Administrator
313 State House
Indianapolis, Indiana
46204
Telephone: (317)

232-2540

TDD: (317) 233-6110

Former Form 4 amended and redesignated as present Form 5 effective Jan. 1, 1994; amended effective May 3, 2006.

FORM 6.   CERTIFICATE OF SERVICE FORM

CERTIFICATE OF SERVICE

I certify that on the ___ day of _____, 20 ___, service was made of a copy of the foregoing Notice of Hearing by *[here insert method of service]* on *[here*

insert the name and address for mailing purposes of the respondent judge, each party opposing Relator in the respondent court, and the Attorney General, if service on him is required by Orig. Act. R. 6(D)].

_____

(Name of attorney for Relator)

Adopted effective Jan. 1, 1994.   Amended effective May 3, 2006.

INDIANA RULES FOR TRIAL DE NOVO FOLLOWING JUDGMENT IN CITY OR TOWN COURT

Adopted Effective November 25, 1997

Including Amendments Received Through November 1, 2013

Rule 1. Trial de Novo Following Civil Judgment

(A) Application. A party who has a statutory right to a trial *de novo* in circuit or superior court after entry of a judgment in a civil action by a city court or an appeal after entry of a judgment in a civil action by a town court described in IC 33–35–2–5 may request and shall receive the trial *de novo* as provided in this Rule. As used in Rule 1, all references to a city court shall also include a town court described in IC 33–35–2–5.

(B) Demand.

(1) Within fifteen (15) days after the city court enters its judgment, the party seeking the trial *de novo* shall file a written "Request for Trial *de Novo*" with the clerk of the circuit court in the county in which the city court is located.

(2) The request for trial *de novo* shall:

(a) state the requesting party's name, address, and telephone number;

(b) state the requesting party's attorney's name, address, and telephone number;

(c) state the opposing party or parties' names, addresses, and telephone numbers;

(d) state the opposing party's or parties' attorneys' names, addresses, and telephone numbers;

(e) state the name of the city court in which judgment was entered against the defendant;

(f) state the date on which judgment was entered in the city court;

(g) request a new trial in the circuit or superior court; and

(h) indicate whether the party filing the request demands or waives the right to have the new trial be by jury.

(3) The party filing the Request for Trial *de novo* shall attach to it:

(a) a copy of the original complaint filed with the city court;

(b) a copy of each responsive pleading filed with the city court; and

(c) a copy of the judgment entered by the city court.

(4) Except as ordered by the circuit or superior court, the clerk of the circuit court shall not accept or file a Request for Trial *de novo* for filing:

(a) without the copies of the original complaint, responsive pleadings, and city court judgment;

(b) more than fifteen (15) days after the date the city court entered its judgment; and

(c) without the bond or other undertaking, or affidavit of indigency required by Subsection (C) of this rule.

(C) Bond or Other Undertaking and Affidavit of Indigency.

(1) The party filing the Request shall file with the clerk of the circuit court a surety bond or cash deposit, payable to the party's opponent or parties' opponent, in an amount sufficient to secure the opponent's or opponents' claims and interest and court costs, and undertaking both the litigation of the trial *de novo* to a final judgment and payment of any judgment entered against the party filing the request by the trial *de novo* court.

(2) If unable to afford a surety bond or cash deposit, the party filing the request may instead file an affidavit of indigency setting forth information which establishes that the party is unable to afford the required surety bond or cash deposit. The party shall attach to the affidavit of indigency that party's personal undertaking, in writing, to prosecute the trial *de novo* to final judgment and to pay any judgment which might be entered against that party.

(D) Belated Request for Trial de Novo. When circumstances beyond a party's control prevent the party from filing a timely and complete request for trial *de novo*, the party may apply for an order from the circuit or superior court directing the clerk of the circuit court to accept and file the party's belated Request for Trial *de novo*. The application to the circuit or superior court for the order shall be verified under Trial Rule 11 and shall state facts which demonstrate that the applying party's failure to file a timely and complete request for trial *de novo* was due to circumstances beyond the party's control. The court shall rule on the application without a hearing after giving the opposing parties fifteen (15) days to file written objections.

(E) Filing and Court Assignment. The clerk of the circuit court shall docket the Request for Trial *de novo* and the copies of the complaint and any responsive pleadings as a civil action in a circuit or superior court in the county. The court to which the request is assigned has full jurisdiction of the case and of the parties from the time the request for the trial *de novo* is filed with the clerk of the circuit court.

(F) Notice to Party or Parties' Opponent. Promptly after the request for trial *de novo* is filed, the clerk of the circuit court shall send notice of the request to the party or parties' opponent named in the request.

(G) Notice to City Court of De Novo Filing. Upon the filing of a request for trial *de novo*, the clerk of the circuit court shall promptly send notice of the filing of the request with a copy of the city court's judgment to the city court from which the trial *de novo* is taken. The city court shall within fifteen (15) days of its receipt of the notice vacate its judgment and shall send notice of the vacation of the judgment to any agency or entity to which it had sent notice of its judgment.

(H) Withdrawal or Dismissal of Request for Trial De Novo.

(1) The party who files the request for trial *de novo* may at any time prior to the trial *de novo* in circuit or superior court withdraw the request by filing a written motion of withdrawal with the circuit or superior court. The court shall grant the motion and shall send notice of its order dismissing the proceeding *de novo* to the city court with an order to the city court to reinstate its judgment.

(2) The circuit or superior court may, on its own motion or on the motion of the party or parties who did not request the trial *de novo*, for good cause dismiss a request for trial *de novo* and order the city court to reinstate its judgment.

(I) Pleadings and Pretrial Procedures.

(1) The Indiana Small Claims Rules shall apply to the trial *de novo* unless:

(a) the request for trial *de novo* demands that the trial be by jury;

(b) the party opponent files within fifteen days of the filing of the request for trial *de novo* a demand for trial by jury; or

(c) the party opponent, if that party was the plaintiff or claimant in the city court, demands within fifteen (15) days of the filing of the

request that the trial be pursuant to the Indiana Rules of Trial Procedure.

(2) Whether the trial *de novo* is subject to Small Claims Rules or Trial Rules, the copies of the original complaint and any responsive pleadings filed with the request for trial *de novo* shall serve as the pleadings for the action in circuit or superior court. In trials *de novo* to which the Trial Rules apply, both the original complaint and responsive pleadings will be considered pleadings to which no responsive pleading is required or permitted.

(J) Limit on De Novo Trial Judgment. The court trying the case *de novo* shall not enter judgment in an amount higher than the statutory maximum limit on judgments which applied in the city court from which the trial *de novo* was taken, to which may be added, without it counting toward the statutory limit, interest on the *de novo* court's judgment beginning from the date the city court's judgment was entered.

Adopted Nov. 25, 1997, effective Jan. 1, 1998. Amended Sept. 21, 2010, effective Jan. 1, 2011.

Rule 2. Trial de Novo Following Infraction or Ordinance Violation Judgment in City or Town Court

(A) Application.

(1) A defendant who has a statutory right to an appeal after a trial for an infraction or ordinance violation in a city or town court may request and shall receive the trial *de novo* as provided in this rule.

(2) A city or town court defendant who admitted committing an infraction or ordinance violation and therefore had no trial in city or town court may request as provided in this rule that the circuit or superior court either:

(a) permit the defendant to withdraw the admission and have a trial *de novo*; or

(b) provide a trial *de novo* on the sanctions.

(B) Demand.

(1) Within fifteen (15) days of the entry of judgment for the infraction or ordinance violation, the defendant shall file a written "Request for Trial *de Novo*" with the clerk of the circuit court in the county in which the city or town court is located.

(2) The Request for Trial *de novo* shall state the defendant's name, address, and telephone number; the city or town court in which judgment was entered against the defendant; the date on which judgment was entered in the city or town court; and whether the judgment was entered on a trial or on an admission of the violation. If the city or town court judgment was entered after a trial, the Request shall request a new trial in the circuit or superior court. If the city or town court judgment was entered after an admission of the violation, the Request shall either:

(a) request permission to withdraw the admission of the violation and have a trial *de novo*; or

(b) request a reassessment of the sanctions imposed in city or town court and a judgment *de novo* as to sanctions.

(C) Filing and Court Assignment. The clerk of the circuit court shall docket and assign the request to a circuit or superior court as an infraction or ordinance violation proceeding. The court to which the request is assigned has full jurisdiction of the case and of the person of the defendant from the time the request for the trial *de novo* is filed with the clerk of the circuit court.

(D) Bond.

(1) The defendant filing the Request shall also file with the clerk of the circuit court a surety bond or cash deposit, payable to the State or municipality, in an amount sufficient to secure the State's or municipality's claims and interest and court costs, and undertaking both the litigation of the trial *de novo* to a final judgment and payment of any judgment entered against the party filing the Request by the trial *de novo* court.

(2) If unable to afford a surety bond or cash deposit, the party filing the Request may instead file an affidavit of indigency setting forth information which establishes that the party is unable to afford the required surety bond or cash deposit. The party shall attach to the affidavit of indigency that party's personal undertaking, in writing, to prosecute the trial *de novo* to final judgment and to pay any judgment which might be entered against that party.

(3) If the party filing the *de novo* Request does not also file the bond or pretrial undertaking or an affidavit of indigency, the clerk of the circuit court shall not docket and file the defendant's Request for trial *de novo*.

(E) Notice to Prosecutor or Municipal Counsel of Trial de Novo. Promptly after the Request for Trial *de novo* is filed, the clerk of the circuit court shall send notice of the Request to the prosecuting attorney or the municipal counsel with an order from the trial *de novo* court that the prosecuting attorney or municipal counsel file a duplicate infraction or ordinance complaint and summons with the clerk of the circuit court charging the infraction or ordinance violation as originally filed with the city or town court. Upon receiving the notice of the Request, the prosecutor or municipal counsel shall within fifteen (15) days file the duplicate summons and complaint or, in the prosecutor's or municipal counsel's discretion, notify the clerk in writing that no proceeding will be filed. If the clerk is notified that no proceeding will be filed, the clerk shall bring the case to the attention of the judge who shall issue an order of dismissal.

(F) Notice to City or Town Court of De Novo Filing and Vacation of City or Town Court Judgment.

(1) Upon the filing of a Request for Trial *de novo*, the clerk of the circuit court shall promptly send notice of the filing of the Request to the city or town court from which the trial *de novo* is taken. The city or town court shall within fifteen (15) days of its receipt of the notice vacate its judgment against the defendant and shall send notice of the vacation of the judgment to any agency or entity to which it had sent notice of the prosecution or the judgment. If the defendant paid an infraction or ordinance violation judgment to the city or town court, the city or town court shall send the payment, after deducting city or town court costs, to the clerk of the circuit court.

(2) The clerk of the circuit court shall hold any payment received from the city or town court pending the outcome of the trial *de novo* and shall apply the payment to any judgment imposed by the circuit or superior court following the trial *de novo*. If any amount of the original payment remains after application to judgments or orders imposed by the trial *de novo* court, the clerk of the circuit court shall refund the balance to the defendant. If the case is dismissed in the *de novo* court by the State or the municipality, the clerk of the circuit court shall refund the entire amount to the defendant.

Adopted Nov. 25, 1997, effective Jan. 1, 1998. Amended Sept. 21, 2010, effective Jan. 1, 2011.

Rule 3. Trial de Novo Following Misdemeanor Trial in City or Town Court

(A) Application.

(1) A defendant who has a statutory right to an appeal after a trial for a misdemeanor in a city or town court may request and shall receive the trial *de novo* as provided in this Rule.

(2) A defendant who entered a plea of guilty to a misdemeanor charge in a city or town court may request as provided in this rule that a circuit or superior court either:

(a) permit the defendant to withdraw the guilty plea and have a trial *de novo*; or

(b) resentence and enter a new judgment of conviction and sentence.

(B) Demand.

(1) Within fifteen (15) days of the hearing at which the city or town court imposed sentence for the misdemeanor, the defendant shall file a written "Request for Trial *de Novo*" with the clerk of the circuit court in the county in which the city or town court is located.

(2) The Request for Trial *de Novo* shall:

(a) state the defendant's name, address, and telephone number;

(b) state the city or town court in which judgment was entered against the defendant;

(c) state the date on which judgment was entered in the city or town court;

(d) state whether the city or town court judgment was entered after a trial or after a guilty plea;

(e) state the name of the penal facility in which the defendant is being held if applicable; and

(f) shall request a new trial in the circuit or superior court.

(C) Filing and Court Assignment.

(1) If the trial *de novo* is taken from a city or town court, the clerk of the circuit court shall docket and assign the request as a misdemeanor in circuit or superior court in accordance with the county criminal case assignment plan established under Indiana Rule of Criminal Procedure 2.2.

(2) The court to which the request is assigned has full jurisdiction of the case and of the person of the defendant from the time the request for the trial *de novo* is filed with the clerk of the circuit court.

(D) Bail or Incarceration. At the time the Request for Trial *de novo* is filed, the defendant may also file with the clerk of the circuit court a surety bond or other pretrial bail undertaking, conditioned on appearance for trial and sentencing as required by the statutes on bail in criminal prosecutions, of the type and in the amount required by a written trial *de novo* bail schedule provided to the clerk by the circuit or superior court. Filing of the bond or undertaking stays the judgment of the city or town court, and during the period of the stay the defendant shall not be subject to incarceration or probation orders of the city or town court. The defendant, if incarcerated pursuant to the judgment of the city or town court, shall be released under a standing order made by the circuit and superior courts for such cases. If the defendant does not file the bond or bail undertaking, the judgment of the city or town court is not stayed and the defendant will remain incarcerated or subject to probation orders of the city or town court.

(E) Notice to Prosecutor of Trial de Novo. Promptly after the Request for Trial *de novo* is filed, the clerk of the circuit court shall send notice of the Request to the prosecuting attorney with an order from the trial *de novo* court that the prosecutor file a duplicate charging instrument with the clerk charging the offense or offenses as originally filed with the city or town court. Upon receiving the notice of the Request, the prosecutor shall within fifteen (15) days file the duplicate charging instrument with the clerk of the circuit court. Failure of the prosecutor to file within the fifteen (15) day period is not a grounds for dismissal of the charges.

(F) Notice to City or Town Court of de Novo Filing.

(1) Upon the filing of a Request for Trial *de Novo*, the clerk of the circuit court shall promptly send notice of the filing of the Request to the city or town court from which the trial *de novo* is taken. Within fifteen (15) days of its receipt of the notice of the Request the city or town court shall stay its judgment of sentence and conviction against the defendant and shall send notice of the stay of the judgment to any agency or entity to which it had sent notice of the prosecution or the judgment.

(2) If the defendant paid a fine and costs to the city or town court as part of the misdemeanor sentence it imposed, the city or town court shall send the fine only to the clerk of the circuit court. The clerk of the circuit court shall hold any fine or payment received from the city or town court pending the outcome of the trial *de novo* and shall apply the payment to any judgment for a fine or costs imposed by the circuit or superior court following the trial *de novo* or to any order for probation users' fees or recoupment of trial expenses otherwise authorized by law and ordered by the *de novo* court. If any amount of the original fine payment remains after application to judgments or orders imposed by the trial *de novo* court, the clerk shall refund the balance to the defendant.

(G) Procedure When Plea of Guilty Was Entered in City or Town Court. If the defendant entered a plea of guilty in the city or town court, the *de novo* court shall resolve any request for permission to withdraw the plea. If the plea is allowed to be withdrawn, procedure shall be as provided in Subsection H of this Rule. If the plea is not allowed to be withdrawn, the *de novo* court shall conduct a sentencing hearing *de novo* and enter its judgment of conviction and sentence. Upon entering its judgment of conviction and sentence, the *de novo* court shall send an order to the city or town court to vacate its judgment of conviction and sentence.

(H) Procedure When Plea of Not Guilty Was Entered in City or Town Court. If the defendant entered a plea of not guilty in the city or town court, the *de novo* court shall provide the defendant with a new trial. Following the trial, upon entering its judgment either of acquittal or of conviction and sentence, the *de novo* court shall send an order to the city or town court to vacate its judgment of conviction and sentence.

Adopted Nov. 25, 1997, effective Jan. 1, 1998. Amended Sept. 21, 2010, effective Jan. 1, 2011.

Rule 4. Documents and Information Excluded from Public Access and Confidential Pursuant to Administrative Rule 9(G)(1).

Documents and information excluded from public access pursuant to Administrative Rule 9(G)(1) shall be filed in accordance with Trial Rule 5(G).

Adopted Sept. 30, 2004, effective Jan. 1, 2005.

INDIANA CHILD SUPPORT RULES AND GUIDELINES

Adopted Effective October 1, 1989

Including Amendments Received Through November 1, 2013

CHILD SUPPORT RULES

Support Rule 1. Adoption of Child Support Rules and Guidelines

The Indiana Supreme Court hereby adopts the Indiana Child Support Guidelines, as drafted by the Judicial Administration Committee and adopted by the Board of the Judicial Conference of Indiana and all subsequent amendments thereto presented by the Domestic Relations Committee of the Judicial Conference of Indiana, as the Child Support Rules and Guidelines of this Court.

Adopted effective Oct. 1, 1989. Amended effective March 1, 1993; amended May 27, 1998, effective July 1, 1998; Sept. 10, 2003, effective Jan. 1, 2004; Sept. 15, 2009, effective Jan. 1, 2010; Dec. 18, 2009, effective Jan. 1, 2010.

Support Rule 2. Presumption

In any proceeding for the award of child support, there shall be a rebuttable presumption that the amount of the award which would result from the application of the Indiana Child Support Guidelines is the correct amount of child support to be awarded.

Adopted effective Oct. 1, 1989.

Support Rule 3. Deviation from Guideline Amount

If the court concludes from the evidence in a particular case that the amount of the award reached through application of the guidelines would be unjust, the court shall enter a written finding articulating the factual circumstances supporting that conclusion.

Adopted effective Oct. 1, 1989.

INDIANA CHILD SUPPORT GUIDELINES

GUIDELINE 1. PREFACE

Guidelines to determine levels of child support were developed by the Judicial Administration Committee of the Judicial Conference of Indiana and adopted by the Indiana Supreme Court. The guidelines are consistent with the provisions of Indiana Code Title 31 which place a duty for child support upon parents based upon their financial resources and needs, the standard of living the child would have enjoyed had the marriage not been dissolved or had the separation not been ordered, the physical or mental condition of the child, and the child's educational needs.

The Guidelines have three objectives:

(1) To establish as state policy an appropriate standard of support for children, subject to the ability of parents to financially contribute to that support;

(2) To make awards more equitable by ensuring more consistent treatment of people in similar circumstances; and,

(3) To improve the efficiency of the court process by promoting settlements and giving courts and the parties guidelines in settling the level of awards.

The Indiana Child Support Guidelines are based on the Income Shares Model, developed by the Child Support Project of the National Center for State Courts. The Income Shares Model is predicated on the concept that the child should receive the same proportion of parental income that he or she would have received if the parents lived together. Because household spending on behalf of children is intertwined with spending on behalf of adults for most expenditure categories, it is difficult to determine the proportion allocated to children in individual cases, even with exhaustive financial information. However, a number of authoritative economic studies provide estimates of the average amount of household expenditure on children in intact households. These studies have found the proportion of household spending devoted to children is related to the level of household income and to the number and ages of children. The Indiana Child Support Guidelines relate the level of child support to income and the number of children. In order to provide simplicity in the use of the Guidelines, however, child support figures reflect a blend of all age categories weighted toward school age children.

Based on this economic evidence, the Indiana Child Support Guidelines calculate child support as the share of each parent's income estimated to have been spent on the child if the parents and child were living in an intact household. The calculated amount establishes the level of child support for both the custodial and non-custodial parent. Absent grounds for a deviation, the custodial parent should be required to make monetary payments of child support, if application of the parenting time credit would so require.

Adopted effective Oct. 1, 1989. Amended effective March 1, 1993; amended May 27, 1998, effective July 1, 1998; Sept. 15, 2009, effective Jan. 1, 2010.

Commentary

History of Development. In June of 1985, the Judicial Reform Committee (now the Judicial Administration Committee) of the Judicial Conference of Indiana undertook the task of developing child support guidelines for use by Indiana judges. While the need had been long recognized in Indiana, the impetus for this project came from federal statutes requiring guidelines to be in place no later than October 1, 1987. P.L. 98–378. Paradoxically, guidelines did not need to be mandatory under the 1984 federal legislation to satisfy federal requirements; they were only required to be made available to judges and other officials with authority to establish child support awards. 45 CFR Ch. III, § 302.56.

The final draft was completed by the Judicial Reform Committee on July 24, 1987, and was presented to the Judicial Conference of Indiana Board of Directors on September 17, 1987. The Board accepted the report of the Reform Committee, approved the Guidelines and recommended their use to the judges of Indiana in all matters of child support.

Family Support Act of 1988. On October 13, 1988, the United States Congress passed the "Family Support Act of 1988," P.L. 100–485 amending the Social Security Act by deleting the original language which made application of the guideline discretionary and inserted in its place the following language:

"There shall be a rebuttable presumption, in any judicial or administrative proceeding for the award of child support, that the amount of the award which would result from the application of such guidelines is the correct amount of child support to be awarded. A written finding or specific finding on the record that the application of the guidelines would be unjust or inappropriate in a particular case, as determined under criteria established by the State, shall be sufficient to rebut the presumption in that case." P.L. 100–485, § 103(a)(2).

The original Guidelines that went into effect October 1, 1987 and their commentary were revised by the Judicial Administration Committee to reflect the requirement that child support guidelines be a rebuttable presumption. The requirement applies to all cases where support is set after October 1, 1989, including actions brought under Title IV–D of the Social Security Act (42 U.S.C.A. § 651–669). Also, after October 1, 1989, counties and individual courts may not opt to use alternate methods of establishing support. The Indiana Child Support Guidelines were required to be in use in all Indiana courts in all proceedings where child support is established or modified on and after October 1, 1989.

Periodic Review of Guidelines and Title IV–D Awards. The "Family Support Act of 1988" also requires that the Guidelines be reviewed at least every four years "to assure their application results in the determination of appropriate child support award amounts." P.L. 100–485, § 103(b). Further, each state must develop a procedure to ensure that all Title IV–D awards are periodically reviewed to ensure that they comply with the Guidelines. P.L. 100–485, § 103(c).

Compliance With State Law. The Child Support Guidelines were developed specifically to comply with federal requirements, as well as Indiana law.

Objectives of the Indiana Child Support Guidelines. The following three objectives are specifically articulated in the Indiana Child Support Guidelines:

1. *To establish as state policy an appropriate standard of support for children, subject to the ability of parents to financially contribute to that support.* When the Guidelines were first recommended for use by the Indiana Judicial Conference on September 17, 1987, many courts in the state had no guideline to establish support. Many judges had expressed the need for guidelines, but few had the resources to develop them for use in a single court system. The time, research and economic understanding necessary to develop meaningful guidelines were simply beyond the resources of most individual courts.

2. *To make awards more equitable by ensuring more consistent treatment of people in similar circumstances.* This consistency can be expected not only in the judgments of a particular court, but between jurisdictions as well. What is fair for a child in one court is fair to a similarly situated child in another court.

3. *To improve the efficiency of the court process by promoting settlements and giving courts and the parties guidelines in settling the level of awards.* In other words, when the outcome is predictable,

there is no need to fight. Because the human experience provides an infinite number of variables, no guideline can cover every conceivable situation, so litigation is not completely forestalled in matters of support. If the guidelines are consistently applied, however, those instances should be minimized.

Economic Data Used in Developing Guidelines. What does it take to support a child? The question is simple, but the answer is extremely complex. Yet, the question must be answered if an adequate amount of child support is to be ordered by the court. Determining the cost attributable to children is complicated by intertwined general household expenditures. Rent, transportation, and grocery costs, to mention a few, are impossible to accurately apportion between family members. In developing these Guidelines, a great deal of reliance was placed on the research of Thomas J. Espenshade, (Investing In Children, Urban Institute Press, 1984) generally considered the most authoritative study of household expenditure patterns. Espenshade used data from 8,547 households and from that data estimated average expenditures for children present in the home. Espenshade's estimates demonstrate that amounts spent on the children of intact households rise as family income increases. They further demonstrate at constant levels of income that expenditures decrease for each child as family size increases. These principles are reflected in the Guideline Schedules for Weekly Support Payments, which are included in the Indiana Child Support Guidelines. By demonstrating how expenditures for each child decrease as family size increases, Espenshade should have put to rest the previous practice of ordering equal amounts of support per child when two or more children are involved. Subsequent guidelines reviews have considered more current economic studies of child-rearing expenditures (e.g., Mark Lino, Expenditures on Children by Families: 2006 Annual Report, United States Department of Agriculture, 2007; David Betson, State of Oregon Child Support Guidelines Review: Updated Obligation Scales and Other Considerations, report to State of Oregon Department of Justice, 2006). These periodic guidelines reviews have concluded that the Indiana Guidelines based on the Espenshade estimates are generally within the range of more current estimates of child-rearing expenditures. A notable exception at high incomes leveled off the child support schedule for combined weekly adjusted incomes above $4,000. In 2009 this exception was removed. The increase is now incorporated into the schedule up to combined weekly adjusted incomes of $10,000 and a formula is provided for incomes above that amount. Previously, a formula was provided for combined weekly adjusted incomes above $4,000.

Income Shares Model. After review of five approaches to the establishment of child support, the Income Shares Model was selected for the Indiana Guidelines. This model was perceived as the fairest approach for children because it is based on the premise that children should receive the same proportion of parental income after a dissolution that they would have received if the family had remained intact. Because it then apportions the cost of children between the parents based on their means, it is also perceived as being fair to parents. In applying the Guidelines, the following steps are taken:

1. The gross income of both parents is added together after certain adjustments are made. A percentage share of income for each parent is then determined.

2. The total is taken to the support tables, referred to in the Indiana Guidelines as the Guideline Schedules for Weekly Support Payments, to determine the total cost of supporting a child or children.

3. Work–related child care expenses and the weekly costs of health insurance premiums for the child(ren) are then added to the basic child support obligation.

4. The child support obligation is then prorated between the parents, based on their proportionate share of the weekly adjusted income, hence the name "income shares."

The Income Shares Model was developed by The Institute for Court Management of the National Center for State Courts under the Child Support Guidelines Project. This approach was designed to be consistent with the Uniform Marriage and Divorce Act, the principles of which are consistent with IC 31–16–6–1. Both require the court to consider the financial resources of both parents and the standard of living the child would have enjoyed in an intact family.

Gross Versus Net Income. One of the policy decisions made by the Judicial Administration Committee in the early stages of developing the Guidelines was to use a gross income approach as opposed to a net income approach. Under a net income approach, extensive discovery is often required to determine the validity of deductions claimed in arriving at net income. It is believed that the use of gross income reduces discovery. (See Commentary to Guideline 3A). While the use of gross income has proven controversial, this approach is used by the majority of jurisdictions and, after a thorough review, is considered the best reasoned.

The basic support obligation would be the same whether gross income is reduced by adjustments built into the Guidelines or whether taxes are taken out and a net income option is used. A support guideline schedule consists of a column of income figures and a column of support amounts. In a gross income methodology, the tax factor is reflected in the support amount column, while in a net income guideline, the tax factor is applied to the income column. In devising the Indiana Guidelines, an average tax factor of 21.88 percent was used to adjust the support column.

Of course, taxes vary for different individuals. This is the case whether a gross or net income approach is used. Under the Indiana Guideline, where taxes vary significantly from the assumed rate of 21.88 percent, a trial court may choose to deviate from the guideline amount where the variance is substantiated by evidence at the support hearing.

Flexibility Versus the Rebuttable Presumption. Although application of the Guideline yields a figure that becomes a rebuttable presumption, there is room for flexibility. Guidelines are not immutable, black letter law. A strict and totally inflexible application of the Guidelines to all cases can easily lead to harsh and unreasonable results. If a judge believes that in a particular case application of the Guideline amount would be unreasonable, unjust, or inappropriate, a finding must be made that sets forth the reason for deviating from the Guideline amount. The finding need not be as formal as Findings of Fact and Conclusions of Law; the finding need only articulate the judge's reasoning. For example, if under the facts and circumstances of the case, the noncustodial parent would bear an inordinate financial burden, the following finding would justify a deviation:

"Because the noncustodial parent suffers from a chronic medical condition requiring uninsured medical expenses of $357.00 per month, the Court believes that setting child support in the Guideline amount would be unjust and instead sets support in the amount of $ ___ per week."

Agreed Orders submitted to the court must also comply with the "rebuttable presumption" requirement; that is, the order must recite why the order deviates from the Guideline amount.

1. *Phasing in Support Orders.* Some courts may find it desirable in modification proceedings to gradually implement the Guideline order over a period of time, especially where support computed under the Guideline is considerably higher than the amount previously paid. Enough flexibility exists in the Guidelines to permit that approach, as long as the judge's rationale is explained with an entry such as:

"The Guideline's support represents an increase of 40%, and the court finds that such an abrupt change in support obligation would render the obligor incapable of meeting his/her other established obligations. Therefore, the Court sets support in the amount of $ ___ and, on October 1, 20 ___, it shall increase to $ ___ and, on September 1, 20 ___, obligor shall begin paying the Guideline amount of $ ___."

2. *Situations Calling for Deviation.* An infinite number of situations may prompt a judge to deviate from the Guideline amount. For illustration only, and not as a complete list, the following examples are offered:

· One or both parties pay union dues as a condition of employment.

· A party provides support for an elderly parent.

· The noncustodial parent purchases school clothes.

· The noncustodial parent has extraordinary medical expenses for himself or herself.

· Both parents are members of the armed forces and the military provides housing.

· The obligor is still making periodic payments to a former spouse pursuant to a prior Dissolution Decree.

· One of the parties is required to travel an unusually long distance in the course of employment on a regular or daily basis and incurs an unusually large expense for such travel, and

· The custodial or noncustodial parent incurs significant travel expense in exercising parenting time.

Again, no attempt has been made to define every possible situation that could conceivably arise when determining child support and to prescribe a specific method of handling each of them. Practitioners must keep this in mind when advising clients and when arguing to the court. Many creative suggestions will undoubtedly result. Judges must also avoid the pitfall of blind adherence to the computation for support without giving careful consideration to the variables that require changing the result in order to do justice.

Amended effective March 1, 1993; amended May 27, 1998, effective July 1, 1998; Sept. 10, 2003, effective Jan. 1, 2004; Sept. 15, 2009, effective Jan. 1, 2010; Dec. 18, 2009, effective Jan. 1, 2010.

GUIDELINE 2.   USE OF THE GUIDELINES

The Guideline Schedules provide calculated amounts of child support. For obligors with a combined weekly adjusted income, as defined by these Guidelines, of less than $100.00, the Guidelines provide for case-by-case determination of child support. When a parent has extremely low income the amount of child support recommended by use of the Guidelines should be carefully scrutinized. The court should consider the obligor's income and living expenses to determine the maximum amount of child support that can reasonably be ordered without denying the obligor the means for self-support at a minimum subsistence level. The court may consider $12.00 as a minimum child support order; however, there are situations where a $0.00 support order is appropriate. A numeric amount of child support shall be ordered.

Temporary maintenance may be awarded by the court not to exceed thirty-five percent (35%) of the obligor's weekly adjusted income. In no case shall child support and temporary maintenance exceed fifty percent (50%) of the obligor's weekly adjusted income. Temporary maintenance and/or child support may be ordered by the court either in dollar payments or "in-kind" payments of obligations.

These guidelines are to be used in paternity cases and all other child support actions.

Adopted effective Oct. 1, 1989. Amended effective March 1, 1993; amended May 27, 1998, effective July 1, 1998; Sept. 15, 2009, effective Jan. 1, 2010.

Commentary

Minimum Support. The Guideline's schedules for weekly support payments do not provide an amount of support for couples with combined weekly adjusted income of less than $100.00. Consequently, the Guidelines do not establish a minimum support obligation. Instead the facts of each individual case must be examined and support set in such a manner that the obligor is not denied a means of self-support at a subsistence level. For example, (1) a parent who has a high parenting time credit; (2) a parent who suffers from debilitating mental illness; (3) a parent caring for a disabled child; (4) an incarcerated parent; (5) a parent or a family member with a debilitating physical health issue; or, (6) a natural disaster are significant but not exclusive factors for the court to consider in setting a child support order. The court should not automatically attribute minimum wage to parents who, for a variety of factors, are not capable of earning minimum wage.

Where parents live together with the child and share expenses, a child support worksheet shall be completed and a $0.00 order may be entered as a deviation.

Economic data indicate one hundred dollars ($100.00), which is half of the 2008 federal poverty level for one person, is not sufficient for a person to live at a subsistence level today. The prior obligation amounts at combined incomes of $100.00 per week are $25.00 per week for one child and $50.00 per week for two children. These amounts absorb 25 and 50 percent, respectively, of the parents' gross income. Most states set their minimum child support order at $50.00 per month, which is about $12.00 per week. Therefore, the revised low-income adjustment sets the obligation amount for combined weekly incomes of $100.00 at $12.00 for one child.

Temporary Maintenance. It is recommended that temporary maintenance not exceed thirty-five percent (35%) of the obligor's weekly adjusted income. The maximum award should be reserved for those instances where the custodial spouse has no income or no means of support, taking into consideration that spouse's present living arrangement (i.e., whether or not he or she lives with someone who shares or bears the majority of the living expense, lives in the marital residence with little or no expense, lives in military housing, etc.).

It is further recommended that the total of temporary maintenance and child support should not exceed fifty percent (50%) of the obligor's weekly adjusted income. In computing temporary maintenance, in-kind payments, such as the payment of utilities, house payments, rent, etc., should also be included in calculating the percentage limitations. Care must also be taken to ensure that the obligor is not deprived of the ability to support himself or herself.

Spousal Maintenance. It should also be emphasized that the recommendations concerning maintenance apply only to temporary maintenance, not maintenance in the Final Decree. An award of spousal maintenance in the Final Decree must, of course, be made in accordance with Indiana statute. These Guidelines do not alter those requirements. Theoretically, when setting temporary maintenance, child support should come first. That is, if child support is set at forty percent (40%) of the obligor's weekly adjusted income, only a maximum of ten percent (10%) of the obligor's income would be available for maintenance. That distinction, however, makes little practical difference. As with temporary maintenance, care should be taken to leave the obligor with adequate income for subsistence. In many instances the court will have to review the impact of taxes on the obligor's income before entering an order for spousal maintenance in addition to child support to avoid injustice to the obligor.

The worksheet provides a deduction for spousal maintenance paid as a result of a former marriage (Line 1D). Caution should be taken to assure that any credit taken is for maintenance and not for periodic payments as the result of a property settlement. No such deduction is given for amounts paid by an obligor as the result of a property settlement resulting from a former marriage, although that is a factor the court may wish to consider in determining the obligor's ability to pay the scheduled amount of support at the present time. Again, flexibility was intended throughout the Guidelines and they were not intended to place the obligor in a position where he or she loses all incentive to comply with the orders of the court.

Guidelines to be Applied in all Matters of Child Support. Federal law now requires that the Indiana Child Support Guidelines be applied in every instance in which child support is established including, but not limited to, dissolutions of marriage, legal separations, paternity actions, juvenile proceedings, petitions to establish support and Title IV–D proceedings.

The Indiana legislature requires the Indiana Child Support Guidelines be applied and the Child Support Worksheet be used in determining the manner in which financial services to children that are CHINS (Child in Need of Services) or delinquent are to be repaid. Similarly, the legislature requires the court to use the Guidelines to determine the financial contribution required from each parent of a child or the guardian of the child's estate for costs associated with the institutional placement of a child.

Amended Sept. 15, 2009, effective Jan. 1, 2010; Dec. 18, 2009, effective Jan. 1, 2010.

GUIDELINE 3. DETERMINATION OF CHILD SUPPORT AMOUNT

A. Definition of Weekly Gross Income.

1. *Definition of Weekly Gross Income (Line 1 of Worksheet).* For purposes of these Guidelines, "weekly gross income" is defined as actual Weekly Gross Income of the parent if employed to full capacity, potential income if unemployed or underemployed, and imputed income based upon "in-kind" benefits. Weekly Gross Income of each parent includes income from any source, except as excluded below, and includes, but is not limited to, income from salaries, wages, commissions, bonuses, overtime, partnership distributions, dividends, severance pay, pensions, interest, trust income, annuities, capital gains, social security benefits, workmen's compensation benefits, unemployment insurance benefits, disability insurance benefits, gifts, inheritance, prizes, and alimony or maintenance received from other marriages. Social Security disability benefits paid for the benefit of the child must be included in the disabled parent's gross income. The disabled parent is entitled to a

credit for the amount of Social Security disability benefits paid for the benefit of the child. Specifically excluded are benefits from means-tested public assistance programs, including, but not limited to, Temporary Aid To Needy Families (TANF), Supplemental Security Income, and Food Stamps. Also excluded are survivor benefits received by or for other children residing in either parent's home.

2. *Self–Employment, Business Expenses, In-Kind Payments and Related Issues.* Weekly Gross Income from self-employment, operation of a business, rent, and royalties is defined as gross receipts minus ordinary and necessary expenses. In general, these types of income and expenses from self-employment or operation of a business should be carefully reviewed to restrict the deductions to reasonable out-of-pocket expenditures necessary to produce income. These expenditures may include a reasonable yearly deduction for necessary capital expenditures. Weekly Gross Income from self-employment may differ from a determination of business income for tax purposes.

Expense reimbursements or in-kind payments received by a parent in the course of employment, self-employment, or operation of a business should be counted as income if they are significant and reduce personal living expenses. Such payments might include a company car, free housing, or reimbursed meals.

The self-employed shall be permitted to deduct that portion of their FICA tax payment that exceeds the FICA tax that would be paid by an employee earning the same Weekly Gross Income.

3. *Unemployed, Underemployed and Potential Income.* If a court finds a parent is voluntarily unemployed or underemployed without just cause, child support shall be calculated based on a determination of potential income. A determination of potential income shall be made by determining employment potential and probable earnings level based on the obligor's work history, occupational qualifications, prevailing job opportunities, and earnings levels in the community. If there is no work history and no higher education or vocational training, the facts of the case may indicate that Weekly Gross Income be set at least at the federal minimum wage level.

Commentary to Guideline 3A
Weekly Gross Income.

1. *Child Support Calculations Generally.* Weekly Gross Income, potential income, weekly adjusted income and basic child support obligation have very specific and well-defined meanings within the Indiana Child Support Guidelines. Their definitions are not repeated in the Commentary, but further explanation follows.

2. *Determination of Weekly Gross Income.* Weekly Gross Income is the starting point in determining the child support obligation, and it must be

calculated for both parents. If one or both parents have no income, then potential income may be calculated and used as Weekly Gross Income. Likewise, imputed income may be substituted for, or added to, other income in arriving at Weekly Gross Income. It includes such items as free housing, a company car that may be used for personal travel, and reimbursed meals or other items received by the obligor that reduce his or her living expenses.

The Child Support Obligation Worksheet does not include space to calculate Weekly Gross Income. It must be calculated separately and the result entered on the worksheet.

In calculating Weekly Gross Income, it is helpful to begin with total income from all sources. This figure may not be the same as gross income for tax purposes. Internal Revenue Code of 1986, § 61. Means-tested public assistance programs (those based on income) are excluded from the computation of Weekly Gross Income, but other government payments, such as Social Security benefits and veterans pensions, should be included. However, survivor benefits paid to or for the benefit of their children are not included. In cases where a custodial parent is receiving, as a representative payee for a prior born child, Social Security survivor benefits because of the death of the prior born child's parent, the court should carefully consider Line 1 C of the basic child support obligation worksheet, Legal Duty of Support for Prior-born Children. Because the deceased parent's contribution for the support of the prior born child is being partially paid by Social Security survivor benefits that are excluded from Weekly Gross Income, the court should not enter, on Line 1C, an amount that represents 100% of the cost of support for the prior born child. The income of the spouses of the parties is not included in Weekly Gross Income.

a. Self–Employment, Rent and Royalty Income. Calculating Weekly Gross Income for the self-employed or for those who receive rent and royalty income presents unique problems, and calls for careful review of expenses. The principle involved is that actual expenses are deducted, and benefits that reduce living expenses (i.e. company cars, free lodging, reimbursed meals, etc.) should be included in whole or in part. It is intended that actual out-of-pocket expenditures for the self-employed, to the extent that they are reasonable and necessary for the production of income, be deducted. Reasonable deductions for capital expenditures may be included. While income tax returns may be helpful in arriving at Weekly Gross Income for a self-employed person, the deductions allowed by the Guidelines may differ significantly from those allowed for tax purposes.

The self-employed pay FICA tax at twice the rate that is paid by employees. At present rates, the self-employed pay fifteen and thirty one-hundredths percent (15.30%) of their gross income to a designated maximum, while employees pay seven and sixty-five one-hundredths percent (7.65%) to the same maximum. The self-employed are therefore permitted to deduct one-half of their FICA payment when calculating Weekly Gross Income.

b. Overtime, Commissions, Bonuses and Other Forms of Irregular Income. There are numerous forms of income that are irregular or nonguaranteed, which cause difficulty in accurately determining the gross income of a party. Overtime, commissions, bonuses, periodic partnership distributions, voluntary extra work and extra hours worked by a professional are all illustrations, but far from an all-inclusive list, of such items. Each is includable in the total income approach taken by the Guidelines, but each is also very fact-sensitive.

Each of the above items is sensitive to downturns in the economy. The fact that overtime, for example, has been consistent for three (3) years does not guarantee that it will continue in a poor economy. Further, it is not the intent of the Guidelines to require a party who has worked sixty (60) hour weeks to continue doing so indefinitely just to meet a support obligation that is based on that higher level of earnings. Care should be taken to set support based on dependable income, while at the same time providing children with the support to which they are entitled.

When the court determines that it is not appropriate to include irregular income in the determination of the child support obligation, the court should express its reasons. When the court determines that it is appropriate to include irregular income, an equitable method of treating such income may be to require the obligor to pay a fixed percentage of overtime, bonuses, etc., in child support on a periodic but predetermined basis (weekly, bi-weekly, monthly, quarterly) rather than by the process of determining the average of the irregular income by past history and including it in the obligor's gross income calculation.

One method of treating irregular income is to determine the ratio of the basic child support obligation (line 4 of the worksheet) to the combined weekly adjusted income (line 3 of the worksheet) and apply this ratio to the irregular income during a fixed period. For example, if the basic obligation was $110.00 and the combined income was $650.00, the ratio would be .169 ($110.00 / $650.00). The order of the court would then require the obligor to make a lump sum payment of .169 of the obligor's irregular income received during the fixed period.

The use of this ratio will not result in an exact calculation of support paid on a weekly basis. It will result in an overstatement of the additional support due, and particularly so when average irregular income exceeds $250.00 per week or exceeds 75% of the regular adjusted Weekly Gross Income. In these latter cases the obligor may seek to have the irregular income calculation redetermined by the court.

Another form of irregular income may exist when an obligor takes a part-time job for the purpose of meeting financial obligations arising from a subsequent marriage, or other circumstances. Modification of the support order to include this income or any portion of it may require that the obligor continue with that employment just to meet an increased support obligation, resulting in a disincentive to work.

Judges and practitioners should be innovative in finding ways to include income that would have benefited the family had it remained intact, but be receptive to deviations where reasons justify them. The foregoing discussion should not be interpreted to exclude consideration of irregular income of the custodial parent.

c. Potential Income. Potential income may be determined if a parent has no income, or only means-tested income, and is capable of earning income or capable of earning more. Obviously, a great deal of discretion will have to be used in this determination. One purpose of potential income is to discourage a parent from taking a lower paying job to avoid the payment of significant support. Another purpose is to fairly allocate the support obligation when one parent remarries and, because of the income of the new spouse, chooses not to be employed. However, attributing potential income that results in an unrealistic child support obligation may cause the accumulation of an excessive arrearage, and be contrary to the best interests of the child(ren). Research shows that on average more noncustodial parental involvement is associated with greater child educational attainment and lower juvenile delinquency. Ordering support for low-income parents at levels they can reasonably pay may improve noncustodial parent-child contact; and in turn, the outcomes for their children. The six examples which follow illustrate some of the considerations affecting attributing potential income to an unemployed or underemployed parent.

(1) When a custodial parent with young children at home has no significant skills or education and is unemployed, he or she may not be capable of entering the work force and earning enough to even cover the cost of child care. Hence, it may be inappropriate to attribute any potential income to that parent. It is not the intention of the Guidelines to force all custodial parents into the work force. Therefore, discretion must be exercised on an individual case basis to determine if it is fair under the circumstances to attribute potential income to a particular nonworking or underemployed custodial parent. The need for a custodial parent to contribute to the financial support of a child must be carefully balanced against the need for the parent's full-time presence in the home.

(2) When a parent has some history of working and is capable of entering the work force, but without just cause voluntarily fails or refuses to work or to be employed in a capacity in keeping with his or her capabilities, such a parent's potential income shall be included in the gross income of that parent. The amount to be attributed as potential income in such a case may be the amount that the evidence demonstrates he or she was capable of earning in the past. If for example the custodial parent had been a nurse or a licensed engineer, it may be unreasonable to determine his or her potential at the minimum wage level. Discretion must be exercised on an individual case basis to determine whether under the circumstances there is just cause to attribute potential income to a particular unemployed or underemployed parent.

(3) Even though an unemployed parent has never worked before, potential income should be considered for that parent if he or she voluntarily remains unemployed without justification. Absent any other evidence of potential earnings of such a parent, the federal minimum wage should be used in calculating potential income for that parent. However, the court should not add child care expense that is not actually incurred.

(4) When a parent is unemployed by reason of involuntary layoff or job termination, it still may be appropriate to include an amount in gross income representing that parent's potential income. If the involuntary layoff can be reasonably expected to be brief, potential income should be used at or near that parent's historical earning level. If the involuntary layoff will be extensive in duration, potential income may be determined based upon such factors as the parent's unemployment compensation, job capabilities, education and whether other employment is available. Potential income equivalent to the federal minimum wage may be attributed to that parent.

(5) When a parent is unable to obtain employment because that parent suffers from debilitating mental illness, a debilitating health issue, or is caring for a disabled child, it may be inappropriate to attribute any potential income to that parent. Another example may be when the cost of child care makes employment economically unreasonable.

(6) When a parent is incarcerated and has no assets or other source of income, potential income should not be attributed.

d. Imputing Income. Whether or not income should be imputed to a parent whose living expenses have been substantially reduced due to financial resources other than the parent's own earning capabilities is also a fact-sensitive situation requiring careful consideration of the evidence in each case. It may be inappropriate to include as gross income occasional gifts received. However, regular and continuing payments made by a family member, subsequent spouse, roommate or live-in friend that reduce the parent's costs for rent, utilities, or groceries, may be the basis for imputing income. The marriage of a parent to a spouse with sufficient affluence to obviate the necessity for the parent to work may give rise to a situation where either potential income or imputed income or both should be considered in arriving at gross income.

e. Return from Individual Retirement Accounts and other retirement plans. The annual return of an IRA, 401(K) or other retirement plan that is automatically reinvested does not constitute income. Where previous withdrawals from the IRA or 401(K) have been made to fund the parent's lifestyle choices or living expenses, these withdrawals may be considered "actual income" when calculating the parent's child support obligation. The withdrawals must have been received by the parent and immediately available for his or her use. The court should consider whether the early withdrawal was used to reduce the parent's current living expenses, whether it was utilized to satisfy on-going financial obligations, and whether the sums are immediately available to the parent. This is a fact-sensitive situation. Retirement funds which were in existence at the time of a dissolution and which were the subject of the property division would not be considered "income" when calculating child support.

B. Income Verification.

1. *Submitting Worksheet to Court.* In all cases, a copy of the worksheet which accompanies these Guidelines shall be completed and filed with the court when the court is asked to order support. This includes cases in which agreed orders are submitted. Worksheets shall be signed by both parties, not their counsel, under penalties for perjury.

2. *Documenting Income.* Income statements of the parents shall be verified with documentation of both current and past income. Suitable documentation of current earnings includes paystubs, employer statements, or receipts and expenses if self-employed. Documentation of income may be supplemented with copies of tax returns.

Commentary to Guideline 3B
Worksheet Documentation.

1. *Worksheet Requirement.* Submission of the worksheet became a requirement in 1989 when use of the Guidelines became mandatory. The Family Support Act of 1988 requires that a written finding be made when establishing support. In Indiana, this is accomplished by submission of a child support worksheet. The worksheet memorializes the basis upon which the support order is established. Failure to submit a completed child support worksheet may, in the court's discretion, result in the court refusing to approve a child support order or result in a continuance of a hearing regarding child support until a completed worksheet is provided. At subsequent modification hearings the court will then have the ability to accurately determine the income claimed by each party at the time of the prior hearing.

If the parties disagree on their respective gross incomes, the court should include in its order the gross income it determines for each party. When the court deviates from the Guideline amount, the order or decree should also include the reason or reasons for deviation. This information becomes the starting point to determine whether or not a substantial and continuing change of circumstance occurs in the future.

2. *Verification of Income.* The requirement of income verification is not a change in the law but merely a suggestion to judges that they take care in determining the income of each party. One pay stub standing alone can be very misleading, as can other forms of documentation. This is particularly true for salesmen, professionals and others who receive commissions or bonuses, or others who have the ability to defer payments, thereby distorting the true picture of their income in the short term. When in doubt, it is suggested that income tax returns for the last two or three years be reviewed.

C. Computation of Weekly Adjusted Income (Line 1E of Worksheet). After Weekly Gross Income is determined, certain reductions are allowed in computing weekly adjusted income which is the

amount on which child support is based. These reductions are specified below.

1. *Adjustment for Subsequent born or Adopted Child(ren) (Line 1A of Worksheet).* In determining a support order, there should be an adjustment to Weekly Gross Income of parents who have a legal duty or court order to support children who were naturally born or legally adopted subsequent to the existing support order and that parent is actually meeting or paying that obligation.

2. *Court Orders for Prior-born Child(ren) (Line 1B of Worksheet).* The amount(s) of any court order(s) for child support for prior-born children should be deducted from Weekly Gross Income. This should include court ordered post-secondary education expenses calculated on an annual basis divided by 52 weeks.

3. *Legal Duty of Support for Prior-born Child(ren) (Line 1C of Worksheet).* Where a party has a legal support duty for children born prior to the child(ren) for whom support is being established, not by court order, an amount reasonably necessary for such support shall be deducted from Weekly Gross Income to arrive at weekly adjusted income. This deduction is not allowed for step-children. (See line 1C of worksheet)

4. *Alimony or Maintenance From Prior Marriage (Line 1D of Worksheet).* The amount(s) of alimony ordered in decrees from foreign jurisdictions or maintenance arising from a prior marriage should be deducted from Weekly Gross Income.

Commentary to Guideline 3C

Determining Weekly Adjusted Income. After Weekly Gross Income is determined, the next step is to compute weekly adjusted income (Line 1E of the Worksheet). Certain deductions, discussed below, are allowed from Weekly Gross Income in arriving at weekly adjusted income.

1. *Adjustment of Weekly Gross Income for Subsequent Child(ren).* In determining support orders, an adjustment should be made in arriving at Weekly Gross Income of the parents in instances where either or both have natural or legally adopted child(ren) who were born or adopted subsequent to the prior support order. The adjustment should be computed as follows:

STEP 1: Determine the number of natural or legally adopted children born or adopted by the parents subsequent to entry of the present support order, and for whom the parent has a legal duty or court order to support. The parent seeking the adjustment has the burden to prove the support is actually paid if the subsequent child does not live in the respective parent's household.

STEP 2: Calculate the subsequent child credit by multiplying the parent's Weekly Gross Income by the appropriate factor listed in the table below and enter the product on Line 1A on the Worksheet.

Appropriate factors are:

1	Subsequent child	.065
2	Subsequent children	.097
3	Subsequent children	.122
4	Subsequent children	.137
5	Subsequent children	.146
6	Subsequent children	.155
7	Subsequent children	.164
8	Subsequent children	.173

EXAMPLE: A noncustodial parent has a Weekly Gross Income, before adjustment of $500.00. The custodial parent has a Weekly Gross Income, before adjustment, of $300.00. In considering a modification request, an adjustment should be made to the parents' respective Weekly Gross Incomes for the two (2) natural children born to the noncustodial parent since entry of the present support order and the one (1) adopted child of the custodial parent, adopted since entry of the present order. The respective subsequent child credit to be entered on Line 1A of the Worksheet would be as follows:

Noncustodial . . . . . . $500.00 × .097 = $48.50
credit
Custodial . . . . $300.00 × .065 = $19.50
credit

2. *Modification of Support in Prior Marriage.* When considering a petition to modify support arriving out of a prior marriage, no deduction is allowed for support ordered as the result of a second or subsequent marriage. Establishment of a support order in a second marriage should not constitute a change in circumstance in the first marriage which would lead to modification of the support order from the prior marriage. Each child is being supported from the money from which they could have expected to be supported had the dissolution not occurred.

Likewise, if support is being established or modified for a child born out of wedlock, the date of birth of the child would determine whether or not a deduction for the support of other children is allowed in arriving at weekly adjusted income. If a child is born out of wedlock before the children of the marriage, no deduction for the children of the marriage is allowed. A deduction for children of the marriage is allowed in establishing support for a child born out of wedlock after the children of the marriage.

3. *Legal Duty to Support for Prior Born Children.* A deduction is allowed for support actually paid, or funds actually expended, for children born prior to the children for whom support is being established. This is true even though that obligation has not been reduced to a court order. The obligor bears the burden of proving the obligation and payment of the obligation.

A custodial parent should be permitted to deduct his or her portion of the support obligation for prior-born children living in his or her home. It is recommended that these guidelines be used to compute support.

EXAMPLE: In establishing support for children of a subsequent marriage, the custodial spouse should be permitted to deduct the support he or she would pay in the prior marriage (pursuant to Line 6

of Worksheet) if custody had been placed with the former spouse.

This necessitates the computation in the second dissolution of the support that would be paid by each spouse in the former marriage. This amount is inserted on Line 1C of the Worksheet.

4. *Alimony or Maintenance From Prior Marriage.* The final allowable deduction from Weekly Gross Income in arriving at weekly adjusted income is for alimony ordered in decrees from foreign jurisdictions or spousal maintenance arising from a prior marriage. These amounts are allowable only if they arise as the result of a court order. This deduction is intended only for spousal maintenance, not for periodic payments from a property settlement although the court may consider periodic payments when determining whether or not to deviate from the guideline amount when ordering support. Refer to the discussion of temporary maintenance earlier in this commentary. (Line 1D of Worksheet).

D. Basic Child Support Obligation (Worksheet Line 4). The Basic Child Support Obligation should be determined using the attached Guideline Schedules for Weekly Support Payments. For combined weekly adjusted income amounts falling between amounts shown in the schedule, basic child support amounts should be rounded to the nearest amount. The number of children refers to children for whom the parents share joint legal responsibility and for whom support is being sought, excluding children for whom a Post-Secondary Education Worksheet is used to determine support. Work-related child care expense for these children is to be deducted from total weekly adjusted income in determining the combined weekly adjusted income that is used in selecting the appropriate basic child support obligation.

Commentary to Guideline 3D
Use of Guideline Schedules.
Combined Weekly Adjusted Income . After reducing Weekly Gross Income by the deductions allowed above, weekly adjusted income is computed. The next step is to add the weekly adjusted income of both parties and take the combined weekly adjusted income to the Guideline schedules for weekly support payments. In selecting the appropriate column for the determination of the basic child support obligation, it should be remembered that the number of children refers only to the number of children of this marriage for whom support is being computed, excluding children for whom a Post-Secondary Education Worksheet is used to determine support.

E. Additions to the Basic Child Support Obligation.

1. *Work–Related Child Care Expense (Worksheet Line 4A).* Child care costs incurred due to employment or job search of both parent(s) should be added to the basic obligation. It includes the separate cost of a sitter, day care, or like care of a child or children while the parent works or actively seeks employment. Such child care costs must be

reasonable and should not exceed the level required to provide quality care for the children. Continuity of child care should be considered. Child care costs required for active job searches are allowable on the same basis as costs required in connection with employment.

The parent who contracts for the child care shall be responsible for the payment to the provider of the child care. For the purpose of designating this expense on the Child Support Obligation Worksheet (Line 4A), each parent's expense shall be calculated on an annual basis divided by 52 weeks. The combined amount shall be added to the Basic Child Support Obligation and each parent shall receive a credit equal to the expense incurred by that parent as an Adjustment (Line 7 of the Worksheet).

When potential income is attributed to a party, the court should not also attribute work-related child care expense which is not actually incurred.

2. *Cost of Health Insurance For Child(ren) (Worksheet Line 4B)*. The weekly cost of health insurance premiums for the child(ren) should be added to the basic obligation whenever either parent actually incurs the premium expense or a portion of such expense. (Please refer to Guideline 7 for additional information regarding the treatment of Health Care Expenses)

3. *Extraordinary Health Care Expense*. Please refer to Support Guideline 7 for treatment of this issue.

4. *Extraordinary Educational Expense*. Please refer to Support Guideline 8 for treatment of this issue.

Commentary to Guideline 3E

Additions to the Basic Child Support Obligation.

1. *Work–Related Child Care Expense (Worksheet Line 4A)*. One of the additions to the basic child support obligation is a reasonable child care expense incurred due to employment, or an attempt to find employment. This amount is added to the basic child support obligation in arriving at the total child support obligation.

Work-related child care expense is an income-producing expense of the parent. Presumably, if the family remained intact, the parents would treat child care as a necessary cost of the family attributable to the children when both parents work. Therefore, the expense is one that is incurred for the benefit of the child(ren) which the parents should share.

In circumstances where a parent claims the work-related child care credit for tax purposes, it would be appropriate to reduce the amount claimed as work-related child care expense by the amount of tax saving to the parent. The exact amount of the credit may not be known at the time support is set, but counsel should be able to make a rough calculation as to its effect.

When potential income is attributed to a party, the court should not also attribute a work-related child care expense which is not actually incurred because this expense is highly speculative and difficult to adequately verify.

2. *Cost of Health Insurance For Child(ren) (Worksheet Line 4B)*. The weekly costs of health insurance premiums only for the child(ren) should be added to the basic obligation so as to apportion that cost between the parents. The parent who actually pays that cost then receives a credit towards his or her child support obligation on Line 7 of the Worksheet. (See Support Guideline 3G. Adjustments to Parent's Child Support Obligation). Only that portion of the cost actually paid by a parent is added to the basic obligation. If health insurance coverage is provided through an employer, only the child(ren)'s portion should be added and only if the parent actually incurs a cost for it.

3. *Total Child Support Obligation (Worksheet Line 5)*. Adding work-related child care costs, and the weekly cost of health insurance premiums for the child(ren) to the basic child support obligation results in a figure called Total Child Support Obligation. This is the basic obligation of both parents for the support of the child(ren) of the marriage, or approximately what it would cost to support the child(ren) in an intact household, excluding extraordinary health care and/or extraordinary education expenses.

F. Computation of Parent's Child Support Obligation (Worksheet Line 6).

Each parent's child support obligation is determined by multiplying his or her percentage share of total weekly adjusted income (Worksheet Line 2) times the Total Child Support Obligation (Worksheet Line 5).

1. *Division of Obligation Between Parents (Worksheet Line 6)*. The total child support obligation is divided between the parents in proportion to their weekly adjusted income. A monetary obligation is computed for each parent. The custodial parent's share is presumed to be spent directly on the child. When there is near equal parenting time, and the custodial parent has significantly higher income than the noncustodial parent, application of the parenting time credit should result in an order for the child support to be paid from a custodial parent to a noncustodal parent, absent grounds for a deviation.

2. *Deviation From Guideline Amount*. If, after consideration of the factors contained in IC 31–16–6–1 and IC 31–16–6–2, the court finds that the Guideline amount is unjust or inappropriate in a particular case, the court may state a factual basis for the deviation and proceed to enter a support amount that is deemed appropriate.

Commentary to Guideline 3F
Computation of Child Support.

1. *Apportionment of Support Between Parents*. After the total child support obligation is determined, it is necessary to apportion that obligation

between the parents based on their respective weekly adjusted incomes. First, a percentage is formed by dividing the weekly adjusted income of each parent by the total weekly adjusted income (Line 1E of the Worksheet). The percentages are entered on Line 2 of the Worksheet. The total child support obligation is then multiplied by the percentages on Line 2 (the percentage of total weekly adjusted income that the weekly adjusted income of each parent represents) and the resulting figure is the child support obligation of each parent. The noncustodial parent is ordered to pay his or her proportionate share of support as calculated on Line 6 of the Worksheet. Custodial parents are presumed to be meeting their obligations by direct expenditures on behalf of the child, so a support order is not entered against the custodial parent.

2. *Apportionment of Support When Incapacitated Adult Child Has Earned Income.* Under certain circumstances the earned income of a child may be considered in apportioning support. In calculating a support obligation with respect to an incapacitated adult child with earned income, the support obligation may be determined by apportioning the support based upon the relative amount earned by the parents and the child.

3. *Deviation From Guideline Amount.* If the court determines that the Guideline amount is unjust or inappropriate, a written finding shall be made setting forth the factual basis for deviation from the Guideline amount. A simple finding such as the following is sufficient: "The court finds that the presumptive amount of support calculated under the Guidelines has been rebutted for the following reasons." A pro forma finding that the Guidelines are not appropriate does not satisfy the requirement for a specific finding of inappropriateness in a particular case, which is required in an order to deviate from the Guideline amount. For further discussion of deviation from the Guideline amount, see also the Commentary to Support Guideline 1.

G. Adjustments to Parent's Child Support Obligation (Worksheet Line 7)

The parent's child support obligation (Worksheet Line 7) may be subject to four (4) adjustments.

1. *Obligation From Post–Secondary Education Worksheet.* If the parents have a child who is living away from home while attending school, his or her child support obligation will reflect the adjustment found on Line J of the Post–Secondary Education Worksheet (See Support Guideline 8).

2. *Weekly Cost of Work-related Child Care Expenses.* A parent who pays a weekly child care expense should receive a credit towards his or her child support obligation. This credit is entered on the space provided on the Worksheet Line 7. The total credits claimed by the parents must equal the total amount on Line 4A. (See Support Guideline 3E Commentary).

3. *Weekly Cost of Health Insurance Premiums For Child(ren).* The parent who pays the weekly premium cost for the child(ren)'s health insurance should receive a credit towards his or her child support obligation in most circumstances. This credit is entered on the space provided on the Worksheet Line 7 and will be in an amount equal to that entered on the Worksheet Line 4B (See Support Guideline 3E Commentary).

4. *Parenting Time Credit.* The court should grant a credit toward the total amount of calculated child support for either "duplicated" or "transferred" expenses incurred by the noncustodial parent. The proper allocation of these expenses between the parents shall be based on the calculation from a Parenting Time Credit Worksheet. (See Support Guideline 6 Commentary).

5. *Effect of Social Security Benefits.*

a. *Current Support Obligation*

1. Custodial parent: Social Security benefits received for a child based upon the disability of the custodial parent are not a credit toward the child support obligation of the noncustodial parent. It is a credit to the custodial parent's child support obligation.

2. Noncustodial parent: Social Security benefits received by a custodial parent, as representative payee of the child, based upon the earnings or disability of the noncustodial parent shall be considered as a credit to satisfy the noncustodial parent's child support obligation as follows:

i. Social Security Retirement benefits may, at the court's discretion, be credited to the noncustodial parent's current child support obligation. The credit is not automatic. The presence of Social Security Retirement benefits is merely one factor for the court to consider in determining the child support obligation or modification of the obligation. Stultz v. Stultz, 659 N.E.2d 125 (Ind. 1995).

ii. Social Security Disability benefits shall be included in the Weekly Gross Income of the noncustodial parent and applied as a credit to the noncustodial parent's current child support obligation. The credit is automatic.

iii. Any portion of the benefit that exceeds the child support obligation shall be considered a gratuity for the benefit of the child(ren), unless there is an arrearage.

3. The filing of a petition to modify on grounds a Social Security Disability determination has been requested will not relieve the parent's obligation to pay the current support order while the disability application is pending. Filing of the petition to modify support entitles the noncustodial parent to a retroactive reduction in support to the date of filing of the petition for modification and not the date of filing for the benefits. If the modification of support is granted, any lump sum payment of retroactive Social Security Disability benefits

paid shall be credited toward the modified support obligation.

b. *Arrearages*

1. Credit for retroactive lump sum payment. A lump sum payment of retroactive Social Security Disability benefits shall be applied as a credit against an existing child support arrearage if the custodial parent, as representative payee, received a lump sum retroactive payment, without the requirement of a filing of a Petition to Modify Child Support. However, no credit should be allowed under the following circumstances:

i. A custodial parent should never be required to pay restitution to a disabled noncustodial parent for lump sum retroactive Social Security Disability benefits which exceed the amount of "court-ordered" child support. Any portion of lump sum payments of retroactive Social Security Disability benefits paid to children not credited against the existing child support arrearage is properly treated as a gratuity to the children. No credit toward future support should be granted.

ii. No credit shall be given for a lump sum disability payment paid directly to a child who is over the age of eighteen (18). The dependency benefits paid directly to a child who has reached the age of majority under the Social Security law, rather than to the custodial parent, as representative payee, do not fulfill the obligations of court-ordered child support.

2. Application of current Social Security Disability benefits. The amount of the benefit which exceeds the child support order may be treated as an ongoing credit toward an existing arrearage.

3. In Title IV–D cases there is no credit toward the monies owed to the State of Indiana unless the retroactive benefit is actually paid to the State of Indiana. The child's Social Security benefits received and used by the custodial parent will not reduce or be credited against the noncustodial parent's obligation to reimburse the State of Indiana for Title IV–A or Title IV–E benefits previously paid on behalf of the children.

4. Modification. The award of Social Security Disability benefits retroactive to a specific date does not modify a noncustodial parent's child support obligation to the same date. The noncustodial parent's duty to pay support cannot be retroactively modified earlier than the filing date of a petition to modify child support. IC § 31–16–16–6.

Commentary to Guideline 3G

It is important to remember the amount of Social Security Disability benefit that exceeds the current child support order will not be re-flected in ISETS as a credit toward an existing arrearage unless specified in the court order. Unless the credit is recognized in ISETS, there is a chance that an arrearage notice may be issued administratively and sanctions could be entered on that arrearage.

Social Security benefits paid to a parent for the benefit of a minor child are included in the disabled parent's Gross Weekly Income for purposes of determining child support regardless of which parent actually receives the payment. (See Guideline 3A). This section, 3G, and its commentary, address adjustments to the recommended child support obligation. Although Social Security benefits are not reflected on Line 7 of the child support Worksheet, the benefit should be considered, and its effect and application shall be included in the written order for support of that child.

The revised Guidelines make no change in the law regarding an adjustment for Social Security Retirement benefits or Supplemental Security Income (SSI). The court has discretion to allow an adjustment to a parent's child support obligation based on the amount of Social Security Retirement benefits paid for the benefit of the child due to that parent's retirement. The retirement benefit is merely one of the factors that the court should consider when making an adjustment to the child support obligation. SSI is a means-tested program and the benefit is not included in either parent's gross income. It therefore should not be considered an adjustment to either parent's child support obligation.

In Brown v. Brown, 849 N.E.2d 610 (Ind. 2006), Social Security Disability (SSD) benefits paid to a child were clearly recognized as earnings of the disabled parent. Id. at 614. Under the new Guidelines, Social Security Disability benefits paid for a child are now recognized as income of the disabled parent who earned the benefits and those benefits are included in the Weekly Gross Income of that parent. See Guideline 3A. It follows then that the payment received for the benefit of the child should be applied to satisfy the disabled parent's support obligation. The child support order should state that the SSD benefit received for the child is credited as payment toward the support obligation. Any portion of the SSD benefit in excess of the current support obligation is a gratuity, unless there is an arrearage.

The new language in Guideline 3G5 directs that the excess SSD benefit shall be applied as payment toward an existing arrearage. Once the arrearage is satisfied, any portion of the SSD benefit that exceeds the current support obligation is considered a gratuity. The new Guidelines also change the application of a lump sum SSD payment. SSD is, by definition, a substitution for a person's income lost due to a recognized disability. Further, under the Act, that individual may be entitled to a lump sum benefit retroactive to the date that his or her disability occurred and that caused the disruption in earnings. This lump sum payment is unique to SSD. The Guidelines now allow the courts to apply the lump sum SSD benefits toward an existing child support arrearage if the custodial parent, as representative payee, receives a lump sum payment. This credit is appropriate without the requirement of a filing of a Petition to Modify Child Support.

The revised Guidelines change the law regarding the application of SSD benefits. The holding in Hieston v. State, 885 N.E.2d 59 (Ind. Ct. App. 2008) and its progeny has been superseded by this change. The rationale is that the lump sum payment is merely a method of payment applied to a past support obligation not paid. The distinction is between modification of support which changes the rate of support, e.g. from $100.00 per week to $50.00 per week, as opposed to credit for an indirect payment. Modification of a child support obligation still requires the filing of a petition for modification as set forth in Guideline 4.

The lump sum payment is a method of payment that may not be specifically authorized by express court order but which should be recognized as a payment of support. Indiana case law establishes that credit can be allowed for payments that do not technically conform to the original support decree. For example, where the obligated parent makes payments directly to the custodial parent rather than through the clerk of the court, the Supreme Court has recognized these payments when there was sufficient proof to convince a trier of fact that the required payments were actually made. O'Neil v. O'Neil, 535 N.E.2d 523 (Ind. 1989), Nill v. Martin, 686 N.E.2d 116 (Ind. 1997). Proof of the lump sum SSD benefit payment is not difficult because the Social Security award certificate is a record easily admitted into evidence as an exception to the hearsay rule under IRE 803(6) and (8) (reports of a public agency setting forth its regularly recorded activity) and trial courts are rarely burdened with an evidentiary dispute about what was paid, when or to whom, once the Social Security records are shared. By contrast, the informal arrangement disputes between parties to modify and reduce the actual amount of weekly support below that ordered in the divorce decree are actual attempts to retroactively modify the amount of support, which are prohibited. Similar to the nonconforming payment, the lump sum payment shall be applied as a credit to an existing child support arrearage.

If there is no child support arrearage, the lump sum payment is considered gratuity. As long as there is an existing support order, there should never be an order entered that requires any excess payment of SSD or the lump sum payment to be paid back to the disabled parent.

The revised Guidelines exclude from the parent's Weekly Gross Income any survivor benefits received by or for other children residing in either parent's home based on the Social Security death benefits of a deceased parent of a prior-born child. See Commentary to Guideline 3(A).

Adopted effective Oct. 1, 1989. Amended effective March 1, 1993; amended May 27, 1998, effective July 1, 1998; Sept. 10, 2003, effective Jan. 1, 2004; Sept. 15, 2009, effective Jan. 1, 2010; Dec. 18, 2009, effective Jan. 1, 2010.

GUIDELINE 4.   MODIFICATION

The provisions of a child support order may be modified only if there is a substantial and continuing change of circumstances.

Adopted effective Oct. 1, 1989. Amended effective March 1, 1993.

Commentary

Substantial and Continuing Change of Circumstances. Before a child support order may be modified in Indiana, it is necessary for a party to demonstrate a substantial and continuing change in circumstances that makes the present order unreasonable or that the amount of support ordered at least twelve (12) months earlier differs from the Guideline amount presently computed by more than twenty percent (20%), see IC 31–16–8–1 regarding dissolution of marriage actions or IC 31–14–11–8 regarding paternity actions. A change in circumstances may include a change in the income of the parents, the application of a parenting plan, the failure to comply with a parenting plan or a change in the expense of child rearing specifically considered in the Guidelines.

If the amount of support computed at the time of modification is significantly higher or significantly lower than that previously ordered and would require a drastic reduction in a parent's standard of living, consideration may be given to phasing in the change in support. This approach would allow the parent affected by the change time to make adjustments in his or her standard of living. Again, it is not the intent of the Guidelines to drive the parents into noncompliance by reducing their spendable income below subsistence level.

Retroactive Modification. The modification of a support obligation may only relate back to the date the petition to modify was filed, and not an earlier date, subject to two exceptions: (1) when the parties have agreed to and carried out an alternative method of payment which substantially complies with the spirit of the decree; or (2) the obligated parent takes the child into the obligated parent's home and assumes custody, provides necessities, and exercises parental control for a period of time that a permanent change of custody is exercised.

Emancipation: Support Orders for Two or More Children. Support orders for two or more children, under the Guidelines, are stated as an in gross or total amount rather than on a per child basis. The total obligation will not decrease when the oldest child reaches twenty-one (21) years of age, or upon the occurrence of some other series of events that gives rise to emancipation, absent judicial modification of the order. Conversely, the law recognizes that where an order is framed in terms of an amount per child, an abatement of respective shares will occur upon each child's emancipation.

The concept of a pro rata delineation of support is generally inconsistent with the economic policy underlying the Guidelines (See "Economic Data Used in Developing Guidelines" in "Commentary" to Support Guideline 1). That policy recognizes that the amount of support required for two children is 1.5

times that required to support one child. The multiplication factor decreases as the number of children increases. If support were reduced by one half when the first of two children was emancipated, the remaining amount of support would be significantly below the Guideline amount for one child at the same parental income levels.

Support orders may, however, be framed to allow for automatic abatement of support upon the emancipation of the first child if that emancipation is by reaching age twenty-one (21) or by virtue of some other significant event that will not be disputed between the parties.

EXAMPLE: Assume a combined weekly adjusted income of $1,000.00 provided solely by the noncustodial parent, and an order for support of three children. No other factors being considered, a support order would provide for payment of $285.00 per week for three children; $228.00 weekly upon the oldest child reaching age twenty-one (21) years of age; and $152.00 per week after the second oldest child reaches twenty-one (21), to and until the youngest child's twenty-first birthday, unless otherwise modified by the court.

It is recommended that such a delineation should be an exception and not the rule. It is incumbent upon counsel who represent parents to attempt to familiarize them with the need to judicially amend the order of support when children are emancipated and to discuss with the parties what constitutes emancipation.

Amended May 27, 1998, effective July 1, 1998; Sept. 10, 2003, effective Jan. 1, 2004; Sept. 15, 2009, effective Jan. 1, 2010; Dec. 18, 2009, effective Jan. 1, 2010.

GUIDELINE 5. FEDERAL STATUTES

These Guidelines have been drafted in an attempt to comply with, and should be construed to conform with applicable federal statutes.

Adopted effective Oct. 1, 1989. Amended effective March 1, 1993.

Commentary

Every attempt was made to draft Guidelines for the State of Indiana that would comply with applicable federal statutes and regulations. Likewise, careful attention was paid to state law.

Amended May 27, 1998, effective July 1, 1998; Dec. 18, 2009, effective Jan. 1, 2010.

GUIDELINE 6. PARENTING TIME CREDIT

A credit should be awarded for the number of overnights each year that the child(ren) spend with the noncustodial parent.

Adopted effective March 1, 1993. Amended Sept. 15, 2009, effective Jan. 1, 2010; Dec. 18, 2009, effective Jan. 1, 2010.

Commentary

Analysis of Support Guidelines. The Indiana Child Support Guidelines are based on the assumption the child(ren) live in one household with primary physical custody in one parent who undertakes all of the spending on behalf of the child(ren).

There is a rebuttable presumption the support calculated from the Guideline support schedule is the correct amount of weekly child support to be awarded. The total amount of the anticipated average weekly spending is the Basic Child Support Obligation (Line 4 of the Worksheet).

The Guideline support schedules do not reflect the fact, however, when both parents exercise parenting time, out-of-pocket expenses will be incurred for the child(ren)'s care. These expenses were recognized previously by the application of a 10% visitation credit and a 50% abatement of child support during periods of extended visitation. The visitation credit was based on the regular exercise of alternate weekend visitation which is equivalent to approximately 14% of the annual overnights. With the adoption of the Indiana Parenting Time Guidelines, the noncustodial parent's share of parenting time, if exercised, is equivalent to approximately 27% of the annual overnights. As a result, these revisions provide a parenting credit based upon the number of overnights with the noncustodial parent ranging from 52 overnights annually to equal parenting time. As parenting time increases, a proportionally larger increase in the credit will occur.

Analysis of Parenting Time Costs. An examination of the costs associated with the sharing of parenting time reveals two types of expenses are incurred by both parents, transferred and duplicated expenses. A third category of expenses is controlled expenses, such as the 6% uninsured health care expense that remains the sole obligation of the parent for whom the parenting time credit is not calculated. This latter category is assumed to be equal to 15% of the Basic Child Support Obligation.

Transferred Expenses. This type of expense is incurred only when the child(ren) reside(s) with a parent and these expenses are "transferred" with the child(ren) as they move from one parent's residence to the other. Examples of this type of expense are food and the major portion of spending for transportation. When spending is transferred from one parent to the other parent, the other parent should be given a credit against that parent's child support obligation since this type of expense is included in the support calculation schedules. When parents equally share in the parenting, an assumption is made that 35% of the Basic Child Support Obligation reflects "transferred" expenses. The amount of expenses transferred from one parent to the other will depend upon the number of overnights the child(ren) spend(s) with each parent.

Duplicated Fixed Expenses. This type of expense is incurred when two households are maintained for the child(ren). An example of this type of expense is shelter costs which are not transferred when the child(ren) move(s) from one parent's residence to the other but remain fixed in each parent's household and represent duplicated expenditures. The fixed expense of the parent who has primary physical custody is included in the Guideline support schedules. However, the fixed expense of the other parent is not included in the support schedules but represents an increase in the total cost of raising the child(ren) attributed to the parenting time plan. Both parents should share in these additional costs.

When parents equally share in the parenting, an assumption is made that 50% of the Basic Child Support Obligation will be "duplicated." When the child(ren) spend(s) less time with one parent, the percentage of duplicated expenses will decline.

Controlled Expenses. This type of expense for the child(ren) is typically paid by the custodial parent and is not transferred or duplicated. Controlled expenses are items like clothing, education, school books and supplies, ordinary uninsured health care and personal care. For example, the custodial parent buys a winter coat for the child. The noncustodial parent will not buy another one. The custodial parent controls this type of expense. The controlled expenses account for 15% of the cost of raising the child. The parenting time credit is based on the more time the parents share, the more expenses are duplicated and transferred. The controlled expenses are not shared and remain with the parent that does not get the parenting time credit. Controlled expenses are generally not a consideration unless there is equal parenting time. These categories of expenses are not pertinent for litigation. They are presented only to explain the factors used in developing the parenting time credit formula. The percentages were assigned to these categories after considering the treatment of joint custody by other states and examining published data from the Bureau of Labor Statistics' Consumer Expenditure Survey.

Computation of Parenting Time Credit. The computation of the parenting time credit will require a determination of the annual number of overnights of parenting time exercised by the parent who is to pay child support, the use of the standard Child Support Obligation Worksheet, a Parenting Time Table, and a Parenting Time Credit Worksheet.

An overnight will not always translate into a twenty-four hour block of time with all of the attendant costs and responsibilities. It should include, however, the costs of feeding and transporting the child, attending to school work and the like. Merely providing a child with a place to sleep in order to obtain a credit is prohibited.

The Parenting Time Table (Table PT) begins at 52 overnights annually or the equivalent of alternate weekends of parenting time only. If the parenting plan is for fewer overnights because the child is an infant or toddler (Section II A of the Parenting Time Guidelines), the court may consider granting the noncustodial parent an appropriate credit for the expenses incurred when caring for the child. If the parenting plan is for fewer overnights due to a significant geographical distance between the parties, the court may consider granting an appropriate credit. The actual cost of transportation should be treated as a separate issue.

If the parents are using the Parenting Time Guidelines without extending the weeknight period into an overnight, the noncustodial parent will be exercising approximately 98 overnights.

Parenting Time Table. The TOTAL column represents the anticipated total out-of-pocket expenses expressed as a percentage of the Basic Child Support Obligation that will be incurred by the parent who will pay child support. The total expenses are the sum of transferred and duplicated expenses. The DUPLICATED column represents the duplicated expenses and reflects the assumption that when there is an equal sharing of parenting time, 50% of the Basic Child Support Obligation will be duplicated. The Number of Annual Overnights column will determine the particular fractions of TOTAL and DUPLICATED to be used in the Parenting Time Credit Worksheet.

Table PT

ANNUAL	OVERNIGHTS		
FROM	TO	TOTAL	DUPLICATED
1	51	0.000	0.000
52	55	0.062	0.011
56	60	0.070	0.014
61	65	0.080	0.020
66	70	0.093	0.028
71	75	0.108	0.038
76	80	0.127	0.052
81	85	0.150	0.070
86	90	0.178	0.093
91	95	0.211	0.122
96	100	0.250	0.156
101	105	0.294	0.195
106	110	0.341	0.237
111	115	0.388	0.280
116	120	0.434	0.321
121	125	0.476	0.358
126	130	0.513	0.390
131	135	0.544	0.417
136	140	0.570	0.438
141	145	0.591	0.454
146	150	0.609	0.467
151	155	0.623	0.476
156	160	0.634	0.483
161	165	0.644	0.488
166	170	0.652	0.491
171	175	0.660	0.494
176	180	0.666	0.495
181	183	0.675	0.500

Parenting Time Credit Worksheet (Credit Worksheet). In determining the credit, take the following steps:

1. Complete the Child Support Obligation Worksheet through Line 6.

2. Enter on Line 1PT of the Credit Worksheet the annual number of overnights exercised by the parent who will pay child support.

3. Enter on Line 2PT of the Credit Worksheet the Basic Child Support Obligation (Line 4 from the Child Support Obligation Worksheet).

4. Enter on Line 3PT of the Credit Worksheet the figure from the TOTAL column that corresponds to the annual overnights exercised by the parent who will pay child support.

5. Enter on Line 4PT of the Credit Worksheet the figure from the DUPLICATED column that corresponds to the annual number of overnights exercised by the parent who will pay child support.

6. Enter on Line 5PT of the Credit Worksheet the percentage share of the Combined Weekly Income of the parent who will pay child support (Line 2 of the Child Support Obligation Worksheet).

7. Complete Lines 6PT through 9PT to determine the allowable credit.

8. Enter the result from Line 9PT on Line 7 of the Child Support Obligation Worksheet as the Parenting Time Credit.

9. Apply the Line 7 Adjustments to determine the recommended Child Support Obligation (Line 8 of the Child Support Obligation Worksheet).

Parenting Time Credit Worksheet

Line:		
1PT	Enter Annual Number of Overnights	
2PT	Enter Weekly Basic Child Support Obligation – BCSO (Enter Line 4 from Child Support Worksheet)	
3PT	Enter Total Parenting Time Expenses as a Percentage of the BCSO (Enter Appropriate TOTAL Entry from Table PT)	
4PT	Enter Duplicated Expenses as a Percentage of the BCSO (Enter Appropriate DUPLICATED Entry from Table PT)	
5PT	Parent's Share of Combined Weekly Income (Enter Line 2 from Child Support Worksheet)	
6PT	Average Weekly Total Expenses during Parenting Time (Multiply Line 2PT times Line 3PT)	
7PT	Average Weekly Duplicated Expenses (Multiply Line 2PT times Line 4PT)	
8PT	Parent's Share of Duplicated Expenses (Multiply Line 5PT times Line 7PT)	
9PT	Allowable Expenses during Parenting Time (Line 6PT – Line 8PT)	
	Enter Line 9PT on Line 7 of the Child Support Worksheet as the Parenting Time Credit	

Application of Parenting Time Credit. Parenting Time Credit is not automatic. The court should determine if application of the credit will jeopardize a parent's ability to support the child(ren). If such is the case, the court should consider a deviation from the credit.

The Parenting Time Credit is earned by performing parental obligations as scheduled and is an advancement of weekly credit. The granting of the credit is based on the expectation the parties will comply with a parenting time order.

A parent who does not carry out the parenting time obligation may be subject to a reduction or loss of the credit, financial restitution, or any other appropriate remedy. However, missed parenting time because of occasional illness, transportation problems or other unforeseen events should not constitute grounds for a reduction or loss of the credit, or financial restitution.

Consistent with Parenting Time Guidelines, if court action is initiated to reduce the parenting time credit because of a failure to exercise scheduled parenting time, the parents shall enter mediation unless otherwise ordered by the court.

Contents of Agreements/Decrees. Orders establishing custody and child support shall set forth the specifics of the parties' parenting time plan in all cases. A reference to the Indiana Parenting Time Guidelines will suffice if the parties intend to follow the Guidelines. All such entries shall be accompanied by a copy of the Child Support Obligation Worksheet and the Parenting Time Credit Worksheet.

In every instance the court shall designate one parent who is receiving support and shall be responsible for payment of the uninsured health care expenses up to 6% of the Basic Child Support Obligation.

If the court determines it is necessary to deviate from the parenting time credit, it shall state its reasons in the order.

Split Custody and Child Support. In those situations where each parent has physical custody of one or more children (split custody), it is suggested that support be computed by completing the Child Support Obligation Worksheets in the following manner:

1. Compute the support a father would pay to a mother for the children in her custody as if they were the only children of the marriage.

2. Compute the support a mother would pay to a father for the children in his custody as if they were the only children of the marriage.

3. Subtract the lesser from the greater support amount. The parent who owes the remaining amount pays the difference to the other parent on a weekly basis.

This method of computation takes into account the fact that the first child in each home is the most expensive to support, as discussed in the Commentary to Guideline 1.

Child Support When Parenting Time is Equally Shared. A frequent source of confusion in determining child support arises in cases where parents equally share the parenting time with the children. Parenting time is considered equally shared when it is 181 to 183 overnights per year. To determine child support in these cases, either the mother or father must be designated as the parent who will pay the controlled expenses. Then, the other parent is given the parenting time credit. The controlled expenses remain the sole obligation of the parent for whom the parenting time credit is not calculated.

When both parents equally share parenting time, the court must determine which parent will pay the controlled expenses. If, for example, father is the parent paying controlled expenses, the parenting time credit will be awarded to the mother.

Factors courts should use in assigning the controlled expenses to a particular parent include the following areas of inquiry:

- Which parent has traditionally paid these expenses.
- Which parent is more likely to be able to readily pay the controlled expenses.
- Which parent more frequently takes the child to the health care provider.
- Which parent has traditionally been more involved in the child's school activities (since much of the controlled expenses concern school costs, such as clothes, fees, supplies, and books).

This determination requires a balancing of these and other factors. Once the court assigns responsibility for these controlled expenses, the court should award the other parent the parenting time credit. When the assignment of the controlled expenses occurs, calculation of the child support in shared custody situations is fairly basic, and is completed by application of the remainder of these Guidelines.

Cost of Transportation for Parenting Time. The Parenting Time Guidelines require the noncustodial parent to provide transportation for the child(ren) at the start of the scheduled parenting time, and the custodial parent to provide transportation for the child(ren) at the end of the scheduled parenting time. There is no specific provision in the Child Support Guidelines for an assignment of costs or a credit for transportation on the child support Worksheet. Transportation costs are part of the transferred expenses. When transportation costs are significant, the court may address transportation costs as a deviation from the child support calculated by the Worksheet, or may address transportation as a separate issue from child support. Consideration should be given to the reason for the geographic distance between the parties and the financial resources of each party. The relocation statute provides that one factor in modifying child support in conjunction with parent relocation is the hardship and expense involved for the nonrelocating individual to exercise parenting time.

Amended May 27, 1998, effective July 1, 1998; Sept. 10, 2003, effective Jan. 1, 2004; Sept. 15, 2009, effective Jan. 1, 2010; Dec. 18, 2009, effective Jan. 1, 2010.

GUIDELINE 7. HEALTH CARE/MEDICAL SUPPORT

The court shall order one or both parents to provide private health care insurance when accessible to the child at a reasonable cost.

Accessibility. Private insurance is accessible if it covers the geographic area in which the child lives. The court may consider other relevant factors such as the managed care regions used by Hoosier Healthwise, the accessibility and comprehensiveness of covered services and likely continuation of coverage.

Reasonable cost. The cost of private health insurance for child(ren) is considered reasonable, if it does not exceed five percent (5%) of the Weekly Gross Income of the parent obligated to provide medical support. The cost of private health insurance for the child(ren) is not considered reasonable when it is combined with that party's share of the total child support obligation (Line 4 of the Worksheet) and that sum exceeds fifty percent (50%) of the gross income of the parent responsible for providing medical support.

A consideration of the foregoing factors is addressed in the Health Insurance Premium Worksheet (HIPW), which should be utilized in determining the appropriate adjustments for the child(ren)'s health insurance on the Child Support Obligation Worksheet.

Cash medical support. When private health care insurance is not accessible to the child(ren) at a reasonable cost, federal law requires the court to order the parties to pay cash medical support. Cash medical support is an amount ordered for medical costs not covered by insurance. The uninsured medical expense apportionment calculation on the Child Support Obligation Worksheet, "the 6% rule," satisfies this federal requirement for a cash medical support order, when incorporated into the court order.

Explanation of 6% rule/uninsured health care expenses. The data upon which the Guideline schedules are based include a component for ordinary health care expenses. Ordinary uninsured health care expenses are paid by the parent who is assigned to pay the controlled expenses (the parent for whom the parenting time credit is not calculated) up to six percent (6%) of the basic child support obligation (Line 4 of the Child Support Obligation Worksheet.) Extraordinary health care expenses are those uninsured expenses which are in excess of six percent (6%) of the basic obligation, and would include uninsured expenses for chronic or long term conditions of a child. Calculation of the apportionment of the health care expense obligation is a matter separate from the determination of the weekly child support obligation. These calculations shall be inserted in the space provided on the Worksheet.

Birth expense. The court may order the father to pay a percentage of the reasonable and necessary expenses of the mother's pregnancy and childbirth, as part of the court's decree in child support actions. The costs to be included in apportionment are prenatal care, delivery, hospitalization, and post-natal care. The paternity statutes require the father to pay at least fifty percent (50%) of the mother's pregnancy and childbirth expenses.

Commentary

Health Insurance Premiums.

The court is federally mandated to order accessible private health care insurance if the cost is at or below 5% of the Weekly Gross Income of a parent as indicated in the Child Support Obligation Worksheet. If above 5% of Weekly Gross Income, the court has discretion to require the health insurance premium be paid by a parent if the court indicates the reason for the deviation.

The 50% cap is not a federal requirement. The basis is the Consumer Credit Protection Act (CCPA) income withholding limits. The 50% cap places less burden on employers when they do income withholding. Without the cap, they would have to figure out whether to withhold child support or health insurance first and how to divide what they can legally withhold. One of the most common questions employers ask child support agencies in states without a cap concerns cases where the combined amount does exceed the CCPA cap. In addition to being less burdensome on employers, it is also commonsense not to set child support at more than what can be legally withheld. Indiana already has that attribute as evident in the last column of the schedule.

When parents agree one or both parents will provide private health insurance, the HIPW need not be completed and filed.

Private health insurance coverage should normally be provided by the parent who can obtain the most comprehensive coverage at the least cost. If a separate policy of private insurance is purchased for the children, determining the weekly cost should be no problem, but in the most common situation coverage for the child(ren) will occur through an employer group plan. If the employer pays the entire cost of coverage, no addition to the basic obligation will occur. If there is an employee cost, it will be necessary for the parent to contact his or her employer or insurance provider to obtain appropriate documentation of the parent's cost for the child(ren)'s coverage.

At low income levels, giving the noncustodial parent credit for payment of the private health insurance premium may reduce support to an unreasonably low amount. In such instance the court may, in the exercise of its discretion, deny or reduce the credit.

A number of different circumstances may exist in providing private health insurance coverage, such as a situation in which a subsequent spouse or child(ren) are covered at no additional cost to the parent who is paying for the coverage. The treatment of these situations rests in the sound discretion of the court, including such options as prorating the cost.

There may be situations where neither parent has the opportunity or ability to afford private health insurance. In those cases, the court may direct the parties to investigate the cost of health insurance and/or may require the parties to obtain health insurance when it is reasonable and accessible.

Where one or both parents have a history of changing jobs and/or health insurance providers both parents may be ordered to carry health insurance when it becomes available at reasonable cost to the parent. Where one parent has a history of maintaining consistent insurance coverage for the child(ren), there is no need to order both parents to provide health insurance for the child(ren).

The court may order both parents to provide health insurance and in those cases both parents should have the cost of the child(ren)'s portion of the health insurance premium included in the calculation of the support order. In such cases both parents receive a credit.

Completion of the Health Insurance Premium Worksheet (HIPW).

Section One: Calculation of Reasonable Cost Threshold.

Line A: Enter each parent's Weekly Gross Income in the appropriate columns, carrying the numbers from Line 1 of the Child Support Obligation Worksheet (CSOW).

Line B: Calculate the reasonable cost threshold by multiplying the amount on Line A times five percent (.05%). This amount becomes the "reasonableness" threshold against which the weekly health insurance premium is compared.

Section Two: Determination of Private Health Insurance Available to the Parents.

Line C: This line is intended to record, for each parent, whether private health insurance is available. Availability is not strictly limited to insurance available through employment. For example, insurance may be available through a union or another group insurance plan, through COBRA, or obtained as an individual private insurance plan. If insurance is not available, the rest of the HIPW need not be completed. However, the court has discretion to order one or both parties to provide health insurance if it becomes available and meets the tests of reasonableness and accessibility.

Section Three: Determination of Whether Premium is Reasonable in Cost.

There are two tests to determine if the cost of the health insurance premium is reasonable to a parent. Both tests must be satisfied for the cost to be reasonable. The first test determines whether the health insurance premium cost exceeds five percent (5%) of the parent's Weekly Gross Income. The second test determines whether the parent's portion of the child support obligation plus the health insurance premium cost exceeds fifty percent (50%) of the parent's Weekly Gross Income.

Line D: Each party should have determined the weekly cost of premiums prior to completing the Worksheet. The cost should be for the "child's portion only." This is the cost of the child's portion, if known, or the difference between the cost of insuring a single party versus the cost of family coverage.

Line E, Test One: The first test of reasonableness compares the cost of the weekly premium with the "reasonable cost threshold." The cost of the health insurance premium cannot exceed five percent (5%) of the parent's Weekly Gross Income. For each parent, compare the amount on Line D to the amount on Line B. If the amount on Line D is less than the amount on Line B, mark "yes" and proceed to Line F. If the amount on Line D is not less than the amount on Line B, mark "no" and the rest of the HIPW for that parent need not be completed.

Line F, Test Two: The second test of reasonableness ensures that a parent's cost of his or her child support obligation added to any health insurance premium that is ordered does not exceed fifty percent (50%) of the his or her gross income. For this test, add the Basic Child Support Obligation amount from Line 4 of the CSOW to the weekly health insurance premium cost from Line D of the HIPW. If this amount is equal to or less than fifty percent (50%) of the parent's Weekly Gross Income, mark "yes" and proceed to Line G. If this amount is more than fifty percent (50%) of the parent's Weekly Gross Income, mark "no" and the rest of the HIPW need not be completed for that parent.

Section Four: Accessibility of the Insurance.

Line G: This line indicates whether the health insurance coverage is accessible for the child(ren). For example, this line tests the geographical coverage of the health insurance. If parents live in different states or different areas of the same state, health insurance that one parent has may not be accessible to the child. See Guideline 7 for more information. For each parent, mark "yes" or "no."

Section Five: Parent(s) Ordered to Provide Health Insurance.

Line H: On this line, mark the parent or parents where "yes" is marked for Lines C, E, F and G.

Line I: Mark the parent or parents who are ordered to provide health insurance. If both parents are ordered, mark both boxes. Enter the amount from Line D in the box next to the parent(s) who are ordered to provide the insurance, and indicate the "Total Ordered." Please note that the court may use its discretion to order or not order health insurance coverage even when all tests are met or not met.

Apportionment of Uninsured Health Care Expenses. Six percent (6%) of the support amount is for health care. The noncustodial parent is, in effect, prepaying health care expenses every time a support payment is made. Consequently, the Guidelines require that custodial parent bear the cost of uninsured health care expenses up to six percent (6%) of the Basic Child Support Obligation found on Line 4 of the Child Support Obligation Worksheet and, if applicable, the child support obligation attributable to a student living away from home (Section Two Line I of the Post-Secondary Education Worksheet).

That computation is made by multiplying the total of Line 4 and Line I by 52 (weeks) and multiplying the product of that multiplication by .06 to arrive at the amount the custodial parent must spend on the uninsured health care costs of the parties' child(ren) in any calendar year before the non-custodial parent is required to contribute toward payment of those uninsured costs. For example, if Line 4 is $150.00 per week and Line I is $25.00 per week, the calcula-

tion would be as follows: $150.00 + $25.00 = $175.00 × 52 = $9,100.00 × .06 = $546.00.

Thus, on an annual basis, the custodial parent is required to spend $546.00 for health care of the child(ren) before the non-custodial parent is required to contribute. The custodial parent must document the $546.00 spent on health care and provide the documentation to the noncustodial parent.

After the custodial parent's obligation for ordinary uninsured health care expenses is computed, provision should be made for the uninsured health care expenses that may exceed that amount. The excess costs should be apportioned between the parties according to the Percentage Share of Income computed on Line 2 of the Worksheet. Where imposing such percentage share of the uninsured costs may work an injustice, the court may resort to the time-honored practice of splitting uninsured health care costs equally, or by using other methods. The court may prorate the custodial parent's uninsured health care expense contribution when appropriate.

As a practical matter, it may be wise to spell out with specificity in the order what uninsured expenses are covered and a schedule for the periodic payment of these expenses. For example, a chronic long-term condition might necessitate weekly payments of the uninsured expense. The order may include any reasonable medical, dental, hospital, pharmaceutical and psychological expenses deemed necessary for the health care of the child(ren). If it is intended that such things as aspirin, vitamins and band-aids be covered, the order should specifically state that such non-prescription health care items are covered.

There are also situations where major health care costs are incurred for a single event such as orthodontics or major injuries. For financial reasons, this may require the custodial parent to pay the provider for the amount not covered by insurance over a number of years. The 6% rule applies to expenses actually paid by the custodial parent each year.

Birth expenses. There is no statute of limitations barring recovery of birthing expenses, providing the paternity, Title IV–D or child support action is timely filed. The court should be very careful to be sure the claimed expenses are both reasonable and necessary. Birthing expenses include both the expenses incurred by the child as well as by the mother, providing they are directly related to the child's birth. The court should distinguish between "postpartum expenses" and "postnatal expenses." "Postpartum" expenses are mother's expenses following the birth of the child. "Postnatal" expenses of the child are those expenses directly related to the child's birth. Between the two, only "postnatal" expenses are reimbursable.

Adopted Sept. 15, 2009, effective Jan. 1, 2010. Amended Dec. 18, 2009, effective Jan. 1, 2010.

GUIDELINE 8.   EXTRAORDINARY EXPENSES
Extraordinary Educational Expenses.

The data upon which the Guideline schedules are based include a component for ordinary educational expenses. Any extraordinary educational expenses incurred on behalf of a child shall be considered apart from the total Basic Child Support Obligation.

Extraordinary educational expenses may be for elementary, secondary or post-secondary education, and should be limited to reasonable and necessary expenses for attending private or special schools, institutions of higher learning, and trade, business or technical schools to meet the particular educational needs of the child.

a. Elementary and Secondary Education. If the expenses are related to elementary or secondary education, the court may want to consider whether the expense is the result of a personal preference of one parent or whether both parents concur; if the parties would have incurred the expense while the family was intact; and whether or not education of the same or higher quality is available at less cost.

b. Post-Secondary Education. The authority of the court to award post-secondary educational expenses is derived from IC 31–16–6–2. It is discretionary with the court to award post-secondary educational expenses and in what amount. In making such a decision, the court should consider post-secondary education to be a group effort, and weigh the ability of each parent to contribute to payment of the expense, as well as the ability of the student to pay a portion of the expense.

If the court determines that an award of post-secondary educational expenses is appropriate, it should apportion the expenses between the parents and the child, taking into consideration the incomes and overall financial condition of the parents and the child, education gifts, education trust funds, and any other education savings program. The court should also take into consideration scholarships, grants, student loans, summer and school year employment and other cost-reducing programs available to the student. These latter sources of assistance should be credited to the child's share of the educational expense unless the court determines that it should credit a portion of any scholarships, grants and loans to either or both parents' share(s) of the education expense.

Current provisions of the Internal Revenue Code provide tax credits and preferences which will subsidize the cost of a child's post-secondary education. While tax planning on the part of all parties will be needed to maximize the value of these subsidies, no one party should disproportionately benefit from the tax treatment of post-secondary expenses. Courts may consider who may be entitled to claim various education tax benefits and tax exemptions for the minor child(ren) and the total value of the tax subsidies prior to assigning the financial responsibility of post-secondary expenses to the parents and the child.

A determination of what constitutes educational expenses will be necessary and will generally include tuition, books, lab fees, supplies, student activity fees and the like. Room and board will also be included when the student resides on campus or otherwise is not with the custodial parent.

The impact of an award of post-secondary educational expenses is substantial upon the custodial and non-custodial parent and a reduction of the Basic Child Support Obligation attributable to the child in question will be required when The child resides on campus or otherwise is not with the custodial parent.

A consideration of the foregoing factors is addressed in the Worksheet on post–secondary education expense which should be utilized in making a fair distribution of this expense.

The court should require that a student maintain a certain minimum level of academic performance to remain eligible for parental assistance and should include such a provision in its order. The court should also consider requiring the student or the custodial parent provide the non-custodial parent with a copy of the child's high school transcript and each semester or trimester post-secondary education grade report.

The court may limit consideration of college expenses to the cost of state supported colleges and universities or otherwise may require that the income level of the family and the achievement level of the child be sufficient to justify the expense of private school.

The court may wish to consider in the category of "Other" educational costs (Line B(5) of the Worksheet) such items as transportation, car insurance, clothing, entertainment and incidental expenses.

c. Use of Post-Secondary Education Worksheet

The Worksheet makes two determinations. Section One determines the obligation of each parent for payment of post-secondary education expenses based upon his or her pro-rata share of the weekly adjusted income from the Child Support Obligation Worksheet after contribution from the student toward those costs. The method of paying such obligation should be addressed in the court's order. When the student remains at home with the custodial parent while attending an institution of higher learning, generally no reduction to the non-custodial parent's support obligation will occur and Section Two of the Worksheet need not be completed.

Section Two determines the amount of each parent's weekly support obligation for the student who does not live at home year round. The amount attributable to the student while at home has been annualized to avoid weekly variations in the order. It further addresses the provisions of IC 31–16–6–2(b) which require a reduction in the child support obligation when the court orders the payment of educational expenses which are duplicated or would otherwise be paid to the custodial parent. In determining the reduction, the student is treated as emancipated. This treatment recognizes that the diminishing marginal effect of additional children is due to economies of scale in consumption and not the age of the children. A second child becomes the "first child" in terms of consumption and the custodial parent will receive Guideline child support on that basis.

Section Two applies when the parties' only child attending school does not reside with the custodial parent while attending school, as well as when the parties have more than one child and one resides away from home while attending school and the other child(ren) remain at home.

Line E of the Worksheet determines the percentage of the year the student lives at home. Line F is used to enter the Basic Child Support Obligation, from the Guideline Schedules for all of the children of the parties including the student who does not live at home year round. Line G is used to enter the amount of support for those children who are not living away from home. If the student is the only child, Line G will be $0.00. The difference between Lines F and G is the total support obligation attributable to the student. This is entered on Line H. By multiplying the percentage of the year the student lives at home, times the support obligation attributable to the student, the worksheet pro rates to a weekly basis the total support obligation attributed to the student. This is computed on Line I and the result is included in the uninsured health care expense calculation. The parents' pro rata share of this obligation is computed in Line J. This result is included in section 7 of the Child Support Obligation Worksheet.

1. *The One Child Situation*. When the parties' only child is a student who does not live at home with the custodial parent while attending school, Section Two establishes the weekly support obligation for that child on Line I. The regular Child Support Obligation Worksheet should be completed through Line 5 for that child and the annualized obligation from Line J of the Post–secondary Education Worksheet is entered on Line 7 with an explanation of the deviation in the order or decree.

2. *The More Than One Child Situation*. When the parties have more than one child, Section Two requires the preparation of a regular Child Support Obligation Worksheet applicable only to the child(ren) who regularly reside with the custodial parent, and for a determination of that support obligation. The annualized obligation from Line J of the Post–Secondary Education Worksheet is then inserted on Line 7 of the regular support Worksheet as an addition to the Parent's Child Support Obligation on Line 6. An explanation of the increase in the support obligation should then appear in the order or decree.

In both situations the Child Support Obligation Worksheet and the Post–Secondary Education Work-

sheet must be filed with the court. This includes cases in which agreed orders are submitted.

When more than one child lives away from home while attending school, Section One of the Post–Secondary Education Worksheet should be prepared for each child. However, Section Two should be completed once for all children living away from home while attending school. The number used to fill in the blank in Line E should be the average number of weeks these children live at home. For example, if one child lives at home for ten (10) weeks and another child lives at home for sixteen (16) weeks, the average number of weeks will be thirteen (13). This number would then be inserted in the blank on Line E which is then divided by 52 (weeks).

Other Extraordinary Expenses. The economic data used in developing the Child Support Guideline Schedules do not include components related to those expenses of an "optional" nature such as costs related to summer camp, soccer leagues, scouting and the like. When both parents agree that the child(ren) may participate in optional activities, the parents should pay their pro rata share of these expenses. In the absence of an agreement relating to such expenses, assigning responsibility for the costs should take into account factors such as each parent's ability to pay, which parent is encouraging the activity, whether the child(ren) has/have historically participated in the activity, and the reasons a parent encourages or opposes participation in the activity. If the parents or the court determine that the child(ren) may participate in optional activities, the method of sharing the expenses shall be set forth in the entry.

Adopted Sept. 15, 2009, effective Jan. 1, 2010.

GUIDELINE 9. ACCOUNTABILITY, TAX EXEMPTIONS, ROUNDING SUPPORT AMOUNTS

Accountability of the Custodial Parent for Support Received. Quite commonly noncustodial parents request, or even demand, that the custodial parent provide an accounting for how support money is spent. While recognizing that in some instances an accounting may be justified, the Committee does not recommend that it be routinely used in support orders. The Indiana Legislature recognized that an accounting may sometimes be needed when it enacted IC 31–16–9–6.

At the time of entering an order for support, or at any time thereafter, the court may make an order, upon a proper showing of the necessity therefore, requiring the spouse or other person receiving such support payments to render an accounting to the court of future expenditures upon such terms and conditions as the court shall decree.

It is recommended that an accounting be ordered upon a showing of reasonable cause to believe that child support is not being used for the support of the child. This provision is prospective in application and discretionary with the court. An accounting may not be ordered as to support payments previously paid.

A custodial parent may be able to account for direct costs (clothing, school expenses, music lessons, etc.) but it should be remembered that it is extremely difficult to compile indirect costs (a share of housing, transportation, utilities, food, etc.) with any degree of accuracy. If a court found that a custodial parent was diverting support for his or her own personal use, the remedy is not clear. Perhaps, the scrutiny that comes with an accounting would itself resolve the problem.

Tax Exemptions. Development of these Guidelines did not take into consideration the awarding of the income tax exemption. Instead, it is recommended that each case be reviewed on an individual basis and that a decision be made in the context of each case. Judges and practitioners should be aware that under current law the court cannot award an exemption to a parent, but the court may order a parent to release or sign over the exemption for one or more of the children to the other parent pursuant to Internal Revenue Code § 152(e). To effect this release, the parent releasing the exemption must sign and deliver to the other parent I.R.S. Form 8332, Release of Claim to Exemption for Child of Divorced or Separated Parents. The parent claiming the exemption must then file this form with his or her tax return. The release may be made, pursuant to the Internal Revenue Code, annually, for a specified number of years or permanently. Judges may wish to consider ordering the release to be executed on an annual basis, contingent upon support being current at the end of the calendar year for which the exemp-

tion is ordered as an additional incentive to keep support payments current. It may also be helpful to specify a date by which the release is to be delivered to the other parent each year. Shifting the exemption for minor children does not alter the filing status of either parent.

The noncustodial parent must demonstrate the tax consequences to each parent as a result of releasing the exemption and how the release would benefit the child(ren). In determining when to order a release of exemptions, it is recommended that at minimum the following factors be considered:

(1) the value of the exemption at the marginal tax rate of each parent;

(2) the income of each parent;

(3) the age of the child(ren) and how long the exemption will be available;

(4) the percentage of the cost of supporting the child(ren) borne by each parent;

(5) the financial aid benefit for post-secondary education for the child(ren); and

(6) the financial burden assumed by each parent under the property settlement in the case.

Rounding child support amounts. The amount of child support entered as an order may be expressed as an even amount, by rounding to the nearest dollar. For example, $50.50 is rounded to $51.00 and $50.49 is rounded to $50.00.

Adopted Sept. 15, 2009, effective Jan. 1, 2010. Amended Dec. 18, 2009, effective Jan. 1, 2010.

Worksheet -- Child Support Obligation

Worksheet – Child Support Obligation

Each party shall complete that portion of the worksheet that applies to him or her, sign the form and file it with the court. This worksheet is required in all proceedings establishing or modifying child support.

IN RE: CASE NO:
                                                FATHER:
                                                MOTHER:

CHILD SUPPORT OBLIGATION WORKSHEET (CSOW)

Children	DOB	Children	DOB

		FATHER	MOTHER	
1.	**WEEKLY GROSS INCOME**			
A.	Subsequent Children Multiplier Credit (.065 .097 .122 .137 .146 .155 .164 .173)			
B.	Child Support (Court Order for Prior Born)			
C.	Child Support (Legal Duty for Prior Born)			
D.	Maintenance Paid			
E.	WEEKLY ADJUSTED INCOME (WAI) Line 1 minus 1A, 1B, 1C and 1D			
2.	**PERCENTAGE SHARE OF TOTAL WAI**	%	%	
3.	**COMBINED WEEKLY ADJUSTED INCOME** (Line 1E)			
4.	**BASIC CHILD SUPPORT OBLIGATION** Apply CWAI to Guideline Schedules			
A.	Weekly Work-Related Child Care Expense of each parent			
B.	Weekly Health Insurance Premium – Total from HIPW, Line I			
5.	**TOTAL CHILD SUPPORT OBLIGATION** (Line 4 plus 4A and 4B)			
6.	**PARENT'S CHILD SUPPORT OBLIGATION** (Line 2 times Line 5)			
7.	**ADJUSTMENTS**			
	( ) Obligation from Post-Secondary Education Worksheet Line J.	+	+	
	( ) Payment of work-related child care by each parent. (Same amount as Line 4A)	-	-	
	( ) Child(ren)'s Portion of Weekly Health Insurance Premium for parent(s) ordered to provide health insurance.	-	-	
	( ) Parenting Time Credit	-	-	
8.	**RECOMMENDED CHILD SUPPORT OBLIGATION**			

I affirm under penalties for perjury that the foregoing representations are true.

Father: _____

Dated: _____   Mother: _____

UNINSURED HEALTH CARE EXPENSE CALCULATION

A. Custodial Parent Annual Obligation: (CSOW Line 4 Total) $_____ + (PSEW § Two, Line I) $_____ = $_____ x 52 weeks x .06 = $_____ .

B. Balance of Annual Expenses to be Paid: (Line 2) _____ % by Father; _____ % by Mother.

Amended effective March 1, 1993; amended May 27, 1998, effective July 1, 1998; Sept. 10, 2003, effective Jan. 1, 2004; Sept. 15, 2009, effective Jan. 1, 2010.

Worksheet -- Health Insurance Premium Worksheet (HIPW)

IN RE:	CASE NO:	
	FATHER:	
	MOTHER:	

HEALTH INSURANCE PREMIUM WORKSHEET (HIPW)		
SECTION ONE: CALCULATION OF REASONABLE COST THRESHOLD	**FATHER**	**MOTHER**
A. Parent's Weekly Gross Income (from Line 1 of Child Support Worksheet)	$	$
B. Weekly Reasonable Cost Threshold (Line A x .05)	$	$
SECTION TWO: DETERMINATION OF PRIVATE HEALTH INSURANCE AVAILABLE TO THE PARENTS		
C. Does the parent have private health insurance, for example, employer sponsored, available for the children? If the answer is **No** for a parent, **STOP** for that parent.	☐ YES ☐ NO	☐ YES ☐ NO
SECTION THREE: DETERMINATION OF WHETHER PREMIUM IS REASONABLE IN COST		
D. What is the weekly premium for the children's portion only?	$	$
E. TEST ONE: Is Amount on Line D equal to or less than the Amount on Line B? If the answer is **No** for a parent, **STOP** for that parent. If the answer is **Yes** for at least one parent, proceed to Line F for that parent(s).	☐ **YES** ⊲The premium may be reasonable in cost. ☐ **NO** ⊲The premium on Line D *is not* reasonable in cost.	☐ **YES** ⊲The premium may be reasonable in cost. ☐ **NO** ⊲The premium on Line D *is not* reasonable in cost.
F. TEST TWO: Is the parent's child support obligation from Line 4 of the Basic CSOW plus the weekly premium from Line D of the HIPW equal to or less than 50% of the Parent's Weekly Gross Income on Line A of the HIPW? Formula: Father: Line 4, CSOW ($_____) + Line D, HIPW, ($_____) = $_____ is equal to or less than Line A, HIPW $_____ X .5 = $_____ Mother: Line 4, CSOW ($_____) + Line D, HIPW, ($_____) = $_____ is equal to or less than Line A, HIPW $_____ X .5 = $_____	☐ **YES** ⊲The premium *is* reasonable in cost. Father may be ordered to provide health insurance. ☐ **NO** ⊲The premium on Line D *is not* reasonable in cost.	☐ **YES** ⊲The premium *is* reasonable in cost. Mother may be ordered to provide health insurance. ☐ **NO** ⊲The premium on Line D *is not* reasonable in cost.
SECTION FOUR: ACCESSIBILITY OF THE INSURANCE		
G. Is the insurance coverage accessible to the children? (See Guideline 7 for definition of accessible)	☐ YES ☐ NO	☐ YES ☐ NO
SECTION FIVE: PARENT(S) ORDERED TO PROVIDE HEALTH INSURANCE		
H. Parent(s) for whom health insurance is reasonable and accessible	☐ FATHER ☐ MOTHER	
I. Parent(s) ordered to provide health insurance for children.	☐ FATHER ☐ MOTHER TOTAL ORDERED:	$ $ $

Adopted Sept. 15, 2009, effective Jan. 1, 2010. Amended Dec. 18, 2009, effective Jan. 1, 2010.

Worksheet -- Post-Secondary Education (PSEW)
Worksheet – Child Support Obligation

IN RE:		CASE NO:		
		FATHER:		
		MOTHER:		

POST-SECONDARY EDUCATION WORKSHEET (PSEW)				
Child:		DOB		
SECTION ONE: DETERMINATION OF EDUCATION EXPENSE		**FATHER**	**MOTHER**	
A. Parents' Percentage Share of Total Weekly Adjusted Income From Line 2 of Child Support Worksheet		%	%	
B. Educational Costs:				
(1) Tuition				
(2) Room & Board				
(3) Books				
(4) Fees				
(5) Other				
TOTAL EDUCATIONAL COSTS (Part B – Lines 1-5)				
C. Child's Share of Costs				
(1) Scholarships				
(2) Grants in Aid				
(3) Student Loans				
(4) Child's Cash Share				
(5) Other				
TOTAL CREDITS (Part C – Line 1-5))				
D. Parents Total Obligations: Subtract Total Credits From Total Costs				
Parents' Share: Line A x Line D		$	$	
SECTION TWO: DETERMINATION OF SUPPORT WHILE STUDENT AT HOME				
E. Weeks Student Lives at Home _____ Divided by 52 =				%
F. Basic Child Support Obligation For All Children,. Including Student (Apply CWAI from Line 3 of Child Support Worksheet to Guideline Schedule)				
G. Basic Child Support Obligation for Children Living with Custodial Parent from Line 4 of Child Support Worksheet.; If student is only child, this amount is $0				
H. Weekly Child Support Obligation Attributable to Student Living Away From Home (Subtract Line G From Line F)				
I. Calculation of Support Obligation For Student (Multiply Line H ____ x Line E ____)				
J. Parent's Weekly Child Support Obligation: (Line A x Line I)		$	$	

Line J of section Two will be reflected in Section 7 of the Child Support Worksheet resulting in the Recommended Support Obligation.

Adopted May 27, 1998, effective July 1, 1998. Amended Sept. 10, 2003, effective Jan. 1, 2004.

Worksheet -- Parenting Time Credit
Worksheet – Child Support Obligation

IN RE:	CASE NO: FATHER: MOTHER:

PARENTING TIME CREDIT WORKSHEET

Children	DOB	Children	DOB

Line:		
1PT	Enter Annual Number of Overnights	
2PT	Enter Weekly Basic Child Support Obligation – BCSO (Enter Line 4 from Child Support Worksheet)	
3PT	Enter Total Parenting Time Expenses as a Percentage of the BCSO (Enter Appropriate TOTAL Entry from Table PT)	
4PT	Enter Duplicated Expenses as a Percentage of the BCSO (Enter Appropriate DUPLICATED Entry from Table PT)	
5PT	Parent's Share of Combined Weekly Income (Enter Line 2 from Child Support Worksheet)	
6PT	Average Weekly Total Expenses during Parenting Time (Multiply Line 2PT times Line 3PT)	
7PT	Average Weekly Duplicated Expenses (Multiply Line 2PT times Line 4PT)	
8PT	Parent's Share of Duplicated Expenses (Multiply Line 5PT times Line 7PT)	
9PT	Allowable Expenses during Parenting Time (Line 6PT – Line 8PT)	
	Enter Line 9PT on Line 7 of the Child Support Worksheet as the Parenting Time Credit	

Adopted effective March 1, 1993. Amended May 27, 1998, effective July 1, 1998; Sept. 10, 2003, effective Jan. 1, 2004.

State of Indiana Guideline Schedules for Weekly Support Payments

Guideline Schedules for Weekly Support Payments

Combined Weekly Adjusted Income	One Child	Two Children	Three Children	Four Children	Five Children	Six Children	Seven Children	Eight Children	Maximum Spouse and Child (50%)
100	12	18	22	24	25	27	29	31	50
110	14	20	25	27	28	31	33	35	55
120	16	23	27	30	32	34	37	40	60
130	18	25	30	33	35	38	41	44	65
140	20	28	33	36	38	41	45	48	70
150	22	30	35	39	41	45	48	52	75
160	24	33	38	42	45	48	52	56	80
170	26	35	41	45	48	52	56	60	85
180	28	38	43	47	51	56	60	64	90
190	30	40	46	50	54	59	64	68	95
200	32	43	49	53	58	63	68	72	100
210	34	45	51	56	61	66	71	76	105
220	36	48	54	59	64	70	75	80	110
230	39	50	57	62	67	73	79	85	115
240	41	53	59	65	71	77	83	89	120
250	43	55	62	68	74	80	87	93	125
260	45	58	65	71	77	84	90	97	130
270	47	60	67	74	80	88	94	101	135
280	49	63	70	77	84	91	98	105	140
290	51	65	73	80	87	95	102	109	145
300	56	71	79	86	93	101	109	117	150
310	61	77	85	92	99	108	116	124	155
320	66	83	91	98	105	114	123	132	160
330	68	89	97	104	111	121	130	139	165
340	71	95	103	110	117	127	137	147	170
350	73	101	109	116	123	134	144	154	175
360	74	107	115	122	129	140	151	162	180
370	75	113	121	128	135	147	158	169	185
380	77	116	127	134	141	153	165	177	190
390	78	117	133	140	147	160	172	184	195
400	79	119	139	146	153	166	179	192	200
410	81	122	145	152	159	173	186	199	205
420	82	123	151	158	165	179	193	207	210
430	83	125	156	164	171	186	200	214	215
440	84	126	158	170	177	192	207	220	220
450	86	129	161	176	183	199	214	225	225
460	87	131	164	182	189	206	222	230	230
470	88	132	165	186	195	212	229	235	235
480	89	134	168	189	201	219	236	240	240
490	91	137	171	192	204	222	239	245	245
500	92	138	173	195	207	225	243	250	250
510	93	140	175	197	209	227	245	255	255

1

271

Guideline Schedules for Weekly Support Payments

Combined Weekly Adjusted Income	One Child	Two Children	Three Children	Four Children	Five Children	Six Children	Seven Children	Eight Children	Maximum Spouse and Child (50%)
520	94	141	176	198	210	228	246	260	260
530	96	144	180	203	216	235	253	265	265
540	97	146	183	206	219	238	257	270	270
550	98	147	184	207	220	239	258	275	275
560	99	149	186	209	222	241	260	278	280
570	101	152	190	214	227	247	266	285	285
580	102	153	191	215	228	248	267	286	290
590	103	155	194	218	232	252	272	291	295
600	104	156	195	219	233	253	273	292	300
610	105	158	198	223	237	258	278	297	305
620	107	161	201	226	240	261	281	301	310
630	108	162	203	228	242	263	284	303	315
640	109	164	205	231	245	266	287	307	320
650	110	165	206	232	247	269	289	310	325
660	111	167	209	235	250	272	293	314	330
670	113	170	213	240	255	277	299	320	335
680	114	171	214	241	256	278	300	321	340
690	115	173	216	243	258	281	302	324	345
700	116	174	218	245	260	283	305	326	350
710	117	176	220	248	264	287	309	331	355
720	119	179	224	252	268	291	314	336	360
730	120	180	225	253	269	293	315	337	365
740	121	182	228	257	273	297	320	342	370
750	122	183	229	258	274	298	321	344	375
760	123	185	231	260	276	300	323	346	380
770	125	188	235	264	281	306	329	352	385
780	126	189	236	266	283	308	332	355	390
790	127	191	239	269	286	311	335	359	395
800	128	192	240	270	287	312	336	360	400
810	129	194	243	273	290	315	340	364	405
820	131	197	246	277	294	320	345	369	410
830	132	198	248	279	296	322	347	371	415
840	133	200	250	281	299	325	350	375	420
850	134	201	251	282	300	326	352	376	425
860	135	203	254	286	304	331	356	381	430
870	137	206	258	290	308	335	361	386	435
880	138	207	259	291	309	336	362	388	440
890	139	209	261	294	312	339	366	391	445
900	140	210	263	296	315	343	369	395	450
910	141	212	265	298	317	345	372	398	455
920	142	213	266	299	318	346	373	399	460
930	144	216	270	304	323	351	379	405	465

2

Guideline Schedules for Weekly Support Payments

Combined Weekly Adjusted Income	One Child	Two Children	Three Children	Four Children	Five Children	Six Children	Seven Children	Eight Children	Maximum Spouse and Child (50%)
940	145	218	273	307	326	355	382	409	470
950	146	219	274	308	327	356	383	410	475
960	147	221	276	311	330	359	387	414	480
970	148	222	278	313	333	362	390	418	485
980	149	224	280	315	335	364	393	420	490
990	151	227	284	320	340	370	398	426	495
1000	152	228	285	321	341	371	400	428	500
1010	153	230	288	324	344	374	403	431	505
1020	154	231	289	325	345	375	404	433	510
1030	155	233	291	327	347	377	407	435	515
1040	156	234	293	330	351	382	411	440	520
1050	158	237	296	333	354	385	415	444	525
1060	159	239	299	336	357	388	418	448	530
1070	160	240	300	338	359	390	421	450	535
1080	161	242	303	341	362	394	424	454	540
1090	162	243	304	342	363	395	425	455	545
1100	163	245	306	344	366	398	429	459	550
1110	165	248	310	349	371	403	435	465	555
1120	166	249	311	350	372	405	436	467	560
1130	167	251	314	353	375	408	440	470	565
1140	168	252	315	354	376	409	441	472	570
1150	169	254	318	358	380	413	445	477	575
1160	170	255	319	359	381	414	447	478	580
1170	172	258	323	363	386	420	452	484	585
1180	173	260	325	366	389	423	456	488	590
1190	174	261	326	367	390	424	457	489	595
1200	175	263	329	370	393	427	461	493	600
1210	176	264	330	371	394	428	462	494	605
1220	177	266	333	375	398	433	466	499	610
1230	179	269	336	378	402	437	471	504	615
1240	180	270	338	380	404	439	474	507	620
1250	181	272	340	383	407	443	477	510	625
1260	182	273	341	384	408	444	478	512	630
1270	183	275	344	387	411	447	482	515	635
1280	184	276	345	388	412	448	483	517	640
1290	186	279	349	393	418	455	490	524	645
1300	187	281	351	395	420	457	492	527	650
1310	188	282	353	397	422	459	495	529	655
1320	189	284	355	399	424	461	497	532	660
1330	190	285	356	401	426	463	499	534	665
1340	191	287	359	404	429	467	503	538	670
1350	193	290	363	408	434	472	509	544	675

3

Guideline Schedules for Weekly Support Payments

Combined Weekly Adjusted Income	One Child	Two Children	Three Children	Four Children	Five Children	Six Children	Seven Children	Eight Children	Maximum Spouse and Child (50%)
1360	194	291	364	410	436	474	511	547	680
1370	195	293	366	412	438	476	513	549	685
1380	196	294	368	414	440	478	516	552	690
1390	197	296	370	416	442	481	518	554	695
1400	198	297	371	417	443	482	519	556	700
1410	200	300	375	422	448	487	525	562	705
1420	201	302	378	425	452	492	530	567	710
1430	202	303	379	426	453	493	531	568	715
1440	203	305	381	429	456	496	534	572	720
1450	204	306	383	431	458	498	537	574	725
1460	205	308	385	433	460	500	539	577	730
1470	207	311	389	438	465	506	545	583	735
1480	208	312	390	439	466	507	546	584	740
1490	209	314	393	442	470	511	551	589	745
1500	210	315	394	443	471	512	552	591	750
1510	211	317	396	446	474	515	556	594	755
1520	212	318	398	448	476	518	558	597	760
1530	214	321	401	451	479	521	561	601	765
1540	215	323	404	455	483	525	566	606	770
1550	216	324	405	456	485	527	568	608	775
1560	217	326	408	459	488	531	572	612	780
1570	218	327	409	460	489	532	573	613	785
1580	219	329	411	462	491	534	575	616	790
1590	221	332	415	467	496	539	581	622	795
1600	222	333	416	468	497	540	583	623	800
1610	223	335	419	471	500	544	586	627	805
1620	224	336	420	473	503	547	590	631	810
1630	225	338	422	476	506	550	593	635	815
1640	226	339	424	477	507	551	594	636	820
1650	228	342	428	482	512	557	600	642	825
1660	229	344	430	484	514	559	602	645	830
1670	230	345	431	485	515	560	604	646	835
1680	231	347	434	488	519	564	608	651	840
1690	232	348	435	489	520	565	609	652	845
1700	233	350	438	493	524	570	614	657	850
1710	235	353	441	496	527	573	618	661	855
1720	236	354	443	498	529	575	620	663	860
1730	237	356	445	501	532	579	624	667	865
1740	238	357	446	502	533	580	625	668	870
1750	239	359	449	505	537	584	629	673	875
1760	240	360	450	506	538	585	631	675	880
1770	242	363	454	511	543	591	636	681	885

4

Guideline Schedules for Weekly Support Payments

Combined Weekly Adjusted Income	One Child	Two Children	Three Children	Four Children	Five Children	Six Children	Seven Children	Eight Children	Maximum Spouse and Child (50%)
1780	243	365	456	513	545	593	639	683	890
1790	244	366	458	515	547	595	641	686	895
1800	245	368	460	518	550	598	645	690	900
1810	246	369	461	519	551	599	646	691	905
1820	247	371	464	522	555	604	650	696	910
1830	249	374	468	527	560	609	656	702	915
1840	250	375	469	528	561	610	658	704	920
1850	251	377	471	530	563	612	660	706	925
1860	252	378	473	532	565	614	662	709	930
1870	253	380	475	534	567	617	665	711	935
1880	254	381	476	536	570	620	668	715	940
1890	256	384	480	540	574	624	673	720	945
1900	257	386	483	543	577	627	676	724	950
1910	258	387	484	545	579	630	679	726	955
1920	259	389	486	547	581	632	681	729	960
1930	260	390	488	549	583	634	683	731	965
1940	261	392	490	551	585	636	686	734	970
1950	263	395	494	556	591	643	693	741	975
1960	264	396	495	557	592	644	694	742	980
1970	265	398	498	560	595	647	697	746	985
1980	266	399	499	561	596	648	699	747	990
1990	267	401	501	564	599	651	702	751	995
2000	268	402	503	566	601	654	704	754	1000
2010	269	404	505	568	604	657	708	757	1005
2020	269	404	505	568	604	657	708	757	1010
2030	270	405	506	569	605	658	709	759	1015
2040	270	405	506	569	605	658	709	759	1020
2050	271	407	509	573	609	662	714	764	1025
2060	271	407	509	573	609	662	714	764	1030
2070	272	408	510	574	610	663	715	765	1035
2080	272	408	510	574	610	663	715	765	1040
2090	272	408	510	574	610	663	715	765	1045
2100	273	410	513	577	613	667	718	769	1050
2110	273	410	513	577	613	667	718	769	1055
2120	274	411	514	578	614	668	720	770	1060
2130	274	411	514	578	614	668	720	770	1065
2140	275	413	516	581	617	671	723	774	1070
2150	275	413	516	581	617	671	723	774	1075
2160	275	413	516	581	617	671	723	774	1080
2170	276	414	518	583	619	673	725	776	1085
2180	276	414	518	583	619	673	725	776	1090
2190	277	416	520	585	622	676	729	780	1095

5

Guideline Schedules for Weekly Support Payments

Combined Weekly Adjusted Income	One Child	Two Children	Three Children	Four Children	Five Children	Six Children	Seven Children	Eight Children	Maximum Spouse and Child (50%)
2200	277	416	520	585	622	676	729	780	1100
2210	277	416	520	585	622	676	729	780	1105
2220	278	417	521	586	623	677	730	781	1110
2230	278	417	521	586	623	677	730	781	1115
2240	279	419	524	590	627	682	735	786	1120
2250	279	419	524	590	627	682	735	786	1125
2260	279	419	524	590	627	682	735	786	1130
2270	280	420	525	591	628	683	736	788	1135
2280	280	420	525	591	628	683	736	788	1140
2290	281	422	525	594	631	686	740	791	1145
2300	281	422	528	594	631	686	740	791	1150
2310	281	422	528	594	631	686	740	791	1155
2320	282	423	529	595	632	687	741	793	1160
2330	282	423	529	595	632	687	741	793	1165
2340	283	425	531	597	634	689	743	795	1170
2350	283	425	531	597	634	689	743	795	1175
2360	283	425	531	597	634	689	743	795	1180
2370	284	426	533	600	638	694	748	800	1185
2380	284	426	533	600	638	694	748	800	1190
2390	284	426	533	600	638	694	748	800	1195
2400	285	428	535	602	640	696	750	803	1200
2410	285	428	535	602	640	696	750	803	1205
2420	286	429	536	603	641	697	751	804	1210
2430	286	429	536	603	641	697	751	804	1215
2440	286	429	536	603	641	697	751	804	1220
2450	287	431	539	606	644	700	755	808	1225
2460	287	431	539	606	644	700	755	808	1230
2470	287	431	539	606	644	700	755	808	1235
2480	288	432	540	608	646	703	757	810	1240
2490	288	432	540	608	646	703	757	810	1245
2500	288	432	540	608	646	703	757	810	1250
2510	289	434	543	611	649	706	761	814	1255
2520	289	434	543	611	649	706	761	814	1260
2530	289	434	543	611	649	706	761	814	1265
2540	290	435	544	612	650	707	762	815	1270
2550	290	435	544	612	650	707	762	815	1275
2560	291	437	546	614	652	709	764	818	1280
2570	291	437	546	614	652	709	764	818	1285
2580	291	437	546	614	652	709	764	818	1290
2590	292	438	548	617	656	713	769	823	1295
2600	292	438	548	617	656	713	769	823	1300
2610	292	438	548	617	656	713	769	823	1305

6

276

Guideline Schedules for Weekly Support Payments

Combined Weekly Adjusted Income	One Child	Two Children	Three Children	Four Children	Five Children	Six Children	Seven Children	Eight Children	Maximum Spouse and Child (50%)
2620	293	440	550	619	658	716	771	825	1310
2630	293	440	550	619	658	716	771	825	1315
2640	293	440	550	619	658	716	771	825	1320
2650	294	441	551	620	659	717	772	826	1325
2660	294	441	551	620	659	717	772	826	1330
2670	294	441	551	620	659	717	772	826	1335
2680	295	443	554	623	662	720	776	830	1340
2690	295	443	554	623	662	720	776	830	1345
2700	295	443	554	623	662	720	776	830	1350
2710	296	444	555	624	663	721	777	831	1355
2720	296	444	555	624	663	721	777	831	1360
2730	296	444	555	624	663	721	777	831	1365
2740	297	446	558	628	667	725	782	836	1370
2750	297	446	558	628	667	725	782	836	1375
2760	297	446	558	628	667	725	782	836	1380
2770	298	447	559	629	668	726	783	838	1385
2780	298	447	559	629	668	726	783	838	1390
2790	298	447	559	629	668	726	783	838	1395
2800	299	449	561	631	670	729	785	840	1400
2810	299	449	561	631	670	729	785	840	1405
2820	299	449	561	631	670	729	785	840	1410
2830	300	450	563	633	673	732	789	844	1415
2840	300	450	563	633	673	732	789	844	1420
2850	300	450	563	633	673	732	789	844	1425
2860	300	450	563	633	673	732	789	844	1430
2870	301	452	565	636	676	735	792	848	1435
2880	301	452	565	636	676	735	792	848	1440
2890	301	452	565	636	676	735	792	848	1445
2900	302	453	566	637	677	736	793	849	1450
2910	302	453	566	637	677	736	793	849	1455
2920	302	453	566	637	677	736	793	849	1460
2930	303	455	569	640	680	739	797	853	1465
2940	303	455	569	640	680	739	797	853	1470
2950	303	455	569	640	680	739	797	853	1475
2960	304	456	570	641	681	741	798	854	1480
2970	304	456	570	641	681	741	798	854	1485
2980	304	456	570	641	681	741	798	854	1490
2990	304	456	570	641	681	741	798	854	1495
3000	305	458	573	645	685	745	803	859	1500
3010	305	458	573	645	685	745	803	859	1505
3020	305	458	573	645	685	745	803	859	1510
3030	306	459	574	646	686	746	804	860	1515

7

Guideline Schedules for Weekly Support Payments

Combined Weekly Adjusted Income	One Child	Two Children	Three Children	Four Children	Five Children	Six Children	Seven Children	Eight Children	Maximum Spouse and Child (50%)
3040	306	459	574	646	686	746	804	860	1520
3050	306	459	574	646	686	746	804	860	1525
3060	306	459	574	647	686	746	804	860	1530
3070	307	461	576	648	689	749	808	864	1535
3080	307	461	576	648	689	749	808	864	1540
3090	307	461	576	648	689	749	808	864	1545
3100	308	462	578	650	691	751	810	867	1550
3110	308	462	578	650	691	751	810	867	1555
3120	308	462	578	650	691	751	810	867	1560
3130	309	464	580	653	694	755	813	870	1565
3140	309	464	580	653	694	755	813	870	1570
3150	309	464	580	653	694	755	813	870	1575
3160	309	464	580	653	694	755	813	870	1580
3170	310	465	581	654	695	756	815	872	1585
3180	310	465	581	654	695	756	815	872	1590
3190	310	465	581	654	695	756	815	872	1595
3200	310	465	581	654	695	756	815	872	1600
3210	311	467	584	657	698	759	818	875	1605
3220	311	467	584	657	698	759	818	875	1610
3230	311	467	584	657	698	759	818	875	1615
3240	312	468	585	658	699	760	819	877	1620
3250	312	468	585	658	699	760	819	877	1625
3260	312	468	585	658	699	760	819	877	1630
3270	312	468	585	658	699	760	819	877	1635
3280	313	470	588	662	703	764	824	882	1640
3290	313	470	588	662	703	764	824	882	1645
3300	313	470	588	662	703	764	824	882	1650
3310	314	471	589	663	704	766	825	883	1655
3320	314	471	589	663	704	766	825	883	1660
3330	314	471	589	663	704	766	825	883	1665
3340	314	471	589	663	704	766	825	883	1670
3350	315	473	591	665	707	769	829	887	1675
3360	315	473	591	665	707	769	829	887	1680
3370	315	473	591	665	707	769	829	887	1685
3380	315	473	591	665	707	769	829	887	1690
3390	316	474	593	667	709	771	831	889	1695
3400	316	474	593	667	709	771	831	889	1700
3410	316	474	593	667	709	771	831	889	1705
3420	316	474	593	667	709	771	831	889	1710
3430	317	476	595	669	711	773	833	892	1715
3440	317	476	595	669	711	773	833	892	1720
3450	317	476	595	669	711	773	833	892	1725

8

Guideline Schedules for Weekly Support Payments

Combined Weekly Adjusted Income	One Child	Two Children	Three Children	Four Children	Five Children	Six Children	Seven Children	Eight Children	Maximum Spouse and Child (50%)
3460	317	476	595	669	711	773	833	892	1730
3470	318	477	596	671	713	775	836	894	1735
3480	318	477	596	674	713	775	836	894	1740
3490	318	477	596	674	713	775	836	894	1745
3500	319	479	599	674	716	779	839	898	1750
3510	319	479	599	674	716	779	839	898	1755
3520	319	479	599	674	716	779	839	898	1760
3530	319	479	599	674	716	779	839	898	1765
3540	320	480	600	675	717	780	840	899	1770
3550	320	480	600	675	717	780	840	899	1775
3560	320	480	600	675	717	780	840	899	1780
3570	320	480	600	675	717	780	840	899	1785
3580	321	482	603	678	720	783	844	903	1790
3590	321	482	603	678	720	783	844	903	1795
3600	321	482	603	678	720	783	844	903	1800
3610	321	482	603	678	720	783	844	903	1805
3620	322	483	604	680	723	786	847	907	1810
3630	322	483	604	680	723	786	847	907	1815
3640	322	483	604	680	723	786	847	907	1820
3650	322	483	604	680	723	786	847	907	1825
3660	323	485	606	682	725	788	850	909	1830
3670	323	485	606	682	725	788	850	909	1835
3680	323	485	606	682	725	788	850	909	1840
3690	323	485	606	682	725	788	850	909	1845
3700	323	485	606	682	725	788	850	909	1850
3710	324	486	608	684	727	791	852	912	1855
3720	324	486	608	684	727	791	852	912	1860
3730	324	486	608	684	727	791	852	912	1865
3740	324	486	608	684	727	791	852	912	1870
3750	325	488	610	686	729	793	854	914	1875
3760	325	488	610	686	729	793	854	914	1880
3770	325	488	610	686	729	793	854	914	1885
3780	325	488	610	686	729	793	854	914	1890
3790	326	489	611	687	730	794	856	915	1895
3800	326	489	611	687	730	794	856	915	1900
3810	326	489	611	687	730	794	856	915	1905
3820	326	489	611	687	730	794	856	915	1910
3830	327	491	614	691	734	798	860	920	1915
3840	327	491	614	691	734	798	860	920	1920
3850	327	491	614	691	734	798	860	920	1925
3860	327	491	614	691	734	798	860	920	1930
3870	327	491	614	691	734	798	860	920	1935

9

Guideline Schedules for Weekly Support Payments

Combined Weekly Adjusted Income	One Child	Two Children	Three Children	Four Children	Five Children	Six Children	Seven Children	Eight Children	Maximum Spouse and Child (50%)
3880	328	492	615	692	735	799	861	922	1940
3890	328	492	615	692	735	799	861	922	1945
3900	328	492	615	692	735	799	861	922	1950
3910	328	492	615	692	735	799	861	922	1955
3920	329	494	618	695	738	803	865	925	1960
3930	329	494	618	695	738	803	865	925	1965
3940	329	494	618	695	738	803	865	925	1970
3950	329	494	618	695	738	803	865	925	1975
3960	330	495	619	696	740	805	867	928	1980
3970	330	495	619	696	740	805	867	928	1985
3980	330	495	619	696	740	805	867	928	1990
3990	330	495	619	696	740	805	867	928	1995
4000	330	495	619	696	740	805	867	928	2000
4010	331	496	620	697	741	806	868	929	2005
4020	332	497	620	697	742	807	869	930	2010
4030	332	498	621	698	743	808	870	931	2015
4040	333	499	621	698	744	809	871	932	2020
4050	334	499	622	699	744	810	873	934	2025
4060	335	500	622	699	745	811	874	935	2030
4070	336	501	623	700	746	812	875	936	2035
4080	337	502	623	701	747	812	876	937	2040
4090	337	503	624	701	748	813	877	938	2045
4100	338	504	625	702	749	814	878	939	2050
4110	339	505	625	702	750	815	879	940	2055
4120	340	506	626	703	751	816	880	941	2060
4130	341	507	626	704	752	817	881	943	2065
4140	342	508	627	704	752	818	882	944	2070
4150	342	508	627	705	753	819	883	945	2075
4160	343	509	628	705	754	820	884	946	2080
4170	344	510	629	706	755	821	885	947	2085
4180	345	511	629	706	756	822	886	948	2090
4190	346	512	630	707	757	823	887	949	2095
4200	347	513	630	708	758	824	888	950	2100
4210	347	514	631	708	759	825	889	951	2105
4220	348	515	631	709	760	826	890	953	2110
4230	349	516	632	709	760	827	891	954	2115
4240	350	517	632	710	761	828	892	955	2120
4250	351	517	633	710	762	829	893	956	2125
4260	351	518	634	711	763	830	894	957	2130
4270	352	519	634	712	764	831	896	958	2135
4280	353	520	635	712	765	832	897	959	2140
4290	354	521	635	713	766	833	898	960	2145

10

Guideline Schedules for Weekly Support Payments

Combined Weekly Adjusted Income	One Child	Two Children	Three Children	Four Children	Five Children	Six Children	Seven Children	Eight Children	Maximum Spouse and Child (50%)
4300	355	522	636	713	767	834	899	962	2150
4310	356	523	636	714	768	835	900	963	2155
4320	356	524	637	715	769	836	901	964	2160
4330	357	525	637	715	769	837	902	965	2165
4340	358	526	638	716	770	838	903	966	2170
4350	359	526	639	716	771	839	904	967	2175
4360	360	527	639	717	772	840	905	968	2180
4370	361	528	640	717	773	841	906	969	2185
4380	361	529	640	718	774	842	907	970	2190
4390	362	530	641	719	775	843	908	972	2195
4400	363	531	641	719	776	843	909	973	2200
4410	364	532	642	720	777	844	910	974	2205
4420	365	533	642	720	777	845	911	975	2210
4430	366	534	643	721	778	846	912	976	2215
4440	366	534	644	722	779	847	913	977	2220
4450	367	535	644	722	780	848	914	978	2225
4460	368	536	645	723	781	849	915	979	2230
4470	369	537	645	723	782	850	916	981	2235
4480	370	538	646	724	783	851	917	982	2240
4490	370	539	646	724	784	852	918	983	2245
4500	371	540	647	725	785	853	920	984	2250
4510	372	541	648	726	785	854	921	985	2255
4520	373	542	648	726	786	855	922	986	2260
4530	374	543	649	727	787	856	923	987	2265
4540	375	543	649	727	788	857	924	988	2270
4550	375	544	650	728	789	858	925	989	2275
4560	376	545	650	728	790	859	926	991	2280
4570	377	546	651	729	791	860	927	992	2285
4580	378	547	651	730	792	861	928	993	2290
4590	379	548	652	730	793	862	929	994	2295
4600	380	549	653	731	793	863	930	995	2300
4610	380	550	653	731	794	864	931	996	2305
4620	381	551	654	732	795	865	932	997	2310
4630	382	552	654	733	796	866	933	998	2315
4640	383	552	655	733	797	867	934	1000	2320
4650	384	553	655	734	798	868	935	1001	2325
4660	385	554	656	734	799	869	936	1002	2330
4670	385	555	656	735	800	870	937	1003	2335
4680	386	556	657	735	801	871	938	1004	2340
4690	387	557	658	736	801	872	939	1005	2345
4700	388	558	658	737	802	873	940	1006	2350
4710	389	559	659	737	803	874	941	1007	2355

11

Guideline Schedules for Weekly Support Payments

Combined Weekly Adjusted Income	One Child	Two Children	Three Children	Four Children	Five Children	Six Children	Seven Children	Eight Children	Maximum Spouse and Child (50%)
5140	420	594	685	765	842	915	986	1055	2570
5150	420	595	686	766	842	916	987	1056	2575
5160	420	595	686	767	843	917	988	1057	2580
5170	421	596	687	767	844	918	989	1058	2585
5180	421	596	688	768	845	919	990	1059	2590
5190	422	597	688	769	846	920	991	1061	2595
5200	422	598	689	770	846	921	992	1062	2600
5210	423	598	690	770	847	921	993	1063	2605
5220	423	599	690	771	848	922	994	1064	2610
5230	423	599	691	772	849	923	995	1065	2615
5240	424	600	692	773	850	924	996	1066	2620
5250	424	601	692	773	851	925	997	1067	2625
5260	425	601	693	774	851	926	998	1068	2630
5270	425	602	694	775	852	927	999	1069	2635
5280	426	602	694	776	853	928	1000	1070	2640
5290	426	603	695	776	854	929	1001	1071	2645
5300	426	604	696	777	855	930	1002	1072	2650
5310	427	604	696	778	856	930	1003	1073	2655
5320	427	605	697	779	856	931	1004	1074	2660
5330	428	605	698	779	857	932	1005	1075	2665
5340	428	606	698	780	858	933	1006	1076	2670
5350	429	607	699	781	859	934	1007	1077	2675
5360	429	607	700	782	860	935	1008	1078	2680
5370	429	608	700	782	861	936	1009	1079	2685
5380	430	608	701	783	861	937	1010	1080	2690
5390	430	609	702	784	862	938	1010	1081	2695
5400	431	610	702	785	863	938	1011	1082	2700
5410	431	610	703	785	864	939	1012	1083	2705
5420	432	611	704	786	865	940	1013	1084	2710
5430	432	611	704	787	865	941	1014	1085	2715
5440	432	612	705	788	866	942	1015	1086	2720
5450	433	613	706	788	867	943	1016	1087	2725
5460	433	613	706	789	868	944	1017	1088	2730
5470	434	614	707	790	869	945	1018	1089	2735
5480	434	614	708	791	870	946	1019	1091	2740
5490	435	615	708	791	870	947	1020	1092	2745
5500	435	615	709	792	871	947	1021	1093	2750
5510	436	616	710	793	872	948	1022	1094	2755
5520	436	617	710	794	873	949	1023	1095	2760
5530	436	617	711	794	874	950	1024	1096	2765
5540	437	618	712	795	875	951	1025	1097	2770
5550	437	618	712	796	875	952	1026	1098	2775

13

Guideline Schedules for Weekly Support Payments

Combined Weekly Adjusted Income	One Child	Two Children	Three Children	Four Children	Five Children	Six Children	Seven Children	Eight Children	Maximum Spouse and Child (50%)
5560	438	619	713	797	876	953	1027	1099	2780
5570	438	620	714	797	877	954	1028	1100	2785
5580	439	620	714	798	878	955	1029	1101	2790
5590	439	621	715	799	879	956	1030	1102	2795
5600	439	621	716	800	879	956	1031	1103	2800
5610	440	622	716	800	880	957	1032	1104	2805
5620	440	623	717	801	881	958	1033	1105	2810
5630	441	623	718	802	882	959	1034	1106	2815
5640	441	624	718	803	883	960	1035	1107	2820
5650	442	624	719	803	884	961	1036	1108	2825
5660	442	625	720	804	884	962	1037	1109	2830
5670	442	626	720	805	885	963	1038	1110	2835
5680	443	626	721	806	886	964	1039	1111	2840
5690	443	627	722	806	887	964	1039	1112	2845
5700	444	627	723	807	888	965	1040	1113	2850
5710	444	628	723	808	889	966	1041	1114	2855
5720	445	629	724	809	889	967	1042	1115	2860
5730	445	629	725	809	890	968	1043	1116	2865
5740	445	630	725	810	891	969	1044	1117	2870
5750	446	630	726	811	892	970	1045	1118	2875
5760	446	631	727	812	893	971	1046	1119	2880
5770	447	632	727	812	894	972	1047	1121	2885
5780	447	632	728	813	894	973	1048	1122	2890
5790	448	633	729	814	895	973	1049	1123	2895
5800	448	633	729	815	896	974	1050	1124	2900
5810	448	634	730	815	897	975	1051	1125	2905
5820	449	635	731	816	898	976	1052	1126	2910
5830	449	635	731	817	898	977	1053	1127	2915
5840	450	636	732	818	899	978	1054	1128	2920
5850	450	636	733	818	900	979	1055	1129	2925
5860	451	637	733	819	901	980	1056	1130	2930
5870	451	638	734	820	902	981	1057	1131	2935
5880	452	638	735	821	903	982	1058	1132	2940
5890	452	639	735	821	903	982	1059	1133	2945
5900	452	639	736	822	904	983	1060	1134	2950
5910	453	640	737	823	905	984	1061	1135	2955
5920	453	641	737	824	906	985	1062	1136	2960
5930	454	641	738	824	907	986	1063	1137	2965
5940	454	642	739	825	908	987	1064	1138	2970
5950	455	642	739	826	908	988	1065	1139	2975
5960	455	643	740	827	909	989	1066	1140	2980
5970	455	644	741	827	910	990	1067	1141	2985

14

Guideline Schedules for Weekly Support Payments

Combined Weekly Adjusted Income	One Child	Two Children	Three Children	Four Children	Five Children	Six Children	Seven Children	Eight Children	Maximum Spouse and Child (50%)
5980	456	644	741	828	911	991	1068	1142	2990
5990	456	645	742	829	912	991	1068	1143	2995
6000	457	645	743	830	912	992	1069	1144	3000
6010	457	646	743	830	913	993	1070	1145	3005
6020	458	647	744	831	914	994	1071	1146	3010
6030	458	647	745	832	915	995	1072	1147	3015
6040	458	648	745	833	916	996	1073	1148	3020
6050	459	648	746	833	917	997	1074	1149	3025
6060	459	649	747	834	917	998	1075	1151	3030
6070	460	650	747	835	918	999	1076	1152	3035
6080	460	650	748	836	919	999	1077	1153	3040
6090	461	651	749	836	920	1000	1078	1154	3045
6100	461	651	749	837	921	1001	1079	1155	3050
6110	461	652	750	838	922	1002	1080	1156	3055
6120	462	653	751	839	922	1003	1081	1157	3060
6130	462	653	751	839	923	1004	1082	1158	3065
6140	463	654	752	840	924	1005	1083	1159	3070
6150	463	654	753	841	925	1006	1084	1160	3075
6160	464	655	753	842	926	1007	1085	1161	3080
6170	464	656	754	842	927	1008	1086	1162	3085
6180	464	656	755	843	927	1008	1087	1163	3090
6190	465	657	755	844	928	1009	1088	1164	3095
6200	465	657	756	845	929	1010	1089	1165	3100
6210	466	658	757	845	930	1011	1090	1166	3105
6220	466	658	757	846	931	1012	1091	1167	3110
6230	467	659	758	847	931	1013	1092	1168	3115
6240	467	660	759	848	932	1014	1093	1169	3120
6250	468	660	759	848	933	1015	1094	1170	3125
6260	468	661	760	849	934	1016	1095	1171	3130
6270	468	661	761	850	935	1017	1096	1172	3135
6280	469	662	761	851	936	1017	1097	1173	3140
6290	469	663	762	851	936	1018	1098	1174	3145
6300	470	663	763	852	937	1019	1098	1175	3150
6310	470	664	763	853	938	1020	1099	1176	3155
6320	471	664	764	854	939	1021	1100	1177	3160
6330	471	665	765	854	940	1022	1101	1178	3165
6340	471	666	765	855	941	1023	1102	1179	3170
6350	472	666	766	856	941	1024	1103	1181	3175
6360	472	667	767	857	942	1025	1104	1182	3180
6370	473	667	767	857	943	1025	1105	1183	3185
6380	473	668	768	858	944	1026	1106	1184	3190
6390	474	669	769	859	945	1027	1107	1185	3195

15

Guideline Schedules for Weekly Support Payments

Combined Weekly Adjusted Income	One Child	Two Children	Three Children	Four Children	Five Children	Six Children	Seven Children	Eight Children	Maximum Spouse and Child (50%)
6400	474	669	769	860	945	1028	1108	1186	3200
6410	474	670	770	860	946	1029	1109	1187	3205
6420	475	670	771	861	947	1030	1110	1188	3210
6430	475	671	772	862	948	1031	1111	1189	3215
6440	476	672	772	863	949	1032	1112	1190	3220
6450	476	672	773	863	950	1033	1113	1191	3225
6460	477	673	774	864	950	1034	1114	1192	3230
6470	477	673	774	865	951	1034	1115	1193	3235
6480	477	674	775	866	952	1035	1116	1194	3240
6490	478	675	776	866	953	1036	1117	1195	3245
6500	478	675	776	867	954	1037	1118	1196	3250
6510	479	676	777	868	955	1038	1119	1197	3255
6520	479	676	778	869	955	1039	1120	1198	3260
6530	480	677	778	869	956	1040	1121	1199	3265
6540	480	678	779	870	957	1041	1122	1200	3270
6550	481	678	780	871	958	1042	1123	1201	3275
6560	481	679	780	872	959	1043	1124	1202	3280
6570	481	679	781	872	960	1043	1125	1203	3285
6580	482	680	782	873	960	1044	1126	1204	3290
6590	482	681	782	874	961	1045	1127	1205	3295
6600	483	681	783	875	962	1046	1127	1206	3300
6610	483	682	784	875	963	1047	1128	1207	3305
6620	484	682	784	876	964	1048	1129	1208	3310
6630	484	683	785	877	964	1049	1130	1209	3315
6640	484	684	786	878	965	1050	1131	1211	3320
6650	485	684	786	878	966	1051	1132	1212	3325
6660	485	685	787	879	967	1052	1133	1213	3330
6670	486	685	788	880	968	1052	1134	1214	3335
6680	486	686	788	881	969	1053	1135	1215	3340
6690	487	687	789	881	969	1054	1136	1216	3345
6700	487	687	790	882	970	1055	1137	1217	3350
6710	487	688	790	883	971	1056	1138	1218	3355
6720	488	688	791	884	972	1057	1139	1219	3360
6730	488	689	792	884	973	1058	1140	1220	3365
6740	489	690	792	885	974	1059	1141	1221	3370
6750	489	690	793	886	974	1060	1142	1222	3375
6760	490	691	794	887	975	1060	1143	1223	3380
6770	490	691	794	887	976	1061	1144	1224	3385
6780	490	692	795	888	977	1062	1145	1225	3390
6790	491	693	796	889	978	1063	1146	1226	3395
6800	491	693	796	890	978	1064	1147	1227	3400
6810	492	694	797	890	979	1065	1148	1228	3405

16

Guideline Schedules for Weekly Support Payments

Combined Weekly Adjusted Income	One Child	Two Children	Three Children	Four Children	Five Children	Six Children	Seven Children	Eight Children	Maximum Spouse and Child (50%)
6820	492	694	798	891	980	1066	1149	1229	3410
6830	493	695	798	892	981	1067	1150	1230	3415
6840	493	696	799	893	982	1068	1151	1231	3420
6850	493	696	800	893	983	1069	1152	1232	3425
6860	494	697	800	894	983	1069	1153	1233	3430
6870	494	697	801	895	984	1070	1154	1234	3435
6880	495	698	802	896	985	1071	1155	1235	3440
6890	495	699	802	896	986	1072	1156	1236	3445
6900	496	699	803	897	987	1073	1156	1237	3450
6910	496	700	804	898	988	1074	1157	1238	3455
6920	497	700	804	899	988	1075	1158	1239	3460
6930	497	701	805	899	989	1076	1159	1241	3465
6940	497	702	806	900	990	1077	1160	1242	3470
6950	498	702	806	901	991	1078	1161	1243	3475
6960	498	703	807	902	992	1078	1162	1244	3480
6970	499	703	808	902	993	1079	1163	1245	3485
6980	499	704	808	903	993	1080	1164	1246	3490
6990	500	704	809	904	994	1081	1165	1247	3495
7000	500	705	810	905	995	1082	1166	1248	3500
7010	521	734	842	941	1035	1125	1213	1298	3505
7020	521	734	843	941	1035	1126	1214	1299	3510
7030	522	735	843	942	1036	1127	1215	1300	3515
7040	522	736	844	943	1037	1128	1216	1301	3520
7050	523	736	845	944	1038	1129	1217	1302	3525
7060	523	737	845	944	1039	1130	1217	1303	3530
7070	523	737	846	945	1040	1131	1218	1304	3535
7080	524	738	847	946	1040	1131	1219	1305	3540
7090	524	739	848	947	1042	1133	1221	1306	3545
7100	525	740	849	948	1043	1134	1222	1308	3550
7110	526	741	850	949	1044	1136	1224	1310	3555
7120	526	742	851	951	1046	1137	1225	1311	3560
7130	527	743	852	952	1047	1138	1227	1313	3565
7140	528	744	853	953	1048	1140	1229	1315	3570
7150	528	744	854	954	1050	1141	1230	1316	3575
7160	529	745	855	955	1051	1143	1232	1318	3580
7170	530	746	856	957	1052	1144	1233	1319	3585
7180	530	747	857	958	1053	1146	1235	1321	3590
7190	531	748	858	959	1055	1147	1236	1323	3595
7200	532	749	860	960	1056	1148	1238	1324	3600
7210	532	750	861	961	1057	1150	1239	1326	3605
7220	533	751	862	962	1059	1151	1241	1328	3610
7230	534	752	863	964	1060	1153	1242	1329	3615

17

287

Guideline Schedules for Weekly Support Payments

Combined Weekly Adjusted Income	One Child	Two Children	Three Children	Four Children	Five Children	Six Children	Seven Children	Eight Children	Maximum Spouse and Child (50%)
7240	534	753	864	965	1061	1154	1244	1331	3620
7250	535	754	865	966	1063	1156	1246	1333	3625
7260	536	755	866	967	1064	1157	1247	1334	3630
7270	536	756	867	968	1065	1159	1249	1336	3635
7280	537	757	868	970	1067	1160	1250	1338	3640
7290	538	758	869	971	1068	1161	1252	1339	3645
7300	538	758	870	972	1069	1163	1253	1341	3650
7310	539	759	871	973	1071	1164	1255	1343	3655
7320	540	760	872	974	1072	1166	1256	1344	3660
7330	540	761	873	976	1073	1167	1258	1346	3665
7340	541	762	875	977	1075	1169	1259	1348	3670
7350	542	763	876	978	1076	1170	1261	1349	3675
7360	542	764	877	979	1077	1171	1262	1351	3680
7370	543	765	878	980	1078	1173	1264	1352	3685
7380	544	766	879	982	1080	1174	1266	1354	3690
7390	544	767	880	983	1081	1176	1267	1356	3695
7400	545	768	881	984	1082	1177	1269	1357	3700
7410	546	769	882	985	1084	1179	1270	1359	3705
7420	546	770	883	986	1085	1180	1272	1361	3710
7430	547	771	884	988	1086	1181	1273	1362	3715
7440	548	772	885	989	1088	1183	1275	1364	3720
7450	548	772	886	990	1089	1184	1276	1366	3725
7460	549	773	887	991	1090	1186	1278	1367	3730
7470	550	774	888	992	1092	1187	1279	1369	3735
7480	550	775	890	994	1093	1189	1281	1371	3740
7490	551	776	891	995	1094	1190	1283	1372	3745
7500	552	777	892	996	1096	1191	1284	1374	3750
7510	552	778	893	997	1097	1193	1286	1376	3755
7520	553	779	894	998	1098	1194	1287	1377	3760
7530	554	780	895	1000	1100	1196	1289	1379	3765
7540	554	781	896	1001	1101	1197	1290	1381	3770
7550	555	782	897	1002	1102	1199	1292	1382	3775
7560	556	783	898	1003	1104	1200	1293	1384	3780
7570	556	784	899	1004	1105	1201	1295	1386	3785
7580	557	785	900	1006	1106	1203	1296	1387	3790
7590	558	786	901	1007	1107	1204	1298	1389	3795
7600	558	786	902	1008	1109	1206	1300	1390	3800
7610	559	787	903	1009	1110	1207	1301	1392	3805
7620	560	788	905	1010	1111	1209	1303	1394	3810
7630	560	789	906	1012	1113	1210	1304	1395	3815
7640	561	790	907	1013	1114	1211	1306	1397	3820
7650	562	791	908	1014	1115	1213	1307	1399	3825

18

Guideline Schedules for Weekly Support Payments

Combined Weekly Adjusted Income	One Child	Two Children	Three Children	Four Children	Five Children	Six Children	Seven Children	Eight Children	Maximum Spouse and Child (50%)
7660	562	792	909	1015	1117	1214	1309	1400	3830
7670	563	793	910	1016	1118	1216	1310	1402	3835
7680	564	794	911	1018	1119	1217	1312	1404	3840
7690	564	795	912	1019	1121	1219	1313	1405	3845
7700	565	796	913	1020	1122	1220	1315	1407	3850
7710	566	797	914	1021	1123	1222	1317	1409	3855
7720	566	798	915	1022	1125	1223	1318	1410	3860
7730	567	799	916	1024	1126	1224	1320	1412	3865
7740	567	800	917	1025	1127	1226	1321	1414	3870
7750	568	800	918	1026	1129	1227	1323	1415	3875
7760	569	801	920	1027	1130	1229	1324	1417	3880
7770	569	802	921	1028	1131	1230	1326	1419	3885
7780	570	803	922	1030	1132	1232	1327	1420	3890
7790	571	804	923	1031	1134	1233	1329	1422	3895
7800	571	805	924	1032	1135	1234	1330	1423	3900
7810	572	806	925	1033	1136	1236	1332	1425	3905
7820	573	807	926	1034	1138	1237	1333	1427	3910
7830	573	808	927	1035	1139	1238	1335	1428	3915
7840	574	809	928	1036	1140	1240	1336	1430	3920
7850	575	810	929	1038	1141	1241	1338	1431	3925
7860	575	811	930	1039	1143	1243	1339	1433	3930
7870	576	811	931	1040	1144	1244	1341	1435	3935
7880	577	812	932	1041	1145	1245	1342	1436	3940
7890	577	813	933	1042	1147	1247	1344	1438	3945
7900	578	814	934	1043	1148	1248	1345	1439	3950
7910	578	815	935	1045	1149	1250	1347	1441	3955
7920	579	816	936	1046	1150	1251	1348	1443	3960
7930	580	817	937	1047	1152	1252	1350	1444	3965
7940	580	818	938	1048	1153	1254	1351	1446	3970
7950	581	819	939	1049	1154	1255	1353	1447	3975
7960	582	820	940	1050	1155	1256	1354	1449	3980
7970	582	820	941	1052	1157	1258	1356	1451	3985
7980	583	821	942	1053	1158	1259	1357	1452	3990
7990	584	822	943	1054	1159	1261	1359	1454	3995
8000	584	823	945	1055	1161	1262	1360	1455	4000
8010	585	824	946	1056	1162	1263	1362	1457	4005
8020	586	825	947	1057	1163	1265	1363	1459	4010
8030	586	826	948	1058	1164	1266	1365	1460	4015
8040	587	827	949	1060	1166	1268	1366	1462	4020
8050	587	828	950	1061	1167	1269	1368	1463	4025
8060	588	829	951	1062	1168	1270	1369	1465	4030
8070	589	830	952	1063	1169	1272	1371	1467	4035

19

289

Guideline Schedules for Weekly Support Payments

Combined Weekly Adjusted Income	One Child	Two Children	Three Children	Four Children	Five Children	Six Children	Seven Children	Eight Children	Maximum Spouse and Child (50%)
8080	589	830	953	1064	1171	1273	1372	1468	4040
8090	590	831	954	1065	1172	1275	1374	1470	4045
8100	591	832	955	1067	1173	1276	1375	1471	4050
8110	591	833	956	1068	1175	1277	1377	1473	4055
8120	592	834	957	1069	1176	1279	1378	1475	4060
8130	593	835	958	1070	1177	1280	1380	1476	4065
8140	593	836	959	1071	1178	1281	1381	1478	4070
8150	594	837	960	1072	1180	1283	1383	1479	4075
8160	595	838	961	1074	1181	1284	1384	1481	4080
8170	595	839	962	1075	1182	1286	1386	1483	4085
8180	596	839	963	1076	1183	1287	1387	1484	4090
8190	596	840	964	1077	1185	1288	1389	1486	4095
8200	597	841	965	1078	1186	1290	1390	1487·	4100
8210	598	842	966	1079	1187	1291	1392	1489	4105
8220	598	843	967	1080	1189	1293	1393	1490	4110
8230	599	844	968	1082	1190	1294	1394	1492	4115
8240	600	845	969	1083	1191	1295	1396	1494	4120
8250	600	846	970	1084	1192	1297	1397	1495	4125
8260	601	847	971	1085	1194	1298	1399	1497	4130
8270	602	848	972	1086	1195	1299	1400	1498	4135
8280	602	848	974	1087	1196	1301	1402	1500	4140
8290	603	849	975	1089	1197	1302	1403	1502	4145
8300	603	850	976	1090	1199	1304	1405	1503	4150
8310	604	851	977	1091	1200	1305	1406	1505	4155
8320	605	852	978	1092	1201	1306	1408	1506	4160
8330	605	853	979	1093	1203	1308	1409	1508	4165
8340	606	854	980	1094	1204	1309	1411	1510	4170
8350	607	855	981	1096	1205	1311	1412	1511	4175
8360	607	856	982	1097	1206	1312	1414	1513	4180
8370	608	857	983	1098	1208	1313	1415	1514	4185
8380	609	858	984	1099	1209	1315	1417	1516	4190
8390	609	858	985	1100	1210	1316	1418	1518	4195
8400	610	859	986	1101	1211	1317	1420	1519	4200
8410	611	860	987	1102	1213	1319	1421	1521	4205
8420	611	861	988	1104	1214	1320	1423	1522	4210
8430	612	862	989	1105	1215	1322	1424	1524	4215
8440	612	863	990	1106	1217	1323	1426	1526	4220
8450	613	864	991	1107	1218	1324	1427	1527	4225
8460	614	865	992	1108	1219	1326	1429	1529	4230
8470	614	866	993	1109	1220	1327	1430	1530	4235
8480	615	867	994	1111	1222	1329	1432	1532	4240
8490	616	867	995	1112	1223	1330	1433	1534	4245

20

Guideline Schedules for Weekly Support Payments

Combined Weekly Adjusted Income	One Child	Two Children	Three Children	Four Children	Five Children	Six Children	Seven Children	Eight Children	Maximum Spouse and Child (50%)
8500	616	868	996	1113	1224	1331	1435	1535	4250
8510	617	869	997	1114	1225	1333	1436	1537	4255
8520	618	870	998	1115	1227	1334	1438	1538	4260
8530	618	871	999	1116	1228	1335	1439	1540	4265
8540	619	872	1000	1118	1229	1337	1441	1542	4270
8550	620	873	1002	1119	1231	1338	1442	1543	4275
8560	620	874	1003	1120	1232	1340	1444	1545	4280
8570	621	875	1004	1121	1233	1341	1445	1546	4285
8580	621	876	1005	1122	1234	1342	1447	1548	4290
8590	622	876	1006	1123	1236	1344	1448	1550	4295
8600	623	877	1007	1124	1237	1345	1450	1551	4300
8610	623	878	1008	1126	1238	1347	1451	1553	4305
8620	624	879	1009	1127	1239	1348	1453	1554	4310
8630	625	880	1010	1128	1241	1349	1454	1556	4315
8640	625	881	1011	1129	1242	1351	1456	1558	4320
8650	626	882	1012	1130	1243	1352	1457	1559	4325
8660	627	883	1013	1131	1245	1353	1459	1561	4330
8670	627	884	1014	1133	1246	1355	1460	1562	4335
8680	628	885	1015	1134	1247	1356	1462	1564	4340
8690	629	886	1016	1135	1248	1358	1463	1566	4345
8700	629	886	1017	1136	1250	1359	1465	1567	4350
8710	630	887	1018	1137	1251	1360	1466	1569	4355
8720	630	888	1019	1138	1252	1362	1468	1570	4360
8730	631	889	1020	1140	1253	1363	1469	1572	4365
8740	632	890	1021	1141	1255	1365	1471	1574	4370
8750	632	891	1022	1142	1256	1366	1472	1575	4375
8760	633	892	1023	1143	1257	1367	1474	1577	4380
8770	634	893	1024	1144	1259	1369	1475	1578	4385
8780	634	894	1025	1145	1260	1370	1477	1580	4390
8790	635	895	1026	1146	1261	1371	1478	1582	4395
8800	636	895	1027	1148	1262	1373	1480	1583	4400
8810	636	896	1028	1149	1264	1374	1481	1585	4405
8820	637	897	1030	1150	1265	1376	1483	1586	4410
8830	637	898	1031	1151	1266	1377	1484	1588	4415
8840	638	899	1032	1152	1267	1378	1486	1590	4420
8850	639	900	1033	1153	1269	1380	1487	1591	4425
8860	639	901	1034	1155	1270	1381	1489	1593	4430
8870	640	902	1035	1156	1271	1383	1490	1594	4435
8880	641	903	1036	1157	1273	1384	1492	1596	4440
8890	641	904	1037	1158	1274	1385	1493	1597	4445
8900	642	904	1038	1159	1275	1387	1495	1599	4450
8910	643	905	1039	1160	1276	1388	1496	1601	4455

21

Guideline Schedules for Weekly Support Payments

Combined Weekly Adjusted Income	One Child	Two Children	Three Children	Four Children	Five Children	Six Children	Seven Children	Eight Children	Maximum Spouse and Child (50%)
8920	643	906	1040	1162	1278	1389	1497	1602	4460
8930	644	907	1041	1163	1279	1391	1499	1604	4465
8940	645	908	1042	1164	1280	1392	1500	1605	4470
8950	645	909	1043	1165	1282	1394	1502	1607	4475
8960	646	910	1044	1166	1283	1395	1503	1609	4480
8970	646	911	1045	1167	1284	1396	1505	1610	4485
8980	647	912	1046	1168	1285	1398	1506	1612	4490
8990	648	913	1047	1170	1287	1399	1508	1613	4495
9000	648	914	1048	1171	1288	1401	1509	1615	4500
9010	649	914	1049	1172	1289	1402	1511	1617	4505
9020	650	915	1050	1173	1290	1403	1512	1618	4510
9030	650	916	1051	1174	1292	1405	1514	1620	4515
9040	651	917	1052	1175	1293	1406	1515	1621	4520
9050	652	918	1053	1177	1294	1407	1517	1623	4525
9060	652	919	1054	1178	1296	1409	1518	1625	4530
9070	653	920	1055	1179	1297	1410	1520	1626	4535
9080	654	921	1056	1180	1298	1412	1521	1628	4540
9090	654	922	1057	1181	1299	1413	1523	1629	4545
9100	655	923	1059	1182	1301	1414	1524	1631	4550
9110	655	923	1060	1184	1302	1416	1526	1633	4555
9120	656	924	1061	1185	1303	1417	1527	1634	4560
9130	657	925	1062	1186	1304	1419	1529	1636	4565
9140	657	926	1063	1187	1306	1420	1530	1637	4570
9150	658	927	1064	1188	1307	1421	1532	1639	4575
9160	659	928	1065	1189	1308	1423	1533	1641	4580
9170	659	929	1066	1190	1310	1424	1535	1642	4585
9180	660	930	1067	1192	1311	1425	1536	1644	4590
9190	661	931	1068	1193	1312	1427	1538	1645	4595
9200	661	932	1069	1194	1313	1428	1539	1647	4600
9210	662	932	1070	1195	1315	1430	1541	1649	4605
9220	662	933	1071	1196	1316	1431	1542	1650	4610
9230	663	934	1072	1197	1317	1432	1544	1652	4615
9240	664	935	1073	1199	1318	1434	1545	1653	4620
9250	664	936	1074	1200	1320	1435	1547	1655	4625
9260	665	937	1075	1201	1321	1437	1548	1657	4630
9270	666	938	1076	1202	1322	1438	1550	1658	4635
9280	666	939	1077	1203	1324	1439	1551	1660	4640
9290	667	940	1078	1204	1325	1441	1553	1661	4645
9300	668	941	1079	1206	1326	1442	1554	1663	4650
9310	668	942	1080	1207	1327	1443	1556	1665	4655
9320	669	942	1081	1208	1329	1445	1557	1666	4660
9330	670	943	1082	1209	1330	1446	1559	1668	4665

22

Guideline Schedules for Weekly Support Payments

Combined Weekly Adjusted Income	One Child	Two Children	Three Children	Four Children	Five Children	Six Children	Seven Children	Eight Children	Maximum Spouse and Child (50%)
9340	670	944	1083	1210	1331	1448	1560	1669	4670
9350	671	945	1084	1211	1332	1449	1562	1671	4675
9360	671	946	1085	1212	1334	1450	1563	1673	4680
9370	672	947	1087	1214	1335	1452	1565	1674	4685
9380	673	948	1088	1215	1336	1453	1566	1676	4690
9390	673	949	1089	1216	1338	1455	1568	1677	4695
9400	674	950	1090	1217	1339	1456	1569	1679	4700
9410	675	951	1091	1218	1340	1457	1571	1681	4705
9420	675	951	1092	1219	1341	1459	1572	1682	4710
9430	676	952	1093	1221	1343	1460	1574	1684	4715
9440	677	953	1094	1222	1344	1461	1575	1685	4720
9450	677	954	1095	1223	1345	1463	1577	1687	4725
9460	678	955	1096	1224	1346	1464	1578	1689	4730
9470	679	956	1097	1225	1348	1466	1580	1690	4735
9480	679	957	1098	1226	1349	1467	1581	1692	4740
9490	680	958	1099	1228	1350	1468	1583	1693	4745
9500	680	959	1100	1229	1352	1470	1584	1695	4750
9510	681	960	1101	1230	1353	1471	1586	1697	4755
9520	682	960	1102	1231	1354	1473	1587	1698	4760
9530	682	961	1103	1232	1355	1474	1589	1700	4765
9540	683	962	1104	1233	1357	1475	1590	1701	4770
9550	684	963	1105	1234	1358	1477	1592	1703	4775
9560	684	964	1106	1236	1359	1478	1593	1704	4780
9570	685	965	1107	1237	1360	1479	1595	1706	4785
9580	686	966	1108	1238	1362	1481	1596	1708	4790
9590	686	967	1109	1239	1363	1482	1597	1709	4795
9600	687	968	1110	1240	1364	1484	1599	1711	4800
9610	687	969	1111	1241	1366	1485	1600	1712	4805
9620	688	970	1112	1243	1367	1486	1602	1714	4810
9630	689	970	1113	1244	1368	1488	1603	1716	4815
9640	689	971	1114	1245	1369	1489	1605	1717	4820
9650	690	972	1116	1246	1371	1491	1606	1719	4825
9660	691	973	1117	1247	1372	1492	1608	1720	4830
9670	691	974	1118	1248	1373	1493	1609	1722	4835
9680	692	975	1119	1250	1374	1495	1611	1724	4840
9690	693	976	1120	1251	1376	1496	1612	1725	4845
9700	693	977	1121	1252	1377	1497	1614	1727	4850
9710	694	978	1122	1253	1378	1499	1615	1728	4855
9720	695	979	1123	1254	1380	1500	1617	1730	4860
9730	695	979	1124	1255	1381	1502	1618	1732	4865
9740	696	980	1125	1256	1382	1503	1620	1733	4870
9750	696	981	1126	1258	1383	1504	1621	1735	4875

23

Guideline Schedules for Weekly Support Payments

Combined Weekly Adjusted Income	One Child	Two Children	Three Children	Four Children	Five Children	Six Children	Seven Children	Eight Children	Maximum Spouse and Child (50%)
9760	697	982	1127	1259	1385	1506	1623	1736	4880
9770	698	983	1128	1260	1386	1507	1624	1738	4885
9780	698	984	1129	1261	1387	1509	1626	1740	4890
9790	699	985	1130	1262	1388	1510	1627	1741	4895
9800	700	986	1131	1263	1390	1511	1629	1743	4900
9810	700	987	1132	1265	1391	1513	1630	1744	4905
9820	701	988	1133	1266	1392	1514	1632	1746	4910
9830	702	989	1134	1267	1394	1515	1633	1748	4915
9840	702	989	1135	1268	1395	1517	1635	1749	4920
9850	703	990	1136	1269	1396	1518	1636	1751	4925
9860	704	991	1137	1270	1397	1520	1638	1752	4930
9870	704	992	1138	1272	1399	1521	1639	1754	4935
9880	705	993	1139	1273	1400	1522	1641	1756	4940
9890	705	994	1140	1274	1401	1524	1642	1757	4945
9900	706	995	1141	1275	1402	1525	1644	1759	4950
9910	707	996	1142	1276	1404	1527	1645	1760	4955
9920	707	997	1144	1277	1405	1528	1647	1762	4960
9930	708	998	1145	1278	1406	1529	1648	1764	4965
9940	709	998	1146	1280	1408	1531	1650	1765	4970
9950	709	999	1147	1281	1409	1532	1651	1767	4975
9960	710	1000	1148	1282	1410	1533	1653	1768	4980
9970	711	1001	1149	1283	1411	1535	1654	1770	4985
9980	711	1002	1150	1284	1413	1536	1656	1772	4990
9990	712	1003	1151	1285	1414	1538	1657	1773	4995
10000	712	1004	1152	1287	1415	1539	1659	1775	5000

The following percentages shall be applied to calculate basic child support when the parties' combined weekly adjusted income is above $10,000 per week.

	7.1%	10.0%	11.5%	12.9%	14.2%	15.4%	16.6%	17.7%	50.0%

24

Amended effective Jan. 1, 2010.

INDIANA PARENTING TIME GUIDELINES

Adopted December 22, 2000, Effective March 31, 2001

Including Amendments Received Through November 1, 2013

Rule

Parenting Time Rule. Adoption of Parenting Time Rule
and Guidelines

Preamble

I. General Rules Applicable to Parenting Time

II. Specific Parenting Time Provisions

III. Parenting Time When Distance Is A Major Factor

IV. Parallel Parenting

Appendix. Model Parallel Parenting Plan Order

PARENTING TIME RULE. ADOPTION OF PARENTING TIME RULE AND GUIDELINES

The Indiana Supreme Court hereby adopts the Indiana Parenting Time Guidelines, as drafted by the Domestic Relations Committee and adopted by the Board of the Judicial Conference of Indiana and all subsequent amendments thereto presented by the Domestic Relations Committee of the Judicial Conference of Indiana, as the Parenting Time Rule and Guidelines of this Court.

Adopted Jan. 4, 2013, effective March 1, 2013.

PREAMBLE

The Indiana Parenting Time Guidelines are based on the premise that it is usually in a child's best interest to have frequent, meaningful and continuing contact with each parent. It is assumed that both parents nurture their child in important ways, significant to the development and well being of the child. The Guidelines also acknowledge that scheduling parenting time is more difficult when separate households are involved and requires persistent effort and communication between parents to promote the best interest of the children involved. The purpose of these guidelines is to provide a model which may be adjusted depending upon the unique needs and circumstances of each family. These guidelines are based upon the developmental stages of children. The members of the Domestic Relations Committee of the Judicial Conference of Indiana developed the guidelines after reviewing the current and relevant literature concerning visitation, the visitation guidelines of other geographic areas, and the input of child development experts and family law practitioners. Committee members also relied upon data from surveys of judges, attorneys, and mental health professionals who work with children, reviews of court files, and a public hearing.

A child whose parents live apart has special needs related to the parent-child relationship. A child's needs and ability to cope with the parent's situation change as the child matures. Parents should consider these needs as they negotiate parenting time. They should be flexible and create a parenting time agreement which addresses the unique needs of the child and their circumstances. Parents and attorneys should always demonstrate a spirit of cooperation. The Indiana Parenting Time Guidelines are designed to assist parents and courts in the development of their own parenting plans. In the event the parties cannot create their own parenting time agreement, these guidelines represent the minimum time a parent should have to maintain frequent, meaningful, and continuing contact with a child.

A. A CHILD'S BASIC NEEDS

To insure more responsible parenting and to promote the healthy adjustment and growth of a child each parent should recognize and address a child's basic needs:

1. To know that the parents' decision to live apart is not the child's fault.

2. To develop and maintain an independent relationship with each parent and to have the continuing care and guidance from each parent.

3. To be free from having to side with either parent and to be free from conflict between the parents.

4. To have a relaxed, secure relationship with each parent without being placed in a position to manipulate one parent against the other.

5. To enjoy regular and consistent time with each parent.

6. To be financially supported by each parent, regardless of how much time each parent spends with the child.

7. To be physically safe and adequately supervised when in the care of each parent and to have a stable, consistent and responsible child care arrangement when not supervised by a parent.

8. To develop and maintain meaningful relationships with other significant adults (grandparents, stepparents and other relatives) as long as these

relationships do not interfere with or replace the child's primary relationship with the parents.

B. PURPOSE OF COMMENTARY FOLLOWING GUIDELINE.

Many of the guidelines are followed by a commentary further explaining the guideline or setting forth the child centered philosophy behind the guideline. The commentary is not an enforceable rule but provides guidance in applying the guideline.

Commentary

1. Use of Term "Parenting Time." Throughout these Guidelines the words "parenting time" have been used instead of the word "visitation" so as to emphasize the importance of the time a parent spends with a child. The concept that a non-custodial parent "visits" with a child does not convey the reality of the continuing parent-child relationship.

2. Minimum Time Concept. The concept that these Guidelines represent the minimum time a non-custodial parent should spend with a child when the parties are unable to reach their own agreement. These guidelines should not be interpreted as a limitation of time imposed by the court. They are not meant to foreclose the parents from agreeing to, or the court from granting, such additional or reduced parenting time as may be in the best interest of the child in any given case. In addressing all parenting time issues, both parents should exercise sensibility, flexibility and reasonableness.

3. Parenting Time Plans or Calendars. It will often be helpful for the parents to actually create a year-long parenting time calendar or schedules. This may include a calendar in which the parties have charted an entire year of parenting time. Forecasting a year ahead helps the parents anticipate and plan for holidays, birthdays, and school vacations. The parenting time calendar may include agreed upon deviations from the Guidelines, which recognize the specialized needs of the children and parents. Parenting Time Calendars may be helpful in arranging holidays, extended summer, and/or when the parents live at a distance and frequent travel arrangements are needed. Indiana's family resource website, which includes information to develop Parenting Time Plans is http://courts.in.gov/selfservice/2332.htm.

C. SCOPE OF APPLICATION

1. Generally. These Guidelines are applicable to all child custody situations, including paternity cases and cases involving joint legal custody where one person has primary physical custody. However, they are not applicable to situations involving family violence, substance abuse, risk of flight with a child, or any other circumstances the court reasonably believes endanger the child's physical health or safety, or significantly impair the child's emotional development. In such cases one or both parents may have legal, psychological, substance abuse or emotional problems that may need to be addressed before these Guidelines can be employed. The type of help that is needed in such cases is beyond the scope of these Guidelines.

2. Amendments. Existing parenting time orders on the date of adoption of these amendments shall be enforced according to the parenting time guidelines that were in effect on the date the parenting time order was issued. Changes to the Indiana Parenting Time Guidelines do not alone constitute good cause for amendment of an existing parenting time order; however, a court or parties to a proceeding may refer to these guidelines in making changes to a parenting time order after the effective date of the guidelines.

Commentary

Parents who agree that current changes to the Indiana Parenting Time Guidelines are in their child's best interests should file their written agreement with the court for approval . Parents may agree to some or all of the changes to the Indiana Parenting Time Guidelines and should be specific in their written agreement.

3. Presumption. There is a presumption that the Indiana Parenting Time Guidelines are applicable in all cases. Deviations from these Guidelines by either the parties or the court that result in parenting time less than the minimum time set forth below must be accompanied by a written explanation indicating why the deviation is necessary or appropriate in the case. A court is not required to give a written explanation as to why a parent is awarded more time with the child than the minimum in these guidelines.

Commentary

The written explanation need not be as formal as Findings of Fact and Conclusions of Law; however, it must state the reason(s) for the deviation. Because the parenting time guidelines are minimum standards, it is recommended parents and courts not "default" to these guidelines in lieu of a consideration of the best parenting time plan.

Adopted Dec. 22, 2000, effective March 31, 2001. Amended Jan. 4, 2013, effective March 1, 2013; Aug. 26, 2013.

SECTION I. GENERAL RULES APPLICABLE TO PARENTING TIME

A. COMMUNICATIONS

1. Between Parents. Parents shall at all times keep each other advised of their home and work addresses, telephone numbers and email addresses. Notice of any change in this information shall be given to the other parent in writing. All communications concerning a child shall be conducted between the parents. Any communication shall occur at reasonable times and places unless circumstances require otherwise. A child shall not be used to exchange documents or financial information between parents.

2. With A Child Generally. A child and a parent shall be entitled to private communications without interference from the other parent. A child shall never be used by one parent to spy or report on the other. Each parent shall encourage the child to respect and love the other parent. Parents shall at all times avoid speaking negatively about each other in or near the presence of the child, and they shall firmly discourage such conduct by relatives or friends.

3. With A Child By Telephone. Both parents shall have reasonable phone access to their child. Telephone communication with the child by either parent to the residence where the child is located shall be conducted at reasonable hours, shall be of reasonable duration, and at reasonable intervals, without interference from the other parent.

If a parent uses an answering machine, voice mail or a pager, messages left for a child shall be promptly communicated to the child and the call returned.

Commentary:

Parents should agree on a specified time for telephone calls so that a child will be available to receive the call. The parent initiating the call should bear the expense of the call. A child may, of course, call either parent, though at reasonable hours, frequencies, and at the cost of the parent called if it is a long distance call.

Examples of unacceptable interference with communication include a parent refusing to answer a phone or refusing to allow the child or others to answer; a parent recording phone conversations between the other parent and the child; turning off the phone or using a call blocking mechanism or otherwise denying the other parent telephone contact with the child.

4. With A Child By Mail. A parent and a child shall have a right to communicate privately by email and faxes, and by cards, letters, and packages, without interference by the other parent.

Commentary:

A parent should not impose obstacles to mail communications. For example, if a custodial parent has a rural address, the parent should maintain a mailbox to receive mail at that address. A parent who receives a communication for a child shall promptly deliver it to the child.

5. Electronic Communication. The same provisions above apply to electronic communications of any kind. However, these provisions shall not be construed to interfere with the authority of either parent to impose reasonable restrictions to a child's access to the Internet.

6. Emergency Notification. For emergency notification purposes, whenever a child travels out of the area with either parent, one of the following shall be provided to the other parent: An itinerary of travel dates, destinations, and places where the child or the traveling parent can be reached, or the name and telephone number of an available third person who knows where the child or parent may be located.

7. Communication between parent and child. Each parent is encouraged to promote a positive relationship between the children and the other parent. It is important, therefore, that communication remain open, positive and frequent. Regular phone contact is an important tool in maintaining a parent/child relationship as well as other forms of contact such as letter, e-mail and other more technologically advanced communications systems such as video chat and Skype. No person shall block reasonable phone or other communication access between a parent and child or monitor such communications. A parent who receives a communication for a child shall promptly deliver it to the child. Both parents shall promptly provide the other parent with updated cell and landline phone numbers and e-mail addresses when there has been a change.

Commentary:

It is important for a child to have as much contact with both parents as possible. Interference with reasonable communication between a parent and child, including monitoring of that communication is destructive not only to the child's relationship with the other parent, but is also destructive to the child. Attempts to block access to and contact with the other parent may violate these parenting time guidelines. These types of behaviors may lead to sanctions, a change of parenting time, or in some cases, a change of custody. The prohibition applies equally to both parents.

B. IMPLEMENTING PARENTING TIME

1. Transportation Responsibilities. Unless otherwise agreed between the parents, the parent receiving the child shall provide transportation for the child at the start of the scheduled parenting time and the other parent shall provide transportation for the child at the end of the scheduled parenting time.

Commentary:

1. Presence Of Both Parents. Both parents should be present at the time of the exchange and should make every reasonable effort to personally transport the child. On those occasions when a parent is unable to be present at the time of the exchange or it becomes necessary for the child to be transported by someone other than a parent, this should be communicated to the other parent in advance if possible. In such cases, the person present at the exchange, or transporting the child, should be a responsible adult with whom the child is familiar and comfortable.

2. Distance/Cost As Factors. Where the distance between the parents' residences is such that extended driving time is necessary, the parents should agree on a location for the exchange of the child. The cost of transportation should be shared based on consideration of various factors, including the distance involved, the financial resources of the parents, the reason why the distances exist, and the family situation of each parent at that time.

*3. **Parental Hostility.** In a situation where hostility between parents makes it impracticable to exchange a child at the parents' residences, the exchange of the child should take place at a neutral site.*

2. Punctuality. Each parent shall have the child ready for exchange at the beginning and at the end of the scheduled parenting time and shall be on time in picking up and returning the child. The parents shall communicate as early as possible regarding any situation that would interfere with the timely exchange of the child. Both parents have a duty to communicate any time the exchange is delayed. When no communication is initiated by the delaying parent, and pick up or return of a child does not occur within a reasonable time, the time and conditions of the exchange may be rescheduled at the discretion of the parent not responsible for the delay.

Commentary:

Punctuality is a matter of courtesy to the child and impacts the child's sense of security and well-being. Parents should make every effort to pick up and return a child at the agreed time, and not substantially earlier or later. Parents should recognize, however, that circumstances occur that require leeway in the scheduled times. What constitutes unreasonable time is fact sensitive. Parents are encouraged to include in their parenting plans what constitutes an unreasonable time.

3. Clothing. The custodial parent shall send an appropriate and adequate supply of clean clothing with the child and the non-custodial parent shall return such clothing in a clean condition. Each parent shall advise the other, as far in advance as possible, of any special activities so that the appropriate clothing may be available to the child.

Commentary:

It is the responsibility of both parents to ensure their child is properly clothed. The non-custodial parent may wish to have a basic supply of clothing available for the child at his or her home.

4. Privacy of Residence. A parent may not enter the residence of the other, except by express invitation permission of the other parent, regardless of whether a parent retains a property interest in the residence of the other. Accordingly, the child shall be picked up at the front entrance of the appropriate residence unless the parents agree otherwise. The person delivering the child shall not leave until the child is safely inside.

C. CHANGES IN SCHEDULED PARENTING TIME

Introduction

Parents should recognize there will be occasions when modification of the existing parenting schedule will be necessary. Parents should exercise reasonable judgment in their dealings with each other and with their child. Parents should be flexible in scheduling parenting time and should consider the benefits to the child of frequent, meaningful and regular contact with each parent and the schedules of the child and each parent.

1. Scheduled Parenting Time To Occur As Planned. Parenting time is both a right and a responsibility, and scheduled parenting time shall occur as planned. Both parents are jointly responsible for following the parenting time orders. A child shall not make parenting time decisions. If a parent is unable to provide personal care for the child during scheduled parenting time, then that parent shall provide alternate child care or pay the reasonable costs of child care caused by the failure to exercise the scheduled parenting time.

Commentary:

Parents should understand it is important for a child to experience consistent and ongoing parenting time. A child is entitled to rely on spending time with each parent in a predictable way and adjusts better after a routine has been established and followed. A parent who consistently cancels scheduled parenting time sends a very harmful message to the child that the child is not a priority in that parent's life. In addition to disappointing a child, the voluntary cancellation of scheduled parenting time by one parent may interfere with the plans of the other parent or cause the other parent to incur child care and other costs.

Parents share a joint and equal responsibility for following parenting time orders. A child shares none of this responsibility and should not be permitted to shoulder the burden of this decision. See also Section E. 3.

Unacceptable excuses for denying parenting time include the following:

The child unjustifiably hesitates or refuses to go.

The child has a minor illness.

The child has to go somewhere.

The child is not home.

The noncustodial parent is behind in support.

The custodial parent does not want the child to go.

The weather is bad (unless the weather makes travel unsafe).

The child has no clothes to wear.

The other parent failed to meet preconditions established by the custodial parent.

2. Adjustments to Schedule / "Make Up" Time. Whenever there is a need to adjust the established parenting schedules because of events outside the normal family routine, the parent who becomes aware of the circumstance shall notify the other parent as far in advance as possible. Both parents shall then attempt to reach a mutually acceptable adjustment to the parenting schedule.

If an adjustment results in one parent losing scheduled parenting time with the child, "make-up" time should be exercised as soon as possible. If the parents cannot agree on "make-up" time, the parent who lost the time shall select the "make-up" time within one month of the missed time.

Commentary:

There will be occasions when scheduled parenting times may need to be adjusted because of illnesses or special family events such as weddings, funerals, reunions, and the like. Each parent should accommodate the other in making the adjustment so that the child may attend the family event. After considering the child's best interests, the parent who lost parenting time may decide to forego the "make-up" time.

3. Opportunity for Additional Parenting Time. When it becomes necessary that a child be cared for by a person other than a parent or a responsible household family member, the parent needing the child care shall first offer the other parent the opportunity for additional parenting time, if providing the child care by the other parent is practical considering the time available and the distance between residences. The other parent is under no obligation to provide the child care. If the other parent elects to provide this care, it shall be done at no cost and without effecting child support. The parent exercising additional parenting time shall provide the necessary transportation unless the parties otherwise agree.

Commentary:

The rule providing for opportunities for additional parenting time promotes the concept that a child receives greater benefit from being with a parent rather than a child care provider who is not a household family member. The household family member is defined as an adult person residing in the household, who is related to the child by blood, marriage or adoption. The rule is also intended to be practical. When a parent's work schedule or other regular activities require hiring or arranging for a child care provider who is not a household family member, the other parent should be given the opportunity to provide the care. Distance, transportation or time may make the rule impractical. The period of absence which triggers the exchange will vary depending upon the circumstances of the parties. Parents should agree on the amount of child care time and the circumstances that require the offer be made. It is presumed that this rule applies in all cases which the guidelines cover; however, the parties or a trial court may, within discretion, determine that a deviation is necessary or appropriate. Any such deviation must be accompanied by a written explanation. See Shelton v. Shelton, 840 N.E.2d 835 (Ind. 2006).

This section is sometimes mistakenly referred to as the "right of first refusal." It is more accurate

to refer to this section as an opportunity to exercise additional parenting time.

D. EXCHANGE OF INFORMATION

Introduction

Parents should obtain and share information about their children. Parents should take the initiative to obtain information about their child from the various providers of services. Each parent is responsible to establish a relationship with the child's school, health care provider and other service provider. A child may suffer inconvenience, embarrassment, and physical or emotional harm when parents fail to actively obtain and share information.

1. School Records. Under Indiana law, both parents are entitled to direct access to their child's school records, Indiana Code § 20–33–7–2. Each parent should obtain school information on their own without depending on the other parent. A parent shall not interfere with the right of the other parent to communicate directly with school personnel concerning a child. The noncustodial parent shall be listed as an emergency contact unless there are special circumstances concerning child endangerment.

2. School Activities. Each parent shall promptly notify the other parent of all information about school activities, which is not accessible to the other parent. A parent shall not interfere with the right of the other parent to communicate directly with school personnel concerning a child's school activities. The parent exercising parenting time shall be responsible to transport the child to school related activities.

Commentary:

Each parent with knowledge of the child's event should promptly inform the other parent of the date, time, place and event. The opportunity for a child to attend a school function should not be denied solely because a parent is not able to attend the function. The child should be permitted to attend the function with the available parent. Scheduled parenting time should not be used as an excuse to deny the child's participation in school related activities, including practices and rehearsals.

3. Other Activities. Each parent shall promptly notify the other parent of all organized events in a child's life which permit parental and family participation. A parent shall not interfere with the opportunity of the other parent to volunteer for or participate in a child's activities.

Commentary:

Each parent should have the opportunity to participate in other activities involving the child even if that activity does not occur during his or her parenting time. This includes activities such as church functions, athletic events, scouting and the like. It is important to understand that a child is more likely to enjoy these experiences when supported by both parents.

4. Health Information. Under Indiana law, both parents are entitled to direct access to their child's medical records, Indiana Code § 16–39–1–7; and mental health records. Indiana Code § 16–39–2–9.

    a. If a child is undergoing evaluation or treatment, the custodial parent shall communicate that fact to the non-custodial parent.

    b. Each parent shall immediately notify the other of any medical emergencies or illness of the child that requires medical attention.

    c. If a child is taking prescription medication or under a health care directive, the custodial parent shall provide the noncustodial parent with a sufficient amount of medication and instructions whenever the noncustodial parent is exercising parenting time. Medical instructions from a health care provider shall be followed.

    d. If required by the health care provider. the custodial parent shall give written authorization to the child's health care providers, permitting an ongoing release of all information regarding the child to the non-custodial parent including the right of the provider to discuss the child's situation with the non-custodial parent.

Commentary:

    Each parent has the responsibility to become informed and participate in ongoing therapies and treatments prescribed for a child and to ensure that medications are administered as prescribed. An evaluation or treatment for a child includes medical, dental, educational, and mental health services.

5. Insurance. A parent who has insurance coverage on the child shall supply the other parent with current insurance cards, an explanation of benefits, and a list of insurer-approved or HMO–qualified health care providers in the area where each parent lives. If the insurance company requires specific forms, the insured parent shall provide those forms to the other parent.

Commentary:

    Qualified health care orders may permit the parent to communicate with the medical health care insurance provider.

E. RESOLUTION OF PROBLEMS AND RELOCATION

1. Disagreements Generally. When a disagreement occurs regarding parenting time and the requirements of these Guidelines, both parents shall make every effort to discuss options, including mediation, in an attempt to resolve the dispute before going to court.

2. Mediation. If court action is initiated, the parents shall enter into mediation unless otherwise ordered by the court.

3. Child Hesitation. If a child is reluctant to participate in parenting time, each parent shall be responsible to ensure the child complies with the scheduled parenting time. In no event shall a child be allowed to make the decision on whether scheduled parenting time takes place.

Commentary:

    In most cases, when a child hesitates to spend time with a parent, it is the result of naturally occurring changes in the life of a child. The child can be helped to overcome hesitation if the parents listen to the child, speak to each other and practically address the child's needs.

    Parents should inquire why a child is reluctant to spend time with a parent. If a parent believes that a child's safety is compromised in the care of the other parent, that parent should take steps to protect the child, but must recognize the rights of the other parent. This situation must be promptly resolved by both parents. Family counseling may be appropriate, If the parents cannot resolve the situation, either parent may seek the assistance of the court.

4. Relocation. When either parent or other person who has custody or parenting time considers a change of residence, a 90 day advance notice of the intent to move must be provided to the other parent or person.

Commentary:

    1. Impact Of Move. Parents should recognize the impact that a change of residence may have on a child and on the established parenting time. The welfare of the child should be a priority in making the decision to move.

    2. Indiana Law. Indiana law (Ind. Code § 31–17–2.2) requires all individuals who have (or who are seeking) child custody or parenting time, and who intend to relocate their residence to provide notice to an individual who has (or is seeking) child custody, parenting time or grandparent visitation. The notice must be made by registered or certified mail not later than 90 days before the individual intends to move. The relocating party's notice must provide certain specified and detailed information about the move. This information includes: the new address; new phone numbers; the date of the proposed move; a stated reason for the move; a proposed new parenting time schedule; and must include certain statements regarding the rights of the non-relocating party. The notice must also be filed with the court. The notice is required for all proposed moves by custodial and non custodial parents in all cases when the proposed move involves a change of the primary residence for a period of at least sixty (60) days. This is true even when a person plans to move across the street or across town, and when a party plans on moving across the state or the country, or to another country.

5. Withholding Support or Parenting Time. Neither parenting time nor child support shall be withheld because of either parent's failure to comply with a court order. Only the court may enter sanctions for noncompliance. A child has the right both to support and parenting time, neither of which is dependent upon the other. If there is a violation of either requirement, the remedy is to apply to the court for appropriate sanctions.

6. Enforcement of Parenting Time.

A. *Contempt Sanctions.* Court orders regarding parenting time must be followed by both parents. Unjustified violations of any of the provisions contained in the order may subject the offender to contempt sanctions. These sanctions may include fine, imprisonment, and/or community service.

B. *Injunctive Relief.* Under Indiana law, a noncustodial parent who regularly pays support and is barred from parenting time by the custodial parent may file an application for an injunction to enforce parenting time under Ind. Code § 31–17–4–4.

C. *Criminal Penalties.* Interference with custody or visitation rights may be a crime. Ind. Code § 35–42–3–4.

D. *Attorney Fees.* In any court action to enforce an order granting or denying parenting time, a court may award reasonable attorney fees and expenses of litigation. A court may consider whether the parent seeking attorney fees substantially prevailed and whether the parent violating the order did so knowingly or intentionally. A court can also award attorney fees and expenses against a parent who pursues a frivolous or vexatious court action.

Adopted Dec. 22, 2000, effective March 31, 2001; amended Sept. 10, 2007, effective Jan. 1, 2008; amended and effective March 28, 2008; amended Jan. 4, 2013, effective March 1, 2013; Aug. 26, 2013.

SECTION II. SPECIFIC PARENTING TIME PROVISIONS

A. INTRODUCTION

The best parenting plan is one created by parents which fulfills the unique needs of the child and the parents. Parents should attempt to create their own parenting plan which is in the best interests of the child. If an agreement is reached, the parenting plan shall be reduced to writing, signed by both parties, and filed for approval by the court in order to be enforceable. When the parties cannot reach an agreement on a parenting plan, the specific provisions which follow are designed to assist parents and the court in the development of a parenting plan. They represent the minimum recommended time a parent should have to maintain frequent, meaningful, and continuing contact with a child.

For identification purposes, the following provisions set forth parenting time for the non-custodial parent and assume the other parent has sole custody or primary physical custody in a joint legal custody situation. These identifiers are not meant to diminish or raise either person's status as a parent.

B. OVERNIGHT PARENTING TIME.

Unless it can be demonstrated by the custodial parent that the non-custodial parent has not had regular care responsibilities for the child, parenting time shall include overnights. If the non-custodial parent has not previously exercised regular care responsibilities for the child, then parenting time shall not include overnights prior to the child's third birthday, except as provided in subsection C. below.

Commentary

*1. **Assumptions.** The provisions identify parenting time for the non-custodial parent and assume that one parent has sole custody or primary physical custody of a child, that both parents are fit and proper, that both parents have adequately bonded with the child, and that both parents are willing to parent the child. They further assume that the parents are respectful of each other and will cooperate with each other to promote the best interests of the child. Finally, the provisions assume that each parent is responsible for the nurturing and care of the child. Parenting time is both a right and a trust and parents are expected to assume full responsibility for the child during their individual parenting time.*

*2. **Lack of Contact.** Where there is a significant lack of contact between a parent and a child, there may be no bond, or emotional connection, between the parent and the child. It is recommended that scheduled parenting time be "phased in" to permit the parent and child to adjust to their situation. It may be necessary for an evaluation of the current relationship (or lack thereof) between the parent and the child in order to recommend a parenting time plan. A guardian ad litem, a mental health professional, a representative from a domestic relations counseling bureau or any other neutral evaluator may be used for this task.*

*3. **Age Categories.** The chronological age ranges set forth in the specific provisions are estimates of the developmental stages of children since children mature at different times.*

*4. **Multiple Children of Different Ages.** When a family has children of different ages, the presumption is that all the children should remain together during the exercise of parenting time. However, the standards set for a young child should not be ignored, and there will be situations where not all of the children participate in parenting time together. On the other hand, when there are younger and older children, it will generally be appropriate to accelerate, to some extent, the time when the younger children move into overnight or weekend parenting time, to keep sibling relationships intact.*

*5. **Non-traditional Work Schedules.** For parents with non-traditional work schedules, who may regularly work weekends, weekday parenting time should be substituted for the weekend time designated in these rules. Similar consideration should* *also be given to parents with other kinds of non-traditional work hours.*

C. INFANTS AND TODDLERS

1. Introduction

The first few years of a child's life are recognized as being critical to that child's ultimate development. Infants (under eighteen months) and toddlers (eighteen months to three years) have a great need for continuous contact with the primary care giver who provides a sense of security, nurturing and predictability. It is thought best if scheduled parenting time in infancy be minimally disruptive to the infant's schedule.

Commentary

*1. **Both Parents Necessary.** It is critical that a child be afforded ample opportunity to bond with both parents. A young child thrives when both parents take an active role in parenting. There is a positive relationship between the degree of involvement of mothers and fathers and the social, emotional, and cognitive growth of a child. Both parents can care for their child with equal effectiveness and their parenting styles may make significant contributions to the development of the child. Parents, therefore, must be flexible in creating for each other opportunities to share both the routine and special events of their child's early development.*

*2. **Frequency Versus Duration.** Infants and young children have a limited but evolving sense of time. These children also have a limited ability to recall persons not directly in front of them. For infants, short frequent visits are much better than longer visits spaced farther apart. From the vantage point of the young child, daily contact with each parent is ideal. If workable, it is recommended that no more than two days go by without contact with the noncustodial parent. A parent who cannot visit often may desire to increase the duration of visits but this practice is not recommended for infants. Frequent and predictable parenting time is best.*

3. Overnight contact between parents and very young children can provide opportunities for them to grow as a family. At the same time, when very young children experience sudden changes in their night time care routines, especially when these changes include separation from the usual caretaker, they can become frightened and unhappy. Under these circumstances, they may find it difficult to relax and thrive, even when offered excellent care.

4. When a very young child is accustomed to receiving regular, hands-on care from both parents, the child should continue to receive this care when the parents separate. Regardless of custodial status, a parent who has regularly cared for the child prior to separation should exercise overnight parenting time. When a parent has not provided regular hands-on care for the child prior to separation, overnight parenting time is not recommended until the parent and the child have developed a

predictable and comfortable daytime care taking routine.

2. Parenting Time In Early Infancy. (Birth through Age 9 Months)

(A) Birth through Age 4 Months:

(1) Three (3) non-consecutive "days" per week of two (2) hours in length.

(2) All scheduled holidays of two (2) hours in length.

(3) Overnight if he noncustodial parent has exercised regular care responsibilities for the child but not to exceed one (1) 24 hour period per week.

Commentary:

Parenting time should occur in a stable place and without disruption of an infant's established routine.

(B) Age 5 Months through Age 9 Months:

(1) Three (3) non-consecutive "days" per week of three (3) hours per day. The child is to be returned at least one (1) hour before evening bedtime.

(2) All scheduled holidays of three (3) hours in length. The child is to be returned at least one (1) hour before evening bedtime.

(3) Overnight if the noncustodial parent has exercised regular care responsibilities for the child but not to exceed one (1) 24 hour period per week.

3. Parenting Time In Later Infancy (Age 10 Months through Age 36 Months)

(A) Age 10 Months through Age 12 Months:

(1) Three (3) non-consecutive "days" per week, with one day on a "non-work" day for eight (8) hours. The other days shall be for three (3) hours each day. The child is to be returned at least one (1) hour before evening bedtime.

(2) All scheduled holidays for eight (8) hours. The child is to be returned at least one (1) hour before evening bedtime.

(3) Overnight if the noncustodial parent has exercised regular care responsibilities for the child but not to exceed one (1) 24 hour period per week.

(B) Age 13 Months through Age 18 Months:

(1) Three (3) non-consecutive "days" per week, with one day on a "non-work" day for ten (10) hours. The other days shall be for three (3) hours each day. The child is to be returned at least one (1) hour before evening bedtime.

(2) All scheduled holidays for eight (8) hours. The child is to be returned at least (1) hour before evening bedtime.

(3) Overnight if the noncustodial parent has exercised regular care responsibilities for the child but not to exceed one (1) 24 hour period per week.

(C) Age 19 Months through 36 Months:

(1) Alternate weekends on Saturdays for ten (10) hours and on Sundays for ten (10) hours. The child is to be returned at least one hour before bedtime, unless overnight is appropriate.

(2) One (1) "day" preferably in mid-week for three (3) hours, the child to be returned at least one (1) hour before evening bedtime, unless overnight during the week is appropriate.

(3) All scheduled holidays for ten (10) hours. The child is to be returned one hour before bedtime.

(4) If the non-custodial parent who did not initially have regular care responsibilities has exercised the scheduled parenting time under these guidelines for at least nine (9) continuous months, regular parenting time as indicated in section II. D. 1. below may take place.

Commentary:

Parenting Time Guideline II. C. 3. (C) (4) is intended to provide a way to shorten the last age-based parenting time stage when the infant is sufficiently bonded to the non-custodial parent so that the infant is able to regularly go back and forth, and particularly wake-up in a different place, without development-retarding strain. If this is not occurring, the provision should not be utilized. The nine (9) month provision is applicable only within the 19 to 36 month section. Therefore, as a practical matter, the provision could not shorten this stage until the infant is at least 28 months old. The provision applies equally to all non-custodial parents.

D. PARENTING TIME—CHILD 3 YEARS OF AGE AND OLDER

1. Regular Parenting Time

(a.) On alternating weekends from Friday at 6:00 P.M. until Sunday at 6:00 P.M. (the times may change to fit the parents' schedules);

(b.) One (1) evening per week, preferably in mid-week, for a period of up to four hours but the child shall be returned no later than 9:00 p.m.; and,

(c.) On all scheduled holidays.

Commentary:

Where the distance from the non-custodial parent's residence makes it reasonable, the weekday period may be extended to an overnight stay. In such circumstances, the responsibility of feeding the child the next morning, getting the child to school or day care, or returning the child to the residence of the custodial parent, if the child is not in school, shall be on the non-custodial parent.

2. Extended Parenting Time (Child 3 through 4 Years Old)

The noncustodial parent shall have up to four (4) non-consecutive weeks during the year beginning at 4:00 P.M. on Sunday until 4:00 P.M. on the following Sunday. The non-custodial parent shall give at least sixty (60) days advance notice of the use of a particular week.

3. Extended Parenting Time (Child 5 and older)

One-half of the Summer Vacation. The summer vacation begins the day after school lets out for the summer, and ends the day before school resumes for the new school year. The time may be either consecutive or split into two (2) segments. The noncustodial parent shall give notice to the custodial parent of the selection by April 1 of each year. If such notice is not given, the custodial parent shall make the selection and notify the other parent. All notices shall be given in writing and verbally. A timely selection may not be rejected by the other parent. Notice of an employer's restrictions on the vacation time of either parent shall be delivered to the other parent as soon as that information is available. In scheduling parenting time the employer imposed restrictions on their parent's time shall be considered by the parents in arranging their time with their child.

If a child attends a school that has a year-round or balanced calendar, the noncustodial parent's extended parenting time shall be one-half of the time for fall and spring school breaks. Unless otherwise agreed to by the parents or ordered by the trial court, the noncustodial parent shall exercise parenting time the first half of school break in odd years, and the second half of school break in even years. Absent an agreement of the parties, the first half of the break will begin two hours after the child is released from the school, and the second half of the period will end at 6:00 p.m. on the day before school begins again. Summer Vacation should be shared equally between parents as provided in the paragraph above. Winter break/Christmas vacation should be shared as provided in the Holiday Parenting Time Schedule.

If a child attends summer school, the parent exercising parenting time shall be responsible for the child's transportation to and attendance at school.

During any extended summer period of more than two (2) consecutive weeks with the non-custodial parent, the custodial parent shall have the benefit of the regular parenting time schedule set forth above, which includes alternating weekends and mid-week parenting time, unless impracticable because of distance created by out of town vacations.

Similarly, during the summer period when the children are with the custodial parent for more than two (2) consecutive weeks, the non-custodial parent's regular parenting time continues, which includes alternating weekends and mid-week parenting time, unless impracticable because of distance created by out of town vacations.

The selection of a parent's summer parenting time shall not deprive the other parent of the Holiday Parenting Time Schedule below. See Section II. F.

E. PARENTING TIME FOR THE ADOLESCENT AND TEENAGER

1. Regular Parenting Time. Regular parenting time by the noncustodial parent on alternating weekends, during holidays, and for an extended time during the summer months as set forth in the Parenting Time Guidelines (Section II. D.) shall apply to the adolescent and teenager.

Commentary

1. A Teenager Needs Both Parents. Adolescence is a stage of child development in which parents play an extremely important role. The single most important factor in keeping a teenager safe is a strong connection to the family. The responsibility to help a teenager maintain this connection to the family rests with the parents, regardless of their relationship. The parents must help the teenager balance the need for independence with the need to be an active part of the family. To accomplish this, they must spend time with the teenager. Parents must help the adolescent become a responsible adult. A teenager should safely learn life's lessons if the parents provide the rules which prevent dangerous mistakes.

2. Anchors of Adolescence. Regardless of whether the parents live together or apart, an adolescent can be made to feel part of a supportive, helpful family. Things that can help this occur include:

Regular time spent in the company of each parent. Parents need to be available for conversation and recreation. They need to teach a teenager skills that will help the teen in adult life.

Regular time spent in the company of siblings. Regardless of personality and age differences, siblings who spend time together can form a family community that can be a tremendous support in adult life. If the children do not create natural opportunities for them to want to do things together, the parents will need to create reasons for this to occur.

Emphasis on worthwhile values. Parent and teens together should invest time in wholesome activities that teach a teenager important lessons. If a teenager identifies with worthwhile values, the teen is more likely to have a positive self-image.

Time spent with good friends. A parent's expectations can influence a teenager's choice of friends. Meet your teenager's friends and their parents and interact with them as guests in your home. This will increase the likelihood that your teenager's friends will be people who are comfortable in the environment that is good for the teen.

Clear rules that are agreed upon by both parents. As a child matures, it is very important that the teen knows rules of acceptable behavior. The chances of this occurring are much better if both parents agree in these important areas. When parents jointly set the standard of behavior for their teen, the chances of the child accepting those values are greatly increased.

Good decisions/greater freedoms. A teenager who does what is expected should be offered more freedom and a wider range of choices. It is helpful if a teenager is reminded of the good decisions that have caused the teen to be given more privileges. If a teen is helped to see that privileges are earned and not natural "rights" he or she will be more likely to realize that the key to getting more freedom is to behave well. If rules are not followed, appropriate consequences should result. A teenager who does not make good use of independence should have less of it.

3. Decision Making In Parenting A Teenager. The rearing of a teenager requires parents to make decisions about what their teen should be allowed to do, when, and with whom. At the same time, parents who live apart may have difficulty communicating with each other.

If parents are not able to agree, the teenager, who very much wants freedom from adult authority, should never be used as the "tie breaker." When parents live apart, it is more likely that a child will be required to make decisions, not as a healthy part of development, but simply to resolve disagreements between the parents.

As a general rule, a teenager should be involved in making important decisions if the parents agree the opportunity to make the decision is valuable, and the value of that opportunity outweighs any possible harm of a poor decision. If the parents feel the welfare of the child is dependent on the decision made, and if they allow the child to make a decision simply because they cannot agree, the parents are in danger of failing the child.

Example #1

Mary Jones and John Jones disagree as to whether or not their daughter, Sally, should study a foreign language in middle school. Mary feels that this early exposure to a foreign language will offer Sally an advantage when she continues this study in high school. John would like Sally to have the opportunity to develop her artistic talents through electives in drawing and painting. The Jones agree that Sally's success and happiness will in large part be determined by her motivation. They agree that Sally should decide between a foreign language and art, and that they will support whatever decision she makes.

Comment: Mary and John feel that Sally is mature enough to think about what interests her and makes her happy. They feel that an opportunity to do this in choosing an elective will be an important experience for Mary—more important than the relative merits of foreign language or art study to Sally's academic career. This is a good example of parents agreeing to involve the adolescent in making a decision that resolves their own disagreement.

Example #2

Tom Smith and Sue Smith cannot come to a visitation agreement. Tom believes their 17 year old son, Pete, should have visitation at a time to be

determined by Pete. Tom feels that, if Pete is given
a visitation schedule, he will feel that he is being
forced to see his father. Tom further believes this
will weaken his relationship with his son. Sue
believes a clear plan regarding the time Tom and
Pete spend together should be established. She
says if Pete is not given a firm expectation of when
he will be with Tom, it will be too easy for other
activities in Pete's life to crowd out this priority.
Unable to resolve this question, Tom and Sue give
Pete the option of deciding if he would like a
visitation schedule or if he would like to be free to
see his father whenever he pleases.

Comment: Tom and Sue each feel the quality of
Pete's relationship with Tom will depend on the
way that visitation is structured. Each believes
that, if Pete makes the wrong choice, the problems
that follow could impact him throughout his adult
life. They have placed the responsibility for the
decision on Pete, not because the chance to make
such a decision will help him, but because they
cannot resolve the matter between themselves. This
is a poor reason for entrusting an adolescent with
such an important decision.

2. Special Considerations. In exercising parenting time with a teenager, the non-custodial parent shall make reasonable efforts to accommodate a
teenager's participation in his or her regular academic, extracurricular and social activities.

Commentary:

Making Regular Parenting Time Workable.
Parents must develop a parenting plan that evolves
or changes as the teen matures. The needs of the
child at age thirteen will be very different from the
needs of that same child at age seventeen. Parents
also must develop a parenting plan that assures
regular involvement of both parents. This can be a
particular challenge when the teen is involved with
school, activities, and friends, and becomes even
more difficult when the parents live some distance
apart.

When parents differ in their views of which free-
doms should be given and which should be with-
held, the parents must be sufficiently united to keep
the teenager from assuming responsibilities when
the child is not ready. At the same time, the
parents must respect that they will run their homes
differently because they are living apart.

Living apart challenges parents to teach their
child that different ways of doing things can work
for different parents. They must see that their
child needs to work especially hard to adapt to two
distinct ways of doing things. Not all differences
mean that one parent is right and one parent is
wrong. The key is for parents to realize different
homes can produce a well-adjusted teen.

Example: The Student Athlete
Jim Doe and Jane Doe have been divorced for 3
years. Their oldest child, Jeremy, is beginning
high school. Throughout his middle school years,
Jeremy was active in football. Practices were held
after school and games took place on weekends.
Jeremy had spent alternating weekends and one
night each week with his noncustodial parent. The

parent who had Jeremy took him to practices and
games during the time they were together. On
week nights with the noncustodial parent, this usu-
ally consisted of dinner and conversation. Week-
ends with both parents included homework, chores,
play, and family outings.

Jeremy's high school coach is serious about foot-
ball. Jeremy loves the sport. Coach expects Jere-
my to work out with teammates throughout the
early summer. In August, practice occurs three
times a day. Once school begins, Jeremy will
practice after school for several hours each day. In
addition, he is taking some difficult courses and
expects that several hours of study will be needed
each night. Jeremy will have games on Friday
nights. Because of his busy weekend schedule, he
expects that Saturdays will be his only time to be
with friends.

Discussion
On the surface, a traditional parenting plan,
placing Jeremy with his noncustodial parent on
alternating weekends and one night each week,
would not seem to work. Jeremy's athletic and
academic demands will require him to work hard
on weeknight evenings. Jeremy's parents agree he
needs time to be with friends and he should be
allowed to make social plans on Saturdays. They
recognize Sundays will often need to be devoted to
homework projects which do not fit into the busy
weekday schedule.

A Possible Solution
Jeremy's parents want him to enjoy sports and
have friends. Yet, they also want him to have the
benefits of being actively raised by two parents.
They want him to grow to become an adult who
sees that balancing family, work, and play is im-
portant. They want to teach him how to do this.

Jeremy's parents have agreed to maintain their
previous supervision plan. However, they have
also agreed on some changes. Jeremy's noncusto-
dial parent will come to the community of the
custodial parent for midweek visitation. Regard-
less of how busy he is, Jeremy needs to eat. The
noncustodial parent plans to take Jeremy to dinner
at a restaurant that offers quick but healthy meals.
They will spend the rest of the time at a local
library where Jeremy can study. The noncustodial
parent can offer help as needed or simply enjoy a
good book. Jeremy's parents plan to purchase an
inexpensive laptop computer to assist him when he
works at the library.

Jeremy's parents plan that alternating weekends
will continue to be spent with the noncustodial
parent. They, like many parents of adolescents,
understand Jeremy wants to be with his friends
more than he wants to be with them. They recog-
nize that, on weekends, they are offering more
supervision and Jeremy's friends are getting more
time. Yet, they also see the need to help Jeremy
establish active family membership as one of his
priorities.

F. HOLIDAY PARENTING TIME SCHEDULE

**1. Conflicts Between Regular and Holiday
Weekends.**

The Holiday Parenting Time Schedule shall take precedence over regularly scheduled and extended parenting time. Extended parenting time takes precedence over regular parenting time unless otherwise indicated in these Guidelines.

Alternating weekends shall be maintained throughout the year as follows. If a parent misses a regular weekend because it is the other parent's holiday, it will be lost. If a parent receives two consecutive weekends because of a holiday, that parent shall have the third weekend also. Regular alternating weekends shall continue throughout the year.

Commentary:

A parent may receive three (3) consecutive weekends due to a holiday. It is anticipated that missed weekends due to holidays will balance out for each parent given the alternating schedule for the holidays provided for in these guidelines.

When the court orders a change of physical custody, the court should consider whether the Holiday Schedule change should start at the beginning of the calendar year, at the beginning or the end of the child's school year, or immediately.

2. **Holiday Schedule.** The following parenting times are applicable in all situations referenced in these Guidelines as "scheduled holidays" with the limitations applied as indicated for children under the age of three (3) years.

A. Special Days.

[1] Mother's Day. With the child's mother from Friday at 6:00 P.M. until Sunday at 6:00 P.M.

[2] Father's Day. With the child's father from Friday at 6:00 P.M. until Sunday at 6:00 P.M.

[3] Child's Birthday. In even numbered years the non-custodial parent shall have all of the children on each child's birthday from 9:00 A.M. until 9:00 P.M. However, if the birthday falls on a school day, then from 5:00 P.M. until 8:00 P.M.

In odd numbered years the non-custodial parent shall have all of the children on each child's birthday on the day before the child's birthday from 9:00 A.M. until 9:00 P.M., however, if such day falls on a school day, then from 5:00 P.M. until 8:00 P.M.

[4] Parent's Birthday. From 9:00 A.M. until 9:00 P.M. with that parent, however, if the parent's birthday falls on a school day, then from 5:00 P.M. until 8:00 P.M.

[5] When the child's birthday falls within a Special Day, Holiday, or Christmas vacation, the child's birthday shall be celebrated with the parent having the child during that time period.

When the parent's birthday falls within a Special Day, Holiday or Christmas vacation, the Special Day, Holiday or Christmas vacation takes precedence.

B. Christmas Vacation.

The Christmas vacation shall be defined as beginning on the last day of school and ending the last day before school begins again. Absent agreement of the parties, the first half of the period will begin two hours after the child is released from school. The second half of the period will end at 6:00 p.m. on the day before school begins again.

Each party will receive one half ($\frac{1}{2}$) of the total days of the Christmas vacation, on an alternating basis as follows:

1. In even numbered years, the custodial parent shall have the first one half ($\frac{1}{2}$) of the Christmas vacation and non-custodial parent shall have the second one half ($\frac{1}{2}$) of the Christmas vacation.

2. In odd numbered years, the non-custodial parent shall have the first one half ($\frac{1}{2}$) of the Christmas vacation and custodial parent shall have the second one half ($\frac{1}{2}$) of the Christmas vacation.

3. In those years when Christmas does not fall in a parent's week, that parent shall have the child from Noon to 9:00 P.M. on Christmas Day.

4. No exchanges under this portion of the rule shall occur after 9:00 p.m. and before 8:00 a.m., absent agreement of the parties.

New Year's Eve and New Year's Day shall not be considered separate holidays under the Parenting Time Guidelines.

C. Holidays.

The following holidays shall be exercised by the noncustodial parent in even numbered years and the custodial parent in odd numbered years:

[1] Martin Luther King Day. If observed by the child's school from Friday at 6:00 P.M. until Monday at 7:00 P.M.

[2] Presidents' Day. If observed by the child's school, from Friday at 6:00 P.M. until Monday at 7:00 P.M.

[3] Memorial Day. From Friday at 6.00 P.M. until Monday at 7:00 P.M.

[4] Labor Day. From Friday at 6:00 P.M. until Monday at 7:00 P.M.

[5] Thanksgiving. From 6:00 P.M. on Wednesday until 7:00 P.M. on Sunday.

The following holidays shall be exercised by the noncustodial parent in odd numbered years and the custodial parent in even numbered years:

[1] Spring Break. From two hours after the child is released from school on the child's last day of school before Spring Break and ending 7:00 p.m. on the last day before school begins again.

[2] Easter. From Friday at 6:00 P.M. until Sunday at 7:00 P.M.

[3] Fourth of July. From 6:00 P.M. on July 3rd until 10:00 A.M. on July 5th.

[4] Fall Break. From two hours after the child is released from school on the child's last day of school before Fall Break and ending 7:00 p. m. of the last day before school begins again.

[5] Halloween. On Halloween evening from 6:00 P.M. until 9:00 P.M. or at such time as coincides with the scheduled time for trick or treating in the community where the non-custodial parent resides.

3. **Religions Holidays.** Religious based holidays shall be considered by the parties and added to the foregoing holiday schedule when appropriate. The addition of such holidays shall not affect the Christmas vacation parenting time, however, they may affect the Christmas day and Easter parenting time

Commentary:

Recognizing there are individuals of varying faiths who celebrate holidays other than those set out in the guidelines, the parties should try to work out a holiday visitation schedule that fairly divides the holidays which they celebrate over a two-year period in as equal a manner as possible.

Adopted Dec. 22, 2000, effective March 31, 2001. Amended Jan. 4, 2013, effective March 1, 2013; Aug. 26, 2013.

SECTION III. PARENTING TIME WHEN DISTANCE IS A MAJOR FACTOR

Where there is a significant geographical distance between the parents, scheduling parenting time is fact sensitive and requires consideration of many factors which include: employment schedules, the costs and time of travel, the financial situation of each parent, the frequency of the parenting time and others.

1. **General Rules Applicable.** The general rules regarding parenting time as set forth in Section 1 of these guidelines shall apply.

2. **Parenting Time Schedule.** The parents shall make every effort to establish a reasonable parenting time schedule.

Commentary

When distance is a major factor, the following parenting time schedule may be helpful:

(A) Child Under 3 Years Of Age. For a child under 3 years of age, the noncustodial parent shall have the option to exercise parenting time, in the community of the custodial parent, up to two five hour periods each week. The five hour period may occur on Saturday and Sunday on alternate weekends only.

(B) Child 3 and 4 Years of Age. For a child 3 and 4 years of age, up to six (6) one week segments annually, each separated by at least (6) weeks.

Including the pickup and return of the child, no segment shall exceed eight (8) days.

(C) Child 5 Years of Age and Older. For a child 5 years of age and older who attends a school with a traditional school calendar, seven (7) weeks of the school summer vacation period and seven (7) days of the school winter vacation plus the entire spring break, including both weekends if applicable. Such parenting time, however, shall be arranged so that the custodial parent shall have religious holidays, if celebrated, in alternate years.

If the child attends a school with a year-round or balanced calendar, the noncustodial parent's parenting time should be adjusted so that the noncustodial parent and child spend at least as much time together as they would under a traditional school calendar.

3. **Priority of Summer Visitation.** Summer parenting time with the non-custodial parent shall take precedence over summer activities (such as Little League) when parenting time cannot be reasonably scheduled around such events. Under such circumstances, the non-custodial parent shall attempt to enroll the child in a similar activity in his or her community.

4. **Extended Parenting Time Notice.** The non-custodial parent shall give notice to the custodial parent of the selection by April 1 of each year. If such notice is not given, the custodial parent shall make the selection.

5. **Special Notice of Availability.** When the non-custodial parent is in the area where the child resides, or when the child is in the area where the non-custodial parent resides, liberal parenting time shall be allowed. The parents shall provide notice to each other, as far in advance as possible, of such parenting opportunities.

Adopted Dec. 22, 2000, effective March 31, 2001. Amended Jan. 4, 2013, effective March 1, 2013.

SECTION IV. PARALLEL PARENTING

Scope. Parallel parenting is a deviation from the parenting time guidelines, Sections I, II, and III. Its application should be limited to cases where the court determines the parties are high conflict and a Parallel Parenting Plan Court Order is necessary to stop ongoing high conflict that is endangering the well-being of the child. "High conflict parents" mean parties who demonstrate a pattern of ongoing litigation, chronic anger and distrust, inability to communicate about and cooperate in the care of the child, or other behaviors placing the child's well-being at risk. In such cases the court may deviate from the parenting time guidelines to reduce the adverse effects on the children. The contact between high conflict parents should be minimized or eliminated, at least until the parent conflict is under control.

In parallel parenting, each parent makes day-to-day decisions about the child while the child is with the parent. With parallel parenting, communication between the parents is limited, except in emergencies, and the communication is usually in writing. Appropriate counseling professionals are recommended to help parents handle parallel parenting arrangements. Parallel parenting may also be appropriate to phase out supervised parenting time. Parallel parenting is not a permanent arrangement.

Commentary:

High conflict parents constantly argue with each other in the presence of the children. They often blame the other parent for their problems. Some parents make negative comments to the children about the other parent. Children of high conflict parents may develop emotional and behavioral problems. For example, they may become fearful, develop low self-esteem, think they are the cause of their parents' fighting or find themselves having to choose between their parents. Parallel parenting may be used to bridge between supervised parenting time and guideline parenting time. Of course, the best interests and safety of the children are paramount in all situations.

The court should recognize the danger that one parent could unilaterally create a high conflict situation. This behavior should not be rewarded by limiting the parenting time of the other parent.

1. Limitations of Parallel Parenting. Joint legal custody of children is normally inappropriate in parallel parenting situations. Rather, sole legal custody is the norm in parallel parenting cases. Additionally, mid week parenting time is not usually proper in parallel parenting cases, due to the higher level of contact and cooperation that is required to implement mid week parenting time. Similarly, in parallel parenting cases, "Make Up" time and the "Opportunity for Additional Parenting Time" are generally inappropriate.

2. Education. In some communities, parents can attend high conflict resolution classes or cooperative parenting classes. In these classes, parents learn that any continuing conflict between them will likely have a long-term negative effect on their children. They also learn skills to be better co-parents.

3. Parallel Parenting Plan Court Order. In ordering the parties to parent according to a parallel parenting plan, the court must enter a written explanation regardless if the parties agree, indicating why the deviation from the regular Indiana Parenting Time Guidelines is necessary or appropriate. The court order shall detail the specific provisions of the plan.

Commentary:

The specific court order for parallel parenting in any individual case should include a consideration of the topics in the Appendix, which is a recommended model parallel parenting plan court order. This order should address "hot topic" issues for each family, and should also include any other provisions the court deems appropriate to the family. Several of the provisions in the model order would be applicable to nearly all cases where parallel parenting is appropriate. Other provisions would be applicable only in certain circumstances. Some of these provisions require the court to make and enter a choice among various options, including Section 2.2 of the model order. The court would modify the order to fit the circumstances of the parties and needs of the children.

4. Mandatory Review Hearing. In all cases, a hearing must be held to review a parallel parenting court order at least every 180 days. At this hearing, the court shall hear evidence and determine whether the parallel parenting plan order should continue, be modified or ended.

Adopted Jan. 4, 2013, effective March 1, 2013.

APPENDIX.   MODEL PARALLEL PARENTING PLAN ORDER

The following is a suggested Model Order For Parallel Parenting, which may be used in implementing these rules.

MODEL PARALLEL PARENTING PLAN ORDER

The court concludes the parties are high conflict parents, as defined in the Indiana Parenting Time Guidelines. The court finds high conflict because of the following behavior(s):

_____ a pattern of ongoing litigation;

_____ chronic anger and distrust;

_____ inability to communicate about the child;

_____ inability to cooperate in the care of the child; or

_____ other behaviors placing the child's well-being at risk:

_____

[OR The court finds parallel parenting is appropriate to phase out supervised parenting time.]

Accordingly, the court deviates from the Indiana Parenting Time Guidelines, and now Orders the following Parallel Parenting Plan.

1. RESPONSIBILITIES AND DECISION–MAKING

1.1 Each parent has a responsibility to provide for the physical and emotional needs of the child. Both parents are very important to the child and the child needs both parents to be active parents throughout their lives. Both parents must respect each parent's separate role with the child. Each parent must put the child's needs first in planning and making arrangements involving the child.

1.2 When the child is scheduled to be with Father, then Father is the "on-duty" parent. When the child is scheduled to be with Mother, then Mother is the "on-duty" parent.

1.3 The on-duty parent shall make decisions about the day to day care and control of the child.

1.4 This decision making is not to be confused with legal custody decision making concerning education, health care and religious upbringing of the child. These more significant decisions continue to be the exclusive responsibility of the parent who has been designated as the sole custodial parent.

1.5 In making decisions about the day to day care and control of the child, neither parent shall schedule activities for the child during the time the other parent is on-duty without prior agreement of the on-duty parent.

1.6 Parents share a joint and equal responsibility for following parenting time orders. The child shares none of this responsibility and should not be permitted to shoulder the burden of this decision.

1.7 Unacceptable excuses for one parent denying parenting time to the other include the following:

The child unjustifiably hesitates or refuses to go.

The child has a minor illness.

The child has to go somewhere.

The child is not home.

The noncustodial parent is behind in support.

The custodial parent does not want the child to go.

The weather is bad.

The child has no clothes to wear.

The other parent failed to meet preconditions established by the custodial parent.

2. REGULAR PARENTING TIME

2.1 The parents shall follow this specific schedule so the child understands the schedule.

2.2 [ ] Mother, *or* [ ] Father has sole custody of the child. The noncustodial parent shall have regular contact with the child as listed below:

[ ] Every other weekend, from 6:00 p.m. on Friday until 6:00 p.m. on Sunday.

[ ] Every other Saturday, from ___ a.m. until ___ p.m.

[ ] Every other Saturday and Sunday from ___ a.m. until ___ p.m. each day.

[ ] _____

[ ] _____

3. SUMMER PARENTING TIME SCHEDULE *(use only if summer is different than the Regular Parenting Time outlined above.)*

3.1 Mother shall be on-duty and the child will be with Mother as follows:

_____

_____

3.2 Father shall be on duty and the child will be with Father as follows:

_____

_____

4. HOLIDAY SCHEDULE

4.1 Holiday Schedule Priority. The below detailed holiday schedule overrides the above Regular Parenting Time Schedule. For listed holidays other than Spring Break and Christmas Break, when a holiday falls on a weekend, the parent who is on-duty for that holiday will be on-duty for the entire weekend unless specifically stated otherwise. It is possible under some circumstances that the holiday schedule could result in the child spending three (3) weekends in a row with the same parent.

4.2 On New Year's Eve/Day, Martin Luther King Day, President's Day, Easter, Memorial Day, 4th of July, Labor Day, Halloween, Fall Break, birthdays of the child and parents, and all other holidays / special days not specifically listed below, the child shall remain with the parent they are normally scheduled to be with that day, as provided in the Regular Parenting Time Schedule.

4.3 Spring Break. The child shall spend Spring Break with Father in odd numbered years and with Mother in even numbered years. This period shall be from two hours after the child is released from school before Spring Break, and ending at 7:00 pm of the last day before school begins again.

4.4 Mother's Day and Father's Day. The child shall spend Mother's Day weekend with Mother, and Father's Day weekend with Father each year. These periods shall be from Friday at 6:00 p.m. until Sunday at 6:00 p.m.

4.5 Thanksgiving. The child shall spend the Thanksgiving holiday, from two hours after the child is released from school Wednesday until Sunday at 7:00 p.m. with Father in odd numbered years, and with Mother in even numbered years.

4.6 Christmas.

a.   The Christmas vacation shall be defined as beginning on the last day of school and ending the last day before school begins again. Absent agreement of the parties, the first half of the period will begin two hours after the child is released from school. The second half of the period will end at 6:00 p.m. on the day before school begins again.

Each party will receive one half (½) of the total days of the Christmas vacation, on an alternating basis as follows:

1.   In even numbered years, the custodial parent shall have the first one half (½) of the Christmas vacation and non-custodial parent shall have the second one half (½) of the Christmas vacation.

2.   In odd numbered years, the non-custodial parent shall have the first one half (½) of the Christmas vacation and custodial parent shall have the second one half (½) of the Christmas vacation.

3.   In those years when Christmas does not fall in a parent's week, that parent shall have the child from Noon to 9:00 P.M. on Christmas Day.

4.   No exchanges under this portion of the rule shall occur after 9:00 p. m. and before 8:00 a.m., absent agreement of the parties.

Or

b.   The child shall celebrate Christmas Eve, December 24, from 9:00 a.m. until 9:00 p.m. with Mother in odd numbered years, and with Father in even numbered years. The child shall celebrate Christmas Day, December 25, from 9:00 p.m. on December 24 until 6:00 p.m. on December 25 with Father in odd numbered years, and with Mother in even numbered years. At 6:00 p.m. on December 25, the Regular Parenting Time Schedule resumes.

Or

c.   Other: _____

5.   TRANSPORTATION OF THE CHILD

5.1 The parents shall arrive on time to drop off and pick up the child. The parents shall deliver the child's clothing, school supplies and belongings at the same time they deliver the child. The parents shall always attempt to return the child's clothing in a clean condition.

5.2 When the child is scheduled to return to Father, then Father shall pick the child up at [ ] Mother's home or [ ] _____.

5.3 When the child is scheduled to return to Mother, then Mother shall pick the child up at [ ] Father's home *or* [ ] _____.

5.4 Special Provisions Regarding Exchange Participation: *(if necessary)*

Other than the parents, only _____ shall be present when the child is exchanged. _____.

5.5 A parent may not enter the residence of the other, except by express invitation, regardless of whether a parent retains a property interest in the residence of the other. Accordingly, the child shall be picked up at the front entrance of the appropriate residence or other location unless the parents agree otherwise. The person delivering the child shall not leave until the child is safely inside.

6. EMERGENCY CHANGES IN THE REGULAR PARENTING TIME SCHEDULE

6.1 Although the child needs living arrangements that are predictable, if an unexpected or unavoidable emergency comes up, the parents shall give each other as much notice as possible.

6.2 If unable to agree on a requested change to the schedule, the Regular Parenting Time Schedule shall be followed. If an emergency results in the need for child care, the on-duty parent shall make the child care arrangements and pay for the cost of child care, unless otherwise agreed.

6.3 Unless the parents agree, any missed parenting time shall not later be made up.

7. COMMUNICATION

7.1 Communication Book. The parents shall always use a "communication book" to communicate with each other on the child's education, health care, and activities. The communication book should be a spiral or hardbound notebook. The communication book will travel with the child, so that information about the child will be transmitted between the parents with minimal contact between parents.

7.2 Neutrality of the Child. To keep the child out of the middle of the parents' relationship and any conflict that may arise between the parents, the parents shall not:

Ask the child about the other parent.

Ask the child to give messages to the other parent.

Make unkind or negative statements about the other parent around the child.

Allow other people to make unkind or negative statements about the other parent around the child.

7.3 Dignity and Respect. The parents shall treat each other with dignity and respect in the presence of the child. The parents shall keep conversations short and calm when exchanging the child so the child will not become afraid or anxious.

7.4 Telephone Contact. The child may have private telephone access to the other parent [ ] at all times *or* [ ] between the hours of ___ and ___. The parents shall encourage and help the child stay in touch with the other parent.

7.5 The parents shall not interfere with communication between the child and the other parent by actions such as: refusing to answer a phone or refusing to allow the child or others to answer; recording phone conversations between the other parent and the child; turning off the phone or using a call blocking mechanism or otherwise denying the other parent telephone or electronic contact with the child.

7.6 Notice of Travel. Before leaving on out of town travel, the parents shall provide each other the address and phone number where the child can be reached if they will be away from home for more than 48 hours.

7.7 The parents shall at all times keep each other advised of their home and work addresses and telephone numbers. Notice of any change in this information shall be given to the other parent in the communication book at the next exchange.

8. SAFETY *(use the following provisions only as necessary)*

8.1 Neither parent shall operate a vehicle when impaired by use of alcohol or drugs.

8.2 [] Mother []Father [] Both parents shall not use alcohol or non-prescribed drugs when they are the on-duty parent.

8.3 The parents shall not leave the child ___ unattended at any time.

8.4 [] Mother []Father [] Both parents shall not use, nor allow anyone else to use, physical discipline with the child.

8.5 _____ shall not use physical discipline with the child.

8.6 All contact between the child and _____ shall be supervised by _____.

8.7 Neither parent shall allow the child to be in the presence of _____

9. EDUCATION

9.1 The custodial parent shall determine where the child attends school.

9.2 Both parents shall instruct the child's schools to list each parent and their respective addresses and telephone numbers on the school's records.

9.3 Each parent will maintain contact with the child's schools to find out about the child's needs, progress, grades, parent-teacher conferences, and other special events.

9.4 The parents shall use the "communication book" to share information about the child's school progress, behavior and events.

10. EXTENDED FAMILY

10.1 The child will usually benefit from maintaining ties with grandparents, relatives and people important to them. The parents shall help the child continue to be in contact with these people.

10.2 However, as provided above at "SAFETY," [ ] all contact between the child and _____ shall be supervised by _____

[ ] neither parent shall allow the child to be in the presence of _____

11. CHILD CARE

11.1 Arranging for normal, day-to-day work-related child care for the child is the responsibility of the [ ] custodial parent [ ] on-duty parent.

11.2 When occasional other situations require child care for the child when the child is with the on-duty parent, the on-duty parent is not required to offer the other parent the chance to provide this care before seeking someone else to care for the child. However, in such situations, the on-duty parent shall make any needed occasional child care arrangements, and the on-duty parent shall pay the cost of that child care.

11.3 Only the following listed persons may provide occasional child care for the child: _____.

11.4 If the [ ] Mother [ ] Father anticipates being unable to personally supervise the child during the parent's entire scheduled on-duty time, the [ ] Mother [ ] Father must notify the other parent as soon as possible, and that parent's on-duty time for that [ ] day [ ] weekend will be cancelled, and not made up at any later time.

12. HEALTH CARE

12.1 Major decisions about health care (such as the need for surgery, glasses, contacts, prescription medications, orthodontia, etc., and the need for regular, on-going medical appointments and treatments, etc.) shall be made by the custodial parent.

12.2 Each parent has a right to the child's medical, dental, optical and other health care information and records. Each parent will contact the child's health care providers to find out about the child's health care needs, treatments and progress. The custodial parent shall give written authorization to the child's health care providers, permitting an ongoing release of all information regarding the child to the non-custodial parent including the right of the provider to discuss the child's situation with the non-custodial parent.

12.3 The parents shall use the "communication book" to communicate with each other on all health care issues for the child.

12.4 The on-duty parent shall make sure the child takes all prescription medication and follow all prescribed health care treatments.

12.5 In medical emergencies concerning the child, the on-duty parent shall notify the other parent of the emergency as soon as it is possible. In such emergencies, each parent can consent to emergency medical treatment for the child, as needed.

13.   RELOCATION FROM CURRENT RESIDENCE

13.1 When either parent considers a change of residence, a 90 day advance notice of the intent to move must be provided to the other parent and filed with the court.

13.2 The Indiana Parenting Time Guidelines have a more detailed discussion of the statutory notice requirements at Section I.E.4, "Relocation."

14.   EVENT ATTENDANCE

14.1 When the child is participating in a sports team, club, religious, or other such event at school or elsewhere, [ ] only the on-duty parent [ ] both parents may attend the event.

14.2 The custodial parent is permitted to enroll the child in _____ extracurricular activity. The non-custodial parent shall encourage this participation.

15.   A CHILD'S BASIC NEEDS

To insure more responsible parenting and to promote the healthy adjustment and growth of the child, each parent should recognize and address the child's basic needs. Those needs include the following:

15.1 To know that the parents' decision to live apart is not the child's fault.

15.2 To develop and maintain an independent relationship with each parent and to have the continuing care and guidance from each parent.

15.3 To be free from having to side with either parent and to be free from conflict between the parents.

15.4 To have a relaxed, secure relationship with each parent without being placed in a position to manipulate one parent against the other.

15.5 To enjoy consistent time with each parent.

15.6 To be financially supported by each parent, regardless of how much time each parent spends with the child.

15.7 To be physically safe and adequately supervised when in the care of each parent and to have a stable, consistent and responsible child care arrangement when not supervised by a parent.

15.8 To develop and maintain meaningful relationships with other significant adults (grandparents, stepparents and other relatives) as long as these relationships do not interfere with or replace the child's primary relationship with the parents.

16.   RESOLVING DISPUTES

16.1 Because this is an Order of the court, both parents must continue to follow this Parallel Parenting Plan even if the other parent does not.

16.2 When the parents cannot agree on the meaning or application of some part of this Parallel Parenting Plan, or if a significant change (such as a move or remarriage) causes conflict between the parents, both parents shall make a good faith effort to resolve those differences before returning to the court for relief. In most situations, the court will require the parents to attend mediation before any court hearing will be conducted.

16.3 The parties shall attend _____ counseling / parenting education program.

17.   MANDATORY REVIEW HEARING

17.1 A mandatory review hearing is set on _____, 20 ___, at ___ a.m./p.m. in this court. Both parents shall appear at this hearing with counsel of record. [Note: The date shall be set within 180 days of the entry of this order]

DATE: _____, 20 ___   _____

COMMISSIONER/MAGISTRATE/JUDGE

The above entry is adopted as the Order of the Court on this same date.

_____

JUDGE

Copies to: Attorney for Petitioner,
              Attorney for Respondent,
              Mediator:

DATE OF NOTICE:
INITIAL OF PERSON WHO NOTIFIED PARTIES: COURT CLERK OTHER

Adopted Jan. 4, 2013, effective March 1, 2013. Amended effective Aug. 26, 2013.

INDIANA RULES FOR ADMISSION TO THE BAR AND THE DISCIPLINE OF ATTORNEYS

Including Amendments Received Through November 1, 2013

Rule 1. The Bar of Indiana

The bar of this state shall consist of all attorneys in good standing who, prior to July 1, 1931, were duly admitted to practice law by the circuit courts of this state, and all attorneys in good standing who, subsequently thereto, have been or hereafter shall be admitted to practice by this court.

Rule 2. Registration and Fees

(a) **Name and Address.** All attorneys in active or inactive good standing, duly admitted to the practice of law in the State of Indiana shall file with the Clerk of the Supreme Court, 216 State House, Indianapolis, Indiana 46204, their correct name, office and residence address, office telephone number, electronic mail address, and county of residence. Said attorneys shall notify the Clerk of the Supreme Court of any change of address (including electronic mail address), change of telephone number, or change of name within thirty (30) days of such change. A notice of a change of name shall be accompanied by a copy of the court record or an affidavit that states the name change. The names and addresses so filed shall be effective for all notices involving licenses as attorneys and/or disciplinary matters, and a failure to file same shall be a waiver of notice involving licenses as attorneys and/or disciplinary matters. The Clerk shall annually send a certified list of attorneys, together with their addresses on file to the Indiana State Bar Association.

(b) **Annual Registration Fee—Active Attorneys.** Except as provided in sections (c) or (d), each attorney who is a member of the bar of this Court on August 1 of each year shall, so long as the attorney is a member of the Bar of this Court, pay a registration fee of one hundred forty-five dollars ($145.00) on or before October 1 of such year. A delinquent fee in the amount of ninety-five dollars ($95.00) shall be added to the registration fee for fees paid after October 1 and on or before October 15 of each year; a delinquent fee in the amount of one hundred forty-five dollars ($145.00) shall be added to the registration fee for fees paid after October 15 and on or before December 31 of each year; and a delinquent fee in the amount of two hundred ninety-five dollars ($295.00) shall be added to the registration fee for fees paid after December 31 of each year. An attorney who has paid the registration fee under this subsection and any applicable delinquent fees and who is otherwise eligible to practice law in this state shall be considered to be in active good standing.

Any attorney admitted to practice law in this State on a date subsequent to August 1 of each year shall, within ten (10) days of the date of his or her admission to the Bar of the Court, or by October 1 of said year, whichever date is later, pay a registration fee of one hundred forty-five dollars ($145.00).

(c) Annual Registration Fee—Inactive Attorneys. One-half (1/2) of the registration fee referred to in section (b) shall be required of an attorney who files with the Clerk, on or before October 1 of each year, an affidavit of inactivity, stating that he or she is currently in active good standing or wishes to retain inactive standing, and that he or she neither holds judicial office nor is engaged in the practice of law in this state. A delinquent fee in the amount of fifty dollars ($50.00) shall be added to the registration fee for fees paid after October 1 and on or before October 15 of each year; and a delinquent fee in the amount of one hundred dollars ($100.00) shall be added to the registration fee for fees paid after October 15 of each year. An attorney who has paid the registration fee under this section and any applicable delinquent fees shall be considered to be in inactive good standing. An inactive attorney shall promptly notify the Clerk of a desire to return to active status, and pay the applicable registration fee for the current year, prior to any act of practicing law.

(d) Annual Registration Fee—Retired Attorneys. No registration fee shall be required of an attorney who is sixty-five (65) years old or older and files with the Clerk, by October 1 of any year, an affidavit of retirement, stating that he or she is currently in active or inactive good standing, neither holds judicial office nor is engaged in the practice of law in this state, and does not plan to return to the practice of law. An affidavit of retirement, once filed, shall be effective for each succeeding year or until the attorney is reinstated pursuant to section (e).

(e) Reinstatement of Retired Attorneys. In the event there is no basis for the suspension of the attorney's license to practice law, a retired attorney's privilege to practice law shall be reinstated upon submitting to the Clerk a written application for reinstatement and payment of:

(1) the unpaid registration fee for the year of reinstatement;

(2) registration fees, including delinquent fees, in the amount referred to in section (b) for each year of retirement; and

(3) an administrative reinstatement fee of two hundred dollars ($200.00).

The Clerk shall deposit the administrative reinstatement fee referred to in subsection (e)(3) into the "Clerk of the Courts–Annual Fees" account, described in section (m).

(f) IOLTA Certification. On or before October 1 of each year, every attorney admitted to practice law in this state shall certify to the Clerk of this Court that all client funds that are nominal in amount or to be held for a short period of time by the attorney so that they could not earn income for the client in excess of the costs incurred to secure such income are held in an IOLTA account (as that term is defined in Indiana Rules of Professional Conduct, Rule 1.15(f)) of the attorney or law firm or that the attorney is exempt under the provisions of Prof. Cond. R. 1.15(g)(2). Any attorney who fails to make an IOLTA certification on or before October 1 of each year shall be assessed a delinquent fee according to the schedule set forth in section (b) if the attorney is active or section (c) if the attorney is inactive.

(g) Annual Registration Notice. On or before August 1 of each year, the Clerk of this Court shall mail a notice to or notify via electronic mail each attorney then admitted to the bar of this Court who is in active or inactive good standing that: (i) a registration fee must be paid on or before October 1; and (ii) the certification required by section (f) of this rule and by Ind. Prof. Cond. R. 1.15(g) must be filed with the Clerk on or before October 1. The Clerk shall also send such notice to the Clerk for each circuit and superior court in this State for posting in a prominent place in the courthouse, the Indiana State Bar Association, and such print and other media publishers of legal information as the Clerk reasonably determines appropriate. Provided, however, that the failure of the Clerk to send such notice will not mitigate the duty to pay the required fee and file the required certification.

(h) Failure to Pay Registration Fee; Reinstatement. Any attorney who fails to pay a registration fee required under section (b) or (c) or fails to file the certification required by section (f) of this rule and by Ind.Prof. Cond. R. 1.15(g) shall be subject to suspension from the practice of law and sanctions for contempt of this Court in the event he or she thereafter engages in the practice of law in this State. In the event there is no basis for the continued suspension of the attorney's license to practice law, such an attorney's privilege to practice law shall be reinstated upon submitting to the Clerk a written application for reinstatement and payment of:

(1) the applicable unpaid registration fee for the year of suspension;

(2) any delinquent fees for the year of suspension due pursuant to section (b) or (c);

(3) the applicable unpaid registration fee for the year of reinstatement, if different from the year of suspension;

(4) a registration fee, including delinquent fees, in the amount referred to in section (c) for all intervening years of suspension;

(5) an administrative reinstatement fee of two hundred dollars ($200.00); and

(6) the certification required by section (f) of this rule.

The Clerk shall deposit the administrative reinstatement fee referred to in subsection (h)(5) in to the "Clerk of the Courts-Annual Fees" account, described in section (m).

(i) Certification of Good Standing. The Clerk of this Court shall issue a certificate of active good standing or inactive good standing approved by this Court to any attorney upon the receipt of the annual registration fee and any applicable delinquent fees referred to in sections (b) and (c), respectively. The certificate of active good standing shall include a statement to the effect that the lawyer has filed the certification required by section (f) of this rule.

(j) Annual Continuing Education Fee — Non-attorney Judges.

(1) On or before August 1, of each year, the Clerk shall mail to each non-attorney judge a notice that an education fee of forty-five dollars ($45.00) must be paid on or before the first day of October. Failure to pay the education fee on or before October 1, will result in the imposition of a delinquency fee of forty-five dollars ($45.00).

(2) Any non-attorney judge who fails to pay the education fee shall be automatically suspended from judicial office. A non-attorney judge may resume office upon written application, payment of unpaid education fees and payment of the delinquency fee set out in subsection (1).

(k) Effective Dates.

(1) The requirement in section (c) that inactive attorneys pay an annual registration fee shall apply to all inactive attorneys and shall be effective for the annual fee due on or before October 1, 2002. Notwithstanding any other provision in this rule, any inactive attorney who filed an affidavit of inactivity on or before October 1, 2001 and who, after suspension for nonpayment of the annual registration fee referred to in section (c), thereafter seeks reinstatement to active or inactive attorney status pursuant to section (h), shall not be required to pay unpaid registration or delinquent fees pursuant to (h)(4) for any year prior to October 1, 2002.

(2) Notwithstanding any other provision in this rule, any attorney who, after suspension for nonpayment of the annual registration fee referred to in section (b), thereafter seeks reinstatement to active or inactive attorney status pursuant to section (h), shall not be required to pay unpaid registration or delinquent fees pursuant to section (h)(4) for any year prior to October 1, 2002.

(3) Notwithstanding any other provision in this rule, any retired attorney who seeks reinstatement to active attorney status pursuant to section (e) shall not be required to pay unpaid registration or delinquent fees pursuant to (e)(2) for any year prior to October 1, 2002.

(*l*) Affidavit of Permanent Withdrawal. An attorney in good standing, who is current in payment of all applicable registration fees and other financial obligations imposed by these rules, and who is not the subject of an investigation into, or a pending proceeding involving, allegations of misconduct, who desires to relinquish permanently his or her license to practice law in the State of Indiana may do so by tendering an Affidavit of Permanent Withdrawal from the practice of law in this State to the Executive Secretary of the Indiana Supreme Court Disciplinary Commission. The Executive Secretary shall promptly verify the eligibility of the attorney to resign under this section, and if eligible, forward a certification of eligibility, together with the Affidavit of Permanent Withdrawal to the Clerk of the Indiana Supreme Court, and the Clerk shall show on the roll of attorneys that the attorney's Indiana law license has been relinquished permanently and that the lawyer is no longer considered an attorney licensed to practice law in the State of Indiana. An attorney who permanently withdraws under this section shall not be eligible for reinstatement under section (e) or (h), but may apply for admission under Admission and Discipline Rules 3 through 21. In the event the attorney is not eligible to permanently withdraw under this section, the Executive Secretary shall promptly notify the attorney of all reasons for ineligibility.

(m) Deposit and Use of Funds.

(1) Deposit of Funds. All funds collected by the Clerk under this rule shall be deposited in an account to be maintained by the Clerk and designated "Clerk of the Courts–Annual Fees." The Clerk shall thereafter issue those funds as directed by the Indiana Supreme Court.

(2) Use of Funds. The Indiana Supreme Court shall periodically apportion the registration fees collected pursuant to this rule for the operation of the Indiana Supreme Court Disciplinary Commission, the Indiana Commission for Continuing Legal Education, and the Judges and Lawyers Assistance Committee.

Amended Oct. 15, 1986, effective Jan. 1, 1987; Nov. 30, 1989, effective Jan. 1, 1990; Dec. 21, 2001, effective April 1, 2002; Aug. 15, 2006, effective Jan. 1, 2007; Sept. 10, 2007, effective Jan. 1, 2008; Sept. 15, 2009, effective Jan. 1, 2010; July 30, 2010, effective Aug. 1, 2010; July 28, 2011, effective Aug. 1, 2011; Sept. 20, 2011, effective Jan. 1, 2012; Oct. 7, 2011, effective Jan. 1, 2012.

Rule 2.1.   Legal Interns

Section 1.   Requirements.

(a) A law student may serve as a legal intern when the following requirements are met:

1. The law student is enrolled in a school accredited pursuant to Admission and Discipline Rule 13V(A);

2. The law student has satisfactorily completed one-half of the academic requisite for a first professional degree in law;

3. The law student has received permission of the Dean of the law school to participate in a legal intern program determined to be beneficial to the law student's training pursuant to the guidelines jointly developed by the law schools of this State; and

4. The law student has completed or is enrolled in a legal ethics or professional responsibility course as set forth in Ind.Admission and Discipline Rule 13(V)(C).

(b) A law school graduate may serve as a legal intern when the following requirements are met:

1. The law graduate has received a first professional degree in law from a school accredited pursuant to Admission and Discipline Rule 13(V)(A);

2. The law graduate is eligible to take the Bar examination under Admission and Discipline Rule 13V; and

3. The law graduate has received permission from an attorney who is a member of the Bar of this State to serve as a legal intern under that attorney's direct supervision.

Section 2. Length of Intern Status.

(a) A law student may serve as a legal intern until graduation from law school or for a lesser period if so designated by the Dean of the law school.

(b) A law school graduate may serve as a legal intern from the date of graduation until the graduate has taken and has been notified of the results of the first examination for which the graduate is eligible under Admission and Discipline Rule 13V, or if successful on that examination, until the first opportunity thereafter for formal admission to the Bar of Indiana.

Section 3. Certification.

(a) The Dean of a law school sponsoring a legal intern program shall advise the Indiana Supreme Court Board of Law Examiners of those students who qualify to be legal interns and the length of that internship.

(b) An Attorney, who is a member of the Bar of this State and who wishes to sponsor and supervise a graduate as a legal intern, shall so advise the Indiana Supreme Court Board of Law Examiners; and also, the Dean of the law school from which the graduate received the first professional degree in law shall advise the Indiana Supreme Court Board of Law Examiners of the date of graduation and the date at which such graduate will be first eligible for examination under Admission and Discipline Rule 13V.

Section 4. Scope of Conduct.

A legal intern may interview, advise, negotiate for, and represent parties in any judicial or administrative proceeding in this State, provided all activities undertaken are supervised and approved by an attorney who is a member of the Bar of this State. A legal intern shall inform each client of his or her intern status, and that the intern is not a licensed attorney. A legal intern shall not interview any person represented by an attorney without the express permission of such attorney. In no event may a person (including private corporations) be charged for the services of a legal intern acting in a representative capacity. The personal presence of a supervising attorney is required in any proceeding in open court.

Amended effective Feb. 16, 1972; amended Nov. 24, 1975, effective Jan. 31, 1976; amended Dec. 23, 1976, effective Jan. 1, 1977; amended Nov. 1, 1982, effective Jan. 1, 1983; amended Nov. 16, 1984, effective Jan. 1, 1985; amended Oct. 30, 1992, effective Jan. 1, 1993; amended Dec. 18, 1995, effective Feb. 1, 1996.

Rule 3. Admission of Attorneys

Section 1. Admission of Attorneys.

The Supreme Court shall have exclusive jurisdiction to admit attorneys to practice in Indiana. Admission to practice law by the Court pursuant to Rule 21 shall entitle attorneys to practice in any of the courts of this state.

Section 2. Temporary Admission on Petition.

(a) *Requirements for Temporary Admission on Petition.* Any court of the State of Indiana, in the exercise of discretion, may permit a member of the bar of another state or territory of the United States, or the District of Columbia, not admitted pursuant to Rule 21, to appear in a particular case or proceeding, only if the court before which the attorney wishes to appear or in the case of an administrative proceeding, the Supreme Court, determines that there is good cause for such appearance and that each of the following conditions is met:

(1) A member of the bar of this state has appeared and agreed to act as co- counsel.

(2) The attorney is not a resident of the state of Indiana, regularly employed in the state of Indiana, or regularly engaged in business or professional activities in the state of Indiana.

(3) The attorney has made payment to the Clerk of the Supreme Court an annual registration fee in the amount set forth in Admission and Discipline Rule 2(b), accompanied by a copy of the Verified Petition for Temporary Admission that the attorney intends to file pursuant to subdivision (4) below. Upon receipt of the registration fee and petition, the Clerk of the Supreme Court will issue a temporary admission attorney number and payment re-

ceipt to the attorney seeking admission. If the attorney's verified petition for temporary admission is thereafter denied, the attorney shall provide a copy of the order denying temporary admission to the Clerk of the Supreme Court, and the Clerk shall issue a refund of the registration fee.

(4) The attorney files a verified petition, co-signed by co-counsel designated pursuant to subdivision (a)(1), setting forth:

(i) The attorney's residential address, office address, office telephone number, electronic mail address, and the name and address of the attorney's law firm or employer, if applicable;

(ii) All states or territories in which the attorney has ever been licensed to practice law, including the dates of admission to practice and any attorney registration numbers;

(iii) That the attorney is currently a member in good standing in all jurisdictions listed in (ii);

(iv) That the attorney has never been suspended, disbarred or resigned as a result of a disciplinary charge, investigation, or proceeding from the practice of law in any jurisdiction; or, if the attorney has been suspended, disbarred or resigned from the practice of law, the petition shall specify the jurisdiction, the charges, the address of the court and disciplinary authority which imposed the sanction, and the reasons why the court should grant temporary admission not withstanding prior acts of misconduct;

(v) That no disciplinary proceeding is presently pending against the attorney in any jurisdiction; or, if any proceeding is pending, the petition shall specify the jurisdiction, the charges and the address of the disciplinary authority investigating the charges. An attorney admitted under this rule shall have a continuing obligation during the period of such admission promptly to advise the court of a disposition made of pending charges or the institution of new disciplinary proceedings;

(vi) A list of all cases and proceedings, including caption and case number, in which either the attorney, or any member of a firm with which the attorney is currently affiliated, has appeared in any court or administrative agency of this state during the last five (5) years by temporary admission.

(vii) Absent good cause, repeated appearances by any person or by members of a single law firm pursuant to this rule shall be cause for denial of the petition. A demonstration that good cause exists for the appearance shall include at least one of the following:

(a) the cause in which the attorney seeks admission involves a complex field of law in which the attorney has special expertise,

(b) there has been an attorney-client relationship with the client for an extended period of time,

(c) there is a lack of local counsel with adequate expertise in the field involved,

(d) the cause presents questions of law involving the law of the foreign jurisdiction in which the applicant is licensed, or

(e) such other reason similar to those set forth in this subsection as would present good cause for the temporary admission.

(viii) A statement that the attorney has read and will be bound by the Rules of Professional Conduct adopted by the Supreme Court, and that the attorney consents to the jurisdiction of the State of Indiana, the Indiana Supreme Court, and the Indiana Supreme Court Disciplinary Commission to resolve any disciplinary matter that might arise as a result of the representation.

(ix) A statement that the attorney has paid the registration fee to the Clerk of the Supreme Court in compliance with subdivision (a)(3) of this rule, together with a copy of the payment receipt and temporary admission attorney number issued by the Clerk of the Supreme Court pursuant to subdivision (3).

(b) Notice of Temporary Admission. All attorneys granted temporary admission under the provisions of subsection 2(a) shall file a Notice with the Clerk of the Supreme Court within thirty (30) days after a court grants permission to appear in the case or proceeding. A separate Notice of Temporary Admission must be filed with the Clerk of the Supreme Court for each case or proceeding in which a court grants permission to appear. Failure to file the notice within the time specified shall result in automatic exclusion from practice within this state. The notice shall include the following:

(1) A current statement of good standing issued to the attorney by the highest court in each jurisdiction in which the attorney is admitted to practice law; and

(2) A copy of the verified petition requesting permission to appear along with the order granting permission.

(c) Renewal of Registration for Temporary Admission. If an attorney continues to appear on the basis of a temporary admission in any case or proceeding pending as of the first day of a new calendar year, the attorney shall pay a renewal fee equal to the annual registration fee set out in Admission and Discipline Rule 2(b). This renewal fee shall be due within thirty (30) days of the start of that calendar year and shall be tendered to the Clerk of the Supreme Court, accompanied by a copy of the Notice of Temporary Admission for each continuing case or proceeding in which a court has granted permission to appear. Failure to pay the required renewal fee within the time specified shall result in automatic exclusion from practice within this state. The Clerk of the Indiana Supreme Court shall notify the trial court or administrative agency of the attorney's exclusion. If the

proceeding has concluded or if the attorney has withdrawn his or her appearance, the attorney must so notify the Clerk of the Supreme Court by the deadline for renewal of registration.

(d) Responsibilities of Attorneys. Members of the bar of this state serving as co-counsel under this rule shall sign all briefs, papers and pleadings in the cause and shall be jointly responsible therefore. The signature of co-counsel constitutes a certificate that, to the best of co-counsel's knowledge, information and belief, there is good ground to support the signed document and that it is not interposed for delay or any other improper reason. Unless ordered by the trial court, local counsel need not be personally present at proceeding before the court.

(e) Failure to Register, Renew, or Otherwise Perform as Required. Any foreign attorney who fails to register or pay the registration fee as required under subsection (a), fails to file a Notice of Temporary Admission under subsection (b), or fails to pay a renewal registration fee required under subsection (c) shall be subject to discipline in this state. Members of the bar of this state serving as co-counsel under this rule shall be subject to discipline if the attorney admitted under this rule fails to pay the required fees or otherwise fails to satisfy the requirements of this rule.

(f) Scope and Effect of Automatic Exclusion from Practice Within the State.

(1) When an attorney is automatically excluded from practice within the state under Section 2(b) or (c), any further action taken by that attorney in any case or proceeding in the state shall constitute the unauthorized practice of law.

(2) An attorney may seek relief from the automatic exclusion from practice within the state by filing a "Petition for Relief from Automatic Exclusion" with the Supreme Court. The petition shall be captioned: "In re Temporary Admission of [Attorney's name]." The petition shall describe the circumstances causing the exclusion, shall list all pending cases or proceedings, including court or administrative agency and case number, in which the attorney had been granted temporary admission prior to the automatic exclusion, and shall be accompanied by a "Notice of Temporary Admission" if the exclusion is under Section 2(b) or a renewal admission fee, together with a delinquent fee in the amount of one hundred and forty-five dollars ($145.00), if the exclusion is under Section 2(c).

(3) If the Supreme Court grants the petition, the exclusion from practice shall be lifted and the Clerk of the Supreme Court shall notify all courts and administrative agencies in which the attorney had been granted temporary admission to practice in cases or proceedings pending at the time of the automatic exclusion. Unless the Supreme Court directs otherwise, all actions taken by the attorney

during the period of automatic exclusion from practice shall be deemed valid to the extent the actions would have been valid if the attorney had not been subject to automatic exclusion. However, the attorney remains subject to a charge of the unauthorized practice of law for actions taken during the automatic exclusion.

The amendments apply only to requests for Temporary Admission on Petition filed on or after January 1, 2007.

If an attorney files the notice with the Clerk of the Supreme Court and pays the fee required by subpart (b) of the Rule in one case or proceeding in any given calendar year, the attorney need not pay another fee for any other case in which the attorney seeks Temporary Admission on Petition during that same calendar year.

If an attorney files the notice with the Clerk of the Supreme Court and pays the fee required by subparts (a) and (b) of the Rule in a particular calendar year, and a new calendar year begins and the attorney is still appearing in any case or proceeding pursuant to a Temporary Admission on Petition, the attorney must file a new notice and pay a fee within 30 days of the start of the new calendar year.

If more than one (1) attorney from one firm is appearing pursuant to a Temporary Admission on Petition in a particular case or proceeding on behalf of the same client, each attorney appearing nevertheless has an individual obligation to comply with the Rule as amended.

Amended effective April 14, 1965; amended Nov. 30, 1989, effective Jan. 1, 1990; Dec. 4, 1998, effective Jan. 1, 1999; Dec. 21, 2001, effective April 1, 2002; July 1, 2003, effective Jan. 1, 2004; Sept. 30, 2004, effective Jan. 1, 2005; Aug. 15, 2006, effective Jan. 1, 2007; Sept. 10, 2007, effective Jan. 1, 2008; Sept. 9, 2008, effective Jan. 1, 2009; amended effective Aug. 1, 2010; amended Aug. 25, 2010, effective Jan. 1, 2011; July 28, 2011, effective Aug. 1, 2011; Sept. 20, 2011, effective Jan. 1, 2012.

Rule 4.   Roll of Attorneys

A record shall hereafter be made and entered on the order book of this court of the admission, enrollment, resignation, suspension, disbarment, reinstatement, and recertification of any and all members of the bar of this court. In addition, the clerk of this court shall keep, and from time to time revise, a permanent alphabetical card index roll of the members of the bar of this court who have been enrolled as such, showing the name, address, and date of admission of each living member.

Rule 5.   Foreign Legal Consultants

(1) General Regulation as to Licensing. In its discretion, the Supreme Court may license to practice in Indiana as a foreign legal consultant, without examination, an applicant who:

(a) is a member in good standing of a recognized legal profession in a foreign country, the members of which are admitted to practice as attorneys or counselors at law or the equivalent and are subject to effective regulation and discipline by a duly constituted professional body or a public authority;

(b) for at least five of the seven years immediately preceding his or her application has been a member in good standing of such legal profession and has actually been engaged in the practice of law in the said foreign country or elsewhere substantially involving or relating to the rendering of advice or the provision of legal services concerning the law of the said foreign country;

(c) possesses the good moral character and general fitness requisite for a member of the bar of Indiana; and

(d) intends to practice as a foreign legal consultant in Indiana and to maintain an office in this State for that purpose.

(2) Proof Required. An applicant under this Rule shall file with the State Board of Law Examiners:

(a) a certificate from the professional body or public authority in such foreign country having final jurisdiction over professional discipline, certifying as to the applicant's admission to practice and the date thereof, and as to his or her good standing as such attorney or counselor at law or the equivalent;

(b) a letter of recommendation from one of the members of the executive body of such professional body or public authority or from one of the judges of the highest law court or court of original jurisdiction of such foreign country and a letter of recommendation from at least one attorney who is licensed to practice law in the State of Indiana other than as a foreign legal consultant;

(c) a duly authenticated English translation of such certificate and such letter if, in either case, it is not in English;

(d) the National Conference of Bar Examiners questionnaire and affidavit along with the payment of the requisite fee and such other evidence as to the applicant's educational and professional qualifications, good moral character and general fitness, and compliance with the requirements of Section 1 of this Rule as the State Board of Law Examiners may require;

(e) a copy or summary of the law and customs of the foreign country that describes the opportunity afforded to members of the Bar of Indiana to establish offices for the giving of legal advice to clients in such foreign country, together with an authenticated English translation if it is not in English; and

(f) the requisite documentation evidencing compliance with the immigration laws of the United States.

(3) Reciprocal Treatment of Members of the Bar of Indiana. In considering whether to license an applicant to practice as a foreign legal consultant, the Supreme Court may in its discretion take into account whether a member of the bar of Indiana would have a reasonable and practical opportunity to establish an office for the giving of legal advice to clients in the applicant's country of admission. Any member of the bar who is seeking or has sought to establish an office in that country may request the court to consider the matter, or the Court may do so *sua sponte.*

(4) Scope of Practice. A person licensed to practice as a foreign legal consultant under this Rule shall be limited to rendering professional legal advice on the law of the foreign country where the foreign legal consultant is admitted to practice. A foreign legal consultant shall not:

(a) appear for a person other than himself or herself as attorney in any court, or before any magistrate or other judicial officer, in this State other than upon admission *pro hac vice;*

(b) prepare any instrument effecting the transfer or registration of title to real estate located in the United States of America;

(c) prepare:

(i) any will or trust instrument effecting the disposition on death of any property located in the United States of America and owned by a resident thereof; or

(ii) any instrument relating to the administration of a decedent's estate in the United States of America;

(d) prepare any instrument in respect of the marital or parental relations, rights or duties of a resident of the United States of America, or the custody or care of the children of such a resident;

(e) render professional legal advice on the law of this State or of the United States of America (whether rendered incident to the preparation of legal instruments or otherwise) except on the basis of advice from a person duly qualified and entitled (otherwise than by virtue of having been licensed under this Rule) to render professional legal advice in this State;

(f) be, or in any way hold himself or herself out as, a member of the bar of Indiana; or

(g) use any title other than "foreign legal consultant" and affirmatively state in conjunction therewith the name of the foreign country in which he or she is admitted to practice (although he or she may additionally identify the name of the foreign or domestic firm with which he or she is associated).

(5) Rights and Obligations. Subject to the limitations set forth in Section 4 of this Rule, a person licensed as a legal consultant under this Rule shall be considered a lawyer affiliated with the bar of this State and shall be entitled and subject to:

(a) the rights and obligations set forth in the Indiana Rules of Professional Conduct or arising from the other conditions and requirements that apply to a member of the bar of Indiana under the Indiana Rules of Court; and

(b) the rights and obligations of a member of the bar of Indiana with respect to:

(i) affiliation in the same law firm with one or more members of the bar of Indiana with respect to:

(A) employing one or more members of the bar of Indiana;

(B) being employed by one or more members of the bar of Indiana or by any partnership or professional corporation which includes members of the bar of this State or which maintains an office in this State;

(C) being a partner in any partnership or shareholder in any professional corporation which includes members of the bar of Indiana or which maintains an office in this State; and

(ii) attorney-client privilege, work product privilege and similar professional privileges.

(6) Disciplinary Provisions. A person licensed to practice as a legal consultant under this Rule shall be subject to professional discipline in the same manner and to the same extent as members of the bar of Indiana and to this end:

(a) every person licensed to practice as a foreign legal consultant under these Rules:

(i) shall be subject to control by the Supreme Court and to censure, suspension, removal or revocation of his or her license to practice by the Supreme Court and shall otherwise be governed by the Admission and Discipline Rules; and

(ii) shall execute and file with the Supreme Court, in such form and manner as such court may prescribe:

(A) his or her commitment to observe the Rules of Professional Conduct and the Indiana Rules of Court to the extent applicable to the legal services authorized under Section 4 of this Rule;

(B) a written undertaking to notify the court of any change in such person's good standing as a member of the foreign legal profession referred to in Section 1(a) of this Rule and of any final action of the professional body or public authority referred to in Section 2(a) of this Rule imposing any disciplinary censure, suspension, or other sanction upon such person; and

(C) a duly acknowledged instrument, in writing, setting forth his or her address in this State and designation the clerk of such court as his or her agent upon whom process may be

served, with like effect as if served personally upon him or her, in any action or proceeding thereafter brought against him or her and arising out of or based upon any legal services rendered or offered to be rendered by him or her within or to residents of Indiana, whenever after due diligence service cannot be made upon him or her at such address or at such new address in this State as he or she shall have filed in the office of such clerk by means of a duly acknowledged supplemental instrument in writing.

(b) service of process on such clerk, pursuant to the designation filed as aforesaid, shall be made by personally delivering to and leaving with such clerk, or with a deputy or assistant authorized by him or her to receive such service, at his or her office, duplicate copies of such process together with a fee of ten dollars ($10). Service of process shall be complete when such clerk has been so served. Such clerk shall promptly send one of such copies to the foreign legal consultant to whom the process is directed, by certified mail, return receipt requested, addressed to such foreign legal consultant at the address specified by him or her as aforesaid.

(7) Application and Renewal Fees. An applicant for a license as a foreign legal consultant under this Rule shall pay an application fee which shall be equal to the fee required to be paid by a person applying for admission as a member of the bar of Indiana under Ind.Admission and Discipline Rule 6. A person licensed as a foreign legal consultant shall pay the annual registration fee required by Admis.Disc.R. 23(21).

(8) Revocation of License. In the event that a person licensed as a legal consultant under this Rule no longer meets the requirements for licensure set forth in Section 1(a) or 1(c) of this rule, the license granted to such person hereunder is revoked.

(9) Admission to Bar. In the event that a person licensed as a foreign legal consultant under this Rule is subsequently admitted as a member of the bar of Indiana under the provisions of the Rules governing such admissions, the license granted to such person hereunder shall be deemed superseded by the license granted to such person to practice law as a member of the bar of Indiana.

(10) Application for Waiver of Provisions. The Supreme Court, upon application, may in its discretion vary the application of or waive any provision of this Rule where strict compliance will cause undue hardship to the applicant. Such application shall be in the form of a verified petition setting forth the applicant's name, age and residence address, the facts relied upon and a prayer for relief.

Adopted effective Jan. 1, 1994.

Rule 6. Admission on Foreign License

Section 1. Provisional License

A person who has been admitted to practice law in the highest court of law in any other state (herein defined as state or territory of the United States or the District of Columbia), may be granted a provisional license to practice law in Indiana upon a finding by the State Board of Law Examiners that said person has met each of the following conditions:

(a) The applicant has actively engaged in the practice of law for a period of at least five (5) of the seven (7) years immediately preceding the date of application. "Actively engaged in the practice of law" shall mean:

(i) performing legal services for the general public as a lawyer for at least 1,000 hours per year; or

(ii) employment by a state or local governmental or business entity as a lawyer performing duties for which admission to the practice of law is a prerequisite for at least 1,000 hours per year; or

(iii) performing the duties of a teacher of law on a full-time basis in an ABA accredited law school; or

(iv) serving as a judge of a court of record on a full-time basis; or

(v) serving on a full-time salaried basis as an attorney with the federal government or a federal governmental agency including service as a member of the Judge Advocate General's Department of one of the military branches of the United States; or

(vi) a combination of the above.

(b) The practice of law must have been in the state where the applicant is licensed and during the period of licensure unless the practice falls under (iii) or (v) above. Practice under a business counsel license admission as defined in Section 2 may apply toward years of practice for a maximum of five (5) years so long as the applicant meets all of the requirements of this Section 1 and the application for provisional license admission is made within seven (7) years of the grant of the initial business counsel license.

(c) The applicant is a member in good standing of the bar(s) of admission.

(d) The admission of the applicant is in the public interest.

(e) The applicant meets the character and fitness requirements of Indiana.

(f) The applicant has paid or tendered the required fee.

(g) The applicant has not failed the Indiana Bar Examination within five (5) years of the date of application.

(h) The applicant has graduated from an ABA accredited law school.

(i) The applicant has filed an affidavit of the applicant's intent to engage in the practice of law as defined in Section 1(a) predominantly in Indiana. "Predominantly" means that the applicant's practice in Indiana must exceed, or be equal to, his or her practice in all other jurisdictions combined.

Section 2. Business Counsel License

A person who establishes an office or other systematic and continuous presence in Indiana in order to accept or continue employment by a person or entity engaged in business in Indiana other than the practice of law may be granted a business counsel license to practice law in Indiana without examination so long as granting the license is in the public interest and such person:

a. is admitted:

1. to practice law in the highest court of law in any other state, or

2. to practice law in a foreign country and fulfills the requirements set forth in 5(1)(a);

b. complies with Section 1(a)(ii) and is or will be devoted solely to the business of such employer and who receives or will receive his or her entire compensation from such employer for applicants legal service, and remains in such employment;

c. is a member in good standing of the bar(s) of admission;

d. meets the character and fitness requirement;

e. pays or tenders the required fee; and

f. has not failed the Indiana Bar Examination within five (5) years of the date of the application.

A person granted a business counsel license under this Rule based upon admission to the practice of law only in a foreign country shall be subject to the limitations on scope of practice set forth in paragraphs (a)–(d) of Rule 5(4).

Upon the transfer of such employment outside the State of Indiana, the right to practice law in Indiana pursuant to a business counsel license shall terminate. Upon the termination of such employment, the right to practice law in Indiana shall terminate unless 1) such business counsel license admittee has secured employment from another person or entity within three (3) months of their termination, which employment meets the criteria of Section 2; or 2) such business counsel license admittee shall have been admitted to practice law in this state pursuant to some other rule.

Section 3. Fees

The applicant shall submit his application accompanied by a fee of eight hundred seventy-five dollars ($875.00). The Executive Director of the Board may refer said application to the National Conference of Bar Examiners for investigation and report. The Board is authorized to pay all expenses incident to the investigation of the qualifications of the applicant.

However, in the event said application is considered and denied by the Board prior to referral to the National Conference, the Board is authorized to refund to the applicant one half (1/2) of the application fee. No part of the application fee shall otherwise be refunded.

Section 4. Renewal of Provisional License and Business License

(a) Renewal of Provisional License. A provisional license admission on a foreign license may continue in force for one year, and may be renewed for a like period upon the submission of such verified individualized information as will demonstrate to the satisfaction of the Board that the applicant has during the past year been both (a) engaged in the practice of law as defined in Section 1(a), and (b) predominantly in Indiana. At the time of the first renewal request, the applicant must also submit verified information to demonstrate compliance with the educational requirements of Section 5. Upon the fifth consecutive renewal of the provisional license granted to the applicant, the admission to practice shall be permanent.

(b) Renewal of Business Counsel License. A business counsel license may continue in force for one year, and may be renewed for a like period upon the submission of such verified individualized information as will demonstrate to the satisfaction of the Board that the applicant has during the past year been employed under the terms of the business counsel license and will continue to be so employed. At the time of the first renewal request, the applicant must also submit verified information to demonstrate compliance with the educational requirements of Section 5.

(c) Annual Renewal Fee—Provisional License and Business Counsel License. Each attorney who is licensed pursuant to this Rule shall pay a renewal fee of $50.00 on or before November 1 of each year; a delinquent fee in the amount of $25.00 shall be added to the renewal fee for fees paid after November 1 and on or before November 15 of each year; a delinquent fee in the amount of $50.00 shall be added to the renewal fee for fees paid after November 15 and on or before December 31 of each year; a delinquent fee in the amount of $150.00 shall be added to the renewal fee for fees paid after December 31 of each year. Additionally, a $100.00 surcharge will be added to the late fee for each consecutive year for which the attorney fails to timely file the renewal form. This renewal fee is in addition to any annual registration and fees paid under Admission and Discipline Rule 2.

(d) Failure to Pay Renewal Fee or Comply with Educational Requirements of Section 5; Revocation of License. Any attorney who fails to pay the renewal fee required under Section 4(c) or fails to file the affidavit required under Section 4(f) or fails to comply with the educational requirements of Section 5 shall be subject to revocation of his or her license to practice law and sanctions for contempt of this Court in the event he or she thereafter engages in the practice of law in this State.

(e) Annual Renewal Notice. On or before September 1 of each year, the Executive Director of the State Board of Law Examiners shall mail a notice to each attorney admitted to practice pursuant to this Rule that (i) a renewal fee must be paid on or before November 1; and (ii) the attorney must (a) affirm compliance with eligibility requirements to maintain the license or (b) submit the signed relinquish affidavit to the State Board of Law Examiners on or before November 1. Notice sent pursuant to this section shall be sent to the name and address maintained by the Clerk of the Supreme Court pursuant to Admission and Discipline Rule 2.

(f) Relinquishing of License. Any attorney who is licensed pursuant to this Rule who is in good standing, who is current in payment of all applicable registration fees and other financial obligations imposed by these rules, who is not the subject of an investigation into or a pending proceeding involving allegations of misconduct, and who no longer is able to meet the requirements to maintain his or her license pursuant to this Rule may voluntarily relinquish his or her license to practice law in the State of Indiana by tendering the renewal form with the relinquish affidavit signed to the Executive Director of the State Board of Law Examiners. The Executive Director shall promptly verify the eligibility of the attorney to relinquish under this section and if eligible, forward a certification of eligibility to the Clerk of the Indiana Supreme Court, and the Clerk shall show on the Roll of Attorneys that the attorney's Indiana law license has been relinquished permanently and that the lawyer is no longer considered an attorney licensed to practice law in the State of Indiana. An attorney who relinquishes his license pursuant to this provision may apply for admission under Admission and Discipline Rules 3 through 21. In the event the attorney is not eligible to relinquish under this section, the Executive Director shall promptly notify the attorney of all reasons for ineligibility.

Section 5. Education Requirements for Provisional License and Business Counsel License

(a) In addition to any requirements found in Rule 29, within twelve (12) months of an applicant's initial provisional license or business counsel license admission, the applicant shall attend an annual Indiana law update seminar, which seminar shall provide a minimum of 12 hours of continuing legal education which has been approved by the Indiana Commission For Continuing Legal Education. The Board of Law Examiners shall publish a list of approved seminars that meet the requirements of this Rule.

(b) Applicants admitted on provisional license or business counsel license are subject to, and shall comply with, the Indiana Rules For Admission to the Bar and the Discipline of Attorneys, the Rules of

Professional Conduct, and all other requirements of statute and Supreme Court Rules.

Section 6. Application of Rules and Appearance Before Board

The provisions of Rule 12, Sections 7, 8, and 9 apply to admission under this Rule. An applicant for admission on foreign license who is denied admission may request an appearance before the Board and a hearing thereafter.

Amended effective May 10, 1961; Oct. 25, 1963; Jan. 8, 1970; Oct. 27, 1971; Jan. 24, 1972; Feb. 16, 1972; July 30, 1973; Oct. 1, 1973; Aug. 31, 1976; amended Dec. 30, 1976, effective Jan. 1, 1977; Dec. 14, 1977, effective Jan. 1, 1978; amended effective Dec. 4, 1980; Nov. 1, 1985; amended April 14, 1988, effective Jan. 1, 1989; Nov. 30, 1989, effective Jan. 1, 1990; Dec. 23, 1996, effective March 1, 1997; July 1, 2003, effective Jan. 1, 2004; Sept. 30, 2004, effective Jan. 1, 2005; Sept. 9, 2008, effective Jan. 1, 2009; Sept. 15, 2009, effective Jan. 1, 2010; May 15, 2012, effective July 1, 2012; Oct. 26, 2012, effective Jan. 1, 2013.

Rule 7. Certificates

An applicant admitted through examination shall be entitled to a certificate of his admission upon taking the oath of attorneys and being entered on the roll of attorneys by the clerk of this court.

Amended Nov. 4, 1991, effective Jan. 1, 1992; amended Feb. 12, 1992, effective Jan. 1, 1992.

Rule 8. [Vacated effective June 23, 1971]

Rule 9. State Board of Law Examiners

The State Board of Law Examiners of the State of Indiana shall consist of ten (10) members of the bar, two (2) from each Supreme Court judicial district, who shall be appointed by this Court to serve for terms of five (5) years and until their successors are appointed. The terms of two (2) members of such Board shall expire on December 1 of each year. The Board shall elect annually, a president, a vice-president, a secretary, and a treasurer. These officers shall take office on December 1. The Board shall maintain its office in a location determined by the Indiana Supreme Court. The Court shall appoint a person to serve as Executive Director to said Board.

Amended Oct. 15, 1986, effective Jan. 1, 1987.

Rule 10. Expenses and Compensation of Members of Board

The board shall have authority to prescribe such forms and adopt such rules as are necessary, not inconsistent herewith. The board shall maintain in a separate fund the fees received under these rules which shall be expended only upon the approval of the Supreme Court. The members of the board of law examiners shall be allowed their necessary expenses and a reasonable compensation which shall be fixed from time to time by the court.

Amended effective Jan. 24, 1972; amended effective Sept. 24, 1974; amended effective Aug. 31, 1976.

Rule 11. Forms

Application for admission and all information in reference thereto shall be upon forms furnished by the secretary of the board.

Rule 12. Committee on Character and Fitness

Section 1. The State Board of Law Examiners shall inquire into and determine the character, fitness and general qualifications to be admitted to practice law as a member of the bar of the Supreme Court of Indiana. It is a condition precedent to admission, whether on examination or upon foreign license, that the Board report and certify to the Supreme Court that the applicant, after due inquiry, has been found to possess the necessary good moral character and fitness to perform the obligations and responsibilities of an attorney practicing law in the State of Indiana, and has satisfied all general qualifications for admission.

Section 2. The applicant must be at least 21 years of age and possess good moral character and fitness to practice law. The applicant shall have the burden of proving that he or she possesses the requisite good moral character and fitness to practice law. The applicant has the absolute duty to inform the Board with full candor of any facts which bear, even remotely, upon the question of the applicant's character and fitness and general qualifications to practice law, which obligation continues from the date of application to the time of admission, and includes the obligation to promptly and to fully inform the Board of any such facts occurring or discovered prior to admission. The term "good moral character" includes, but is not limited to, the qualities of honesty, fairness, candor, trustworthiness, observance of fiduciary responsibility, and of the laws of this State and of the United States, and a respect for the rights of other persons and things, and the judicial process. Anyone who has been convicted of a felony *prima facie* shall be deemed lacking the requisite of good moral character as defined in this section. The term "fitness" includes, but is not limited to, the physical and mental suitability of the applicant to practice law in Indiana. In satisfying the requirements of good moral character and fitness, applicants should be persons whose record of conduct justifies the trust of clients, adversaries, courts and others with respect to the professional duties owed to them, and whose record demonstrates the qualities of honesty, trustworthiness, diligence, or reliability. In the determination of good moral character and fitness, relevant considerations may include, but are not limited to the following: unlawful conduct; academic misconduct; making of false statements, including omissions; misconduct in employment; acts involving dishonesty, fraud, deceit or misrepresentation; abuse of legal process; neglect of financial responsibilities; violation of an order of a court; evidence of mental or emotional instability; evidence of drug or alcohol dependency;

denial of admission to the bar in another jurisdiction on character and fitness grounds; and disciplinary action by a lawyer disciplinary agency or other professional disciplinary agency of any jurisdiction. ·

General qualifications are those requirements to be admitted to the practice of law established by these rules, other than those dealing with examinations and character and fitness.

Section 3. No person who advocates the overthrow of the government of the United States or this state by force, violence or other unconstitutional or illegal means, shall be certified to the Supreme Court of Indiana for admission to the bar of the court and a license to the practice of law.

Section 4. There shall be appointed by this Court a Committee on Character and Fitness in each Supreme Court judicial district, consisting of at least one attorney-at-law from each county in such district. The members of such committee shall continue in office until their successors are appointed. The State Board of Law Examiners shall send a copy of each application for admission to the bar of this state to the local member of the Committee on Character and Fitness in the Indiana county which the applicant selects. A member of the committee, or some member designated by the State Board of Law Examiners, shall require the personal attendance of each applicant before the member, and inquire into the question as to whether or not the applicant is possessed of those requisites of good moral character and fitness, has adequate knowledge of the standards and ideals of the profession, and is familiar with and agrees to be bound by the Indiana Supreme Court Rules of Professional Conduct, all as necessary to qualify him to serve as an attorney. The member of the committee shall make such further inquiry into the matter as the member sees fit. At least thirty (30) days before the examination, the member of the committee conducting the inquiry, or promptly, if upon application for admission upon foreign license, the Board member conducting the inquiry shall make a finding: (1) That the applicant is familiar with and agrees to be bound by the Indiana Supreme Court Rules of Professional Conduct and that such Applicant is a person of good moral character and is fit to practice law in Indiana; or (2) That the member is unable to certify that the Applicant is a person of good moral character and is fit to practice law in Indiana, setting forth the reasons for this conclusion; or (3) That there is some question as to the Applicant's good moral character and/or fitness to practice law in Indiana and therefore recommends that the State Board of Law Examiners conduct a personal inquiry with the Applicant, stating the reasons for the member's conclusion. The committee member shall forward such findings and recommendations and all papers filed in connection therewith to the State Board of Law Examiners, which Board shall at its next meeting review said findings, make such

further inquiry as it sees fit, and take such action as the matter requires.

Section 5. The Board may, upon its own motion, require an applicant to appear before the full Board, or a committee composed of members of the Board, for inquiry into the applicant's character and fitness. The Board may continue such appearance and require that the applicant submit additional information, evaluations or proofs before concluding such appearance.

Section 6. The Board of Law Examiners shall make a finding regarding each applicant:

(a) That the applicant possesses the requisite good moral character and fitness and has satisfied the general qualifications to be eligible to be admitted to practice law in Indiana, subject to continued qualification; or

(b) That the applicant has failed to sustain his or her burden of proof that the applicant possesses good moral character and fitness, and has satisfied all of the general qualifications to be admitted to the practice of law, in which case the Board may find that the applicant should not be permitted to reapply for admission to practice law or should be permitted to reapply only after a specific period of time; or

(c) That the Board has special concerns about the proof of applicant's moral character and fitness based upon evidence of drug, alcohol, psychological or behavioral problems, but in lieu of denying admission to the bar finds that the applicant has satisfied the Board as to his or her character and fitness, and has also satisfied the general qualifications, sufficiently to be eligible for conditional admission upon such terms and conditions as specified by the Board, said conditional admission to be administered by the Board over a period of time not to exceed five (5) years. The conditional admission shall be governed by Internal Rules and Policies adopted by the Board. The fact that the admission is conditional shall be confidential; or

(d) That the Board has special concerns about the proof of applicant's moral character and fitness based upon evidence of drug, alcohol, psychological or behavioral problems, but in lieu of denying admission to the bar finds that the applicant's admission be withheld for a specified period of time, not to exceed two (2) years, to allow the applicant to establish and prove rehabilitation. If at the end of the specified period of time the applicant shall have satisfied requirements to be eligible for admission to practice law, barring subsequent disclosure of matters adversely reflecting upon the applicant's character and fitness, the applicant will be eligible for admission upon passing the examination requirements. The Board may permit the applicant to take any examination administered during that period; or

(e) That the Board has special concerns about the proof of applicant's moral character and fitness based upon evidence of drug, alcohol, psychological or behavioral problems, but in lieu of denying admission to the bar finds that the behavior giving rise to the special concern has occurred of such recent date to prevent the Board from determining whether the applicant has sufficiently established his or her qualifications and the Board extends the time for further inquiry for a reasonable time, not to exceed one (1) year, and the Board may permit the applicant to take any examination administered during that period.

Section 7. If the Board finds that the applicant is not eligible for admission, or if the Board finds that an applicant is eligible for admission only upon condition under Section 6(c), whether after inquiry into the applicant's character and fitness to practice law, or determination that the applicant has failed to establish satisfaction of general qualifications, or in the case of an applicant for admission on foreign license, failure to prove that he or she has met the requirements of Rule 6, Sections 1 through 3, or if a conditional admittee has violated the terms of conditional admission, the applicant or conditional admittee may request a hearing under Section 9 of this Rule by filing a written request for such hearing with the Board within thirty (30) days of mailing of notice to the applicant of the finding of the Board.

Section 8. The necessity of a hearing as provided in Section 9 of this Rule may be dispensed with by the Board where the evidence is not in dispute and the subject matter of the hearing may be submitted to the Supreme Court upon written findings and specifications adopted by the Board.

Section 9. If the applicant or conditional admittee timely requests a hearing, or if the State Board of Law Examiners in connection with further inquiry shall deem it advisable to hold a hearing, the State Board of Law Examiners will schedule a hearing pursuant to the provisions of this Section.

(a) In such event, the Board may appoint a hearing panel from the members of the Board, consisting of three members. Said panel shall select from among its members a presiding officer and shall schedule and conduct such hearing. All of the above rules and regulations with respect to the action of the Board shall apply at said hearing.

(b) If, in connection with said further inquiry, the State Board of Law Examiners shall deem it advisable to hold a hearing, the applicant or conditional admittee shall be informed of the substance of the matter to be inquired into by written notice served on the applicant or conditional admittee by mailing such notice to the applicant or conditional admittee at such person's last known address as shown by the Board's record by certified mail, return receipt requested, at least ten (10) days before the date set for said hearing.

(c) A record of the proceedings shall be taken by electronic recording equipment provided by the

Board. If necessary this record shall be transcribed by the staff of the Executive Director.

(d) The panel shall report its findings to the Board for consideration and decision.

(e) The State Board of Law Examiners, at any such hearing, or otherwise, shall have the power to administer oaths, to issue subpoenas to require attendance at said hearing and for the production of documentary or other evidence. In case of the refusal of a witness to attend said hearing, to produce documentary or other evidence or to testify, the said Board shall certify such failure to the Court, and such witness shall be dealt with as for a contempt. Witnesses shall receive the fees and mileage provided by law for witnesses in civil cases. The Board may employ outside legal counsel to represent the interest of the State of Indiana at such hearing.

(f) The applicant or conditional admittee shall have the right to attend such hearing in person, to examine and cross-examine witnesses and otherwise participate in said hearing and to require the attendance of witnesses and production of documentary and other evidence by subpoena. An applicant or conditional admittee may be represented by counsel at such person's expense.

(g) Upon the conclusion of said hearing, the State Board of Law Examiners shall enter findings as provided in Section 6 (a) through (e) of this Rule.

(h) In the event the Board makes a finding other than that the applicant or conditional admittee does possess good moral character and fitness and has satisfied the general qualifications to be admitted to practice as provided in Section 6 (a) of this Rule, a final report of the proceedings, including specific findings of fact, conclusion and recommendations shall be prepared. The Board shall notify the applicant or conditional admittee and all counsel of record of the action of the Board, including with such notice a copy of the final report.

Section 10. If, after following the hearing procedures in Section 5, 8 & 9 of this Rule, the Board determines that a conditional admittee has violated any of the conditions of the admission, or if the Board determines that any applicant admitted under these rules falsified or failed to fully inform the Board of facts bearing upon the applicant's character and fitness and general qualifications to practice law prior to admission, the Board may impose additional conditions, including without limitation, an additional term of conditional admission for up to five (5) years, or the Board may certify such findings to the Supreme Court of Indiana with the recommendation that the Court revoke such admission, along with a recommended period of time before the conditional admittee can submit a new application for admission. A conditional admittee whose conditional admission has been revoked by the Supreme Court shall not be readmitted, except upon a new application and examination, after the expiration of the revocation period set by order of the Supreme Court.

Section 11. Any person who has been accepted for admission to a law school accredited as required in Rule 13V may file an application with the State Board of Law Examiners, on such forms as the Board shall provide, for determination of his character and fitness to practice law in the State of Indiana in advance of the completion of his legal education. His application shall be processed and the final determination made through the same procedures set out above for the handling of submissions by applicants who have completed or are about to complete their formal legal education. Each application shall be accompanied by a fee of fifty dollars ($50.00). Thereafter, upon filing an application for admission to the Bar of this State, said person shall again be screened by a member of the Committee on Character and Fitness in the proper county as required by this Rule 12, to determine the applicant's continued qualification for admission to the Bar of Indiana as far as his character and fitness is concerned.

Amended effective June 2, 1970; Nov. 24, 1975, effective Jan. 31, 1976; Dec. 23, 1976, effective Jan. 1, 1977; Nov. 30, 1989, effective Jan. 1, 1990; Dec. 23, 1996, effective March 1, 1997; amended effective November 13, 2002; Aug. 15, 2006, effective Jan. 1, 2007.

Rule 13. Educational Requirements For Admission To Examination

Section 1. Authority. Constitution of Indiana, Article 7, Section 4, and this court's inherent power.

Section 2. Purpose. The purpose of this rule is to establish minimal educational prerequisites for the effective assistance of counsel in civil or criminal matters and cases in the State of Indiana, which minimal educational prerequisites shall be held by all persons admitted to the bar of this Court by written examination after the effective date of this rule.

Section 3. Notice. Notice is hereby given to all persons who seek admission to the bar of this Court by written examination, after the effective date of this Rule, that minimal educational prerequisites for the effective assistance of counsel in civil or criminal matters and cases are established by this rule.

Section 4. Educational Qualifications. Each applicant for admission to the bar of this Court by written examination shall be required to establish to the satisfaction of the State Board of Law Examiners that the applicant is:

(A) A graduate of a law school located in the United States which at the time of the applicant's graduation was on the approved list of the Council of Legal Education and Admission to the Bar of the American Bar Association (the Supreme Court of Indiana reserves the right to disapprove any school regardless of ABA approval);

(B) A person who satisfactorily has completed the law course required for graduation and furnishes to the Board of Law Examiners a certificate from the Dean thereof, or a person designated by the Dean, that the applicant will receive the degree as a matter of course at a future date, pursuant to Indiana Rules of Admission and Discipline, Rule 15; and

(C) A person who has completed in an approved school of law two cumulative semester hours of legal ethics or professional responsibility.

Section 5. Early Examination Rule. An applicant, who has fewer than five (5) hours to complete and is within one hundred (100) days of graduation from an approved law school, satisfactorily has passed work in the subject matter as set forth in the provisions of this section, and otherwise has completed all requirements for admission to the bar, shall be entitled to take the examination for admission to the bar, but may not be admitted to the bar of the Court until said applicant has met all other requirements for admission and has graduated from an approved law school.

Section 6. Certification of Educational Qualifications. Certification of the completion of the subject matter requirements under the provision of section 4 of this rule shall be made by the dean of the law school, or his designee, who shall have faculty status. Said certification shall be filed with the board twenty (20) days prior to the date of the examination.

Amended effective Feb. 15, 1954; amended effective Oct. 25, 1963; amended effective Oct. 27, 1971; amended effective July 30, 1973; amended Dec. 18, 1973, effective Feb. 1, 1974; amended effective Feb. 19, 1974; amended effective March 6, 1974; amended Nov. 24, 1975, effective Jan. 31, 1976; amended Dec. 23, 1976, effective Jan. 1, 1977; amended Dec. 30, 1976, effective Jan. 1, 1977; amended Dec. 14, 1977, effective Jan. 1, 1978; amended Nov. 1, 1982, effective Jan. 1, 1983; amended Oct. 15, 1986, effective Jan. 1, 1987; amended April 14, 1988, effective Jan. 1, 1989; amended Nov. 30, 1989, effective Jan. 1, 1990; amended effective Jan. 8, 1990; amended Oct. 30, 1992, effective Jan. 1, 1993; amended Dec. 18, 1995, effective Feb. 1, 1996; amended effective Jan. 24, 1996; Amended Dec. 23, 1996, effective March 1, 1997.

Rule 14. Review

Review of final action by the State Board of Law Examiners shall be as follows:

Section 1. The State Board of Law Examiners shall adopt such procedure for review of an applicant, aggrieved by failure of said board to award said applicant a satisfactory grade upon the bar examination, as shall be approved by the Supreme Court of Indiana. All applicants who have achieved a combined scaled score of 255 to 263 shall be eligible to appeal. The eligible examinees must make a written request to appeal on forms provided by the Board within fourteen (14) days of the date of mailing by the Board of the eligible examinee's results. No response other than the written request to appeal is permitted. The President of the Board shall designate certain of the Board's members as "Appeals Reviewers." The Appeals Reviewers shall consider and decide all appeals of bar examination results. In the appeals process, all of an eligible examinee's responses shall be subject to review by the Appeals Reviewers. Multistate Bar Examination scores will also be available to the Appeals Reviewers. Eligible examinees that are deemed to have passed after review shall be treated as having passed that administration of the Indiana Bar Examination. No change in score shall be effectuated. The determination by the Appeals Reviewers whether to treat an appealing applicant as having passed the bar examination shall be final, subject to general principles of procedural due process.

Section 2. Any applicant aggrieved by the final action of the State Board of Law Examiners in refusing to recommend to the Supreme Court of Indiana the admission of the applicant to practice law in Indiana for any reason other than the failure to pass any examination as set forth in section (1) may, within twenty (20) days of receipt of notification setting forth the reason for refusal, file a petition with the Supreme Court of Indiana requesting review by this Court of such final determination. The notification referenced herein shall be sent to the applicant by certified mail with return receipt requested. In the petition the applicant shall set forth specifically the reasons, in fact or law, assigned as error in the Board's determination. The Court may order further consideration of the application, in which event the State Board of Law Examiners shall promptly transmit to the Court the complete file relating to such applicant and his or her application, including the transcript of the record of any hearing held by the State Board of Law Examiners relating thereto. The Court shall enter such order as in its judgment is proper, which shall thereupon become final. The petition for review must be accompanied by a fifty dollar ($50.00) filing fee unless the petitioner previously paid an application fee to the State Board of Law Examiners as provided in these rules.

Adopted effective March 10, 1953; amended effective Feb. 9, 1971. Amended Aug. 21, 1972, effective Sept. 1, 1972. Amended effective March 5, 1973. Amended Nov. 24, 1975, effective Jan. 31, 1976; Dec. 5, 1994, effective Feb. 1, 1995; Dec. 22, 2000, effective Jan. 1, 2001; Sept. 30, 2004, effective Jan. 1, 2005; Sept. 7, 2012, effective Jan. 1, 2013.

Rule 15. Applications, Filing Dates and Fees for Examination and Re–Examination

Application for admission on first examination must be made on forms prescribed by the State Board of Law Examiners and filed with the Executive Director of the Board. The application shall be in such form and shall request such information as may be required by the Board of Law Examiners. Form applications shall be prepared by the State Board of Law Examiners and furnished to applicants upon request. The Board of Law Examiners may require additional information as is deemed by it to be necessary.

An affidavit of the dean of the applicant's law school, or the dean's designee, to the effect that there is nothing in the school records or personal knowledge of the dean or faculty of such school to indicate that the applicant is not of good moral character or that the applicant is not fit for admission to the practice of law must be filed with the State Board of Law Examiners. The Board shall provide forms for such certification.

A certified transcript of the law school record of the applicant showing the date of graduation and the degree conferred must be filed with the Board of Law Examiners before the applicant can be admitted to the bar.

Filing of applications may be made by personal delivery to the office of the Board of Law Examiners or by regular, certified or registered United States mail. If filing is made by personal delivery, the date of filing is determined by the date of the Received stamp of the Board office. If filing is made by mail, the application shall be deposited in the United States mail with postage prepaid. The United States mail postmark will determine the filing date. Facsimile filing is not permitted. No requests for filing past the stated deadlines or for waiver of filing deadlines will be accepted by the Board of Law Examiners or by the Supreme Court.

Applications for admission on first examination for the July examination must be filed by April 1, and accompanied by a filing fee of two hundred fifty dollars ($250). A late filing period is permitted until April 15. The filing fee for late filing is five hundred dollars ($500).

The deadline filing date for the February examination is November 15 of the previous year. The filing fee is two hundred fifty dollars ($250). The late filing period is from that date to November 30 of the previous year. The late filing fee is five hundred dollars ($500).

If an applicant fails to pass the first examination and is permitted to take further examinations, the application for re-examination must be made on forms prescribed by the Board and filed with the Executive Director by the following dates. Applications for re-examination for the July examination must be filed by May 30 and accompanied by a filing fee of two hundred fifty dollars ($250). The late filing deadline is June 15 and the late filing fee is five hundred dollars ($500). Applications for re-examination for the February examination must be filed by December 15 of the previous year. The regular filing fee is two hundred fifty dollars ($250). The late filing deadline is December 30 of the previous year. The late filing fee is five hundred dollars ($500).

There are no other provisions for or consideration of requests for late filing by the Board or by the Indiana Supreme Court.

Applicants who have a petition before the Board or an appeal before the Supreme Court of the grading of their examination will be required to meet all filing deadlines for re-examination. If an applicant is successful on petition or on appeal, the applicant will receive a full refund of any re-examination fee.

If an applicant whose application has been approved and processed fails to take the examination first following its approval, such applicant shall have the privilege of having that application held in abeyance and of taking the next regularly scheduled examination given by the Board without payment of any additional fee. Any applicant whose application has been approved and processed who fails to take that examination, or the next following examination, shall have that application dismissed. The applicant will be entitled to a refund of one-half (½) of the fee paid.

If an applicant applies to sit for a first examination after his or her application has been dismissed, a new application must be filed and a two hundred fifty dollar ($250) filing fee must be paid and the first examination deadlines must be met. If an applicant applies to sit for a re-examination after his or her application has been dismissed, a new application must be filed and a two hundred fifty dollar ($250) filing fee must be paid, but these applicants will be permitted to file by the re-examination time deadline and will have the opportunity to file within that late filing period. All applicants applying after dismissal must meet the regular deadlines or late filing deadlines and pay the regular fee or the late fee as they apply to those deadlines.

Amended Nov. 30, 1989, effective Jan. 1, 1990; amended Nov. 25, 1997, effective Jan. 1, 1998; amended effective Sept. 11, 2000; amended Sept. 30, 2004, effective Jan. 1, 2005.

Rule 16. [Vacated effective January 1, 1998]

Rule 17. Examinations

Section 1. No person shall be licensed to practice law in this state who has not taken and passed a Bar examination as provided in these rules, except attorneys who are licensed in another jurisdiction and who qualify for admission without examination under the provisions of Admission and Discipline Rule 6.

Section 2. In addition, each applicant for admission upon examination, before being admitted, must pass the Multistate Professional Responsibility Examination (MPRE). The passing score for the MPRE shall be a scaled score of eighty (80) and must be achieved within two (2) years before or after the date the applicant successfully takes the Indiana two-day essay bar examination.

Section 3. An applicant who successfully passes the Bar examination must complete all requirements for, and receive, a law degree and be admitted to the practice of law before the Court within two (2) years of the last date of the applicant's bar examination, or the bar examination must be repeated.

Section 4. The bar examination shall be administered with the identity of the applicant remaining anonymous throughout the examination, grading and review. The Executive Director shall adopt such procedures necessary for the identity of all applicants by number only. It shall be a violation of these Rules for the applicant, or anyone upon the applicant's behalf, to attempt to reveal the identity, origin, gender or race of the applicant at any time throughout the examination and review process.

Section 5. The Executive Director of the Board of Law Examiners shall notify each applicant, promptly after request for application, of the subject matter which the applicants may expect to be covered in the bar examination interrogatories.

Since the bar examination attempts to establish the applicant's ability to practice law in the State of Indiana, questions requiring answers determining an understanding of Indiana law will be expected. From time to time, the Board shall publish a listing of subject matters to be covered on examinations.

Amended effective March 23, 1970; amended effective July 30, 1973; amended Oct. 15, 1986, effective Jan. 1, 1987; amended effective Sept. 3, 1991; Amended Dec. 23, 1996, effective March 1, 1997; amended Dec. 22, 2000, effective Jan. 1, 2001.

Rule 18. Report on Examinations

Section 1. Unless otherwise ordered by the Court, there shall be two (2) bar examinations held annually, in February and July. The examination shall be supervised by the Board. The number and form of the questions and the subject matter tested shall be determined by the Board of Law Examiners with the approval of the Supreme Court.

Section 2. The Board of Law Examiners shall act on and report passing or failing to the applicant on all bar examinations within one hundred (100) days after the final day of the examination, and may inform interested news media of the names of the applicants successfully passing the bar examination.

Section 3. The Board shall certify to the Court the applicants for admission who have passed the bar examination and the Multistate Professional Responsibility Examination (MPRE), and its recommendations for admission based upon the applicant's satisfaction of the provisions and requirements of these Rules.

Amended effective Jan. 1, 1968; amended Oct. 30, 1972, effective Nov. 1, 1972; amended Oct. 15, 1986, effective Jan. 1, 1987; Amended Dec. 23, 1996, effective March 1, 1997; amended Dec. 22, 2000, effective Jan. 1, 2001.

Rule 19. Confidentiality

Section 1. All information and all records obtained and maintained by the Board of Law Examiners in the performance of its duty under these rules and as delegated by the Supreme Court of Indiana shall be confidential, except as otherwise provided by these rules, or by order of (or as otherwise authorized by) the Supreme Court of Indiana.

Section 2. All materials and information in the possession or knowledge of the Board of Law Examiners, its Executive Director, or its agents or employees, shall be the property of the Supreme Court of Indiana, and the Board shall serve as custodian of such materials and information. This shall include, but not be limited to, the applications and files of all the applicants, reports and correspondence regarding investigation of applicants, inter-office and inter-member memoranda, minutes and records of all meetings and hearings, and all examination materials and results.

Section 3. The Board is authorized to disclose information relating to applicants or members of the bar only as follows:

(a) The names of applicants successfully passing the law examination.

(b) The name of any applicant admitted to the practice of law at any admission ceremony.

(c) The name, date of birth, Social Security number, and other information relating to a bar application, an applicant, and the result of the bar application for placement in a national data bank operated by or on behalf of the National Conference of Bar Examiners.

(d) Upon request of any law school, the names of each of its graduating students that took the law examination and whether each passed or failed the exam.

(e) Information requests by the National Conference of Bar Examiners or from a foreign bar admitting agency, when accompanied by a written authorization and release duly executed by the person about whom such information is sought, providing, however, that no information received by the Board under an agreement of confidentiality or designation of confidentiality or otherwise restricted by law or these rules shall be disclosed.

(f) Information relating to a violation of the Indiana Rules of Professional Conduct or to the unauthorized practice of law may be supplied to the Indiana Disciplinary Commission, either at the request of the Disciplinary Commission or on the Board's own motion, except that information received by the Board under an agreement of confidentiality or otherwise restricted by law shall not be disclosed.

(g) Copies of documents previously filed by an applicant may be provided upon the applicant's written request. Copies of documents submitted by other parties regarding an applicant may be supplied to the applicant only upon written consent by the party submitting such documents. The com-

plete record of any hearing, including any and all documents or exhibits formally introduced into the record, and any transcript of such hearings may be made available to the applicant who was a party to the hearing pursuant to other provisions of these rules.

Adopted Dec. 23, 1996, effective March 1, 1997. Amended Dec. 22, 2000, effective Jan. 1, 2001; amended July 19, 2002, effective Jan. 1, 2003; amended Sept. 15, 2009, effective Jan. 1, 2010.

Rule 20. Immunity

Section 1. Persons Providing Information to the State Board of Law Examiners.

Every person or entity shall be immune from civil liability for providing, in good faith, documents, statements of opinion, records, or other information regarding an applicant or potential applicant for admission to the bar of this State to the State Board of Law Examiners; to its officers, Executive Director, staff, employees or agents; or to the Committees on Character and Fitness and their members and agents.

Section 2. Immunity for Board, Staff and Character and Fitness Committee.

The State Board of Law Examiners and its officers, members, Executive Director, staff, employees and agents, and the Committees on Character and Fitness and their members and agents, are immune from all civil liability for acts performed in the course of their official duties relating to the examination, character and fitness qualification, and licensing of persons seeking to be admitted to the practice of law.

Adopted July 1, 2003, effective Jan. 1, 2004.

Rule 21. Admissions

An applicant who is eligible for admission under the foregoing rules may be admitted by appearing in person before the bar of this Court and by taking the oath hereinafter set forth after establishing to the satisfaction of the Court that the applicant is a person of good moral character and fitness.

Amended effective Oct. 27, 1971; amended effective Dec. 18, 1973; amended Dec. 30, 1976, effective Jan. 1, 1977; amended Dec. 14, 1977, effective Jan. 1, 1978; amended April 14, 1988, effective Jan. 1, 1989; amended Nov. 30, 1989, effective Jan. 1, 1990.

Rule 22. Oath of Attorneys

Upon being admitted to practice law in the state of Indiana, each applicant shall take and subscribe to the following oath or affirmation:

"I do solemnly swear or affirm that: I will support the Constitution of the United States and the Constitution of the State of Indiana; I will maintain the respect due to courts of justice and judicial officers; I will not counsel or maintain any action, proceeding, or defense which shall appear to me to be unjust, but this obligation shall not prevent me from defending a person charged with crime in any case; I will employ for the purpose of maintaining the causes confided to me, such means only as are consistent with truth, and never seek to mislead the court or jury by any artifice or false statement of fact or law; I will maintain the confidence and preserve inviolate the secrets of my client at every peril to myself; I will abstain from offensive personality and advance no fact prejudicial to the honor or reputation of a party or witness, unless required by the justice of the cause with which I am charged; I will not encourage either the commencement or the continuance of any action or proceeding from any motive of passion or interest; I will never reject, from any consideration personal to myself, the cause of the defenseless, the oppressed or those who cannot afford adequate legal assistance; so help me God."

Amended effective Feb. 15, 1954; amended effective June 19, 1985; amended Sept. 30, 2004, effective Jan. 1, 2005.

Rule 23. Disciplinary Commission and Proceedings

Section 1.   General Principles

Each person granted the privilege to practice law in this State has the obligation to behave at all times in a manner consistent with the trust and confidence reposed in him or her by this Court and in a manner consistent with the duties and responsibilities as an officer or judge of the courts of this State. The Supreme Court has exclusive jurisdiction of all cases in which an attorney who is admitted to the bar of this Court or who practices law in this State (hereinafter referred to as "attorney") is charged with misconduct. The procedures hereinafter set forth shall be employed and construed to protect the public, the court and the members of the bar of this State from misconduct on the part of attorneys and to protect attorneys from unwarranted claims of misconduct.

The term "attorney" as used in this rule shall include, in addition to all persons admitted to the bar of this Court, or who practice law in this State, any and all judges of any and all courts of this State now in existence or hereafter created or established.

Unless otherwise specified, the term "Clerk" as used in this rule shall mean the Clerk of the Indiana Supreme Court, Court of Appeals and Tax Court.

Section 2.   Grounds for Discipline or Suspension

(a) Any conduct that violates the Rules of Professional Conduct or the Code of Judicial Conduct heretofore adopted or as hereafter amended by this Court or any standards or rules of legal and judicial ethics or professional responsibility then in effect or hereafter adopted by this Court shall constitute grounds for discipline.

(b) If an attorney admitted to practice in this State who is also admitted to practice in any other state should be disbarred or suspended by the proper authority of such other state, such disbarment or sus-

pension shall constitute sufficient grounds for disbarment or suspension of said attorney in this State.

(c) Any attorney who becomes disabled by reason of physical or mental illness or infirmity or because of the use of or addiction to intoxicants or drugs shall be subject to suspension by reason of such disability.

Section 3.   Types of Discipline and Suspension

(a) One of the following types of discipline may be imposed upon any attorney found guilty of misconduct: permanent disbarment from the practice of law; suspension for a definite or an indefinite period from the practice of law subject to reinstatement as hereinafter provided; suspension for a definite period, not to exceed six (6) months, from the practice of law with provision for automatic reinstatement upon such conditions as the Court shall specify in the order of suspension; a public reprimand; a private reprimand; or a private administrative admonition.

(b) Any attorney found disabled by reason of physical or mental illness or infirmity or by use of or addiction to any intoxicants or drugs shall be suspended for the duration of such disability.

(c) In cases of misconduct or disability, this Court may, in lieu of permanent disbarment or suspension, place an attorney on probation and permit such attorney to continue practicing law if in its opinion such action is appropriate and desirable. In such event, the attorney will be subject to such conditions, limitations and restrictions as this Court may see fit to impose, and upon a violation of such conditions, restrictions or limitations, said attorney may be suspended or disbarred.

(d) Notice of permanent disbarment, resignation under Section 17, suspension, reinstatement (except automatic reinstatement), revocation of probation, release from probation, or public reprimand shall be communicated to the parties to the proceeding, the Clerk of this Court; the Clerk of the United States Court of Appeals for the Seventh Circuit; the Clerk of each of the Federal District Courts in this State; the Clerk of the United States Bankruptcy Courts in this State; the Clerk of the Court, Circuit and Superior Court judges, and Bar Association of each county in which the attorney maintains an office; the Clerk of the Court, Circuit and Superior Court judges, and Bar Association of each contiguous county; a newspaper of general circulation in each county in which the attorney maintains an office; the official publication of the Indiana State Bar Association; and the American Bar Association. In addition, notice of disbarment, resignation under Section 17 or suspension of one year or more shall be communicated to the Clerk of the United States Supreme Court. Notice of private reprimand shall be communicated to the parties to the proceeding and the Clerk of this Court. In cases where probation is imposed by this Court, the Clerk shall notify such persons as the Court may direct of the action taken and of the restriction, conditions or limitations.

Section 4. Reinstatement

(a) A person who has been suspended from the practice of law may petition for reinstatement when the term of suspension prescribed in the order of suspension has elapsed. A person who has resigned as a member of the bar may petition for reinstatement when five (5) years have elapsed since the date of the order accepting the resignation. If costs have been imposed as part of an order of suspension or an order accepting an affidavit of resignation, those costs must be paid before a petition for reinstatement is filed.

(b) A petition for reinstatement may be granted if the petitioner establishes by clear and convincing evidence before the disciplinary commission of this Court that:

(1) The petitioner desires in good faith to obtain restoration of his or her privilege to practice law;

(2) The petitioner has not practiced law in this State or attempted to do so since he or she was disciplined;

(3) The petitioner has complied fully with the terms of the order for discipline;

(4) The petitioner's attitude towards the misconduct for which he or she was disciplined is one of genuine remorse;

(5) The petitioner's conduct since the discipline was imposed has been exemplary and above reproach;

(6) The petitioner has a proper understanding of and attitude towards the standards that are imposed upon members of the bar and will conduct himself or herself in conformity with such standards;

(7) The petitioner can safely be recommended to the legal profession, the courts and the public as a person fit to be consulted by others and to represent them and otherwise act in matters of trust and confidence, and in general to aid in the administration of justice as a member of the bar and an officer of the Courts;

(8) The disability has been removed, if the discipline was imposed by reason of physical or mental illness or infirmity, or for use of or addiction to intoxicants or drugs;

(9) The petitioner has taken the Multistate Professional Responsibility Examination (MPRE) within six (6) months before or after the date the petition for reinstatement is filed and passed with a scaled score of eighty (80) or above.

(c) Whenever a person is suspended for a definite period not to exceed six (6) months with provision for automatic reinstatement, the commission shall have the right to file written objections to such automatic reinstatement, setting forth its reasons for such objections, which shall be limited to:

(1) failure to comply with the terms of the order;

(2) pendency of other complaints;

(3) failure to comply with the terms of Section 26, infra; and

(4) failure to satisfy fully the costs of the proceeding assessed pursuant to Section 16.

Such objections must be filed with the Court at least fifteen (15) days prior to the expiration of such period of suspension, and a copy of such objections shall be mailed to the suspended attorney. The Court shall conduct a hearing on such objections and upon the question of reinstatement of such attorney, except that the Court need not conduct a hearing when the reason for the objections is the respondent's failure to satisfy fully the costs of the proceeding assessed pursuant to Section 16. After such hearing, the Court shall determine whether or not such suspended attorney shall be reinstated. If the Court determines that such attorney should not then be reinstated, the Court shall, in its order, specify when such attorney shall be eligible to apply for reinstatement pursuant to subsection (a) of this section.

If the Court determines that the respondent has failed to satisfy fully the costs assessed against him or her, the Court may enter an order staying the automatic reinstatement until the suspended attorney satisfies fully the costs of the proceeding assessed against such attorney or until further order of the Court.

(d) The Court may provide for reinstatement on other terms and by other procedures than those set forth above, such as reinstatement conditioned only on the attorney's submission of proof of compliance with a requirement for reinstatement.

Section 5. Role of Bar Association

(a) Bar associations in this State shall not conduct proceedings for the imposition of discipline as defined in this rule. Such bar associations shall take all necessary action to resolve attorney-client disputes which do not involve claims of misconduct upon request by the Disciplinary Commission. Such bar associations and the members of the bar shall also assist the Disciplinary Commission in the investigation of claims of misconduct upon request by the Disciplinary Commission.

(b) Bar associations of this State may take reasonable action to resolve attorney-client disputes where the dispute is limited to the amount of compensation being charged by the attorney independently of any request by the Disciplinary Commission and without referring such dispute to the Disciplinary Commission. Such action by the bar associations may include but shall not be limited to mediation or arbitration of the amounts to be charged for an attorney's services.

In cases where a bar association attempts to resolve an attorney-client dispute as to compensation charged for the attorney's services, any person dissatisfied with such attempt at resolution shall have a right to file a formal complaint with the Disciplinary Commission if the amount charged by the attorney is so completely excessive in relation to the services performed and to the usual considerations taken into account in determining an attorney's charges as to constitute misconduct in itself, or if other misconduct on the part of the attorney is claimed.

(c) A bar association of this State shall be permitted to prepare and file a claim of misconduct with the Disciplinary Commission under the following circumstances:

(1) The decision to prepare and file such claim of misconduct shall be taken at a regular or special meeting of said bar association after notice has been given to the members of such association or

Where such association has a governing Board of Managers or Board of Directors, such decision may be taken at a regular or special meeting of such Board of Managers or Board of Directors after notice to such managers or directors.

(2) A quorum of the members of such association, or of the Board of Managers or Board of Directors thereof shall be in attendance at the meeting.

(3) The decision to file a claim of misconduct shall be made by a roll call vote of the members, managers or directors in attendance at such meeting, with the vote of each member present being recorded.

Section 6. Composition of Supreme Court Disciplinary Commission

(a) A Disciplinary Commission to be known as the "Disciplinary Commission of the Supreme Court of Indiana" (hereinafter referred to as "the commission") is hereby created and shall have the powers and duties hereinafter set forth.

(b) The Disciplinary Commission shall consist of nine (9) members appointed by the Supreme Court of Indiana, seven (7) of whom shall be admitted to the Bar of the Supreme Court and two (2) of whom shall be lay persons. Those who are not members of the Bar must take and subscribe to an oath of office which shall be filed and maintained by the Clerk. A reasonable effort shall be made to provide a geographical representation of the State. The term of each member shall be for five (5) years. Provided, however, upon the effective date of this rule, two (2) members shall be appointed for a term of two (2) years, two (2) members for a term of three (3) years, two (2) members for a term of four (4) years and one (1) member for a term of five (5) years. The initial term of the two additional members authorized by the amendment of this subsection effective February 1, 1996, shall be for two (2) and four (4) years, respectively. Thereafter, the terms of each appointee shall be for five (5) years, or in the case of an appointee to fill the vacancy of an unexpired term, until the end of such unexpired

term. Any member may be terminated by the Court for good cause.

(c) Commission members who are not admitted to the Bar shall not be eligible for appointment as hearing officers under Section 18(b) of this rule.

Section 7. Organization of the Disciplinary Commission

(a) The Commission shall annually elect from among its membership a Chairman who shall preside at all meetings, a Vice Chairman who shall preside in the absence of the Chairman, and a Secretary who shall keep the minutes of the meetings of the Commission.

(b) Five (5) Commissioners shall constitute a quorum of the Commission and the Commission shall act by a vote of a majority of Commissioners present.

(c) The Commission shall meet monthly at a time and place designated by the Chairman who may also convene special meetings of the Commission in his or her discretion. The members of the Commission shall be allowed their necessary expenses and such reasonable compensation as the Supreme Court shall fix from time to time.

Section 8. Powers and Duties of the Disciplinary Commission

In addition to the powers and duties set forth in this Rule, the Commission shall have the power and duty to:

(a) appoint with the approval of the Supreme Court an Executive Secretary of the Commission who shall be a member of the Bar of this State and who shall serve at the pleasure of the Commission;

(b) prepare and furnish a form of request for investigation to each person who claims that an attorney is guilty of misconduct and to each Bar Association in this State for distribution to such persons;

(c) supervise the investigation of claims of misconduct;

(d) issue subpoenas, including subpoenas duces tecum; the failure to obey such subpoena may be punished as contempt of this Court or, in the case of an attorney under investigation, shall subject the attorney to suspension under the procedures set forth in subsection 10(f) of this Rule;

(e) do all things necessary and proper to carry out its powers and duties under these Rules;

(f) the right to bring an action in the Supreme Court to enjoin or restrain the unauthorized practice of law.

Section 9. Powers and Duties of the Executive Secretary

In addition to the powers and duties set forth in this Rule, the Executive Secretary shall have the power and duty to:

(a) administer the Commission's work;

(b) appoint, with the approval of the Commission, such staff as may be necessary to assist the Commission to carry out its powers and duties under this Rule;

(c) supervise and direct the work of the Commission's staff;

(d) appoint and assign duties to investigators;

(e) supervise the maintenance of the Commission's records;

(f) issue subpoenas in the name of the Commission, including subpoenas duces tecum. The failure to obey such a subpoena shall be punished as a contempt of this Court or, in the case of an attorney under investigation, shall subject the attorney to suspension under the procedures set forth in subsection 10(f) of this Rule;

(g) enforce the collection of the registration fee provided in Ind. Admission and Discipline Rule 2 against delinquent members of the Bar;

(h) notwithstanding Section 22, cooperate with the attorney disciplinary enforcement agencies of other jurisdictions, including, upon written request, the release of any documents or records that are in the control of the Executive Secretary to the chief executive of an attorney disciplinary enforcement agency in any jurisdiction in which an Indiana attorney is also admitted; and

(i) do all things necessary and proper to carry out the Executive Secretary's duties and powers under this Rule.

Section 10. Investigatory Procedures

(a) Upon receipt of a written, verified claim of misconduct (hereinafter referred to as "the grievance"), from a member of the public, a member of this bar, a member of the Commission, or a Bar Association (hereinafter referred to as "the grievant") and completion of such preliminary investigation as may be deemed appropriate, the Executive Secretary shall:

(1) Dismiss the claim, with the approval of the Commission, if the Executive Secretary determines that it raises no substantial question of misconduct; or

(2) If the Executive Secretary determines that it does raise a substantial question of misconduct, send a copy of the grievance by certified mail to the attorney against whom the grievance is filed (hereinafter referred to as "the respondent") and shall demand a written response. The respondent shall respond within twenty (20) days, or within such additional time as the Executive Secretary may allow, after the respondent receives a copy of the grievance. In the event of a dismissal as provided herein, the person filing the grievance and the respondent shall be given written notice of the Executive Secretary's determination. In the event of a determination that a substantial question exists,

the matter shall proceed to subsection (b) hereinafter.

(b) Thereafter, if the Executive Secretary, upon consideration of the grievance, any response from the respondent, and any preliminary investigation, determines there is a reasonable cause to believe that the respondent is guilty of misconduct the grievance shall be docketed and investigated. If the Executive Secretary determines that no such reasonable cause exists, the grievance shall be dismissed with the approval of the Commission. In either event, the person filing the grievance (hereinafter referred to as "the grievant") and the respondent shall be given written notice of the Executive Secretary's determination.

(c) If the grievance is docketed for investigation, the Executive Secretary shall conduct an investigation of the grievance. Upon completion of the investigation the Executive Secretary shall promptly make a report of the investigation and a recommendation to the Commission at its next meeting.

(d) In conducting an investigation of any grievance, or in considering the same, the Executive Secretary or the Commission shall not be limited to an investigation or consideration of only matters set forth in the grievance, but shall be permitted to inquire into the professional conduct of the attorney generally. In the event that the Executive Secretary or the Commission should consider any charges of misconduct against an attorney not contained in the grievance, the Executive Secretary shall notify the attorney of the additional charges under consideration, and the attorney shall make a written response to the additional charges under consideration within twenty (20) days after the receipt of such notification, or within such additional time as the Executive Secretary shall allow.

Any additional charges of misconduct against an attorney, after such notice has been given by the Executive Secretary and the attorney has had an opportunity to reply thereto, may be the subject of a count of any complaint filed against the attorney pursuant to Sections 11 and 12 of this Rule.

(e) It shall be the duty of every attorney against whom a grievance is filed under this Section to cooperate with the Commission's investigation, accept service, comply with the provisions of these rules, and when notice is given by registered or certified mail, claim the same in a timely manner either personally or through an authorized agent. Every attorney is obligated under the terms of Admission and Discipline Rule 2 to notify the Clerk of any change of address or name within thirty (30) days of such change, and a failure to file the same shall be a waiver of notice involving licenses as attorneys or disciplinary matters.

(f) An attorney who is the subject of an investigation by the Disciplinary Commission may be suspended from the practice of law upon a finding that the attorney has failed to cooperate with the investigation.

(1) Such a finding may be based upon the attorney's failure to submit a written response to pending allegations of professional misconduct, to accept certified mail from the Disciplinary Commission that is sent to the attorney's official address of record with the Clerk and that requires a written response under this Rule, or to comply with any lawful demand for information made by the Commission or its Executive Secretary in connection with any investigation, including failure to comply with a subpoena issued pursuant to sections 8(d) and 9(f) or unexcused failure to appear at any hearing on the matter under investigation.

(2) Upon the filing with this Court of a petition authorized by the Commission, the Court shall issue an order directing the attorney to respond within ten (10) days of service of the order and show cause why the attorney should not be immediately suspended for failure to cooperate with the disciplinary process. Service upon the attorney shall be made pursuant to sections 12(g) and (h). The suspension shall be ordered upon this Court's finding that the attorney has failed to cooperate, as outlined in subsection (f)(1), above. An attorney suspended from practice under this subsection shall comply with the requirements of sections 26(b) and (c) of this rule.

(3) Such suspension shall continue until such time as (a) the Executive Secretary certifies to the Court that the attorney has cooperated with the investigation; (b) the investigation or any related disciplinary proceeding that may arise from the investigation is disposed; or (c) until further order of the Court.

(4) On motion by the Commission and order of the Court, suspension that lasts for more than six (6) months may be converted into indefinite suspension.

(5) Upon the disposition of any show cause petition filed pursuant to paragraph (f)(2), above, due to dismissal because the respondent cooperated, or due to suspension, disbarment, or resignation in any proceeding, the Commission may seek an order reimbursing the Commission in the amount of $500 plus out-of-pocket expenses for its time and effort in seeking the order in addition to all other costs and expenses provided for by Section 16 of this rule. An attorney who fails to pay the reimbursements, costs, or expenses assessed pursuant to this paragraph by the due date of the annual registration fee required by Admission and Discipline Rule 2(b) shall be subject to an order of suspension from the practice of law pursuant to Indiana Admission and Discipline Rule 2(h), and shall be reinstated only upon paying the outstanding reimbursements, costs and expenses and submitting to the Clerk a written application for reinstatement and payment of an administrative reinstatement fee of two hundred dollars ($200).

Section 11. Pre-hearing Procedures

(a) The members of the Commission shall consider and make a determination of the report and recommendations of the Executive Secretary not later than the meeting following the submission of the report. If the Commission determines that there is not reasonable cause to believe that the respondent is guilty of misconduct the grievance shall be dismissed, and the grievant and the respondent shall be given written notice of the Commission's determination.

(b) If after such consideration, the Commission determines there is a reasonable cause to believe the respondent is guilty of misconduct which would warrant disciplinary action, it shall file with the Clerk a complaint as provided in Section 12. Upon the filing of a complaint, the Supreme Court shall appoint a hearing officer or officers, not to exceed three (3) in number, who shall be members of the Bar of this Court, none of whom shall be members of the Disciplinary Commission, to hear and determine said charges. A respondent may on a showing of good cause petition the Court for a change of hearing officer within ten (10) days after the appointment of such hearing officer.

(c) After the filing of a complaint with the Clerk, the parties (commission and respondent) may conditionally agree upon the discipline to be imposed, in which event they shall jointly submit to the Division of Supreme Court Administration Office a statement of circumstances which shall contain the charges, the facts agreed to, the facts in dispute, the evidence the parties separately believe would be adduced in a hearing, the charge(s) which the parties agree are established, and the discipline with which the parties are in conditional agreement. Said statement shall also contain an affidavit executed by the respondent stating that the respondent consents to the agreed discipline and that:

(1) The respondent's consent is freely and voluntarily rendered; the respondent is not being subjected to coercion or duress; the respondent is fully aware of the implications of submitting his or her consent;

(2) The respondent is aware that there is a presently pending proceeding involving allegations that there exist grounds for his or her discipline the nature of which shall be specifically set forth;

(3) The respondent acknowledges that the material facts set forth in the conditional agreement are true; and

(4) The respondent submits his or her agreement because the respondent knows that if charges were predicated upon matters under investigation, or if the proceeding were prosecuted, the respondent could not successfully defend himself or herself. Said statement may also contain any other information that the parties deem relevant, other than statements by witnesses attesting to the character or repu-

tation of the respondent, which statements may not be submitted.

Upon such submission, the Court will consider the same and (1) enter an order for the discipline conditionally agreed to or (2) submit to the parties a proposed disposition for such discipline as the Court shall deem appropriate, or (3) notify the parties that it declines to approve the agreement or recommend a disposition.

In the event an order is entered as set forth under (1) above, such order shall be a final disposition of the matter. In the event the Court submits a proposed disposition as set forth under (2) above, and the parties shall desire to agree to such disposition, they shall, within sixty (60) days following the submission of such proposed disposition, file with the Clerk a statement of agreement, verified by the respondent and by a member of the Commission or the Executive Secretary thereof. Said statement of agreement shall reflect the prior conditional agreement, the prior action of the Court thereon and the agreement of the parties thereto. Upon such filing, the Court shall enter its disposition accordingly, which shall conclude the matter. In the event the parties do not desire to agree to such proposed disposition or in the event the Court proceeds as set forth under (3) above, the parties shall proceed as if no conditional agreement had been filed.

It is the intent of this rule to encourage appropriate agreed dispositions of disciplinary matters. A conditional agreement shall not be admitted into evidence at any hearing of the matter.

Section 11.1. Interim and Summary Suspensions

(a) Upon finding that an attorney has been found guilty of a crime punishable as a felony, the Supreme Court may suspend such attorney from the practice of law pending further order of the Court or final determination of any resulting disciplinary proceeding.

(1) The judge of any court in this state in which an attorney is found guilty of a crime shall, within ten (10) days after the finding of guilt, transmit a certified copy of proof of the finding of guilt to the Executive Secretary of the Indiana Supreme Court Disciplinary Commission.

(2) An attorney licensed to practice law in the state of Indiana who is found guilty of a crime in any state or of a crime under the laws of the United States shall, within ten (10) days after such finding of guilt, transmit a certified copy of the finding of guilt to the Executive Secretary of the Indiana Supreme Court Disciplinary Commission.

(3) Upon receipt of information indicating that an attorney has been found guilty of a crime punishable as a felony under the laws of any state or of the United States, the Executive Secretary shall verify the information, and, in addition to any other proceeding initiated pursuant to this Rule, shall file

with the Supreme Court a Notice of Finding of Guilt and Request for Suspension, and shall forward notice to the attorney by certified mail. The attorney shall have fifteen (15) days thereafter to file any response to the request for suspension. Thereafter, the Supreme Court may issue an order of suspension upon notice of finding of guilt which order shall be effective until further order of the Court.

(b) If it appears to the Disciplinary Commission upon the affirmative vote of two-thirds (2/3) of its membership, that: (i) the continuation of the practice of law by an attorney during the pendency of a disciplinary investigation or proceeding may pose a substantial threat of harm to the public, clients, potential clients, or the administration of justice, and (ii) the alleged conduct, if true, would subject the respondent to sanctions under this Rule, the Executive Secretary shall petition the Supreme Court for an order of interim suspension from the practice of law or imposition of temporary conditions of probation on the attorney.

(1) A petition to the Supreme Court for interim relief under this subsection shall set forth the specific acts and violations of the Rules of Professional Conduct submitted by the Commission as grounds for the relief requested. The petition shall be verified and may be supported by documents or affidavits. A copy of the petition, along with a notice to answer, shall be served by the Commission on the attorney in the same manner as provided in sections 12(g) and (h) of this rule. The Executive Secretary shall file a return on service, setting forth the method of service and the date on which the respondent was served with the petition and notice to answer. The attorney shall file an answer to the Commission's petition with the Supreme Court within fourteen (14) days of service. The answer shall be verified and may be supported by documents or affidavits. The attorney shall mail a copy of the answer to the Executive Secretary and file proof of mailing with the court.

(2) The failure of the respondent to answer the Commission's petition within the time granted by this rule for an answer shall constitute a waiver of the attorney's right to contest the petition, and the Supreme Court may enter an order of interim suspension or imposition of temporary conditions of probation in conformity with subsection (b)(5) either upon the record before it, or at the discretion of the Court, after a hearing ordered by the Court.

(3) Upon the filing of the respondent's answer and upon consideration of all of the pleadings, the Court may:

(i) order interim suspension or imposition of temporary conditions of probation upon the petition and answer in conformity with subsection (b)(5);

(ii) deny the petition upon the petition and answer; or

(iii) refer the matter to a hearing officer, who shall proceed consistent with the procedures set forth in subsection (b)(4).

(4) Upon referral to a hearing officer of an interim relief matter from the Supreme Court, the hearing officer shall hold a hearing thereon within thirty (30) days of the date of referral and render a report to the Court containing findings of fact and a recommendation within fourteen (14) days of the hearing. The Court shall thereafter act promptly on the hearing officer's report, findings and recommendation.

(5) The Supreme Court, upon the record before it or after receiving a hearing officer's report, shall enter an appropriate order. If the Court finds that the Commission has shown by a preponderance of the evidence that:

(i) the continuation of the practice of law by the respondent during the pendency of a disciplinary investigation or proceeding may pose a substantial threat of harm to the public, clients, potential clients, or the administration of justice; and

(ii) the conduct would subject the respondent to sanctions under this rule;

the Court shall grant the petition and enter an order of interim suspension or imposition of temporary conditions of probation. The order shall set forth an effective date and remain in effect until disposition of any related disciplinary proceeding or further order of the court.

(6) In the event the Court issues an order of interim relief pursuant to subsection (b)(5), the respondent may file a verified motion with the Supreme Court at any time for dissolution or amendment of the interim order by verified motion that sets forth specific facts demonstrating good cause. A copy of the motion shall be served on the Executive Secretary. Successive motions for dissolution or amendment of an interim order may be summarily dismissed by the Supreme Court to the extent they raise issues that were or with due diligence could have been raised in a prior motion. If the motion is in proper form, the Court may refer the matter to a hearing officer, who shall proceed consistent with the procedures set forth in subsection (b)(4).

(7) In the event a verified complaint for disciplinary action has not been filed by the time an order of interim relief is entered, the Disciplinary Commission shall file a formal complaint within sixty (60) days of the interim relief order. When a respondent is subject to an order of interim relief, the hearing officer shall conduct a final hearing of the underlying issues and report thereon to the Court without undue delay.

(8) An attorney suspended from practice under this section shall comply with the requirements of subsections 26(b) and (c) of this rule.

(c) Upon receipt of an order from a court pursuant to IC 31–16–12–8 or IC 31–14–12–5 stating finding that an attorney has been found to be delinquent in the payment of child support as a result of an intentional violation of an order for support, the Executive Secretary shall file with the Supreme Court a Notice of Intentional Violation of Support Order and Request for Suspension, and shall forward notice to the attorney by certified mail. The attorney shall have fifteen (15) days thereafter to file any response to the request for suspension. Thereafter, the Supreme Court may issue an order of suspension. Such order shall be effective until further order of the Court.

Section 11.2. Filing and Service of Pleadings and Other Papers

(a) Filing.

(1) Except as otherwise provided in subsection (2) hereof, all pleadings and papers subsequent to the complaint which are required to be served upon a party shall be filed with the Clerk.

(2) No deposition or request for discovery or response thereto shall be filed with the Court unless required under circumstances set forth in Trial Rule 5(D)(2).

(3) Original depositions shall be maintained according to the procedures set forth in Trial Rule 5(D)(3).

(4) In the event it is made to appear to the satisfaction of the hearing officer that the original of a deposition or request for discovery or response thereto cannot be filed with the Court when required, the Court may allow use of a copy instead of the original.

(5) The filing of any deposition shall constitute publication.

(b) Filing With the Court Defined. All papers will be deemed filed with the Clerk when they are:

(1) personally delivered to the Clerk;

(2) deposited in the United States Mail, postage prepaid, properly addressed to the Clerk; or

(3) deposited with any third-party commercial carrier for delivery to the Clerk within three (3) calendar days, cost prepaid, properly addressed.

(c) Filing; Number of Copies. Except as otherwise provided in this rule, the following shall be filed with the Clerk:

(1) An original and one (1) copy of any pleading, motion or other paper directed to the attention of the hearing officer that is filed between the date the Court appoints the hearing officer and the date the hearing officer files written findings of fact.

(2) An original and one (1) copy of a motion for extension of time, an appearance, a motion to with-

draw appearance, a petition by the Commission for an order to show cause under Rule 23(10)(f), and a motion by the Commission to dismiss a show cause proceeding under Rule 23(10)(f).

(3) An original and five (5) copies of all other documents filed with the Clerk.

(d) Required Service. All documents tendered to the Clerk for filing must be served upon all parties or their counsel and the hearing officer, after one has been appointed.

(e) Time for Service. A party shall serve a document no later than the date the document is filed.

(f) Manner and Date of Service. Unless otherwise provided in this rule, all papers will be deemed served when they are:

(1) personally delivered;

(2) deposited in the United States Mail, postage prepaid, properly addressed; or

(3) deposited with any third-party commercial carrier for delivery within three (3) calendar days, cost prepaid, properly addressed.

(g) Certificate of Service. An attorney or unrepresented party tendering a document to the Clerk for filing shall certify that service has been made, list the parties or others served, and specify the date and means of service. The certificate of service shall be placed at the end of the documents and shall not be separately filed. The separate filing of a certificate of service, however, shall not be grounds for rejecting a document for filing. The Clerk may permit documents to be filed without a certificate of service but shall require prompt filing of a separate certificate of service.

Section 11.3.   Computation of Time

(a) *Non-Business and Business Days.* For purposes of this rule, a non-business day shall mean a Saturday, a Sunday, a legal holiday as defined by state statute, or a day the Office of the Clerk is closed during regular business hours. A business day shall mean all other days.

(b) *Counting Days.* In computing any period of time allowed by these Rules, by order of the court, or by any applicable statute, the day of the act, event, or default from which the designated period of time begins to run shall not be included. The last day of the period so computed is to be included unless it is a non-business day. If the last day is a non-business day, the period runs until the end of the next business day. When the time allowed is less than seven (7) days, all non-business days shall be excluded from the computation.

(c) *Extension of Time When Served by Mail or Carrier.* When a party serves a document by mail or third-party commercial carrier, the time period for filing any response or reply to the document shall be extended automatically for an additional three (3) days from the date of deposit in the mail or with the carrier. This Rule does not extend any time period that is not triggered by a party's service of a document, such as the time for filing a petition for review.

Section 12.   Prosecution of Grievances

(a) If the Commission determines that there is reasonable cause to believe respondent is guilty of misconduct and the misconduct would not likely result in a sanction greater than a public reprimand if successfully prosecuted, and if the respondent and the Commission agree to an administrative resolution of the complaint, the Commission may resolve and dispose of minor misconduct by private administrative admonition without filing a verified complaint with the Court. Without limitation, misconduct shall not be regarded as minor if any of the following conditions exist:

(1) The misconduct involves misappropriation of funds or property;

(2) The misconduct resulted in or is likely to result in material prejudice (loss of money, legal rights or valuable property rights) to a client or other person;

(3) The respondent has been publicly disciplined in the past three (3) years;

(4) The misconduct involved is of the same nature as misconduct for which the respondent has been publicly or privately disciplined in the past five (5) years;

(5) The misconduct includes dishonesty, misrepresentation, deceit, or fraud on the part of the respondent; or

(6) The misconduct constitutes the commission of a felony under applicable law.

(b) An administrative admonition shall be issued in the form of a letter from the Executive Secretary to the respondent summarizing the facts and setting out the applicable violations of the Rules of Professional Conduct. A copy of the admonition letter shall first be sent to each Justice of the Supreme Court and to the Supreme Court Administration Office. The administrative admonition shall be final within thirty (30) days thereafter, unless set aside by the Court. If not set aside by the Court, the admonition shall be sent to the respondent, and notice of the fact that a respondent has received a private administrative admonition shall be given by the Executive Secretary to the grievant. The fact that an attorney has received a private administrative admonition shall be a public record, which shall be filed with the Clerk and shall be kept by the Executive Secretary.

(c) In the event the Commission determines that the misconduct, if proven, would warrant disciplinary action and should not be disposed of by way of an administrative admonition, the Executive Secretary shall prepare a verified complaint which sets forth the misconduct with which the respondent is charged and shall prosecute the case.

(d) The complaint shall be entitled "In the Matter of," naming the respondent. Six (6) copies shall be filed with this Court. The complaint may be verified on the basis of information and belief.

(e) Contemporaneously with the filing of the complaint, the Commission shall promptly prepare and furnish to the Clerk as many copies of the complaint and summons as are necessary. The Clerk shall examine, date, sign and affix his/her seal to the summons and thereupon issue and deliver the papers to the appropriate person for service. Separate or additional summons shall be issued by the Clerk at any time upon proper request by the Commission.

(f) The summons shall contain:

(1) The name and address of the person on whom the service is to be effected;

(2) The Supreme Court cause number assigned to the case;

(3) The title of the case as shown by the complaint;

(4) The name, address, and telephone number of the Disciplinary Commission;

(5) The time within which this rule requires the person being served to respond, and a clear statement that in case of his or her failure to do so, the allegations in the complaint shall be taken as true.

The summons may also contain any additional information that will facilitate proper service.

(g) Upon the filing of such complaint, the summons and complaint shall be served upon the respondent by delivering a copy of them to the respondent personally or by sending a copy of them by registered or certified mail with return receipt requested and returned showing the receipt of the letter.

In the event the personal service or service by registered or certified mail cannot be obtained upon any respondent attorney, said summons and complaint shall be served on the Clerk as set forth in Section 12(h) of this rule.

(h) Each attorney admitted to practice law in this State shall be deemed to have appointed the Clerk as his or her agent to receive service of any and all papers, processes or notices which may be called for by any provision of this rule. Such papers, process or notice may be served by filing the same with the Clerk as the agent for said attorney, together with an affidavit setting forth the facts necessitating this method of service. Upon receipt of such papers, process or notice together with such affidavit, the Clerk shall immediately mail such papers, process or notice to such attorney at the attorney's office address, or if unavailable the attorney's residence address, as shown upon the records of the Clerk, and the Clerk shall file a written certification showing the mailing of such papers, process or notice to said attorney. Upon the completion of this procedure, said attorney shall be deemed to have been served with such papers, process or notice.

Section 13. Hearing Officers

In addition to the powers and duties set forth in the rule, hearing officers shall have the power and duty to:

(a) Conduct a hearing on a complaint of misconduct;

(b) Administer oaths to witnesses;

(c) Receive evidence and file a "Hearing Officer's Report" making written findings of fact and conclusions of law; and

(d) Do all things necessary and proper to carry out their responsibilities under this rule.

Section 14. Proceedings Before the Hearing Officer

(a) The rules of pleading and practice in civil cases shall not apply. No motion to dismiss or dilatory motions shall be entertained. The case shall be heard on the complaint and an answer which shall be filed by the respondent within thirty (30) days after service of the summons and complaint, or such additional time as may be allowed upon written application to the hearing officer that sets forth good cause. A written application for enlargement of time to answer shall be automatically allowed for an additional thirty (30) days from the original due date without a written order of the Hearing Officer. Any motion for automatic enlargement of time filed pursuant to this rule shall state the date when such answer is due and the date to which time is enlarged. The motion must be filed on or before the original due date or this provision shall be inapplicable. All subsequent motions shall be so designated and shall be granted by the hearing officer only for good cause shown.

(b) The answer shall admit or controvert the averments set forth in the complaint by specifically denying designated averments or paragraphs or generally denying all averments except such designated averments or paragraphs as the respondent expressly admits. If the respondent lacks knowledge or information sufficient to form a belief as to the truth of an averment, he or she shall so state and his statement shall be considered a denial. If in good faith the respondent intends to deny only a part of an averment, he or she shall specify so much of it as is true and material and deny the remainder. All denials shall fairly meet the substance of the averments denied. Averments in a complaint are admitted when not denied in the answer. The answer shall assert any legal defense.

(c) When a respondent has failed to answer a complaint as required by this section and that fact is made to appear by affidavit and an application for judgment on the complaint, the allegations set forth in the complaint shall be taken as true. If a respondent who has failed to answer has appeared in the action, he or she (or, if appearing by counsel, his or her counsel) shall be served with written notice of the application for judgment on the complaint at least seven (7) days prior to the hearing on such application. Upon application for judgment on the complaint and in the absence of any answer by the respondent, the hearing officer shall take the facts alleged in the complaint as true and promptly tender a report to the Supreme Court in conformity with subsection (h). If a hearing officer has not been appointed by the time an application for judgment on the complaint is filed and no appearance has been filed by or on behalf of the respondent, the Supreme Court shall act directly on the application for judgment on the complaint.

(d) Discovery shall be available to the parties on terms and conditions that, as nearly as practicable, follow the Indiana Rules of Civil Procedure pertaining to discovery proceedings.

(e) At the discretion of the hearing officer, or upon the request of either party, a pre-hearing conference shall be ordered for the purpose of obtaining admissions, narrowing the issues presented by the pleadings, requiring an exchange of the names and addresses of prospective witnesses and the general nature of their expected testimony, considering the necessity or desirability of amendments to the verified complaint and answer thereto, and such other matters as may aid in the disposition of the action.

(f) Within thirty (30) days after the hearing officer is appointed and has qualified, the hearing officer shall schedule a date for a final hearing on the complaint, which date, absent good cause to the contrary, shall be within ninety (90) days of the same.

(g) The grievant, the respondent, and the Commission shall be given not less than fifteen (15) days written notice of the hearing date. The respondent shall have the right to attend the hearing in person, to be represented by counsel, to cross-examine the witnesses testifying against him or her and to produce at the hearing and require the production of evidence and witnesses in his or her own behalf at the hearing, as in civil proceedings. All notices connected with processing of such complaint shall be issued only under the direction of the hearing officer or hearing officers, and no other court or judicial officer of this State shall have jurisdiction to issue any orders or processes in connection with a disciplinary complaint. Upon request of a party, the hearing officer may issue a subpoena, or a subpoena for the production of documentary evidence, signed and sealed but otherwise in blank, to a party requesting it or his or her attorney, who shall fill it in before service. The hearing officer may also authorize an attorney admitted to practice law in this state who has appeared for a party, as an officer of the court, to issue and sign such subpoena. Subpoenas for the attendance of witnesses and production of documentary evidence shall conform to the provisions of Trial Rule 45. The hearing officer or officers shall have authority to enforce, quash or modify subpoenas upon proper application by an interested party or witness.

(h) The proceedings may be summary in form and shall be without the intervention of a jury and shall be conducted on the record.

(i) Within thirty (30) days after the conclusion of the hearing, the hearing officer shall determine whether misconduct has been proven by clear and convincing evidence and shall file with the Clerk a written "Hearing Officer's Report" with findings of fact and conclusions of law. Either party may request or the hearing officer at his or her own motion may make a recommendation concerning the disposition of the case and the discipline to be imposed. Such recommendation is not binding on the Supreme Court. A copy of the report shall be served by the hearing officer on the respondent and the Executive Secretary of the Disciplinary Commission at the time the report is filed with the Clerk.

Section 15. Supreme Court Review

(a) The respondent or Commission shall have thirty (30) days after the filing of the Hearing Officer's Report to petition for a review of the same before the Supreme Court. Instead of a petition for review, the respondent or the Commission may file a brief on sanctions. If no petition for review or brief on sanctions is filed within thirty (30) days of the filing of the Hearing Officer's Report, the Supreme Court shall enter judgment or such other appropriate order.

(b) In the event a party does not concur in a factual finding made by the hearing officer and asserts error in such finding in the petition for review, such party shall file with the petition for review a record of all the evidence before the hearing officer relating to this factual issue. Within thirty (30) days of the filing of the transcript, opposing parties may file such additional transcript as deemed necessary to resolve the factual issue so raised in the petition for review. Any transcript filed must be settled, signed and certified as true and correct by the hearing officer. The cost of procuring a transcript shall be borne by the party obtaining it for purposes of seeking review.

(c) The respondent or Commission may file a brief at the time a petition for review is filed. Opposing parties shall have thirty (30) days from the date of service of the petition for review or brief on sanctions to file a response brief. The party opposing a petition for review may raise in its brief any issues for review that were not raised in the brief of the party filing the petition for review. The party filing the petition for review or brief on sanctions shall then have fifteen (15) days from the date of service of the response brief to file a reply brief. The briefs filed under the provisions of this rule need not conform to the Rules of Appellate Procedure adopted by this Court.

Section 16. Expenses

The judgment of this Court imposing discipline will normally include an order that the respondent pay the costs and expenses of the proceeding. The Executive Secretary shall prepare an itemized statement of expenses allocable to each case, including expenses incurred by the Commission in the course of the investigatory, hearing or review procedures under this rule and costs attributable to the services of the hearing officer. The Executive Secretary shall include in the itemized statement of expenses a fee of two hundred fifty dollars ($250) payable to the Clerk, as reimbursement for the Clerk's processing of all papers in connection with the proceeding. Proceedings for the collection of the costs taxed against the respondent may be initiated by the Executive Secretary on the order approving expenses and costs entered by this Court. An attorney who fails to pay costs and expenses assessed pursuant to this section by the due date of the annual registration fee required by Admission and Discipline Rule 2(b) shall be subject to an order of suspension from the practice of law pursuant to Indiana Admission and Discipline Rule 2(h), and shall be reinstated only upon paying the outstanding costs and expenses and submitting to the Clerk a written application for reinstatement and payment of an administrative reinstatement fee of two hundred dollars ($200).

Section 17.   Resignations and Consents to Discipline on Admission of Misconduct

(a) An attorney who is the subject of an investigation into, or a pending proceeding involving, allegations of misconduct may resign as a member of the bar of this Court, or may consent to discipline, but only by delivering an affidavit and five copies to the Supreme Court Administration Office and providing a copy to the Commission. The affidavit shall state that the respondent desires to resign or to consent to discipline and that:

(1) The respondent's consent is freely and voluntarily rendered; he or she is not being subjected to coercion or duress; he or she is fully aware of the implications of submitting his or her consent;

(2) The respondent is aware that there is a presently pending investigation into, or proceeding involving, allegations that there exist grounds for his or her discipline the nature of which shall be specifically set forth;

(3) The respondent acknowledges that the material facts so alleged are true; and

(4) The respondent submits his or her resignation or consent because the respondent knows that if charges were predicated upon the matters under investigation, or if the proceeding were prosecuted, he or she could not successfully defend himself or herself.

(b) Upon receipt of the required affidavit in support of resignation, this Court may enter an order approving the resignation. In the case of consent to discipline, the Commission and the respondent may file a brief regarding an appropriate sanction within thirty

(30) days of delivery of the required affidavit. The Court shall then enter an order imposing a disciplinary sanction on consent.

(c) An order entered under (b) above shall be a matter of public record. However, the affidavit required under the provisions of (a) above shall not be publicly disclosed or made available for use in any other proceeding except upon order of this Court.

Section 17.1   Termination of Probation

(a) Unless provided in the order of probation, disciplinary probation shall remain in effect until terminated pursuant to this rule or by Court order.

(b) At any time after fifteen (15) days prior to expiration of a period of probation, an attorney on probation may file with the Clerk and shall serve on the Commission (i) a "Petition for Termination of Probation," and (ii) an affidavit by the attorney attesting to successful compliance with all terms of probation.

(c) The Commission shall have fifteen (15) days after service of a petition for termination of probation to file with the Clerk and serve on the attorney an objection to the petition. If such an objection is filed, the order of probation and all related obligations shall continue until further order of the Court. The attorney shall have fifteen (15) days after service of an objection to file a response. The Commission shall have ten (10) days after service of a response to file a reply.

(d) If no objection to a petition for termination of probation is filed, the petition shall be deemed granted with no further action required by the Court, effective fifteen (15) days after the petition was filed, and the Clerk shall adjust the attorney's status on the Roll of Attorneys to reflect that the attorney is no longer on probation.

Section 17.2.   Revocation of Probation

(a) *Motion to Revoke.* If the Executive Secretary receives information that an attorney on probation may have violated any condition of probation, the Executive Secretary may file a verified motion to revoke probation with the Court, setting forth specific facts in support of the motion. A motion for revocation of an attorney's probation shall not preclude the Commission from filing independent disciplinary charges based on the same conduct alleged in the motion.

(b) *Response to Motion.* Within ten (10) days after service of a petition under subparagraph (a), the attorney shall file an answer under penalties of perjury admitting or controverting each of the allegations contained in the revocation motion. A general denial shall not be allowed and, if filed, will be taken as a failure to answer. The attorney's failure to answer timely will be deemed to be an admission to the averments in the motion to revoke probation, unless the Court in its discretion elects to give consideration to any answer that is filed before the Court acts on the revocation motion.

(c) *Burden of Proof and Matters Considered.* The Executive Secretary has the burden of establishing by a preponderance of the evidence any violations of conditions of probation. Any reliable evidence of probative value may be considered regardless of its admissibility under rules of evidence so long as the opposing party is accorded a fair opportunity to controvert it.

(d) *Disposition.* After the time for filing an answer has expired, the Court may dispose of the matter on the pleadings and supportive materials or, in the event there are material factual disputes, may refer it to a hearing officer who shall hold a hearing on the revocation motion within fourteen (14) days of the date the hearing officer is appointed. The hearing officer shall file with the Clerk findings and a recommendation within ten (10) days of the hearing. Following receipt of the hearing officer's findings and recommendation, the Court shall enter an order granting or denying the revocation motion and entering an appropriate disposition consistent with the Court's ruling in the matter.

Section 17.3. Service in Termination and Revocation of Probation Matters

Service upon the attorney and the Executive Secretary shall be made by personal service or by certified mail, return receipt requested. Service shall be complete and sufficient upon mailing when served upon the attorney at his current address of record on the roll of attorneys, regardless of whether the attorney claims the mail.

Section 17.4. Immediate Suspension

In addition to a motion for revocation of probation, the Executive Secretary may also file a verified motion setting forth good cause for the immediate suspension of the attorney's license to practice. Upon a showing of good cause, the Court may order the attorney's license suspended immediately until such time as the revocation motion has been determined.

Section 18. Petitions for Reinstatement

(a) A person who has been suspended from the practice of law under the provisions of this rule, except pursuant to Section 11.1(c) of this rule, may apply for reinstatement by filing with the Clerk a petition conforming with the requirements of Section 4 of this rule. Nine (9) copies of such petition shall be filed with the Clerk, together with a filing fee of five hundred dollars ($500).

A person who has been suspended pursuant to Section 11.1(c) of this rule may petition for reinstatement and pay a filing fee pursuant to subsection (c) of this section. If costs have been imposed as part of an order of suspension, those costs must be paid before any petition for reinstatement is filed.

Upon the filing of such petition and filing fee under this subsection, the commission shall schedule a hearing. After such hearing, the commission shall determine whether the petitioner has met the requirements set forth in Section 4 of this rule and may recommend that the Supreme Court enter an order continuing the suspension or reinstating the petitioner as a member of the Bar of this Court on such terms and conditions as the Supreme Court may deem proper. The applicant for reinstatement may petition this Court for a review of the recommendation of the Commission within thirty (30) days of the entry thereof.

(b) For the purpose of conducting hearings on petitions for reinstatement, the Commission may request the appointment of a hearing officer or hearing officers, who may but shall not be required to be members of the Commission. Such hearing officers shall have the same powers as the hearing officers provided for in Section 13, and shall hear such petition for reinstatement and make written findings of fact and recommendations to the Commission. Following the receipt of the findings and recommendations of the hearing officer or officers, the Commission shall make its recommendation to this Court on such petition, as set forth in subsection (a) above.

(c) An attorney suspended pursuant to Section 11.1(c) of this rule may be automatically reinstated by the Supreme Court upon filing a petition for reinstatement and presenting therewith a certified copy of a court order stating that the attorney is no longer in intentional violation of an order for child support. Nine (9) copies of such petition shall be filed with the Clerk together with a filing fee of two hundred dollars ($200).

(d) Any person filing a petition for reinstatement shall be responsible for the payment of any and all costs incurred by the Commission in conducting a hearing upon said petition for reinstatement which exceed the amount of the filing fee provided for in subsection (a) above. Any such costs shall be paid by the petitioner within ten (10) days of the receipt of a statement therefor from the Commission. In no event will there be any refund or rebate of any part of the filing fee as provided for in subsection (a) above.

Section 19. Assistance of Law Enforcement Agencies and to Lawyer Disciplinary Agencies in Other Jurisdictions

(a) The Commission, or the Executive Secretary, may request any law enforcement agency or office to assist in an investigation. Such assistance shall include the furnishing of all available information about the respondent.

(b) The Supreme Court may order a person domiciled or found within this state to give testimony or a statement or to produce documents or other things for use in an attorney discipline or disability proceeding in another state. The order may be made upon the application of any interested person or in response to a letter rogatory, and may prescribe the practice and procedure, which may be wholly or in part the practice and procedure of a tribunal outside this state, for the taking of the testimony or statement or producing the documents or other things. To the extent that the order does not prescribe otherwise, the practice and procedure shall be in accordance with the applicable provisions of the Indiana Rules of Trial Procedure. The order may direct that the testimony or statement be given, or document or other thing be produced, before a person appointed by the Court. A person may be required to give testimony or a statement only in the county wherein he or she resides or is employed or transacts business in person, or at such other convenient place as is fixed in the order. The person appointed shall have the power to administer any necessary oath. Any order to testify or to produce documents or other things issued as prescribed in this subsection may be enforced in the circuit court of the county wherein the person commanded to appear is domiciled, upon petition of any party interested in the subject attorney discipline or disability proceeding.

Section 20. Immunity

Each person shall be absolutely immune from civil suit for all of his or her oral or written statements intended for transmittal either: a) to the Commission, the Executive Secretary, or the Commission staff, or made in the course of investigatory, hearing or review proceedings under this rule; or b) to a Lawyers Assistance Program approved by the Supreme Court. Oral or written statements made to others which are not intended for such transmittal have no immunity under this Section. The Executive Secretary, his staff, counsel, investigators, hearing officers, and the commissioners shall be immune from suit for any conduct arising out of the performance of their duties.

Section 21. Sources and Uses of Funds

(a) The Indiana Supreme Court shall periodically designate a portion of the registration fees charged to attorneys pursuant to Admission and Discipline Rule 2 to be used for the operations of the Disciplinary Commission. The Executive Secretary of the Disciplinary Commission shall deposit such funds into an account designated "Supreme Court Disciplinary Commission Fund."

(b) Disbursements from the fund shall be made solely upon vouchers signed by or pursuant to the direction of the Chief Justice of this Court.

(c) The Supreme Court shall specifically approve all salaries to be paid out of the Disciplinary Commission Fund.

(d) Not later than May 1 of each year, the Commission shall submit for approval by the Supreme Court an operating budget for July 1 to June 30 of the following fiscal year.

Section 22. Public Disclosure

(a) Except as provided in Section 22(b), after a verified complaint has been filed with the Court, all proceedings, except for adjudicative deliberations, and all papers filed of record with the Clerk shall be open and available to the public. Proceedings and papers that relate to matters that have not resulted in the filing of a verified complaint shall not be open and available to the public. Investigative reports and other work product of the Executive Secretary or his or her agents, and statements of circumstances conditionally agreeing to discipline submitted pursuant to Section 11(c), shall be confidential and not open to public inspection.

(b) Hearings before hearing officers shall be open to the public. However, hearing officers may, in the exercise of sound discretion, order a closed hearing or other appropriate relief on the motion of the hearing officer, or at the request of the Commission or the respondent if, in the opinion of such hearing officer, the conduct of a closed hearing is necessary for any of the following purposes:

(1) For the protection of witnesses;

(2) To prevent likely disruption of the proceedings;

(3) For the security of the hearing officer, or any of the parties to the proceedings;

(4) To prevent the unauthorized disclosure of attorney-client confidences not at issue in the proceeding;

(5) For any other good cause shown which in the judgment of the hearing officer requires such hearing to be closed.

Section 23. Annual Report

The commission shall make an annual report of its activities to the Supreme Court and the Indiana State Bar Association. The report shall include a statement of income and expenses for the year.

Section 24. Rules of Procedure

The Commission may adopt rules and regulations for the efficient discharge of its power and duties. Such rules and regulations shall become effective upon approval by a majority of this Court.

Section 25. Proceedings to Determine Disability

(a) A member of the Commission, a member of the Bar of this Court, the Executive Secretary, any individual or any bar association of this State, may at any time file a verified petition with the Commission alleging that an attorney is disabled and should be suspended from the practice of law by reason of physical or mental illness or infirmity, or because of the use of or addiction to intoxicants or drugs.

(b) If such petition is filed by a member of the Bar of this Court, by any other person or by a bar association, the Executive Secretary shall conduct an investigation of the facts stated in said petition and make a report with a recommendation to the Commission at its next meeting.

(c) If the petition is filed by a member of the Commission or the Executive Secretary, or if after the investigation by the Executive Secretary, the Commission determines that there is good reason to believe that disability exists which would justify suspension of the attorney named in said petition, the Commission shall hold a hearing to determine if said attorney should be suspended because of such disability. For the purpose of conducting such hearing, the Commission may request the appointment of a hearing officer or hearing officers as provided in Section 18(b). The Commission shall report its findings and recommendations to this Court. The findings and recommendations to this Court may include a written recommendation for suspension pending final determination of the petition, and may also include a recommendation that the Court appoint a member of the Bar of this Court to inventory the client file of said attorney and to report to the Court the status of said matters, and this Court may forthwith enter an order of suspension upon such recommendation. The respondent shall have fifteen (15) days thereafter to petition this Court for a review and a dissolution of such order.

(d) If the Commission recommends suspension, the respondent attorney shall have thirty (30) days after the filing of the report and recommendations of the commission to petition this Court for a review of the same. If no petition for review is filed within thirty (30) days of the findings and recommendations of the Commission, this Court shall enter an order of suspension of said attorney for the duration of such disability.

(e) In the event that this Court grants a petition under this section, briefs may be filed and oral arguments heard, as this Court shall determine. Such briefs need not conform to the rules of this Court. Upon a review, this Court shall determine whether the findings and recommendations of the Commission are supported by sufficient evidence, and shall enter its judgment, with or without opinion, as this Court shall determine.

(f) Any attorney suspended for disability as provided in this section shall have the right to petition for reinstatement upon the termination of such disability in accordance with sections 4 and 18 of this rule.

Section 26. Duties of Disbarred or Suspended Attorneys, and Attorneys who have Resigned

(a) *Duties of Disbarred Attorneys.*

(1) In any case where an attorney has been disbarred under the provisions of this rule, said attorney shall promptly notify or cause to be notified by registered or certified mail, return receipt requested, all clients being represented by him or her in pending matters, of the disbarment and the attorney's consequent inability to act as an attorney. Such notice shall advise said clients to seek legal advice of the client's own choice elsewhere.

(2) In addition to notifying clients as set forth above, the attorney who has been disbarred shall move in the Court or agency in which any proceeding is pending for leave to withdraw as such attorney, shall notify all attorneys for adverse parties in such proceedings, and shall furnish the address of the client involved to the Court or agency and to the attorneys for adverse parties.

(3) Any attorney who has been disbarred under the provisions of this rule shall make available to any of his or her clients, to new counsel for any of said clients or to any other person designated by the Court having appropriate jurisdiction all papers, documents, files or information which may be in his or her possession.

(4) Within thirty (30) days after the effective date of the disbarment order, the disbarred attorney shall file with this Court an affidavit showing that he or she has fully complied with the provisions of the order and with these rules and also stating all other State, Federal and Administrative jurisdictions to which the attorney has been admitted to practice. The disbarred attorney shall also serve a copy of such affidavit upon the Executive Secretary and shall set forth the address where communications may thereafter be directed to him or her.

(b) *Duties of Disbarred and Suspended Attorneys.* Upon receiving notice of the order of suspension or disbarment, the respondent shall not undertake any new legal matters between service of the order and the effective date of the discipline. Upon the effective date of the order, the respondent shall not maintain a presence or occupy an office where the practice of law is conducted. A respondent suspended for more than six (6) months or disbarred shall take such action as is necessary to cause the removal of any indicia of lawyer, counselor at law, legal assistant, law clerk or similar title.

(c) *Duties of Suspended Attorneys.* The suspended attorney shall, within twenty (20) days from the date of the notice of the suspension, file with the Court an affidavit showing that:

(1) All clients being represented by the attorney in pending matters have been notified by certified mail, return receipt requested, of the nature and duration of the suspension, and all pending matters of clients requiring the attorney's services during the period of suspension have been placed in the hands and care of an attorney admitted to practice before the Supreme Court of Indiana with the consent of the client.

(2) Clients not consenting to be represented by substitute counsel have been advised to seek the services of counsel of their own choice.

(3) Proof of compliance with this section of the rule shall be a condition precedent to reinstatement.

(d) *Duties of Attorneys who have Resigned.* An attorney whose resignation from the Bar has been accepted pursuant to Section 17 of this rule shall comply with the provisions of this section applicable to a disbarred attorney.

Section 27. Attorney Surrogates

(a) *Definitions for purposes of this section only:*

"Attorney Surrogate" means a senior judge certified by the Indiana Judicial Nominating Commission or another member of the bar of this State, in good standing, who has been appointed by a court of competent jurisdiction to act as an attorney surrogate for a lawyer.

"Court of competent jurisdiction" means a court of general jurisdiction in the county in which a Lawyer maintains or has maintained a principal office.

"Disabled" means that a Lawyer has a physical or mental condition resulting from accident, injury, disease, chemical dependency, mental health problems or age that significantly impairs the Lawyer's ability to practice law.

"Fiduciary Entity" means a partnership, limited liability company, professional corporation, or a limited liability partnership, in which entity a Lawyer is practicing with one or more other members of the Bar of this State who are partners, shareholders or owners.

"Lawyer" means a member of the Bar of this State who is engaged in the private practice of law in this State. "Lawyer" does not include a member of the Bar whose practice is solely as an employee of another Lawyer, a Fiduciary Entity or an organization that is not engaged in the private practice of law.

(b) *Designation of Attorney Surrogate*

(1) At the time of completing the annual registration required by Ind. Admission and Discipline Rule 2(b), a Lawyer may designate an attorney surrogate in the Clerk of Courts Portal (www.in.gov/judiciary/cofc/license) provided by the Clerk of the Supreme Court by specifying the attorney number of the attorney surrogate and certifying that the attorney surrogate has agreed to the designation in a writing in possession of both the lawyer and the surrogate. The designation of an attorney surrogate shall remain in effect until revoked by either the designated attorney surrogate or the Lawyer designating the attorney surrogate. The Lawyer who designates the attorney surrogate shall notify the Clerk of the Supreme Court of any change of designated attorney surrogate within thirty (30) days of such change. The Clerk shall keep a list of designated attorney surrogates and their addresses.

(2) A Lawyer, practicing in a Fiduciary Entity, shall state the name and address of the Fiduciary Entity where indicated in the attorney surrogate designation section of the Clerk of Courts Portal (www.in.gov/judiciary/cofc/license). Because of the ongoing responsibility of the Fiduciary Entity to the clients of the Lawyer, no attorney surrogate shall be appointed for a Lawyer practicing in a Fiduciary Entity.

(3) A lawyer not practicing in a Fiduciary Entity who does not designate an attorney surrogate pursuant to subsection (1) above, will be deemed to designate a senior judge or other suitable member of the bar of this State in good standing appointed by a court of competent jurisdiction to perform the duties of an attorney surrogate.

(c) *Role of Attorney Surrogate*

(1) Upon notice that a Lawyer has:

(a) died;

(b) disappeared;

(c) become disabled; or

(d) been disbarred or suspended and has not fully complied with the provisions of Ind. Admission and Discipline Rule 23, Section 26

any interested person (including a local bar association) or a designated attorney surrogate may file in a court of competent jurisdiction a verified petition (1) informing the court of the occurrence and (2) requesting appointment of an attorney surrogate.

(2) A copy of the verified petition shall be served upon the Lawyer at the address on file with the Clerk of the Supreme Court of Indiana or, in the event the Lawyer has died, upon the personal representative, if one has been appointed. Upon the filing of the verified petition, the court shall, after notice and opportunity to be heard (which in no event shall be longer than ten (10) days from the date of service of the petition), determine whether there is an occurrence under (a), (b), (c) or (d), and an attorney surrogate needs to be appointed to act as custodian of the law practice. If the court finds that an attorney surrogate should be appointed then the court shall appoint as attorney surrogate either the designated attorney surrogate as set forth pursuant to subsection (b)(1), a suitable member of the Bar of this State in good standing or a senior judge.

(3) Upon such appointment, the attorney surrogate may:

(a) take possession of and examine the files and records of the law practice, and obtain information as to any pending matters which may require attention;

(b) notify persons and entities who appear to be clients of the Lawyer that it may be in their best interest to obtain replacement counsel;

(c) apply for extensions of time pending employment of replacement counsel by the client;

(d) file notices, motions and pleadings on behalf of the client where jurisdictional time limits are involved and other legal counsel has not yet been obtained;

(e) give notice to appropriate persons and entities who may be affected, other than clients, that the attorney surrogate has been appointed;

(f) arrange for the surrender or delivery of clients' papers or property;

(g) as approved by the court, take possession of all trust accounts subject to Ind. Prof. Cond. R. 1.15(a), and take all appropriate actions with respect to such accounts;

(h) deliver the file to the client; make referrals to replacement counsel with the agreement of the client; or accept representation of the client with the agreement of the client; and

(i) do such other acts as the court may direct to carry out the purposes of this section.

(4) If the attorney surrogate determines that conflicts of interest exist between the attorney surrogate's clients and the clients of the Lawyer, the attorney surrogate shall notify the court of the existence of the conflict of interest with regard to the particular cases or files and the attorney surrogate shall take no action with regard to those cases or files

(d) *Jurisdiction of Court*

A court of competent jurisdiction that has granted a verified petition for appointment under this section shall have jurisdiction over the files, records and property of clients of the Lawyer and may make orders necessary or appropriate to protect the interests of the Lawyer, the clients of the Lawyer and the public. The court shall also have jurisdiction over closed files of the clients of the Lawyer and may make appropriate orders regarding those files including, but not limited to, destruction of the same.

(e) *Time Limitations Suspended.*

Upon the granting of a verified petition for appointment under this section, any applicable statute of limitations, deadline, time limit or return date for a filing as it relates to the Lawyer's clients (except as to a response to a request for temporary emergency relief) shall be extended automatically to a date 120 days from the date of the filing of the petition, if it would otherwise expire on or after the date of filing of the petition and before the extended date.

(f) *Applicability of Attorney–Client Rules.*

Persons examining the files and records of the law practice of the Lawyer pursuant to this section shall observe the attorney-client confidentiality requirements set out in Ind. Professional Conduct Rule 1.6 and otherwise may make disclosures in camera to the court only to the extent necessary to carry out the purposes of this section. The attorney-client privilege shall apply to communications by or to the attorney surrogate to the same extent as it would have applied to communications by or to the Lawyer. However, the attorney surrogate relationship does not create an attorney/client relationship between the attorney surrogate and the client of the Lawyer.

(g) *Final Report of Attorney Surrogate: Petition for Compensation; Court Approval.*

When the purposes of this section have been accomplished with respect to the law practice of the Lawyer, the attorney surrogate shall file with the court a final report and an accounting of all funds and property coming into the custody of the attorney surrogate. The attorney surrogate may also file with the court a petition for reasonable fees and expenses in compensation for performance of the attorney surrogate's duties. Notice of the filing of the final report and accounting and a copy of any petition for fees and expenses shall be served as directed by the court. Upon approval of the final report and accounting, the court shall enter a final order to that effect and discharging the attorney surrogate from further duties. Where applicable, the court shall also enter an order fixing the amount of fees and expenses allowed to the attorney surrogate. The amount of fees and expenses allowed shall be a judgment against the Lawyer or the estate of the Lawyer. The judgment is a lien upon all assets of the Lawyer (except trust funds) retroactive to the date of filing of the verified petition for appointment under this section. The judgment lien is subordinate to nonpossessory liens and security interests created prior to its taking effect and may be foreclosed upon in the manner prescribed by law.

(h) *Immunity*

Absent intentional wrongdoing, an attorney surrogate shall be immune from civil suit for damages for all actions and omissions as an attorney surrogate under this section. This immunity shall not apply to an employment after acceptance of representation of a client with the agreement of the client under subsection (c)(3)(h) above.

Section 28. Discipline Imposed by Other Jurisdictions

(a) Within fifteen (15) days of the issuance of any final order in another jurisdiction imposing a public disciplinary sanction, an attorney admitted to practice in this state shall notify the Executive Secretary in writing of the discipline. Upon notification from any source that an attorney admitted to practice in Indiana has been publicly disciplined in another jurisdiction, the Executive Secretary shall obtain a certified copy of the order of discipline.

(b) Upon receipt of a certified copy of an order demonstrating that an attorney admitted to practice in Indiana has been disciplined in another jurisdiction, resulting in suspension or revocation of the attorney's license to practice law in that jurisdiction, disbarment or acceptance of resignation with an admission of misconduct, the Executive Secretary shall file a notice with the Court, attaching a certified copy of the order of discipline, and request the issuance of an order to the Executive Secretary and the attorney directing them to show cause in writing within thirty (30) days from service of the order why the imposition of reciprocal discipline in this state would be unwarranted.

(c) Upon the expiration of thirty (30) days from service of the order set out in subsection (b), this Court shall suspend the attorney from the practice of law in this state indefinitely unless the Executive Secretary or the attorney demonstrate, or this Court finds that it clearly appears upon the face of the record from which the discipline is predicated, that:

(1) The procedure was so lacking in notice or opportunity to be heard as to constitute a deprivation of due process;

(2) There was such infirmity of proof establishing the misconduct as to give rise to the clear conviction that the Court could not, consistent with its duty, accept as final the conclusion on that subject;

(3) The imposition of suspension by the Court would be inconsistent with standards governing sanctions in this rule or would result in grave injustice; or

(4) The misconduct established warrants substantially different discipline in this state.

If this Court determines that any of those elements exists, this Court shall enter such other order of discipline as it deems appropriate. The burden is on the party seeking different discipline in this state to demonstrate that the imposition of the same discipline is unwarranted.

(d) In all other aspects, a final adjudication in another jurisdiction that an attorney has been guilty of misconduct shall establish conclusively the misconduct for purposes of a disciplinary proceeding in this state.

(e) An attorney suspended under this section may file a "Motion for Reinstatement" in this state only after the attorney is reinstated to the practice of law in the jurisdiction that imposed the discipline and after the attorney has paid all costs assessed by the Court against him or her. However, regardless of the attorney's date of reinstatement in the foreign jurisdiction, the attorney's suspension in this state shall not be lifted until the attorney has been suspended at least as long as the attorney was suspended in the foreign jurisdiction.

(1) The suspension in this state shall be deemed to begin on the date the foreign suspension begins only if the attorney promptly notifies the Commission of the foreign suspension and states that the attorney has suspended his or her practice in Indiana as of the date the foreign suspension began.

(2) The motion for reinstatement shall be verified, shall be accompanied by certified proof of reinstatement in the foreign jurisdiction, and shall state the length of time the attorney was suspended in the foreign jurisdiction and the date on which the length of the attorney's Indiana suspension equals the length of the attorney's foreign suspension.

(3) The Court may grant the motion without appointment of a hearing officer, and the provisions of Admission and Discipline Rules 23(4) and (18) shall not apply.

(4) If the attorney's reinstatement in the foreign jurisdiction is subject to terms of probation, the attorney's reinstatement in Indiana shall be subject to compliance with those terms as determined by the disciplinary authorities in the foreign jurisdiction.

Section 29. Maintenance Of Trust Funds In Approved Financial Institutions; Overdraft Notification.

(a) *Clearly Identified Trust Accounts In Approved Financial Institutions And Related Recordkeeping Requirements.*

(1) Attorneys shall deposit all funds held in trust in accounts clearly identified as "trust" or "escrow" accounts, referred to herein as "trust accounts" and shall inform the depository institution of the purpose and identity of the accounts. Funds held in trust include funds held in any fiduciary capacity in connection with a representation, whether as trustee, agent, guardian, executor or otherwise. Attorney trust accounts shall be maintained only in financial institutions approved by the Commission.

(2) Every attorney shall maintain and preserve for a period of at least five (5) years, after final disposition of the underlying matter, the records of trust accounts, including checkbooks, canceled checks, check stubs, written withdrawal authorizations, vouchers, ledgers, journals, closing statements, accounting or other statements of disbursements rendered to clients or other parties with regard to trust funds or similar equivalent records clearly and expressly reflecting the date, amount, source, and explanation for all receipts, withdrawals, deliveries and disbursements of the funds or other property held in trust.

(3) The "ledger" required by this rule shall set forth a separate record of each trust, client or beneficiary, the source of all funds deposited in that account, the names of all persons for whom the funds are, or were, held, the amount of such funds, the description and the amounts of charges or withdrawals, and the names of all persons to whom such funds were disbursed.

(4) All receipts shall be deposited intact, funds shall not be commingled with other funds of the attorney or firm, and records or deposits shall be sufficiently detailed to identify each item.

(5) Withdrawals shall be based upon a written withdrawal authorization stating the amount of the withdrawal, the purpose of the withdrawal, and the

payee. The authorization shall contain the signed approval of an attorney. Withdrawals shall be made only by wire transfer or by check payable to a named payee and not to "cash". Wire transfers shall be authorized by written withdrawal authorization and evidenced by a document from the financial institution indicating the date of the transfer, the payee and the amount.

(6) Only an attorney admitted to practice law in this jurisdiction or his or her designee shall be an authorized signatory on the account.

(7) Records required by this rule may be maintained by electronic, photographic, computer or other media provided they otherwise comply with this rule and provided further that printed copies can be produced.

(8) Upon dissolution of any partnership of attorneys or of any professional corporation of attorneys, the partners or shareholders shall make appropriate written arrangements for the maintenance of the records specified under this rule.

(9) Upon the disposition of a law practice, appropriate written arrangements for the maintenance of the records specified in this rule shall be made.

(b) *Overdraft Notification Agreement Required.* A financial institution shall be approved as a depository for trust accounts if it files with the Commission an agreement, in a form provided by the Commission, to report to the Commission whenever any properly payable instrument is presented against an attorney trust account containing insufficient funds, irrespective of whether or not the instrument is honored. The Commission shall establish rules governing approval and termination of approved status for financial institutions, and shall annually publish a list of approved financial institutions. No trust account shall be maintained in any financial institution that does not agree so to report. Any such agreement shall apply to all branches of the financial institution and shall not be canceled except upon thirty (30) days' notice in writing to the Commission.

(c) *Overdraft Reports.* The overdraft notification agreement shall provide that all reports made by the financial institution shall be in the following format:

(1) In the case of a dishonored instrument, the report shall be identical to the overdraft notice customarily forwarded to the depositor, and should include a copy of the dishonored instrument, if such a copy is normally provided to depositors.

(2) In the case of instruments that are presented against insufficient funds but which instruments are honored, the report shall identify the financial institution, the attorney or law firm, the account number, the date of presentation for payment, and the

date paid, as well as the amount of overdraft created thereby.

(d) *Timing of Reports.* Reports under subsection (c) shall be made simultaneously with, and within the time provided by law for, notice of dishonor, if any. If an instrument presented against insufficient funds is honored, then the report shall be made within five (5) banking days of the date of presentation for payment against insufficient funds.

(e) *Consent By Attorneys.* Every attorney practicing or admitted to practice in this jurisdiction shall, as a condition thereof, be conclusively deemed to have consented to the reporting and production requirements mandated by this rule.

(f) *Costs.* Nothing herein shall preclude a financial institution from charging a particular attorney or law firm for the reasonable cost of producing the reports and records required by this rule.

(g) *Definitions.* For purposes of this rule:

(1) "Financial institution" means a bank, savings and loan association, credit union, savings bank, and any other business or person that accepts for deposit funds held in trust by attorneys.

(2) "Properly payable" means an instrument which, if presented in the normal course of business, is in a form requiring payment under the laws of this jurisdiction.

(3) "Notice of dishonor" means the notice that a financial institution is required to give, under the laws of this jurisdiction, upon presentation of an instrument that the institution dishonors.

(4) "Trust account" means any account maintained by an attorney admitted to practice law in the State of Indiana for the purpose of keeping funds belonging to clients or third parties separate from the attorney's own funds as required by Indiana Rule of Professional Conduct 1.15(a). It also means any account maintained by an attorney for funds held in trust in connection with a representation in any other fiduciary capacity, including as trustee, agent, guardian, executor, or otherwise.

Section 30. Audits of Trust Accounts

(a) *Generally.* Whenever the Executive Secretary has probable cause to believe that a trust account of an attorney contains, should contain, or has contained funds belonging to a client that have not been properly maintained or properly handled pursuant to Section 29, the Executive Secretary shall request the approval of the Commission to audit the accuracy and integrity of all trust accounts maintained by the attorney. In the event that the Commission approves, the Executive Secretary shall proceed to audit the accounts.

(b) *Confidentiality.* Investigations, examinations, and audits shall be conducted so as to preserve the private and confidential nature of the attorney's records insofar as is consistent with these rules.

Amended effective April 1, 1967; June 23, 1971; July 13, 1971; Nov. 30, 1971; March 15, 1972; March 14, 1973; June 11, 1975. Amended Nov. 24, 1975, effective Jan. 31, 1976; Dec. 23, 1976, effective Jan. 1, 1977; Dec. 14, 1977, effective Jan. 1, 1978; Dec. 13, 1979, effective Jan. 1, 1980; Nov. 20, 1980, effective Jan. 1, 1981. Amended effective April 22, 1981; Jan. 29, 1985; July 1, 1986; Sept. 9, 1986. Amended Oct. 15, 1986, effective Jan. 1, 1987; Nov. 25, 1986, effective Jan. 1, 1987. Amended effective Nov. 12, 1987; Nov. 10, 1988. Amended Nov. 27, 1990, effective Jan. 1, 1991; March 11, 1991, effective July 1, 1991; Sept. 9, 1991, effective Jan. 1, 1992; Oct. 30, 1992, effective Jan. 1, 1993. Amended effective May 25, 1993. Amended Dec. 5, 1994, effective Feb. 1, 1995. Amended effective Feb. 1, 1996 (except section 29, amended effective Jan. 1, 1997). Amended Dec. 23, 1996, effective March 1, 1997. Amended effective July 1, 1997. Amended June 27, 1997, effective Aug. 1, 1997; Nov. 25, 1997, effective Jan. 1, 1998; Oct. 22, 1997, effective Feb. 1, 1998; Jan. 16, 1998, effective Feb. 1, 1998. Amended effective Sept. 30, 1998; Oct. 29, 1999; Feb. 4, 2000. Amended Dec. 22, 2000, effective Jan. 1, 2001; May 4, 2001, effective Jan. 1, 2001; Dec. 21, 2001, effective April 1, 2002; July 19, 2002, effective Jan. 1, 2003; July 1, 2003, effective Aug. 1, 2003; Sept. 30, 2004, effective Jan. 1, 2005; Feb. 9, 2005, effective July 1, 2005; June 20, 2005, effective July 1, 2005; July 1, 2005, effective Jan. 1, 2006. Amended effective May 3, 2006. Amended Aug. 15, 2006, effective Jan. 1, 2007; Sept. 10, 2007, effective Jan. 1, 2008; Sept. 9, 2008, effective Jan. 1, 2009; Sept. 15, 2009, effective Jan. 1, 2010; Aug. 25, 2010, effective Jan. 1, 2011. Amended effective Sept. 20, 2011. Amended Sept. 7, 2012, effective Jan. 1, 2013; Sept. 18, 2012, effective Jan. 1, 2013.

Rule 24. Rules Governing the Unauthorized Practice of Law

Original actions, under I.C. 33–24–1–2, to restrain or enjoin the unauthorized practice of law in this state may be brought in this court by the attorney general, the Indiana Supreme Court Disciplinary Commission, the Indiana State Bar Association or any duly authorized committee thereof, without leave of court, and by any duly organized local bar association by leave of court. The action against any person, firm, association or corporation, shall be brought by verified petition, in the name of the state of Indiana, on the relation of the authorized person or association or committee, and shall charge specifically the acts constituting the unauthorized practice.

Within time allowed, a respondent may file a verified return showing any reason in law or fact why an injunction should not issue. No other pleading in behalf of a respondent will be entertained. All allegations of fact in the petition and return shall be specific and not by way of ultimate fact or conclusion. The return shall specifically deny or admit each allegation of fact in the petition, and it may allege new facts in mitigation or avoidance of the causes alleged in the petition.

The parties shall file an original and five [5] copies of all pleadings, including exhibits, plus an additional copy for each adverse party. If any exhibit shall be a matter of public record one [1] certified copy thereof shall be filed with the original petition or return. No pleading or exhibit thereto will be considered which has words or figures on both sides of the same sheet of paper.

No restraining order will issue without notice except upon the filing of an undertaking with conditions and surety to the approval of the court. Notice of the filing of the petition will be given and served upon any respondent as may be directed by the court, such notice to be accompanied by a copy of the petition. The clerk will mail a copy of any return to the relator.

The verified petition and return shall constitute the evidence upon which the issues are decided, unless the court shall deem it necessary to, and shall appoint, a commissioner, in which event such commissioner, who shall have full authority to subpoena witnesses and records, shall hear the evidence and report his findings of fact to the court.

A copy of any pertinent agreement, made by any recognized bar association concerning the unauthorized practice of law, may be attached to and made a part of any pleading and unless denied under oath shall be deemed to be a true copy without further proof of the execution thereof.

The costs and expenses incurred by such hearing shall be borne by the losing party. Briefs need not conform to requirements of Appellate Rules 43-48. Arguments will not be heard as of right.

Adopted effective Oct. 21, 1952. Renumbered effective June 23, 1971; readopted April 24, 1973, effective June 23, 1971; amended Dec. 21, 2001, effective April 1, 2002; amended effective Feb. 5, 2007.

Rule 25. Judicial Disciplinary Proceedings

Preamble. The regulation of judicial conduct is critical to the integrity of the judiciary and to public confidence in the judicial system. The purpose of this rule is to provide a mechanism for the discipline of judicial officers of the State of Indiana.

I. Jurisdiction.

A. Pursuant to Article 7, Section 4 of the Constitution of Indiana, the Supreme Court of Indiana (the Supreme Court) has exclusive, original jurisdiction for the discipline, removal, and retirement of all judicial officers of this state.

B. The Indiana Commission on Judicial Qualifications (the Commission), established by Article 7, Section 9 of the Constitution of Indiana, shall receive and investigate complaints against all judicial officers of the state, regardless of the origin of such judicial position, and shall, in accordance with the procedures established under these rules, forward to the Supreme Court of Indiana any recommendation for the discipline, removal, or retirement of any judicial officer of this state. This provision shall not in any way curtail the authority of Judicial Nominating Commissions appointed in any county of this state.

C. The Commission shall have jurisdiction over conduct committed by a judicial officer, whether or not related to the judicial office and whether or not committed during the judicial officer's term of office.

D. The Commission may refer to the Indiana Supreme Court Disciplinary Commission allegations of misconduct committed by a judicial officer while an attorney and not during the judicial officer's term of office.

E. The Commission shall have jurisdiction over violations of Canon 4 of the Code of Judicial Conduct committed by a candidate for judicial office.

F. The jurisdiction of the Commission survives the resignation or retirement of a judicial officer.

II. Application and Definitions. These rules shall apply to all judicial officers of the State of Indiana regardless of the origin of their judicial office.

For the purposes of this rule the following definitions shall apply:

"Deferred Resolution"—A confidential agreement between the Commission and a judicial officer entered into prior to the filing of formal proceedings which defers the resolution of a complaint for a specific period of time upon condition that the judicial officer take appropriate specified corrective action.

"Judicial Officer"—A Justice of the Indiana Supreme Court, Judge of the Indiana Court of Appeals, Judge of the Indiana Tax Court, Judge of any Circuit, Superior, County, City or Town Court of the State, and a pro tempore or senior judge, magistrate, commissioner, master or referee thereof, and any person eligible to perform a judicial function, whether or not a lawyer, whether part-time or full-time, temporary or permanent, excluding mediators and arbitrators and administrative law judges of independent state agencies. This rule applies to candidates for judicial office who are subject to the jurisdiction of the Commission as if they were judicial officers.

"Private Caution"—A confidential statement from the Commission to a judicial officer stating that the Commission has inquired into or investigated a complaint and has considered the judicial officer's written response to the allegations, and has voted to close the inquiry or investigation by cautioning the judicial officer that misconduct was established which, in light of all the circumstances, does not warrant further inquiry.

"Public Admonition"—A public statement from the Commission concluding that misconduct occurred, which is issued by the Commission after a determination that formal proceedings are warranted and which is issued in lieu of formal proceedings and with the written consent of the judicial officer.

"Settlement Agreement"—A written agreement submitted to the Supreme Court after the Commission has filed charges, and after the judicial officer has had an opportunity to answer, in which the parties agree to facts which establish grounds for discipline under this rule and to an appropriate sanction.

III. Grounds for Discipline or Involuntary Retirement.

A. Any judicial officer may be disciplined for any of the following acts:

(1) conviction of any felony, or any crime which involves moral turpitude or conduct that adversely affects the ability to perform the duties of judicial office;

(2) willful and persistent failure to perform duties;

(3) willful misconduct in office;

(4) willful misconduct unrelated to the judicial office that brings such office into disrepute;

(5) habitual intemperance;

(6) conduct prejudicial to the administration of justice, including the repeated failure to adhere to the rules of procedure; or

(7) a violation of the Code of Judicial Conduct, the Rules of Professional Conduct, or other professional rules duly adopted by the Indiana Supreme Court.

B. A judicial officer may be involuntarily retired when a physical or mental disability seriously interferes with the performance of judicial duties.

C. A judicial officer involuntarily retired by the Supreme Court shall be considered to have retired voluntarily. A judicial officer removed from office by the Supreme Court under an order of discipline, excluding retirement or disability, shall be ineligible for judicial office and, pending further order of the Supreme Court, shall be suspended from the practice of law in the State of Indiana.

D. These rules shall not be construed to impair any vested right or benefit of a judicial officer, now or hereafter existing as provided by law.

IV. Sanctions. Upon a finding of misconduct pursuant to Section III A. or disability pursuant to Section III B., the Supreme Court may impose any of the following:

(1) removal;

(2) retirement;

(3) suspension;

(4) discipline as an attorney;

(5) limitations or conditions on the performance of judicial duties;

(6) private or public reprimand or censure;

(7) fine;

(8) assessment of reasonable costs and expenses; or

(9) any combination of the above sanctions.

V.   Interim Suspension.

A.   A judicial officer shall be suspended with pay by the Supreme Court without the necessity of action by the Commission upon the filing of an indictment or information charging the judicial officer in any court in the United States with a crime punishable as a felony under the laws of Indiana or the United States.

B.   A judicial officer shall be suspended with pay while there is pending before the Supreme Court a recommendation from the Commission for the retirement or removal of the judicial officer.

C.   Upon a finding of guilty, plea of guilty, or plea of no contest to a crime punishable as a felony under the laws of Indiana or the United States, or any crime that involves moral turpitude under the law, a judicial officer may be suspended without pay by the Supreme Court.

D.   A judicial officer may be suspended with pay by the Supreme Court without the necessity of action by the Commission upon the filing of an indictment or information charging the judicial officer with a misdemeanor which suggests conduct that adversely affects the ability to perform the duties of the judicial office. In the event the Supreme Court suspends a judicial officer under this provision without a hearing, the suspended judicial officer shall thereafter be permitted a hearing and review of the basis for the suspension.

E.   Upon petition by the Commission, the Supreme Court may impose, pending the disposition of formal charges, an interim suspension with pay if the Court deems the interim suspension necessary to protect public confidence in the integrity of the judiciary. This provision is applicable in proceedings involving the disability of the judge as well as proceedings involving discipline.

VI.   Staff.

A.   The Division of State Court Administration shall serve the Commission in the performance of the Commission's constitutional and statutory duties. Any attorney specifically appointed by the Supreme Court for such purpose may serve as Counsel for the Commission in the course of a judicial disciplinary proceeding. In the event a judicial disciplinary proceeding involves a current member of the Supreme Court, a regular employee of the Supreme Court shall not serve as Counsel.

B.   A quorum of the Commission shall have the authority to employ investigators and such experts and staff as the Commission, in its discretion, determines necessary to the performance of its duties.

VII.   Immunity.
Members of the Commission, Masters, Commission Counsel, and staff are absolutely immune from suit for all conduct in the course of their official duties.

VIII.   Disciplinary Procedure.

A.   *Meetings of Commission.*

(1) The Commission shall meet from time to time as may be necessary to discharge its responsibilities. The Commission shall elect a Vice–Chair to perform the duties of the Chair when the Chair is absent or unable to act by reason of unavailability or disqualification. Meetings of the Commission shall be called by the Chair, or the Vice–Chair, whenever deemed necessary or upon the request of any four members of the Commission, and each member of the Commission shall be given at least five days' written notice by mail of the time and place of every meeting, unless the Commission at its previous meeting designated the time and place of its next meeting. A quorum for the transaction of business shall be four members of the Commission.

(2) Meetings of the Commission are to be held at such place in Indiana as the Chair of the Commission, or the Vice–Chair, may arrange.

(3) The Commission shall act only at a meeting. Meetings may be conducted by telephone conference, electronic mail, written and facsimile communication, or other means of communication, on all matters that do not involve deliberating and voting on whether to file formal charges, when the Commission shall meet in person. The Commission shall have the power to adopt reasonable and proper rules and regulations for the conduct of its meeting and the discharge of its duties.

B.   *Confidentiality.*

(1) Before the filing and service of formal charges, the Commission shall not publicly disclose information relating to a complaint, inquiry, or investigation, except that the Commission may disclose information:

(a) upon waiver or agreement by the judicial officer; or

(b) where the Commission has determined that there is a need to notify another person or agency in order to protect the public or to assure the proper administration of justice; or

(c) where the Commission elects to respond to publicly disseminated statements by a complainant or a judicial officer.

(2) After the filing of formal charges, all pleadings and proceedings are public unless the Masters or Supreme Court find extraordinary circumstances warranting limitations on the public nature of the proceedings.

(3) Commission deliberations, settlement conferences, and proposed settlement agreements shall remain confidential. Settlement agreements submitted to the Supreme Court for approval shall become public when the Supreme Court accepts the agreement in whole or in part and issues an order or opinion resolving the judicial disciplinary case.

C. *Civil Immunity.* Each person shall be immune from civil suit for all sworn or written statements, if made without malice, and intended for transmittal only to the Commission, Counsel, or staff, or made in the course of investigatory, hearing, or review proceedings under this rule.

D. *Complaint.* Any person may file a complaint with the Commission about the judicial activities, fitness, or qualifications of any judicial officer. Complaints directed to the Commission or to any member of the Commission concerning a judicial officer shall be in writing and verified. No specified form of complaint shall be required.

E. *Consideration of Complaint.*

(1) The Commission shall provide written acknowledgment of the complaint and shall notify the complainant in writing of its final disposition.

(2) The Commission shall make such initial inquiry as is necessary to determine if the complaint is founded and within the jurisdiction of the Commission. The Commission, without receiving a complaint, may make such an initial inquiry on its own motion. The Commission shall dismiss any complaint or inquiry which is frivolous, groundless, not within the Commission's jurisdiction, or upon a finding that no misconduct occurred. The notification of dismissal to the complainant shall contain the basis for the Commission's decision. The Commission may also conduct further inquiry, begin an investigation, agree to a deferred resolution, or issue a private caution. If the final disposition is by deferred resolution or private caution, the judicial officer shall have had the opportunity to respond to the allegations in writing and the complainant shall be notified that appropriate action was taken without specifying the nature of the disposition.

(3) If the Commission deems it necessary as the result of its initial inquiry to conduct an investigation, the judicial officer involved shall be notified of the investigation, the nature of the charge, and the name of the person making the complaint, if any, or that the investigation is on the Commission's own motion, and shall be afforded a reasonable opportunity in the course of the investigation to present such matters as the judicial officer may choose. Such notice shall be given by certified mail addressed to the judicial officer's chambers or address of record and shall be clearly marked "Personal and Confidential." Delivery of all other papers or notices shall be made in accordance with the Rules of Procedure.

(4) The Commission shall have such jurisdiction and powers as are necessary to conduct the proper and speedy disposition of any investigation, including the power to compel the attendance of witnesses, to take or cause to be taken the deposition of witnesses, and to order the production of books, records, or other documentary evidence. Any member of the Commission shall have the power to subpoena witnesses or the production of evidence and may administer oaths and affirmations to witnesses in any matter within the jurisdiction of the Commission. The quashing and enforcement of subpoenas, and the enforcement of any other power delegated to the Commission shall be upon application to the Supreme Court or to the Masters, if appointed.

(5) If the investigation does not disclose probable cause to warrant further proceedings, the Commission may dismiss the complaint with a finding that no misconduct occurred, may conduct further investigation, or may issue a deferred resolution or private caution, and the judicial officer shall be so notified. Where a deferred resolution or private caution is imposed, the judicial officer shall have had an opportunity to respond in writing to the allegations. The Commission shall have the power to make investigations by members of the Commission, staff, or by special investigators employed by the Commission and to hold confidential hearings with the judicial officer involved.

(6) During the course of an investigation by the Commission, the judicial officer whose conduct is being investigated may demand, in writing, that the Commission either institute formal proceedings or enter a formal finding that there is not probable cause to believe that the judicial officer is guilty of misconduct, and the Commission shall, within sixty days after such demand, comply therewith.

(7) If, upon the conclusion of a full investigation, the Commission does not find probable cause to believe that misconduct has occurred, the Commission shall dismiss the complaint. If the Commission determines the existence of probable cause, the Commission may vote that one or more of the following is appropriate:

(a) dismissal;

(b) deferred resolution or private caution;

(c) formal charges;

(d) petition for suspension;

(e) a stay.

At any time after the Commission has determined the existence of probable cause to file charges, the judicial officer may demand that the charges be filed within sixty days rather than consent to a private caution, a public admonition, deferred resolution, or a stay.

If the Commission votes to file formal charges against a judicial officer, it may, with the judicial officer's written consent, dismiss the complaint after issuing a public admonition of the judicial officer's conduct.

F. *Notice of Formal Proceedings.*

(1) After the investigation has been completed and the Commission concludes that there is proba-

ble cause to believe in the existence of grounds for discipline or involuntary retirement under Section III of this Rule and that formal proceedings should be instituted, it shall give written notice to the judicial officer advising of the institution of formal proceedings. This notice shall be filed as an original action in the Supreme Court.

(2) The notice shall be issued in the name of the Commission, shall specify in ordinary and concise language the charges against the judicial officer and the alleged facts upon which such charges are based, and shall advise the judicial officer of the right to file a written answer to the charges within twenty days after service of notice. No charge shall be sufficient if it merely recites the general language of the original complaint, but must specify the facts relied upon to support a particular charge.

(3) The notice shall be made by certified mail to the judicial officer's chambers or address of record and shall be clearly marked "Personal and Confidential".

(4) In the event the notice filed under Rule VII-IF(1) is directed toward a member of the Supreme Court, the provisions of this paragraph shall apply.

(a) At the time the notice is filed, all Justices of the Supreme Court, except the Chief Justice, shall recuse themselves from the proceedings. Should the Chief Justice, for any reason, be unable to participate in such proceedings, the most senior member of the Supreme Court, not otherwise disqualified, shall continue to serve. The Chief Justice or the member of the Supreme Court continuing to serve under this provision shall be the presiding member of the Supreme Court for all proceedings relating to the notice.

(b) The vacancies on the Supreme Court created by the above procedure shall be filled for the limited purpose of the judicial disciplinary proceedings by members of the Indiana Court of Appeals chosen pursuant to this provision. Six Judges of the Court of Appeals shall be randomly selected by the Clerk of the Supreme Court and Court of Appeals. Advisement of the members of the Court of Appeals selected under this procedure shall be given to the Commission and the judicial officer. Within seven days after advisement of the selection is issued, the Commission shall strike one judge selected and within seven days after the judge is stricken by the Commission, the judicial officer shall strike one judge. If the Commission or the judicial officer fails to strike a judge under this procedure, the Clerk of the Supreme Court shall strike at random in their stead.

(c) In the event all members of the Supreme Court are unable to participate in a judicial disciplinary proceeding, the Clerk of the Supreme Court and Court of Appeals shall randomly select seven members of the Indiana Court of Appeals to serve in such proceedings and each side shall strike one judge under the procedure set forth in Rule VIIIF(4)(b) above.

G. *Answer.* Within twenty days after service of the notice of formal proceedings, the judicial officer may file with the Supreme Court, under the cause initiated by the filing of the notice of formal proceedings, an answer, and serve a copy of the answer on Counsel for the Commission by mail.

All pleadings shall be filed with the Clerk of the Supreme Court and shall be served to the Commission at its published address.

H. *Settlement Agreements.* The Commission and the judicial officer may enter into a settlement agreement, either prior to the appointment of Masters, or at any time prior to a final disposition by the Supreme Court. The Supreme Court may accept the agreement resolving the case or it may reject the agreement and return the matter to the Commission for further action.

I. *Masters.* Upon the filing of an answer or upon the expiration of the time for its filing, the Supreme Court shall, within thirty days, appoint three Masters and designate a Presiding Master. Each Master shall be an active or retired member of a court of record in the State of Indiana. The Masters shall hear and take evidence in the judicial disciplinary proceeding and report thereon to the Supreme Court. The appointed Masters shall set a time and place for a hearing, to be conducted within ninety days of their appointment, and shall give notice of such hearing to the judicial officer charged and Counsel for the Commission at least twenty days prior to the date set. At the discretion of the Masters, the cause may be set for a pretrial conference or such other hearing as may be deemed necessary under the circumstances. Continuances shall be granted only by agreement or upon good cause shown. All differences of opinion by the Masters shall be resolved by majority vote, except that a minority opinion may be submitted to the Supreme Court with the final report and the recommended findings of fact and conclusions of law.

J. *Pretrial Procedure.*

(1) In all formal proceedings, discovery shall be available to the Commission and to the judicial officer in accordance with the Indiana Rules of Trial Procedure. Any motions requesting court orders for discovery shall be made to the Masters appointed to hear the case.

(2) In all formal proceedings, Counsel for the Commission shall furnish to the judicial officer not less than twenty days prior to any hearing the following, unless modified by agreement or by an order on discovery:

(a) The names and addresses of all witnesses whose testimony Counsel expects to offer at the hearing, together with copies of all written statements and transcripts of testimony of such witnesses in the possession of Counsel or the Commission and copies of all documentary evidence which Counsel expects to offer in evidence at the hearing. The testimony of any witness whose name and address has not been furnished to the judicial officer, and documentary evidence copies of which have not been furnished to the judicial officer, as provided above, shall not be admissible in evidence at said hearing over objection.

(b) After formal proceedings have been instituted, Counsel shall furnish to the judicial officer, within ten days, the names and addresses of all witnesses, then or thereafter known to Counsel, who have information which may be relevant to any charge against the judicial officer, and to any defense. Counsel shall also furnish copies of such written statements, transcripts of testimony, and documentary evidence as are then or thereafter in the possession of Counsel for the Commission, which are relevant to any such charge or defense and which have not previously been furnished to the judicial officer.

K. *Hearing.*

(1) At the time and place set for hearing, the Masters may proceed with the hearing whether or not the judicial officer has filed an answer or appears at the hearing.

(2) The failure of the judicial officer to answer or to appear at the hearing, standing alone, shall not be taken as evidence of the facts alleged or constitute grounds for discipline, retirement, or removal, however the failure to cooperate in the prompt resolution of a complaint by the refusal to respond to Commission requests or by the use of dilatory practices, frivolous or unfounded arguments, or other obdurate behavior may be considered as aggravating factors affecting sanctions or may be the basis for the filing of separate counts of judicial misconduct.

(3) In any proceeding for involuntary retirement for disability, the failure of the judicial officer to testify in his or her own behalf or to submit to medical examination requested by the Commission or Masters may be considered, unless it appears that such failure was due to circumstances beyond the judicial officer's control.

(4) The proceedings shall be reported verbatim.

(5) At the hearing before the Masters for the taking of testimony with regard to the pending charges, the Indiana Rules of Evidence shall apply.

(6) The Commission shall have the burden to prove misconduct on the part of the judicial officer by clear and convincing evidence.

(7) Whenever a witness invokes the privilege against self-incrimination as a basis for refusing to answer a question or to produce other evidence that may be relevant to a disciplinary or disability proceeding, the Commission may apply in a court of record for a grant of immunity from criminal prosecution, and shall give notice of the application to the judicial officer and to the prosecuting attorney of the jurisdiction. If the court grants the order, the witness may not refuse to comply with the order on the basis of the privilege of the witness against self-incrimination, but no testimony or other evidence compelled under such an order shall be used against the witness in any criminal case. The witness may be prosecuted for perjury or contempt committed in answering or failing to answer in accordance with the order.

(8) The Masters shall have such jurisdiction and powers as are necessary to conduct a hearing, including the power to compel the attendance of witnesses, to administer oaths and affirmations, to make findings and issue sanctions for contempt, to take or cause to be taken the deposition of witnesses, and to order the production of books, records, or other documentary evidence. The quashing and enforcement of subpoenas shall be upon application to the Masters.

L. *Defense Rights of Judicial Officer.*

(1) In formal proceedings involving discipline, retirement, or removal, a judicial officer shall have the right to defend against the charges by the introduction of evidence, to be represented by counsel, and to examine and cross-examine witnesses. A judicial officer shall also have the right to the issuance of subpoenas for the attendance of witnesses to testify or to produce books, papers, and other evidentiary matters.

(2) Whenever a transcript of any proceedings hereunder is requested by the judicial officer, the Commission or Commission Counsel, the Masters or the Supreme Court, it shall be produced promptly, and it shall be provided to the judicial officer without cost.

(3) If the judicial officer has been adjudicated incompetent, the Supreme Court shall appoint an attorney ad litem unless a guardian has been appointed. The guardian or attorney ad litem shall exercise any right and privilege , make any defense and receive process for the judicial officer.

M. *Amendments to Notice or Answer.* The Masters, at any time prior to the conclusion of the hearing, may allow or require amendments to the notice of formal proceedings and may allow amendments to the answer. The notice may be amended to conform to proof or to set forth additional facts, whether occurring before or after the commencement of the hearing. In case such an amendment is made, the judicial officer shall be given reasonable time both to answer the amendment and to prepare and present a defense against the matters charged thereby.

N. *Report of Hearing by Masters.*

(1) After the conclusion of the hearing, the Masters shall, within forty-five days, file with the Supreme Court a report which shall contain a brief statement of the proceedings, recommended findings of fact and conclusions of law, and any minority opinion. The recommended findings of fact and conclusions of law are not binding upon the Supreme Court. An original and six copies of the report and the original transcript of the testimony together with all exhibits shall be filed with the Supreme Court.

(2) The Masters may include a recommendation in the report to the Supreme Court as to the discipline, removal, or retirement of the judicial officer involved in the proceeding. The recommended sanction is not binding on the Supreme Court.

(3) At the time the report and transcript is filed with the Supreme Court, the Masters shall serve a copy of the report and transcript on the judicial officer and Counsel for the Commission.

O. *Recommendation of Commission.* Within twenty days of the filing of the report by the Masters, the Commission shall make a recommendation to the Supreme Court as to the disposition of the judicial disciplinary proceeding under consideration. If the Commission does not concur in the proposed findings of fact, conclusions of law, and, if appropriate, the recommended sanction, the Commission's recommendation as to disposition shall specifically set forth all objections to the report of the Masters and shall be accompanied by a memorandum brief in support of the recommended disposition.

P. *Petition for Review.*

(1) Within twenty days of the filing of the Commission's recommendation, the judicial officer may file with the Supreme Court a petition for review setting forth all objections to the report or recommendation and the reasons in opposition to the recommended findings of fact, conclusions of law, and, if appropriate, the recommended sanction contained in the report and recommendation. A copy of the petition for review shall be served on all other parties to the proceeding.

(2) The petition shall be verified, shall be based on the record, shall specify the grounds relied on, and shall be accompanied by a brief in support of the arguments offered. Within ten days of service of the petition for review and brief, the Commission may file a reply brief.

(3) Failure to file a petition for review within the time provided may be deemed by the Supreme Court as agreement on the Commission's recommendation. The Supreme Court, however, conducts its review *de novo* and retains the discretion to adopt or reject all or part of the proposed findings

of fact, conclusions of law, or recommended disposition with or without objection by a party.

(4) To the extent necessary to implement this provision and if not inconsistent with this provision, the Indiana Rules of Appellate Procedure shall be applicable to reviews by the Supreme Court in judicial disciplinary proceedings.

Adopted Nov. 24, 1975, effective Jan. 31, 1976. Amended effective March 2, 1989; Nov. 30, 1989, effective Jan. 1, 1990; Dec. 23, 1996, effective March 1, 1997; Nov. 25, 1997, effective Jan. 1, 1998; July 1, 2005, effective Jan. 1, 2006; Sept. 10, 2007, effective Jan. 1, 2008; Sept. 15, 2009, effective Jan. 1, 2010.

Rule 26. Group Legal Service Plans

(A) A "group legal service plan" is a plan or arrangement by which legal services are rendered (1) to individual members of a group identifiable in terms of substantial common interest; (2) by a lawyer provided, secured, recommended or otherwise selected by: (a) the group, its organization, or its officers; (b) some other agency having an interest in obtaining legal services for members of the group; or (c) the individual members. Not-for-profit legal services programs funded through governmental appropriations are excluded from this rule.

(B) A lawyer may not render legal services pursuant to a group legal service plan unless the following conditions have been satisfied:

(1) The entire plan has been reduced to writing and a description of its terms has been distributed to the Indiana members or beneficiaries thereof;

(2) The plan and description clearly describe and specify:

(a) the benefits to be provided, exclusions therefrom and conditions thereto,

(b) the extent of the undertaking to provide benefits and reveal such facts as will indicate the ability of the plan to meet the undertaking,

(c) that there shall be no infringement upon the independent exercise of professional judgment of any lawyer furnishing service under the plan,

(d) that a lawyer providing legal service under the plan shall not be required to act in derogation of his professional responsibilities,

(e) the procedures for the objective review and resolution of disputes arising under the plan,

(f) that the plan shall provide for an advisory group which should include members of the Bar and members of the plan who shall meet periodically to review and evaluate the organization and operation of the plan and to offer suggestions for its improvement, and

(g) that the plan shall state in writing that the satisfaction of the conditions under this rule shall not be construed as an approval of such plan by the Supreme Court of Indiana;

(3) A copy of the group legal service plan has been filed with the Clerk of the Supreme Court and Court of Appeals together with a one hundred dollar ($100) filing fee; and

(4) The requirements, as appropriate, for an initial disclosure statement or annual report have been met.

(**C**) Concurrent with the filing of the plan, an initial disclosure statement, relating to the first year of operation or any portion thereof, also must be filed. This initial disclosure statement shall state:

(1) The names and addresses of all the attorneys who will be rendering any legal service for Indiana residents for the coming year or part thereof ending January 31st;

(2) All relevant financial data including any projected income from fees, dues, premiums, or subscriptions to be collected from Indiana group members or beneficiaries for the first year of operation or part thereof, ending January 31st and the period of time covered by such fee, dues, premium or subscription charge;

(3) The total number of hours of legal service projected to be provided to Indiana members;

(4) The number of Indiana members in the plan or projected to be in the plan for the first year or part thereof, ending January 31st; and

(5) Whether legal service provided under the plan is to be funded, in any part, on an actuarial basis.

(**D**) Every group legal services plan shall file an annual report with the Clerk of the Supreme Court. A fifty dollar ($50) annual fee shall accompany the report. The annual report shall be filed between February 1st and March 31st of each year. A copy of said annual report shall be sent to plan members by March 31st of each year. An additional twenty-five dollar ($25) late fee shall accompany all annual reports filed after March 31st. The annual report shall update any information regarding the plan as originally filed and shall specifically set forth:

(1) The names and addresses of all attorneys under the plan who will be rendering any legal service to Indiana residents for the year, ending on January 31st; and

(2) All relevant financial data, including:

(a) the actual gross income generated by fees, dues, premiums, or subscriptions, paid by Indiana members of the group for the past year or part thereof, ending on January 31st;

(b) the number of hours of legal service provided to Indiana members during the past year, and ending January 31st;

(c) the number of Indiana members of the plan as of January 31st;

(d) the projected gross income, expected to be generated from fees, dues, premiums or sub-

scriptions from Indiana group members during the coming year (February 1st through January 31st); and

(e) the amount each Indiana group member will pay as a fee, dues, premium or subscription charge for the next year (February 1st through January 31st).

An annual report form may be obtained from the Clerk of the Supreme Court and Court of Appeals to assist in the filing of the annual report.

(**E**) A group legal service plan which discontinues operation, shall file a final report so stating. There shall be no filing fee for such report.

(**F**) Whenever a new attorney is employed by any plan, the plan shall, within ten days of the employment, transmit to the Clerk of the Supreme Court and Court of Appeals the name of such attorney so employed.

(**G**) No representation that a plan has been filed or approved shall be made. If such representation is made, all function under the plan shall cease.

(**H**) Any lawyer rendering legal services in Indiana pursuant to a group legal service plan shall be found by and comply with the Rules of Professional Conduct adopted January 1, 1987, as amended.

(**I**) Failure to comply with the above requirements could subject plans and individuals involved to legal action. In addition, if a plan member represented by a plan attorney is a party in an action in a court of this State, any other party to the action may file a motion to dismiss the action if the plan has not filed its initial disclosure statement or its annual report as required under Subsections C and D of this Rule. Provided, however, that the motion to dismiss shall only dismiss the case, after hearing, if the initial disclosure statement and plan or the annual report are not filed with the Clerk of the Supreme Court and Court of Appeals within sixty (60) days after the filing of the motion to dismiss.

ADMISSION AND DISCIPLINE
RULE 26. GROUP
LEGAL SERVICE PLAN DISCLOSURE
STATEMENT

1. Date of Statement _____.
2. Name of the Group Legal Services Plan and address of administrator.
3. Names and addresses of all attorneys who will be rendering any legal service under the plan to Indiana residents this year (year ends January 31st of following year):

Name	Address
1.	
2.	
3.	
4.	

5.

6.

7.

8.

9.

10.

(Use additional sheets if necessary).

4. Relevant Financial Data—Income Projection:

   (a) Gross income actually received in the form of fees, dues, premiums, or subscriptions from Indiana members for the past year or part of year (February 1, 19___ to January 31, 19___): $_____.

   (b) Number of hours of legal service provided to Indiana members during past year: _____.

   (c) Number of Indiana members of plan as of January 31, 19___.

5. Projections:

   (a) Projected gross income expected from fees, dues, premiums or subscription charges from Indiana members during the coming year (February 1, 19___ to January 31, 19___): $_____.

   (b) Projected amount each Indiana group member will pay as a fee, dues, premium or subscription charge for the coming year (February 1, 19___ to January 31, 19___).

6. Names and addresses of plan advisory group members:

      Name   Address

   1.

   2.

   3.

   4.

   5.

7. Attach one copy of plan as revised during the past year (or revisions).

Submitted By:

_____

Plan Administrator

Adopted Nov. 24, 1975, effective Jan. 31, 1976. Amended Dec. 23, 1976, effective Jan. 1, 1977; amended Dec. 13, 1979, effective Jan. 1, 1980; amended Nov. 12, 1986, effective Jan. 1, 1987; amended Jan. 26, 1987, effective Jan. 1, 1987; amended effective Nov. 10, 1988; amended Sept. 15, 2009, effective Jan. 1, 2010.

Rule 27. Professional Corporations, Limited Liability Companies and Limited Partnerships

Section 1. General Provisions. One or more lawyers may form a professional corporation, limited liability company or a limited liability partnership for the practice of law under Indiana Code 23–1.5–1, IC 23–18–1 and IC 23–4–1, respectively.

(a) The name of the professional corporation, limited liability company or limited liability partnership shall contain the surnames of some of its members, partners or other equity owners followed by the words "Professional Corporation," "PC," "P.C.," "Limited Liability Company," "L.L.C.," "LLC," "Limited Liability Partnership," "L.L.P.," or "LLP," as appropriate. Such a professional corporation, limited liability company, or limited liability partnership shall be permitted to use as its name the name or names of one or more deceased or retired members of a predecessor law firm in a continuing line of succession, subject to Rule of Professional Conduct 7.2.

(b) The professional corporation, limited liability company or limited liability partnership shall be organized solely for the purpose of conducting the practice of law, and, with respect to the practice of law in Indiana, shall conduct such practice only through persons licensed by the Supreme Court of Indiana to do so.

(c) Each officer, director, shareholder, member, partner or other equity owner shall be an individual who shall at all times own his or her interest in the professional corporation, limited liability company or limited liability partnership in his or her own right and, except for illness, accident, time spent in the armed services or during vacations and/or leaves of absence, shall be actively engaged in the practice of law through such professional corporation, limited liability company or limited liability partnership.

(d) The practice of law in Indiana as a professional corporation, limited liability company or limited liability partnership shall not modify any law applicable to the relationship between the person or persons furnishing professional legal services and the person or entity receiving such services, including, but not limited to, laws regarding privileged communications.

(e) The practice of law in Indiana as a professional corporation, limited liability company or limited liability partnership shall not relieve any lawyer of or diminish any obligation of a lawyer under the Rules of Professional Conduct or under these rules.

(f) Each officer, director, shareholder, member, partner or other equity owner of a professional corporation, limited liability company, or limited liability partnership shall be liable for his or her own acts of fraud, defalcation or theft or errors or omissions committed in the course of rendering professional legal services as provided by law including, but not limited to, liability arising out of the acts of fraud, defalcation or theft or errors or omissions of another lawyer over whom such officer, director, shareholder, member, partner or other equity owner has supervisory responsibilities under Rule 5.1 of the Rules of Professional Conduct, without prejudice to any contractual or other right that the aggrieved party may be entitled to assert against a professional corporation, limited liability company, limited liability partnership, an insurance carrier, or other third party.

(g) A professional corporation, limited liability company or limited liability partnership shall maintain adequate professional liability insurance or other form of adequate financial responsibility for any liability of the professional corporation, limited liability company, or limited liability partnership arising from acts of fraud, defalcation or theft or errors or omissions committed in the rendering of professional legal services by an officer, director, shareholder, member, partner, other equity owner, agent, employee or manager of the professional corporation, limited liability company or limited liability partnership.

(1) "Adequate professional liability insurance" means one or more policies of attorneys' professional liability insurance or other form of adequate financial responsibility that insure the professional corporation, limited liability company or limited liability partnership or both;

(i) in an amount for each claim, in excess of any insurance deductible or deductibles, of fifty thousand dollars ($50,000), multiplied by the number of lawyers practicing with the professional corporation, limited liability company or limited liability partnership; and

(ii) in an amount of one hundred thousand dollars ($100,000) in excess of any insurance deductible or deductibles for all claims during the policy year, multiplied by the number of lawyers practicing with the professional corporation, limited liability company or limited liability partnership.

However, no professional corporation, limited liability company or limited liability partnership shall be required to carry insurance or other form of adequate financial responsibility of more than five million dollars ($5,000,000) per claim, in excess of any insurance deductibles, or more than ten million dollars ($10,000,000) for all claims during the policy year, in excess of any insurance deductible.

The maximum amount of any insurance deductible under this Rule shall be as prescribed from time to time by the Board of Law Examiners.

(2) "Other form of adequate financial responsibility" means funds, in an amount not less than the amount of professional liability insurance applicable to a professional corporation, limited liability company or limited liability partnership under section (g)(1) of this Rule, available to satisfy any liability of the professional corporation, limited liability company or limited liability partnership arising from acts of fraud, defalcation or theft or errors or omissions committed in the rendering of professional legal services by an officer, director, shareholder, other equity owner, member, partner, agent, employee or manager of the professional corporation, limited liability company or limited liability partnership. These funds shall be available in the form of a deposit in trust of cash, bank certificates of deposit, United States Treasury obligations, bank letters of credit or surety bonds, segregated from all other funds of the professional corporation, limited liability company or limited liability partnership and held for the exclusive purpose of protecting any aggrieved party of the professional corporation, limited liability company or limited partnership in compliance with this Rule.

(h) Each officer, director, shareholder, member, partner or other equity owner of a professional corporation, limited liability company or limited liability partnership shall be jointly and severally liable for any liability of the professional corporation, limited liability company or limited liability partnership based upon a claim arising from acts of fraud, defalcation or theft or errors or omissions committed in the rendering of professional legal services while he or she was an officer, director, member, shareholder, partner or other equity owner, in an amount not to exceed the aggregate of both of the following:

(1) The per claim amount of professional liability insurance or other form of adequate financial responsibility applicable to the professional corporation, limited liability company or limited liability partnership under this Rule, but only to the extent that the professional corporation, limited liability company or limited liability partnership fails to have the professional liability insurance or other form of adequate financial responsibility required by this Rule; and

(2) The deductible amount of the professional liability insurance applicable to the claim.

The joint and several liability of the shareholder, member, partner or other equity owner shall be reduced to the extent that the liability of the professional corporation, limited liability company or limited liability partnership has been satisfied by the assets of the professional corporation, limited liability company or limited liability partnership.

(i) Lawyers seeking to organize or practice by means of a professional corporation, limited liability company or limited liability partnership shall obtain applications to do so and instructions for preparing and submitting these applications from the State Board of Law Examiners. Applications shall be upon a form prescribed by the State Board of Law Examiners. Two copies of the application for a certificate of registration shall be delivered to the State Board of Law Examiners, accompanied by a registration fee of two hundred dollars ($200.00), plus ten dollars ($10.00) for each officer, director, shareholder, member, partner, other equity owner or lawyer employee licensed to practice law in Indiana of the professional corporation, limited liability company or limited liability partnership, two copies of a certification of the Clerk of the Supreme Court and Court of Appeals of Indiana that each officer, director, shareholder, member, partner, other equity owner or lawyer employee who will practice law in Indiana holds an unlimited license to practice law in Indiana, and two copies of a certification of the Indiana Disciplinary Commission that each officer, director, shareholder, member, partner, other equity owner or lawyer employee licensed to practice in Indiana has no disciplinary complaints pending against him or her and if he or she does, what the nature of each such complaint is. Applications must be accompanied by four copies of the Articles of Incorporation, Articles of Organization or Registration of the professional corporation, limited liability company or limited liability partnership with appropriate fees for the Secretary of State. All forms are to be filed with the State Board of Law Examiners.

Upon receipt of such application form and fees, the State Board of Law Examiners shall make an investigation of the professional corporation, limited liability company or limited liability partnership in regard to finding that all officers, directors, shareholders, members, partners, other equity owners, managers of lawyer employees licensed to practice law in Indiana are each duly licensed to practice law in Indiana and that all hereinabove outlined elements of this Rule have been fully complied with, and the Clerk of the Supreme Court and Court of Appeals shall likewise certify this fact. The Executive Secretary of the Indiana Disciplinary Commission shall certify whether a disciplinary action is pending against any of the officers, directors, shareholders, members, partners, other equity owners, managers or lawyer employees licensed to practice law in Indiana. If it appears that no such disciplinary action is pending and that all officers, directors, shareholders, members, partners, other equity owners, managers of lawyer employees required to be are duly licensed to practice law in Indiana are, and that all hereinabove outlined elements of this Rule have been fully complied with, the Board shall issue a certificate of registration which will remain effective until January 1st of the year following the date of such registration.

Upon written application of the holder, upon a form prescribed by the State Board of Law Examiners, accompanied by a fee of fifty dollars ($50.00), the Executive Director of the Board shall annually renew the certificate of registration, if the Board finds that the professional corporation, limited liability company or limited liability partnership has complied with the provisions of the statute under which it was formed and this Rule. Such application for renewal shall be filed each year on or before June 30th. Within ten (10) days after any change in the officers, directors, shareholders, members, partners, other equity owners or lawyer employees licensed to practice law in Indiana, a written listing setting forth the names and addresses of each shall be filed with the State Board of Law Examiners with a fee of ten dollars ($10.00) for each new person listed.

Copies of any amendments to the Articles of Incorporation, Articles of Organization or Registration of the professional corporation, limited liability company or limited liability partnership thereafter filed with the Secretary of State's office shall also be filed with the State Board of Law Examiners.

Section 2. Applications for Registration

(a) Lawyers seeking to organize or practice by means of a professional corporation, limited liability company or limited liability partnership shall submit an application for a certificate of registration to the State Board of Law Examiners.

(b) The Board of Law Examiners shall publish instructions for submission of the application and a prescribed form for use by all lawyers seeking to organize under this Rule. The application shall include, at a minimum, the following:

(1) Two copies of the application for a certificate of registration shall be delivered to the State Board of Law Examiners; and,

(2) A registration fee of two hundred dollars ($200.00), plus ten dollars ($10.00) for each officer, director, shareholder, member, partner, other equity owner or lawyer employee licensed to practice law in Indiana of the professional corporation, limited liability company or limited liability partnership; and,

(3) Two copies of a certification of the Clerk of the Supreme Court and Court of Appeals of Indiana that each officer, director, shareholder, member, partner, other equity owner or lawyer employee who will practice law in Indiana holds an unlimited license to practice law in Indiana; and,

(4) Two copies of a certification of the Indiana Disciplinary Commission that each officer, director, shareholder, member, partner, other equity owner or lawyer employee licensed to practice in Indiana has no disciplinary complaints pending against him or her and if he or she does, what the nature of each such complaint is; and,

(5) Four copies of the Articles of Incorporation, Articles of Organization or Registration of the professional corporation, limited liability company or limited liability partnership with appropriate fees for the Secretary of State.

(c) Upon receipt of such application form and fees, the State Board of Law Examiners shall make an investigation of the professional corporation, limited liability company or limited liability partnership in regard to finding that all officers, directors, shareholders, members, partners, other equity owners, managers of lawyer employees licensed to practice law in Indiana are each duly licensed to practice law in Indiana and that all hereinabove outlined elements of this Rule have been fully complied with, and the Clerk of the Supreme Court and Court of Appeals shall likewise certify this fact. The Executive Secretary of the Indiana Disciplinary Commission shall certify whether a disciplinary action is pending against any of the officers, directors, shareholders, members, partners, other equity owners, managers or lawyer employees licensed to practice in Indiana. If it appears that no such disciplinary action is pending and that all officers, directors, shareholders, members, partners, other equity owners, managers of lawyer employees required to be are duly licensed to practice law in Indiana are, and that all hereinabove outlined elements of this Rule have been fully complied with, the Board shall issue a certificate of registration which will remain effective until June 30th of the year following the date of such registration.

Section 3. Renewal of Certificate of Registration; Fees

(a) A certificate of registration shall continue in force for one year (July 1 thru the following June 30), and may be renewed for a like period upon the submission of such verified information to the Board of Law Examiners as will demonstrate that the professional corporation, limited liability company or limited liability partnership has complied with the provisions of the statute under which it was formed and this Rule.

(b) Each professional corporation, limited liability company or limited liability partnership formed pursuant to this Rule shall pay a renewal fee of fifty dollars ($50.00) on or before June 30 of each year; a delinquent fee in the amount of twenty-five dollars ($25.00) shall be added to the renewal fee for fees paid after June 30 and on or before July 15 of each year; a delinquent fee in the amount of fifty dollars ($50.00) shall be added to the renewal fee for fees paid after July 15 and on or before August 31 of each year; a delinquent fee in the amount of one hundred fifty dollars ($150.00) shall be added to the renewal fee for fees paid after August 31 of each year. Additionally, a one hundred dollar ($100.00) surcharge will be added to the late fee for each consecutive year for which the attorney fails to timely file the renewal form. This renewal fee is in addition to any annual registration and fees paid under Rule 2 and/or Rule 6.

Section 4. Registration of Changes; Fees

(a) Within thirty (30) days after any change in the officers, directors, shareholders, members, partners, other equity owners or lawyer employees licensed to practice in Indiana, a written listing setting forth the names and addresses of each shall be filed with the State Board of Law Examiners with a fee often dollars ($10.00) for each new person listed

(b) A delinquent fee of ten dollars ($10.00) for each new person listed shall be added to the Registration Change Fee for fees paid after the 30th day. Additionally, a twenty-five dollar ($25.00) surcharge will be added to the late fee for each consecutive time for which the Registration of Changes fails to be timely filed. This Registration of Changes fee is in addition to any annual registration and fees paid under Rule 2, Rule 6 or otherwise in this Rule.

(c) Copies of any amendments to the Articles of Incorporation, Articles of Organization or Registration of the professional corporation, limited liability company or limited liability partnership thereafter filed with the Secretary of State's office shall also be filed with the State Board of Law Examiners.

Section 5. Failure to Pay Renewal Fee; Revocation of Certificate of Registration

(a) Any lawyer practicing under a certificate of registration who fails to pay the renewal fee required under Section 3(b) or fails to file the affidavit required under Section 7 shall be subject to revocation of the certificate of registration and sanctions for contempt of this Court in the event he or she thereafter engages in the practice of law under the professional corporation, limited liability company or limited liability partnership in this State.

(b) Any lawyer whose certificate of registration has been revoked pursuant to this provision and wishes to engage in the practice of law under the professional corporation, limited liability company or limited liability partnership in this State may apply for a new certificate of registration pursuant to Section 2 of this Rule.

Section 6. Annual Renewal Notice.

On or before May 1 of each year, the Executive Director of the State Board of Law Examiners shall mail a notice to each professional corporation, limited liability company or limited liability partnership registered pursuant to this Rule that (i) a renewal fee must be paid on or before June 30; and (ii) the attorney must (a) affirm continued compliance with this Rule to maintain the certificate of registration or (b) submit the signed relinquish affidavit to the State Board of Law Examiners on or before June 30. Notice sent pursuant to this section shall be sent to the name and address maintained by the Clerk of the Supreme Court pursuant to Admission & Discipline Rule 2 for the attorney listed as the registered agent pursuant to the records previously filed with the State Board of Law Examiners.

Section 7. Relinquishing of Certificate of Registration.

Any lawyer who is registered to practice law pursuant to this Rule who is current in payment of all applicable registration fees and other financial obligations imposed by this rule who no longer is able to meet the requirements to maintain such registration or who no longer practices under the professional corporation, limited liability company or limited liability partnership may voluntarily relinquish his or her certificate of registration by tendering a signed relinquish affidavit to the Executive Director of the State Board of Law Examiners no later than June 30 of the reporting year (July 1 through June 30). The Executive Director shall promptly verify the eligibility of the lawyer to relinquish the certificate of registration under this section and if eligible, forward a notice of the relinquishment to the Secretary of State. In the event that the lawyer is not eligible to relinquish under this section, the Executive Director shall promptly notify the lawyer of all reasons for ineligibility.

Adopted Nov. 24, 1976, effective Jan. 1, 1976. Amended effective Aug. 31, 1976; Dec. 4, 1980; amended Nov. 16, 1984, effective Jan. 1, 1985; Oct. 15, 1986, effective Jan. 1, 1987; amended effective Sept. 13, 1991; amended Nov. 25, 1997, effective Jan. 1, 1998; Sept. 15, 2009, effective Jan. 1, 2010; Aug. 25, 2010, effective Jan. 1, 2011.

Rule 28. Mandatory Continuing Judicial Education

Section 1. Purpose.

It is essential to the public that Judges continue their education in order to maintain and increase their professional competence, to fulfill their obligations under the Indiana Code of Judicial Conduct, and to ensure the delivery of quality judicial services to the people of the State of Indiana. The purpose of this Rule is to establish minimum continuing judicial education requirements for each Judge in the State of Indiana.

Section 2. Definitions.

As used in this Rule:

(a) *Approved Courses* shall mean those Substantive Continuing Judicial and Legal Education Courses and those Non Legal Subject Matter Courses which are approved under the Commission's Accreditation Policies in the Guidelines to this Rule. Any course approved for continuing legal education credit under the Commission's Accreditation Policies is also approved for continuing judicial education credit.

(b) *Attorney* shall mean a person who has been admitted to practice law in the State of Indiana and whose name appears in the files of the Board of Law Examiners as provided under Admission and Discipline Rule 4.

(c) *Bar* shall mean the Indiana Bar and includes those persons who are Attorneys under subsection (b) above.

(d) *Business Day* shall mean Monday, Tuesday, Wednesday, Thursday, and Friday of each week but shall not include Federal or Indiana state holidays.

(e) *Clerk* shall mean Clerk of the Indiana Supreme Court, Court of Appeals and Tax Court.

(f) *Commission* shall mean the Indiana Commission For Continuing Legal Education created by Section 4 of Rule 29.

(g) *Commissioner* shall mean a person who is a member of the Commission.

(h) *Educational Period* shall mean a three-year period during which a Senior Judge, City or Town Court Judge, Marion County Small Claims Court Judge, or a part-time Court Commissioner or Referee must complete thirty-six (36) hours of Approved Courses. Educational Periods shall be sequential, in that once a particular three-year period terminates, a new three-year period and thirty-six (36) hour minimum shall commence.

(i) *Full-time Court Commissioner or Referee* shall mean an attorney serving as a court commissioner or referee in a circuit, superior or probate court and who does not practice law regardless of the number of hours worked per week for the court.

Text of Section 2(j) effective until January 1, 2015. See also text of Section 2(j) effective January 1, 2015.

(j) *Judge* shall mean a regularly sitting Justice of the Indiana Supreme Court, Judge of the Indiana Court of Appeals or Tax Court, Judge of an Indiana circuit, superior or probate court, Magistrate, court commissioner or referee of any such court, Judge of an Indiana city or town court including non-attorney judges, and Senior Judge certified by the Indiana Supreme Court Division of State Court Administration. The term Judge does not include state or federal administrative law judges. State and federal administrative law judges are governed by the provisions of Admission and Discipline Rule 29.

Text of Section 2(j) effective January 1, 2015. See also text of Section 2(j) effective until January 1, 2015.

(j) *Judge* shall mean a regularly sitting Justice of the Indiana Supreme Court, Judge of the Indiana Court of Appeals or Tax Court, Judge of an Indiana circuit, superior or probate court, Magistrate, court commissioner or referee of any such court, Judge of an Indiana city or town court including non-attorney Judges, and Senior Judge certified by the Indiana Supreme Court Division of State Court Administration. The term Judge does not include state or federal administrative law Judges. State and federal administrative law Judges are governed by the provisions of Admission and Discipline Rule 29.

(k) *Judicial Officer Educational Period* shall mean a three-year period during which a State Level Judicial Officer (as defined below) must complete fifty-four (54) hours of Approved Courses. Judicial Officer Education Periods shall be sequential in that once a particular three-year period terminates, a new three-year period and fifty-four (54) hour minimum shall commence.

Text of Section 2(l) effective until January 1, 2015. See also text of Section 2(l) effective January 1, 2015.

(l) *Non-attorney Judge* shall mean a person who has been elected or appointed to serve as the judge of a city or town court and who is not required by statute to be a licensed attorney to hold the office of city or town court judge.

Text of Section 2(l) effective January 1, 2015. See also text of Section 2(l) effective until January 1, 2015.

(*l*) *Non-attorney Judge* shall mean a person who has been elected or appointed to serve as the Judge of a city or town court and who is not required by statute to be a licensed attorney to hold the office of city or town court Judge.

(m) *Non Legal Subject Matter (NLS) Courses* shall mean courses that the Commission approves for Non Legal Subject Matter credit pursuant to the Commission's Accreditation Policies in the Guidelines to this Rule because, even though they lack substantive judicial or legal content, they nonetheless enhance an attendee's proficiency in the management or administration of a court.

(n) *Part–time Court Commissioner or Referee* shall mean an attorney serving as a court commissioner or referee in a circuit, superior or probate court and who continues to practice law regardless of the number of hours worked per week for the court.

(*o*) *State Level Judicial Officer* shall mean a sitting Justice of the Indiana Supreme Court, Judge of the Indiana Court of Appeals or Tax Court, Judge of a circuit, superior or probate court, magistrate, and a full-time court commissioner or referee of a circuit, superior or probate court.

(p) *Substantive Continuing Judicial and Legal Education Courses* shall mean courses that the Commission approves for credit pursuant to the Commission's Accreditation Policies in the Guidelines to this Rule because the course pertains to subject matter having significant intellectual or practical content relating to the administration of justice, the adjudication of cases, the management of cases or court operations by the judicial officer or to the education of judicial officers with respect to their professional or ethical obligations.

(q) *Supreme Court* shall mean the Supreme Court of the State of Indiana.

(r) *Year* shall mean calendar year unless otherwise specified in this Rule.

(s) *Professional Responsibility Credits* shall mean credits for topics that specifically address judicial ethics or professional responsibility. Any course that is approved for ethics or professional responsibility under the Commission's accreditation policies is also approved for judicial ethics credit.

(t) *Distance Education* shall mean instructional delivery that does not constrain the student to be physically present in the same location as the instructor and does not require an attendant at the learning site to monitor attendance.

(u) *New Judge Orientation Program* shall mean the General Jurisdiction Orientation Program conducted by the Indiana Judicial Center.

Section 3.   Education Requirements.

(a) Every State Level Judicial Officer shall complete no less than fifteen (15) hours of Approved Courses each year and shall complete no less than fifty-four (54) hours of Approved Courses each Judicial Officer Educational Period as defined in Section 2(k). At least five (5) hours of Approved Courses in Professional Responsibility, either as a free standing program or integrated as part of a substantive program, shall be included within the hours of continuing education required during each three (3) year Judicial Officer Educational Period. No more than eighteen (18) hours of the Judicial Officer Educational Period requirement shall be filled by Non Legal Subject Matter Courses. No more than nine (9) hours of the Judicial Officer Educational Period requirement shall be filled through interactive Distance Education. All credits for a single educational activity will be applied in one (1) calendar year.

(b) Any judge not covered by (a) shall complete no less than six (6) hours of Approved Courses each year and shall complete no less than thirty-six (36) hours of Approved Courses each Educational Period as defined in Section 2(h). At least three (3) hours of Approved Courses in Professional Responsibility, either as a free standing program or integrated as part of a substantive program, shall be included within the hours of continuing education required during each three (3) year Educational Period. No more than twelve (12) hours of the Educational Period requirement shall be filled by Non Legal Subject Matter Courses. No more than six (6) hours of the Educational Period requirement shall be filled through interactive Distance Education. No more than three (3) hours of the Educational Period Requirement shall be filled through in-house education programs in accordance with the Guidelines. All credits for a single educational activity will be applied in one (1) calendar year.

Text of Section 3(c) effective until January 1, 2015. See also text of Section 3(c) effective January 1, 2015.

(c) Every Judge of a circuit, superior or probate court first elected or appointed to the bench after January 1, 2006 shall attend the next regularly scheduled New Judge Orientation Program following the date of the judge's election or appointment unless the Chief Justice of Indiana, for good cause shown in a written request, excuses attendance.

Text of Section 3(c) effective January 1, 2015. See also text of Section 3(c) effective until January 1, 2015.

(c) Every Judge of a circuit, superior or probate court first elected or appointed to the bench after January 1, 2006 shall attend the next regularly scheduled New Judge Orientation Program following the date of the Judge's election or appointment unless the Chief Justice of Indiana, for good cause shown in a written request, excuses attendance.

(d) For all current sitting State Level Judicial Officers, their existing three-year Continuing Legal Education cycle under Rule 29 terminates as of December 31, 2010. A State Level Judicial Officer's first three (3) year Judicial Officer Educational Period as defined in Section 2(k) of this Rule shall commence on January 1, 2011 with no carry-over hours.

(e) An Attorney serving as a Senior Judge, City or Town Court Judge, Marion County Small Claims Court Judge or a part-time Court Commissioner or Referee shall remain in their current three (3) year cycle established under Section 3(b) of Rule 29. For Non-attorney Judges, the first three year Educational Period shall commence on January 1 of the first full calendar year in office.

(f) In the event an Attorney becomes a State Level Judicial Officer during a three (3) year Educational Period as defined in Section 2(h) of Rule 29, the State Level Judicial Officer must complete the year of appointment with the same requirements as those of an Attorney under Rule 29. Thereafter, a State Level Judicial Officer's Educational Period shall commence January 1 of the first full calendar year in office.

(g) In the event a State Level Judicial Officer ceases to be such an officer within a State Level Judicial Officer Educational Period, the former officer must complete the year and three (3) year Educational Period with the same requirements as those of an Attorney as required by Rule 29 or those of a Senior Judge under Section 3(b) of this Rule if senior judge status is obtained. Hours earned during the State Level Judicial Officer Educational Period will be converted to CLE hours for the remainder of the three year Educational Period.

(h) Educational seminars or programs conducted by the Indiana Judicial Center shall be approved for Substantive Continuing Judicial and Legal Education credit.

(i) A Judge who fails to comply with the educational requirements of this rule shall be subject to suspension from office and to all sanctions under Section 7. A Judge so suspended shall be automatically reinstated upon compliance with Section 7(b) "Reinstatement Procedures". The Commission shall issue a statement reflecting reinstatement which shall also be sent to the Clerk to show on the Roll of Attorneys that the Judge is in good standing.

(j) For an attorney newly admitted to the bar, at least six (6) hours of the educational requirements of Sections (a) or (b) above shall be satisfied by attending an applied professionalism program that has been accredited by the Commission.

Section 4. Powers and Duties of the Indiana Commission for Continuing Legal Education and Executive Director.

The powers and duties of the Indiana Commission for Continuing Legal Education and its Executive Director under this Rule shall be the same as under Sections 6 and 7 of Rule 29.

Section 5. Exemptions and Other Relief From the Rule.

Text of Section 5(a) effective until January 1, 2015. See also text of Section 5(a) effective January 1, 2015.

(a) United States Supreme Court Justices, United States Court of Appeals Judges, United States District Court Judges and full-time Magistrates, and United States Bankruptcy Court Judges are exempt from this Rule and Rule 29 on Mandatory Continuing Legal Education. The educational requirements imposed on such judges and full-time magistrates by federal rules are deemed to satisfy the requirements of this Rule and Rule 29.

Text of Section 5(a) effective January 1, 2015. See also text of Section 5(a) effective until January 1, 2015.

(a) United States Supreme Court Justices, United States Court of Appeals Judges, United States District Court Judges and full-time Magistrates, and United States Bankruptcy Court Judges are exempt from this Rule and Rule 29 on Mandatory Continuing Legal Education. The educational requirements imposed on such Judges and full-time magistrates by federal rules are deemed to satisfy the requirements of this Rule and Rule 29.

(b) A Judge shall be exempted from the educational requirements of the Rule for such period of time as shall be deemed reasonable by the Commission upon the filing of a verified petition with the Commission and a finding by the Commission that special circumstances unique to the petitioning Judge have created undue hardship. Subsequent exemptions may be granted.

(c) A Judge who is physically impaired shall be entitled to establish an alternative method of completing the educational requirements of this Rule upon the filing of a verified petition with the Commission and a finding by the Commission that the alternative method proposed is necessary and consistent with the educational intent of this Rule. Any petition filed under this subsection shall contain a description of the physical impairment, a statement from a physician as to the nature and duration of the impairment, a waiver of any privileged information as to the impairment and a detailed proposal for an alternative educational method.

(d) A Judge who believes that he or she will be unable to make timely compliance with the educational requirements imposed by this Rule may seek relief from a specific compliance date by filing a verified petition with the Commission. The petition shall set forth reasons from which the Commission can determine whether to extend such compliance date. A petition seeking such an extension of time must be filed as much in advance of the applicable compliance date as the reasons which form the basis of the request afford. The Commission, upon receipt and consideration of such petition, shall decide if sufficient reasons exist, and may grant an extension for such period of time as shall be deemed reasonable by the Commission. In no event shall such an extension be granted beyond the time when the next compliance date, as required by the Rule, occurs.

Section 6.   Annual Reporting to Judges.

Text of Section 6(a) effective until January 1, 2015. See also text of Section 6(a) effective January 1, 2015.

(a) On or before September 1 of each year, the Commission shall mail or electronically transmit to each Judge, a statement showing the Approved Courses which the Judge is credited on the records of the Commission with having attended during the current year and the current Educational Period. This statement will be sent to the mailing or e-mail address for the Judge listed on the Roll of Attorneys maintained by the Clerk. A Judge shall at all times keep his or her address and e-mail address current with the Roll of Attorneys. If the Judge has completed the minimum hours for the year or Educational Period, the statement will so reflect and inform the Judge that he or she is currently in compliance with the education requirements of the Rule. It shall not be a defense to noncompliance that a Judge has not received an annual statement. Additional statements will be provided to a Judge upon written request and a five dollar ($5.00) fee made payable to the Continuing Legal Education Fund.

If the statement shows the Judge is deficient in educational hours, but the Judge believes he or she is in compliance for the year or Educational Period the Judge shall file a letter of explanation, a Sponsor certification of course attendance, a personal affidavit of attendance, and an application for course accreditation. The documents required by this subsection shall be filed by December 31 of the year or Educational Period in question unless an extension of time to file the same has been granted by the Commission. When a Judge has resolved the above discrepancies, the Commission shall issue a statement showing that the Judge is in compliance with the Rule for the year or Educational Period. In the event credit is not granted, the Judge shall have thirty (30) days after written notification of that fact to comply with the educational requirements. Failure to do so will result in referral to the Supreme Court for suspension.

Text of Section 6(a) effective January 1, 2015. See also text of Section 6(a) effective until January 1, 2015.

(a) On or before September 1 of each year, the Commission shall mail or electronically transmit to each Judge, a statement showing the Approved Courses which the Judge is credited on the records of the Commission with having attended during the current year and the current Educational Period. This statement will be sent to the mailing or e-mail address for the Judge listed on the Roll of Attorneys maintained by the Clerk. A Judge shall at all times keep his or her address and e-mail address current with the Roll of Attorneys. If the Judge has completed the minimum hours for the year or Educational Period, the statement will so reflect and inform the Judge that he or she is currently in compliance with the education requirements of the Rule. It shall not be a defense to noncompliance that a Judge has not received an annual statement. Additional statements will be provided to a Judge upon written request and a five dollar ($5.00) fee made payable to the Continuing Legal Education Fund.

If the statement shows the Judge is deficient in educational hours, but the Judge believes he or she is in compliance for the year or Educational Period the Judge shall file a letter of explanation, a Sponsor certification of course attendance, a personal affidavit of attendance, and an application for course accreditation. All fees must be included with the submission. The documents required by this subsection shall be filed by December 31 of the year or Educational Period in question unless an extension of time to file the same has been granted by the Commission. When a Judge has resolved the above discrepancies, the Commission shall issue a statement showing that the Judge is in compliance with the Rule for the year or Educational Period. In the event credit is not granted, the Judge shall have thirty (30) days after written notification of that fact to comply with the educational requirements or appeal the determination pursuant to Section 8. Failure to do so will result in referral to the Supreme Court for suspension.

(b) If the statement incorrectly reflects that the Judge has completed the minimum hours for the year or the Educational Period, then it shall be the duty of the Judge to notify the Commission and to complete the educational requirements mandated by this Rule.

Text of Section 6(c) effective January 1, 2015.

(c) All fees must be paid in order for a Judge to be considered in compliance with this Rule.

Text of Section 7 effective until January 1, 2015. See also text of Section 7 effective January 1, 2015.

Section 7.   Sanctions and Reinstatements.

(a) *Sanctions.* On January 1, a one-hundred fifty dollar ($150.00) late fee accrues against each Judge who has not met his/her yearly or Educational Period requirements for the period ending December 31st of the previous year. On February 1 of each year the Commission shall mail or electronically transmit a notice assessing a one-hundred fifty dollar ($150.00) late fee to those Judges who are shown as not having completed the yearly or Educational Period requirements. The Commission will consider the Judge delinquent for Continuing Judicial Education (CJE) until both certification of attendance at an approved program and payment of the late fee are received. Late fees and surcharges are to be deposited by the Commission immediately upon receipt. If the delinquent Judge has not fulfilled the yearly or Educational Period requirements at the time the Court issues an order suspending that Judge from office and the practice of law, the delinquency fee is forfeited. If the Judge is reinstated to the office and the practice of law pursuant to the provisions of this Section within one year of suspension, any forfeited late fee shall be credited toward the reinstatement fee. A one hundred dollar ($100.00) surcharge will be added to the late fee for each consecutive year for which a Judge fails to timely comply with CJE requirements.

On May 1 of each year, a list of those Judges still failing to complete the yearly or Educational Period requirements will be submitted to the Supreme Court for immediate suspension from the practice of law and suspension from the office of judge. These Judges will suffer the suspension of their license to practice law and suspension from the office of judge and all related penalties until they are reinstated.

(b) *Reinstatement Procedures.* A Judge suspended shall be automatically reinstated upon petition to the Commission and payment of a two hundred dollar ($200.00) reinstatement fee in addition to any applicable surcharge. The petition must demonstrate the petitioner's compliance according to the following reinstatement schedule:

(1) for a suspension of one (1) year or less the petitioner must, between the date of suspension and the date of the petition for reinstatement:

(i) complete the hours required to satisfy the deficiency which resulted in the suspension; and

(ii) complete six (6) additional hours of Approved Courses in a separate course or courses;

(2) for a suspension of more than one (1) year a petitioner must, between the date of suspension and the date of the petition for reinstatement:

(i) complete the hours required to satisfy the deficiency which resulted in the suspension;

(ii) complete thirty-six (36) hours of Approved Courses, twelve (12) hours of which must have been completed within the last twelve (12) month period prior to the date of the petition; and

(iii) begin a new Educational Period as of January 1st of the year of reinstatement pursuant to Section 3(a) of this Rule.

The Commission shall issue a statement reflecting reinstatement which shall also be sent to the Clerk to show on the Roll of Attorneys that the Judge is in good standing. A Judge suspended by the Supreme Court who continues to hold office or practice law shall be subject to sanctions by the Supreme Court.

Extensions to provide course attendance certifications for courses which were timely taken may be granted for good cause shown; extensions of time to complete educational requirements are not permitted except under Section 5 of this Rule. Providing or procuring of false certifications of attendance at educational courses shall be subject to appropriate discipline under the Admission and Discipline Rules.

Text of Section 7 effective January 1, 2015. See also text of Section 7 effective until January 1, 2015.

Section 7.   Sanctions and Reinstatements.

(a) *Sanctions.* On January 1, a one-hundred fifty dollar ($150.00) late fee accrues against each Judge who has not met his/her yearly or Educational Period requirements for the period ending December 31st of the previous year. On February 1 of each year the Commission shall mail or electronically transmit a notice assessing a one-hundred fifty dollar ($150.00) late fee to those Judges who are shown as not having completed the yearly or Educational Period requirements. The Commission will consider the Judge delinquent for Continuing Judicial Education (CJE) until both certification of attendance at an approved program and payment of the late fee are received. Late fees and surcharges are to be deposited by the Commission immediately upon receipt. If the delinquent Judge has not fulfilled the yearly or Educational Period requirements at the time the Court issues an order suspending that Judge from office and the practice of law, the delinquency fee is forfeited. If the Judge is reinstated to the office and the practice of law pursuant to the provisions of this Section within one year of suspension, any forfeited late fee shall be credited toward the reinstatement fee. A one hundred dollar ($100.00) surcharge will be added to the late fee for each consecutive year for which a Judge fails to timely comply with CJE requirements.

On May 1 of each year, a list of those Judges still failing to complete the yearly or Educational Period requirements will be submitted to the Supreme Court for immediate suspension from the practice of law and suspension from the office of judge. These Judges will suffer the suspension of their license to practice law and suspension from the office of Judge and all related penalties until they are reinstated.

(b) *Reinstatement Procedures.* A Judge suspended shall be automatically reinstated upon petition to the Commission and payment of a two hundred dollar ($200.00) reinstatement fee in addition to any applicable surcharge. The petition must demonstrate the petitioner's compliance according to the following reinstatement schedule:

(1) for a suspension of one (1) year or less the petitioner must, between the date of suspension and the date of the petition for reinstatement:

(i) complete the hours required to satisfy the deficiency which resulted in the suspension; and

(ii) complete six (6) additional hours of Approved Courses in a separate course or courses;

(2) for a suspension of more than one (1) year a petitioner must, between the date of suspension and the date of the petition for reinstatement:

(i) complete the hours required to satisfy the deficiency which resulted in the suspension;

(ii) complete thirty-six (36) hours of Approved Courses, twelve (12) hours of which must have been completed within the last twelve (12) month period prior to the date of the petition; and

(iii) begin a new Educational Period as of January 1st of the year of reinstatement pursuant to Section 3(a) of this Rule.

The Commission shall issue a statement reflecting reinstatement which shall also be sent to the Clerk to show on the Roll of Attorneys that the Judge is in good standing. A Judge suspended by the Supreme Court who continues to hold office or practice law shall be subject to sanctions by the Supreme Court.

Extensions to provide course attendance certifications for courses which were timely taken may be granted for good cause shown; extensions of time to complete educational requirements are not permitted except under Section 5 of this Rule. Providing or procuring of false certifications of attendance at educational courses shall be subject to appropriate discipline under the Admission and Discipline Rules. All fees must be paid in order for a Judge to be considered in compliance with this Rule.

Text of Section 8 effective until January 1, 2015. See also text of Section 8 effective January 1, 2015.

Section 8. Disputes Regarding Commission Records.

Any Judge who disagrees with the records of the Commission in regard to the credits recorded for the Judge during the current year or Educational Period and is unable to resolve the disagreement pursuant to Section 6 of this Rule, may petition the Commission for a determination as to the credits to which the Judge is entitled. Petitions pursuant to this Section shall be considered by the Commission at its next regular or special meeting, provided that the petition is received by the Commission at least ten (10) business days before such meeting. The Judge filing the petition shall have the right to attend the Commission meeting at which the petition is considered and to present relevant evidence and arguments to the Commission. The rules of pleading and practice in civil cases shall not apply, and the proceedings shall be informal. The determination of the Commission shall be final as to the number of credits for the Judge and shall be appealable directly to the Supreme Court. In the event of a good faith dispute which is not resolved pursuant to Section 6, the educational and reporting deadlines of this Rule shall be extended until thirty (30) days after the full Commission has ruled on the disputed issue, or if an appeal is taken, until thirty (30) days after the Supreme Court has ruled on the disputed issue.

Text of Section 8 effective January 1, 2015. See also text of Section 8 effective until January 1, 2015.

Section 8. Appeals Regarding Commission Records.

Any Judge who disagrees with the records of the Commission in regard to the credits recorded for the Judge during the current year or Educational Period and is unable to resolve the disagreement pursuant to Section 6 of this Rule, may petition the Commission for a determination as to the credits to which the Judge is entitled. Petitions pursuant to this Section must be received by the Commission within thirty (30) days of the Commission's written notification that credit has not been granted and shall be considered by the Commission at its next regular or special meeting, provided that the petition is received by the Commission at least ten (10) business days before such meeting. The Judge filing the petition shall have the right to attend the Commission meeting at which the petition is considered and to present relevant evidence and arguments to the Commission. The rules of pleading and practice in civil cases shall not apply, and the proceedings shall be informal. The determination of the Commission shall be final as to the number of credits for the Judge and shall be appealable directly to the Supreme Court. In the event of a good faith dispute pursuant to this Section, the educational and reporting deadlines of this Rule shall be extended until thirty (30) days after the full Commission has ruled on the disputed issue, or if an appeal is taken, until thirty (30) days after the Supreme Court has ruled on the disputed issue.

Section 9. Petitions.

Any petition filed with the Commission pursuant to this Rule shall be in writing and shall be signed and verified by the Judge seeking relief. The petition shall be sent by registered or certified mail to the attention of the Executive Director at the Commission's offices at the address shown on the most recent statements or on the Commission's web page pursuant to Section 6 of this Rule.

Section 10. Confidentiality.

Unless otherwise directed by the Supreme Court or by another court having jurisdiction, the files, records and proceedings of the Commission, as they may relate to or arise out of a Judge or Sponsor attempting to satisfy the continuing judicial educational requirements of this Rule shall be confidential and shall not be disclosed except in furtherance of the duties of the Commission or upon the request of the Judge or Sponsor affected.

Section 11. Conflict of Interest.

A member, agent or administrator of the Commission shall abstain from participating in any decision involving a sponsor or provider of educational services of which he or she is an officer. A member, agent or administrator of the Commission shall not be an employee of an entity principally engaged in sponsoring or providing continuing legal education services.

Adopted Aug. 25, 2010, effective Jan. 1, 2011. Amended September 21, 2010, effective Jan. 1, 2011; Sept. 13, 2013, effective Jan. 1, 2015.

Rule 29. Mandatory Continuing Legal Education

Section 1. Purpose.

The purpose of this Rule is to establish minimum continuing legal education requirements for each Attorney admitted to the Bar of the State of Indiana. The minimum continuing education requirements for an Attorney who serves as a Judge in the State of Indiana shall be governed by the provisions of Admission and Discipline Rule 28.

Section 2. Definitions.

As used in this Rule:

(a) *Approved Courses* shall mean those Substantive Legal Courses and those Non Legal Subject Matter Courses (as defined below) which are approved under the Commission's Accreditation Policies in the Guidelines to this Rule.

(b) *Attorney* shall mean a person who has been admitted to practice law in the State of Indiana and whose name appears in the files of the Board of Law Examiners as provided under Admission and Discipline Rule 4. The term Attorney includes a state or federal administrative law judge.

(c) *Bar* shall mean the Indiana Bar and includes those persons who are Attorneys under subsection (b) above.

(d) *Business Day* shall mean Monday, Tuesday, Wednesday, Thursday, and Friday of each week but shall not include Federal or Indiana state holidays.

(e) *Clerk* shall mean Clerk of the Indiana Supreme Court, Court of Appeals and Tax Court.

(f) *Commission* shall mean the Indiana Commission For Continuing Legal Education created by Section 4 of this Rule.

(g) *Commissioner* shall mean a person who is a member of the Commission.

(h) *Educational Period* shall mean a three-year period during which an Attorney must complete thirty-six (36) hours of Approved Courses. Educational Periods shall be sequential, in that once an

Attorney's particular three-year period terminates, a new three-year period and thirty-six hour minimum shall commence.

(i) [Deleted.]

(j) *Non Legal Subject Matter (NLS) Courses* shall mean courses that the Commission approves for Non Legal Subject Matter credit pursuant to Section 3(a) of this Rule because, even though they lack substantive legal content, they nonetheless enhance an attendee's proficiency in the attorney's practice of law.

(k) *Supreme Court* shall mean the Supreme Court of the State of Indiana.

(*l*) *Year* shall mean calendar year unless otherwise specified in this Rule.

(m) *Professional Responsibility Credits* shall mean credits for topics that specifically address legal ethics or professional responsibility.

(n) *Distance Education* shall mean instructional delivery that does not constrain the student to be physically present in the same location as the instructor and does not require an attendant at the learning site to monitor attendance.

Text of Section 3 effective until January 1, 2015. See also text of Section 3 effective January 1, 2015.

Section 3. Education Requirements.

(a) Every Attorney, except as provided below, shall complete no less than six (6) hours of Approved Courses each year and shall complete no less than thirty-six (36) hours of Approved Courses each Educational Period. At least three (3) hours of Approved Courses in professional responsibility shall be included within the hours of continuing legal education required during each three-year Educational Period. Such hours may be integrated as part of a substantive program or as a free standing program. No more than twelve (12) hours of the Educational Period requirement shall be filled by Non Legal Subject Matter Courses. No more than six (6) hours of the Educational Period requirement shall be filled through interactive Distance Education. No more than three (3) hours of the Educational Period requirement shall be filled through in-house education programs in accordance with the Guidelines. All credits for a single educational activity will be applied in one (1) calendar year.

(b) [Deleted, effective Jan. 1, 2011]

(c) Attorneys admitted to the Indiana Bar before December 31, 1998, on the basis of successfully passing the Indiana Bar examination, shall have a grace period of three (3) years commencing on January 1 of the year of admission and then shall commence meeting the minimum yearly and Educational Period requirements thereafter. Attorneys admitted after December 31, 1998, shall commence meeting the yearly and Educational Period requirements starting on January 1 after the year of their admission by completing programs designated by the Commission as appropriate for new lawyers.

For Attorneys admitted after December 31, 1998, at least six (6) of the thirty-six (36) Educational Period requirements shall be satisfied by attending an Applied Professionalism Program for Newly Admitted Attorneys which has been accredited by the Commission.

(d) Attorneys admitted on foreign license or Attorneys who terminate their inactive status shall have no grace period. Their first three-year Educational Period shall commence on January 1 of the year of admission or termination of inactive status.

(e) [Deleted, effective Jan. 1, 2011]

(f) In recognition of the nature of the work, commitment of time, and the benefit of Attorney participation in the Indiana General Assembly, during an Attorney's Educational Period, for each calendar year in which the Attorney serves as a member of the Indiana General Assembly for more than six (6) months, the Attorney's minimum number of continuing legal education hours for that Educational Period shall be reduced by six (6) hours.

Text of Section 3 effective January 1, 2015. See also text of Section 3 effective until January 1, 2015.

Section 3.   Education Requirements.

(a) Every Attorney, except as provided below, shall complete no less than six (6) hours of Approved Courses each year and shall complete no less than thirty-six (36) hours of Approved Courses each Educational Period. At least three (3) hours of Approved Courses in professional responsibility shall be included within the hours of continuing legal education required during each three-year Educational Period. Such hours may be integrated as part of a substantive program or as a free standing program. No more than twelve (12) hours of the Educational Period requirement shall be filled by Non Legal Subject Matter Courses. No more than six (6) hours of the Educational Period requirement shall be filled through interactive Distance Education. No more than three (3) hours of the Educational Period requirement shall be filled through in-house education programs in accordance with the Guidelines. All credits for a single educational activity will be applied in one (1) calendar year.

(b) Attorneys admitted to the Indiana Bar before December 31, 1998, on the basis of successfully passing the Indiana Bar examination, shall have a grace period of three (3) years commencing on January 1 of the year of admission and then shall commence meeting the minimum yearly and Educational Period requirements thereafter. Attorneys admitted after December 31, 1998, shall commence meeting the yearly and Educational Period requirements starting on January 1 after the year of their

admission by completing programs designated by the Commission as appropriate for new lawyers.

For Attorneys admitted after December 31, 1998, at least six (6) of the thirty-six (36) Educational Period requirements shall be satisfied by attending an Applied Professionalism Program for Newly Admitted Attorneys which has been accredited by the Commission.

(c) Attorneys admitted on foreign license or Attorneys who terminate their inactive status shall have no grace period. Their first three-year Educational Period shall commence on January 1 of the year of admission or termination of inactive status.

(d) In recognition of the nature of the work, commitment of time, and the benefit of Attorney participation in the Indiana General Assembly, during an Attorney's Educational Period, for each calendar year in which the Attorney serves as a member of the Indiana General Assembly for more than six (6) months, the Attorney's minimum number of continuing legal education hours for that Educational Period shall be reduced by six (6) hours.

Section 4.   Commission for Continuing Legal Education.

(a) *Creation of the Commission.* A commission to be known as the Indiana Commission For Continuing Legal Education is hereby created and shall have the powers and duties hereinafter set forth. The Commission shall consist of eleven (11) Commissioners.

(b) *Appointment of Commissioners and Executive Director.* All Commissioners and the Executive Director shall be appointed by the Supreme Court.

(c) *Diversity of Commissioners.* It is generally desirable that the Commissioners be selected from various geographic areas and types of practice in order to reflect the diversity of the Bar and consideration should be given to the appointment of one (1) non-lawyer public member. The three (3) geographic divisions used for selecting Judges for the Indiana Court of Appeals in the First, Second and Third Districts may be used as a model for achieving geographic diversity.

(d) *Terms of Commissioners.* Commissioners shall be appointed for five (5) year terms. All terms shall commence on January 1 and end on December 31. Any Commissioner who has served for all or part of two (2) consecutive terms shall not be reappointed to the Commission for at least three (3) consecutive years.

Section 5.   Organization of the Commission.

Text of Section 5(a) effective until January 1, 2015. See also text of Section 5(a) effective January 1, 2015.

(a) *Election of Officers.* At the first meeting of the Commission after each October 1, the Commissioners shall elect from the membership of the Commission a Chair who shall preside at all meetings, a Vice Chair who shall preside in the absence of the Chair, a Secretary who shall be responsible for giving notices and keeping the minutes of the meetings of the Commission and a Treasurer who shall be responsible for keeping the records of account of the Commission.

Text of Section 5(a) effective January 1, 2015. See also text of Section 5(a) effective until January 1, 2015.

(a) *Election of Officers.* At the first meeting of the Commission after each December 1, the Commissioners shall elect from the membership of the Commission a Chair who shall preside at all meetings, a Vice Chair who shall preside in the absence of the Chair, a Secretary who shall be responsible for giving notices and keeping the minutes of the meetings of the Commission and a Treasurer who shall be responsible for keeping the records of account of the Commission.

(b) *Meetings.* The Commission shall meet at least twice each year at times and places designated by the Chair. The Chair, the Executive Committee or any six (6) Commissioners may call special meetings of the Commission.

(c) *Notices.* The Secretary shall send notice of each meeting of the Commission, stating the purposes of the meeting, to all Commissioners at least five (5) business days before the meeting. Commissioners may waive notice of a meeting by attending the meeting or by delivering a written waiver to the Secretary either before or after the meeting.

(d) *Quorum.* Six (6) Commissioners shall constitute a quorum for the transaction of business. The Commission shall act by a majority of the Commissioners constituting the quorum. Commissioners may participate in meetings of the Commission and committees thereof by telephone or other similar device.

(e) *Vacancies.* Any vacancy on the Commission shall be filled as soon as practical and the new Commissioner so appointed shall serve out the unexpired term of the Commissioner being replaced.

(f) *Executive Committee.* The officers of the Commission described in subsection (a) of this Section shall comprise the Executive Committee which shall have the power to conduct all necessary business of the Commission that may arise between meetings of the full Commission. Three (3) officers of the Commission shall constitute a quorum of the Executive Committee, and the Executive Committee shall act by a vote of a majority of the officers constituting the quorum. All action taken by the Executive Committee shall be reported to the full Commission at its next meeting.

(g) *Other Committees.* The Commission may appoint such other committees having such powers and duties as the Commission may determine from time to time.

Section 6. Powers and Duties of the Commission and Executive Director.

(a) In addition to the powers and duties set forth in this Rule or Rule 28, the Commission shall have the power and duty to:

(1) Approve all or portions of individual educational activities which satisfy the legal education requirements of this Rule.

(2) Approve Sponsors who meet the Requirements of Section 4 of the Commission's Guidelines and whose educational activities satisfy the legal education requirements of this Rule. The Judicial Conference and all seminars conducted by the Judicial Center shall be approved for credit.

(3) Determine the number of credit hours allowed for each educational activity.

(4) Establish an office to provide administrative and financial record-keeping support of the Commission and to employ such persons, sponsors, or providers as the Commission may in its discretion determine to be necessary to assist in administering matters solely of a ministerial nature under this Rule.

(5) Review this Rule and Commission Guidelines from time to time and make recommendations to the Supreme Court for changes.

(6) Upon approval of the Supreme Court publish proposed guidelines and procedures through West Publishing Company and Res Gestae and file the proposed guidelines and procedures with the Clerk.

(7) Provide quarterly financial reports and an annual report of the Commission activity to the Chief Justice of the Supreme Court. A proposed budget for the coming fiscal year (July 1-June 30) shall be submitted to the Chief Justice no later than May 1 of each year.

(8) Do all other things necessary and proper to carry out its powers and duties under this Rule.

(9) Perform all other duties as set forth in Indiana Admission and Discipline Rule 30 and the Indiana Alternative Dispute Resolution Rules.

(b) In addition to the powers and duties set forth in this Rule, the Executive Director shall have the power and the duty to:

(1) Administer the Commission's work.

(2) Appoint, with the approval of the Commission, such staff as may be necessary to assist

the Commission to carry out its powers and duties under this Rule.

(3) Supervise and direct the work of the Commission's staff.

(4) Supervise the maintenance of the Commission's records.

Text of Section 6(b)(5) effective until January 1, 2015. See also text of Section 6(b)(5) effective January 1, 2015.

(5) Enforce the collection of fees attorneys, mediators and independent certifying organizations must pay pursuant to this Rule, Admission and Discipline Rule 30 and the Indiana Alternative Dispute Resolution Rules.

Text of Section 6(b)(5) effective January 1, 2015. See also text of Section 6(b)(5) effective until January 1, 2015.

(5) Enforce the collection of fees that attorneys, sponsors, mediators and independent certifying organizations must pay pursuant to this Rule, Admission and Discipline Rule 28, Admission and Discipline Rule 30 and the Indiana Alternative Dispute Resolution Rules.

(6) Enforce the continuing legal education requirements of Judges and Attorneys under this Rule.

(7) Assist the Commission in developing guidelines.

(8) Perform such other duties as may be assigned by the Commission in the furtherance of its responsibilities hereunder.

Section 7.   Sources and Uses of Funds.

(a) The Indiana Supreme Court shall periodically designate a portion of the registration fee charged to attorneys pursuant to Admission and Discipline Rule 2 to be used for the operations of the Commission on Continuing Legal Education. The Executive Director of the Commission shall deposit such funds into an account designated "Supreme Court Continuing Legal Education Fund."

(b) Disbursements from the fund shall be made solely upon vouchers signed by or pursuant to the direction of the Chief Justice of this Court.

(c) The Supreme Court shall specifically approve all salaries to be paid out of Continuing Legal Education Fund.

(d) Not later than May 1 of each year, the Commission shall submit for approval by the Supreme Court an operating budget for July 1 to June 30 of the following fiscal year.

(e) Commissioners shall be paid one hundred dollars ($100) for each meeting of the Commission they attend and be reimbursed for expenses in accordance with guidelines established by the State of Indiana.

Text of Section 8 effective until January 1, 2015. See also text of Section 8 effective January 1, 2015.

Section 8.   Exemptions and Other Relief from the Rule.

(a) An Attorney shall be exempted from the educational requirements of the Rule for such period of time as shall be deemed reasonable by the Commission upon the filing of a verified petition with the Commission and a finding by the Commission that special circumstances unique to the petitioning Attorney have created undue hardship. Subsequent exemptions may be granted.

(b) [Deleted, effective Jan. 1, 2011]

(c) An Attorney who is physically impaired shall be entitled to establish an alternative method of completing the educational requirements of this Rule upon the filing of a verified petition with the Commission and a finding by the Commission that the alternative method proposed is necessary and consistent with the educational intent of this Rule. Any petition filed under this subsection shall contain a description of the physical impairment, a statement from a physician as to the nature and duration of the impairment, a waiver of any privileged information as to the impairment, and a detailed proposal for an alternative educational method.

(d) An Attorney shall be exempt from the educational and reporting requirements of this Rule if the Attorney has filed an affidavit of inactivity or a retirement affidavit under Sections (c) or (d) of Rule 2. An Attorney who has been inactive for less than a year, and desires to resume active status, shall complete any balance of his or her yearly Educational Period requirements as of the date of inactive status.

(e) An Attorney who believes that he or she will be unable to make timely compliance with the educational requirements imposed by this Rule may seek relief from a specific compliance date by filing a verified petition with the Commission. The petition shall set forth reasons from which the Commission can determine whether to extend such compliance date. A petition seeking such an extension of time must be filed as much in advance of the applicable compliance date as the reasons which form the basis of the request afford. The Commission, upon receipt and consideration of such petition, shall decide if sufficient reasons exist, and may grant an extension for such period of time as shall be deemed reasonable by the Commission. In no event shall such an extension be granted beyond the time when the next compliance date, as required by the Rule, occurs.

Text of Section 8 effective January 1, 2015. See also text of Section 8 effective until January 1, 2015.

Section 8. Exemptions and Other Relief from the Rule.

(a) An Attorney shall be exempted from the educational requirements of the Rule for such period of time as shall be deemed reasonable by the Commission upon the filing of a verified petition with the Commission and a finding by the Commission that special circumstances unique to the petitioning Attorney have created undue hardship. Subsequent exemptions may be granted.

(b) An Attorney who is physically impaired shall be entitled to establish an alternative method of completing the educational requirements of this Rule upon the filing of a verified petition with the Commission and a finding by the Commission that the alternative method proposed is necessary and consistent with the educational intent of this Rule. Any petition filed under this subsection shall contain a description of the physical impairment, a statement from a physician as to the nature and duration of the impairment, a waiver of any privileged information as to the impairment, and a detailed proposal for an alternative educational method.

(c) An Attorney shall be exempt from the educational and reporting requirements of this Rule if the Attorney has filed an affidavit of inactivity or a retirement affidavit under Section 21(b) of Rule 23 of the Supreme Court. An Attorney who has been inactive for less than a year, and desires to resume active status, shall complete any balance of his or her yearly Educational Period requirements as of the date of inactive status.

(d) An Attorney who believes that he or she will be unable to make timely compliance with the educational requirements imposed by this Rule may seek relief from a specific compliance date by filing a verified petition with the Commission. The petition shall set forth reasons from which the Commission can determine whether to extend such compliance date. A petition seeking such an extension of time must be filed as much in advance of the applicable compliance date as the reasons which form the basis of the request afford. The Commission, upon receipt and consideration of such petition, shall decide if sufficient reasons exist, and may grant an extension for such period of time as shall be deemed reasonable by the Commission. In no event shall such an extension be granted beyond the time when the next compliance date, as required by the Rule, occurs.

Text of Section 9 effective until January 1, 2015. See also text of Section 9 effective January 1, 2015.

Section 9. Annual Reporting to Attorneys and Judges.

(a) On or before September 1 of each year, the Commission shall mail or electronically transmit to each Attorney, a statement showing the Approved Courses which the Attorney is credited on the records of the Commission with having attended during the current year and the current Educational Period. This statement will be sent to the mail or e-mail address for the Attorney listed on the Roll of Attorneys maintained by the Clerk. An Attorney shall at all times keep his or her mailing or e-mail address current with the Roll of Attorneys. If the Attorney has completed the minimum hours for the year or Educational Period, the statement will so reflect and inform the Attorney that he or she is currently in compliance with the education requirements of the Rule. It shall not be a defense to noncompliance that an Attorney has not received an annual statement. Additional statements will be provided to an Attorney upon written request and a five dollar ($5.00) fee made payable to the Continuing Legal Education Fund.

If the statement shows the Attorney is deficient in educational hours, but the Attorney believes he or she is in compliance for the year or Educational Period the Attorney shall file a letter of explanation, a Sponsor certification of course attendance, a personal affidavit of attendance, and an application for course accreditation. The documents required by this subsection shall be filed by December 31 of the year or Educational Period in question unless an extension of time to file the same has been granted by the Commission. When an Attorney has resolved the above discrepancies, the Commission shall issue a statement showing that the Attorney is in compliance with the Rule for the year or Educational Period. In the event credit is not granted, the Attorney shall have thirty (30) days after written notification of that fact to comply with the educational requirements. Failure to do so will result in referral to the Supreme Court for suspension.

(b) If the statement incorrectly reflects that the Attorney has completed the minimum hours for the year or the Educational Period, then it shall be the duty of the Attorney to notify the Commission and to complete the educational requirements mandated by this Rule.

Text of Section 9 effective January 1, 2015. See also text of Section 9 effective until January 1, 2015.

Section 9. Annual Reporting to Attorneys.

(a) On or before September 1 of each year, the Commission shall mail or electronically transmit to each Attorney, a statement showing the Approved Courses which the Attorney is credited on the records of the Commission with having attended during the current year and the current Educational Period. This statement will be sent to the mail or e-mail address for the Attorney listed on the Roll of Attorneys maintained by the Clerk. An Attorney shall at all times keep his or her mailing or e-mail address current with the Roll of Attorneys. If the Attorney has completed the minimum hours for the year or Educational Period, the statement will so reflect and inform the Attorney that he or she is currently in compliance with the education requirements of the Rule. It shall not be a defense to noncompliance that an Attorney has not received an annual statement. Additional statements will be provided to an Attorney upon written request and a five dollar ($5.00) fee made payable to the Continuing Legal Education Fund.

If the statement shows the Attorney is deficient in educational hours, but the Attorney believes he or she is in compliance for the year or Educational Period the Attorney shall file a letter of explanation, a Sponsor certification of course attendance, a personal affidavit of attendance, and an application for course accreditation. All fees must be included with the submission. The documents required by this subsection shall be filed by December 31 of the year or Educational Period in question unless an extension of time to file the same has been granted by the Commission. When an Attorney has resolved the above discrepancies, the Commission shall issue a statement showing that the Attorney is in compliance with the Rule for the year or Educational Period. In the event credit is not granted, the Attorney shall have thirty (30) days after written notification of that fact to comply with the educational requirements or appeal the determination pursuant to Section 11. Failure to do so will result in referral to the Supreme Court for suspension.

(b) If the statement incorrectly reflects that the Attorney has completed the minimum hours for the year or the Educational Period, then it shall be the duty of the Attorney to notify the Commission and to complete the educational requirements mandated by this Rule.

(c) All fees must be paid in order for an Attorney to be considered in compliance with this Rule.

Section 10. Sanctions and Reinstatements.

Text of Section 10(a) effective until January 1, 2015. See also text of Section 10(a) effective January 1, 2015.

(a) *Sanctions.* On January 1, a one hundred fifty dollar ($150.00) late fee accrues against each Attorney who has not met his/her yearly or Educational Period requirements for the period ending December 31st of the previous year. On February 1 of each year the Commission shall mail a notice assessing a one hundred fifty dollar ($150.00) late fee to those Attorneys who are shown as not having completed the yearly or Educational Period requirements. The Commission will consider the Attorney delinquent for CLE until both certification of attendance at a CLE program and payment of the late fee are received. Late fees and surcharges are to be deposited by the Commission immediately upon receipt. If the delinquent Attorney has not fulfilled the yearly or Educational Period requirements at the time the Court issues an order suspending that Attorney, the delinquency fee is forfeited. If the Attorney is reinstated to the practice of law pursuant to the provisions of Admission and Discipline Rule 29(10) within one (1) year of suspension, any forfeited late fee shall be credited toward the reinstatement fee. A one hundred dollar ($100.00) surcharge will be added to the late fee for each consecutive year for which an Attorney fails to timely comply with CLE requirements.

On May 1 of each year, a list of those Attorneys still failing to complete the yearly or Educational Period requirements will be submitted to the Supreme Court for immediate suspension from the practice of law. These Attorneys will suffer the suspension of their license to practice law and all related penalties until they are reinstated.

Text of Section 10(a) effective January 1, 2015. See also text of Section 10(a) effective until January 1, 2015.

(a) *Sanctions.* On January 1, a one hundred fifty dollar ($150.00) late fee accrues against each Attorney who has not met his/her yearly or Educational Period requirements for the period ending December 31st of the previous year. On February 1 of each year the Commission shall mail or electronically transmit a notice assessing a one hundred fifty dollar ($150.00) late fee to those Attorneys who are shown as not having completed the yearly or Educational Period requirements. The Commission will consider the Attorney delinquent for CLE until both certification of attendance at a CLE program and payment of the late fee are received. Late fees and surcharges are to be deposited by the Commission immediately upon receipt. If the delinquent Attorney has not fulfilled the yearly or Educational Period requirements at the time the Court issues an order suspending that Attorney, the delinquency fee is forfeited. If the Attorney is reinstated to the practice of law pursuant to the provisions of Admission and Discipline Rule 29(10) within one (1) year of suspension, any forfeited late fee shall be credited toward the reinstatement fee. A one hundred dollar ($100.00) surcharge will be added to the late fee for each consecutive year for which an Attorney fails to timely comply with CLE requirements.

On May 1 of each year, a list of those Attorneys still failing to complete the yearly or Educational Period requirements will be submitted to the Supreme Court for immediate suspension from the practice of law. These Attorneys will suffer the suspension of their license to practice law and all related penalties until they are reinstated.

(b) *Reinstatement Procedures.* An Attorney suspended shall be automatically reinstated upon petition to the Commission and payment of a two hundred dollar ($200.00) reinstatement fee in addition to any applicable surcharge. The petition must demonstrate the petitioner's compliance according to the following reinstatement schedule:

(1) for a suspension of one (1) year or less the petitioner must, between the date of suspension and the date of the petition for reinstatement:

(i) complete the hours required to satisfy the deficiency which resulted in the suspension; and

(ii) complete six (6) additional hours of Approved Courses in a separate course or courses;

(2) for a suspension of more than one (1) year a petitioner must, between the date of suspension and the date of the petition for reinstatement:

(i) complete the hours required to satisfy the deficiency which resulted in the suspension;

(ii) complete thirty-six (36) hours of Approved Courses, twelve (12) hours of which must have been completed within the last twelve (12) month period prior to the date of the petition; and

(iii) begin a new Educational Period as of January 1st of the year of reinstatement pursuant to Section 3(a) of this Rule.

The Commission shall issue a statement reflecting reinstatement which shall also be sent to the Clerk to show on the Roll of Attorneys that the Attorney is in good standing. An Attorney suspended by the Supreme Court who continues to practice law shall be subject to the sanctions for the unauthorized practice of law.

Extensions to provide course attendance certifications for courses which were timely taken may be granted for good cause shown; extensions of time to complete educational requirements are not permitted except under Section 8 of this Rule. Providing or procuring of false certifications of attendance at educational courses shall be subject to appropriate discipline under the Admission and Discipline Rules.

Text of Section 11 effective until January 1, 2015. See also text of Section 11 effective January 1, 2015.

Section 11. Disputes Regarding Commission Records.

Any Attorney who disagrees with the records of the Commission in regard to the credits recorded for the Attorney during the current year or Educational Period and is unable to resolve the disagreement pursuant to Section 9 of this Rule, may petition the Commission for a determination as to the credits to which the Attorney is entitled. Peti-

tions pursuant to this Section shall be considered by the Commission at its next regular or special meeting, provided that the petition is received by the Commission at least ten (10) business days before such meeting. The Attorney filing the petition shall have the right to attend the Commission meeting at which the petition is considered and to present relevant evidence and arguments to the Commission. The rules of pleading and practice in civil cases shall not apply, and the proceedings shall be informal. The determination of the Commission shall be final as to the number of credits for the Attorney and shall be appealable directly to the Supreme Court. In the event of a good faith dispute which is not resolved pursuant to Section 9, the educational and reporting deadlines of this Rule shall be extended until thirty (30) days after the full Commission has ruled on the disputed issue, or if an appeal is taken, until thirty (30) days after the Supreme Court has ruled on the disputed issue.

Text of Section 11 effective January 1, 2015. See also text of Section 11 effective until January 1, 2015.

Section 11. Appeals Regarding Commission Records.

Any Attorney who disagrees with the records of the Commission in regard to the credits recorded for the Attorney during the current year or Educational Period and is unable to resolve the disagreement pursuant to Section 9 of this Rule, may petition the Commission for a determination as to the credits to which the Attorney is entitled. Petitions pursuant to this Section must be received by the Commission within thirty (30) days of the Commission's written notification that credit has not been granted and shall be considered by the Commission at its next regular or special meeting, provided that the petition is received by the Commission at least ten (10) business days before such meeting. The Attorney filing the petition shall have the right to attend the Commission meeting at which the petition is considered and to present relevant evidence and arguments to the Commission. The rules of pleading and practice in civil cases shall not apply, and the proceedings shall be informal. The determination of the Commission shall be final as to the number of credits for the Attorney and shall be appealable directly to the Supreme Court. In the event of a good faith dispute pursuant to this Section, the educational and reporting deadlines of this Rule shall be extended until thirty (30) days after the full Commission has ruled on the disputed issue, or if an appeal is taken, until thirty (30) days after the Supreme Court has ruled on the disputed issue.

Section 12. Petitions.

Any petition filed with the Commission pursuant to this Rule shall be in writing and shall be signed and verified by the Attorney seeking relief. The petition shall be sent by registered or certified mail to the attention of the Executive Director at the Commission's offices at the address shown on the most recent statements or Commission's web page pursuant to Section 9 of this Rule.

Section 13. Confidentiality.

Unless otherwise directed by the Supreme Court or by another court having jurisdiction, the files, records, and proceedings of the Commission, as they may relate to or arise out of an Attorney, Mediator, or Sponsor attempting to satisfy the continuing legal educational requirements of this Rule, or the requirements of the Indiana Alternative Dispute Resolution Rules shall be confidential and shall not be disclosed except in furtherance of the duties of the Commission or upon the request of the Attorney, Mediator, or Sponsor affected.

Section 14. Conflict of Interest.

A member, agent or administrator of the Commission shall abstain from participating in any decision involving a sponsor or provider of educational services of which he or she is an officer. A member, agent or administrator of the Commission shall not be an employee of an entity principally engaged in sponsoring or providing continuing legal education services.

Adopted effective October 1, 1986. Amended effective April 16, 1987; Oct. 15, 1987; June 8, 1988; July 28, 1989; amended Nov. 30, 1989, effective Jan. 1, 1990; amended effective Jan. 16, 1990; May 11, 1990; Jan. 1, 1991; May 23, 1991; Sept. 21, 1993; Sept. 22, 1993; Feb. 1, 1996; amended Dec. 23, 1996, effective March 1, 1997; Nov. 25, 1997, effective Jan. 1, 1998; amended effective Jan. 23, 1998; Feb. 4, 2000; May 31, 2001; amended Dec. 21, 2001, effective April 1, 2002; July 19, 2002, effective Jan. 1, 2003; amended effective Nov. 12, 2002; amended Sept. 30, 2004, effective Jan. 1, 2005; amended effective Oct. 4, 2004; amended July 1, 2005, effective Jan. 1, 2006; Aug. 15, 2006, effective Jan. 1, 2007; Sept. 10, 2007, effective Jan. 1, 2008; Sept. 9, 2008, effective Jan. 1, 2009; Aug. 25, 2010, effective Jan. 1, 2011; Oct. 7, 2011, effective Jan. 1, 2012; Sept. 13, 2013, effective Jan. 1, 2015.

MANDATORY CONTINUING LEGAL EDUCATION AND MANDATORY JUDICIAL EDUCATION GUIDELINES

SECTION 1. AUTHORITY AND PUBLICATION OF GUIDELINES.

These guidelines have been adopted by the Court under Section 4 of Rule 28 and Section 6(a) of Rule 29 in furtherance of the efficient discharge of the Commission's duties. The Commission shall:

(a) file a copy of these guidelines with the Clerk;

(b) cause these guidelines to be published from time to time as revised in a pamphlet, brochure, or the Internet along with the full text of the Rule 28 and 29 and any other materials deemed useful by the Commission in assisting Attorneys, Judges, and Sponsors to understand and comply with the Rule;

(c) cause these guidelines and the full text of the Rules to be sent to the West Publishing Company of St. Paul, Minnesota, with a request that they be published in the *Northeast Reporter*; and

(d) cause these guidelines and the full text of the Rules to be sent to the Editors of *Res Gestae* with a request that they be published.

SECTION 2. DEFINITIONS.

All of the definitions found in Section 2 of the Rule 28 and 29 are applicable in these guidelines. In addition, as used in these guidelines:

(a) *Approved Courses* means any course, approved by the Commission under Section 3 of these Guidelines, or conducted by an Approved Sponsor which meets the requirements of Section 3 of these Guidelines.

(b) *Approved Sponsor* means any person approved under Section 4 of these Guidelines.

(c) *Course* means any educational seminar, institute, or program which is designed to contribute to the continuing legal education of Attorneys and the continuing judicial and legal education of Judges.

(d) *Enroll* means registration for and attendance at a course.

(e) *Person* means an individual, partnership, corporation, or any other organization.

(f) *Rule* means Admission and Discipline Rule 28 on Mandatory Continuing Judicial Education and Admission and Discipline Rule 29 on Mandatory Continuing Legal Education.

(g) *Sponsor* means a Person who conducts or presents a course.

Text of Section 2(h) effective January 1, 2015.

(h) *Application* means a completed application form, with all required attachments and fees, signed and dated by the applicant.

Text of Section 2(i) effective January 1, 2015.

(i) *Received*, in the context of an application, document(s), and/or other item(s) which is or are requested by or submitted to the Commission, means delivery to the Commission; mailed to the Commission by registered, certified or express mail return receipt requested or deposited with any third-party commercial carrier for delivery to the Commission within three (3) calendar days, cost prepaid, properly addressed. Sending by registered or certified mail and by third-party commercial carrier shall be complete upon mailing or deposit.

SECTION 3. ACCREDITATION POLICIES.

(a) **Approval of Courses.** The Commission shall approve the course if it determines that the course will make a significant contribution to the professional competency of Attorneys or Judges who enroll. In determining if a course meets this standard the Commission shall consider whether:

(1) the course has substantial legal content.

(2) the course has substantial judicial content and constitutes an organized program of learning which contributes directly to the professional competency of a Judge.

(3) the course deals with matters related directly to the practice of law or the professional responsibility of Attorneys or Judges.

(4) the course pertains to subject matter having significant intellectual or practical content relating to the administration of justice, the adjudication of cases, the management of case or court operations by a Judge, or to the education of Judges with respect to their professional or ethical obligations.

(5) each faculty member who has teaching responsibility in the course is qualified by academic work or practical experience to teach the assigned subject.

(6) the physical setting for the course is suitable, including the availability of a writing surface and accessibility to persons with disabilities.

(7) high quality written materials including notes and outlines are available at or prior to the time the course is offered to all Attorneys or Judges who enroll.

(8) the course is of sufficient length to provide a substantial educational experience. Courses of less than one (1) hour will be reviewed carefully to determine if they furnish a substantial educational experience.

(9) there are live presentations; or there is a licensed Indiana Attorney, whose function shall be to certify attendance to accompany the replaying of tapes.

(10) the applicant has sufficiently identified those portions of a seminar that should be accredited. It shall be the duty of an applicant to apply separately for accreditation of the legal portions of a seminar, where the substance of a seminar is not entirely legal. The Commission may deny accreditation for an entire program where separate application is not made and where a significant portion of the program is not continuing legal education.

(11) the course is designed for and targeted to Attorneys or Judges.

(12) any attendance restrictions are grounded in a bona fide educational objective to enhance the Continuing Judicial Education or Continuing Legal Education activity. The Commission may deny accreditation to any course that restricts or that a reasonable person would perceive to restrict attendance based upon a classification protected by Indiana state law, federal law or by the Indiana Rules of Professional Conduct.

(b) Approval of Other Educational Activities.

(1) Credit may be given for the following legal subject matter courses:

(i) *Law School Courses.* An Attorney or Judge who attends a regularly conducted class at a law school approved by the American Bar Association. The number of credits may not exceed twenty-four (24) hours for a single law school activity.

(ii) *Bar Review Courses.* An Attorney or Judge who completes a bar review course may apply for continuing legal education credit. The number of credits may not exceed twenty-four (24) hours for the course.

(iii) *Commission–Accredited Basic Mediation Training Course.* An Attorney or Judge who completes a basic mediation training course approved by the Commission for mediation training shall receive twenty-four (24) hours.

(iv) *Court Administration Courses.* Courses directed at improving docket management and court administration shall be approved.

(v) *Ethics Concentrated Law Firm Management Courses.* An Attorney or Judge who attends a law firm management course with a concentration on: Trust accounting, ethical client contact, and ethical use of staff and resources, may apply for credit. Any portion of the course dealing with marketing of services or profit enhancement will be denied credit.

(vi) *Teaching Approved Courses.* An Attorney or Judge who participates as a teacher, lecturer, panelist, or author in an approved course will receive credit for:

(A) Four (4) hours of either approved continuing legal education or continuing judicial education, as applicable, for every hour spent in presentation.

(B) One (1) hour of either continuing legal education credit or continuing judicial education, as applicable, for every four (4) hours of preparation time (up to a maximum of six (6) hours of credit) for a contributing author who does not make a presentation relating to the materials prepared.

(C) One (1) hour of either approved continuing legal education or continuing judicial education, as applicable, for every hour the Attorney or Judge spends in attendance at sessions of a course other than those in which the Attorney or Judge participates as a teacher, lecturer or panel member.

(D) Attorneys or Judges will not receive credit for acting as a speaker, lecturer, or panelist on a program directed to non-attorneys.

(2) Subject to the 12–hour limitation set forth in Rule 28, Section 3(b) and Rule 29, Section 3(a) and the 18–hour limitation set forth in Rule 28, Section

3(a), credit may also be given for Non Legal Subject Matter (NLS) Courses.

(i) *Sponsor Applications for NLS Course Approval.* A sponsor may apply for and receive accreditation of an NLS course. An NLS course may be approved without reference to Section 3(a)(1) of these guidelines. The following is a non-exclusive list of courses that may be accredited under this section:

Text of Section 3(b)(2)(i)(A) effective until January 1, 2015. See also text of Section 3(b)(2)(i)(A) effective January 1, 2015.

(A) *Law Firm Management Courses.* A Sponsor may apply for accreditation of a law office management course that does not meet the criteria of (b)(1)(v) Ethics Concentrated Law Firm Management courses (above). To be accredited, the course must deal with law firm management as opposed to office management in general. Further, the course must be directed to Attorneys or law office administrators. Any portions of the course dealing mainly with profit enhancement or marketing of services will be denied credit.

Text of Section 3(b)(2)(i)(A) effective January 1, 2015. See also text of Section 3(b)(2)(i)(A) effective until January 1, 2015.

(A) *Law Firm Management Courses.* A Sponsor may apply for accreditation of a law office management course that does not meet the criteria of (b)(1)(v) Ethics Concentrated Law Firm Management courses (above). To be accredited, the course must deal with law firm management as opposed to office management in general. Further, the course must be directed to Attorneys or law office administrators. Any portions of the course dealing mainly with profit enhancement or marketing of services will be denied credit.

(B) *Medicine.* Orthopaedics or Anatomy for Lawyers.

(C) *Accounting for Lawyers.*

(D) *Teaching Administration Skills for Law School Teachers.*

(E) *Wellness Courses specifically targeted to Attorneys and Judges.*

(ii) *Attorney Application for NLS Course Approval.* In addition, individual Attorneys and Judges may apply for NLS credit for a course that does not deal with matters directly related to the practice of law. NLS credit may be approved without reference to Sections 3 (a)(1), (3), and (11) of these guidelines if the course directly related to a subject matter directly applicable to the applicant's practice. The following are non-exclusive examples of courses for which individual credit may be awarded under this provision:

(A) Courses in anatomy or other fields of medicine, when credit is sought by an Attorney whose practice includes medical malpractice.

(B) Courses in construction, engineering, or architecture, when credit is sought by an Attorney whose practice includes construction contracting or litigation.

(C) Courses in financial planning, when credit is sought by an Attorney whose practice includes estate planning.

(3) Professional Responsibility Credit shall be given when a topic has professional responsibility or ethics as its main focus, and the course has at least one-half (½) hour of professional responsibility content.

(i) An Approved Sponsor must separately designate Professional Responsibility Credits when certifying attendance to the Commission.

(ii) A Non–Approved Sponsor must separately request Professional Responsibility Credits on an application provided by the Commission.

(4) *Approved In-house education.* In–house programs include those primarily designed for the exclusive benefit of Attorneys employed by a private organization or law firm. In-house programs also include those programs presented only to those Attorneys and/or their clients, even if the program was not designed for those Attorneys. Attorneys within related companies are considered to be employed by the same organization or law firm for purposes of this Rule. In-house education programs may become approved where the education is provided by a Judge, Attorney or Sponsor of legal education who is not a member, employee or acting of counsel of the participating organization or law firm. In-house CLE is subject to the following limitations and requirements:

(i) Limited credit may be given for courses taught in-house. Non-governmental or non-academic Attorneys may report up to three (3) hours per three-year educational period for in-house programs that have been accredited by the Commission. Governmental or academic Attorney employees may receive unlimited CLE for these courses sponsored by their employers for the exclusive benefit of their Attorney employees.

(ii) To be accredited, the Attorney or Sponsor must apply for accreditation at least thirty (30) days before the course is presented, using an Application for Accreditation. Additionally, the Sponsor or Attorney must demonstrate the facts set forth in paragraph 6 below.

(5) *Distance education courses.* Limited credit may be given for courses taken through distance education methods. Subject to the six (6) hour limitation found in Rule 28, Section 3(b) and Rule 29, Section 3(a) and the nine (9) hour limitation found in Rule 28, Section 3(a), an Attorney or Judge may receive CLE or CJE through interactive dis-

tance education during an educational period. To be accredited, the Attorney, Judge or Sponsor must apply for accreditation at least 30 days before the course is presented using an Application for Accreditation. Additionally, the Sponsor, Attorney or Judge must demonstrate the facts set forth in paragraph 6 below.

(6) *Accreditation of in-house and distance education courses.* The Sponsor, Attorney, or Judge must demonstrate that:

(i) the course is designed for and targeted to Attorneys or Judges;

Text of Section 3(b)(6)(ii) effective until January 1, 2015. See also text of Section 3(b)(6)(ii) effective January 1, 2015.

(ii) continuing attendance is monitored and evidence of continuing attendance and/or participation is provided by the Sponsor to the Commission in conformance with such guidelines as the Commission may develop;

Text of Section 3(b)(6)(ii) effective January 1, 2015. See also text of Section 3(b)(6)(ii) effective until January 1, 2015.

(ii) continuing attendance is monitored and evidence of continuing attendance and/or participation is provided by the Sponsor to the Commission in conformance with such guidelines as the Commission may develop. In the case of distance education, the sponsor or Attorney must provide evidence that attendance is monitored by randomly polling or testing of participants during the program to ensure their participation;

(iii) the Sponsor will provide a certificate of continuing attendance to the Commission;

(iv) in content and style the program meets standards of educational quality as determined by the Commission;

(v) in the case of distance education courses, meaningful technical assistance will be provided at times and in ways reasonable to the attendee;

(vi) the course has substantial legal or judicial content (non legal subject credit is not available through in-house programs);

(vii) the course deals with matters related directly to the practice of law, management or administration of court, the adjudication of cases, or the professional responsibility of Attorneys or Judges;

(viii) each faculty member who has teaching responsibility in the course is qualified by academic work or practical experience to teach the assigned subject;

(ix) high quality written materials are available either through paper format or electronic format to accompany the instruction either at or prior to the time the course is offered;

(x) in the case of distance education courses, the program is not text-based;

(xi) in the case of distance education courses, either audio or video or both are provided; and,

(xii) the Sponsor will allow the Commission and its Executive Director or designated appointee to audit the course for regulation purposes.

(7) Credit will be denied for the following activities:

(i) Legislative, lobbying or other law-making activities; and,

(ii) Self-study activities. Courses or activities completed by self-study will be denied credit unless approved under Section 8(c) of this rule.

(c) **Procedure for Sponsors.** Any Sponsor may apply to the Commission for approval of a course. The application must:

Text of Section 3(c)(1) effective until January 1, 2015. See also text of Section 3(c)(1) effective January 1, 2015.

(1) be submitted to the Commission at least thirty (30) days before the first date on which the course is to be offered;

Text of Section 3(c)(1) effective January 1, 2015. See also text of Section 3(c)(1) effective until January 1, 2015.

(1) be received by the Commission at least thirty (30) days before the first date on which the course is to be offered; The [1] applicant must include the nonrefundable application fee in order for the application to be reviewed by the Commission.

Courses presented by non-profit sponsors which do not require a registration fee are eligible for an application fee waiver.

Courses presented by bar associations, Indiana Continuing Legal Education Forum (ICLEF) and government or academic entities will not be assessed an application fee, but are subject to late processing fees.

Applications received less than thirty (30) days before a course is presented must also include a late processing fee in order to be processed by the Commission.

Either the provider or the attendee must pay all application and late processing fees before an attorney may receive credit.

Fees may be waived in the discretion of the Commission upon a showing of good cause.

(2) contain the information required by and be in the form approved by the Commission and available upon request; and

(3) be accompanied by the written course outline and brochure used to furnish information about the course to Attorneys or Judges.

Text of Section 3(d) effective until January 1, 2015. See also text of Section 3(d) effective January 1, 2015.

(d) Procedure for Attorneys and Judges. An Attorney or Judge may apply for credit of a course either before or after the date on which it is offered. Application for accreditation of a distance education course or in-house course must be made at least 30 days prior to the Course. The application must:

(1) contain the information required by and be in the form set forth in the application approved by the Commission and available upon request;

(2) be accompanied by the written course outline and brochure used by the Sponsor to furnish information about the course to Attorneys or Judges; and

(3) be accompanied by an affidavit of the Attorney or Judge attesting that the Attorney or Judge attended the course together with a certification of the course Sponsor as to the Attorney's or Judge's attendance. If the application for course approval is made before attendance, this affidavit and certification requirement shall be fulfilled within thirty (30) days after course attendance.

Text of Section 3(d) effective January 1, 2015. See also text of Section 3(d) effective until January 1, 2015.

(d) Procedure for Attorneys and Judges. Except for distance education and in-house courses, an Attorney or Judge may apply for credit of a course either before or after the date on which it is offered. Application for accreditation of a distance education course or in-house course must be received at least thirty (30) days prior to the Course. The application must:

(1) include the nonrefundable application fee in order for the application to be reviewed by the Commission. Courses presented by non-profit sponsors which do not require a registration fee are eligible for an application fee waiver.

Either the provider or the attendee must pay all application and late fees before an Attorney may receive credit.

Fees may be waived in the discretion of the Commission upon a showing of good cause;

(2) contain the information required by and be in the form set forth in the application approved by the Commission and available upon request;

(3) be accompanied by the written course outline and brochure used by the Sponsor to furnish information about the course to Attorneys or Judges; and

(4) be accompanied by an affidavit of the Attorney or Judge attesting that the Attorney or Judge attended the course together with a certification of the course Sponsor as to the Attorney's or Judge's attendance. If the application for course approval is made before attendance, this affidavit and certification requirement shall be fulfilled within thirty (30) days after course attendance. Attendance reports received more than thirty (30) days after the

conclusion of a course must include a late processing fee.

Course applications received more than one-year after a course is presented may be denied as untimely.

Text of Section 3(e) effective until January 1, 2015. See also text of Section 3(e) effective January 1, 2015.

(e) Executive Director's Discretionary Powers. The Executive Director of the Indiana Commission for Continuing Legal Education may use discretion in waiving the 30-day pre-program application requirements of b (4) (b), b (5), and (d) of Section 3 of these Guidelines upon a showing of good cause by the applicant.

Text of Section 3(e) effective January 1, 2015. See also text of Section 3(e) effective until January 1, 2015.

(e) Executive Director's Discretionary Powers. The Executive Director of the Indiana Commission for Continuing Legal Education may use discretion in waiving the 30–day pre-program application requirements of these Guidelines upon a showing of good cause by the applicant and may waive application or late processing fees.

SECTION 4.   APPROVAL OF SPONSORS.

(a) Procedure. A Person may apply to the Commission for approval as a Sponsor of continuing legal or judicial education activity. The application submitted to the Commission must contain the information required by and be in the form approved by the Commission and available upon request in the Commission office. A Person becomes an Approved Sponsor when the Commission places a Person's name on the list of Approved Sponsors.

(b) Standard for Approval. The Commission shall approve the Person as a Sponsor if the Commission finds that the Person has conducted and is prepared to conduct on a regular basis programs which, if considered on an individual basis, would satisfy the standards for course approval set out in Section 3(a) of these Guidelines.

In order to determine whether a Sponsor should be granted Approved Sponsor status, the Commission may consider the following:

(1) Whether the Sponsor has presented a minimum of an average of five (5) Approved Courses per year for the previous three (3) years.

(2) Whether the courses within the previous three (3) years were substantively legal or judicial in nature and primarily targeted to Attorneys or Judges.

(3) Whether the Sponsor has observed Commission Rules, Guidelines and Policies with regard to advertising, application requirements and attendance reporting.

(4) Whether courses within the previous three (3) years were high quality and advanced the education of Attorneys or Judges.

(5) Whether the Sponsor has substantially complied with requests from the Commission.

(6) Whether courses have been denied accreditation by the Commission during the previous three (3) years and the reasons for the denials.

(c) Review of Approved Sponsors. The Commission shall periodically audit Approved Sponsors. If the Person fails to conduct approvable courses on a regular basis, the Person shall be removed from the Commission's list of Approved Sponsors. In order to remain an Approved Sponsor, a Sponsor must certify to the Commission the name and attorney number of all Indiana Attorneys and Judges who attend any Continuing Legal Education Program or Continuing Judicial Education Program.

(d) Presumption of Course Accreditation. Courses presented by an Approved Sponsor are presumed to satisfy the education requirements of Section 3 of Rule 28 and Rule 29; provided however, courses which do not meet requirements of Section 3(a) of these Guidelines will be denied credit. Approved Sponsors must seek approval of courses of less than one (1) hour duration under Section 3 of these Guidelines.

Text of Section 4(e) effective January 1, 2015.

(e) Fees. Approved sponsors need not pay application fees. Approved sponsors must pay a late processing fee for attendance reports received more than thirty (30) days after conclusion of a course.

Text of Section 5 effective until January 1, 2015. See also text of Section 5 effective January 1, 2015.

SECTION 5. PROCEDURE FOR RESOLVING DISPUTES.

Any Person who disagrees with a decision of the Commission and is unable to resolve the disagreement informally, may petition the Commission for a resolution of the dispute. Petitions pursuant to this Section shall be considered by the Commission at its next regular meeting, provided that the petition is received by the Commission at least ten (10) business days before such meeting. The Person filing the petition shall have the right to attend the Commission meeting at which the petition is considered and to present relevant evidence and arguments to the Commission. The rules of pleading and practice in civil cases shall not apply, and the proceedings shall be informal as directed by the Chair. The determination of the Commission shall be final subject to appeal directly to the Supreme Court.

Text of Section 5 effective January 1, 2015. See also text of Section 5 effective until January 1, 2015.

SECTION 5. PROCEDURE FOR APPEALS.

Any Person who disagrees with a decision of the Commission and is unable to resolve the disagreement informally, may petition the Commission for a resolution of the dispute. Petitions pursuant to this Section must be received by the Commission within thirty (30) days of the Commission's written notification giving rise to the disagreement and shall be considered by the Commission at its next regular meeting, provided that the petition is received by the Commission at least ten (10) business days before such meeting. The Person filing the petition shall have the right to attend the Commission meeting at which the petition is considered and to present relevant evidence and arguments to the Commission. The rules of pleading and practice in civil cases shall not apply, and the proceedings shall be informal as directed by the Chair. The determination of the Commission shall be final subject to appeal directly to the Supreme Court.

SECTION 6. CONFIDENTIALITY.

Filings with the Commission shall be confidential. These filings shall not be disclosed except in furtherance of the duties of the Commission or upon the request, by the Attorney, Judge or Sponsor involved, or as directed by the Supreme Court.

SECTION 7. RULES FOR DETERMINING EDUCATION COMPLETED.

(a) Formula. The number of hours of continuing legal or judicial education completed in any course by an Attorney or Judge shall be computed by:

(1) Determining the total instruction time expressed in minutes;

(2) Dividing the total instruction time by sixty (60); and

(3) Rounding the quotient up to the nearest one-tenth ($\frac{1}{10}$).

Stated in an equation the formula is:

$$\frac{\text{Total Instruction Time (in minutes)}}{\text{Sixty (60)}} = \text{Hours completed (rounded up to nearest 1/10)}$$

(b) Instruction Time Defined. Instruction time is the amount of time when a course is in session and presentations or other educational activities are in progress. Instruction time does not include time spent on:

(1) Introductory remarks;

(2) Breaks; or

(3) Business meetings.

SECTION 8. REPORT OF SPONSOR.

Text of Section 8 effective until January 1, 2015. See also text of Section 8 effective January 1, 2015.

The Sponsor shall, within thirty (30) days after the course is presented, submit to the Commission an alphabetical list including attorney numbers of all Attorneys admitted in Indiana and Indiana Judges who have attended the course. This list shall be certified by the Sponsor and include the hours to be credited to each Attorney and Judge for attendance and speaking.

If the course is presented by an Approved Sponsor under Section 4 of these Guidelines, the Sponsor shall submit a copy of the outline and brochure by which information about the program was furnished to Attorneys or Judges.

Text of Section 8 effective January 1, 2015. See also text of Section 8 effective until January 1, 2015.

The Sponsor shall, within thirty (30) days after the course is presented, submit to the Commission an alphabetical list including attorney numbers of all Attorneys admitted in Indiana and Indiana Judges who have attended the course. This list shall be certified by the Sponsor and include the hours to be credited to each Attorney and Judge for attendance and speaking. Attendance reports received more than thirty (30) days after the conclusion of a course must include a late processing fee.

If the course is presented by an Approved Sponsor under Section 4 of these Guidelines, the Sponsor shall submit a copy of the outline and brochure by which information about the program was furnished to Attorneys or Judges.

SECTION 9. USE OF THE OFFICIAL LEGEND OF THE COMMISSION.

(a) Legend of the Commission. The Commission has adopted the official legend set forth in subsection (c) of this Section as a symbol of approval of continuing legal education activity. This legend is the subject of copyright and may not be used in advertisement or publicity for a course unless the Sponsor complies with the requirements of subsection (b) of this Section.

(b) A Sponsor of Approved Courses may use the legend set forth in subsection (c) of this Section if the Sponsor agrees to report hours of credit and submit materials under Section 8 of these Guidelines.

(c) This legend which may be utilized by Sponsors is:

THIS COURSE HAS BEEN APPROVED BY THE COMMISSION FOR CONTINUING LEGAL EDUCATION OF THE STATE OF INDIANA. ATTORNEYS OR JUDGES WHO COMPLETE THIS COURSE SHALL RECEIVE

1. ___ HOURS OF SUBSTANTIVE CONTINUING EDUCATION, INCLUDING ___ HOURS OF ETHICS, OR

2. ___ HOURS OF NLS CONTINUING EDUCATION HOURS

UNDER INDIANA SUPREME COURT ADMISSION AND DISCIPLINE RULE 29 ON MANDA-

TORY CONTINUING LEGAL EDUCATION AND/OR ADMISSION AND DISCIPLINE RULE 28 ON MANDATORY CONTINUING JUDICIAL EDUCATION. THE SPONSOR OF THIS COURSE IS OBLIGATED TO REPORT THE HOURS OF CONTINUING EDUCATION COMPLETED BY AN ATTORNEY OR JUDGE.

Adopted effective October 1, 1986. Amended effective April 16, 1987; June 8, 1988; amended Nov. 30, 1989, effective Jan. 1, 1990; May 23, 1991, effective Jan. 1, 1992; Dec. 23, 1996, effective March 1, 1997; Jan. 14, 2002, effective Jan. 1, 2003; Sept. 30 and Oct. 29, 2004, effective Jan. 1, 2005; Sept. 9, 2008, effective Jan. 1, 2009; Aug. 25, 2010, effective Jan. 1, 2011; amended effective Jan. 6, 2011; Sept. 13, 2013, effective Jan. 1, 2015.

1 So in original.

Rule 30. Indiana Certification Review Plan

Section 1. Purpose. The purpose of this rule is to regulate the certification of lawyers as specialists by independent certifying organizations (ICO's) to:

(a) enhance public access to and promote efficient and economic delivery of appropriate legal services;

(b) assure that lawyers claiming special competence in a field of law have satisfied uniform criteria appropriate to the field;

(c) facilitate the education, training and certification of lawyers in limited fields of law;

(d) facilitate lawyer access to certifying organizations;

(e) expedite consultation and referral; and

(f) encourage lawyer self-regulation and organizational diversity in defining and implementing certification of lawyers in limited fields of law.

Section 2. Power of Indiana Commission for Continuing Legal Education (CLE). CLE shall review, approve and monitor organizations (ICO's) which issue certifications of specialization to lawyers practicing in the State of Indiana to assure that such organizations satisfy the standards for qualification set forth in this rule.

Section 3. Authority and Discretion of CLE. In furtherance of the foregoing powers and subject to the supervision of and, where appropriate, appeal to the Supreme Court of Indiana, CLE shall have authority and discretion to:

(a) approve or conditionally approve appropriate organizations as qualified to certify lawyers as specialists in a particular field or closely related group of fields of law;

(b) adopt and interpret rules and policies reasonably needed to implement this rule and which are not inconsistent with its purposes;

(c) review and evaluate the programs of ICO's to assure continuing compliance with the purposes of this rule, the rules and policies of CLE, and the qualification standards set forth in Section 4;

(d) deny, suspend or revoke the approval of an ICO upon CLE's determination that the ICO has failed to comply with the qualification standards or rules and policies of CLE;

(e) keep appropriate records of those lawyers certified by ICO's approved under this rule;

(f) cooperate with other organizations, boards and agencies engaged in the field of lawyer certification;

(g) enlist the assistance of advisory committees to advise CLE; and

(h) make recommendations to the Indiana Supreme Court concerning:

(1) the need for and appointment of a Director and other staff, their remuneration and termination;

(2) an annual budget;

(3) appropriate fees for applicant organizations, qualified organizations and certified specialists; and

(4) any other matter the Indiana Supreme Court requests.

Section 4. Qualification Standards for Independent Certifying Agencies.

(a) The ICO shall encompass a comprehensive field or closely related group of fields of law so delineated and identified (1) that the field of certification furthers the purpose of the rule; and (2) that lawyers can, through intensive training, education and work concentration, attain extraordinary competence and efficiency in the delivery of legal services within the field or group.

(b) The ICO shall be a non-profit entity whose objectives and programs foster the purpose of this rule. A majority of the body within an Applicant organization reviewing applicants for certification of lawyers as specialists in a particular area of law shall consist of lawyers who, in the judgment of CLE, are experts in the field of certification.

(c) The ICO shall have a substantial continuing existence and demonstrable administrative capacity to perform the tasks assigned it by this rule and the rules and policies of CLE.

(d) The ICO shall adopt, publish and enforce open membership and certifications standards and procedures which do not unfairly discriminate against members of the Bar of Indiana individually or collectively.

(e) The ICO shall provide the following assurance to the continuing satisfaction of CLE with respect to its certified practitioners:

(1) that certified practitioners have a demonstrated proficiency in the field of certification that is;

   i.   comprehensive;

   ii. objectively demonstrated;

   iii. peer recognized; and

   iv. reevaluated at appropriate intervals;

(2) that members actively and effectively pursue the field of certification as demonstrated by continuing education and substantial involvement; and

(f) The ICO shall cooperate at all times with CLE and perform such tasks and duties as CLE may require to implement, enforce and assure compliance with and effective administration of this rule.

Section 5. Qualification Standards for Certification.

(a) To be recognized as certified in a field of law in the State of Indiana, the lawyer must be duly admitted to the bar of this state, in active status, and in good standing, throughout the period for which the certification is granted.

(b) The lawyer must be certified by an ICO approved by CLE, and must be in full compliance with the Indiana Bar Certification Review Plan, the rules and policies of the ICO and the rules and policies of CLE.

Section 6. Privileges Conferred and Limitations Imposed.

(a) A lawyer who is certified under this rule may communicate the fact that the lawyer is certified by the ICO as a specialist in the area of law involved. The lawyer shall not represent, either expressly or impliedly, that the lawyer's certification has been individually recognized by the Indiana Supreme Court or CLE, or by an entity other than the ICO.

(b) Certification in one or more fields of law, shall not limit a lawyer's right to practice in other fields of law.

(c) Absence of certification in a field of law shall not limit the right of a lawyer to practice in that field of law. Participation in the Indiana Bar Certification Review Plan shall be on a voluntary basis.

(d) The number of certifications which a lawyer may hold shall be limited only by the practical limits of the qualification standards imposed by this rule and the rules and policies of the ICO.

(e) An ICO shall not be precluded from issuing certificates in more than one area of certification but in such event, the ICO's qualifications shall be judged and determined separately as to each such area of certification. To the extent consistent with the purpose of the Indiana Bar Certification Review Plan, any number of ICO's may be approved to issue certifications in the same or overlapping fields or groups of closely related fields of law.

Section 7. Fees.
To defray expenses of the Indiana Bar Certification Review program, the Indiana Supreme Court may establish and collect reasonable and periodic fees from the ICO's and from applicants and lawyers certified under the Indiana Bar Certification Review program.

Section 8. Appeal.
CLE action or inaction may be appealed as abuse of authority under the Rules of

Procedure applicable to original actions in the Indiana Supreme Court.

Adopted Dec. 5, 1994, effective Feb. 1, 1995. Amended Sept. 10, 2007, effective Jan. 1, 2008.

Rule 31. Judges and Lawyers Assistance Program
Section 1. Establishment.

The Judges and Lawyers Assistance Committee is created and shall have the powers and duties set out below. The Committee shall be composed of Committee members, an Executive Director, and such other persons as shall from time to time be approved by the Supreme Court and who are necessary to carry out the Committee's work.

Section 2. Purpose.

The purpose of the Judges and Lawyers Assistance Program is assisting impaired members in recovery; educating the bench and bar; and reducing the potential harm caused by impairment to the individual, the public, the profession, and the legal system. Through the Judges and Lawyers Assistance Program, the Committee will provide assistance to judges, lawyers and law students who suffer from physical or mental disabilities that result from disease, chemical dependency, mental health problems or age that impair their ability to practice; and will support other programs designed to increase awareness about the problems of impairment among lawyers and judges.

Section 3. Committee Members.

(a) The Committee shall consist of fifteen (15) Committee members, all of whom shall be appointed by the Supreme Court. Members shall have experience with the problems of chemical dependency and/or mental health problems. Seven (7) members shall be practicing lawyers; five (5) shall be judges; one (1) shall be a law school administrator or law school faculty member employed by, or a law student enrolled in, an Indiana law school at the time of appointment; two (2) members may be filled by judges, lawyers, and/or law student(s). A reasonable effort shall be made to provide geographical representation of the State.

(b) Members shall be appointed for three-year terms. All terms shall commence on January 1 and end on December 31. Any member who has served three (3) consecutive terms, exclusive of filling out an unexpired term, shall not be reappointed to the Committee for at least three (3) consecutive years. Any vacancy on the Committee shall be filled as soon as practicable and the new member so appointed shall serve the unexpired term of the member being replaced. Any member may be removed by the Supreme Court for a good cause.

(c) *Election of Officers.* The members shall elect from the membership a Chair who shall preside at all meetings, a Vice-Chair who shall preside in the absence of the Chair, a Secretary who shall be responsible for giving notices and keeping the Committee's minutes, and a Treasurer who shall be responsible for keeping the Committee's record of account.

(d) *Executive Committee.* The Officers shall comprise the Executive Committee, which shall have the power to conduct all necessary business that may arise between meetings of the full Committee. Three (3) Officers shall constitute a quorum. The Executive Committee shall act by a vote of a majority of the Officers. All action taken by the Executive Committee shall be reported to the full Committee at its next meeting.

(e) *Meetings.* The Committee shall meet at least twice each year at times and places designated by the Chair. The Chair, the Executive Committee or any six Committee members may call special meetings of the Committee.

(f) *Notices.* The Secretary shall send notice of each Committee meeting, which states the meeting's purpose, to all members at least five (5) business days before the meeting.

(g) *Quorum.* Six (6) members shall constitute a quorum for the transaction of business. The Committee shall act by majority of the members constituting the quorum. Members may participate in meetings by telephone or other similar device.

Section 4. Powers and Duties of the Committee.

In addition to the powers and duties set forth elsewhere in this Rule, the Committee shall have the power and duty to:

(a) Adopt rules and regulations, to be known as the Judges and Lawyers Assistance Program Guidelines, for the efficient discharge of its powers and duties. The Guidelines shall become effective when approved by the Supreme Court.

(b) Establish an office to provide administrative and financial record keeping support for the Committee.

(c) Establish a mechanism, subject to Court approval, to arrange loans or other financial assistance to members of the bar for recovery related expenses.

(d) Review this Rule and Guidelines from time to time and make recommendations to the Supreme Court for changes.

(e) Publish proposed Guidelines and procedures through West Publishing Company and Res Gestae and file them with the Clerk of the Supreme and Appellate Courts.

(f) Appoint subcommittees having such powers and duties as the Committee may determine are necessary to carry out the Committee's work; including trustees of any organization created to receive and distribute or spend grants, bequests, gifts and other monies for loans or other financial assistance to members of the bar for recovery related expenses.

(g) Provide financial reports to the Chief Justice.

(h) Make an annual report of its activities to the Supreme Court each year. The report shall include a statement of income and expenses for the year.

(i) Recruit and train volunteers, as defined by the Guidelines, to assist the Committee's work with impaired members of the legal profession.

(j) Do all other things necessary and proper to carry out its powers and duties under this Rule.

Section 5. Executive Director. With the assistance of the Committee members, the Chief Justice shall hire an Executive Director.

Section 6. Powers and Duties of the Executive Director. In addition to the powers and duties set forth in this Rule or otherwise defined by the Committee or the Supreme Court, the Executive Director shall have the power and duty to:

(a) Administer the Committee's work.

(b) Appoint, with approval of the Committee, such staff as may be necessary to assist the Committee to carry out its powers and duties under this Rule.

(c) Supervise and direct the work of the Committee's staff and volunteers.

(d) Assist the Committee in developing Guidelines.

(e) Supervise the maintenance of the Committee's records.

(f) Assist judges, courts, lawyers, law firms and law schools to identify and intervene with impaired members of the legal profession.

(g) Do all things necessary and proper to carry out the Executive Director's duties and powers under this Rule.

Section 7. Sources and Uses of Funds.

(a) The Indiana Supreme Court shall periodically designate a portion of the registration fee charged to attorneys pursuant to Admission and Discipline Rule 2 to be used for the operations of the Judges and Lawyers Assistance Committee. The Executive Director shall deposit such funds into an account designated "Supreme Court Judges and Lawyers Assistance Committee Fund.".

(b) The Supreme Court shall specifically approve the salaries to be paid out of the Judges and Lawyers Committee Fund.

(c) Not later than May 1 of each year, the Committee shall submit for approval by the Supreme Court an operating budget for July 1 to June 30 of the following fiscal year.

Section 8. Referrals.

(a) Any judge, lawyer, or law student may contact the Committee seeking assistance.

(b) Any person may report to the Committee that a judge, lawyer, or law student needs the Committee's assistance. The Committee shall then take such action as authorized by the Guidelines.

(c) The Supreme Court, the Indiana Commission on Judicial Qualifications, the Disciplinary Commission, the Board of Law Examiners, and the Administration of any Indiana law school may refer judges, lawyers, or law students to the Committee for assessment or treatment upon such terms authorized by the Guidelines.

(d) The Committee may refer judges, lawyers, and law students to outside agencies, organizations, or individuals for assessment or treatment upon such terms authorized by the Guidelines.

Section 9. Confidentiality.

(a) All information, including records obtained by the Committee in the performance of its duty under these rules and as delegated by the Supreme Court of Indiana, shall be confidential, except as provided by the Program Guidelines.

(b) Nothing in this section prevents the Committee from communicating statistical information which does not divulge the identity of any individual.

(c) Violation of the confidentiality provisions of this rule shall be subject to disciplinary proceeding under Indiana Admission and Discipline Rules 12, 23 and 26.

Section 10. Immunity. The Committee, Executive Director, staff, and volunteers are not subject to civil suit for official acts done in good faith in furtherance of the Committee's work. Absent malice, a person who gives information to the Committee, staff or volunteers about a judge, lawyer or law student thought to be impaired is not subject to civil suit.

Adopted effective Oct. 14, 1997. Amended Dec. 21, 2001, effective April 1, 2002; Aug. 15, 2006, effective Jan. 1, 2007; effective Dec. 16, 2008.

PROGRAM GUIDELINES FOR THE INDIANA JUDGES AND LAWYERS ASSISTANCE PROGRAM

The Indiana Judges and Lawyers Assistance Program (JLAP), established pursuant to Indiana Admission and Discipline Rule 31, provides assistance to judges, lawyers, and law students who suffer from physical or mental disabilities resulting from disease, chemical dependency, mental health problems, or age that impair their ability to practice or serve. JLAP neither engages in punishing nor disciplining members nor does it have the power or authority to do so. These policies and procedures have been adopted by JLAP and constitute guidelines approved by the Committee.

Section 1. Definitions.

The following terms or phrases shall have the meanings assigned in this section.

(a) Chairperson—the person who is currently holding the office of chairperson of the committee.

(b) Clinical director—clinical director of JLAP

(c) Committee—the body comprised of the persons appointed by the Supreme Court of Indiana to administer JLAP pursuant to Admis.Disc.R. 31 § 1.

(d) Confidential information—all information, whether oral, written, or electronically acquired, received by, or held in the possession of a representative, which in any manner (including identity) relates to a member who is impaired, believed to be impaired or possibly has an impairment.

(e) Contract participant—a participant who has entered into a formal, written agreement with JLAP.

(f) Court—the Supreme Court of Indiana

(g) Director—executive director of JLAP

(h) Impaired—having a physical or mental disability resulting from disease, chemical dependency, mental health problems, or age that could affect a member's ability to practice law or serve as a lawyer or judge.

(i) Independent source—any person consulted to verify a JLAP contact who did not initiate the contact.

(j) JLAP—the Indiana Judges and Lawyers Assistance Program as established pursuant to Admis.Disc.R. 31, its staff and volunteers.

(k) Members or members of the legal profession — persons who are judges, lawyers, law students, or have applied for admission to the Indiana bar.

(l) Monitor—Volunteer who oversees a contract participant's compliance with a JLAP monitoring agreement.

(m) Monitoring agreement—a formal written agreement between a participant and JLAP that establishes the obligations of the participant and provides for the monitoring of the participant's compliance.

(n) Official referral—referral of a member to JLAP by:

1) The Indiana Supreme Court Disciplinary Commission;

2) The Indiana Board of Law Examiners;

3) The Indiana Commission on Judicial Qualifications; or

4) Any Indiana law school administration as part of its disciplinary process.

(o) Participant—any member who is referred to JLAP and, as a result thereof, receives a contact or communication from a representative.

(p) Permitted disclosures—disclosure of confidential information

1) Permitted or required pursuant to Rule 31 § 9(c);

2) With the written consent of the participant or contract participant to whom such confidential information relates; or

3) By or among representatives to carry out or accomplish the purposes of JLAP.

(q) Representative—the director, clinical director, any member or employee of the committee or any volunteer.

(r) Self-referral--a member's direct contact with a representative to consider becoming a participant in JLAP not in furtherance of an official referral or a third party referral.

(s) Staff—any and/or all of the employees of JLAP.

(t) Third party referral—any referral of a member to JLAP other than an official referral or self-referral.

(u) Volunteer—any person (including members of the committee) who has entered into an agreement with JLAP to assist in providing services in accordance with JLAP policies and procedures including completing any required application process.

Section 2. Purpose of JLAP.

Pursuant to Admis.Disc.R. 31 § 2, JLAP was established to assist impaired members in recovery; to educate the bench and bar; and to reduce the potential harm caused by impairment to the individual, the public, the profession, and the legal system.

These guidelines have been adopted with these purposes in mind. The work of JLAP is designed to be educational, confidential, and responsive to the special situations faced by impaired members of the legal profession.

The JLAP committee and the executive director may take any other action required to fulfill, yet remains consistent with, the stated purpose.

Section 3. Organization.

JLAP was established pursuant to Admis.Disc.R. 31. The Committee consists of fifteen (15) members appointed by the Court: seven (7) practicing attorneys, five (5) judges, one (1) law student, and two (2) judge(s), lawyer(s), or law student(s). The director operates under the direction of the committee. The clinical director, staff and volunteers operate under the direction of the director.

Section 4. Policies.

(a) JLAP designs and delivers programs to raise the awareness of the legal community about potential types of impairment and the identification, prevention and available resources for treatment and/or support.

(b) JLAP works toward increasing the likelihood of recovery by encouraging early identification, referral and treatment.

(c) Any person may report to the director, clinical director, or any member of the committee that a particular member of the bar needs the assistance of JLAP.

(d) JLAP encourages and welcomes contact by any means. However, the confidentiality of e-mail communications is subject to the limitations inherent in Internet transmissions.

(e) Neither JLAP, nor any representative, in their role as a volunteer, engages in the practice of law while fulfilling their JLAP responsibilities. Upon admission to inpatient or residential treatment, or with a physical disability case, JLAP may:

1) work with the participant to find friends and/or colleagues to assist with the law practice;

2) work with the relevant local and state bar association committees to assist with the practice;

3) should no other arrangements be possible, attempt to facilitate movement of a participant's case files to the respective clients upon receipt of written permission from the participant.

Section 5. Referral Procedures

(a) General Procedures

The state will be divided into geographical areas and a committee member or other designated representative shall serve as the primary contact for each area.

(b) Self–Referrals and Other Referrals

1) When the participant is a self-referral, the following procedures apply:

i. JLAP may conduct an initial consultation to determine the nature of the participant's impairment;

ii. where appropriate, JLAP may make a referral to a qualified medical and/or clinical resource for further evaluation, assessment, and/or treatment;

iii. if appropriate, JLAP may assist in the development of a treatment plan, which may include participation in JLAP;

iv. with the participant's permission, a volunteer will be appointed to provide ongoing support.

2) When the member is referred by a third party the following procedures apply:

i. JLAP will obtain detailed information from the referral source regarding the nature of the impairment, the referral source's relationship to the member, and the circumstances giving rise to the referral. The identity of the referral source shall remain confidential unless the referral source instructs otherwise.

ii. JLAP may conduct further investigations to verify the circumstances that led to the referral by contacting independent sources to determine whether the member may be impaired.

iii. Any independent sources shall be approached in a manner to preserve, as far as possible, the privacy of the member.

iv. If it is determined the member may be impaired, JLAP will determine how the member will be approached with special attention given to involving local volunteers and/or local members of the bar who may already be involved in the case.

v. If the referred member is a judge, every effort shall be made to include at least one judge as a volunteer in the case.

3) If the impaired member agrees to treatment, or other levels of participation in JLAP, further assistance may include:

i. consultation with the participant, in-house assessment/evaluation, or referral for appropriate assessment/evaluation;

ii. assistance in locating treatment resources; and

iii. assistance in development of continuing care including support and referral to JLAP.

4) The director may terminate JLAP's involvement in any case at any time should it be determined that the member does not comply or refuses to participate and will not likely benefit from JLAP services at that time.

(c) Official Referrals

1) Upon receipt of an official referral for assessment/evaluation, JLAP will:

i. Determine if all appropriate releases and/or authorizations have been signed and obtained.

ii. Determine whether the requested assessment/evaluation will be done in house, referred out or a combination.

iii. Contact the official referral source for background information and direction, if necessary.

iv. Coordinate the assessment process with selected provider, participating as deemed appropriate on a case-by-case basis.

v. Release information and/or the final assessment/evaluation as allowed by written release.

2) Upon receipt of an official referral for a monitoring agreement JLAP will:

i. Determine if all appropriate signed releases/authorizations have been obtained.

ii. Review existing assessment(s) and/or determine whether initial or additional assessment(s) are necessary.

iii. Develop a monitoring agreement.

iv. Select and provide a monitor.

v. Meet with the participant, his/her attorney if appropriate, and the monitor prior to execution of the agreement to explain JLAP's role and the agreement terms and conditions.

vi. Report to the official referral source according to the terms of the referral and the monitoring agreement.

Section 6.   Services.

(a) Any member is eligible for assistance and participation in JLAP. JLAP services will be provided without charge for initial consultation, in-house assessment, referral, and peer support.

(b) Referrals for medical and/or clinical evaluations, treatment, therapy and aftercare services will be provided; engagement of, and payment for, such services is solely the responsibility of the participant.

(c) Participants entering into a monitoring agreement with JLAP due to an official referral or upon their own initiative may be charged a monthly fee pursuant to JLAP's fee policy as approved by the Supreme Court from time to time.

Section 7.   Treatment—Medical Assistance.

(a) JLAP endeavors to provide a network of therapeutic resources that includes a broad range of health care providers, therapists, and "self-help" support groups. JLAP will maintain a statewide list of available providers.

(b) With the written consent of the participant, JLAP may maintain contact with, and receive information from, the treatment provider. JLAP may remain involved in support during treatment, and shall endeavor to provide peer support and aftercare assistance in early recovery.

(c) In cases where it is determined the participant is not in need of inpatient or residential treatment, JLAP may provide referrals to outpatient counseling resources and self-help groups such as 12–step programs.

Section 8.   Confidentiality.

(a) JLAP and its representatives will observe anonymity and confidentiality at all times. JLAP is an autonomous program, independent from the administrative offices of the Court or any other board or disciplinary organization, agency or authority.

(b) No disclosure of confidential information will be made by any representative except for permitted disclosures and those identified in Ind. Professional Conduct Rule 8.3.

Section 9.   Role of Program Volunteers..

JLAP will maintain a statewide network of volunteers to assist the committee in carrying out the purposes of JLAP. Volunteers fulfill the following functions:

(a) Assist in investigations, assessments, interventions, monitoring and support;

(b) Appear on behalf of contract participants as witnesses at the discretion of the director;

(c) Attend ongoing training on topics that enhance their ability to assist impaired members of the legal profession; and

(d) Disseminate information about JLAP including the offer of presentations to local and specialty bars.

Adopted Dec. 21, 2001, effective April 1, 2002. Amended July 1, 2003, effective Jan. 1, 2004; Aug. 15, 2006, effective Jan. 1, 2007.

INDIANA SUPREME COURT DISCIPLINARY COMMISSION RULES GOVERNING ATTORNEY TRUST ACCOUNT OVERDRAFT REPORTING

The following rules and procedures, issued pursuant to the authority granted to the Indiana Supreme Court Disciplinary Commission by the Supreme Court of the State of Indiana in Admission and Discipline Rule 23, Sections 24 and 29(b), govern the administration of an attorney trust account overdraft reporting program in the State of Indiana.

Rule 1.   Definitions

As used herein:

A. "Financial institution" means a bank, savings and loan association, credit union, savings bank, and any other business or person that accepts for deposit funds held in trust by attorneys.

B. "Trust account" means any account maintained by an attorney admitted to practice law in the State of Indiana for the purpose of keeping funds belonging to clients or third parties separate from the attorney's own funds as required by Indiana Rule of Professional Conduct 1.15(a). It also means any account maintained by an attorney for funds held in trust in connection with a representation in any other fiduciary capacity, including as trustee, agent, guardian, executor, or otherwise.

C. "IOLTA (Interest on Lawyer Trust Account)" means an attorney trust account in a financial institution pursuant to Professional Conduct Rule 1.15(f).

D. "Properly payable" refers to an instrument which, if presented in the normal course of business, is in a form requiring payment under the laws of the State of Indiana.

Adopted Dec. 23, 1996, effective July 1, 1997. Amended June 20, 2005, effective July 1, 2005; amended effective June 13, 2006.

Rule 2.   Approval of Financial Institutions

A. Indiana Admission and Discipline Rule 23, Section 29(a)(1) requires that attorneys maintain trust accounts only in financial institutions that are approved by the Disciplinary Commission. A financial institution shall be approved by the Disciplinary Commission as a depository for trust accounts if it files with the Disciplinary Commission a written agreement, in the form attached hereto as Exhibit A, whereby it agrees to report to the Disciplinary Commission whenever it has actual notice that any properly payable instrument is presented against a trust account containing insufficient funds, irrespective of whether or not the instrument is honored.

B. The written agreement of any financial institution is binding upon all branches of the financial institution.

C. The Disciplinary Commission will maintain a public listing of all approved financial institutions and will publish it on its website. The names of approved financial institutions will also be available by written or telephone inquiry to the Disciplinary Commission.

D. The written agreement of any financial institution will continue in full force and effect and be binding upon the financial institution until such time as the financial institution gives thirty (30) days notice of cancellation in writing to the Disciplinary Commission, or until such time as its approval is revoked by the Disciplinary Commission.

Adopted Dec. 23, 1996, effective July 1, 1997; amended Sept. 20, 2011, effective Jan. 1, 2012.

Rule 3. Disapproval and Revocation of Approval of Financial Institutions

A. A financial institution shall not be approved in the first instance as a depository for trust accounts unless it submits to the Disciplinary Commission an agreement in the form attached hereto as **Exhibit A** that is binding upon all of its branches and signed by an officer with authority to act on behalf of the institution. The refusal of the Disciplinary Commission to approve a financial institution due to its failure or refusal to submit an executed written agreement in the form attached as **Exhibit A** is not appealable or otherwise subject to challenge.

B. The approval of a financial institution shall be revoked and the institution shall be removed by the Disciplinary Commission from the list of approved financial institutions if it engages in a pattern of neglect or acts in bad faith in not complying with its obligations under the written agreement.

C. The Executive Secretary shall communicate any decision to revoke the approval of a financial institution in writing by certified mail to the institution in care of the officer who signed the written agreement. The notice of revocation shall include a specific statement of facts setting forth the reasons in support of the revocation decision. Thereafter, the financial institution shall have a period of thirty (30) days from the date of receipt of the notice of revocation to file a written request with the Executive Secretary seeking reconsideration of the revocation decision. In the event an institution timely seeks reconsideration, the Disciplinary Commission shall appoint one of its members to act as hearing officer to take evidence. The Executive Secretary or designee shall act to defend the revocation decision. The hearing officer, after taking evidence, shall report findings and conclusions for review by the full Disciplinary Commission, whose decision in the matter shall be final. The approved status of a financial institution shall continue until such time as the reconsideration process is final.

D. Once the approval of a financial institution has been revoked, the institution shall not thereafter be approved as a depository for trust accounts until such time as the institution petitions the Disciplinary Commission for approval and includes within the petition a plan for curing any deficiencies that caused its earlier revocation and for periodically reporting compliance with the plan in the future.

Adopted Dec. 23, 1996, effective July 1, 1997.

Rule 4. Duty to Notify Financial Institutions of Trust Accounts

A. Every attorney shall notify each financial institution in which he or she maintains any trust account, as defined above, that the account is subject to the provisions of overdraft reporting. For each trust account, a lawyer or law firm shall maintain a copy of each such notice throughout the period of time that the account is open and for a period of five (5) years following closure of the account.

  1) For IOLTA accounts as required by Rule 1.15(f), notice by the attorney to the financial institution that the account is an IOLTA account shall constitute notice to the financial institution that the account is subject to overdraft reporting to the Disciplinary Commission.

  2) For non–IOLTA trust accounts as permitted by Rule 1.15(f)(1), every attorney shall notify each financial institution that the account is subject to overdraft reporting to the Disciplinary Commission by submitting a notice in the form attached as **Exhibit B** for each such account to the financial institution in which the account is maintained.

B. In the case of a law firm that maintains one or more trust accounts in the name of the firm, only one notice from a member of the firm need be provided for each such trust account. However, every member of the firm is responsible for insuring that notice of each firm trust account is given to each financial institution wherein an account is maintained.

Adopted Dec. 23, 1996, effective July 1, 1997. Amended June, 20, 2005, effective July 1, 2005; amended effective Dec. 5, 2006.

Rule 5. Duty of Financial Institutions

A. Each financial institution shall report to the Indiana Supreme Court Disciplinary Commission any properly payable attorney IOLTA or non–IOLTA trust account instrument presented against insufficient funds as set forth in Indiana Admission and Discipline Rule 23, Section 29(b) through (g) and these rules irrespective of whether the instrument is honored.

B. No financial institution shall be responsible for forwarding a report of any overdraft on an account about which it has not received notice pursuant to Rule 4(A)(1) or (2) above from the depositor attorney that it is a trust account subject to overdraft reporting.

Adopted June 20, 2005, effective July 1, 2005.

Rule 6. Processing of Overdraft Reports by the Commission

A. Whenever the Disciplinary Commission receives an overdraft notice from a financial institution, the Executive Secretary shall send a letter to the depositor attorney seeking a documented explanation of the overdraft within ten (10) business days. This letter is a demand for information, noncompliance with which is a violation of Professional Conduct Rule 8.1(b). If bank error is claimed by the attorney, a written statement from a bank officer must be submitted with the explanation. If office error is claimed by the attorney, affidavits from the appropriate office personnel must be submitted with the explanation.

B. If the depositor attorney does not provide a timely explanation or if the explanation provided does not document the existence of bank error or isolated office inadvertence, the Executive Secretary shall present the matter to the full Disciplinary Commission to consider the issuance of a grievance pursuant to Indiana Admission and Discipline Rule 23, Section 10(a). Thereafter, the procedures of Admission and Discipline Rule 23 for the processing of grievances shall apply.

Adopted as Rule 5, Dec. 23, 1996, effective July 1, 1997; renumbered as Rule 6, June 20, 2005, effective July 1, 2005.

Rule 7. Miscellaneous Matters

A. Any attorney who is admitted to practice law in another jurisdiction having attorney trust account overdraft notification rules that are substantially similar to the Indiana rules governing attorney trust account overdraft notification may apply to the Disciplinary Commission for exemption from compliance with these rules to the extent that the attorney maintains trust funds belonging to Indiana clients in a trust account in a foreign jurisdiction that is subject to overdraft reporting under the rules of that jurisdiction. Any such application for exemption shall be in writing and shall include:

   1) a copy of the rules from the other jurisdiction governing attorney trust account overdraft notification;

   2) a copy of the agreement between the applicable financial institution and the agency in the foreign jurisdiction that administers the overdraft notification program verifying that the financial institution participates in the foreign jurisdiction's attorney trust account notification program;

   3) a list of the names of all financial institutions, account names, and account numbers of all trust accounts maintained by the attorney in the foreign jurisdiction; and

   4) a certification under oath by the attorney that each such foreign trust account has been properly identified to the foreign financial institution as an attorney trust account subject to overdraft reporting.

Any attorney seeking exemption under the terms of this provision is under a continuing obligation to immediately report any changes in the information provided to the Disciplinary Commission.

B. Admission and Discipline Rule 23, Section 29(a)(6) contemplates that a designee who is not admitted to practice law in Indiana may be an authorized signatory on a trust account. In the event an attorney or law firm delegates trust account signature authority to any person who is not admitted to practice law in Indiana, such delegation shall be accompanied by specific safeguards, including at a minimum the following:.

   1. All periodic account activity statements from the financial institution shall be delivered unopened to and reviewed by an attorney having supervisory authority over the non-attorney signatory; and

   2. Responsibility for conducting periodic reconciliations between internal trust account records and periodic trust account activity statements from the financial institution shall be vested in a person who has no signature authority over the trust account.

C. All communications from financial institutions to the Disciplinary Commission shall be directed to: Executive Secretary, Indiana Supreme Court Disciplinary Commission, 30 South Meridian Street, Suite 850, Indianapolis, Indiana 46204.

Adopted as Rule 6, Dec. 23, 1996, effective July 1, 1997; amended Dec. 4, 1998, effective Jan. 1, 1999; amended and renumbered as Rule 7, June 20, 2005, effective July 1, 2005. Amended Sept. 10, 2007, effective Jan. 1, 2008.

Exhibit A.   Trust Account Overdraft Reporting Agreement

TRUST ACCOUNT OVERDRAFT REPORTING AGREEMENT

TO: INDIANA SUPREME COURT DISCIPLINARY COMMISSION
30 South Meridian Street
Suite 850
Indianapolis, Indiana 46204

The undersigned, being a duly authorized officer of _____ , a financial institution doing business in the State of Indiana, and the agent of the named financial institution specifically authorized to enter into this agreement, hereby applies to be approved to receive attorney trust accounts in the State of Indiana. In consideration of the Indiana Supreme Court Disciplinary Commission's approval of the named financial institution, the institution agrees to comply with the reporting requirements for such institution as set forth in Indiana Admission and Discipline Rule 23, § 29(b) through (g) and the Rules Governing Trust Account Overdraft Reporting promulgated by the Disciplinary Commission, as now in effect and as hereafter amended from time to time.

Specifically, the named financial institution agrees:

(1) To report to the Indiana Supreme Court Disciplinary Commission in the event it has actual notice that any properly payable attorney trust account instrument is presented against insufficient funds, irrespective of whether the instrument is honored. (This obligation applies to both IOLTA trust accounts under Indiana Professional Conduct Rule 1.15(f)(1) and non-IOLTA attorney trust accounts under Indiana Professional Conduct Rule 1.15(f)(1).)

(2) That all such reports shall be in substantially the following format:
    (a) in the case of a dishonored instrument, the report shall be identical to the overdraft notice customarily forwarded to the depositor and should include a copy of the dishonored instrument, if such a copy is normally provided to the depositor;
    (b) in the case of an instrument that is presented against insufficient funds but which instrument is honored, the report shall identify the financial institution, the depositor attorney or law firm, the account number, the date of presentation for payment, the date paid, and the amount of the overdraft created thereby.

(3) That all such reports shall be made within the following time periods:
    (a) in the case of a dishonored instrument, simultaneously with, and within the time provided by law for, notice of dishonor;
    (b) in the case of an instrument that is presented against insufficient funds but which instrument is honored, within five (5) banking days of the date of presentation for payment against insufficient funds.

(4) To provide the Disciplinary Commission with the name and contact information of the financial institution's primary point of contact for matters pertaining to its responsibilities under this agreement, and to promptly update that contact information in the event it changes.

This agreement shall apply to all branches of the named financial institution and shall not be canceled except upon thirty (30) days notice in writing to the Executive Secretary, Indiana Supreme Court Disciplinary Commission, 30 South Meridian Street, Suite 850, Indianapolis, Indiana 46204.

Name, Address, and Telephone Number of Contact Person for Financial Institution:

_____

_____

_____

DATE:_____   _____
                         Signature of Authorized Official

     CORPORATE
                         _____
        SEAL   Printed or Typed Name of Authorized Official

                         _____
                         Title or Position of Authorized Official

ACKNOWLEDGMENT

STATE OF _____)
) ss:
COUNTY OF _____)

On the _____ day of _____, 20___, before me, a Notary Public in and for the State of _____, personally appeared the above-named individual, known to me to be the person executing the foregoing instrument, and acknowledged and executed said instrument as his/her free and voluntary act and deed.

                         _____
                         Notary Public (signature)

                         _____
                         Notary Public (printed or typed)

My Commission Expires:_____   County of Residence:_____

ACCEPTANCE

The named financial institution is hereby approved by the Indiana Supreme Court Disciplinary Commission as a depository for trust accounts in the State of Indiana until such time as this agreement is canceled upon thirty (30) days' written notice to the Commission by the institution or is revoked by action of the Disciplinary Commission.

DATE: _____   _____
                         Executive Secretary
                         Indiana Supreme Court Disciplinary Commission

Adopted Dec. 23, 1996, effective July 1, 1997. Amended June 20, 2005, effective July 1, 2005; amended effective Dec. 5, 2006; amended Sept. 10, 2007, effective Jan. 1, 2008; amended effective Jan. 11, 2008.

Exhibit B. Attorney Trust Account Notification

Attorney Trust Account Notification

Name of Attorney   Attorney Number

Name of Law Firm

Business Address

City   State   Zip Code

Name of Financial Institution

Business Address

City   State   Zip Code

Name of Account

Account Number   _____ New _____ Existing

Type of Account:

_____ Trust   _____ Guardian

_____ Escrow   _____ Estate

_____ Other
                (Please Describe)

The undersigned hereby certifies that he/she is an attorney licensed to practice law in the State of Indiana and that the information indicated above provided to his/her financial institution is accurate. This information is provided to permit the financial institution to report all overdraft or insufficient funds occurrences to the Indiana Supreme Court Disciplinary Commission pursuant to Indiana Admission and Discipline Rule 23, Section 29.

Date:_____

                        Signature

Adopted Dec. 23, 1996, effective July 1, 1997. Amended effective April 20, 2005.

RULES OF PROFESSIONAL CONDUCT

Adopted Effective January 1, 1987

Including Amendments Received Through November 1, 2013

PREAMBLE: A LAWYER'S RESPONSIBILITIES

[1] A lawyer, as a member of the legal profession, is a representative of clients, an officer of the legal system and a public citizen having special responsibility for the quality of justice. Whether or not engaging in the practice of law, lawyers should conduct themselves honorably.

[2] As a representative of clients, a lawyer performs various functions. As advisor, a lawyer provides a client with an informed understanding of the client's legal rights and obligations and explains their practical implications. As advocate, a lawyer asserts the client's position under the rules of the adversary system. As negotiator, a lawyer seeks a result advantageous to the client but consistent with requirements of honest dealings with others. As intermediary between clients, a lawyer seeks to reconcile their divergent interests as an advisor and, to a limited extent, as a spokesperson for each client. As an evaluator, a lawyer acts by examining a client's legal affairs and reporting about them to the client or to others.

[3] In addition to these representational functions, a lawyer may serve as a third-party neutral, a nonrepresentational role helping the parties to resolve a dispute or other matter. Some on these Rules apply directly to lawyers who are or have served as third-party neutrals. See, e.g., Rules 1.12 and 2.4. In addition, there are Rules that apply to lawyers who are not active in the practice of law or to practicing lawyers even when they are acting in a nonprofessional capacity. For example, a lawyer who commits fraud in the conduct of a business is subject to discipline for engaging in conduct involving dishonesty, fraud, deceit, or misrepresentation. See Rule 8.4.

[4] In all professional functions a lawyer should be competent, prompt and diligent. A lawyer should maintain communication with a client concerning the representation. A lawyer should keep in confidence information relating to representation of a client except so far as disclosure is required or permitted by the Rules of Professional Conduct or other law.

[5] A lawyer's conduct should conform to the requirements of the law, both in professional service to clients and in the lawyer's business and personal affairs. A lawyer should use the law's procedures only for legitimate purposes and not to harass or intimidate others. A lawyer should demonstrate respect for the legal system and for those who serve it, including judges, other lawyers and public officials. While it is a lawyer's duty, when necessary, to challenge the rectitude of official action, it is also a lawyer's duty to uphold legal process.

[6] As a public citizen, a lawyer should seek improvement of the law, access to the legal system, the administration of justice and the quality of service rendered by the legal profession. As a member of a learned profession, a lawyer should cultivate knowledge of the law beyond its use for clients, employ that knowledge in reform of the law and work to strengthen legal education. In addition, a lawyer should further the public's understanding of and confidence in the rule of law and the justice system because legal institutions in a constitutional democracy depend on popular participation and support to maintain their authority. A lawyer should be mindful of deficiencies in the administration of justice and of the fact that the poor, and sometimes persons who are not poor, cannot afford adequate legal assistance. Therefore, all lawyers should devote professional time and resources and use civic influence to ensure equal access to our system of justice for all those who because of economic or social barriers cannot afford or secure adequate legal counsel. A lawyer should aid the legal profession in pursuing these objectives and should help the bar regulate itself in the public interest.

[7] Many of a lawyer's professional responsibilities are prescribed in the Rules of Professional Conduct, as well as substantive and procedural law. However, a lawyer is also guided by personal conscience and the approbation of professional peers. A lawyer should strive to attain the highest level of skill, to improve the law and the legal professional and to exemplify the legal profession's ideals of public service.

[8] A lawyer's responsibilities as a representative of clients, an officer of the legal system and a public citizen are usually harmonious. Thus, when an opposing party is well represented, a lawyer can be an effective advocate on behalf of a client and at the same time assume that justice is being done. So also, a lawyer can be sure that preserving client confidences ordinarily serves the public interest because people are more likely to seek legal advice, and thereby heed their legal obligations, when they know their communications will be private.

[9] In the nature of law practice, however, conflicting responsibilities are encountered. Virtually all difficult ethical problems arise from conflict between a lawyer's responsibilities to clients, to the legal system and to the lawyer's own interest in remaining an ethical person while earning a satisfactory living. The Rules of Professional Conduct often prescribe terms for resolving such conflicts. Within the framework of these Rules, however, many difficult issues of professional discretion can arise. Such issues must be resolved through the exercise of sensitive professional and moral judgment guided by the basic principles underlying the Rules. These principles include the lawyer's obligation to protect and pursue a client's legitimate interests, within the bounds of the law, while maintaining a professional, courteous and civil attitude toward all persons involved in the legal system.

[10] The legal profession is largely self-governing. Although other professions also have been granted powers of self-government, the legal profession is unique in this respect because of the close relationship between the profession and the processes of government and law enforcement. This connection is manifested in the fact that ultimate authority over the legal profession is vested largely in the courts.

[11] To the extent that lawyers meet the obligations of their professional calling, the occasion for government regulation is obviated. Self-regulation also helps maintain the legal profession's independence from government domination. An independent legal profession is an important force in preserving government under law, for abuse of legal authority is more readily challenged by a profession whose members are not dependent on government for the right to practice.

[12] The legal profession's relative autonomy carries with it special responsibilities of self-government. The profession has a responsibility to assure that its regulations are conceived in the public interest and not in furtherance of parochial or self-interested concerns of the bar. Every lawyer is responsible for observance of the Rules of Professional Conduct. A lawyer should also aid in securing their observance by other lawyers. Neglect of these responsibilities compromises the independence of the profession and the public interest which it serves.

[13] Lawyers play a vital role in the preservation of society. The fulfillment of this role requires an understanding by lawyers of their relationship to our legal system. The Rules of Professional Conduct, when properly applied, serve to define that relationship.

Adopted effective Jan. 1, 1987. Amended Sept. 30, 2004, effective Jan. 1, 2005.

Scope

[14] The Rules of Professional Conduct are rules of reason. They should be interpreted with reference to the purposes of legal representation and of the law itself. Some of the Rules are imperatives, cast in the terms "shall" or "shall not." These define proper conduct for purposes of professional discipline. Others, generally cast in the term "may," are permissive and define areas under the Rules in which the lawyer has discretion to exercise professional judgment. No disciplinary action should be taken when the lawyer chooses not to act or acts within the bounds of such discretion. Other Rules define the nature of relationships between the lawyer and others. The Rules are thus partly obligatory and disciplinary and partly constitutive and descriptive in that they define a lawyer's professional role. Many of the Comments use the term "should." Comments do not add obligations to the Rules but provide guidance for practicing in compliance with the Rules.

[15] The Rules presuppose a larger legal context shaping the lawyer's role. That context includes court rules and statutes relating to matters of licensure, laws defining specific obligations of lawyers and substantive and procedural law in general. The Comments are sometimes used to alert lawyers to their responsibilities under such other law.

[16] Compliance with the Rules, as with all law in an open society, depends primarily upon understanding and voluntary compliance, secondarily upon reinforcement by peer and public opinion and finally, when necessary, upon enforcement through disciplinary proceedings. The Rules do not, however, exhaust the moral and ethical considerations that should inform a lawyer, for no worthwhile human activity can be completely defined by legal rules. The Rules simply provide a framework for the ethical practice of law.

[17] Furthermore, for purposes of determining the lawyer's authority and responsibility, principles of substantive law external to these Rules determine whether a client-lawyer relationship exists. Most of the duties flowing from the client-lawyer relationship attach only after the client has requested the lawyer to render legal services and the lawyer has agreed to do so. But there are some duties, such as that of confidentiality under Rule 1.6, that attach when the lawyer agrees to consider whether a client-lawyer relationship shall be established. See Rule 1.18. Whether a client-lawyer relationship exists for any specific purpose can depend on the circumstances and may be a question of fact.

[18] Under various legal provisions, including constitutional, statutory and common law, the responsibilities of government lawyers may include authority concerning legal matters that ordinarily reposes in the client in private client-lawyer relationships. For example, a lawyer for a government agency may have authority on behalf of the government to decide upon settlement or whether to appeal from an adverse judgment. Such authority in various respects is generally vested in the attorney general and the state's attorney in state government, and their federal counterparts, and the same may be true of other government law officers. Also, lawyers under the supervision of these officers may be authorized to represent several government agencies in intragovernmental legal controversies in circumstances where a private lawyer could not represent multiple private clients. These Rules do not abrogate any such authority.

[19] Failure to comply with an obligation or prohibition imposed by a Rule is a basis for invoking the disciplinary process. The Rules presuppose that disciplinary assessment of a lawyer's conduct will be made on the basis of the facts and circumstances as they existed at the time of the conduct in question and in recognition of the fact that a lawyer often has to act upon uncertain or incomplete evidence of the situation. Moreover, the Rules presuppose that whether or not discipline should be imposed for a violation, and the severity of a sanction, depend on all the circum-

stances, such as the willfulness and seriousness of the violation, extenuating factors and whether there have been previous violations.

[20] Violation of a Rule should not itself give rise to a cause of action against a lawyer, nor should it create any presumption in such a case that a legal duty has been breached. In addition, violation of a Rule does not necessarily warrant any other nondisciplinary remedy, such as disqualification of a lawyer in pending litigation. The Rules are designed to provide guidance to lawyers and to provide a structure for regulating conduct through disciplinary agencies. They are not designed to be a basis for civil liability, but these Rules may be used as non-conclusive evidence that a lawyer has breached a duty owed to a client. Furthermore, the purpose of the Rules can be subverted when they are invoked by opposing parties as procedural weapons. The fact that a rule is a just basis for a lawyer's self-assessment, or for sanctioning a lawyer under the administration of a disciplinary authority, does not imply that an antagonist in a collateral proceeding or transaction has standing to seek enforcement of the Rule. Nevertheless, since the Rules do establish standards of conduct by lawyers, a lawyer's violation of a Rule may be evidence of breach of the applicable standard of conduct.

[21] The Comment accompanying each Rule explains and illustrates the meaning and purpose of the Rule. The Preamble and this note on Scope provide general orientation. The Comments are intended as guides to interpretation, but the text of each Rule is authoritative.

Adopted effective Jan. 1, 1987; amended Sept. 30, 2004, effective Jan. 1, 2005.

Rule 1.0. Terminology

(a) "Belief" or "believes" denotes that the person involved actually supposed the fact in question to be true. A person's belief may be inferred from circumstances.

(b) "Confirmed in writing," when used in reference to the informed consent of a person, denotes informed consent that is given in writing by the person or a writing that a lawyer promptly transmits to the person confirming an oral informed consent. See paragraph (n) for the definition of "writing." See paragraph (e) for the definition of "informed consent." If it is not feasible to obtain or transmit the writing at the time the person gives informed consent, then the lawyer must obtain or transmit it within a reasonable time thereafter.

(c) "Firm" or "law firm" denotes a lawyer or lawyers in a law partnership, professional corporation, sole proprietorship or other association authorized to practice law; or lawyers employed in a legal services organization or the legal department of a corporation or other organization.

(d) "Fraud" or "fraudulent" denotes conduct that is fraudulent under the substantive or procedural law of the applicable jurisdiction and has a purpose to deceive.

(e) "Informed consent" denotes the agreement by a person to a proposed course of conduct after the lawyer has communicated adequate information and explanation about the material risks of and reasonably available alternatives to the proposed course of conduct.

(f) "Knowingly," "known," or "knows" denotes actual knowledge of the fact in question. A person's knowledge may be inferred from circumstances.

(g) "Partner" denotes a member of a partnership, a shareholder in a law firm organized as a professional corporation, or a member of an association authorized to practice law.

(h) "Reasonable" or "reasonably" when used in relation to conduct by a lawyer denotes the conduct of a reasonably prudent and competent lawyer.

(i) "Reasonable belief" or "reasonably believes" when used in reference to a lawyer denotes that the lawyer believes the matter in question and that the circumstances are such that the belief is reasonable.

(j) "Reasonably should know" when used in reference to a lawyer denotes that a lawyer of reasonable prudence and competence would ascertain the matter in question.

(k) "Screened" denotes the isolation of a lawyer from any participation in a matter through the timely imposition of procedures within a firm that are reasonably adequate under the circumstances to protect information that the isolated lawyer is obligated to protect under these Rules or other law.

(*l*) "Substantial" when used in reference to degree or extent denotes a material matter of clear and weighty importance.

(m) "Tribunal" denotes a court, an arbitrator, or any other neutral body or neutral individual making a decision, based on evidence presented and the law applicable to that evidence, which decision is binding on the parties involved.

(n) "Writing" or "written" denotes a tangible or electronic record of a communication or representation, including handwriting, typewriting, printing, photostatting, photography, audio or videorecording or e-mail. A "signed" writing includes an electronic sound, symbol or process attached to or logically associated with a writing and executed or adopted by a person with the intent to sign the writing.

Adopted effective Jan. 1, 1987. Amended Sept. 30, 2004, effective Jan. 1, 2005.

Comment

Confirmed in Writing

[1] If it is not feasible to obtain or transmit a written confirmation at the time the client gives informed consent, then the lawyer must obtain or transmit it within a reasonable time thereafter. If a lawyer has obtained a client's informed consent, the lawyer may act in reliance on that consent so long as it is confirmed in writing within a reasonable time thereafter.

Firm

[2] Whether two or more lawyers constitute a firm within paragraph (c) can depend on the specific facts. For example, two practitioners who share office space and occasionally consult or assist each other ordinarily would not be regarded as constituting a firm. However, if they present themselves to the public in a way that suggests that they are a firm or conduct themselves as a firm, they should be regarded as a firm for purposes of the Rules. The terms of any formal agreement between associated lawyers are relevant in determining whether they are a firm, as is the fact that they have mutual access to information concerning the clients they serve. Furthermore, it is relevant in doubtful cases to consider the underlying purpose of the Rule that is involved. A group of lawyers could be regarded as a firm for purposes of the Rule that the same lawyer should not represent opposing parties in litigation, while it might not be so regarded for purposes of the Rule that information acquired by one lawyer is attributed to another.

[3] With respect to the law department of an organization, including the government, there is ordinarily no question that the members of the department constitute a firm within the meaning of the Rules of Professional Conduct. There can be uncertainty, however, as to the identity of the client. For example, it may not be clear whether the law department of a corporation represents a subsidiary or an affiliated corporation, as well as the corporation by which the members of the department are directly employed. A similar question can arise concerning an unincorporated association and its local affiliates.

[4] Similar questions can also arise with respect to lawyers in legal aid and legal services organizations. Depending upon the structure of the organization, the entire organization or different components of it may constitute a firm or firms for purposes of these Rules.

Fraud

[5] When used in these Rules, the terms "fraud" or "fraudulent" refer to conduct that is characterized as such under the substantive or procedural law of the applicable jurisdiction and has a purpose to deceive. This does not include merely negligent misrepresentation or negligent failure to apprise another of relevant information. For purposes of these Rules, it is not necessary that anyone has suffered damages or relied on the misrepresentation or failure to inform.

Informed Consent

[6] Many of the Rules of Professional Conduct require the lawyer to obtain the informed consent of a client or other person (e.g., a former client or, under certain circumstances, a prospective client) before accepting or continuing representation or pursuing a course of conduct. See, e.g., Rules 1.2(c), 1.6(a) and 1.7(b). The communication necessary to obtain such consent will vary according to the Rule involved and the circumstances giving rise to the need to obtain informed consent. The lawyer must make reasonable efforts to ensure that the client or other person possesses information reasonably adequate to make an informed decision. Ordinarily, this will require communication that includes a disclosure of the facts and circumstances giving rise to the situation, any explanation reasonably necessary to inform the client or other person of the material advantages and disadvantages of the proposed course of conduct and a discussion of the client's or other person's options and alternatives. In some circumstances it may be appropriate for a lawyer to advise a client or other person to seek the advice of other counsel. A lawyer need not inform a client or other person of facts or implications already known to the client or other person; nevertheless, a lawyer who does not personally inform the client or other person assumes the risk that the client or other person is inadequately informed and the consent is invalid. In determining whether the information and explanation provided are reasonably adequate, relevant factors include whether the client or other person is experienced in legal matters generally and in making decisions of the type involved, and whether the client or other person is independently represented by other counsel in giving the consent. Normally, such persons need less information and explanation than others, and generally a client or other person who is independently represented by other counsel in giving the consent should be assumed to have given informed consent.

[7] Obtaining informed consent will usually require an affirmative response by the client or other person. In general, a lawyer may not assume consent from a client's or other person's silence. Consent may be inferred, however, from the conduct of a client or other person who has reasonably adequate information about the matter. A number of Rules require that a person's consent be confirmed in writing. See Rules 1.7(b) and 1.9(a). For a definition of "writing" and "confirmed in writing," see paragraphs (n) and (b). Other Rules require that a client's consent be obtained in a writing signed by the client. See, e.g., Rules 1.8(a) and (g). For a definition of "signed," see paragraph (n).

Screened

[8] This definition applies to situations where screening of a personally disqualified lawyer is permitted to remove imputation of a conflict of interest under Rules 1.10, 1.11, 1.12 or 1.18.

[9] The purpose of screening is to assure the affected parties that confidential information known by the personally disqualified lawyer remains protected. The personally disqualified lawyer should acknowledge the obligation not to communicate with any of the other lawyers in the firm with respect to

the matter. Similarly, other lawyers in the firm who are working on the matter should be informed that the screening is in place and that they may not communicate with the personally disqualified lawyer with respect to the matter. Additional screening measures that are appropriate for the particular matter will depend on the circumstances. To implement, reinforce and remind all affected lawyers of the presence of the screening, it may be appropriate for the firm to undertake such procedures as a written undertaking by the screened lawyer to avoid any communication with other firm personnel and

any contact with any firm files or other materials relating to the matter, written notice and instructions to all other firm personnel forbidding any communication with the screened lawyer relating to the matter, denial of access by the screened lawyer to firm files or other materials relating to the matter and periodic reminders of the screen to the screened lawyer and all other firm personnel.

[10] In order to be effective, screening measures must be implemented as soon as practical after a lawyer or law firm knows or reasonably should know that there is a need for screening.

CLIENT–LAWYER RELATIONSHIP

Rule 1.1. Competence

A lawyer shall provide competent representation to a client. Competent representation requires the legal knowledge, skill, thoroughness and preparation reasonably necessary for the representation.

Adopted effective Jan. 1, 1987.

Comment
Legal Knowledge and Skill

[1] In determining whether a lawyer employs the requisite knowledge and skill in a particular matter, relevant factors include the relative complexity and specialized nature of the matter, the lawyer's general experience, the lawyer's training and experience in the field in question, the preparation and study the lawyer is able to give the matter and whether it is feasible to refer the matter to, or associate or consult with, a lawyer of established competence in the field in question. In many instances, the required proficiency is that of a general practitioner. Expertise in a particular field of law may be required in some circumstances.

[2] A lawyer need not necessarily have special training or prior experience to handle legal problems of a type with which the lawyer is unfamiliar. A newly admitted lawyer can be as competent as a practitioner with long experience. Some important legal skills, such as the analysis of precedent, the evaluation of evidence and legal drafting, are required in all legal problems. Perhaps the most fundamental legal skill consists of determining what kind of legal problems a situation may involve, a skill that necessarily transcends any particular specialized knowledge. A lawyer can provide adequate representation in a wholly novel field through necessary study. Competent representation can also be provided through the association of a lawyer of established competence in the field in question.

[3] In an emergency a lawyer may give advice or assistance in a matter in which the lawyer does not have the skill ordinarily required where referral to or consultation or association with another lawyer would be impractical. Even in an emergency, however, assistance should be limited to that reasonably necessary in the circumstances, for ill-considered action under emergency conditions can jeopardize the client's interest.

[4] A lawyer may accept representation where the requisite level of competence can be achieved by reasonable preparation. This applies as well to a lawyer who is appointed as counsel for an unrepresented person. See also Rule 6.2.

Thoroughness and Preparation

[5] Competent handling of a particular matter includes inquiry into and analysis of the factual and legal elements of the problem, and use of methods and procedures meeting the standards of competent practitioners. It also includes adequate preparation. The required attention and preparation are determined in part by what is at stake; major litigation and complex transactions ordinarily require more extensive treatment than matters of lesser complexity and consequence. An agreement between the lawyer and the client regarding the scope of the representation may limit the matters for which the lawyer is responsible. See Rule 1.2(c).

Maintaining Competence

[6] To maintain the requisite knowledge and skill, a lawyer should keep abreast of changes in the law and its practice, engage in continuing study and education and comply with all continuing legal education requirements to which the lawyer is subject.

Rule 1.2. Scope of Representation and Allocation of Authority Between Client and Lawyer

(a) Subject to paragraphs (c) and (d), a lawyer shall abide by a client's decisions concerning the objectives of representation and, as required by Rule 1.4, shall consult with the client as to the means by which they are to be pursued. A lawyer may take such action on behalf of the client as is impliedly authorized to carry out the representation. A lawyer shall abide by a client's decision whether to settle a matter. In a criminal case, the lawyer shall abide by the client's decision, after consultation with the lawyer, as to a plea to be entered, whether to waive jury trial and whether the client will testify.

(b) A lawyer's representation of a client, including representation by appointment, does not constitute an endorsement of the client's political, economic, social or moral views or activities.

(c) A lawyer may limit the scope and objectives of the representation if the limitation is reasonable under the circumstances and the client gives informed consent.

(d) A lawyer shall not counsel a client to engage, or assist a client, in conduct that the lawyer knows is criminal or fraudulent, but a lawyer may discuss the legal consequences of any proposed course of conduct with a client and may counsel or assist a client to make a good faith effort to determine the validity, scope, meaning or application of the law.

Adopted effective Jan. 1, 1987; amended Sept. 30, 2004, effective Jan. 1, 2005.

Comment
Allocation of Authority between Client and Lawyer

[1] Paragraph (a) confers upon the client the ultimate authority to determine the purposes to be served by legal representation, within the limits imposed by law and the lawyer's professional obligations. The decisions specified in paragraph (a), such as whether to settle a civil matter, must also be made by the client. See Rule 1.4(a)(1) for the lawyer's duty to communicate with the client about such decisions. With respect to the means by which the client's objectives are to be pursued, the lawyer shall consult with the client as required by Rule 1.4(a)(2) and may take such action as is impliedly authorized to carry out the representation.

[2] On occasion, however, a lawyer and a client may disagree about the means to be used to accomplish the client's objectives. Clients normally defer to the special knowledge and skill of their lawyer with respect to the means to be used to accomplish their objectives, particularly with respect to technical, legal and tactical matters. Conversely, lawyers usually defer to the client regarding such questions as the expense to be incurred and concerns for third persons who might be adversely affected. Because of the varied nature of the matters about which a lawyer and client might disagree and because the actions in question may implicate the interests of a tribunal or other persons, this Rule does not prescribe how such disagreements are to be resolved. Other law, however, may be applicable and should be consulted by the lawyer. The lawyer should also consult with the client and seek a mutually acceptable resolution of the disagreement. If such efforts are unavailing and the lawyer has a fundamental disagreement with the client, the lawyer may withdraw from the representation. See Rule 1.16(b)(4). Conversely, the client may resolve the disagreement by discharging the lawyer. See Rule 1.16(a)(3).

[3] At the outset of a representation, the client may authorize the lawyer to take specific action on the client's behalf without further consultation. Absent a material change in circumstances and subject to Rule 1.4, a lawyer may rely on such an advance authorization. The client may, however, revoke such authority at any time.

[4] In a case in which the client appears to be suffering diminished capacity, the lawyer's duty to abide by the client's decisions is to be guided by reference to Rule 1.14.

Independence from Client's Views or Activities

[5] Legal representation should not be denied to people who are unable to afford legal services or whose cause is controversial or the subject of popular disapproval. By the same token, representing a client does not constitute approval of the client's views or activities.

Agreements Limiting Scope of Representation

[6] The scope of services to be provided by a lawyer may be limited by agreement with the client or by the terms under which the lawyer's services are made available to the client. When a lawyer has been retained by an insurer to represent an insured, for example, the representation may be limited to matters related to the insurance coverage. A limited representation may be appropriate because the client has limited objectives for the representation. In addition, the terms upon which representation is undertaken may exclude specific means that might otherwise be used to accomplish the client's objectives. Such limitations may exclude actions that the client thinks are too costly or that the lawyer regards as repugnant, unethical, or imprudent.

[7] Although this Rule affords the lawyer and client substantial latitude to limit the representation, the limitation must be reasonable under the circumstances. If, for example, a client's objective is limited to securing general information about the law the client needs in order to handle a common and typically uncomplicated legal problem, the lawyer and client may agree that the lawyer's services will be limited to a brief telephone consultation. Such a limitation, however, would not be reasonable if the time allotted was not sufficient to yield advice upon which the client could rely. Although an agreement for a limited representation does not exempt a lawyer from the duty to provide competent representation, the limitation is a factor to be considered when determining the legal knowledge, skill, thoroughness and preparation reasonably necessary for the representation. See Rule 1.1.

[8] All agreements concerning a lawyer's representation of a client must accord with the Rules of Professional Conduct and other law. See, e.g., Rules 1.1, 1.8 and 5.6.

Criminal, Fraudulent and Prohibited Transactions

[9] Paragraph (d) prohibits a lawyer from knowingly counseling or assisting a client to commit a crime or fraud. This prohibition, however, does not preclude the lawyer from giving an honest opinion about the actual consequences that appear likely to result from a client's conduct. Nor does the fact that a client uses advice in a course of action that is criminal or fraudulent of itself make a lawyer a party to the course of action. There is a critical distinction between presenting an analysis of legal aspects of questionable conduct and recommending the means by which a crime or fraud might be committed with impunity.

[10] When the client's course of action has already begun and is continuing, the lawyer's responsibility is especially delicate. The lawyer is required to avoid assisting the client, for example, by drafting or delivering documents that the lawyer knows are fraudulent or by suggesting how the wrongdoing might be concealed. A lawyer may not continue assisting a client in conduct that the lawyer originally supposed was legally proper but then discovers is criminal or fraudulent. The lawyer must, therefore, withdraw from the representation of the client in the matter. See Rule 1.16(a). In some cases, withdrawal alone might be insufficient. It may be necessary for the lawyer to give notice of the fact of withdrawal and to disaffirm any opinion, document, affirmation or the like. See Rule 4.1.

[11] Where the client is a fiduciary, the lawyer may be charged with special obligations in dealings with a beneficiary.

[12] Paragraph (d) applies whether or not the defrauded party is a party to the transaction. Hence, a lawyer must not participate in a transaction to effectuate criminal or fraudulent avoidance of tax liability. Paragraph (d) does not preclude undertaking a criminal defense incident to a general retainer for legal services to a lawful enterprise. The last clause of paragraph (d) recognizes that determining the validity or interpretation of a statute or regulation may require a course of action involving disobedience of the statute or regulation or of the interpretation placed upon it by governmental authorities.

[13] If a lawyer comes to know or reasonably should know that a client expects assistance not permitted by the Rules of Professional Conduct or other law or if the lawyer intends to act contrary to the client's instructions, the lawyer must consult with the client regarding the limitations on the lawyer's conduct. See Rule 1.4(a)(5).

Rule 1.3. Diligence

A lawyer shall act with reasonable diligence and promptness in representing a client.

Adopted effective Jan. 1, 1987.

Comment

[1] A lawyer should pursue a matter on behalf of a client despite opposition, obstruction or personal inconvenience to the lawyer, and may take whatever lawful and ethical measures are required to vindicate a client's cause or endeavor. A lawyer must also act with commitment and dedication to the interests of the client. A lawyer is not bound, however, to press for every advantage that might be realized for a client. For example, a lawyer may have authority to exercise professional discretion in determining the means by which a matter should be pursued. See Rule 1.2. The lawyer's duty to act with reasonable diligence does not require the use of offensive tactics or preclude the treating of all persons involved in the legal process with courtesy and respect.

[2] A lawyer's workload must be controlled so that each matter can be handled competently.

[3] Perhaps no professional shortcoming is more widely resented than procrastination. A client's interests often can be adversely affected by the passage of time or the change of conditions; in extreme instances, as when a lawyer overlooks a statute of limitations, the client's legal position may be destroyed. Even when the client's interests are not affected in substance, however, unreasonable delay can cause a client needless anxiety and undermine confidence in the lawyer's trustworthiness. A lawyer's duty to act with reasonable promptness, however, does not preclude the lawyer from agreeing to a reasonable request for a postponement that will not prejudice the lawyer's client.

[4] Unless the relationship is terminated as provided in Rule 1.16, a lawyer should carry through to conclusion all matters undertaken for a client. If a lawyer's employment is limited to a specific matter, the relationship terminates when the matter has been resolved. If a lawyer has served a client over a substantial period in a variety of matters, the client sometimes may assume that the lawyer will continue to serve on a continuing basis unless the lawyer gives notice of withdrawal. Doubt about whether a client-lawyer relationship still exists should be clarified by the lawyer, preferably in writing, so that the client will not mistakenly suppose the lawyer is looking after the client's affairs when the lawyer has ceased to do so. For example, if a lawyer has handled a judicial or administrative proceeding that produced a result adverse to the client and the lawyer and the client have not agreed that the lawyer will handle the matter on appeal, the lawyer must consult with the client about the possibility of appeal before relinquishing responsibility for the matter. See Rule 1.4(a)(2). Whether the lawyer is obligated to prosecute the appeal for the client depends on the scope of the representation the lawyer has agreed to provide to the client. See Rule 1.2.

[5] To prevent neglect of client matters in the event of a sole practitioner's death or disability, the duty of diligence may require that each sole practitioner prepare a plan, in conformity with applicable rules, that designates another competent lawyer to review client files, notify each client of the lawyer's death or disability, and determine whether there is a need for immediate protective action. Cf. Ind. Admission and Discipline Rule 23, Section 27 (providing for court appointment of a lawyer to inventory files and take other protective action in absence of a plan providing for another lawyer to protect the interests of the clients of a deceased or disabled lawyer).

Rule 1.4. Communication

(a) A lawyer shall:

(1) promptly inform the client of any decision or circumstance with respect to which the client's informed consent, as defined in Rule 1.0(e), is required by these Rules;

(2) reasonably consult with the client about the means by which the client's objectives are to be accomplished;

(3) keep the client reasonably informed about the status of the matter;

(4) promptly comply with reasonable requests for information; and

(5) consult with the client about any relevant limitation on the lawyer's conduct when the lawyer knows that the client expects assistance not permitted by the Rules of Professional Conduct or other law or assistance limited under Rule 1.2(c).

(b) A lawyer shall explain a matter to the extent reasonably necessary to permit the client to make informed decisions regarding the representation.

Adopted effective Jan. 1, 1987. Amended Sept. 30, 2004, effective Jan. 1, 2005.

Comment

[1] Reasonable communication between the lawyer and the client is necessary for the client effectively to participate in the representation.

Communicating with Client

[2] If these Rules require that a particular decision about the representation be made by the client, paragraph (a)(1) requires that the lawyer promptly consult with and secure the client's consent prior to taking action unless prior discussions with the client have resolved what action the client wants the lawyer to take. For example, a lawyer who receives from opposing counsel an offer of settlement in a civil controversy or a proffered plea bargain in a criminal case must promptly inform the client of its substance unless the client has previously indicated that the proposal will be acceptable or unacceptable or has authorized the lawyer to accept or to reject the offer. See Rule 1.2(a).

[3] Paragraph (a)(2) requires the lawyer to reasonably consult with the client about the means to be used to accomplish the client's objectives. In some situations — depending on both the importance of the action under consideration and the feasibility of consulting with the client — this duty will require consultation prior to taking action. In other circumstances, such as during a trial when an immediate decision must be made, the exigency of the situation may require the lawyer to act without prior consultation. In such cases the lawyer must nonetheless act reasonably to inform the client of actions the lawyer has taken on the client's behalf. Additionally, paragraph (a)(3) requires that the lawyer keep the client reasonably informed about the status of the matter, such as significant developments affecting the timing or the substance of the representation.

[4] A lawyer's regular communication with clients will minimize the occasions on which a client will need to request information concerning the representation. When a client makes a reasonable request for information, however, paragraph (a)(4) requires prompt compliance with the request, or if a prompt response is not feasible, that the lawyer, or a member of the lawyer's staff, acknowledge receipt of the request and advise the client when a response may be expected. Client telephone calls should be promptly returned or acknowledged.

Explaining Matters

[5] The client should have sufficient information to participate intelligently in decisions concerning the objectives of the representation and the means by which they are to be pursued, to the extent the client is willing and able to do so. Adequacy of communication depends in part on the kind of advice or assistance that is involved. For example, when there is time to explain a proposal made in a negotiation, the lawyer should review all important provisions with the client before proceeding to an agreement. In litigation a lawyer should explain the general strategy and prospects of success and ordinarily should consult the client on tactics that are likely to result in significant expense or to injure or coerce others. On the other hand, a lawyer ordinarily will not be expected to describe trial or negotiation strategy in detail. The guiding principle is that the lawyer should fulfill reasonable client expectations for information consistent with the duty to act in the client's best interests and the client's overall requirements as to the character of representation. In certain circumstances, such as when a lawyer asks a client to consent to a representation affected by a conflict of interest, the client must give informed consent, as defined in Rule 1.0(e).

[6] Ordinarily, the information to be provided is that appropriate for a client who is a comprehending and responsible adult. However, fully informing the client according to this standard may be impracticable, for example, where the client is a child or suffers from diminished capacity. See Rule 1.14. When the client is an organization or group, it is often impossible or inappropriate to inform everyone of its members about its legal affairs; ordinarily, the lawyer should address communications to the appropriate officials of the organization. See Rule 1.13. Where many routine matters are involved, a system of limited or occasional reporting may be arranged with the client.

Withholding Information

[7] In some circumstances, a lawyer may be justified in delaying transmission of information when the client would be likely to react imprudently to an immediate communication. Thus, a lawyer might withhold a psychiatric diagnosis of a client when the examining psychiatrist indicates that disclosure would harm the client. A lawyer may not withhold information to serve the lawyer's own interest or convenience or the interests or convenience of another person. Rules or court orders governing litigation may provide that information supplied to a lawyer may not be disclosed to the client. Rule 3.4(c) directs compliance with such rules or orders.

Rule 1.5. Fees

(a) A lawyer shall not make an agreement for, charge, or collect an unreasonable fee or an unreasonable amount for expenses. The factors to be considered in determining the reasonableness of a fee include the following:

(1) the time and labor required, the novelty and difficulty of the questions involved, and the skill requisite to perform the legal service properly;

(2) the likelihood, if apparent to the client, that the acceptance of the particular employment will preclude other employment by the lawyer;

(3) the fee customarily charged in the locality for similar legal services;

(4) the amount involved and the results obtained;

(5) the time limitations imposed by the client or by the circumstances;

(6) the nature and length of the professional relationship with the client;

(7) the experience, reputation, and ability of the lawyer or lawyers performing the services; and

(8) whether the fee is fixed or contingent.

(b) The scope of the representation and the basis or rate of the fee and expenses for which the client will be responsible shall be communicated to the client, preferably in writing, before or within a reasonable time after commencing the representation, except when the lawyer will charge a regularly represented client on the same basis or rate. Any changes in the basis or rate of the fee or expenses shall also be communicated to the client.

(c) A fee may be contingent on the outcome of the matter for which the service is rendered, except in a matter in which a contingent fee is prohibited by paragraph (d) or other law. A contingent fee agreement shall be in a writing signed by the client and shall state the method by which the fee is to be determined, including the percentage or percentages that shall accrue to the lawyer in the event of settlement, trial or appeal; litigation and other expenses to be deducted from the recovery; and whether such expenses are to be deducted before or after the contingent fee is calculated. The agreement must clearly notify the client of any expenses for which the client will be liable whether or not the client is the prevailing party. Upon conclusion of a contingent fee matter, the lawyer shall provide the client with a written statement stating the outcome of the matter and, if there is a recovery, showing the remittance to the client and the method of its determination.

(d) A lawyer shall not enter into an arrangement for, charge, or collect:

(1) any fee in a domestic relations matter, the payment or amount of which is contingent upon the securing of a dissolution or upon the amount of maintenance, support, or property settlement, or obtaining custody of a child; or

(2) a contingent fee for representing a defendant in a criminal case.

This provision does not preclude a contract for a contingent fee for legal representation in a domestic relations post-judgment collection action, provided the attorney clearly advises his or her client in writing of the alternative measures available for the collection of such debt and, in all other particulars, complies with *Prof.Cond.R.* 1.5(c).

(e) A division of a fee between lawyers who are not in the same firm may be made only if:

(1) the division is in proportion to the services performed by each lawyer or each lawyer assumes joint responsibility for the representation;

(2) the client agrees to the arrangement, including the share each lawyer will receive, and the agreement is confirmed in writing; and

(3) the total fee is reasonable.

Adopted effective Jan. 1, 1987; amended Dec. 5, 1994, effective Feb. 1, 1995; amended Sept. 30, 2004, effective Jan. 1, 2005.

Comment

Reasonableness of Fee and Expenses

[1] Paragraph (a) requires that lawyers charge fees that are reasonable under the circumstances. The factors specified in (1) through (8) are not exclusive. Nor will each factor be relevant in each instance. Paragraph (a) also requires that expenses for which the client will be charged must be reasonable. A lawyer may seek reimbursement for the cost of services performed in-house, such as copying, or for other expenses incurred in-house, such as telephone charges, either by charging a reasonable amount to which the client has agreed in advance or by charging an amount that reasonably reflects the cost incurred by the lawyer.

Basis or Rate of Fee

[2] When the lawyer has regularly represented a client, they ordinarily will have evolved an understanding concerning the basis or rate of the fee and the expenses for which the client will be responsible. In a new client-lawyer relationship, however, an understanding as to fees and expenses must be promptly established. Generally, it is desirable to furnish the client with at least a simple memorandum or copy of the lawyer's customary fee arrangements that states the general nature of the legal services to be provided, the basis, rate or total amount of the fee and whether and to what extent the client will be responsible for any costs, expenses or disbursements in the course of the representation. A written statement concerning the terms of the engagement reduces the possibility of misunderstanding.

[3] Contingent fees, like any other fees, are subject to the reasonableness standard of paragraph (a) of this Rule. In determining whether a particular contingent fee is reasonable, or whether it is reasonable to charge any form of contingent fee, a lawyer must consider the factors that are relevant under the circumstances. Applicable law may impose limitations on contingent fees, such as a ceiling on the

percentage allowable, or may require a lawyer to offer clients an alternative basis for the fee. Applicable law also may apply to situations other than a contingent fee, for example, government regulations regarding fees in certain tax matters.

Terms of Payment

[4] A lawyer may require advance payment of a fee, but is obliged to return any unearned portion. See Rule 1.16(d). A lawyer may accept property in payment for services, such as an ownership interest in an enterprise, providing this does not involve acquisition of a proprietary interest in the cause of action or subject matter of the litigation contrary to Rule 1.8(i). However, a fee paid in property instead of money may be subject to the requirements of Rule 1.8(a) because such fees often have the essential qualities of a business transaction with the client.

[5] An agreement may not be made whose terms might induce the lawyer improperly to curtail services for the client or perform them in a way contrary to the client's interest. For example, a lawyer should not enter into an agreement whereby services are to be provided only up to a stated amount when it is foreseeable that more extensive services probably will be required, unless the situation is adequately explained to the client. Otherwise, the client might have to bargain for further assistance in the midst of a proceeding or transaction. However, it is proper to define the extent of services in light of the client's ability to pay. A lawyer should not exploit a fee arrangement based primarily on hourly charges by using wasteful procedures.

Prohibited Contingent Fees

[6] Paragraph (d) prohibits a lawyer from charging a contingent fee in a domestic relations matter when payment is contingent upon the securing of a dissolution or obtaining custody of a child or upon the amount of maintenance or support or property settlement to be obtained.

Division of Fee

[7] A division of fee is a single billing to a client covering the fee of two or more lawyers who are not in the same firm. A division of fee facilitates association of more than one lawyer in a matter in which neither alone could serve the client as well, and most often is used when the fee is contingent and the division is between a referring lawyer and a trial specialist. Paragraph (e) permits the lawyers to divide a fee either on the basis of the proportion of services they render or if each lawyer assumes responsibility for the representation as a whole. In addition, the client must agree to the arrangement, including the share that each lawyer is to receive, and the agreement must be confirmed in writing. Contingent fee agreements must be in a writing signed by the client and must otherwise comply with paragraph (c) of this Rule. Joint responsibility for the representation entails financial and ethical responsibility for the representation as if the lawyers were associated in a partnership. A lawyer

should only refer a matter to a lawyer whom the referring lawyer reasonably believes is competent to handle the matter. See Rule 1.1.

[8] Paragraph (e) does not prohibit or regulate division of fees to be received in the future for work done when lawyers were previously associated in a law firm.

Disputes over Fees

[9] If a procedure has been established for resolution of fee disputes, such as an arbitration or mediation procedure established by the bar, the lawyer must comply with the procedure when it is mandatory, and, even when it is voluntary, the lawyer should conscientiously consider submitting to it. Law may prescribe a procedure for determining a lawyer's fee, for example, in representation of an executor or administrator, a class or a person entitled to a reasonable fee as part of the measure of damages. The lawyer entitled to such a fee and a lawyer representing another party concerned with the fee should comply with the prescribed procedure.

Rule 1.6. Confidentiality of Information

(a) A lawyer shall not reveal information relating to representation of a client unless the client gives informed consent, the disclosure is impliedly authorized in order to carry out the representation or the disclosure is permitted by paragraph (b).

(b) A lawyer may reveal information relating to the representation of a client to the extent the lawyer reasonably believes necessary:

(1) to prevent reasonably certain death or substantial bodily harm;

(2) to prevent the client from committing a crime or from committing fraud that is reasonably certain to result in substantial injury to the financial interests or property of another and in furtherance of which the client has used or is using the lawyer's services;

(3) to prevent, mitigate or rectify substantial injury to the financial interests or property of another that is reasonably certain to result or has resulted from the client's commission of a crime or fraud in furtherance of which the client has used the lawyer's services;

(4) to secure legal advice about the lawyer's compliance with these Rules;

(5) to establish a claim or defense on behalf of the lawyer in a controversy between the lawyer and the client, to establish a defense to a criminal charge or civil claim against the lawyer based upon conduct in which the client was involved, or to respond to allegations in any proceeding concerning the lawyer's representation of the client; or

(6) to comply with other law or a court order.

(c) In the event of a lawyer's physical or mental disability or the appointment of a guardian or conservator of an attorney's client files, disclosure of a client's names and files is authorized to the extent necessary to carry out the duties of the person managing the lawyer's files.

Adopted effective Jan. 1, 1987. Amended Oct. 30. 1992, effective Jan. 1, 1993; Sept. 30, 2004, effective Jan. 1, 2005.

Comment

[1] This Rule governs the disclosure by a lawyer of information relating to the representation of a client during the lawyer's representation of the client. See Rule 1.18 for the lawyer's duties with respect to information provided to the lawyer by a prospective client, Rule 1.9(c)(2) for the lawyer's duty not to reveal information relating to the lawyer's prior representation of a former client and Rules 1.8(b) and 1.9(c)(1) for the lawyer's duties with respect to the use of such information to the disadvantage of clients and former clients.

[2] A fundamental principle in the client-lawyer relationship is that, in the absence of the client's informed consent, the lawyer must not reveal information relating to the representation. See Rule 1.0(e) for the definition of informed consent. This contributes to the trust that is the hallmark of the client-lawyer relationship. The client is thereby encouraged to seek legal assistance and to communicate fully and frankly with the lawyer even as to embarrassing or legally damaging subject matter. The lawyer needs this information to represent the client effectively and, if necessary, to advise the client to refrain from wrongful conduct. Almost without exception, clients come to lawyers in order to determine their rights and what is, in the complex of laws and regulations, deemed to be legal and correct. Based upon experience, lawyers know that almost all clients follow the advice given, and the law is upheld.

[3] The principle of client-lawyer confidentiality is given effect by related bodies of law: the attorney-client privilege, the work product doctrine and the rule of confidentiality established in professional ethics. The attorney-client privilege and work-product doctrine apply in judicial and other proceedings in which a lawyer may be called as a witness or otherwise required to produce evidence concerning a client. The rule of client-lawyer confidentiality applies in situations other than those where evidence is sought from the lawyer through compulsion of law. The confidentiality rule, for example, applies not only to matters communicated in confidence by the client but also to all information relating to the representation, whatever its source. A lawyer may not disclose such information except as authorized or required by the Rules of Professional Conduct or other law. See also Scope.

[4] Paragraph (a) prohibits a lawyer from revealing information relating to the representation of a client. This prohibition also applies to disclosures by a lawyer that do not in themselves reveal protected information but could reasonably lead to the discovery of such information by a third person. A lawyer's use of a hypothetical to discuss issues relating to the representation is permissible so long as there is no reasonable likelihood that the listener will be able to ascertain the identity of the client or the situation involved.

Authorized Disclosure

[5] Except to the extent that the client's instructions or special circumstances limit that authority, a lawyer is impliedly authorized to make disclosures about a client when appropriate in carrying out the representation. In some situations, for example, a lawyer may be impliedly authorized to admit a fact that cannot properly be disputed or to make a disclosure that facilitates a satisfactory conclusion to a matter. Lawyers in a firm may, in the course of the firm's practice, disclose to each other information relating to a client of the firm, unless the client has instructed that particular information be confined to specified lawyers.

Disclosure Adverse to Client

[6] Although the public interest is usually best served by a strict rule requiring lawyers to preserve the confidentiality of information relating to the representation of their clients, the confidentiality rule is subject to limited exceptions. Paragraph (b)(1) recognizes the overriding value of life and physical integrity and permits disclosure reasonably necessary to prevent reasonably certain death or substantial bodily harm. Such harm is reasonably certain to occur if it will be suffered imminently or if there is a present and substantial threat that a person will suffer such harm at a later date if the lawyer fails to take action necessary to eliminate the threat. Thus, a lawyer who knows that a client has accidentally discharged toxic waste into a town's water supply may reveal this information to the authorities if there is a present and substantial risk that a person who drinks the water will contract a life-threatening or debilitating disease and the lawyer's disclosure is necessary to eliminate the threat or reduce the number of victims.

[7] Paragraph (b)(2) is a limited exception to the rule of confidentiality that permits the lawyer to reveal information to the extent necessary to enable affected persons or appropriate authorities to prevent the client from committing a crime or from committing fraud, as defined in Rule 1.0(d), that is reasonably certain to result in substantial injury to the financial or property interests of another and in furtherance of which the client has used or is using the lawyer's services. Such a serious abuse of the client-lawyer relationship by the client forfeits the protection of this Rule. The client can, of course, prevent such disclosure by refraining from the wrongful conduct. Although paragraph (b)(2) does not require the lawyer to reveal the client's misconduct, the lawyer may not counsel or assist the client in conduct the lawyer knows is criminal or fraudulent. See Rule 1.2(d). See also Rule 1.16 with respect to the lawyer's obligation or right to withdraw from the representation of the client in such circumstances, and Rule 1.13(c), which permits the lawyer, where the client is an organization, to reveal information relating to the representation in limited circumstances.

[8] Paragraph (b)(3) addresses the situation in which the lawyer does not learn of the client's crime or fraud until after it has been consummated. Although the client no longer has the option of preventing disclosure by refraining from the wrongful conduct, there will be situations in which the loss suffered by the affected person can be prevented, rectified or mitigated. In such situations, the lawyer may disclose information relating to the representation to the extent necessary to enable the affected persons to prevent or mitigate reasonably certain losses or to attempt to recoup their losses. Paragraph (b)(3) does not apply when a person who has committed a crime or fraud thereafter employs a lawyer for representation concerning that offense.

[9] A lawyer's confidentiality obligations do not preclude a lawyer from securing confidential legal advice about the lawyer's personal responsibility to comply with these Rules. In most situations, disclosing information to secure such advice will be impliedly authorized for the lawyer to carry out the representation. Even when the disclosure is not impliedly authorized, paragraph (b)(4) permits disclosure because of the importance of a lawyer's compliance with the Rules of Professional Conduct.

[10] Where a legal claim or disciplinary charge alleges complicity of the lawyer in a client's conduct or other misconduct of the lawyer involving representation of the client, the lawyer may respond to the extent the lawyer reasonably believes necessary to establish a defense. The same is true with respect to a claim involving the conduct or representation of a former client. Such a charge can arise in a civil, criminal, disciplinary or other proceeding and can be based on a wrong allegedly committed by the lawyer against the client or on a wrong alleged by a third person, for example, a person claiming to have been defrauded by the lawyer and client acting together. The lawyer's right to respond arises when an assertion of such complicity has been made. Paragraph (b)(5) does not require the lawyer to await the commencement of an action or proceeding that charges such complicity, so that the defense may be established by responding directly to a third party who has made such an assertion. The right to defend also applies, of course, where a proceeding has been commenced.

[11] A lawyer entitled to a fee is permitted by paragraph (b)(5) to prove the services rendered in an action to collect it. This aspect of the rule expresses the principle that the beneficiary of a fiduciary relationship may not exploit it to the detriment of the fiduciary.

[12] Other law may require that a lawyer disclose information about a client. Whether such a law supersedes Rule 1.6 is a question of law beyond the scope of these Rules. When disclosure of information relating to the representation appears to be required by other law, the lawyer must discuss the matter with the client to the extent required by Rule 1.4. If, however, the other law supersedes this Rule and requires disclosure, paragraph (b)(6) permits the lawyer to make such disclosures as are necessary to comply with the law.

[13] A lawyer may be ordered to reveal information relating to the representation of a client by a court or by another tribunal or governmental entity claiming authority pursuant to other law to compel the disclosure. Absent informed consent of the client to do otherwise, the lawyer should assert on behalf of the client all nonfrivolous claims that the order is not authorized by other law or that the information sought is protected against disclosure by the attorney-client privilege or other applicable law. In the event of an adverse ruling, the lawyer must consult with the client about the possibility of appeal to the extent required by Rule 1.4. Unless review is sought, however, paragraph (b)(6) permits the lawyer to comply with the court's order.

[14] Paragraph (b) permits disclosure only to the extent the lawyer reasonably believes the disclosure is necessary to accomplish one of the purposes specified. Where practicable, the lawyer should first seek to persuade the client to take suitable action to obviate the need for disclosure. In any case, a disclosure adverse to the client's interest should be no greater than the lawyer reasonably believes necessary to accomplish the purpose. If the disclosure will be made in connection with a judicial proceeding, the disclosure should be made in a manner that limits access to the information to the tribunal or other persons having a need to know it and appropriate protective orders or other arrangements should be sought by the lawyer to the fullest extent practicable.

[15] Paragraph (b) permits but does not require the disclosure of information relating to a client's representation to accomplish the purposes specified in paragraphs (b)(1) through (b)(6). In exercising the discretion conferred by this Rule, the lawyer may consider such factors as the nature of the lawyer's relationship with the client and with those who might be injured by the client, the lawyer's own involvement in the transaction and factors that may extenuate the conduct in question. A lawyer's decision not to disclose as permitted by paragraph (b) does not violate this Rule. Disclosure may be required, however, by other Rules. Some Rules require disclosure only if such disclosure would be permitted by paragraph (b). See Rules 1.2(d), 4.1(b), 8.1 and 8.3. Rule 3.3, on the other hand, requires disclosure in some circumstances regardless of whether such disclosure is permitted by this Rule. See Rule 3.3(c).

Acting Competently to Preserve Confidentiality

[16] A lawyer must act competently to safeguard information relating to the representation of a client against inadvertent or unauthorized disclosure by the lawyer or other persons who are participating in the representation of the client or who are subject to the lawyer's supervision. See Rules 1.1, 5.1 and 5.3.

[17] When transmitting a communication that includes information relating to the representation of a client, the lawyer must take reasonable precautions to prevent the information from coming into the hands of unintended recipients. This duty, however, does not require that the lawyer use special security measures if the method of communication affords a reasonable expectation of privacy. Special circumstances, however, may warrant spe-

cial precautions. Factors to be considered in determining the reasonableness of the lawyer's expectation of confidentiality include the sensitivity of the information and the extent to which the privacy of the communication is protected by law or by a confidentiality agreement. A client may require the lawyer to implement special security measures not required by this Rule or may give informed consent to the use of a means of communication that would otherwise be prohibited by this Rule.

Former Client

[18] The duty of confidentiality continues after the client-lawyer relationship has terminated. See Rule 1.9(c)(2). See Rule 1.9(c)(1) for the prohibition against using such information to the disadvantage of the former client.

Disability of an Attorney

[19] Paragraph (c) is intended to operate in conjunction with Ind. Admission and Discipline Rule 23, Section 27, as well as such other arrangements as may be implemented by agreement to deal with the physical or mental disability of a lawyer.

Rule 1.7.   Conflict of Interest: Current Clients

(a) Except as provided in paragraph (b), a lawyer shall not represent a client if the representation involves a concurrent conflict of interest. A concurrent conflict of interest exists if:

(1) the representation of one client will be directly adverse to another client; or

(2) there is a significant risk that the representation of one or more clients will be materially limited by the lawyer's responsibilities to another client, a former client or a third person or by a personal interest of the lawyer.

(b) Notwithstanding the existence of a concurrent conflict of interest under paragraph (a), a lawyer may represent a client if:

(1) the lawyer reasonably believes that the lawyer will be able to provide competent and diligent representation to each affected client;

(2) the representation is not prohibited by law;

(3) the representation does not involve the assertion of a claim by one client against another client represented by the lawyer in the same litigation or other proceeding before a tribunal; and

(4) each affected client gives informed consent, confirmed in writing.

Adopted effective Jan. 1, 1987; amended Sept. 30, 2004, effective Jan. 1, 2005.

Comment
General Principles

[1] Loyalty and independent judgment are essential elements in the lawyer's relationship to a client. Concurrent conflicts of interest can arise from the lawyer's responsibilities to another client, a former client or a third person or from the lawyer's own interests. For specific Rules regarding certain concurrent conflicts of interest, see Rule 1.8. For former client conflicts of interest, see Rule 1.9. For conflicts of interest involving prospective clients, see Rule 1.18. For definitions of "informed consent" and "confirmed in writing," see Rule 1.0(e) and (b).

[2] Resolution of a conflict of interest problem under this Rule requires the lawyer to: 1) clearly identify the client or clients; 2) determine whether a conflict of interest exists; 3) decide whether the representation may be undertaken despite the existence of a conflict, i.e., whether the conflict is consentable; and 4) if so, consult with the clients affected under paragraph (a) and obtain their informed consent, confirmed in writing. The clients affected under paragraph (a) include both of the clients referred to in paragraph (a)(1) and the one or more clients whose representation might be materially limited under paragraph (a)(2).

[3] A conflict of interest may exist before representation is undertaken, in which event the representation must be declined, unless the lawyer obtains the informed consent of each client under the conditions of paragraph (b). To determine whether a conflict of interest exists, a lawyer should adopt reasonable procedures, appropriate for the size and type of firm and practice, to determine in both litigation and non-litigation matters the persons and issues involved. See also Comment to Rule 5.1. Ignorance caused by a failure to institute such procedures will not excuse a lawyer's violation of this Rule. As to whether a client-lawyer relationship exists or, having once been established, is continuing, see Comment to Rule 1.3 and Scope.

[4] If a conflict arises after representation has been undertaken, the lawyer ordinarily must withdraw from the representation, unless the lawyer has obtained the informed consent of the client under the conditions of paragraph (b). See Rule 1.16. Where more than one client is involved, whether the lawyer may continue to represent any of the clients is determined both by the lawyer's ability to comply with duties owed to the former client and by the lawyer's ability to represent adequately the remaining client or clients, given the lawyer's duties to the former client. See Rule 1.9. See also Comments [5] and [29].

[5] Unforeseeable developments, such as changes in corporate and other organizational affiliations or the addition or realignment of parties in litigation, might create conflicts in the midst of a representation, as when a company sued by the lawyer on behalf of one client is bought by or merged with another client represented by the lawyer in an unrelated matter. Depending on the circumstances, the lawyer may have the option to withdraw from one of the representations in order to avoid the conflict. The lawyer must seek court approval where necessary and take steps to minimize harm to the clients. See Rule 1.16. The lawyer must continue to protect the confidences of the client from whose representation the lawyer has withdrawn. See Rule 1.9(c).

Identifying Conflicts of Interest: Directly Adverse

[6] Loyalty to a current client prohibits undertaking representation directly adverse to that client without that client's informed consent. Thus, absent consent, a lawyer may not act as an advocate in one matter against a person the lawyer represents in some other matter, even when the matters are wholly unrelated. The client as to whom the representation is directly adverse is likely to feel betrayed, and the resulting damage to the client-lawyer relationship is likely to impair the lawyer's ability to represent the client effectively. In addition, the client on whose behalf the adverse representation is undertaken reasonably may fear that the lawyer will pursue that client's case less effectively out of deference to the other client, i.e., that the representation may be materially limited by the lawyer's interest in retaining the current client. Similarly, a directly adverse conflict may arise when a lawyer is required to cross-examine a client who appears as a witness in a lawsuit involving another client, as when the testimony will be damaging to the client who is represented in the lawsuit. On the other hand, simultaneous representation in unrelated matters of clients whose interests are only economically adverse, such as representation of competing economic enterprises in unrelated litigation, does not ordinarily constitute a conflict of interest and thus may not require consent of the respective clients.

[7] Directly adverse conflicts can also arise in transactional matters. For example, if a lawyer is asked to represent the seller of a business in negotiations with a buyer represented by the lawyer, not in the same transaction but in another, unrelated matter, the lawyer could not undertake the representation without the informed consent of each client.

Identifying Conflicts of Interest: Material Limitation

[8] Even where there is no direct adverseness, a conflict of interest exists if there is a significant risk that a lawyer's ability to consider, recommend or carry out an appropriate course of action for the client will be materially limited as a result of the lawyer's other responsibilities or interests. For example, a lawyer asked to represent several individuals seeking to form a joint venture is likely to be materially limited in the lawyer's ability to recommend or advocate all possible positions that each might take because of the lawyer's duty of loyalty to the others. The conflict in effect forecloses alternatives that would otherwise be available to the client. The mere possibility of subsequent harm does not itself require disclosure and consent. The critical questions are the likelihood that a difference in interests will eventuate and, if it does, whether it will materially interfere with the lawyer's independent professional judgment in considering alternatives or foreclose courses of action that reasonably should be pursued on behalf of the client.

Lawyer's Responsibilities to Former Clients and Other Third Persons

[9] In addition to conflicts with other current clients, a lawyer's duties of loyalty and independence may be materially limited by responsibilities to former clients under Rule 1.9 or by the lawyer's responsibilities to other persons, such as fiduciary duties arising from a lawyer's service as a trustee, executor or corporate director.

Personal Interest Conflicts

[10] The lawyer's own interests should not be permitted to have an adverse effect on representation of a client. For example, if the probity of a lawyer's own conduct in a transaction is in serious question, it may be difficult or impossible for the lawyer to give a client detached advice. Similarly, when a lawyer has discussions concerning possible employment with an opponent of the lawyer's client, or with a law firm representing the opponent, such discussions could materially limit the lawyer's representation of the client. In addition, a lawyer may not allow related business interests to affect representation, for example, by referring clients to an enterprise in which the lawyer has an undisclosed financial interest. See Rule 1.8 for specific Rules pertaining to a number of personal interest conflicts, including business transactions with clients. See also Rule 1.10 (personal interest conflicts under Rule 1.7 ordinarily are not imputed to other lawyers in a law firm).

[11] When lawyers representing different clients in the same matter or in substantially related matters are closely related by blood or marriage, there may be a significant risk that client confidences will be revealed and that the lawyer's family relationship will interfere with both loyalty and independent professional judgment. As a result, each client is entitled to know of the existence and implications of the relationship between the lawyers before the lawyer agrees to undertake the representation. Thus, a lawyer related to another lawyer, e.g., as parent, child, sibling or spouse, ordinarily may not represent a client in a matter where that lawyer is representing another party, unless each client gives informed consent. The disqualification arising from a close family relationship is personal and ordinarily is not imputed to members of firms with whom the lawyers are associated. See Rule 1.10.

[12] A lawyer is prohibited from engaging in sexual relationships with a client unless the sexual relationship predates the formation of the client-lawyer relationship. See Rule 1.8(j).

Interest of Person Paying for a Lawyer's Service

[13] A lawyer may be paid from a source other than the client, including a co-client, if the client is informed of that fact and consents and the arrangement does not compromise the lawyer's duty of loyalty or independent judgment to the client. See Rule 1.8(f). If acceptance of the payment from any other source presents a significant risk that the lawyer's representation of the client will be materially limited by the lawyer's own interest in accommodating the person paying the lawyer's fee or by the lawyer's responsibilities to a payer who is also a co-client, then the lawyer must comply with the

requirements of paragraph (b) before accepting the representation, including determining whether the conflict is consentable and, if so, that the client has adequate information about the material risks of the representation.

Prohibited Representations

[14] Ordinarily, clients may consent to representation notwithstanding a conflict. However, as indicated in paragraph (b), some conflicts are nonconsentable, meaning that the lawyer involved cannot properly ask for such agreement or provide representation on the basis of the client's consent. When the lawyer is representing more than one client, the question of consentability must be resolved as to each client.

[15] Consentability is typically determined by considering whether the interests of the clients will be adequately protected if the clients are permitted to give their informed consent to representation burdened by a conflict of interest. Thus, under paragraph (b)(1), representation is prohibited if in the circumstances the lawyer cannot reasonably conclude that the lawyer will be able to provide competent and diligent representation. See Rule 1.1 (competence) and Rule 1.3 (diligence).

[16] Paragraph (b)(2) describes conflicts that are nonconsentable because the representation is prohibited by applicable law. For example, in some states substantive law provides that the same lawyer may not represent more than one defendant in a capital case, even with the consent of the clients, and under federal criminal statutes certain representations by a former government lawyer are prohibited, despite the informed consent of the former client. In addition, decisional law in some states limits the ability of a governmental client, such as a municipality, to consent to a conflict of interest.

[17] Paragraph (b)(3) describes conflicts that are nonconsentable because of the institutional interest in vigorous development of each client's position when the clients are aligned directly against each other in the same litigation or other proceeding before a tribunal. Whether clients are aligned directly against each other within the meaning of this paragraph requires examination of the context of the proceeding. Although this paragraph does not preclude a lawyer's multiple representation of adverse parties to a mediation (because mediation is not a proceeding before a "tribunal" under Rule 1.0(m)), such representation may be precluded by paragraph (b)(1).

Informed Consent

[18] Informed consent requires that each affected client be aware of the relevant circumstances and of the material and reasonably foreseeable ways that the conflict could have adverse effects on the interests of that client. See Rule 1.0(e) (informed consent). The information required depends on the nature of the conflict and the nature of the risks involved. When representation of multiple clients in a single matter is undertaken, the information must include the implications of the common representation, including possible effects on loyalty, confidentiality and the attorney-client privilege and the advantages and risks involved. See Comments [30] and [31] (effect of common representation on confidentiality).

[19] Under some circumstances it may be impossible to make the disclosure necessary to obtain consent. For example, when the lawyer represents different clients in related matters and one of the clients refuses to consent to the disclosure necessary to permit the other client to make an informed decision, the lawyer cannot properly ask the latter to consent. In some cases the alternative to common representation can be that each party may have to obtain separate representation with the possibility of incurring additional costs. These costs, along with the benefits of securing separate representation, are factors that may be considered by the affected client in determining whether common representation is in the client's interests.

Consent Confirmed in Writing

[20] Paragraph (b) requires the lawyer to obtain the informed consent of the client, confirmed in writing. Such a writing may consist of a document executed by the client. In the alternative, the lawyer shall promptly transmit a writing to the client confirming the client's oral consent. See Rule 1.0(b). See also Rule 1.0(n) (writing includes electronic transmission). If it is not feasible to obtain or transmit the writing at the time the client gives informed consent, then the lawyer must obtain or transmit it within a reasonable time thereafter. See Rule 1.0(b). The requirement of a writing does not supplant the need in most cases for the lawyer to talk with the client, to explain the risks and advantages, if any, of representation burdened with a conflict of interest, as well as reasonably available alternatives, and to afford the client a reasonable opportunity to consider the risks and alternatives and to raise questions and concerns. Rather, the writing is required in order to impress upon clients the seriousness of the decision the client is being asked to make and to avoid disputes or ambiguities that might later occur in the absence of a writing.

Revoking Consent

[21] A client who has given consent to a conflict may revoke the consent and, like any other client, may terminate the lawyer's representation at any time. Whether revoking consent to the client's own representation precludes the lawyer from continuing to represent other clients depends on the circumstances, including the nature of the conflict, whether the client revoked consent because of a material change in circumstances, the reasonable expectations of the other client and whether material detriment to the other clients or the lawyer would result.

Consent to Future Conflict

[22] Whether a lawyer may properly request a client to waive conflicts that might arise in the future is subject to the test of paragraph (b). The effectiveness of such waivers is generally determined by the extent to which the client reasonably

understands the material risks that the waiver entails. The more comprehensive the explanation of the types of future representations that might arise and the actual and reasonably foreseeable adverse consequences of those representations, the greater the likelihood that the client will have the requisite understanding. Thus, if the client agrees to consent to a particular type of conflict with which the client is already familiar, then the consent ordinarily will be effective with regard to that type of conflict. If the consent is general and open-ended, then the consent ordinarily will be ineffective, because it is not reasonably likely that the client will have understood the material risks involved. On the other hand, if the client is an experienced user of the legal services involved and is reasonably informed regarding the risk that a conflict may arise, such consent is more likely to be effective, particularly if, e.g., the client is independently represented by other counsel in giving consent and the consent is limited to future conflicts unrelated to the subject of the representation. In any case, advance consent cannot be effective if the circumstances that materialize in the future are such as would make the conflict nonconsentable under paragraph (b).

Conflicts in Litigation

[23] Paragraph (b)(3) prohibits representation of opposing parties in the same litigation, regardless of the clients' consent. On the other hand, simultaneous representation of parties whose interests in litigation may conflict, such as coplaintiffs or codefendants, is governed by paragraph (a)(2). A conflict may exist by reason of substantial discrepancy in the parties' testimony, incompatibility in positions in relation to an opposing party or the fact that there are substantially different possibilities of settlement of the claims or liabilities in question. Such conflicts can arise in criminal cases as well as civil. The potential for conflict of interest in representing multiple defendants in a criminal case is so grave that ordinarily a lawyer should decline to represent more than one codefendant. On the other hand, common representation of persons having similar interests in civil litigation is proper if the requirements of paragraph (b) are met.

[24] Ordinarily a lawyer may take inconsistent legal positions in different tribunals at different times on behalf of different clients. The mere fact that advocating a legal position on behalf of one client might create precedent adverse to the interests of a client represented by the lawyer in an unrelated matter does not create a conflict of interest. A conflict of interest exists, however, if there is a significant risk that a lawyer's action on behalf of one client will materially limit the lawyer's effectiveness in representing another client in a different case; for example, when a decision favoring one client will create a precedent likely to seriously weaken the position taken on behalf of the other client. Factors relevant in determining whether the clients need to be advised of the risk include: where the cases are pending, whether the issue is substantive or procedural, the temporal relationship between the matters, the significance of the issue to the immediate and long term interests of the clients

involved, and the clients' reasonable expectations in retaining the lawyer. If there is significant risk of material limitation, then absent informed consent of the affected clients, the lawyer must refuse one of the representations or withdraw from one or both matters.

[25] When a lawyer represents or seeks to represent a class of plaintiffs or defendants in a class-action lawsuit, unnamed members of the class are ordinarily not considered to be clients of the lawyer for purposes of applying paragraph (a)(1) of this Rule. Thus, the lawyer does not typically need to get the consent of such a person before representing a client suing the person in an unrelated matter. Similarly, a lawyer seeking to represent an opponent in a class action does not typically need the consent of an unnamed member of the class whom the lawyer represents in an unrelated matter.

Nonlitigation Conflicts

[26] Conflicts of interest under paragraphs (a)(1) and (a)(2) arise in contexts other than litigation. For a discussion of directly adverse conflicts in transactional matters, see Comment [7]. Relevant factors in determining whether there is significant potential for material limitation include the duration and intimacy of the lawyer's relationship with the client or clients involved, the functions being performed by the lawyer, the likelihood that disagreements will arise and the likely prejudice to the client from the conflict. The question is often one of proximity and degree. See Comment [8].

[27] For example, conflict questions may arise in estate planning and estate administration. A lawyer may be called upon to prepare wills for several family members, such as husband and wife, and, depending upon the circumstances, a conflict of interest may be present. In estate administration the identity of the client may be unclear under the law of a particular jurisdiction. Under one view, the client is the fiduciary; under another view the client is the estate or trust, including its beneficiaries. In order to comply with conflict of interest rules, the lawyer should make clear the lawyer's relationship to the parties involved.

[28] Whether a conflict is consentable depends on the circumstances. For example, a lawyer may not represent multiple parties to a negotiation whose interests are fundamentally antagonistic to each other, but common representation is permissible where the clients are generally aligned in interest even though there is some difference in interest among them. Thus, a lawyer may seek to establish or adjust a relationship between clients on an amicable and mutually advantageous basis; for example, in helping to organize a business in which two or more clients are entrepreneurs, working out the financial reorganization of an enterprise in which two or more clients have an interest or arranging a property distribution in settlement of an estate. The lawyer seeks to resolve potentially adverse interests by developing the parties' mutual interests. Otherwise, each party might have to obtain separate representation, with the possibility of incurring additional cost, complication or even litigation. Given these and other relevant factors, the

clients may prefer that the lawyer act for all of them.

Special Considerations in Common Representation

[29] In considering whether to represent multiple clients in the same matter, a lawyer should be mindful that if the common representation fails because the potentially adverse interests cannot be reconciled, the result can be additional cost, embarrassment and recrimination. Ordinarily, the lawyer will be forced to withdraw from representing all of the clients if the common representation fails. In some situations, the risk of failure is so great that multiple representation is plainly impossible. For example, a lawyer cannot undertake common representation of clients where contentious litigation or negotiations between them are imminent or contemplated. Moreover, because the lawyer is required to be impartial between commonly represented clients, representation of multiple clients is improper when it is unlikely that impartiality can be maintained. Generally, if the relationship between the parties has already assumed antagonism, the possibility that the clients' interests can be adequately served by common representation is not very good. Other relevant factors are whether the lawyer subsequently will represent both parties on a continuing basis and whether the situation involves creating or terminating a relationship between the parties.

[30] A particularly important factor in determining the appropriateness of common representation is the effect on client-lawyer confidentiality and the attorney-client privilege. With regard to the attorney-client privilege, the prevailing rule is that, as between commonly represented clients, the privilege does not attach. Hence, it must be assumed that if litigation eventuates between the clients, the privilege will not protect any such communications, and the clients should be so advised.

[31] As to the duty of confidentiality, continued common representation will almost certainly be inadequate if one client asks the lawyer not to disclose to the other client information relevant to the common representation. This is so because the lawyer has an equal duty of loyalty to each client, and each client has the right to be informed of anything bearing on the representation that might affect that client's interests and the right to expect that the lawyer will use that information to that client's benefit. See Rule 1.4. The lawyer should, at the outset of the common representation and as part of the process of obtaining each client's informed consent, advise each client that information will be shared and that the lawyer may have to withdraw from representing one or more or all of the common clients if one client decides that some matter material to the representation should be kept from the others. In limited circumstances, it may be appropriate for the lawyer to proceed with the representation when the clients have agreed, after being properly informed, that the lawyer will keep certain information confidential. For example, the lawyer may reasonably conclude that failure to disclose one client's trade secrets to another client will not adversely affect representation involving a

joint venture between the clients and agree to keep that information confidential with the informed consent of both clients.

[32] When seeking to establish or adjust a relationship between clients, the lawyer should make clear that the lawyer's role is not that of partisanship normally expected in other circumstances and, thus, that the clients may be required to assume greater responsibility for decisions than when each client is separately represented. Any limitations on the scope of the representation made necessary as a result of the common representation should be fully explained to the clients at the outset of the representation. See Rule 1.2(c) and 2.2

[33] Subject to the above limitations, each client in the common representation has the right to loyal and diligent representation and the protection of Rule 1.9 concerning the obligations to a former client. The client also has the right to discharge the lawyer as stated in Rule 1.16.

Organizational Clients

[34] A lawyer who represents a corporation or other organization does not, by virtue of that representation, necessarily represent any constituent or affiliated organization, such as a parent or subsidiary. See Rule 1.13(a). Thus, the lawyer for an organization is not barred from accepting representation adverse to an affiliate in an unrelated matter, unless the circumstances are such that the affiliate should also be considered a client of the lawyer, there is an understanding between the lawyer and the organizational client that the lawyer will avoid representation adverse to the client's affiliates, or the lawyer's obligations to either the organizational client or the new client are likely to limit materially the lawyer's representation of the other client.

[35] A lawyer for a corporation or other organization who is also a member of its board of directors should determine whether the responsibilities of the two roles may conflict. The lawyer may be called on to advise the corporation in matters involving actions of the directors. Consideration should be given to the frequency with which such situations may arise, the potential intensity of the conflict, the effect of the lawyer's resignation from the board and the possibility of the corporation's obtaining legal advice from another lawyer in such situations. If there is material risk that the dual role will compromise the lawyer's independence of professional judgment, the lawyer should not serve as a director or should cease to act as the corporation's lawyer when conflicts of interest arise. The lawyer should advise the other members of the board that in some circumstances matters discussed at board meetings while the lawyer is present in the capacity of director might not be protected by the attorney-client privilege and that conflict of interest considerations might require the lawyer's recusal as a director or might require the lawyer and the lawyer's firm to decline representation of the corporation in a matter.

Rule 1.8. Conflict of Interest: Current Clients: Specific Rules

(a) A lawyer shall not enter into a business transaction with a client or knowingly acquire an ownership, possessory, security or other pecuniary interest adverse to a client unless:

(1) the transaction and terms on which the lawyer acquires the interest are fair and reasonable to the client and are fully disclosed and transmitted in writing in a manner that can be reasonably understood by the client;

(2) the client is advised in writing of the desirability of seeking and is given a reasonable opportunity to seek the advice of independent legal counsel on the transaction; and

(3) the client gives informed consent, in a writing signed by the client, to the essential terms of the transaction and the lawyer's role in the transaction, including whether the lawyer is representing the client in the transaction.

(b) A lawyer shall not use information relating to representation of a client to the disadvantage of the client unless the client gives informed consent, except as permitted or required by these Rules.

(c) A lawyer shall not solicit any substantial gift from a client, including a testamentary gift, or prepare on behalf of a client an instrument giving the lawyer or a person related to the lawyer any substantial gift unless the lawyer or other recipient of the gift is related to the client. For purposes of this paragraph, related persons include a spouse, child, grandchild, parent, grandparent or other relative or individual with whom the lawyer or the client maintains a close, familial relationship.

(d) Prior to the conclusion of representation of a client, a lawyer shall not make or negotiate an agreement giving the lawyer literary or media rights to a portrayal or account based in substantial part on information relating to the representation.

(e) A lawyer shall not provide financial assistance to a client in connection with pending or contemplated litigation, except that:

(1) a lawyer may advance court costs and expenses of litigation, the repayment of which may be contingent on the outcome of the matter; and

(2) a lawyer representing an indigent client may pay court costs and expenses of litigation on behalf of the client.

(f) A lawyer shall not accept compensation for representing a client from one other than the client unless:

(1) the client gives informed consent;

(2) there is no interference with the lawyer's independence of professional judgment or with the client-lawyer relationship; and

(3) information relating to representation of a client is protected as required by Rule 1.6.

(g) A lawyer who represents two or more clients shall not participate in making an aggregate settlement of the claims of or against the clients, or in a criminal case an aggregated agreement as to guilty or nolo contendere pleas, unless each client gives informed consent, in a writing signed by the client. The lawyer's disclosure shall include the existence and nature of all the claims or pleas involved and of the participation of each person in the settlement.

(h) A lawyer shall not:

(1) make an agreement prospectively limiting the lawyer's liability to a client for malpractice unless the client is independently represented in making the agreement; or

(2) settle a claim or potential claim for such liability with an unrepresented client or former client unless that person is advised in writing of the desirability of seeking and is given a reasonable opportunity to seek the advice of independent legal counsel in connection therewith.

(i) A lawyer shall not acquire a proprietary interest in the cause of action or subject matter of litigation the lawyer is conducting for a client, except that the lawyer may:

(1) acquire a lien authorized by law to secure the lawyer's fee or expenses; and

(2) contract with a client for a reasonable contingent fee in a civil case.

(j) A lawyer shall not have sexual relations with a client unless a consensual sexual relationship existed between them when the client-lawyer relationship commenced.

(k) While lawyers are associated in a firm, a prohibition in paragraphs (a) through (i) and (l) that applies to any one of them shall apply to all of them.

(l) A part-time prosecutor or deputy prosecutor authorized by statute to otherwise engage in the practice of law shall refrain from representing a private client in any matter wherein exists an issue upon which said prosecutor has statutory prosecutorial authority or responsibilities. This restriction is not intended to prohibit representation in tort cases in which investigation and any prosecution of infractions has terminated, nor to prohibit representation in family law matters involving no issue subject to prosecutorial authority or responsibilities. Upon a prior, express written limitation of responsibility to exclude prosecutorial authority in matters related to family law, a part-time deputy prosecutor may fully represent private clients in cases involving family law.

Adopted effective Jan. 1, 1987. Amended effective Sept. 4, 1987; amended Dec. 15, 1995, effective Feb. 1, 1996; Sept. 30, 2004, effective Jan. 1, 2005; amended effective May 3, 2006.

Comment
Business Transactions Between Client and Lawyer

[1] A lawyer's legal skill and training, together with the relationship of trust and confidence between lawyer and client, create the possibility of overreaching when the lawyer participates in a business, property or financial transaction with a client, for example, a loan or sales transaction or a lawyer investment on behalf of a client. The requirements of paragraph (a) must be met even when the transaction is not closely related to the subject matter of the representation, as when a lawyer drafting a will for a client learns that the client needs money for unrelated expenses and offers to make a loan to the client. The Rule applies to lawyers engaged in the sale of goods or services related to the practice of law, for example, the sale of title insurance or investment services to existing clients of the lawyer's legal practice. See Rule 5.7. It also applies to lawyers purchasing property from estates they represent. It does not apply to ordinary initial fee arrangements between client and lawyer, which are governed by Rule 1.5, although its requirements must be met when the lawyer accepts an interest in the client's business or other nonmonetary property as payment of all or part of a fee. Paragraph (a) applies when a lawyer seeks to renegotiate the terms of the fee arrangement with the client after representation begins in order to reach a new agreement that is more advantageous to the lawyer than the initial fee arrangement. In addition, the Rule does not apply to standard commercial transactions between the lawyer and the client for products or services that the client generally markets to others, for example, banking or brokerage services, medical services, products manufactured or distributed by the client, and utilities' services. In such transactions, the lawyer has no advantage in dealing with the client, and the restrictions in paragraph (a) are unnecessary and impracticable.

[2] Paragraph (a)(1) requires that the transaction itself be fair to the client and that its essential terms be communicated to the client, in writing, in a manner that can be reasonably understood. Paragraph (a)(2) requires that the client also be advised, in writing, of the desirability of seeking the advice of independent legal counsel. It also requires that the client be given a reasonable opportunity to obtain such advice. Paragraph (a)(3) requires that the lawyer obtain the client's informed consent, in a writing signed by the client, both to the essential terms of the transaction and to the lawyer's role. When necessary, the lawyer should discuss both the material risks of the proposed transaction, including any risk presented by the lawyer's involvement, and the existence of reasonably available alternatives and should explain why the advice of independent legal counsel is desirable. See Rule 1.0(e) (definition of informed consent).

[3] The risk to a client is greatest when the client expects the lawyer to represent the client in the transaction itself or when the lawyer's financial interest otherwise poses a significant risk that the lawyer's representation of the client will be materially limited by the lawyer's financial interest in the transaction. Here the lawyer's role requires that the lawyer must comply, not only with the requirements of paragraph (a), but also with the requirements of Rule 1.7. Under that Rule, the lawyer must disclose the risks associated with the lawyer's dual role as both legal adviser and participant in the transaction, such as the risk that the lawyer will structure the transaction or give legal advice in a way that favors the lawyer's interests at the expense of the client. Moreover, the lawyer must obtain the client's informed consent. In some cases, the lawyer's interest may be such that Rule 1.7 will preclude the lawyer from seeking the client's consent to the transaction.

[4] If the client is independently represented in the transaction, paragraph (a)(2) of this Rule is inapplicable, and the paragraph (a)(1) requirement for full disclosure is satisfied either by a written disclosure by the lawyer involved in the transaction or by the client's independent counsel. The fact that the client was independently represented in the transaction is relevant in determining whether the agreement was fair and reasonable to the client as paragraph (a)(1) further requires.

Use of Information Related to Representation

[5] Use of information relating to the representation to the disadvantage of the client violates the lawyer's duty of loyalty. Paragraph (b) applies when the information is used to benefit either the lawyer or a third person, such as another client or business associate of the lawyer. For example, if a lawyer learns that a client intends to purchase and develop several parcels of land, the lawyer may not use that information to purchase one of the parcels in competition with the client or to recommend that another client make such a purchase. The Rule does not prohibit uses that do not disadvantage the client. For example, a lawyer who learns a government agency's interpretation of trade legislation during the representation of one client may properly use that information to benefit other clients. Paragraph (b) prohibits disadvantageous use of client information unless the client gives informed consent, except as permitted or required by these Rules. See Rules 1.2(d), 1.6, 1.9(c), 3.3, 4.1(b), 8.1 and 8.3.

Gifts to Lawyers

[6] A lawyer may accept a gift from a client, if the transaction meets general standards of fairness. For example, a simple gift such as a present given at a holiday or as a token of appreciation is permitted. If a client offers the lawyer a more substantial gift, paragraph (c) does not prohibit the lawyer from accepting it, although such a gift may be voidable by the client under the doctrine of undue influence, which treats client gifts as presumptively fraudulent. In any event, due to concerns about overreaching and imposition on clients, a lawyer may not suggest that a substantial gift be made to the lawyer or for the lawyer's benefit, except where the lawyer is related to the client as set forth in paragraph (c).

[7] If effectuation of a substantial gift requires preparing a legal instrument such as a will or conveyance the client should have the detached advice that another lawyer can provide. The sole exception to this Rule is where the client is a relative of the donee.

[8] This Rule does not prohibit a lawyer from seeking to have the lawyer or a partner or associate of the lawyer named as executor of the client's estate or to another potentially lucrative fiduciary position. Nevertheless, such appointments will be subject to the general conflict of interest provision in Rule 1.7 when there is a significant risk that the lawyer's interest in obtaining the appointment will materially limit the lawyer's independent professional judgment in advising the client concerning the choice of an executor or other fiduciary. In obtaining the client's informed consent to the conflict, the lawyer should advise the client concerning the nature and extent of the lawyer's financial interest in the appointment, as well as the availability of alternative candidates for the position.

Literary Rights

[9] An agreement by which a lawyer acquires literary or media rights concerning the conduct of the representation creates a conflict between the interests of the client and the personal interests of the lawyer. Measures suitable in the representation of the client may detract from the publication value of an account of the representation. Paragraph (d) does not prohibit a lawyer representing a client in a transaction concerning literary property from agreeing that the lawyer's fee shall consist of a share in ownership in the property, if the arrangement conforms to Rule 1.5 and paragraphs (a) and (i).

Financial Assistance

[10] Lawyers may not subsidize lawsuits or administrative proceedings brought on behalf of their clients, including making or guaranteeing loans to their clients for living expenses, because to do so would encourage clients to pursue lawsuits that might not otherwise be brought and because such assistance gives lawyers too great a financial stake in the litigation. These dangers do not warrant a prohibition on a lawyer lending a client court costs and litigation expenses, including the expenses of medical examination and the costs of obtaining and presenting evidence, because these advances are virtually indistinguishable from contingent fees and help ensure access to the courts. Similarly, an exception allowing lawyers representing indigent clients to pay court costs and litigation expenses regardless of whether these funds will be repaid is warranted.

Person Paying for a Lawyer's Services

[11] Lawyers are frequently asked to represent a client under circumstances in which a third person will compensate the lawyer, in whole or in part. The third person might be a relative or friend, an indemnitor (such as a liability insurance company) or a co-client (such as a corporation sued along with

one or more of its employees). Because third-party payers frequently have interests that differ from those of the client, including interests in minimizing the amount spent on the representation and in learning how the representation is progressing, lawyers are prohibited from accepting or continuing such representations unless the lawyer determines that there will be no interference with the lawyer's independent professional judgment and there is informed consent from the client. See also Rule 5.4(c) (prohibiting interference with a lawyer's professional judgment by one who recommends, employs or pays the lawyer to render legal services for another).

[12] Sometimes, it will be sufficient for the lawyer to obtain the client's informed consent regarding the fact of the payment and the identity of the third-party payer. If, however, the fee arrangement creates a conflict of interest for the lawyer, then the lawyer must comply with Rule 1. 7. The lawyer must also conform to the requirements of Rule 1.6 concerning confidentiality. Under Rule 1.7(a), a conflict of interest exists if there is significant risk that the lawyer's representation of the client will be materially limited by the lawyer's own interest in the fee arrangement or by the lawyer's responsibilities to the third-party payer (for example, when the third-party payer is a co-client). Under Rule 1.7(b), the lawyer may accept or continue the representation with the informed consent of each affected client, unless the conflict is nonconsentable under that paragraph. Under Rule 1.7(b), the informed consent must be confirmed in writing.

Aggregate Settlements

[13] Differences in willingness to make or accept an offer of settlement are among the risks of common representation of multiple clients by a single lawyer. Under Rule 1.7, this is one of the risks that should be discussed before undertaking the representation, as part of the process of obtaining the clients' informed consent. In addition, Rule 1.2(a) protects each client's right to have the final say in deciding whether to accept or reject an offer of settlement and in deciding whether to enter a guilty or nolo contendere plea in a criminal case. The rule stated in this paragraph is a corollary of both these Rules and provides that, before any settlement offer or plea bargain is made or accepted on behalf of multiple clients, the lawyer must inform each of them about all the material terms of the settlement, including what the other clients will receive or pay if the settlement or plea offer is accepted. See also Rule 1.0(e) (definition of informed consent). Lawyers representing a class of plaintiffs or defendants, or those proceeding derivatively, may not have a full client-lawyer relationship with each member of the class; nevertheless, such lawyers must comply with applicable rules regulating notification of class members and other procedural requirements designed to ensure adequate protection of the entire class.

Limiting Liability and Settling Malpractice Claims

[14] Agreements prospectively limiting a lawyer's liability for malpractice are prohibited unless the

client is independently represented in making the agreement because they are likely to undermine competent and diligent representation. Also, many clients are unable to evaluate the desirability of making such an agreement before a dispute has arisen, particularly if they are then represented by the lawyer seeking the agreement. This paragraph does not, however, prohibit a lawyer from entering into an agreement with the client to arbitrate legal malpractice claims, provided such agreements are enforceable and the client is fully informed of the scope and effect of the agreement. Nor does this paragraph limit the ability of lawyers to practice in the form of a limited-liability entity, where permitted by law, provided that each lawyer remains personally liable to the client for his or her own conduct and the firm complies with any conditions required by law, such as provisions requiring client notification or maintenance of adequate liability insurance. Nor does it prohibit an agreement in accordance with Rule 1.2 that defines the scope of the representation, although a definition of scope that makes the obligations of representation illusory will amount to an attempt to limit liability.

[15] Agreements settling a claim or a potential claim for malpractice are not prohibited by this Rule. Nevertheless, in view of the danger that a lawyer will take unfair advantage of an unrepresented client or former client, the lawyer must first advise such a person in writing of the appropriateness of independent representation in connection with such a settlement. In addition, the lawyer must give the client or former client a reasonable opportunity to find and consult independent counsel.

Acquiring Proprietary Interest in Litigation

[16] Paragraph (i) states the traditional general rule that lawyers are prohibited from acquiring a proprietary interest in litigation. Like paragraph (e), the general rule has its basis in common law champerty and maintenance and is designed to avoid giving the lawyer too great an interest in the representation. In addition, when the lawyer acquires an ownership interest in the subject of the representation, it will be more difficult for a client to discharge the lawyer if the client so desires. The Rule is subject to specific exceptions developed in decisional law and continued in these Rules. The exception for certain advances of the costs of litigation is set forth in paragraph (e). In addition, paragraph (i) sets forth exceptions for liens authorized by law to secure the lawyer's fees or expenses and contracts for reasonable contingent fees. The law of each jurisdiction determines which liens are authorized by law. These may include liens granted by statute, liens originating in common law and liens acquired by contract with the client. When a lawyer acquires by contract a security interest in property other than that recovered through the lawyer's efforts in the litigation, such an acquisition is a business or financial transaction with a client and is governed by the requirements of paragraph (a). Contracts for contingent fees in civil cases are governed by Rule 1.5.

Client–Lawyer Sexual Relationships

[17] The relationship between lawyer and client is a fiduciary one in which the lawyer occupies the highest position of trust and confidence. The relationship is almost always unequal; thus, a sexual relationship between lawyer and client can involve unfair exploitation of the lawyer's fiduciary role, in violation of the lawyer's basic ethical obligation not to use the trust of the client to the client's disadvantage. In addition, such a relationship presents a significant danger that, because of the lawyer's emotional involvement, the lawyer will be unable to represent the client without impairment of the exercise of independent professional judgment. Moreover, a blurred line between the professional and personal relationships may make it difficult to predict to what extent client confidences will be protected by the attorney-client evidentiary privilege, since client confidences are protected by privilege only when they are imparted in the context of the client-lawyer relationship. Because of the significant danger of harm to client interests and because the client's own emotional involvement renders it unlikely that the client could give adequate informed consent, this Rule prohibits the lawyer from having sexual relations with a client regardless of whether the relationship is consensual and regardless of the absence of prejudice to the client.

[18] Sexual relationships that predate the client-lawyer relationship are not prohibited. Issues relating to the exploitation of the fiduciary relationship and client dependency are diminished when the sexual relationship existed prior to the commencement of the client-lawyer relationship. However, before proceeding with the representation in these circumstances, the lawyer should consider whether the lawyer's ability to represent the client will be materially limited by the relationship. See Rule 1.7(a)(2).

[19] When the client is an organization, paragraph (j) of this Rule prohibits a lawyer for the organization (whether inside counsel or outside counsel) from having a sexual relationship with a constituent of the organization who supervises, directs or regularly consults with that lawyer concerning the organization's legal matters.

Imputation of Prohibitions

[20] Under paragraph (k), a prohibition on conduct by an individual lawyer in paragraphs (a) through (i) and (l) also applies to all lawyers associated in a firm with the personally prohibited lawyer. For example, one lawyer in a firm may not enter into a business transaction with a client of another member of the firm without complying with paragraph (a), even if the first lawyer is not personally involved in the representation of the client. The prohibition set forth in paragraph (j) is personal and is not applied to associated lawyers.

Part–time Prosecutor or Deputy Prosecutor

[21] Under paragraph (l) special rules are provided for part-time prosecutors and deputy prosecutors.

Rule 1.9. Duties to Former Clients

(a) A lawyer who has formerly represented a client in a matter shall not thereafter represent another person in the same or a substantially related matter in which that person's interests are materially adverse to the interests of the former client unless the former client gives informed consent, confirmed in writing.

(b) A lawyer shall not knowingly represent a person in the same or a substantially related matter in which a firm with which the lawyer formerly was associated had previously represented a client

(1) whose interests are materially adverse to that person; and

(2) about whom the lawyer had acquired information protected by Rules 1. 6 and 1.9(c) that is material to the matter; unless the former client gives informed consent, confirmed in writing.

(c) A lawyer who has formerly represented a client in a matter or whose present or former firm has formerly represented a client in a matter shall not thereafter:

(1) use information relating to the representation to the disadvantage of the former client except as these Rules would permit or require with respect to a client, or when the information has become generally known; or

(2) reveal information relating to the representation except as these Rules would permit or require with respect to a client.

Adopted effective Jan. 1, 1987. Amended Dec. 15, 1995, effective Feb. 1, 1996; Sept. 30, 2004, effective Jan. 1, 2005.

Comment

[1] After termination of a client-lawyer relationship, a lawyer has certain continuing duties with respect to confidentiality and conflicts of interest and thus may not represent another client except in conformity with this Rule. Under this Rule, for example, a lawyer could not properly seek to rescind on behalf of a new client a contract drafted on behalf of the former client. So also a lawyer who has prosecuted an accused person could not properly represent the accused in a subsequent civil action against the government concerning the same transaction. Nor could a lawyer who has represented multiple clients in a matter represent one of the clients against the others in the same or a substantially related matter after a dispute arose among the clients in that matter, unless all affected clients give informed consent. See Comment [9]. Current and former government lawyers must comply with this Rule to the extent required by Rule 1.11.

[2] The scope of a "matter" for purposes of this Rule depends on the facts of a particular situation or transaction. The lawyer's involvement in a matter can also be a question of degree. When a lawyer has been directly involved in a specific transaction, subsequent representation of other clients with materially adverse interests in that transaction clearly is prohibited. On the other

hand, a lawyer who recurrently handled a type of problem for a former client is not precluded from later representing another client in a factually distinct problem of that type even though the subsequent representation involves a position adverse to the prior client. Similar considerations can apply to the reassignment of military lawyers between defense and prosecution functions within the same military jurisdictions. The underlying question is whether the lawyer was so involved in the matter that the subsequent representation can be justly regarded as a changing of sides in the matter in question.

[3] Matters are "substantially related" for purposes of this Rule if they involve the same transaction or legal dispute or if there otherwise is a substantial risk that confidential factual information as would normally have been obtained in the prior representation would materially advance the client's position in the subsequent matter. For example, a lawyer who has represented a businessperson and learned extensive private financial information about that person may not then represent that person's spouse in seeking a divorce. Similarly, a lawyer who has previously represented a client in securing environmental permits to build a shopping center would be precluded from representing neighbors seeking to oppose rezoning of the property on the basis of environmental considerations; however, the lawyer would not be precluded, on the grounds of substantial relationship, from defending a tenant of the completed shopping center in resisting eviction for nonpayment of rent. Information that has been disclosed to the public or to other parties adverse to the former client ordinarily will not be disqualifying. Information acquired in a prior representation may have been rendered obsolete by the passage of time, a circumstance that may be relevant in determining whether two representations are substantially related. In the case of an organizational client, general knowledge of the client's policies and practices ordinarily will not preclude a subsequent representation; on the other hand, knowledge of specific facts gained in a prior representation that are relevant to the matter in question ordinarily will preclude such a representation. A former client is not required to reveal the confidential information learned by the lawyer in order to establish a substantial risk that the lawyer has confidential information to use in the subsequent matter. A conclusion about the possession of such information may be based on the nature of the services the lawyer provided the former client and information that would in ordinary practice be learned by a lawyer providing such services.

Lawyers Moving Between Firms

[4] When lawyers have been associated within a firm but then end their association, the question of whether a lawyer should undertake representation is more complicated. There are several competing considerations. First, the client previously represented by the former firm must be reasonably assured that the principle of loyalty to the client is not compromised. Second, the rule should not be so broadly cast as to preclude other persons from

having reasonable choice of legal counsel. Third, the rule should not unreasonably hamper lawyers from forming new associations and taking on new clients after having left a previous association. In this connection, it should be recognized that today many lawyers practice in firms, that many lawyers to some degree limit their practice to one field or another, and that many move from one association to another several times in their careers. If the concept of imputation were applied with unqualified rigor, the result would be radical curtailment of the opportunity of lawyers to move from one practice setting to another and of the opportunity of clients to change counsel.

[5] Paragraph (b) operates to disqualify the lawyer only when the lawyer involved has actual knowledge of information protected by Rules 1.6 and 1.9(c). Thus, if a lawyer while with one firm acquired no knowledge or information relating to a particular client of the firm, and that lawyer later joined another firm, neither the lawyer individually nor the second firm is disqualified from representing another client in the same or a related matter even though the interests of the two clients conflict. See Rule 1.10(b) for the restrictions on a firm once a lawyer has terminated association with the firm.

[6] Application of paragraph (b) depends on a situation's particular facts, aided by inferences, deductions or working presumptions that reasonably may be made about the way in which lawyers work together. A lawyer may have general access to files of all clients of a law firm and may regularly participate in discussions of their affairs; it should be inferred that such a lawyer in fact is privy to all information about all the firm's clients. In contrast, another lawyer may have access to the files of only a limited number of clients and participate in discussions of the affairs of no other clients; in the absence of information to the contrary, it should be inferred that such a lawyer in fact is privy to information about the clients actually served but not those of other clients. In such an inquiry, the burden of proof should rest upon the firm whose disqualification is sought.

[7] Independent of the question of disqualification of a firm, a lawyer changing professional association has a continuing duty to preserve confidentiality of information about a client formerly represented. See Rules 1.6 and 1.9(c).

[8] Paragraph (c) provides that information acquired by the lawyer in the course of representing a client may not subsequently be used or revealed by the lawyer to the disadvantage of the client. However, the fact that a lawyer has once served a client does not preclude the lawyer from using generally known information about that client when later representing another client.

[9] The provisions of this Rule are for the protection of former clients and can be waived if the client gives informed consent, which consent must be confirmed in writing under paragraphs (a) and (b). See Rule 1.0(e). With regard to the effectiveness of an advance waiver, see Comment [22] to Rule 1.7. With regard to disqualification of a firm with which a lawyer is or was formerly associated, see Rule 1.10.

Rule 1.10. Imputation of Conflicts of Interest: General Rule

(a) While lawyers are associated in a firm, none of them shall knowingly represent a client when any one of them practicing alone would be prohibited from doing so by Rules 1.7, 1.9, or 2.2 unless the prohibition is based on a personal interest of the prohibited lawyer and does not present a significant risk of materially limiting the representation of the client by the remaining lawyers in the firm.

(b) When a lawyer has terminated an association with a firm, the firm is not prohibited from thereafter representing a person with interests materially adverse to those of a client represented by the formerly associated lawyer and not currently represented by the firm unless:

(1) the matter is the same or substantially related to that in which the formerly associated lawyer represented the client; and

(2) any lawyer remaining in the firm has information protected by Rules 1.6 and 1.9(c) that is material to the matter.

(c) When a lawyer becomes associated with a firm, no lawyer associated in the firm shall knowingly represent a person in a matter in which that lawyer is disqualified under Rule 1.9 unless:

(1) the personally disqualified lawyer did not have primary responsibility for the matter that causes the disqualification under Rule 1.9;

(2) the personally disqualified lawyer is timely screened from any participation in the matter and is apportioned no part of the fee therefrom; and

(3) written notice is promptly given to any affected former client to enable it to ascertain compliance with the provisions of this rule.

(d) A disqualification prescribed by this rule may be waived by the affected client under the conditions stated in Rule 1.7.

(e) The disqualification of lawyers associated in a firm with former or current government lawyers is governed by Rule 1.11.

Adopted effective Jan. 1, 1987; amended Dec. 5, 1994, effective Feb. 1, 1995; amended Sept. 30, 2004, effective Jan. 1, 2005.

Comment

Definition of "Firm"

[1] For purposes of the Rules of Professional Conduct, the term "firm" denotes lawyers in a law partnership, professional corporation, sole proprietorship or other association authorized to practice law; or lawyers employed in a legal services organization or the legal department of a corporation or other organization. See Rule 1.0(c). Whether two or more lawyers constitute a firm within this definition can depend on the specific facts. See Rule 1.0, Comments [2]—[4].

Principles of Imputed Disqualification

[2] The rule of imputed disqualification stated in paragraph (a) gives effect to the principle of loyalty to the client as it applies to lawyers who practice in a law firm. Such situations can be considered from the premise that a firm of lawyers is essentially one lawyer for purposes of the rules governing loyalty to the client, or from the premise that each lawyer is vicariously bound by the obligation of loyalty owed by each lawyer with whom the lawyer is associated. Paragraph (a) operates only among the lawyers currently associated in a firm. When a lawyer moves from one firm to another, the situation is governed by Rules 1.9(b), and 1.10(b) and 1.10(c).

[3] The rule in paragraph (a) does not prohibit representation where neither questions of client loyalty nor protection of confidential information are presented.

[4] The rule in paragraph (a) also does not prohibit representation by others in the law firm where the person prohibited from involvement in a matter is a nonlawyer, such as a paralegal or legal secretary. Nor does paragraph (a) prohibit representation if the lawyer is prohibited from acting because of events before the person became a lawyer, for example, work that the person did while a law student. Such persons, however, ordinarily must be screened from any personal participation in the matter to avoid communication to others in the firm of confidential information that both the nonlawyers and the firm have a legal duty to protect. See Rules 1.0(k) and 5.3.

[5] Rule 1.10(b) operates to permit a law firm, under certain circumstances, to represent a person with interests directly adverse to those of a client represented by a lawyer who formerly was associated with the firm. The Rule applies regardless of when the formerly associated lawyer represented the client. However, the law firm may not represent a person with interests adverse to those of a present client of the firm, which would violate Rule 1.7. Moreover, the firm may not represent the person where the matter is the same or substantially related to that in which the formerly associated lawyer represented the client and any other lawyer currently in the firm has material information protected by Rules 1.6 and 1.9(c).

[6] Where the conditions of paragraph (c) are met, imputation is removed, and consent to the new representation is not required. Lawyers should be aware, however, that courts may impose more stringent obligations in ruling upon motions to disqualify a lawyer from pending litigation. Requirements for screening procedures are stated in Rule 1.0(k). Paragraph (c)(2) does not prohibit the screened lawyer from receiving a salary or partnership share established by prior independent agreement, but that lawyer may not receive compensation directly related to the matter in which the lawyer is disqualified. Notice, including a description of the screened lawyer's prior representation and of the screening procedures employed, generally should be given as soon as practicable after the need for screening becomes apparent.

[7] Rule 1.10(d) removes imputation with the informed consent of the affected client or former client under the conditions stated in Rule 1.7. The conditions stated in Rule 1.7 require the lawyer to determine that the representation is not prohibited by Rule 1.7(b) and that each affected client or former client has given informed consent to the representation, confirmed in writing. In some cases, the risk may be so severe that the conflict may not be cured by client consent. For a discussion of the effectiveness of client waivers of conflicts that might arise in the future, see Rule 1.7, Comment [22]. For a definition of informed consent, see Rule 1.0(e).

[8] Where a lawyer has joined a private firm after having represented the government, imputation is governed by Rule 1.11(b) and (c), not this Rule. Under Rule 1.11(d), where a lawyer represents the government after having served clients in private practice, nongovernmental employment or in another government agency, former-client conflicts are not imputed to government lawyers associated with the individually disqualified lawyer.

[9] Where a lawyer is prohibited from engaging in certain transactions under Rule 1.8, paragraph (k) of that Rule, and not this Rule, determines whether that prohibition also applies to other lawyers associated in a firm with the personally prohibited lawyer.

Rule 1.11. Special Conflicts of Interest for Former and Current Government Officers and Employees

(a) Except as law may otherwise expressly permit, a lawyer who has formerly served as a public officer or employee of the government:

(1) is subject to Rule 1.9(c); and

(2) shall not otherwise represent a client in connection with a matter in which the lawyer participated personally and substantially as a public officer or employee, unless the appropriate government agency gives its informed consent, confirmed in writing to the representation.

(b) When a lawyer is disqualified from representation under paragraph (a), no lawyer in the firm with which that lawyer is associated may knowingly undertake or continue representation in such a matter unless:

(1) the disqualified lawyer is timely screened from any participation in the matter and is apportioned no part of the fee therefrom; and

(2) written notice is promptly given to the appropriate government agency to enable it to ascertain compliance with the provisions of this rule.

(c) Except as law may otherwise expressly permit, a lawyer having information that the lawyer knows is confidential government information about a person acquired when the lawyer was a public officer or employee, may not represent a private client whose interests are adverse to that person in a matter in which the information could be used to the material disadvantage of that person. As used in this Rule, the term "confidential government information" means information that has been obtained under governmental authority and which, at the time this Rule is applied, the government is prohibited by law from disclosing to the public or has a legal privilege not to disclose and which is not otherwise available to the public. A firm with which that lawyer is associated may undertake or continue representation in the matter only if the disqualified lawyer is timely screened from any participation in the matter and is apportioned no part of the fee therefrom.

(d) Except as law may otherwise expressly permit, a lawyer currently serving as a public officer or employee:

(1) is subject to Rules 1.7 and 1.9; and

(2) shall not:

(i) participate in a matter in which the lawyer participated personally and substantially while in private practice or nongovernmental employment, unless the appropriate government agency gives its informed consent, confirmed in writing; or

(ii) negotiate for private employment with any person who is involved as a party or as lawyer for a party in a matter in which the lawyer is participating personally and substantially, except that a lawyer serving as a law clerk to a judge, other adjudicative officer, or arbitrator may negotiate for private employment as permitted by Rule 1.12(b) and subject to the conditions stated in Rule 1.12(b).

(e) As used in this Rule, the term "matter" includes:

(1) any judicial or other proceeding, application, request for a ruling or other determination, contract, claim, controversy, investigation, charge, accusation, arrest or other particular matter involving a specific party or parties; and

(2) any other matter covered by the conflict of interest rules of the appropriate government agency.

Adopted effective Jan. 1, 1987; amended Dec. 15, 1995, effective Feb. 1,1996; amended Sept. 30, 2004, effective Jan. 1, 2005.

Comment

[1] A lawyer who has served or is currently serving as a public officer or employee is personally subject to the Rules of Professional Conduct, including the prohibition against concurrent conflicts of interest stated in Rule 1.7. In addition, such a lawyer may be subject to statutes and government regulations regarding conflict of interest. Such statutes and regulations may circumscribe the extent to which the government agency may give consent under this Rule. See Rule 1.0(e) for the definition of informed consent.

[2] Paragraphs (a)(1), (a)(2) and (d)(1) restate the obligations of an individual lawyer who has served or is currently serving as an officer or employee of the government toward a former government or private client. Rule 1.10 is not applicable to the conflicts of interest addressed by this Rule. Rather, paragraph (b) sets forth a special imputation rule for former government lawyers that provides for screening and notice. Because of the special problems raised by imputation within a government agency, paragraph (d) does not impute the conflicts of a lawyer currently serving as an officer or employee of the government to other associated government officers or employees, although ordinarily it will be prudent to screen such lawyers.

[3] Paragraphs (a)(2) and (d)(2) apply regardless of whether a lawyer is adverse to a former client and are thus designed not only to protect the former client, but also to prevent a lawyer from exploiting public office for the advantage of another client. For example, a lawyer who has pursued a claim on behalf of the government may not pursue the same claim on behalf of a later private client after the lawyer has left government service, except when authorized to do so by the government agency under paragraph (a). Similarly, a lawyer who has pursued a claim on behalf of a private client may not pursue the claim on behalf of the government, except when authorized to do so by paragraph (d). As with paragraphs (a)(1) and (d)(1), Rule 1.10 is not applicable to the conflicts of interest addressed by these paragraphs.

[4] This Rule represents a balancing of interests. On the one hand, where the successive clients are a government agency and another client, public or private, the risk exists that power or discretion vested in that agency might be used for the special benefit of the other client. A lawyer should not be in a position where benefit to the other client might affect performance of the lawyer's professional functions on behalf of the government. Also, unfair advantage could accrue to the other client by reason of access to confidential government information about the client's adversary obtainable only through the lawyer's government service. On the other hand, the rules governing lawyers presently or formerly employed by a government agency should not be so restrictive as to inhibit transfer of employment to and from the government. The government has a legitimate need to attract qualified lawyers as well as to maintain high ethical standards. Thus a former government lawyer is disqualified only from particular matters in which the lawyer participated personally and substantially. The provisions for screening and waiver in paragraph (b) are necessary to prevent the disqualification rule from imposing too severe a deterrent against entering public service. The limitation of disqualification in paragraphs (a)(2) and (d)(2) to matters involving a specific party or parties, rather than extending disqualification to all substantive issues on which the lawyer worked, serves a similar function.

[5] When a lawyer has been employed by one government agency and then moves to a second government agency, it may be appropriate to treat

that second agency as another client for purposes of this Rule, as when a lawyer is employed by a city and subsequently is employed by a federal agency. However, because the conflict of interest is governed by paragraph (d), the latter agency is not required to screen the lawyer as paragraph (b) requires a law firm to do. The question of whether two government agencies should be regarded as the same or different clients for conflict of interest purposes is beyond the scope of these Rules. See Rule 1.13 Comment [6].

[6] Paragraphs (b) and (c) contemplate a screening arrangement. See Rule 1.0(k) (requirements for screening procedures). These paragraphs do not prohibit a lawyer from receiving a salary or partnership share established by prior independent agreement, but that lawyer may not receive compensation directly relating the lawyer's compensation to the fee in the matter in which the lawyer is disqualified.

[7] Notice, including a description of the screened lawyer's prior representation and of the screening procedures employed, generally should be given as soon as practicable after the need for screening becomes apparent.

[8] Paragraph (c) operates only when the lawyer in question has knowledge of the information, which means actual knowledge; it does not operate with respect to information that merely could be imputed to the lawyer.

[9] Paragraphs (a) and (d) do not prohibit a lawyer from jointly representing a private party and a government agency when doing so is permitted by Rule 1.7 and is not otherwise prohibited by law.

[10] For purposes of paragraph (e) of this Rule, a "matter" may continue in another form. In determining whether two particular matters are the same, the lawyer should consider the extent to which the matters involve the same basic facts, the same or related parties, and the time elapsed.

Rule 1.12. Former Judge, Arbitrator, Mediator or Other Third-Party Neutral

(a) Except as stated in paragraph (d), a lawyer shall not represent anyone in connection with a matter in which the lawyer participated personally and substantially as a judge or other adjudicative officer, arbitrator, mediator or other third-party neutral, or law clerk to such a person, unless all parties to the proceeding give informed consent, confirmed in writing.

(b) A lawyer shall not negotiate for employment with any person who is involved as a party or as lawyer for a party in a matter in which the lawyer is participating personally and substantially as a judge or other adjudicative officer or as an arbitrator, mediator or other third-party neutral. A lawyer serving as a law clerk to any such person may negotiate for employment with a party or lawyer involved in a matter in which the clerk is participating personally and substantially, but only after the lawyer has notified the law clerk's employer.

(c) If a lawyer is disqualified by paragraph (a), no lawyer in a firm with which that lawyer is associated may knowingly undertake or continue representation in the matter unless:

(1) the disqualified lawyer is timely screened from any participation in the matter and is apportioned no part of the fee therefrom; and

(2) written notice is promptly given to the parties and any appropriate tribunal to enable them to ascertain compliance with the provisions of this rule.

(d) An arbitrator selected as a partisan of a party in a multi-member arbitration panel is not prohibited from subsequently representing that party.

Adopted effective Jan. 1, 1987. Amended Dec. 15, 1995, effective Feb. 1, 1996; Sept. 30, 2004, effective Jan. 1, 2005.

Comment

[1] This Rule generally parallels Rule 1.11. The term "personally and substantially" signifies that a judge who was a member of a multimember court, and thereafter left judicial office to practice law, is not prohibited from representing a client in a matter pending in the court, but in which the former judge did not participate. So also the fact that a former judge exercised administrative responsibility in a court does not prevent the former judge from acting as a lawyer in a matter where the judge had previously exercised remote or incidental administrative responsibility that did not affect the merits. Compare the Comment to Rule 1.11. The term "adjudicative officer" includes such officials as judges pro tempore, referees, special masters, hearing officers and other parajudicial officers, and also lawyers who serve as part-time judges. The Indiana Code of Judicial Conduct provides that a part-time judge, judge pro tempore or retired judge recalled to active service, may not "act as a lawyer in any proceeding in which he served as a judge or in any other proceeding related thereto." Although phrased differently from this Rule, those rules correspond in meaning.

[2] Like former judges, lawyers who have served as arbitrators, mediators or other third-party neutrals may be asked to represent a client in a matter in which the lawyer participated personally and substantially. This Rule forbids such representation unless all of the parties to the proceedings give their informed consent, confirmed in writing. See Rule 1.0(e) and (b). Other law or codes of ethics governing third-party neutrals may impose more stringent standards of personal or imputed disqualification. See Rule 2.4.

[3] Although lawyers who serve as third-party neutrals do not have information concerning the parties that is protected under Rule 1.6, they typically owe the parties an obligation of confidentiality under law or codes of ethics governing third-party neutrals. Thus, paragraph (c) provides that conflicts of the personally disqualified lawyer will be imputed to other lawyers in a law firm unless the conditions of this paragraph are met.

[4] Requirements for screening procedures are stated in Rule 1.0(k). Paragraph (c)(1) does not

prohibit the screened lawyer from receiving a salary or partnership share established by prior independent agreement, but that lawyer may not receive compensation directly related to the matter in which the lawyer is disqualified.

[5] Notice, including a description of the screened lawyer's prior representation and of the screening procedures employed, generally should be given as soon as practicable after the need for screening becomes apparent.

Rule 1.13.   Organization as Client

(a) A lawyer employed or retained by an organization represents the organization acting through its duly authorized constituents.

(b) If a lawyer for an organization knows that an officer, employee or other person associated with the organization is engaged in action, intends to act or refuses to act in a matter related to the representation that is a violation of a legal obligation to the organization, or a violation of law which reasonably might be imputed to the organization, and that is likely to result in substantial injury to the organization, then the lawyer shall proceed as is reasonably necessary in the best interest of the organization. Unless the lawyer reasonably believes that it is not necessary in the best interest of the organization to do so, the lawyer shall refer the matter to higher authority in the organization, including, if warranted by the circumstances to the highest authority that can act on behalf of the organization as determined by applicable law.

(c) Except as provided in paragraph (d), if

(1) despite the lawyer's efforts in accordance with paragraph (b) the highest authority that can act on behalf of the organization insists upon or fails to address in a timely and appropriate manner an action, or a refusal to act, that is clearly a violation of law and

(2) the lawyer reasonably believes that the violation is reasonably certain to result in substantial injury to the organization, then the lawyer may reveal information relating to the representation whether or not Rule 1.6 permits such disclosure, but only if and to the extent the lawyer reasonably believes necessary to prevent substantial injury to the organization.

(d) Paragraph (c) shall not apply with respect to information relating to a lawyer's representation of an organization to investigate an alleged violation of law, or to defend the organization or an officer, employee or other constituent associated with the organization against a claim arising out of an alleged violation of law.

(e) A lawyer who reasonably believes that he or she has been discharged because of the lawyer's actions taken pursuant to paragraphs (b) or (c), or who withdraws under circumstances that require or permit the lawyer to take action under either of those paragraphs, shall proceed as the lawyer reasonably believes necessary to assure that the organization's highest authority is informed of the lawyer's discharge or withdrawal.

(f) In dealing with an organization's directors, officers, employees, members, shareholders or other constituents, a lawyer shall explain the identity of the client when the lawyer knows or reasonably should know that the organization's interests are adverse to those of the constituents with whom the lawyer is dealing.

(g) A lawyer representing an organization may also represent any of its directors, officers, employees, members, shareholders or other constituents, subject to the provisions of Rule 1.7. If the organization's consent to the dual representation is required by Rule 1.7, the consent shall be given by an appropriate official of the organization other than the individual who is to be represented, or by the shareholders.

Adopted effective Jan. 1, 1987. Amended Sept. 30, 2004, effective Jan. 1, 2005.

Comment

The Entity as the Client

[1] An organizational client is a legal entity, but it cannot act except through its officers, directors, employees, shareholders and other constituents. Officers, directors, employees and shareholders are the constituents of the corporate organizational client. The duties defined in this Comment apply equally to unincorporated associations. "Other constituents" as used in this Comment means the positions equivalent to officers, directors, employees and shareholders held by persons acting for organizational clients that are not corporations.

[2] When one of the constituents of an organizational client communicates with the organization's lawyer in that person's organizational capacity, the communication is protected by Rule 1.6. Thus, by way of example, if an organizational client requests its lawyer to investigate allegations of wrongdoing, interviews made in the course of that investigation between the lawyer and the client's employees or other constituents are covered by Rule 1.6. This does not mean, however, that constituents of an organizational client are the clients of the lawyer. The lawyer may not disclose to such constituents information relating to the representation except for disclosures explicitly or impliedly authorized by the organizational client in order to carry out the representation or as otherwise permitted by Rule 1. 6.

[3] When constituents of the organization make decisions for it, the decisions ordinarily must be accepted by the lawyer even if their utility or prudence is doubtful. Decisions concerning policy and operations, including ones entailing serious risk, are not as such in the lawyer's province. Paragraph (b) makes clear, however, that when the lawyer knows that the organization is likely to be substantially injured by action of an officer or other constituent that violates a legal obligation to the organization or is in violation of law that might be imputed to the organization, the lawyer must pro-

ceed as is reasonably necessary in the best interest of the organization. As defined in Rule 1.0(f), knowledge can be inferred from circumstances, and a lawyer cannot ignore the obvious.

[4] In determining how to proceed under paragraph (b), the lawyer should give due consideration to the seriousness of the violation and its consequences, the responsibility in the organization and the apparent motivation of the person involved, the policies of the organization concerning such matters, and any other relevant considerations. Ordinarily, referral to a higher authority would be necessary. In some circumstances, however, it may be appropriate for the lawyer to ask the constituent to reconsider the matter; for example, if the circumstances involve a constituent's innocent misunderstanding of law and subsequent acceptance of the lawyer's advice, the lawyer may reasonably conclude that the best interest of the organization does not require that the matter be referred to higher authority. If a constituent persists in conduct contrary to the lawyer's advice, it will be necessary for the lawyer to take steps to have the matter reviewed by a higher authority in the organization. If the matter is of sufficient seriousness and importance or urgency to the organization, referral to higher authority in the organization may be necessary even if the lawyer has not communicated with the constituent. Any measures taken should, to the extent practicable, minimize the risk of revealing information relating to the representation to persons outside the organization. Even in circumstances where a lawyer is not obligated by Rule 1.13 to proceed, a lawyer may bring to the attention of an organizational client, including its highest authority, matters that the lawyer reasonably believes to be of sufficient importance to warrant doing so in the best interest of the organization.

[5] Paragraph (b) also makes clear that when it is reasonably necessary to enable the organization to address the matter in a timely and appropriate manner, the lawyer must refer the matter to higher authority, including, if warranted by the circumstances, the highest authority that can act on behalf of the organization under applicable law. The organization's highest authority to whom a matter may be referred ordinarily will be the board of directors or similar governing body. However, applicable law may prescribe that under certain conditions the highest authority reposes elsewhere, for example, in the independent directors of a corporation.

Relation to Other Rules

[6] The authority and responsibility provided in this Rule are concurrent with the authority and responsibility provided in other Rules. In particular, this Rule does not limit or expand the lawyer's responsibility under Rules 1.8, 1.16, 3.3 or 4.1. Paragraph (c) of this Rule supplements Rule 1.6(b) by providing an additional basis upon which the lawyer may reveal information relating to the representation, but does not modify, restrict, or limit the provisions of Rule 1.6(b)(1)—(6). Under paragraph (c) the lawyer may reveal such information only when the organization's highest authority insists

upon or fails to address threatened or ongoing action that is clearly a violation of law, and then only to the extent the lawyer reasonably believes necessary to prevent reasonably certain substantial injury to the organization. It is not necessary that the lawyer's services be used in furtherance of the violation, but it is required that the matter be related to the lawyer's representation of the organization. If the lawyer's services are being used by an organization to further a crime or fraud by the organization, Rules 1.6(b)(2) and 1.6(b)(3) may permit the lawyer to disclose confidential information. In such circumstances Rule 1.2(d) may also be applicable, in which event, withdrawal from the representation under Rule 1.16(a)(1) may be required.

[7] Paragraph (d) makes clear that the authority of a lawyer to disclose information relating to a representation in circumstances described in paragraph (c) does not apply with respect to information relating to a lawyer's engagement by an organization to investigate an alleged violation of law or to defend the organization or an officer, employee or other person associated with the organization against a claim arising out of an alleged violation of law. This is necessary in order to enable organizational clients to enjoy the full benefits of legal counsel in conducting an investigation or defending against a claim.

[8] A lawyer who reasonably believes that he or she has been discharged because of the lawyer's actions taken pursuant to paragraph (b) or (c), or who withdraws in circumstances that require or permit the lawyer to take action under either of these paragraphs, must proceed as the lawyer reasonably believes necessary to assure that the organization's highest authority is informed of the lawyer's discharge or withdrawal.

Government Agency

[9] The duty defined in this Rule applies to governmental organizations. Defining precisely the identity of the client and prescribing the resulting obligations of such lawyers may be more difficult in the government context and is a matter beyond the scope of these Rules. See Scope [18]. Although in some circumstances the client may be a specific agency, it may also be a branch of government, such as the executive branch, or the government as a whole. For example, if the action or failure to act involves the head of a bureau, either the department of which the bureau is a part or the relevant branch of government may be the client for purposes of this Rule. Moreover, in a matter involving the conduct of government officials, a government lawyer may have authority under applicable law to question such conduct more extensively than that of a lawyer for a private organization in similar circumstances. Thus, when the client is a governmental organization, a different balance may be appropriate between maintaining confidentiality and assuring that the wrongful act is prevented or rectified, for public business is involved. In addition, duties of lawyers employed by the government or lawyers in military service may

be defined by statutes and regulation. This Rule does not limit that authority. See Scope.

Clarifying the Lawyer's Role

[10] There are times when the organization's interest may be or become adverse to those of one or more of its constituents. In such circumstances the lawyer should advise any constituent, whose interest the lawyer finds adverse to that of the organization of the conflict or potential conflict of interest, that the lawyer cannot represent such constituent, and that such person may wish to obtain independent representation. Care must be taken to assure that the individual understands that, when there is such adversity of interest, the lawyer for the organization cannot provide legal representation for that constituent individual, and that discussions between the lawyer for the organization and the individual may not be privileged.

[11] Whether such a warning should be given by the lawyer for the organization to any constituent individual may turn on the facts of each case.

Dual Representation

[12] Paragraph (g) recognizes that a lawyer for an organization may also represent a principal officer or major shareholder.

Derivative Actions

[13] Under generally prevailing law, the shareholders or members of a corporation may bring suit to compel the directors to perform their legal obligations in the supervision of the organization. Members of unincorporated associations have essentially the same right. Such an action may be brought nominally by the organization, but usually is, in fact, a legal controversy over management of the organization.

[14] The question can arise whether counsel for the organization may defend such an action. The proposition that the organization is the lawyer's client does not alone resolve the issue. Most derivative actions are a normal incident of an organization's affairs, to be defended by the organization's lawyer like any other suit. However, if the claim involves serious charges of wrongdoing by those in control of the organization, a conflict may arise between the lawyer's duty to the organization and the lawyer's relationship with the board. In those circumstances, Rule 1.7 governs who should represent the directors and the organization.

Rule 1.14. Client with Diminished Capacity

(a) When a client's capacity to make adequately considered decisions in connection with a representation is diminished, whether because of minority, mental impairment or for some other reason, the lawyer shall, as far as reasonably possible, maintain a normal client-lawyer relationship with the client.

(b) When the lawyer reasonably believes that the client has diminished capacity, is at risk of substantial physical, financial or other harm unless action is taken and cannot adequately act in the client's own interest,

the lawyer may take reasonably necessary protective action, including consulting with individuals or entities that have the ability to take action to protect the client and, in appropriate cases, seeking the appointment of a guardian ad litem, conservator or guardian.

(c) Information relating to the representation of a client with diminished capacity is protected by Rule 1.6. When taking protective action pursuant to paragraph (b), the lawyer is impliedly authorized under Rule 1.6(a) to reveal information about the client, but only to the extent reasonably necessary to protect the client's interests.

(d) This Rule is not violated if the lawyer acts in good faith to comply with the Rule.

Adopted effective Jan. 1, 1987; amended Sept. 30, 2004, effective Jan. 1, 2005.

Comment

[1] The normal client-lawyer relationship is based on the assumption that the client, when properly advised and assisted, is capable of making decisions about important matters. When the client is a minor or suffers from a diminished mental capacity, however, maintaining the ordinary client-lawyer relationship may not be possible in all respects. In particular, a severely incapacitated person may have no power to make legally binding decisions. Nevertheless, a client with diminished capacity often has the ability to understand, deliberate upon, and reach conclusions about matters affecting the client's own well-being. For example, children as young as five or six years of age, and certainly those of ten or twelve, are regarded as having opinions that are entitled to weight in legal proceedings concerning their custody. So also, it is recognized that some persons of advanced age can be quite capable of handling routine financial matters while needing special legal protection concerning major transactions.

[2] The fact that a client suffers a disability does not diminish the lawyer's obligation to treat the client with attention and respect. Even if the person has a legal representative, the lawyer should as far as possible accord the represented person the status of client, particularly in maintaining communication.

[3] The client may wish to have family members or other persons participate in discussions with the lawyer. When necessary to assist in the representation, the presence of such persons generally does not affect the applicability of the attorney-client evidentiary privilege. Nevertheless, the lawyer must keep the client's interests foremost and, except for protective action authorized under paragraph (b), must look to the client, and not family members, to make decisions on the client's behalf.

[4] If a legal representative has already been appointed for the client, the lawyer should ordinarily look to the representative for decisions on behalf of the client. In matters involving a minor, whether the lawyer should look to the parents as natural guardians may depend on the type of proceeding or matter in which the lawyer is representing the

minor. If the lawyer represents the guardian as distinct from the ward, and is aware that the guardian is acting adversely to the ward's interest, the lawyer may have an obligation to prevent or rectify the guardian's misconduct. See Rule 1.2(d).

Taking Protective Action

[5] If a lawyer reasonably believes that a client is at risk of substantial physical, financial or other harm unless action is taken, and that a normal client-lawyer relationship cannot be maintained as provided in paragraph (a) because the client lacks sufficient capacity to communicate or to make adequately considered decisions in connection with the representation, then paragraph (b) permits the lawyer to take protective measures deemed necessary. Such measures could include: consulting with family members, using a reconsideration period to permit clarification or improvement of circumstances, using voluntary surrogate decision making tools such as durable powers of attorney or consulting with support groups, professional services, adult-protective agencies or other individuals or entities that have the ability to protect the client. In taking any protective action, the lawyer should be guided by such factors as the wishes and values of the client to the extent known, the client's best interests and the goals of intruding into the client's decision making autonomy to the least extent feasible, maximizing client capacities and respecting the client's family and social connections.

[6] In determining the extent of the client's diminished capacity, the lawyer should consider and balance such factors as: the client's ability to articulate reasoning leading to a decision, variability of state of mind and ability to appreciate consequences of a decision; the substantive fairness of a decision; and the consistency of a decision with the known long-term commitments and values of the client. In appropriate circumstances, the lawyer may seek guidance from an appropriate diagnostician.

[7] If a legal representative has not been appointed, the lawyer should consider whether appointment of a guardian ad litem, conservator or guardian is necessary to protect the client's interests. Thus, if a client with diminished capacity has substantial property that should be sold for the client's benefit, effective completion of the transaction may require appointment of a legal representative. In addition, rules of procedure in litigation sometimes provide that minors or persons with diminished capacity must be represented by a guardian or next friend if they do not have a general guardian. In many circumstances, however, appointment of a legal representative may be more expensive or traumatic for the client than circumstances in fact require. Evaluation of such circumstances is a matter entrusted to the professional judgment of the lawyer. In considering alternatives, however, the lawyer should be aware of any law that requires the lawyer to advocate the least restrictive action on behalf of the client.

Disclosure of the Client's Condition

[8] Disclosure of the client's diminished capacity could adversely affect the client's interests. For example, raising the question of diminished capacity could, in some circumstances, lead to proceedings for involuntary commitment. Information relating to the representation is protected by Rule 1.6. Therefore, unless authorized to do so, the lawyer may not disclose such information. When taking protective action pursuant to paragraph (b), the lawyer is impliedly authorized to make the necessary disclosures, even when the client directs the lawyer to the contrary. Nevertheless, given the risks of disclosure, paragraph (c) limits what the lawyer may disclose in consulting with other individuals or entities or seeking the appointment of a legal representative. At the very least, the lawyer should determine whether it is likely that the person or entity consulted with will act adversely to the client's interests before discussing matters related to the client. The lawyer's position in such cases is an unavoidably difficult one.

Emergency Legal Assistance

[9] In an emergency where the health, safety or a financial interest of a person with seriously diminished capacity is threatened with imminent and irreparable harm, a lawyer may take legal action on behalf of such a person even though the person is unable to establish a client-lawyer relationship or to make or express considered judgments about the matter, when the person or another acting in good faith on that person's behalf has consulted with the lawyer. Even in such an emergency, however, the lawyer should not act unless the lawyer reasonably believes that the person has no other lawyer, agent or other representative available. The lawyer should take legal action on behalf of the person only to the extent reasonably necessary to maintain the status quo or otherwise avoid imminent and irreparable harm. A lawyer who undertakes to represent a person in such an exigent situation has the same duties under these Rules as the lawyer would with respect to a client.

[10] A lawyer who acts on behalf of a person with seriously diminished capacity in an emergency should keep the confidences of the person as if dealing with a client, disclosing them only to the extent necessary to accomplish the intended protective action. The lawyer should disclose to any tribunal involved and to any other counsel involved the nature of his or her relationship with the person. The lawyer should take steps to regularize the relationship or implement other protective solutions as soon as possible. Normally, a lawyer would not seek compensation for such emergency actions taken.

Rule 1.15. Safekeeping Property

(a) A lawyer shall hold property of clients or third persons that is in a lawyer's possession in connection with a representation separate from the lawyer's own property. Funds shall be kept in a separate account maintained in the state where the lawyer's office is situated, or elsewhere with the consent of the client or third person. Other property shall be identified as such and appropriately safeguarded. Complete records of such account funds and other property shall be kept by the lawyer and shall be preserved for a period of five years after termination of the representation.

(b) A lawyer may deposit his or her own funds reasonably sufficient to maintain a nominal balance in a client trust account.

(c) A lawyer shall deposit into a client trust account legal fees and expenses that have been paid in advance, to be withdrawn by the lawyer only as fees are earned or expenses incurred.

(d) Upon receiving funds or other property in which the client or third person has an interest, a lawyer shall promptly notify the client or third person. Except as stated in this rule or otherwise permitted by law or by agreement with the client, a lawyer shall promptly deliver to the client or third person any funds or other property that the client or third person is entitled to receive and, upon request by the client or third person, shall promptly render a full accounting regarding such property.

(e) When in the course of representation a lawyer is in possession of property in which two or more persons (one of whom may be the lawyer) claim interests, the property shall be kept separate by the lawyer until the dispute is resolved. The lawyer shall promptly distribute all portions of the property as to which the interests are not in dispute.

(f) Except as provided in paragraph (g) of this rule, a lawyer or law firm shall create and maintain an interest-bearing trust account for clients' funds which are nominal in amount or to be held for a short period of time so that they could not earn income for the client in excess of the costs incurred to secure such income (hereinafter sometimes referred to as an "IOLTA account") in compliance with the following provisions:

(1) Client funds shall be deposited in a lawyer's or law firm's IOLTA account unless the funds can earn income for the client in excess of the costs incurred to secure such income. A lawyer or law firm shall establish a separate interest-bearing trust account for clients' funds which are neither nominal in amount nor to be held for a short period of time and which could earn income for the client in excess of costs for a particular client or client's matter. All of the interest on such account, net of any transaction costs, shall be paid to the client, and no earnings from such account shall be made available to a lawyer or law firm.

(2) No earnings from such an IOLTA account shall be made available to a lawyer or law firm.

(3) The IOLTA account shall include all clients' funds which are nominal in amount or to be held for a short period of time.

(4) An IOLTA account may be established with any financial institution (i) authorized by federal or state law to do business in Indiana, (ii) insured by the Federal Deposit Insurance Corporation or its equivalent, and (iii) approved as a depository for trust accounts pursuant to *Indiana Admission and Discipline Rules*, Rule 23, Section 29. Funds in each IOLTA account shall be subject to withdrawal upon request and without delay and without risk to principal by reason of said withdrawal.

(5) Participating financial institutions shall maintain IOLTA accounts which pay the highest interest rate or dividend generally available from the institution to its non–IOLTA account customers when IOLTA accounts meet or exceed the same minimum balance or other account eligibility qualifications, if any. In determining the highest interest rate or dividend generally available from the institution to its non–IOLTA accounts, eligible institutions may consider factors, in addition to the IOLTA account balance, customarily considered by the institution when setting interest rates or dividends for its customers, provided that such factors do not discriminate between IOLTA accounts and accounts of non–IOLTA customers, and that these factors do not include that the account is an IOLTA account. All interest earned net of fees or charges shall be remitted to the Indiana Bar Foundation (the "Foundation"), which is designated in paragraph (i) of this rule to organize and administer the IOLTA program, and the depository institution shall submit reports thereon as set forth below.

(6) Lawyers or law firms depositing client funds in an IOLTA account established pursuant to this rule shall, on forms approved by the Foundation, direct the depository institution:

(A) to remit all interest or dividends, net of reasonable service charges or fees, if any, on the average monthly balance in the account, or as otherwise computed in accordance with the institution's standard accounting practice, at least quarterly, solely to the Foundation. The depository institution may remit the interest or dividends on all of its IOLTA accounts in a lump sum; however, the depository institution must provide, for each individual IOLTA account, the information to the lawyer or law firm and to the Foundation required by subparagraphs (f)(6)(B) and (f)(6)(C) of this rule;

(B) to transmit with each remittance to the Foundation a statement showing the name of the lawyer or law firm for whom the remittance is sent, the rate of interest applied, and such other information as is reasonably required by the Foundation;

(C) to transmit to the depositing lawyer or law firm a periodic account statement for the IOLTA account reflecting the amount of interest paid to the Foundation, the rate of interest applied, the average account balance for the period for which the interest was earned, and such other information as is reasonably required by the Foundation; and

(D) to waive any reasonable service charge that exceeds the interest earned on any IOLTA account during a reporting period ("excess charge"), or bill the excess charge to the Foundation.

(7) Any IOLTA account which has or may have the net effect of costing the IOLTA program more in fees than earned in interest over a period of time may, at the discretion of the Foundation, be exempted from and removed from the IOLTA program. Exemption of an IOLTA account from the IOLTA program revokes the permission to use the Foundation's tax identification number for that account. Exemption of such account from the IOLTA program shall not relieve the lawyer and/or law firm from the obligation to maintain the property of clients and third persons separately, as required above, in a non-interest bearing account.

(8) The IOLTA program will issue refunds when interest has been remitted in error, whether the error is the bank's or the lawyer's. Requests for refunds must be submitted in writing by the bank, the lawyer, or the law firm on a timely basis, accompanied by documentation that confirms the amount of interest paid to the IOLTA program. As needed for auditing purposes, the IOLTA program may request additional documentation to support the request. The refund will be remitted to the appropriate financial institution for transmittal at the lawyer's direction after appropriate accounting and reporting. In no event will the refund exceed the amount of interest actually received by the IOLTA program.

(9) All interest transmitted to the Foundation shall be held, invested and distributed periodically in accordance with a plan of distribution which shall be prepared by the Foundation and approved at least annually by the Supreme Court of Indiana, for the following purposes:

(A) to pay or provide for all costs, expenses and fees associated with the administration of the IOLTA program;

(B) to establish appropriate reserves;

(C) to assist or establish approved pro bono programs as provided in Rule 6.6;

(D) for such other programs for the benefit of the public as are specifically approved by the Supreme Court from time to time.

(10) The information contained in the statements forwarded to the Foundation under subparagraph (f)(6) of this rule shall remain confidential and the provisions of Rule 1.6 (Confidentiality of Information), are not hereby abrogated; therefore the Foundation shall not release any information contained in any such statement other than as a compilation of data from such statements, except as directed in writing by the Supreme Court.

(11) The Foundation shall have full authority to and shall, from time to time, prepare and submit to the Supreme Court for approval, forms, procedures, instructions and guidelines necessary and appropriate to implement the provisions set forth in this rule and, after approval thereof by the Court, shall promulgate same.

(g) Every lawyer admitted to practice in this State shall annually certify to this Court, pursuant to Ind.Admis.Disc.R. 2(f), that all client funds which are nominal in amount or to be held for a short period of time by the lawyer or the lawyer's law firm so that they could not earn income for the client in excess of the costs incurred to secure such income are held in an IOLTA account, or that the lawyer is exempt because:

(1) the lawyer or law firm's client trust account has been exempted and removed from the IOLTA program by the Foundation pursuant to subparagraph (f)(7) of this rule; or

(2) the lawyer:

(A) is not engaged in the private practice of law;

(B) is not engaged in the private practice of law in Indiana that involves holding client or third party funds in trust;

(C) does not have an office within the State of Indiana;

(D) is a judge, attorney general, public defender, U.S. attorney, district attorney, on duty with the armed services or employed by a local, state or federal government, and is not otherwise engaged in the private practice of law;

(E) is a corporate counsel or teacher of law and is not otherwise engaged in the private practice of law;

(F) has been exempted by an order of general or special application of this Court which is cited in the certification; or

(G) compliance with paragraph (f) would work an undue hardship on the lawyer or would be extremely impractical, based either on the geographic distance between the lawyer's principal office and the closest depository institution which is participating in the IOLTA program, or on other compelling and necessitous factors.

(h) In the exercise of a lawyer's good faith judgment in determining whether funds of a client can earn income in excess of costs, a lawyer shall take into consideration the following factors:

(1) the amount of interest which the funds would earn during the period they are expected to be deposited;

(2) the cost of establishing and administering the account, including the cost of the lawyer's services,

accounting fees, and tax reporting costs and procedures;

(3) the capability of a financial institution, a lawyer or a law firm to calculate and pay income to individual clients;

(4) any other circumstances that affect the ability of the client's funds to earn a net return for the client; and

(5) the nature of the transaction(s) involved. The determination of whether a client's funds are nominal or short-term so that they could not earn income in excess of costs shall rest in the sound judgment of the lawyer or law firm. No lawyer shall be charged with an ethical impropriety or other breach of professional conduct based on the good faith exercise of such judgment.

(i) The Foundation is hereby designated as the entity to organize and administer the IOLTA program established by paragraph (f) of this rule in accordance with the following provisions:

(1) The Board of Directors of the Foundation (the "Board") shall have general supervisory authority over the administration of the IOLTA program, subject to the continuing jurisdiction of the Supreme Court.

(2) The Board shall receive the net earnings from IOLTA accounts established in accordance with paragraph (f) of this rule and shall make appropriate temporary investments of IOLTA program funds pending disbursement of such funds.

(3) The Board shall, by grants, appropriations and other appropriate measures, make disbursements from the IOLTA program funds, including current and accumulated net earnings, in accordance with the plan of distribution approved by the Supreme Court from time to time referenced in subparagraph (f)(9) of this rule.

(4) The Board shall maintain proper records of all IOLTA program receipts and disbursements, which records shall be audited or reviewed annually by a certified public accountant selected by the Board. The Board shall annually cause to be presented to the Supreme Court a reviewed or audited financial statement of its IOLTA program receipts and expenditures for the prior year. The report shall not identify any clients of lawyers or law firms or reveal confidential information. The statement shall be filed with the Clerk of the Supreme Court and a summary thereof shall be published in the next available issue of one or more state-wide publications for attorneys, such as Res Gestae and The Indiana Lawyer.

(5) The president and other members of the Board shall administer the IOLTA program without compensation, but may be reimbursed for their reasonable and necessary expenses incurred in the performance of their duties, and shall be indemni-

fied by the Foundation against any liability or expense arising directly or indirectly out of the good faith performance of their duties.

(6) The Board shall monitor attorney compliance with the provisions of this rule and periodically report to the Supreme Court those attorneys not in compliance with the provisions of Rule 1.15.

(7) In the event the IOLTA program or its administration by the Foundation is terminated, all assets of the IOLTA program, including any program funds then on hand, shall be transferred in accordance with the Order of the Supreme Court terminating the IOLTA program or its administration by the Foundation; provided, such transfer shall be to an entity which will not violate the requirements the Foundation must observe regarding transfer of its assets in order to retain its tax-exempt status under the Internal Revenue Code of 1986, as amended, or similar future provisions of law.

Amended Oct. 22, 1997, Subds. (a) - (c) effective Feb. 1, 1998; Subds. (d) - (h) held in abeyance until further order of Court per court order filed and effective Sept. 30, 1998; order of Sept. 30, 1998, holding Subds. (d) - (h) in abeyance, is terminated, and effective date for declining participation in IOLTA program for calendar years 1999 and 2000 pursuant to Subd. (f) is Nov. 30, 1999, per court order filed and effective Oct. 29, 1999; amended Sept. 30, 2004, effective Jan. 1, 2005; Feb. 9, 2005, effective July 1, 2005; Aug. 15, 2006, effective Jan. 1, 2007; Sept. 15, 2009, effective Jan. 1, 2010.

Comment

[1] A lawyer should hold property of others with the care required of a professional fiduciary. Securities should be kept in a safe deposit box, except when some other form of safekeeping is warranted by special circumstances. All property that is the property of clients or third persons, including prospective clients, must be kept separate from the lawyer's business and personal property and, if monies, in one or more trust accounts. Separate trust accounts may be warranted when administering estate monies or acting in similar fiduciary capacities. A lawyer should maintain on a current basis books and records in accordance with generally accepted accounting practice and comply with any recordkeeping rules established by law or court order. See, e.g., ABA Model

Financial Recordkeeping Rule.

[2] While normally it is impermissible to commingle the lawyer's own funds with client funds, paragraph (b) provides that it is permissible when necessary to maintain a nominal balance in the account. Accurate records must be kept regarding which part of the funds are the lawyer's.

[3] Lawyers often receive funds from which the lawyer's fee will be paid. The lawyer is not required to remit to the client, funds that the lawyer reasonably believes represent fees owed. However, a lawyer may not hold funds to coerce a client into accepting the lawyer's contention. The disputed

portion of the funds must be kept in a trust account and the lawyer should suggest means for prompt resolution of the dispute, such as arbitration. The undisputed portion of the funds shall be promptly distributed.

[4] Paragraph (e) also recognizes that third parties may have lawful claims against specific funds or other property in a lawyer's custody, such as a client's creditor who has a lien on funds recovered in a personal injury action. A lawyer may have a duty under applicable law to protect such third-party claims against wrongful interference by the client. In such cases, when the third-party claim is not frivolous under applicable law, the lawyer must refuse to surrender the property to the client until the claims are resolved. A lawyer should not unilaterally assume to arbitrate a dispute between the client and the third party, but, when there are substantial grounds for dispute as to the person entitled to the funds, the lawyer may file an action to have a court resolve the dispute.

[5] The obligations of a lawyer under this Rule are independent of those arising from activity other than rendering legal services. For example, a lawyer who serves only as an escrow agent is governed by the applicable law relating to fiduciaries even though the lawyer does not render legal services in the transaction and is not governed by this Rule.

[6] A lawyers' fund for client protection provides a means through the collective efforts of the bar to reimburse persons who have lost money or property as a result of dishonest conduct of a lawyer. Where such a fund has been established, a lawyer must participate where it is mandatory, and, even when it is voluntary, the lawyer should participate.

Rule 1.16.   Declining or Terminating Representation

(a) Except as stated in paragraph (c), a lawyer shall not represent a client or, where representation has commenced, shall withdraw from the representation of a client if:

(1) the representation will result in violation of the Rules of Professional Conduct or other law;

(2) the lawyer's physical or mental condition materially impairs the lawyer's ability to represent the client; or

(3) the lawyer is discharged.

(b) Except as stated in paragraph (c), a lawyer may withdraw from representing a client if:

(1) withdrawal can be accomplished without material adverse effect on the interests of the client;

(2) the client persists in a course of action involving the lawyer's services that the lawyer reasonably believes is criminal or fraudulent;

(3) the client has used the lawyer's services to perpetrate a crime or fraud;

(4) a client insists upon taking action that the lawyer considers repugnant or with which the lawyer has a fundamental disagreement;

(5) the client fails substantially to fulfill an obligation to the lawyer regarding the lawyer's services and has been given reasonable warning that the lawyer will withdraw unless the obligation is fulfilled;

(6) the representation will result in an unreasonable financial burden on the lawyer or has been rendered unreasonably difficult by the client; or

(7) other good cause for withdrawal exists.

(c) A lawyer must comply with applicable law requiring notice to or permission of a tribunal when terminating a representation. When ordered to do so by a tribunal, a lawyer shall continue representation notwithstanding good cause for terminating the representation.

(d) Upon termination of representation, a lawyer shall take steps to the extent reasonably practicable to protect a client's interests, such as giving reasonable notice to the client, allowing time for employment of other counsel, surrendering papers and property to which the client is entitled and refunding any advance payment of fee or expense that has not been earned or incurred. The lawyer may retain papers relating to the client to the extent permitted by other law.

Adopted effective Jan. 1, 1987; amended Sept. 30, 2004, effective Jan. 1, 2005.

Comment

[1] A lawyer should not accept representation in a matter unless it can be performed competently, promptly, without improper conflict of interest and to completion. Ordinarily, a representation in a matter is completed when the agreed-upon assistance has been concluded. See Rules 1.2(c) and 6.5. See also Rule 1.3, Comment [4].

Mandatory Withdrawal

[2] A lawyer ordinarily must decline or withdraw from representation if the client demands that the lawyer engage in conduct that is illegal or violates the Rules of Professional Conduct or other law. The lawyer is not obliged to decline or withdraw simply because the client suggests such a course of conduct; a client may make such a suggestion in the hope that a lawyer will not be constrained by a professional obligation.

[3] When a lawyer has been appointed to represent a client, withdrawal ordinarily requires approval of the appointing authority. See also Rule 6.2. Similarly, court approval or notice to the court is often required by applicable law before a lawyer withdraws from pending litigation. Difficulty may be encountered if withdrawal is based on the client's demand that the lawyer engage in unprofessional conduct. The court may request an explanation for the withdrawal, while the lawyer may be bound to keep confidential the facts that would constitute such an explanation. The lawyer's statement that professional considerations require termination of the representation ordinarily should be accepted as sufficient.. Lawyers should be mindful of their

obligations to both clients and the court under Rules 1.6 and 3.3.

Discharge

[4] A client has a right to discharge a lawyer at any time, with or without cause, subject to liability for payment for the lawyer's services. Where future dispute about the withdrawal may be anticipated, it may be advisable to prepare a written statement reciting the circumstances.

[5] Whether a client can discharge appointed counsel may depend on applicable law. A client seeking to do so should be given a full explanation of the consequences. These consequences may include a decision by the appointing authority that appointment of successor counsel is unjustified, thus requiring self-representation by the client.

[6] If the client has severely diminished capacity, the client may lack the legal capacity to discharge the lawyer, and in any event the discharge may be seriously adverse to the client's interests. The lawyer should make special effort to help the client consider the consequences and may take reasonably necessary protective action as provided in Rule 1.14.

Optional Withdrawal

[7] A lawyer may withdraw from representation in some circumstances. The lawyer has the option to withdraw if it can be accomplished without material adverse effect on the client's interests. Withdrawal is also justified if the client persists in a course of action that the lawyer reasonably believes is criminal or fraudulent, for a lawyer is not required to be associated with such conduct even if the lawyer does not further it. Withdrawal is also permitted if the lawyer's services were misused in the past even if that would materially prejudice the client. The lawyer may also withdraw where the client insists on taking action that the lawyer considers repugnant or with which the lawyer has a fundamental disagreement.

[8] A lawyer may withdraw if the client refuses to abide by the terms of an agreement relating to the representation, such as an agreement concerning fees or court costs or an agreement limiting the objectives of the representation.

Assisting the Client upon Withdrawal

[9] Even if the lawyer has been unfairly discharged by the client, a lawyer must take all reasonable steps to mitigate the consequences to the client. The lawyer may retain papers as security for a fee only to the extent permitted by law. See Rule 1.15.

Rule 1.17.   Sale of Law Practice

A lawyer or a law firm may sell or purchase a law practice, or an area of law practice, including goodwill, if the following conditions are satisfied:

(a) The seller ceases to engage in the private practice of law, or in the area of practice that has been sold, in the geographic area in which the practice has been conducted.

(b) The entire practice, or the entire area of practice, is sold to one or more lawyers or law firms.

(c) The seller gives written notice to each of the seller's clients regarding:

(1) the proposed sale;

(2) the client's right to retain other counsel or to take possession of the file; and

(3) the fact that the client's consent to the transfer of the client's files will be presumed if the client does not take any action or does not otherwise object within ninety (90) days of receipt of the notice.

If a client cannot be given notice, the representation of that client may be transferred to the purchaser only upon entry of an order so authorizing by a court having jurisdiction. The seller may disclose to the court in camera information relating to the representation only to the extent necessary to obtain an order authorizing the transfer of a file.

(d) The fees charged clients shall not be increased by reason of the sale.

Adopted Nov. 25, 1997, effective Jan. 1, 1998. Amended Sept. 30, 2004, effective Jan. 1, 2005.

Comment

[1] The practice of law is a profession, not merely a business. Clients are not commodities that can be purchased and sold at will. Pursuant to this Rule, when a lawyer or an entire firm ceases to practice, or ceases to practice in an area of law, and other lawyers or firms take over the representation, the selling lawyer or firm may obtain compensation for the reasonable value of the practice as may withdrawing partners of law firms. See Rules 5.4 and 5.6.

Termination of Practice by the Seller

[2] The requirement that all of the private practice, or all of an area of practice, be sold is satisfied if the seller in good faith makes the entire practice, or the area of practice, available for sale to the purchasers. The fact that a number of the seller's clients decide not to be represented by the purchasers but take their matters elsewhere, therefore, does not result in a violation. Return to private practice as a result of an unanticipated change in circumstances does not necessarily result in a violation. For example, a lawyer who has sold the practice to accept an appointment to judicial office does not violate the requirement that the sale be attendant to cessation of practice if the lawyer later resumes private practice upon being defeated in a contested or a retention election for the office or resigns from a judiciary position.

[3] The requirement that the seller cease to engage in the private practice of law does not prohibit employment as a lawyer on the staff of a public agency or a legal services entity that provides legal services to the poor, or as in-house counsel to a business.

[4] This Rule also permits a lawyer or law firm to sell an area of practice. If an area of practice is sold and the lawyer remains in the active practice of law, the lawyer must cease accepting any matters in the area of practice that has been sold, either as counsel or co-counsel or by assuming joint responsibility for a matter in connection with the division of a fee with another lawyer as would otherwise be permitted by Rule 1.5(e). For example, a lawyer with a substantial number of estate planning matters and a substantial number of probate administration cases may sell the estate planning portion of the practice but remain in the practice of law by concentrating on probate administration; however, that practitioner may not thereafter accept any estate planning matters. Although a lawyer who leaves a jurisdiction or geographical area typically would sell the entire practice, this Rule permits the lawyer to limit the sale to one or more areas of the practice, thereby preserving the lawyer's right to continue practice in the areas of the practice that were not sold.

Sale of Entire Practice or Entire Area of Practice

[5] The Rule requires that the seller's entire practice, or an entire area of practice, be sold. The prohibition against sale of less than an entire practice area protects those clients whose matters are less lucrative and who might find it difficult to secure other counsel if a sale could be limited to substantial fee-generating matters. The purchasers are required to undertake all client matters in the practice or practice area, subject to client consent. This requirement is satisfied, however, even if a purchaser is unable to undertake a particular client matter because of a conflict of interest.

Client Confidences, Consent and Notice

[6] Negotiations between seller and prospective purchaser prior to disclosure of information relating to a specific representation of an identifiable client no more violate the confidentiality provisions of Rule 1. 6 than do preliminary discussions concerning the possible association of another lawyer or mergers between firms, with respect to which client consent is not required. Providing the purchaser access to client-specific information relating to the representation and to the file, however, requires client consent. The Rule provides that before such information can be disclosed by the seller to the purchaser the client must be given actual written notice of the contemplated sale, including the identity of the purchaser, and must be told that the decision to consent or make other arrangements must be made within 90 days. If nothing is heard from the client within that time, consent to the sale is presumed.

[7] A lawyer or law firm ceasing to practice cannot be required to remain in practice because some clients cannot be given actual notice of the proposed purchase. Since these clients cannot themselves consent to the purchase or direct any other disposition of their files, the Rule requires an order from a court having jurisdiction authorizing their transfer or other disposition. The Court can be expected to determine whether reasonable efforts to locate the client have been exhausted, and whether the absent client's legitimate interests will be served by authorizing the transfer of the file so that the purchaser may continue the representation. Preservation of client confidences requires that the petition for a court order be considered in camera.

[8] All elements of client autonomy, including the client's absolute right to discharge a lawyer and transfer the representation to another, survive the sale of the practice or area of practice.

Fee Arrangements Between Client and Purchaser

[9] The sale may not be financed by increases in fees charged the clients of the practice. Existing arrangements between the seller and the client as to fees and the scope of the work must be honored by the purchaser.

Other Applicable Ethical Standards

[10] Lawyers participating in the sale of a law practice or a practice area are subject to the ethical standards applicable to involving another lawyer in the representation of a client. These include, for example, the seller's obligation to exercise competence in identifying a purchaser qualified to assume the practice and the purchaser's obligation to undertake the representation competently (see Rule 1.1); the obligation to avoid disqualifying conflicts, and to secure the client's informed consent for those conflicts that can be agreed to (see Rule 1.7 regarding conflicts and Rule 1.0(e) for the definition of informed consent); and the obligation to protect information relating to the representation (see Rules 1.6 and 1.9).

[11] If approval of the substitution of the purchasing lawyer for the selling lawyer is required by the rules of any tribunal in which a matter is pending, such approval must be obtained before the matter can be included in the sale (see Rule 1.16).

Applicability of the Rule

[12] This Rule applies to the sale of a law practice of a deceased, disabled or disappeared lawyer. Thus, the seller may be represented by a non-lawyer representative not subject to these Rules. Since, however, no lawyer may participate in a sale of a law practice which does not conform to the requirements of this Rule, the representatives of the seller as well as the purchasing lawyer can be expected to see to it that they are met.

[13] Admission to or retirement from a law partnership or professional association, retirement plans and similar arrangements, and a sale of tangible assets of a law practice, do not constitute a sale or purchase governed by this Rule.

[14] This Rule does not apply to the transfers of legal representation between lawyers when such transfers are unrelated to the sale of a practice or an area of practice.

Rule 1.18. Duties to Prospective Client

(a) A person who discusses with a lawyer the possibility of forming a client-lawyer relationship with respect to a matter is a prospective client.

(b) Even when no client-lawyer relationship ensues, a lawyer who has had discussions with a prospective client shall not use or reveal information learned in the consultation, except as Rule 1.9 would permit with respect to information of a former client.

(c) A lawyer subject to paragraph (b) shall not represent a client with interests materially adverse to those of a prospective client in the same or a substantially related matter if the lawyer received information from the prospective client that could be significantly harmful to that person in the matter, except as provided in paragraph (d). If a lawyer is disqualified from representation under this paragraph, no lawyer in a firm with which that lawyer is associated may knowingly undertake or continue representation in such a matter, except as provided in paragraph (d).

(d) When a lawyer has received disqualifying information as defined in paragraph (c), representation is permissible if:

(1) both the affected client and the prospective client have given informed consent, confirmed in writing, or:

(2) the lawyer who received the information took reasonable measures to avoid exposure to more disqualifying information than was reasonably necessary to determine whether to represent the prospective client; and

(i) the disqualified lawyer is timely screened from any participation in the matter and is apportioned no part of the fee therefrom; and

(ii) written notice is promptly given to the prospective client.

Adopted Sept. 30, 2004, effective Jan. 1, 2005.

Comment

[1] Prospective clients, like clients, may disclose information to a lawyer, place documents or other property in the lawyer's custody, or rely on the lawyer's advice. A lawyer's discussions with a prospective client usually are limited in time and depth and leave both the prospective client and the lawyer free (and sometimes required) to proceed no further. Hence, prospective clients should receive some but not all of the protection afforded clients.

[2] Not all persons who communicate information to a lawyer are entitled to protection under this Rule. A person who communicates information unilaterally to a lawyer, without any reasonable expectation that the lawyer is willing to discuss the possibility of forming a client-lawyer relationship, is not a "prospective client" within the meaning of paragraph (a).

[3] It is often necessary for a prospective client to reveal information to the lawyer during an initial consultation prior to the decision about formation of a client-lawyer relationship. The lawyer often must learn such information to determine whether there is a conflict of interest with an existing client and whether the matter is one that the lawyer is willing to undertake. Paragraph (b) prohibits the lawyer from using or revealing that information, except as permitted by Rule 1.9, even if the client or lawyer decides not to proceed with the representation. The duty exists regardless of how brief the initial conference may be.

[4] In order to avoid acquiring disqualifying information from a prospective client, a lawyer considering whether or not to undertake a new matter should limit the initial interview to only such information as reasonably appears necessary for that purpose. Where the information indicates that a conflict of interest or other reason for non-representation exists, the lawyer should so inform the prospective client or decline the representation. If the prospective client wishes to retain the lawyer, and if consent is possible under Rule 1.7, then consent from all affected present or former clients must be obtained before accepting the representation.

[5] A lawyer may condition conversations with a prospective client on the person's informed consent that no information disclosed during the consultation will prohibit the lawyer from representing a different client in the matter. See Rule 1.0(e) for the definition of informed consent.

[6] Even in the absence of an agreement, under paragraph (c), the lawyer is not prohibited from representing a client with interests adverse to those of the prospective client in the same or a substantially related matter unless the lawyer has received from the prospective client information that could be significantly harmful if used in the matter.

[7] Under paragraph (c), the prohibition in this Rule is imputed to other lawyers as provided in Rule 1.10, but, under paragraph (d)(1), imputation may be avoided if the lawyer obtains the informed consent, confirmed in writing, of both the prospective and affected clients. In the alternative, imputation may be avoided if the conditions of paragraph (d)(2) are met and all disqualified lawyers are timely screened and written notice is promptly given to the prospective client. See Rule 1.0(k) (requirements for screening procedures). Paragraph (d)(2)(i) does not prohibit the screened lawyer from receiving a salary or partnership share established by prior independent agreement, but that lawyer may not receive compensation directly related to the matter in which the lawyer is disqualified.

[8] Notice, including a general description of the subject matter about which the lawyer was consulted, and of the screening procedures employed, generally should be given as soon as practicable after the need for screening becomes apparent.

[9] For the duty of competence of a lawyer who gives assistance on the merits of a matter to a prospective client, see Rule 1.1. For a lawyer's duties when a prospective client entrusts valuables or papers to the lawyer's care, see Rule 1.15.

[10] Paragraph (d) also applies to other lawyers in the firm with whom the receiving lawyer actually shared disqualifying information.

COUNSELOR

Rule 2.1. Advisor

In representing a client, a lawyer shall exercise independent professional judgment and render candid advice. In rendering advice, a lawyer may refer not only to law but to other considerations such as moral, economic, social and political factors, that may be relevant to the client's situation.

Adopted effective Jan. 1, 1987.

Comment

Scope of Advice

[1] A client is entitled to straightforward advice expressing the lawyer's honest assessment. Legal advice often involves unpleasant facts and alternatives that a client may be disinclined to confront. In presenting advice, a lawyer endeavors to sustain the client's morale and may put advice in as acceptable a form as honesty permits. However, a lawyer should not be deterred from giving candid advice by the prospect that the advice will be unpalatable to the client.

[2] Advice couched in narrow legal terms may be of little value to a client, especially where practical considerations, such as cost or effects on other people, are predominant. Purely technical legal advice, therefore, can sometimes be inadequate. It is proper for a lawyer to refer to relevant moral and ethical considerations in giving advice. Although a lawyer is not a moral advisor as such, moral and ethical considerations impinge upon most legal questions and may decisively influence how the law will be applied.

[3] A client may expressly or impliedly ask the lawyer for purely technical advice. When such a request is made by a client experienced in legal matters, the lawyer may accept it at face value. When such a request is made by a client inexperienced in legal matters, however, the lawyer's responsibility as advisor may include indicating that more may be involved than strictly legal considerations.

[4] Matters that go beyond strictly legal questions may also be in the domain of another profession. Family matters can involve problems within the professional competence of psychiatry, clinical psychology or social work; business matters can involve problems within the competence of the accounting profession or of financial specialists. Where consultation with a professional in another field is itself something a competent lawyer would recommend, the lawyer should make such a recommendation. At the same time, a lawyer's advice at its best often consists of recommending a course of action in the face of conflicting recommendations of experts.

Offering Advice

[5] In general, a lawyer is not expected to give advice until asked by the client. However, when a lawyer knows that a client proposes a course of action that is likely to result in substantial adverse legal consequences to the client, the lawyer's duty to the client under Rule 1.4 may require that the lawyer offer advice if the client's course of action is related to the representation. Similarly, when a matter is likely to involve litigation, it may be necessary under Rule 1.4 to inform the client of forms of dispute resolution that might constitute reasonable alternatives to litigation. A lawyer ordinarily has no duty to initiate investigation of a client's affairs or to give advice that the client has indicated is unwanted, but a lawyer may initiate advice to a client when doing so appears to be in the client's interest.

Rule 2.2. Intermediary

(a) A lawyer may act as intermediary between clients if:

(1) the lawyer consults with each client concerning the implications of the common representation, including the advantages and risks involved, and the effect on the attorney-client privileges, and obtains each client's consent to the common representation;

(2) the lawyer reasonably believes that the matter can be resolved on terms compatible with the clients' best interests, that each client will be able to make adequately informed decisions in the matter and that there is little risk of material prejudice to the interests of any of the clients if the contemplated resolution is unsuccessful; and

(3) the lawyer reasonably believes that the common representation can be undertaken impartially and without improper effect on other responsibilities the lawyer has to any of the clients.

(b) While acting as intermediary, the lawyer shall consult with each client concerning the decisions to be made and the considerations relevant in making them, so that each client can make adequately informed decisions.

(c) A lawyer shall withdraw as intermediary if any of the clients so requests, or if any of the conditions stated in paragraph (a) is no longer satisfied. Upon withdrawal, the lawyer shall not continue to represent any of the clients in the matter that was the subject of the intermediation.

Adopted effective Jan. 1, 1987.

Comment

[1] A lawyer acts as intermediary under this rule when the lawyer represents two or more parties with potentially conflicting interests. A key factor in defining the relationship is whether the parties share responsibility for the lawyer's fee, but the common representation may be inferred from other circumstances. Because confusion can arise as to the lawyer's role where each party is not separately

represented, it is important that the lawyer make clear the relationship.

[2] The Rule does not apply to a lawyer acting as arbitrator or mediator between or among parties who are not clients of the lawyer, even where the lawyer has been appointed with the concurrence of the parties. In performing such a role the lawyer may be subject to applicable codes of ethics, such as the Code of Ethics for Arbitration in Commercial Disputes prepared by a joint Committee of the American Bar Association and the American Arbitration Association.

[3] A lawyer acts as intermediary in seeking to establish or adjust a relationship between clients on an amicable and mutually advantageous basis; for example, in helping to organize a business in which two or more clients are entrepreneurs, working out the financial reorganization of an enterprise in which two or more clients have an interest, arranging a property distribution in settlement of an estate or mediating a dispute between clients. The lawyer seeks to resolve potentially conflicting interests by developing the parties' mutual interests. The alternative can be that each party may have to obtain separate representation, with the possibility in some situations of incurring additional cost, complication or even litigation. Given these and other relevant factors, all the clients may prefer that the lawyer act as intermediary.

[4] In considering whether to act as intermediary between clients, a lawyer should be mindful that if the intermediation fails the result can be additional cost, embarrassment and recrimination. In some situations the risk of failure is so great that intermediation is plainly impossible. For example, a lawyer cannot undertake common representation of clients between whom contentious litigation is imminent or who contemplate contentious negotiations. More generally, if the relationship between the parties has already assumed definite antagonism, the possibility that the clients' interests can be adjusted by intermediation ordinarily is not very good.

[5] The appropriateness of intermediation can depend on its form. Forms of intermediation range from informal arbitration, where each client's case is presented by the respective client and the lawyer decides the outcome, to mediation, to common representation where the clients' interests are substantially though not entirely compatible. One form may be appropriate in circumstances where another would not. Other relevant factors are whether the lawyer subsequently will represent both parties on a continuing basis and whether the situation involves creating a relationship between the parties or terminating one.

Confidentiality and Privilege

[6] A particularly important factor in determining the appropriateness of intermediation is the effect on client-lawyer confidentiality and the attorney-client privilege. In a common representation, the lawyer is still required both to keep each client adequately informed and to maintain confidentiality of information relating to the representation. See Rules 1.4 and 1.6. Complying with both requirements while acting as intermediary requires a delicate balance. If the balance cannot be maintained, the common representation is improper. With regard to the attorney-client privilege, the prevailing rule is that as between commonly represented clients the privilege does not attach. Hence, it must be assumed that if litigation eventuates between the clients, the privilege will not protect any such communications, and the clients should be so advised.

[7] Since the lawyer is required to be impartial between commonly represented clients, intermediation is improper when that impartiality cannot be maintained. For example, a lawyer who has represented one of the clients for a long period and in a variety of matters might have difficulty being impartial between that client and one to whom the lawyer has only recently been introduced.

Consultation

[8] In acting as intermediary between clients, the lawyer is required to consult with the clients on the implications of doing so, and proceed only upon consent based on such a consultation. The consultation should make clear that the lawyer's role is not that of partisanship normally expected in other circumstances.

[9] Paragraph (b) is an application of the principle expressed in Rule 1.4. Where the lawyer is intermediary, the clients ordinarily must assume greater responsibility for decisions than when each client is independently represented.

Withdrawal

[10] Common representation does not diminish the rights of each client in the client-lawyer relationship. Each has the right to loyal and diligent representation, the right to discharge the lawyer as stated in Rule 1.16, and the protection of Rule 1.9 concerning obligations to a former client.

Rule 2.3.   Evaluation for Use by Third Persons

(a) A lawyer may provide an evaluation of a matter affecting a client for the use of someone other than the client if the lawyer reasonably believes that making the evaluation is compatible with other aspects of the lawyer's relationship with the client.

(b) When the lawyer knows or reasonably should know that the evaluation is likely to affect the client's interests materially and adversely, the lawyer shall not provide the evaluation unless the client gives informed consent.

(c) Except as disclosure is authorized in connection with a report of an evaluation, information relating to the evaluation is otherwise protected by Rule 1.6.

Adopted effective Jan. 1, 1987; amended Sept. 30, 2004, effective Jan. 1, 2005.

Comment

Definition

[1] An evaluation may be performed at the client's direction or when impliedly authorized in order to carry out the representation. See Rule 1.2. Such an evaluation may be for the primary purpose of establishing information for the benefit of third parties; for example, an opinion concerning the title of property rendered at the behest of a vendor for the information of a prospective purchaser, or at the behest of a borrower for the information of a prospective lender. In some situations, the evaluation may be required by a government agency; for example, an opinion concerning the legality of the securities registered for sale under the securities laws. In other instances, the evaluation may be required by a third person, such as a purchaser of a business.

[2] A legal evaluation should be distinguished from an investigation of a person with whom the lawyer does not have a client-lawyer relationship. For example, a lawyer retained by a purchaser to analyze a vendor's title to property does not have a client-lawyer relationship with the vendor. So also, an investigation into a person's affairs by a government lawyer, or by special counsel by a government lawyer, or by special counsel employed by the government, is not an evaluation as that term is used in this Rule. The question is whether the lawyer is retained by the person whose affairs are being examined. When the lawyer is retained by that person, the general rules concerning loyalty to client and preservation of confidences apply, which is not the case if the lawyer is retained by someone else. For this reason, it is essential to identify the person by whom the lawyer is retained. This should be made clear not only to the person under examination, but also to others to whom the results are to be made available.

Duties Owed to Third Person and Client

[3] When the evaluation is intended for the information or use of a third person, a legal duty to that person may or may not arise. That legal question is beyond the scope of this Rule. However, since such an evaluation involves a departure from the normal client-lawyer relationship, careful analysis of the situation is required. The lawyer must be satisfied as a matter of professional judgment that making the evaluation is compatible with other functions undertaken in behalf of the client. For example, if the lawyer is acting as advocate in defending the client against charges of fraud, it would normally be incompatible with that responsibility for the lawyer to perform an evaluation for others concerning the same or a related transaction. Assuming no such impediment is apparent, however, the lawyer should advise the client of the implications of the evaluation, particularly the lawyer's responsibilities to third persons and the duty to disseminate the findings.

Access to and Disclosure of Information

[4] The quality of an evaluation depends on the freedom and extent of the investigation upon which it is based. Ordinarily a lawyer should have whatever latitude of investigation seems necessary as a matter of professional judgment. Under some circumstances, however, the terms of the evaluation may be limited. For example, certain issues or sources may be categorically excluded, or the scope of search may be limited by time constraints or the noncooperation of persons having relevant information. Any such limitations that are material to the evaluation should be described in the report. If after a lawyer has commenced an evaluation, the client refuses to comply with the terms upon which it was understood the evaluation was to have been made, the lawyer's obligations are determined by law, having reference to the terms of the client's agreement and the surrounding circumstances. In no circumstances is the lawyer permitted to knowingly make a false statement of material fact or law in providing an evaluation under this Rule. See Rule 4.1.

Obtaining Client's Informed Consent

[5] Information relating to an evaluation is protected by Rule 1.6. In many situations, providing an evaluation to a third party poses no significant risk to the client; thus, the lawyer may be impliedly authorized to disclose information to carry out the representation. See Rule 1.6(a). Where, however, it is reasonably likely that providing the evaluation will affect the client's interests materially and adversely, the lawyer must first obtain the client's consent after the client has been adequately informed concerning the important possible effects on the client's interests. See Rules 1.6(a) and 1.0(e).

Financial Auditors' Requests for Information

[6] When a question concerning the legal situation of a client arises at the instance of the client's financial auditor and the question is referred to the lawyer, the lawyer's response may be made in accordance with procedures recognized in the legal profession. Such a procedure is set forth in the American Bar Association Statement of Policy Regarding Lawyers' Responses to Auditors' Requests for Information, adopted in 1975.

Rule 2.4. Lawyer Serving as Third-Party Neutral

(a) A lawyer serves as a third-party neutral when the lawyer assists two or more persons who are not clients of the lawyer to reach a resolution of a dispute or other matter that has arisen between them. Service as a third-party neutral may include service as an arbitrator, a mediator or in such other capacity as will enable the lawyer to assist the parties to resolve the matter.

(b) A lawyer serving as a third-party neutral shall inform unrepresented parties that the lawyer is not representing them. When the lawyer knows or reasonably should know that a party does not understand the lawyer's role in the matter, the lawyer shall explain the difference between the lawyer's role as a third-party neutral and a lawyer's role as one who represents a client.

Adopted Sept. 30, 2004, effective Jan. 1, 2005.

Comment

[1] Alternative dispute resolution has become a substantial part of the civil justice system. Aside from representing clients in dispute-resolution processes, lawyers often serve as third-party neutrals. A third-party neutral is a person, such as a mediator, arbitrator, conciliator or evaluator, who assists the parties, represented or unrepresented, in the resolution of a dispute or in the arrangement of a transaction. Whether a third-party neutral serves primarily as a facilitator, evaluator or decision maker depends on the particular process that is either selected by the parties or mandated by a court.

[2] The role of a third-party neutral is not unique to lawyers, although, in some court-connected contexts, only lawyers are allowed to serve in this role or to handle certain types of cases. In performing this role, the lawyer may be subject to court rules or other law that apply either to third-party neutrals generally or to lawyers serving as third-party neutrals. Lawyer–neutrals may also be subject to various codes of ethics, such as the Code of Ethics for Arbitration in Commercial Disputes prepared by a joint committee of the American Bar Association and the American Arbitration Association or the Model Standards of Conduct for Mediators jointly prepared by the American Bar Association, the American Arbitration Association and the Society of Professionals in Dispute Resolution.

[3] Unlike nonlawyers who serve as third-party neutrals, lawyers serving in this role may experience unique problems as a result of differences between the role of a third-party neutral and a lawyer's service as a client representative. The potential for confusion is significant when the parties are unrepresented in the process. Thus, paragraph (b) requires a lawyer-neutral to inform unrepresented parties that the lawyer is not representing them. For some parties, particularly parties who frequently use dispute-resolution processes, this information will be sufficient. For others, particularly those who are using the process for the first time, more information will be required. Where appropriate, the lawyer should inform unrepresented parties of the important differences between the lawyer's role as third-party neutral and a lawyer's role as a client representative, including the inapplicability of the attorney-client evidentiary privilege. The extent of disclosure required under this paragraph will depend on the particular parties involved and the subject matter of the proceeding, as well as the particular features of the dispute-resolution process selected.

[4] A lawyer who serves as a third-party neutral subsequently may be asked to serve as a lawyer representing a client in the same matter. The conflicts of interest that arise for both the individual lawyer and the lawyer's law firm are addressed in Rule 1.12.

[5] Lawyers who represent clients in alternative dispute-resolution processes are governed by the Rules of Professional Conduct. When the dispute-resolution process takes place before a tribunal, as in binding arbitration (see Rule 1.0(m)), the lawyer's duty of candor is governed by Rule 3.3. Otherwise, the lawyer's duty of candor toward both the third-party neutral and other parties is governed by Rule 4.1.

ADVOCATE

Rule 3.1. Meritorious Claims and Contentions

A lawyer shall not bring or defend a proceeding, or assert or controvert an issue therein, unless there is a basis in law and fact for doing so that is not frivolous, which includes a good faith argument for an extension, modification or reversal of existing law. A lawyer for the defendant in a criminal proceeding, or the respondent in a proceeding that could result in incarceration, may nevertheless so defend the proceeding as to require that every element of the case be established.

Adopted effective Jan. 1, 1987. Amended Sept. 30, 2004, effective Jan. 1, 2005.

Comment

[1] The advocate has a duty not to abuse legal procedure. The law, both procedural and substantive, establishes the limits within which an advocate may proceed. However, the law is not always clear and never is static. Accordingly, in determining the proper scope of advocacy, account must be taken of the law's ambiguities and potential for change.

[2] The filing of an action or defense or similar action taken for a client is not frivolous merely because the facts have not first been fully substantiated or because the lawyer expects to develop vital evidence only by discovery. What is required of lawyers, however, is that they inform themselves about the facts of their clients' cases and the applicable law and determine that they can make good faith arguments in support of their clients' positions. Such action is not frivolous even though the lawyer believes that the client's position ultimately will not prevail. The action is frivolous, however, if the lawyer is unable either to make a good faith argument on the merits of the action taken or to support the action taken by a good faith argument for an extension, modification or reversal of existing law.

[3] The lawyer's obligations under this Rule are subordinate to federal or state constitutional law that entitles a defendant in a criminal matter to the assistance of counsel in presenting a claim or contention that otherwise would be prohibited by this Rule.

Rule 3.2. Expediting Litigation

A lawyer shall make reasonable efforts to expedite litigation consistent with the interests of the client.

Adopted effective Jan. 1, 1987.

Comment

[1] Dilatory practices bring the administration of justice into disrepute. Although there will be occa-

sions when a lawyer may properly seek a postponement for personal reasons, it is not proper for a lawyer to routinely fail to expedite litigation solely for the convenience of the advocates. Nor will a failure to expedite be reasonable if done for the purpose of frustrating an opposing party's attempt to obtain rightful redress or repose. It is not a justification that similar conduct is often tolerated by the bench and bar. The question is whether a competent lawyer acting in good faith would regard the course of action as having some substantial purpose other than delay. Realizing financial or other benefit from otherwise improper delay in litigation is not a legitimate interest of the client.

Rule 3.3. Candor Toward the Tribunal

(a) A lawyer shall not knowingly:

(1) make a false statement of fact or law to a tribunal or fail to correct a false statement of material fact or law previously made to the tribunal by the lawyer;

(2) fail to disclose to the tribunal legal authority in the controlling jurisdiction known to the lawyer to be directly adverse to the position of the client and not disclosed by opposing counsel; or

(3) offer evidence that the lawyer knows to be false. If a lawyer, the lawyer's client, or a witness called by the lawyer, has offered material evidence and the lawyer comes to know of its falsity, the lawyer shall take reasonable remedial measures, including, if necessary, disclosure to the tribunal. A lawyer may refuse to offer evidence, other than the testimony of a defendant in a criminal matter, that the lawyer reasonably believes is false.

(b) A lawyer who represents a client in an adjudicative proceeding and who knows that a person intends to engage, is engaging or has engaged in criminal or fraudulent conduct related to the proceeding shall take reasonable remedial measures, including, if necessary, disclosure to the tribunal.

(c) The duties stated in paragraphs (a) and (b) continue to the conclusion of the proceeding, and apply even if compliance requires disclosure of information otherwise protected by Rule 1.6.

(d) In an ex parte proceeding, a lawyer shall inform the tribunal of all material facts known to the lawyer which will enable the tribunal to make an informed decision, whether or not the facts are adverse.

Adopted effective Jan. 1, 1987. Amended Sept. 30, 2004, effective Jan. 1, 2005.

Comment

[1] This Rule governs the conduct of a lawyer who is representing a client in the proceedings of a tribunal. See Rule 1.0(m) for the definition of "tribunal." It also applies when the lawyer is representing a client in an ancillary proceeding conducted pursuant to the tribunal's adjudicative authority, such as a deposition. Thus, for example, paragraph (a)(3) requires a lawyer to take reasonable remedial measures if the lawyer comes to know that a client who is testifying in a deposition has offered evidence that is false.

[2] This Rule sets forth the special duties of lawyers as officers of the court to avoid conduct that undermines the integrity of the adjudicative process. A lawyer acting as an advocate in an adjudicative proceeding has an obligation to present the client's case with persuasive force. Performance of that duty while maintaining confidences of the client, however, is qualified by the advocate's duty of candor to the tribunal. Consequently, although a lawyer in an adversary proceeding is not required to present an impartial exposition of the law or to vouch for the evidence submitted in a cause, the lawyer must not allow the tribunal to be misled by false statements of law or fact or evidence that the lawyer knows to be false.

Representations by a Lawyer

[3] An advocate is responsible for pleadings and other documents prepared for litigation, but is usually not required to have personal knowledge of matters asserted therein, for litigation documents ordinarily present assertions by the client, or by someone on the client's behalf, and not assertions by the lawyer. Compare Rule 3.1. However, an assertion purporting to be on the lawyer's own knowledge, as in an affidavit by the lawyer or in a statement in open court, may properly be made only when the lawyer knows the assertion is true or believes it to be true on the basis of a reasonably diligent inquiry. There are circumstances where failure to make a disclosure is the equivalent of an affirmative misrepresentation. The obligation prescribed in Rule 1.2(d) not to counsel a client to commit or assist the client in committing a fraud applies in litigation. Regarding compliance with Rule 1.2(d), see the Comment to that Rule. See also the Comment to Rule 8.4(b).

Legal Argument

[4] Legal argument based on a knowingly false representation of law constitutes dishonesty toward the tribunal. A lawyer is not required to make a disinterested exposition of the law, but must recognize the existence of pertinent legal authorities. Furthermore, as stated in paragraph (a)(2), an advocate has a duty to disclose directly adverse authority in the controlling jurisdiction that has not been disclosed by the opposing party. The underlying concept is that legal argument is a discussion seeking to determine the legal premises properly applicable to the case.

Offering Evidence

[5] Paragraph (a)(3) requires that the lawyer refuse to offer evidence that the lawyer knows to be false, regardless of the client's wishes. This duty is premised on the lawyer's obligation as an officer of the court to prevent the trier of fact from being misled by false evidence. A lawyer does not violate this Rule if the lawyer offers the evidence for the purpose of establishing its falsity.

[6] If a lawyer knows that the client intends to testify falsely or wants the lawyer to introduce false evidence, the lawyer should seek to persuade the client that the evidence should not be offered. If the persuasion is ineffective and the lawyer continues to represent the client, the lawyer must refuse to offer the false evidence. If only a portion of a witness's testimony will be false, the lawyer may call the witness to testify but may not elicit or otherwise permit the witness to present the testimony that the lawyer knows is false.

[7] The duties stated in paragraphs (a) and (b) apply to all lawyers, including defense counsel in criminal cases. In some jurisdictions, however, courts have required counsel to present the accused as a witness or to give a narrative statement if the accused so desires, even if counsel knows that the testimony or statement will be false. The obligation of the advocate under the Rules of Professional Conduct is subordinate to such requirements. See also Comment [9].

[8] The prohibition against offering false evidence only applies if the lawyer knows that the evidence is false. A lawyer's reasonable belief that evidence is false does not preclude its presentation to the trier of fact. A lawyer's knowledge that evidence is false, however, can be inferred from the circumstances. See Rule 1.0(f). Thus, although a lawyer should resolve doubts about the veracity of testimony or other evidence in favor of the client, the lawyer cannot ignore an obvious falsehood.

[9] Although paragraph (a)(3) only prohibits a lawyer from offering evidence the lawyer knows to be false, it permits the lawyer to refuse to offer testimony or other proof that the lawyer reasonably believes is false. Because of the special protections historically provided criminal defendants, however, this Rule does not permit a lawyer to refuse to offer the testimony of such a client where the lawyer reasonably believes but does not know that the testimony will be false. Unless the lawyer knows the testimony will be false, the lawyer must honor the client's decision to testify. See also Comment [7].

Remedial Measures

[10] Having offered material evidence in the belief that it was true, a lawyer may subsequently come to know that the evidence is false. Or, a lawyer may be surprised when the lawyer's client, or another witness called by the lawyer, offers testimony the lawyer knows to be false, either during the lawyer's direct examination or in response to cross-examination by the opposing lawyer. In such situations or if the lawyer knows of the falsity of testimony elicited from the client during a deposition, the lawyer must take reasonable remedial measures. In such situations, the advocate's proper course is to remonstrate with the client confidentially, advise the client of the lawyer's duty of candor to the tribunal and seek the client's cooperation with respect to the withdrawal or correction of the false statements or evidence. If that fails, the advocate must take further remedial action. If withdrawal from the representation is not permitted or will not undo the effect of the false evidence, the advocate

must make such disclosure to the tribunal as is reasonably necessary to remedy the situation, even if doing so requires the lawyer to reveal information that otherwise would be protected by Rule 1.6. It is for the tribunal then to determine what should be done — making a statement about the matter to the trier of fact, ordering a mistrial or perhaps nothing.

[11] The disclosure of a client's false testimony can result in grave consequences to the client, including not only a sense of betrayal but also loss of the case and perhaps a prosecution for perjury. But the alternative is that the lawyer cooperate in deceiving the court, thereby subverting the truth-finding process which the adversary system is designed to implement. See Rule 1.2(d). Furthermore, unless it is clearly understood that the lawyer will act upon the duty to disclose the existence of false evidence, the client can simply reject the lawyer's advice to reveal the false evidence and insist that the lawyer keep silent. Thus the client could in effect coerce the lawyer into being a party to fraud on the court.

Preserving Integrity of Adjudicative Process

[12] Lawyers have a special obligation to protect a tribunal against criminal or fraudulent conduct that undermines the integrity of the adjudicative process, such as bribing, intimidating or otherwise unlawfully communicating with a witness, juror, court official or other participant in the proceeding, unlawfully destroying or concealing documents or other evidence or failing to disclose information to the tribunal when required by law to do so. Thus, paragraph (b) requires a lawyer to take reasonable remedial measures, including disclosure if necessary, whenever the lawyer knows that a person, including the lawyer's client, intends to engage, is engaging or has engaged in criminal or fraudulent conduct related to the proceeding.

Duration of Obligation

[13] A practical time limit on the obligation to rectify false evidence or false statements of law and fact has to be established. The conclusion of the proceeding is a reasonably definite point for the termination of the obligation. A proceeding has concluded within the meaning of this Rule when a final judgment in the proceeding has been affirmed on appeal or the time for review has passed.

Ex Parte Proceedings

[14] Ordinarily, an advocate has the limited responsibility of presenting one side of the matters that a tribunal should consider in reaching a decision; the conflicting position is expected to be presented by the opposing party. However, in any ex parte proceeding, such as an application for a temporary restraining order, there is no balance of presentation by opposing advocates. The object of an ex parte proceeding is nevertheless to yield a substantially just result. The judge has an affirmative responsibility to accord the absent party just consideration. The lawyer for the represented party has the correlative duty to make disclosures of material facts known to the lawyer and that the

lawyer reasonably believes are necessary to an informed decision.

Withdrawal

[15] Normally, a lawyer's compliance with the duty of candor imposed by this Rule does not require that the lawyer withdraw from the representation of a client whose interests will be or have been adversely affected by the lawyer's disclosure. The lawyer may, however, be required by Rule 1.16(a) to seek permission of the tribunal to withdraw if the lawyer's compliance with this Rule's duty of candor results in such an extreme deterioration of the client-lawyer relationship that the lawyer can no longer competently represent the client. Also see Rule 1.16(b) for the circumstances in which a lawyer will be permitted to seek a tribunal's permission to withdraw. In connection with a request for permission to withdraw that is premised on a client's misconduct, a lawyer may reveal information relating to the representation only to the extent reasonably necessary to comply with this Rule or as otherwise permitted by Rule 1.6.

Rule 3.4. Fairness to Opposing Party and Counsel

A lawyer shall not:

(a) unlawfully obstruct another party's access to evidence or unlawfully alter, destroy or conceal a document or other material having potential evidentiary value. A lawyer shall not counsel or assist another person to do any such act;

(b) falsify evidence, counsel or assist a witness to testify falsely, or offer an inducement to a witness that is prohibited by law;

(c) knowingly disobey an obligation under the rules of a tribunal except for an open refusal based on an assertion that no valid obligation exists;

(d) in pretrial procedure, make a frivolous discovery request or fail to make reasonably diligent effort to comply with a legally proper discovery request by an opposing party;

(e) in trial, allude to any matter that the lawyer does not reasonably believe is relevant or that will not be supported by admissible evidence, assert personal knowledge of facts in issue except when testifying as a witness, or state a personal opinion as to the justness of a cause, the credibility of a witness, the culpability of a civil litigant or the guilt or innocence of an accused; or

(f) request a person other than a client to refrain from voluntarily giving relevant information to another party unless:

(1) the person is a relative or an employee or other agent of a client; and

(2) the lawyer reasonably believes that the person's interests will not be adversely affected by refraining from giving such information.

Adopted effective Jan. 1, 1987.

Comment

[1] The procedure of the adversary system contemplates that the evidence in a case is to be marshaled competitively by the contending parties. Fair competition in the adversary system is secured by prohibitions against destruction or concealment of evidence, improperly influencing witnesses, obstructive tactics in discovery procedure, and the like.

[2] Documents and other items of evidence are often essential to establish a claim or defense. Subject to evidentiary privileges, the right of an opposing party, including the government, to obtain evidence through discovery or subpoena is an important procedural right. The exercise of that right can be frustrated if relevant material is altered, concealed or destroyed. Applicable law in many jurisdictions makes it an offense to destroy material for purpose of impairing its availability in a pending proceeding or one whose commencement can be foreseen. Falsifying evidence is also generally a criminal offense. Paragraph (a) applies to evidentiary material generally, including computerized information. Applicable law may permit a lawyer to take temporary possession of physical evidence of client crimes for the purpose of conducting a limited examination that will not alter its potential evidentiary value. In such a case, applicable law may require the lawyer to turn the evidence over to the police or prosecuting authority, depending on the circumstances.

[3] With regard to paragraph (b), it is not improper to pay a witness's expenses or to compensate an expert witness on terms permitted by law. The common law rule in most jurisdictions is that it is improper to pay an occurrence witness any fee for testifying and that it is improper to pay an expert witness a contingent fee.

[4] Paragraph (f) permits a lawyer to advise employees of a client to refrain from giving information to another party, for the employees may identify their interests with those of the client. See also Rule 4.2.

Rule 3.5. Impartiality and Decorum of the Tribunal

A lawyer shall not:

(a) seek to influence a judge, juror, prospective juror or other official by means prohibited by law;

(b) communicate ex parte with such a person during the proceeding unless authorized to do so by law or court order;

(c) communicate with a juror or prospective juror after discharge of the jury if:

(1) the communication is prohibited by law or court order;

(2) the juror has made known to the lawyer a desire not to communicate; or

(3) the communication involves misrepresentation, coercion, duress or harassment.

(d) engage in conduct intended to disrupt a tribunal.

Adopted effective Jan. 1, 1987; amended Sept. 30, 2004, effective Jan. 1, 2005.

Comment

[1] Many forms of improper influence upon a tribunal are proscribed by criminal law. Others are specified in the ABA Model Code of Judicial Conduct, with which an advocate should be familiar. A lawyer is required to avoid contributing to a violation of such provisions.

[2] During a proceeding a lawyer may not communicate ex parte with persons serving in an official capacity in the proceeding, such as judges, masters or jurors, unless authorized to do so by law or court order.

[3] A lawyer may on occasion want to communicate with a juror or prospective juror after the jury has been discharged. The lawyer may do so unless the communication is prohibited by law or a court order but must respect the desire of the juror not to talk with the lawyer. The lawyer may not engage in improper conduct during the communication.

[4] The advocate's function is to present evidence and argument so that the cause may be decided according to law. Refraining from abusive or obstreperous conduct is a corollary of the advocate's right to speak on behalf of litigants. A lawyer may stand firm against abuse by a judge but should avoid reciprocation; the judge's default is no justification for similar dereliction by an advocate. An advocate can present the cause, protect the record for subsequent review and preserve professional integrity by patient firmness no less effectively than by belligerence or theatrics.

[5] The duty to refrain from disruptive conduct applies to any proceeding of a tribunal, including a deposition. See Rule 1.0(m).

Rule 3.6. Trial Publicity

(a) A lawyer who is participating or has participated in the investigation or litigation of a matter shall not make an extrajudicial statement that the lawyer knows or reasonably should know will be disseminated by means of public communication and will have a substantial likelihood of materially prejudicing an adjudicative proceeding in the matter.

(b) Notwithstanding paragraph (a), a lawyer may state:

(1) the claim, offense or defense involved and, except when prohibited by law, the identity of the persons involved;

(2) information contained in a public record;

(3) that an investigation of a matter is in progress;

(4) the scheduling or result of any step in litigation;

(5) a request for assistance in obtaining evidence and information necessary thereto;

(6) a warning of danger concerning the behavior of a person involved, when there is reason to believe that there exists the likelihood of substantial harm to an individual or to the public interest; and

(7) in a criminal case, in addition to subparagraphs (1) through (6):

(i) the identity, residence, occupation and family status of the accused;

(ii) if the accused has not been apprehended, information necessary to aid in apprehension of that person;

(iii) the fact, time and place of arrest; and

(iv) the identity of investigating and arresting officers or agencies and the length of the investigation.

(c) Notwithstanding paragraph (a), a lawyer may make a statement that a reasonable lawyer would believe is required to protect a client from the substantial undue prejudicial effect of recent publicity not initiated by the lawyer or the lawyer's client. A statement made pursuant to this paragraph shall be limited to such information as is necessary to mitigate the recent adverse publicity.

(d) A statement referred to in paragraph (a) will be rebuttably presumed to have a substantial likelihood of materially prejudicing an adjudicative proceeding when it refers to that proceeding and the statement is related to:

(1) the character, credibility, reputation or criminal record of a party, suspect in a criminal investigation or witness, or the identity of a witness, or the expected testimony of a party or witness;

(2) in a criminal case or proceeding that could result in incarceration, the possibility of a plea of guilty to the offense or the existence or contents of any confession, admission, or statement given by a defendant or suspect or that person's refusal or failure to make a statement;

(3) the performance or results of any examination or test or the refusal or failure of a person to submit to an examination or test, or the identity or nature of physical evidence expected to be presented;

(4) any opinion as to the guilt or innocence of a defendant or suspect in a criminal case or proceeding that could result in incarceration;

(5) information that the lawyer knows or reasonably should know is likely to be inadmissible as evidence in a trial and would if disclosed create a substantial risk of prejudicing an impartial trial; or

(6) the fact that a defendant has been charged with a crime, unless there is included therein a statement explaining that the charge is merely an accusation and that the defendant is presumed innocent until and unless proven guilty.

(e) No lawyer associated in a firm or government agency with a lawyer subject to paragraph (a) shall make a statement prohibited by paragraph (a).

Adopted effective Jan. 1, 1987; amended Sept. 30, 2004, effective Jan. 1, 2005.

Comment

[1] It is difficult to strike a balance between protecting the right to a fair trial and safeguarding the right of free expression. Preserving the right to a fair trial necessarily entails some curtailment of the information that may be disseminated about a party prior to trial, particularly where trial by jury is involved. If there were no such limits, the result would be the practical nullification of the protective effect of the rules of forensic decorum and the exclusionary rules of evidence. On the other hand, there are vital social interests served by the free dissemination of information about events having legal consequences and about legal proceedings themselves. The public has a right to know about threats to its safety and measures aimed at assuring its security. It also has a legitimate interest in the conduct of judicial proceedings, particularly in matters of general public concern. Furthermore, the subject matter of legal proceedings is often of direct significance in debate and deliberation over questions of public policy.

[2] Special rules of confidentiality may validly govern proceedings in juvenile, domestic relations and mental disability proceedings, and perhaps other types of litigation. Rule 3.4(c) requires compliance with such rules.

[3] The Rule sets forth a basic general prohibition against a lawyer's making statements that the lawyer knows or should know will have a substantial likelihood of materially prejudicing an adjudicative proceeding. Recognizing that the public value of informed commentary is great and the likelihood of prejudice to a proceeding by the commentary of a lawyer who is not involved in the proceeding is small, the rule applies only to lawyers who are, or who have been involved in the investigation or litigation of a case, and their associates.

[4] Paragraph (b) identifies specific matters about which a lawyer's statements would not ordinarily be considered to present a substantial likelihood of material prejudice, and should not in any event be considered prohibited by the general prohibition of paragraph (a). Paragraph (b) is not intended to be an exhaustive listing of the subjects upon which a lawyer may make a statement, but statements on other matters may be subject to paragraph (a).

[5] Another relevant factor in determining prejudice is the nature of the proceeding involved. Criminal jury trials will be most sensitive to extra-judicial speech. Civil trials may be less sensitive. Non–jury hearings and arbitration proceedings may be even less affected. The Rule will still place limitations on prejudicial comments in these cases, but the likelihood of prejudice may be different depending on the type of proceeding.

[6] See Rule 3.8(f) for additional duties of prosecutors in connection with extrajudicial statements about criminal proceedings.

[7] Finally, extrajudicial statements that might otherwise raise a question under this Rule may be permissible when they are made in response to statements made publicly by another party, another party's lawyer, or third persons, where a reasonable lawyer would believe a public response is required in order to avoid prejudice to the lawyer's client. When prejudicial statements have been publicly made by others, responsive statements may have the salutary effect of lessening any resulting adverse impact on the adjudicative proceeding. Such responsive statements should be limited to contain only such information as is necessary to mitigate undue prejudice created by the statements made by others.

Rule 3.7. Lawyer as Witness

(a) A lawyer shall not act as advocate at a trial in which the lawyer is likely to be a necessary witness unless:

(1) the testimony relates to an uncontested issue;

(2) the testimony relates to the nature and value of legal services rendered in the case; or

(3) disqualification of the lawyer would work substantial hardship on the client.

(b) A lawyer may act as advocate in a trial in which another lawyer in the lawyer's firm is likely to be called as a witness unless precluded from doing so by Rule 1.7 or Rule 1.9.

Adopted effective Jan. 1, 1987; amended Sept. 30, 2004, effective Jan. 1, 2005.

Comment

[1] Combining the roles of advocate and witness can prejudice the tribunal and the opposing party and can also involve a conflict of interest between the lawyer and client.

Advocate-Witness Rule

[2] The tribunal has proper objection when the trier of fact may be confused or misled by a lawyer serving as both advocate and witness. The opposing party has proper objection where the combination of roles may prejudice that party's rights in the litigation. A witness is required to testify on the basis of personal knowledge, while an advocate is expected to explain and comment on evidence given by others. It may not be clear whether a statement by an advocate-witness should be taken as proof or as an analysis of the proof.

[3] To protect the tribunal, paragraph (a) prohibits a lawyer from simultaneously serving as advocate and necessary witness except in those circumstances specified in paragraphs (a)(1) through (a)(3). Paragraph (a)(1) recognizes that if the testimony will be uncontested, the ambiguities in the dual role are purely theoretical. Paragraph (a)(2) recognizes that where the testimony concerns the extent and value of legal services rendered in the action in

which the testimony is offered, permitting the lawyers to testify avoids the need for a second trial with new counsel to resolve that issue. Moreover, in such a situation the judge has firsthand knowledge of the matter in issue; hence, there is less dependence on the adversary process to test the credibility of the testimony.

[4] Apart from these two exceptions, paragraph (a)(3) recognizes that a balancing is required between the interests of the client and those of the tribunal and the opposing party. Whether the tribunal is likely to be misled or the opposing party is likely to suffer prejudice depends on the nature of the case, the importance and probable tenor of the lawyer's testimony, and the probability that the lawyer's testimony will conflict with that of other witnesses. Even if there is risk of such prejudice, in determining whether the lawyer should be disqualified, due regard must be given to the effect of disqualification on the lawyer's client. It is relevant that one or both parties could reasonably foresee that the lawyer would probably be a witness. The conflict of interest principles stated in Rules 1.7, 1.9 and 1.10 have no application to this aspect of the problem.

[5] Because the tribunal is not likely to be misled when a lawyer acts as advocate in a trial in which another lawyer in the lawyer's firm will testify as a necessary witness, paragraph (b) permits the lawyer to do so except in situations involving a conflict of interest.

Conflict of Interest

[6] In determining if it is permissible to act as advocate in a trial in which the lawyer will be a necessary witness, the lawyer must also consider that the dual role may give rise to a conflict of interest that will require compliance with Rules 1.7 or 1.9. For example, if there is likely to be substantial conflict between the testimony of the client and that of the lawyer the representation involves a conflict of interest that requires compliance with Rule 1.7. This would be true even though the lawyer might not be prohibited by paragraph (a) from simultaneously serving as advocate and witness because the lawyer's disqualification would work a substantial hardship on the client. Similarly, a lawyer who might be permitted to simultaneously serve as an advocate and a witness by paragraph (a)(3) might be precluded from doing so by Rule 1.9. The problem can arise whether the lawyer is called as a witness on behalf of the client or is called by the opposing party. Determining whether or not such a conflict exists is primarily the responsibility of the lawyer involved. If there is a conflict of interest, the lawyer must secure the client's informed consent, confirmed in writing. In some cases, the lawyer will be precluded from seeking the client's consent. See Rule 1.7. See Rule 1.0(b) for the definition of "confirmed in writing" and Rule 1.0(e) for the definition of "informed consent."

[7] Paragraph (b) provides that a lawyer is not disqualified from serving as an advocate because a lawyer with whom the lawyer is associated in a firm is precluded from doing so by paragraph (a). If,

however, the testifying lawyer would also be disqualified by Rule 1.7 or Rule 1.9 from representing the client in the matter, other lawyers in the firm will be precluded from representing the client by Rule 1.10 unless the client gives informed consent under the conditions stated in Rule 1.7.

Rule 3.8.   Special Responsibilities of a Prosecutor

The prosecutor in a criminal case shall:

(a) refrain from prosecuting a charge that the prosecutor knows is not supported by probable cause;

(b) make reasonable efforts to assure that the accused has been advised of the right to, and the procedure for obtaining, counsel and has been given reasonable opportunity to obtain counsel;

(c) not seek to obtain from an unrepresented accused a waiver of important pretrial rights, such as the right to a preliminary hearing;

(d) make timely disclosure to the defense of all evidence or information known to the prosecutor that tends to negate the guilt of the accused or mitigates the offense, and, in connection with sentencing, disclose to the defense and to the tribunal all unprivileged mitigating information known to the prosecutor, except when the prosecutor is relieved of this responsibility by a protective order of the tribunal;

(e) not subpoena a lawyer in a grand jury or other criminal proceeding to present evidence about a past or present client unless the prosecutor reasonably believes:

(1) the information sought is not protected from disclosure by any applicable privilege;

(2) the evidence sought is essential to the successful completion of an ongoing investigation or prosecution; and

(3) there is no other feasible alternative to obtain the information;

(f) except for statements that are necessary to inform the public of the nature and extent of the prosecutor's action and that serve a legitimate law enforcement purpose, refrain from making extrajudicial comments that have a substantial likelihood of heightening public condemnation of the accused and exercise reasonable care to prevent investigators, law enforcement personnel, employees or other persons assisting or associated with the prosecutor in a criminal case from making an extrajudicial statement that the prosecutor would be prohibited from making under Rule 3.6 or this Rule.

Adopted effective Jan. 1, 1987; amended Sept. 30, 2004, effective Jan. 1, 2005.

Comment

[1] A prosecutor has the responsibility of a minister of justice and not simply that of an advocate. This responsibility carries with it specific obli-

gations to see that the defendant is accorded procedural justice and that guilt is decided upon the basis of sufficient evidence. Applicable law may require other measures by the prosecutor and knowing disregard of those obligations or a systematic abuse of prosecutorial discretion could constitute a violation of Rule 8.4.

[2] In some jurisdictions, a defendant may waive a preliminary hearing and thereby lose a valuable opportunity to challenge probable cause. Accordingly, prosecutors should not seek to obtain waivers of preliminary hearings or other important pretrial rights from unrepresented accused persons. Paragraph (c) does not apply, however, to an accused appearing *pro se* with the approval of the tribunal. Nor does it forbid the lawful questioning of an uncharged suspect who has knowingly waived the rights to counsel and silence.

[3] The exception in paragraph (d) recognizes that a prosecutor may seek an appropriate protective order from the tribunal if disclosure of information to the defense could result in substantial harm to an individual or to the public interest.

[4] Paragraph (e) is intended to limit the issuance of lawyer subpoenas in grand jury and other criminal proceedings to those situations in which there is a genuine need to intrude into the client-lawyer relationship.

[5] Paragraph (f) supplements Rule 3.6, which prohibits extrajudicial statements that have a substantial likelihood of prejudicing an adjudicatory proceeding. In the context of a criminal prosecution, a prosecutor's extrajudicial statement can create the additional problem of increasing public condemnation of the accused. Although the announcement of an indictment, for example, will necessarily have severe consequences for the accused, a prosecutor can, and should, avoid comments which have no legitimate law enforcement purpose and have a substantial likelihood of increasing public opprobrium of the accused. Nothing in this Comment is intended to restrict the statements which a prosecutor may make which comply with Rule 3.6(b), 3.6(c) or 3.6(d).

[6] Like other lawyers, prosecutors are subject to Rules 5.1 and 5.3, which relate to responsibilities regarding lawyers and nonlawyers who work for or are associated with the lawyer's office. Paragraph (f) reminds the prosecutor of the importance of these obligations in connection with the unique dangers of improper extrajudicial statements in a criminal case. In addition, paragraph (f) requires a prosecutor to exercise reasonable care to prevent persons assisting or associated with the prosecutor from making improper extrajudicial statements,

even when such persons are not under the direct supervision of the prosecutor. Ordinarily, the reasonable care standard will be satisfied if the prosecutor issues the appropriate cautions to law-enforcement personnel and other relevant individuals.

Rule 3.9. Advocate in Nonadjudicative Proceedings

A lawyer representing a client before a legislative body or administrative agency in a nonadjudicative proceeding shall disclose that the appearance is in a representative capacity and shall conform to the provisions of Rules 3.3(a) through (c), 3.4(a) through (c), and 3.5.

Adopted effective Jan. 1, 1987. Amended Sept. 30, 2004, effective Jan. 1, 2005.

Comment

[1] In representation before bodies such as legislatures, municipal councils, and executive and administrative agencies acting in a rule-making or policy-making capacity, lawyers present facts, formulate issues and advance argument in the matters under consideration. The decision-making body, like a court, should be able to rely on the integrity of the submissions made to it. A lawyer appearing before such a body must deal with it honestly and in conformity with applicable rules of procedure. See Rules 3.3(a) through (c), 3.4(a) through (c) and 3.5.

[2] Lawyers have no exclusive right to appear before nonadjudicative bodies, as they do before a court. The requirements of this Rule therefore may subject lawyers to regulations inapplicable to advocates who are not lawyers. However, legislatures and administrative agencies have a right to expect lawyers to deal with them as they deal with courts.

[3] This Rule only applies when a lawyer represents a client in connection with an official hearing or meeting of a governmental agency or a legislative body to which the lawyer or the lawyer's client is presenting evidence or argument. It does not apply to representation of a client in a negotiation or other bilateral transaction with a governmental agency or in connection with an application for a license or other privilege or the client's compliance with generally applicable reporting requirements, such as the filing of income-tax returns. Nor does it apply to the representation of a client in connection with an investigation or examination of the client's affairs conducted by government investigators or examiners. Representation in such matters is governed by Rules 4.1 through 4.4.

TRANSACTIONS WITH PERSONS OTHER THAN CLIENTS

Rule 4.1. Truthfulness in Statements to Others

In the course of representing a client a lawyer shall not knowingly:

(a) make a false statement of material fact or law to a third person; or

(b) fail to disclose a material fact to a third person when disclosure is necessary to avoid assisting a criminal or fraudulent act by a client, unless disclosure is prohibited by Rule 1.6.

Adopted effective Jan. 1, 1987. Amended Oct. 23, 1987, effective Jan. 1, 1998; Sept. 30, 2004, effective Jan. 1, 2005.

Comment

Misrepresentation

[1] A lawyer is required to be truthful when dealing with others on a client's behalf, but generally has no affirmative duty to inform an opposing party of relevant facts. A misrepresentation can occur if the lawyer incorporates or affirms a statement of another person that the lawyer knows is false. Misrepresentations can also occur by partially true but misleading statements or omissions that are the equivalent of affirmative false statements. For dishonest conduct that does not amount to a false statement or for misrepresentations by a lawyer other than in the course of representing a client, see Rule 8.4.

Statements of Fact

[2] This Rule refers to statements of fact. Whether a particular statement should be regarded as one of fact can depend on the circumstances. Under generally accepted conventions in negotiation, certain types of statements ordinarily are not taken as statements of material fact. Estimates of price or value placed on the subject of a transaction and a party's intentions as to an acceptable settlement of a claim are ordinarily in this category, and so is the existence of an undisclosed principal except where nondisclosure of the principal would constitute fraud. Lawyers should be mindful of their obligations under applicable law to avoid criminal and tortious misrepresentation.

Crime or Fraud by Client

[3] Under Rule 1.2(d), a lawyer is prohibited from counseling or assisting a client in conduct that the lawyer knows is criminal or fraudulent. Paragraph (b) states a specific application of the principle set forth in Rule 1.2(d) and addresses the situation where a client's crime or fraud takes the form of a lie or misrepresentation. Ordinarily, a lawyer can avoid assisting a client's crime or fraud by withdrawing from the representation. Sometimes it may be necessary for the lawyer to give notice of the fact of withdrawal and to disaffirm an opinion, document, affirmation or the like. In extreme cases, substantive law may require a lawyer to disclose information relating to the representation to avoid being deemed to have assisted the client's crime or fraud. If the lawyer can avoid assisting a client's crime or fraud only by disclosing this information, then under paragraph (b) the lawyer is required to do so, unless the disclosure is prohibited by Rule 1.6.

Rule 4.2. Communication with Person Represented by Counsel

In representing a client, a lawyer shall not communicate about the subject of the representation with a person the lawyer knows to be represented by another lawyer in the matter, unless the lawyer has the consent of the other lawyer or is authorized by law or a court order.

Adopted effective Jan. 1, 1987. Amended Sept. 30, 2004, effective Jan. 1, 2005.

Comment

[1] This Rule contributes to the proper functioning of the legal system by protecting a person who has chosen to be represented by a lawyer in a matter against possible overreaching by other lawyers who are participating in the matter, interference by those lawyers with the client-lawyer relationship and the uncounseled disclosure of information relating to the representation.

[2] This Rule applies to communications with any person who is represented by counsel concerning the matter to which the communication relates.

[3] The Rule applies even though the represented person initiates or consents to the communication. A lawyer must immediately terminate communication with a person if, after commencing communication, the lawyer learns that the person is one with whom communication is not permitted by this Rule.

[4] This Rule does not prohibit communication with a represented person, or an employee or agent of such a person, concerning matters outside the representation. For example, the existence of a controversy between a government agency and a private party, or between two organizations, does not prohibit a lawyer for either from communicating with nonlawyer representatives of the other regarding a separate matter. Nor does this Rule preclude communication with a represented person who is seeking advice from a lawyer who is not otherwise representing a client in the matter. A lawyer may not make a communication prohibited by this Rule through the acts of another. See Rule 8.4(a). Parties to a matter may communicate directly with each other, and a lawyer is not prohibited from advising a client concerning a communication that the client is legally entitled to make. Also, a lawyer having independent justification or legal authorization for communicating with a represented person is permitted to do so.

[5] Communications authorized by law may include communications by a lawyer on behalf of a client who is exercising a constitutional or other legal right to communicate with the government. Communications authorized by law may also include investigative activities of lawyers representing governmental entities, directly or through investigative agents, prior to the commencement of criminal or civil enforcement proceedings. When communicating with the accused in a criminal matter, a government lawyer must comply with this Rule in addition to honoring the constitutional rights of the accused. The fact that a communication does not violate a state or federal constitutional right is insufficient to

establish that the communication is permissible under this Rule.

[6] A lawyer who is uncertain whether a communication with a represented person is permissible may seek a court order. A lawyer may also seek a court order in exceptional circumstances to authorize a communication that would otherwise be prohibited by this Rule, for example, where communication with a person represented by counsel is necessary to avoid reasonably certain injury.

[7] In the case of a represented organization, this Rule prohibits communications with a constituent of the organization who supervises, directs or regularly consults with the organization's lawyer concerning the matter or has authority to obligate the organization with respect to the matter or whose act or omission in connection with the matter may be imputed to the organization for purposes of civil or criminal liability. Consent of the organization's lawyer is not required for communication with a former constituent. If a constituent of the organization is represented in the matter by his or her own counsel, the consent by that counsel to a communication will be sufficient for purposes of this Rule. Compare Rule 3.4(f). In communicating with a current or former constituent of an organization, a lawyer must not use methods of obtaining evidence that violate the legal rights of the organization. See Rule 4.4.

[8] The prohibition on communications with a represented person only applies in circumstances where the lawyer knows that the person is in fact represented in the matter to be discussed. This means that the lawyer has actual knowledge of the fact of the representation; but such actual knowledge may be inferred from the circumstances. See Rule 1.0(f). Thus, the lawyer cannot evade the requirement of obtaining the consent of counsel by closing eyes to the obvious.

[9] In the event the person with whom the lawyer communicates is not known to be represented by counsel in the matter, the lawyer's communications are subject to Rule 4.3.

Rule 4.3. Dealing with Unrepresented Persons

In dealing on behalf of a client with a person who is not represented by counsel, a lawyer shall not state or imply that the lawyer is disinterested. When the lawyer knows or reasonably should know that the unrepresented person misunderstands the lawyer's role in the matter, the lawyer shall make reasonable efforts to correct the misunderstanding. The lawyer shall not give legal advice to an unrepresented person, other than the advice to secure counsel, if the lawyer knows or reasonably should know that the interests of such person are or have a reasonable possibility of being in conflict with the interests of the client.

Adopted effective Jan. 1, 1987. Amended Sept. 30, 2004, effective Jan. 1, 2005.

Comment

[1] An unrepresented person, particularly one not experienced in dealing with legal matters, might assume that a lawyer is disinterested in loyalties or is a disinterested authority on the law even when the lawyer represents a client. In order to avoid a misunderstanding, a lawyer will typically need to identify the lawyer's client and, where necessary, explain that the client has interests opposed to those of the unrepresented person. For misunderstandings that sometimes arise when a lawyer for an organization deals with an unrepresented constituent, see Rule 1.13(d).

[2] The Rule distinguishes between situations involving unrepresented persons whose interests may be adverse to those of the lawyer's client and those in which the person's interests are not in conflict with the client's. In the former situation, the possibility that the lawyer will compromise the unrepresented person's interests is so great that the Rule prohibits the giving of any advice, apart from the advice to obtain counsel. Whether a lawyer is giving impermissible advice may depend on the experience and sophistication of the unrepresented person, as well as the setting in which the behavior and comments occur. This Rule does not prohibit a lawyer from negotiating the terms of a transaction or settling a dispute with an unrepresented person. So long as the lawyer has explained that the lawyer represents an adverse party and is not representing the person, the lawyer may inform the person of the terms on which the lawyer's client will enter into an agreement or settle a matter, prepare documents that require the person's signature and explain the lawyer's own view of the meaning of the document or the lawyer's view of the underlying legal obligations.

Rule 4.4. Respect for Rights of Third Persons

(a) In representing a client, a lawyer shall not use means that have no substantial purpose other than to embarrass, delay, or burden a third person, or use methods of obtaining evidence that violate the legal rights of such a person.

(b) A lawyer who receives a document relating to the representation of the lawyer's client and knows or reasonably should know that the document was inadvertently sent shall promptly notify the sender.

Adopted effective Jan. 1, 1987. Amended Sept. 30, 2004, effective Jan. 1, 2005.

Comment

[1] Responsibility to a client requires a lawyer to subordinate the interests of others to those of the client, but that responsibility does not imply that a lawyer may disregard the rights of third persons. It is impractical to catalogue all such rights, but they include legal restrictions on methods of obtaining evidence from third persons and unwarranted intrusions into privileged relationships, such as the client-lawyer relationship.

[2] Paragraph (b) recognizes that lawyers sometimes receive documents that were mistakenly sent or produced by opposing parties or their lawyers. If a lawyer knows or reasonably should know that such a document was sent inadvertently, then this

Rule requires the lawyer to promptly notify the sender in order to permit that person to take protective measures. Whether the lawyer is required to take additional steps, such as returning the original document, is a matter of law beyond the scope of these Rules, as is the question of whether the privileged status of a document has been waived. Similarly, this Rule does not address the legal duties of a lawyer who receives a document that the lawyer knows or reasonably should know may have been wrongfully obtained by the sending person.

For purposes of this Rule, "document" includes e-mail or other electronic modes of transmission subject to being read or put into readable form.

[3] Some lawyers may choose to return a document unread, for example, when the lawyer learns before receiving the document that it was inadvertently sent to the wrong address. Where a lawyer is not required by applicable law to do so, the decision to voluntarily return such a document is a matter of professional judgment ordinarily reserved to the lawyer. See Rules 1.2 and 1.4.

LAW FIRMS AND ASSOCIATIONS

Rule 5.1. Responsibilities of a Partner or Supervisory Lawyer

(a) A partner in a law firm, and a lawyer who individually or together with other lawyers possess comparable managerial authority in a law firm, shall make reasonable efforts to ensure that the firm has in effect measures giving reasonable assurance that all lawyers in the firm conform to the Rules of Professional Conduct.

(b) A lawyer having direct supervisory authority over another lawyer shall make reasonable efforts to ensure that the other lawyer conforms to the Rules of Professional Conduct.

(c) A lawyer shall be responsible for another lawyer's violation of the Rules of Professional Conduct if:

(1) the lawyer orders or, with knowledge of the specific conduct, ratifies the conduct involved; or

(2) the lawyer is a partner or has comparable managerial authority in the law firm in which the other lawyer practices, or has direct supervisory authority over the other lawyer, and knows of the conduct at a time when its consequences can be avoided or mitigated but fails to take reasonable remedial action.

Adopted effective Jan. 1, 1987; amended Sept. 30, 2004, effective Jan. 1, 2005.

Comment

[1] Paragraph (a) applies to lawyers who have managerial authority over the professional work of a firm. See Rule 1.0(c). This includes members of a partnership, the shareholders in a law firm organized as a professional corporation, and members of other associations authorized to practice law; lawyers having comparable managerial authority in a legal services organization or a law department of an enterprise or government agency; and lawyers who have intermediate managerial responsibilities in a firm. Paragraph (b) applies to lawyers who have supervisory authority over the work of other lawyers in a firm.

[2] Paragraph (a) requires lawyers with managerial authority within a firm to make reasonable efforts to establish internal policies and procedures designed to provide reasonable assurance that all lawyers in the firm will conform to the Rules of Professional Conduct. Such policies and procedures may include those designed to detect and resolve conflicts of interest, identify dates by which actions must be taken in pending matters, account for client funds and property and ensure that inexperienced lawyers are properly supervised.

[3] Other measures that may be required to fulfill the responsibility prescribed in paragraph (a) can depend on the firm's structure and the nature of its practice. In a small firm of experienced lawyers, informal supervision and periodic review of compliance with the required systems ordinarily will suffice. In a large firm, or in practice situations in which difficult ethical problems frequently arise, more elaborate measures may be necessary. Some firms, for example, have a procedure whereby junior lawyers can make confidential referral of ethical problems directly to a designated senior partner or special committee. See Rule 5.2. Firms, whether large or small, may also rely on continuing legal education in professional ethics. In any event, the ethical atmosphere of a firm can influence the conduct of all its members and the partners may not assume that all lawyers associated with the firm will inevitably conform to the Rules.

[4] Paragraph (c) expresses a general principle of personal responsibility for acts of another. See also Rule 8.4(a).

[5] Paragraph (c)(2) defines the duty of a partner or other lawyer having comparable managerial authority in a law firm, as well as a lawyer who has direct supervisory authority over performance of specific legal work by another lawyer. Whether a lawyer has supervisory authority in particular circumstances is a question of fact. Partners and lawyers with comparable authority have at least indirect responsibility for all work being done by the firm, while a partner or manager in charge of a particular matter ordinarily also has supervisory responsibility for the work of other firm lawyers engaged in the matter. Appropriate remedial action by a partner or managing lawyer would depend on the immediacy of that lawyer's involvement and the seriousness of the misconduct. A supervisor is required to intervene to prevent avoidable consequences of misconduct if the supervisor knows that the misconduct occurred. Thus, if a supervising lawyer knows that a subordinate misrepresented a matter to an opposing party in negotiation, the supervisor as well as the subordinate has a duty to correct the misrepresentation.

[6] Professional misconduct by a lawyer under supervision could reveal a violation of paragraph (b) on the part of the supervisory lawyer even though it does not entail a violation of paragraph (c) because there was no direction, ratification or knowledge of the violation.

[7] Apart from this Rule and Rule 8.4(a), a lawyer does not have disciplinary liability for the conduct of a partner, associate or subordinate. Whether a lawyer may be liable civilly or criminally for another lawyer's conduct is a question of law beyond the scope of these Rules.

[8] The duties imposed by this Rule on managing and supervising lawyers do not alter the personal duty of each lawyer in a firm to abide by the Rules of Professional Conduct. See Rule 5.2(a).

Rule 5.2. Responsibilities of a Subordinate Lawyer

(a) A lawyer is bound by the Rules of Professional Conduct notwithstanding that the lawyer acted at the direction of another person.

(b) A subordinate lawyer does not violate the Rules of Professional Conduct if that lawyer acts in accordance with a supervisory lawyer's reasonable resolution of an arguable question of professional duty.

Adopted effective Jan. 1, 1987.

Comment

[1] Although a lawyer is not relieved of responsibility for a violation by the fact that the lawyer acted at the direction of a supervisor, that fact may be relevant in determining whether a lawyer had the knowledge required to render conduct a violation of the Rules. For example, if a subordinate filed a frivolous pleading at the direction of a supervisor, the subordinate would not be guilty of a professional violation unless the subordinate knew of the document's frivolous character.

[2] When lawyers in a supervisor-subordinate relationship encounter a matter involving professional judgment as to ethical duty, the supervisor may assume responsibility for making the judgment. Otherwise a consistent course of action or position could not be taken. If the question can reasonably be answered only one way, the duty of both lawyers is clear and they are equally responsible for fulfilling it. However, if the question is reasonably arguable, someone has to decide upon the course of action. That authority ordinarily reposes in the supervisor, and a subordinate may be guided accordingly. For example, if a question arises whether the interests of two clients conflict under Rule 1.7, the supervisor's reasonable resolution of the question should protect the subordinate professionally if the resolution is subsequently challenged.

Rule 5.3. Responsibilities Regarding Nonlawyer Assistants

With respect to a nonlawyer employed or retained by or associated with a lawyer:

(a) a partner, and a lawyer who individually or together with other lawyers possess comparable managerial authority in a law firm shall make reasonable efforts to ensure that the firm has in effect measures giving reasonable assurance that the person's conduct is compatible with the professional obligations of the lawyer;

(b) a lawyer having direct supervisory authority over the nonlawyer shall make reasonable efforts to ensure that the person's conduct is compatible with the professional obligations of the lawyer; and

(c) a lawyer shall be responsible for conduct of such a person that would be a violation of the Rules of Professional Conduct if engaged in by a lawyer if:

(1) the lawyer orders or, with the knowledge of the specific conduct, ratifies the conduct involved; or

(2) the lawyer is a partner or has comparable managerial authority in the law firm in which the person is employed, or has direct supervisory authority over the person, and knows of the conduct at a time when its consequences can be avoided or mitigated but fails to take reasonable remedial action.

Adopted effective Jan. 1, 1987; amended Sept. 30, 2004, effective Jan. 1, 2005.

Comment

[1] Lawyers generally employ assistants in their practice, including secretaries, investigators, law student interns, paralegals and other paraprofessionals. Such assistants, whether employees or independent contractors, act for the lawyer in rendition of the lawyer's professional services. A lawyer must give such assistants appropriate instruction and supervision concerning the ethical aspects of their employment, particularly regarding the obligation not to disclose information relating to representation of the client, and should be responsible for their work product. The measures employed in supervising nonlawyers should take account of the fact that they may not have legal training and are not subject to professional discipline.

[2] Paragraph (a) requires lawyers with managerial authority within a law firm to make reasonable efforts to establish internal policies and procedures designed to provide reasonable assurance that nonlawyers in the firm will act in a way compatible with the Rules of Professional Conduct. See Comment [1] to Rule 5.1. Paragraph (b) applies to lawyers who have supervisory authority over the work of a nonlawyer. Paragraph (c) specifies the circumstances in which a lawyer is responsible for conduct of a nonlawyer that would be a violation of the Rules of Professional Conduct if engaged in by a lawyer.

Rule 5.4. Professional Independence of a Lawyer

(a) A lawyer or law firm shall not share legal fees with a nonlawyer, except that:

(1) an agreement by a lawyer with the lawyer's firm, partner, or associate may provide for the payment of money, over a reasonable period of time after the lawyer's death, to the lawyer's estate or to one or more specified persons;

(2) a lawyer who purchases the practice of a deceased, disabled, or disappeared lawyer may, pursuant to the provisions of Rule 1.17, pay to the estate or other representative of that lawyer the agreed upon purchase price; and

(3) a lawyer or law firm may include nonlawyer employees in a compensation or retirement plan, even though the plan is based in whole or in part on a profit-sharing arrangement.

(b) A lawyer shall not form a partnership with a nonlawyer if any of the activities of the partnership consist of the practice of law.

(c) A lawyer shall not permit a person who recommends, employs, or pays the lawyer to render legal services for another to direct or regulate the lawyer's professional judgment in rendering such legal services.

(d) A lawyer shall not practice with or in the form of a professional corporation or association authorized to practice law for a profit, if:

(1) a nonlawyer owns any interest therein, except that a fiduciary representative of the estate of a lawyer may hold the stock or interest of the lawyer for a reasonable time during administration;

(2) a nonlawyer is a corporate director or officer thereof or occupies the position of similar responsibility in any form of association other than a corporation; or

(3) a nonlawyer has the right to direct or control the professional judgment of a lawyer.

Adopted effective Jan. 1, 1987; amended Sept. 30, 2004, effective Jan. 1, 2005.

Comment

[1] The provisions of this Rule express traditional limitations on sharing fees. These limitations are to protect the lawyer's professional independence of judgment. Where someone other than the client pays the lawyer's fee or salary, or recommends employment of the lawyer, that arrangement does not modify the lawyer's obligation to the client. As stated in paragraph (c), such arrangements should not interfere with the lawyer's professional judgment.

[2] This Rule also expresses traditional limitations on permitting a third party to direct or regulate the lawyer's professional judgment in rendering legal services to another. See also Rule 1.8(f) (lawyer may accept compensation from a third party as long as there is no interference with the lawyer's independent professional judgment and the client gives informed consent).

Rule 5.5. Unauthorized Practice of Law; Multijurisdictional Practice of Law

(a) A lawyer shall not practice law in a jurisdiction in violation of the regulation of the legal profession in that jurisdiction, or assist another in doing so.

(b) A lawyer who is not admitted to practice in this jurisdiction shall not:

(1) except as authorized by these Rules or other law, establish an office or other systematic and continuous presence in this jurisdiction for the practice of law; or

(2) hold out to the public or otherwise represent that the lawyer is admitted to practice law in this jurisdiction.

(c) A lawyer who is not admitted to practice in this jurisdiction, but is admitted in another United States jurisdiction, and not disbarred or suspended from practice in any jurisdiction, may provide legal services on a temporary basis in this jurisdiction that:

(1) are undertaken in association with a lawyer who is admitted to practice in this jurisdiction and who actively participates in the matter;

(2) are in or reasonably related to a pending or potential proceeding before a tribunal in this or another jurisdiction, if the lawyer, or a person the lawyer is assisting, is authorized by law or order to appear in such proceeding or reasonably expects to be so authorized;

(3) are in or reasonably related to a pending or potential arbitration, mediation, or other alternative dispute resolution proceeding in this or another jurisdiction, if the services arise out of or are reasonably related to the lawyer's practice in a jurisdiction in which the lawyer is admitted to practice and are not services for which the forum requires temporary admission; or

(4) are not within paragraphs (c)(2) or (c)(3) and arise out of or are reasonably related to the lawyer's practice in a jurisdiction in which the lawyer is admitted to practice.

(d) A lawyer who is not admitted to practice in this jurisdiction, but is admitted in another United States jurisdiction, or in a foreign jurisdiction, and not disbarred or suspended from practice in any jurisdiction, may provide legal services in this jurisdiction if:

(1) the lawyer does not establish an office or other systematic and continuous presence in this jurisdiction for the practice of law and the legal services are provided to the lawyer's employer or its organizational affiliates and are not services for which the forum requires temporary admission; or

(2) the services are services that the lawyer is authorized to provide by federal law or other law of this jurisdiction.

Adopted effective Jan. 1, 1987. Amended Sept. 30, 2004, effective Jan. 1, 2005; Oct. 26, 2012, effective Jan. 1, 2013.

Comment

[1] A lawyer may practice law only in a jurisdiction in which the lawyer is authorized to practice. A lawyer may be admitted to practice law in a jurisdiction on a regular basis or may be authorized by court rule or order or by law to practice for a limited purpose or on a restricted basis. Paragraph (a) applies to unauthorized practice of law by a lawyer, whether through the lawyer's direct action or by the lawyer assisting another person.

[2] The definition of the practice of law is established by law and varies from one jurisdiction to another. Whatever the definition, limiting the practice of law to members of the bar protects the public against rendition of legal services by unqualified persons. This Rule does not prohibit a lawyer from employing the services of paralegals and other paraprofessionals and delegating functions to them, so long as the lawyer supervises the delegated work and retains responsibility for their work. See Rule 5.3.

[3] A lawyer may provide professional advice and instruction to nonlawyers whose employment requires knowledge of the law; for example, claims adjusters, employees of financial or commercial institutions, social workers, accountants and persons employed in government agencies. Lawyers also may assist independent nonlawyers, such as paralegals and other paraprofessionals, who are authorized by the law of a jurisdiction to provide particular law-related services. In addition, a lawyer may counsel nonlawyers who wish to proceed pro se.

[4] Other than as authorized by law or this Rule, a lawyer who is not admitted to practice generally in the State of Indiana violates paragraph (b) if the lawyer establishes an office or other systematic and continuous presence in the State of Indiana for the practice of law. Presence may be systematic and continuous even if the lawyer is not physically present here. For example, advertising in media specifically targeted to Indiana residents or initiating contact with Indiana residents for solicitation purposes could be viewed as systematic and continuous presence. In any event, such a lawyer must not hold out to the public or otherwise represent that the lawyer is admitted to practice law in the State of Indiana. See also Rules 7.1(a) and 7.5(b).

[5] There are occasions in which a lawyer admitted to practice in another United States jurisdiction, and not disbarred or suspended from practice in any jurisdiction, may provide legal services on a temporary basis in this jurisdiction under circumstances that do not create an unreasonable risk to the interests of his or her clients, the public or the courts. Paragraph (c) identifies four such circumstances. The fact that conduct is not so identified does not imply that the conduct is or is not authorized. With the exception of paragraph (d)(2), this Rule does not authorize a U.S. or foreign lawyer to establish an office or other systematic and continuous presence in this jurisdiction without being admitted to practice generally here or licensed pursuant to Admission and Discipline Rule 6.

[6] There is no single test to determine whether a lawyer's services are provided on a "temporary basis" in this jurisdiction, and may therefore be permissible under paragraph (c). Services may be "temporary" even though the lawyer provides services in this jurisdiction on a recurring basis, or for an extended period of time, as when the lawyer is representing a client in a single lengthy negotiation or litigation.

[7] Paragraph (c) applies to lawyers who are admitted to practice law in any United States jurisdiction, which includes the District of Columbia and any state, territory or commonwealth of the United States. The word "admitted" in paragraph (c) contemplates that the lawyer is authorized to practice in the jurisdiction in which the lawyer is admitted and excludes a lawyer who while technically admitted is not authorized to practice, because, for example, the lawyer is on inactive status. Paragraph (d) applies to lawyers admitted to practice in a United States jurisdiction and to lawyers admitted in a foreign jurisdiction.

[8] Paragraph (c)(1) recognizes that the interests of clients and the public are protected if a lawyer admitted only in another jurisdiction associates with a lawyer licensed to practice in this jurisdiction. For this paragraph to apply, however, the lawyer admitted to practice in this jurisdiction must actively participate in and share responsibility for the representation of the client.

[9] Lawyers not admitted to practice generally in a jurisdiction may be authorized by law or order of a tribunal or an administrative agency to appear before the tribunal or agency. This authority may be granted pursuant to formal rules governing admission pro hac vice or pursuant to informal practice of the tribunal or agency. Under paragraph (c)(2), a lawyer does not violate this Rule when the lawyer appears before a tribunal or agency pursuant to such authority. To the extent that a court rule or other law of this jurisdiction requires a lawyer who is not admitted to practice in this jurisdiction to obtain admission pro hac vice before appearing before a tribunal or administrative agency, this Rule requires the lawyer to obtain that authority.

[10] Paragraph (c)(2) also provides that a lawyer rendering services in this jurisdiction on a temporary basis does not violate this Rule when the lawyer engages in conduct in anticipation of a proceeding or hearing in a jurisdiction in which the lawyer is authorized to practice law or in which the lawyer reasonably expects to be admitted pro hac vice. Examples of such conduct include meetings with the client, interviews of potential witnesses, and the review of documents. Similarly, a lawyer admitted only in another jurisdiction may engage in conduct temporarily in this jurisdiction in connection with pending litigation in another jurisdiction in which the lawyer is or reasonably expects to be authorized to appear, including taking depositions in this jurisdiction.

[11] When a lawyer has been or reasonably expects to be admitted to appear before a court or administrative agency, paragraph (c)(2) also permits conduct by lawyers who are associated with that lawyer in the matter, but who do not expect to appear before the court or administrative agency.

For example, subordinate lawyers may conduct research, review documents, and attend meetings with witnesses in support of the lawyer responsible for the litigation.

[12] Paragraph (c)(3) permits a lawyer admitted to practice law in another jurisdiction to perform services on a temporary basis in this jurisdiction if those services are in or reasonably related to a pending or potential arbitration, mediation, or other alternative dispute resolution proceeding in this or another jurisdiction, if the services arise out of or are reasonably related to the lawyer's practice in a jurisdiction in which the lawyer is admitted to practice. The lawyer, however, must obtain admission pro hac vice in the case of a court-annexed arbitration or mediation or otherwise if court rules or law so require.

[13] Paragraph (c)(4) permits a lawyer admitted in another jurisdiction to provide certain legal services on a temporary basis in this jurisdiction that arise out of or are reasonably related to the lawyer's practice in a jurisdiction in which the lawyer is admitted but are not within paragraphs (c)(2) or (c)(3). These services include both legal services and services that nonlawyers may perform but that are considered the practice of law when performed by lawyers.

[14] Paragraphs (c)(3) and (c)(4) require that the services arise out of or be reasonably related to the lawyer's practice in a jurisdiction in which the lawyer is admitted. A variety of factors evidence such a relationship. The lawyer's client may have been previously represented by the lawyer, or may be resident in or have substantial contacts with the jurisdiction in which the lawyer is admitted. The matter, although involving other jurisdictions, may have a significant connection with that jurisdiction. In other cases, significant aspects of the lawyer's work might be conducted in that jurisdiction or a significant aspect of the matter may involve the law of that jurisdiction. The necessary relationship might arise when the client's activities or the legal issues involve multiple jurisdictions, such as when the officers of a multinational corporation survey potential business sites and seek the services of their lawyer in assessing the relative merits of each. In addition, the services may draw on the lawyer's recognized expertise developed through the regular practice of law on behalf of clients in matters involving a particular body of federal, nationally uniform, foreign, or international law.

[15] Paragraph (d) identifies two circumstances in which a lawyer who is admitted to practice in another United States or a foreign jurisdiction, and is not disbarred or suspended from practice in any jurisdiction, may establish an office or other systematic and continuous presence in this jurisdiction for the practice of law as well as provide legal services on a temporary basis. Except as provided in paragraphs (d)(1) and (d)(2), a lawyer who is admitted to practice law in another jurisdiction and who establishes an office or other systematic or continuous presence in this jurisdiction must become admitted to practice law generally in this jurisdiction.

[16] Paragraph (d)(1) applies to a United States or foreign lawyer who is employed by a client to provide legal services to the client or its organizational affiliates, i.e., entities that control, are controlled by, or are under common control with the employer. This paragraph does not authorize the provision of personal legal services to the employer's officers or employees. The paragraph applies to in-house corporate lawyers, government lawyers and others who are employed to render legal services to the employer. The lawyer's ability to represent the employer outside the jurisdiction in which the lawyer is licensed generally serves the interests of the employer and does not create an unreasonable risk to the client and others because the employer is well situated to assess the lawyer's qualifications and the quality of the lawyer's work.

[17] If an employed lawyer establishes an office or other systematic presence in this jurisdiction for the purpose of rendering legal services to the employer, the lawyer shall be subject to registration or other requirements, including assessments for client protection funds and mandatory continuing legal education. See, Ind. Admission and Discipline Rule 6, sections 2 through 5.

[18] Paragraph (d)(2) recognizes that a lawyer may provide legal services in a jurisdiction in which the lawyer is not licensed when authorized to do so by federal or other law, which includes statute, court rule, executive regulation or judicial precedent.

[19] A lawyer who practices law in the State of Indiana pursuant to paragraphs (c) or (d) or otherwise is subject to the disciplinary authority of the State of Indiana. See Rule 8.5(a).

[20] In some circumstances, a lawyer who practices law in the State of Indiana pursuant to paragraphs (c) or (d) may have to inform the client that the lawyer is not licensed to practice law in the State of Indiana. For example, that may be required when the representation occurs primarily in the State of Indiana and requires knowledge of the law of the State of Indiana. See Rule 1.4(b).

[21] Paragraphs (c) and (d) do not authorize communications advertising legal services to prospective clients in the State of Indiana by lawyers who are admitted to practice in other jurisdictions. Whether and how lawyers may communicate the availability of their services to prospective clients in the State of Indiana is governed by Rules 7.2 to 7.5.

Rule 5.6. Restrictions on Right to Practice

A lawyer shall not participate in offering or making:

(a) a partnership, shareholder, operating, employment, or other similar type of agreement that restricts the rights of a lawyer to practice after termination of the relationship, except an agreement concerning benefits upon retirement; or

(b) an agreement in which a restriction on the lawyer's right to practice is part of the settlement of a client controversy.

Adopted effective Jan. 1, 1987; amended Sept. 30, 2004, effective Jan. 1, 2005.

Comment

[1] An agreement restricting the right of lawyers to practice after leaving a firm not only limits their professional autonomy but also limits the freedom of clients to choose a lawyer. Paragraph (a) prohibits such agreements except for restrictions incident to provisions concerning retirement benefits for service with the firm.

[2] Paragraph (b) prohibits a lawyer from agreeing not to represent other persons in connection with settling a claim on behalf of a client.

[3] This Rule does not apply to prohibit restrictions that may be included in the terms of the sale of a law practice pursuant to Rule 1.17.

Rule 5.7   Responsibilities Regarding Law-Related Services

(a) A lawyer shall be subject to the Rules of Professional Conduct with respect to the provision of law-related services, as defined in paragraph (b), if the law-related services are provided:

(1) by the lawyer in circumstances that are not distinct from the lawyer's provision of legal services to clients; or

(2) in other circumstance by an entity controlled by the lawyer individually or with others if the lawyer fails to take reasonable measures to assure that a person obtaining the law-related services knows that the services are not legal services and that the protections of the client-lawyer relationship do not exist.

(b) The term "law-related services" denotes services that might reasonably be performed in conjunction with and in substance are related to the provision of legal services, and that are not prohibited as unauthorized practice of law when provided by a nonlawyer.

Adopted Dec. 23, 1996, effective March 1, 1997. Amended Sept. 30, 2004, effective Jan. 1, 2005.

Comment

[1] When a lawyer performs law-related services or controls an organization that does so or uses a law license to promote an organization or otherwise creates a basis for a belief that the client may be dealing with an attorney (such as where a person uses "J.D." on business cards or stationary or hangs framed law degrees or court admissions on office walls), there exists the potential for ethical problems. Principal among these is the possibility that the person for whom the law-related services are performed fails to understand that the services may not carry with them the protections normally afforded as part of the client-lawyer relationship. The recipient of the law-related services may expect, for example, that the protection of client confidences, prohibitions against representation of persons with conflicting interests, and obligations of a lawyer to maintain professional independence apply to the provision of law-related services when that may not be the case.

[2] Rule 5.7 applies to the provision of law-related services by a lawyer even when the lawyer does not provide any legal services to the person for whom the law-related services are performed and whether the law-related services are performed through a law firm or a separate entity. The Rule identifies the circumstances in which all of the Rules of Professional Conduct apply to the provision of law-related services. Even when those circumstances do not exist, however, the conduct of a lawyer involved in the provision of law-related services is subject to those Rules that apply generally to lawyer conduct, regardless of whether the conduct involves the provision of legal services. See, e.g., Rule 8.4.

[3] When law-related services are provided by a lawyer under circumstances that are not distinct from the lawyer's provision of legal services to clients, the lawyer in providing the law-related services must adhere to the requirements of the Rules of Professional Conduct as provided in paragraph (a)(1). Even when the law-related and legal services are provided in circumstances that are distinct from each other, for example through separate entities or different support staff within the law firm, the Rules of Professional Conduct apply to the lawyer as provided in paragraph (a)(2) unless the lawyer takes reasonable measures to assure that the recipient of the law-related services knows that the services are not legal services and that the protections of the client-lawyer relationship do not apply.

[4] Law–related services also may be provided through an entity that is distinct from that through which the lawyer provides legal services. If the lawyer individually or with others has control of such an entity's operations, the Rule requires the lawyer to take reasonable measures to assure that each person using the services of the entity knows that the services provided by the entity are not legal services and that the Rules of Professional Conduct that relate to the client-lawyer relationship do not apply. A lawyer's control of an entity extends to the ability to direct its operation. Whether a lawyer has such control will depend upon the circumstances of the particular case.

[5] When a client-lawyer relationship exists with a person who is referred by a lawyer to a separate law-related service entity controlled by the lawyer, individually or with others, the lawyer must comply with Rule 1.8(a).

[6] In taking the reasonable measures referred to in paragraph (a)(2) to assure that a person using law-related services understands the practical effect or significance of the inapplicability of the Rules of Professional Conduct, the lawyer should communicate to the person receiving the law-related services, in a manner sufficient to assure that the person understands the significance of the fact, that the relationship of the person to the business entity will not be a client-lawyer relationship. The communication should be made before entering into an agreement for provision of or providing law-related services, and preferably should be in writing.

[7] The burden is upon the lawyer to show that the lawyer has taken reasonable measures under

the circumstances to communicate the desired understanding. For instance, a sophisticated user of law-related services, such as a publicly held corporation, may require a lesser explanation than someone unaccustomed to making distinctions between legal services and law-related services, such as an individual seeking tax advice from a lawyer-accountant or investigative services in connection with a lawsuit.

[8] Regardless of the sophistication of potential recipients of law-related services, a lawyer should take special care to keep separate the provision of law-related and legal services in order to minimize the risk that the recipient will assume that the law-related services are legal services. The risk of such confusion is especially acute when the lawyer renders both types of services with respect to the same matter. Under some circumstances the legal and law-related services may be so closely entwined that they cannot be distinguished from each other, and the requirement of disclosure and consultation imposed by paragraph (a)(2) of the Rule cannot be met. In such a case a lawyer will be responsible for assuring that both the lawyer's conduct and, to the extent required by Rule 5.3, that of nonlawyer employees in the distinct entity that the lawyer controls complies in all respects with the Rules of Professional Conduct.

[9] A broad range of economic and other interests of clients may be served by lawyers' engaging in the delivery of law-related services. Examples of law-related services include providing title insurance, financial planning, accounting, real estate counseling, legislative lobbying, economic analysis, social work, psychological counseling, tax preparation, and medical or environmental consulting.

[10] When a lawyer is obliged to accord the recipients of such services the protections of those Rules that apply to the client-lawyer relationship, the lawyer must take special care to heed the proscriptions of the Rules addressing conflict of interest (Rules 1.7 through 1.11, especially Rules 1.7(a)(2) and 1.8(a), (b) and (f)), and to scrupulously adhere to the requirements of Rule 1.6 relating to disclosure of confidential information. Where the provision of law-related services is subject to these Rules, the promotion of the law-related services must also in all respects comply with Rules 7.2, through 7.5, dealing with advertising and solicitation. In that regard, lawyers should take special care to identify the obligations that may be imposed as a result of a jurisdiction's decisional law.

[11] When the full protections of all of the Indiana Rules of Professional Conduct do not apply to the provision of law-related services, principles of law external to the Rules, for example, the law of principal and agent, govern the legal duties owed to those receiving the services. Those other legal principles may establish a different degree of protection for the recipient with respect to confidentiality of information, conflicts of interest and permissible business relationships with clients. See also Rule 8.4 (Misconduct).

PUBLIC SERVICE

Rule 6.1. Pro Bono Publico Service

A lawyer should render public interest legal service. A lawyer may discharge this responsibility by providing professional services at no fee or a reduced fee to persons of limited means or to public service or charitable groups or organizations, by service in activities for improving the law, the legal system or the legal profession, and by financial support for organizations that provide legal services to persons of limited means.

Adopted effective Jan. 1, 1987. Amended Sept. 15, 2009, effective Jan. 1, 2010.

Comment

[1] The American Bar Association House of Delegates has formally acknowledged "the basic responsibility of each lawyer engaged in the practice of law to provide public interest legal services" without fee, or at a substantially reduced fee, in one or more of the following areas: poverty law, civil rights law, public rights law, charitable organization representation and the administration of justice. The Indiana State Bar Association's House of Delegates has declared that "all Indiana lawyers have an ethical and a social obligation to provide uncompensated legal assistance to poor persons" and adopted an aspirational goal of fifty hours a year, or an equivalent financial contribution, for each member of the bar.

For purposes of this paragraph:

(a) Poverty law means legal representation of a client who does not have the financial resources to compensate counsel.

(b) Civil rights (including civil liberties) law means legal representation involving a right of an individual that society has a special interest in protecting.

(c) Public rights law means legal representation involving an important right belonging to a significant segment of the public.

(d) Charitable organization representation means legal service to or representation of charitable, religious, civic, governmental and educational institutions in matters in furtherance of the organization's purpose, where the payment of customary legal fees would significantly deplete the organization's economic resources or where it would be inappropriate.

(e) Administration of justice means activity, whether under bar association auspices or otherwise, which is designed to increase the availability of legal representation, or otherwise improve the administration of justice. This may include increasing the availability of legal resources to individuals or groups, improving the judicial system, or reforming legal institutions that significantly affect the lives of disadvantaged individuals and groups.

[2] The rights and responsibilities of individuals and organizations in the United States are increasingly defined in legal terms. As a consequence, legal assistance in coping with the web of statutes, rules and regulations is imperative for persons of modest and limited means, as well as for the relatively well-to-do.

[3] The basic responsibility for providing legal services for those unable to pay ultimately rests upon the individual lawyer, and personal involvement in the problems of the disadvantaged can be one of the most rewarding experiences in the life of a lawyer. Every lawyer, regardless of professional prominence or professional workload, should find time to participate in or otherwise support the provision of legal services to the disadvantaged. The provision of free legal services to those unable to pay reasonable fees continues to be an obligation of each lawyer as well as the profession generally, but the efforts of individual lawyers are often not enough to meet the need. Thus, it has been necessary for the profession and government to institute additional programs to provide legal services. Accordingly, legal aid offices, lawyer referral services and other related programs have been developed, and others will be developed by the profession and government. Every lawyer should support all proper efforts to meet this need for legal services.

[4] Typically, to fulfill the aspirational goals in Comment 1, legal services should be performed without the expectation of compensation. If, during the course of representation, a paying client is no longer able to afford a lawyer's legal services, and the lawyer continues to represent the client at no charge, any work performed with the knowledge and intent of no compensation may be considered pro bono legal service.

The award of attorney's fees in a case originally accepted as pro bono does not disqualify such services from fulfilling the foregoing aspirational goals. However, lawyers who receive attorney's fees in pro bono cases are strongly encouraged to contribute an appropriate portion of such fees to organizations or projects that benefit persons of limited means, or that promote access to justice for persons of limited means.

[5] Typically, the following would not fulfill the aspirational goals in Comment 1:

(a) Legal services written off as bad debts.

(b) Legal services performed for family members.

(c) Legal services performed for political organizations for election purposes.

(d) Activities that do not involve the provision of legal services, such as serving on the board of a charitable organization.

Rule 6.2. Accepting Appointments

A lawyer shall not seek to avoid appointment by a tribunal to represent a person except for good cause, such as when:

(a) representing the client is likely to result in violation of the Rules of Professional Conduct or other law;

(b) representing the client is likely to result in an unreasonable financial burden on the lawyer; or

(c) the client or the cause is so repugnant to the lawyer as to be likely to impair the client-lawyer relationship or the lawyer's ability to represent the client.

Adopted effective Jan. 1, 1987; amended Sept. 30, 2004, effective Jan. 1, 2005.

Comment

[1] A lawyer ordinarily is not obliged to accept a client whose character or cause the lawyer regards as repugnant. The lawyer's freedom to select clients is, however, qualified. All lawyers have a responsibility to assist in providing pro bono publico service. See Rule 6.1. An individual lawyer may fulfill this responsibility by accepting a fair share of unpopular matters or indigent or unpopular clients. A lawyer may also be subject to appointment by a court to serve unpopular clients or persons unable to afford legal services.

Appointed Counsel

[2] For good cause a lawyer may seek to decline an appointment to represent a person who cannot afford to retain counsel or whose cause is unpopular. Good cause exists if the lawyer could not handle the matter competently, see Rule 1.1, or if undertaking the representation would result in an improper conflict of interest, for example, when the client or the cause is so repugnant to the lawyer as to be likely to impair the client-lawyer relationship or the lawyer's ability to represent the client. A lawyer may also seek to decline an appointment if acceptance would be unreasonably burdensome, for example, when it would impose a financial sacrifice so great as to be unjust.

[3] An appointed lawyer has the same obligations to the client as retained counsel, including the obligations of loyalty and confidentiality, and is subject to the same limitations on the client-lawyer relationship, such as the obligation to refrain from assisting the client in violation of the Rules.

Rule 6.3. Membership in Legal Service Organization

A lawyer may serve as a director, officer or member of a legal services organization, apart from the law firm in which the lawyer practices, notwithstanding that the organization serves persons having interests adverse to a client of the lawyer. The lawyer shall not knowingly participate in a decision or action of the organization:

(a) if participating in the decision or action would be incompatible with the lawyer's obligations to a client under Rule 1.7; or

(b) where the decision or action could have a material adverse effect on the representation of a client of the organization whose interests are adverse to a client of the lawyer.

Adopted effective Jan. 1, 1987; amended Dec. 15, 1995, effective Feb. 1, 1996.

Comment

[1] Lawyers should be encouraged to support and participate in legal service organizations. A lawyer who is an officer or a member of such an organization does not thereby have a client-lawyer relationship with persons served by the organization. However, there is potential conflict between the interests of such persons and the interests of the lawyer's clients. If the possibility of such conflict disqualified a lawyer from serving on the board of a legal services organization, the profession's involvement in such organizations would be severely curtailed.

[2] It may be necessary in appropriate cases to reassure a client of the organization that the representation will not be affected by conflicting loyalties of a member of the board. Established, written policies in this respect can enhance the credibility of such assurances.

Rule 6.4. Law Reform Activities Affecting Client Interests

A lawyer may serve as a director, officer or member of an organization involved in reform of the law or its administration notwithstanding that the reform may affect the interests of a client of the lawyer. When the lawyer knows that the interests of a client may be materially benefited by a decision in which the lawyer participates, the lawyer shall disclose that fact but need not identify the client.

Adopted effective Jan. 1, 1987.

Comment

[1] Lawyers involved in organizations seeking law reform generally do not have a client-lawyer relationship with the organization. Otherwise, it might follow that a lawyer could not be involved in a bar association law reform program that might indirectly affect a client. See also Rule 1.2(b). For example, a lawyer specializing in antitrust litigation might be regarded as disqualified from participating in drafting revisions of rules governing that subject. In determining the nature and scope of participation in such activities, a lawyer should be mindful of obligations to clients under other Rules, particularly Rule 1.7. A lawyer is professionally obligated to protect the integrity of the program by making an appropriate disclosure within the organization when the lawyer knows a private client might be materially benefited.

Rule 6.5 Nonprofit and Court-Annexed Limited Legal Services Programs

(a) A lawyer who, under the auspices of a program sponsored by a nonprofit organization or court, provides short-term limited legal services to a client without expectation by either the lawyer or the client that the lawyer will provide continuing representation in the matter:

(1) is subject to Rules 1.7 and 1.9(a) only if the lawyer knows that the representation of the client involves a conflict of interest; and

(2) is subject to Rule 1.10 only if the lawyer knows that another lawyer associated with the lawyer in a law firm is disqualified by Rule 1.7 or 1.9(a) with respect to the matter.

(b) Except as provided in paragraph (a)(2), Rule 1.10 is inapplicable to a representation governed by this Rule.

Adopted Sept. 30, 2004, effective Jan. 1, 2005.

Comment

[1] Legal services organizations, courts and various nonprofit organizations have established programs through which lawyers provide short-term limited legal services — such as advice or the completion of legal forms — that will assist persons to address their legal problems without further representation by a lawyer. In these programs, such as legal-advice hotlines, advice-only clinics or pro se counseling programs, a client-lawyer relationship is established, but there is no expectation that the lawyer's representation of the client will continue beyond the limited consultation. Such programs are normally operated under circumstances in which it is not feasible for a lawyer to systematically screen for conflicts of interest as is generally required before undertaking a representation. See, e.g., Rules 1.7, 1.9 and 1.10.

[2] A lawyer who provides short-term limited legal services pursuant to this Rule must secure the client's informed consent to the limited scope of the representation. See Rule 1.2(c). If a short-term limited representation would not be reasonable under the circumstances, the lawyer may offer advice to the client but must also advise the client of the need for further assistance of counsel. Except as provided in this Rule, the Rules of Professional Conduct, including Rules 1.6 and 1.9(c), are applicable to the limited representation.

[3] Because a lawyer who is representing a client in the circumstances addressed by this Rule ordinarily is not able to check systematically for conflicts of interest, paragraph (a) requires compliance with Rules 1.7 or 1. 9(a) only if the lawyer knows that the representation presents a conflict of interest for the lawyer, and with Rule 1.10 only if the lawyer knows that another lawyer in the lawyer's firm is disqualified by Rules 1.7 or 1.9(a) in the matter.

[4] Because the limited nature of the services significantly reduces the risk of conflicts of interest with other matters being handled by the lawyer's firm, paragraph (b) provides that Rule 1.10 is inapplicable to a representation governed by this Rule except as provided by paragraph (a)(2). Paragraph (a)(2) requires the participating lawyer to comply with Rule 1.10 when the lawyer knows that the lawyer's firm is disqualified by Rules 1.7 or 1.9(a). By virtue of paragraph (b), however, a lawyer's

participation in a short-term limited legal services program will not preclude the lawyer's firm from undertaking or continuing the representation of a client with interests adverse to a client being represented under the program's auspices. Nor will the personal disqualification of a lawyer participating in the program be imputed to other lawyers participating in the program.

[5] If, after commencing a short-term limited representation in accordance with this Rule, a lawyer undertakes to represent the client in the matter on an ongoing basis, Rules 1.7, 1.9(a) and 1.10 become applicable.

Rule 6.6. Voluntary Attorney Pro Bono Plan

(a) The purpose of this voluntary attorney pro bono plan is to promote equal access to justice for all Indiana residents, regardless of economic status, by creating and promoting opportunities for attorneys to provide pro bono civil legal services to persons of limited means, as determined by each district pro bono committee. The voluntary pro bono attorney plan has the following goals:

(1) To enable Indiana attorneys to discharge their professional responsibilities to provide pro bono services;

(2) To improve the overall delivery of civil legal services to persons of limited means by facilitating the integration and coordination of services provided by pro bono organizations and other legal assistance organizations throughout the State of Indiana.

(3) To ensure statewide access to high quality and timely pro bono civil legal services for persons of limited means by (i) fostering the development of new pro bono programs where needed and (ii) supporting and improving the quality of existing pro bono programs.

(4) To foster the growth of a public service culture within the Indiana Bar which values pro bono publico service.

(5) To promote the ongoing development of financial and other resources for pro bono organizations in Indiana.

(b) There is created a twenty-one (21) member Indiana Pro Bono Commission (the "Commission") the members of which shall be appointed by the Supreme Court and the President of the Indiana Bar Foundation ("Foundation"). In appointing members to the Commission, the Supreme Court and the Foundation should seek to ensure that members of the Commission are representative of the different geographic regions and judicial districts of the state, and that the members possess skills and experience relevant to the needs of the Commission.

(1) The Supreme Court shall appoint eleven (11) members as follows:

(i) One (1) trial judge and one (1) appellate judge;

(ii) Two (2) representatives of pro bono organizations or other legal assistance organizations;

(iii) Three (3) representatives from local bar associations; including one representative from a minority bar association;

(iv) One (1) representative each from two of the four (4) Indiana law schools accredited by the American Bar Association;

(v) One (1) representative of a certified provider of continuing legal education services in the state;

(vi) One (1) representative from the community-at-large with experience in assisting persons of limited means.

(2) The President of the Indiana Bar Foundation shall appoint ten (10) members as follows:

(i) Three (3) members of the Indiana State Bar Association;

(ii) Two (2) members of the Indiana Bar Foundation;

(iii) One (1) representative each from two of the four (4) Indiana law schools accredited by the American Bar Association;

(iv) One (1) member of the Indiana State Bar Association Pro Bono Committee;

(v) Two (2) representatives of pro bono organizations or other civil legal assistance organizations;

(3) No more than three of these appointments under (1) and three under (2) may be officers, directors or employees of organizations organized primarily for providers of pro bono legal services or other legal services for the indigent.

(4) The Supreme Court shall designate the chair of the Commission from among the appointed members. The Executive Director of the Indiana Bar Foundation shall serve as a non-voting ex-officio member of the Commission.

(5) The Commission shall operate as a program within the Foundation. Members of the Commission shall serve for three (3)-year terms, except that for the initial appointments, four (4) members appointed by the Supreme Court shall serve for one (1)-year terms, four (4) members appointed by the president shall serve for one (1)-year terms, four (4) members appointed by the Supreme Court shall serve for two (2)-year terms, and three (3) members appointed by the president shall serve for two (2)-year terms. Members may be removed by the appointing authority. The appointing authority shall fill any vacancy caused by resignation, removal or otherwise, as it occurs, for the remainder of the vacated term. Members shall not serve for more than two (2) consecutive terms.

(c) The Foundation shall have the overall responsibility and authority for management of the voluntary attorney pro bono plan. The Foundation's authority and responsibility shall include making funding decisions and disbursing available funds to pro bono organizations/projects upon recommendations of the Commission.

(d) The Commission shall undertake those tasks delegated to it by the Foundation which are reasonable and necessary to the fulfillment of the Commission's purpose. The Commission, subject to the approval of the Foundation, shall have the responsibility and authority to supervise the district pro bono committees. The Commission shall make funding recommendations to the Foundation in response to district committee pro bono plans and funding requests. The Commission may, with the consent of the Foundation, incorporate as a non-profit corporation.

(e) The Commission is not authorized to raise funds for itself, other than from IOLTA, in a manner which adversely affects the fund-raising capabilities or reduces the funding of any civil legal assistance provider. With the consent of the Foundation, the Commission is authorized to raise funds for itself, other than from IOLTA, in order to fund its usual and reasonable start-up expenses.

(f) There shall be one district pro bono committee in each of the twelve districts set forth below:

District A, consisting of the counties of Lake, Porter, Jasper, and Newton;

District B, consisting of the counties of LaPorte, St. Joseph, Elkhart, Marshall, Starke, and Kosciusko;

District C, consisting of the counties of LaGrange, Adams, Allen, DeKalb, Huntington, Noble, Steuben, Wells, and Whitley;

District D, consisting of the counties of Clinton, Fountain, Montgomery, Tippecanoe, Warren, Benton, Carroll, Vermillion, Parke, Boone, and White;

District E, consisting of the counties of Cass, Fulton, Howard, Miami, Tipton, Pulaski, Grant, and Wabash;

District F, consisting of the counties of Blackford, Delaware, Henry, Jay, Madison, Hamilton, Hancock, and Randolph;

District G, consisting of the county of Marion;

District H, consisting of the counties of Greene, Lawrence, Monroe, Putnam, Hendricks, Clay, Morgan, and Owen;

District I, consisting of the counties of Bartholomew, Brown, Decatur, Jackson, Johnson, Shelby, Rush, and Jennings;

District J, consisting of the counties of Dearborn, Jefferson, Ohio, Ripley, Franklin, Wayne, Union, Fayette, and Switzerland;

District K, consisting of the counties of Daviess, Dubois, Gibson, Knox, Martin, Perry, Pike, Posey, Spencer, Vanderburgh, Sullivan, Vigo, and Warrick; and,

District L, consisting of the counties of Clark, Crawford, Floyd, Harrison, Orange, Scott, and Washington.

The pro bono committee in each of the above districts shall appoint its chair, in accordance with the following provisions:

(1) Each district pro bono committee shall be composed of:

(A) a judge from the district as designated by the Supreme Court to preside;

(B) to the extent feasible, one or more representatives from each voluntary bar association in the district, one representative from each pro bono and legal assistance provider in the district, and one representative from each law school in the district; and

(C) at least two (2) community-at-large representatives, one of whom shall be a present or past recipient of pro bono publico legal services.

(2) Governance of each district pro bono committee and terms of service of the members thereof shall be determined by each committee. Replacement and succession members shall be appointed by the judge designated by the Supreme Court.

(g) To ensure an active and effective district pro bono program each district committee shall do the following:

(1) prepare in written form, on an annual basis, a district pro bono plan, including any county subplans if appropriate, after evaluating the needs of the district and making a determination of presently available pro bono services;

(2) select and employ a plan administrator to provide the necessary coordination and administrative support for the district pro bono committee;

(3) implement the district pro bono plan and monitor its results;

(4) submit an annual report to the Commission;

(5) submit the plan and funding requests for individual pro bono organizations/projects to the Commission; and

(6) forward to the Pro Bono Commission for review and consideration any requests which were presented as formal proposals to be included in the district plan but were rejected by the district committee, provided the group asks for review by the Pro Bono Commission.

(h) To encourage more lawyers to participate in pro bono activities, each district pro bono plan should provide various support and educational services for participating pro bono attorneys, which, to the extent possible, should include:

(1) providing intake, screening, and referral of prospective clients;

(2) matching cases with individual attorney expertise, including the establishment of specialized panels;

(3) providing resources for litigation and out-of-pocket expenses for pro bono cases;

(4) providing legal education and training for pro bono attorneys in specialized areas of law useful in providing pro bono civil legal service;

(5) providing the availability of consultation with attorneys who have expertise in areas of law with respect to which a volunteer lawyer is providing pro bono civil legal service;

(6) providing malpractice insurance for volunteer pro bono lawyers with respect to their pro bono civil legal service;

(7) establishing procedures to ensure adequate monitoring and follow-up for assigned cases and to measure client satisfaction;

(8) recognizing pro bono civil legal service by lawyers; and

(9) providing other support and assistance to pro bono lawyers.

(i) The district pro bono plan may include opportunities such as the following:

(1) representing persons of limited means through case referral;

(2) representing persons of limited means through direct contact with a lawyer when the lawyer, before undertaking the representation, first

determines client eligibility based on standards substantially similar to those used by legal assistance providers;

(3) representing community groups serving persons of limited means through case referral;

(4) interviewing and determining eligibility of prospective pro bono clients;

(5) acting as co-counsel on cases or matters with civil legal assistance providers and other pro bono lawyers;

(6) providing consultation services to civil legal assistance providers for case reviews and evaluations;

(7) providing training to the staff of civil legal assistance providers and other volunteer pro bono attorneys;

(8) making presentations to persons of limited means regarding their rights and obligations under the law;

(9) providing legal research;

(10) providing guardian *ad litem* services;

(11) serving as a mediator or arbitrator to the client-eligible party; and

(12) providing such other pro bono service opportunities as appropriate.

Adopted as Rule 6.5, Oct. 22, 1997, effective Feb. 1, 1998. Amended, and renumbered as Rule 6.6, Sept. 30, 2004, effective Jan. 1, 2005; amended Sept. 21, 2010, effective Jan. 1, 2011; Sept. 20, 2011, effective Jan. 1, 2012.

INFORMATION ABOUT LEGAL SERVICES

RULE 7.1. Communications Concerning a Lawyer's Services

A lawyer shall not make a false or misleading communication about the lawyer or the lawyer's services. A communication is false or misleading if it contains a material misrepresentation of fact or law, or omits a fact necessary to make the statement considered as a whole not materially misleading.

Adopted Oct. 14, 2010, effective Jan. 1, 2011.

Commentary

[1] This Rule governs all communications about a lawyer's services, including advertising permitted by Rule 7.2. Whatever means are used to make known a lawyer's services, statements about them must be truthful.

[2] Truthful statements that are misleading are also prohibited by this Rule. In the absence of special circumstances that serve to protect the probable targets of a communication from being misled or deceived, a communication will violate Rule 7.1 if it:

(1) is intended or is likely to result in a legal action or a legal position being asserted merely to harass or maliciously injure another;

(2) contains statistical data or other information based on past performance or an express or implied prediction of future success;

(3) contains a claim about a lawyer, made by a third party, that the lawyer could not personally make consistent with the requirements of this rule;

(4) appeals primarily to a lay person's fear, greed, or desire for revenge;

(5) compares the services provided by the lawyer or a law firm with other lawyers' services, unless the comparison can be factually substantiated;

(6) contains any reference to results obtained that may reasonably create an expectation of similar results in future matters;

(7) contains a dramatization or recreation of events unless the advertising clearly and conspicuously discloses that a dramatization or recreation is being presented;

(8) contains a representation, testimonial, or endorsement of a lawyer or other statement that, in light of all the circumstances, is intended or is likely to create an unjustified expectation about a lawyer or law firm or a person's legal rights;

(9) states or implies that a lawyer is a certified or recognized specialist other than as permitted by Rule 7.4;

(10) is prohibited by Rule 7.3.

[3] See also Rule 8.4(e) for the prohibition against stating or implying an ability to influence improperly a government agency or official or to achieve results by means that violate the Rules of Professional Conduct or other law.

Rule 7.2.   Advertising

(a) Subject to the requirements of this rule, lawyers and law firms may advertise their professional services and law related services. The term "advertise" as used in these Indiana Rules of Professional Conduct refers to any manner of public communication partly or entirely intended or expected to promote the purchase or use of the professional services of a lawyer, law firm, or any employee of either involving the practice of law or law-related services.

(b) A lawyer shall not give anything of value to a person for recommending or advertising the lawyer's services except that a lawyer may:

(1) pay the reasonable costs of advertisements or communications permitted by this Rule;

(2) pay the usual charges of a legal service plan or a not-for-profit or qualified lawyer referral service described in Rule 7.3(d);

(3) pay for a law practice in accordance with Rule 1.17; and

(4) refer clients to another lawyer or a non-lawyer professional pursuant to an agreement not otherwise prohibited under these Rules that provides for the other person to refer clients or customers to the lawyer, if

(i) the reciprocal referral agreement is not exclusive, and

(ii) the client is informed of the existence and nature of the agreement.

(c) Any communication subject to this rule shall include the name and office address of at least one lawyer or law firm responsible for its content. The lawyer or law firm responsible for the content of any communication subject to this rule shall keep a copy or recording of each such communication for six years after its dissemination.

Adopted as Rule 7.1, effective Jan. 1, 1987. Renumbered as Rule 7.2, Sept. 30, 2004, effective Jan. 1, 2005; amended Oct. 14, 2010, effective Jan. 1, 2011.

Commentary

[1] To assist the public in obtaining legal services, lawyers should be allowed to make known their services not only through reputation but also through organized information campaigns in the form of advertising. Advertising involves an active quest for clients, contrary to the tradition that a lawyer should not seek clientele. However, the public's need to know about legal services can be fulfilled in part through advertising.

[2] Provided that the advertising otherwise complies with the requirements of the Rules of Professional Conduct, permissible subjects of advertising include:

(1) name and contact information, including the name and contact information for an attorney, a law firm, and professional associates;

(2) one or more fields of law in which the lawyer or law firm practices, using commonly accepted and understood definitions and designations;

(3) date and place of birth;

(4) date and place of admission to the bar of state and federal courts;

(5) schools attended, with dates of graduation, degrees, and other scholastic distinctions;

(6) academic, public or quasi-public, military, or professional positions held;

(7) military service;

(8) legal authorship;

(9) legal teaching position;

(10) memberships, offices, and committee assignments, in bar professional, scientific, or technical associations or societies;

(11) memberships and offices in legal fraternities and legal societies;

(12) technical and professional licenses;

(13) memberships in scientific, technical, and professional associations and societies;

(14) foreign language ability;

(15) names and addresses of bank references;

(16) professional liability insurance coverage;

(17) prepaid or group legal services programs in which the lawyer participates as allowed by Rule 7.3(d);

(18) whether credit cards or other credit arrangements are accepted;

(19) office and telephone answering service hours; and

(20) fees charged and other terms of service pursuant to which an attorney is willing to provide legal or law-related services.

[3] Neither this Rule nor Rule 7.3 prohibits communications authorized by law, such as notice to members of a class in class action litigation.

[4] Lawyers are not permitted to pay others for channeling professional work. Paragraph (b)(1), however, allows a lawyer to pay for advertising and communications permitted by this Rule, including the costs of print directory listings, on-line directory listings, newspaper ads, television and radio airtime, domain-name registrations, sponsorship fees, banner ads, and group advertising. A lawyer may compensate employees, agents, and vendors who are engaged to provide marketing or client-development services, such as publicists, public-relations personnel, business-development staff, and website designers. See Rule 5.3 for the duties of lawyers and law firms with respect to the conduct of non-lawyers who prepare marketing materials for them.

Rule 7.3.   Direct Contact with Prospective Clients

(a) A lawyer (including the lawyer's employee or agent) shall not by in-person, live telephone, or real-time electronic contact solicit professional employment from a prospective client when a significant motive for the lawyer's doing so is the lawyer's pecuniary gain, unless the person contacted:

(1) is a lawyer; or

(2) has a family, close personal, or prior professional relationship with the lawyer.

(b) A lawyer shall not solicit professional employment from a prospective client by in-person or by written, recorded, audio, video, or electronic communication, including the Internet, if:

(1) the prospective client has made known to the lawyer a desire not to be solicited by the lawyer;

(2) the solicitation involves coercion, duress or harassment;

(3) the solicitation concerns an action for personal injury or wrongful death or otherwise relates to an accident or disaster involving the person to whom the solicitation is addressed or a relative of that person, unless the accident or disaster occurred more than 30 days prior to the initiation of the solicitation;

(4) the solicitation concerns a specific matter and the lawyer knows, or reasonably should know, that the person to whom the solicitation is directed is represented by a lawyer in the matter; or

(5) the lawyer knows, or reasonably should know, that the physical, emotional, or mental state of the person makes it unlikely that the person would exercise reasonable judgment in employing a lawyer.

(c) Every written, recorded, or electronic communication from a lawyer soliciting professional employment from a prospective client potentially in need of legal services in a particular matter shall include the words "Advertising Material" conspicuously placed both on the face of any outside envelope and at the beginning of any written communication, and both at the beginning and ending of any recorded or electronic communication, unless the recipient of the communication is a person specified in paragraphs (a)(1) or (a)(2). A copy of each such communication shall be filed with the Indiana Supreme Court Disciplinary Commission at or prior to its dissemination to the prospective client. A filing fee in the amount of fifty dollars ($50.00) payable to the "Supreme Court Disciplinary Commission Fund" shall accompany each such filing. In the event a written, recorded, or electronic communication is distributed to multiple prospective clients, a single copy of the mailing less information specific to the intended recipients, such as name, address (including email address) and date of mailing, may be filed with the Commission. Each time any such communication is changed or altered, a copy of the new or modified communication shall be filed with the Disciplinary Commission at or prior to the time of its mailing or distribution. The lawyer shall retain a list containing the names and addresses, including email addresses, of all persons or entities to whom each communication has been mailed or distributed for a period of not less than one (1) year following the last date of mailing or distribution. Communications filed pursuant to this subdivision shall be open to public inspection.

(d) A lawyer shall not accept referrals from, make referrals to, or solicit clients on behalf of any lawyer referral service unless such service falls within clauses (1)–(4) below. A lawyer or any other lawyer affiliated with the lawyer or the lawyer's law firm may be recommended, employed, or paid by, or cooperate with, one of the following offices or organizations that promote the use of the lawyer's services or those of the lawyer's firm, if there is no interference with the exercise of independent professional judgment on behalf of a client of the lawyer or the lawyer's firm:

(1) A legal office or public defender office:

(A) operated or sponsored on a not-for-profit basis by a law school accredited by the American Bar Association Section on Legal Education and Admissions to the Bar;

(B) operated or sponsored on a not-for-profit basis by a bona fide non-profit community organization;

(C) operated, or sponsored on a not-for-profit basis by a governmental agency;

(D) operated, sponsored, or approved in writing by the Indiana State Bar Association, the Indiana Trial Lawyers Association, the Defense Trial Counsel of Indiana, any bona fide county or city bar association within the State of Indiana, or any other bar association whose lawyer referral service has been sanctioned for operation in Indiana by the Indiana Disciplinary Commission; and

(E) operated by a Circuit or Superior Court within the State of Indiana.

(2) A military legal assistance office;

(3) A lawyer referral service operated, sponsored, or approved by any organization listed in clause (1)(D); or

(4) Any other non-profit organization that recommends, furnishes, or pays for legal services to its members or beneficiaries, but only if the following conditions are met:

(A) the primary purposes of such organization do not include the rendition of legal services;

(B) the recommending, furnishing, or paying for legal services to its members is incidental and reasonably related to the primary purposes of such organization;

(C) such organization does not derive a financial benefit from the rendition of legal services by the lawyer; and

(D) the member or beneficiary for whom the legal services are rendered, and not such organization, is recognized as the client of the lawyer in the matter.

(e) A lawyer shall not compensate or give anything of value to a person or organization to recommend or secure the lawyer's employment by a client, or as a reward for having made a recommendation resulting in the lawyer's employment by a client, except that the lawyer may pay for public communication permitted by Rule 7.2 and the usual and reasonable fees or dues charged by a lawyer referral service falling within the provisions of paragraph (d) above.

(f) A lawyer shall not accept employment when the lawyer knows, or reasonably should know, that the person who seeks the lawyer's services does so as a result of lawyer conduct prohibited under this Rule 7.3.

Adopted effective Jan. 1, 1987. Amended effective Jan. 19, 1989; amended Nov. 30, 1989, effective Jan. 1, 1990; Dec. 4, 1998, effective Jan. 1, 1999; Sept. 30, 2004, effective Jan. 1, 2005; Oct. 14, 2010, effective Jan. 1, 2011; December 22, 2010, effective Jan. 1, 2011.

Commentary

[1] There is a potential for abuse inherent in direct in-person, live telephone or real-time electronic contact by a lawyer with a prospective client known to need legal services. These forms of contact between a lawyer and a prospective client subject the layperson to the private importuning of the trained advocate in a direct interpersonal encounter. The prospective client, who may already feel overwhelmed by the circumstances giving rise to the need for legal services, may find it difficult fully to evaluate all available alternatives with reasoned judgment and appropriate self-interest in the face of the lawyer's presence and insistence upon being retained immediately. The situation is fraught with the possibility of undue influence, intimidation, and overreaching.

[2] This potential for abuse inherent in direct in-person, live telephone or real-time electronic solicitation of prospective clients justifies its prohibition, particularly since lawyer advertising and written and recorded communication permitted under Rule 7.2 offer alternative means of conveying necessary information to those who may be in need of legal services.

[3] The use of general advertising and written, recorded, or electronic communications to transmit information from lawyer to prospective client, rather than direct in-person, live telephone or real-time electronic contact, will help to assure that the information flows cleanly as well as freely. The contents of advertisements and communications permitted under Rule 7.2 can be permanently recorded so that they cannot be disputed and may be shared with others who know the lawyer. This potential for informal review is itself likely to help guard against statements and claims that might constitute false and misleading communications, in violation of Rule 7.1. The contents of direct in-person, live tele-

phone, or real-time electronic conversations between a lawyer and a prospective client can be disputed and may not be subject to third-party scrutiny. Consequently, they are much more likely to approach (and occasionally cross) the dividing line between accurate representations and those that are false and misleading.

[4] There is far less likelihood that a lawyer would engage in abusive practices against an individual who is a former client, or with whom the lawyer has close personal or family relationship, or in situations in which the lawyer is motivated by considerations other than the lawyer's pecuniary gain. Nor is there a serious potential for abuse when the person contacted is a lawyer. Consequently, the general prohibition in Rule 7.3(a) and the requirements of Rule 7.3(c) are not applicable in those situations. Also, paragraph (a) is not intended to prohibit a lawyer from participating in constitutionally protected activities of public or charitable legal-service organizations or bona fide political, social, civic, fraternal, employee, or trade organizations whose purposes include providing or recommending legal services to its members or beneficiaries.

[5] But even permitted forms of solicitation can be abused. Thus, any solicitation which contains information which is false or misleading within the meaning of Rule 7.1, which involves coercion, duress, or harassment within the meaning of Rule 7.3(b)(2), or which involves contact with a prospective client who has made known to the lawyer a desire not to be solicited by the lawyer within the meaning of Rule 7.3(b)(1) is prohibited. Moreover, if after sending a letter or other communication to a client as permitted by Rule 7.2, the lawyer receives no response, any further effort to communicate with the prospective client may violate the provisions of Rule 7.3(b).

[6] This rule allows targeted solicitation of potential plaintiffs or claimants in personal injury and wrongful death causes of action or other causes of action that relate to an accident, disaster, death, or injury, but only if such solicitation is initiated no less than 30 days after the incident. This restriction is reasonably required by the sensitized state of the potential clients, who may be either injured or grieving over the loss of a family member, and the abuses that experience has shown exist in this type of solicitation.

Rule 7.4. Communication of Fields of Practice and Specialization

(a) A lawyer may communicate the fact that the lawyer does or does not practice in particular fields of law.

(b) A lawyer admitted to engage in patent practice before the United States Patent and Trademark Office may use the designation "Patent Attorney" or a substantially similar designation.

(c) A lawyer engaged in Admiralty practice may use the designation "Admiralty," "Proctor in Admiralty" or a substantially similar designation.

(d) A lawyer shall not state or imply that the lawyer is a specialist in a particular field of law, unless:

(1) The lawyer has been certified as a specialist by an Independent Certifying Organization accredited by the Indiana Commission for Continuing Legal Education pursuant to Admission and Discipline Rule 30; and,

(2) The certifying organization is identified in the communication.

(e) Pursuant to rule-making powers inherent in its ability and authority to police and regulate the practice of law by attorneys admitted to practice law in the State of Indiana, the Indiana Supreme Court hereby vests exclusive authority for accreditation of Independent Certifying Organizations that certify specialists in legal practice areas and fields in the Indiana Commission for Continuing Legal Education. The Commission shall be the exclusive accrediting body in Indiana, for purposes of Rule 7.4(d)(1), above; and shall promulgate rules and guidelines for accrediting Independent Certifying Organizations that certify specialists in legal practice areas and fields. The rules and guidelines shall include requirements of practice experience, continuing legal education, objective examination; and, peer review and evaluation, with the purpose of providing assurance to the consumers of legal services that the attorneys attaining certification within areas of specialization have demonstrated extraordinary proficiency within those areas of specialization. The Supreme Court shall retain review oversight with respect to the Commission, its requirements, and its rules and guidelines. The Supreme Court retains the power to alter or amend such requirements, rules and guidelines; and, to review the actions of the Commission in respect to this Rule 7.4.

Adopted effective Jan. 1, 1987. Amended Nov. 27, 1990, effective Jan. 1, 1991; Dec. 5, 1994, effective Feb. 1, 1995; Nov. 25, 1997, effective Jan. 1, 1998; Oct. 15, 1998, effective Oct. 1, 1998; Sept. 30, 2004, effective Jan. 1, 2005; Oct. 14, 2010, effective Jan. 1, 2011.

Commentary

[1] Paragraph (a) of this Rule permits a lawyer to indicate areas of practice in communications about the lawyer's services. If a lawyer practices only in certain fields, or will not accept matters except in a specified field or fields, the lawyer is permitted to so indicate.

[2] Paragraph (b) recognizes the long-established policy of the Patent and Trademark Office for the designation of lawyers practicing before the Office. Paragraph (c) recognizes that designation of Admiralty practice has a long historical tradition associated with maritime commerce and the federal courts.

Rule 7.5. Firm Names and Letterheads

(a) Firm names, letterheads, and other professional designations are subject to the following requirements:

(1) A lawyer shall not use a firm name, letterhead or other professional designation that violates Rule 7.1.

(2) The name of a professional corporation, professional association, limited liability partnership, or limited liability company may contain, "P.C.," "P.A.," "LLP," or "LLC" or similar symbols indicating the nature of the organization.

(3) If otherwise lawful a firm may use as, or continue to include in, its name, the name or names of one or more deceased or retired members of the firm or of a predecessor firm in a continuing line of succession. See Admission & Discipline Rule 27.

(4) A trade name may be used by a lawyer in private practice subject to the following requirements:

(i) the name shall not imply a connection with a government agency or with a public or charitable legal services organization and shall not otherwise violate Rule 7.1.

(ii) the name shall include the name of a lawyer (or the name of a deceased or retired member of the firm, or of a predecessor firm in a manner that complies with subparagraph (2) above).

(iii) the name shall not include words other than words that comply with clause (ii) above and words that:

(A) identify the field of law in which the firm concentrates its work, or

(B) describe the geographic location of its offices, or

(C) indicate a language fluency.

(b) A law firm with offices in more than one jurisdiction may use the same name or other professional designation in Indiana if the name or other designation does not violate paragraph (a) and the identification of the lawyers in an office of the firm indicates the jurisdictional limitations on those not licensed to practice in Indiana.

(c) The name of a lawyer holding a public office shall not be used in the name of a law firm, or in communications on its behalf, during any substantial period in which the lawyer is not actively and regularly practicing with the firm. A member of a part-time legislative body such as the General Assembly, a county or city council, or a school board is not subject to this rule.

(d) Lawyers may state or imply that they practice in a partnership or other organization only when they in fact do so.

Adopted as Rule 7.2, effective Jan. 1, 1987. Renumbered as Rule 7.5, Sept. 30, 2004, effective Jan. 1, 2005; amended July 1, 2005, effective Jan. 1, 2006; Oct. 14, 2010, effective Jan. 1, 2011; Dec. 22, 2010, effective Jan. 1, 2011.

Commentary

[1] A firm may be designated by the names of all or some of its members, by the names of deceased members where there has been a continuing succession in the firm's identity, or by a trade name that complies with the requirements of the Rules of Professional Conduct. A lawyer or law firm may also be designated by a distinctive website address or comparable professional designation. The use of a trade name in law practice is acceptable so long as it is not misleading and otherwise complies with the requirements of paragraph (a)(4). A firm name that includes the name of a deceased partner is,

strictly speaking, a trade name. The use of such names to designate law firms has proven a useful means of identification. However, it is misleading to use the name of a lawyer not associated with the firm or a predecessor of the firm, or the name of a non-lawyer.

[2] With regard to paragraph (d), lawyers sharing office facilities, but who are not in fact associated with each other in a law firm, may not denominate themselves as, for example, "Smith and Jones," for that title suggests that they are practicing law together in a firm.

MAINTAINING THE INTEGRITY
OF THE PROFESSION

Rule 8.1.   Bar Admission and Disciplinary Matters

An applicant for admission to the bar, or a lawyer in connection with a bar admission application or in connection with a disciplinary matter, shall not:

(a) knowingly make a false statement of material fact; or

(b) fail to disclose a fact necessary to correct a misapprehension known by the person to have arisen in the matter, or knowingly fail to respond to a lawful demand for information from an admissions or disciplinary authority, except that this Rule does not require disclosure of information otherwise protected by Rule 1.6.

Adopted effective Jan. 1, 1987.

Comment

[1] The duty imposed by this Rule extends to persons seeking admission to the bar as well as to lawyers. Hence, if a person makes a material false statement in connection with an application for admission, it may be the basis for subsequent disciplinary action if the person is admitted, and in any event may be relevant in a subsequent admission application. The duty imposed by this Rule applies to a lawyer's own admission or discipline as well as that of others. Thus, it is a separate professional offense for a lawyer to knowingly make a misrepresentation or omission in connection with a disciplinary investigation of the lawyer's own conduct. Paragraph (b) of this Rule also requires correction of any prior misstatement in the matter that the applicant or lawyer may have made and affirmative clarification of any misunderstanding on the part of the admissions or disciplinary authority of which the person involved becomes aware.

[2] This Rule is subject to the provisions of the Fifth Amendment of the United States Constitution and corresponding provisions of state constitutions. A person relying on such a provision in response to a question, however, should do so openly and not use the right of nondisclosure as a justification for failure to comply with this Rule.

[3] A lawyer representing an applicant for admission to the bar, or representing a lawyer who is the

subject of a disciplinary inquiry or proceeding, is governed by the rules applicable to the client-lawyer relationship, including Rule 1.6 and, in some cases, Rule 3.3.

Rule 8.2.   Judicial and Legal Officials

(a) A lawyer shall not make a statement that the lawyer knows to be false or with reckless disregard as to its truth or falsity concerning the qualifications or integrity of a judge, adjudicatory officer or public legal officer, or of a candidate for election or appointment to judicial or legal office.

(b) A lawyer who is a candidate for judicial office shall comply with the applicable provisions of the Code of Judicial Conduct.

Adopted effective Jan. 1, 1987; amended Sept. 30, 2004, effective Jan. 1, 2005.

Comment

[1] Assessments by lawyers are relied on in evaluating the professional or personal fitness of persons being considered for election or appointment to judicial office and to public legal offices, such as attorney general, prosecuting attorney and public defender. Expressing honest and candid opinions on such matters contributes to improving the administration of justice. Conversely, false statements by a lawyer can unfairly undermine public confidence in the administration of justice.

[2] When a lawyer seeks judicial office, the lawyer should be bound by applicable limitations on political activity.

[3] To maintain the fair and independent administration of justice, lawyers are encouraged to continue traditional efforts to defend judges and courts unjustly criticized.

Rule 8.3.   Reporting Professional Misconduct

(a) A lawyer who knows that another lawyer has committed a violation of the Rules of Professional Conduct that raises a substantial question as to that lawyer's honesty, trustworthiness or fitness as a lawyer in other respects, shall inform the appropriate professional authority.

(b) A lawyer who knows that a judge has committed a violation of applicable rules of judicial conduct that raises a substantial question as to the judge's fitness for office shall inform the appropriate authority.

(c) This Rule does not require reporting of a violation or disclosure of information if such action would involve disclosure of information that is otherwise protected by Rule 1.6, or is gained by a lawyer while providing advisory opinions or telephone advice on legal ethics issues as a member of a bar association committee or similar entity formed for the purposes of providing such opinions or advice and designated by the Indiana Supreme Court.

(d) The relationship between lawyers or judges acting on behalf of a judges or lawyers assistance program approved by the Supreme Court, and lawyers or judges who have agreed to seek assistance from and participate in any such programs, shall be considered one of attorney and client, with its attendant duty of confidentiality and privilege from disclosure.

Adopted effective Jan. 1, 1987; amended Oct. 30. 1992, effective Jan. 1, 1993; amended Sept. 30, 2004, effective Jan. 1, 2005.

Comment

[1] Self–regulation of the legal profession requires that members of the profession initiate disciplinary investigation when they know of a violation of the Rules of Professional Conduct. Lawyers have a similar obligation with respect to judicial misconduct. An apparently isolated violation may indicate a pattern of misconduct that only a disciplinary investigation can uncover. Reporting a violation is especially important where the victim is unlikely to discover the offense.

[2] A report about misconduct is not required where it would involve violation of Rule 1.6. However, a lawyer should encourage a client to consent to disclosure where prosecution would not substantially prejudice the client's interests.

[3] If a lawyer were obliged to report every violation of the Rules, the failure to report any violation would itself be a professional offense. Such a requirement existed in many jurisdictions but proved to be unenforceable. This Rule limits the reporting obligation to those offenses that a self-regulating profession must vigorously endeavor to prevent. A measure of judgment is, therefore, required in complying with the provisions of this Rule. The term "substantial" refers to the seriousness of the possible offense and not the quantum of evidence of which the lawyer is aware. A report should be made to the bar disciplinary agency unless some other agency, such as a peer review agency, is more appropriate in the circumstances. Similar considerations apply to the reporting of judicial misconduct.

[4] The duty to report professional misconduct does not apply to a lawyer retained to represent a lawyer whose professional conduct is in question. Such a situation is governed by the rules applicable to the client-lawyer relationship.

[5] Information about a lawyer's or judge's misconduct or fitness may be received by a lawyer in the course of that lawyer's participation in an approved lawyers or judges assistance program. In that circumstance, providing for an exception to the reporting requirements of paragraphs (a) and (b) of this Rule encourages lawyers and judges to seek treatment through such a program. Conversely, without such an exception, lawyers and judges may hesitate to seek assistance from these programs, which may then result in additional harm to their professional careers and additional injury to the welfare of clients and the public. These Rules do not otherwise address the confidentiality of information received by a lawyer or judge participating in an approved lawyers assistance program; such an obligation, however, may be imposed by the rules of the program or other law.

Rule 8.4. Misconduct

It is professional misconduct for a lawyer to:

(a) violate or attempt to violate the Rules of Professional Conduct, knowingly assist or induce another to do so, or do so through the acts of another;

(b) commit a criminal act that reflects adversely on the lawyer's honesty, trustworthiness or fitness as a lawyer in other respects;

(c) engage in conduct involving dishonesty, fraud, deceit or misrepresentation;

(d) engage in conduct that is prejudicial to the administration of justice;

(e) state or imply an ability to influence improperly a government agency or official or to achieve results by means that violate the Rules of Professional Conduct or other law;

(f) knowingly assist a judge or judicial officer in conduct that is a violation of applicable rules of judicial conduct or other law; or

(g) engage in conduct, in a professional capacity, manifesting, by words or conduct, bias or prejudice based upon race, gender, religion, national origin, disability, sexual orientation, age, socioeconomic status, or similar factors. Legitimate advocacy respecting the foregoing factors does not violate this subsection. A trial judge's finding that preemptory challenges were exercised on a discriminatory basis does not alone establish a violation of this Rule.

Adopted effective Jan. 1, 1987. Amended Dec. 21, 2001, effective April 1, 2002; Sept. 30, 2004, effective Jan. 1, 2005.

Comment

[1] Lawyers are subject to discipline when they violate or attempt to violate the Rules of Professional Conduct, knowingly assist or induce another to do so or do so through the acts of another, as when they request or instruct an agent to do so on the

lawyer's behalf. Paragraph (a), however, does not prohibit a lawyer from advising a client concerning action the client is legally entitled to take.

[2] Many kinds of illegal conduct reflect adversely on fitness to practice law, such as offenses involving fraud and the offense of willful failure to file an income tax return. However, some kinds of offenses carry no such implication. Traditionally, the distinction was drawn in terms of offenses involving "moral turpitude." That concept can be construed to include offenses concerning some matters of personal morality, such as adultery and comparable offenses, that have no specific connection to fitness for the practice of law. Although a lawyer is personally answerable to the entire criminal law, a lawyer should be professionally answerable only for offenses that indicate lack of those characteristics relevant to law practice. Offenses involving violence, dishonesty, breach of trust, or serious interference with the administration of justice are in that category. A pattern of repeated offenses, even ones of minor significance when considered separately, can indicate indifference to legal obligation.

[3] A lawyer may refuse to comply with an obligation imposed by law upon a good faith belief that no valid obligation exists. The provisions of Rule 1.2(d) concerning a good faith challenge to the validity, scope, meaning or application of the law apply to challenges of legal regulation of the practice of law.

[4] Lawyers holding public office assume legal responsibilities going beyond those of other citizens. A lawyer's abuse of public office can suggest an inability to fulfill the professional role of lawyers. The same is true of abuse of positions of private trust such as trustee, executor, administrator, guardian, agent and officer, director or manager of a corporation or other organization.

Rule 8.5. Disciplinary Authority: Choice of Law

(a) Disciplinary Authority. A lawyer admitted to practice in this jurisdiction is subject to the disciplinary authority of this jurisdiction, regardless of where the lawyer's conduct occurs. A lawyer not admitted in this jurisdiction is also subject to the disciplinary authority of this jurisdiction if the lawyer provides or offers to provide any legal services in this jurisdiction. A lawyer may be subject to the disciplinary authority of both this jurisdiction and another jurisdiction for the same conduct.

(b) Choice of Law. In any exercise of the disciplinary authority of this jurisdiction, the rules of professional conduct to be applied shall be as follows:

(1) for conduct in connection with a matter pending before a tribunal, the rules of the jurisdiction in which the tribunal sits, unless the rules of the tribunal provide otherwise; and

(2) for any other conduct, the rules of the jurisdiction in which the lawyer's conduct occurred, or, if the predominant effect of the conduct is in a differ-

ent jurisdiction, the rules of that jurisdiction shall be applied to the conduct.

Adopted effective Jan. 1, 1987; amended Sept. 30, 2004, effective Jan. 1, 2005.

Comment

Disciplinary Authority

[1] It is longstanding law that the conduct of a lawyer admitted to practice in this jurisdiction is subject to the disciplinary authority of this jurisdiction. Extension of the disciplinary authority of this jurisdiction to other lawyers who provide or offer to provide legal services in this jurisdiction is for the protection of the citizens of this jurisdiction. Reciprocal enforcement of a jurisdiction's disciplinary findings and sanctions will further advance the purposes of this Rule. A lawyer who is subject to the disciplinary authority of this jurisdiction under Rule 8.5(a) appoints an official to be designated by this Court to receive service of process in this jurisdiction. The fact that the lawyer is subject to the disciplinary authority of this jurisdiction may be a factor in determining whether personal jurisdiction may be asserted over the lawyer for civil matters.

Choice of Law

[2] A lawyer may be potentially subject to more than one set of rules of professional conduct which impose different obligations. The lawyer may be licensed to practice in more than one jurisdiction with differing rules, or may be admitted to practice before a particular court with rules that differ from those of the jurisdiction or jurisdictions in which the lawyer is licensed to practice. Additionally, the lawyer's conduct may involve significant contacts with more than one jurisdiction.

[3] Paragraph (b) seeks to resolve such potential conflicts. Its premise is that minimizing conflicts between rules, as well as uncertainty about which rules are applicable, is in the best interest of both clients and the profession (as well as the bodies having authority to regulate the profession). Accordingly, it takes the approach of (i) providing that any particular conduct of a lawyer shall be subject to only one set of rules of professional conduct and (ii) making the determination of which set of rules applies to particular conduct as straightforward as possible, consistent with recognition of appropriate regulatory interests of relevant jurisdictions.

[4] Paragraph (b)(1) provides that as to a lawyer's conduct relating to a proceeding pending before a tribunal, the lawyer shall be subject only to the rules of the jurisdiction in which the tribunal sits unless the rules of the tribunal, including its choice of law rule, provide otherwise. As to all other conduct, including conduct in anticipation of a proceeding not yet pending before a tribunal, paragraph (b)(2) provides that a lawyer shall be subject to the rules of the jurisdiction in which the lawyer's conduct occurred, or, if the predominant effect of the conduct is in another jurisdiction, the rules of that jurisdiction shall be applied to the conduct. In the case of conduct in anticipation of a proceeding that is likely to be before a tribunal, the predomi-

nant effect of such conduct could be where the conduct occurred, where the tribunal sits or in another jurisdiction.

[5] If two admitting jurisdictions were to proceed against a lawyer for the same conduct, they should, applying this rule, identify the same governing ethics rules. They should take all appropriate steps to see that they do apply the same rule to the same

conduct, and in all events should avoid proceeding against a lawyer on the basis of two inconsistent rules.

[6] The choice of law provision applies to lawyers engaged in transnational practice, unless international law, treaties or other agreements between competent regulatory authorities in the affected jurisdictions provide otherwise.

USE OF NON-LAWYER ASSISTANTS

Introduction

Subject to the provisions in Rule 5.3, all lawyers may use non-lawyer assistants in accordance with the following guidelines.

Adopted effective Jan. 1, 1994; amended Sept. 30, 2004, effective Jan. 1, 2005.

Guideline 9.1. Supervision

A non-lawyer assistant shall perform services only under the direct supervision of a lawyer authorized to practice in the State of Indiana and in the employ of the lawyer or the lawyer's employer. Independent non-lawyer assistants, to-wit, those not employed by a specific firm or by specific lawyers are prohibited. A lawyer is responsible for all of the professional actions of a non-lawyer assistant performing services at the lawyer's direction and should take reasonable measures to insure that the non-lawyer assistant's conduct is consistent with the lawyer's obligations under the Rules of Professional Conduct.

Adopted effective Jan. 1, 1994; amended Sept. 30, 2004, effective Jan. 1, 2005.

Guideline 9.2. Permissible Delegation

Provided the lawyer maintains responsibility for the work product, a lawyer may delegate to a non-lawyer assistant or paralegal any task normally performed by the lawyer; however, any task prohibited by statute, court rule, administrative rule or regulation, controlling authority, or the *Indiana Rules of Professional Conduct* may not be assigned to a non-lawyer.

Adopted effective Jan. 1, 1994; amended Sept. 30, 2004, effective Jan. 1, 2005.

Guideline 9.3. Prohibited Delegation

A lawyer may not delegate to a non-lawyer assistant:

(a) responsibility for establishing an attorney-client relationship;

(b) responsibility for establishing the amount of a fee to be charged for a legal service; or

(c) responsibility for a legal opinion rendered to a client.

Adopted effective Jan. 1, 1994; amended Sept. 30, 2004, effective Jan. 1, 2005.

Guideline 9.4. Duty to Inform

It is the lawyer's responsibility to take reasonable measures to ensure that clients, courts, and other lawyers are aware that a non-lawyer assistant, whose services are utilized by the lawyer in performing legal services, is not licensed to practice law.

Adopted effective Jan. 1, 1994; amended Sept. 30, 2004, effective Jan. 1, 2005.

Guideline 9.5. Identification on Letterhead

A lawyer may identify non-lawyer assistants by name and title on the lawyer's letterhead and on business cards identifying the lawyer's firm.

Adopted effective Jan. 1, 1994; amended Sept. 30, 2004, effective Jan. 1, 2005.

Guideline 9.6. Client Confidences

It is the responsibility of a lawyer to take reasonable measures to ensure that all client confidences are preserved by non-lawyer assistants.

Adopted effective Jan. 1, 1994; amended Sept. 30, 2004, effective Jan. 1, 2005.

Guideline 9.7. Charge for Services

A lawyer may charge for the work performed by non-lawyer assistants.

Adopted effective Jan. 1, 1994; amended Sept. 30, 2004, effective Jan. 1, 2005.

Guideline 9.8. Compensation

A lawyer may not split legal fees with a non lawyer assistant nor pay a non-lawyer assistant for the referral of legal business. A lawyer may compensate a non-lawyer assistant based on the quantity and quality of the non-lawyer assistant's work and the value of that work to a law practice, but the non-lawyer assistant's compensation may not be contingent, by advance agreement, upon the profitability of the lawyer's practice.

Adopted effective Jan. 1, 1994; amended Sept. 30, 2004, effective Jan. 1, 2005.

Guideline 9.9. Continuing Legal Education

A lawyer who employs a non-lawyer assistant should facilitate the non-lawyer assistant's participation in appropriate continuing education and pro bono publico activities.

Adopted effective Jan. 1, 1994; amended Sept. 30, 2004, effective Jan. 1, 2005.

Guideline 9.10.   Legal Assistant Ethics

All lawyers who employ non-lawyer assistants in the State of Indiana shall assure that such non-lawyer assistants conform their conduct to be consistent with the following ethical standards:

(a) A non-lawyer assistant may perform any task delegated and supervised by a lawyer so long as the lawyer is responsible to the client, maintains a direct relationship with the client, and assumes full professional responsibility for the work product.

(b) A non-lawyer assistant shall not engage in the unauthorized practice of law.

(c) A non-lawyer assistant shall serve the public interest by contributing to the delivery of quality legal services and the improvement of the legal system.

(d) A non-lawyer assistant shall achieve and maintain a high level of competence, as well as a high level of personal and professional integrity and conduct.

(e) A non-lawyer assistant's title shall be fully disclosed in all business and professional communications.

(f) A non-lawyer assistant shall preserve all confidential information provided by the client or acquired from other sources before, during, and after the course of the professional relationship.

(g) A non-lawyer assistant shall avoid conflicts of interest and shall disclose any possible conflict to the employer or client, as well as to the prospective employers or clients.

(h) A non-lawyer assistant shall act within the bounds of the law, uncompromisingly for the benefit of the client.

(i) A non-lawyer assistant shall do all things incidental, necessary, or expedient for the attainment of the ethics and responsibilities imposed by statute or rule of court.

(j) A non-lawyer assistant shall be governed by the Indiana Rules of Professional Conduct.

(k) For purposes of this Guideline, a non-lawyer assistant includes but shall not be limited to: paralegals, legal assistants, investigators, law students and paraprofessionals.

Adopted effective Jan. 1, 1994; amended Sept. 30, 2004, effective Jan. 1, 2005.

CODE OF JUDICIAL CONDUCT

Adopted Effective March 1, 1993

Including Amendments Received Through November 1, 2013

Preamble

[1] An independent, fair and impartial judiciary is indispensable to our system of justice. The United States legal system is based upon the principle that an independent, impartial, and competent judiciary, composed of men and women of integrity, will interpret and apply the law that governs our society. Thus, the judiciary plays a central role in preserving the principles of justice and the rule of law. Inherent in all the Rules contained in this Code are the precepts that judges, individually and collectively, must respect and honor the judicial office as a public trust and strive to maintain and enhance confidence in the legal system.

[2] Judges should maintain the dignity of judicial office at all times, and avoid both impropriety and the appearance of impropriety in their professional and personal lives. They should aspire at all times to conduct that ensures the greatest possible public confidence in their independence, impartiality, integrity, and competence.

[3] The Code of Judicial Conduct establishes standards for the ethical conduct of judges and judicial candidates. It is not intended as an exhaustive guide for the conduct of judges and judicial candidates, who are governed in their judicial and personal conduct by general ethical standards as well as by the Code. The Code is intended, however, to provide guidance and assist judges in maintaining the highest standards of judicial and personal conduct, and to provide a basis for regulating their conduct through disciplinary agencies.

Scope

[1] The Code of Judicial Conduct consists of four Canons, numbered Rules under each Canon, and Comments that generally follow and explain each Rule. Scope and Terminology sections provide additional guidance in interpreting and applying the Code. An Application section establishes when the various Rules apply to a judge or judicial candidate.

[2] The Canons state overarching principles of judicial ethics that all judges must observe. Although a judge may be disciplined only for violating a Rule, the Canons provide important guidance in interpreting the Rules. Where a Rule contains a permissive term, such as "may" or "should," the conduct being addressed is committed to the personal and professional discretion of the judge or candidate in question, and no disciplinary action should be taken for action or inaction within the bounds of such discretion.

[3] The Comments that accompany the Rules serve two functions. First, they provide guidance regarding the purpose, meaning, and proper application of the Rules. They contain explanatory material and, in some instances, provide examples of permitted or prohibited conduct. Comments neither add to nor subtract from the binding obligations set forth in the Rules. Therefore, when a Comment contains the term "must," it does not mean that the Comment itself is binding or enforceable; it signifies that the Rule in question, properly understood, is obligatory as to the conduct at issue.

[4] Second, the Comments identify aspirational goals for judges. To implement fully the principles of this Code as articulated in the Canons, judges should strive to exceed the standards of conduct established by the Rules, holding themselves to the highest ethical standards and seeking to achieve those aspirational goals, thereby enhancing the dignity of the judicial office.

[5] The Rules of the Code of Judicial Conduct are rules of reason that should be applied consistent with constitutional requirements, statutes, other court rules, and decisional law, and with due regard for all relevant circumstances. The Rules should not be interpreted to impinge upon the essential independence of judges in making judicial decisions.

[6] Although the black letter of the Rules is binding and enforceable, it is not contemplated that every transgression will result in the imposition of discipline. Whether discipline should be imposed should be determined through a reasonable and reasoned application

of the Rules, and should depend upon factors such as the seriousness of the transgression, the facts and circumstances that existed at the time of the transgression, the extent of any pattern of improper activity, whether there have been previous violations, and the effect of the improper activity upon the judicial system or others.

[7] The Code is not designed or intended as a basis for civil or criminal liability. Neither is it intended to be the basis for litigants to seek collateral remedies against each other or to obtain tactical advantages in proceedings before a court.

Terminology

The first time any term listed below is used in a Rule in its defined sense, it is followed by an asterisk (*).

"Appropriate authority" means the authority having responsibility for initiation of disciplinary process in connection with the violation to be reported. See Rules 2.14 and 2.15.

"Contribution" means both financial and in-kind contributions, such as goods, professional or volunteer services, advertising, and other types of assistance, which, if obtained by the recipient otherwise, would require a financial expenditure. See Rules 3.7, 4.1, and 4.4.

"De minimis" in the context of interests pertaining to disqualification of a judge, means an insignificant interest that could not raise a reasonable question regarding the judge's impartiality. See Rule 2.11.

"Domestic partner" means a person with whom another person maintains a household and an intimate relationship, other than a person to whom he or she is legally married. See Rules 2.11, 2.13, 3.13, and 3.14.

"Economic interest" means ownership of more than a de minimis legal or equitable interest. Except for situations in which the judge participates in the management of such a legal or equitable interest, or the interest could be substantially affected by the outcome of a proceeding before a judge, it does not include:

(1) an interest in the individual holdings within a mutual or common investment fund;

(2) an interest in securities held by an educational, religious, charitable, fraternal, or civic organization in which the judge or the judge's spouse, domestic partner, parent, or child serves as a director, an officer, an advisor, or other participant;

(3) a deposit in a financial institution or deposits or proprietary interests the judge may maintain as a member of a mutual savings association or credit union, or similar proprietary interests; or

(4) an interest in the issuer of government securities held by the judge. See Rules 1.3 and 2.11.

"Fiduciary" includes relationships such as executor, administrator, trustee, or guardian. See Rules 2.11, 3.2, and 3.8.

"Impartial," "impartiality," and **"impartially"** mean absence of bias or prejudice in favor of, or against, particular parties or classes of parties, as well as maintenance of an open mind in considering issues that may come before a judge. See Canons 1, 2, and 4, and Rules 1.2, 2.2, 2.10, 2.11, 2.13, 3.1, 3.12, 3.13, 4.1, and 4.2.

"Impending matter" is a matter that is imminent or expected to occur in the near future. See Rules 2.9, 2.10, 3.13, and 4.1.

"Impropriety" includes conduct that violates the law, court rules, or provisions of this Code, and conduct that undermines a judge's independence, integrity, or impartiality. See Canon 1 and Rule 1.2.

"Independence" means a judge's freedom from influence or controls other than those established by law. See Canons 1 and 4, and Rules 1.2, 3.1, 3.12, 3.13, and 4.2.

"Integrity" means probity, fairness, honesty, uprightness, and soundness of character. See Canon 1 and Rule 1.2.

"Judicial candidate" means any person, including a sitting judge, who is seeking selection for or retention in judicial office by election or appointment. A person becomes a candidate for judicial office as soon as he or she makes a public announcement of candidacy, declares or files as a candidate with the election or appointment authority, authorizes or, where permitted, engages in solicitation or acceptance of contributions or support, or is nominated for election or appointment to office. See Rules 2. 11, 4.1, 4.2, and 4.4.

"Knowingly," "knowledge," "known," and **"knows"** mean actual knowledge of the fact in question. A person's knowledge may be inferred from circumstances. See Rules 2.11, 2.13, 2.15, 2.16, 3.6, and 4.1.

"Law" encompasses court rules as well as statutes, constitutional provisions, and decisional law. See Rules 1.1, 2.1, 2.2, 2.6, 2.7, 2.9, 3.1, 3.2, 3.4, 3.9, 3.12, 3.13, 3.14, 3.15, 4.1, 4.2, 4.4, and 4.5.

"Member of the candidate's family" means a spouse, domestic partner, child, grandchild, parent, grandparent, or other relative or person with whom the candidate maintains a close familial relationship.

"Member of the judge's family" means a spouse, domestic partner, child, grandchild, parent, grandparent, or other relative or person with whom the judge maintains a close familial relationship. See Rules 3.7, 3.8, 3.10, and 3.11.

"Member of a judge's family residing in the judge's household" means any relative of a judge by blood or marriage, or a person treated by a judge as a member of the judge's family, who resides in the judge's household. See Rules 2.11 and 3.13.

"Nonpublic information" means information that is not available to the public. Nonpublic information may include, but is not limited to, information that is sealed by statute or court order or impounded or communicated in camera, and information offered in grand jury proceedings, presentencing reports, dependency cases, or psychiatric reports. See Rule 3. 5.

"Pending matter" is a matter that has commenced. A matter continues to be pending through any appellate process until final disposition. See Rules 2.9, 2.10, 3.13, and 4.1.

"Personally solicit" means a direct request made by a judge or a judicial candidate for financial support or in-kind services, whether made by letter, telephone, or any other means of communication. See Rule 4.1.

"Political organization" means a political party or other group sponsored by or affiliated with a political party or candidate, the principal purpose of which is to further the election or appointment of candidates for political office. For purposes of this Code, the term does not include a judicial candidate's campaign committee created as authorized by Rule 4.4. See Rules 4.1 and 4.2.

"Public election" includes primary and general elections, partisan elections, nonpartisan elections, and retention elections. See Rules 4.2 and 4.4.

"Third degree of relationship" includes the following persons: great-grandparent, grandparent, parent, uncle, aunt, brother, sister, child, grandchild, great-grandchild, nephew, and niece. See Rule 2.11.

Application

I. Applicability of This Code

(A) A judge, within the meaning of this Code, is anyone who is authorized to perform judicial functions within the courts of the Indiana judiciary, including an officer such as a magistrate, commissioner, or referee. Administrative law judges and hearing officers of State agencies are not judges within the meaning of this Code.

(B) All the provisions of the Code apply to full-time judges. Parts II through V of this section identify those provisions that apply to the distinct categories of part-time judges. The categories of judicial service in other than a full-time capacity are necessarily defined in general terms because of the widely varying forms of judicial service. Canon 4 applies to judicial candidates.

COMMENT

[1] The Rules in this Code have been formulated to address the ethical obligations of any person who serves a judicial function, and are premised upon the supposition that a uniform system of ethical principles should apply to all those authorized to perform judicial functions.

[2] The determination of which category and, accordingly, which specific Rules apply to an individu-

al judicial officer, depends upon the facts of the particular judicial service.

[3] In recent years many jurisdictions have created what are often called "problem solving" courts, in which judges are authorized by court rules to act in nontraditional ways. For example, judges presiding in drug courts and monitoring the progress of participants in those courts' programs may be authorized and even encouraged to communicate directly with social workers, probation officers, and others outside the context of their usual judicial role as independent decision makers on issues of fact and law. When local rules specifically authorize conduct not otherwise permitted under these Rules, they take precedence over the provisions set forth in the Code. Nevertheless, judges serving on "problem solving" courts shall comply with this Code except to the extent local rules provide and permit otherwise.

II. Senior Judge

A senior judge is considered to be a periodic part-time judge subject to Part IV of this Application Section.

III. Continuing Part-Time Judge

A judge who serves on a part-time basis by election or under a continuing appointment (a "continuing part-time judge")

(A) is not required to comply:

(1) with Rules 2.10(A) and 2.10(B) (Judicial Statements on Pending and Impending Cases), except while serving as a judge; or

(2) at any time with Rules 3.4 (Appointments to Governmental Positions), 3.8 (Appointments to Fiduciary Positions), 3.9 (Service as Arbitrator or Mediator), 3.10 (Practice of Law), 3.11 (Financial, Business, or Remunerative Activities), 3.14 (Reimbursement of Expenses and Waivers of Fees or Charges), and 3.15 (Financial Reporting Requirements); and

(B) shall not practice law in the court on which the judge serves or in any court subject to the appellate jurisdiction of the court on which the judge serves, and, except as permitted by the Indiana Rules of Professional Conduct, shall not act as a lawyer in a proceeding in which the judge has served as a judge or in any other proceeding related thereto.

IV. Periodic Part–Time Judge

A judge, including a senior judge, who serves or expects to serve repeatedly on a part-time basis but under a separate appointment for each limited period of service or for each matter (a "periodic part-time judge")

(A) is not required to comply:

(1) with Rule 2.10 (Judicial Statements on Pending and Impending Cases), except while serving as a judge; or

(2) at any time with Rules 3.4 (Appointments to Governmental Positions), 3.7 (Participation in Educational, Religious, Charitable, Fraternal, or Civic Organizations and Activities), 3.8 (Appointments to Fiduciary Positions), 3.9 (Service as Arbitrator or Mediator), 3.10 (Practice of Law), 3.11 (Financial, Business, or Remunerative Activities), 3. 13 (Acceptance and Reporting of Gifts, Loans, Bequests, Benefits, or Other Things of Value), 3.15 (Financial Reporting Requirements), 4.1 (Political and Campaign Activities of Judges and Judicial Candidates in General), and 4. 5 (Activities of Judges Who Become Candidates for Nonjudicial Office); and

(B) shall not represent any client in any court on which the judge serves or in any court subject to the appellate jurisdiction of a court on which the judge serves, and, except as permitted by the Indiana Rules of Professional Conduct, shall not act as a lawyer or ADR neutral in a proceeding in which the judge has served as a judicial officer or in any other proceeding related thereto.

V. Pro Tempore Part–Time Judge

A judge who serves or expects to serve once or only sporadically on a part-time basis under a separate appointment for each period of service or for each case heard (a "pro tempore part-time judge") is not required to comply:

(A) except while serving as a judge, with Rules 1.2 (Promoting Confidence in the Judiciary), 2.4 (External Influences on Judicial Conduct), 2.10 (Judicial Statements on Pending and Impending Cases), or 3.2 (Appearances before Governmental Bodies and Consultation with Government Officials); or

(B) at any time with Rules 3.4 (Appointments to Governmental Positions), 3.6 (Affiliation with Discriminatory Organizations), 3.7 (Participation in Educational, Religious, Charitable, Fraternal, or Civic Organizations and Activities), 3.8 (Appointments to Fiduciary Positions), 3.9 (Service as Arbitrator or Mediator), 3.10 (Practice of Law), 3.11 (Financial, Business, or Remunerative Activities), 3.13 (Acceptance and Reporting of Gifts, Loans, Bequests, Benefits, or Other Things of Value), 3.15 (Financial Reporting Requirements), 4.1 (Political and Campaign Activities of Judges and Judicial Candidates in General), and 4.5 (Activities of Judges Who Become Candidates for Nonjudicial Office), and

(C) shall not act as a lawyer in a proceeding in which the judge has served as a judge or in any proceeding related thereto except as permitted by the Indiana Rules of Professional Conduct.

VI. Time For Compliance

A person to whom this Code becomes applicable shall comply immediately with its provisions, except that those judges to whom Rules 3.8 (Appointments to Fiduciary Positions) and 3.11 (Financial, Business, or Remunerative Activities) apply shall comply with those Rules as soon as reasonably possible, but in no event later than one year after the Code becomes applicable to the judge.

COMMENT

[1] If serving as a fiduciary when selected as judge, a new judge may, notwithstanding the prohibitions in Rule 3.8, continue to serve as fiduciary, but only for that period of time necessary to avoid serious adverse consequences to the beneficiaries of the fiduciary relationship and in no event longer than one year. Similarly, if engaged at the time of judicial selection in a business activity, a new judge may, notwithstanding the prohibitions in Rule 3.11, continue in that activity for a reasonable period but in no event longer than one year.

Amended Sept. 21, 2010, effective Jan. 1, 2011.

CANON 1. A Judge Shall Uphold and Promote the Independence, Integrity, and Impartiality of the Judiciary, and Shall Avoid Impropriety and the Appearance of Impropriety

RULE 1.1 : *Compliance with the Law*

A judge shall comply with the law,* including the Code of Judicial Conduct.

RULE 1.2 : *Promoting Confidence in the Judiciary*

A judge shall act at all times in a manner that promotes public confidence in the independence,* integrity,* and impartiality* of the judiciary, and shall avoid impropriety and the appearance of impropriety.

Comment

[1] Public confidence in the judiciary is eroded by improper conduct and conduct that creates the appearance of impropriety. This principle applies to both the professional and personal conduct of a judge.

[2] A judge should expect to be the subject of public scrutiny that might be viewed as burdensome if applied to other citizens, and must accept the restrictions imposed by the Code.

[3] Conduct that compromises or appears to compromise the independence, integrity, and impartiality of a judge undermines public confidence in the judiciary. Because it is not practicable to list all such conduct, the Rule is necessarily cast in general terms.

[4] Judges should participate in activities that promote ethical conduct among judges and lawyers, support professionalism within the judiciary and the legal profession, and promote access to justice for all.

[5] Actual improprieties include violations of law, court rules, or provisions of this Code. The test for appearance of impropriety is whether the conduct would create in reasonable minds a perception that the judge violated this Code or engaged in other conduct that reflects adversely on the judge's honesty, impartiality, temperament, or fitness to serve as a judge.

[6] A judge should initiate and participate in community outreach activities for the purpose of promoting public understanding of and confidence in the administration of justice. In conducting such activities, the judge must act in a manner consistent with this Code.

RULE 1.3 : *Avoiding Abuse of the Prestige of Judicial Office*

A judge shall not abuse the prestige of judicial office to advance the personal or economic interests* of the judge or others, or allow others to do so.

Comment

[1] It is improper for a judge to use or attempt to use his or her position to gain personal advantage or deferential treatment of any kind. For example, it would be improper for a judge to allude to his or her judicial status to gain favorable treatment in encounters with traffic officials. Similarly, a judge must not use judicial letterhead to gain an advantage in conducting his or her personal business.

[2] A judge may provide a reference or recommendation for an individual based upon the judge's personal knowledge and may use official letterhead, but may not provide a reference or recommendation if there is a likelihood that it would reasonably be perceived as an attempt to exert pressure by reason of the judicial office.

[3] Judges may participate in the process of judicial selection by initiating communication, writing letters of recommendation, and otherwise cooperating with appointing authorities and screening committees, and by responding to inquiries from such entities concerning the professional qualifications of a person being considered for judicial office.

[4] Special considerations arise when judges write or contribute to publications of for-profit entities, whether related or unrelated to the law. A judge should not permit anyone associated with the publication of such materials to exploit the judge's office in a manner that violates this Rule or other applicable law. In contracts for publication of a judge's writing, the judge should retain sufficient control over the advertising to avoid such exploitation.

Adopted effective March 1, 1993; amended effective Jan.1, 2009.

CANON 2. A Judge Shall Perform the Duties of Judicial Office Impartially, Competently, and Diligently

RULE 2.1 : *Giving Precedence to the Duties of Judicial Office*

The duties of judicial office, as prescribed by law,* shall take precedence over all of a judge's personal and extrajudicial activities.

Comment

[1] To ensure that judges are available to fulfill their judicial duties, judges must conduct their personal and extrajudicial activities to minimize the risk of conflicts that would result in frequent disqualification. See Canon 3.

[2] Although it is not a duty of judicial office unless prescribed by law, judges are encouraged to participate in activities that promote public understanding of and confidence in the justice system.

RULE 2.2 : *Impartiality and Fairness*

A judge shall uphold and apply the law,* and shall perform all duties of judicial office fairly and impartially.*

Comment

[1] To ensure impartiality and fairness to all parties, a judge must be objective and open-minded.

[2] Although each judge comes to the bench with a unique background and personal philosophy, a judge must interpret and apply the law without regard to whether the judge approves of or disapproves of the law in question.

[3] When applying and interpreting the law, a judge sometimes may make good-faith errors of fact or law. Errors of this kind do not violate this Rule.

[4] It is not a violation of this Rule for a judge to make reasonable accommodations to ensure pro se litigants the opportunity to have their matters fairly heard.

RULE 2.3 : *Bias, Prejudice, and Harassment*

(A) A judge shall perform the duties of judicial office, including administrative duties, without bias or prejudice.

(B) A judge shall not, in the performance of judicial duties, by words or conduct manifest bias or prejudice, or engage in harassment, including but not limited to bias, prejudice, or harassment based upon race, sex, gender, religion, national origin, ethnicity, disability, age, sexual orientation, marital status, socioeconomic status, or political affiliation, and shall not permit court staff, court officials, or others subject to the judge's direction and control to do so.

(C) A judge shall require lawyers in proceedings before the court to refrain from manifesting bias or prejudice, or engaging in harassment, based upon attributes including but not limited to race, sex, gender, religion, national origin, ethnicity, disability, age, sexual orientation, marital status, socioeconomic status, or political affiliation, against parties, witnesses, lawyers, or others.

(D) The restrictions of paragraphs (B) and (C) do not preclude judges or lawyers from making legitimate reference to the listed factors, or similar factors, when they are relevant to an issue in a proceeding.

Comment

[1] A judge who manifests bias or prejudice in a proceeding impairs the fairness of the proceeding and brings the judiciary into disrepute.

[2] Examples of manifestations of bias or prejudice include but are not limited to epithets; slurs; demeaning nicknames; negative stereotyping; attempted humor based upon stereotypes; threatening, intimidating, or hostile acts; suggestions of connections between race, ethnicity, or nationality and crime; and irrelevant references to personal

characteristics. Even facial expressions and body language can convey to parties and lawyers in the proceeding, jurors, the media, and others an appearance of bias or prejudice. A judge must avoid conduct that may reasonably be perceived as prejudiced or biased.

[3] Harassment, as referred to in paragraphs (B) and (C), is verbal or physical conduct that denigrates or shows hostility or aversion toward a person on bases such as race, sex, gender, religion, national origin, ethnicity, disability, age, sexual orientation, marital status, socioeconomic status, or political affiliation.

[4] Sexual harassment includes but is not limited to sexual advances, requests for sexual favors, and other verbal or physical conduct of a sexual nature that is unwelcome.

RULE 2.4 : *External Influences on Judicial Conduct*

(A) A judge shall not be swayed by public clamor or fear of criticism.

(B) A judge shall not permit family, social, political, financial, or other interests or relationships to influence the judge's judicial conduct or judgment.

(C) A judge shall not convey or permit others to convey the impression that any person or organization is in a position to influence the judge.

Comment

[1] An independent judiciary requires that judges decide cases according to the law and facts, without regard to whether particular laws or litigants are popular or unpopular with the public, the media, government officials, or the judge's friends or family. Confidence in the judiciary is eroded if judicial decision making is perceived to be subject to inappropriate outside influences.

RULE 2.5 : *Competence, Diligence, and Cooperation*

(A) A judge shall perform judicial and administrative duties competently, diligently, and promptly.

(B) A judge shall cooperate with other judges and court officials in the administration of court business.

Comment

[1] Competence in the performance of judicial duties requires the legal knowledge, skill, thoroughness, and preparation reasonably necessary to perform a judge's responsibilities of judicial office.

[2] A judge should seek the necessary docket time, court staff, expertise, and resources to discharge all adjudicative and administrative responsibilities.

[3] Prompt disposition of the court's business requires a judge to devote adequate time to judicial duties, to be punctual in attending court and expeditious in determining matters under submission, and to take reasonable measures to ensure that court officials, litigants, and their lawyers cooperate with the judge to that end.

[4] In disposing of matters promptly and efficiently, a judge must demonstrate due regard for

the rights of parties to be heard and to have issues resolved without unnecessary cost or delay. A judge should monitor and supervise cases in ways that reduce or eliminate dilatory practices, avoidable delays, and unnecessary costs.

RULE 2.6 : *Ensuring the Right to Be Heard*

(A) A judge shall accord to every person who has a legal interest in a proceeding, or that person's lawyer, the right to be heard according to law.*

(B) A judge may encourage parties to a proceeding and their lawyers to settle matters in dispute but shall not act in a manner that coerces any party into settlement.

Comment

[1] The right to be heard is an essential component of a fair and impartial system of justice. Substantive rights of litigants can be protected only if procedures protecting the right to be heard are observed.

[2] The judge plays an important role in overseeing the settlement of disputes, but should be careful that efforts to further settlement do not undermine any party's right to be heard according to law. The judge should keep in mind the effect that the judge's participation in settlement discussions may have, not only on the judge's own views of the case, but also on the perceptions of the lawyers and the parties if the case remains with the judge after settlement efforts are unsuccessful. Among the factors that a judge should consider when deciding upon an appropriate settlement practice for a case are (1) whether the parties have requested or voluntarily consented to a certain level of participation by the judge in settlement discussions, (2) whether the parties and their counsel are relatively sophisticated in legal matters, (3) whether the case will be tried by the judge or a jury, (4) whether the parties participate with their counsel in settlement discussions, (5) whether any parties are unrepresented by counsel, and (6) whether the matter is civil or criminal.

[3] Judges must be mindful of the effect settlement discussions can have, not only on their objectivity and impartiality, but also on the appearance of their objectivity and impartiality. Despite a judge's best efforts, there may be instances when information obtained during settlement discussions could influence a judge's decision making during trial, and, in such instances, the judge should consider whether disqualification may be appropriate. See Rule 2.11(A)(1).

RULE 2.7 : *Responsibility to Decide*

A judge shall hear and decide matters assigned to the judge, except when disqualification is required by Rule 2.11 or other law.*

Comment

[1] Judges must be available to decide the matters that come before the court. Although there are times when disqualification is necessary to protect the rights of litigants and preserve public confidence in the independence, integrity, and impartiality of the judiciary, judges must be available to

decide matters that come before the courts. Unwarranted disqualification may bring public disfavor to the court and to the judge personally. The dignity of the court, the judge's respect for fulfillment of judicial duties, and a proper concern for the burdens that may be imposed upon the judge's colleagues require that a judge not use disqualification to avoid cases that present difficult, controversial, or unpopular issues.

RULE 2.8 : *Decorum, Demeanor, and Communication with Jurors*

(A) A judge shall require order and decorum in proceedings before the court.

(B) A judge shall be patient, dignified, and courteous to litigants, jurors, witnesses, lawyers, court staff, court officials, and others with whom the judge deals in an official capacity, and shall require similar conduct of lawyers, court staff, court officials, and others subject to the judge's direction and control.

(C) A judge shall not commend or criticize jurors for their verdict other than in a court order or opinion in a proceeding.

> **Comment**
>
> [1] The duty to hear all proceedings with patience and courtesy is not inconsistent with the duty imposed in Rule 2.5 to dispose promptly of the business of the court. Judges can be efficient and businesslike while being patient and deliberate.
>
> [2] Commending or criticizing jurors for their verdict may imply a judicial expectation in future cases and may impair a juror's ability to be fair and impartial in a subsequent case.
>
> [3] A judge may meet with jurors who choose to remain after trial but should be careful not to discuss the merits of the case.

RULE 2.9 : *Ex Parte Communications*

(A) A judge shall not initiate, permit, or consider ex parte communications, or consider other communications made to the judge outside the presence of the parties or their lawyers, concerning a pending* or impending matter,* except as follows:

(1) When circumstances require it, ex parte communication for scheduling, administrative, or emergency purposes, which does not address substantive matters, is permitted, provided:

(a) the judge reasonably believes that no party will gain a procedural, substantive, or tactical advantage as a result of the ex parte communication; and

(b) the judge makes provision promptly to notify all other parties of the substance of the ex parte communication, and gives the parties an opportunity to respond.

(2) A judge may obtain the written advice of a disinterested expert on the law applicable to a proceeding before the judge, if the judge gives advance notice to the parties of the person to be consulted and the subject matter of the advice to be solicited, and affords the parties a reasonable opportunity to object and respond to the notice and to the advice received.

(3) A judge may consult with court staff and court officials whose functions are to aid the judge in carrying out the judge's adjudicative responsibilities, or with other judges, provided the judge makes reasonable efforts to avoid receiving factual information that is not part of the record, and does not abrogate the responsibility personally to decide the matter.

(4) A judge may, with the consent of the parties, confer separately with the parties and their lawyers in an effort to settle matters pending before the judge.

(5) A judge may initiate, permit, or consider any ex parte communication when expressly authorized by law* to do so.

(B) If a judge inadvertently receives an unauthorized ex parte communication bearing upon the substance of a matter, the judge shall make provision promptly to notify the parties of the substance of the communication and provide the parties with an opportunity to respond.

(C) A judge shall not investigate facts in a matter independently, and shall consider only the evidence presented and any facts that may properly be judicially noticed.

(D) A judge shall make reasonable efforts, including providing appropriate supervision, to ensure that this Rule is not violated by court staff, court officials, and others subject to the judge's direction and control.

> **Comment**
>
> [1] To the extent reasonably possible, all parties or their lawyers shall be included in communications with a judge.
>
> [2] Whenever the presence of a party or notice to a party is required by this Rule, it is the party's lawyer, or if the party is unrepresented, the party, who is to be present or to whom notice is to be given.
>
> [3] The proscription against communications concerning a proceeding includes communications with lawyers, law teachers, and other persons who are not participants in the proceeding, except to the limited extent permitted by this Rule.
>
> [4] A judge may initiate, permit, or consider ex parte communications expressly authorized by law, such as when serving on therapeutic or problem-solving courts, mental health courts, or drug courts. In this capacity, judges may assume a more interactive role with parties, treatment providers, probation officers, social workers, and others.
>
> [5] A judge may consult with other judges on pending matters, but must avoid ex parte discussions of a case with judges who have previously been disqualified from hearing the matter, and with judges who have appellate jurisdiction over the matter.

[6] The prohibition against a judge investigating the facts in a matter extends to information available in all mediums, including electronic.

[7] A judge may consult ethics advisory committees, outside counsel, or legal experts concerning the judge's compliance with this Code. Such consultations are not subject to the restrictions of paragraph (A)(2).

[8] A judge is permitted by Rule 2.9(A)(3) to consult about legal and procedural issues with the Indiana Judicial Center or Indiana Supreme Court Division of State Court Administration.

RULE 2.10 : *Judicial Statements on Pending and Impending Cases*

(A) A judge shall not make any public statement that might reasonably be expected to affect the outcome or impair the fairness of a matter pending* or impending* in any court, or make any nonpublic statement that might substantially interfere with a fair trial or hearing.

(B) A judge shall not, in connection with cases, controversies, or issues that are likely to come before the court, make pledges, promises, or commitments that are inconsistent with the impartial* performance of the adjudicative duties of judicial office.

(C) A judge shall require court staff, court officials, and others subject to the judge's direction and control to refrain from making statements that the judge would be prohibited from making by paragraphs (A) and (B).

(D) Notwithstanding the restrictions in paragraph (A), a judge may make public statements in the course of official duties, may explain court procedures, and may comment on any proceeding in which the judge is a litigant in a personal capacity.

(E) Subject to the requirements of paragraph (A), a judge may respond directly or through a third party to allegations in the media or elsewhere concerning the judge's conduct in a matter.

Comment

[1] This Rule's restrictions on judicial speech are essential to the maintenance of the independence, integrity, and impartiality of the judiciary.

[2] This Rule does not prohibit a judge from commenting on proceedings in which the judge is a litigant in a personal capacity. In cases in which the judge is a litigant in an official capacity, such as a writ of mandamus, the judge must not comment publicly.

[3] Depending upon the circumstances, the judge should consider whether it may be preferable for a third party, rather than the judge, to respond or issue statements in connection with allegations concerning the judge's conduct in a matter.

RULE 2.11 : *Disqualification*

(A) A judge shall disqualify himself or herself in any proceeding in which the judge's impartiality* might reasonably be questioned, including but not limited to the following circumstances:

(1) The judge has a personal bias or prejudice concerning a party or a party's lawyer, or personal knowledge* of facts that are in dispute in the proceeding.

(2) The judge knows* that the judge, the judge's spouse or domestic partner,* or a person within the third degree of relationship* to either of them, or the spouse or domestic partner of such a person is:

(a) a party to the proceeding, or an officer, director, general partner, managing member, or trustee of a party;

(b) acting as a lawyer in the proceeding;

(c) a person who has more than a de minimis* interest that could be substantially affected by the proceeding; or

(d) likely to be a material witness in the proceeding.

(3) The judge knows that he or she, individually or as a fiduciary,* or the judge's spouse, domestic partner, parent, or child, or any other member of the judge's family residing in the judge's household,* has an economic interest* in the subject matter in controversy or in a party to the proceeding that could be substantially affected by the proceeding.

(4) [Reserved]

(5) The judge, while a judge or a judicial candidate,* has made a public statement, other than in a court proceeding, judicial decision, or opinion, that commits or appears to commit the judge to reach a particular result or rule in a particular way in the proceeding or controversy.

(6) The judge:

(a) served as a lawyer in the matter in controversy, or was associated with a lawyer who participated substantially as a lawyer in the matter during such association;

(b) served in governmental employment, and in such capacity participated personally and substantially as a lawyer or public official concerning the proceeding, or has publicly expressed in such capacity an opinion concerning the merits of the particular matter in controversy;

(c) was a material witness concerning the matter; or

(d) previously presided as a judge over the matter in another court.

(B) A judge shall keep informed about the judge's personal and fiduciary economic interests, and make a reasonable effort to keep informed about the personal economic interests of the judge's spouse or domestic partner and minor children residing in the judge's household.

Comment

[1] Under this Rule, a judge is disqualified whenever the judge's impartiality might reasonably be questioned, regardless of whether any of the specif-

ic provisions of paragraphs (A)(1) through (6) apply. In many jurisdictions, the term "recusal" is used interchangeably with the term "disqualification."

[2] A judge's obligation not to hear or decide matters in which disqualification is required applies regardless of whether a motion to disqualify is filed.

[3] The rule of necessity may override the rule of disqualification. For example, a judge might be required to participate in judicial review of a judicial salary statute, or might be the only judge available in a matter requiring immediate judicial action, such as a hearing on probable cause or a temporary restraining order. In matters that require immediate action, the judge must disclose on the record the basis for possible disqualification and make reasonable efforts to transfer the matter to another judge as soon as practicable.

[4] The fact that a lawyer in a proceeding is affiliated with a law firm with which a relative of the judge is affiliated does not itself disqualify the judge. If, however, the judge's impartiality might reasonably be questioned under paragraph (A), or the relative is known by the judge to have an interest in the law firm that could be substantially affected by the proceeding under paragraph (A)(2)(c), the judge's disqualification is required.

[5] A judge should disclose on the record information that the judge believes the parties or their lawyers might reasonably consider relevant to a possible motion for disqualification, even if the judge believes there is no basis for disqualification.

[6] "Economic interest," as set forth in the Terminology section, means ownership of more than a de minimis legal or equitable interest. Except for situations in which a judge participates in the management of such a legal or equitable interest, or the interest could be substantially affected by the outcome of a proceeding before a judge, it does not include:

(1) an interest in the individual holdings within a mutual or common investment fund;

(2) an interest in securities held by an educational, religious, charitable, fraternal, or civic organization in which the judge or the judge's spouse, domestic partner, parent, or child serves as a director, officer, advisor, or other participant;

(3) a deposit in a financial institution or deposits or proprietary interests the judge may maintain as a member of a mutual savings association or credit union, or similar proprietary interests; or

(4) an interest in the issuer of government securities held by the judge.

[7] A statement that "appears to commit" a judge within the meaning of Rule 2.11 (A)(5) is one that a reasonable person would believe from the judge's public statement that the judge has specifically undertaken to reach a particular result.

RULE 2.12 : *Supervisory Duties*

(A) A judge shall require court staff, court officials, and others subject to the judge's direction and control to act in a manner consistent with the judge's obligations under this Code.

(B) A judge with supervisory authority for the performance of other judges shall take reasonable measures to ensure that those judges properly discharge their judicial responsibilities, including the prompt disposition of matters before them.

Comment

[1] A judge is responsible for his or her own conduct and for the conduct of others, such as staff, when those persons are acting at the judge's direction or control. A judge may not direct court personnel to engage in conduct on the judge's behalf or as the judge's representative when such conduct would violate the Code if undertaken by the judge.

[2] Public confidence in the judicial system depends upon timely justice. To promote the efficient administration of justice, a judge with supervisory authority must take the steps needed to ensure that judges under his or her supervision administer their workloads promptly.

RULE 2.13 : *Hiring and Administrative Appointments*

(A) In hiring court employees and making administrative appointments, a judge:

(1) shall exercise the power of appointment impartially* and on the basis of merit; and

(2) shall avoid nepotism, favoritism, and unnecessary appointments.

(B) [Reserved]

(C) A judge shall not approve compensation of appointee beyond the fair value of services rendered.

COMMENT

[1] "Appointees of a judge" includes but is not limited to assigned counsel, officials such as referees, commissioners, special masters, receivers, special advocates, and guardians, and personnel such as clerks, secretaries, and bailiffs.

[2] Unless otherwise defined by law, nepotism is the appointment or hiring of any relative within the third degree of relationship of either the judge or the judge's spouse or domestic partner, or the spouse or domestic partner of such relative.

[3] A judge should consult the staff of the Indiana Commission on Judicial Qualifications or its advisory opinions to determine whether hiring or appointing a relative as defined by Comment [2] may be justifiable under the circumstances.

[4] Consent by the parties to an appointment or an award of compensation does not relieve the judge of the obligation prescribed by paragraphs (A) and (C).

RULE 2.14 : *Disability and Impairment*

A judge having a reasonable belief that the performance of a lawyer or another judge is impaired by drugs or alcohol, or by a mental, emotional, or physical condition, shall take appropriate action, which may include a confidential referral to a lawyer or judicial assistance program.

Comment

[1] "Appropriate action" means action intended and reasonably likely to help the judge or lawyer in question address the problem and prevent harm to the justice system. Depending upon the circumstances, appropriate action may include but is not limited to speaking directly to the impaired person, notifying an individual with supervisory responsibility over the impaired person, or making a referral to an assistance program.

[2] Taking or initiating corrective action by way of referral to an assistance program may satisfy a judge's responsibility under this Rule. Assistance programs have many approaches for offering help to impaired judges and lawyers, such as intervention, counseling, or referral to appropriate health care professionals. Depending upon the gravity of the conduct that has come to the judge's attention, however, the judge may be required to take other action, such as reporting the impaired judge or lawyer to the appropriate authority, agency, or body. See Rule 2.15.

RULE 2.15 : *Responding to Judicial and Lawyer Misconduct*

(A) A judge having knowledge* that another judge has committed a violation of this Code that raises a substantial question regarding the judge's honesty, trustworthiness, or fitness as a judge in other respects shall inform the appropriate authority.*

(B) A judge having knowledge that a lawyer has committed a violation of the Rules of Professional Conduct that raises a substantial question regarding the lawyer's honesty, trustworthiness, or fitness as a lawyer in other respects shall inform the appropriate authority.

(C) A judge who receives credible information indicating a substantial likelihood that another judge has committed a violation of this Code shall take appropriate action.

(D) A judge who receives credible information indicating a substantial likelihood that a lawyer has committed a violation of the Rules of Professional Conduct shall take appropriate action.

Comment

[1] Taking action to address known misconduct is a judge's obligation. Paragraphs (A) and (B) impose an obligation on the judge to report to the appropriate disciplinary authority the known misconduct of another judge or a lawyer that raises a substantial question regarding the honesty, trustworthiness, or fitness of that judge or lawyer. Ignoring or denying known misconduct among one's judicial colleagues or members of the legal profession undermines a judge's responsibility to participate in efforts to ensure public respect for the justice system. This Rule limits the reporting obligation to those offenses that an independent judiciary must vigorously endeavor to prevent.

[2] A judge who does not have actual knowledge that another judge or a lawyer may have committed misconduct, but who receives credible information indicating a substantial likelihood of such misconduct, is required to take appropriate action under

paragraphs (C) and (D). Appropriate action may include, but is not limited to, communicating directly with the judge who may have violated this Code, communicating with a supervising judge, or reporting the suspected violation to the appropriate authority or other agency or body. Similarly, actions to be taken in response to information indicating that a lawyer has committed a violation of the Rules of Professional Conduct may include but are not limited to communicating directly with the lawyer who may have committed the violation, or reporting the suspected violation to the appropriate authority or other agency or body.

[3] The provisions of this Rule do not require the reporting of information received while acting on behalf of an impaired judges or lawyers assistance program approved by the Indiana Supreme Court.

RULE 2.16 : *Cooperation with Disciplinary Authorities*

(A) A judge shall cooperate and be candid and honest with judicial and lawyer disciplinary agencies.

(B) A judge shall not retaliate, directly or indirectly, against a person known* or suspected to have assisted or cooperated with an investigation of a judge or a lawyer.

Comment

[1] Cooperation with investigations and proceedings of judicial and lawyer discipline agencies, as required in paragraph (A), instills confidence in judges' commitment to the integrity of the judicial system and the protection of the public.

RULE 2.17 : *Prohibiting Broadcasting of Proceedings*

Except with prior approval of the Indiana Supreme Court, a judge shall prohibit broadcasting, televising, recording, or taking photographs in the courtroom and areas immediately adjacent thereto during sessions of court or recesses between sessions, except that a judge may authorize:

(1) the use of electronic or photographic means for the presentation of evidence, for the perpetuation of a record, or for other purposes of judicial administration;

(2) the broadcasting, televising, recording, or photographing of investitive, ceremonial, or naturalization proceedings;

(3) the photographic or electronic recording and reproduction of appropriate court proceedings under the following conditions:

(a) the means of recording will not distract participants or impair the dignity of the proceedings;

(b) the parties have consented, and the consent to being depicted or recorded has been obtained from each witness appearing in the recording and reproduction;

(c) the reproduction will not be exhibited until after the proceeding has been concluded and all direct appeals have been exhausted; and

(d) the reproduction will be exhibited only for instructional purposes in educational institutions.

Adopted effective March 1, 1993. Amended effective Jan. 1, 2009.

CANON 3. A Judge Shall Conduct the Judge's Personal and Extrajudicial Activities to Minimize the Risk of Conflict with the Obligations of Judicial Office

RULE 3.1 : *Extrajudicial Activities in General*

A judge may engage in extrajudicial activities, except as prohibited by law* or this Code. However, when engaging in extrajudicial activities, a judge shall not:

(A) participate in activities that will interfere with the proper performance of the judge's judicial duties;

(B) participate in activities that will lead to frequent disqualification of the judge;

(C) participate in activities that would appear to a reasonable person to undermine the judge's independence,* integrity,* or impartiality;*

(D) engage in conduct that would appear to a reasonable person to be coercive; or

(E) make use of court premises, staff, stationery, equipment, or other resources, except for incidental use or for activities that concern the law, the legal system, or the administration of justice.

Comment

[1] To the extent that time permits, and judicial independence and impartiality are not compromised, judges are encouraged to engage in appropriate extrajudicial activities. Judges are uniquely qualified to engage in extrajudicial activities that concern the law, the legal system, and the administration of justice, such as by speaking, writing, teaching, or participating in scholarly research projects. In addition, judges are permitted and encouraged to engage in educational, religious, charitable, fraternal or civic extrajudicial activities not conducted for profit, even when the activities do not involve the law. See Rule 3.7.

[2] Participation in both law-related and other extrajudicial activities helps integrate judges into their communities, and furthers public understanding of and respect for courts and the judicial system.

[3] Discriminatory actions and expressions of bias or prejudice by a judge, even outside the judge's official or judicial actions, are likely to appear to a reasonable person to call into question the judge's integrity and impartiality. Examples include jokes or other remarks that demean individuals based upon their race, sex, gender, religion, national origin, ethnicity, disability, age, sexual orientation, or socioeconomic status. For the same reason, a judge's extrajudicial activities must not be conducted in connection or affiliation with an organization that practices invidious discrimination. See Rule 3.6.

[4] While engaged in permitted extrajudicial activities, judges must not coerce others or take action that would reasonably be perceived as coercive. For example, depending upon the circumstances, a judge's solicitation of contributions or memberships for an organization, even as permitted by Rule 3.7(A), might create the risk that the person solicited would feel obligated to respond favorably, or would do so to curry favor with the judge.

RULE 3.2 : *Appearances before Governmental Bodies and Consultation with Government Officials*

A judge shall not appear voluntarily at a public hearing before, or otherwise consult with, an executive or a legislative body or official, except:

(A) in connection with matters concerning the law,* the legal system, or the administration of justice;

(B) in connection with matters about which the judge acquired knowledge or expertise in the course of the judge's judicial duties; or

(C) when the judge is acting pro se in a matter involving the judge's legal or economic interests or those of members of the judge's family residing in the judge's household, or when the judge is acting in a fiduciary* capacity.

Comment

[1] Judges possess special expertise in matters of law, the legal system, and the administration of justice, and may properly share that expertise with governmental bodies and executive or legislative branch officials.

[2] In appearing before governmental bodies or consulting with government officials, judges must be mindful that they remain subject to other provisions of this Code, such as Rule 1.3, prohibiting judges from using the prestige of office to advance their own or others' interests, Rule 2.10, governing public comment on pending and impending matters, and Rule 3.1(C), prohibiting judges from engaging in extrajudicial activities that would appear to a reasonable person to undermine the judge's independence, integrity, or impartiality.

[3] In general, it would be an unnecessary and unfair burden to prohibit judges from appearing before governmental bodies or consulting with government officials on matters that are likely to affect them as private citizens, such as zoning proposals affecting their real property. In engaging in such activities, however, judges must not refer to their judicial positions, and must otherwise exercise caution to avoid using the prestige of judicial office.

[4] A judge is not prohibited under this Rule from appearing before an executive or legislative body or official in connection with an extrajudicial position held in accordance with Rule 3.4.

RULE 3.3 : *Testifying as a Character Witness*

A judge shall not testify as a character witness in a judicial, administrative, or other adjudicatory proceeding or otherwise vouch for the character of a person in a legal proceeding, except when duly summoned.

Comment

[1] A judge who, without being subpoenaed, testifies as a character witness abuses the prestige of judicial office to advance the interests of another. See Rule 1.3. Except in unusual circumstances where the demands of justice require, a judge should discourage a party from requiring the judge to testify as a character witness.

[2] This Rule does not prohibit judges from writing letters of recommendation in non-adjudicatory proceedings pursuant to Rule 1.3, Comments [2] and [3].

[3] This Rule applies to attorney and judicial disciplinary proceedings, including reinstatements.

RULE 3.4 : *Appointments to Governmental Positions*

A judge shall not accept appointment to a governmental committee, board, commission, or other governmental position except with prior approval of the Indiana Supreme Court, unless it is one that concerns the law,* the legal system, or the administration of justice.

COMMENT

[1] Rule 3.4 implicitly acknowledges the value of judges accepting appointments to entities that concern the law, the legal system, or the administration of justice. Even in such instances, however, a judge should assess the appropriateness of accepting an appointment, paying particular attention to the subject matter of the appointment and the availability and allocation of judicial resources, including the judge's time commitments, and giving due regard to the requirements of the independence and impartiality of the judiciary.

[2] A judge may represent his or her country, state, or locality on ceremonial occasions or in connection with historical, educational, or cultural activities. Such representation does not constitute acceptance of a government position.

RULE 3.5 : *Use of Nonpublic Information*

A judge shall not intentionally disclose or use nonpublic information* acquired in a judicial capacity for any purpose unrelated to the judge's judicial duties.

Comment

[1] In the course of performing judicial duties, a judge may acquire information of commercial or other value that is unavailable to the public. The judge must not reveal or use such information for personal gain or for any purpose unrelated to his or her judicial duties.

[2] This rule is not intended, however, to affect a judge's ability to act on information as necessary to protect the health or safety of the judge or a member of a judge's family, court personnel, or other judicial officers if consistent with other provisions of this Code.

RULE 3.6 : *Affiliation with Discriminatory Organizations*

(A) A judge shall not hold membership in any organization that practices invidious discrimination on the basis of race, sex, gender, religion, national origin, ethnicity, or sexual orientation.

(B) A judge shall not use the benefits or facilities of an organization if the judge knows* or should know that the organization practices invidious discrimination on one or more of the bases identified in paragraph (A). A judge's attendance at an event in a facility of an organization that the judge is not permitted to join is not a violation of this Rule when the judge's attendance is an isolated event that could not reasonably be perceived as an endorsement of the organization's practices.

COMMENT

[1] A judge's public manifestation of approval of invidious discrimination on any basis gives rise to the appearance of impropriety and diminishes public confidence in the integrity and impartiality of the judiciary. A judge's membership in an organization that practices invidious discrimination creates the perception that the judge's impartiality is impaired.

[2] An organization is generally said to discriminate invidiously if it arbitrarily excludes from membership on the basis of race, sex, gender, religion, national origin, ethnicity, or sexual orientation persons who would otherwise be eligible for admission. Whether an organization practices invidious discrimination is a complex question to which judges should be attentive. The answer cannot be determined from a mere examination of an organization's current membership rolls, but rather, depends upon how the organization selects members, as well as other relevant factors, such as whether the organization is dedicated to the preservation of religious, ethnic, or cultural values of legitimate common interest to its members, or whether it is an intimate, purely private organization whose membership limitations could not constitutionally be prohibited.

[3] When a judge learns that an organization to which the judge belongs engages in invidious discrimination, the judge must resign immediately from the organization.

[4] A judge's membership in a religious organization as a lawful exercise of the freedom of religion is not a violation of this Rule.

[5] This Rule does not apply to national or state military service.

RULE 3.7 : *Participation in Educational, Religious, Charitable, Fraternal, or Civic Organizations and Activities*

(A) Except as provided by Rule 3.7(A)(2), a judge may not directly solicit funds for an organization. However, subject to the requirements of Rule 3.1, a judge may participate in activities sponsored by organizations or governmental entities concerned with the law, the legal system, or the administration of justice, and those sponsored by or on behalf of educational, religious, charitable, fraternal, or civic organizations not conducted for profit, including but not limited to the following activities:

(1) assisting such an organization or entity in planning related to fund-raising, volunteering services or goods at fund-raising events, and participat-

ing in the management and investment of the organization's or entity's funds;

(2) soliciting* contributions* for such an organization or entity, but only from members of the judge's family,* or from judges over whom the judge does not exercise supervisory or appellate authority;

(3) soliciting membership for such an organization or entity, even though the membership dues or fees generated may be used to support the objectives of the organization or entity, but only if the organization or entity is concerned with the law, the legal system, or the administration of justice;

(4) appearing or speaking at, receiving an award or other recognition at, being featured on the program of, and permitting his or her title to be used in connection with an event of such an organization or entity, but if the event serves a fund-raising purpose, the judge may not be a featured speaker or guest of honor;

(5) making recommendations to such a public or private fund-granting organization or entity in connection with its programs and activities, but only if the organization or entity is concerned with the law, the legal system, or the administration of justice; and

(6) serving as an officer, director, trustee, or nonlegal advisor of such an organization or entity, unless it is likely that the organization or entity:

(a) will be engaged in proceedings that would ordinarily come before the judge; or

(b) will frequently be engaged in adversary proceedings in the court of which the judge is a member, or in any court subject to the appellate jurisdiction of the court of which the judge is a member.

(B) A judge may encourage lawyers to provide pro bono publico legal services.

Comment

[1] The activities permitted by paragraph (A) generally include those sponsored by or undertaken on behalf of public or private not-for-profit educational institutions, and other not-for-profit organizations, including law-related, charitable, and other organizations.

[2] Even for law-related organizations, a judge should consider whether the membership and purposes of the organization, or the nature of the judge's participation in or association with the organization, would conflict with the judge's obligation to refrain from activities that reflect adversely upon a judge's independence, integrity, and impartiality.

[3] Attendance at fund-raising events and volunteering services or goods at or in support of fund-raising events do not present an element of coercion or abuse the prestige of judicial office and are not prohibited by this Rule.

[4] Identification of a judge's position in educational, religious, charitable, fraternal, or civic or-

ganizations on letterhead used for fund-raising or membership solicitation does not violate this Rule. The letterhead may list the judge's title or judicial office if comparable designations are used for other persons.

[5] In addition to appointing lawyers to serve as counsel for indigent parties in individual cases, a judge may promote broader access to justice by encouraging lawyers to participate in pro bono publico legal services, if in doing so the judge does not employ coercion, or abuse the prestige of judicial office. Such encouragement may take many forms, including providing lists of available programs, training lawyers to do pro bono publico legal work, and participating in events recognizing lawyers who have done pro bono publico work.

[6] Judges, as parents, may assist their children in their fund-raising activities if the procedures employed are not coercive and the sums nominal.

RULE 3.8 : *Appointments to Fiduciary Positions*

(A) A judge shall not accept appointment to serve in a fiduciary* position, such as executor, administrator, trustee, guardian, attorney in fact, or other personal representative, except for the estate, trust, or person of a member of the judge's family,* and then only if such service will not interfere with the proper performance of judicial duties.

(B) A judge shall not serve in a fiduciary position if the judge as fiduciary will likely be engaged in proceedings that would ordinarily come before the judge, or if the estate, trust, or ward becomes involved in adversary proceedings in the court on which the judge serves, or one under its appellate jurisdiction.

(C) A judge acting in a fiduciary capacity shall be subject to the same restrictions on engaging in financial activities that apply to a judge personally.

(D) If a person who is serving in a fiduciary position becomes a judge, he or she must comply with this Rule as soon as reasonably practicable, but in no event later than one year after becoming a judge.

Comment

[1] A judge should recognize that other restrictions imposed by this Code may conflict with a judge's obligations as a fiduciary; in such circumstances, a judge should resign as fiduciary. For example, serving as a fiduciary might require frequent disqualification of a judge under Rule 2.11 because a judge is deemed to have an economic interest in shares of stock held by a trust if the amount of stock held is more than de minimis.

RULE 3.9 : *Service as Arbitrator or Mediator*

A judge shall not act as an arbitrator or a mediator or perform other judicial functions apart from the judge's official duties unless expressly authorized by law.*

Comment

[1] This Rule does not prohibit a judge from participating in arbitration, mediation, or settlement conferences performed as part of assigned judicial duties. Rendering dispute resolution services apart

from those duties, whether or not for economic gain, is prohibited unless it is expressly authorized by law.

RULE 3.10 : *Practice of Law*

A judge shall not practice law. A judge may act pro se and may, without compensation, give legal advice to and draft or review documents for a member of the judge's family,* but is prohibited from serving as the family member's lawyer before a tribunal. This Rule does not prohibit the practice of law pursuant to military service.

Comment

[1] A judge may act pro se in all legal matters, including matters involving litigation and matters involving appearances before or other dealings with governmental bodies. A judge must not use the prestige of office to advance the judge's personal or family interests. See Rule 1.3.

[2] A judge's assistance to a family member in legal matters may not include signing pleadings or appearing before a tribunal for a family member.

RULE 3.11 : *Financial, Business, or Remunerative Activities*

(A) A judge shall not engage in any business, financial, or other remunerative activity if engaging in the activity would:

(1) interfere with the proper performance of judicial duties;

(2) lead to frequent disqualification of the judge;

(3) involve the judge in frequent transactions or continuing business relationships with lawyers or other persons likely to come before the court on which the judge serves; or

(4) result in violations of other provisions of this Code.

Comment

[1] Judges generally are permitted to engage in financial and business activities subject to the requirements of this Rule and all other provisions of the Code. For example, it would be improper for a judge to spend so much time on business activities that it interferes with the performance of judicial duties. See Rule 2.1. Similarly, it would be improper for a judge to use his or her official title or appear in judicial robes in business advertising, to conduct his or her business or financial affairs in such a way that disqualification is frequently required, or to use or permit the use of the judicial position in the judge's extrajudicial financial activities. See Rules 1.3 and 2.11.

[2] As soon as practicable without serious financial detriment, the judge must divest himself or herself of investments and other financial interests that might require frequent disqualification or otherwise violate this Rule.

RULE 3.12 : *Compensation for Extrajudicial Activities*

A judge may accept reasonable compensation for extrajudicial activities permitted by this Code or other law* unless such acceptance would appear to a reasonable person to undermine the judge's independence,* integrity,* or impartiality.*

Comment

[1] A judge is permitted to accept honoraria, stipends, fees, wages, salaries, royalties, or other compensation for speaking, teaching, writing, and other extrajudicial activities, provided the compensation is reasonable and commensurate with the task performed. The judge should be mindful, however, that judicial duties must take precedence over other activities. See Rule 2.1.

[2] Compensation derived from extrajudicial activities is subject to public reporting. See Rule 3.15.

RULE 3.13 : *Acceptance and Reporting of Gifts, Loans, Bequests, Benefits, or Other Things of Value*

(A) A judge shall not accept any gifts, loans, bequests, benefits, or other things of value, if acceptance is prohibited by law* or would appear to a reasonable person to undermine the judge's independence,* integrity,* or impartiality.*

(B) Unless otherwise prohibited by law, or by paragraph (A), a judge may accept the following without publicly reporting such acceptance:

(1) items with little intrinsic value, such as plaques, certificates, trophies, and greeting cards;

(2) gifts, loans, bequests, benefits, or other things of value from friends, relatives, or other persons, including lawyers, whose appearance or interest in a proceeding pending* or impending* before the judge would in any event require disqualification of the judge under Rule 2.11;

(3) ordinary social hospitality;

(4) commercial or financial opportunities and benefits, including special pricing and discounts, and loans from lending institutions in their regular course of business, if the same opportunities and benefits or loans are made available on the same terms to similarly situated persons who are not judges;

(5) rewards and prizes given to competitors or participants in random drawings, contests, or other events that are open to persons who are not judges;

(6) scholarships, fellowships, and similar benefits or awards, if they are available to similarly situated persons who are not judges, based upon the same terms and criteria;

(7) books, magazines, journals, audiovisual materials, and other resource materials supplied by publishers on a complimentary basis for official use; or

(8) gifts, awards, or benefits associated with the business, profession, or other separate activity of a spouse, a domestic partner,* or other family member of a judge residing in the judge's household,* but that incidentally benefit the judge;

(9) gifts incident to a public testimonial;

(10) invitations to the judge and the judge's spouse, domestic partner, or guest to attend without charge:

(a) an event associated with a bar-related function or other activity relating to the law, the legal system, or the administration of justice; or

(b) an event associated with any of the judge's educational, religious, charitable, fraternal or civic activities permitted by this Code, if the same invitation is offered to nonjudges who are engaged in similar ways in the activity as is the judge.

(C) Unless otherwise prohibited by law or by paragraph (A), a judge may accept any other gift, loan, bequest, benefit, or other thing of value but must report such acceptance to the extent required by Rule 3.15.

Comment

[1] Whenever a judge accepts a gift or other thing of value without paying fair market value, there is a risk that the benefit might be viewed as intended to influence the judge's decision in a case. Rule 3.13 imposes restrictions upon the acceptance of such benefits, according to the magnitude of the risk. Paragraph (B) identifies circumstances in which the risk that the acceptance would appear to undermine the judge's independence, integrity, or impartiality is low, and explicitly provides that such items need not be publicly reported. As the value of the benefit or the likelihood that the source of the benefit will appear before the judge increases, the judge is either prohibited under paragraph (A) from accepting the gift, or required under paragraph (C) to publicly report it.

[2] Gift-giving between friends and relatives is a common occurrence, and ordinarily does not create an appearance of impropriety or cause reasonable persons to believe that the judge's independence, integrity, or impartiality has been compromised. In addition, especially when the appearance of friends or relatives in a case would require the judge's disqualification under Rule 2.11, there would be no opportunity for a gift to influence the judge's decision making. Paragraph (B)(2) places no restrictions upon the ability of a judge to accept gifts or other things of value from friends or relatives under these circumstances, and does not require public reporting.

Similarly, the receipt of ordinary social hospitality, commensurate with the occasion, is not likely to undermine the integrity of the judiciary. However, the receipt of other gifts and things of value, not listed in Rule 3.13(B), presents the greatest risk. Under Rule 3.13(C), a judge may accept and report other gifts and things of value only after careful scrutiny in light of Rule 3.13(A). Where the donor is an attorney or party who has or is likely to come before the judge, the exchange will be appropriate only in the rarest of circumstances, and only after the judge has determined under Rule 3.13(A) that the receipt would not appear to a reasonable person to undermine the judge's integrity, impartiality, or

independence, and only if reported pursuant to Rule 3.15. For example, if a substantial period of time has elapsed since the judge presided over a case involving the donor and, in the interim, there has occurred a significant change of personal circumstances between the two, the judges may be permitted to accept the gift or loan or other thing of value, subject to the reporting requirements.

[3] Businesses and financial institutions frequently make available special pricing, discounts, and other benefits, either in connection with a temporary promotion or for preferred customers, based upon longevity of the relationship, volume of business transacted, and other factors. A judge may freely accept such benefits if they are available to the general public, or if the judge qualifies for the special price or discount according to the same criteria as are applied to persons who are not judges. As an example, loans provided at generally prevailing interest rates are not gifts, but a judge could not accept a loan from a financial institution at below-market interest rates unless the same rate was being made available to the general public for a certain period of time or only to borrowers with specified qualifications that the judge also possesses.

[4] Rule 3.13 applies only to acceptance of gifts or other things of value by a judge. Nonetheless, if a gift or other benefit is given to the judge's spouse, domestic partner, or member of the judge's family residing in the judge's household, it may be viewed as an attempt to evade Rule 3.13 and influence the judge indirectly. Where the gift or benefit is being made primarily to such other persons, and the judge is merely an incidental beneficiary, this concern is reduced. A judge should, however, remind family and household members of the restrictions imposed upon judges, and urge them to take these restrictions into account when making decisions about accepting such gifts or benefits.

[5] Rule 3.13 does not apply to contributions to a judge's campaign for judicial office. Such contributions are governed by Rule 4.4.

RULE 3.14 : *Reimbursement of Expenses and Waivers of Fees or Charges*

(A) Unless otherwise prohibited by Rules 3.1 and 3.13(A) or other law,* a judge may accept reimbursement of necessary and reasonable expenses for travel, food, lodging, or other incidental expenses, or a waiver or partial waiver of fees or charges for registration, tuition, and similar items, from sources other than the judge's employing entity, if the expenses or charges are associated with the judge's participation in extrajudicial activities permitted by this Code.

(B) Reimbursement of expenses for necessary travel, food, lodging, or other incidental expenses shall be limited to the actual costs reasonably incurred by the judge and, when appropriate to the occasion, by the judge's spouse, domestic partner,* or guest.

(C) A judge who accepts reimbursement of expenses or waivers or partial waivers of fees or charges on behalf of the judge or the judge's spouse, domestic partner, or guest shall publicly report such acceptance as required by Rule 3.15.

Comment

[1] Educational, civic, religious, fraternal, and charitable organizations often sponsor meetings, seminars, symposia, dinners, awards ceremonies, and similar events. Judges are encouraged to attend educational programs, as both teachers and participants, in law-related and academic disciplines, in furtherance of their duty to remain competent in the law. Participation in a variety of other extrajudicial activity is also permitted and encouraged by this Code.

[2] Not infrequently, sponsoring organizations invite certain judges to attend seminars or other events on a fee-waived or partial-fee-waived basis, and sometimes include reimbursement for necessary travel, food, lodging, or other incidental expenses. A judge's decision whether to accept reimbursement of expenses or a waiver or partial waiver of fees or charges in connection with these or other extrajudicial activities must be based upon an assessment of all the circumstances. The judge must undertake a reasonable inquiry to obtain the information necessary to make an informed judgment about whether acceptance would be consistent with the requirements of this Code.

[3] A judge must assure himself or herself that acceptance of reimbursement or fee waivers would not appear to a reasonable person to undermine the judge's independence, integrity, or impartiality. The factors that a judge should consider when deciding whether to accept reimbursement or a fee waiver for attendance at a particular activity include:

(a) whether the sponsor is an accredited educational institution or bar association rather than a trade association or a for-profit entity;

(b) whether the funding comes largely from numerous contributors rather than from a single entity and is earmarked for programs with specific content;

(c) whether the content is related or unrelated to the subject matter of litigation pending or impending before the judge, or to matters that are likely to come before the judge;

(d) whether the activity is primarily educational rather than recreational, and whether the costs of the event are reasonable and comparable to those associated with similar events sponsored by the judiciary, bar associations, or similar groups;

(e) whether information concerning the activity and its funding sources is available upon inquiry;

(f) whether the sponsor or source of funding generally associated with particular parties or interests currently appearing or likely to appear in the judge's court, thus possibly requiring disqualification of the judge under Rule 2.11;

(g) whether differing viewpoints are presented; and

(h) whether a broad range of judicial and nonjudicial participants are invited, whether a large number of participants are invited, and whether the program is designed specifically for judges.

[4] Rule 3.14(C) does not require judges to report expenses paid by governmental entities, colleges and universities, or the following local, state, and national judicial and bar organizations or their subdivisions: Indiana Judges Association, Indiana State Bar Association, National Association of Women Judges, Indiana Continuing Legal Education Forum, American Bar Association, National Bar Association, National Center for State Courts, Conference of Chief Justices, National Conference of Bar Examiners, Seventh Circuit Bar Association, any Indiana city or county local bar association, or any other organization designated by the Indiana Supreme Court as an exempted source of reimbursement.

RULE 3.15 : *Financial Reporting Requirements*

(A) A judge shall publicly report the amount or value of:

(1) compensation received for extrajudicial activities whether or not permitted by Rule 3.12;

(2) gifts and other things of value as permitted by Rule 3.13(C), unless the value of such items, alone or in the aggregate with other items received from the same source in the same calendar year, does not exceed $150.00; and

(3) reimbursement of expenses and waiver of fees or charges permitted by Rule 3.14(A), unless the amount of reimbursement or waiver, alone or in the aggregate with other reimbursements or waivers received from the same source in the same calendar year, does not exceed $150.00.

(B) When public reporting is required by paragraph (A), a judge shall report the date, place, and nature of the activity for which the judge received any compensation; the description of any gift, loan, bequest, benefit, or other thing of value accepted; and the source of reimbursement of expenses or waiver or partial waiver of fees or charges.

(C) The public report required by paragraph (A) shall be made annually on the Statement of Economic Interests.

Comment

[1] Compensation from the performance of marriage ceremonies or from a prior law practice may be reported in lump sums and need not include the identities of individual payors or clients.

Adopted effective March 1, 1993; amended Jan. 14, 2002, effective April 1, 2002; amended effective January 1, 2009.

CANON 4. A Judge or Candidate for Judicial Office Shall Not Engage in Political or Campaign Activity That is Inconsistent with the Independence, Integrity, or Impartiality of the Judiciary

RULE 4.1 : *Political and Campaign Activities of Judges and Judicial Candidates in General*

(A) Except as permitted by law,* or by Rules 4.1(B), 4.1(C), 4.2, 4.3, and 4.4, a judge or a judicial candidate* shall not:

(1) act as a leader in or hold an office in a political organization;*

(2) make speeches on behalf of a political organization;

(3) publicly endorse or oppose a candidate for any public office;

(4) solicit funds for, pay an assessment to, or make a contribution* to a political organization or a candidate for public office;

(5) attend or purchase tickets for dinners or other events sponsored by a political organization or a candidate for public office;

(6) publicly identify himself or herself as a member or candidate of a political organization;

(7) seek, accept, or use endorsements from a political organization;

(8) personally solicit* or accept campaign contributions other than through a campaign committee authorized by Rule 4.4;

(9) use or permit the use of campaign contributions for the private benefit of the judge, the candidate, or others;

(10) use court staff, facilities, or other court resources in a campaign for judicial office or for any political purpose;

(11) knowingly,* or with reckless disregard for the truth, make any false or misleading statement;

(12) make any statement that would reasonably be expected to affect the outcome or impair the fairness of a matter pending* or impending* in any court; or

(13) in connection with cases, controversies, or issues that are likely to come before the court, make pledges, promises, or commitments that are inconsistent with the impartial* performance of the adjudicative duties of judicial office.

(B) A judge or judicial candidate shall take reasonable measures to ensure that other persons do not undertake, on behalf of the judge or judicial candidate, any activities prohibited under paragraph (A).

(C) A judge in an office filled by partisan election, a judicial candidate seeking that office, and a judicial officer serving for a judge in office filled by partisan election may at any time:

(1) identify himself or herself as a member of a political party;

(2) voluntarily contribute to and attend meetings of political organizations; and

(3) attend dinners and other events sponsored by political organizations and may purchase a ticket for such an event and a ticket for a guest.

(D) A judge in an office filled by nonpartisan election other than a retention election, a judicial candidate seeking that office, and a judicial officer serving for a judge in an office filled by nonpartisan election may at any time attend dinners and other events sponsored by political organizations and may purchase a ticket for such an event and a ticket for a guest.

Comment

GENERAL CONSIDERATIONS

[1] Even when subject to public election, a judge plays a role different from that of a legislator or executive branch official. Rather than making decisions based upon the expressed views or preferences of the electorate, a judge makes decisions based upon the law and the facts of every case. Public confidence in the independence and impartiality of the judiciary is eroded if judges or judicial candidates are perceived to be subject to political influence. In furtherance of this interest, judges and judicial candidates must, to the greatest extent possible, be free, and appear to be free, from political influence and partisan interests. Therefore, this Canon permits only narrowly-tailored exceptions to the prohibitions against political activities of judges and judicial candidates, taking into account the different methods of judicial selection and the role of the electorate in selecting and retaining its judiciary.

[2] When a person becomes a judicial candidate, this Canon becomes applicable to his or her conduct.

PARTICIPATION IN POLITICAL ACTIVITIES

[3] Public confidence in the independence and impartiality of the judiciary is eroded if judges or judicial candidates are perceived to be subject to political influence. Although judges and judicial candidates may register to vote as members of a political party, they are prohibited by paragraph (A)(1) from assuming leadership roles in political organizations.

[4] Paragraphs (A)(2) and (A)(3) prohibit judges and judicial candidates from making speeches on behalf of political organizations or, except as permitted by Rule 4.2, from publicly endorsing or opposing candidates for public office to prevent them from abusing the prestige of judicial office to advance the interests of others. See Rule 1.3. These Rules do not prohibit candidates from campaigning on their own behalf.

[5] Family members of judges and judicial candidates are not bound by the Code of Judicial Conduct, and are free to engage in their own political activities, including running for public office. Nonetheless, a judge or judicial candidate must not be publicly associated with a family member's political activity or campaign for public office except that a judge may, as a family member, accompany a member of the judge's family* at events related directly and solely to that person's candidacy for public office. To avoid public misunderstanding, judges and judicial candidates should take, and should urge members of their families to take, reasonable steps to avoid any implication that the prestige of judicial office is being used to support any family member's candidacy or other political activity.

[6] Judges and judicial candidates retain the right to participate in the political process as voters in both primary and general elections.

[7] Full-time and continuing part-time judicial officers who are employed by or appointed to serve on behalf of an elected or appointed judge are bound by Rule 4.1 and, therefore, may not endorse or contribute to candidates for public office. However, as a limited exception to the restrictions in Rule 4.1, a judicial officer who serves for or is employed by a judge who is a candidate for judicial office publicly may endorse that judicial candidate by attending the candidate's fundraisers and purchasing a ticket for such an event and a ticket for a guest.

[8] Generally, taking part in ceremonies and similar public events with other public officials, such as riding in parades or participating in public inaugural activities, does not constitute political conduct.

STATEMENTS AND COMMENTS MADE DURING A CAMPAIGN FOR JUDICIAL OFFICE

[9] Judicial candidates must be scrupulously fair and accurate in all statements made by them and by their campaign committees. Paragraph (A)(11) obligates candidates and their committees to refrain from making statements that are false or misleading, or that omit facts necessary to make the communication considered as a whole not materially misleading.

[10] Judicial candidates are sometimes the subject of false, misleading, or unfair allegations made by opposing candidates, third parties, or the media. For example, false or misleading statements might be made regarding the identity, present position, experience, qualifications, or judicial rulings of a candidate. In other situations, false or misleading allegations may be made that bear upon a candidate's integrity or fitness for judicial office. As long as the candidate does not violate paragraphs (A)(11), (A)(12), or (A)(13), the candidate may make a factually accurate public response. In addition, when an independent third party has made unwarranted attacks on a candidate's opponent, the candidate may disavow the attacks, and request the third party to cease and desist.

[11] Subject to paragraph (A)(12), a judicial candidate is permitted to respond directly to false, misleading, or unfair allegations made against him or her during a campaign, although it is preferable for someone else to respond if the allegations relate to a pending case.

[12] Paragraph (A)(12) prohibits judicial candidates from making comments that might impair the fairness of pending or impending judicial proceedings. This provision does not restrict arguments or statements to the court or jury by a lawyer who is a judicial candidate, or rulings, statements, or instructions by a judge that may appropriately affect the outcome of a matter.

PLEDGES, PROMISES, OR COMMITMENTS INCONSISTENT WITH IMPARTIAL PERFORMANCE OF THE ADJUDICATIVE DUTIES OF JUDICIAL OFFICE

[13] The role of a judge is different from that of a legislator or executive branch official, even when the judge is subject to public election. Campaigns for judicial office must be conducted differently from campaigns for other offices. The narrowly drafted restrictions upon political and campaign activities of judicial candidates provided in Canon 4 allow candidates to conduct campaigns that provide voters with sufficient information to permit them to distinguish between candidates and make informed electoral choices.

[14] Paragraph (A)(13) makes applicable to both judges and judicial candidates the prohibition that applies to judges in Rule 2.10(B), relating to pledges, promises, or commitments that are inconsistent with the impartial performance of the adjudicative duties of judicial office.

[15] The making of a pledge, promise, or commitment is not dependent upon, or limited to, the use of any specific words or phrases; instead, the totality of the statement must be examined to determine if a reasonable person would believe that the candidate for judicial office has specifically undertaken to reach a particular result. Pledges, promises, or commitments must be contrasted with statements or announcements of personal views on legal, political, or other issues, which are not prohibited. When making such statements, a judge should acknowledge the overarching judicial obligation to apply and uphold the law, without regard to his or her personal views.

[16] A judicial candidate may make campaign promises related to judicial organization, administration, and court management, such as a promise to dispose of a backlog of cases, start court sessions on time, or avoid favoritism in appointments and hiring. A candidate may also pledge to take action outside the courtroom, such as working toward an improved jury selection system, or advocating for more funds to improve the physical plant and amenities of the courthouse.

[17] Judicial candidates may receive questionnaires or requests for interviews from the media and from issue advocacy or other community organizations that seek to learn their views on disputed or controversial legal or political issues. Paragraph (A)(13) does not specifically address judicial responses to such inquiries. Depending upon the wording and format of such questionnaires, candidates' responses might be viewed as pledges, promises, or commitments to perform the adjudicative duties of office other than in an impartial way. To avoid violating paragraph (A)(13), therefore, candidates who respond to media and other inquiries should also give assurances that they will keep an open mind and will carry out their adjudicative duties faithfully and impartially if elected. Candidates who do not respond may state their reasons for not responding, such as the danger that answering might be perceived by a reasonable person as undermining a successful candidate's independence or impartiality, or that it might lead to frequent disqualification. See Rule 2.11.

RULE 4.2 : *Political and Campaign Activities of Judicial Candidates in Public Elections*

(A) A judicial candidate* in a partisan, nonpartisan, or retention public election* shall:

(1) act at all times in a manner consistent with the independence,* integrity,* and impartiality* of the judiciary;

(2) comply with all applicable election, election campaign, and election campaign fund-raising laws and regulations;

(3) review and approve the content of all campaign statements and materials produced by the candidate or his or her campaign committee, as authorized by Rule 4.4, before their dissemination;

(4) take reasonable measures to ensure that other persons do not undertake on behalf of the candidate activities, other than those described in Rule 4.4, that the candidate is prohibited from doing by Rule 4.1; and

(5) notify the Indiana Commission on Judicial Qualifications in writing, within one week after becoming a candidate, of the office sought and of the candidate's address and telephone number.

(B) A candidate for partisan elective judicial office may, in addition to those activities permitted at any time under Rule 4.1(C) and unless prohibited by law,* and not earlier than one (1) year before the primary or general election in which the candidate is running:

(1) establish a campaign committee and accept campaign contributions pursuant to the provisions of Rule 4.4;

(2) speak on behalf of his or her candidacy through any medium, including but not limited to advertisements, websites, or other campaign literature;

(3) publicly endorse and contribute to candidates for election to public office running in the same election cycle;

(4) attend dinners, fundraisers, or other events for candidates for public office running in the same election cycle and purchase a ticket for such an event and a ticket for a guest;

(5) seek, accept, or use endorsements from any person or organization, including a political organization; and

(6) identify himself or herself as a candidate of a political organization.

(C) A candidate for nonpartisan elective judicial office may, in addition to those activities permitted at any time under Rule 4.1(D) and unless prohibited by law, and not earlier than one (1) year before the primary or general election in which the candidate is running:

(1) establish a campaign committee and accept campaign contributions pursuant to the provisions of Rule 4.4;

(2) speak on behalf of his or her candidacy through any medium, including but not limited to advertisements, websites, or other campaign literature;

(3) publicly endorse, contribute to, and attend functions for other candidates running for the same judicial office for which he or she is running; and

(4) seek, accept, and use endorsements from any appropriate person or organization other than a political organization.

(D) A candidate for retention to judicial office whose candidacy has drawn active opposition may campaign in response and may:

(1) establish a campaign committee and accept campaign contributions pursuant to the provisions of Rule 4.4;

(2) speak on behalf of his or her candidacy through any medium, including but not limited to advertisements, websites, or other campaign literature; and

(3) seek, accept, and use endorsements from any appropriate person or organization other than a political organization.

Comment

[1] Paragraphs (B), (C), and (D) permit judicial candidates in public elections to engage in some political or campaign activities otherwise prohibited by Rule 4.1. Candidates in partisan and nonpartisan elections may not engage in these activities earlier than one year before the first applicable electoral event. Candidates for retention to judicial office may engage in certain campaign activities only if their retention actively is opposed.

[2] Despite paragraphs (B) and (C), and (D), judicial candidates for public election remain subject to many of the provisions of Rule 4.1. For example, a candidate continues to be prohibited from soliciting funds for a political organization, knowingly making false or misleading statements during a campaign, or making certain promises, pledges, or commitments related to future adjudicative duties. See Rule 4.1(A), paragraphs (4), (11), and (13).

[3] In partisan public elections for judicial office, a candidate may be nominated by, affiliated with, or otherwise publicly identified as a candidate of a political organization.

[4] In nonpartisan public elections or retention elections, candidates are prohibited from seeking, accepting, or using nominations or endorsements from partisan political organizations.

[5] Judicial candidates in partisan and nonpartisan elections are permitted to attend dinners and other events sponsored by political organizations and may purchase a ticket for such an event and a ticket for a guest.

[6] For purposes of paragraph (C)(3), nonpartisan candidates are considered to be running for the same judicial office if several judgeships on the same court are to be filled as a result of the election. In endorsing another candidate for a position on the same court, a judicial candidate must abide by the same rules governing campaign conduct and speech as apply to the candidate's own campaign.

[7] Although judicial candidates in nonpartisan public elections are prohibited from running on a ticket or slate associated with a political organization, they may group themselves into slates or other alliances to conduct their campaigns more effectively. Candidates who have grouped themselves together are considered to be running for the same judicial office if they satisfy the conditions described in Comment [6].

RULE 4.3 : *Activities of Candidates for Appointive Judicial Office*

A candidate for appointment to judicial office may:

(A) communicate with the appointing or confirming authority, including any selection, screening, or nominating commission or similar agency;

(B) seek endorsements for the appointment from any person or organization other than a partisan political organization; and

(C) otherwise engage only in those political activities permissible at any time under Rule 4.1 for judges holding the type of judicial office sought.

Comment

[1] When seeking support or endorsement, or when communicating directly with an appointing or confirming authority, a candidate for appointive judicial office must not make any pledges, promises, or commitments that are inconsistent with the impartial performance of the adjudicative duties of the office. See Rule 4.1(A)(13).

[2] Candidates for appointive judicial office may arrange for letters of recommendation to nominating commissions or the Governor in support of their candidacies from friends, relatives, colleagues, and other members of the candidate's community, including lawyers. However, a judicial candidate, particularly a judge seeking another judicial appointment, must be cautious about from whom and how these letters are obtained, and must not misuse the court's power.

[3] This Rule does not apply to a candidate for appointment to a judicial office subject to partisan or nonpartisan election.

RULE 4.4 : *Campaign Committees*

(A) A judicial candidate* subject to partisan or nonpartisan election*, and a candidate for retention who has met active opposition, may establish a campaign committee to manage and conduct a campaign for the candidate, subject to the provisions of this Code. The candidate is responsible for ensuring that his or her campaign committee complies with applicable provisions of this Code and other applicable law.*

(B) A judicial candidate shall direct his or her campaign committee:

(1) to solicit and accept only such campaign contributions* as are reasonable;

(2) not to solicit or accept contributions for a candidate's current campaign more than one (1) year before the applicable primary election, caucus, or general or retention election, nor more than

ninety (90) days after the last election in which the candidate participated; and

(3) to comply with all applicable statutory requirements for disclosure and divestiture of campaign contributions.

Comment

[1] Judicial candidates are prohibited from personally soliciting campaign contributions or personally accepting campaign contributions. See Rule 4.1(A)(8). This Rule recognizes that in many jurisdictions, judicial candidates must raise campaign funds to support their candidacies, and permits candidates, other than candidates for appointive judicial office or candidates for retention who have not met active opposition, to establish campaign committees to solicit and accept reasonable financial contributions or in-kind contributions.

[2] Campaign committees may solicit and accept campaign contributions, manage the expenditure of campaign funds, and generally conduct campaigns. Candidates are responsible for compliance with the requirements of election law and other applicable law, and for the activities of their campaign committees.

[3] At the start of a campaign, the candidate must instruct the campaign committee to solicit or accept only such contributions as are reasonable in amount, appropriate under the circumstances, and in conformity with applicable law. Although lawyers and others who might appear before a successful candidate for judicial office are permitted to make campaign contributions, the candidate should instruct his or her campaign committee to be especially cautious in connection with such contributions, so they do not create grounds for disqualification if the candidate is elected to judicial office. See Rule 2.11.

RULE 4.5 : *Activities of Judges Who Become Candidates for Nonjudicial Office*

(A) Upon becoming a candidate for a nonjudicial elective office, a judge shall resign from judicial office, unless permitted by law* to continue to hold judicial office.

(B) Upon becoming a candidate for a nonjudicial appointive office, a judge is not required to resign from judicial office, provided that the judge complies with the other provisions of this Code.

Comment

[1] In campaigns for nonjudicial elective public office, candidates may make pledges, promises, or commitments related to positions they would take and ways they would act if elected to office. Although appropriate in nonjudicial campaigns, this manner of campaigning is inconsistent with the role of a judge, who must remain fair and impartial to all who come before him or her. The potential for misuse of the judicial office, and the political promises that the judge would be compelled to make in the course of campaigning for nonjudicial elective office, together dictate that a judge who wishes to run for such an office must resign upon becoming a candidate.

[2] The "resign to run" rule set forth in paragraph (A) ensures that a judge cannot use the judicial office to promote his or her candidacy, and prevents post-campaign retaliation from the judge in the event the judge is defeated in the election. When a judge is seeking appointive nonjudicial office, however, the dangers are not sufficient to warrant imposing the "resign to run" rule.

[3] For purposes of this Rule, the office of Prosecuting Attorney is a nonjudicial office.

RULE 4.6 : *Political Activities of Nonjudicial Court Employees*

(A) An appointed judge in an office filled by retention election must require nonjudicial court employees to abide by the same standards of political conduct which bind the judge.

(B) A judge in an office filled by partisan or nonpartisan election must not permit nonjudicial court employees to run for or hold nonjudicial partisan elective office or to hold office in a political party's central committee.

Comment

[1] Limitations on political activities by court employees are necessary to protect the public's confidence in the independence and impartiality of the judicial system.

[2] Unlike appointed judges subject to retention, judges in partisan and nonpartisan elective office are not required to hold their employees to the same limitations on political conduct which apply to the judges.

[3] The standards for employees of retention judges set out in Rule 4.6(A) are those which apply to the judges when they are not running in an election.

[4] Unlike nonjudicial court employees, court employees who perform judicial functions are bound directly by the Code of Judicial Conduct unless exempted under the Application Section.

Adopted effective March 1, 1993. Amended Jan. 14, 2002, effective April 1, 2002; July 1, 2005, effective Jan. 1, 2006; amended effective May 3, 2006; Jan. 1, 2009; amended Sept. 21, 2010, effective Jan. 1, 2011.

CANONS 6, 7. [Vacated effective March 1, 1993]

INTERPRETER CODE OF CONDUCT AND PROCEDURE

Adopted Effective September 24, 2008

Including Amendments Received Through November 1, 2013

Rule

Rule I. Preamble

Many persons who come before the courts are partially or completely excluded from full participation in the proceedings due to limited English proficiency. It is essential that the resulting communication barrier be removed, as far as possible, so that these persons are placed in the same position as similarly situated persons for whom there is no such barrier.

As officers of the court, interpreters help ensure that non-English speakers may enjoy equal access to justice and that court proceedings and court support services function efficiently and effectively. Interpreters are highly skilled professionals who fulfill an essential role in the administration of justice.

However, the opportunity for any specific interpreter to provide services to the Indiana courts is at the Indiana Supreme Court's complete and continuing discretion because of the critical reliance the trial courts must have on the skills, performance, and integrity of the interpreter in performing duties for the courts. This Code sets forth the minimum standard of conduct the Indiana Supreme Court expects from any interpreter providing services for Indiana courts, but it is not intended to be a vehicle for complaints about interpreting errors made by interpreters during the course of a proceeding, unless there is an allegation of gross incompetence or knowing misinterpretation or misrepresentation. In those circumstances, complaints should be made pursuant to the procedures outlined in the Indiana Supreme Court Disciplinary Process for Certified Court Interpreters and Candidates for Interpreter Certification.

1. Purpose.

These Standards seek to:

a) Ensure meaningful access to all trial courts and court services for non-English speakers;

b) Protect the constitutional rights of criminal defendants to the assistance of court interpreters during court proceedings;

c) Ensure due process in all phases of litigation for non-English speakers;

d) Ensure equal protection of the law for non-English speakers;

e) Increase efficiency, quality, and uniformity in handling proceedings which involve a court interpreter;

f) Encourage the broadest use of professional language interpreters by all those in need of such services within the trial courts.

2. Scope.

a) These Standards define and govern the practice of court interpretation in Indiana trial courts.

3. Applicability.

a) This Code shall guide and be binding upon all persons, agencies and organizations who administer, supervise, use, or deliver spoken foreign language interpreting services to the judicial system.

b) Violations of this Code may result in the interpreter being removed from a case, denied future appointments by the courts or losing credentials if the interpreter has been certified pursuant to the rules of the Indiana Supreme Court.

c) The Standards and any subparts are mandatory requirements for those who are bound by this Code. The commentary is not mandatory and exists to provide guidance in interpreting the Code.

d) These Standards apply to court interpreters appearing:

1) In any proceeding before any trial court of the state;

2) Before any attorney, court, or agency in connection with any matter that is, or may be, brought before a court;

3) In any other activity ordered by the court or conducted under the supervision of a court.

Adopted effective September 24, 2008.

Rule II. Definitions

For the purposes of this Code, the following words shall have the following meaning:

Interpretation

The unrehearsed transmission of the spoken word or message from one language to another.

Translation

The conversion of a written text from one language into written text in another language.

Sight Translation

The reading of written text of one language, translated orally into another language.

Simultaneous Interpretation

The rendering of an interpretation for a party at the same time someone is speaking, usually heard only by the person receiving the interpretation; this form of interpretation may be accomplished using equipment specially designed for the purpose.

Consecutive Interpretation

Relaying a message from one language into another in a sequential manner after the speaker has completed a thought. The speaker may pause at regular intervals to facilitate the conveyance of his or her statements through the interpreter.

Certified Interpreter

An interpreter who has been duly trained and certified under the direction of the Indiana Supreme Court Division of State Court Administration.

Interpreter

One who is readily able to interpret spoken language, sign language, or written language.

Non-English Speaker

A person who uses only, or primarily, a spoken or signed language other than English.

Cultural Fluency

Awareness and full comprehension of cross-cultural factors including but not limited to expectations, attitudes, values, roles, institutions, and linguistic differences and similarities.

Summarize

Make a summary of the chief points or thoughts of the speaker; *e.g.*, summary interpretation, a non-verbatim account of the statements made by the speaker.

Consortium

The Consortium for State Court Interpreter Certification, operated by the National Center for State Courts, is an organization responsible for facilitating court interpretation test development and administration standards, providing testing materials, developing educational programs and standards, and facilitating communication among member states and entities in order for individual member states and entities to have the necessary tools and guidance to implement certification programs.

Adopted effective September 24, 2008.

Rule III. Standards

1. Representation of Qualifications.

a) Interpreters shall accurately and completely represent their certifications, training and pertinent experience.

Commentary 1. Acceptance of a case by an interpreter is a representation to the court of linguistic competency in legal settings. Withdrawing or being asked to withdraw from a case after it begins causes a disruption of court proceedings and is wasteful of scarce public resources. It is therefore essential that interpreters present a complete and truthful account of their training, certification and experience prior to appointment so the officers of the court can fairly evaluate their qualifications for delivering interpreting services.

Commentary 2. Interpreters should know and observe the established protocol, rules, and procedures for delivering interpreting services. When interpreting testimony or making comments to be included in the record, interpreters should speak at a rate and volume that enable them to be heard and understood throughout the courtroom, but the interpreter's presence should otherwise be as unobtrusive as possible. Interpreters should work without drawing undue or inappropriate attention to themselves. Interpreters should dress in a manner that is consistent with the dignity of the proceedings of the court. Interpreters should avoid obstructing the view of any of the individuals involved in the proceedings. Interpreters are encouraged to avoid personal or professional conduct that could discredit the court.

2. Accuracy.

a) Each court interpreter shall faithfully and accurately interpret what is said without embellishment or omission while preserving the language level of the speaker to the best of said interpreter's skill and ability.

b) Each court interpreter shall provide the most accurate form of a word in spite of a possible vulgar meaning. Colloquial, slang, obscene or crude language as well as sophisticated and scholarly language shall be conveyed in accordance with the usage of the speaker. An interpreter is not to tone down, improve, or edit any statements.

c) A court interpreter shall speak in a clear, firm, and well-modulated voice that conveys the inflections, tone, and emotions of the speaker.

d) A court interpreter shall not simplify statements for a non-English speaker even when the interpreter believes the non-English speaker cannot understand the speaker's language level. The non-English speaker may request an explanation or simplification, if necessary, from the court or counsel through the interpreter.

Commentary 1. Interpreters are obligated to apply their best skills and judgment to preserve faithfully the meaning of what is said in court, including the style or register of speech. Verbatim, "word for word," or literal oral interpretations are not appropriate when they distort the meaning of the source language, but every spoken statement, even if it appears nonresponsive, obscene, rambling, or incoherent should be interpreted. This includes apparent misstatements.

Commentary 2. Interpreters should never interject their own words, phrases, or expressions. If the need arises to explain an interpreting problem (*e.g.*, a term or phrase with no direct equivalent in the target language or a misunderstanding that only the interpreter can clarify), the interpreter should ask the court's permission to provide an explanation. Interpreters should convey the emotional emphasis of the speaker without re-enacting or mimicking the speaker's emotions or dramatic gestures.

3. Impartiality.

a) Each court interpreter shall maintain an impartial attitude at all times and avoid unnecessary discussions with counsel, parties, witnesses, and interested parties, either inside or outside the courtroom, to avoid any appearance of partiality.

4. Confidentiality.

a) Each court interpreter shall guard confidential information and not betray the confidences which may have been entrusted to him or her by any parties concerned.

b) Disclosures made out of court by communication of a non-English speaker through an interpreter to another person shall be privileged communication and said interpreter shall not disclose such communication without permission of said non-English speaker; provided, however, that such non-English speaker had a reasonable expectation or intent that such communication would not be so disclosed.

Commentary 1. The interpreter must protect and uphold the confidentiality of all privileged information obtained during the course of his/her duties. It is especially important that the interpreter understands and upholds the attorney-client privilege, which requires confidentiality with respect to any communication between attorney and client. It is equally important for the interpreter to be aware that when the attorney is not present, there is no attorney-client privilege and the interpreter may be held to divulge any information gained. The interpreter, therefore, must avoid that situation. This rule also applies to other types of privileged communications such as spousal privilege, clergymen-parishioner privilege, and doctor-patient privilege.

Commentary 2. Interpreters must also refrain from repeating or disclosing information obtained by them in the course of their employment that may be relevant to the legal proceeding.

Commentary 3. In the event that an interpreter becomes aware of information that suggests the threat of imminent harm to someone or relates to a crime being committed during the course of the proceedings, the interpreter should immediately disclose the information to an appropriate authority within the judicial system and seek advice in regard to the potential conflict in professional responsibility.

5. Proficiency.

a) Each court interpreter shall provide professional services only in matters or areas in which the interpreter can perform accurately.

b) Each court interpreter shall continuously improve language skills and cultural fluency and increase knowledge of the various areas within the judiciary which may be encountered in court interpretation. An interpreter should attend workshops, seminars, conferences, or courses to keep current in the changes of the law as well as interpretation and translation theories and techniques, to receive updates to existing glossaries of technical terms, and to exchange information with colleagues.

c) A court interpreter is responsible for having the proper legal and bilingual dictionaries readily available for consultation.

d) A court interpreter shall withdraw from any case in which his/her performance will be adversely affected due to lack of proficiency, preparation or difficulty in understanding the speaker for any reason, including insurmountable linguistic and/or cultural differences or complexity of conceptual or technical terms to be used in the proceedings. Such withdrawal may be made at the time of the pre-appearance interview with the non-English speaker or at any other appropriate time.

6. Demeanor.

a) Each court interpreter shall maintain a low profile, speak at audible volumes appropriate to the context, and be as unobtrusive as possible. The positioning in the courtroom and the style of work shall contribute to maintaining a natural atmosphere as there would be if no language barrier existed.

b) The court interpreter shall be positioned in full view of the person testifying or specially situated to ensure proper communication but shall not obstruct the view of the judge, jury or counsel. The interpreter shall always be positioned so that the non-English speaker can hear or see everything the court interpreter says or signs and so that the interpreter can hear or see everything that is said or signed during the proceedings.

c) The court interpreter shall be familiar with the courtroom layout, particularly the location of the microphones for the electronic recording of the proceedings.

d) Each court interpreter shall appear on time and report immediately upon arrival to the clerk of the court.

7. Case Preparation.

a) Each court interpreter shall prepare for the case, whenever possible, and particularly with respect to lengthy and complex criminal and civil trials, by reviewing the case material including the charges, police or other reports, complaints or indictments, transcripts of interviews, motions, or any other documentation to be used in the case. The court interpreter especially should review these items if counsel plans to quote directly from them. Requests for case material shall be made to the attorney processing the case with the awareness and consent of both parties. The information is to be used solely for the technical preparation of the court interpreter.

b) Counsel and/or the court shall interview the non-English speaker prior to the initial court appearance in order to instruct the speaker as to the proper role of the court interpreter during the proceeding.

c) The non-English speaker will be instructed by the court interpreter as follows:

1) The non-English speaker will be advised that the court interpreter will interpret any statements or comments at all times.

2) The non-English speaker shall be instructed not to ask direct questions of the court interpreter or initiate any independent dialogue with the interpreter, including legal advice or explanations of any statement made during the proceedings. The non-English speaker shall be instructed to direct all questions to counsel or court when necessary.

3) The court interpreter shall familiarize himself/herself with the speech pattern or sign language communication, cultural background, and native language level of proficiency of the non-English speaker.

4) The court interpreter shall familiarize the non-English speaker with the interpretation mode to be used and with the hand technique used in interpretation for segmenting lengthy testimony.

5) The non-English speaker shall be instructed to wait for the full interpretation of the English before responding to a question.

6) The non-English speaker shall be instructed not to maintain eye contact with the interpreter except in the case where the non-English speaker is deaf. Eye contact is crucial in this case.

8. Oath or Affirmation.

a) All interpreters, before commencing their duties, shall take an oath that they will make a true and impartial interpretation using their best skills and judgment in accordance with the standards and ethics of the interpreter profession. The court shall use the following oath:

Do you solemnly swear (or affirm) that you will justly, truly, and impartially interpret to ___ the oath about to be administered to him (her), and the questions which may be asked him (her), and the answers that he (she) shall give to such questions, relative to the cause now under consideration before this court so help you God (or under the pains and penalties of perjury)? Ind. Code § 34–45–1–5

b) All interpreters, before commencing their duties in any court proceeding, shall take an oath that they have reviewed and will abide by the Indiana Supreme Court Interpreter Code of Conduct and Procedure.

9. Modes of Court Interpreting.

a) The simultaneous mode of court interpretation requires the interpreter to speak contemporaneously with the speaker whose statements are being heard. This mode shall be used when a non-English speaker is in the position of a third person vis-à-vis the proceedings; *e.g.*, at counsel table.

b) The consecutive mode of court interpretation requires the interpreter to allow the speaker to complete his/her thought or statement before attempting its interpretation. This mode shall be used when a non-English speaker is giving testimony or when the judge, counsel, or officer of the court is in direct dialogue with the speaker.

c) A court interpreter shall not summarize court proceedings at any time unless instructed to do so by the court (*e.g.*, sidebar conference, jury selection, charge to the jury).

10. Modes of Address.

a) Each court interpreter shall use the first person singular when interpreting for a non-English speaker giving testimony or in dialogue with another person. Persons addressing the non-English speaker (*e.g.*, attorneys, judges, probation officers, and clerks) shall use the second person.

b) A court interpreter shall address the court and identify himself/herself as the interpreter using the third person singular to protect the record from confusion (*e.g.*, the interpreter requests a break).

11. Language and/or Hearing Difficulties.

a) Whenever there is a word, phrase or concept that the court interpreter does not understand, the interpreter shall so inform the court so that, at its discretion, it may order an explanation, rephrasing, or repetition of the statement. The interpreter may request time to look up an unfamiliar word in a dictionary.

b) Whenever the court or counsel uses a word, phrase, or concept which the court interpreter finds may confuse the non-English speaker, particularly when a concept has no cultural equivalent in the non-English speaker's language or when it may prove ambiguous in translation, the interpreter shall so inform the court.

c) Whenever a court interpreter has difficulty interpreting for a particular speaker or the proceeding in general due to the noise level in the courtroom, the speaker's voice level, or because there may be more than one person speaking at the same time, the court interpreter shall so inform the court so that the judge, at his/her discretion, may order the speaker to repeat the statement, raise his/her voice, modulate better. The judge, at his/her discretion, also may rectify the situation by ordering the interpreter to change positioning in the courtroom.

12. Errors.

a) Whenever a court interpreter discovers his/her own error, the interpreter shall, if still at the witness stand, correct the error at once after first identifying himself/herself for the record. If the error is perceived after testimony has been completed, the court interpreter shall request a bench or sidebar conference with judge and counsel, explain the problem, and make the correction on the record.

b) Whenever an alleged error is perceived by someone other than the court interpreter, that person should, if testimony is still being taken from the stand, bring the allegation to the attention of the court. If the error occurs in a jury trial, the allegation should not be brought to the attention of the jury. A sidebar should be requested so that the matter may be brought to the attention of the court. At that time the court will determine first whether the issue surrounding the allegedly inaccurate interpretation is substantial enough to warrant correction. If the court agrees that the error could be prejudicial, then the court shall hear evidence as to what the correct interpretation should be from information submitted by both counsel, from the court interpreter (who is already an expert witness), and from any other experts selected by the judge. The judge shall make a final determination in view of the evidence as to the correct interpretation. If the determination is different from the original interpretation, then the court shall amend the record accordingly and so instruct the jury, if necessary.

13. Difficulties While Interpreting.

a) Each court interpreter shall interpret the exact response of the witness or speaker even if the answer to a question is nonresponsive, leaving issues of admissibility of the response to the court and counsel.

b) If a witness testifying in a foreign language occasionally uses a few words in English, the court interpreter shall repeat such words for the record so that a person listening to the recorded proceeding may continue following the interpreter's voice. However, should the witness utter a full English response, the interpreter will not ask the witness to respond in his/her native language. Rather, the interpreter will stand back so that the parties are aware of the English response and await the court's direction.

c) Whenever an objection is made, the court interpreter shall interpret everything that was said up to the objection and instruct the witness by hand gesture not to speak until the court has ruled on the objection.

d) Whenever a serious communication problem arises between the interpreter and the non-English speaker (*e.g.*, person is being disruptive or does not allow the interpreter to speak), or whenever there is a need to instruct the witness as to proper usage of the interpreter by the non-English speaker, the court interpreter shall bring such matter to the immediate attention of the court or counsel so that time may be allowed to solve the problem.

e) A court interpreter shall not characterize or give gratuitous explanation of testimony. The court or counsel will request clarification from the non-English speaker through the interpreter when necessary. Except in the case of certain gestures or grimaces that may have a cultural significance, the interpreter shall not offer an explanation or repeat a speaker's gesture or grimace which has been seen.

f) A court interpreter shall not correct erroneous facts posed in questions to non-English speakers. Similarly, the interpreter shall never correct the testimony of non-English speakers, even if errors are obvious. A response of a non-English speaker shall never be inferred; *e.g.*, if the witness is asked to clarify his/her prior answer regarding direction or place, the interpreter shall pose the question as asked and not volunteer what the interpreter thought the speaker meant.

14. Fatigue Factor.

a) If a court interpreter believes that the quality of the interpretation is about to falter due to fatigue, the interpreter shall so inform the court.

b) For any proceeding that will require in excess of two hours of continuous simultaneous interpretation, two court interpreters should, when practical, be assigned so that they can relieve each other at periodic intervals and prevent fatigue and delays.

15. Availability of Court Interpreter.

a) A court interpreter shall not leave the courtroom until the proceedings are terminated or he/she is excused by the presiding judge, magistrate, or their designee. During brief recesses, an interpreter shall be available to court and counsel as necessary.

16. Conflicts of Interest.

a) A court interpreter shall not engage in nor have any interest, direct or indirect, in any business or transaction, nor incur any obligation which is in conflict with the proper discharge of official duties in the court or which impairs independence of judgment in the discharge of those duties.

b) A court interpreter shall not derive personal profit or advantage from any confidential information acquired while acting in his/her professional capacity.

c) A court interpreter shall not accept money or consideration or favors from anyone other than the court for the performance of an act the interpreter would be required or expected to perform in the regular course of assigned duties. A court interpreter also shall not accept any gifts, gratuities, or favors of any kind that might be construed as an attempt to influence the interpreter's actions with respect to the court.

d) A court interpreter shall not use, for private gain or advantage, the court's time, facilities, equipment, or supplies, nor shall the interpreter use or attempt to use his/her position to secure unwarranted privileges or exemptions for himself/herself or others.

e) A court interpreter shall not serve in any proceeding in which:

1) The interpreter, his/her spouse or child is a party to the proceeding or has a financial interest or any other interest that would be affected by the outcome of the proceeding; or

2) The interpreter is an associate, friend or relative of a party, of counsel for a party, or a witness; or

3) The interpreter has been involved in the selection of counsel; or

4) The interpreter has any other interest that would prevent him/her from being impartial.

f) Prior to providing services in a proceeding in court, a court interpreter shall disclose on the record any services that the interpreter may have previously provided on a private basis to any of the parties involved in the matter as well as anything else that could be reasonably construed as affecting his/her ability to serve impartially or as constituting a conflict of interest. This disclosure shall not include confidential information.

g) During the course of a trial, a court interpreter shall not discuss the case with parties, jurors, attorneys, or with friends or relatives of any party, except in the discharge of official functions.

Commentary 1. The interpreter acts as an officer of the court, and the interpreter's duty in a court proceeding is to serve the court and the public to which the court is a servant. This is true regardless of whether the interpreter is publicly retained at government expense or retained privately at the expense of one of the parties.

Commentary 2. During the course of the proceedings, interpreters should not converse with parties, witnesses, jurors, attorneys, or with friends or relatives of any party, except in the discharge of their official functions. It is especially important that interpreters, who are often familiar with attorneys or other members of the courtroom work group, including law enforcement officers, refrain from casual and personal conversations with anyone in court that may convey an appearance of a special relationship or partiality to any of the court participants.

Commentary 3. The interpreter should strive for professional detachment. Verbal and nonverbal displays of personal attitudes, prejudices, emotions, or opinions should be avoided at all times.

Commentary 4. An interpreter who is also an attorney should not serve in both capacities in the same matter.

Commentary 5. A court interpreter may not interpret for any bail bondsman. Not only should the prohibition stand for same case situations but also when the bail bondsman is different than the one whom the defendant is using. The knowledge that a particular person interprets for a bail bondsman may chill a defendant's capacity to alert the court to any improprieties.

Commentary 6. Court interpreters may not leave their business cards in court buildings, police stations, clerks' offices, or jails to solicit business. Indiana courts and other justice system offices are not venues for marketing services.

Commentary 7. Particular attention should be given to interpreters who have knowledge in sensitive criminal cases about codefendants and fail to keep confidentiality. Judicial officers should screen potential conflict of interest cases for relatives interpreting in those cases when conflict of interests would arise. Disqualification should ensue upon the discovery of conflicts.

Commentary 8. A court interpreter may not interpret for the court and interpret privately in the same court. Individuals pose as the "access person" for certain courts in the eyes of particular non-English-speaking communities. The potential problems are the interpreter "explaining the legal process" to unsuspecting individuals and appearing before court to "plead people."

Commentary 9. Court interpreters may not refer cases to any particular attorney.

Commentary 10. Particular attention should be given to actual conflicts of interest or the appearance of conflicts with respect to interpreters employed by law enforcement agencies or prosecutors' offices who are asked to interpret for the official court record in a criminal proceeding. Every effort should be made to ensure that the criminal defendant is aware that the interpreter is employed by a law enforcement agency or a prosecutor's office and waives any potential conflict prior to the interpreter providing interpretation for the court record.

17. Public Comments.

a) Interpreters shall not publicly discuss, report or offer an opinion concerning a matter in which they are or have been engaged professionally, even when that information is not privileged by law to be confidential.

18. Legal Advice.

a) A court interpreter shall not give any legal advice of any kind to anyone whether solicited or not. In all instances, the non-English speaker shall be referred to counsel or to the court. An interpreter may give only information to a non-English speaker regarding the time, place, and nature of the court proceedings. All other matters shall be referred to the court or counsel.

b) A court interpreter shall never act as an individual referral service for any attorney. When asked to refer a non-English speaker to an attorney, the interpreter shall refer the individual to the local bar association in civil and criminal matters if the individual indicates that he/she can afford private counsel.

19. Scope of Practice.

a) While serving in their interpreter capacity, court interpreters shall limit themselves to interpreting or translating and shall not give legal advice, express personal opinions to individuals for whom they are interpreting or engage in any other activities which may be construed to constitute a service other than interpreting or translating.

Commentary 1. Since interpreters are responsible only for enabling others to communicate, they should limit themselves to the activity of interpreting or translating only. Interpreters should refrain from initiating communications while interpreting unless it is necessary for assuring an accurate and faithful interpretation or except as set out below.

Commentary 2. Interpreters may be required to initiate communications during a proceeding when they find it necessary to seek assistance in performing their duties. Examples of these circumstances include seeking direction when unable to understand or express a word or thought, requesting speakers to moderate their rate of communication or repeat or rephrase something, correcting their own interpreting errors or notifying the court of reservations about their ability to satisfy an assignment competently. In these instances they should refer to themselves in the third person as "the interpreter," making clear on the record that they are speaking for themselves.

Commentary 3. At no time can an interpreter give legal advice, but an interpreter may interpret legal advice from an attorney to any party only while that attorney is giving it. An interpreter should not explain the purpose of forms, services, or otherwise act as a counselor or advisor unless interpreting for someone who is acting in that official capacity. An interpreter may translate the language on a form for the person who is filling out the form but may not explain the form or its purpose for the person except when interpreting in the presence of an attorney or authorized legal personnel.

Commentary 4. The interpreter should not personally serve to perform acts that are the responsibility of other court officials including but not limited to court clerks, pretrial release investigators or interviewers, or probation officers, except as required by and in the presence of these officials.

20. Compliance.

a) A court interpreter who discovers anything which would impede full compliance with this Code shall immediately report the matter to the court.

b) A court interpreter shall immediately report to the presiding judge any solicitations or efforts by another to induce or encourage the interpreter to violate any law, standard of this Code, or any other provision governing interpretation promulgated by the judiciary.

c) A court interpreter may be removed by the court from his/her participation in a particular assignment if that interpreter is unable to interpret the proceedings adequately including an instance when the interpreter self-reports such inability.

d) Should a court interpreter feel harassed or intimidated by an officer of the court, the interpreter shall so inform the presiding judge.

Commentary 1. Interpreters must continually strive to increase their knowledge of the languages in which they professionally interpret, including past and current trends in technical, vernacular, and regional terminology as well as their application within court proceedings.

Commentary 2. Interpreters should keep informed of all statutes, rules of courts and policies of the judicial system that relate to the performance of their professional duties.

Commentary 3. An interpreter should seek to elevate the standards of the profession through participation in workshops, professional meetings, interaction with colleagues, and reading current literature in the field.

21. Reporting Impediments to Performance.

a) Interpreters shall assess at all times their ability to deliver their services. When interpreters have any reservation about their ability to satisfy an assignment competently, they shall immediately convey that reservation to the appropriate judicial authority.

Commentary 1. If the communication mode or language of the non-English speaker cannot be readily interpreted, the interpreter should notify the appropriate judicial authority.

Commentary 2. Interpreters should notify the appropriate judicial authority of any environmental or physical limitation that impedes or hinders their ability to deliver interpreting services adequately (e.g., the courtroom is not quiet enough for the interpreter to hear or be heard by the non-English speaker, more than one person is speaking at a time, or principals or witnesses of the court are speaking at a rate of speed that is too rapid for the interpreter to adequately interpret). Sign language interpreters must ensure that they can both see and convey the full range of visual language elements that are necessary for communication including facial expressions and body movement as well as hand gestures.

Commentary 3. Interpreters are encouraged to make inquiries as to the nature of a case whenever possible before accepting an assignment. This enables interpreters to match more closely their professional qualifications, skills and experience to potential assignments and more accurately assess their ability to satisfy those assignments competently.

Commentary 4. Interpreters should refrain from accepting a case if they feel the language and subject matter of that case is likely to exceed their skills or capacities. Interpreters should feel no reluctance about notifying the court or presiding officer if they feel unable to perform competently due to lack of familiarity with terminology, preparation, or difficulty in understanding a witness or defendant.

Commentary 5. Interpreters should notify the court or the presiding officer of any personal bias they may have involving any aspect of the proceedings (*e.g.*, an interpreter who has been the victim of a sexual assault may wish to be excused from interpreting in cases involving similar offenses).

Commentary 6. Interpreters should notify the presiding officer of the need to take periodic breaks to maintain mental and physical alertness and prevent interpreter fatigue. Interpreters should recommend and encourage the use of team interpreting whenever necessary such as trials, complex and technical proceedings, proceedings over two hours in length and testimony lasting one hour or more (keeping in mind that the consecutive interpreting mode doubles the length of time of the testimony).

Commentary 7. Even competent and experienced interpreters may encounter cases when routine proceedings suddenly involve technical or specialized terminology unfamiliar to the interpreter (*e.g.*, the unscheduled testimony of an expert witness). When these instances occur, interpreters should request a brief recess to familiarize themselves with the subject matter. If familiarity with the terminology requires extensive time or more intensive research, interpreters should inform the presiding officer.

Commentary 8. Court personnel and parties are encouraged to provide interpreters with copies of all documents referred to in a proceeding such as witness lists, indictments, exhibit lists, criminal complaints, investigative reports, tape transcripts, telephone logs and bank records.

22. Duty to Report Ethical Violations.

a) Interpreters shall report to the proper judicial authority any effort to impede their compliance with any law, any provision of this Code or any other official policy governing court interpreting and legal translating.

Commentary 1. Because the users of interpreting services frequently misunderstand the proper role of the interpreter, they may ask or expect the interpreter to perform duties or engage in activities that run counter to the provisions of this Code or other laws, regulations or policies governing court interpreters. It is incumbent upon the interpreter to inform these persons of the interpreter's professional obligations. If, after having been apprised of these obligations, the person persists in demanding that the interpreter violate them, the interpreter should turn to a supervisory interpreter, a judge or another official with jurisdiction over interpreter matters to resolve the situation.

Adopted effective September 24, 2008.

Rule IV. Procedures

1. Determining Need for Interpretation.

a) Appointing an interpreter is a matter of judicial discretion. It is the responsibility of the court to determine whether a participant in a legal proceeding has a limited ability to understand and communicate in English.

b) An interpreter should be appointed in a ***criminal case*** when the defendant:

1) Is unable to accurately describe persons, places, and events that affect his or her defense;

2) Is unable to tell the court "what happened" over a period of time;

3) Is unable to request clarification when statements are vague or misleading, particularly during cross-examination, to defend his/her position, or otherwise to participate in his/her defense;

4) Is not on an equal footing with an English-speaking defendant with an equivalent education and background.

c) The court shall use the services of multiple interpreters when necessary to aid interpretation in court proceedings.

Commentary 1. Recognition of the need for an interpreter may arise from: a request by a party or counsel for the services of an interpreter, from the court's own *voir dire* of a party or witness, or from disclosures made to the court by parties, counsel, court employees or other persons familiar with the ability of the person to understand and communicate in English.

Commentary 2. The court may wish to consider using multiple interpreters in legal proceedings when one or more of the following situations exist: (1) For proceedings lasting longer than thirty minutes of continuous interpreting, regular breaks should be allowed every thirty minutes. A similar standard should be maintained for lengthy or continuous witness interpreting; (2) Legal proceedings lasting more than two hours—generally, in legal proceedings lasting more than two hours, a team of two interpreters should be designated to ensure the accuracy and completeness of the record by allowing interpreters to alternate work and rest in short shifts, thus avoiding fatigue; (3) Multiple defendants—one or more interpreters may be appointed (apart from the interpreter(s) who are interpreting the legal proceedings) in order to provide interpreting services for attorney-client communications during the proceeding.

Commentary 3. The interpreter's role is an exacting one, physically and mentally. There is evidence that an interpreter's performance deteriorates after thirty minutes of continuous interpreting. Studies show that the deterioration is not gradual but a steep plummeting.

Commentary 4. If team interpreting is simply impossible, the court has an obligation to provide regular breaks (every thirty minutes for ten-minute intervals). A qualified interpreter has the obligation to inform the court whenever fatigue is beginning to interfere with the accuracy of the interpretation.

2. Waiver of Interpreter.

a) A non-English speaker may at any point in the proceeding waive the services of an interpreter. The waiver of the interpreter's services must be knowing and voluntary, and with the approval of the court. Granting this waiver is a matter of judicial discretion.

1) Procedure.

i) The waiver is approved by the court after explaining in open court to the non-English speaker, through an interpreter, the nature and effect of the waiver; and

ii) The court determines in open court that the waiver has been made knowingly, intelligently, and voluntarily.

iii) If the non-English speaker is the defendant in a criminal matter, the court must further determine that the defendant has been afforded the opportunity to consult with his or her attorney.

2) At any point in any proceeding, for good cause shown, a non-English speaker may retract his/her waiver and request an interpreter.

3. Interpreter Oath.

a) All interpreters, before commencing their duties, shall take an oath that they will make a true and impartial interpretation using their best skills and judgment in accordance with the standards and ethics of the interpreter profession. *See* Section III, 8, (a).

4. Audio Recording.

a) All interpreted proceedings shall be recorded to preserve the original source and target language as well as interpretation.

Commentary 1. A proper record of the interpretation will allow for an accurate record in case of appeal. This will also allow interpreters to document their interpretation in the event of any challenges.

Adopted effective September 24, 2008.

Rule V. State Certified Court Interpreters

1. To receive Indiana Court Interpreter Certification status, the candidate shall:

a) Submit to a criminal background check. Conviction for any felony or for a misdemeanor involving dishonesty or false statement shall disqualify a candidate from certification if the conviction is ten years old or less.

b) Attend an approved orientation seminar.

c) Pass an approved criterion-referenced written examination with at least a 70% score on the multiple-choice portion and a score of "borderline" or better on the translation portion of the examination.

d) Attend an approved skills building workshop.

e) Pass all three parts of the oral exam individually with at least a 70% score in each section of the examination.

f) Complete any required application forms and pay any required fees.

2. Candidates will be granted two years from the skills building program to take and pass the oral exam. If more than two years elapse without the candidate passing the oral exam, the skills building portion must be retaken.

3. Interpreters with certification as a federal court interpreter or certified in another Consortium state shall be certified as an Indiana state court interpreter after completing any required reciprocity application, paying any required fees, and submitting to a criminal background check.

Adopted effective September 24, 2008.

DISCIPLINARY PROCESS FOR CERTIFIED COURT INTERPRETERS AND CANDIDATES FOR INTERPRETER CERTIFICATION

Adopted Effective September 24, 2008

Including Amendments Received Through November 1, 2013

Rule

Rule 1.　Purpose

This policy seeks to:

a) Assure quality interpretation within Indiana courts for non-English speakers by allowing the Division of State Court Administration to control the quality of interpreting services offered in the Indiana courts and probation departments;

b) Assist the Division of State Court Administration with quality control by allowing for discipline, up to and including revocation of certification.

Adopted effective September 24, 2008.

Rule 2.　Applicability

a) This policy applies to interpreters who are certified in foreign language interpretation by the Indiana Supreme Court.

b) This policy applies to interpreter candidates who are seeking to be certified in foreign language interpretation by the Indiana Supreme Court.

Adopted effective September 24, 2008.

Rule 3.　Possible Reasons for Discipline

Disciplinary complaints may be filed against court interpreters who have been certified or are seeking certification by the Indiana Supreme Court for the following reasons:

a) Conviction of a felony or a misdemeanor involving moral turpitude, dishonesty, or false statements;

b) Fraud, dishonesty, or corruption, whether or not related to the functions and duties of a court interpreter;

c) Continued false or deceptive advertising after receipt of notification to discontinue;

d) Knowing and willful disclosure of confidential or privileged information obtained while serving in an official capacity;

e) Gross incompetence;

f) Failing to appear as scheduled without good cause;

g) Noncompliance with any existing continuing education requirements;

h) Nonpayment of any required renewal fees; or

i) Violation of the Indiana Supreme Court Interpreter's Code of Conduct and Procedure or any other judicial department policies or procedures.

Adopted effective September 24, 2008.

Rule 4.　Complaint Process

a) Any person may initiate a complaint within 180 days of the egregious act by filing it with the Division of State Court Administration. All complaints must be in writing, must be signed, and must describe the alleged inappropriate conduct and the date(s) when the conduct occurred.

b) Upon receipt of a complaint, the Program Manager of the Indiana Court Interpreter Certification Program will review the complaint to determine whether the allegations, if true, would constitute grounds for discipline. If no grounds are found, then the Program Manager will dismiss the complaint with a notification of the reasons for dismissing the complaint and will notify the complainant and interpreter. If the complaint alleges conduct that would constitute grounds for discipline, the interpreter will be provided with written notice of the allegations and asked to provide a written response to the complaint within thirty (30) days of this notification. The Program Manager shall investigate the allegations and may consider information obtained from sources other than the complaint and response. If the Program Manager is unavailable for any reason, the Executive Director of the Division of State Court Administration may designate any attorney within the Division to fulfill any and all of the Program Manager's duties under the Disciplinary Code.

c) If the Program Manager determines that there is probable cause to believe that conduct constituting grounds for discipline occurred, then the Program Manager shall submit a report of findings to the Executive Director for review. If the investigation reveals that there is not probable cause to believe that the conduct occurred, then the complaint will be dismissed and the complainant and interpreter will be so notified.

Adopted effective September 24, 2008.

Rule 5.   Determination of Need of Discipline

a) If probable cause is found, the Executive Director of the Division of State Court Administration will review the report of the Program Manager and determine what further action is required. The Executive Director may set a hearing to review the complaint or review the matter by considering the information as submitted. If a hearing is set, the interpreter shall be notified by certified mail of the time and date of the hearing, which shall be set no later than thirty (30) days after a determination that probable cause exists.

b) Efforts to resolve the complaint informally may be initiated by any of the parties to the complaint at any time. Any resolution reached must be submitted to the Executive Director of the Division of State Court Administration for approval. Upon approval of any resolution reached informally, or subsequent to any review without a hearing, the Executive Director or the Executive Director's designee will notify the complainant and the court interpreter of the decision in writing.

c) All hearings will be reported or recorded electronically and shall be private and confidential, except upon request of the interpreter facing the allegations. Strict rules of evidence shall not apply. The Program Manager may, in his/her discretion, call witnesses or clarify any evidence presented (including affidavits). The Executive Director or the Executive Director's designee (a person different from the individual presenting the charges) shall preside over the hearing and give all evidence the weight deemed appropriate. The interpreter may be represented by counsel and shall be able to testify, comment on the allegations, and call witnesses. Testimony shall be under oath.

d) If the Executive Director or the Executive Director's designee finds that there is clear and convincing evidence that the court interpreter has violated the Indiana Supreme Court Interpreter Code of Conduct and Procedure or these rules, the Executive Director or his/her designee shall impose such discipline or sanctions as deemed appropriate.

Adopted effective September 24, 2008.

Rule 6.   Possible Sanctions

a) All disciplinary sanctions imposed shall become public unless dismissed, resolved informally and/or by stipulation, or if the sanction is a private reprimand.

The Executive Director of the Division of State Court Administration or his/her designee shall issue his/her decision, including findings and the sanctions to be imposed, if any, within thirty (30) days from the conclusion of the hearing. Time limits may be extended by mutual agreement in writing when an extension is necessary to ensure the fairness and/or sufficiency of the process.

b) Sanctions may consist of but are not limited to one or more of the following:

1) A private reprimand;

2) A public reprimand;

3) Imposition of costs and expenses incurred by the Division of State Court Administration in connection with the proceeding including investigative costs, if any;

4) Restitution;

5) Requiring that specified education courses be taken;

6) Requiring that one or more parts of the interpreter certification examination be retaken;

7) Modification or suspension from the list of interpreters eligible to work in the courts;

8) Requiring that work be supervised;

9) Suspension of certification for a specified period of time;

10) Revocation of certification;

11) Requiring a period of probation in which the interpreter will not be eligible to seek certification.

c) The specific disciplinary action and the degree of discipline to be imposed should depend upon factors such as the seriousness of the violation, the intent of the interpreter, whether there is a pattern of improper activity, and the effect of the improper activity on others or on the judicial system.

Adopted effective September 24, 2008.

Rule 7.   Appeal

The interpreter may appeal the decision of the Executive Director of State Court Administration to a three-member panel of the Indiana Supreme Court Interpreter Advisory Board [1] no later than twenty (20) days after the decision is mailed to the interpreter. The appeal shall include the interpreter's written objections to the decision. The three-member panel of the Indiana Supreme Court Advisory Board shall review the record of the hearing to determine whether the decision reached and sanctions imposed were appropriate, or whether the Division of State Court Administration abused its discretion.

[1] The Indiana Supreme Court Interpreter Advisory Board was created by the Commission on Race and Gender Fairness in June 2003. The Board's membership includes judicial officers, attorneys, interpreters, and other public officials. Members serve staggered terms of one (1) to three (3) years.

Adopted effective September 24, 2008.

ADMINISTRATIVE RULES

Effective January 1, 1976

Including Amendments Received Through November 1, 2013

Rule 1. Preparation and Filing of Statistical Reports

(A) **Preparation of Forms.** The Division of State Court Administration (Division), pursuant to these rules and IC 33–24–6–3, shall draft forms to be used in the gathering of statistical data and other information and shall submit the proposed forms to the Supreme Court for approval. After the Supreme Court approves the forms the Division shall distribute the forms to all courts to be used in preparation of reports.

(B) **Quarterly Case Status Reports.**

(1) All trial courts shall prepare quarterly case status reports, on forms approved under the provisions of Administrative Rule 1(A), concerning the judicial work of their respective courts. The last day of the reporting period for the quarterly case status reports shall be March 31, June 30, September 30, and December 31.

(2) The judge of the trial court may require clerks, court reporters, or any other officer or employee of the court to furnish the information needed to prepare the reports.

(3) The judge of the trial court shall cause the quarterly case status reports to be filed with the Division no later than ten (10) calendar days after the end of the reporting period in electronic format as established by the Division.

(4) The method for assigning case numbers set out below is intended for all purposes, including court costs, but it does not affect the court's ability to waive multiple court costs in selected cases or to try related cases as one.

(a) Criminal Cases and Infractions. The clerk shall assign one case number to each defendant charged with one or more criminal offenses or infractions arising out of the same incident, or multiple incidents occurring on the same date, to be tried as one case, regardless of the number of counts or citations charged against the defendant. The case shall be designated as a MR—Murder, FA—Class A Felony, FB—Class B Felony, FC—Class C Felony, FD—Class D Felony, CM—Criminal Misdemeanor, MC—Miscellaneous Criminal, or IF—Infraction, and shall be counted as one case on the quarterly case status report. When the defendant is charged with multiple charges involving different case type categories, the case number shall be designated so as to reflect only the most serious charge.

(b) Ordinance Violations. Counts or citations charging ordinance violations shall not be included in the criminal case. The clerk shall assign one case number designated as an OV—Local Ordinance Violation, or OE—Exempted Ordinance Violation case type to each defendant charged with one or more ordinance violations arising out of the same incident, or multiple incidents occurring on the same date, to be tried as one case, regardless of the number of counts or citations charged against the defendant, and the case shall be counted as one case on the quarterly case status report.

(c) Juvenile Cases. The clerk shall assign a separate case number to each juvenile who is the subject of a Juvenile CHINS—JC, Juvenile

Delinquency—JD, Juvenile Status—JS, Juvenile Termination of Parental Rights—JT, Juvenile Paternity—JP and Juvenile Miscellaneous—JM case, for all events and conduct that arise out of the same incident. Each juvenile case number shall be counted as a case on the court's quarterly case status reports.

(C) Probation Reports.

(1) All probation officers or probation departments shall compile and prepare reports on the information required by IC 11-13-1-4 concerning the work of the respective office. All probation officers or probation departments shall file, on forms approved pursuant to the provisions of Administrative Rule 1(A), the following reports:

(a) Quarterly statistical reports. The last day of the reporting period for the quarterly reports shall be March 31, June 30, September 30, and December 31.

(b) An annual operations report. The reporting period for the annual operations report begins on January 1 and ends on December 31.

(2) The quarterly statistical reports and the annual operations report shall be filed with the Division no later than ten (10) calendar days after the end of the reporting period, in electronic format as established by the Division.

(3) Every trial judge or chief judge of a unified court system shall require the probation officer or probation department subject to the judge's direction and control to comply with these reporting requirements.

(D) Judge's Confirmation of Reporting. The judge of the court or the chief judge of a unified court system shall review all reports and confirm, through a process established by the Division, the completion and filing of all reports,.

(E) County Caseload Plans. The courts of record in a county shall, by a local rule, implement a caseload allocation plan for the county that ensures an even distribution of judicial workload among the courts of record in the county.

(1) Schedule for Plans. The Indiana Supreme Court Division of State Court Administration (Division), with Supreme Court approval, shall prepare and publish a schedule for the submission and approval of such local caseload allocation plans. The schedule shall ensure that the courts of record in each county must review and submit a new plan or re-submit an existing plan not less than once every two (2) years.

(2) Weighted Caseload Measures and Caseload Variance. Based on the statistical reports submitted pursuant to this rule and a weighted caseload measures system, the Division shall prepare and publish annually a weighted caseload report on the caseload of the Indiana trial courts of record.

The caseload allocation plans required under this section must ensure that the variance, or difference, in utilization between any two courts of record in the county does not exceed 0.40 based on a weighted caseload measures system.

(3) Approval of Plans. With Supreme Court approval, the Division may approve a county plan that complies with the 0.40 utilization variance, return a plan that does not comply and request revisions, grant an exception for good cause shown, or reject a plan for not complying with the utilization variance. Should a county fail to adopt such a plan, the Supreme Court shall prescribe a plan for use by the county.

(F) Reporting of Performance Measures in Juvenile Cases

(1) All trial courts exercising jurisdiction over Children in Need of Services (CHINS) and Termination of Parental Rights (TPR) cases shall annually compile and report on court performance measures for all qualifying cases in their jurisdiction. The Division of State Court Administration shall draft forms to be used in the gathering of statistical data and other information to the Supreme Court for approval. After the Supreme Court approves the forms the Division shall distribute the forms to all courts to be used in the preparation of reports.

(2) All trial courts exercising jurisdiction over child in need of services and termination of parent-child relationship cases shall prepare an annual summary report of the court performances measures for their respective court to the Division of State Court Administration on the forms provided by the Division of State Court Administration.

(3) The reporting period for Court Performance Measures under this rule shall be the fiscal year for the federal government, October 1 of the prior year through September 30 of the year being described. Beginning in federal fiscal year 2014 (October 1, 2013–September 30, 2014), trial courts subject to this rule shall file the required reports within thirty (30) days after the close of the reporting period.

(4) *Qualifying Cases.* All CHINS and TPR cases that were opened not more than five years prior to the beginning of the reporting period and which were closed in the reporting period shall be included in the Court Performance Measures report for that reporting period. All cases filed more than five years prior to October 1 of the reporting year shall be excluded from the report.

(5) *Court Performance Measures:* Effective for the federal fiscal year of October 1, 2013–September 30, 2014, and annually for the same period thereafter, trial courts subject to this rule shall report the statistics and data requested by the State Court Administration for the following defined court performance measures:

a. Time to Permanent Placement: This measure is defined as the median number of days from the filing of the original CHINS petition to permanency. Permanency for the purposes of this measurement is defined as the date that wardship is terminated. This Measure is limited to those cases in which the child was removed from the original parent guardian, or custodian at any time during the pendency of the case.

b. Time to First Permanency Hearing: This measure is defined as the median number of days from the filing of the original CHINS petition to the date the first permanency hearing is held on the case as defined by of IC 31–34–21–7

c. Time to Termination of Parental Rights Petition: This measure is defined as the median number of days from the filing of the original CHINS petition to the filing of the petition for termination of parental rights. This measure excludes automatic petitions for termination of parental rights that are filed under IC 31–35–2–4 and 31–35–2–4.5, and such petitions should not be counted in this measure.

d. Time to Termination of Parental Rights: This measure is defined as the median number of days from the filing of the original CHINS petition to the day that the last order on the termination of parental rights is entered with regard to the child.

e. Time to all Subsequent Permanency Hearings: This measure is defined as the median number of days between all subsequent permanency hearings in a case as defined by IC 31–34–21–7.

This Rule is drafted to conform with the requirements of the Program Instructions for the Court Improvement Program as published by the Administration for Children and Families, U.S Department of Health and Human Services, Log. No: ACYF–CB–PI–12–02.

Adopted effective Jan. 1, 1976. Amended June 16, 1976, effective June 30, 1976; amended effective Jan. 1, 1980; amended Dec. 7, 1987, effective Jan. 1, 1988, in Allen, Kosciusko, Miami, Morgan, Rush, Shelby, and Union Counties, and effective in other counties upon subsequent designation by the Supreme Court; Nov. 10, 1988, effective Jan. 1, 1989; Nov. 30, 1989, effective Jan. 1, 1990; Nov. 1, 1991, effective Jan. 1, 1992; Dec. 5, 1994, effective Feb. 1, 1995; July 1, 2003, effective Aug. 1, 2003; July 1, 2005, effective Jan. 1, 2006; amended effective Jan. 30, 2007; Feb. 1, 2007; amended Sept. 10, 2007, effective Jan. 1, 2008; Sept. 9, 2008, effective Jan. 1, 2009; Sept. 21, 2010, effective Jan. 1, 2011; April 15, 2013, effective Oct. 1, 2013.

Appendix. Schedule and Format for Adoption of County Caseload Allocation Plans

<u>Schedule and Format for Adoption of County Caseload Allocation Plans</u>

The Indiana Supreme Court Division of State Court Administration, an office of the Chief Justice of Indiana, is charged pursuant to Administrative Rule 1 of the Indiana Rules of Court with establishing and publishing a schedule for the submission and approval of local court rules implementing caseload allocation plans.

Administrative Rule 1(E) requires the courts of record in a county to develop and implement caseload allocation plans that ensure an even distribution of judicial workload among the courts in the county. The plans must reduce disparity in caseloads and judicial resources so that the utilization variance among the courts in the county, based on a weighted caseload measures system, does not exceed 0.40 points. Courts must submit new plans or re-submit existing plans, if no changes are required, every other year.

Further, Trial Rule 81(C) requires that the Division of State Court Administration develop and publish a schedule for the adoption of all local court rules.

Pursuant to Admin. R. 1(E) and T.R. 81(C), the following schedule shall apply for the submission and approval of local rules governing caseload allocation plans.

1. Year Plans Must Be Developed

Courts must develop and submit caseload allocation plans every two (2) years.

Submission of caseload allocation plans shall follow the schedule for submission of caseload allocation which is set out in **Section 10**.

If the weighted caseload statistics for the calendar year immediately preceding the year in which a caseload allocation plan is due indicate that the courts of record within the county are within a utilization variance of 0.40 from each other, the courts may revalidate their plan and request that their existing plan be re-adopted.

2. Schedule

The schedule for submitting caseload allocation plans shall follow the schedule for adoption of all local rules under Trial Rule 81 and is as follows:

April 15—Division of State Court Administration shall publish the WCL report based on the prior year caseload statistics.

June 1—Courts of record in the counties who are due to file caseload plans that year pursuant to **Section 10** below shall submit their plans to the Division of State Court Administration for publication and shall publish notice for comment pursuant to T.R. 81.

July 1—Close of comment period.

July 2 to July 31—Final approval of caseload plans by local courts.

August 1—Submission of locally approved caseload plans to Division of State Court Administration for approval pursuant to Administrative Rule 1 (E)(3).

October 1—Supreme Court action—approval, return with request for revisions, or rejection.

November 1—Revised plans due before Supreme Court.

November 15—Final Supreme Court action on resubmitted plans.

January 1 of following calendar year—effective date of caseload plan.

3. Content of the Notice

Not later than June 1 of each year, those courts obligated to prepare a caseload reallocation plan shall give notice to the bar and the public of the content of their proposed caseload allocation plan. The notice shall include:

(a) Whether the plan is new or a resubmitted pre-existing plan;

(b) The address to which comments should be sent;

(c) That comments by the bar and public will be received until July 1;

(d) That the trial courts will adopt, modify, or reject the plan by July 31;

(e) That the plan will be submitted to the Indiana Supreme Court by August 1;

(f) That the plan shall not be effective until approved by the Supreme Court; and

(g) That the effective date of the caseload plan shall be January 1 of the following year.

4. Publication of the Notice

Publication of the notice is accomplished when the courts of a county provide the text of the caseload allocation plan to the county clerk and to the Division of State Court Administration in digital format. The county clerk shall post the notice in the county clerk's office(s) and on the county clerk's website, if any. The Division of State Court Administration shall post the proposal on the Indiana Judicial website for public inspection and comment. The trial courts shall also give notice to the president and secretary (or similar officers) of any local bar association.

5. Close of Comment Period

The courts of the county shall accept comments for 30 days, until July 1. After July 1, the courts shall review and study the comments received and make any advisable changes to the proposed allocation plan.

6. Adoption of Plan

The courts of record in the county shall approve a single final caseload allocation plan for the courts on or before July 31.

7. Supreme Court Approval

(a) Not later than August 1, the courts shall submit to the Supreme Court's Division of State Court Administration all newly adopted and re-adopted case allocation plans by sending a Request for Approval of Local Rules to the Clerk of the Indiana Supreme Court. The Clerk shall enter the Request in the Supreme Court Chronological Case Summary and shall forward the Request to the Division of State Court Administration. **(See Appendix A for a form Request for Approval of Local Rules.)**

(b) The Division of State Court Administration, with Supreme Court approval, will act upon Requests not later than October 1. The Division, with Supreme Court approval, may approve the proposal as submitted, approve a modified version, or reject the proposal.

Courts whose plans are rejected or returned with request for revisions shall have until November 1 to resubmit corrected plans.

(c) The Supreme Court order approving the Request for Approval of Caseload Allocation Plan shall be entered in the Record of Judgments and Orders of each local court in which it is effective.

(d) A Caseload Allocation Plan is not effective until the Supreme Court enters an order approving it.

8. Effective Date Of Allocation Plans

All caseload allocation plans shall become effective January 1 of the following year.

9. Plans for Courts that Fail to Develop Plan.

Not later than December 1, The Division shall report to the Supreme Court the counties, if any, where the courts have failed to develop a caseload allocation plan or the plan does not meet the requirements of Administrative Rule 1 so that the Court may determine a plan for such a county pursuant to Admin.R. 1(E).

10. Year Caseload Plans Must Be Developed

a) 2011: The following counties must review their caseload allocation plans and either: (1) revalidate their current plan and submit a request to readopt the current plan; or (2) submit a new caseload allocation plan in 2011, and in each odd-numbered year thereafter. Districts 10, 11, 12, 13, 14, 16, 17, 18, 19, 20, 22, 23 & 24 (As established in Administrative Rule 3, amended effective January 1, 2011)

| Boone | Harrison | Ripley |

Carroll	Hendricks	Rush
Clark	Jefferson	Scott
Clay	Johnson	Shelby
Clinton	Lawrence	Sullivan
Crawford	Madison	Switzerland
Dearborn	Marion	Tippecanoe
Fayette	Monroe	Tipton
Floyd	Montgomery	Union
Fountain	Morgan	Vermillion
Franklin	Ohio	Vigo
Grant	Orange	Warren
Greene	Owen	Washington
Hamilton	Parke	Wayne
Hancock	Putnam	White

b) 2012: The following counties must review their caseload allocation plans and either: (1) revalidate their current plan and submit a request to readopt the current plan; or (2) submit a new caseload allocation plan in 2012, and in each even-numbered year thereafter.

Districts 1, 2, 3, 4, 5, 6, 7, 8, 9, 15, 21, 25 & 26 (As established in Administrative Rule 3, amended effective January 1, 2011.)

Adams	Huntington	Perry
Allen	Jackson	Pike
Bartholomew	Jasper	Porter
Benton	Jay	Posey
Blackford	Jennings	Pulaski
Brown	Knox	Randolph
Cass	Kosciusko	Spencer
Daviess	LaGrange	St. Joseph
Decatur	Lake	Starke
DeKalb	LaPorte	Steuben
Delaware	Marshall	Vanderburgh
Dubois	Martin	Wabash
Elkhart	Miami	Warrick
Fulton	Newton	Wells
Gibson	Noble	Whitley
Grant		
Henry		
Howard		

These standards shall remain in effect until amended.

February 1, 2011.

Lilia Judson

Executive Director

Indiana Supreme Court Division of State Court Administration

Adopted Dec. 22, 2005, effective Jan. 1, 2006. Amended effective Feb. 1, 2011.

Rule 2. Reporting Fiscal Matters

(A) Preparation of Fiscal Reporting Forms. The Division of State Court Administration (Division), pursuant to these rules and IC 33-24-6-3, shall draft forms to be used in the gathering of revenue, budget and expenditure data from the courts and shall submit the proposed forms to the Supreme Court for approval. The revenue report forms shall collect data on the revenues generated by the operation of the courts within the county, the categories for which monies were collected, the amounts collected in each category, and how the collected funds were distributed. The budget and expenditure forms shall collect data on the requested budgets of the courts and their offices for the upcoming calendar year, the approved budgets for the courts and their offices for the upcoming year, the actual expenditures of the court and their offices during the previous calendar year, specifying the categories for which funds were requested, approved and spent.

After the Supreme Court approves the forms the Division shall distribute the forms to all courts to be used in preparation of reports. All trial courts shall prepare, on forms approved under the provisions of this rule, fiscal reports on the receipt and expenditure of public money by and for the operation of the courts.

(B) Report of Clerk on Revenues. Within ten (10) days after the close of the calendar year, the Clerk of the Court shall report to the judge of the court, or chief judge of a unified court system, all information necessary for the completion of the revenue report form. In the case of a City or Town Court, if there is no clerk, the judge of a City or Town Court shall prepare such report.

(C) Report of Judge. The judge of the trial court or the chief judge of a unified court system shall cause the fiscal reports to be filed with the Division no later than twenty (20) days after the end of the calendar year for the reporting period in electronic format as established by the Division.

(D) Judge's Confirmation of Reporting. The judge of the court or the chief judge of a unified court system shall review all reports and confirm, through a process established by the Division, the completion and filing of all reports.

Amended effective Jan. 1, 1980; amended Nov. 30, 1989, effective Jan. 1, 1990; Sept. 10, 2007, effective Jan. 1, 2008; Sept. 9, 2008, effective Jan. 1, 2009.

Rule 3. Administrative Districts

(A) The State of Indiana is hereby divided into twenty-six (26) administrative districts as follows:

(1) District 1, consisting of Lake County;

(2) District 2, consisting of Porter, Newton, Jasper and Benton Counties;

(3) District 3, consisting of LaPorte, Starke and Pulaski Counties;

(4) District 4, consisting of St. Joseph County;

(5) District 5, consisting of Elkhart, Marshall and Kosciusko Counties;

(6) District 6, consisting of LaGrange, Steuben, Noble, DeKalb and Whitley Counties;

(7) District 7, consisting of Allen County;

(8) District 8, consisting of Fulton, Miami, Cass and Howard Counties;

(9) District 9, consisting of Wabash, Huntington, Wells and Adams Counties;

(10) District 10, consisting of White, Carroll and Tippecanoe Counties;

(11) District 11, consisting of Warren, Fountain, Montgomery, Vermillion and Parke Counties;

(12) District 12, consisting of Clinton, Boone, Tipton and Hamilton Counties;

(13) District 13, consisting of Marion County;

(14) District 14, consisting of Grant and Madison Counties;

(15) District 15, consisting of Blackford, Jay, Delaware, Randolph and Henry Counties;

(16) District 16, consisting of Hendricks and Morgan Counties;

(17) District 17, consisting of Hancock, Shelby and Johnson Counties;

(18) District 18, consisting of Wayne, Rush, Fayette, Union and Franklin Counties;

(19) District 19, consisting of Vigo, Clay, Putnam and Sullivan Counties;

(20) District 20, consisting of Owen, Greene, Monroe and Lawrence Counties;

(21) District 21, consisting of Brown, Bartholomew, Decatur, Jackson and Jennings Counties;

(22) District 22, consisting of Ripley, Dearborn, Ohio, Jefferson and Switzerland Counties;

(23) District 23, consisting of Scott, Clark and Floyd Counties;

(24) District 24, consisting of Orange, Washington, Crawford and Harrison Counties;

(25) District 25, consisting of Knox, Daviess, Martin, Pike, Dubois, Perry and Spencer Counties; and,

(26) District 26, consisting of Gibson, Posey, Vanderburgh and Warrick Counties.

(B) The Board of Directors of the Judicial Conference of Indiana shall, by rule, establish a structure for the governance, management and administration of the judicial districts.

Amended effective Aug. 17, 1990; Aug. 29, 1990; Aug. 6, 1996; November 18, 1999; amended Sept. 21, 2010, effective Jan. 1, 2011.

Rule 4. Committees

(A) Records Management Committee.

(1) *Creation and Members.* There is hereby created a committee to be known as the Records Management Committee. The Records Management Committee shall consist of not more than twenty-seven (27) members representative of the agencies responsible for the management and maintenance of the records of the courts throughout the State of Indiana. The members of the Records Management Committee shall be appointed by the Supreme Court and shall serve at the pleasure of the Court. With the exception of the permanent members, each member shall serve a staggered term of three (3) years. A member may serve two

(2) consecutive terms, plus any unexpired term of a previous member. A vacancy on the Committee shall be filled by the Supreme Court for the unexpired term of the departing member. Permanent members shall consist of a member of the Supreme Court, appointed by the Supreme Court, who shall serve as chair of the Committee; the State Public Defender; the Executive Director of the Prosecuting Attorneys Council; the Clerk of the Supreme Court, Court of Appeals, and Tax Court; and the Executive Director of the Division of State Court Administration. The remaining membership shall consist of eleven (11) trial court judges and judicial officers; three (3) members from the staff or administrative agencies of the Indiana Supreme Court and the Court of Appeals; three (3) circuit court clerks; three (3) court administrators; and two (2) practicing attorneys. The staff of the Division of State Court Administration shall assist the Committee in the performance of its duties. In making appointments to the Committee, the Supreme Court should seek to ensure that the members represent the geographic, ethnic, racial, and gender diversity of Indiana.

(2) *Duties of the Committee.* The Records Management Committee shall conduct a continuous study of the practices, procedures, and systems for the maintenance, management and retention of court records employed by the courts and offices serving the courts of this State. Such study may include micrographics, imaging, copiers, fax machines, courtroom security and disaster prevention planning. The committee shall submit to the Supreme Court from time to time recommendations for the modernization, improvement and standardization of such practices, procedures and systems.

(3) *Meetings and Compensation.* The Records Management Committee shall meet at the call of the chair. The Records Management Committee shall act by vote of a majority of the members present at a committee meeting. All members who are public employees shall serve without compensation. Members who are not public employees shall receive a per diem compensation as the Supreme Court shall fix from time to time. All members shall receive mileage and reimbursement for reasonable expenses necessary for the performance of any duty incidental to service on the Records Management Committee.

(4) *Suggestions for Improvement.* The Committee shall encourage suggestions from all interested parties and the public for the improvement of the records management system employed by the courts and court agencies. These recommendations should be submitted in writing to the Division of State Court Administration.

(B) Judicial Technology and Automation Committee.

(1) *Creation and Members.* In order to develop a uniform policy on implementation of information technology by the Indiana judicial system, there is hereby created a committee to be known as the Indiana Judicial Technology and Automation Committee. The members of the Committee shall be appointed by the Supreme Court and shall serve at the pleasure of the Court. A member of the Supreme Court shall serve as chair of the Committee. The Executive Director and staff of the Division of State Court Administration shall assist the Committee in the performance of its duties.

(2) *Duties of the Committee.* The Judicial Technology and Automation Committee shall conduct a continuous study of information technology applications for Indiana's judicial system. The Committee's charge includes but is not limited to the development of a long-range strategy for technology and automation in Indiana's judicial system. Such strategy may involve approaches for funding and implementation as well as the development of standards for judicial information case management systems, judicial data processing, electronic filling, deployment and use of judicial information on the Internet, and for all related technologies used in the courts. The Committee shall from time to time recommend to the Supreme Court the implementation of policies, standards and rules which promote effective use of technology and automation in the courts.

(3) *Meetings and Compensation.* The Committee shall meet at the call of the chair. The Committee shall act by a vote of a majority of the members present at a committee meeting. All members who are public employees shall serve without compensation. Members who are not public employees shall receive a per diem compensation as the Supreme Court shall fix from time to time. All members shall receive mileage and reimbursement for reasonable expenses necessary for the performance of any duty incidental to service on the Committee.

(C) Indiana Supreme Court Commission on Race and Gender Fairness.

(1) *Creation and Members.* There is hereby created a commission to be known as the Indiana Supreme Court Commission on Race and Gender Fairness. The commission shall consist of not less than ten (10) and no more than twenty-five (25) members representative of the Indiana judiciary, the practicing bar, academia, state and local government, public organizations, law enforcement, and corrections. The members of the commission shall be appointed by the Supreme Court and shall serve for a period of five (5) years each at the pleasure of the Supreme Court. The Supreme Court shall appoint a chair of the commission. A member of the commission shall serve as secretary. The Executive Director and staff of the Division of State Court

Administration shall assist the commission in performance of its duties.

(2) *Duties of the Commission.* The Indiana Supreme Court Commission on Race and Gender Fairness shall study the status of race and gender fairness in Indiana's justice system and shall investigate ways to improve race and gender fairness in the courts, legal system, among legal service providers, state and local government, and among public organizations. The Commission shall from time to time recommend to the Supreme Court the implementation of policies and procedures which promote race and gender fairness in the courts, among legal service providers in state and local government and by public organizations.

(3) *Meetings and Compensation.* The commission shall meet at the call of the chair. The commission shall act by vote of a majority of the members present at a commission meeting. All members who are public employees shall serve without compensation. Members who are not public employees shall receive a per diem compensation as the Supreme Court shall fix from time to time. All members shall receive mileage and reimbursement for reasonable expenses necessary for the performance of any duty incidental to service on the Commission.

(D) Indiana Supreme Court Committee on Unrepresented Litigants.

(1) *Creation, Members and Staff Support.* There is hereby created a committee to be known as the Indiana Supreme Court Committee on Unrepresented Litigants. The committee shall consist of members representative of the Indiana judiciary, the practicing bar, academia, state and local government and public organizations. The Supreme Court shall appoint the members and shall appoint one of them as chair of the Committee. Except for initial terms, which shall be staggered, the term of each member and chair shall be three (3) years. The members shall serve at the pleasure of the Supreme Court. The Executive Director and staff of the Division of State Court Administration shall assist the Committee in the performance of its duties.

(2) *Duties of the Committee.* The Indiana Supreme Court Committee on Unrepresented Litigants shall conduct a continuous study of the practices, procedures, and systems for serving unrepresented litigants in Indiana courts. The Committee's charge includes but is not limited to providing a long-range strategy for improving access to justice for unrepresented litigants. Such strategy may involve development of protocols for judges, clerks, and their staffs in addition to providing general guidance to the courts, legal service providers, and public organizations through training about meeting the needs of unrepresented litigants. The Committee shall from time to time recommend to the Supreme Court the implemen-

tation of policies and procedures that promote access to justice in the courts for unrepresented litigants.

(3) *Meetings and Compensation.* The Indiana Supreme Court Committee on Unrepresented Litigants shall meet not less than four times per year and other times at the call of the chair. The Committee shall act by vote of a majority of the members present at a committee meeting. All members who are public employees shall serve without compensation. Members who are not public employees shall receive a per diem compensation, as the Supreme Court shall fix from time to time. All members shall receive mileage and reimbursement for reasonable expenses necessary for the performance of any duty incidental to service on the Committee.

(E) Indiana Supreme Court Advisory Commission on Guardian ad Litem ("GAL")/Court Appointed Special Advocate ("CASA")

(1) *Creation, Members and Staff Support.* There is hereby created a commission to be known as the Indiana Supreme Court Advisory Commission on GAL/CASA. The Commission shall consist of eighteen (18) members representative of the Indiana judiciary and directors of certified, volunteer based GAL/CASA programs. The Commission shall include three GAL/CASA program directors and one member of the judiciary each from four regions of Indiana (North, South, East, West) and two at-large members of the judiciary. The Indiana Supreme Court shall appoint the members. The term of each member and the chair shall be three (3) years. The terms of the program directors shall be staggered so that one representative is appointed from each region every year. The terms of the judicial representatives shall also be staggered so that two judicial representatives are appointed each year. All members shall serve at the pleasure of the Supreme Court. The Commission members shall elect a Chair, Vice-Chair and other officers at the first meeting of the year. The Executive Director of the Division of State Court Administration, the Division's GAL/CASA Director and Division staff shall assist the Commission in the performance of its duties. The Division GAL/CASA Director shall serve as ex-officio member of the Commission.

(2) *Duties of the Commission.* The Indiana Supreme Court Advisory Commission on GAL/CASA shall conduct a continuous study of the GAL/CASA services in Indiana and shall provide support and guidance to the Indiana Supreme Court on how best to provide GAL/CASA services. The Commission's charge includes but is not limited to providing a long-range strategy for promoting, expanding and training child advocacy GAL/CASA programs. The Commission shall from time to time review the GAL/CASA Program Standards and Code of Ethics and make recommendations to the Supreme Court for their improvement.

(3) *Meetings and Compensation.* The Commission shall meet at least quarterly and at such other times as called by the chair. The Commission shall act by a vote of a majority. For voting purposes, a simple majority of a nine-member quorum is required. All members who are public employees shall serve without compensation. Members who are not public employees shall receive a per diem compensation, as the Supreme Court shall fix from time to time. All members shall receive mileage and reimbursement for reasonable expenses for the performance of any duty incidental to service on the Commission.

Adopted effective Sept. 19, 1983; amended Nov. 1, 1991, effective Jan. 1, 1992; Dec. 5, 1994, effective Feb. 1, 1995; effective Nov. 18, 1999; Sept. 10, 2007, effective Jan. 1, 2008; Sept. 20, 2011, effective Jan. 1, 2012; Sept. 13, 2013, effective Jan. 1, 2014.

Rule 5. Payment and Notification Procedures

(A) Special Judge Fees. The Division of State Court Administration shall administer the payment procedure for special judge fees in accordance with this provision.

(1) *Entitlement.* As provided in Trial Rule 79(P), all persons other than a full-time judge, magistrate, or other employee of the judiciary who serve as special judge are entitled to a fee of twenty-five dollars ($25.00) per day for each jurisdiction served for the entry of judgments and orders and hearings incidental to such entries. Persons residing outside the county where service is rendered shall be entitled to mileage and reimbursement paid in accordance with standards set for other public officials of the State. Senior Judges who serve as special judges shall be paid in accordance with a schedule published by the Executive Director of State Court Administration. Senior Judges are not entitled to compensation for special judge service when the service is performed on the same day he or she serves as a senior judge.

(2) *Procedure for Payment.* A special judge shall file his or her claim for compensation with the Division of State Court Administration on forms provided by such agency as prescribed by the State Board of Accounts. Any claim for services as special judge shall encompass a specified period of time and shall include all such services rendered during such period of time. The Division of State Court Administration shall present the claim form to the Auditor of the State for payment.

(3) *Timely Filing of Claims.* Claims for compensation shall be filed by the special judge no later than ninety (90) days from the date of service.

(B) Senior Judges. The Division of State Court Administration shall administer the payment proce-

dures for senior judges in accordance with the provisions set forth in this rule.

(1) *Appointment.* The Court of Appeals, the Tax Court, a circuit, superior or probate court may request that the Supreme Court provide senior judge services. The request must contain the reasons for the request and the estimated duration of the need for senior judge services. Upon approving the request, the Supreme Court may appoint one or all senior judges currently certified by the Judicial Nominating Commission to serve the requesting court consistent with this rule. The Supreme Court shall fix the term or period of time for the senior judge appointment.

(2) *Number of Senior Judge Days for Requesting Court.* Each year, the Supreme Court shall fix, based upon the recommendation of the Executive Director of the Indiana Supreme Court Division of State Court Administration, who shall use the Indiana Weighted Caseload Measures System, the annual statistical reports, and other relevant criteria, the number of senior judge days that each court may use. Every court authorized in this rule to use senior judges will be entitled to a minimum of ten (10) days of senior judge service during the year of appointment. If a senior judge serves as a Mediator under Rule 5(B)(9) or as an Attorney Surrogate under Rule 5(B)(10), those days of service shall not count as service days against the appointing court's allotment under this rule.

(3) *Qualification for Senior Judge Status.* A person who is certified by the Indiana Judicial Nominating Commission may serve as senior judge. Each year the Indiana Judicial Nominating Commission shall certify to the Supreme Court that a person who is certified:

(a)(i) has served in their judicial capacity for at least four (4) years and (ii) at least one of those years was within five (5) years of the application or, in the event the four years of service was more than five (5) years prior to the application, has served at least thirty (30) days as a senior judge during a calendar year within five (5) years of the application; except that the Indiana Judicial Nominating Commission may, upon the finding of exceptional circumstances, waive the foregoing criteria and certify a senior judge with less service than specified above;

(b) agrees to serve as a senior judge for at least thirty (30) days in the year of appointment and has not in any previous year of service failed to serve for at least thirty (30) days without good cause as determined by the Indiana Judicial Nominating Commission.

(c) agrees to comply with the Code of Judicial Conduct; further agrees to not serve as an elected official or employee of a governmental entity or subdivision except with Supreme Court permission;

(d) agrees to serve where assigned; and that the service shall be substantially equivalent to the daily calendar of the court to which the senior judge is assigned;

(e) agrees to continue to serve in all special judge cases in which the person who is certified was serving as a special judge at the time the person left office, but will receive senior judge credit for such service; provided however, if the circumstances that led to the person who is certified being appointed as special judge no longer exist, and no other disqualification exists, then the case may be returned to the regular judge of the court where the case is pending.

(f) agrees,

(i) in the case of a senior judge appointed or assigned to serve a trial court, not to represent any client in any case before a court in which the senior judge is appointed or assigned as senior judge and to disclose to the parties coming before him in his capacity as a senior judge whenever, within the previous one (1) year, he has served as an ADR neutral for: 1) a lawyer or lawyer's firm of a party to the case, or 2) a party currently before the court. Following the disclosure, unless all parties agree on the record that the senior judge may hear the case, the senior judge must recuse; and,

(ii) in the case of a senior judge appointed or assigned to serve an appellate court, (1) not to represent any client in any case before an Indiana appellate court, (2) not to serve as an ADR neutral in any case in which he or she participated as a judicial officer, (3) not to serve as a judicial officer in any case in which he or she participated as an ADR neutral, and (4) not to represent any client in any case before a tribunal whose decisions are subject to review by an Indiana appellate court.

(g) is fit to serve as a senior judge.

(4) *Jurisdiction.* A presiding judge wishing to use a senior judge shall issue an order naming the senior judge who will serve the court. The order shall specify the day(s) the senior judge is to serve the court and whether the service is limited to the regular business hours of the court or is for the full twenty-four (24) hours. The senior judge shall provide to the presiding judge, and the presiding judge shall attach to the order, a verified written statement from the senior judge that the senior judge does not practice law in the court. The order shall be filed in the Record of Judgments and Orders of the court and a copy sent to the Division of State Court Administration. A senior judge shall have the same jurisdiction as the presiding judge of the court where the senior judge is serving but only during the time specified in the order naming the senior judge to serve the court. A senior judge who

has been certified by the Judicial Nominating Commission shall have jurisdiction at any time during the certification to officiate at marriages and administer oaths. A senior judge retains jurisdiction in an individual case on the order of the presiding judge of the court in which the case is pending;

(5) *Oath of Office.* Upon initial certification as a senior judge, the senior judge shall take an oath of office and shall file it with the Clerk of the Indiana Supreme Court.

(6) *Per Diem Allowance.* As provided by statute, a senior judge is entitled to senior judge service credit and a per diem allowance of one hundred dollars ($100.00) per day for the first thirty (30) days of service in a calendar year. Pursuant to statute, the Indiana Supreme Court may adjust the per diem rate and increase it to not more than two hundred fifty dollars ($250.00) for each day of service after the first thirty (30) days. A senior judge shall report only the portion of the day served for payment and credit. However, in exceptional circumstances, upon joint application to the Supreme Court by a senior judge and the judge of the trial court, the Supreme Court, in its discretion, may grant additional senior judge credit to the senior judge and additional senior judge service time to the trial court. A senior judge residing outside of the county where service is rendered is entitled to reimbursement for mileage at a rate equal to other public officials as established by state law and reasonable expenses incurred in performing the duties of senior judge for each day served, all as provided by state travel guidelines. A senior judge may not be compensated as such for more than one hundred (100) calendar days in the aggregate during any one calendar year.

(7) *Procedure for Payment.* A senior judge shall file a claim for compensation with the Division of State Court Administration (Division) on forms provided by such agency as prescribed by the State Board of Accounts. The Division shall promptly present the claim to the Auditor of State for payment. Claims for compensation shall be filed no later than thirty (30) days from the date of service.

(8) *Qualification for Benefits.* As provided by statute, a senior judge who is appointed by the Supreme Court to serve for a period equal to or greater than thirty (30) working days is a state employee for purposes for state insurance benefits. A senior judge becomes eligible for state insurance upon appointment. In the event a senior judge fails to serve at least thirty (30) days during any year of appointment, that senior judge's eligibility to state insurance benefits based on senior judge service shall cease and terminate at the end of that year. A senior judge whose eligibility to state insurance benefits has terminated under this subsection may become eligible again if the judge is certified by the Judicial Nominating Commission pursuant to Sec-

tion (B)(3) of this Rule and is appointed to serve in a court, but only after serving as a senior judge a minimum of thirty (30) days during the year of appointment. A senior judge who waives per diem pay is entitled to receive senior judge service credit and to state insurance benefits for service that substantially complies with the appointment of the Supreme Court. As used in this rule, term "state insurance benefits" includes group health, life, dental, and vision insurance benefits and other benefits offered by the State of Indiana to its elected officials from time to time.

(9) *Senior Judge Serving as Mediator.* A senior judge who is also a registered mediator and serves as a mediator in court-ordered mediation pursuant to IC 33–23–3–3, or on a pro bono basis, may receive senior judge service credit for said mediation service provided that the senior judge is not compensated at a rate greater than the per diem rate for senior judges.

(10) *Senior Judge Serving as an Attorney Surrogate.* A senior judge who is appointed and serves as an Attorney Surrogate under Admission and Discipline Rule 23 § 27 may receive senior judge credit and compensation at the per diem rate for senior judges so long as the senior judge is not being compensated for the services under Admission and Discipline Rule 23 § 27(g). The senior judge shall make the election to receive senior judge credit and compensation within sixty days of the appointment as Attorney Surrogate by filing a notice with the appointing court.

(C) Notice of Commencement or Termination of Term in Office and Employment.

(1) *Notice by Judges.* Each elected or appointed circuit, superior, county, probate, city, town or small claims court judge shall give notice to the Indiana Supreme Court Division of State Court Administration of:

(a) the commencement and termination of the judge's term of office;

(b) the employment or termination of any magistrate, referee, commissioner, hearing officer, or other appointed judicial officer, whether such judicial officer is paid by the State of Indiana or by another entity. This notice must designate the position as full or part time, state the number of hours per week that the position requires and identify all court(s) in which such appointed judicial officer shall serve.

(2) *Notice by Prosecuting Attorneys.* Each elected or appointed prosecuting attorney shall give notice to the Indiana Supreme Court Division of State Court Administration of:

(a) the commencement and termination of the prosecuting attorney's term of office and, pursuant to statute, whether the position will be full or part time;

(b) the employment or termination of a deputy prosecuting attorney whose salary is paid by the State of Indiana and, pursuant to statute, whether the position will be full or part time.

(3) *Content and Time of Notice.* The notice must be given at least two (2) weeks in advance of the beginning or termination of the term in office or employment on forms designed by the Division of State Court Administration.

Adopted Nov. 16, 1984, effective Jan. 1, 1985. Amended Oct. 29, 1993, effective Jan. 1, 1994; Dec. 5, 1994, effective Feb. 1, 1995; Dec. 15, 1995, effective Feb. 1, 1996; Nov. 25, 1997, effective Jan. 1, 1998; Dec. 21, 2001, effective April 1, 2002; amended effective Dec. 3, 2003; amended Sept. 30, 2004, effective Jan. 1, 2005; amended effective Jan. 14, 2005; amended July 1, 2005, effective Jan. 1, 2006; Aug. 15, 2006, effective Jan. 1, 2007; amended effective Feb. 1, 2007; amended Sept. 10, 2007, effective Jan. 1, 2008; amended effective Feb. 22, 2008; amended June 23, 2010, effective July 1, 2010; Sept. 21, 2010, effective Jan. 1, 2011; Sept. 20, 2011, effective Jan. 1, 2012; Oct. 11, 2012, effective Jan. 1, 2013; Oct. 26, 2012, effective Jan. 1, 2013.

Appendix. Schedule for Payment of Senior Judges

ATTACHMENT A

**Schedule for Payment of Senior Judges Who Serve as Special Judges
And
Senior Judges Who Serve as Mediators**

This Schedule shall take effect September 1, 2005. Revised January 15, 2009

Pursuant to Administrative Rule 5(A)(1), senior judges who serve as special judges are to be paid in accordance with a Schedule published by the Executive Director of the Indiana Supreme Court Division of State Court Administration.

The Trial Rules and Administrative Rules contain four sections which relate to the payment of senior judges who serve as special judges. They are:

1. Trial Rule 79(J), which qualifies a senior judge to serve as a special judge pursuant to local rule;

2. Administrative Rule 5(A)(1), which prohibits a senior judge from collecting special judge pay on the same day he serves as a senior judge;

3. Administrative Rule 5(B)(3)(e), which provides that a former judge serving as a senior judge must retain his/her pre-retirement special judge cases, without senior judge credit, unless specifically approved by the Supreme Court; and

4. Administrative Rule 5(A)(1), which provides that a senior judge who serves as special judges shall be paid in accordance with a Schedule published by the Executive Director of State Court Administration.

The foregoing rules treat a senior judge who has special judge cases in two ways, depending on whether the senior judge acquired jurisdiction of the special judge cases before or after retirement.

In light of the foregoing provisions, the Executive Director, Lilia Judson, now submits this Schedule, in a question and answer format, to the Supreme Court for its approval.

I. Payment Schedule for Senior Judges Who Serve as Special Judges

A. How will a senior judge who hears a "pre-retirement" special judge case be compensated?

If the special judge case predates the senior judge's retirement, the senior judge retains the case as special judge [Admin. R. 5(B)(3)(e)] and receives no senior judge credit for his/her post-retirement service (except when specifically requested of and approved by the Supreme Court). The senior judge will receive compensation for this service only as a special judge.

However, if the "pre-retirement" special judge case comes before the senior judge on a day the senior judge is serving as a senior judge on other matters assigned by the trial court, the senior judge could claim senior judge pay and credit for that day of service, but not special judge pay. Admin. R. 5(A)(1).

B. How will a senior judge who hears a "post-retirement" special judge case be compensated?

A senior judge who hears a special judge case which he/she received after retiring, may claim senior judge pay and credit for the case under Admin.R. 5(B)(6). Such "post retirement" special judge cases will be treated the same as other senior judge work and "a senior judge who serves substantially shorter time than the daily calendar of the court where the judge is serving may, with the permission of the Executive Director, accumulate and consolidate such service times into a day's credit."

C. How will senior judge days be counted by the court in which a senior judge hears special judge cases?

If the senior judge claims senior judge pay and/or credit time while serving on special judge cases in a particular court, that time will be counted toward that court's senior judge day allotment.

D. How will a senior judge be compensated when he/she serves as a special judge in a court in which he/she is not appointed as a senior judge?

A senior judge who serves as a special judge in a court in which he/she is not appointed as a senior judge cannot receive senior judge pay or senior judge credit for service in that court. He/she can only receive special judge pay.

E. May a senior judge claim service time and/or per diem for traveling to and from a court where he/she serves?

No. A senior judge may claim credit only for actual time served in a court.

F. May a senior judge claim service time and/or per diem for scheduled senior judge service which is canceled through no fault of the senior judge?

No. A senior judge may claim credit only for actual time served in a court.

II. Schedule for Payment of Senior Judges Serving as Mediators.

Indiana Code 33-23-3-3 provides that senior judges may serve as domestic relations mediators but they cannot receive a senior judge per diem as provided in IC 33-23-3-5. A senior judge serving as a domestic relations mediator may receive compensation from the alternative dispute resolution fund under IC 33-23-6 in accordance with the county domestic relations alternative dispute resolution plan. Administrative Rule 5(B)(9) further provides that a senior judge who is also a registered mediator and serves as a mediator in a court-ordered mediation pursuant to IC 33-23-3-3, or on a pro bono basis, may receive senior judge service credit for said mediation service provided that, the senior judge is not compensated at a rate greater than the per diem rate for senior judges.

In light of the foregoing, the Executive Director, Lilia Judson, now submits this Schedule, in question and answer format, for Supreme Court approval.

A. Can a senior judge who mediates pro bono for a court in which he also practices law receive senior judge credit for the mediation?

No. In order to serve as a senior judge, a person must be appointed by the Supreme Court as a senior judge in a particular court. The senior judge cannot be appointed as a senior judge in any court in which the judge practices law.

B. Can a senior judge receive senior judge credit for service as a mediator in a court in which he has not been appointed to serve as a senior judge by the Supreme Court?

No. A senior judge must be appointed to a particular court in order to receive credit and/or per diem for senior judge service in that court.

Adopted effective Sept. 1, 2005. Amended Sept. 15, 2009, effective Jan. 1, 2010.

Rule 6. Court Case Records Media Storage Standards

(A) Application of Standards. All courts and clerks of court in the State of Indiana shall meet the standards set forth under this rule regarding the use of: (1) microfilm for the preservation of any record of a court or a court agency; (2) digital imaging technology for the storage and preservation of any record of a court or of a court agency; (3) hybrid systems producing both digital images and microfilm; and, (4) any related system created by advances in technology for the preservation of any record of a court or of a court agency. These standards shall apply to all records, regardless of medium, kept by courts, their clerks, and court agencies, including the methods used to reproduce or create records electronically and to the methods, systems, and formats used to store, archive, and reproduce records electronically for the purpose of maintenance and preservation of records. Only those records or record series which have been approved for microfilming under Administrative Rule 7 shall be eligible for microfilming.

(B) Definitions. The following definitions shall apply to this Administrative Rule 6:

(1) *"Archival,"* as this term applies to records maintained in electronic form, means that point at which a document is no longer subject to modification and is maintained to ensure reasonably its preservation according to the appropriate record retention schedule as found in Administrative Rule 7.

(2) *"Clerk"* means the Clerk of the Indiana Supreme Court, Court of Appeals, and Tax Court, the Clerk of a Circuit, Superior, Probate, or County Court, the Clerk of a City or Town Court, and the Clerk of a Marion County Small Claims Court, including staff.

(3) *"Court"* means the Indiana Supreme Court, Court of Appeals, Tax Court, and all Circuit, Superior, Probate, City, Town, or Small Claims Courts.

(4) *"Court Agency"* means a section, division, or department performing duties for the Court or Clerk and which has been created by statute or court rule or works at the direction of the court or clerk of court.

(5) *"Court Case Record"* has the same meaning as "Case Record" that is defined in Administrative Rule 9(C)(2).

(6) *"Digital Image"* means an electronic file consisting of digital data, which, when reconstructed on a display screen, a hard copy print, or on microfilm, appears as the original document.

(7) *"Digital Imaging"* means the process by which a document or photograph is scanned by a computer and converted from analog format to a computer-readable digital format.

(8) *"Digital Duplicate"* means any copy of digital images used for reference or communication.

(9) *"Digital Imaging File Format"* means the program used to store Digital Masters of Digital Images.

(10) *"Digital Master"* means the record copy of an electronic record transferred directly from a computer onto an electronic storage medium.

(11) *"Digital Media"* refers to the physical method for storing digital records and images. There are two types: magnetic and optical. Examples of the former are magnetic disks, tape, and Digital Audio Tape (DAT). Examples of optical media include Compact Disk (C–D, CD–ROM), Write-Once, Read–Many (WORM) disk, Erasable Optical Disk (EO), and Digital Versatile Disk (DVD).

(12) *"Division"* means the Division of State Court Administration.

(13) *"DPI"* means dots per inch and is used as a measure of the number of dots recorded in either a vertical or horizontal plane for each inch. It is used to measure scanning resolution.

(14) *"Hybrid Imaging System"* means a system that produces both micrographic and digital images, either simultaneously or one from the other.

(15) *"Image Enhancement"* means the process of manipulating a scanned image with software, to lighten or darken the image, to increase sharpness, alter contrast, or to filter out data elements appearing on the document.

(16) *"Index"* means descriptive locator information attached to a digital image that enables a requestor to identify the file and retrieve it from the electronic storage medium.

(17) *"In electronic Form"* means any information in a court record in a form that is readable through the use of an electronic device, regardless of the manner in which it was created.

(18) *"ISO"* means International Standards Organization.

(19) *"Metadata"* means a standardized structure format and control vocabulary which allows for the precise description of record content, location, and value.

(20) *"Microfilm"* means a photographic film containing an image greatly reduced in size from the original, or the process of generating microphotographs on film.

(21) *"Microform"* means any form, usually film, which contains microphotographs.

(22) *"Migration"* means the process of upgrading electronic systems to new technologies while preserving accessibility to existing records. It includes transferring one electronic data format to another when a new computer or data management system is incompatible with its existing system. It also means the process of moving electronic data from one storage device or medium to another.

(23) *"Noise"* means background discoloration of paper and stains on paper caused by aging, handling, and accidental spilling of fluids.

(24) *"Open System Standard"* means a published and commonly available interface specification that describes services provided by a software product. Such specifications are available to anyone and have evolved through consensus and are open to the entire industry.

(25) *"Record Series"* means a group of related documents, either as to form or content, which are arranged under a single filing system; are kept together as a unit because they consist of the same form, relate to the same subject, result from the same activity; or which have certain similar physical characteristics such as computer magnetic tapes or disks, or as microforms.

(26) *"Record Retention Schedules"* means a series of documents governing, on a continuing basis, the retention and disposal of records of a Court, Clerk, or Court Agency.

(27) *"Refreshing"* means the copying of an image or of a whole storage medium for the purpose of preserving or enhancing the quality of a digital image.

(28) *"Reproduction"* means the process of making an exact copy from an existing document in the same or a different medium.

(29) *"Scanning Resolution"* means the quality of a digital image resulting from its initial scanning. It is represented in the number of dots per inch ("dpi"), used to represent the image.

(30) *"Specifications"* means a set of requirements to be satisfied, and whenever appropriate, the procedure by which it may be determined whether the given requirements are satisfied.

(31) *"Standard"* means a uniformly accepted set of specifications for a predefined norm. "ANSI/AIIM" means the American National Standards Institute and the Association for Information and Imaging Management. "CCITT" means the Consultative Committee on International Telegraphy and Telephony. Specific standards appear both by number and by name.

(32) *"Target"* means any document or chart containing identification information, coding or test criteria used in conjunction with microfilming. A target is an aid to technical or bibliographical control, which is photographed on the film preceding or following a document or series of documents.

(33) *"Thresholding"* refers to the level at which data elements are removed from the scanned document. During thresholding, individual pixels in an image are marked as object pixels if their value is greater than some threshold value and as background pixels otherwise. Thresholding is used in eliminating background discoloration of paper and stains on paper caused by aging, handling, and accidental spilling of fluids.

(34) *"WORM"* means Write–Once, Read–Many.

(C) Official Case Record.

(1) A microfilm record produced and documented in accordance with the provisions of this rule, or a duplicate copy of such microform kept by the court, is the official record of the Court or Court Agency, regardless of whether or not an original paper document exists.

(2) A document generated from a digital image produced in accordance with the provisions of this rule is the official record of the Court or Court Agency, regardless of whether or not an original paper document exists.

(D) Microfilm Specifications. Specifications for microfilm equipment, film, and photographic chemicals

must meet appropriate standards referenced in section (G) of this rule. However, before a court, clerk, or court agency shall install such a system to create an official record, systems specifications must be forwarded to the Division, in writing, to determine compliance with Trial Rule 77(J).

(E) Digital Imaging Specifications. Specifications for digital imaging systems must meet appropriate standards referenced in section (H) of this rule. However, before a court, clerk, or court agency shall install such a system to create an official record, systems specifications must be forwarded to the Division, in writing, to determine compliance with Trial Rule 77(J).

(F) General Standards.

(1) Courts, Clerks and Court Agencies shall ensure that records generated by, or received by, the courts are preserved in accordance with the applicable record retention schedules in Administrative Rule 7.

(2) Records required to be placed in the Record of Judgments and Orders (RJO) as paper or in electronic format, and records with a retention schedule of fifteen (15) years or more, are classified as permanent. Such records must be scanned using a dpi as specified in Administrative Rule 6 (H)(2)(a)(ii).

(3) Microform and Digital Media used for the storage of court records shall be inspected at least annually to verify that no deterioration has occurred, incorporating the appropriate ANSI/AIIM standard for microfilm or for digital data deterioration in accordance with Administrative Rule 6 (H)(3)(i). Such inspection results shall be forwarded to the Division on a form available from the Division.

(G) Microfilm Standards.

(1) *Documentation.* A formal written documentation file shall be created by the Clerk or the appropriate public agency and retained for the microfilm process, incorporating the following:

(a) That every stage of the microfilm process is covered by a written procedure and kept in the documentation file including:

(i) Authority to microfilm specific records;

(ii) A preparation guide concerning the arrangement of the originals on microfilm;

(iii) Any policy to select which filed documents will be placed on microfilm;

(iv) Any contracts with in-house record custodians or agents of vendors who will perform the actual microfilming (either in-house or through a vendor);

(v) Maintenance of the "Certificate of Destruction" form and approval correspondence from the Division.

(b) The reproduction processes employed to assure accuracy.

(c) Verification of each microfilm image against the original for completeness and legibility. The verification process shall be part of the certification procedure submitted to the Division.

(d) The justification for the microfilming of originals (i.e., space reduction, security) and the written process for the destruction of originals as authorized by an approved retention schedule.

(e) The identity of supervisors of the microfilming procedures who are capable of giving evidence of these procedures.

(f) The retention schedule from Administrative Rule 7 for the documentation matching the expected longevity of the microform.

(g) Certification of compliance with this documentation procedure to the Division.

(2) *Legibility.*

(a) If a standard is updated or superseded, the most current one applies to those records preserved after its effective date.

(b) Resolution. A microform system for source documents shall be tested for resolution capability under procedures set forth in the appropriate section of ANSI/AIIM MS23–2004, both upon installation of the system and at the beginning and end of each roll of microfilm, by use of a camera test chart, such as the "Rotary Camera Test Chart," ANSI/AIIM MS 17–2001; "The Planetary Camera Test Chart," ANSI/ISO Test Chart No. 2, arranged one in each of the four corners of the image area and one in the center; or any equivalent chart incorporating the appropriate camera test charts. Where camera-generated roll microfilm is not used, a microform of the appropriate camera test chart must be generated weekly. Micrographic systems used for court records must meet the following standards for resolution:

(i) A micrographic system for source documents must produce a quality index level of not less than 5.0 for third-generation microfilm as measured according to *American National Standard Practice for Operational Procedures/Inspection and Quality Control of First–Generation, Silver–Gelatin Microfilm of Documents.* ANSI/AIIM MS23- 2004. In applying this standard, a lower-case letter "e" height of 1.4 millimeters or less must be used;

(ii) All pattern groups on the camera test chart must be read. The smallest line pattern (highest numerical designation) in which both horizontal and vertical line direction is clearly discernible is the resolving power of that pattern group. The lowest numerical resolving power of all the pattern groups on the camera test chart is the resolving power of the micrographic system;

(iii) The film used in reading the camera test chart must be processed to the density standard of Administrative Rule 6 (G)(2)(c)(i);

(iv) A computer-output microfilm system must produce quality index of not less than 5.0 for third-generation microfilm as measured according to *American National Standard Practice for Operational Practices/Inspection and Quality Control for Alphanumeric Computer–Output Microforms.* ANSI/AIIM MS1–1996.

(v) Conversion of archival data stored on a Digital Master [(H) (1) (g)], may occur at a quality index level of 4.0, upon written pre-approval from the Division.

(c) Density. Microfilm systems used for court records must meet the following density standards:

(i) The background ISO standard visual diffuse transmission density on microforms shall be appropriate to the type of documents being filmed. The procedure for density measurement is described in ANSI/AIIM MS23-2004 and the densitometer shall be in accordance with ANSI/NAPM 18–1996, for spectral conditions and ANSI/NAPM IT2.19–1994, for geometric conditions for transmission density. Recommended visual diffuse transmission background densities for images of documents are as follows:

Class	Description of documents	Background Density
Group 1	High-quality, high-contrast printed books, periodicals, and black typing	1.3–1.5
Group 2	Fine-line originals, black opaque pencil writing, and documents with small high-contrast printing.	1.15–1.4
Group 3	Pencil and ink drawings, faded printing, and very small printing such as footnotes at the bottom of a printed page.	1.0–1.2
Group 4	Low-contrast manuscripts and drawing, graph paper with pale, fine-colored lines; letters typed with worn ribbon; and poorly printed, faint documents.	0.8–1.0

(ii) Background density in first-generation computer-output microfilm must meet ANSI/AIIM MS1–1996.

(iii) Base Plus Fog Density of Films. The base plus fog density of unexposed, processed films should not exceed 0.10. When a tinted base film is used, the density will be increased. The difference must be added to the values given in the tables in Administrative Rule 6 (G)(2)(c)(i).

(iv) Line or Stroke Width. Due to optical limitations in most photographic systems, film images of thin lines appearing in the original document will tend to fill in as a function of their width and density. Therefore, as the reduction ratio of a given system is increased, the background density shall be reduced as needed to ensure that the copies produced will contain legible characters.

(d) Reduction Ratio. Microfilm systems used for court records shall meet the following reduction ratio standards:

(i) A reduction ratio for microfilm of documents of 25 to 1 or 24 to 1 or less is required;

(ii) A reduction ratio for microfilm of documents of greater than 25 to 1 may be used only if the micrographics system can maintain the required quality index at the higher reduction;

(iii) Computer-output microfilm must be at a reduction ratio ranging from 48 to 1 to 24 to 1.

(3) *Permanency.* For records requiring retention of over fifteen years based on an approved retention schedule under Administrative Rule 7, the following standards shall apply:

(a) Raw stock microfilm shall be of safety-based permanent record film meeting specification of ANSI/NAPM IT9.6–1991 (R 1996).

(b) The camera generated master negative microfilm shall be silver-halide silver gelatin, meeting the permanency requirements of ANSI/NAPM IT9.1–1996. Microforms shall be processed in accordance with ANSI/NAPM IT 9.1–1996 and in accordance with processing procedures in ANSI/ AIIM MS196 and ANSI/AIIM MS23–2004.

(c) The master microfilm record meeting the above standards shall be stored at a site other than the producing Clerk, Court, or Court Agency's structure, in a fireproof vault, meeting ISO 18911:2010.

(d) In addition to the master microfilm record, which is a security copy, the Clerk, Court, or Court Agency may provide working copies of the microfilm. These may be on silver, diazo, vesicular, dry silver, or transparent electro-photograph film on a safety base of cellulose ester or polyester material.

(H) Digital Imaging Standards.

(1) *Documentation.* A formal written documentation file shall be created by the Clerk or the appropriate public agency and retained for the life of the information stored on the digital medium based upon an approved record retention schedule documenting the following:

(a) that every stage of the digital imaging process is covered by a written procedure and kept in the documentation file, including:

(i) authority to implement digital imaging technology.

(ii) any selection policy to determine what documents from any file will be imaged. The indexing process shall also identify documents which are subject to approved criteria for purging prior to conversion to a permanent storage medium, and

(iii) any contracts with agents of record custodians who will perform the actual digital imaging process;

(iv) the metadata for each digital record.

(b) the imaging process employed to assure accuracy;

(c) verification of the image on a computer screen against the original for completeness and legibility;

(d) definition of the indexing system employed with storage in multiple places on the optical disk for security and integrity;

(e) the identity of supervisors of the digital imaging procedures who are capable of giving evidence of these procedures; and

(f) written certification of compliance with this documentation procedure to the Division.

(g) Archival data stored on a digital master shall be converted to microfilm. Retention schedules will be applied to all documents prior to conversion to microfilm.

(2) *Legibility.* The following standards on legibility apply for digital imaging. If a standard is updated or superseded, the most current one applies to those records preserved after its effective date.

(a) Scanner input shall:

(i) Scan office documents at a density of at least 200 dpi.

(ii) Scan records deemed permanent according to the retention schedule and as required for placement in the Record of Judgments and Orders, at a minimum of 300 dpi; and

(iii) Use a higher scanning resolution, as needed, for poor contrast documents, those containing faded text and those containing fine handwriting or lines, based upon a verification test that includes hard copy reproduction from such scanned documents at various densities, and

(iv) Scanning quality must adhere to the standards presented in *Recommended Practices for Quality Control of Image Scanners* ANSI/AIIM MS44–1988 (R1993), incorporating scanner resolution target X441 or X443, depending upon the application.

(b) Image enhancement is permissible for lightening or darkening a digital image, improving sharpness or contrast, but applying threshold software to eliminate noise requires prior approval of the Division.

(3) *Permanency.* The following standards on permanency shall apply for digital imaging: Storage and quality control standards apply only to Digital Masters and not to digital duplicates.

(a) Digital imaging systems will be built from hardware and software components that are non-proprietary and are based upon open systems architecture.

(b) Digital imaging systems will use the Digital Imaging File Format known as TIFF Group 4 digital imaging file format meeting ISO Standard 12639: 2004, (or as updated or superseded.)

(c) Data will be scanned using SCSI [small computer system interface] command "write and verify."

(d) System upgrades will provide backward compatibility to existing system or digital data will be converted to the upgrade at the time of such upgrade.

(e) The digital master will employ WORM technology as the digital medium.

(f) If a CD–ROM is used as a storage medium, it must comply with ISO 9660–1988, *Volume and File Structure of CD–ROM for Information Interchange*. CD–ROM, EO, and DVD media shall not be used for storage of the digital master but may be used for digital duplicates.

(g) Digital media will have a pre-write shelf life of at least five years and post-write life of twenty years based upon accelerated aging test results that reports on specific disk areas.

(h) The digital master shall be stored in a dust-free, temperature and humidity-controlled environment, meeting ANSI/AIIM TR25–1995, *Use of Optical Disks for Public Records*.

(i) The digital media shall be monitored for deterioration using ANSI/AIIM MS59–1996 *Media Error Monitoring and Reporting Techniques for Verification of Stored Data on Optical Digital Data Disks*, and duplicating data to a new or replacement medium when data deterioration reaches the point of loss as described in this standard.

(I) Hybrid Systems. That portion of a hybrid system producing microforms will be governed by Section (G) of this rule; that portion of a hybrid system producing digital images will be governed by Section (H) of this rule.

(J) Access. Access to a court record created or stored in either or both a microfilm or digital format will be governed according to Administrative Rule 9.

(K) Disposal of Records. Court records which have been preserved in accordance with the standards set out in this rule may be destroyed or otherwise disposed but only after the court or its clerk files a "Destruction Certificate" with the Division certifying that the records have been microfilmed or digitized in accordance with the standards set out in this rule, and the Division issues a written authorization for the destruction of such records. The Division shall make available a form "Destruction Certificate" for this purpose.

Adopted Nov. 4, 1985, effective Jan. 1, 1986. Amended Oct. 30, 1986, effective Jan. 1, 1987; Dec. 7, 1987, effective Jan. 1, 1988; Nov. 10, 1988, effective Jan. 1, 1989; Nov. 13, 1990, effective Jan. 1, 1991; Dec. 15, 1995, effective Feb. 1, 1996; amended effective Nov. 18, 1999; Sept. 30, 2004, effective Jan. 1, 2005; amended effective Feb. 1, 2007; amended Sept. 10, 2007, effective Jan. 1, 2008; Sept. 20, 2011, effective Jan. 1, 2012.

Rule 7. Judicial Retention Schedules

I. GENERAL

A. Authority to Dispose of Records.

Clerks of Circuit Court, Judges and other court officers shall dispose of records in the manner set out in this Rule and in accordance with the retention schedules specified herein. The retention schedules set out in this Rule should be presented to the appropriate county records commission, one time only for informational purposes, before disposal of the records. Prior to disposal of judicial records not listed on this schedule, or if special circumstances necessitate the retention or disposal of judicial records in a manner not set forth in this Rule, a circuit court clerk, judge or other officer of the court must seek written authorization from the Division of State Court Administration to maintain or destroy such records.

B. Records Authorized to Be Microfilmed.

Records which call for microfilming under this Rule must be microfilmed in accordance with the provisions of Administrative Rule 6. The following are the only record series which are authorized to be microfilmed:

(1) Records whose retention requires microfilming;

(2) Records which may be maintained in original or microform, as provided in the retention schedules;

(3) Records which must be retained permanently, as provided in the retention schedules;

Microfilming other records is not authorized because the cost of microfilming exceeds the costs of storage for the duration of the retention period. If special circumstances arise, a circuit court clerk, judge, or other officer of the court may seek written authorization from the Division of State Court Administration to microfilm records other than those herein authorized.

C. Records Authorized for Transfer. Records deemed permanent or authorized for transfer to the Indiana State Archives. Indiana Commission on Public Records, must follow the Commission's written procedures and use its approved forms before transfer can occur. With the written approval of the Indiana Supreme Court, records authorized for transfer to the Archives Division of the Indiana Commission on Public Records may be deposited by said Commission with a local repository, such as a historical society, library, archives, or university, as designated by the Commission and meeting the archival standards of the Commission.

D. Retention Schedules.

These retention schedules are based upon assumptions that because certain records exist, others may be destroyed. Due to fire disasters, or other causes, this may not be true for all Indiana counties. Therefore, the first step is to conduct an inventory to determine if records requiring permanent retention or transfer do indeed exist before destroying records by series whose authority for destruction is based on the fact that other records exist.

The list of retention schedules is arbitrarily arranged by type of jurisdiction and not by court, since jurisdictions overlap from court to court with original, concurrent and exclusive jurisdictions. Different courts in different counties can exercise the same jurisdiction. The date of 1790 means that the record potentially could date from the formation of the county.

The format includes a number, as 85–4.3–04, which gives the year of the schedules (1985), the jurisdiction (4.3, or family law/adoptions) and the record series item (04). As new record series are added, additional numbers will be assigned. If a series is amended, it will be followed by an "R" for "revised." The jurisdictions, which can be the same for a number of courts, are classified as:

85–1   CIVIL
      85–1.1   Civil
      85–1.2   Chancery
      85–1.3   Lis Pendens Series
      85–1.4   Partitions
      85–1.5   Dissolution of Marriage
85–2   CRIMINAL
85–3   ESTATES
      85–3.1   Wills
      85–3.2   Estates
      85–3.3   Guardianships
      85–3.4   Trusts
85–4   FAMILY LAW
      85–4.1   Juvenile
      85–4.2   Paternity
      85–4.3   Adoption
      85–4.4   Birth Certificate Record
85–5   COUNTY COURT/MUNICIPAL COURT/SMALL CLAIMS
      Small Claims
      Misdemeanors
      Traffic Infractions
      Plenary Civil
      City Civil Jurisdiction
85–6   NATURALIZATION
85–7   CONCILIATION
85–8   SPECIAL JUDICIAL FUNCTIONS
      85–8.1   Insanity/Mental Health
      85–8.2   Epileptic Hearings

II. PROCEDURE

It is critically important that these schedules be carried out exactly as approved since this is your legal authority to do so, and only for the records so listed. Once a record is destroyed, its information is lost. Do not assume that the record under consideration is the record actually authorized for destruction. You must compare both the title and content before a record series can be destroyed. Work in a spirit of caution. If in doubt, save until you can get advice from the Division of State Court Administration or the Indiana Commission on Public Records.

CIVIL (1)

85–1.1–01R	Entry Docket	1790–c. 1913	maintain permanently in original or in microform meeting the standards of Admin.R. 6.
85–1.1–02	Issue Docket	1790–c. 1913	destroy.
85–1.1–03R	Entry, Issue Docket & Fee Book (Civil Docket, 1970 +)	c. 1913–1990	maintain permanently in original or in microfilm (microfilm after 20 years).
85–1.1–04	Change of Venue Record	c. 1873 +	maintain permanently in original, or microfilm after 20 years and destroy original.
85–1.1–05	Judge's/Bench/Court Docket	1790–c. 1918	destroy.
85–1.1–06	Clerk's Docket Day Book/Scratch Book	1790–c. 1918	destroy.
85–1.1–07	Sheriff's Docket (rare)	1790–c. 1918	destroy.
85–1.1–08	Bar Docket (cases arranged by attorney; not Entry Docket)	1790– +	destroy.
85–1.1–09	Summons Docket (rare)	c. 1790– +	destroy 6 years after date of last entry.
85–1.1–10	Sheriff's Summons Docket (rare)	c. 1790– +	destroy 6 years after date of last entry.
85–1.1–11	Witness Docket/Witness Affidavit Docket	c. 1860's– +	destroy 3 years after date of last entry and audit by State Board of Accounts.
85–1.1–12	Stamp Tax Docket	c. 1933–1965	destroy.
85–1.1–13	Bond Register (bonds filed in civil actions)	c. 1880's– +	destroy 20 years after date of last entry.
85–1.1–14	Misc. Bond Record (bonds filed in civil actions)	c. 1880's– +	destroy 20 years after date of last entry.
85–1.1–15	Recognizance Bond Record–Civil	varies as separate ledger	destroy 20 years after date of last entry.
85–1.1–16	Record of Assignments (rare)	1870's– +	destroy 20 years after date of last entry.
85–1.1–17R	Civil Order Book	1790–1990	maintain permanently in original or microform meeting standards of Admin.R. 6. Microfilm after 20 years and transfer originals to the Indiana Commission on Public Records or otherwise dispose of upon approval of the Division of State Court Administration.

85–1.1–18	Index to Civil Cases/General Index to Civil Order Book/ Gen. Index Plaintiff and Gen. Index, Defendant	1790–1990	maintain permanently in original or microfilm 20 years after date of last entry, using microfilm system meeting standards set by Supreme Court.
85–1.1–19R	Misc. Order Book	varies, usually 20th Century	maintain permanently in original or in microform meeting standards of Admin.R. 6. Microfilm after 20 years and transfer originals to the Indiana Commission on Public Records or otherwise dispose of upon approval of the Division of State Court Administration.
85–1.1–19.1R	Nonjudicial Order Book (Certifications and Statutorily Directed Matters)	1989– +	maintain permanently in original or in microform meeting the standards set by the Supreme Court (microfilm after 20 years).
85.1.1–20	Civil Order Book Complete; Final Order Book Civil	1790–1990, usually 19th Century	transfer to Archives Division, Indiana Commission on Public Records.
85–1.1–21	General Index to Complete Order Book, Civil	1790–1990	transfer to Archives Division, Indiana Commission on Public Records.
85–1.1–22	Depositions, opened	1790– +	maintain as part of Civil Case File.
85–1.1–23	Depositions Not Admitted Into Evidence or for Dismissed Cases	1790– +	return to attorney at disposition of case or destroy 1 year after final disposition of case.
85–1.1–24	Docket Sheets	c. 1910–1990	maintain permanently in original, or microfilm and destroy original 3 years after final disposition of case, unless dissolution of marriage, then microfilm and destroy original 21 years after disposition.
85–1.1–25R	Plenary Civil Case Files Designated as CP, CT, MT, PL, CC, MF	1790–9/1881	transfer to Archives Division, Indiana Commission on Public Records.
		9/1881–1990	maintain all divorce/dissolution cases; cases where title to real property is in issue; public sector cases; and pre–1941 adoption and bastardy cases in original or in microfilm. For remaining cases, maintain a 2% statistical sample, which is determined by the Division of State Court Administration with transfer to the Archives Division, Indiana Commission on Public Records. Destroy remaining files 20 years after final disposition.
90–1.1–25.1R	Civil Miscellaneous Case Files (MI)	1/01/1987– +	retain for 5 years and upon review of trial court. Maintain permanently all tax deed MI cases ordered upon IC 6–1.1–25–4.6.
85–1.1–26R	Dismissed Civil Case Files Designated as CP, CT, MI, RS, DR, MH, PO, PL, CC, MF	9/1881– +	Unless relief granted under TR 60(B): (a) those dismissed before trial, destroy 2 years after dismissal; (b) those dismissed during or after trial, destroy 2 years after order to dismiss is given under TR 41.
89–1.1–26.1R	Shorthand Notes/ Tapes/ Disks Not Transcribed	1873– +	destroy 3 years after date of trial for CP, CT, MI, RS, DR, MH, PO, CC, MF.
91–1.1–61	Protective Order Case Files With PO	1/1/1992– +	destroy 3 years after date Order has been entered.

	Designation Under Administrative Rule 8		
91–1.1–62	Notice and Release of Lien for Medical Assistance (IC 12–1–7–24.6)(c)(1)	1982– +	for those liens formally released by Dept. of Public Welfare, destroy notice and Lien 2 years after release filed.
91–1.1–63	Hardship Driver's License (Emergency Order for Restricted Hardship License) (MI Case # Only)	varies	for independent court action, not a part of a larger case, and if original order in RJO, destroy Case File 2 years after judgment.

JUDGMENTS AND EXECUTIONS

85–1.1–27	Judgment Dockets	1790– + pre–1853	transfer to Archives Division, Indiana Commission on Public Records.
		post 1852	destroy docket 20 years after date of last entry.
85–1.1–28	Transcribed Judgment Docket (copy of deteriorated original)	varies	destroy 20 years after date of last entry.
85–1.1–29	Judgment Docket Release	c. 20th Century	destroy 20 years after date of last entry.
85–1.1–30	Record of Delinquent Tax/Delinquent Tax Judgment Record IC 6–1–55–1 IC 6–1.1–23–9	1964– +	destroy 20 years after date of last entry.
85–1.1–31	Judgment Docket: Statements and Transcripts (orig. statements of judgment of court w. ref. to Judgment Docket) (ledger) ACTS 1929:83:1 IC 34–1–43–1 (not all courts created this ledger)	1929– +	destroy 20 years after date of last entry.
85–1.1–32	Judgment Statements and Transcripts (originals)	varies, usually after 1929– +	destroy 20 years after filing.
90–1.1–32.1	Collection Warrant Under Employment Security Act (IC 22–4–29–7)	varies	destroy after 20 years.
85–1.1–33	Judgment Docket Index	varies	destroy 20 years after date of last entry.
85–1.1–34	Praecipe/Certified Copy Praecipe (ledger)	1790– +	destroy 20 years after date of last entry.
85–1.1–35	Praecipes	1790– +	destroy 20 years after filing, if filed separately.
85–1.1–36	Executions	1790– + pre–1853	transfer to Archives Division, Indiana Commission on Public Records.
		post 1852	destroy 20 years after date of last entry.
85–1.1–37	Execution Dockets	1790– + pre–1853	transfer to Archives Division, Indiana Commission on Public Records.
		post 1852	destroy 20 years after date of last entry.
85–1.1–38	Sheriff's Execution Docket (rare)	c. 1853– +	destroy 20 years after date of last entry.

85–1.1–39	Register of Executions (rare)	c. 1870's– +	destroy 20 years after date of last entry.
85–1.1–40	Supplement to Execution Docket (rare)	c. 1870's– +	destroy 20 years after date of last entry.
85–1.1–41	Executions: Order of Sale (original pleadings)	c. 1790– +	destroy 20 years after date of issue.
85–1.1–42	Executions: Order of Sale (ledger)	c. 1790's– +	destroy 20 years after date of last entry.
85–1.1–43	Stay of Execution (original pleadings)	c. 1790's– +	destroy 20 years after date of issue.
85–1.1–44	Index to Execution Docket	varies	destroy 20 years after date of last entry.
85–1.1–45	Fee Bills (original filings)	1790– +	destroy after 20 years.
85–1.1–46	Fee Bill Record	varies, usually 20th Century	destroy 20 years after date of last entry.
85–1.1–47	Sheriff's Fee Bill Docket	varies, usually 20th Century	destroy 20 years after date of last entry.
85–1.1–48	Fee Bill Index	varies, usually 20th Century	destroy when last entry becomes 20 years old.
85–1.1–49	Tax Warrants IC 6–8–7–1 (1976)	1933–1980	destroy after 20 years.
85–1.1–50	Alias Tax Warrants IC 6–8–7–2 and IC 6–8–7–3 (1976)	1933–1980	destroy after 20 years.
85–1.1–51	Tax Warrants	1980– +	maintain 3 years after payment and audit by State Board of Accounts.
85–1.1–52	Alias Tax IC 6–8.1–8–2(e)	1980– +	maintain 3 years after payment and audit by State Board of Accounts.

NOTE: REVENUE DEPARTMENT MAY "RENEW A LIEN FOR ADDITIONAL TEN (10) YEAR PERIODS BY FILING AN ALIAS TAX WARRANT..."

85–1.1–53	Power of Attorney Filings	1790– + pre–9/1881 post 9/1881	transfer to Archives Division, Indiana Commission on Public Records. destroy after 20 years.
85–1.1–54	Power of Attorney Record (not all courts created)	c. 1881– + varies	destroy 20 years after date of last entry.
85–1.1–55	Power of Attorney Index (rare)	c. 1881– + varies	destroy 20 years after date of last entry.
85–1.1–56	Index to Misc. Court Records	c. 1853/81– + varies	maintain for period in which records are referred to.
85–1.1–57	Subpoena Docket (rare)	1790– +	destroy 20 years after date of last entry.
85–1.1–58	Sheriff's Subpoena Docket (rare)	1790– +	destroy 20 years after date of last entry.
87–1.1–59	Sheriff Foreign Service	varies	destroy 3 years after date of last entry.
88–1.1–60	Civil Fee Books	1790–c. 1913 +	destroy upon written approval of the Division of State Court Administration.

CHANCERY

85–1.2–01	Chancery Order Book	1843–1852	maintain permanently in original or in microform.
85–1.2–02	Case Files, Chancery	to 1853	transfer to Archives Division, Indiana Commission on Public Records.

LIS PENDENS

85–1.3–01	Lis Pendens Record (Complaints) IC 32–30–11–11	1877– +	destroy 20 years after date of last entry.
85–1.3–02	Lis Pendens - Complaint Files IC 32–30–11–1	1877– +	destroy 20 years after filing.
85–1.3–03	Lis Pendens Record - Sheriff's Notice of Attachment IC 32–30–11	1877– +	destroy 20 years after date of last entry.
85–1.3–04	Lis Pendens - Sheriff's Notice of Attachment IC 32–30–11	1877– +	destroy 20 years after filing.
85–1.3–05	Lis Pendens Record— Sheriff's Certificates of Sale IC 34–2–29–1	1881–1987	destroy 20 years after date of entry.
85–1.3–06	Lis Pendens—Sheriff's Certificates of Sale IC 34–2–29–1	1881–1987	destroy 20 years after filing.
85–1.3–07	Lis Pendens— Redemption Record IC 34–2–29–3	1881–1987	destroy 20 years after date of last entry.
85–1.3–08	Lis Pendens— Redemptions IC 34–2–29–3	1881–1987	destroy 20 years after filing.

NOTE: IC 34–2–29–1 et seq. was repealed by P.L. 309–1987.

85–1.3–09	Index—Lis Pendens Record (discretionary)	1877– +	destroy 20 years after date of last entry.
85–1.3–10	Transcript Order Book (to collect judgments)	JP to 1976 City 1847– + Gen.Cts. to current	destroy 20 years after date of last entry.
85–1.3–11	Transcripts (to collect judgments)	JP to 1976 City 1847– +	destroy 20 years after filing.
87–1.3–12	Transcript and Insurance Order Book (see also 85–1.3–10) (rare)	1877–1935	destroy.

NOTE: ACTS 1877(r): 43:1 required foreign insurance companies to file certain statements with the Auditor of State and Clerk of the Circuit Court, the latter to note "in vacation of entries of the order book of such court" the name of the company and its agent and the date of filing. Some courts created separate "order books" for this purpose.

87–1.3–13	Foreign Insurance Company Statements	1877–1935	destroy.

PARTITIONS

85–1.4–01	Partition Record	1853–1869 (& later)	maintain permanently in original or in microform.
85–1.4–02	Partition Record Complete	1853–1869 (& later)	maintain permanently in original or in microform.
85–1.4–03	Case Files, Partitions	1853– +	maintain in accordance with Plenary Civil Case Files, 85–1.1–25R.

DISSOLUTION OF MARRIAGE

Some courts maintain separate filing systems and have created separate "Domestic Relations" records for divorce/dissolution of marriage.

85–1.5–01R	Entry Docket, Issue Docket & Fee Book	c. 1973– +	maintain permanently in original or in microform (microfilm after 20 years).

85–1.5–02R	Order Book, Domestic Relations	c. 1973– +	maintain permanently in original or in microform meeting the standards of Admin.R. 6. Microfilm after 20 years and transfer originals to the Indiana Commission on Public Records or otherwise dispose of upon approval of the Division of State Court Administration.
85–1.5–03R	Divorce Case Files	to 8/31/1973	maintain in accordance with schedule 85–1.1–25R.
85–1.5–04	Judgment Docket	c. 1973– +	destroy 20 years after date of last entry.
85–1.5–05	Execution Docket	c. 1973– +	destroy 20 years after date of last entry.
85–1.5–06	Domestic Relations Index	c. 1973– +	maintain permanently in original or in microform. Microfilm 6 years after ledger is filled.
88–1.5–07	Dissolution of Marriage Case Files	9/01/1973– +	maintain in accordance with Plenary Civil Case Files, 85–1.1–25R.
90–1.5–07.1	Dismissed Divorce/Dissolution of Marriage Case Files	9/1881– +	destroy in accordance with Dismissed Plenary Civil Case Files 85–1.1–26R.
91–1.5–0.8	UIRESA Uniform Support, Petition, Certificate and Order as Initiating Court Under IC 31–18–3–4	7/01/1951- +	maintain 2 years after order is entered if copy of petition is maintained by prosecuting attorney. (Docket Sheet/CCS is maintained).
01–1.5–10	Reciprocal Support (RS) Case files as Responding Court under IC 31–18–3–5		destroy case files 21 years after date of last action (Applies to both adjudicated and dismissed case files.)
93–1.5–09	Court Referral Case Files (IC 31–1–23); (IC 31–1–24)	1971 – +	Domestic Relations Counseling Bureau Files. Destroy files 21 years after date of last entry.

CRIMINAL (2)

85–2–01	Indictment Record—Grand Jury (ledger)	1853–1973	transfer to Archives Division, Indiana Commission on Public Records.
85–2–02	Indictments/Grand Jury Reports	1790– +	transfer to Archives Division, Indiana Commission on Public Records after 20 years.
85–2–03R	Information Record	1853–1905	transfer to Archives Division, Indiana Commission on Public Records.
87–2–33	Affidavit Record	1905–1973	transfer to Archives Division, Indiana Commission on Public Records
87–2–34	Indictment/Information Record IC 35–34–1–1	1973– +	transfer to Archives Division, Indiana Commission on Public Records after 20 years.
85–2–04	Informations/Affidavits (1905–1973)	1853 - +	transfer to Archives Division, Indiana Commission on Public Records after 20 years.
85–2–05	Arrest Warrants	1790 - +	file with Criminal Case File.
85–2–06	Recognizance Bonds, Criminal	1790– +	transfer bonds prior to 9–01–1881 to Archives Division, Indiana Commission on Public Records; destroy post 1881 bonds after 6 years.
85–2–07	Criminal Recognizance Bond Record (discretionary)	1790– +	transfer ledgers prior to 9–01–1881 to Archives Division, Indiana Commission on Public Records; destroy post 9/1881 ledgers 6 years after date of last entry.

85–2–08	Continuing Recognizance Bond Record (discretionary) (rare)	1790 - +	destroy 6 years after date of last entry.
85–2–09	Habeas Corpus	1790 - +	transfer to Archives Division, Indiana Commission on Public Records 6 years after date of issue, if filed separately.
85–2–10	Habeas Corpus (ledger)	1790- +	transfer to Archives Division, Indiana Commission on Public Records 6 years after date of last entry.
85–2–11R	Entry Docket	1790–1913	maintain permanently in original or in microform meeting the standards of Admin. R. 6.
85–2–12	Entry Docket & Fee Book	1913–1990	maintain permanently in original or in microform; microfilm 20 years after date of last entry.
90–2–12.1	Issue Docket, Criminal	1790–c. 1915	destroy.
85–2–13	Fee Book, Criminal	to 1913	destroy if separate Entry Docket exists. If not, maintain permanently in original or in microform.
85–2–14	Clerk's Docket, Criminal (discretionary)	1790–1920's	destroy.
85–2–15	Judge's/Bench/Court Docket, Criminal	1790–1920's	destroy.
85–2–16	State Docket	c. 1880's	destroy.
85–2–17	Sheriff's State Docket	c. 1880's	destroy.
85–2–18	Docket Sheets, Criminal	c. 1910's–1990	maintain permanently in original or in microform. Microfilm original 3 years after case is disposed of.
85–2–19R	Order Book, Criminal	c. 1860's–1990 (varies)	maintain permanently in original or in microform meeting the standards of Admin.R. 6. Microfilm after 20 years and transfer original to the Indiana Commission on Public Records or otherwise dispose of upon approval of the Division of State Court Administration.
85–2–20	Order Book Complete, Criminal (rare)	c. 1860's– c. 1880's	maintain permanently in original or in microform.
85–2–21R	Felony Criminal Case Files	1790- to 9–01–1881	transfer all files prior to 9–01–1881 to Archives Division, Indiana Commission on Public Records.
		9/1881–1990	Maintain a 2% statistical sample, which is determined by the Division of State Court Administration with transfer to the Archives Division, Indiana Commission on Public Records. Destroy remaining files 55 years after final disposition. Maintain packet for post- conviction relief.
87–2–21.1R	Dismissed Felony Case Files	9/1881– +	destroy 2 years after order to dismiss is given.
90–2–21.2	Misdemeanor Criminal Case Files (CM)	1790- to 9/1881	transfer all files prior to 9–01–1881 to Archives Division, Indiana Commission on Public Records.

		9/1881 +	Maintain a 2% statistical sample, which is determined by the Division of State Court Administration with transfer to the Archives Division, Indiana Commission on Public Records. Destroy remaining files 10 years after final disposition.
		1990- +	handgun possession maintain fifteen years.
85–2–22	Judgment Docket Criminal	rare as separate volume	destroy 20 years after date of last entry.
85–2–23	Disfranchisement Record (rare)	1920's	destroy.
85–2–24	Suspended Sentence Docket	1919–1977	destroy 55 years after date of last entry.
85–2–25	Judgment Withheld Docket	1919–1977	destroy 55 years after date of last entry.
85–2–26R	Depositions Published or Unpublished	1790– +	destroy after 55 years if unopened and not filed with court packet.
95–2–26.1	Misdemeanor Depositions Published or Unpublished	1852– +	destroy after 10 years if unopened and not filed in court packet.
85–2–27R	Shorthand Notes/ Tapes/Disks Not Transcribed—Felonies	1873- +	destroy 55 years after date of trial. [Criminal Rule 5]
89–2–27.1	Shorthand Notes/ Tapes/Disks Not Transcribed–Misdemeanors (CM)	1873– +	destroy 10 years after date of trial.
85–2–28	Transcripts for Appeals	1790– +	file in Criminal Case File if copy is maintained.
85–2–29	Probation Files	1907– +	destroy 6 years after release of individual from final discharge.
95–2–29.1	Court Administered Alcohol Program (CAAP)	1974– +	destroy 6 years after release of individual from final discharge (Probation Department Files).
95–2–29.2	Alternative Sentencing Case Files (Work Release Files)	1991– +	destroy 6 years after release of individual from final discharge (Probation Department Files).
85–2–30	General Index, Criminals	varies	transfer to Archives Division, Indiana Commission on Public Records after 55 years.
85–2–31R	Restitution Record IC 35–38–2–2	(1927) 1976– +	destroy 6 years after date of last entry.
89–2–32R	Search Warrants (Executed and Unexecuted) and not associated with a specific criminal case file	1790– +	place in separate case file and assign a criminal miscellaneous case number. Destroy 20 years after issuance of warrant. (The prosecuting attorney may request a longer retention period by filing a written request specifying the length of the extended retention period).
09–2–32.1	Search Warrant Executed and associated with specific criminal case file	1790– +	place in separate case file and assign a criminal miscellaneous case number. Destroy at the same time as the associated criminal case. If there is more than one associated criminal case, destroy at the same time as the case with the longest retention period. An association

			with a specific criminal case is created when a notice is filed with the court by the prosecuting attorney stating that a filed criminal case is associated with the executed search warrant. Upon the filing of such a notice, an entry shall be made on the CCS in both cases noting the association.
09–2–32.2	Search Warrants Denied or Not Executed	1790– +	destroy 2 years after order denying issuance of search warrant or if search is not executed (No return filed within the 2 year period presumes that warrant was not executed).
89–2–33R	Certificates on Standards for Breath Test Operators, Equipment & Chemicals (IC 9–30–6–5)	1983— +	destroy 10 years after filing or upon recordation in Nonjudicial Order Book 89–1.1-19.1.
05–2–34	Dismissed Misdemeanor Case Files	9/1881	destroy 1 year after order to dismiss is given.
05–2–35	Forensic Diversion Program	2004— +	destroy 6 years after release of individual from final discharge.
05–2–36	Wiretap recordings Under IC 35–33.5–5–2	1990— +	Destroy after ten (10) years only upon an order of the court that issued the warrant.
05–2–37	Applications for wiretaps and corresponding warrants under IC 35–33.5–5–2	1990— +	Destroy after ten (10) years only upon an order of the court that issued the warrant.
09–2–38	Grand Jury Recordings and Transcriptions—felonies	1881 +	Destroy 55 years after date of final disposition.
09–2–38.1	Grand Jury Recordings and Transcriptions—dismissed felony cases	1881 +	Destroy 2 years after order to dismiss granted
05–2–38.2	Grand Jury Recordings and Transcriptions—misdemeanors	1881 +	Destroy 10 years after date of final disposition
09–2–38.3	Grand Jury Recordings and Transcriptions—dismissed misdemeanors	1881— +	Destroy 1 year after order to dismiss granted
12–2–39	Problem–Solving Court Case Files	2002–+	Destroy no earlier than 6 years after discharge from problem-solving court or completion of probation whichever is later

ESTATES (3)

WILLS

85–3.1–01R	Recorded Original Wills	1790– +	maintain permanently in original or in microform (as a part of the Estate Case File, or as a separate series if filed separately). Microfilm after 5 years.
85–3.1–02	Will Record	1790– +	maintain permanently in original format; microfilm as a critical record, for security.
85–3.1–03	Transcript Will Record/original Will Record Ledger (a copy of an original ledger,	varies	maintain both versions permanently in original format; microfilm as a critical record, for security.

copied for preservation)

85–3.1.04	Clerk's Report of Wills Probated in Vacation	discretionary, usually from 1881, little used thereafter	maintain permanently in original format; microfilm as a critical record, for security.
85–3.1–05	Index to Will Record	discretionary	maintain permanently in original format, microfilm as a critical record, for security.

ESTATES

85–3.2–01	Appearance Docket	to c. 1881	maintain permanently in original or in microform.
85–3.2–02	Allowance Docket	to c. 1879	destroy.
85–3.2–03	Estate Entry Docket	to c. 1879	maintain permanently in original or in microform.
85–3.2–04	General Entry Claim and Allowance Docket	c. 1879 c.	maintain permanently in original or in microform.
85–3.2–05	Estate Entry Claim and Allowance Docket & Fee Book (Form 42)	c. 1911- +	maintain permanently; microfilm and destroy original 3 years after date of last entry.
85–3.2–06	Vacation Entries in Estates and Guardianships	discretionary c. 1881–c. 1920's	maintain permanently in original or in microform.
85–3.2–07	Probate Claim Docket	discretionary c. 1853–c. 1879	destroy.
85–3.2–08	Clerk's Minute Book, Probate/Clerk's Docket	discretionary	destroy.
85–3.2–09	Clerk's Docket, Sale of Real Estate	discretionary	destroy.
85–3.2–10	Bar Docket, Probate	discretionary to c. 1920's	destroy.
85–3.2–11	Bench/Estate/Judge's Docket, Probate	to c. 1920's	destroy.
85–3.2–12	Issue Docket, Probate	discretionary to c.1913	destroy.
85–3.2–13	Transfer Docket, Probate	discretionary to c. 1920's	destroy.
85–3.2–14	Docket Sheets, Estate	c. 1910–1990	maintain permanently in original, or microfilm 3 years after close of case.
85–3.2–15R	Probate/ Estate Case Files	1790–1990	maintain permanently in original or in microform (microfilm 2 years after order of final discharge of personal representative).
85–3.2–16	Accounts Current Reports IC 29–1–1–23(f)	c. 1860's–	maintain as part of Probate Case File.
85–3.2–17	Claims Against the Estate	1790– +	maintain as part of Probate Case File.
85–3.2–18	Sale of Real Estate, Probate	1790– +	maintain as part of Probate Case File.
85–3.2–19	Settled Assignment of Estates, Probate	1790– +	maintain as part of Probate Case File.
85–3.2–20	Executor's Oath & Letters (ledger)	c. 1840's–1953	destroy ledger 20 years after disposal of last case.
85–3.2–21	Administrator's Oaths & Letters (ledger)	c. 1840's–1953	destroy ledger 20 years after disposal of last case.

85–3.2–22	Executor's Bond Record IC 29–1–1–23(d)	1840's–6/30/1991	destroy ledger 20 years after disposal of last case.
85–3.2–23	Administrator's Bond Record IC 29–1–1–23(d)	1840's–6/30/1991	destroy 20 years after disposal of last case.
88–3.2–51	Personal Representatives Bonds (ledger) per IC 29–1–1–23(d) (discretionary)	1/01/1954–6/30/1991	destroy 20 years after disposal of last entry.
85–3.2–24	Executor's Bond to Sell Real Estate (ledger)	1853–c. 1881	destroy.
85–3.2–25	Administrator's Bond to Sell Real Estate (ledger)	1853–c. 1881	destroy.
85–3.2–26	Commissioner's Bond to Sell Real Estate (ledger)	1853–1881	destroy.
85–3.2–27	Record of Additional Bonds, Estates (discretionary)	c. 1853–c. 1881	destroy.
85–3.2–28	Commissioner's Bond Record (discretionary)	c. 1853–c. 1881	destroy.
85–3.2–29	Executor's Bonds Oaths & Letters (ledger)	c. 1853–1953	destroy 20 years after disposal of last case.
85–3.2–30	Administrator's Bonds, Oaths & Letters (ledger)	c. 1853–1953	destroy 20 years after disposal of last case.
85–3.2–31	Administrator's Executor's and Guardian's Bonds to Sell Real Estate	1853 - c. 1881	destroy.

NOTE: ORIGINAL BONDS, OATHS, & LETTERS ARE APPROVED BY THE COURT, ARE ENTERED IN THE ORDER BOOK WITH ORIGINALS FILED IN THE ESTATE CASE FILES.

85–3.2–32	Record of Inventories IC 29–1–1–23(e)	1853–6/30/1991	destroy 20 years after disposal of last case.
85–3.2–33	Inventory of Surviving Partners (ledger)	post 1853, discretionary	destroy 20 years after disposal of last case.
85–3.2–34	Record of Inventory & Sale Bills	1853–6/30/1991	destroy 20 years after disposal of last case.
85–3.2–35	Record of Sale Bills/Account Sale of Personal Property	1853–1953	destroy.
85–3.2–36R	Probate Order Book	1790–1990	maintain permanently in original or in microform meeting the standards of Admin.R. 6. Microfilm after 20 years and transfer originals to the Indiana Commission on Public Records or otherwise dispose of upon approval of the Division of State Court Administration.
85–3.2–37R	Probate Order Book, Complete	c. 1829–c. 1920's	maintain permanently in original or in microform meeting the standards of Admin.R. 6. Microfilm after 20 years and transfer originals to the Indiana Commission on Public Records or otherwise dispose of upon approval of the Division of State Court Administration.
85–3.2–38	Order Book Estates, Vacation Entries	c. 1881–c. 1969	maintain permanently in original or in microform.

85–3.2–39	Assignment Order Book	discretionary	maintain permanently in original or in microform.
85–3.2–40	Probate Order Book, Transcript of Original	discretionary	maintain permanently in original or in microform.
85–3.2–41	Record of Administrator's Accounts IC 29–1–1–23(f)	c. 1860's–+ 6/30/1991	maintain permanently in original or in microform.
85–3.2–42	Inheritance Tax Files	1913– +	maintain as part of Probate Case File.
85–3.2–43	Inheritance Tax Ledger	1913– +	maintain permanently in original or microfilm & destroy original 15 years after date of last entry.
85–3.2–44	Judgment Docket, Probate (rare)	1790– +	destroy 20 years after date of last entry.
85–3.2–45	Praecipe Book, Probate (rare)	1790– +	destroy 20 years after date of last entry.
85–3.2–46	Execution Docket, Probate (rare)	1790– +	destroy 20 years after date of last entry.
85–3.2–47	General Index to Estates/Probate IC 29–1–1–23	1790–1990	maintain permanently - microfilm for security purposes.
85–3.2–48	General Index to Probate Complete Record	to c. 1920's	maintain permanently in original or in microform.
85–3.2–49	Index to Administrator's & Executor's Bonds IC 29–1–1–23	1840's– 6/20/1991	destroy when last corresponding bond ledger is destroyed.
88–3.2–50	Fee Books, Probate	1790–c. 1913	destroy upon written approval of Division of State Court Administration.

GUARDIANSHIPS

85–3.3–01	Guardianship Docket	c. 1853–c. 1913	maintain permanently.
88–3.3–18	Guardianship Docket & Fee Book IC 29–1–1–23	1913– +	microfilm and destroy original 20 years after date of last entry/close of guardianship.
85–3.3–02	Clerk's Guardianship Docket	c. 1853–c. 1913	destroy.
85–3.3–03	Bar Docket, Guardianships	c. 1853–c. 1920's	destroy.
85–3.3–04	Bench/Judge's Docket, Guardianships	1790–c. 1920	destroy.
85–3.3–05	Guardianship Docket Sheets	c. 1910–1990	microfilm and destroy original 20 years after close of case.
85–3.3–06R	Case Files, Guardianships	1790–1990	maintain permanently in original or in microform (microfilm 5 years after order of final discharge of guardian).
85–3.3–07	Guardianship Accounts Current Reports	c. 1860's– 6/30/1991	maintain permanently in original or in microform. Maintain as part of Guardianship Case File.
94–3.3–18	Record of Guardianship Accounts Current IC 29–1–1–23(f)	c. 1860's– 6/30/1991	maintain permanently in original or in microform.
85–3.3–08	Guardian's Oaths & Letters Record	1847– +	destroy ledger 20 years after close of last case.
85–3.3–09	Guardian's Bond Record	1847– 6/30/1991	destroy ledger 20 years after close of last case.
85–3.3–10	Guardian's Bond Record to Sell Real Estate	1853–c. 1881	destroy.
85–3.3–11	Guardian's Bond, Oath & Letter Record	c. 1853–1953	destroy ledger 20 years after close of last case.

NOTE: ORIGINAL BONDS, OATHS & LETTERS ARE APPROVED BY THE COURT,
ARE ENTERED IN THE ORDER BOOK WITH ORIGINALS FILED IN THE
GUARDIANSHIP CASE FILES.

85–3.3–12R	Inventory Record, Guardianships	1853– +	destroy 20 years after disposal of last case.
85–3.3–13	Record of Sale Bills, Guardianships	1853–1953	destroy.
85–3.3–14R	Order Book, Guardianships	discretionary	maintain permanently in original or in microform meeting the standards of Admin.R. 6. Microfilm after 20 years and transfer original to the Indiana Commission on Public Records or otherwise dispose of upon approval of the Division of State Court Administration.
85–3.3–15	General Index Guardianships	discretionary	maintain permanently.
85–3.3–16	Index to Guardianship Bonds	discretionary to 6/30/1991	destroy filled ledger 20 years after entry of last case.
88–3.3–17	Fee Books, Guardianships	1790–c. 1913– +	destroy upon written approval of Division of State Court Administration.

TRUSTS
(Separate record series from probate, estates)

85–3.4–01R	Trust Entry Docket Book/Trust Estate Fee Book [not required by IC 30–4–4–4(a)]	–to current	maintain permanently, in original or in microform (microfilm after 20 years).
85–3.4–02	Trust Case Files	–to current	maintain permanently, in original or in microform (microfilm 3 years after disposal).
85–3.4–03	Record of Trust Company Oaths (ledger)	varies	destroy 4 years after date of last entry.
85–3.4–04	Record of Delinquent Trust Records (ledger)	varies	maintain permanently in original or in microform.
85–3.4–05	Trustee's Miscellaneous Record of Reports (ledger)	varies	maintain permanently in original or in microform.

FAMILY LAW (4)
JUVENILE COURT

85–4.1–01	Record of Affidavit for Prosecution of Juvenile (discretionary)	1903– +	destroy 20 years after date of last entry.
85–4.1–02	Entry Docket/Juvenile Entry Docket, Issue Docket & Fee Book (ledger)	1903–1990	destroy 20 years after date of last entry.
85–4.1–03	Juvenile Court Docket/Judge's Docket (replaced by Docket Sheets)	1903–c. 1930's	destroy 20 years after date of last entry.
85–4.1–04	Docket Sheets	c. 1910–1990	destroy 20 years after last entry or 20 years after time when minor reaches majority unless expunged.
85–4.1–05	Investigator's Case Reports (ledger)	1903– +	destroy 20 years after date of last entry.
85–4.1–06R	Master Card Index File	1903– +	destroy 20 years from date of last entry or all born prior to 12–31 of year when child is 18 years of age.

85–4.1–07	Society History Case Files	1903– +	destroy 12 years after last entry or 12 years after time when minor reaches majority unless expunged.
85–4.1–08R	Juvenile Order Book (ledger)	1903–1990	maintain permanently in original or in microform meeting the standards of Admin.R. 6, except individual records expunged. Microfilm after 20 years and transfer original to the Indiana Commission on Public Records or otherwise dispose of upon approval of the Division of State Court Administration.
01–4.1–29	JD case files	IC 31–30–1–4 felonies committed by a juvenile under 16 years of age	destroy 12 years after juvenile reaches 18th birthdate.
01–4.1–30	JD, JC, JM and JS case files	Delinquency cases not under IC 31–30–1–4 for under 16 years of age and all CHINS, status and miscellaneous case files	destroy 12 years after juvenile reaches 18th birthdate.
01–4.1–31	JT case files	Termination of parental rights	destroy 5 years after juvenile reaches 18th birthdate.
01–4.1–32	Juvenile CCS	Official Chronological Case Summary	maintain permanently in original or in microfilm meeting AR 6 and upon written approval of the Division of State Court Administration
01–4.1–33	Juvenile RJO	Record of Judgments and Orders	maintain permanently in original or in microfilm meeting AR 6 and upon written approval of the Division of State Court Administration
87–4.1–21	Dismissed Juvenile Case Files	1903– +	destroy 2 years after order to dismiss is given.
85–4.1–10	Adult Causes, Contributing to Delinquency of Minor (Case Files)	1905– +	destroy 20 years from final judgment/order.
85–4.1–11	Bonds	1903– +	destroy 3 years after disposal of case, if such bonds are filed separately.
85–4.1–12	Record of Commitments (ledger)	1869– +	destroy 7 years after release of last person named in ledger.
85–4.1–13	Record of Releases (ledger)	1869– +	destroy 7 years after release of last person named in ledger.
85–4.1–14	Record or Reports from Juvenile Institutions (ledger)	1869– +	destroy 7 years after release of last person named in ledger.
85–4.1–15	Juvenile Institutional Report (Case Files)	1869– +	destroy 7 years after individual is released from probation.
85–4.1–16R	Probation Case Files/Folders	1903– +	destroy 7 years after individual is released from probation or informal adjustment and after child reaches 18th birthday.
88–4.1–23	Juvenile Probation Officer's Copy of Report Where no Delinquency is Filed	varies	destroy after compilation of statistics.
88–4.1–24	No Probable Cause Files	varies	destroy after 2 years of filing.
88–4.1–25	Statistical Sheets	varies	destroy upon compilation of statistics.

88–4.1–26R	Shorthand Notes/ Tapes/Disks Not Transcribed	varies	destroy 7 years after date of trial and final judgment.
88–4.1–27	Court Reporter Calendars "Court Reporter's Call Sheets"	varies	maintain current year and previous year and discard earlier years.
85–4.1–17	Judgment Docket, Juvenile Court	1903– +	maintain for 20 years from date of last entry.
85–4.1–18	Juvenile Fee Book/Juvenile Fine and Fee Docket (ledger)	1903– +	destroy 6 years after date of last entry.
85–4.1–19	General Index, Juvenile Court (ledger or card file) (discretionary)	1903–1990	destroy 20 years after date of last entry.
85–4.1–20	Juvenile Restitution Record (ledger) IC 35–7–2–1	1976– +	destroy 7 years after termination of probation of last person entered.
88–4.1–22	Fee Books, Juvenile	1903–c. 1913	destroy upon written approval of Division of State Court Administration.
91–4.1–28	Juvenile Wardship Case Files	1903– +	maintain under 01–4.1–30.

Note: Under ACTS 1936(ss): 3:26(b), IC 12–1–3–10, 1976, County Boards of Welfare filed for "the dismissal of such guardianships". These Case Files are not dismissed but such agency is ending its jurisdiction in such cases.

PATERNITY

85–4.2–01R	Paternity Book	1941- +	maintain Order permanently in court; microfilm filled ledger for security.
85–4.2–02R	Docket Sheets	1941- +	maintain permanently in court; microfilm 3 years after disposition using standards of Admin. R. 6.
85–4.2–03R	Paternity Case Files	1941- +	maintain permanently (microfilm after 5 years). If court has an approved imaging system under Admin. R. 6, scan after 1 year, destroy hard copy and convert scanned images to microfilm after 5 years.
87–4.2–04R	Dismissed Paternity Case Files	1941- +	maintain permanently in hard copy or microfilm after 2 years from order of dismissal.
91–4.2–05	Shorthand Notes/ Tapes/Disks Not Transcribed	1941- +	maintain permanently.

ADOPTIONS

85–4.3–01R	Adoption Order Book/Record	1941- +	maintain permanently in original or in microform meeting the standards of Admin.R. 6. Microfilm after 20 years and transfer originals to the Indiana Commission on Public Records or otherwise dispose of upon approval of the Division of State Court Administration.

85–4.3–02R	Adoption Case Files	1941- +	maintain permanently in hardcopy or in microform (microfilm after 5 years). If court has an approved imaging system under Admin. R. 6, scan after 1 year, destroy hard copy and convert scanned images to microfilm after 5 years.
95–4.3–02.1	Dismissed Adoption Case Files	1941- +	maintain permanently in hard copy or microform (microfilm after 2 years from order of dismissal).
85–4.3–03	Adoption Docket Sheets	1941– +	file with Adoption Case File.
85–4.3–04	Adoption General Index	1941– +	maintain permanently in original format.
91–4.3–05	Shorthand Notes/ Tapes/Disks Not Transcribed	1941– +	maintain permanently.

COURT–ORDERED BIRTH CERTIFICATES

85–4.4–01R	Birth Certificate Record (Order Book Index of Judicial Judgment & Decree)	1941– +	maintain permanently in original or microform meeting the standards of Admin.R. 6. Microfilm after 20 years and transfer originals to the Indiana Commission on Public Records or otherwise dispose of upon approval of the Division of State Court Administration.
85–4.4–02	Birth Certificate Record—Original Pleadings	1941– +	destroy 5 years after hearing.

COUNTY COURT AND COURTS

PERFORMING COUNTY COURT FUNCTIONS (5)

85–5.1–01R	Small Claims Docket and Fee Book	1976–1990	destroy after 20 years if not used as substitute Order Book (see 85–5.1–02R).
85–5.1–02R	Civil Order Book – Small Claims/ Small Claims Docket	1976–1990	maintain permanently in original or in microfilm meeting the standards of Admin.R. 6. Microfilm after 20 years and transfer originals to the Indiana Commission on Public Records or otherwise dispose of upon approval of the Division of State Court Administration.
85–5.1–03R	Small Claims Docket Sheets	1976–1990	maintain permanently microfilm 3 years after disposition using standards of Admin. R. 6.
90–5.1–03.1R	Small Claims Shorthand Notes/Tapes/ Disks Not Transcribed	1971- +	destroy or reuse 3 years after date of trial. S ee 89–1.1–26.1R for CP cases.

85–5.1–04	Judgment Docket Small Claims Rule 11	1976– +	destroy 20 years after date of last entry.
85–5.1–05R	Small Claims Case Files	1976–1990	destroy 5 years after order releasing judgment; or 10 years where judgment has not been ordered released or where no discharge in bankruptcy is filed.
87–5.1–21R	Dismissed Small Claims Case Files	1976– +	destroy 2 years after order to dismiss is given or after discharge in bankruptcy is filed.
85–5.1–06R	Civil Order Book— Plenary/Plenary Docket	1976–1990	maintain permanently in original or in microform meeting the standards of Admin.R. 6. Microfilm after 20 years and transfer originals to the Indiana Commission on Public Records or otherwise dispose of upon approval of the Division of State Court Administration.
85–5.1–07R	Plenary Case Files	1976–1990	maintain in accordance with 85–1.125R
85–5.1–08R	Criminal Entry Docket and Fee Book	1976–1990	maintain 55 years in original or microfilm 10 years after last entry and destroy original.
85–5.1–09	Traffic Violation Docket	1976–1981	destroy.
85–5.1–10R	Infractions Order Book	1981–1990	destroy 10 years after date of last entry.
85–5.1–11R	Criminal and Traffic Docket	1976–1981	if it contains Class D Felonies, maintain 55 years; if misdemeanor only, destroy after 10 years.
85–5.1–12R	Criminal Order Book/Criminal & Misdemeanors	1976–1990	maintain permanently in original or in microform meeting the standards of Admin.R. 6. Microfilm after 20 years and transfer originals to the Indiana Commission on Public Records or otherwise dispose of upon approval of the Division of State Court Administration.
85–5.1–13R	Case Packets, Traffic Infractions	1977–1990	destroy 10 years prior to 1981; after 9–01–1981 destroy after 2 years if court complies with IC 9–30–3–11(c), (d).
85–5.1–13.1R	Traffic Non-moving Violations	1979–1990	destroy 3 years after end of calendar year and after audit by State Board of Accounts.
87–5.1–22R	Case Packets, Non-Traffic Infractions	1977–1990	destroy 10 years after final judgment.
87–5.1–23R	Case Packets, Ordinance Violations	1976–1990	destroy 10 years after final judgment.
90–5.1–23.1R	Infraction/Ordinance Violations Shorthand Notes/Tapes/Disks Not Transcribed	1971– +	destroy or reuse 2 years after final judgment. For felony and misdemeanors see 85–2–27R and 89–2–27.1.
85–5.1–14	Case Files—Criminal & Misdemeanor	1976–1990	destroy misdemeanor case files 10 years after final disposition; maintain Class D Felonies for 55 years–1979 +. Sample CM case files in accordance with 90–2–21–2; sample felony cases in accordance with 85–2–21R.
90–5.1–14.1	Copy of Pretrial Diversion Contract and Papers Filed in County of Residence, Different From County of Conviction	1976– +	retain for 2 years after contract's termination date.
85–5.1–15	General Indices	1976– +	maintain for life of ledger they index.

| 85–5.1–16 | Jury Record | 1976– + | destroy 3 years after date of final entry and audit by State Board of Accounts. |

JUSTICE OF THE PEACE JURISDICTION

85–5.1–17	Civil Docket	to 1976	destroy.
85–5.1–18	Civil Case Files	to 1976	destroy.
85–5.1–19R	Criminal Docket	to 1976	destroy.
85–5.1–20R	Criminal Case Files	to 1976	destroy.

NOTE: Includes Lake County JP courts through 1978. For records prior to 1941, offer to local repository or Archives Division, Indiana Commission on Public Records before destruction.

TOWN COURT AND CITY CRIMINAL JURISDICTION

| 91–5.1–29 | Criminal Docket | varies | destroy 10 years after last entry. |
| 91–5.1–30 | Criminal Case Files | varies | destroy 10 years after final entry. |

CITY CIVIL JURISDICTION

88–5.1–24	Civil Entry Dockets	1875–1905; 1917– +	destroy after 20 years by petition to county records commission.
88–5.1–25	Civil Docket Ledgers/Sheets	1875–1905; 1917– +	destroy after 10 years.
88–5.1–26R	Order Books ("Minute Books" Lake County)	1875–1905; 1917– +	maintain permanently in original or microform meeting the standards of Admin.R. 6. Microfilm after 20 years and transfer originals to the Indiana Commission on Public Records or otherwise dispose of upon approval of the Division of State Court Administration.
88–5.1–27	Civil Case Files	1875–1905; 1917– +	destroy after 5 years from date of final judgment.
88–5.1–28	Fee Books, Civil	1875–1905; 1917– +	destroy 10 years after completion of volume.

NATURALIZATIONS (6)

(Formerly schedules 85–6–1 through 12). Transfer any and all naturalization records immediately to the Archives Division, Indiana Commission on Public Records through the Division of State Court Administration. See Indiana Rules of Court, 1991, page 675 for list.

COURT OF CONCILIATION (7)

| 85–7–01 | Order Book | 1853–1865 | transfer to Archives Division, Indiana Commission on Public Records. |
| 85–7–02 | Case Files | 1853–1865 | transfer to Archives Division, Indiana Commission on Public Records. |

SPECIAL JUDICIAL FUNCTIONS (8)

| 85–8.1–01R | Insane Record/Mental Health Record | 1848– + | maintain permanently in original or in microform meeting the standards of Admin.R. 6. Microfilm after 20 years and transfer originals to the Indiana Commission on Public Records or otherwise dispose of upon approval of the Division of State Court Administration. |
| 85–8.1–02 | Insanity Inquests/M.H. Hearing, Case Files | 1848–1990 | destroy 7 years after discharge. |

85–8.1–03R	Proceedings to Re-commit to a Hospital for Insane	1881–1927	maintain permanently in original or in microform meeting the standards of Admin.R. 6. Microfilm after 20 years and transfer originals to the Indiana Commission on Public Records or otherwise dispose of upon approval of the Division of State Court Administration.
85–8.1–04R	Gen. Index to In-sane/Mental Health Record (discretion-ary)	–1990	maintain permanently in original or in microform meeting the standards of Admin.R. 6. Microfilm after 20 years and transfer originals to the Indiana Commission on Public Records or otherwise dispose of upon approval of the Division of State Court Administration.
94–8.1–05	Commitment Files, Alcoholism	1929– +	destroy 7 years after discharge.
85–8.2–01	Commitment Order Book, Epilepsy IC 16–14–9.1	1907–1990	transfer to Archives Division, Indiana Commission on Public Records 20 years after last entry.
85–8.2–02	Commitment Files, Epilepsy IC 16–14–9.1	1907–1990	destroy 2 years after discharge of patient.
85–8.3–01	Commitment Order Book, Feeble-minded IC 16–15–1–2	1901–1990	transfer to Archives Division, Indiana Commission on Public Records 20 years after last entry.
85–8.3–02	Commitment Files, Feeble-minded IC 16–15–1–2	1901–1990	destroy 2 years after discharge of patient.
85–8.4–01	Riley Hosp'l Order Book	1924–1943	transfer to Archives Division, Indiana Commission on Public Records.
85–8.4–02	Case Files, Riley Hosp'l	1924–1943	destroy.
85–8.5–01	Commitment Files, Children to Public Hospitals	1933–1943	destroy.
85–8.6–01	IU Medical Center Order Book	1939–1943	destroy.
85–8.6–02	Case Files, IU Medi-cal Center	1939–1943	destroy.
85–8.7–01	Record of Receiver-ships IC 34–2–6–1	1911–1990	destroy 20 years after date of last entry.
85–8.7–02	Files, Receivership Affidavit of Assets and Liabilities	1911–1990	destroy 20 years after filing.
85–8.7–03	Files, Receivership Claims	1911–1990	destroy 20 years after filing.
85–8.8–01R	Drainage Petitions and Case Files	1881–1990	maintain permanently in original or in microform (microfilm after 10 years).
85–8.8–02R	Drainage Order Book	1881–1990	maintain permanently in original or in microform meeting standards of Admin.R. 6. Microfilm after 20 years and transfer of originals to the Indiana Commission on Public Records or otherwise dispose of upon approval of the Division of State Court Administration.

GENERAL SCHEDULES (9)

87–9–01	Jury Lists (name slips and lists)	1790– +	maintain for 10 years unless entered in order book. If entered in order book, destroy 2 years after drawing.

87–9–02R	Order Book, Appellate Court Decisions	c. 1880– + varies	maintain permanently in original or in microform meeting the standards of Admin.R. 6. Microfilm after 20 years and transfer originals to the Indiana Commission on Public Records or otherwise dispose of upon approval of the Division of State Court Administration.
87–9–03R	Appellate Court Decisions	1790– +	maintain permanently in original or in microform meeting the standards of Admin.R. 6. Microfilm after 20 years and transfer originals to the Indiana Commission on Public Records or otherwise dispose of upon approval of the Division of State Court Administration.
90–9–04	Jury Record (List of Jurors) Serving on Specific Cases/Time Book (ledger)	1853– +	destroy 3 years after volume is filled and after audit by State Board of Accounts.
90–9–05	Jury Questionnaire Forms	1881– +	destroy after 2 years from date of creation.
05–9–06	Documentation supporting juror disqualifications, exemptions, and deferrals	2003—+	retain for a minimum of two (2) years.
05–9–07	Digital Master created in accordance with Administrative Rule 6	2005—+	deposit digital master (regardless of medium [used for generation of microfilm]) with the Indiana Commission on Public Records Vault for security backup.

TRIAL RULE 77 SCHEDULES (10)

94–10–01	Case Files	1991– +	Apply existing schedules for each jurisdiction, adjudicated & dismissed.
94–10–02	Indexes	1991– +	Apply existing schedules for each jurisdiction.
94–10–03	Chronological Case Summary (CCS)	1991– +	For all types (except for IF/OV), maintain permanently. Microfilm 5 years after final disposition. If maintained electronically, guarantee capacity to generate hard copy at any time. For IF/OV, destroy 10 years after final disposition.
94–10–04	Record of Designated Judgments and Orders (RJO)	1991– +	Maintain each type permanently. Microfilm 2 years after completion of volume in accordance with standards set in Administrative Rule 6. If maintained electronically, guarantee capacity to generate hard copy at any time.

Adopted Nov. 4, 1985, effective Jan. 1, 1988. Amended Oct. 30, 1986, effective Jan. 1, 1987; Dec. 7, 1987, effective Jan. 1, 1988; Nov. 10, 1988, effective Jan. 1, 1989; amended effective Feb. 16, 1989; Nov. 30, 1989, effective Jan. 1, 1990; Nov. 13, 1990, effective Jan. 1, 1991; Nov. 1, 1991, effective Jan. 1, 1992; Oct. 30, 1992, effective Jan. 1, 1993; Oct. 29, 1993, effective Jan. 1, 1994; Dec. 5, 1994, effective Feb. 1, 1995; Dec. 15, 1995, effective Feb. 1, 1996; July 1, 2003, effective Aug. 1, 2003; Sept. 30, 2004, effective Jan. 1, 2005; July 1, 2005, effective Jan. 1, 2006; Aug. 15, 2006, effective Jan. 1, 2007; Sept. 10, 2007, effective Jan. 1, 2008; Sept. 15, 2009, effective Jan. 1, 2010; Oct. 11, 2012, effective Jan. 1, 2013.

Rule 8. Uniform Case Numbering System

(A) Application. All trial courts in the State of Indiana shall use the uniform case numbering system as set forth under this rule.

(B) Numbering System. The uniform case numbering system shall consist of four groups of characters arranged in a manner to identify the court, the year/month of filing, the case type and the filing sequence. The following is an example of the case number to be employed:

55C01–1101–CF–000123

(1) *Court Identifier.* The first group of five characters shall constitute the county and court identifier. The first and second character in this group shall represent the county of filing employing the following code:

01	Adams County
02	Allen County
03	Bartholomew County
04	Benton County
05	Blackford County
06	Boone County
07	Brown County
08	Carroll County
09	Cass County
10	Clark County
11	Clay County
12	Clinton County
13	Crawford County
14	Daviess County
15	Dearborn County
16	Decatur County
17	DeKalb County
18	Delaware County
19	Dubois County
20	Elkhart County
21	Fayette County
22	Floyd County
23	Fountain County
24	Franklin County
25	Fulton County
26	Gibson County
27	Grant County
28	Greene County
29	Hamilton County
30	Hancock County
31	Harrison County
32	Hendricks County
33	Henry County
34	Howard County
35	Huntington County
36	Jackson County
37	Jasper County
38	Jay County
39	Jefferson County
40	Jennings County
41	Johnson County
42	Knox County
43	Kosciusko County
44	LaGrange County
45	Lake County
46	LaPorte County
47	Lawrence County
48	Madison County
49	Marion County
50	Marshall County
51	Martin County
52	Miami County
53	Monroe County
54	Montgomery County
55	Morgan County
56	Newton County
57	Noble County
58	Ohio County
59	Orange County
60	Owen County
61	Parke County
62	Perry County
63	Pike County
64	Porter County
65	Posey County
66	Pulaski County
67	Putnam County
68	Randolph County
69	Ripley County
70	Rush County
71	St. Joseph County
72	Scott County
73	Shelby County
74	Spencer County
75	Starke County
76	Steuben County
77	Sullivan County
78	Switzerland County
79	Tippecanoe County
80	Tipton County
81	Union County
82	Vanderburgh County
83	Vermillion County
84	Vigo County
85	Wabash County
86	Warren County
87	Warrick County
88	Washington County
89	Wayne County
90	Wells County
91	White County
92	Whitley County

The third character in the first group shall represent the court of filing employing the following code:

C	Circuit Court
D	Superior Court
E	County Court
F	Superior Municipal Division
G	Superior Court/Criminal Division
H	City Court
I	Town Court
J	Probate Court
K	Township Small Claims Court

The last two characters of the first group shall distinguish between courts in counties having more than one court of a specific type. The following code sets forth the county and court identifier for all courts:

01C01	Adams Circuit Court
01D01	Adams Superior Court
02C01	Allen Circuit Court
02D01	Allen Superior Court
02D02	Allen Superior Court
02D03	Allen Superior Court
02D04	Allen Superior Court
02D05	Allen Superior Court
02D06	Allen Superior Court
02D07	Allen Superior Court
02D08	Allen Superior Court
02D09	Allen Superior Court

02H01	Allen/New Haven City Court
03C01	Bartholomew Circuit Court
03D01	Bartholomew Superior Court 1
03D02	Bartholomew Superior Court 2
04C01	Benton Circuit Court
05C01	Blackford Circuit Court
05D01	Blackford Superior Court
05E01	Blackford County Court (abolished)
05H01	Blackford/Hartford City City Court (abolished)
05H02	Blackford/Montpelier City Court (abolished)
06C01	Boone Circuit Court
06D01	Boone Superior Court 1
06D02	Boone Superior Court 2
06H01	Boone/Lebanon City Court
06I01	Boone/Thorntown Town Court
06I02	Boone/Zionsville Town Court
06I03	Boone/Jamestown Court
06I04	Boone/Whitestown Town Court
07C01	Brown Circuit Court
08C01	Carroll Circuit Court
08D01	Carroll Superior Court
08H01	Carroll/Delphi City Court
08I01	Carroll/Burlington Town Court
09C01	Cass Circuit Court
09D01	Cass Superior Court 1
09D02	Cass Superior Court 2
10C01	Clark Circuit Court 1
10C02	Clark Circuit Court 2 (effective January 1, 2012, formerly Clark Superior Court 2)
10C03	Clark Circuit Court 3 (effective January 1, 2012, formerly Clark Superior Court 3)
10C04	Clark Circuit Court 4 (effective January 1, 2012, formerly Clark Superior Court 1)
10D01	Clark Superior Court 1 (abolished effective January 1, 2012)
10D02	Clark Superior Court 2 (abolished effective January 1, 2012)
10D03	Clark Superior Court 3 (abolished effective January 1, 2012)
10E01	Clark County Court (abolished)
10H01	Clark/Charlestown City Court (abolished effective January 1, 2012)
10H02	Clark/Jeffersonville City Court
10I01	Clark/Clarksville Town Court
10I02	Clark/Sellersburg Town Court (abolished effective January 1, 2012)
11C01	Clay Circuit Court
11D01	Clay Superior Court
12C01	Clinton Circuit Court
12D01	Clinton Superior Court
12E01	Clinton County Court (abolished)
12H01	Clinton/Frankfort City Court
13C01	Crawford Circuit Court
14C01	Daviess Circuit Court
14D01	Daviess Superior Court
14E01	Daviess County Court (abolished)
15C01	Dearborn Circuit Court
15D01	Dearborn Superior Court
15D02	Dearborn Superior Court 2
15E01	Dearborn County Court (abolished)
15H01	Dearborn/Aurora City Court (abolished effective January 1, 2012)
15H02	Dearborn/Lawrenceburg City Court
16C01	Decatur Circuit Court
16D01	Decatur Superior Court
16E01	Decatur County Court (abolished)
17C01	DeKalb Circuit Court

17D01	DeKalb Superior Court
17D02	DeKalb Superior Court 2
17H01	DeKalb/Butler City Court
18C01	Delaware Circuit Court
18C02	Delaware Circuit Court 2
18C03	Delaware Circuit Court 3
18C04	Delaware Circuit Court 4
18C05	Delaware Circuit Court 5
18D01	Delaware Superior Court 1 (abolished)
18D02	Delaware Superior Court 2 (abolished)
18D03	Delaware Superior Court 3 (abolished)
18D04	Delaware Superior Court 4 (abolished)
18H01	Delaware/Muncie City Court
18I01	Delaware/Yorktown Town Court
19C01	Dubois Circuit Court
19D01	Dubois Superior Court
20C01	Elkhart Circuit Court
20D01	Elkhart Superior Court 1
20D02	Elkhart Superior Court 2
20D03	Elkhart Superior Court 3
20D04	Elkhart Superior Court 4 [Goshen]
20D05	Elkhart Superior Court 5 [Elkhart]
20D06	Elkhart Superior Court 6 [Elkhart]
20E01	Elkhart County Court 1 in Elkhart (abolished)
20E02	Elkhart County Court 2 in Goshen (abolished)
20H01	Elkhart/Elkhart City Court
20H02	Elkhart/Goshen City Court
20H03	Elkhart/Nappanee City Court
21C01	Fayette Circuit Court
22C01	Floyd Circuit Court
22D01	Floyd Superior Court 1
22D02	Floyd Superior Court 2 (effective January 1, 2009, formerly Floyd County Court)
22D03	Floyd Superior Court 3 (effective January 1, 2009)
22E01	Floyd County Court (abolished January 1, 2009)
21D01	Fayette Superior Court
23C01	Fountain Circuit Court
23H01	Fountain/Attica City Court
24C01	Franklin Circuit Court 1
24C02	Franklin Circuit Court 2
25C01	Fulton Circuit Court
25D01	Fulton Superior Court
25E01	Fulton County Court (abolished)
26C01	Gibson Circuit Court
26D01	Gibson Superior Court
27C01	Grant Circuit Court
27D01	Grant Superior Court 1
27D02	Grant Superior Court 2
27D03	Grant Superior Court 3
27E01	Grant County Court (abolished)
27H01	Grant/Gas City City Court
27H02	Grant/Marion City Court
28C01	Greene Circuit Court
28D01	Greene Superior Court
28E01	Greene County Court (abolished)
29C01	Hamilton Circuit Court
29D01	Hamilton Superior Court 1
29D02	Hamilton Superior Court 2
29D03	Hamilton Superior Court 3
29D04	Hamilton Superior Court 4
29D05	Hamilton Superior Court 5
29D06	Hamilton Superior Court 6
29E01	Hamilton County Court (abolished)
29H01	Hamilton/Carmel City Court
29H02	Hamilton/Noblesville City Court

29I01	Hamilton/Fishers Town Court (effective January 1, 2012)
30C01	Hancock Circuit Court
30D01	Hancock Superior Court 1
30D02	Hancock Superior Court 2
30E01	Hancock county Court (abolished)
31C01	Harrison Circuit Court
31D01	Harrison Superior Court
31E01	Harrison County Court (abolished)
32C01	Hendricks Circuit Court
32D01	Hendricks Superior Court 1
32D02	Hendricks Superior Court 2
32D03	Hendricks Superior Court 3
32D04	Hendricks Superior Court 4
32D05	Hendricks Superior Court 5
32I01	Hendricks/Plainfield Town Court
32I02	Hendricks/Brownsburg Town Court
32I03	Hendricks/Avon Town Court
33C01	Henry Circuit Court 1
33C02	Henry Circuit Court 2 (effective July 1, 2011, formerly Henry Superior Court 1)
33C03	Henry Circuit Court 3 (effective July 1, 2011, formerly Henry Superior Court 2)
33D01	Henry Superior Court 1 (abolished effective July 1, 2011)
33D02	Henry Superior Court 2 (abolished effective July 1, 2011)
33E01	Henry County Court (abolished)
33H01	New Castle City Court
33I01	Henry/Knightstown Town Court (abolished effective October 31, 2011)
34C01	Howard Circuit Court
34D01	Howard Superior Court 1
34D02	Howard Superior Court 2
34D03	Howard Superior Court 3
34D04	Howard Superior Court 4
34E01	Howard County Court (abolished)
35C01	Huntington Circuit Court
35D01	Huntington Superior Court
35E01	Huntington County Court (abolished)
35I01	Huntington/Roanoke Town Court (abolished)
36C01	Jackson Circuit Court
36D01	Jackson Superior Court 1
36D02	Jackson Superior Court 2 (effective January 1, 2008)
36E01	Jackson County Court (abolished)
37C01	Jasper Circuit Court
37D01	Jasper Superior Court
37D02	Jasper Superior Court 2 (abolished)
37I01	Jasper/DeMotte Town Court
37I02	Jasper/Wheatfield Town Court (abolished)
38C01	Jay Circuit Court
38D01	Jay Superior Court
38E01	Jay County Court (abolished)
38H01	Jay/Dunkirk City Court
38H02	Jay/Portland City Court
39C01	Jefferson Circuit Court
39D01	Jefferson Superior Court
39E01	Jefferson County Court (abolished)
40C01	Jennings Circuit Court
40D01	Jennings Superior Court
40H01	Jennings/North Vernon city Court (abolished)
41C01	Johnson Circuit Court
41D01	Johnson Superior Court 1
41D02	Johnson Superior Court 2
41D03	Johnson Superior Court 3
41H01	Johnson/Franklin City Court
41H02	Johnson/Greenwood City Court
41I01	Johnson/New Whiteland Town Court (abolished)
42C01	Knox Circuit Court
42D01	Knox Superior Court 1
42D02	Knox Superior Court 2
42E01	Knox County Court (abolished)
42H01	Knox/Bicknell City Court
43C01	Kosciusko Circuit Court
43D01	Kosciusko Superior Court 1
43D02	Kosciusko Superior Court 2
43D03	Kosciusko Superior Court 3
43E01	Kosciusko County Court (abolished)
44C01	LaGrange Circuit Court
44D01	LaGrange Superior Court
44E01	LaGrange County Court (abolished)
45C01	Lake Circuit Court
45D01	Lake Superior Court, Civil Division 1
45D02	Lake Superior Court, Civil Division 2
45D03	Lake Superior Court, Civil Division 3
45D04	Lake Superior Court, Civil Division 4
45D05	Lake Superior Court, Civil Division 5
45D10	Lake Superior Court, Civil Division 6
45D11	Lake Superior Court, Civil Division 7
45D06	Lake Superior Court, Juvenile Division
45D07	Lake Superior Court, County Division 1
45D08	Lake Superior Court, County Division 2
45D09	Lake Superior Court, County Division 3
45D12	Lake Superior Court, County Division 4
45G01	Lake Superior Court, Criminal Division 1
45G02	Lake Superior Court, Criminal Division 2
45G03	Lake Superior Court, Criminal Division 3
45G04	Lake Superior Court, Criminal Division 4
45E01	Lake County Court (abolished)
45E02	Lake County Court (abolished)
45E03	Lake County Court (abolished)
45H01	Lake/Crown Point City Court
45H02	Lake/East Chicago City Court
45H03	Lake/Gary City Court
45H04	Lake/Hammond City Court
45H05	Lake/Hobart City Court
45H06	Lake/Lake Station City Court
45H07	Lake/Whiting City Court
45I01	Lake/Merrillville Town Court
45I02	Lake/Schererville Town Court
45I03	Lake/Lowell Town Court
46C01	LaPorte Circuit Court
46D01	LaPorte Superior Court 1
46D02	LaPorte Superior Court 2
46D03	LaPorte Superior Court 3 in LaPorte
46D04	LaPorte Superior Court 4 in Michigan City
47C01	Lawrence Circuit Court
47D01	Lawrence Superior Court 1
47D02	Lawrence Superior Court 2
47E01	Lawrence County Court (abolished)
48C01	Madison Circuit Court 1
48C02	Madison Circuit Court 2 (effective July 1, 2011, formerly Madison Superior Court 2)
48C03	Madison Circuit Court 3 (effective July 1, 2011, formerly Madison Superior Court 3)
48C04	Madison Circuit Court 4 (effective July 1, 2011, formerly Madison Superior Court 4)
48C05	Madison Circuit Court 5 (effective July 1, 2011, formerly Madison Superior Court 5)
48C06	Madison Circuit Court 6 (effective July 1, 2011, formerly Madison Superior Court 1)

48D01	Madison Superior Court 1 (abolished effective July 1, 2011)
48D02	Madison Superior Court 2 (abolished effective July 1, 2011)
48D03	Madison Superior Court 3 (abolished effective July 1, 2011)
48D04	Madison Superior Court 4 (effective January 1, 2009, formerly Madison County Court 1) (abolished effective July 1, 2011)
48D05	Madison Superior Court 5 (effective January 1, 2009, formerly Madison County Court 2) (abolished effective July 1, 2011)
48E01	Madison County Court 1 (abolished effective January 1, 2009)
48E02	Madison County Court 2 (abolished effective January 1, 2009)
48H01	Madison/Alexandria City Court (abolished)
48H02	Madison/Anderson City Court
48H03	Madison/Elwood City Court
48I01	Madison/Edgewood Town Court
48I02	Madison/Pendleton Town Court
49C01	Marion Circuit Court
49D01	Marion Superior Court, Civil Division 1
49D02	Marion Superior Court, Civil Division 2
49D03	Marion Superior Court, Civil Division 3
49D04	Marion Superior Court, Civil Division 4
49D05	Marion Superior Court, Civil Division 5
49D06	Marion Superior Court, Civil Division 6
49D07	Marion Superior Court, Civil Division 7
49D08	Marion Superior Court, Probate Division
49D09	Marion Superior Court, Juvenile Division
49D10	Marion Superior Court, Civil Division 10
49D11	Marion Superior Court, Civil Division 11
49D12	Marion Superior Court, Civil Division 12
49D13	Marion Superior Court, Civil Division 13
49D14	Marion Superior Court, Civil Division 14
49F07	Marion Superior Court, Criminal Division 7
49F08	Marion Superior Court, Criminal Division 8
49F09	Marion Superior Court, Criminal Division 9
49F10	Marion Superior Court, Criminal Division 10
49F11	Initial Hearing Court
49F12	Marion Superior Court, Environmental/Community Court
49F13	Marion Superior Court, Criminal Division 13
49F15	Marion Superior Court, Criminal Division 15
49F16	Marion Superior Court, Criminal Division 16 (renumbered 49G16 effective 2/1/07)
49F17	Marion Superior Court, Criminal Division 17 (renumbered 49G17 effective 2/1/07)
49F18	Marion Superior Court, Criminal Division 18
49F19	Marion Superior Court, Criminal Division 19
49F24	Marion Superior Court, Criminal Division 24
49F25	Marion Superior Court, Criminal Division 25 (effective 1/1/2013)
49G01	Marion Superior Court, Criminal Division 1
49G02	Marion Superior Court, Criminal Division 2
49G03	Marion Superior Court, Criminal Division 3
49G04	Marion Superior Court, Criminal Division 4
49G05	Marion Superior Court, Criminal Division 5
49G06	Marion Superior Court, Criminal Division 6
49G13	Marion Superior Court, Criminal Division 13
49G14	Marion Superior Court, Criminal Division 14
49G16	Marion Superior Court, Criminal Division 16
49G17	Marion Superior Court, Criminal Division 17
49G20	Marion Superior Court, Criminal Division 20
49G21	Marion Superior Court, Criminal Division 21
49G22	Marion Superior Court, Criminal Division 22 (renumbered 49F25 effective 1/1/13)
49G23	Marion Superior Court, Criminal Division 23
49H01	Marion/Beech Grove City Court
49I01	Marion/Cumberland Town Court
49K01	Marion County Small Claims Court, Center Division
49K02	Marion County Small Claims Court, Decatur Division
49K03	Marion County Small Claims Court, Lawrence Division
49K04	Marion County Small Claims Court, Perry Division
49K05	Marion County Small Claims Court, Pike Division
49K06	Marion County Small Claims Court, Warren Division
49K07	Marion County Small Claims Court, Washington Division
49K08	Marion County Small Claims Court, Wayne Division
49K09	Marion County Small Claims Court, Franklin Township
50C01	Marshall Circuit Court
50D01	Marshall Superior Court 1
50D02	Marshall Superior Court 2
50E01	Marshall County Court (abolished)
50H01	Marshall/Plymouth City Court (abolished)
50I01	Marshall/Argos Town Court (abolished)
51C01	Martin Circuit Court
51H01	Martin/Loogootee City Court (abolished)
52C01	Miami Circuit Court
52D01	Miami Superior Court 1
52D02	Miami Superior Court 2
52H01	Miami/Peru City Court
52I01	Miami/Bunker Hill Town Court
53C01	Monroe Circuit Court 1
53C02	Monroe Circuit Court 2
53C03	Monroe Circuit Court 3
53C04	Monroe Circuit Court 4
53C05	Monroe Circuit Court 5
53C06	Monroe Circuit Court 6
53C07	Monroe Circuit Court 7
53C08	Monroe Circuit Court 8
53C09	Monroe Circuit Court 9
53D01	Monroe Superior Court (abolished)
53D02	Monroe Superior Court (abolished)
53D03	Monroe Superior Court (abolished)
53D04	Monroe Superior Court (abolished)
53D05	Monroe Superior Court (abolished)
54C01	Montgomery Circuit Court
54D01	Montgomery Superior Court
54D02	Montgomery Superior Court 2
54E01	Montgomery County Court (abolished)
54H01	Montgomery/Crawfordsville City Court (abolished)
55C01	Morgan Circuit Court
55D01	Morgan Superior Court 1
55D02	Morgan Superior Court 2
55D03	Morgan Superior Court 3
55E01	Morgan County Court (abolished)
55H01	Morgan/Martinsville City Court
55I01	Morgan/Mooresville Town Court
56C01	Newton Circuit Court
56D01	Newton Superior Court

57C01	Noble Circuit Court
57D01	Noble Superior Court 1
57D02	Noble Superior Court 2 7/1/1999
57E01	Noble County Court (to be abolished) 7/1/1999
57I01	Noble/Avilla Town Court (abolished)
57I02	Noble/Cromwell Town Court (abolished)
58C01	Ohio Circuit Court
58D01	Ohio Superior Court (abolished effective January 1, 2009)
59C01	Orange Circuit Court
59D01	Orange Superior Court
59E01	Orange County Court (abolished)
60C01	Owen Circuit Court
61C01	Parke Circuit Court
62C01	Perry Circuit Court
62H01	Perry/Cannelton Town Court (abolished)
62H02	Perry/Tell City City Court (abolished)
63C01	Pike Circuit Court
63H01	Pike/Petersburg City Court (abolished)
64C01	Porter Circuit Court
64D01	Porter Superior Court 1
64D02	Porter Superior Court 2
64D03	Porter Superior Court 3
64D04	Porter Superior Court 4
64D05	Porter Superior Court 5 (Circuit Judge)
64D06	Porter Superior Court 6
64E01	Porter County Court (abolished)
64I01	Porter/Chesterton Town Court (abolished)
65C01	Posey Circuit Court
65D01	Posey Superior Court
65E01	Posey County Court (abolished)
66C01	Pulaski Circuit Court
66D01	Pulaski Superior Court
66E01	Pulaski County Court (abolished)
67C01	Putnam Circuit Court
67D01	Putnam Superior Court
67E01	Putnam County Court (abolished)
68C01	Randolph Circuit Court
68D01	Randolph Superior Court
68E01	Randolph County Court (abolished)
68H01	Randolph/Winchester City Court
68H02	Randolph/Union City City Court
69C01	Ripley Circuit Court
69D01	Ripley Superior Court
69H01	Ripley/Batesville City Court
69I01	Ripley/Versailles Town court
70C01	Rush Circuit Court
70D01	Rush Superior Court
70E01	Rush County Court (abolished)
71C01	St. Joseph Circuit Court
71D01	St. Joseph Superior Court
71D02	St. Joseph Superior Court
71D03	St. Joseph Superior Court
71D04	St. Joseph Superior Court
71D05	St. Joseph Superior Court
71D06	St. Joseph Superior Court
71D07	St. Joseph Superior Court
71D08	St. Joseph Superior Court
71I01	St. Joseph/Walkerton Town Court
71I02	St. Joseph/Lakeville Town Court
71J01	St. Joseph Probate Court
72C01	Scott Circuit Court
72D01	Scott Superior Court
72E01	Scott County Court (abolished)
73C01	Shelby Circuit Court
73D01	Shelby Superior Court 1
73D02	Shelby Superior Court 2
73E01	Shelby County Court (abolished)
74C01	Spencer Circuit Court
74H01	Spencer/Rockport City Court (abolished)
75C01	Starke Circuit Court
75H01	Starke/Knox City Court
76C01	Steuben Circuit Court
76D01	Steuben Superior Court
76E01	Steuben County Court (abolished)
76I01	Steuben/Fremont Town Court
77C01	Sullivan Circuit Court
77D01	Sullivan Superior Court
77E01	Sullivan County Court (abolished)
78C01	Switzerland Circuit Court
78D01	Switzerland Superior Court (abolished effective January 1, 2009)
79C01	Tippecanoe Circuit Court
79D01	Tippecanoe Superior Court 1
79D02	Tippecanoe Superior Court 2
79D03	Tippecanoe Superior Court 3
79D04	Tippecanoe Superior Court 4
79D05	Tippecanoe Superior Court 5
79D06	Tippecanoe Superior Court 6
79H01	Tippecanoe/West Lafayette City Court
80C01	Tipton Circuit Court
80H01	Tipton/Tipton City Court
80I01	Tipton/Sharpsville Town Court
81C01	Union Circuit Court
82C01	Vanderburgh Circuit Court
82D01	Vanderburgh Superior Court
82D02	Vanderburgh Superior Court
82D03	Vanderburgh Superior Court
82D04	Vanderburgh Superior Court
82D05	Vanderburgh Superior Court
82D06	Vanderburgh Superior Court
82D07	Vanderburgh Superior Court
83C01	Vermillion Circuit Court
83H01	Vermillion/Clinton City Court
84C01	Vigo Circuit Court
84D01	Vigo Superior Court 1
84D02	Vigo Superior Court 2
84D03	Vigo Superior Court 3 (Circuit Judge)
84D04	Vigo Superior Court 4
84D05	Vigo Superior Court 5
84D06	Vigo Superior Court 6
84E04	Vigo County Court, Division 4 (abolished)
84E05	Vigo County Court, Division 5 (abolished)
(84E01, 84E02, and 84E03 not used)	
84H01	Vigo/Terre Haute City Court
85C01	Wabash Circuit Court
85D01	Wabash Superior Court
85E01	Wabash County Court (abolished)
85H01	Wabash/Wabash City Court
85I01	Wabash/N. Manchester Town Court (abolished effective January 1, 2012)
86C01	Warren Circuit Court
87C01	Warrick Circuit Court
87D01	Warrick Superior Court 1
87D02	Warrick Superior Court 2
88C01	Washington Circuit Court
88D01	Washington Superior Court
88H01	Washington/Salem City Court (abolished)
89C01	Wayne Circuit Court
89D01	Wayne Superior Court 1
89D02	Wayne Superior Court 2
89D03	Wayne Superior Court 3
89D03	Wayne Superior Court 4 (transfer judge)
89I01	Wayne/Hagerstown Town Court
90C01	Wells Circuit Court
90D01	Wells Superior Court
90H01	Wells/Bluffton City Court
91C01	White Circuit Court
91D01	White Superior Court

91I01   White/Monon Town Court (abolished effective
   January 1, 2011)
92C01   Whitely Circuit Court
92D01   Whitley Superior Court

(2) *Year/Month of filing.* The second group of four characters shall represent the year and month of filing. As shown above, digits one and two of this group denote the last two digits of the calendar year and digits three and four reflect the month of filing.

(3) *Case type.* The third group of two characters shall designate the type of proceeding utilizing the following case classification code:

MR-- Murder
CF-- Criminal Felony (New CF case numbers shall not be issued after 12/31/2001. CF cases filed prior to 1/1/2002 shall continue to bear the CF case type designation.
FA-- Class A Felony
FB-- Class B Felony
FC-- Class C Felony
FD-- Class D Felony
PC-- Post Conviction Relief Petition
CM-- Criminal Misdemeanor
MC-- Miscellaneous Criminal
IF-- Infraction
OV-- Local Ordinance Violation
OE-- Exempted Ordinance Violation
CT-- Civil Tort
CP-- Civil Plenary () (New CP case numbers shall not be issued after 12/31/2001. CP cases filed before 1/1/2002 shall continue to bear the CP case type.)
PL-- Civil Plenary (Civil Plenary cases filed after 1/1/2002—All Civil cases except those otherwise specifically designated)
CC-- Civil Collection
MF-- Mortgage Foreclosure
MI-- Miscellaneous (Civil cases other than those specifically identified--i.e. change of name, appointment of appraisers, marriage waivers, etc.)
CB-- court business record--i.e. court orders that refer to non-case matters such as the appointment of judge pro tem, drawing the jury, etc.
RS-- Reciprocal Support
SC-- Small Claim
DR-- Domestic Relation (Includes Dissolution of Marriage, Annulment, and Legal Separation)
MH-- Mental Health
AD-- Adoption
ES-- Estate, Supervised
EU-- Estate, Unsupervised
EM-- Estate, Miscellaneous
GU-- Guardianship
TR-- Trust
JC-- Juvenile CHINS
JD-- Juvenile Delinquency

JS-- Juvenile Status
JT-- Juvenile Termination of Parental Rights
JP-- Juvenile Paternity
JM-- Juvenile Miscellaneous
PO-- Order of Protection

Separate dockets need not be maintained for each type.

(4) *Filing sequence.* The fourth group shall consist of six (6) characters assigned sequentially to a case when it is filed. It shall begin with a "000001" at the beginning of each year for each case classification (or for each docket book or case pool if more than one case classification is grouped within a single docket or case pool) and continue sequentially until the end of the year. No court is required to change to using six (6) characters in the fourth group to the extent that it requires re-programming that court's existing electronic case management system. The same sequence for each case classification (or for each docket book or case pool if more than one case classification is grouped within a single docket or case pool) shall be used in common for all circuit, probate and superior courts within a county using the same case management system. No court is required to use the same sequence in common to the extent that it requires re-programming that court's existing electronic case management system.

(C) **Transferring Cases Between Courts Within County.** Whenever a case is transferred between circuit, probate or superior courts within the same county, only the court identifier in the first group of characters in the case number shall be changed. No change shall be made to the fourth group of characters in the case number. The following is an example of how a case number should appear before and after the case has been transferred from one court to another:

55C01–1101–CF–000123 (Case number as it appears in originating court).

55D02–1101–CF–000123 (Case number as it appears in court to which case transferred).

The restriction prohibiting a change to the fourth group of characters does not apply to the extent that implementation of this restriction would require re-programming of the court's existing electronic case management system.

Commentary

The following changes to the uniform case numbering system shall take effect January 1, 2011:

1. Administrative Rule 8(2) is amended to require that any case number must contain the month in which a case is filed. (Previously, including the month of filing was optional.) The reason for this change is to facilitate the collection of case filing statistics for periods of time of less than one year.

2. Administrative Rule 8(4) is amended to require that the fourth group of characters (the "filing sequence") in a case number consist of six (6) characters. (Previously, the filing sequence could contain any number of characters up to six (6)). The reasons for this change are to, first, facilitate on-line searches for cases and, second, achieve greater statewide uniformity in the case numbering system. No court is required to comply with this change to the extent that it would require re-programming of that court's existing electronic case management system. In the process of converting a court's legacy data to a new case management system, the filing sequence may be expanded to consist of six (6) characters.

*   3.   Administrative Rule 8(4) is further amended to require that the same sequence for each case classification (or for each docket book or case pool if more than one case classification is grouped within a single docket or case pool) shall be used in common for all circuit and superior courts within a county using the same case management system. (Previously, each court could use its own filing sequence). In addition, Administrative Rule 8 is further amended by adding a new paragraph "C" providing that when a case is transferred between any circuit, probate, and superior court in the same county, only the court identifier is to be changed; the filing sequence is to remain the same. The reason for these changes is to facilitate the transfer of cases between courts in the same county. Without this change, two cases may, after a transfer, have the same case number, requiring a new filing sequence to be assigned. For example, under current practice, C Felony cases could be filed in Circuit and Superior Courts in Morgan County under case numbers 55C01–1101–CF–000123 and 55D01–1101–CF–000123. Absent this amendment, if the case in Circuit Court is transferred to Superior Court, there would be two cases in Superior Court with the case number 55C01–1101–CF–000123. This change will also achieve greater statewide uniformity in the case numbering system. No court is required to comply with this change to the extent that it would require re-programming of that court's existing electronic case management system.*

Adopted Oct. 15, 1986, effective Jan. 1, 1987. Amended Dec. 8, 1986, effective Jan. 1, 1987; Nov. 10, 1988, effective Jan. 1, 1989; Nov. 30, 1989, effective Jan. 1, 1990; Nov. 13, 1990, effective Jan. 1, 1991; Oct. 25, 1991, effective Jan. 1, 1992; Oct. 29, 1993, effective Jan. 1, 1994; Nov. 9, 1993, effective Jan. 1, 1994; Dec. 5, 1994, effective Feb. 1, 1995; Dec. 15, 1995, effective Feb. 1, 1996; amended effective Dec. 23, 1996; Feb. 17, 1997; April 6, 1999; June 30, 1999; Nov. 18, 1999; April 28, 2000; amended Dec. 22, 2000, effective Jan. 1, 2001; amended effective Feb. 23, 2001; amended Dec. 22, 2000, effective Jan. 1, 2002; Jan. 23, 2001, effective Jan. 1, 2002; amended effective Dec. 21, 2001; amended Sept. 30, 2004, effective Jan. 1, 2005; amended effective Sept. 9, 2005; Feb. 1, 2007; amended Sept. 10, 2007, effective Jan. 1, 2008; amended effective Jan. 9, 2008; amended Sept. 9, 2008, effective Jan. 1, 2009; Sept. 15, 2009, effective Jan. 1, 2010; Sept. 21, 2010, effective Jan. 1, 2011; June 6, 2011, effective July 1, 2011; July 13, 2011, effective July 1, 2011; Sept. 20, 2011, effective Jan. 1, 2012; Oct. 11, 2012, effective Jan. 1, 2013; Jan. 11, 2013; Sept. 13, 2013, effective Jan. 1, 2014.

Rule 8.1.   Uniform Appellate Case Numbering System

(A) **Application.** The Clerk of the Supreme Court shall use the uniform case numbering system set forth below for cases filed in the Supreme Court, Court of Appeals and Tax Court.

(B) **Numbering System.** The uniform appellate case numbering system shall consist of four groups of characters arranged in a manner to identify the court, the year/month of filing, the case type and the filing sequence. The following is an example of the case number to be employed:

    55S00–0804–SJ–001

(1) *Court Identifier.* In cases filed in the Supreme Court and the Court of Appeals, and in inheritance tax cases and original tax appeals filed in the Tax Court, the first group of five characters shall constitute the county and the court identifier. The first and second character in this group shall represent the county of the court from which the case is being appealed or the original action arose; the county where the original inheritance tax action arose; or the county designated in the written election filed by the taxpayer in an original tax appeal, or otherwise designated as set forth in Indiana Tax Rule 8(A), employing the same code set forth in Administrative Rule 8(B)(1). For the cases noted below, the following topic codes will be used in place of county codes:

93   Appeals from agency actions pursuant to IC 4–21.5–5 et seq.

94   Certified Questions, Rule Amendments, and other miscellaneous matters

98   Disciplinary matters involving out-of-state attorneys.

The third character in the first group shall represent the court in which the proceeding is being filed employing the following codes:

S   Supreme Court
A   Court of Appeals
T   Tax Court

The last two characters of the first group shall distinguish between geographical districts set forth in IC 33–25–1–2 from which the case is being appealed or being assigned in the Court of Appeals, and additional cases and other matters handled by the Supreme Court and the Tax Court, employing the following codes:

00 Administrative/Other matters handled by the Supreme Court, including, but not limited to, Attorney Disciplinary matters, Judicial Disciplinary matters, Special Judge assignments, Senior Judge assignments and Rule amendments.

01 First District: Bartholomew, Boone, Brown, Clark, Clay, Crawford, Daviess, Dearborn, Decatur, Dubois, Fayette, Floyd, Fountain, Franklin, Gibson, Greene, Hancock, Harrison, Hendricks, Henry, Jackson, Jefferson, Jennings, Johnson, Knox, Lawrence, Martin, Monroe, Montgomery, Morgan, Ohio, Orange, Owen, Parke, Perry, Pike, Posey, Putnam, Randolph, Ripley, Rush, Scott, Shelby, Spencer,

Sullivan, Switzerland, Union, Vanderburgh, Vermillion, Vigo, Warrick, Washington, and Wayne.

02 Second District: Adams, Blackford, Carroll, Cass, Clinton, Delaware, Grant, Hamilton, Howard, Huntington, Jay, Madison, Marion, Miami, Tippecanoe, Tipton, Wabash, Wells, and White.

03 Third District: Allen, Benton, DeKalb, Elkhart, Fulton, Jasper, Kosciusko, LaGrange, Lake, LaPorte, Marshall, Newton, Noble, Porter, Pulaski, St. Joseph, Starke, Steuben, Warren, and Whitley.

04 The entire state constitutes the Fourth District.

05 The entire state constitutes the Fifth District.

10 Cases appealed to the Tax Court.

(2) *Year/Month of Filing.* The second group of four characters shall represent the year and month of filing. As shown above, the first and second characters of this group denote the last two digits of the calendar year and the third and fourth characters reflect the month of filing.

(3) *Case Type.* The third group of two characters shall designate the type of proceeding.

i.   The following codes shall be used for matters originating in the Supreme Court:

BL	Board of Law Examiners
CQ	Certified Questions
DI	Attorney Discipline
JD	Judicial Discipline
MS	Miscellaneous Matters
OR	Original Actions
SJ	Special Judges

ii.   In appeals, the same case type code used in the lower court, as specified in Administrative Rule 8(B)(3), shall be used except as indicated below:

EX	Appeals in certain administrative proceedings
TA	Appeals from the Tax Court
DP	Direct capital appeals
PD	Post-conviction capital appeals
LW	Direct Life without Parole (LWOP) appeals
CR	Direct appeals (non-capital, non-LWOP)
PC	Post–conviction appeals (non-capital)
SD	Requests to file successive capital post-conviction petitions
SP	Requests to file successive post-conviction petitions (non-capital)
JV	Juvenile delinquency appeals with a trial court designation of " JD".

(4) *Filing Sequence.* The fourth group may consist of any number of characters assigned sequentially to a case when it is filed. It shall begin with "1" at the beginning of each year for each case classification and continue sequentially until the end of the year. The number of cases filed within a given classification will determine the number of digits in this group.

Adopted effective Jan. 1, 2010. Amended Sept. 21, 2010, effective Jan. 1, 2011.

Rule 9.   Access to Court Records

(A) Scope and Purposes.

(1) Pursuant to the inherent authority of the Indiana Supreme Court and pursuant to Indiana Code § 5–14–3–4(a)(8), this rule governs public access to, and confidentiality of, court records. Except as otherwise provided by this rule, access to court records shall be governed by the Indiana Access to Public Records Act (Indiana Code § 5–14–3–1, et. seq.).

(2) The purposes of this rule are to:

(a) Promote accessibility to court records;

(b) Support the role of the judiciary;

(c) Promote governmental accountability;

(d) Contribute to public safety;

(e) Minimize the risk of injury to individuals;

(f) Protect individual privacy rights and interests;

(g) Protect proprietary business information;

(h) Minimize reluctance to use the court system;

(i) Make the most effective use of court and clerk of court staff;

(j) Provide excellent customer service; and

(k) Avoid unduly burdening the ongoing business of the judiciary.

(3) This rule applies only to court records as defined in this rule and does not authorize or prohibit access to information gathered, maintained, or stored by a non-judicial governmental agency or other entity.

(4) Disputes arising under this rule shall be determined in accordance with this and, to the extent not inconsistent with this rule, by all other rules of procedure, evidence, and appeal.

(5) This rule applies to all court records; however clerks and courts need not redact or restrict information that was otherwise public in case records and administrative records created before January 1, 2005.

Commentary

The objective of this rule is to provide maximum public accessibility to court records, taking into account public policy interests that are not always fully compatible with unrestricted access. The public policy interests listed above are in no particular order. This rule attempts to balance competing interests and recognizes that unrestricted access to certain information in court records could result in an unwarranted invasion of personal privacy or unduly increase the risk of injury to individuals and businesses. This rule recognizes there are strong societal reasons for allowing public access to court records and denial of access could compromise the judiciary's role in society, inhibit accountability, and endanger public safety.

This rule starts from the presumption of open public access to court records. In some circumstances; however, there may be sound reasons for restricting access to these records. This rule recognizes that there are times when access to information may lead to, or increase the risk of, harm to individuals. However, given the societal interests in access to court records, this rule also reflects the view that any restriction to access must be implemented in a manner tailored to serve the interests in open access. It is also important to remember that, generally, at least some of the parties in a court case are not in court voluntarily, but rather have been brought into court by plaintiffs or by the government. A person who is not a party to the action may also be mentioned in the court record. Care should be taken that the privacy rights and interests of such involuntary parties or 'third' persons are not unduly compromised.

Subsection (A)(3) is intended to assure that public access provided under this Rule does not apply to information gathered, maintained or stored by other agencies or entities that is not necessary to, or is not part of the basis of, a court's decision or the judicial process. Access to this information is governed by the law and the access policy of the agency collecting and maintaining such information. The ability of a computer in a court or clerk's office to access the information because the computer uses shared software and databases does not, by itself, make the information subject to this rule.

The Division of State Court Administration may provide advisory information to individuals or entities about the provisions, restrictions, and limitations of this rule.

(B) Who Has Access Under This Rule.

(1) All persons have access to court records as provided in this rule, except as provided in section (B)(2) of this rule.

(2) The following persons, in accordance with their functions within the judicial system, may have greater access to court records:

    (a) court, court agency or clerk of court employees;

    (b) private or governmental persons or entities who assist a court in providing court services;

    (c) public agencies whose access to court records is defined by other statutes, rules, orders or policies; and

    (d) the parties to a case or their lawyers with respect to their own case.

Commentary

Subsection (B)(1) provides the general rule that all persons, including members of the general public, the media, and commercial and noncommercial entities, are entitled to the same basic level of access to court records. Access to court records is not determined by who is seeking access or the purpose for seeking access, although some users, such as court employees or the parties to a particular case, may have greater access to those particular records than is afforded the general public.

Subsection (B)(2) provides the exception to the general rule and specifies the entities and persons for whom courts may provide greater access. This greater level of access is a result of the need for effective management of the judicial system and the protection of the right to a fair trial.

The means of access may depend upon the form in which the court record exists. Certain circumstances relating to compilation or bulk distribution of information gleaned from court records may affect access to court records.

(C) Definitions. For purpose of this rule:

(1) "Court Record" means both case records and administrative records.

(2) "Case Record" means any document, information, data, or other item created, collected, received, or maintained by a court, court agency or clerk of court in connection with a particular case.

(3) "Administrative Record" means any document, information, data, or other item created, collected, received, or maintained by a court, court agency, or clerk of court pertaining to the administration of the judicial branch of government and not associated with any particular case.

(4) "Court" means the Indiana Supreme Court, Court of Appeals, Tax Court, and all Circuit, Superior, Probate, County, City, Town, or Small Claims Courts.

(5) "Clerk of Court" means the Clerk of the Indiana Supreme Court, Court of Appeals, and Tax Court, the Clerk of a Circuit, Superior, Probate, or County Court, the Clerk of a City or Town court, and the Clerk of a Marion County Small Claims Court, including staff.

(6) "Public access" means the process whereby a person may inspect and copy the information in a court record.

(7) "Remote access" means the ability of a person to inspect and copy information in a court record in electronic form through an electronic means.

(8) "In electronic form" means any information in a court record in a form that is readable through the use of an electronic device, regardless of the manner in which it was created.

(9) "Bulk Distribution" means the distribution of all, or a significant subset of the information in court records in electronic form, as is, and without modification or compilation.

(10) "Compiled Information" means information that is derived from the selection, aggregation or reformulation of some of all or a subset of all the information from more than one individual court record in electronic form.

Commentary

"Case record" refers to records connected with a particular case. It does not include other records maintained by the clerk of court, including, but not limited to, election records, marriage and other license functions; copies of notary bonds; oaths and certificates of public officials other than oaths of judicial officers and attorneys; lists, including those for distressed sales, licensed child placing agencies; reports of perpetual care of cemetery endowment accounts; and certificates of inspection and compliance of chemicals and chemical tests results and certifications of breath test operators; delinquency personal property taxes; hunting and fishing licenses; conflict of interest statements; passports; and the filing of reports from state agencies, such as the Alcohol Licensing Board.

The definition of case record is medium neutral and access neutral, and is intended to apply to every case record, regardless of the manner in which it was created, the form(s) in which it is stored, or other form(s) in which the information may exist.

An "administrative record" may include, but not be limited to, the roll of attorneys, rosters of medical review panels and group legal services, records relating to elections to the Judicial Nominating Commission, statistical reports, local court rules, jury pool list records, general court orders, budget and expenditure records, and record of receipts of funds. The term "court agency" in subsection (C)(3) includes without limitation the Indiana Judicial Center and the Judicial Conference of Indiana.

(D) General Access Rule.

(1) A court record is accessible to the public except as provided in sections (G) and (H) of this rule, or as otherwise ordered sealed by the trial court.

(2) This rule applies to all court records, regardless of the manner of creation, method of collection, form of storage, or the form in which the record is maintained.

(3) If a court record, or portion thereof, is excluded from public access, there shall be a publicly accessible indication of the fact of exclusion but not the content of the exclusion. This sub-section (3) does not apply to court proceedings or administrative records which are confidential pursuant to law.

(4) A court may manage access to audio and video recordings of its proceedings to the extent appropriate to avoid substantial interference with the resources or normal operation of the court and to comply with Indiana Judicial Conduct Rule 2.17 *[former Canon 3(B)(13)]*. This provision does not operate to deny to any person the right to access a court record under Rule 9(D)(1).

Commentary

The objective of this section is to make it clear that this rule applies to information in the court record regardless of the manner in which the information was created, collected or submitted to the court. Application of this rule is not affected by the means of storage, manner of presentation or the form in which information is maintained. To support the general principle of open access, the application of the rule is independent of the technology or the format of the information.

Subsection (D)(3) requires that any and all redactions be identified. The phrase "not-public information" or an equivalent designation may be used.

(E) Remote Access and Fees. Courts should endeavor to make at least the following information, when available in electronic form, remotely accessible to the public unless public access is restricted pursuant to sections (G) or (H):

(1) Litigant/party indexes to cases filed with the court;

(2) Listings of new case filings, including the names of the parties;

(3) The chronological case summary of cases;

(4) Calendars or dockets of court proceedings, including case numbers and captions, date and time of hearings, and location of hearings;

(5) Judgments, orders, or decrees.

Upon the request and at an amount approved by the majority of judges of courts of record in the county, the County Board of Commissioners may adopt an electronic system fee to be charged in conjunction with electronic access to court records. The fee must be approved by the Division of State Court Administration. In the instance of records from multiple courts, the Supreme Court may adopt such a fee. The method of the fee's collection, deposit, distribution and accounting must be approved by the Indiana State Board of Accounts.

Commentary

In addition to any fees charged under this rule, Sections (C)(9) and (10) provide that courts may charge for the fair market value of bulk and compiled information This rule does not impose an affirmative obligation to preserve information or data or to transform information or data received into a format or medium that is not otherwise routinely maintained by the court. While this section encourages courts to make the designated information available to the public through remote access, this is not required, even if the information already exists in an electronic format.

(F) Bulk Distribution and Compiled Information.

(1) Upon written request as provided in this Section (F), bulk distribution or compiled information that is not excluded by Section (G) or (H) of this rule may be provided.

(2) Requests for bulk distribution or compiled information shall be made to the Executive Director of the Division of State Court Administration or other designee of the Indiana Supreme Court. The Executive Director or other designee may forward such request to a court exercising jurisdiction over the records, and in the instance of records from multiple courts, to the Indiana Supreme Court, for further action. Requests will be acted upon or responded to within a reasonable period of time.

(3) With respect to requests for case record information not excluded from public access by Sections (G) or (H) of this rule, the request for bulk distribution or compiled information may be granted upon determination that the information sought is consistent with the purposes of this rule, that resources are available to prepare the information, and that fulfilling the request is an appropriate use of public resources. The grant of said request may be made contingent upon the requestor paying an amount which the court determines is the fair market value of the information.

(4) With respect to requests for bulk distribution or compiled information that include information excluded from public access pursuant to Sections (G) or (H) of this rule:

    (a) such requests must be verified and can only be made by individuals or entities having a substantial interest or a bona fide research activity for scholarly, journalistic, political, governmental, research, evaluation or statistical purposes, and wherein the identification of specific individuals is ancillary to the purpose of the inquiry. Each request under this subsection (4) must:

        (i) fully identify the requestor and describe the requestor's interest and purpose of the inquiry;

        (ii) identify what information is sought;

        (iii) describe the purpose for requesting the information and explain how the information will benefit the public interest or public education;

        (iv) explain provisions for the secure protection of any information requested to which public access is restricted or prohibited;

        (v) provide for individual notice to all persons affected by the release of information, unless, upon prior notice to the Indiana Attorney General and a reasonable opportunity to respond, such individual notice requirement is waived by the Supreme Court;

        (vi) demonstrate by clear and convincing evidence that the public interest will be served by allowing access, that denying access will create a serious and imminent danger to the public interest, or that denying access will cause a substantial harm to a person or third parties.

    (b) Upon receiving a request pursuant to this sub-section (F)(4), the Supreme Court may permit objections by persons affected by the release of information, unless individual notice required under (F)(4)(a)(v) is waived by the Supreme Court.

    (c) The request may be granted only upon determination by the Supreme Court that the information sought is consistent with the purposes of this rule, that resources are available to prepare the information, and that fulfilling the request is an appropriate use of public resources, and further upon finding by clear and convincing evidence that the requestor satisfies the requirements of subsection (F)(4)(a), and that the purposes for which the information is sought substantially outweighs the privacy interests protected by this rule. An order granting a request under this subsection may specify particular conditions or requirements for use of the information, including without limitation:

        (i) The confidential information will not be sold or otherwise distributed, directly or indirectly, to third parties;

        (ii) The confidential information will not be used directly or indirectly to sell a product or service to an individual or the general public;

        (iii) The confidential information will not be copied or duplicated other than for the stated scholarly, journalistic, political, governmental, research, evaluation, or statistical purpose; and

        (iv) The requestor must pay reasonable costs of responding to the request, as determined by the court.

    (d) When the request includes release of social security numbers, dates of birth, or addresses, the information provided may include only the last four digits of social security numbers, only the year of birth, and only the zip code of addresses. The restrictions on release of social security numbers, dates of birth, and addresses may be waived only upon a petition to the Executive Director of the Division of State Court Administration and a finding of exceptional circumstances by the Indiana Supreme Court.

Commentary

Section (F)(3) authorizes courts, in their discretion, to provide access to bulk distribution and compiled information that is accessible to the public. It does not require that such information be made available. Permitting bulk distribution or compiled information should not be authorized if providing the data will interfere with the normal operations of the court.

In allowing bulk or compiled data requests, courts must limit bulk data to court records, even if those requesting this information are seeking other information which is governed by other agencies' policies.

Generating compiled data may require court resources and generating the complied information may compete with the normal operations of the court for resources, which may be a reason for the court not to compile the information. However, it may be less demanding on court resources to instead provide bulk distribution of the requested information pursuant to section (D)(3), and let the requestor, rather than the court, compile the information. Courts may charge for the fair market value of bulk or compiled information provided under Section (F)(3).

Section (F)(4) allows only the Supreme Court to grant requests for bulk or compiled information that is excluded from public access and only when the request is made by research and/or governmental entities. The general intent of (F)(4)(d) is that the last four digits of social security numbers and years of birth, rather than entire birth dates and social security numbers, are sufficient for matching records and to ensure that someone is correctly identified in bulk or compiled records. Courts should provide more complete social security numbers or other identifying information only in extraordinary circumstances.

(G) Court Records Excluded From Public Access.

(1) *Case records.* The following information in case records is excluded from public access and is confidential:

(a) Information that is excluded from public access pursuant to federal law;

(b) Information that is excluded from public access as declared confidential by Indiana statute or other court rule, including without limitation:

(i) All adoption records created after July 8, 1941, as declared confidential by Ind. Code § 31–19–19–1 *et. seq.*, except those specifically declared open by Ind. Code § 31–19–13–2(2);

(ii) All records relating to chancroid, chlamydia, gonorrhea, hepatitis, human immunodeficiency virus (HIV), Lymphogranuloma venereum, syphilis, tuberculosis, as declared confidential by Ind. Code § 16–41–8–1 *et. seq.*;

(iii) All records relating to child abuse as declared confidential by Ind. Code § 31–33–18 *et. seq.*;

(iv) All records relating to drug tests as declared confidential by Ind. Code § 5–14–3–4(a)(9);

(v) Records of grand jury proceedings as declared confidential by Ind. Code § 35–34–2–4;

(vi) Records of juvenile proceedings as declared confidential by Ind. Code § 31–39–1–2, except those specifically open under statute;

(vii) All paternity records created after July 1, 1941 as declared confidential by Ind. Code §§ 31–14–11–15, 31–19–5–23, 31–39–1–1 and 31–39–1–2;

(viii) All pre-sentence reports as declared confidential by Ind. Code § 35–38–1–13;

(ix) Written petitions to permit marriages without consent and orders directing the Clerk of Court to issue a marriage license to underage persons, as declared confidential by Ind. Code § 31–11–1–6;

(x) Only those arrest warrants, search warrants, indictments and informations ordered confidential by the trial judge, prior to return of duly executed service as declared confidential by Ind. Code § 5–14–3–4(b)(1);

(xi) All medical, mental health, or tax records unless determined by law or regulation of any governmental custodian not to be confidential, released by the subject of such records, or declared by a court of competent jurisdiction to be essential to the resolution of litigation as declared confidential by Ind. Code §§ 16–39–3–10, 6–4.1–5–10, 6–4.1–12–12, and 6–8.1–7–1;

(xii) Personal information relating to jurors or prospective jurors, other than for the use of the parties and counsel, pursuant to Jury Rule 10;

(xiii) Information relating to protection from abuse orders, no-contact orders and workplace violence restraining orders as declared confidential by Ind. Code § 5–2–9–6 *et. seq.*;

(xiv) Mediation proceedings pursuant to Alternative Dispute Resolution Rule 2.11, Mini-Trial proceedings pursuant to Alternative Dispute Resolution Rule 4.4(C), and Summary Jury Trials pursuant to Alternative Dispute Resolution Rule 5.6;

(xv) Information in probation files pursuant to the Probation Standards promulgated by the Judicial Conference of Indiana pursuant to Ind. Code § 11–13–1–8(b);

(xvi) Information deemed confidential pursuant to the Rules for Court Administered Alcohol and Drug Programs promulgated by the Judicial Conference of Indiana pursuant to Ind. Code § 12–23–14–13;

(xvii) Information deemed confidential pursuant to the Problem–Solving Court Rules promulgated by the Judicial Conference of Indiana pursuant to Ind. Code § 33–23–16–16.

(xviii) All records of the Department of workforce Development as declared confidential by Ind. Code § 22–4–19–6.

(xix) Information regarding interception of electronic communications that is sealed or deemed confidential as set forth in Ind. Code § 35–33.5 et seq.

(c) Information excluded from public access by specific court order;

(d) Complete Social Security Numbers of living persons;

(e) With the exception of names, information such as addresses, phone numbers, and dates of birth which explicitly identifies:

(i) natural persons who are witnesses or victims (not including defendants) in criminal, domestic violence, stalking, sexual assault, juvenile, or civil protection order proceedings, provided that juveniles who are victims of sex crimes shall be identified by initials only;

(ii) places of residence of judicial officers, clerks and other employees of courts and clerks of court;

unless the person or persons about whom the information pertains waives confidentiality;

(f) Complete account numbers of specific assets, loans, bank accounts, credit cards, and personal identification numbers (PINs);

(g) All orders of expungement entered in criminal or juvenile proceedings, orders to restrict access to criminal history information pursuant to Ind. Code § 35–38–5–5.5 or Ind. Code § 35–38–8–5 and records excluded from public access by such orders, and information related to infractions that is excluded from public access pursuant to Ind. Code § 34–28–5–15 or Ind. Code § 34–28–5–16;

(h) All personal notes and e-mail, and deliberative material, of judges, jurors, court staff and judicial agencies, and information recorded in personal data assistants (PDA's) or organizers and personal calendars.

(1.1) *Court Proceedings Closed to the Public.* During court proceedings that are closed to the public by statute or court order, when information in case records that is excluded from public access pursuant to this rule is admitted into evidence, the information shall remain excluded from public access.

(1.2) *Court Proceedings Open to the Public.* During court proceedings that are open to the public, when information in case records that is excluded from public access pursuant to this rule is admitted into evidence, the information shall remain excluded from public access only if a party or a person affected by the release of the information, prior to or contemporaneously with its introduction into evidence, affirmatively requests that the information remain excluded from public access.

(1.3) *Access to Excluded Information.* Access to information excluded from public access under sub-

sections 1.1 and 1.2 may be granted after a hearing pursuant to Administrative Rule 9(I).

(2) *Administrative records.* The following information in administrative records is excluded from public access and is confidential:

(a) All information excluded in sub-sections (a) through (h) of section (G)(1);

(b) Information that is excluded from public access to the extent provided by Indiana statute or other court rule, including without limitation:

(i) the work product of an attorney representing, pursuant to state employment or appointment, a public agency, the state, or an individual, pursuant to Ind. Code § 5–14–3–4(b)(2);

(ii) test questions, scoring keys, and other examination data used in administering a licensing examination, examination for employment before the examination is given or if it is to be given again, pursuant to Ind. Code § 5–14–3–4(b)(3);

(iii) test scores of a person if a person is identified by name and has not consented to the release of the person's scores, pursuant to Ind. Code § 5–14–3–4(b)(4);

(iv) records that are intra-agency or inter-agency advisory or deliberative material, including material developed by a private contractor under a contract with a public agency, that are expressions of opinion or are of a speculative nature, and that are communicated for the purpose of decision making, pursuant to Ind. Code § 5–14–3–4(b)(6);

(v) diaries, journals, or other personal notes serving as the functional equivalent of a diary or journal, pursuant to Ind. Code § 5–14–3–4(b)(7);

(vi) personnel files of employees and files of applicants for employment, except for the name, compensation, job title, business address, business telephone number, job description, education and training background, previous work experience, and dates of first and last employment of present or former officers or employees of the agency; information relating to the status of any formal charges against the employee; and information concerning disciplinary actions in which final action has been taken and that resulted in the employee being suspended, demoted, or discharged, pursuant to Ind. Code § 5–14–3–4(b)(8);

(vii) administrative or technical information that would jeopardize a record keeping, security system or court security plan described in Indiana Administrative Rule 19, pursuant to Ind. Code § 5–14–3–4(b)(10);

(viii) computer programs, computer codes, computer filing systems, and other software that are owned by the public agency or entrusted to it, pursuant to Ind. Code § 5–14–3–4(b)(11);

(ix) lists of employees of court, court agency, or clerk offices, which may not be disclosed to commercial entities for commercial purposes and may not be used by commercial entitles for commercial purposes, pursuant to Ind. Code § 5–14–3–4(c)(1);

(x) all information and all records obtained and maintained by the Board of Law Examiners in the performance of its duty pursuant to Admission and Discipline Rule 19, except as otherwise required by court rule or order of the Indiana Supreme Court;

(xi) proceedings and papers in attorney disciplinary matters that relate to matters that have not resulted in the filing of a verified complaint, investigative reports and other work product of the Executive Secretary, employees or agents of the Disciplinary Commission, statements of circumstances conditionally agreeing to discipline, and affidavits of resignation or consenting to discipline pursuant to Admission and Discipline Rules 23;

(xii) files, records and proceedings of the Continuing Legal Education Commission, as they may relate to or arise out of an attorney, judge, mediator, or sponsor attempting to satisfy continuing legal educational requirements pursuant to Admission and Discipline Rule 29;

(xiii) all information, including records obtained by the Judges and Lawyers Assistance Program Committee in the performance of its duty and as delegated by the Indiana Supreme Court, with the exception of statistical data, pursuant to Admission and Discipline Rule 31;

(xiv) before the filing and service of formal charges, Judicial Qualifications Commission complaints, inquiries, investigations, or Commission deliberations, settlement conferences and proposed settlement agreements pursuant to Admission and Discipline Rule 25.

(3) Information in a case record that is otherwise excluded from public access may be made accessible if the information is declared by a court with jurisdiction over the case to be essential to the resolution of litigation, or, if the information is released by each person to whom such information pertains.

(4) *Appellate Proceedings.* In appellate proceedings pending as of or commencing after January 1, 2009, parties, counsel, the courts on appeal, and the Clerk of the Supreme Court, Court of Appeals, and Tax Court ("Clerk") shall have the following obligations:

(a) *Cases in which the entire record is excluded from public access by statute or by rule.* In any case in which all case records are excluded from public access by statute or by rule of the Supreme Court,

(i) the Clerk shall make the appellate chronological case summary for the case publicly accessible but shall identify the names of the parties and affected persons in a manner reasonably calculated to provide anonymity and privacy; and

(ii) the parties and counsel, at any oral argument and in any public hearing conducted in the appeal, shall refer to the case and parties only as identified in the appellate chronological case summary and shall not disclose any matter excluded from public access.

(b) *Cases in which a portion of the record is excluded from public access by statute or by rule.* In any case in which a portion (but less than all) of the record in the case has been excluded from public access by statute or by rule of the Supreme Court,

(i) the parties and counsel shall not disclose any matter excluded from public access in any document not itself excluded from public access; to the extent it is necessary to refer to excluded information in briefs or other documents that are not excluded from public access, the reference shall be made in a separate document filed in compliance with Trial Rule 5(G); and

(ii) the parties, counsel, and the Clerk shall have the respective obligations set forth in (a)(i) and (a)(ii) to the extent necessary to comply with the statute or rule.

(c) *Cases in which any public access is excluded by trial court order.* In any case in which all or any portion of the record in the case has been excluded from public access by trial court order ("TCO"),

(i)(A) the appellant shall provide notice in the appropriate place on the Notice of Appeal (see Ind. Appellate Rule 9) that all or a portion of the record in the case has been excluded from public access by TCO, and attach to the appellant's case summary all TCOs concerning each exclusion; and

(B) the parties, counsel, and the Clerk shall have the respective obligations set forth in (a)(i), (a)(ii), and (b)(i) to the extent necessary to comply with the TCO.

(ii) if the notice and supporting orders referred to in (i)(A) are supplied, then the Clerk shall exclude the information from public access to the extent necessary to comply with the TCO unless the court on appeal determines that

(A) the TCO was improper or is no longer appropriate,

(B) public disclosure of the information is essential to the resolution of litigation, or

(C) disclosure is appropriate to further the establishment of precedent or the development of the law;

(iii) any party may supplement or challenge the appellant's notice or attachments supplied under (i)(A) or request a determination from the court on appeal under (ii); and

(iv) if the appellant does not notify the court on appeal that all or a portion of the record in the case has been excluded from public access by TCO, and attach to the Notice of Appeal all TCOs concerning each exclusion, as required by (i)(A),

(A) the Clerk shall be under no obligation to exclude the information from public access; and

(B) the appellant and appellant's counsel shall be subject to sanctions.

(d) Orders, decisions, and opinions issued by the court on appeal shall be publicly accessible, but each court on appeal should endeavor to exclude the names of the parties and affected persons, and any other matters excluded from public access, except as essential to the resolution of litigation or appropriate to further the establishment of precedent or the development of the law.

Subsection (1)(a) Federal Law: There are several types of information that are commonly but possibly incorrectly, considered to be protected from public disclosure by federal law. Although there may be restrictions on federal agencies disclosing Social Security Numbers, they may not apply to state or local agencies such as courts. While federal law prohibits disclosure of tax returns by federal agencies or employees, but this prohibition may not extend to disclosure by others. The Health Insurance Portability and Accountability Act of 1996 (HIPAA) and regulations adopted pursuant to it limits disclosure of certain health related information. Whether the limitation extends to state court records is not clear. There are also federal restrictions regarding information in alcohol and drug abuse patient records and requiring confidentiality of information acquired by drug court programs. This rule does not supersede any federal law or regulation requiring privacy or non-disclosure of information.

This section does not limit the authority of a judge in a particular case to order the sealing of particular records or to exclude from public access during the pendency of a case motions to suppress or motions otherwise seeking to limit or exclude matters from presentation at a jury trial, and all proceedings and rulings thereon. Such exclusion of public access to pre-trial proceedings should be invoked sparingly and only when the court is convinced that admonitions to prospective jurors and the jury selection process will likely be inadequate to assure a fair trial.

The prohibition of access to addresses under this section includes, without limitation, mail and e-mail addresses.

With respect to expungement orders excluded from public access under section (G)(1)(g) of this rule, an interested person may seek a copy or other verification of an expungement order by filing a request under section (I) of this rule.

In addition to deliberative material excluded under this rule, a court may exclude from public access materials generated or created by a court reporter with the exception of the official transcript.

Several state statutes address access to certain confidential court records, including but not limited to Ind. Code § 31–39–2–10 (involving access to juvenile records) and Ind. Code § 16–41–8–1 et seq., (involving procedures for handling medical records of persons accused of a "potentially disease causing offense"). Indiana Administrative Rule 9 and its requirements concerning access to confidential records should guide the actions of judicial officers when considering granting access to records made confidential by statute.

(H) Prohibiting Public Access to Information in Court Records.

(1) A verified written request to prohibit public access to information in a court record, may be made by any person affected by the release of the information. The request shall demonstrate that:

(a) The public interest will be substantially served by prohibiting access;

(b) Access or dissemination of the information will create a significant risk of substantial harm to the requestor, other persons or the general public;

(c) A substantial prejudicial effect to on-going proceedings cannot be avoided without prohibiting public access, or;

(d) The information should have been excluded from public access under section (G) of this rule.

The person seeking to prohibit access has the burden of providing notice to the parties and such other persons as the court may direct, providing proof of notice to the court or the reason why notice could not or should not be given, demonstrating to the court the requestor's reasons for prohibiting access to the information. A party or person to whom notice is given shall have twenty (20) days from receiving notice to respond to the request.

(2) A court may deny a request to prohibit public access without a hearing. If the court does not initially deny the request, it shall post advance public notice of the hearing. A court may grant a request to prohibit public access following a hearing if the requestor demonstrates by clear and convincing evidence that any one or more of the requirements of (H)(1)(a) through (H)(1)(d) have been satisfied. An order prohibiting public access to information in a court record may be issued by the

court having jurisdiction over the record. An order prohibiting public access to information in bulk or compiled records, or in records under the jurisdiction of multiple courts may be issued only by the Supreme Court.

(3) The court shall balance the public access interests served by this rule and the grounds demonstrated by the requestor. In its order, the court shall state its reasons for granting or denying the request. If the court prohibits access, it will use the least restrictive means and duration. When a request is made to prohibit public access to information in a court record at the time of case initiation, the request and the case information will remain confidential for a reasonable period of time until the court rules on the request. When a request is made to prohibit public access to information in court records that are already publicly accessible, the information may be rendered confidential for a reasonable period of time until the court rules on the request.

(4) This section does not limit the authority of a court to seal court records pursuant to Ind. Code § 5–14–3–5.5.

Commentary

This section is intended to address those extraordinary circumstances in which information that is otherwise publicly accessible is to be excluded from public access. This section generally incorporates a presumption of openness, and the need for demonstrating compelling grounds to overcome the presumption.

Parties should be aware that their request is not retroactive. Copies of the public record may have been disseminated prior to any request, and corrective action taken under the provisions of this rule will not affect those records.

Notice requirements for this section correspond to those requirements found in Trial Rule 65(b) and are intended to be consistent with T.R. 65(b), Posted notice requirements correspond and are intended to be consistent with those found in Ind. Code § 5–14–2–5 which requires that: "[t]he court shall notify the parties of the hearing date and shall notify the general public by posting a copy of the hearing notice at a place within the confines of the court accessible to the general public".

(I) Obtaining Access to Information Excluded from Public Access.

(1) A verified written request to obtain access to information in a case or administrative record to which public access is prohibited under this Rule may be made by any person to the court having jurisdiction over the record. The request shall demonstrate that:

(a) Extraordinary circumstances exist which requires deviation from the general provisions of this rule;

(b) The public interest will be served by allowing access;

(c) Access or dissemination of the information creates no significant risk of substantial harm to any party, to third parties, or to the general public, and;

(d) The release of information creates no prejudicial effect to on-going proceedings, or;

(e) The information should not be excluded for public access under Section (G) of this Rule.

The person seeking access has the burden of providing notice to the parties and such other persons as the court may direct, providing proof of notice to the court or the reason why notice could not or should not be given, demonstrating to the court the requestor's reasons for prohibiting access to the information. A party or person to whom notice is given shall have twenty (20) days from receiving notice to respond to the request.

(2) A court may deny a request to provide access without a hearing. If the court does not initially deny the request, it shall post advance public notice of the hearing. A court may grant a request to allow access following a hearing if the requestor demonstrates by clear and convincing evidence that the requirements of (I)(1) have been satisfied. An order allowing public access to information excluded from public access may be issued by the court having jurisdiction over the record. An order permitting access to information excluded from public access in bulk or compiled records, or in records under the jurisdiction of multiple courts may be issued only by the Supreme Court.

(3) A court shall consider the public access and the privacy interests served by this rule and the grounds demonstrated by the requestor. In its order, the court shall state its reasons for granting or denying the request, When a request is made for access to information excluded from public access, the information will remain confidential while the court rules on the request.

(4) A court may place restrictions on the use or dissemination of the information to preserve confidentiality.

Commentary

This section is intended to address those extraordinary circumstances in which confidential information or information which is otherwise excluded from public access is to be included in a release of information. In some circumstances, the nature of the information contained in a record and the restrictions placed on the accessibility of the information contained in that record may be governed by federal or state law. This section is not intended to modify or overrule any federal or state law governing such records or the process for releasing information.

Information excluded from public access that is sought in a request for bulk or compiled records request is governed by section (F) of this rule.

(J) When Court Records May Be Accessed.

(1) Court records which are publicly accessible will be available for public access in the courthouse during regular business hours established by the court. Court records in electronic form to which the court allows remote access under this policy will be available for access during hours established by the court, subject to unexpected technical failures or normal system maintenance announced in advance.

(2) Upon receiving a request pursuant to section (F)(4), (H), or (I) of this rule, a court will respond within a reasonable period of time.

Commentary

This section does not preclude or require "after hours" access to court records in electronic form. Courts are encouraged to provide access to records in electronic form beyond the hours access is available at the courthouse, however, it is not the intent of this rule to compel such additional access.

(K) Contracts With Vendors Providing Information Technology Services Regarding Court Records.

(1) If a court or other private or governmental entity contracts with a vendor to provide information technology support to gather, store, or make accessible court records, the contract will require the vendor to comply with the intent and provisions of this access policy. For purposes of this section, the term "vendor" also includes a state, county or local governmental agency that provides information technology services to a court.

(2) Each contract shall require the vendor to assist the court in its role of educating litigants and the public about this rule. The vendor shall also be responsible for training its employees and subcontractors about the provisions of this rule.

(3) Each contract shall prohibit vendors from disseminating bulk or compiled information, without first obtaining approval as required by this Rule.

(4) Each contract shall require the vendor to acknowledge that court records remain the property of the court and are subject to the directions and orders of the court with respect to the handling and access to the court records, as well as the provisions of this rule.

(5) These requirements are in addition to those otherwise imposed by law.

Commentary

This section is intended to apply when information technology services are provided to a court by an agency outside the judicial branch, or by outsourcing of court information technology services to non-governmental entities. Implicit in this rule is the concept that all court records are under the authority of the judiciary, and that the judiciary

has the responsibility to ensure public access to court records and to restrict access where appropriate. This applies as well to court records maintained in systems operated by a clerk of court or other non-judicial governmental department or agency.

This section does not supercede or alter the requirements of Trial Rule 77(K) which requires that, before court records may be made available through the internet or other electronic method, the information to be posted, its format, pricing structure, method of dissemination, and changes thereto must receive advance approval by the Division of State Court Administration.

(L) Immunity for Disclosure of Protected Information.

A court, court agency, or clerk of court employee, official, or an employee or officer of a contractor or subcontractor of a court, court agency, or clerk of court who unintentionally and unknowingly discloses confidential or erroneous information is immune from liability for such a disclosure.

Commentary

This immunity provision is consistent with the immunity and protections provided by Indiana statute as found at IC 5–14–3–10(c).

Adopted Nov. 10, 1988, effective Jan. 1, 1989. Amended Nov. 1, 1991, effective Jan. 1, 1992; Dec. 21, 2001, effective Jan. 1, 2003; amended effective July 19, 2002; amended Feb. 25, 2004, effective Jan. 1, 2005; Sept. 30, 2004, effective Jan. 1, 2005; July 1, 2005, effective Jan. 1, 2006; Aug. 15, 2006, effective Jan. 1, 2007; Sept. 9, 2008, effective Jan. 1, 2009; Oct. 6, 2008, effective Jan. 1, 2009; Sept. 15, 2009, effective Jan. 1, 2010; Sept. 21, 2010, effective Jan. 1, 2011; Sept. 13, 2011, effective Oct. 1, 2011; Sept. 20, 2011, effective Jan. 1, 2012; Oct. 11, 2012, effective Jan. 1, 2013; Sept. 13, 2013, effective Jan. 1, 2014.

Rule 10. Security of Court Records

(A) **Court Responsibilities.** Each judge is administratively responsible for the integrity of the judicial records of the court and must ensure that measures and procedures are employed to protect such records from mutilation, false entry, theft, alienation, and any unauthorized alteration, addition, deletion, or replacement of items or data elements.

Commentary

The court is required to preserve the integrity of audio and video recordings of court proceedings. The judge may employ various methods for ensuring the recording is not altered, including but not limited to supervised playback for listening or copying, creating a copy of the recording for use during said playback, serving notice to the parties that the recording is being accessed, and providing a copy, clearly identified as such. As prescribed by Indiana Judicial Conduct Rule 2.17 [former Canon 3(B)(13)], because the court is further required to prohibit broadcasting or televising court proceedings, the court may employ methods to restrict publication of copies of court proceedings made during the pendency of the case.

(B) Clerk Responsibilities. Each Clerk is responsible for the maintenance of court records in a manner consistent with the directives of the Supreme Court of Indiana, judge of court, and other pertinent authority. In all instances, the Clerk of the court must safeguard the integrity and security of all court records in his or her custody and diligently guard against any prohibited practice.

(C) Prohibited Practices. The following practices are prohibited and may subject an individual to contempt of court or constitute damage to a public record under IC 35–43–1–2(a):

(1) Mutilation, vandalism, or theft;

(2) False entry, unauthorized alterations, additions, or deletions or replacement of item or data elements;

(3) Alienation or any unauthorized release of court records;

(4) Use of non-reversible lamination; and

(5) Use of unauthorized repair procedures on records deemed permanent under Administrative Rule 7.

(D) Reconstruction of Records. Trial courts of this state, after a hearing, may reconstruct judicial records that have been lost or destroyed. A judicial officer whose court exercised jurisdiction of a case whose records have been lost or destroyed may reconstruct the lost or destroyed records, under the procedures set forth in this rule, and any party or interested person, for good cause shown, may file a verified petition seeking a judicial ruling on reconstruction from the best available sources. Notice of the petition shall be given by the petitioner in accordance with the Indiana Rules of Trial Procedure to all parties and any other interested persons in advance of the hearing, which shall take place no sooner than sixty (60) days after the petition is filed, unless good cause exists for a shorter period. Unless determined otherwise by the court, costs of notice shall be borne by the petitioner. Interested persons include the custodian of the lost or destroyed records and any person the court so designates, considering the facts and nature of the case. Certified copies of original records shall be as acceptable to such reconstruction as the original. "Best available sources" are the most credible sources to determine the contents of the lost or destroyed records and include, without limitation, certified copies, copies accompanied by verified statements, and verified statements. The court shall settle and reconstruct the lost or destroyed records following the hearing unless parties and any interested persons file a verified waiver of the hearing. Within one (1) year of the date of the court's settlement and reconstruction of a record, any party or interested person not receiving notice of the proceedings may seek to set aside the court's order, provided, however, that any

reconstruction shall be conclusively presumed to be final following this period.

Adopted Nov. 10, 1988, effective Jan. 1, 1989. Amended July 1, 2005, effective Jan. 1, 2006. Amended Oct. 6, 2008, effective Jan. 1, 2009; Oct. 11, 2012 , effective Jan. 1, 2013.

Rule 11. Paper Size

Effective January 1, 1992, all pleadings, copies, motions and documents filed with any trial court or appellate level court, typed or printed, with the exception of exhibits and existing wills, shall be prepared on 8 ½″ × 11″ size paper. Through December 31, 1991, such papers and records will be accepted on either 8 ½″ × 11″ or 8 ½″ × 14″ size paper.

Adopted Nov. 13, 1990, effective Jan. 1, 1991.

Rule 12. Facsimile Transmission

(A) Definitions. For the purposes of this rule, the definitions set forth in this paragraph shall apply:

(1) *Cover Sheet* means a descriptive initial page that accompanies an electronic facsimile transmission;

(2) *Electronic Facsimile Transmission*, commonly referred to as "FAX," means a method of transmitting and receiving information in paper medium over telephone lines or other forms of electronic transmissions;

(3) *Original Document* means the initially prepared written document or any counterpart intended to have the same effect by the creator; and

(4) *Duplicate Document* means a written counterpart of the original produced by the same impression as the original or from the same matrix or by digitized electronic transmission, readable by sight, which accurately reproduces the original.

(B) Filing by Electronic Facsimile Transmission. In counties where a majority of judges of the courts of record, by posted local rule, have authorized electronic facsimile filing and designated a telephone number to receive such transmissions, pleadings, motions, and other papers may be sent to the Clerk of Circuit Court by electronic facsimile transmission for filing in any case, provided:

(1) such matter does not exceed ten (10) pages, including the cover sheet;

(2) such matter does not require the payment of fees other than the electronic facsimile transcription fee set forth in paragraph (E) of this rule;

(3) the sending party creates at the time of transmission a machine generated log for such transmission; and

(4) the original document and the transmission log are maintained by the sending party for the duration of the litigation.

(C) Time of Filing. During normal, posted business hours, the time of filing shall be the time the duplicate document is produced in the office of the

Clerk of the Circuit Court. Duplicate documents received at all other times shall be filed as of the next normal business day.

If the receiving FAX machine endorses its own time and date stamp upon the transmitted documents and the receiving machine produces a delivery receipt which is electronically created and transmitted to the sending party, the time of filing shall be the date and time recorded on the transmitted document by the receiving FAX machine.

(D) Cover Sheet. Any document sent to the Clerk of the Circuit Court by electronic facsimile transmission shall be accompanied by a cover sheet which states the title of the document, case number, number of pages, identity and voice telephone number of the sending party and instructions for filing. The cover sheet shall contain the signature of the attorney or party, pro se, authorizing the filing.

(E) Electronic Facsimile Transmission Fee. Upon request and at an amount approved by the majority of judges of courts of record in the county, the County Board of Commissioners may adopt an electronic facsimile transmission fee not to exceed ten dollars ($10.00) per transmission.

(F) Standards. Electronic facsimile transmission equipment used by courts and their offices under this rule shall comply with "Group III" level equipment standards established by the CCITT (Consultative Committee International Telegraph and Telephone of the International Telecommunications Union), which provides standards for operating speed and image resolution available for use over public telephone networks. Pleadings and papers filed by electronic facsimile transmission shall be letter size.

Adopted effective Jan. 1, 1992; amended Dec. 5, 1994, effective Feb. 1, 1995.

Rule 13. [Vacated]
Vacated Sept. 30, 2004, effective Jan. 1, 2005.

Rule 14. Use of Telephone and Audiovisual Telecommunication

(A) Authority. A trial court may, in its discretion, use telephone or audiovisual telecommunication pursuant to the provisions of this rule as follows:

(1) A trial court may use telephone or audiovisual telecommunication to conduct:

(a) Pre-trial conferences;

(b) Proceedings where only the attorneys are present;

(c) Proceedings during a declared emergency under Ind. Administrative Rule 17; and,

(d) Proceedings where a party or witness is unavailable due to quarantine.

(2) A trial court may use audiovisual telecommunication to conduct:

(a) Initial hearings pursuant to IC 35–33–7–1, 3, 3.5, 4 and 5, including any probable cause hearing pursuant to IC 35–33–7–2; determination of indigence and assignment of counsel pursuant to IC 35–33–7–6; amount and conditions of bail pursuant to IC 35–33–7–5(4), 35–33–8–3.1 and 4; and the setting of omnibus date pursuant to IC 35–36–8–1;

(b) The taking of a plea of guilty to a misdemeanor charge, pursuant to IC 35–35–1–2;

(c) Sentencing hearings pursuant to IC 35–38–1–2 when the defendant has given a written waiver of his or her right to be present in person and the prosecution has consented;

(d) Post–conviction hearings pursuant to Ind. Post–Conviction Rule 1(5), with the written consent of the parties;

(e) Preliminary hearings in mental health emergency detention proceedings pursuant to IC 12–26–5–10;

(f) Review hearings in mental health commitment proceedings pursuant to IC 12–26–15–2;

(g) When a child is alleged to be a delinquent child, for a detention hearing pursuant to IC 31–37–6 or a periodic review hearing pursuant to IC 31–37–20–2;

(h) When a child is alleged to be a child in need of service, for a detention hearing pursuant to IC 31–34–5 or a periodic review hearing pursuant to IC 31–34–21–2.

(B) Other Proceedings. In addition, in any conference, hearing or proceeding not specifically enumerated in Section (A) of this rule, with the exception of criminal proceedings involving the right of confrontation or the right to be present, a trial court may use telephone or audiovisual communications subject to:

(1) the written consent of all the parties, entered on the Chronological Case Summary; or

(2) upon a trial court's finding of good cause, upon its own motion or upon the motion of a party. The following factors shall be considered in determining "good cause":

(a) Whether, after due diligence, the party has been unable to procure the physical presence of the witness;

(b) Whether effective cross-examination of the witness is possible, considering the availability of documents and exhibits to counsel and the witness;

(c) The complexity of the proceedings and the importance of the offered testimony in relation to the convenience to the party and the proposed witness;

(d) The importance of presenting the testimony of the witness in open court, where the fact finder may observe the demeanor of the witness and impress upon the witness the duty to testify truthfully;

(e) Whether undue surprise or unfair prejudice would result; and

(f) Any other factors a trial court may determine to be relevant in an individual case.

(3) A party or a trial court if it is acting on its own motion must give notice of the motion to use telephone or audiovisual telecommunication as follows:

(a) Any motion for testimony to be presented by telephone or audiovisual telecommunication shall be served not less than thirty (30) days before the time specified for hearing of such testimony;

(b) Opposition to a motion for testimony to be presented by telephone or audiovisual telecommunication shall be made by written objection within seven (7) days after service;

(c) A trial court may hold an expedited hearing no later than ten (10) days before the scheduled hearing of such testimony to determine if good cause has been shown to present testimony by telephone or audiovisual telecommunication;

(d) A trial court shall make written findings of fact and conclusions of law within its order on the motion for testimony to be presented by telephone or audiovisual telecommunication; and

(e) For cause found, a trial court may alter the time deadlines set forth in paragraphs (a) through (c) upon motion made prior to the expiration of the time for the required action.

(C) **Facilities and Equipment.** In relation to any hearing or proceeding conducted under this rule, the court shall assure that:

(1) The facility and equipment provide counsel with the ability to confer privately with an out of court party, or with other counsel, off the record, before, during, and immediately following the hearing or proceeding. Mental health care providers, employees of the Indiana Family and Social Services Administration and its county offices of Family and Children, and county probation officers who appear as witnesses are not parties for the purposes of this section.

(2) When using telephonic and audiovisual telecommunication:

(a) All participants are able to fully view and/or converse with each other simultaneously.

(b) The facilities have the capacity for contemporaneous transmission of documents and exhibits.

(c) Audiovisual images are in color and monitor screens are of sufficient quality, design, and architecture as to allow all parties to observe the demeanor and non-verbal communication of the other parties.

(d) The telephonic or audiovisual transmission is of sufficient quality, design, and archi-

tecture to allow easy listening and/or viewing of all public proceedings.

(e) The use of telephonic or audiovisual technology in conducting hearings and proceedings shall in no way abridge any right of the public.

(3) Application may be made to the Indiana Supreme Court, through the Division of State Court Administration, for approval of a plan that uses alternative procedures and technology that meet the intent and objective of this rule.

(4) The confidentiality accorded to attorney-client communications, and all other privileges applicable under Indiana law, apply.

(5) When using audiovisual telecommunication, images shall be in color; monitor screens shall be no smaller than twenty-five (25) inches.

(6) When using telephonic or audiovisual transmission, such transmission shall be of such quality, design and architecture as to allow easy listening and/or viewing of all public proceedings. The use of telephonic or audiovisual technology in conducting hearings and proceedings shall in no way abridge any right that the public may have to access to the courtroom and or jail.

(7) A trial court may apply to the Indiana Supreme Court, through the Division of State Court Administration, for approval of a plan that uses alternative procedures and technology that meet the intent and objective of this rule.

Adopted Dec. 20, 1995, effective Feb. 1, 1996. Amended July 1, 2003, effective Aug. 1, 2003; amended effective March 2, 2004; amended effective Sept. 30, 2004; Sept. 30, 2004, effective Dec. 31, 2005; July 1, 2005, effective Jan. 1, 2006; Sept. 10, 2007, effective Jan. 1, 2008; Sept. 9, 2008, effective Jan. 1, 2009; Sept. 20, 2011, effective Jan. 1, 2012.

Rule 15 Court Reporters

A. Application of Rule. All courts of record in each county of the State of Indiana shall adopt for approval by the Indiana Supreme Court a local rule by which all court reporter services shall be governed. Should a county fail to adopt such a plan, the Supreme Court shall prescribe a plan for use by the county. The local rule shall be in substantial compliance with the provisions of this rule.

B. Definitions. The following definitions shall apply under this administrative rule:

(1) A **Court reporter** is a person who is specifically designated by a court to perform the official court reporting services for the court including preparing a transcript of the record.

(2) **Equipment** means all physical items owned by the court or other governmental entity and used by a court reporter in performing court reporting services. Equipment shall include, but not be limited to, telephones, computer hardware, software programs, disks, tapes, and any other device used for recording and storing, and transcribing electronic data.

(3) **Work space** means that portion of the court's facilities dedicated to each court reporter, including but not limited to actual space in the courtroom and any designated office space.

(4) **Page** means the page unit of transcript which results when a recording is transcribed in the form required by Indiana Rule of Appellate Procedure 7.2.

(5) **Recording** means the electronic, mechanical, stenographic or other recording made as required by Indiana Rule of Trial Procedure 74.

(6) **Regular hours worked** means those hours which the court is regularly scheduled to work during any given work week. Depending on the particular court, these hours may vary from court to court and county to county, but remain the same for each work week.

(7) **Gap hours worked** means those hours worked that are in excess of the regular hours worked but hours not in excess of forty (40) hours per work week.

(8) **Overtime hours worked** means those hours worked in excess of forty (40) hours per work week.

(9) **Work week** means a seven (7) consecutive day week that consistently begins and ends on the same days throughout the year; i.e. Sunday through Saturday, Wednesday through Tuesday, Friday through Thursday.

(10) **Court** means the particular court for which the court reporter performs services. Depending upon the county, Court may also mean a group of courts; i.e. "X County Courts".

(11) **County indigent transcript** means a transcript that is paid for from county funds and is for the use on behalf of a litigant who has been declared indigent by a court.

(12) **State indigent transcript** means a transcript that is paid for from state funds and is for the use on behalf of a litigant who has been declared indigent by a court.

(13) **Private Transcript** means a transcript, including but not limited to a deposition transcript, that is paid for by a private party.

C. Court Reporter Models. The court or courts of each county shall uniformly adopt by local court rule one of the following Court Reporter Models:

(1) *Model Option One.* The local rule shall:

(a) designate that a court reporter shall be paid an annual salary for time spent working under the control, direction and direct supervision of the court during any regular work hours, gap hours or overtime hours;

(b) designate a per page fee for county indigent transcript preparation;

(c) designate that the court reporter shall submit directly to the county a claim for the preparation of the county indigent transcript;

(d) designate a maximum per page fee that the court reporter may charge for a state indigent transcript;

(e) designate a maximum per page fee that the court reporter may charge for a private transcript;

(f) require the court reporter to report at least on an annual basis to the Indiana Supreme Court Division of State Court Administration, on forms prescribed by the Division, all transcript fees (either county indigent, state indigent, or private) received by the court reporter;

(g) designate that if a court reporter elects to engage in private practice through recording of a deposition and/or preparing of a deposition transcript, and the court reporter desires to utilize the court's equipment, work space and supplies, and the court agrees to the use of court equipment for such purpose, the court and the court reporter shall enter into a written agreement which must, at a minimum, designate the following:

(1) the reasonable market rate for the use of equipment, work space and supplies;

(2) the method by which records are to be kept for the use of equipment, work space and supplies;

(3) the method by which the court reporter is to reimburse the court for the use of the equipment, work space and supplies;

(h) designate that if a court reporter elects to engage in private practice through recording a deposition and/or the preparing of a deposition transcript, that such private practice shall be conducted outside of regular working hours; and

(i) designate that the court shall enter into a written agreement with the court reporter which outlines the manner in which the court reporter is to be compensated for gap and overtime hours; i.e. either monetary compensation or compensatory time off regular work hours.

(2) *Model Option Two.* The local rule shall:

(a) designate that a court reporter shall be paid an annual salary for time spent working under the control, direction and direct supervision of the court during any regular work hours, gap hours or overtime hours;

(b) designate that subject to the approval of each county's fiscal body, the amount of the annual salary shall be set by the court;

(c) designate that the annual salary paid to the court reporter shall be for a fixed schedule of regular working hours;

(d) designate that a court reporter shall, if requested or ordered, prepare any transcript during regular working hours;

(e) designate that in the event that preparing a transcript cannot be completed during regular hours worked, a court reporter shall be entitled to additional compensation beyond regular salary under one of the two options set forth as follows:

(1)(a) Gap hours shall be paid in the amount equal to the hourly rate of the annual salary; and

(b) Overtime hours shall be paid in the amount of one and one-half (1½) times the hourly rate of the annual salary; or,

(2)(a) Compensatory time off from regular work hours shall be given in the amount equal to the number of gap hours worked; and

(b) Compensatory time off from regular work hours shall be given in the amount of one and one-half (1½) times the number of overtime hours worked;

(f) designate that the court and each court reporter may freely negotiate between themselves as to which of the preceding two (2) options in (e) shall be utilized and that the court and court reporter shall enter into a written agreement designating the terms of such agreement;

(g) designate that if a court reporter elects to engage in private practice through recording a deposition and/or preparing a deposition transcript, that such private practice shall be conducted outside of regular working hours;

(h) designate that if a court reporter elects to engage in private practice through recording a deposition and/or preparing of a deposition transcript, and the court reporter desires to utilize the court's equipment, work space and supplies, and the court agrees to the use of court equipment for such purposes, the court and the court reporter shall enter into a written agreement which must at a minimum designate the following:

(1) the reasonable market rate for the use of equipment, work space and supplies;

(2) the method by which records are to be kept for the use of equipment, work space and supplies;

(3) the method by which the court reporter is to reimburse the court for the use of the equipment, work space and supplies.

(i) designate a maximum per page fee that a court reporter may charge for private practice work;

(j) designate a maximum per page fee that the court reporter may charge for a private transcript; and

(k) require the court reporter to report at least on an annual basis to the State Court Administrator all transcript fees (either county indigent, state indigent or private) received by the court reporter.

(3) *Model Option Three.* The court(s) may, by adopting a local rule to that effect, elect to procure all court reporter services by private contract and submit such contract for approval by the Indiana Supreme Court in accordance with Section A of this rule. Any

such procedure must conform with all applicable state and local statutes, rules and regulations.

Adopted Nov. 25, 1997, effective Jan. 1, 1998.

Rule 16. Electronic Filing and Electronic Service Pilot Projects

(A) Definitions. The following definitions shall apply to this rule:

(1) E–Filing System. An E-filing system is a system approved by the Indiana Supreme Court for filing and service of pleadings, motions and other papers ("documents") or information via an electronic means such as the Internet, a court-authorized remote service provider, or through other remote means to and from the trial court's case management system.

(2) Electronic Filing. Electronic filing ("E-filing") is a method of filing court documents or information with the Clerk of the Court by electronic transmission utilizing the E-filing system.

(3) Electronic Service. Electronic service ("E-service") is a method of serving documents or information by electronic transmission on any User in a case via the E-filing system.

(4) User Agreement. A user agreement is an agreement that establishes obligations and responsibilities of the User and the Court and provides guidelines for proper use of the E-filing system.

(5) User. A User is an individual that has received authorization from the trial court administering an E-filing system to use that E-filing system by remote access.

(B) Approval. Courts wishing to establish an electronic filing or an electronic service pilot project pursuant to these rules must submit a written request for approval and a plan to the Division of State Court Administration. The Division shall define the necessary elements of the plan. At a minimum, the plan must state if and how the system is compatible with the clerk's office and other court users, if it is accessible to the public, if it is accessible to unrepresented litigants, if and what sort of fees will be charged, and all technical details relevant to the approval process. The plan must also include a process for archival record retention that meets the permanent and other record retention requirements of the Indiana Rules of Court.

(C) User Agreements. The User Agreement must be approved by the Division of State Court Administration. The User and the Court must execute the User Agreement before the User may use the E–filing system. The User must file the executed User Agreement, and the clerk must note the filing of the agreement on the Chronological Case Summary (CCS) and enter it into the Record of Orders and Judgments (RJO) of the case in which the User is appearing. In the User Agreement, the User must agree to receive service of Documents through the E–filing system.

In the User Agreement, the Court shall issue to the User distinct remote access with a unique password and user identification. The trial court may enter into a User Agreement with any attorney licensed to practice law in Indiana, an individual designated pursuant to Ind. Small Claims Rule 8(C) to appear for a corporation, partnership or sole proprietorship in small claims cases, and with any party in a particular case.

(D) Fees. Upon the request and at an amount approved by the majority of judges of courts of record in the county, the County Board of Commissioners may adopt, in accordance with Ind. Administrative Rule 9(E), an electronic system fee to be charged in conjunction with the use of the E-filing system The fees must be included in the User Agreement and in the plan submitted pursuant to section (B) of this rule.

(E) Signature. The filing of documents and information through the E-filing system by use of a valid username and password is presumed to have been authorized by the User to whom that username and password have been issued and documents filed through the E-filing system are presumed to have been signed by the same User.

(F) Commencement of an Action. An action may be commenced by E-filing only in a court which has adopted a pilot project plan approved by the Division of State Court Administration pursuant to this rule.

(G) Time of Filing. Documents or information may be filed through an E-filing system at any time. Documents or information filed through the E-filing system are deemed filed as of the time shown on the time stamp issued by the E-filing system.

(H) Original Document. Until such time that a Court implements a process approved by the Division of State Court Administration for the permanent retention of electronically transmitted, served or maintained documents, the Court must maintain a traditional paper copy of all electronic documents required to be maintained pursuant to the Indiana Rules of Court in the medium required. Upon the approval by the Division of State Court Administration of a permanent record retention process for electronically filed and served documents, a Document filed or served through an E-filing system shall be deemed an original record. Attorneys and unrepresented parties must retain signed copies of such electronically filed documents and, upon the Court's request, must provide such documents to the Court.

(I) Request for Changes to the System. A Court authorized to administer an E–filing system must seek approval from the Division of State Court Administration for any changes to the E-filing system that the Court wishes to implement after the initial approval.

Adopted July 1, 2005, effective Jan. 1, 2006. Amended Aug. 15, 2006, effective Jan. 1, 2007; Sept. 15, 2009, effective Jan. 1, 2010; Sept. 21, 2010, effective Jan. 1, 2011; Sept. 13, 2013, effective Jan. 1, 2014.

Appendix. The Necessary Elements of a Proposed Plan to Implement Electronic Filing or An Electronic Service Pilot Project Pursuant to Administrative Rule 16

Pursuant to Administrative Rule 16(B), the following provisions relate to the necessary elements required in any written request for approval of an electronic filing or an electronic service pilot project. The Division of State Court Administration may modify these provisions at any time.

I. Definitions

(a) "Filing User" refers to attorneys who have an electronic case filing log-in and password to file documents electronically, or the agent an attorney has expressly designated to make a filing on his or her behalf.

(b) "Electronic Case Filing System" (ECF) refers to the court's system that receives in electronic form documents or information via the Internet, a court-authorized remote service provider, or through other remote means to and from the trial court's case management system.

(c) "Notice of Electronic Filing" refers to the notice that is automatically generated by the Electronic Case Filing System at the time a document is filed with the system, setting forth the time of filing, the name of the party and attorney filing the document, the type of document, the text of the docket entry, and the name of the attorney(s) receiving the notice.

(d) "Archival Retention" refers to permanent records retention pursuant to Administrative Rule 7.

(e) "Registration" refers to the execution of the User Agreement (see below) by a Filing User.

II. Elements

A proposed plan submitted pursuant to Administrative Rule 16(B) must contain the following elements:

A. System Compatibility

A detailed description of how the proposed system is compatible with the clerk's office and the current technology in use in the court and court offices.

B. User Hardware and Software Requirements
The specific hardware and software users will need to electronically file documents and information and receive notice of case activity.

C. System Users
An identification of other court users, including the public, and a description of how the proposed system would be compatible with their use. Any proposed system must allow members of the public to view electronic and hard copy documents, unless they are deemed confidential by statute, court rule, or court order.

D. Eligible Cases
A description of what cases may be filed electronically, what cases must be filed electronically and what cases cannot be filed electronically.

E. Fees
What fees will be charged, if any, including those applicable to filing, serving, viewing and/or copying court documents. Proposals also must include a discussion of how fees will be collected and a comparison of the proposed fees to the existing (pre-electronic) fee structure. All fees must comply with the provisions of Administrative Rule 16(D).

F. Document Preservation
A description of the process for archival retention that satisfies permanent records retention and other requirements of the Indiana Rules of Court.

G. Local Rules
Any proposed local rules that the court intends to adopt to aid in the implementation of the Plan or the ECF.

H. Forms
Any forms that the court has developed to aid in the implementation of the Plan or the ECF, such as:
    Attorney Registration Form
    Notice of Manual Filing
    Notice of Signature Endorsement
    Declaration that Party Was Unable to File in a Timely Manner Due to Technical Difficulties.
    Notice of Filing Sealed/Confidential Document Manually

I. Security
The measures that the court or its vendor would employ to protect the security of the ECF.

J. Proof of Service
A detailed description of how the system will accomplish service of process pursuant to Trial Rule 5 through electronic means. Return receipt email will not be considered adequate proof of service of process. In addition, the plan must describe how the court and other users may verify the service in the future.

K. Legal XML Compliance
A description of how the system will comply with the Legal XML E-Filing Standard. Compliance with this standard will help ensure compatibility with the future statewide CMS.

L. Proposed User Agreement(s), Forms, Other Documents

A sample of the proposed User Agreement(s) required by Administrative Rule 16(C), accompanied by a detailed description its components, the procedure for its use and the method by which the unique password and user identification will be assigned. In addition, any forms and other generic documents to be incorporated must be provided.

M. A Proposed Implementation Plan and Schedule

A detailed description of when and how the Plan and system will be implemented, including anticipated training arrangements.

N. Accessibility by Unrepresented Litigants

A detailed description of whether unrepresented litigants are permitted to use the system, and if so, how they will be accommodated. In addition, the plan must describe how documents filed in hard copy by unrepresented litigants will be served to the other parties.

O. Performance Measurements

A detailed description of how the Court will determine if the pilot project meets expectations. These measurements may be a combination of reports and user queries. Some examples may be the equivalent of "comment cards" sent to the users and returned to the Court, error reporting by the user when he or she encounters a difficulty, the error being returned to the court, reports of downtime (maintenance) and system failures (i.e. crash) monthly or quarterly, and routine reviews by the system administrator for feature or software upgrades.

III. Content/Substantive Requirements

In addition to the elements outlined above, any proposed Plan shall include the following content:

A. Eligible Users

Attorneys admitted to the Indiana bar and in good standing are eligible to register as Filing Users of a court's Electronic Case Filing system. Registration via the User Agreement should require the Filing User's name, address, telephone number, Internet e-mail address, and a declaration that the attorney is admitted to the bar. Filing Users must notify the clerk of the court in writing within 30 days of any change of address, electronic or otherwise.

B. Registration Obligations

Registration as a Filing User constitutes consent to electronic service of all documents in accordance with the Indiana Rules of Court. Filing Users must agree to protect the security of their passwords and immediately notify the clerk if they learn that their password has been compromised.

C. Public Accessibility

Members of the public may review at the clerk's office filings that have not been sealed by the court. A person who has system access may retrieve docket sheets and documents. Only a Filing User may file documents and information electronically.

D. General Format Requirements

Formatting requirements for all documents filed electronically must comply with the format and procedures set forth in the Indiana Rules of Court and the local rules for the county in which the electronic filing occurs. (If the court intends to create local rules specifically applicable to electronic filing, a copy of such proposed local rules must be included with the proposed plan).

E. Initial Pleadings

With the exception of cases involving infractions, the initial pleading and accompanying documents, including the complaint and service of the summons, must be served in the traditional manner on paper. The plan must describe the method by which proof of service of process pursuant to Trial Rule 4 will be reflected on the electronic docket. In the event a case is initiated electronically, the plan shall include a description of the method by which the relevant filing and service fees are collected and remitted to the Clerk's office.

F. Appearance

The filing of a Notice of Appearance shall act to establish the filing attorney as an attorney of record representing a designated party in a particular cause of action.

G. Format of Attachments and Exhibits

Filing Users must submit in electronic form all documents referenced as exhibits or attachments, except as specifically permitted by court rule or order.

Exceptions to the electronic filing requirement include the following documents:

> a.   Exhibits in a format that does not readily permit electronic filing, such as videotapes, x-rays and similar materials;
>
> b.   Paper documents that are illegible when scanned into PDF format; and
>
> c.   Documents filed under seal or information not for public access as defined in Administrative Rule 9(G)(1).

Such components shall not be filed electronically, but instead shall be manually filed on paper with the clerk, and served upon the parties in accordance with the applicable Indiana Rules of Court and local rules for filing and service of non-electronic documents. Parties making a manual filing of a component must file electronically, in place of the manually filed component, a Notice of Manual Filing setting forth the reason(s) why the component cannot be filed electronically. The manually filed component must be presented to the clerk within 24 hours after the electronic submission of the Notice of Manual Filing. A paper copy of the electronically filed Notice of Manual Filing must accompany the component at the time of manual filing.

H. Certificate of Service

A certificate of service, if required by the Rules of Trial Procedure, must be included with all documents and information filed electronically. The certificate shall indicate that service was accomplished pursuant to the court's electronic filing procedures. The party effectuates service on all registered parties by filing electronically. Those parties or attorneys who have been permitted by the court to be exempt from the electronic filing requirement must be provided the documents in paper form in accordance with the Indiana Rules of Court.

I. Electronic Copies and Electronic File–Stamps

When a document or information is filed electronically, the official record is the electronic recording of the document as stored by the court. The system will generate a Notice of Electronic Filing, which will be transmitted via e-mail to the filer and all attorneys of record in the matter. The Notice of Electronic Filing serves as the court's date-stamp and proof of filing.

J. Password Serves as Signature

No Filing User or other person may knowingly permit or cause to permit a Filing User's password to be used by anyone other than an authorized agent of the Filing User. A Filing User has responsibility for all transactions under his or her password and is obligated to notify the clerk if his or her password is compromised.

The log-in and password required to submit documents and information to the Electronic Case Filing System shall serve, in part, as the Filing User's signature on all electronic documents filed with the Court, and as the Filing User's authorization for filing information with the Court. They also serve as a signature for purposes of the Indiana Rules of Court, the local rules of the court, and any other purpose for which a signature is required in connection with proceedings before a court.

K. Signatures Other Than Filing User

Documents requiring signatures for two or more parties represented by different counsel must be electronically filed either by: (a) representing the consent of the other attorney(s) on the signature line where the other attorney's handwritten signature would otherwise appear; (b) identifying in the signature block attorneys whose signatures are required and by the submission of a notice of endorsement by the other attorneys no later than three business days after filing; (c) submitting a scanned document containing all necessary signatures; or (d) in any other manner approved by the court.

L. Filing Consequences

Electronic transmission of a document or information to the Electronic Case Filing System consistent with these rules, together with the transmission of a Notice of Electronic Filing from the court, constitutes filing of the document or information for all purposes of the Indiana Rules of Court and the local rules of the court, and constitutes entry of the filing on the court's docket. When a document or information has been filed electronically, the official record is the electronic recording of the document or information as stored by the court, and the filing party is bound by the document or information as filed.

Filing a document or information electronically does not alter the filing deadline for that document or information . Filing must be completed before midnight local time of the court in order to be considered timely filed that day.

When a document or information is filed electronically, the court's system must generate a Notice of Electronic Filing, which will be transmitted via e-mail to the filer and all attorneys of record in the matter who are Filing Users. The party submitting the filing should retain a paper or electronic copy of the Notice of Electronic Filing, which serves as the court's date-stamp and proof of filing. Transmission of the Notice of Electronic Filing to an attorney's registered e-mail address constitutes service upon the attorney. Only the Notice of Electronic Filing, generated and transmitted by the court's system, is sufficient to constitute electronic service of an electronically filed document. Those parties or attorneys who have been permitted by the court to be exempt from the electronic filing requirement must be provided notice of the filing in paper form in accordance with the Indiana Rules of Court.

M. Sealed Documents

The provider of the electronic filing system must certify a level of security for sealed documents that demonstrates the ability to comply with the Indiana Rules of Court, especially Administrative Rule 9. The party filing a sealed document also must electronically file a Notice of Manual Filing.

No document will be maintained under seal in the absence of an authorizing statute, court rule, or court order.

N. Court Orders

Immediately upon the entry of an order or judgment in an action assigned to the Electronic Filing System, the clerk will transmit to Filing Users in the case, in electronic form, a Notice of Electronic Filing. Electronic transmission of the Notice of Electronic Filing constitutes the notice required by Indiana Rule of Trial Procedure 77(D). If a party is not represented by at least one attorney who is a Filing User, the court must give notice in paper form in accordance with the Indiana Rules of Court.

O. Technical Difficulties

Parties are encouraged to file documents and information electronically during normal business hours, in case a problem is encountered. In the event a technical failure occurs, and despite the best efforts of the filing party a document or information cannot be filed electronically, the party should print (if possible) a copy of the error message received. In addition, as soon as practically possible, the party should file a Declaration that Party was Unable to File in a Timely Manner Due to Technical Difficulties.

If a party is unable to file electronically and, as a result, may miss a filing deadline, the party must contact the designated Electronic Filing System Administrator. If a party misses a filing deadline due to an inability to file electronically, the party may submit the untimely-filed document, accompanied by a declaration stating the reason(s) for missing the deadline. The document and declaration must be filed no later than 12:00 noon of the first day on which the court is open for business following the original filing deadline.

P. Retention of Documents in Cases Filed Electronically

Filing Users must retain signed copies of electronically filed documents until two (2) years after all time periods for appeals expire. Documents that are electronically filed and require original signatures other than that of the Filing User must be maintained in paper form. On request of the court, the Filing User must provide original documents for review.

Originals of documents filed electronically which require scanning (*e.g.* documents that contain signatures, such as affidavits) must be retained by the filing party and made available, upon request, to the Court and other parties for a period of two years following the expiration of all time periods for appeals.

Q. Entry of Court Orders

All signed orders must be filed electronically by the court or court personnel. All orders, decrees, judgments, and proceedings of the court filed electronically will constitute entry on the court's docket. A hardcopy version of all judgments shall be entered in the Court's Record of Judgments and Orders, pursuant to Trial Rule 77(D).

IV. Exemption Requests

Any court tendering a Plan for approval may seek exemption from including or complying with one or more of the elements or content requirements specified in this Appendix by identifying:
- (1) The specific requirement from which the applying court seeks to be exempted;
- (2) The basis for seeking the exemption; and
- (3) What the applying court shall do in lieu of or to serve the underlying purpose of the specified requirement.

The Division of State Court Administration shall consider Requests for Exemption from the specifications of this Appendix on a case-by-case basis. In the event that the Request for Exemption is denied, such determination shall not preclude approval of the remainder of a court's tendered Plan.

Adopted Oct. 6, 2006, effective Jan. 1, 2007. Amended Sept. 15, 2009, effective Jan. 1, 2010; Sept. 13, 2013, effective Jan. 1, 2014.

Rule 17. Emergency Petition for Administrative Orders

(A) Supreme Court Authority. Under the authority vested in the Indiana Supreme Court to provide by rule for the procedure employed in all courts of this state and the Court's inherent authority to supervise the administration of all courts of this state, the Court has the power upon petition from any trial court as set forth herein, or sua sponte, in the event of natural disaster, civil disobedience, wide spread disease outbreak, or other exigent circumstances requiring the closure of courts or inhibiting the ability of litigants and courts to comply with statutory deadlines and rules of procedure applicable in courts of this state, to enter such order or orders as may be appropriate to ensure the orderly and fair administration of justice. This order shall include, without limitation, those rules and procedures affecting time limits currently imposed for speedy trials in criminal and juvenile proceedings, public health, mental health, appellate, and all other civil and criminal matters.

The Court also may authorize any petitioning court to move its location from its statutory location to any location the Court deems appropriate, and the Court may authorize any judge of a Circuit or Superior Court to exercise general jurisdiction over any civil or criminal matter.

(B) Trial court petition. When it becomes apparent to the local trial court(s) that an emergency exists, the local trial court(s) shall:

1. Confer with the clerk, bar representative and local official, as the trial court(s) deem necessary and appropriate.

2. Petition the Supreme Court for emergency relief stating: the emergency, the effect it is having or will have on the local administration of justice, the anticipated duration, and any additional information that would aid the Court in its decision making process.

3. Submit the trial court's plan for all civil and criminal matters during the emergency.

The petition shall be filed with the Clerk of the Court, with a copy provided to the Division of State Court Administration. The Division of State Court Administration shall create form petitions available for trial court use.

(C) When the Supreme Court determines that the petition is made for good cause shown, the Supreme Court may promptly issue an administrative order addressing the emergency on such terms and conditions as it deems appropriate.

Adopted Sept. 10, 2007, effective Jan. 1, 2008.

Appendix 17A. Sample Administrative Rule 17 Petition.

APPENDIX 17A SAMPLE ADMINISTRATIVE RULE 17 PETITION

Come now the Courts of _____ County and petition the Supreme Court for relief under Ind. Administrative Rule 17. In Support of this petition, the courts inform the Supreme Court as follows:

1. The courts of _____ County have convened in banc and have determined:

   A. That of the fifteen (15) staff personnel, of all the courts combined, nine (9) are absent because of the _____ virus and are expected to be absent for up to four (4) weeks.

   B. That of the ten (10) clerk staff personnel, six (6) are absent because of virus and are expected to be absent for up to four (4) weeks.

   C. That three (3) of the five (5) judges are absent because of the virus and are expected to be absent for up to four (4) weeks.

   D. That the _____ County health department has declared a local health emergency, closed all local schools, banned all public gathering, and has issued quarantine orders.

   E. That the local courts have appointed Judge _____ as the presiding Judge for this emergency.

The judges of _____ County request that the Supreme Court declare that an emergency exists in _____ County under the authority of Ind. Admin. R. 17, and to make appropriate emergency orders for _____ County directing and allowing the courts and clerk of _____ County to alter, modify, and suspend necessary procedures as provided in the emergency plan submitted herewith, so as to appropriately address this emergency.

DONE at Indianapolis, Indiana, this ___ day of _____, 20 ___.

_____

Judge

Adopted Sept. 10, 2007, effective Jan. 1, 2008.

Rule 18. County Probation Departments

(A) Application of Rule. The courts of record in a county that are authorized to impose probation shall adopt a plan by which the county will operate a unified or consolidated probation department.

(B) The management and governance of the department and any divisions within the department is to be determined by the supervising judge, and may include arrangements on who shall have the authority to appoint probation officers, assign probation officers to a particular court, and remove probation officers.

(C) Definitions. The following definitions shall apply under this administrative rule:

(1) *Chief probation officer* means a probation officer designated to direct and supervise the work of the probation department.

(2) *Separate juvenile probation* department means a probation department established before January 1, 2010, with a chief probation officer that supervises only juvenile probation officers and probation officers that supervise only juvenile offenders.

(3) *Supervising judge* means the judge, judges, board of judges, or chief judge responsible for the governance/oversight of the probation department.

(4) *Unified or Consolidated probation department* means a single, county-funded probation department that is directed by a single chief probation officer. A unified or consolidated probation department may contain separate divisions such as felony, misdemeanor, adult, juvenile, Court Alcohol & Drug, or pre-trial divisions.

(D) Annual Certification Reports. A report certifying that a county has adopted a plan for a unified or consolidated probation department, or has adopted a plan for a unified or consolidated adult probation department and a separate juvenile probation department, shall be filed with the Indiana Judicial Center by March 1 annually. The annual report shall be submitted on a form drafted by the Indiana Judicial Center and shall also include certification of department compliance with education and salary standards for probation officers.

(E) Judge's Confirmation of Reporting. The supervising judge of the unified or consolidated probation department shall review and confirm, through a process established by the Indiana Judicial Center, the completion and filing of the annual certification report.

(F) Plan for Unified or Consolidated Probation Department.

(1) *Counties in which only one court of record is authorized to impose probation.* Counties in which only one court of record is authorized to impose probation shall certify to the Indiana Judicial Center by October 1, 2011 that the county operates a unified or consolidated probation department.

(2) *Counties in which more than one court of record is authorized to impose probation.* Counties in which more than one court of record is authorized to impose probation shall certify to the Indiana Judicial Center that the county operates a unified or consolidated probation department or file an initial plan for the implementation of a unified or consolidated probation department by October 1, 2011. The initial plan shall be filed with the Indiana Judicial Center and shall consist of information on, including but not limited to, judicial governance/oversight of the probation department, any assignment of probation officers to a specific court or division, any divisions created within the consolidated department (such as circuit, superior, felony, misdemeanor, adult, juvenile, Court Alcohol & Drug, pre-trial or any other divisions agreed upon by the supervising judges), judicial oversight of any divisions within the department, appointment of a chief probation officer, appointment of assistant chief probation officers/supervisors assigned to a specific court or division, and probation officer salaries. The plan must be implemented by January 1, 2012. An extension for filing the plan and implementation may be granted at the discretion of the Judicial Conference Board of Directors for good cause shown. Any amendments to the initial plan after the implementation date shall be reported in the annual certification report.

(3) *Counties in which the circuit, superior, or probate court has established a separate juvenile probation department.* Counties in which the circuit, superior, or probate court has established a separate juvenile probation department before January 1, 2010, may elect to operate a unified or consolidated adult probation department and a separate juvenile probation department. These counties shall certify to the Indiana Judicial Center by October 1, 2011 that the county operates a unified or consolidated adult probation department and a separate juvenile probation department.

(4) *Review and Approval of Plans.* The Judicial Conference shall review plans submitted pursuant to standards adopted by the Conference. The Judicial Conference may approve the plan in whole or in part, may modify the plan, or deny the plan in whole or in part. If the Judicial Conference denies a plan in whole or in part, the Judicial Conference may require all or part of the plan to be resubmitted and may approve or reject the resubmitted plan in whole or in part. Should a county fail to submit a plan for review, the Judicial Conference may prescribe a plan for use by the county.

(G) Preparation of Forms. The Indiana Judicial Center shall draft forms to be used in filing initial plans, certification reports, and annual reports.

Adopted Sept. 21, 2010, effective Jan. 1, 2011.

Rule 19. Court Security Plans

Each court shall develop and implement a court security plan to ensure security in court facilities. If more than one court occupies a court facility, the courts shall collectively develop and implement a single court security plan. The plan shall give due consideration to the provisions of the Indiana Courthouse Security Minimum Standards unanimously adopted by the Judicial Conference of Indiana in 2002 and any other provisions necessary to satisfy court facility safety and security.

To ensure security in court facilities, a court security plan, including any security policy and procedures manual adopted as part of the security plan, shall be excluded from public access pursuant to Admin. R 9(G)(2)(b)vii.

Adopted Sept. 13, 2013, effective Jan. 1, 2014.

INDIANA RULES CUMULATIVE INDEX

INTERPRETERS AND TRANSLATORS—Cont'd
Court proceedings—Cont'd
Position in courtroom, **Interpret Rule III**
Practice, scope, **Interpret Rule III**
Procedures, **Interpret Rule IV**
Proficiency, **Interpret Rule III**
Public comments, **Interpret Rule III**
Purpose of standards, **Interpret Rule I**
Qualifications, **REV Rule 604**
Accurate representation, **Interpret Rule III**
Reciprocity, state certification, **Interpret Rule V**
Sanctions, certified interpreters, **Inter Disc Rule 6**
Simplifying statements, **Interpret Rule III**
Simultaneous translation,
Definitions, **Interpret Rule II**
Use, **Interpret Rule III**
Summarizing statements,
Definitions, **Interpret Rule II**
Use, when, **Interpret Rule III**
Vulgar meaning of words, **Interpret Rule III**
Waiver, **Interpret Rule IV**
Withdrawal from case, when, **Interpret Rule III**
Witnesses, **REV Rule 604**
Reprimands, disciplinary process, certified interpreters, **Inter Disc Rule 6**
Witnesses, opinion and expert testimony, **REV Rule 604**

INTERROGATORIES
Generally, **Trial P Rule 26**
Answers, **Trial P Rule 33**
Business records, option to produce, **Trial P Rule 33**
Failure to answer, **Trial P Rule 37**
Format, **Trial P Rule 33**
Jury, interrogatories to, abolished, **Trial P Rule 49**
Objections and exceptions, **Trial P Rule 33**
Response, time, **Trial P Rule 33**
Sanctions, **Trial P Rule 33**
Scope, **Trial P Rule 33**
Service, time, **Trial P Rule 33**
Time for service, response, **Trial P Rule 33**
Use at trial, **Trial P Rule 33.1**

INTERVENTION
Motions, **Trial P Rule 24**
Parties, **Trial P Rule 24**
Appearance, commencement of action, **Trial P Rule 3.1**

INTESTATE SUCCESSION
Probate Proceedings, generally, this index

INVESTMENTS
Judges, restrictions, **CJC Canon 3**

ISSUE
Children and Minors, generally, this index

JEFFERSON COUNTY
Tax Court, generally, this index

JOINDER OF CAUSES OF ACTION
Actions and Proceedings, this index

JOINDER OF PARTIES
Parties, this index

JOINT APPEALS
Initiation, **RAP Rule 9**

JOINT OBLIGATIONS
Joinder of parties, **Trial P Rule 19**

JUDGES
Abuse of office, avoiding, **CJC Canon 1**
Accreditation, continuing professional education, **Admis and Disc Guidelines**
Adverse or pecuniary interest, **CJC Canon 1 et seq.**
Continuing professional education, **Admis and Disc Rule 28**
Disqualification, **CJC Canon 2**
Personal economic interests, duty to stay informed, **CJC Canon 2**
Use of office to gain personal advantage or preferential treatment, **CJC Canon 1**
Appeal and review, continuing professional education, **Admis and Disc Guidelines**
Records and recordation, **Admis and Disc Rule 28**
Appointment, governmental positions, **CJC Canon 3**
Assignment of cases to judges, availability, **CJC Canon 2**
Assistance, judges and lawyers assistance program, **Admis and Disc Rule 31; Admis and Disc JLAP Guidelines**
Referrals to, **CJC Canon 2**
Associations and societies, discriminatory organizations, membership, **CJC Canon 3**
Attorneys,
Communications with, **CJC Canon 2**
False statements, **RPC Rule 8.2**
Misconduct, duty to inform, **CJC Canon 2**
Referral to assistance program, **CJC Canon 2**
Benefits, reports, **CJC Canon 3**
Bequests, reports, **CJC Canon 3**
Bias or prejudice, **CJC Canon 2**
Broadcasting, court proceedings, **CJC Canon 2**
Business and commerce, engaging in, **CJC Canon 3**
Campaign committees, **CJC Canon 4**
Candidates,
Conduct, **CJC Canon 4**
Public statements, disqualification, **CJC Canon 2**
Caseload reports, **Admin Rule 1**
Certificates and certification. Senior Judges, this index
Change of judges, **Trial P Rules 79, 79.1**
Family procedures, **Trial P Rule 81.1**
Charitable organizations, membership, **CJC Canon 3**
Circuit Court Judges, generally, this index
Civic organizations, membership, **CJC Canon 3**
Code of Judicial Conduct, **CJC Canon 1 et seq.**
Commercial information, disclosure, **CJC Canon 3**
Communication with jurors, **CJC Canon 2**
Community outreach, **CJC Canon 1**
Compensation and salaries,
Extrajudicial activities, **CJC Canon 3**
Senior Judges, this index
Competence, **CJC Canon 2**
Competency as witnesses, **REV Rule 605**
Complaints against, **Admis and Disc Rule 25**
Confidential or privileged information,
Continuing professional education, **Admis and Disc Rule 28**
Disciplinary proceedings, **Admis and Disc Rule 25**
Consultations,
Other judges or experts, **CJC Canon 2**
Public officials, **CJC Canon 3**
Continuing professional education, **Admis and Disc Rule 28; Admis and Disc Guidelines**
Nonattorney judges, fees, **Admis and Disc Rule 2**
Cooperation, **CJC Canon 2**